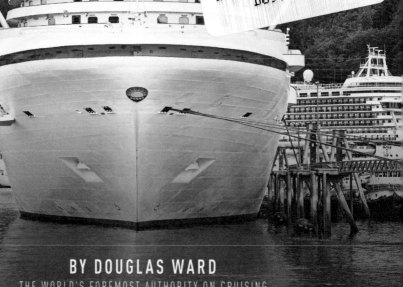

Berlitz

CRUISING
& CRUISE SHIPS
2018

D0976392

BY DOUGLAS WARD
THE WORLD'S FOREMOST AUTHORITY ON CRUISING

◎ Walking Eye App

Your Berlitz Cruising and Cruise Ships guide now includes a free app and eBook version of the book, all included for the same great price as before. They are available to download from the free Insight Guides Walking Eye app, found in the App Store and Google Play. Simply download the Walking Eye container app to access the eBook and app.

Multiple eBooks & apps available

Now that you've bought this book you can download the accompanying app and eBook for free. Inside the Walking Eye container app, you'll also find the whole range of other Insight Guides destination apps and eBooks, all available for purchase.

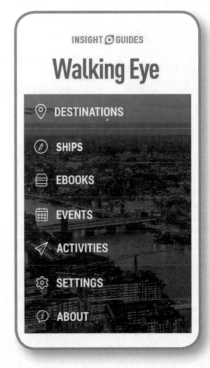

Events & activities

Free access to information on a range of local guided tours, sightseeing activities and local events in any destination, with the option to book.

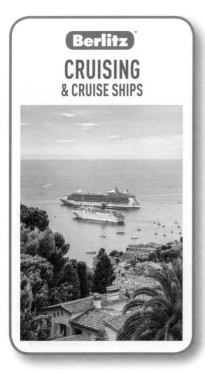

Berlitz
CRUISING
& CRUISE SHIPS

Berlitz Cruising and Cruise Ships app

The app has been designed to give you quick and easy access to insightful ship reviews. The app search function makes it easy to find out which ships are best for you. You will be able to highlight your favourite cruise ships for future reference, and share with friends and family.

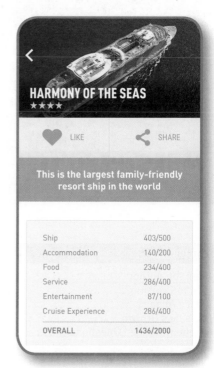

HARMONY OF THE SEAS
★★★★

♥ LIKE   ⦔ SHARE

This is the largest family-friendly resort ship in the world

Ship	403/500
Accommodation	140/200
Food	234/400
Service	286/400
Entertainment	87/100
Cruise Experience	286/400
OVERALL	1436/2000

Cruise ship descriptions

The app also includes descriptions of the facilities and cruise experience on every one of the 300 ships featured.

HOW TO DOWNLOAD THE WALKING EYE APP

1. Download the Walking Eye App from the App Store or Google Play.
2. Open the app and select the scanning function from the main menu.
3. Scan the QR code on this page – you will then be asked a security question to verify ownership of the book.
4. Once this has been verified, you will see your eBook and destination content in the purchased ebook and destination sections, where you will be able to download them.

Other destination apps and eBooks are available for purchase separately or are free with the purchase of the Insight Guide book.

GET IT ON
Google Play

Download on the
App Store

TABLE OF CONTENTS

Practical Information

The Ships and Their Ratings

The Ship Listings 179

YOUR FREE WALKING EYE APP

When you buy this book, you get access to the free Insight Guides Walking Eye app, which contains an eBook version of Cruising and Cruise Ships 2018 as well as all the ship listings in handy app form. Insight Guides is the sister brand of Berlitz Publishing, both owned by Apa Publications. See page 3 for more information on how to get your app.

Tables and Charts

FROM THE AUTHOR

Welcome to the 2018 edition of Berlitz Cruising & Cruise Ships – the book's 33rd year of continuous publication.

The cruise industry is a fiercely competitive business, and one within which any marketing opportunity is seized upon and hyped to the utmost. Cruise industry awards – often in the form of magazine or online readers' polls – provide a perfect such opportunity and are extremely valuable to the cruise companies.

Yet these polls are only ever as good as the number of people who vote in them, the number and types of ships, and the criteria established for measuring quality. For example, if a magazine initiates a readers' poll, and no readers have cruised aboard a French-speaking cruise ship, that ship will receive no votes. So, votes go to the most-traveled ships, that are not necessarily the best. The magazines never state the criteria. The results are therefore unreliable.

At Berlitz, we always state our criteria, clearly and honestly. That's why the Berlitz Cruising & Cruise Ships 2018 is the most authoritative and dependable guide on the market. What's more, this book is totally independent, and unconnected or influenced by sponsorship.

My 6,200-plus days at sea

In welcoming new readers, I should mention my qualifications for assessing cruise ships on your behalf. I first fell in love with ships when, in 1965, I sailed aboard Cunard Line's 83,673-ton ocean liner RMS *Queen Elizabeth* – at that time the world's largest passenger ship. Coincidentally, it was also the year that The Beatles had a hit with *Ticket to Ride*.

To date, I have completed over 6,200 days at sea, participating in more than 1,100 cruises, 159 transatlantic crossings, and countless Panama Canal transits, plus shipyard visits, numerous ship-naming ceremonies, and maiden voyages.

The first edition of this book, reviewing, testing, and evaluating 120 ships, was published in 1985, when cruising was viewed as an expensive, rarefied experience. Today, the book is the most highly regarded source of comparative information not only for cruise purchasers, but also for cruise industry executives, travel agents, and crew members.

This book is a tribute to everyone who has made my seafaring experiences possible, especially my mother and father, and I thank the cruise lines for their assistance during the complex scheduling, sailing, inspection, evaluation, and rating processes.

How to use this book

This book is divided into two main parts. The first helps you to define what you are looking for in a cruise vacation and advises on how to find it; it provides a wealth of information. Specialist cruises are discussed, too, culminating with that ultimate travel experience: the around-the-world cruise.

The book's main section profiles 300 ocean-going cruise and expedition ships. From large to small, from unabashed luxury and exclusivity to ships for the budget-minded, they are all here.

The ratings and evaluations are a painstaking documentation of my personal work. I travel throughout the world, and I sail for up to 200 days each year and take more than 50 flights. All evaluations are made objectively, without bias, partiality, or prejudice.

My intention has always been to make this the most informative and useful guidebook possible, and to help you to make informed decisions about the ship(s) you choose for your next cruise(s).

Although price indicators are given for some things such as alternative restaurants, spa treatments, and other items, prices may have changed since this book went to press. Check all prices with your cruise line.

Most of the statistical information contained in the ship profiles has been supplied by the cruise companies. You are welcome to send details of any errors or any updated information to me at: shipratings@hotmail.com.

My constant travel and ship inspection schedule means I am frequently at sea, and I no longer answer mailed letters.

Enjoying the view from a cabin balcony.

New to Cruising?

Are you all at sea about cruises, when it seems like everyone around you has taken one, but you haven't? Here's what you'll need to know before you first step aboard.

About 75 cruise companies operate around 350 ocean-going cruise ships and provide cruise vacations, and so the choice is huge.

You see them all the time – those online advertisements that shout 'Only $49 per day per person.' Well, take them with a pinch of salt! What you'll end up with is basic, basic, basic, with a left-over cabin in the worst location, and then, once aboard, you'll need to spend money at every turn.

It's a bit of an obstacle course, like trying to choose between different models of car, starting with a base price, and deciding on all the optional extras before getting the model you want. In other words, it's *not* the inclusive vacation that you thought you were buying, but an 'unbundled' product that requires you to make decisions, some of which cost extra.

The good news is that an ocean cruise can offer variety, excellent value for money, and a memorable vacation, and, with a little planning, it should all go smoothly. And, after your first cruise, be prepared for the feeling of addiction that so often hits.

You'll need to find the right ship and cruise to suit your needs – whether you are a solo traveler, a young couple, a family with children, or well-traveled seniors.

What exactly is a cruise?

A cruise is a change from everyday life on land. It is a (mostly) pre-paid, hassle-free vacation. You sleep in the same bed each night, the ship takes you from destination to destination, and only one currency is used on board.

Everything's close at hand and there are always polite people to help you explore new places. It facilitates multi-generational togetherness, solo adventuring, and total escapism. And, some of the world's most beautiful places are best seen from the deck of a cruise ship.

Why take a cruise?

Value for money. A cruise represents excellent value for money, considering everything that is provided. As it's mostly pre-paid, you don't have to constantly make financial decisions once on board.

Convenience. You may be able to drive to your port of embarkation (doorstep cruising). If not, the cruise line or your booking agent can make all the arrangements, including flights, baggage handling, and transfers to and from the ship. And you only have to unpack once!

Comfort. A suite or cabin is your home away from home. It can be as small as a tent (at about 60 sq ft/6

sq m), as large as a villa (at over 4,000 sq ft/372 sq m), or anything in between.

Good food. Dining is one of the pleasures of ship life, and all your meals are included from breakfast through to late-night snacks; most ships can accommodate specific dietary needs.

Family togetherness. Cruising offers a safe, family-friendly environment, and many ships have good children's facilities and well-supervised activities for kids. It is also an excellent way for groups of friends to vacation together.

Learning experience. Most ships have guest speakers/lecturers, so you can learn something new while you cruise.

Adventure. A cruise can be an adventure. It can take you to places that are impossible to reach by almost any other means, such as the Antarctic Peninsula, the Arctic, or to remote islands with no access by air.

Staying healthy. You can pamper yourself in a spa, although body-pampering treatments are at extra cost. And, with all the available food, learn to pace yourself to stay healthy.

The words say it all!

The stylish *Europa 2*, by Hapag-Lloyd Cruises.

Entertainment. Cruise ships provide a wide range of professional entertainment, from colorful large-cast productions and acrobatic shows to intimate classical instrumental recitals and jazz. And during the day, there are activities galore – enough to keep even the most active occupied.

About the price

The amount you can spend will determine the length of the cruise, and the size, location and style of your accommodation.

Will I need a passport?

Yes. You'll need to ensure that any appropriate authorizations and visas are obtained ahead of your cruise. If you already have a valid passport, ensure that you have at least six months left on it at the *end* of the cruise. In some ports (such as Venice, Italy, and all ports in Russia) you are required to carry your passport when ashore.

10 steps to a good first cruise experience

1. Find a cruise-booking specialist. Although the internet is a popular research tool, it pays to find a specialist (note that some internet-only 'agencies' with slick websites have been known to disappear without trace – with your money).

Describe your preferences (relaxation, visiting destinations, adventure, activities, entertainment, etc.), so that your agent can find a cruise and ship

that is right for you, for the right reasons, and at the right price.

They can guide you through all the important details, such as choice of cabin and dining arrangements. They may also have insider tips, knowledge about upgrades, and pre- and post-cruise programs.
2. Where to? Choose where you want to cruise: Alaska, Australia/New Zealand, the Bahamas, the Baltic, Bermuda, the Caribbean, Hawaii, Indian Ocean, the Mediterranean, Northern Europe, South Africa, South America, South Pacific, Southeast Asia, the US East Coast, etc. When you want to cruise: Alaska, for example, is not available during the winter; the Caribbean may be too hot for you in summer; Northern Europe is best in the summer, while South America and Southeast Asia are best in the winter. If you are interested in a special theme, such as Carnival in Rio or Formula One racing in Monte Carlo, this will determine the date of your cruise.
3. How long? Decide on the length of cruise you want. Allow traveling time to get to and from your ship, particularly if it is in an area far from home, or during winter. The standard Caribbean cruise length, for example, is seven days, although you could try a three- or four-day short-break Bahamas or Mexican Riviera cruise. In Northern Europe 12–14 days are more typical, while for an around-South America cruise, you'll need 30 days or more. For visiting the Antarctic Peninsula, allow 14–21 days, while an around-the-world cruise will take 90–120 days.
4. Choose the right ship. Size matters! Choose the right size ship for your needs. Do you want to be with 100, 500, 1,000, or 5,000-plus others on your vacation? Generally speaking, the larger the ship, the greater the focus on it as the destination.

Or perhaps you would like to experience cruising under sail; or with specialist lecturers; or an adventure/expedition cruise; or a coastal/inland waterways cruise.
5. Choose the right cabin. For a first cruise, choose an outside-view cabin. In an interior ('no-view') cabin you won't know how to dress when you wake up, because you can't see the weather outside. However, interior no-view cabins are good if you like to sleep in

a dark room. If you are concerned about motion sickness (it's not common, but it can happen), choose a cabin in the ship's center.

The average cabin size aboard a large resort ship is 180–200 sq ft (17–18.5 sq m); anything less and you will feel cramped. With limited closet space, you'll need fewer clothes than you might think. The more space you want, the more it will cost. Balcony cabins cost a little more than non-balcony cabins.

6. Dining. If there are two seatings for dinner, it could be wise to choose the later seating (typically at 8:30pm), so that you have enough time ashore in port without having to rush back to shower and change for the first seating (typically at 6:30pm).

Most ships have several dining venues, and you go where and when and with whom you like, though venues some cost extra.

7. Health and fitness. If you like body-pampering treatments, check that your ship has the right facilities. Aboard large resort ships you can also sign up for some exercise classes.

Book early for spa treatments, as appointment slots go quickly. Some cruise companies allow you to book online, but this means planning your time in advance.

8. Families. It's important to choose a family-friendly ship. Most large resort ships have very good facilities for youngsters; mid-size and small ships have more limited facilities, and some ships have none. Children usually love cruising, finding it educational, fun, sociable, and safe.

For those who don't want children around them, there are several child-free ships from which to choose.

9. Dress codes. Dress codes today are mostly casual aboard the large resort ships. In general, no formal attire is needed, although there are exceptions to this, such as on a transatlantic crossing aboard Cunard's *Queen Mary 2*, where formality is part of the tradition. It sounds obvious, but ships move around, so flat or low-heeled shoes are strongly recommended for women.

10. Extra expenses. Finally, do budget for extra-cost items such as shore excursions, drinks (unless they are included), and drink 'packages,' meals in extra-cost dining venues, spa treatments, casino gaming, and other personal items. Allow additional money,

Sunrise in the southern Atlantic Ocean.

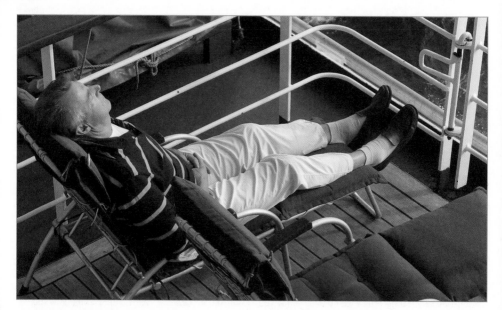

Relaxing on a deckchair on a transatlantic crossing with Cunard.

too, for souvenirs and gifts. Finally, make sure you have full insurance cover for your vacation.

Digital details

Today, most people use cell phones, tablets, or laptops and expect to be able to use them during their cruise.

You can use your device aboard ship, but once you leave port your cell phone will automatically lock into a ship's digital marine network, incurring a charge. At sea, your cell is out of range with land-based carriers, and will be slower than normal.

Note that some ships have notices outside their restaurants prohibiting the use of cell phones (for social etiquette).

What to expect

Stepping aboard for the first time? Here is what you need to know about a typical embarkation.

You've arrived at the airport closest to your ship's embarkation point, and retrieved your luggage. A cruise company representative will be holding a sign with the company's name on it. Your luggage – make sure it has your cabin number displayed clearly on it – is placed in a cluster together with that of other passengers. The next time you see your bags should be in your cabin.

You'll find check-in desks in the passenger terminal. If you have suite-grade accommodation, there should be a separate check-in facility. (Note: don't buy liquor to take on board – it will be confiscated.)

Getting aboard

You'll go through security screening, just as at airports. Then it's a few paces to reach the gangway.

You will probably be greeted by the ship's snap-happy photographers, ready to take your portrait, bedraggled as you may appear after having traveled for hours. Just say no (firmly) if you don't want your photograph taken.

At the ship end of the gangway, you will find staff to welcome you aboard.

THE BRIDGE

A ship's navigation bridge is manned at all times, both at sea and in port. Besides the captain, who is master of the vessel, other senior officers take 'watch' turns for four- or eight-hour periods. In addition, junior officers are continually honing their skills as experienced navigators, waiting for the day when they will be promoted to master.

The captain is always in command at times of high risk, such as when the ship is entering or leaving a port, when the density of traffic is particularly high, or when visibility is severely restricted by poor weather.

Navigation has come a long way since the days of the ancient mariners, who used only the sun and the stars to calculate their course across the oceans. The space-age development of sophisticated navigation devices (using satellites) has enabled us to eliminate the guesswork of early navigation (the first global mobile satellite system was introduced in 1979).

A ship's navigator today uses a variety of sophisticated instruments to pinpoint the ship's position at any time and establish its course.

Things to check

Once inside your cabin, check to see that it's clean and tidy? Are the beds properly made? Is there ice in the ice container? Check the bathroom; make sure there are towels and soap. If there are problems, tell your cabin steward.

Memorize the telephone number for medical emergencies, so you know how to call for help.

Your luggage probably will not have arrived yet – especially if it is a large resort ship – but don't sit in the cabin waiting for it...take a walk. If you're hungry, head to the self-serve buffet.

Familiarize yourself with the ship's layout. Learn which way is forward and aft, and how to reach your cabin from the main stairways. This is also a good time to learn how to get from your cabin to the outside decks in an emergency.

Control that thirst

Picture the scenario: you're thirsty when you arrive in your cabin. You see a bottle of water with a tab around its neck. Be sure to read the notice on the tab: 'This bottle is provided for your convenience. If you open it, your account will be charged $4.50.'

On deck, you are greeted by a smiling waiter offering you a colorful drink. But, put your fingers on the glass as he hands it to you and he'll also ask for your cruise card. There, you've just paid $6.95 for a drink full of ice worth 5¢.

The cost of drinks soon adds up. Note that aboard some ships mixers such as tonic for gin may be charged separately.

The safety drill

A Passenger Safety Drill must take place before a ship sails from the embarkation port. (This was introduced following the *Costa Concordia* tragedy in 2012.) It is mandatory that you attend the drill, and do pay attention – it could save your life. Directions to your assembly station are posted on the back of the cabin door. By now, your luggage probably will have arrived.

Titanic-style stairway aboard *Insignia*.

Today's activities.

6am

6.00am Good Morning Queen Mary 2
Your guide to today's entertainment and activities with Entertainment Director Jo Haley.
Stateroom TV, Channel 23
(repeated continuously until 12.00pm)

7am

7.30am Canyon Ranch Fitness
Stretch and relax - Full body stretch. Previous sign-up required.
Queens Room, Deck 3, D Stairway

8am

8.15am Canyon Ranch Fitnes
Powerful Pilates (All levels). $12 fitness pass and previous sign up required.
Queens Room, Deck 3, D Stairway

8.30am Catholic Mass
Illuminations, Deck 3, B Stairway

9am

9.00am Fencing (Group B)
Limited to 16 people, first come first served. With your Sports Host Dave. (Over 18s only)
Queens Room, Deck 3, D Stairway

9.00am Christian Fellowship
The Boardroom, Deck 9, A Stairway
(unhosted)

9.15am Canyon Ranch Lecture
Decreased mobility in shoulders and neck, causes and solutions. Join our physiotherapist Dragan and find ways how to improve mobility, decrease the pain and stregthen your muscles.
Chelsea Room, Deck 1, B Stairway

9.30am Golf Putting Competition
Pavilion Pool, Deck 12, B Stairway

9.30am Talent Show Sign Up & Rehearsal
Now is your time to shine. Meet your entertainment staff and be part of a special talent show. You must attend the rehearsal in order to take part.
Chart Room, Deck 3, C Stairway
(until 10.00am)

9.30am iStudy: Next Steps Workshop
Part 2 of 2: Adobe Photoshop Elements. A $15 fee applies.
ConneXions Room 6, Deck 2, A Stairway

9.30am Beginners' Bridge Class - Day 5
Atlantic Room, Deck 11, A Stairway

10am

10.00am Cunard Insights:
Dr. William Fowler
Recorded and broadcast on TV Ch. 44 from 5.00pm onwards.
'The War on Pirates.'
Despite their romantic image, by whatever name they were called – freebooters, buccaneers, scavenging sharks – pirates were murderous rogues. The eighteenth century was the heyday for the 'Jolly Roger.' It was a time when notorious captains, including William Kidd and Blackbeard, amassed fortunes and struck terror at sea and along the coasts.
Illuminations, Deck 3, B Stairway

10.00am Watercolour Art Class
There will be a one-time fee of $35 for supplies. Limited to 25 guests.
Britannia Restaurant, Deck 3, C Stairway, port side

10.00am Canyon Ranch Lecture
Living with Arthritis? - Learn about the most common forms of arthritis and how with a proper diet and exercise you can rejuvenate affected joints and relieve inflammation and pain.
Chelsea Room, Deck 1, B Stairway

10am

10.00am Retired Veterans and Military
Personnel Meeting
The Boardroom, Deck 9, A Stairway

10.00am Ballroom Dance Class
Beginners' Tango class with your dance instructors Volodymyr and Nadiya.
Queens Room, Deck 3, D Stairway

10.30am Morning Trivia
Golden Lion Pub, Deck 2, C Stairway

10.30am Intermediate Bridge Class
Atlantic Room, Deck 11, A Stairway

10.30am 'Sailing Solo' Coffee Get Together
Meet other independent guests, with your Social Hostess Ruth and the dance hosts.
Chef's Galley, Deck 7, C Stairway
(until 11.15am)

11am

11.00am Line Dance Class
With your Entertainment Host Claire. Please wear appropriate footwear.
Queens Room, Deck 3, D Stairway

11.00am Meet and Greet with
Susan Branch
A chance to meet with best selling Author and Artist Susan Branch.
The Boardroom, Deck 9, A Stairway

11.00am Cunard Insights:
Giancarlo Impiglia
Recorded and broadcast on TV Ch. 44 from 5.00pm onwards.
'The Birth of Modern Art: The Visual Revolution of Impressionism, from Claude Monet to Vincent Van Gogh.'
The history of the struggle of the revolutionary group of artists, named "The Impressionists," who in the second half of 19th Century, in the Paris of Napoleon III, changed the course of history, fighting and suffering to affirm their conviction. This presentation recounts Monet and his fellow Impressionists' new way of interpreting life and nature, which created scandal among the bourgeoisies in Paris. We touch on the visions of Vincent Van Gogh and possible explanations for his tragic suicide, as well as recounting Paul Gauguin's escape from western civilization, and his search for primitive culture in the Pacific island of Tahiti. The dramatic and colorful story of these famous artists will unfold with mostly unknown anecdotes.
Illuminations, Deck 3, B Stairway

11.00am Shuffleboard Tournament
Deck 13, A Stairway (over 18s only)

11.00am Canyon Ranch Lecture
Healthy Feet, Healthy Posture.
Chelsea Room, Deck 1, B Stairway

11.15am Harpist Magdalena Reising
Carinthia Lounge, Deck 7, B Stairway
(until 12.00pm)

11.15am Darts Competition
Golden Lion Pub, Deck 2, C Stairway
(over 18s only)

11.45am Canyon Ranch Lecture
Maybe she is born with it. Maybe it is Botox! - Eliminate the myths and learn the real facts about Botox with Dr. Claudia. Complimentary facial assessments for anyone who attends.
Chelsea Room, Deck 1, B Stairway

12pm

12.00pm Navigational Announcement
Public Address System

12pm

12.00pm Time Change
Today at midday the ships clocks will be SET FORWARD BY ONE HOUR. Please set your watches FORWARD at 12 noon today.

1pm

1.00pm Blackjack Tournament
Empire Casino, Deck 2, B Stairway

1.00pm Low Limit Afternoon Sea Days
Play your favorite Poker Games for $3 and Roulette for 50 cents until 5.00pm.
Empire Casino, Deck 2, B Stairway

1.15pm Pianist/ Vocalist Gavin Burke
Golden Lion Pub, Deck 2, C Stairway
(until 2.00pm)

1.15pm Canyon Ranch Lecture
Change your style, change your life. Hair seminar - Join Louise and discuss the latest trends and styles. Does your hair compliment your face shape?
Chelsea Room, Deck 1, B Stairway

1.30pm Poolside Music With Vibz
Pavilion Pool, Deck 12, B Stairway
(until 2.30pm)

1.30pm Napkin Folding Class
With your Social Hostess Ruth.
G32, Deck 3, D Stairway (until 2.00pm)

1.30pm Film: 'Dark Horse'
An inspirational documentary of a group of friends from a working men's club who decide to take on the elite 'sport of kings' and breed themselves a racehorse. Starring Jan Voxes, Brian Vokes, Howard Davies and Angela Davies. Rated PG.
Illuminations, Deck 3, B Stairway
(duration 87 minutes)

1.45pm Afternoon Classical Concert:
Michael Christian Durrant
Join the international classical guitarist Michael Christian Durrant for a dramatic matinée performance in which you will be guided through a captivating programme of the evocative music of Spain. This afternoon's concert programme includes a selection of stirring works by the Spanish composers Francisco Tárrega, Enriqué Granados and Joaquín Rodrigo – not to be missed!
Queens Room, Deck 3, D Stairway

2pm

2.00pm Canyon Ranch Lecture
Burn Fat Faster. Educational Seminar.
Chelsea Room, Deck 1, B Stairway

2.30pm Darts Competition
Golden Lion Pub, Deck 2, C Stairway
(over 18s only)

2.30pm iStudy: iPad Workshop
Part 4 of 5: iPad Cameras, Photos & Video. A $15 fee applies.
ConneXions Room 6, Deck 2, A Stairway

2.30pm Dixieland Jazz
Join the Royal Court Theatre Orchestra, under the musical direction of Jeff Hughes, for some fantastic Dixieland (Traditional Jazz) music.
Carinthia Lounge, Deck 7, B Stairway

2.30pm Watercolour Art Class
There will be a one-time fee of $35 for supplies. Limited to 25 guests.
Britannia Restaurant, Deck 3, C Stairway, Port side

2.30pm Duplicate Bridge Tournament
Atlantic Room, Deck 11, A Stairway

This is an example of a full day at sea aboard Cunard Line's *Queen Mary 2*. So, there really is plenty of life on a day at sea and absolutely no time to become bored.

Today's activities.

2pm

2.30pm Deck Quoits Competition ●
Deck 12, B Stairway (over 18s only)

2.45pm Canyon Ranch Lecture
Acupuncture for back pain and arthritis. Acupuncture is most effective for the treatment for back pain, sciatic pain, neck pain, shoulder pain and arthritis. To know more about acupuncture we welcome all to join our licensed acupuncturist onboard. Complimentary acupuncture health assessment for those who attend this seminar .
Chelsea Room, Deck 1, B Stairway

3pm

3.00pm Champagne Afternoon Tea
If you wish to take part in this exclusive event please call the Commodore Club on 29000 or contact any of our bar staff. Prices begin at $30 per guest.
Champagne Bar, Deck 3, Grand Lobby

3.00pm Snowball Jackpot Bingo
Tickets on sale at the Golden Lion Pub from 1.00pm to 3.00pm.
Golden Lion Pub, Deck 2, C Stairway

3.00pm Hostess Corner: Needlework & Knitting
With your Social Hostess Ruth. Bring your own projects. This is not a class.
Chart Room, Deck 3, C Stairway
(until 4.00pm)

3.30pm Afternoon Tea
With Pianist Nick Lido.
Queens Room ♪, Deck 3, D Stairway
(until 4.30pm)

3.30pm Cunard Insights: Susan Branch
Recorded and broadcast on TV Ch. 44 from 5.00pm onwards.
'A Fine Romance: Falling in Love with the English Countryside'.
Watercolor artist, cookbook writer, home and garden guru, blogger and New York Times Bestselling Author, Susan Branch talks about how she kept a diary of her two-month ramble through the back roads of rural England, through hedgerows and bluebells, visiting homes and gardens of her literary and artistic heroes including Beatrix Potter, Jane Austen and William Morris (to name a few) ~ and then made a bestselling hand-written book about it. Susan will demonstrate how easy it is to create a charming handmade travel book, a keepsake to last a lifetime, and discuss her upcoming BYO Picnic Basket Party in Wiltshire. There will be a book signing.
Illuminations ♪, Deck 3, B Stairway

3.30pm Complimentary Golf Competition ●
Longest drive. Places are limited sign up is required.
The Fairways, Deck 12, B Stairway
(over 18s only, sign up from 9.30am)

3.30pm Canyon Ranch Lecture
Sciatica, arthritis and disc problems. Join our Chiropractor Dr. Sarah as she discusses the root and management of it all.
Chelsea Room, Deck 1, B Stairway

3.30pm Book Club Meeting
Boardroom, Deck 9, A Stairway

4pm

4.00pm Pub Team Trivia ●
Golden Lion Pub, Deck 2, C Stairway
(over 18s only)

4pm

4.00pm Canyon Ranch Fitness
Indoor Cycling. A $12 fitness pass applies.
Knightsbridge Room, Deck 1, C Stairway

4.00pm iStudy: iPad Workshop
Part 4 of 5: iPad Cameras, Photos & Video. A $15 fee applies.
ConneXions Room 6, Deck 2, A Stairway

4.00pm Mask Sales
Grand Lobby, Deck 3, B Stairway
(until 4.45pm)

4.30pm Friends of Bill W.
The Boardroom, Deck 9, A Stairway

5pm

5.00pm National Symphony Orchestra Auction
Please see the back page of the Daily Programme for further information.
Royal Court Theatre ♪, Decks 2 & 3, B Stairway

5.00pm Charity Chart Auction
Assistant Entertainment Director Edward James Moffat will auction the chart used on this voyage. Proceeds are donated to the Prince's Trust.
Queens Room ♪, Deck 3, D Stairway

followed by Guest Talent Show
Now is your time to shine. You must have attended the earlier rehearsal in order to take part.
Queens Room ♪, Deck 3, D Stairway

5.00pm Film: 'Dark Horse'
An inspirational documentary of a group of friends from a working men's club who decide to take on the elite 'sport of kings' and breed themselves a racehorse. Starring Jan Voxes, Brian Vokes, Howard Davies and Angela Davies. Rated PG.
Illuminations, Deck 3, B Stairway
(duration 87 minutes)

5.00pm Friends Of Dorothy LGBT
Commodore Club, Deck 9, A Stairway

5.00pm Canyon Ranch Fitness
Abs express. Previous sign up required.
Knightsbridge Room, Deck 1, C Stairway

5.15pm Pianist Nick Lido
Chart Room, Deck 3, C Stairway
(until 6.00pm)

5.30pm Pianist/ Vocalist Gavin Burke
Golden Lion Pub, Deck 2, C Stairway
(until 6.00pm)

5.30pm Formal Portrait Studios
Decks 2 & 3, between B & C Stairways
(until 6.15pm)

5.30pm Canyon Ranch Fitness
Foot Fitness. Previous sign up required.
Knightsbridge Room, Deck 1, C Stairway

6pm

6.00pm Original art work for sale at Clarendon Fine Art
Join your Art Dealers Taja and Katie this evening to acquire original artwork from our eclectic portfolio of international and highly acclaimed artists. From the new and emerging to the very well established, we have something for you. Take advantage of 5% off all original artwork exhibited only exclusive to guests on board the prestigious Queen Mary 2.
Clarendon Fine Art, Deck 3L, C or D Stairway
(until 9.00pm)

7pm

7.30pm Formal Portrait Studios
Decks 2 & 3, between B & C Stairways
(until 8.45pm)

7.30pm Pianist Nick Lido
Commodore Club, Deck 9, A Stairway
(until 8.30pm)

7.45pm Pianist & Musical Director Jeff Hughes
Chart Room, Deck 3, C Stairway
(until 8.30pm)

8pm

8.00pm Early Evening Trivia ●
Golden Lion Pub, Deck 2, C Stairway

8.00pm Film: 'Dark Horse'
Illuminations, Deck 3, B Stairway
(duration 87 minutes)

8.30pm Last Night Of The Cunard Proms
With the National Symphony Orchestra.
Royal Court Theatre ♪, Decks 2 & 3, B Stairway

9pm

9.00pm Recorded Strict Tempo Music
Queens Room ♪, Deck 3, D Stairway
(until 9.45pm)

9.30pm Formal Portrait Studios
Decks 2 & 3, between B & C Stairways
(until 10.30pm)

9.30pm Pianist/ Vocalist Gavin Burke
Golden Lion Pub, Deck 2, C Stairway
(until 10.00pm)

9.30pm The Jazz Club
With the Mark Hodgson Trio.
Chart Room, Deck 3, C Stairway
(until late)

9.45pm Pianist Nick Lido
Carinthia Lounge, Deck 7, B Stairway
(until 10.30pm)

9.45pm Masquerade Ball
With the Queens Room Orchestra and Vocalist Damian Dowd.
Queens Room, Deck 3, D Stairway
(until 12.00am)

9.45pm International Band Vibz
G32, Deck 3, D Stairway
(until 10.45pm)

10pm

10.00pm Karaoke
Golden Lion Pub, Deck 2, C Stairway

10.00pm Pianist Geza Torocsik
Commodore Club, Deck 9, A Stairway
(until 12.00am)

10.30pm Last Night Of The Cunard Proms
With the National Symphony Orchestra.
Royal Court Theatre ♪, Decks 2 & 3, B Stairway

10.30pm Film: 'Dark Horse'
Illuminations ♪, Deck 3, B Stairway
(duration 87 minutes)

10.45pm Abba Night & More with your resident DJ
G32, Deck 3, D Stairway (until 11.30pm)

11pm

11.30pm International Band Vibz
G32, Deck 3, D Stairway
(until 12.30am)

12am

12.00am Dance Music For Enthusiasts
Queens Room ♪, Deck 3, D Stairway
(until 12.30am)

12.30am All Requests Express with your resident DJ
G32, Deck 3, D Stairway (until late)

What's Ahead

A record number of new ships is on order, as cruise companies battle it out to provide facilities to woo newcomers to cruising.

A multitude of new ships is coming your way! In 2018 and 2019, some 35 new ships of various sizes are scheduled to debut, with some stunning new facilities and features.

In 2017 the new ships delivered varied in size from Lindblad Expeditions' 100-passenger *National Geographic Quest* to MSC Cruises' 5,400-passenger *MSC Seaside*. In 2018 the trend continues. The smallest ship is Ponant's 180-passenger *Le Champlain*, while the largest is Royal Caribbean International's *Symphony of the Seas* (the new largest cruise ship in the world). The real drivers of the cruise business are MSC Cruises, Norwegian Cruise Line, and Royal Caribbean International (and, in Asia, Dream Cruises), who are all really creative with their new ships.

Given the economics of scale and shipbuilding costs, the new 'optimum' size for large resort ships is now about 160,000 tons, with a capacity of 3,500–4,500 passengers.

Demand for innovation is propelling new ship orders, and companies are investing billions of dollars in order to compete. Meanwhile experienced passengers are expecting better-quality food and dining experiences, and simplified cruise pricing. Today, you pay only for what you want – I call it the 'pay-more, get-more' principle.

What's the cost of a new cruise ship?
A small ship such as the 604-passenger *Seabourn Encore* would cost about $250 million; the 930-passenger *Viking Sun* would cost around $400 million; the 4,200-passenger *Norwegian Bliss* would cost about $700 million; the 5,496-passenger *Symphony of the Seas* would cost approximately €1.3 billion.

Nonstop refurbishment
Ships no longer in the first flush of youth need cosmetic surgery and regular makeovers in order to keep up their appearance. Items such as balcony door frames need replacing, suites/cabins need updating, and navigational, safety, and technical machinery needs updating.

Cruise companies often add more cabins during refurbishment, bringing additional passengers and increasing occupancy levels and revenue, but meaning a decrease in the amount of space per passenger (passenger space ratio). Usually, there's no corresponding increase in the number of crew, and so the crew to passenger ratio unfortunately decreases. And, because no new elevators are added, there is greater congestion and increased waiting time.

Some companies with older ships tend to sell them off to smaller operators. Some, such as AIDA Cruises'

AIDAcara, would be hard to sell on given the low number of crew cabins.

Stretch marks
For some cruise companies 'stretching' older ships make sense in light of the enormous cost of a new ship and the typical two-year time frame needed for completion and delivery. Even so, refits are expensive, at around $2 million a day, with that figure being pushed up by material, equipment, and labor costs. MSC Cruises, for example, 'stretched' four of its ships (*MSC Armonia, MSC Lirica, MSC Opera, MSC Sinfonia*) in 2014/2015, by adding a new 82-ft (25-m) mid-section in 'cut-and-insert' operations at Fincantieri's shipyard in Palermo, Italy.

All change
In 2017, *Pacific Pearl* (formerly *Ocean Village*) was sold to Cruise & Maritime Voyages (CMV) to become *Columbus*, while *Dawn Princess* was moved to P&O Cruises (Australia) and renamed *Pacific Explorer*.

Celestyal Odyssey moved to China to become *Brilliant of the Seas* for the Chinese company Diamond Cruise International.

AIDAbella was also repositioned to China in 2017, as was *Carnival Miracle* and *Costa neoRomantica. Carnival Splendor* will be transferred to P&O Cruises (Australia) to be based year-round for the Australasian market.

Symphony of the Seas, Royal Caribbean's newest Oasis class ship, under construction at the STX shipyard in France.

New ships to debut

Cruise line	Ship name	Gross tonnage	Debut year	No. of lower beds	Builder
2018					
Carnival Cruise Line	Carnival Horizon	133,500	2018	3,954	Fincantieri (Italy)
Celebrity Cruises	Celebrity Edge	117,000	2018	2,900	STX (France)
Holland America Line	Nieuw Statendam	99,700	2018	2,650	Fincantieri (Italy)
Hurtigruten	Roald Amundsen	25,000	2018	530	Fincantieri (Italy)
Lindblad Expeditions	National Geographic Venture	1,450	2018	100	Nichols Brothers Boat Builders (USA)
MSC Cruises	MSC Seaview	154,000	2018	5,300	Fincantieri (Italy)
Norwegian Cruise Line	TBA	168,800	2018	4,200	Meyer Werft (Germany)
Ponant	Le Champlain	10,000	2018	180	Vard (Norway)
Ponant	Le Laperouse	10,000	2018	180	Vard (Norway)
Royal Caribbean International	Symphony of the Seas	230,000	2018	5,400	STX (France)
Scenic	Scenic Eclipse	16,500	2018	228	Uljanik Group (Croatia)
Seabourn	Seabourn Ovation	40,350	2018	450	Mariotti (Italy)
Star Clippers	Flying Clipper	8,770	2018	300	Brodosplit (Croatia)
TUI Cruises	Mein Schiff 1	111,500	2018	2,894	Meyer Turku (Finland)
Viking Cruises	Viking Spirit	47,800	2018	930	Fincantieri (Italy)
2019					
AIDA Cruises	AIDAperla	183,200	2019	5,000	Meyer Werft (Germany)
Carnival Cruise Line	TBA	135,500	2019	4,200	Fincantieri (Italy)
Costa Cruises (Asia)	TBA	135,500	2019	4,200	Fincantieri (Italy)
Costa Cruises	TBA	180,000	2019	5,000	Meyer Turku (Finland)
Crystal Cruises	Crystal Endeavor	25,000	2019	200	LV Werften (Germany)
Hapag-Lloyd Expedition Cruises	Hanseatic Inspiration	16,100	2019	240	Fincantieri (Italy
Hapag-Lloyd Expedition Cruises	Hanseatic Nature	16,100	2019	240	Fincantieri (Italy
MSC Cruises	MSC Bellissima	167,600	2019	4,200	Fincantieri (Italy)
MSC Cruises	TBA	177,100	2019	4,800	STX (France)
Norwegian Cruise Line	TBA	164,600	2019	4,200	Meyer Werft (Germany)
Ponant	Le Bougainville	10,000	2019	180	Vard (Norway)
Ponant	Le Kerguelen	10,000	2019	180	Vard (Norway)
Princess Cruises	TBA	143,700	2019	3,570	Fincantieri (Italy)
Royal Caribbean International	TBA	168,600	2019	4,180	Meyer Werft (Germany)
SAGA Cruises	Spirit of Discovery	55,900	2019	1,000	Meyer Werft (Germany)
TUI Cruises	Mein Schiff 2	99,700	2019	2,500	Meyer Turku (Finland)
Virgin Voyages	TBA	110,000	2019	2,800	Fincantieri (Italy)

Cruising's Growth

When the first jet aircraft made most former passenger liners redundant, some were scrapped, but others gave birth to the modern cruise industry.

Although Bahamas/Caribbean cruises from Miami resurfaced in the 1950s with a ship named *Nuevo Dominicano* (ex-*New Northland*), it was not until the 1960s that cruising was updated and re-packaged for a society that had an increasing amount of leisure time on its hands.

Thirty three years ago, the first edition of this book listed 120 ships, some of which are still operating in one form or another. Today, that number has grown to over 400, including the small ships operating coastal and inland waterways cruises. But many well-known cruise lines have also gone to the deep blue seabed. Indeed, since 1990 more than 65 cruise companies have either merged, or been taken over, or simply gone out of business, including such well-liked firms as Chandris Cruises, Epirotiki, Renaissance Cruises, Royal Cruise Lines, Royal Viking Line, and Sun Line Cruises.

Some start-up lines, using older ships and aimed at specific markets, also came and went – companies such as American Family Cruises, Festival Cruises, Fiesta Marina Cruises, Premier Cruise Lines, and Regency Cruises. In came new shiny tonnage, complete with vanity logos and adornments painted on all-white hulls – the attributes of the industry's emerging giants. Fresh thinking transformed the design of accommodation, the use of public spaces, and the growing number of food and entertainment venues.

Yield management, a term purloined from the airline industry, was introduced. These days, company executives think of little else, because running a cruise company is all about economics.

Modern cruising is born

In the early 1960s, passenger-shipping directories listed over 100 passenger lines. At that time it was cheaper to cross the Atlantic by ship than by plane, but the introduction of the jet aircraft changed that rapidly, particularly with the appearance of the Boeing 747 in the early 1970s. In 1962, more than 1 million people crossed the North Atlantic by ship; in 1970, that number was down to 250,000.

The success of the jumbo jet created a fleet of unprofitable and out-of-work passenger liners that appeared doomed for the scrapyard. Even the famous big 'Queens,' noted for their regular weekly transatlantic service, were at risk. Cunard White Star Line's *Queen Mary* (81,237 gross tonnage) was withdrawn in September 1967. Cunard tried to fight back with Cunard-Eagle Airways but then formed a short-lived BOAC-Cunard joint venture with the British Overseas Aircraft Corporation, flying 707s and Super VC10s.

Cunard's *Queen Elizabeth,* at 83,673 gross tonnage the largest-ever passenger liner (until 1996), made its final crossing in November 1968.

Ships were sold for a fraction of their value. Many lines went out of business. Those that survived attempted to mix transatlantic crossings with voyages south to the sun. The Caribbean (including the Bahamas) became appealing, cruising became an alternative, and an entire new industry was born, with new lines being formed exclusively for cruising.

Then smaller, more specialized ships arrived, capable of accessing the tiny ports of developing Caribbean islands; there were no commercial airlines taking vacationers to the Caribbean then, and few hotels. Companies established their headquarters in Florida. Cruising was reborn. California became the base for cruises to the Mexican Riviera, while Vancouver was the focus for summer cruises to Alaska.

Flying passengers to embarkation ports was the next logical step, and soon a working relationship emerged between the cruise lines and the airlines. Air/sea and 'sail and stay' packages thrived – joint

Cunard linked up with BOAC in the early 1960s.

Disney Dream features AquaDuck, the first-ever shipboard water coaster.

resort ships that offer ice-skating, rock climbing, golfing, rollerblading, wave surfing, bowling, even 'skydiving,' and so on, as well as dining at fine restaurants that offer varied cuisines, relaxing in luxurious spas, and being entertained by high-quality shows. And there are many more places to visit than ever, from Acapulco to Antarctica, Bergen to Bermuda, Dakar to Dominica, and St Thomas to Shanghai.

The 'small is beautiful' concept has really taken hold in the cruising world, particularly with the more upscale/exclusive brands. Cruise lines with high-quality, low-capacity ships can provide a highly personalized range of services and top-level hospitality. This means better-trained, more-experienced staff serving fewer passengers and higher-quality food, with more meals cooked to order. Small ships can also visit the less-crowded ports.

Some cruise lines have expanded by 'stretching' their ships – accomplished by cutting a ship in half and inserting a newly constructed midsection, thus instantly adding more accommodation and public rooms, while maintaining the same draft.

Ships that have been 'stretched' (with year and length of 'stretch') include: *Albatros* (1983, 91ft/27.7m), *Balmoral* (2007, 98.4ft/30m), *Berlin* (1986, 65.6ft/20m), *Black Watch* (1981, 91ft/27.7m), *Boudicca* (1982, 91ft/27.7m), *Braemar* (2008, 102.4ft/31.2m), *Enchantment of the Seas* (2005, 72.8ft/22.2m), *MSC Armonia* (2014, 82ft/25m), *MSC Lirica* (2015, 82ft/25m), *MSC Opera* (2015, 82ft/25m), *MSC Sinfonia* (2015, 82ft/25m), *SuperStar Aquarius* (1998, 131.2ft/40m), *SuperStar Gemini* (1998, 131.2ft/40m) and *Thomson Dream* (1990, 131.2ft/40m).

cruise and hotel vacations with inclusive pricing. Some old liners came out of mothballs, purchased by emerging cruise lines and refurbished for warm-weather cruising operations with their interiors redesigned and refitted. During the late 1970s, the modern cruise industry grew at a rapid rate.

Cruising today

Today's cruise concept hasn't changed much from that of earlier days, although it has been improved, refined, expanded, and packaged for ease of consumption. Cruising today attracts people of all ages, socio-economic backgrounds, and tastes. It's no longer the shipping business, but the hospitality industry.

When I first started sailing (in 1965, ships had almost no air conditioning, only forced air ventilation), the voltage was direct current (not alternating current, as now), bell boys attended elevators, there were no show lounges, computers, or fresh water pools (or showers), or vacuum toilets. Although ships have long been devoted to eating and relaxation in comfort, they now offer a greater number of activities, and more learning and life-enriching experiences than ever. For the same prices as a quarter of a century ago, you can cruise aboard the latest large

Exclusivity

Exclusive communities at sea are proliferating. These 'gated' areas are for those paying extra to live in a larger suite and gain access to 'private' facilities, concierge lounges, and private sunbathing areas. Ships that have them: *MSC Divina*, *MSC Fantasia*, *MSC Preziosa*, *MSC Splendida*, *Norwegian Breakaway*, *Norwegian Epic*, *Norwegian Escape*, *Norwegian Gem*, *Norwegian Getaway*, *Norwegian Jade*, and *Norwegian Pearl*. Two-class cruising – in some cases, three-class cruising – is very much in vogue.

PIER PRESSURE

Bigger ships can mean overcrowded ports. The most congested ports – where several ships carrying thousands of passengers may be in port at the same time – include the following:
Caribbean/Bahamas: Antigua, Barbados, Grand Cayman, Nassau, St. Maarten, St. Thomas.
Europe/Mediterranean: Barcelona, Civitavecchia (the port for Rome), Kuşadasi, Venice.
Other ports: Cabo San Lucas, Juneau, Ketchikan, Mazatlan, Sydney.

Frequently Asked Questions

Many cruise brochures are hype over reality. We answer the questions about ocean cruising most frequently asked by those new to this type of vacation and by experienced passengers.

Cruises are packaged vacations, offering overall good value for money, with your accommodation, meals, and entertainment included. But it's the little hidden extras that are not made clear in the brochures that you have to look out for. Some ships have 'drinks-inclusive' fares, while others let you choose from one of several 'beverage packages' on offer.

Here are some of the most commonly asked questions, covering those items that the brochures often gloss over.

Is cruising good value?

Yes, it is. In fact, it's never been better, thanks in part to the economic downturn that forced cruise lines to offer more incentives – such as onboard credit, cabin upgrades, and other perks – in an effort to keep their companies afloat and their ships full.

The price of your vacation is protected by advance pricing, so you know before you go that your major outgoings have already been set. A fuel surcharge is the only additional cost that may change at the last minute.

Isn't cruising expensive?

Compare what it would cost on land to have all your meals and entertainment provided, as well as transportation to different destinations, fitness and sports facilities, leisure activities, educational talks, parties, and other social functions, and you'll see the remarkable value of a cruise.

What you pay determines the size, location, and style of accommodation. The choice ranges from basic to luxury, so give yourself a budget, and ask your professional travel supplier how to make the best use of it.

Is the brochure price firm?

Cruise brochure prices are set by cruise line sales and marketing departments. It's the price they would like to achieve to cover themselves against currency fluctuations, international bonding schemes, and the like. But discounts attract business, and so there is always some leeway. Also, travel agents receive a commission. As a consumer, always ask for the 'best price,' watch for special offers in newspapers and magazines, and talk to your travel agent – they may even rebate some of their commission, something they are not allowed to advertise on their websites.

How do I get the best discount?

Book ahead for the best discounts, as they normally decrease closer to the cruise date. You can reserve a cabin grade, but not a specific cabin – 'TBA' (to be assigned). The first cabins to be sold out are usually those at minimum and maximum prices. Note: premium rates usually apply to Christmas/New Year cruises. Make sure that all port charges, government fees, and any additional fuel surcharges are included in the quote.

Although bargains do exist, always check what's included. Highly discounted fares may apply only to certain dates and itineraries; for example, the eastern Caribbean instead of the more popular western Caribbean.

A bargain price may be subject to a booking deadline or may be 'cruise only,' so you must arrange your own air transportation. If air transportation *is* included, changes or deviations may not be possible.

Your accommodation choice, grade, and location may not be available. You could be limited to first seating for dinner aboard a two-seating ship (possibly less convenient, if you are busy with activities or excursions during the day). Also, highly discounted fares may not apply to children, and port charges, handling fees, fuel surcharges, or other taxes may be extra.

Hanseatic passengers exploring a new destination.

Queen Mary 2 has 24 kennels on board.

Should I use the internet or a travel agent?

You've found an ideal cruise online – fine. But, if a cruise line suddenly offers special discounts for your sailing, or cabin upgrades, or if things go wrong with your booking, your internet booking service may prove difficult to access for post-purchase questions. Your travel agent, however, can probably make special discounts work for you and perhaps even provide upgrades.

The internet may be a useful resource tool, but I would not recommend it as the place to book your cruise, unless you know exactly what you want, and can plan ahead – and it doesn't work for groups. You can't ask questions, and much of the information provided is marketing hype. Most websites providing cruise ship reviews have paid advertising, or something to sell, and the sound-bite information can be misleading. Be aware that many internet booking agents are unlicensed and unregulated, and some add a 'booking fee.'

If you book with an internet-based cruise agency, you should confirm with the cruise line that the booking has been made and that any payments have been received. Large travel agency groups and consortiums often reserve large blocks of cabins, while smaller independent agencies can access extensive discounts not available on the internet. Furthermore, cruise lines consider travel agents as their preferred distribution system and provide special discounts and value-added amenities not available online.

Do travel agents charge for their services?

Travel agents do not charge for their services, but they earn a commission from cruise lines. Consider a travel agent as your business advisor, not just a ticket agent. They will handle all matters relevant to your booking including the latest information on changes of itinerary, cruise fares, fuel surcharges, discounts, and travel and cancellation insurance in case you have to cancel for any reason prior to sailing.

Your travel agent should find exactly the right ship for your needs and lifestyle. Some sell only a limited number of cruise lines (known as 'preferred suppliers'), because they receive 'overrides' on top of their normal commission. (They may know their limited number of ships well, however.)

Note that some travel agents may charge for booking airline tickets.

How do I get my tickets?

Most cruise lines have changed to online bookings and check-in. You'll need to print your own boarding passes, travel documents, and luggage tags. If you go through a cruise-travel agent, they can print these for you.

Your printed documents will allow you to pass through the port's security station to get to your ship. Only the more exclusive, upscale cruise lines, expedition companies, and sail-cruise ship lines provide boxes or wallets packed with documents, cruise tickets, leather (or faux-leather) luggage tags, and colorful destination booklets – cruise lines operating large resort ships have all but abandoned such niceties.

Should I purchase cancellation insurance?

Yes, if it is not included, as cruises (and air transportation to/from them) must be paid in full before tickets are issued. If you cancel at the last minute – even for medical reasons – you could lose the whole fare. Pay by credit card, if you have one, as you're then more likely to get your money back if the agency goes bust.

Cruise lines typically accept cancellations more than 30 days before sailing, but all of them charge full fare if you don't turn up on sailing day. Many lines do not return port taxes, which are not part of the cruise fare.

10 QUESTIONS TO ASK A TRAVEL AGENT

1. Is air transportation included in the cabin rate quoted? If not, how much will it be? What other costs will be added – these can include port charges, insurance, gratuities, shore excursions, laundry, and drinks?
2. What is the cruise line's cancellation policy?
3. If I want to make changes to my flight, routing, dates, and so on, are there any extra charges?
4. Does your agency deal with only one, or several different insurance companies?
5. Does the cruise line offer advance booking discounts or other incentives?
6. Do you have preferred suppliers, or do you book any cruise on any cruise ship?
7. Have you sailed aboard the ship I want to book or that you are recommending?
8. Is your agency bonded and insured? If so, by whom?
9. Is insurance included if I book the shore excursions offered by the cruise line?
10. Can I occupy my cabin on the day of disembarkation until I am ready to disembark?

Travel insurance

Cruise lines and travel agents routinely sell travel cover policies that, on close inspection, appear to wriggle out of payment due to a litany of exclusion clauses. Examples include pre-existing medical conditions (ignoring this little gem could cost you dearly) and valuables left unattended on a tour bus, even if the guide says it is safe and that the driver will lock the door.

Won't I get bored?

Whether you want to lie back and be pampered, or be active nonstop, you can do it on a cruise. Just being at sea provides an intoxicating sense of freedom that few places on land can offer. And, in case you think you may feel cut off without contact, almost all large resort ships (those carrying over 2,501 passengers) have ship-wide Wi-Fi, internet access, movies, and digital music libraries.

Why is it so expensive for solo travelers?

Almost all cruise lines base their rates on double occupancy, so when you travel alone the cabin portion of your fare reflects an additional supplement. Although most new ships are built with cabins for double occupancy, some companies may find a cabin mate for you to share with, if you so desire. However, in cabins with three or four berths (two beds plus upper berths), personal privacy doesn't exist. Some companies sell two-bed cabins at a special single rate. Also, some companies schedule a solo travelers get-together, usually on the first or second day of a cruise.

How about holiday season cruises?

Celebrating the festive lifestyle is even more special aboard ship, where decorations add to the sense of occasion. However, the large resort ships are usually full during the main holiday periods. (Don't travel at these busy times, if you want to have the facilities of a large resort ship but want to be able to relax.)

What about 'Spring Break' cruises?

If you take a cruise aboard one of the large resort ships (the most popular brands for these are Carnival Cruise Lines, Norwegian Cruise Line, and Royal Caribbean International) during the annual Spring Break (usually in March) expect to find hordes of students causing mayhem.

Do cruise lines have loyalty programs?

Many companies have loyalty clubs or programs, which offer discounts, credits, and onboard benefits unavailable to non-members. Programs are based either on the number of cruises taken, or, more fairly, on the number of nights sailed. There's no charge to join, but many benefits to gain if you keep cruising with the same line.

Some companies allow you to transfer point levels to a sister brand. There are usually several levels (a maximum of six at present), such as Silver, Gold, Platinum, Diamond, Titanium, etc., depending on the cruise line. Reaching the higher levels requires more effort because the cruise companies are overwhelmed by the sheer number of passengers in their respective clubs/programs.

Father and son playing table tennis aboard a Carnival ship.

A birthday aboard a Carnival Cruise Line ship.

Is there enough to keep kids busy?
Most cruises provide families with more quality time than any other type of vacation, and family cruising is the industry's largest growth segment, with activities tailored to various age groups.

Do we need to take towels and soap?
No. Both of these are provided by the cruise ship. Some ships have individual soaps, and some fit liquid soap and shampoo in wall-mounted dispensers. Towels for the pool deck are provided either in your cabin or by the pool.

Do cruise ship pools have lifeguards?
In general, no, except for Disney Cruise Line, Norwegian Cruise Line and Royal Caribbean International.

Do youth programs operate on port days?
Most cruise lines also operate programs on port days, although they won't be as extensive as on days at sea.

Are there adults-only ships?
Companies that operate small and mid-size adults-only ships include Cruise & Maritime Voyages (Columbus, Magellan, Marco Polo), P&O Cruises (Adonia, Arcadia, Oriana), and Saga Cruises (Saga Pearl II, Saga Sapphire). The minimum age may be different depending on the company, so do check for the latest information.

Can cruise lines provide a daily program for each day at the beginning of the cruise, so that I can plan my stay and activities accordingly?
Apart from minor changes that may need to be made each day (due to weather conditions, or substitutions), there's no reason why this can't be done.

How can I celebrate a birthday or anniversary?
If you have a birthday or anniversary or other special occasion to celebrate during your cruise, let the cruise line know in advance. They should be able to arrange a cake for you, or a special 'Champagne breakfast' in bed. Some cruise lines offer anniversary packages – for a fee – or a meal in an alternative restaurant, where available.

Do cruises suit honeymooners?
Absolutely. A cruise is the ideal setting for romance, for shipboard weddings aboard ships with the right registry (they can also be arranged in some ports, depending on local regulations), receptions, and honeymoons. And for those on a second honeymoon,

10 TIPS TO GET THE BEST TRAVEL INSURANCE

1. Shop around. Don't accept the first travel insurance policy you are offered.
2. If you purchase travel cover online, check the credentials of the company underwriting the scheme. Deal with well-established names instead of automatically taking what appears to be the cheapest deal.
3. Read the contract carefully and make sure you know exactly what you are covered for.
4. Beware the 'box ticking' approach to travel cover, which is often done quickly in lieu of providing proper advice. Insurers should not be allowed to apply exclusions that have not been clearly pointed out to you.
5. Ask for a detailed explanation of all exclusions, excesses, and limitations.
6. If you purchase your own air transportation, check whether your insurance policy covers you if the airline fails, or if bad weather prevents you

from joining your ship on time.
7. Check the procedure you need to follow if you are the victim of a crime, such as your wallet or camera being stolen while on a shore excursion.
8. If you are a crime victim, obtain a police report as soon as possible. Many insurance policies will reimburse you only for the second-hand value of any lost or stolen items, rather than the full cost of replacement, and you may have to produce the original receipt for any such items claimed.
9. Look out for exclusions for 'hazardous sports.' These could include activities offered as shore excursions such as horseback riding, cycling, kayaking, jet skiing, or ziplining.
10. Different countries have different requirements for travel insurance providers. Be sure to check the details in the country where you purchased your policy.

many ships can perform a 'renewal of vows' ceremony; some will make a charge for this service.

Do some people really live on board?

Yes! There are several 'live aboard' passengers who simply love traveling the world continuously – and why not? They sell their house, put possessions into storage, step on board, and disembark only when the ship has to go into dry dock for refits.

Is a repositioning cruise cheaper?

When ships move from one cruise region to another, it is termed repositioning. When ships move between the Caribbean and Europe, typically in April/May, or between Europe and the Caribbean (typically in October/November), for example, the cruise fares are usually discounted. The ships rarely sail full, and offer excellent value for money. Some cruise lines use this time to do essential maintenance work, so always check before you book to make sure that all facilities will be available.

How inclusive is all-inclusive?

It usually means that transportation, accommodation, food, and entertainment are wrapped up in one neat package. If drinks are included, it's mostly a limited range of low-quality brands chosen by the cruise line, and bartenders tend to be overgenerous with ice for cocktails. 'Mostly inclusive' might be a better term to use.

Tell me more about extra costs

While cruise lines offer appealingly low fares, most try hard to maintain revenues by increasing the cost of onboard choices (particularly for specialty restaurants), including beverages. Expect to spend at least $25 a day per person on extras, plus $10–15 a day per person in gratuities (unless they are included). Here are the approximate prices per person for a typical seven-day cruise aboard a well-rated mid-size or large resort ship, based on an outside-view two-bed cabin:

Cruise fare: $1,000
Port charges: $100 (if not included)
Gratuities: $50
Total cost per person: $1,150

This is less than $165 per person per day, which seems reasonable when you consider all it covers.

However, your seven-day cruise can easily become more expensive when you start adding on any extras, such as excursions, cappuccinos, drinks (unless they are included), mineral water, internet access, gratuities, and other items. Allowing about $1,000 extra per person may be a good idea.

More examples of extra-cost items (these are provided only as guidelines, and may have changed since this book was completed, so always check with the cruise line, onboard concession, or your travel provider for the latest prices) may include:

Aqua Spa use: $30–35 per day

Babysitting (per hour): $10
Bottled water: $2.50–7 (per bottle)
Cappuccino/espresso: $2.50–4.50
Cartoon character bedtime 'tuck-in' service: $20–25
Dry-clean dress: $8–10
Dry-clean jacket: $8–10
Golf simulator: $25 (30 minutes)
Group cycling class: $11
Hair wash/set: $40–75
Haircut (men): $30
Ice cream: $2.50–4
In-cabin (on-demand) movies: $6.95–12.95
Internet connection: $0.50–0.95 per minute
Laundry: wash one shirt: $3–4
Laundry soap: $1–1.50
Massage: $3-plus a minute (plus tip)
Satellite phone/fax: $4.95–9.95 per minute
Shuttle bus in ports of call: $3–6
Sodas (soft fizzy drinks): $2–3
Souvenir photograph (8x6in/20x15cm): $10–12
Souvenir photograph (10x8in/25x20cm): $20–30
Specialty dining (cover charge): $15–100 each
Wine/cheese tasting: $10–25
Wine with dinner: $7–500
Yoga or Pilates class: $12

What are port charges?

These are levied by various ports visited, rather like city taxes imposed on hotel guests. They help pay for the infrastructure required to provide facilities including

Outdoor breakfast aboard *Seven Seas Voyager*.

The Haven Courtyard aboard *Norwegian Jade*.

docks, linesmen, security and operations personnel, and porters at embarkation and disembarkation ports.

Do cruise lines have their own credit cards?

Most don't, but those that do include Carnival Cruise Lines, Celebrity Cruises, Disney Cruise Line, Holland America Line, Norwegian Cruise Line, Princess Cruises, Royal Caribbean International, Saga Cruises, and Seabourn. Credits are earned for any spending charged to the card.

Should I take a back-to-back cruise?

If you're considering two seven-day back-to-back cruises, for example eastern Caribbean and western Caribbean, bear in mind that many aspects of the cruise – the seven-day menu cycle, one or more ports, all shows and cabaret entertainment, even the cruise director's jokes and spiel – may be duplicated.

Do ships have different classes?

Gone are the official class distinctions. Differences are now found mainly in the type of accommodation chosen, in the price you pay for a larger cabin (or suite), the location of your cabin (or suite), and whether or not you have butler service.

Some cruise lines, however, have a 'concierge lounge' that can be used only by occupants of accommodation designated as suites, thus reviving the two-class system.

Private areas have been created by Cunard, MSC Cruises (Yacht Club), and Norwegian Cruise Line (The Haven) for occupants of the most expensive suites, in an effort to insulate their occupants from the masses. The result is a 'ship within a ship.'

Most companies, however, have in essence, created two classes: (1) Suite-grade accommodation; (2) Standard cabins (either exterior view or interior – no view).

Cunard has always had several classes for transatlantic travel (just like scheduled airlines), but the company's three ships (*Queen Elizabeth*, *Queen Mary 2*, *Queen Victoria*) are classed according to the restaurant and accommodation grade chosen.

Do ships have deck names or numbers?

Ships can have both names and numbers. Historically, ships used to have only deck names (example: Promenade Deck, 'A' Deck, 'B' Deck, 'C' Deck, Restaurant Deck, and so on). As ships became larger, numbers started appearing, as aboard ferries. Note that some ships don't have a Deck 13 (examples include the ships of AIDA Cruises, Carnival Cruise Line, Celebrity Cruises, P&O Cruises Australia – *Pacific Explorer* – and Princess Cruises) or any cabin with the number ending in 13 in it. Dream Cruises ships don't have a Deck 4 or 14 (the number four is considered unlucky for Chinese passengers – Dream's main clientele), while Italian ships do not have a Deck 17, for the same reason (instead, the numbering moves straight on to Deck 18).

Can I eat when I want to?

Most major cruise lines now offer 'flexible dining', which allows you to choose (with some limitations) when you want to eat, and with whom you dine, during your cruise – or a choice of several restaurants. As with places to eat ashore, reservations may be required, you may also have to wait in line at busy periods, and occupants of the top suites get priority.

Aboard large resort ships (2,501-plus passengers) the big entertainment shows are typically staged twice each evening, so you end up with the equivalent of two-seating dining anyway.

What is specialty dining?

Mass-market dining isn't to everyone's taste, so some ships now have alternative dining spots other than the main restaurant. These à la carte restaurants usually cost extra – typically between $15 and $75 a person – but the food quality, preparation, and presentation are decidedly better, as is service and ambience. You may need to make a reservation.

What's the minimum age for drinking alcohol?

Aboard most ships based in the US and Canada, the minimum drinking age is 21. However, for ships based throughout the rest of the world, it is generally 18. But you should always check with your chosen cruise line.

Are drinks packages good value?

Yes, if you like to drink. Note that they can vary hugely between cruise ships in terms of cost, and some also add a mandatory gratuity. Also, the choice may not include your favorite brands.

Can I bring my own booze on board?

No, at least not aboard the major cruise lines, as it will be confiscated. Some smaller lines might, however, turn a blind eye if you bring your favorite wine or spirit on board for in-cabin consumption.

How about service standards?

You can estimate the standard of service by looking at the crew-to-passenger ratio – provided in the ship profiles in this book. The best service levels are aboard ships that have a ratio of one crew member to every two passengers, or higher. The best ships in the world, from the point of view of crew living and working conditions, also tend to be the most expensive ones – the adage 'you get what you pay for' tends to be all too true.

Do ships have room service?

While most cruise ships provide free 24-hour room service, some ships charge a delivery fee for items such as food and beverages, including tea and coffee (particularly late at night). A room service menu will be in your cabin. Aboard sail-cruise ships such as those of Sea Cloud Cruises or Star Clippers, there's no room service.

If you occupy suite-grade accommodation, you may get additional services such as afternoon tea-trolley service and evening canapés, at no extra cost. Some ships may offer room service specialties, for example a Champagne breakfast, at extra cost (Princess Cruises, for example).

Should I tip for room service?

No. It's part of the normal onboard duties that the hotel staff are paid to carry out. Watch out for staff aboard the large resort ships saying that they don't always get the tips that are 'automatically added' to

A spot of social dancing aboard *Queen Elizabeth*.

---

10 MONEY-SAVING TIPS

1. Research online, but book through a specialist cruise-travel agency.
2. Cut through the sales hype and get to the bottom line.
3. Make sure that all taxes are included.
4. Book early – the most desirable itineraries go soonest. If air travel is involved, remember that air fares tend to rise in peak seasons.
5. The best cabins also go sooner rather than later, so book early to get the best one of these at the lowest prices.
6. Book a cabin on a lower deck – the higher the deck, the more expensive will it be.
7. An interior (no view) cabin is cheaper, if you can live without natural light.
8. Be flexible with your dates – go off-season, when fares will be lower.
9. Book an older (pre-1990) ship – the newest ships are more expensive.
10. Purchase travel cancellation insurance – your cruise is an investment, after all.

onboard accounts – it's a ploy to get you to tip them more in cash.

What does a butler do?
The best ships' butlers will have been in private service on land, or will have been trained at one of the accredited specialist schools in London. A good butler should be educated, able to communicate well, provide unobtrusive service, and anticipate what might be required.

They should learn your likes and dislikes, such as how you want your tea, how you like your fresh juice in the morning, or how you want your ties laid out – whether rolled and placed in a drawer, or hung over a tie rack. And a good butler ought to remember your preferences should you return to the same ship.

Do any special food events take place?
In addition to birthdays, anniversaries and other celebrations, special events, or special celebration dinners, or 'foodertainment' event may be featured once each cruise. Examples of this include a Champagne Waterfall (Princess Cruises) and Rijsttafel (pronounced 'rice-taffle'), rice-based Indonesian food to which small items of meat, seafood, and vegetables are added (Holland America Line).

Some cruise lines feature a British Pub Lunch (featuring fish and chips, or sausages and mash) or late-morning 'Frühschoppen' (German sausages, pretzels, and beer). Others still offer an old standby, the Baked Alaska Parade, also known as 'Flaming Bombé Alaska.' This usually happens on the night before the last night of a typical cruise (also known as 'Comment Form Night'), although some companies have replaced this with a Chef's Parade. Traditionally, February 1 is the official Baked Alaska Day.

Do ships still serve bouillon on sea days?
Some ships carry on the tradition of serving or making bouillon available at 11am each sea day. Examples include the ships of Cunard, Fred. Olsen Cruise Lines, Hapag-Lloyd Cruises, Hebridean Island Cruises, P&O Cruises, Phoenix Reisen, Saga Cruises, and Voyages to Antiquity.

Do all ships have self-service launderettes?
Some cruise lines do (AIDA Cruises, Carnival Cruise Line, Cunard, Holland America Line, Princess Cruises), and some don't (Celebrity Cruises, Costa Cruises, MSC Cruises, Norwegian Cruise Line, Royal Caribbean International). Companies that don't have them may offer 'family bundles' at a special price. Many ships do have a retractable clothesline in the bathroom, however, which is good for those small items.

Do all ships have proper dance floors?
No. For social dancing, a properly 'sprung' wood floor is the best for social (ballroom) dancing. Ships with good, large wooden dance floors include *Asuka II, Aurora, Britannia, Oriana, Queen Elizabeth, Queen Mary 2,* and *Queen Victoria.*

Do all ships have swimming pools?
The largest is the half Olympic size (82ft/25m in length) pool aboard *Mein Schiff 3, Mein Schiff 4, Mein Schiff 5,* and *Mein Schiff 6.* Most, however, are a maximum of just over 56ft (17m) long and 19.6ft (6m) wide. They are usually located on one of the uppermost decks of a ship for stability.

Some ships have multi-pool complexes that include water slides (examples: *Allure of the Seas, Carnival Sunshine, Harmony of the Seas, Norwegian Bliss, Norwegian Breakaway, Norwegian Epic, Norwegian Escape, Norwegian Getaway, Norwegian Joy,* and *Oasis of the Seas*). Some ships have 'infinity' pools on an aft deck, so, when you swim or take a dip, it looks like you're at one with the sea (*MSC Divina, MSC Preziosa, Viking Sea, Viking Sky, Viking Star, and Viking Sun*).

Some ships have completely separate adult-only, family pools, and toddler pools, such as *Disney Dream, Disney Fantasy, Disney Magic,* and *Disney Wonder.* The family-friendly large resort ships usually have separate pools and tubs for children in different

FIVE RIP-OFFS TO WATCH OUT FOR

1. Internet charges. Cruise lines often overcharge for use of the internet (connections are by satellite).

2. Currency conversion. Using a foreign credit card to pay your account means you could incur unseen currency conversion charges, known in the trade as dynamic currency conversion (DCC). When you pay your bill, the price quoted is recalculated into a 'guaranteed' price, often higher than the rate quoted by banks or credit card companies.

3. Double gratuities. Some cruise lines typically imprint an additional gratuity line on signable receipts for such things as spa treatments, extra-cost coffees, and other bar charges, despite a 15 percent gratuity having already been added. Example: for an espresso coffee costing $2.80, a 15 percent tip of 40 cents is added, thus making the total cost $3.22. You sign the receipt, but one line above the signature line says 'Additional Gratuity' – thus inviting you to pay a double gratuity.

4. Transfer buses. The cost of airport transfer buses in some ports, such as Athens and Civitavecchia (the port for Rome). A cheaper option is to take the train instead.

5. Mineral water. The cost of bottled mineral water for shore excursions. Example: one cruise line charges $4.50, but then adds another 15 percent gratuity 'for your convenience.' Budget accordingly.

Poolside movie screens adorn large resort ships, including *Carnival Sunshine*.

age groups located within a children-only zone, or a water park with fabulous water slides.

Some ships have pools that can be covered by retractable glass domes – useful in case of inclement weather; other ships only have open-air pools, yet trade in cold weather areas in winter. A few ships have heated pools – examples include *Freedom of the Seas, Independence of the Seas, Liberty of the Seas,* and *Saga Sapphire*.

While most pools are outside, some ships also have indoor pools set low down in the ship, so that the water doesn't move about when sea conditions are unkind. Examples include *Astor, Deutschland,* and *Saga Sapphire*.

Some of the smaller ships have only a 'dip' pool – just big enough to cool off in on hot days – while others may have hot tubs and no pool.

Note that when there is inclement weather, swimming pools are emptied to avoid the water sloshing around.

Do all ships have freshwater pools?

All the ships of Disney Cruise Line and most of the large resort ships (such as *Allure of the Seas* and *Oasis of the Seas*) have freshwater pools. Some ships, however, do have saltwater pools, with the water for the pools being drawn from the sea, and filtered.

How are swimming pools kept clean?

All shipboard swimming pools have chlorine – a member of the residual halogen group – added (a minimum of 1.0–3.0 ppm in recirculated swimming pools), while some have chemically treated saltwater pools. Pools are regularly checked for water-flow rates, pH balance, alkalinity, and clarity – all of which are entered into a daily log.

Do any ships have walk-in pools (instead of steps)?

Not many, because of space considerations, although they can often be useful for older passengers. Some ships do, however (*Aurora, Crystal Serenity, Crystal Symphony,* and *Oriana,* for example).

What's the difference between an outside and an interior cabin?

An 'outside' (or 'exterior') cabin has a window (or porthole) with a view of the outside, or there is a private balcony for you to step on to to be outside. An 'interior' (or 'inside') cabin means that it doesn't have a view of the outside, although it may have a 'virtual' window or balcony.

Some balcony cabins appear rather cheap. Is there a catch?

It may be cheaper because it has an obstructed view – often because it's in front of a lifeboat. Always check the deck plan, because it may be that it's only partially obstructed.

Can I visit the bridge?

Usually not – for insurance and security reasons – and never when the ship is maneuvering into and out of port. However, some companies, such as Celebrity Cruises, Cunard, NCL, Princess Cruises, and Royal Caribbean International, run extra-cost 'Behind the Scenes' tours. The cost varies, but it can be as much as $150 per person.

Can I bring golf clubs?

Yes, you can. Although cruise lines do not charge for carrying them, some airlines (especially budget ones) do. Some ships cater for golfers with mini-golf courses on deck and electronically monitored practice areas.

Golf-themed cruises are popular, with 'all-in' packages allowing participants to play on some of the world's most desirable courses. Hapag-Lloyd Cruises and Silversea Cruises, for example, operate a number of golf-themed sailings.

Do mobile phones work on board?

Most cruise lines have contracts with maritime phone service companies. Mobile phone signals piggyback off systems that transmit Internet data via satellite. When your ship is in port, the ship's network may be switched off, and you will pay the going local (country-specific) rate for mobile calls if you can manage to access a local network.

Are there any ships without in-cabin WLAN wiring? I am allergic to it.

The 94-passenger Sea Cloud II comes to mind, as well as some of the older ships that have not been retro-fitted with WLAN cabling.

Where can I watch movies?

Some ships have real movie theaters, but most don't. Many large resort ships have large showlounges

Europa provides free bicycles for passengers.

that are also equipped for screening movies (mainly in the afternoons), or open-air movie sceens on the pool deck.

Some ships have small-capacity screening rooms, typically for 100–200 passengers, where movies may be shown several times daily, and special rooms for showing 3D, and 4D movies (these often include fast-paced adventure movies, surround sound, and moving seats). Carnival's 4,000-passenger Carnival Vista was fitted with the first IMAX theater at sea; Carnival Horizon now has one, too.

Movies are provided by a licensed film distribution or leasing service. Many newer ships have replaced or supplemented movie theaters with in-cabin infotainment systems (with pay-on-demand movies).

Do all cabins have flat-screen TV sets?

No. Some older cruise ships still have bulky CRT sets, but these are replaced when a ship goes for refurbishment. All new ships have flat-screen TVs.

Are there any ships without televisions?

Yes – the 64-passenger sailing ship Sea Cloud.

Can I take an iron to use in my cabin?

No. However, some ships have self-service launderettes, which include an ironing area. Check with your cruise line.

What is expedition cruising?

Expedition cruises are operated by specialists such as Quark Expeditions, using small ships that have ice-strengthened hulls or specially constructed icebreakers that enable them to reach areas totally inaccessible to standard cruise ships. These vessels have a relaxed, informal atmosphere, with expert lecturers and expedition leaders accompanying every voyage.

What is a Panamax ship?

This is one that conforms to the maximum dimensions possible for passage through the Panama Ca-

15 THINGS NOT INCLUDED IN 'ALL-INCLUSIVE'

1. Dining in extra-cost restaurants
2. Premium (vintage) wines
3. Specialty ice creams
4. Specialty teas and coffees
5. Wine tastings/seminars
6. Internet and Wi-Fi access
7. Spa treatments
8. Some fitness classes
9. Personal training instruction
10. Use of steam room/saunas
11. Laundry, pressing (ironing), and dry-cleaning
12. Personal shopping
13. Professional souvenir photographs
14. Casino gaming
15. Medical services

MS Astor passing through the Pedro Miguel Locks on the Panama Canal.

nal – useful particularly for around-the-world voyages. The 50-mile (80-km) canal transit takes from eight to nine hours.

Is there a cruise that skips ports?
Yes, but it isn't really a cruise. It's a transatlantic crossing, from New York to Southampton, England (or vice versa), aboard *Queen Mary 2*.

Can I shop in ports of call?
Many passengers embrace retail therapy when visiting ports of call such as Dubai, Hong Kong, St. Maarten, St. Thomas, and Singapore, among many others. However, it's prudent to exercise self-control. Remember that you'll have to carry those purchases home at the end of your cruise.

Do I have to go ashore in each port?
Absolutely not! In fact, many passengers enjoy being aboard 'their' ships when there are virtually no other passengers aboard. Also, if you have a spa treatment, it could be less expensive during this period than when the ship is at sea. Many ships have price differentials for sea days and port days.

Can I bring my pet?
No, with one exception: the regular transatlantic crossings aboard Cunard's ocean liner *Queen Mary 2*, which has carried more than 500 pet animals since its debut in 2004 (the one-way cost is $800–1,000 for a single kennel; cats are required to have two kennels – one as a litter tray – at a cost of $1,600). It has 22 air-conditioned kennels for dogs and cats

(no birds) and dedicated kennel attendants. Pets must have the required certification and vaccination against rabies.

Can I fly in the day before or stay an extra day after the cruise?
Cruise lines often offer pre- and post-cruise stay packages – either included or at additional cost. The advantage is that you don't have to do anything else – all will be taken care of. If you book a hotel on your own, however, you may have to pay an 'air deviation' fee if you don't take the cruise line's air arrangements, or you want to change them.

What are the downsides to cruising?
Much-anticipated ports of call can be aborted or changed due to poor weather or other conditions. Some popular ports (particularly in the Caribbean) can become extremely crowded – there can be up to 12 ships at the same time in Barcelona or St. Thomas, disgorging 20,000-plus people.

Many frequent irritations could be fixed if the cruise lines really tried. Entertainment, for instance, whether production shows or cabaret acts, is always linked to dinner times, which can be inconvenient.

What legal rights do I have?
It would seem almost none! After reading the Passenger Ticket Contract, you'll see why. A 189-word sentence in one contract begins 'The Carrier shall not be liable for ...' and goes on to cover the legal waterfront. Check all your documentation very carefully before you travel.

Where did all the money go?

Apart from the cruise fare itself, incidentals could include government taxes, port charges, air ticket tax, and fuel surcharges. On board, extra costs may include drinks, mini-bar items, cappuccino and espresso coffees, shore excursions (especially those involving flightseeing tours), internet access, beauty treatments, casino gaming, photographs, laundry and dry-cleaning, babysitting services, wine tasting, bottled water placed in your cabin, and medical services.

A cruise aboard a ship belonging to a major cruise line could be compared to buying a car, whereby motor manufacturers offer a basic model and price, and then tempt you with optional extras to inflate the cost. Cruise lines say income generated on board helps to keep the basic cost of a cruise reasonable. In the end, it's up to you to exercise self-restraint to keep those little extras from mounting up to a very large sum.

Does a ship's registry (flag state) matter?

Not really. Some years ago, cruise ships used to be registered in their country of operation, so Italian Line ships (with all-Italian crews) would be registered only in Italy, and Greek ships (with all-Greek crews) would be registered only in Greece, etc. To avoid prohibition, some American-owned ships were re-registered to Panama. Thus was born the flag of convenience, now called the 'Flag State.'

Today's ships no longer have single-nationality crews, however, so where a ship is registered is not of such great importance. Cunard and P&O Cruises ships, for example, are now registered in Bermuda, so that weddings can be performed on board.

Today, the most popular flag registries are (in alphabetical order): the Bahamas, Bermuda, Italy, Japan, Malta, the Marshall Islands, Panama, and The Netherlands. This fragmented authority means that all cruise ships come under the IMO (International Maritime Organization, within the United Nations) when operating in international waters – 12 nautical miles from shore. A country only has authority over the ship when it is either in one of its own ports or within 12 nautical miles offshore.

How are ships weighed?

They aren't. They are measured. Gross tonnage is a measurement of the enclosed space within a ship's hull and superstructure (1 gross ton = 100 cubic ft).

Is anyone building a cruise ship powered by liquefied natural gas (LNG)?

Yes. While the main challenge is space to store the fuel, several LNG-powered ships are on order. Meanwhile, AIDA Cruises has dual fuel capability, including LNG. There's also one nuclear-powered cruise vessel: the Russian Arctic expedition ship *50 Years of Victory*, which debuted in 2008.

Why is a coin laid under the mast of ships as they are built?

According to a 2,000-year old shipbuilding tradition, the coin brings good luck, and also protects the ship's keel.

Ships with a shallow draft, such as *Hanseatic*, can get surprisingly close to shore.

How long do cruise ships last?

In general, a very long time. For example, during the *QE2*'s almost-40-year service for Cunard, the ship sailed more than 5.5 million nautical miles, carried 2.5 million passengers, completed 25 full world cruises, and crossed the Atlantic more than 800 times. But the *QE2* was built with a very thick hull, whereas today's thin-hulled cruise ships probably won't last as long. Even so, the life expectancy is typically a healthy 30 years.

Where do old cruise ships go when they're scrapped?

They go to the beach. Actually, they are driven at speed onto a not very nice beach at Alang in India, or to Chittagong in Bangladesh, or to Pan Yo in China – the main shipbreaking places. Greenpeace has claimed that workers, including children, at some sites have to work under primitive conditions without adequate equipment to protect them against the toxic materials that can be released into the environment. In 2009, a new IMO guideline – the International Convention for the Safe and Environmentally Sound Recycling of Ships – was adopted.

Will I get seasick?

Today's ships have stabilizers – large underwater 'fins' on each side of the hull – to counteract any rolling motion, and most cruises are in warm, calm waters. As a result, fewer than 3 percent of passengers become seasick. Yet it's possible to develop some symptoms – anything from slight nausea to vomiting.

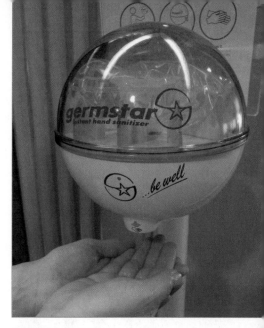

Helping to stop norovirus.

Both old-time sailors and modern physicians have their own remedies, and you can take your choice or try them all, as follows:

When you notice the first movement of a ship, walk back and forth on the deck. You will find that your knees will start to get their feel of balance and counteraction.

Find a place where the sea breeze will blow into your face (fresh air is arguably the best antidote to seasickness), and, if you are nauseous, suck an orange or a lemon.

Eat lightly. Don't make the mistake of thinking a heavy meal will keep your stomach anchored. It won't.

When on deck, focus on a steady point, such as the horizon.

Dramamine (dimenhydrinate, an antihistamine and sedative introduced just after World War II) will be available aboard in tablet (chewable) form. A stronger version (Meclizine) is available on prescription (brand names for this include Antivert, Antizine, Bonine, and Meni-D). Ciba-Geigy's Scopoderm (or Transderm Scop), known as 'The Patch,' contains scopolamine and has proven effective, but possible side effects include dry mouth, blurred vision, drowsiness, and problems with urinating.

If you are really distressed, the ship's doctor can give you, at extra cost, an injection to alleviate discomfort. Note that this may make you drowsy.

A natural preventive for seasickness, said to settle any stomach for up to eight hours, is ginger in powder form. Mix half a teaspoon in a glass of warm water or milk, and drink it before sailing.

'Sea Bands' are a drug-free method of controlling motion sickness. Usually elasticated and available in different colors, they are slim bands that slip onto the wrist. They have a circular 'button' that presses

---

RULES OF THE ROAD

Ships, the largest moving objects made by man, are subject to stringent international regulations. They must keep to the right in shipping lanes, and pass on the right (with certain exceptions). When circumstances raise some doubt, or shipping lanes are crowded, ships use their whistles in the same way that an automobile driver uses directional signals to show which way he will turn. When one ship passes another and gives a single blast on its whistle, this means it is turning to starboard (right). Two blasts mean a turn to port (left).

The other ship acknowledges by repeating the same signal. Ships switch on navigational running lights at night – green for starboard, red for port, plus two white lights on the masts, with the forward one lower than the aft one.

A ship's funnel (smokestack) is one other means of identification, each line having its own design and color scheme. The size, height, and number of funnels were all points worth advertising at the start of the 20th century. Most ocean liners of the time had four funnels and were called 'four-stackers.'

Staring at the horizon helps with seasickness.

against the acupressure point Pericardium 6 (nei guan) on the lower arm. Attach them a few minutes before you step aboard and wear on both wrists throughout the cruise.

Another drug-free remedy is Reletex, a watch-like device worn on the wrist. First used for patients undergoing chemotherapy, it emits a small neuro-modulating current that stops peristaltic waves in the stomach causing nausea and vomiting.

Is having hay fever a problem?

People who suffer from hay fever and pollen allergies benefit greatly from a cruise. Almost all sufferers I have met say that their symptoms simply disappear on a ship – particularly when it is at sea.

Are hygiene standards high enough?

News reports often focus on hygiene and sanitation aboard cruise ships. In the 1980s, the North American cruise industry agreed with the Centers for Disease Control (CDC) that hygiene and sanitation inspections should be carried out once or twice yearly aboard all cruise ships carrying American passengers, and the Vessel Sanitation Program (VSP) was born. The original intention of the VSP was to achieve and maintain a level of sanitation that would lower the risk of gastro-intestinal disease outbreaks and assist the cruise industry to provide a healthy environment for passengers and crew.

It is a voluntary inspection, and cruise lines pay handsomely for each one. For a ship the size of Queen Mary 2, for example, the cost would be $17,940; for a ship the size of Azamara Journey, it would be about $8,970. However, the inspection points are well accepted by the international cruise industry. Inspections cover two main areas: 1) water sanitation, including free chlorine residuals in the potable water system, swimming pool, and hot tub filters; and 2) food sanitation: food storage, preparation, and serving areas, including bars and passenger service pantries.

The ships score extremely well – those that undergo inspections, that is. Some ships that don't regularly call on US ports would possibly not pass the inspections every time. Older ships with outdated galley equipment and poor food-storage facilities would have a harder time complying with the United States Public Health (USPH) inspection standards. Some other countries also have strict health inspection standards. However, if the same USPH inspection standards were applied to restaurants and hotels ashore in the US, it is estimated that at least 95 percent or more would fail.

What about the norovirus?

This temporary but highly contagious condition occurs worldwide. Humans are the only known hosts, and only the common cold is reported more frequently than viral gastroenteritis as a cause of illness in the US. About 23 million Americans each year are diagnosed with the effects of the Norwalk-like virus (NLV gastroenteritis, sometimes known as winter vomiting virus or norovirus). It is more prevalent in adults and older children than in the very young.

Norovirus is part of the 'calicivirus' family. The condition itself is self-limiting, mild, and characterized by nausea, vomiting, diarrhea, and abdominal pain. Although it can be transmitted by person-to-person contact, it is more likely to arrive via contaminated foods and water. Shellfish (most notably clams and oysters), salad ingredients (particular salad dressings), and fruits are the most often implicated in noroviral outbreaks.

A mild and brief illness typically occurs 24 to 48 hours after contaminated food or water has been consumed, and lasts for 24 to 72 hours. If you board a large resort ship after norovirus has struck, bread and bread rolls, butter, and salt and pepper shakers may not be placed on tables, but will be available on request during meals.

When an outbreak occurs, the ship will immediately be sanitized, and affected passengers may be confined to their cabins to stop the condition spreading. Hand gel dispensers are provided at the entrance to all eateries. Crew members and their livelihoods can also be affected, so they will want any outbreak contained as quickly as possible.

Are incidents on the rise? Yes, but so is the number of cruise ships. Should cruise lines pay compensation? I don't think so. In my experience, almost all outbreaks have occurred because someone has brought the condition with them from ashore.

How can you avoid the bug? Don't drink from aircraft water dispensers on the way to join your cruise – they are seldom cleaned thoroughly. And always wash your hands thoroughly after using the toilet, both on the plane and the ship.

Most ships provide liquid gel dispensers as a preventative – at the gangway and outside the dining venues (especially the self-serve buffets). Ships constructed after October 2011 must provide washbasins in buffets (one per 100 seats) under the United States Public Health's Vessel Sanitation Program. Several cruise lines now show a 'Wash Your Hands' video at muster stations following the passenger emergency drill.

What do ships do about garbage?
The newest ships are models of recycling and efficient waste handling. Cooking oil, for example, is turned into biodiesel. Garbage is sorted into dry and wet bins, and the dry garbage is burned on board or compacted for offloading in selected ports. Aluminum cans are offloaded for recycling. As for sewage, ships must be three nautical miles from land before they can dump treated sewage and 12 miles for sewage and food waste.

Where is smoking allowed?
Smoking is generally allowed only in designated areas on open decks. Almost no cruise companies allow smoking in cabins or on balconies. Some lines place a notice in each cabin advising you that a hefty cleaning fee will be added to your onboard account if evidence of smoking in your cabin is found.

Almost all cruise lines prohibit smoking in restaurants and food service areas. Most ships now allow smoking only on the open decks.

What about cigars?
Cigar-smoking lounges are found aboard many ships, but some are now being converted into private lounges for high-rollers (that's gaming, not cigars). These are among the best: *Asuka II, Crystal Serenity, Crystal Symphony, Europa, Europa 2, Seven Seas Explorer, Seven Seas Mariner, and Seven Seas Voyager.* The biggest humidors and the largest selection of cigars can be found aboard *Europa* and *Europa 2.*

Note that the air purification system in a ship's cigar lounge will often not be effective enough if someone comes in to smoke a cigarette, and you may suffer the consequences of inhaling second-hand cigarette smoke.

How about freighter travel?
Slow freighter voyages appeal to independent travelers (about 3,000 passengers annually travel aboard them) who don't require constant entertainment but want comfortable accommodation and the joy of days at sea. For more information, contact the specialists: www.cruisepeople.co.uk/freighters.htm
www.freightertravel.co.nz
www.freightervoyages.eu
www.travltips.com

Collins cigar smokers' lounge aboard *Europa 2.*

Seven Seas Navigator passing the Statue of Liberty

Choose Your Destination

Cruise lines visit around 2,000 destinations, from the Caribbean to Antarctica, from the Mediterranean to the Baltic, and from Northern Europe to the South Pacific.

Where can I go on a cruise? As the saying goes: the world is your oyster. There are more than 30,000 different cruises to choose from each year, and about 2,000 cruise destinations. A cruise can also take you to places inaccessible by almost any other means, such as Antarctica, the North Cape, or the South Sea islands.

Itineraries vary widely, so different companies may offer the same or similar ones simply because these have been tried and tested. Narrow the choice by noting the time spent at each destination call (a few ships may stay overnight in port) and whether the ship docks in port or lies at anchor – it can take time to get ashore by the tender.

Caribbean cruises

There are more than 7,000 islands in the Caribbean Sea, although many are uninhabited. Caribbean cruises are usually destination-intensive, with three or four ports in one week, depending on whether you sail from a Florida port or from a Caribbean port such as Barbados or San Juan. This means you could be visiting at least one port a day, with little time at sea for relaxation, so by the end of the cruise you might need another week to unwind.

June 10 to November 30 is the official Caribbean Atlantic hurricane season (this includes Bermuda, the Bahamas, and Florida). Cruise ships can change course quickly to avoid weather problems, which can also mean a change of itinerary. When that happens, cruise lines will generally not offer compensation, nor will travel insurance providers.

Geographically, the Caribbean region is large enough to be split into sections: eastern, western, and southern.

Eastern Caribbean. Cruises sail to the Leeward and Windward islands, and might include calls at Antigua, Barbados, Dominica, Martinique, Puerto Rico, St. Croix, St. Kitts, St. Maarten, St. Lucia, and St. Thomas.

Western Caribbean. Cruises sail to the Cayman Islands, Mexico, and Jamaica, and might call at Calica, Cozumel, Grand Cayman, Grand Turk, Playa del Carmen, Ocho Rios (Calico), and the island of Roatán.

Southern Caribbean. Cruises might call at Antigua, the Netherlands Antilles (Aruba, Bonaire, Curaçao), Barbados, La Guaira (Venezuela), Tortola, and San Juan.

Cuba, the Caribbean's largest island, which has nine World Heritage sites, holds a fascination for many. Several cruise lines have called there during the past 25 years (examples include Fred. Olsen Cruise Lines, Hapag-Lloyd Cruises, MSC Cruises, Phoenix Cruises, and Thomson Cruises). Cuba now allows a limited number of ships with American passengers.

'Private' island beach days

Several cruise lines with Bahamas/Caribbean itineraries feature a 'private island' day. NCL pioneered the trend when it bought a former military outpost in 1977. So far, it has spent millions upgrading its facilities.

These islands, or secure protected beaches, usually leased from the owning governments, have all that's needed for an all-day beach party. There are no reservations to make, no tickets to buy, no hassles with taxis. But you may be sharing your 'private' island with more than 5,000 others from a single large resort ship.

Such beach days are not all-inclusive, however, and command premium prices for items such as snorkel gear and mandatory swim vest, rental pleasure craft, 'banana' boat fun rides, floating beach mats, private waterfront cabanas for the day, sunfish

Castaway Cay, Disney's private island in the Bahamas.

sailboat rental, floating foam mattresses, and hammock rental. Rent an air-conditioned cabana with private deck and sunbeds for the day (there are just 11 at Harvest Caye, an island base for exploring Belize, at a cost of $499).

One bonus is that such an island will not be cluttered with hawkers and hustlers, as are so many Caribbean beaches. And, because they are 'private,' there is security, and no fear of being mugged.

The most dramatic island experience, however, has as much to do with nature as the beaches. It's MSC Cruises' newly introduced marine reserve island (on a 100-year lease, developed at a cost of $200 million, and open from November 2017). Developed jointly with the Bahamas government and designed by ecologists, it is the most extensive private island experience today.

Alaska cruises

These are popular because Alaska is still a vast, relatively unexplored region. Cruise ships offer the best way to see the state's magnificent shoreline and glaciers. The wide range of shore excursions includes floatplane and helicopter tours, mostly to glaciers and salmon fisheries. Other excursions include 'dome car' rail journeys to Denali National Park to see North America's highest peak, Mt. McKinley.

Pre- and post-cruise journeys to Banff and Jasper National Parks can be made from Vancouver.

There are two popular cruise routes: **The Inside Passage Route**, a 1,000-mile (1,600-km) stretch of protected waterways carved by Ice Age glaciers. This usually includes visits to tidewater glaciers, such as those in Glacier Bay's Hubbard Glacier or Tracy Arm

Crown Princess in Glacier Bay, Alaska.

– just two of the 15 active glaciers along the bay's 60-mile (100-km) coastline. Glacier Bay was established in 1986 as a biosphere reserve, and in 1992 the 3.3-million-acre (1.3-million-hectare) park became a World Heritage Site. Typical ports might include Juneau, Ketchikan, Skagway, and Haines. **The Glacier Route** usually includes the Gulf of Alaska during a one-way cruise between Vancouver and Anchorage. Typical ports might include Seward, Sitka, and Valdez.

Holland America Line and Princess Cruises own many facilities in Alaska (hotels, tour buses, even trains), and between them have invested hundreds of millions of dollars; in fact, Holland America Line is Alaska's largest private employer. Both companies take in excess of 250,000 passengers to Alaska each year. Other lines depend on what's left of the local transportation for their land tours. In ports with limited docking space, some ships anchor rather than dock.

With around one million cruise passengers a year visiting Alaska, and several large resort ships likely to be in port on any given day, there's so much congestion in port that avoiding crowded streets can be difficult. Even nature is retreating; with more people around, wildlife is harder to spot. And many of the same shops found in the Caribbean are now found in Alaska.

The more adventurous might consider one of the more unusual Alaska cruises to the far north, around the Pribilof Islands (superb for bird-watching) and into the Bering Sea.

Alaska can be wet and windy, and excursions may be canceled or changed. Even if it's sunny in port, glaciers have their own weather systems and helicopter flightseeing excursions are vulnerable. Take an Alaska cruise in May or August, when it gets darker earlier, for the best chance of seeing the Northern Lights.

Greenland cruises

The world's largest island, the inappropriately named Greenland, in the Arctic Circle, is around 82 percent covered with ice – actually compressed snow – up to 11,000ft (3,350m) thick. Its rocks are among the world's oldest, yet its ecosystem is one of the newest.

The glacier at Jacobshavn, also known as Ilulissat, is the world's fastest moving, creating a new iceberg every five minutes. Greenland, which was granted home rule by Denmark in 1978, makes a living from fishing. The island is said to have more dogs than people – its population is 68,400 – and dogs are an important means of transport.

Iceland cruises

Cruising around Iceland, located just south of the Arctic Circle, and her fjords is akin to tracing Viking legends across the land of fire and ice. Geysers, lava fields, ice sheets, hot springs, fjords, inlets, remote coastal stretches, waterfalls, snow-clad peaks, and the towering icebergs of Jökulsárlón can all be part of an Icelandic adventure cruise, as can looking for the Northern Lights (Aurea Borealis) at night. Cruis-

A Viking Ocean Cruises ship in Venice.

es typically visit the capital, Reykjavík, and Akureyri, the largest town in the north.

Canada/New England cruises

These 10- to 14-day cruises travel between New York or Boston and Montreal (northbound and southbound). Ports may include Boston; Québec City, Québec; Charlottetown, Prince Edward Island; Sydney and Halifax, Nova Scotia; Bar Harbor, Maine; and Saguenay, Québec.

The ideal time to sail is during the fall, when the leaves dramatically change color. Shorter five-to-seven-day cruises – usually from New York or Boston – go north to take in the fall foliage.

European and Mediterranean cruises

Traveling within Europe (including the Aegean, Baltic, Black Sea, Mediterranean, and Norwegian fjord areas) by cruise ship makes economic sense. Although no single cruise covers every port, cruise ships do offer a comfortable way of exploring a rich mix of destinations, cultures, history, architecture, lifestyles, and cuisines – without you having to pack and unpack each day.

European cruises have become increasingly popular because so many of Europe's major cities – Amsterdam, Athens, Barcelona, Copenhagen, Dubrovnik, Genoa, Helsinki, Lisbon, London, Monte Carlo, Nice, Oslo, St. Petersburg, Stockholm, and Venice – are on the water. It is far less expensive to take a cruise than to fly and stay in decent hotels, paying extra for food and transport. You will not have to try to speak or understand different languages when you are aboard ship (unless you prefer to), as you would ashore – if you choose the right ship. Aboard ship you use a single currency – typically US dollars, British

pounds, or euros. A wide variety of shore excursions are offered. Lecture programs provide insights into a culture before you step ashore.

Small ships are arguably better than large resort ships, as they can obtain berthing space – the large resort ships may have to anchor in more of the smaller ports, so it can take time to get to and from shore, and you'll probably have to wait for shore-tender tickets. Many Greek islands are accessible only by shore tender. Some companies allow more time ashore than others, so compare itineraries in the brochures; it's probably best to choose a regional cruise line (such as Louis Cruises) for these destination-intensive cruises, for example.

Baltic and Northern capitals cruises

A Baltic and Northern capitals cruise is an excellent way to see several countries in a week or so, and enjoy different architecture, cultures, cuisines, history, and stunning scenery. The season for most cruises to this region runs from May to September, when the weather really is at its best.

Copenhagen, Stockholm (the entry through the archipelago is awash with islands and country cottages), Helsinki, Tallinn, and an overnight stay in the treasure chest city of St. Petersburg – for many the highlight of the cruise – with its sumptuous architecture, palaces, and, of course, the Hermitage Museum. Most ships include at least one overnight stay, so that you can also take in a ballet or circus performance.

Norwegian fjords cruises

These cruises usually include a visit to Bergen and a tram ride to the peak of Mt. Floyen, with stunning views over the city and harbor on a good-weather day. A highlight could be a visit to Troldhaugen in

Bergen – the stunning home (and now a museum) of Edvard Grieg, Norway's most famous composer.

However, it's the sheer scenic beauty of cruising through fjords such as Eidfjord, Geirangerfjord, Hardangerfjord, and Sognefjord that inspires travelers. Typical visits will include Bergen, Flåm, Olden, Ålesund, and Oslo.

Around Britain cruises

Traveling around the British Isles' more than 7,455 miles (12,000km) of coastline by cruise ship provides a unique perspective. The major sights – and some unexpected gems – of England, Scotland, Wales, the Republic of Ireland, and Northern Ireland can be covered in a single cruise that typically lasts 10–14 days. Because the British Isles are compact – Great Britain actually consists of thousands of islands – the actual sea time is short. But the range of experiences is vast: the turquoise waters off the Scilly Isles and the coast of Cornwall in England's southwest; the northern highlights in Scotland's more remote, nature-rich islands; the laid-back lifestyle of Ireland; the charm and distinctive voices of Wales; and then there are towering castles, incredible gardens, the England of Shakespeare, and, of course, the coastline itself.

Pride of America sails past the Na Pali coast, Kauai.

Canary Islands cruises

The sun-kissed Islas Canarias, a Spanish archipelago and the outermost region of the European Union, are located just off the northwest coast of mainland Africa – they are actually closer to Africa than Europe. With a year-round temperature of 70 degrees Fahrenheit (21 degrees Celsius) the islands provide a fine setting for a winter escape.

The islands of Gran Canaria, Tenerife, La Gomera, Lanzarote, Fuerteventura, La Palma, and Hierro make up the itinerary of some cruises to the region.

A Canary Islands cruise usually includes a call at Funchal on the Portuguese island of Madeira. Another attraction here is Ponta de São Lourenço, which offers some of the island's most stunning views.

Middle East cruises

The Middle East cruise region includes the Arab countries bordering the Arabian and Red seas, and the southeastern Mediterranean. Countries with cruise facilities and places of historic interest are: Bahrain, Egypt, Iran (one of the author's favorite shore excursions was to the ancient site of Persepolis, near Shiraz), Jordan, Oman, Qatar, and the seven sheikdoms – the governing bodies of the United Arab Emirates (UAE). You will need to carry your passport with you in almost all these countries – it will be available at the ship's reception desk. It is advisable to check current government advice on how safe it is to travel to specific countries in the Middle East – check https://travel.state.gov and www.gov.uk/foreign-travel-advice for further details. Travel warnings can have an impact on your insurance coverage, so it's worth checking. Cruise companies, however, will adjust their itineraries as needed to avoid this being a problem.

Abu Dhabi and Dubai are fast becoming cruise bases, although cruise terminal and handling facilities are still limited. If you visit Dubai, note that displays of affection such as hand-holding or kissing are not permitted in public, and you can't drink alcohol in a public place. If you fly into Dubai with prescription medicines, make sure you have the appropriate, signed prescription.

South Africa and Indian Ocean cruises

Attractions include cosmopolitan cities, wine tours, wildlife safaris, unspoiled landscapes, and uninhabited beaches. Itineraries include sailings starting and finishing in Cape Town, or from Cape Town to East African ports such as Port Elizabeth, Richards Bay, Durban, Zanzibar, and Mombasa (Kenya).

The Mexican Riviera

These typically sail from Los Angeles or San Diego, along Mexico's west coast, calling at ports such as Cabo San Lucas, Mazatlán, Puerto Vallarta, Ixtapa/Zihuatanejo, Manzanillo, and Acapulco. They usually include a stop in the Baja Peninsula, Mexico's northernmost state. Be aware that there has been a

Cruise lines: private islands			
Cruise line	Name of island	Location	First used
Carnival Cruise Line	Amber Cove	Dominican Republic	2015
Celebrity Cruises	Catalina Island	Dominican Republic	1995
Costa Cruises	Serena Cay	Dominican Republic	1996
Disney Cruise Line	Castaway Cay	Bahamas	1998
Holland America Line	Half Moon Cay	Bahamas	1997
MSC Cruises	Ocean Cay Marine Reserve	Bahamas	2017
Norwegian Cruise Line	Great Stirrup Cay	Bahamas	1977
Norwegian Cruise Line	Harvest Caye	Belize	2015
Princess Cruises	Princess Cays	Eleuthera, Bahamas	1992
Royal Caribbean Int.	Coco Cay	Bahamas	1990
Royal Caribbean Int.	Labadee	Haiti	1986

considerable amount of crime even in the most visited ports such as Puerto Vallarta and Manzanillo in the past few years. Also, a number of cruise tourists have been caught out by rip tides and rogue waves when swimming in Cabo San Lucas. There is also a risk of Zika virus transmission in Mexico.

Route Canal (Transcanal cruises)

These take you through the Panama Canal, constructed by the US after the failure of a French effort begun in 1882 with a labor force of over 10,000 but plagued by disease and financial problems – more than 22,000 people died. The US took over the building effort in 1904, and the waterway opened on August 15, 1914, shaving more than 7,900 nautical miles off the distance between New York and San Francisco. The canal runs from *northwest* to *southeast* (not west to east), covering 51 miles (82km) of locks and gates and dams. Control of the canal passed from the US to Panama in 2000.

Between the Caribbean and the Pacific, a ship is lifted 85ft (26m) in a continuous flight of three steps at Gatun Locks to Gatun Lake, through which it travels to Gaillard Cut, where the canal slices through the Continental Divide. It is lowered at Pedro Miguel

PANAMA CANAL LOCKS

While the existing Panama Canal locks measure 963x106ft (293.5x32m), with 39.5ft (12m) maximum draft, the new ones are 1,200x160ft (366x49m), with 49.9ft (15m) maximum draft. They allow almost all cruise ships, including the *Oasis of the Seas*-class and *Queen Mary 2*, to pass through (*Disney Wonder* was the first cruise ship to go through the new locks, in April 2017), although there is still the problem of a bridge at Panama City not being high enough for them to pass underneath. These ships need more than 200ft (61m) of air draft (height from waterline to topmost part of the ship), but the present limit of the Panama Canal is under 190ft (58m).

Locks 31ft (9.4m) in one step to Miraflores Lake, then the remaining two steps to sea level at Miraflores Locks before passing into the Pacific.

Ships move through the locks under their own power, guided by towing locomotives. The 50-mile (80-km) trip takes eight to nine hours. All this effort isn't cheap; cruise ships over 30,000 tons pay a fee of $134 per occupied bed. So, a ship with 3,000 passengers would pay a one-way transit fee of $402,000!

Most Panama Canal cruises depart from Fort Lauderdale or San Juan, calling at islands such as Aruba or Curaçao before entering the canal and ending in Acapulco, Los Angeles, or San Francisco. In 2008, the Inter-American Development Bank approved a $400 million loan to help finance the historic Panama Canal Expansion Program. The new three-step locks feature 16 rolling instead of mitre gates, each weighing around 3,300 tons. It opened in May 2016.

Hawaii and its islands

The islands of Hawaii, America's 50th state, are a tropical feast. Although relatively close together, they have many differences. For example, the lush, Garden-of-Eden-like Kauai is a world away from Oahu, with its urban metropolis of ever-busy Honolulu. The two parts of the Big Island, Kona and Hilo, are really opposites.

Although several cruise lines feature Hawaii once or twice a year, usually on Circle Pacific or special Hawaii sailings, only one ship is allowed to cruise in the state year-round: NCL's US-flagged *Pride of America*. Note that anything purchased aboard, including drinks, is subject to Hawaii sales tax, although this doesn't apply to ships registered outside the US.

South America cruises

Cruises around Cape Horn between Santiago or Valparaíso in Chile and Buenos Aires in Argentina are increasingly popular. The optimum season is November to March, and most cruises last 14 days. However, operating costs are high, because several countries are involved. Pilotage charges, for example, are among the highest in the world. Chile and Peru require compulsory tugs (extra cost). Steep charges for provisioning and supplies, visa complexities, and infrastructure issues all push up the cost.

Sailing southbound, ports might include Puerto Montt (Chile), the magnificent Chilean fjords, Punta Arenas (Chile), and Ushuaia (Argentina), the world's southernmost city and the starting point for many expedition cruises to the Antarctic Peninsula.

Coming up the continent's east coast, ports may include Puerto Madryn (Argentina) and Montevideo (Uruguay). Slightly longer itineraries might include a call at Port Stanley in the Falkland Islands.

A few cruise lines also operate seven-day cruises from Rio de Janeiro, Brazil, mainly for Brazilians – who typically love to dance the night away and don't rise until nearly afternoon. Called 'eat late, sleep late' cruises, these are generally aboard large resort ships chartered to local companies.

For up-to-date information on which countries are affected by the Zika virus, see www.cdc.gov/zika/geo.

Australia and New Zealand

Australia and New Zealand offer a wealth of cruising possibilities, with a growing number of port cities attracting cruise ships. Apart from the major destinations, such as Sydney, Melbourne, Brisbane, and Perth (Australia), and Auckland, Christchurch, and Wellington (New Zealand), there are numerous smaller destinations, such as Adelaide, Cairns, and the Great Barrier Reef.

Then there's Tasmania's Hobart and the stunning former penal colony of Port Arthur, renowned for its beautiful grounds. Scenic cruising along Tasmania's coastline is glorious, particularly in the area such as Wineglass Bay and Great Oyster Bay. The best time to go is November to March, ie summer in Australasia.

The extraordinarily beautiful Kimberley region, in Australia's Northwest Territories, essentially in the area between Broome and Darwin, is a must for chasing waterfalls. The best time to go is in April or May, after the rainy season, for the best waterfall action. Landings are by Zodiac inflatable rubber craft or by helicopter for a visit to the sandstone formation of the 350-million years old Bungle Bungle Range.

Asia cruises

With such a rich tapestry of different countries, cultures, traditions, food, and sights to see, Asia should be high on the list of places to visit for the inquisitive traveler, and what better way to do this than by cruise ship. China, Japan, Indonesia, Malaysia, Singapore, Thailand, and Vietnam can all be visited by cruise ship. Indeed, 'marquee' ports such as Singapore, Hong Kong, Yokohama, and Bangkok are all good points from which to join your cruise. The region has so much to offer that it's worth taking a cruise of 14 days or longer to discover many of the fascinating destinations that await you.

South Pacific cruises

The region is large, and so are the distances between island groups. Still, the area has inspired many people to travel to them to discover the unique lifestyle of its indigenous peoples. The region encompasses French Polynesia, the Marquesas, Trobriand, Pitcairn, and Cook island groups, among others – like string of pearls. Some magical names come to mind – Bora Bora, Moorea, Easter Island, Fiji, and Tonga.

THE OCEANS ON WHICH WE SAIL...

Oceans – large bodies of saline water – form 71 percent of the surface of the earth and are a major component of its hydrosphere. Some 86 percent of the water we drink comes from oceans, and they absorb 48 percent of the carbon that we humans launch into the atmosphere. The world's oceans form an incredible natural recycling organ.

In addition, there are many seas (smaller branches of an ocean). These are often partly enclosed by land, the largest being the South China Sea, the Caribbean Sea, and the Mediterranean Sea.

In size order, the world's five oceans are:
Pacific Ocean. The planet's largest ocean, the Pacific measures a colossal 60,060,700 sq miles (155,557,000 sq km). That equates to some 28 percent of the earth and means it is equal in size to all of the land area of the earth. It is located between the Southern Ocean, Asia, Australia, and the Western Hemisphere.
Atlantic Ocean. The world's second-largest ocean measures 29,637,900 sq miles (76,762,000 sq km) –

a relative puddle compared with the Pacific. Located between Africa, Europe, the Southern Ocean, and the Western Hemisphere, it includes the Baltic Sea, Black Sea, Caribbean Sea, the Gulf of Mexico, the Mediterranean Sea, and the North Sea.
Indian Ocean. Next, at No. 3, is the Indian Ocean, which is just slightly smaller than the Atlantic, at 26,469,900 sq miles (68,566,000 sq km). It is located between Africa, the Southern Ocean, Asia, and Australia.
Southern Ocean. Quite a drop down in size is the world's fourth-largest, and also its newest, ocean, measuring 7,848,000 sq miles (20,320 000 sq km). The Southern Ocean extends from the coast of Antarctica to 60 degrees south latitude.
Arctic Ocean. Finally, there's the Arctic Ocean, which measures some 5,427,000 sq miles (14,056,000 sq km) – a mere baby compared with its big brothers. What it lacks in size (in ocean terms, that is), it makes up for in terms of outreach, extending between Europe, Asia, and North America. Most of its waters are north of the Arctic Circle.

Choose the Right Ship

What's the difference between large and small ships?
Are new ships better than older ones? Here is the latest to
make sure you select the right ship on which to sail away.

There's something to suit virtually all tastes when it comes to which ship to choose. Ships are measured (not weighed) in gross tonnage (GT) and come in four principal size categories, (based on lower bed capacity):

Large resort ships: for 2,501–6,500 passengers (measure 101,001–230,000 gross tonnage).
Think: double-decker bus (with some seats that are better than others).
Mid-size ships: for 751–2,500 passengers (50,001–101,000 gross tonnage).
Think: long-distance coach (comfortable seats).
Small ships: for 251–750 passengers (5,001–50,000 gross tonnage).
Think: mini-van (some are executive types; some are more mainstream).
Boutique ships: 50–250 passengers (1,000–5,000 gross tonnage).
Think: private car (luxury, mid-range, or compact).

Space

For an idea of the amount of the space around you (I call it the 'crowd factor'), check the 'Passenger Space Ratio' given for each ship in the listings section (gross tonnage divided by the number of passengers, based on two lower beds per cabin, plus single-occupancy cabins).
Passenger space ratio:
51 and above: outstanding
31 to 50: very spacious
21 to 30: not very spacious
20 and under: very cramped

Large resort ships (2,501–6,500 passengers)

These ships provide a well-packaged vacation, usually in a seven-day cruise.

However, if you meet someone on the first day and want to meet them again, make it a specific place and time; remember that your new acquaintance may always be at a different meal seating.

It is the standard of service, entertainment, lecture programs, level of communication, and finesse in dining services that can move these ships into high-rating categories. Choose higher-priced suite accommodation, and the service improves. In other words: pay more, get more.

Large resort ships are tightly programmed. It is difficult, for example, to go swimming in the late evening – the decks are cleaned and pools are often netted over by 6pm. Having Champagne delivered to

outdoor hot tubs for a late-night celebration is virtually impossible. The flexibility for which cruise ships were once known has been lost – victims of company 'policy' and insurance regulations. Welcome to 'conveyor-belt' cruising, with few cultural offerings.

Mid-size ships (751–2,500 passengers)

These suit the smaller ports and are more maneuverable than larger ships. Several operate around-the-world cruises and other long-distance itineraries to destinations not really feasible aboard many small ships or large resort ships.

There is a big difference in the amount of space available. Accommodation varies from large 'penthouse suites' with butler service to small interior

Good signage aboard *Celebrity Reflection*.

Advantages and disadvantages of large resort ships	
Advantages	**Disadvantages**
They have the widest range of public rooms and facilities, often a walk-around promenade deck outdoors, and more space (but more passengers).	The itineraries may be limited by ship size, and there may be tender ports where you need to take a number, sit in a lounge, and wait… and wait.
They generally have more dining options.	Room-service breakfast is not generally available on the day of disembarkation.
The newest ships have state-of-the-art electronic interactive entertainment facilities.	They are floating hotels – with many announcements – and many items cost extra. They are like retail parks surrounded by cabins.
You can expect abundant entertainment, including lavish Broadway musicals and Las Vegas-style production shows.	Finding quiet spaces to read a book will be challenging, except in a pay-extra retreat.
There are more facilities and activities for people of all ages, particularly for families with children.	Finding your way around the ship can be frustrating, and signage is often confusing.
Children of all ages will have a whale of a time.	There will be a lack of available elevators at peak times.
They generally sail well in open seas in bad weather.	You may have to use a sign-up sheet to use gym equipment such as treadmills or exercise bikes.
Announcements could be in several languages.	The restaurant service staff is trained to provide fast service, so it's almost impossible to dine at leisure.
The large choice of rooms is likely to mean a large range of price points.	The food is prepared on a large scale – cooking for 5,000 is not quite the same as cooking for a dinner party of eight.
There will be a huge variety of passengers on board – great for socializing.	Telephoning room service can be frustrating due to automatic telephone-answering systems.
There is a wide choice of shopping opportunities for clothing, watches, and jewelry.	There will be lines for embarkation, reception, elevators, buffet meals, shore excursions, security checkpoints, and disembarkation.
The newest ships have large spas with numerous exercise and body-pampering facilities.	In the early evening, deckchairs are taken away, or strapped up, so they can't be used.
There are more outdoor aqua park facilities – popular with families.	The in-cabin music is typically supplied through the television set; it may be impossible to turn off the picture while listening.
There are large casino gaming facilities.	Some large resort ships have only two main passenger stairways.

Royal Caribbean's mega ship *Harmony of the Seas*.

Pool deck aboard *Indepence of the Seas*.

cabins with no view. These ships will generally be more stable at sea than 'small ships,' due to their increased size and draft. They provide more facilities, more entertainment, and more dining options than smaller ships. There is some entertainment and more structured activities than aboard small ships, but less than aboard large resort ships.

Small ships (251–750 passengers) and boutique ships (50–250 passengers)

Choose a small or boutique ship for an intimate cruise experience and a more limited number of passengers. Some of the world's most exclusive cruise ships belong to this group – but so do most of the coastal vessels with basic, unpretentious amenities, sail-cruise ships, and the expedition-style cruise vessels that take passengers to see natural wonders.

Select this size of ship if you don't need much in the way of entertainment, large resort ship facilities, gambling casinos, several restaurants, and if you don't like to wait in lines for anything. If you want to swim in the late evening, or have Champagne in the hot tub at midnight, it's easier aboard boutique or small ships than aboard larger ships, where more rigid programs lead to inflexible, passenger-unfriendly thinking.

What about age?

A ship's condition depends on the level of maintenance it has received, and whether it has operated on short or longer cruises – short cruises cause more wear and tear. Many passengers like older ships, as they tend to have fewer synthetic materials in their interior decor. It's inevitable that most older ships won't match the latest high-tech hardware, but today's ships aren't built with the same loving care as in the past.

Advantages and disadvantages of mid-size ships	
Advantages	**Disadvantages**
They are neither too large, nor too small; their size and facilities often strike a happy balance.	Few have large showlounges for large-scale production shows, so entertainment tends to be more of the cabaret variety.
It is easy to find one's way around.	They don't offer as wide a range of public rooms and facilities as the large resort ships.
They generally sail well in bad weather, being neither high-sided like the large resort ships, nor too shallow draft like some of the small ships.	Most activities will be geared to couples, and single travellers might feel left out.
Lines seldom form, except on ships approaching 1,600 passengers.	Aboard some ships bathrooms may be small and cramped.
They appear more like traditional ships than most of the larger vessels, which tend to be more 'boxy' in shape and profile.	There are fewer opportunities for social gatherings.

An illustrated nature talk aboard *National Geographic Explorer*.

Ships under 10 years old: advantages

Newer ships typically incorporate the latest in high-tech equipment in advanced ship design and construction; they also meet the latest safety and operating regulations.

Many new ships have 'pod' propulsion systems, which have replaced conventional propeller shafts, propellers, and rudders, resulting in little or no vibration, and greater fuel efficiency.

Although the trade-off is debatable, more recent ships have been built with more space given over to the interior public rooms, and less to the topside pool deck, so there's less space for sunbathing.

Newer ships have design advantages as well, including: a shallower draft, which makes it easier for them to enter and leave ports; bow and stern thrusters, so they seldom require tug assistance in many ports, which reduces operating costs; and many have the latest submersible lifeboats, creating a safer operating environment.

Ships under 10 years old: disadvantages

Recent design changes mean that newer ships have thin hulls and do not withstand the bangs and dents as well as older, more heavily plated vessels.

The interior decor is made mostly from synthetic materials, due to stringent regulations, and could cause problems for passengers sensitive to such materials. Most egregiously, newer ships almost always have toilets of the powerful vacuum suction, which I call the 'barking dog' type, due to the noise they make when flushed.

Advantages and disadvantages of small ships/boutique ships	
Advantages	**Disadvantages**
Most provide 'open seating' in the dining room; this means that you can sit with whomever you wish, whenever you wish, for all meals.	They don't have the bulk, length, or beam to sail well in open seas in inclement weather conditions.
They provide a totally unstructured lifestyle, offering a level of service not found aboard most of the larger ships, and no – or almost no – announcements.	They don't have the range of public rooms or open spaces that the large resort ships can provide.
They are at their best in warm-weather areas.	Options for entertainment are more limited than on larger ships.
They are capable of offering true culinary excellence, with fresh foods cooked to order.	The cost – this is the upper end of the market, and doesn't come cheap.
They're more like small inns than mega-resorts.	The size of cabin bathrooms (particularly the shower enclosures) is often disappointing.
It's easy to find your way around, and signage is usually clear and concise.	The range of shore excursion opportunities is more limited.
They provide an 'open bridge' policy, allowing passengers to visit the navigation bridge when it is safe to do so.	Swimming pools will be very small; in fact, they are more like 'dip' pools.
Some small ships have a hydraulic marina water-sports platform at the stern and carry equipment such as jet skis and scuba/snorkeling gear.	Many of the smaller ships do not have balcony cabins because the accommodation decks are too close to the waterline.
They can visit the more off-beat ports of call that larger ships can't.	
When the ship is at anchor, going ashore is easy and speedy, with a continuous tender service and no lines. Access to these less-crowded ports means more exclusivity.	

The biggest of the big

Ship name	Cruise line	Gross tonnage	No. of passengers	Year built
Symphony of the Seas	Royal Caribbean International	227,700	5,488	2018
Harmony of the Seas	Royal Caribbean International	226,963	5,496	2016
Allure of the Seas	Royal Caribbean Int.	225,282	5,400	2010
Oasis of the Seas	Royal Caribbean Int.	225,282	5,400	2009
MSC Meraviglia	MSC Cruises	171,598	4,500	2017
Anthem of the Seas	Royal Caribbean Int.	168,666	4,180	2015
Ovation of the Seas	Royal Caribbean	168,666	4,180	2016
Quantum of the Seas	Royal Caribbean Int.	168,666	4,180	2014
Norwegian Bliss	Norwegian Cruise Line	167,800	4,200	2018
Norwegian Escape	Norwegian Cruise Line LineLineLine	165,157	4,266	2015
Norwegian Joy	Norwegian Cruise Line	165,157	3,900	2017
MSC Seaside	MSC Cruises	160,000	4,140	2017
MSC Seaview	MSC Cruises	160,000	4,140	2018
Norwegian Epic	Norwegian Cruise Line	155,873	4,200	2010
Freedom of the Seas	Royal Caribbean Int.	154,407	3,634	2006
Independence of the Seas	Royal Caribbean Int.	154,407	3,634	2008
Liberty of the Seas	Royal Caribbean Int.	154,407	3,634	2007
Genting Dream	Dream Cruises	151,300	3,360	2016
World Dream	Dream Cruises	151,300	3,360	2017
Queen Mary 2	Cunard	148,528	2,620	2004
Norwegian Getaway	Norwegian Cruise Line	145,655	3,998	2014
Norwegian Breakaway	Norwegian Cruise Line Line	144,017	3,998	2013
Regal Princess	Princess Cruises	142,229	3,600	2014
Royal Princess	Princess Cruises	142,229	3,600	2013
Majestic Princess	Princess Cruises	142,229	3,560	2017
Britannia	P&O Cruises	141,000	3,638	2015
MSC Divina	MSC Cruises	139,400	3,502	2012
MSC Preziosa	MSC Cruises	139,400	3,502	2013
MSC Fantasia	MSC Cruises	137,936	3,274	2008
MSC Splendida	MSC Cruises	137,936	3,274	2009
Explorer of the Seas	Royal Caribbean Int.	137,308	3,634	2000
Voyager of the Seas	Royal Caribbean Int.	137,280	3,634	1999
Adventure of the Seas	Royal Caribbean Int.	137,276	3,634	2001
Mariner of the Seas	Royal Caribbean	137,276	3,634	2004
Navigator of the Seas	Royal Caribbean Int.	137,276	3,634	2003
Carnival Horizon	Carnival Cruise Line	135,000	3,954	2018
Costa Diadema	Costa Cruises	132,500	3,700	2014
Disney Dream	Disney Cruise Line	129,690	2,500	2011
Disney Fantasy	Disney Cruise Line	129,690	2,500	2012
Carnival Breeze	Carnival Cruise Line	128,251	3,646	2012
Carnival Dream	Carnival Cruise Line	128,251	3,646	2009
Carnival Magic	Carnival Cruise Line	128,251	3,646	2011
AIDAperla	AIDA Cruises	124,100	3,286	2017
AIDAprima	AIDA Cruises	124,100	3,286	2015

Quantum of the Seas, Owner's Loft

Choose Your Accommodation

Does cabin size count? Are cabins with an outside view more expensive than interior ones? Are suites sweeter than cabins? How desirable is a balcony (or 'loft') suite? What about location?

Ideally, you should feel at home when at sea, so it is important to choose the right accommodation, even if most of your time in it is spent with your eyes shut. Accommodation sizes range from a very generous 4,390 sq ft (408 sq m) to a minuscule 60 sq ft (5.5 sq m). Choose wisely (dependent on your budget, of course), for if you find that your cabin (incorrectly called a 'stateroom' by some companies) is too small when you get to the ship, it may be impossible to change it, as the ship could be full.

Cruise lines designate cabins only when deposits have been received – they may, however, guarantee the grade and rate requested. If this isn't done, or if you find a disclaimer such as 'All cabin assignments are confirmed upon embarkation of the vessel,' get a guarantee in writing that your cabin will *not* be changed.

There are three main types of accommodation: interior (no-view) cabins, outside-view cabins (with or without balcony), and suites. But, there are many variations on each type (including solo-occupancy cabins).

Cabin sizes

Cabins provide more or less the same facilities as hotel rooms, except space. Most cruise companies favor providing large public rooms over large cabins. In some smaller interior (no-view) cabins, and some outside ones, changing clothes can be a challenge.

Today's ships have more standardized cabin sizes, because they are made in modular form. I consider 180 sq ft (16.7 sq m) to be the *minimum* acceptable size for a 'standard' cabin today. The decor in most, however, is bland, and devoid of personality.

Cabin location

I recommend an 'outside-view' cabin for your first cruise; an 'interior' cabin has no portholes or windows, making it more difficult to get oriented or to gauge the weather.

Cabins in the center of a ship are more stable and tend to be quieter and vibration-free. Ships powered

by diesel engines (i.e., the most modern vessels) create and transmit some vibrations at the stern.

Take into account personal habits or needs when choosing your cabin location. If you like to go to bed early, avoid a cabin close to the disco. If you have trouble walking, choose a cabin close to the elevator.

Generally, the higher the deck, the higher the cabin price, and the better the service (a leftover from transoceanic times, when upper-deck cabins and suites were superior).

Cabins at the front of a ship may be slightly crescent-shaped, given that the outer wall follows the curvature of the ship's hull. But they can be exposed to early-morning noises, such as the anchor being unwound at some ports where the ship is too big to dock.

Cabins with interconnecting doors are fine for families or close friends, but the dividing wall may be so thin that you can hear the conversation next door.

Brochures usually indicate cabins with 'obstructed views.' Cabins on lower decks are closer to engine noise and heat, especially at the stern of the vessel

The lavish Reflection Suite wet room aboard *Celebrity Reflection*.

Seven Seas Explorer suite balcony.

and around the engine casing. In many older ships, elevators may not operate to the lowermost decks.

The suite life

Suites are the most luxurious and spacious of all shipboard accommodation, and typically come with butler service. A suite (in the sense of a 'suite of rooms') should comprise a lounge or sitting room that is separated from a bedroom by a solid door (not just a curtain or half-height room divider), a bedroom with a large bed, one or more bathrooms, and an abundance of closet, drawer, and other storage space. The best suites are in the most desirable position on the ship and have privacy, good views, and the highest-quality bed linen and pillow choice. Many cruise lines inaccurately describe some accommodation as suites, but many are nothing more than large cabins with curtains dividing sitting and sleeping areas.

Be aware that, although large resort ships may devote a whole deck or two to penthouses and suites, their occupants will have to share the rest of the ship with those in lower-priced accommodation. That means there is no preferential seating in the showroom, dining rooms, or on sunbathing decks. Those in suites may get separate check-in facilities and preferential treatment upon disembarkation, but their luggage will be lumped with everyone else's.

'Spa suite' accommodation

Spa suites – not to be confused with the 'thermal spa suites' (comprising sauna, steam room, and herbal showers), which are found in the on-board spa – are usually located adjacent to or near the ship's spa. They often have 'spa-added' features such as a bathroom with window into the sleeping area, bathtub, and mood lighting, and perhaps special health teas or herbal infusions. Some cruise lines may even include a spa treatment such as a massage or facial, in the 'spa suite' package, plus unlimited access to the actual spa.

Examples of ships with spa suites include *Celebrity Reflection*, *Costa Deliziosa*, *Costa Fascinosa*, *Costa Favolosa*, *Costa Luminosa*, *Costa Pacifica*, *Costa Serena*, *Europa*, *Europa 2*, *MSC Divina*, *MSC Fantasia*, *MSC Preziosa*, and *MSC Splendida*. Some ships also have a special spa-food-menu-only restaurant; examples include *Celebrity Eclipse*, *Celebrity Equinox*, *Celebrity Reflection*, *Celebrity Silhouette*, and *Celebrity Solstice*.

Are balconies worth it?

Romeo and Juliet thought so. And they're addictive, too. A private balcony (or veranda, terrace, or lanai), for which you pay a premium, is just that. It is a mini-terrace adjoining your cabin, where you can sit, enjoy the private view, smell the sea, dine, or even have a massage.

Some private balconies aren't so private, though. Balconies not separated by full floor-to-ceiling partitions don't quite cut it (examples include *Carnival Sunshine*, *Carnival Triumph*, *Carnival Victory*, *Oriana*, *Pacific Aria*, *Pacific Eden*, *Queen Mary 2*, *Seven Seas Mariner*, *Seven Seas Voyager*, *Veendam*). You could be disturbed by noise from your neighbor

Many large resort ships have balconies that are too small to accommodate even two reclining chairs; they may have plastic matting or plain painted-steel decking instead of traditional, more expensive hardwood. The average size of a cabin balcony aboard large resort ships is about 9 by 6ft (2.7x1.8m) or about 55 sq ft (5.1 sq m), but they can measure as much as 30 times that.

Suites with forward-facing private balconies may not be so good, as the wind speed can make them all but unusable. Ships with balconies of this kind include *Silver Cloud, Silver Shadow, Silver Spirit, Silver Whisper, Silver Wind, Star Legend, Star Pride,* and *Star Spirit*. And when the ship drops anchor in ports of call, the noise pollution can be irritating – as on *Silver Cloud* and *Silver Wind*, for example.

For the best in privacy, a balcony suite at a ship's stern is hard to beat, and some of the largest afloat can be found there – sheltered from the wind, such as aboard *Marina* and *Riviera* (Oceania Cruises).

The inclusion of a balcony means that space is often taken away from either the cabin or the bathroom, which is why today's bathrooms are smaller and almost none have tubs.

All private balconies have railings to lean on, but some have solid steel plates between the railing and deck, so you can't look out to sea when seated (*Costa neoClassica, Costa neoRomantica, Dawn Princess, Oceana, Sea Princess,* and *Sun Princess*). Better are ships with clear-glass balconies (*Aurora, Brilliance of the Seas, Mein Schiff 3, Mein Schiff 4, Mein Schiff 5, Mein Schiff 6, Radiance of the Seas,* and *Serenade of the Seas*) or ones with horizontal bars.

Balcony doors can be quite heavy and difficult to open. Many ships have doors that slide open (examples: *Crystal Serenity, Grand Princess, Norwegian Gem*); a few have doors that open inward (examples: *Silver Cloud, Silver Wind, Star Breeze, Star Legend, Star Pride*); some have doors that open outward (examples: *Eurodam, Koningsdam, Legend of the Seas, Queen Elizabeth, Queen Victoria*).

French balconies

A 'French' balcony (also called a 'Juliet' or 'Juliette' balcony) is neither French, nor a balcony as such. It is a full floor-to-ceiling sliding door with a tiny ledge that allows you to stick out your toes and smell the fresh air, and with railings for safety.

Interior-view balconies

These are the least expensive balcony options on cruise ships. Aboard Royal Caribbean International's *Allure of the Seas, Harmony of the Seas,* and *Oasis of*

10 THINGS A BUTLER CAN DO

1. Assist with unpacking your suitcase
2. Bring you board games or a pack of cards
3. Bring you menus for dining venues and serve course-by-course meals in your suite
4. Arrange a private cocktail party
5. Arrange for laundry/cleaning items
6. Make dining reservations
7. Provide afternoon tea or canapés
8. Book shore excursions
9. Make your spa reservations
10. Shine your shoes

the Seas, 'interior' balcony cabins are novel. They overlook one of two 'neighborhoods': Central Park, with its trees and plants, or The Boardwalk, at the stern of the ship. However, these really are classed as outside balcony cabins – if it rains, your balcony *can* get wet, but it's unlikely. Also, people scream as they career along the Zipline above the Boardwalk balconies (except on *Harmony of the Seas*), so they can be really noisy by day. And, when no one is zipping, you may have a view of the sea (and perhaps the excellent acrobatic AquaShow) at the ship's stern.

Balconies that lack privacy

If you choose a Riviera Deck (Deck 14) balcony cabin aboard *Azura* or *Ventura*, for example, you can oversee many balconies on the decks below yours – particularly those on C Deck and D Deck – because they are built out to the ship's sides. If you have such a cabin, it would be unwise to sunbathe or sit naked on your balcony. Not only that, but almost *all* balcony cabins can be seen from the navigation bridge, where the staff members are equipped with binoculars (for lookout purposes).

Interior 'virtual' balconies

For the latest in interior design, there's the 'virtual' balcony. Royal Caribbean International's *Anthem of the Seas, Ovation of the Seas,* and *Quantum of the Seas* have them, and so do many interior cabins retrofitted on *Navigator of the Seas*. They give the cabins an 'outside' feel, and feature 6ft 7in (2m) 'screens' with a live video feed from cameras mounted on the front and aft of the ship fed through the ship's computer server and fibre-optic cables. With curtains on either side of the (almost) floor-to-ceiling wall 'screen' (which you can turn off), the 'balcony' is positioned on a forward- or aft-facing cabin wall. Naturally, these cabins command a premium price.

Balconies to covet

Some of my favorite large balcony suites and cabins include Celebrity Cruises' *Celebrity Constellation, Celebrity Infinity, Celebrity Millennium,* and *Celebrity Summit* (6147, 6148, 9096, 9098, 9156, 9197); Cunard's *Queen Mary 2* (9069, 9078, and the Balmoral and Sandringham duplexes at the stern); Hapag-Lloyd Cruises' *Europa* and *Europa 2* (owner's suites 1001, 1002); Oceania Cruises' *Insignia, Nautica,* and *Regatta* (6088, 6091, 7114, 7119, 8064, 8067), *Marina* and *Riviera* (8143, 9147, 10111 – these suites span the ship's entire beam, although the balcony is actually split into two); P&O Cruises *Britannia* (A726, A727; B725, B726; C736, C737; D738, D739; E742, E743; F730, F731; G732, G733); Regent Seven Seas Cruises' *Seven Seas Mariner* (780, 781, 8100, 8101, 988, 989, 1080, 1081), and *Seven Seas Voyager* (673, 674, 781, 782, 970, 971); TUI Cruises' *Mein Schiff 3*, 4, 5, 6 (14000, 14001, 14002, 14003, 14004, 14005, 14006,

14007, 14008, 14009, 14010 – these have a spacious rooftop terrace; also 6176, 6181 'Diamond' suites).

Upstairs and downstairs
Allure of the Seas, Anthem of the Seas, Aurora, Harmony of the Seas, *Oasis of the Seas, Ovation of the Seas, Quantum of the Seas,* and *Queen Mary 2* have 'loft'-style or 'duplex' accommodation, with a living room downstairs and bedroom upstairs.

Family cabins
Although a small number of large resort ships have suites/cabins that can sleep up to 14, the majority of 'Family' cabins accommodate between 3 and 10, with 3 or 4 being the most common (typically these cabins tend to have twin- or queen-sized beds for the adults, and a pull-out sofa bed for the youngsters). In busy school vacation periods, however, these tend to be sold quickly, so try to plan ahead and book early.

An alternative would be to look for cabins with interconnecting doors – good for parents with teenagers, for example; the door can be locked from both sides.

Solo traveler cabins
Solo travelers have long been considered an afterthought by most cruise lines, although some firms are now beginning to appreciate how useful cabins specifically designed for solo travelers can be. Instead of turning away business, companies such as Cunard have retrofitted their ships with several cabins for solos. Interestingly, the now-retired *Queen Elizabeth 2* (or *QE2*, as she was known) had 132 cabins for solo travelers.

Norwegian Cruise Line has approximately 100 trendy, well-designed but small 'studio' cabins for solo travelers aboard *Norwegian Bliss, Norwegian Breakaway, Norwegian Epic, Norwegian Escape, Norwegian Getaway,* and *Norwegian Joy.* SAGA is another company known for its solo traveler cabins. Some cruise lines offer their double-occupancy cabins for solo travelers, but at a special price or at an added percentage – not ideal, but better than nothing.

If you are traveling with friends and in a party of three or more and don't mind sharing a cabin, you'll save money, so you may be able to afford a higher-grade cabin.

How much?
Accommodation cost is related to size, location, facilities, and services. Each line implements its own system according to ship size, age, construction, and profit potential. It may be better to book a low-grade cabin on a good ship than a high-grade cabin on a poor ship, depending on your budget.

Cabin numbers
Nautical tradition aboard ocean-going ships dictates that even-numbered cabins should be on the port side (left when looking forward; the same as the lifeboats), and most companies follow this rule.

Some companies – including Celebrity Cruises, MSC Cruises, and TUI Cruises – have odd-numbered cabins on the port side. Strangely, *Costa neoClassica, Costa neoRiviera, Costa neoRomantica,* and *Costa Victoria* also have odd-numbered cabins on the port side, although all other Costa ships follow nautical tradition. Meanwhile, aboard Royal Caribbean International's *Freedom of the Seas, Independence of the Seas,* and *Liberty of the Seas,* outside cabins have even numbers, and interior cabins have odd numbers. But AIDA Cruises places both even- and odd-numbered cabins on the same side, whether port or starboard side. The admiralty would never approve!

And so to bed
Aboard ship, the bed frames are usually made of steel or tubular aluminum for fire-protection purposes, although some older ships may have (flame-retardant) wood frames. Some have rounded edges, while others have square edges (watch your legs on these), particularly when the mattress is contained within the bed frame.

Some beds have space underneath for your luggage, while others have drawers fitted for additional storage space, so your luggage has to be stored elsewhere in the cabin.

Mattresses
These can be hard, semi-hard, or soft. If your mattress is not to your liking, ask your cabin steward if it can be changed – most ships have spares. Bed boards are also usually available to make the bed firmer.

Some cruise lines provide simple foam mattresses, while others place more emphasis on providing extra comfort. Regent Seven Seas Cruises, for example, provides a custom-designed 'Suite Slumber Bed' – a plush euro-top mattress capped with a dou-

---

10 REASONS WHY PEOPLE LIKE BALCONIES

1. You can access fresh air.
2. You can see the sea.
3. You get the maximum amount of natural light.
4. You can have tea/coffee or breakfast outside.
5. You can see what the weather is like, to decide how to dress.
6. You may see the stars (and shooting stars) at night.
7. You can sunbathe in private – assuming that the ship is in the right position and your balcony isn't overlooked.
8. You can escape from the noise of the entertainment areas.
9. You can take pictures of the sea from within your cabin.
10. You can boast about it to your friends.

SPA suite bathroom aboard *MS Europa.*

ble layer of memory foam and dressed in the finest linens to assure a refreshing sleep.

Ultra-expensive Tempur-Pedic memory mattresses can be found aboard Hapag-Lloyd Cruises (*Europa* and *Europa 2* – on request), and Un-Cruise Adventures (*Safari Endeavor*, *Safari Explorer*, *Safari Legacy*, and *Safari Quest*).

There are differences between mattress sizes in the UK, US, and Europe, depending on which supplier a cruise line specifies when a ship is outfitted or when bed frames and mattresses are replaced.

Duvets

Down duvets, fine bed linens, and plush mattresses are what superior sleeping environments are all about. Duvets are usually goose down or cotton filled, and range from 3.5 togs (thin) to 13.5 togs (thick), the tog rating being the warmth measurement. Anyone with allergies should try a spundown duvet, which is filled with non-allergenic polyester microfiber.

Duvet covers can be for single, double, queen-, or king-size mattresses. If you request a queen-size bed configuration when you book your cruise, request an overlay, otherwise there will be a crack between the beds. Not all ships have these, but the luxury/premium grade ships, and ships with suite-grade accommodation, should do so.

Duvet covers and sheets of 100 percent cotton (up to 400 thread count) are best, but may be more difficult for a ship's laundry to handle. But they do provide those wonderful moments when you slip into bed.

Pillows

Many ships have a 'pillow menu' in suite-grade accommodation. This gives you a choice of several different pillow types, including hop-filled or hypoallergenic, goose down, Hungarian goose down (considered the best), silk-filled, body pillow (as long as an adult body, providing full support at to the head and neck at the top and, lower down, to legs and knees), Tempur-Pedic, isotonic or copycat memory foam.

Facilities

The standard is a small private bathroom with shower, washbasin, and toilet. Higher-grade cabins and suites may have full-size bathtubs. Some have a whirlpool bath and/or bidet, a hairdryer, and more space. Most cabins come with the following: flat-screen television 'infotainment' system or regular television (regular satellite channels or closed circuit); two beds (possibly, another one or two upper berths), or a double, queen- or king-size bed (some twin beds can be pushed together to form a double/queen). Depending on cabin size, they should also have: a chair, or chair and table, or sofa and table, or, in higher grades, even a separate lounge/sitting area; telephone (for inter-cabin or ship-to-shore calls); refrigerator/wet bar (higher grades); electrical outlets for personal appliances, usually 110 and/or 220 volts; vanity/desk unit with chair or stool; personal safe; closet space, drawer space, plus under-bed storage for suitcases; bedside night stand/table unit.

Some older ships may have upper and lower berths. A 'berth' is a nautical term for a bed held in a wooden or metal frame. A 'Pullman berth' tucks away out of sight during the day, usually into the bulkhead or ceiling. You climb up a short ladder at night to get into an upper berth.

Lego Experience on an MSC cruise

Cruising for Families

Cruising can be a great vacation for families, but be sure to choose the right ship for your needs.

More than two *million* under-18s went on a cruise in 2017 – a figure that reflects just how well cruising suits families with children. Cruise ships provide a virtually crime-free, safe, contained environment, and, for younger kids, there are so many fun things to keep them entertained (particularly on the latest ships); for older children and teens, there's plenty to do, giving them a certain level of independence – something that always goes down well. Meanwhile, parents can enjoy vacationing together as a family, and get some well-earned 'me' time. With dining, entertainment, sporting and active outdoor areas, wellness facilities, and more available, it makes it so much easier to combine with parenting. But planning family vacations can be complicated, with so many things to think about. Here's what you need to know.

Family-friendly ships

It goes without saying that you need to choose the right ship. The newest large resort ships have excellent facilities for children of all ages, plus water parks with adrenaline-pumping water slides, rope-climbing courses, and other neat things.

Carnival Cruise Line, Disney Cruise Line, MSC Cruises, Norwegian Cruise Line, and Royal Caribbean International employ whole teams of trained counselors, with special programs off-limits to adults. Other cruise lines may only have token programs in major holidays only, with limited activities and only a few general staff allocated to look after children. Check whether the cruise line offers the right facilities for your needs at other times. Many ships have full programs for children during days at sea, but these may be limited when the ship is in port. If the ship has a playroom, find out if it is open and supervised on every day of the cruise. All programs are included in the cost of your cruise.

Carnival Cruise Line, Disney Cruise Line, MSC Cruises, Norwegian Cruise Line, Princess Cruises, and Royal Caribbean International provide pagers (or wrist bands) for parents; others provide them only for special-needs children. In-cabin telephones aboard some ships can be set to 'in-cabin listening,' allowing parents to call their cabin from any of the ships' telephones, and eavesdrop.

Most cruise lines give children colored bracelets, to be worn at all times. These identify which muster station they belong to in the event of an emergency, as well as showing which children are enrolled in which activity programs.

Some youth programs allow older children (usually 10 and older, but it varies by cruise line) to sign themselves out of youth centers, if authorized to do so by a parent. This makes it easy for children to meet family members somewhere – by the pool or restaurant, for example – or the cabin. If authorization isn't granted, only designated adults can sign them out of programs, typically by showing some ID or by providing a password created at the beginning of the cruise.

Disney Cruise Line, Norwegian Cruise Line, and Royal Caribbean International provide trained lifeguards during pool open hours. Other cruise lines expect parents to watch over their children when using a ship's swimming pools. In 2015, an eight-year-old boy drowned in the pool aboard *Liberty of the Seas*.

Note that a ship's medical department isn't set up for pediatric services, as cruise ship doctors are generalists.

If you book a cruise aboard one of the ships catering to more international passengers, such as Costa Cruises, Dream Cruises, MSC Cruises, or Star Cruises, your youngsters may find themselves surrounded by children speaking other languages. This might be a little confusing to them at first, but in most cases

Noddy aboard *Azura*.

it will prove to be an adventure in learning and communication that adds immensely to their vacation.

Age groups

Cruise lines generally divide young cruisers into distinct age groups. As an example: infants (3 months–up to 3 years); children (3–10); pre-teens (11–12); and teens (13–17).

Cruising with babies and infants

Many new or recent parents want to take their babies with them when they cruise. Check the minimum age requirements for your chosen cruise line and itinerary; they vary according to the cruise, length, and region. By choosing the right ship, a cruise with baby should hopefully be much more enjoyable than most package holidays on land. The biggest attractions include only having to pack and unpack the baby things once, plus the convenience of having everything (food, entertainment, activities, etc.) absolutely on hand. There may also be a crèche/nursery (see below), plus there's always room service, if you prefer to dine in your cabin.

Bottle warmers are available for babies, as are bottle sterilizers – upon request – so there's no need to bring your own. Highchairs are also available upon request for meal times. For babies already on solids, menu items can be pureed and blended for them.

Check the ship's itinerary to see whether the vessel docks alongside in each port. This is easier than being at anchor, when shore tenders must be used; these may require you to go down a rigged ladder to a small boat waiting to take you ashore, which is not easy with an infant in tow.

Check with the cruise line or your travel agent before you book as to what equipment is available, and whether any of it needs to be pre-booked (a refrigerator for milk, for example). Some cruise ships will lend you cribs, strollers (some charge a rental fee), bouncy seats, books, toys, cots, bed guards, and other items.

An inexpensive umbrella-type stroller will prove invaluable in airports, aboard ship (Carnival Cruise Line offers them for rent aboard ship), and ashore. Small is better because it takes up less space in cabins, elevators, and self-serve buffet areas. It will be easier to maneuver at the cruise terminal, and for negotiating open deck areas aboard ship.

Consider taking a car seat for flights, buses, and taxis, and a sling-style baby carrier for hands-free baby carrying when negotiating stairways, and for shore outings.

Request a crib as soon as possible and book as early as you can (ships carry only a limited number). However, while it's fine to order cribs and camp beds, you'll soon find there's little room to move about, so go for as large a cabin as your budget allows. If you have a non-walker, consider a balcony cabin to give you more breathing space – you can relax on the balcony, while your infant naps in the cabin.

Disposable diapers (nappies), wipes, and sterilizing fluid can be purchased aboard most family-friendly ships, but they are expensive, so it's wise to bring your own supplies. If you book a Disney Cruise Line ship, you can order diapers and other products online at www.babiestravellite.com. These will be delivered to your cabin.

SUGGESTED PACKING LISTS FOR INFANTS

Travelling by plane? Suggested items for your carry-on bag.
Diapers (or pull-ups) and changing pad.
Antibacterial wipes (take plenty).
Snacks.
Drinks (small).
Small toys and books to keep your infant happy.
Pacifiers and bibs (if your child uses them).
A camera (or smartphone).
Suggested items for your checked luggage
Diapers/pull-ups, deodorized disposal bags, and wipes, if your child is not potty-trained.
Any toiletries your infant may need, including special baby soap and shampoo (these are not provided by cruise lines), lotions, sunscreen, toothbrush, and toothpaste.
Outlet plugs for childproofing.
Clothes.
Bibs.
Pacifiers.
First-aid kit and any medication such as pain relievers, fever reducers, and the name and contact details of your infant's pediatrician (for comfort).
Plastic bags for any snacks for shore excursions.
Ziplock bags – useful for soiled clothing.
Portable potty seat (if infant is potty-trained).
Swim diapers.
Swim vest: make sure it's of an approved type.
Sunglasses and sun hat (if your cruise is in or to a warm weather area).
Bottles and sip cups: cruise lines don't provide these. They can be washed in your cabin, so a little dish detergent and bottle brush could be useful.
Formula: ready-to-feed variety is convenient but bulky. Alternatively, bring powder and buy bottled mineral water from the ship's bar (a more expensive option).
Utensils.
Medication, such as pain relievers and fever reducers for babies, and the name and contact details of your child's pediatrician – just in case.
Inflatable toys such as beach balls and zoo animals are inexpensive and easy to pack (you won't be able to borrow toys from the ship's playroom).
Picture books to keep baby amused.

In the It's A Small World Nursery aboard *Disney Dream*.

As for laundry, it's best to use the self-service launderette, if your ship has one – not all do, so check before booking. Pack all-detergent sheets (they are easier to transport than liquid detergent). Many ships have laundry 'bundles' (either a set number of items, or all-you-can-bundle into a provided laundry sack), depending on the cruise line, for a special price.

You'll need to look after your child the whole time, unless you choose a ship with a proper nursery and qualified staff to look after infants. Ships with a nursery for ages six months to 36 months include: *Allure of the Seas, Anthem of the Seas, Disney Dream, Disney Fantasy, Disney Magic, Disney Wonder, Harmony of the Seas, Oasis of the Seas,* and *Quantum of the Seas.* Ships with a free night nursery: *Azura, Britannia, Oceana, Queen Elizabeth, Queen Mary 2, Queen Victoria,* and *Ventura.*

Children under three years old need to be potty-trained to take part in any group activities. Check with the cruise line whether babies and infants are allowed in paddling and swimming pools, and whether they must wear swim diapers.

Note that you may have to bathe infants/small children in a cabin with a small shower enclosure, possibly with a fixed-head shower; choosing a cabin with a bathtub makes it easier to do bathtime. Some ships (e.g. those of Costa Cruises) have baby baths available. Make sure you have adequate medical insurance, and take your infant's medical information in case of an emergency.

Minimum age accepted

It's important to check the minimum age requirements for your chosen cruise line and itinerary, because they can vary according to the cruise, length, and region. Here's our list of 12 principal cruise lines and the minimum age allowed for sailing, which was correct at time of going to press.

Carnival Cruise Line
Minimum sailing age: 6 months (12 months on transatlantic, Hawaii, and South America cruises).

Celebrity Cruises
Minimum sailing age: 6 months (12 months for transatlantic and transpacific and some South American cruises).

Costa Cruises
Minimum sailing age: 6 months.

Cunard
Minimum sailing age: 6 months (some sailings); 12 months for transatlantic and transpacific crossings, world cruise segments, and Hawaii cruises.

Disney Cruise Line
Minimum sailing age: 3 months.

Holland America Line
Minimum sailing age: 12 months.

MSC Cruises
Minimum sailing age: 3 months.

Norwegian Cruise Line
Minimum sailing age: 6 months.

P&O Cruises
Minimum sailing age: 6 months (12 months for transatlantic cruises) aboard the family-friendly ships *Aurora, Azura, Britannia, Oceania,* and *Ventura.*

Princess Cruises:
Minimum sailing age: 6 months.

Royal Caribbean International Minimum sailing age: 6 months for many itineraries; 12 months for any cruises with three or more sea days, and for all transatlantic, transpacific, Hawaii, and South Pacific cruises.

Star Cruises
Minimum sailing age: 6 months (note: any child whose travel document is attached to the parent's passport must travel with the accompanying parent).

Fun design in *Europa 2*'s family suites.

Babysitting

If you take baby (or babies) along, and you want some time to yourself, you'll need the services of a babysitter. Some, but not all, ships have babysitting services; some have restricted hours (meaning you'll need to be back by midnight like a grown-up Cinderella); and some have group babysitting, not in-cabin care. In some ships, stewards, stewardesses, and other staff may be available as private babysitters for an hourly charge. For example, *Queen Mary 2* has children's nurses and English nannies. *Aurora, Azura, Oceana,* and *Ventura* have a 'night nursery' for two- to five-year-olds.

Feeding infants under three

Selected baby foods are stocked by ships catering to infants, but ask your booking agent to get confirmation in writing that they'll be provided. Some cruise lines may even mash food up for your child, if you ask. If you need a special brand of baby food, advise your booking agent well in advance, or bring your own. Parents providing organic baby foods, such as those obtained from health-food stores, should be aware that cruise lines buy their supplies from general food suppliers and not from the smaller specialized food houses. You may need to check whether the ship has whole or soy milk available, for example.

Cruising with children ages 3–10

Assuming that they don't get seasick, children of this age should love cruising. They love to get involved right from the planning stages, learning how big the ship is, what facilities it has on board, etc. All very exciting!

One thing to note – if your budget allows, and you think your young children will be happy at sea for this long – is that it's best to avoid cruises of fewer than

seven days, because they tend to attract the party-going types out for a good time.

Once on board, go to the children's clubs and sign in your youngsters – you need to give their name, cabin number, and details of allergies to any foods or materials (this typically applies up to an age according to cruise line). You'll probably be given a pager in case you need instant contact. Children's activities are mostly about team participation events, so they may seem highly programmed to some youngsters used to getting their own way.

In addition to the clubs, there are plenty of other facilities on deck that will appeal to children of this age, from aqua parks to chill-out rooms to sports activities such as rope courses. Most large resort ships close their pools at 6pm, although those of MSC Cruises are exceptions to this – aboard *MSC Preziosa*, for example, a large, covered family pool is open until 9pm.

Barbie steps aboard

Royal Caribbean International and Mattel have free Barbie-related activities in the Adventure Ocean youth club, plus an additional cost ($349 per child) 'Barbie Premium Experience,' with pink cabin decorations, a Barbie doll blanket, tote bag and toothbrush, a special tea with pink cupcakes and dainty dishes, and a mermaid dance class featuring dances from the movie *Barbie in a Mermaid Tale 2*; plus other perks.

Dr. Seuss steps aboard too

Not to be outdone – and a better bet for boys – Carnival Cruise Line's 'Seuss at Sea' program has an array of immersive onboard youth, family, dining, and entertainment experiences featuring the amazing world and words of Dr. Seuss. The main dining room aboard each ship features 'The Green Eggs and

Ham Breakfast' with the Cat in the Hat and Friends. Children (parents can go too) can eat playful foods from Dr. Seuss's imagination, notably green eggs and ham, moose juice, goose juice, fruit and pancake stacks, funky French toast, and more. (Note that traditional breakfast favorites are also available.) Dining room staff members wear Dr. Seuss-inspired uniforms, and characters such as the Cat in the Hat, Thing One and Thing Two, and Sam join families at their tables for interaction and photo opportunities. This takes place on the first sea day of each cruise (cost: $5 per person).

Also, there are Dr. Seuss-themed toys, games, and arts and crafts activities. Some ships have a Dr. Seuss Bookville Seuss-themed play space with iconic decor, colors, shapes, and funky furniture, where families can relax. And movies such as *The Cat in the Hat* and Dr. *Seuss's How the Grinch Stole Christmas* are shown outdoors on Lido Deck Seaside Theater screens.

Carnival also introduced 'Seuss-a-Palooza Story Time,' an interactive reading event that brings the characters of Dr. Seuss to life. It usually takes place inside a tent on the main showlounge stage on a sea day each cruise.

There's also a Character Parade that includes Dr. Seuss characters along the Promenade. Naturally, Dr. Seuss-themed retail items are also available.

Disney goes cruising
In 1998, Disney Cruise Line introduced the first of two large resort ships to cater for families with children, with cruises of three, four, and seven days. *Disney Magic* and *Disney Wonder* were joined by *Disney Dream* in 2011 and by *Disney Fantasy* in 2012. The casino-free ships have ambitious entertainment programs, all centered around Disney and its stable of famous characters. Disney has its own Art Deco passenger terminal at Port Canaveral, Florida, plus a fleet of special motorcoaches.

Each ship carries over 40 children's and youth counselors, plus lifeguards at the family pool. Families preparing to sail with toddlers under three can access an online service to order baby supplies in advance of their cruise and have them delivered to their cabin. The service, exclusive to Disney Cruise Line, is provided by Babies Travel Lite (www.babiestravellite.com), an online retailer with more than 1,000 brand-name baby products including diapers, baby food, infant formula, and specialty travel items. The ships sail in the Caribbean, the Bahamas, Alaska, the Mediterranean, and the Baltic. Disney calls at its own 1,000-acre (405-hectare) private island on Bahamas and Caribbean cruises – about 50 miles (80km) north of Nassau in the Bahamas, Castaway Cay has its own ship-docking pier. Locals say it had a military landing strip that was once used by drug runners. Beaches are divided into family-friendly and adults-only 'quiet' sections.

Cruising with older children (pre-teens 11–12)
Some cruise lines provide extra attention for the 'Tweens.' Supervised group activities and activity/play centers mean that parents won't have to be concerned, and will be able to enjoy themselves, knowing that their children are in good hands, enrolled in special programs. Activities typically include make-up and cookery classes, arts and crafts projects, group games, interactive computer programs, character parades and scavenger hunts, and watching movies and video wall programming. Then there are the outdoor activities such as water slides, miniature golf, and swimming and other sports events for the pre-teens.

Cruising with teenagers (13–17)
Teens love cruising, too, and many large resort ships have dedicated 'no adults allowed' zones and chill-out rooms. Teens-only activities include deck parties, pool parties, sports tournaments, poolside games, karaoke, discos, dances, computer games, video arcades, activity clubs, and talent shows. Some ships provide musical instruments for jam sessions (Royal Caribbean International, for example). Sports activities include rock-climbing, rollerblading, basketball, and riding the wave surfer.

With some cruise lines the fun can extend ashore, with beach barbecues. There's usually almost unlimited food, too, although some of it may not be very nutritious.

SAFETY TIPS AT SEA

In case children get lost or separated from their parents, most cruise lines provide them with colored wristbands, which must be worn at all times. Disney Cruise Line has 'Mickey Bands' – magic bracelets that use radio tracking to locate the exact whereabouts of children at any time.

Young children love to climb, so don't ever leave them on a balcony alone. On the open decks, ships have railings – these are either horizontal bars through which children cannot get their heads, or they are covered in glass/plexiglass under a thick wooden top rail.

It's a good idea to walk your children between your cabin and the playroom/activity center, so that all of you are familiar with the route.

Discuss safety issues with your kids, and, with youngsters who are old enough to read, warn them not to walk into 'Crew Only' areas at any time.

Children's lifejackets are available aboard most cruise ships that carry children. However, check your cabin as soon as you embark. If no child's or infant's life vests are provided, see your steward right away.

Basketball fun aboard a Carnival ship.

Choosing the right cabin

Cruise lines know that 'families who play together want to stay together.' Although connecting cabins and Pullman beds are nothing new on family-friendly ships, brands such as Disney Cruise Line, Norwegian Cruise Lines, and Royal Caribbean International have taken group-friendly accommodations more seriously than some others.

Families cruising together often find that sharing a confined space causes distress. It's best to choose the largest accommodation option you can afford. Before booking, check the size of the cabin and pace it out at home, remembering that the size quoted on ship deck plans includes the bathroom. If you have a large or extended family, cabins with interconnecting doors may be the most practical option.

Certain ships may work best for certain age groups. For example, multigenerational groups might consider large resort ships such as Royal Caribbean International's *Allure of the Seas, Harmony of the Seas,* or *Oasis of the Seas,* or Disney Cruise Line ships thanks to their wide range of facilities and eateries.

If you are a large or extended family, some ships (such as those of Norwegian Cruise Line) have family cabins and suites that can sleep up to 14. Larger cabins or suites simply have more space than standard cabins, and may include sofa beds.

If you are traveling with teens, consider booking them an adjoining cabin or one across the hallway from yours. You get your own space, your teens will have their own bathroom and privacy, and you give them freedom, but at arm's length. If your children are younger, a cabin with an interconnecting door is a good option, if the budget allows. Many ships have cabins with two lower beds and one or two upper berths. In some cabins, the two lower beds can't be pushed together to form a queen-size bed for parents. This means mom and dad and one or two children all have separate beds. Some ships, such as *Disney Dream, Disney Fantasy, Disney Magic, Disney Wonder, Europa 2, Norwegian Bliss, Norwegian Breakaway, Norwegian Epic, Norwegian Escape, Norwegian Getaway,* and *Norwegian Joy* have cabins with two bathrooms, and a privacy curtain to screen off your youngsters.

Dependent on how young your children are (and how safe you feel this would be), you might like to opt for a cabin with a balcony. An interior (no-view) cabin may be adequate for a short cruise, but could be claustrophobic on a longer one. To get access to fresh air without a balcony, you'd have to keep trudging up to the open deck, carrying towels and other paraphernalia. However, if you don't anticipate spending much time in your cabin, an interior (no-

---

SHIPS THAT CATER WELL FOR CHILDREN

These ships have been selected for the quality of their children's programs and facilities:

Aida Cruises: *AIDAbella, AIDAblu, AIDAluna, AIDAmar, AIDAperla, AIDAprima, AIDAsol, AIDAstella*
Carnival Cruise Line: *Carnival Breeze, Carnival Dream, Carnival Freedom, Carnival Horizon, Carnival Magic, Carnival Splendor, Carnival Visa*
Celebrity Cruises: *Celebrity Eclipse, Celebrity Equinox, Celebrity Reflection, Celebrity Solstice*
Costa Cruises: *Costa Atlantica, Costa Deliziosa, Costa Diadema, Costa Fascinosa, Costa Favolosa, Costa Fortuna, Costa Luminosa, Costa Magica, Costa Mediterranea, Costa Pacifica, Costa Serena*
Cunard: *Queen Mary 2*
Disney Cruise Line: *Disney Dream, Disney Fantasy, Disney Magic, Disney Wonder*
Dream Cruises: *Genting Deam, World Dream*

MSC Cruises: *MSC Divina, MSC Fantasia, MSC Preziosa, MSC Meraviglia, MSC Seaside, MSC Splendida*
Norwegian Cruise Line: *Norwegian Bliss, Norwegian Breakaway, Norwegian Epic, Norwegian Escape, Norwegian Getaway, Norwegian Joy*
P&O Cruises: *Aurora, Azura, Britannia, Ventura*
Princess Cruises: *Regal Princess, Royal Princess*
Royal Caribbean International: *Adventure of the Seas, Allure of the Seas, Anthem of the Seas, Explorer of the Seas, Freedom of the Seas, Harmony of the Seas, Independence of the Seas, Liberty of the Seas, Mariner of the Seas, Navigator of the Seas, Oasis of the Seas, Ovation of the Seas, Quantum of the Seas, Voyager of the Seas*
Star Cruises: *SuperStar Virgo*
TUI Cruises: *Mein Schiff 3, Mein Schiff 4, Mein Schiff 5, Mein Schiff 6*

view) cabin is cheaper, although the storage space limitations may prove frustrating.

Try to book an *assigned* cabin rather than a *guaranteed* cabin; the latter means that only the space within a specific category is *ensured* – the room and bed configuration may not be the exact one you want.

Children's fares

Children under two travel free on most cruise lines and airlines. Most cruise lines offer special rates for children sharing their parents' cabin. The cost is often lower than third and fourth person share rates.

Although many adult cruise rates include airfare, most children's rates don't. Also, although some lines say children sail 'free,' they must pay port taxes as well as airfare.

Dining with children

Flexibility is the key. Coaxing children out of a pool and getting them dressed and ready to sit quietly through a four-course dinner every night can be tough. Work out a compromise by eating dinner together occasionally at the buffet. Most ships offer a tempting menu of children's favorites as well as special mealtimes for children.

Children with special needs

If a child has special needs, advise the cruise line before you book. Children needing one-to-one care or assistance must be accompanied by a parent or guardian when in the children's play center.

Practical matters: passports

Note that separate passports are required for all children traveling internationally. If you have an *adopted* child, you may also need Adoption Placement Papers, as well as the child's Birth Certificate.

Confirming a guardian's identity

A Parent and Guardian Consent Form (PGCSA) will be needed at or before embarkation, if you are a parent, grandparent, or guardian with a passport

Junior chefs of Princess Cruises.

surname different from that of any child traveling with you. Without this form, which includes passport information of the child's legal parent, you will be denied boarding. Check with your cruise provider if you are unclear.

Single parents

A few cruise lines have introduced their versions of the 'Single Parent Plan' (e.g., Disney Cruise Line, P&O Cruises). This offers an economical way for single parents to take their children on a cruise, with a parent and one child sharing a two-berth cabin, or a parent with more children sharing a three- or four-berth cabin.

As a single parent with just one child, you may have to pay for two adults (double occupancy), so it's important to check the pricing policy of each cruise line you're interested in. It may also be better to take an adult friend and share the cost (in some cases, your child could travel free).

Family reunions and birthdays

A cruise can provide the ideal place for a family get-together, with or without children, and, because it's an almost all-inclusive vacation, you won't have to haggle about who pays for the extras.

With pricing that includes accommodation, meals, entertainment, use of most of the ship's recreational facilities, and travel to various destinations, a cruise represents very good value for money. Cruise lines also make special offers to groups. Let your travel agent make the arrangements, and ask for a group discount if there are more than 15 of you.

Family groups may have the option to ensure even greater value by purchasing everything in advance, from cruise fares to shore excursions, drinks packages, spa packages, and pre-paid gratuities. Addi-

SHIPS THAT CATER BEST TO INFANTS

Disney Cruise Line: *Disney Dream, Disney Fantasy, Disney Magic, Disney Wonder*
MSC Cruises: *MSC Divina, MSC Fantasia, MSC Meraviglia, MSC Seaside, MSC Preziosa, MSC Splendida*
P&O Cruises: *Azura, Britannia, Ventura*
Royal Caribbean International: *Adventure of the Seas, Allure of the Seas, Explorer of the Seas, Freedom of the Seas, Harmony of the Seas, Independence of the Seas, Liberty of the Seas, Mariner of the Seas, Navigator of the Seas, Oasis of the Seas, Ovation of the Seas, Quantum of the Seas, Voyager of the Seas*
Star Cruises: *SuperStar Virgo*

A family goes snorkeling in the Caribbean.

tional savings can be realized through reduced fares for third and fourth passengers in each cabin, and some cruise lines offer 'kids sail free' programs.

Formal nights

Some ships have nights when traditional 'formal attire' is the suggested dress code. If you don't want your children to dress formally (although some children really enjoy getting dressed up – it's a bit like going to a birthday party or prom night), you can opt out of the festivities, and simply head for one of the casual dining options instead. Or your kids may prefer to opt out and go to the children's clubs or teen rooms and hang out while you go to the captain's cocktail party.

Tips for cruising with children

Take wet wipes for those inevitable clothes stains, and anti-bacterial hand wipes and face wipes to keep you cool when it's hot outside.

Take a highlighter pen – good for marking the daily program and shore excursion literature, so you can focus on what's important to you and the children.

Take an extension cord or power strip (although note that not all cruise lines allow them), because there will be plenty of things to plug in (chargers for games consoles, mobile phone, and iPod/iPad, etc.). Most cabins provide only one electrical outlet.

A pop-up laundry basket could prove useful for keeping everyone's dirty laundry separate from clean items (really useful in small cabins).

Refillable water bottles (empty until you are on board ship) are useful for shore excursions, beach days, and other outings.

Take lots of high-factor sunscreen (SPF50 or above).

A set of walkie-talkie radios can prove useful for keeping track of everyone's whereabouts – if everyone remembers to turn them on!

Glow sticks – kids love them – for use as night lights (they are cheap and come in different colors – one for each night).

Shore excursions

Many cruise ships in the Caribbean visit a 'private' island for a day. Lifeguards will be on duty at assigned swimming locations. Operators take advantage of the captive market, so rental of beach and water-sports items can be expensive.

It's best not to book a long shore excursion if you have an infant, unless you know that they (and you!) can handle it. Diaper-changing facilities are likely to be limited (and non-existent on buses).

Can you cruise when pregnant?

In 2010, a 30-year-old woman on a four-night Baja cruise aboard *Carnival Paradise* gave birth on board to a premature baby. In 2016, a woman who gave birth three weeks early, one day before the ship berthed in Brooklyn, called her baby Benjamin Brooklyn.

It can happen. If your pregnancy is routine and healthy, there's no reason not to go on a cruise, assuming you are within the normal travel limits for pregnant women. Indeed, a cruise could be a great getaway before you deal with the things associated with an upcoming childbirth. First, ask about any restrictions imposed by your chosen cruise line. Some cruise lines may let you sail even in your 27th week of pregnancy (as in the second case above), but most will not accept you from your 24th week onwards. You may be required to produce a doctor's note. (It is advisable to check with your doctor or midwife that you are safe to travel, prior to sailing, anyway.)

Be sure to purchase travel insurance that will cover you for last-minute cancellation and medical treatment due to pregnancy complications, both on board and in ports of call.

How grandparents can bridge the generation gap

Many children love to go cruising with grandparents, perhaps because they anticipate fewer restrictions than they have at home. And busy parents like the idea, too, particularly if the grandparents make a contribution to the cost and offer the possibility of a rest.

Having enrolled their grandchildren in age-related groups for daytime activities aboard ship (note the limitations on activities for children under three, as mentioned above), grandparents will be able to enjoy the adults-only facilities, such as the wellness and spa treatments. Not surprisingly, it's the large resort ships that provide the widest choice of facilities for both age groups. For those not averse to ubiquitous cartoon characters, Disney Cruise Line provides some facilities for adults and children in separate areas, but also allows them to mix in others.

Before you leave home

Grandparents should remember that, in addition to their grandchildren's passports, they should also bring along a letter signed by the parent authorizing any necessary medical attention. A Parent and Guardian Consent Form (PGCSA) will be needed at or before embarkation, if you are a grandparent (or parent or guardian) with a passport surname different from that of any child traveling with you. Check with your cruise provider about this.

Ground rules should be established with a child's parent(s) present to avoid potential problems. An important issue is whether a child will be allowed to roam the ship unsupervised, given that some cruise lines allow children as young as eight to sign themselves out of supervised programs. Walkie-talkies are a good solution to this issue. They work well aboard ships, and allow adults and children to stay in constant touch.

On board

Most cruise lines offer scheduled activities from 9am to noon, 2–5pm, and 7–10pm. This means you can drop your grandchild off after breakfast, relax by the pool, go to a lecture, or take part in other activities, and pick them up for lunch. After a couple of hours together, they can rejoin their friends, while you enjoy an afternoon movie or siesta.

Shore excursions

Consider your grandchild's interests before booking expensive shore excursions (example: flightseeing in Alaska). It's also best to avoid long bus rides, shopping trips, and scenic tours, and better to choose excursions that feature water and/or animals. Examples include snorkeling, aquariums, or nature walks. Remember to pack snacks. In some ports, it may be better to explore on your own. If your grandchildren are really young, full-day shore excursions are a probably bad idea.

Ropes course aboard *Norwegian Breakaway*.

5 BEST SPLASH-TASTIC WATER SLIDES

Water slides are always a highlight for youngsters, who can't wait to go for a ride once they are on board.
Aquaduck (Disney Cruise Line)
This water slide is four decks high and extends over the edge of the ship – scary. You'll find it on *Disney Dream* and *Disney Fantasy*.
Epic Plunge (Norwegian Cruise Line)
This water slide will have your youngsters doing the loop-de-loop down a long slide that ends in – surprise, surprise – a nice big splash.
Kaleid-O-Slide (Carnival Cruise Line)
This water slide ends in a giant funnel that swirls you around and spits you out with a splash! You'll find it on Carnival's newest ship and *Carnival Vista*.
Parthenon Slide (Star Cruises)
The half-million-dollar stainless steel Water Slide aboard SuperStar Virgo starts 34.5ft (10.5m) above the deck and swirls and swoops through over 328ft (100m) before emptying out into a water break.
Vertigo (MSC Cruises)
MSC's Vertigo is presently the longest single-body water slide at sea. You'll find it aboard *MSC Divina*, *MSC Fantasia*, *MSC Preziosa*, and *MSC Splendida*.

Cruising for Solo Travelers

Cruise prices are geared toward couples.
Yet about one in four cruise passengers travels
alone or as a single parent. How do they fare?

Cruising, in general, is designed for couples. Many solo passengers feel that cruising penalizes them, because most lines charge them a solo-occupancy supplement. The reason is that the most precious commodity aboard any ship is space. Since a solo-occupancy cabin is often as large as a double and is just as expensive to build, cruise lines feel the premium price is justified. What's more, because solo-occupancy cabins are at a premium, they are less likely to be discounted.

Solo supplements

If you are not sharing a cabin, you'll be asked to pay either a flat rate or a solo 'supplement' to occupy a double-occupancy cabin by yourself. Some lines charge a fixed amount – $250, for instance – as a supplement, regardless of the cabin category, ship,

Cunard provides dance hosts.

itinerary, or length of cruise. Such rates vary between lines, and sometimes between a particular line's ships. Since there are so few solo-occupancy cabins, it's best to book as far ahead as you can. One notable exception is Norwegian Cruise Line, whose *Norwegian Bliss*, *Norwegian Breakaway*, *Norwegian Epic*, *Norwegian Escape*, and *Norwegian Getaway* all have a special section with Studio cabins. These are small, but excellent, for solo cruisers.

Some cruise lines charge low solo supplements on selected voyages. Saga Cruises has no additional supplements for solo travelers on any cruise, but it offers special fares. Look out for sneaky cruise lines that may try to charge you *twice* for port charges and government taxes by including that non-existent second person in the cabin you occupy as a solo traveler – check your cruise fare invoice carefully.

Guaranteed solo traveler rates

Some lines offer solo travelers a set price for a double cabin but reserve the right to choose the cabin. This means that you could end up with a rotten cabin in a poor location or a wonderful cabin that happened to be unallocated.

Guaranteed share programs

These allow you to pay what it would cost each half of a couple for a double-occupancy cabin, but the cruise line will find another passenger of the same gender (and with preferences such as smoking or non-smoking) to share it with you. If the line doesn't find a cabin-mate, the solo traveler may have the cabin to themselves at no extra charge. Some cruise lines don't advertise a guaranteed share program in their brochures but they will often try to accommodate such bookings at times when demand for space is comparatively light.

Solo dining

A common irritation concerns dining arrangements. Before you take your cruise, make sure that you request a table assignment based on your personal preferences; table sizes are typically for two, four, six, or eight. Do you want to sit with other solo travelers? Or do you like to sit with couples? Or is a mixture of both ok? And are you happy to sit with passengers who might not speak your language?

When you are on board, make sure that you are comfortable with the dining arrangements, particularly in ships with fixed table assignments, or ask the maître d' to move you to a different table. Aboard ships with open seating or with several different dining venues, you can choose which venue you want to eat in, and when; Norwegian Cruise Line (NCL) is an example of this arrangement, with its Freestyle Dining, as is Star Cruises.

Cruising for women traveling solo

A cruise ship is as safe for women as any major vacation destination. It may not, of course, be entirely hassle-free, but it should not be a 'meat market' that keeps you under constant observation.

If you enjoy meeting other solo travelers, the easiest way is to participate in scheduled activities. However, beware of embarking on an affair with a ship's officer or crew member, as you may not be the only one to have done so.

Gentlemen cruise hosts

The female-to-male passenger ratio is typically high, especially among older people, so some cruise lines provide male social hosts. They may host a table in the dining room, appear as dance partners at cocktail parties and dance classes, join bridge games, and accompany women on shore excursions.

A DJ keeps youthful late-night clubbers dancing.

These men, usually over 55 and retired, are outgoing, mingle easily, and are well groomed. First introduced aboard Cunard's *QE2* in the mid-1970s, gentlemen hosts are now employed by a number of cruise lines. Examples include Crystal Cruises, Cunard, Holland America Line, Regent Seven Seas Cruises, Silversea Cruises, and Voyages to Antiquity.

If you think you'd like such a job, do remember that you'll have to dance for several hours most nights, and be proficient in just about every kind of dance.

OPTIONS FOR LGBT TRAVELERS

Several US companies specialize in ship charters or large group bookings for gay and lesbian passengers. These include the California-based Atlantis (www.atlantisevents.com), San Francisco's lesbian specialist Olivia (www.olivia.com), or New York's Pied Piper Travel (www.piedpipertravel.com).

One drawback of LGBT charters is that they're as much as 20 percent more expensive than the equivalent general cruise. Another is that they have been greeted with hostility by church groups on some Caribbean islands such as Grand Cayman, Jamaica, and Bermuda. One Atlantis cruise was even denied the right to dock. But their great advantage is that they provide an accepting environment and gay-oriented entertainment, with some big-name comedians and singers.

Another idea is to join a gay affinity group on a regular cruise at normal prices; these groups may be offered amenities such as private dining rooms and separate shore excursions.

If you are concerned that on a mainstream cruise you might be seated for dinner with unsympathetic companions, opt for a cruise line offering 'open-choice seating' (where you sit where you want, when you want at dinner,

and you can change time you dine), for example Carnival Cruise Line, Celebrity Cruises, Holland America Line, Norwegian Cruise Line, Princess Cruises, and Royal Caribbean International (request this option when you book). That doesn't mean that any of the major cruise companies are not gay-friendly – many hold regular 'Friends of Dorothy' gatherings, sometimes scheduled and sometimes on request – though it would be prudent to realize that Disney Cruise Line, for example, will not really offer the ideal entertainment and ambience. Among the smaller companies, Windstar's sail-powered cruise yachts have a reputation for being gay-friendly.

Gay families are catered to by R Family Vacations (www.rfamilyvacations.com), although it's not essential to bring children. Events may include seminars on adoption and discussion groups for teenagers in gay families.

Transgender passengers may encounter some problems, such as the passport name being of one gender, while appearance and dress reflect another. Ships sometimes encounter problems in some ports when passenger ID cards do not match the gender on the ship's manifest.

Cruising for Romantics

No need to worry about getting to the church on time – you can be married at sea, get engaged, renew your vows, or enjoy a honeymoon.

Two classic TV shows, *The Love Boat* (US) and *Traumschiff* (Germany), boosted the concept of cruising as a romantic vacation, the natural culmination of which would be getting married at sea – the ultimate 'mobile wedding.' Such ceremonies have become such big money-earners that, after 171 years, Cunard changed the registry of its three ships in 2011 from its traditional home port of Southampton to Hamilton, Bermuda, partly because its British registry didn't allow it to perform weddings at sea. As a result, couples can now say 'I do' aboard *Queen Mary 2* in the middle of the North Atlantic; the first such wedding was in May 2012.

Saying 'I do' aboard ship

This increasingly popular option includes a honeymoon conveniently in the same location and a 'wed-

Sunset aboard Cunard's *Queen Mary 2*.

ding planner,' who can sort out all the nitty-gritty details such as arranging flights, hotels, transportation, and packages. For the bride, spa and beauty services are immediately on hand, and you literally can sail into the sunset after the reception.

Check first in your country of domicile whether such a marriage is legal, and ascertain what paperwork and blood tests are needed. It is up to you to prove the validity of such a marriage. The captain could be held legally responsible if he has married a couple not entitled to wed.

It's relatively easy to get married aboard almost any cruise ship when it's alongside in port. Carnival Cruise Line, Celebrity Cruises, Costa Cruises, Holland America Line, Princess Cruises, and Royal Caribbean International, among others, offer special wedding packages. These include the services of a minister to marry you, wedding cake, Champagne, bridal bouquet and matching boutonnière for the bridal party, a band to perform at the ceremony, and an album of wedding pictures. Note that US citizens and 'green card' residents may need to pay sales tax on wedding packages.

Asuka Cruise, Azamara Club Cruises, Celebrity Cruises, Cunard, P&O Cruises, Princess Cruises, Royal Caribbean International, and Sea Cloud Cruises – among others – offer weddings aboard their ships. The ceremonies can be performed by the captain, who is certified as a notary, when the ships' registry – Bermuda, Japan, or Malta, for example – recognizes such unions. Japanese citizens can also be married at sea aboard one of the Japan-registered cruise ships such as *Asuka II*.

Expect to pay about $3,000 plus about $500 for licensing fees. Harbor-side or shore-side packages vary according to the port.

Even if you don't get married aboard ship, you could have your wedding reception on one. Contact the director of hotel services at the cruise line. The cruise line will go out of its way to help, especially if you follow the reception with a honeymoon cruise – and a cruise, of course, also makes a fine, worry-free honeymoon.

UK-based passengers should know that P&O Cruises hosts a series of cruises called the 'Red-Letter Anniversary Collection' for those celebrating 10, 15, 20, 25, 30, 35, 40, 45, 50, 55, or 60 years of marriage. The cruise comes with a complimentary gift, such as a brass carriage clock, leather photograph album, or – less romantic, but very useful – free car parking at Southampton.

Getting married ashore

An alternative is to have a marriage ceremony in an exotic destination with your reception and honeymoon aboard ship afterwards. For example, you could get married on the beach in Barbados or Hawaii; on a glacier in Juneau, Alaska; in a villa in Rome or Venice; in an authentic Tahitian village; in Central Park, New York; or on Disney's Castaway Cay in the Bahamas, with Mickey and Minnie at hand. Note that your marriage license must be from the jurisdiction in which you will be married. If you set your heart on a Bermuda beach wedding, for example, the license to marry must be obtained in Bermuda, no matter what your nationality is.

Carnival Cruise Line's wedding packages, available both aboard ship on embarkation day or in tropical ports of call, are immensely popular, with more than 2,600 ceremonies performed each year.

Getting engaged aboard ship

For those who aren't quite ready to tie the knot, Princess Cruises has a special 'Engagement Under the Stars' package that allows you to propose to your loved one in a personal video that is then screened just before an evening movie at a large outdoor screen aboard some of the company's ships. Current cost: $695.

Renewal of vows

Many cruise lines perform 'renewal of vows' ceremonies. A cruise is a wonderful setting for reaffirming to one's partner the strength of commitment. A handful of ships have a small chapel where this ceremony can take place; otherwise, it can be anywhere aboard ship – a most romantic time is at sunrise or sunset on the open deck. The renewal of vows ceremony is conducted by the ship's captain, using a non-denominational text.

PRACTICAL TIPS FOR HONEYMOONERS

Remember to take a copy of your marriage license or certificate, for immigration (or marriage) purposes, as your passports will not yet have been amended. Since you may well wish to share a large bed with your partner, check with your travel agent and cruise line to make sure the cabin you have booked has such a bed. Better still, book a suite, if the budget allows. It's important to check and double-check to avoid disappointment.

If you plan to combine your honeymoon with getting married along the way – in Hawaii or Bermuda, for example – and need to take your wedding gown aboard, there's usually space to hang it in the dressing room next to the stage in the main showlounge, especially aboard the large resort ships.

A honeymoon couple enjoy being pampered aboard an MSC Cruises ship.

Some companies, such as Carnival Cruise Line, Celebrity Cruises, Cunard, Holland America Line, P&O Cruises, and Princess Cruises, have complete packages for purchase, which include music, Champagne, hors d'oeuvres, certificate, corsages for the women, and so on.

Cruising for honeymooners

There are many advantages in honeymooning at sea: it is a hassle-free and safe environment; and you get special attention, if you want it. It is easy to budget in advance, as one price often includes airfare, cruise, food, entertainment, several destinations, shore excursions, and pre- and post-cruise hotel stays. Also, some cruise lines offer discounts if you book a future cruise to celebrate an anniversary.

Although no ship as yet provides real bridal suites, many ships have suites with king- or queen-size beds. Some also provide tables for two in the dining room, should you wish to dine together without having to make friends with others. A variety of honeymoon packages are available; these might include Champagne and caviar for breakfast, flowers in the suite or cabin, a complimentary cake, and a private captain's cocktail party.

Some cruise ships have Sunday departures, so couples can plan a Saturday wedding and reception before traveling to their ship. Pre- and post-cruise hotel accommodation can also be arranged.

Most large resort ships accommodate honeymoon couples well. However, couples averse to crowds might try one of the smaller cruise ships such as those of Regent Seven Seas Cruises, Sea Cloud Cruises, Seabourn, Silversea Cruises, or Windstar Cruises.

And for quiet moments? The deck to the forward part of a ship, near the bridge, is the most dimly lit part and the quietest – except perhaps for some wind noise.

Cruising for Seniors

People everywhere are living longer and healthier lives, and cruise lines are keen to cater to their particular needs.

Although cruise lines have been striving, with some success, to embrace all age groups, the over-60s remain an important segment of the market. Group cruising for seniors, in fact, is growing in popularity and is a good way for like-minded people to vacation together. Nowhere is this more evident than in Japan's 'Golden Week,' a collection of four national holidays within seven days in late April/early May, when seniors clamor for available cabins.

One trend for seniors is toward longer cruises – even round-the-world cruises, if they can afford them. Some opt for an adults-only ship such as *Magellan* (CMV), *Adonia, Arcadia,* or *Oriana* (P&O Cruises), or *Saga Sapphire* (Saga Cruises), for example. There are bargains to be had, too. Organizations for seniors such as AARP (American Association of Retired Persons) in the US and Saga in the UK often offer discount fares and upgrades.

Some seniors who may have had major surgery or have mobility problems cannot fly, or don't wish to, are helped by the 'Homeland Cruising' trend, which ena-

Making new friends aboard *Oasis of the Seas*.

bles them to embark at and disembark from a nearby port in their home country. In the US, the number of homeland ports increased dramatically following the terrorist attacks of September 2001. In the UK, some cruise ships sail from ports in both the north and south of the country. The same is true elsewhere, as language-specific cruise lines and ships proliferate.

But all is far from perfect. Some cruise lines have yet to recognize that, with seniors as with other groups, one size does *not* fit all. Only a few, for example, take the trouble to provide the kind of items that millions of seniors need, such as large-print editions of daily programs, menus, and other printed matter.

Special diets

While the wide range of cuisine aboard many ships is a big attraction, cruise lines understand that many passengers are on special diets. Lighter menu options are available aboard most ships, as well as vegetarian and vegan choices. Options include low-sodium, low-fat, low-cholesterol, and sugar-free entrées (main courses) and desserts. A booking agent will ensure that special dietary needs are recorded.

Healthier eating

You don't have to put on weight during a cruise. Many health-conscious seniors prefer smaller portions of food with good taste and nutritional value rather than overflowing plates.

Heart-healthy diets are in demand, as are low-fat, low-carbohydrate, salt-free, or low-salt foods. Denture wearers often request food that includes softer items.

Those seeking lighter fare should be aware that most cruise lines have an 'always available' section of heart-healthy items that can be cooked plainly, such as grilled or steamed salmon, skinless chicken breast, lean sirloin steak, or baked potatoes.

Gentlemen hosts

Because more female than male seniors cruise, cruise lines have developed 'gentlemen host' programs. These are gentlemen, typically over 55 years of age, selected for their social skills and competence as dance partners, for dining table conversation, and for accompanying passengers on shore excursions.

Cruise lines with gentlemen hosts include: Celebrity Cruises, Crystal Cruises, Cunard, Holland America Line, P&O Cruises, Princess Cruises, Regent Seven Seas Cruises, Seabourn, Silversea Cruises, Swan Hellenic Cruises, Voyages to Antiquity, and Voyages of Discovery Cruises.

Enrichment programs

Many seniors want to learn about a destination's history and culture rather than be told which shops to visit ashore. Lecturers of academic quality are found aboard some smaller ships such as *Aegean Odyssey* (Voyages to Antiquity), *Minerva* (Swan Hellenic Cruises), and *Saga Sapphire* (Saga Cruises). Some lines, such as Crystal Cruises, have special-interest lecturers on topics such as archaeology, food and wine, ornithology, and military history.

Tips for seniors

If you're traveling solo, it's important to check the price of any single supplements.

If you take medication, make sure you have enough with you. Some ships have a dress-up code, while some are casual. Choose a ship according to your own lifestyle and tastes.

If you have mobility difficulties, choose one of the newer ships that have public rooms with an 'openflow' style of interior design. Examples include *Arcadia, Balmoral, Eurodam, Magellan, Nieuw Amsterdam, Oosterdam, Queen Elizabeth, Queen Mary 2, Queen Victoria, Westerdam,* and *Zuiderdam*. Older ships, such as *Marco Polo,* have 'lips' or doors between public rooms.

Enrichment lecture aboard a small ship.

Best facilities

Among the cruise lines that provide the facilities and onboard environment that seniors tend to enjoy most are: American Cruise Lines, Azamara Club Cruises, Blount Small Ship Adventures, Crystal Cruises, Fred. Olsen Cruise Lines, Hebridean Island Cruises, Holland America Line, Noble Caledonia, Oceania Cruises, P&O Cruises, Pearl Seas Cruises, Regent Seven Seas Cruises, Saga Cruises, Sea Cloud Cruises, Seabourn, Silversea Cruises, Swan Hellenic Cruises, and Voyages to Antiquity.

WHY SENIORS LIKE CRUISING – BUT CAN OFTEN FIND IT FRUSTRATING

Thumbs up

A cruise is an excellent choice for those who like to be independent while having the chance to meet other like-minded people.

Cruising is stress-free and relaxing. You don't have to keep packing and unpacking as you do on a land-based tour.

It's safe. You travel and dine in comfort and safety, while your floating hotel takes you to a choice of around 2,000 destinations all over the world.

Lecturers and lessons in everything from golf to computing provide a chance to learn something new.

There's plenty of entertainment – shows, cinema, casinos, games, dances.

All main and self-serve buffet meals are included in the fare, and those passengers on special diets can be easily accommodated.

Senior singles, in particular, find it easy to meet others in a non-threatening environment. Some ships provide male dance hosts, screened and subject to a strict code of ethics, who can also act as escorts on shore excursions.

Most ships have 24-hour room service and a 24-hour reception desk.

Passengers with disabilities can find ships that cater to their needs.

Ships carry a medical doctor and one or more trained nurses. In an emergency, treatment can be arranged.

Thumbs down

Online check-in procedures, and hard-to-read Passenger Ticket Conditions and Contracts that are provided only online.

Credit card-size electronic key cards to cabins – it is often unclear which end of these to insert, especially for passengers with poor eyesight.

Booking events and meals via the in-cabin 'interactive' television/keypad system; it is user-unfriendly for many seniors. All services should be readily accessible via the telephone.

Poor, difficult-to-read signage such as 'You are here' deck plans unreadable from farther away than an inch (2.5cm).

Menus with small, hard-to-read typefaces, and daily programs that require a magnifying glass to be legible.

Buffets with plates only, requiring several visits, and cutlery too heavy to hold comfortably.

Anything that requires a signature – for example: bar, shore excursions, spa bills with small print.

Libraries with few books, if any, in large-print format – notably recent novels.

The absence of a 'concierge' for seniors.

Public toilets not clearly marked.

The lack of music-free lounges and bars for conversation and drinks.

Cruising to Suit Special Needs

Cruising for those with physical special needs offers one of the most hassle-free vacations possible. But it's important to choose the right ship and to prepare in advance.

If you are mobility-limited or have any other kind of physical disabilities (this includes sight or hearing impairments), do tell the cruise line (or your travel agent) at the time you book; otherwise, you may legally be denied boarding by the cruise line.

Anyone in a wheelchair but considering a cruise may be nervous at the thought of getting around. However, you'll find that crew members aboard most ships are extremely helpful. Indeed, cruise ships have become much more accessible for people with most types of disabilities. Ships built in the past five to 10 years have the most up-to-date suites, cabins, and accessible shipboard facilities for those with special needs. Many new ships also have text telephones and listening device kits for the hearing-impaired (including in showlounges aboard some ships). Special dietary needs can often be met, and many cabins have refrigerators – useful for those with diabetes who need to keep supplies of insulin cool.

Many cruise ships offer an ideal environment for people with special needs.

Special haemodialysis cruises cater for dialysis patients. For the very best in dialysis care and travel arrangements, contact Dr. Peter Rittich at: www.dia care.ch. Other providers include www.dialysisatsea.com and www.dialysis-cruises.com. Typically, a renal care specialist team consisting of a nephrologist, dialysis nurses, and certified technicians will be provided. Some ships (examples include *Astor, Europa,* and *Europa 2*) have first-class dialysis equipment (such as the Fresenius 4008 B) permanently installed in a special dialysis room within the medical center.

If you use a wheelchair, take it with you, as ships carry only a limited number for emergency hospital use only. An alternative is to rent an electric wheelchair, which can be delivered to the ship on your sailing date.

Arguably the weakest point of cruising for the mobility-limited is any shore-tender operation. Ship tenders simply aren't designed properly for the wheelchair-bound – and neither are the landing platforms.

Little problems to consider

Unless cabins and bathrooms are specifically designed, problem areas include the entrance, furniture configuration, closet hanging rails, beds, grab bars, the height of toiletries cabinet, and the wheel-in shower stall. The elevators may present the biggest obstacle, and you may get frustrated at the wait time involved. In older ships, controls often can't be reached from a wheelchair.

Some ships have access-help hoists installed at swimming pools. These include *Celebrity Eclipse, Celebrity Equinox, Celebrity Reflection,* and *Celebrity Silhouette,* the pool in 'The Haven' aboard *Norwegian Breakaway, Norwegian Epic, Norwegian Escape, Norwegian Getaway,* and *Norwegian Gem,* and P&O Cruises' *Aurora, Britannia,* and *Oriana.*

It can be hard to access areas including self-serve buffets, and many large resort ships provide only oval plates (no trays) in their casual eateries. So you may need to ask for help.

Some insurance companies may prohibit smaller ships from accepting passengers with severe disabilities. Some cruise lines will send you a form requesting the dimensions and weight of the wheelchair, stating that it has to fold to be taken inside the cabin.

Note that wheelchairs, mobility scooters, and walking aids must be stored in your cabin – they *cannot* be left in the hallway outside your cabin.

Only five cruise ships have direct wheelchair-access ramps to lifeboats: *Amadea, Asuka II, Crystal Serenity, Crystal Symphony,* and *Europa.*

Avoid pitfalls

Start by planning an itinerary and date, and find a travel agent who is well suited to your needs. You should also follow up on all aspects of the booking yourself to avoid slip-ups; many cruise lines have a department or person to handle requests from disabled passengers.

Choose a cruise line that lets you select a specific cabin, not just a price category.

If the ship doesn't have any specially equipped cabins, book the best outside cabin in your price range, or choose another ship.

Check whether your wheelchair will fit through your cabin's bathroom door or into the shower area and whether there is a 'lip' at the door. Don't accept 'I think so' as an answer. Get specific measurements.

Choose a cabin close to an elevator. Not all elevators go to all decks, so check the deck plan. Smaller and older vessels may not even have elevators, making access to even the dining room difficult.

Avoid, at all costs, a cabin down a little alleyway shared by several other cabins, even if the price is attractive. It's hard to access a cabin in a wheelchair from such an alleyway. Cabins located amidships are less affected by vessel motion, so choose something in the middle of the ship if you are concerned about possible rough seas. The larger – and therefore more expensive – the cabin, the more room you will have to maneuver in.

Hanging rails in the closets on most ships are positioned too high for someone in a wheelchair to reach – even the latest ships seem to repeat this basic error. Many cruise ships, however, have cabins to suit the mobility-limited. They are typically fitted with roll-in closets and have a pull-down facility to bring your clothes down to any height you want.

Meals in some ships may be served in your cabin, on special request, but few ships have enough space in the cabin for dining tables. If you opt for a dining room with two fixed-time seatings for meals, the second is more leisurely. Alert the restaurant manager in advance that you would like a table that leaves plenty of room for your wheelchair.

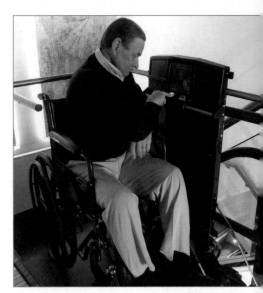
Douglas Ward tests accessibility around a ship.

Make sure that the contract specifically states that if, for any reason, the cabin is not available, that you will get a full refund and transportation back home as well as a refund on any hotel bills incurred.

Advise the cruise line of the need for proper transfer facilities such as buses or vans with wheelchair ramps or hydraulic lifts.

If you live near the port of embarkation, arrange to visit the ship to check its suitability – most cruise lines will be accommodating.

Hand-carry your medical information. Once on board, tell the reception desk help may be needed in an emergency.

Coping with embarkation

The boarding process can pose problems. If you embark at ground level, the gangway may be level or inclined. It will depend on the embarkation deck of the ship and/or the tide in the port.

DOORS CAN PRESENT A PROBLEM FOR WHEELCHAIR USERS

The design of cruise ships has traditionally worked against the mobility-limited. To keep water out or to prevent water escaping from a flooded area, raised edges (lips) – unfriendly to wheelchairs – are often placed in doorways and across exit pathways. Also, cabin doorways, at a standard 24in (60cm) wide, are not big enough for wheelchairs, for which about 30in (76cm) is needed.

Bathroom doors, whether they open outward or inward, similarly hinder maneuverability (an electrically operated sliding door would be better). Bathrooms in some older ships are small and full of plumbing fixtures, often at odd angles – awkward for wheelchair movement. Those aboard new ships are much better, but plumbing may be located beneath the complete prefabricated module, making the floor higher than that in the cabin, so a ramp is needed. Some cruise lines will, if given advance notice, remove a bathroom door and hang a fabric curtain in its place, and provide a ramp for the doorway if needed.

Access to outside decks may be through doors that must be opened manually rather than via automatic electric-eye doors.

A cabin number in Braille aboard *Costa Serena*.

Alternatively, you may be required to embark from an upper level of a terminal, in which case the gangway could well be of the floating loading-bridge type, like those used at major airports. Some have flat floors; others may have raised lips at regular intervals.

Ship-to-shore tenders

Cruise lines should – but don't always – provide an anchor emblem in brochures for those ports of call where a ship will be at anchor instead of alongside. If the ship is at anchor, the crew will lower you and your wheelchair into a waiting tender and then, after a short boat ride, lift you out again onto a rigged gangway or integral platform. If the sea is calm, this maneuver proceeds uneventfully; if the sea is choppy, it could vary from exciting to somewhat harrowing.

This type of embarkation is rare except in a busy port with several ships sailing the same day. Holland America Line is one of the few companies to make shore tenders accessible to the disabled, with a special boarding ramp and scissor lift so that wheelchair passengers can see out of the shore tender's windows.

Help for the hearing-impaired

Difficulties for such passengers include hearing announcements on the public address system, using the telephone, and poor acoustics in key areas such as where shore tenders are boarded.

Some cruise lines have special 'alert kits.' These include 'visual-tactile' devices for those unable to hear a knock on the door, a telephone ringing, or the sound of an alarm clock. Crystal Cruises' *Crystal Serenity* and *Crystal Symphony*, and TUI Cruises' *Mein Schiff 1, Mein Schiff 2, Mein Schiff 3, Mein Schiff 4, Mein Schiff 5,* and *Mein Schiff 6* have movie theaters fitted with special headsets for those with hearing difficulties.

Finally, when going ashore, particularly on organized excursions, be aware that some destinations are simply not equipped to handle people with hearing impairment.

Cruising for the blind and sight-impaired

Any totally or almost-blind persons must be accompanied by a fully able-bodied person, occupying the same cabin. A few cruise lines will allow seeing-eye dogs (guide dogs).

All elevators and cabins have Braille text. Some large resort ships (examples include *Celebrity Reflection, Celebrity Silhouette, MSC Divina, MSC Fantasia, MSC Meraviglia, MSC Preziosa,* and *MSC Splendida*) have Braille pads subtly hidden under each lower section of handrail in the main foyers – very user-friendly, and most welcome.

Recent improvements

Many new ships now provide mobility-limited cabin bathrooms with collapsible shower stools mounted on shower walls, and bathroom toilets have collapsible arm guards and lower washbasins. Other cabin equipment may include a vibrating alarm clock, door beacon (with a light that flashes when someone knocks on the door), television with closed-caption decoders, and a flashing light as fire alarm.

Look out, too, for:
Kits for the hearing-impaired, available on request.
Induction systems for the hearing impaired.
Dedicated wheelchair positions in the showlounge.
Electrical hoists to access pools and hot tubs.

Although public rooms do not have special seating areas, most showlounges do – almost always at the back, adjacent to the elevators – for wheelchair passengers.

Wheelchair accessibility

Each cruise ship reviewed in this book is rated in its data listing for wheelchair accessibility.

QUESTIONS TO ASK BEFORE YOU BOOK

Are any public rooms or public decks inaccessible to wheelchairs?
Will special transportation be provided for the transfer from airport to ship?
Will you need to sign a medical release?
If you need a collapsible wheelchair, can this be provided by the cruise line?
Can the ship supply a raised toilet seat?
Will crew members be on hand to help?
Will you be guaranteed a good viewing place in the showlounge if seated in a wheelchair?
How do you get from your cabin to lifeboats in an emergency, if the elevators are out of action?
Does the cruise line's travel insurance (with a cancellation or trip interruption) cover you for any injuries while you are aboard?
Most disabled cabins have twin beds or one queen-size bed. Anyone with a disabled child should ask whether a suitable portable bed can be installed.

Cruising to a Theme

A whole world of hobby, special-interest, and
lifestyle theme cruises awaits your participation.

What's your interest? Think of it and you'll probably find a special cruise dedicated to it. These are the special theme cruises that don't really fit into the normal range of offerings, although they usually follow the same itinerary.

Theme cruises are primarily 'regular' cruises, but with additional programs, linked to personalities and theme subject specialists. With special seminars and hands-on learning sessions, dances or concerts, sports, activities, and leisure on the menu, the possibilities are endless. Also, you'll be traveling with people who have the same hobbies, interests, or passions, or to increase your knowledge of a particular subject. You could also be close to your favorite celebrity and get to talk to them in person.

Music on the high seas

Music has always been a popular feature of shipboard entertainment, and special-interest music festivals, celebrations, and even competitions at sea have been part of the modern-day cruise scene since the 1960s. It's like having a special backstage pass to be up-close-and-personal with world-class musical talent.

Solo instruments are an unusual item for a theme cruise, but in 1986 the first Accordion Festival at Sea – with over 600 accordionists on board competing for financial and other prizes – took place aboard Chandris Fantasy Cruises' *Galileo*. It was not a full ship charter, so the other passengers were fascinated by the richness of performances of this versatile instrument.

Even before that, however, starting in 1976, a Classical Music Festival At Sea took place annually aboard the Paquet French Cruises' 650-passenger *Mermoz* until the early 1990s (and wine, all other drinks, and shore excursions were included in the fare). The artistic director André Borocz organized the whole event, including booking about 70 musicians who sailed on each of these special cruises (either in the Mediterranean or Caribbean). World-class artists such as James Galway, Barbara Hendricks, Jean-Pierre Rampal, Maurice André, Mstislav Rostropovich, Yo-Yo Ma, Emmanuel Ax, Schlomo Mintz, Bobby McFerrin, and the English Chamber Orchestra sailed aboard the ship, with music concerts performed ashore – usually in the evening – in Caribbean venues such as Papa Doc's Citadelle in Haiti, La Popa Monastery in

Néstor Torres performs as part of The Grammy Experience aboard *Norwegian Getaway*.

Cartagena, or, in Europe, the ancient Greek theatre at Epidaurus, the Teatro Mercadante in Naples, or the ancient open-air theatre at Xanthos, Turkey.

What was unusual, and fun, was to watch these world-famous artistes rehearsing in the daytime – often in their bathrobes – with passengers (also in bathrobes or casual clothing) attending; then, at around 6pm, everyone donned tuxedos for the evening. The close contact and the interaction between performers and the music-loving passengers were wonderful. Suffice it to say that this was indeed a very special theme cruise.

In 1993 Paquet French Cruises was purchased by Costa Cruises, which was itself purchased by the Carnival Corporation in 1996. In 1999 Paquet Cruises was dismantled, and the *Mermoz* ship was scrapped in 2008.

Today, several cruise lines have taken up the Classical Music Festival at Sea theme, with Hapag-Lloyd's annual Ocean Sun Festival the most prestigious and sought-after event.

The company also hosts the annual Stella Maris International Vocal Competition (opera, song, and oratorio) in cooperation with renowned opera houses throughout the world. It is organized under the direction of Canadian tenor Michael Schade aboard *Europa*, with up-and-coming opera singers from around the world competing to win €15,000 and a recording contract with the German classical music record label, Deutsche Grammophon.

Cool jazz

Staying on the music theme, Big Band theme cruises have also always been popular, with bands such as the Glenn Miller Orchestra, Tommy Dorsey Orchestra, Count Basie Orchestra, and the Duke Ellington Orchestra all having been part of the music on the high seas theme. In October 2015, Cunard hosted the first-ever Blue Note-themed crossing aboard *Queen Mary 2* – showcasing Blue Note's 75th anniversary All Star Band. It featured keyboardist Robert Glasper, trumpeter Keyon Harrold, tenor saxophonist Marcus Strickland, guitarist Lionel Loueke, bassist Derrick Hodge, and drummer Kendrick Scott. Herbie Hancock was the headline act on one of two more special Blue Note-themed crossings in 2016, as was jazz vocalist Gregory Porter.

Jazz greats such as Dizzy Gillespie and Clark Terry (trumpet), Woody Herman (clarinet), Benny Carter, Buddy Tate, Gerry Mulligan (saxophone), Junior Mance, Mel Powell, and Paul Broadnax (piano), Howard Alden (guitar), Keter Betts, Major Holley, Milt Hinton, and Kiyoshi Kitagawa (double bass), Chuck Riggs and Louis Bellson (drums), Mel Tormé (voice), the Harlem Blues and Jazz Band, and Joe Williams and the Festival Jazzers have all sailed and played on Norwegian Cruise Line's 'Floating Jazz Festival' cruises aboard the now-scrapped *Norway* and other ships in the fleet (organized by Hank O'Neal).

Today, the Smooth Jazz Cruise (also known as 'The Greatest Party At Sea') has been attracting well-known names such as the jazz violinist Ken Ford, guitarist-vocalist George Benson, bassist Marcus Miller, guitarist Earl Klugh, saxophonists David Sanborn, Mindi Abair, Paul Taylor, and Richard Elliott, and jazz fans – principally aboard Holland America Line ships.

Off your rocker

Today, even rock 'n' roll stars and fans have taken to cruising, with music-themed charters of ships becoming more prevalent.

The Moody Blues with Peter Dalton, The Zombies, Carl Palmer and The Orchestra with ELO, Starship, Little River Band, and Yes have all featured on cruises. Not to be left out, grown-up 'boy bands,' including the Backstreet Boys and New Kids on the Block, have also been cruising.

In 2017, over 20 bands rocked aboard *Carnival Victory* on a four-night cruise, with 44 concerts spread out among five venues, under the brand name ShipRocked. Expect more of the same, as rock 'n' roll and blues bands go cruising to replace the loss of land-based venues and revenue (merchandising aboard a cruise ship with a captive audience is a massive incentive).

Although classical music and jazz cruises tend to last 7 to 14 days, most other music themes, such as rock 'n' roll, or heavy metal ones, tend to be shorter (and less expensive).

Soul train

Usually a full-ship charter, a re-creation of the popular music show *Soul Train* includes artists such as Gladys Knight and Earth, Wind and Fire, together with numerous artists that have been part of the television show, created and hosted by Don Cornelius. The artists, dancers, and fans have a blast, and enjoy the close interaction with each other (www.soultraincruise.com). In 2016, Smokey Robinson performed aboard Celebrity Constellation. The 2018 lineup include Charlie Wilson, Eddie Levert of the O'Jays, and The Pointer Sisters.

Going up country

Country and Western and Gospel music theme cruises also pop up occasionally. Stars who have sailed in the past few years include the country and western band Alabama, Trace Adkins, Montgomery Gentry, Wynonna, Neal McCoy, Love and Theft, Craig Morgan, Lonestar, Kenny Rogers, Vince Gill, Larry Gatlin and the Gatlin Brothers, The Oak Ridge Boys, Mel Tillis, and Kathy Mattea. There are also songwriter workshops and karaoke (judged by the professionals), late-night dance parties, and a little unscheduled jammin' along the way.

Strictly Come Dancing with the stars

Fans of TV's *Strictly Come Dancing* ballroom dancing shows will find special theme cruises with P&O Cruises (www.pocruises.com).

Family themes

Aboard the ships of Disney Cruise Line, *everything* is Disney – every song heard, every game played, every participation event, race, or party – it's the complete Disney at sea package.

Royal Caribbean International has its own star themes at sea, including characters from the Dream-Works Experience such as Alex from *Madagascar*, Fiona and Puss in Boots from *Shrek*, and Po from *Kung Fu Panda*.

Culinary theme cruises

Food and wine cruises have always attracted interest, although some are better than others. Most have tended to be more like presentation lectures at cooking stations set on a large stage, and always seem to leave audiences wanting to ask questions one-on-one rather than as part of a general audience.

Wine-themed cruises are especially popular with oenophiles (wine lovers), who get to meet owners and specialists from various world-famous vineyards with wine talks and wine tasting as part of the pleasure of these special voyages.

Star Wars

In 2016, Disney Cruise Line designated eight sailings aboard *Disney Fantasy* as *Star Wars* cruises. *Star Wars* films were shown, and Darth Vader, Stormtroopers, Chewbacca, Boba Fett, and other characters from across the *Star Wars* galaxy were aboard for meet-and-greet sessions.

A shipboard version of the Jedi Training Academy invited young Jedi hopefuls to learn lightsaber moves from a Jedi master.

Families participated in *Star Wars* trivia games, while themed arts and crafts, games, and activities were featured daily.

In 2017, there were 15 *Star Wars* sailings aboard *Disney Fantasy*; in 2018 there are 15. May the Force be with you!

Not your regular theme cruise

Other unusual theme cruises include naturist vacations – clothing-free vacations. Bare Necessities has been doing it since 1990, although participants do dress to go to the dining room. The Big Nude Boat Cruise 2016 took place aboard *Celebrity Constellation*. Then there's Dream Pleasure Tours (http://dream-pleasuretours.com), founded in 2007 for sensual indulgence. This company charters ships for hedonistic lifestyle cruises, including for the gay, lesbian, and swinger communities. A swingers' (adventurous couples) cruise took place in 2016 aboard *MSC Divina*, with a Bliss Cruise (for couples) aboard *Celebrity Silhouette*.

The Harley-Davidson Motorcycle Rally At Sea has been happening for around 10 years aboard Celebrity Cruises. Dress code: biker attire. There's a belly smacker contest; a treasured chest (women); best beard (men); and a contest for the best tattoo.

Some cruises are just magical adventures in themselves. In 2013, everyone's favorite wizard, the venerable Harry Potter, took to the seas with his own theme cruise.

Other themed cruises include Wellness, Fitness, 'Mind, Body and Spirit,' and 'Life Modification' cruises (the first Holistic Health Cruise at sea was aboard *Cunard Countess* in 1976 and included Ida Rolf – the esteemed creator of the extreme massage technique

A complimentary music class aboard *Crystal Serenity*.

The author taking part in a culinary class aboard *Britannia*.

known as Rolfing – on board). Then there's the Quilting and Girlfriends cruise – for girls who cruise to quilt (https://stitchinheaven.com); castles and gardens cruises (www.hebridean.co.uk); and scrapbooking cruises (www.cruiseandcrop.com).

Several cruise lines also have golf-themed cruises, but perhaps the best packages are put together by companies including Crystal Cruises, Hapag-Lloyd Cruises, Regent Seven Seas Cruises, and SeaDream Yacht Club, all of which operate smaller-size ships for a more personal experience.

Corporate cruising

Corporate incentive organizations and seagoing conferences need to have such elements as accommodation, food, or entertainment for delegates organized as one contract. Cruise companies have specialized departments to deal with all the details. Helpfully, many larger ships have almost identical cabin sizes and configurations.

Once a corporate contract is signed, no refund is possible, so insurance is essential. Although you may need only 70 percent of a ship's capacity for your purposes, you will have to pay for the whole ship if you want an *exclusive* charter.

Although you can contact cruise lines directly, I strongly recommend contacting the Miami-based ship charter specialists Landry & Kling (http://landrykling.com), who can arrange whole-ship charters for theme cruises.

Maiden and inaugural voyages

It can be fun to take part in the maiden voyage of a new cruise ship. Or you could join an inaugural voyage aboard a refurbished, reconstructed, or stretched ship. However, you'll need a degree of tolerance – and be prepared for some inconveniences, such as slow or non-existent service in dining venues.

One thing is certain: any maiden voyage is a collector's item, but Murphy's Law – 'If anything can go wrong, it will' – can prevail. Service aboard new or recently refurbished ships (or a new cruise line) is likely to be uncertain and could be a disaster. An existing cruise line may use experienced crew from its other vessels to help 'bring out' a new ship, but they may be unfamiliar with the ship's layout and may have problems training other staff.

Plumbing and electrical items tend to cause the most problems, particularly aboard reconstructed and refurbished vessels. Examples: toilets that don't flush or don't stop flushing; faucets incorrectly marked, where 'hot' really means 'cold'; and 'automatic' telephones that refuse to function.

In the entertainment department, items such as spare spotlight bulbs may not be in stock. Or what if the pianos arrive damaged, or audio-visual materials for the lecturers haven't been delivered? Manuals for high-tech sound and lighting equipment may be in a foreign language.

Items such as menus, postcards, writing paper, TV remote control units, door keys, towels, pillowcases, glassware, and even toilet paper may be lost in the bowels of the ship, or simply not ordered.

The galley (kitchen) of a new ship is in trouble if the right supplies don't turn up on time.

If you feel any of these mishaps might spoil your cruise, it would probably be better to wait until the ship has been in service for at least three months.

Expedition Cruises

By the beginning of 2017, some 10 new expedition ships were on order due to the upsurge of interest in such voyages, which allow passengers to discover nature in the world's most remote places.

Like sport-utility vehicles, expedition ships offer a very comfortable lifestyle as a base to experience nature safely – no more being squeezed into telephone-box-sized cabins.

Expedition cruising is poles apart from all other types of cruising. It is total immersion in nature and discovery, with a sense of pioneering thrown in. Passengers joining cruise expeditions need to be pretty self-reliant and more interested in doing or learning than in being entertained. They become 'participants' and take very active roles in almost every aspect of a voyage.

Naturalists, historians, and lecturers are aboard each ship to provide background information and observations about wildlife.

Collectible expedition experiences

You can venture right to the North Pole, walk on pack ice in the Arctic Circle, or visit a penguin rookery on an island in the Antarctic Peninsula, the Falkland Islands, and South Georgia. Or, you could go birding in the Aleutian Pribilof Islands, search for 'lost' peoples in Papua New Guinea, explore the Amazon basin, venture to Darwin's laboratory in the Galápagos Islands, or watch real dragons on Komodo island – from a comfortable distance, of course.

Explore in comfort

Briefings and lectures bring cultural and intellectual elements to expedition cruises, which are all about being close to nature. An expedition leader works closely with the ship's captain and marine operations department. The ships are designed and equipped to sail in ice-laden waters, yet they have a shallow-enough draft to glide over coral reefs.

Without traditional cruise ports, ships must be self-sufficient, capable of long-range cruising, and totally environmentally friendly. There's no professional entertainment. Instead, recaps of the day's experiences take place each evening, and board games and library books are always available.

However, the expedition experience itself really comes alive by the use 'Zodiacs' – inflatable but rigid craft that can seat up to a dozen participants (note that landings on icy terrain can be quite demanding). The feel of sea spray and wind on your face gives you a thrill, and the feeling that this really is something different from any cruising you may have done previously.

How expedition cruising developed

Lars-Eric Lindblad pioneered expedition cruising in 1966. The Swedish-American turned travel into ad-

venture by going to parts of the world tourists had not visited. After chartering several vessels for voyages to Antarctica, he organized the construction of a small ship capable of going almost anywhere in comfort and safety. In 1969, *Lindblad Explorer* was launched; it soon earned an enviable reputation in adventure travel. Others followed.

To put together cruise expeditions, companies turn to specialist advisers. Scientific institutions are consulted; experienced world explorers and naturalists provide up-to-date reports on wildlife sightings, migrations, and other natural phenomena. Sea days are usually spent preparing, and participants are kept physically and mentally active. Avoid such an adventure cruise if you are not completely mobile, because getting into and out of Zodiacs (inflatable shore landing craft) can be tricky.

The companies provide expedition parkas and waterproof boots, but you will need to take waterproof trousers for Antarctica and the Arctic.

Most of the present 'expedition' ships are ageing. Some have really passed their sell by date and will not

Typical serene Antarctic scenery.

Hanseatic is equipped with the highest ice class (E4) for passenger ships, enabling it to safely navigate through the ice.

comply with the new Polar Code PC6 requirements, required for ships to cruise in the polar regions during summer and fall in medium 'first-year' ice that is typically off limits to most 'expedition' ships). Hence the orders for new specialist ships. Scenic is first off the mark, with its state-of-the-art Discovery Yacht to be delivered in 2018. In 2019 Crystal Cruises, Hapag-Lloyd (a company with long-standing expedition experience), Hurtigruten, Oceanwide Expeditions, and Ponant all have new ships due for delivery. *Crystal Endeavor* and *Scenic Eclipse* will carry mini-submersible vessels, one or two helicopters (it's not easy to get permits to use them, however, particularly in the Arctic), and other specialist equipment. Meanwhile, the landing craft aboard Hapag-Lloyd's new expedition ships *Hanseatic Nature* and *Hanseatic Inspiration* will be environmentally friendly, electric-powered Zodiacs (but no helicopters or submersibles),

Antarctica

See the 'Frozen Planet' for yourself. While Arctic ice is only a few feet thick, the ice of Antarctica is thousands of feet thick. The continent was first sighted in 1820 by the American sealer Nathaniel Palmer, British naval officer Edward Bransfield, and Russian captain Fabian Bellingshausen.

For most, it is just a windswept frozen wasteland – it has been calculated that the ice mass contains almost 90 percent of the world's snow and ice (and 70 percent of the world's water), while its treeless land

mass is nearly twice the size of Australia. For others, it represents the last pristine place on earth, offering an abundance of marine and bird life.

As many as 36,000 people a year visit Antarctica. In 2014, there were 18,000 expedition cruise visitors to Port Lockroy, the British research station, which has a resident postmaster. There is 24-hour sunshine during the austral summer, but not a single native inhabitant. Its ice is as much as 2 miles (3km) thick, and its total land mass equals more than all the rivers and lakes on earth and exceeds that of China and India combined. Icebergs can easily be the size of Belgium. The region has a raw beauty.

There are two ways to reach the cold continent by sea.

From Ushuaia in Argentina, Punta Arenas, or Puerto Williams in Chile, across the Drake Passage, to the Antarctic Peninsula (the most popular route). The peninsula (sometimes together with South Georgia) is visited by the 'soft' expedition cruise ships and even normal-size cruise ships with ice-hardened hulls. From Ushuaia or Punta Arenas, it takes two days to reach the Antarctic Peninsula, to see the pristine Antarctic ice and observe the wildlife (the best time is mid-November, when penguins come ashore for courtship and nesting). South Georgia is famous, because the explorer Ernest Shackleton is buried in Grytviken – a former Norwegian whaling station.

From Hobart (Australia) or Auckland (New Zealand) to the Ross Ice Shelf, it takes about seven days to reach the eastern side of the continent in the Ross Sea (hence it is more expensive than leaving from Argentina or Chile). This, the more remote 'far side' – the Oates and Scott coasts, McMurdo Sound, and the famous Ross Ice Shelf – can be visited only by genuine icebreakers, as the katabatic winds can easily reach more than 100mph (160kph). However, a highlight will be a visit to Scott's well-preserved hut at Cape Evans on Ross Island. It has been frozen in time since 1912 (with over 8,000 items – including many tins of food). You can also visit Shackleton's hut, at Cape Royds on Ross Island (it contains over 5,000 items), and Mawson's huts at Cape Denison in the eastern sector (a replica of one of Mawson's huts (built by the Mawson's Huts Foundation) opened in December 2013. It sits on the dockside in Hobart, Australia.

The first ship carrying participants on a complete circumnavigation of Antarctica was the 114-passenger *Kapitan Khlebnikov*, operated by Quark Expeditions, in 1996–97.

Only 100 participants *per ship* are now allowed ashore at any given time, so if you cruise aboard one of the larger ships that claim to include Antarctica on their itineraries, it will probably be to view it – but only from the ship. Indeed, since 2011 cruise ships with more than 500 participants have not been allowed to sail in Antarctic waters unless they use lighter-grade distillate fuel. Moreover, the chances of rescue in the event of pack ice crushing a normal cruise ship hull are virtually nil. For real expedition cruising, choose a ship that includes a flotilla of Zodiacs, proper boot-washing stations, expedition equipment, experienced expedition leaders, ice captains, and no extra charges for items such as kayaks. Companies that stand out from the crowd are Hapag-Lloyd, Quark Expeditions, and Poseidon Expeditions.

Most large resort ship operators thankfully exited Antarctica in 2011 due to a ban on carrying or burning heavy fuel oil below 60 degree south latitude, leaving travel mainly in the hands of specialist expedition ship operators. 'Antarctic' fuel (lighter-grade distillate fuel) is the world's highest cost fuel for ship use. However, some large resort ships and mid-size ships also carry the special fuel, which allows them to continue traveling to Antarctica – although these are for cruising only, not passenger landings.

Be aware that you can still get stuck even aboard these specialized expedition ships.

Tip: Wear an ID bracelet or belt at all times while on an Antarctic expedition cruise, and take thermal underwear. Anyone on a special diet should advise the cruise operator as early as possible, so that any necessary items can be obtained.

Wildlife you may see or come into contact with includes orcas, dolphins, the six species of Antarctic seals, penguins, and various species of lichen and flora, depending on the area visited.

Take plastic bags to cover your camera, so that condensation forms inside the bag and not on your camera when changing from the cold of the outside Antarctic air to the warmth of your expedition cruise vessel. Make sure you know how to operate your camera with gloves on – frostbite is a real danger.

The High Arctic

This is an ocean surrounded by continents, whereas Antarctica is an ice-covered continent surrounded by ocean. The Arctic Circle is located at 66 degrees, 33 minutes, 3 seconds North, although this really designates where 24-hour days and nights begin. The High Arctic is best defined as that region north of which no trees grow, and where water is the primary feature of the landscape.

Poseidon Expeditions, the Arctic expedition cruise specialist, operates under the strict guidelines of the Association of Arctic Expedition Cruise Operators (AECO), the body committed to minimizing the impact of visit to the Far North. These expeditions to the North Pole (90 degrees North) are undertaken only at the height of the Arctic summer, in June and July, usually aboard the world's most powerful ice-breaker – the Russian nuclear-powered *50 Years of Victory* – which can crush ice up to 10ft (3m) thick. An onboard helicopter whisks participants between the ship and the North Pole.

This really is a once-in-a-lifetime adventure. Only 250 participants managed to visit the North Pole in 2016.

The Northwest Passage

Passenger ships that have navigated the dangerous Northwest Passage linking the Atlantic and Pacific oceans include *Lindblad Explorer* (1984), *World Discoverer* (1985), *Society Explorer* (1988), *Frontier Spirit* (1992), *Kapitan Khlebnikov* (1994, 1995, 1998, 2006, 2007, 2008), *Hanseatic* (1995, 1996, 1997, 1999, 2007, 2010, 2012), and *Bremen* (2009, 2010). In 2013, 2015, and 2017, unusual double crossings took place; *Hanseatic* went east to west, while *Bremen* went west to east.

The Amazon

The River Amazon is long – around 4,080 miles (6,566km) from close to its source in the Peruvian Andes, to Belém on South America's Atlantic coast – and contains one fifth of the earth's water supply. Home to a tenth of the planet's animal species and plant life, it has thousands of tributaries, and is of-

---

PROTECTING SENSITIVE ENVIRONMENTS

In the future, only ships capable of meeting new 'zero discharge' standards will be allowed to cross environmentally sensitive areas. Expedition cruise companies are concerned about the environment, and they spend a great deal of time and money in educating their crews and participants about safe procedures.

They observe the 'Antarctic Traveler's Code,' based on 1978's Antarctic Conservation Act, designed to protect the region's ecosystem, flora, and fauna.

The Antarctic Treaty Meeting in Kyoto in 1994 made it unlawful, unless authorized by permit, to enter certain special protected areas (SPAs), or discharge or dispose of pollutants. The original Antarctic Treaty, signed in 1959 by 12 nations active in the region, defined Antarctica as all of the land and ice shelves south of 60 degrees South latitude. The signatories: Argentina, Australia, Belgium, Chile, France, Japan, New Zealand, Norway, South Africa, the Soviet Union, the UK, and the US. Some 29 countries now sit on the Antarctic Treaty Consultative committee, with 53 countries acceding to the Treaty.

Ships carrying over 500 participants are not allowed to land and are restricted to 'scenic' cruising, so the likelihood of a large resort ship zooming in on penguins is low. It would not be possible to rescue so many passengers (plus crew) in the event of an emergency. Also, large resort ships burn heavy oil (now banned in the Antarctic) rather than the lighter oil used by the specialist expedition ships, which also have ice-strengthened hulls.

New expedition ships: 2018–2021					
Company	Ship name	Length (m)	Length (ft)	Passengers (approximate)	Due
2018					
Hurtigruten	Roald Amundsen	43	140	530	2018
Ponant	Le Lapérouse	40	131	184	2018
Scenic	Scenic Eclipse	51	168	228	2018
2019					
Hapag-Lloyd Cruises	Hanseatic nature	42	138	230	2019
Hapag-Lloyd Cruises	Hanseatic inspiration	42	138	230	2019
Hurtigruten	Fridtjof Nansen	43	140	530	2019
Oceanwide Expeditions	Hondius				2019
Ponant	Le Bougainville	40	131	184	2019
Ponant	Le Kerguelen	40	131	184	2019
Ponant	Le Champlain	40	131	184	2019

ten so wide you cannot see the riverbank on the opposite side.

Cruises usually start in the Caribbean from ports such as Barbados and end up in Manaus (or vice versa). Starting in Manaus, with its muddy red-brown water, and ending up in the clear blue waters of the Caribbean may be the more appealing option. Calls along the way may be made in Parintins, Alter do Chão, Santarém, and Belém. Few ships venture farther upriver from Manaus to Iquitos.

Manaus, located around 1,000 miles (1,600km) from the ocean, was built by barons of the rubber industry. Today, it really is a gaudy metropolis, but its opera house, built at the end of the 19th cen-

tury, remains a much-visited icon and still stages concerts.

One must-do shore excursion is a rainforest walk with a knowledgeable Brazilian guide to give you an insight into the richest variety of life on the planet. But make sure you have plenty of insect repellent – more than 200 varieties of mosquito inhabit the Amazon Basin.

The Galápagos Islands

These islands, 600 miles (966km) west of Ecuador in the Pacific Ocean, are a microcosm of our planet. Some 13 major and 7 minor islands plus scores of islets make up the Galápagos, which are fed by the nutrient-rich Cromwell and Humboldt currents. The fertile waters can be cold, even on the equator.

The Ecuadorians jealously guard their islands and prohibit the movement of almost all non-Ecuador-registered cruise vessels within its boundaries. The best way to follow in the footsteps of Charles Darwin, who visited the islands in 1835 aboard the Beagle, is to fly to Quito and cruise aboard an Ecuadorian-registered vessel.

The government of Ecuador set aside most of the islands as a wildlife sanctuary in 1934, while uninhabited areas were declared national parks in 1959. The national park includes approximately 97 percent of the islands' landmass, together with 20,000 sq miles (52,000 sq km) of ocean. The Charles Darwin Research Station was established in 1964, and the government created the Galápagos Marine Resources Reserve in 1986.

The Galápagos National Park tax is $100, plus $10 for an Immigration Control Card (this must be obtained before you travel). Smoking is prohibited on the islands, and no more than 50,000 visitors a year are admitted. In 2012 new rules stopped ships from visiting most islands more than once in a 14-day period. Some cruise lines require vaccinations for cruises that include Ecuador, although the World Health Organization does not.

CRACKING THE NORTHWEST PASSAGE

In 1984, Salen Lindblad Cruising made maritime history with Lindblad Explorer by negotiating a westbound voyage through the Northwest Passage, a 41-day epic that started from St. John's, in Newfoundland, Canada, and ended at Yokohama, Japan. The search for a Northwest Passage to the Orient – finding a sea route connecting the Pacific and Atlantic oceans through the treacherous Canadian Arctic archipelago – had attracted brave explorers for more than four centuries, and, despite numerous attempts and loss of life including the English explorer Henry Hudson in 1610, a 'white passage' to the East remained an elusive dream. The Norwegian explorer Roald Amundsen's 47-ton ship Gjoa eventually navigated the route in 1906, taking three years to do so. It was not until 1943 that a Canadian ship, St. Roch, became the first vessel in history to make the passage in a single season. Lindblad Explorer became the 34th vessel, and the first cruise vessel, to complete the Northwest Passage.

Coastal Cruises

Being all at sea doesn't appeal? You can stay close to dry land by journeying round the coasts of Australia, Europe, and North and South America.

The marine wonderland of the Great Barrier Reef, a World Heritage Site off the northeast coast of Australia, is the earth's largest living coral reef – it actually consists of more than 2,800 individual coral reefs. It is visited by around 70 local Australian boutique ship operators, who mostly offer one- to four-night cruises to the reefs and Whitsunday Islands. The area is excellent for scuba diving and snorkeling.

June through September is humpback whale-watching season; the Reef shelters the young whales, while the adults nurture them in the shallow waters. Note that the Australian government levies an environmental charge of A$6.50 per day (A$3.25 for those spending less than three hours in the Marine Park) on everyone over four years of age visiting the Great Barrier Reef and its environs.

Norway

An alternative to traditional cruise ships can be found in the year-round coastal cruising along the shores of Norway to the Land of the Midnight Sun aboard the ships of the Hurtigruten Group. The fleet consists of small, comfortable, working express coastal vessels and contemporary cruise vessels that deliver mail,

small packaged goods, and foodstuffs, and take passengers to the communities spread on the shoreline.

Invariably dubbed 'the world's most beautiful voyage,' this is a 1,250-mile (2,012-km) journey from Bergen in Norway to Kirkenes, close to the Russian border (half of which is north of the Arctic Circle) and takes 12 days. The service started in 1893 to provide connection to communities when there were no roads, and the name Hurtigruten – meaning 'fast route' – reflects the fact that this coastal express was once the most reliable communication link between southern Norway and its remote north. Today the company carries more than 300,000 passengers a year. It's a good way to meet Norwegians, who treat the service like a bus.

You can join it at any of the 34 ports of call and stay as long as you wish because the vessels sail every day of the year (some port calls are of only one hour or so – enough to get off and on and unload freight). Most ports are repeated on the return journey, but stop at different times, so you may get a different feeling for a place, even if you've also visited it.

Note that double beds are available only in suite-grade accommodation (other cabins are dimensionally challenged, with sparse decor, furnishings, and mini-

A Hurtigruten ship on Norway's Arctic coast.

Hebridean Princess in the Scottish islands.

mal luggage storage space); many of the beds are fixed in an L-shape, or in a bed and sofa/bed combination. Note that most of the ships do not have stabilizers, and there is no doctor on board, nor indeed any medical facilities, but all gratuities are included in the fare.

At the height of summer, north of the Arctic Circle, there are almost 24 hours of daylight (there is no sunset between April 19 and August 23). Between November and February, the northern lights – if the atmospheric conditions are right – create spectacular arcs across the sky. Some specialist voyages are aimed at wildlife, birdwatchers, astronomy, and others, while onboard concerts and lectures celebrate the work of Norwegian composer Edvard Grieg.

The ships can accommodate between 144 and 652 passengers. The newest ships have an elevator that can accommodate a wheelchair passenger, but, otherwise, they are plain, basic, practical vessels, with food that is more canteen-style than restaurant. A 24-hour restaurant provides items at extra cost. Note that the price of alcoholic drinks is extremely high (you can take your own on board), as it is throughout Norway, and that the currency is the Norwegian krone.

Archipelago-hopping can be done along Sweden's eastern coast, too, by sailing in the daytime and staying overnight in one of the many small hotels en route. One vessel sails from Norrtalje, north of Stockholm, to Oskarshamn, near the Baltic island of Öland, right through the spectacular Swedish archipelago.

The Hurtigruten Group also operates utilitarian ships for expeditions to the Arctic, Antarctic, and Greenland.

Scotland

The fishing town of Oban, two hours west of Glasgow by road, is the base for one of the world's finest cruise experiences. *Hebridean Princess* is a real gem, with Laura Ashley-style interiors – posh enough to have been chartered by Queen Elizabeth II for a fam-

ily-only celebration of her 80th birthday in 2006. The food is excellent, and includes locally sourced Scottish beef, local seafood, and seasonal vegetables. There's fine personal service.

This ship, owned by Hebridean Island Cruises, carries up to 50 passengers around some of Scotland's most magnificent coastline and islands. If you cruise from Oban, you can be met at Glasgow airport or railway station and taken to the ship by motor coach. Take lots of warm clothing, however (layers are best), as the weather can be changeable and often inclement.

There's also the 54-passenger *Lord of the Glens*, operated by the Magna Carta Steamship Company and with many of its fittings taken from famous ocean liners and trains of yesteryear. It cruises in style through Scotland's lakes and canals, although it's not a steamship but a modern deluxe vessel. Some high-season sailings have historians and guest lecturers on board. Note that the cuisine is not up to the standard of Hebridean Princess, and drinks are very expensive.

North America

Coastal cruise ships flying the American flag offer a complete change of style from the large resort cruise ships. They are American-owned and American-crewed, and very informal. Being US-registered, they can start from and return to a US port without being required to call at a foreign port along the way – which a foreign-flagged cruise ship must do.

Accommodating up to 200 passengers, the ships are rarely out of sight of land. These cruises are low-key, low-pace, and not for active, adventurous types. Their operators seek out lesser-known areas, offering in-depth visits to destinations inaccessible to larger ships, along both the eastern and western seaboards of the US, including Alaska.

Most passengers are of senior years. Many prefer not to fly, and wherever possible drive or take a train to join their ship. During the summer, you might see a couple of children on board, but in general small kids are not allowed. There are no facilities for them, and no staff to look after them.

Destinations. Eastern US and Canadian seaboard cruises include the St. Lawrence River, Atlantic Coastal Waterways, New England (good for fall cruises), Cape Cod and the Islands – and Cape Cod Canal, the Great Lakes – and the Welland Canal, the Colonial Deep South, and Florida waterways.

Western seaboard cruises cover Alaska, the Pacific Northwest, California Wine Country, and Baja California/Sea of Cortez. Cruises focus on historically relevant destinations, nature and wildlife spotting, and coastal viewing. On some cruises, these boutique ships can dock adjacent to a town, allowing easy access on foot.

The ships. These 'D-class' vessels are less than 2,500 gross tonnage, and are subject neither to bureaucratic regulations nor to union rules. They are restricted to cruising no more than 20 miles (32km) offshore. Public room facilities are limited. Because the vessels are US-registered, there is no casino. They really are casual, no-frills ships with basic facilities, no swimming pools, little artwork, and no glitz in terms of the interior decor. They usually have three or four decks and, except for the ships of American Cruise Lines, sister company Pearl Seas Cruises, and Victory Cruise Lines, there is no elevator. Stairs can be steep and are not recommended for anyone with walking difficulties. Because of this, some have an electric chair-lift.

Accommodation is in outside-view cabins, some opening directly onto a walking deck, which is inconvenient when it rains. Each has a picture window and small bathroom. They are basic, with very limited closet space – often just a curtain across a space with a hanging rod for clothes. Many don't have a television set or telephone. There's no room service, and you may have to turn your own bed down. Cabins are closer to the engines and generators than aboard the large resort ships, so the noise of the generator humming can be disturbing at night. The quietest cabins are at the bows – although there could be noise from the bow thruster propeller. Most cruising is, however, done in the early morning, so that passengers can sleep better at night.

Tall passengers should note that the overall length of beds rarely exceeds 6ft (1.8m). Although soap is provided, it's best to bring your own shampoo, conditioner, and other toiletries. The ships of Blount Small Ship Adventures do not have cabin keys. Hot and cold water lines may run close to each other in your bathroom, delivering neither really hot nor really cold water. Sound insulation is quite poor.

Activities. The main evening event is dinner in the dining room, with one seating. This can be a family-style affair, with passengers at long tables, and the food passed around.

The cuisine is decidedly American, with fresh local specialties. Menus aboard the ships of Alaskan Dream Cruises and Blount Small Ship Adventures are quite limited; those aboard the ships of American Cruise Lines offer slightly more variety, includ-

Swimming from *Wilderness Adventurer* in Alaska.

ing seasonal items. You'll probably be asked in the morning to choose which of the two main courses you'd like for dinner.

Evening entertainment consists mainly of after-dinner conversation. Most vessels are in port during the time, so you can easily go ashore for the local nightlife, although most passengers simply go to bed early.

The cost. These cruises are expensive, with an average daily rate of $400–800 a person, plus gratuities of about $125 per person, per seven-day cruise (these are shared by all personnel).

COASTAL CRUISE LINES IN NORTH AMERICA

There are several small ship cruise companies: Alaskan Dream Cruises, American Cruise Lines, Blount Small Ship Adventures, Lindblad Expeditions, Pearl Seas Cruises, Un-Cruise Adventures, and Victory Cruise Lines.

What differentiates them? American Cruise Lines, Pearl Seas Cruises, and Un-Cruise Adventures provide better food and service than the others. American Cruise Lines' and Pearl Seas Cruises' ships have larger cabins, and more public rooms. Drinks are included aboard the ships of American Cruise Lines and Victory Cruise Lines.

Hurtigruten ships			
Ship	Tonnage	Built	Berths
Finnmarken	15,000	2002	638
Fram *	12,700	2007	328
Kong Harald	11,200	1993	490
Lofoten	2,621	1964	147
Midnatsol **	16,053	2003	652
Nordkapp	11,386	1996	464
Nordlys	11,200	1994	482
Nordnorge	11,386	1997	455
Nordstjernen **	2,621	1956	114
Polarlys	12,000	1996	479
Richard With	11,205	1993	483
Spitsbergen	7,025	2009	200
Trollfjord	15,000	2002	648
Vesterålen	6,261	1983	316
* for expedition voyages only ** for 'soft' expedition-style cruises			

Cruising Under Sail

Want to be free as the wind? Think about cruising under sail, with towering masts, the creak of the deck, and gleaming white sails to power the ship along.

There's simply nothing that beats the thrill of being aboard a multi-mast tall ship, sailing under thousands of square feet of canvas through waters that mariners have sailed for centuries. This is cruising in the traditional manner of seafaring, aboard authentic sailing ships, contemporary copies of clipper ships, or high-tech cruise-sail ships, which provides a genuine sailing experience, while keeping creature comforts.

Mealtimes apart, there are no rigid schedules, so life aboard can be liberatingly unstructured. Weather conditions may often dictate whether a scheduled port visit will be made or not, but passengers sailing on these vessels are usually unconcerned. They would rather savor the feeling of being at one with nature, albeit in a comfortable, civilized setting, and without having to do the work themselves. The more luxurious sailing ships are the closest most people will get to owning their own mega-yacht.

Real sail-cruise ships

While we have all been dreaming of adventure, a pocketful of designers and yachtsmen committed

The *Sea Cloud* crew goes up the rigging.

pen to paper, hand in pocket and rigging to mast, and came up with a potpourri of stunning vessels to delight the eye and refresh the spirit. Examples are *Flying Clipper* (new in 2018), *Royal Clipper, Sea Cloud, Sea Cloud II, Star Clipper,* and *Star Flyer* – all of which have beautiful retro decor to convey the feeling of yesteryear and a slower pace of life.

Of these, *Sea Cloud,* built in 1931, restored in 1979, and adapted to satisfy the latest safety regulations of the International Convention for the Safety of Life at Sea (SOLAS), is the most exhilarating and romantic sailing ship afloat. It operates under charter for part of the year, and sails in both the Caribbean and the Mediterranean.

The activities are few, so relaxation is the key, in a stylish but unpretentious setting. The food and service are extremely good, as is the interaction between the

HOW TO MEASURE WIND SPEEDS

Understanding wind patterns is important to sailing ships, but the numbering system for wind velocity can confuse. There are 12 velocities, known as 'force' on the Beaufort scale, devised in 1805 by Sir Francis Beaufort, an Irish-born hydrographer and officer in Britain's Royal Navy. It was adopted internationally in 1874 as the official means of recording wind velocity. They are as follows, with descriptions of the ocean surface:
Force 0 (0–1mph): Calm; glassy (like a mirror).
Force 1 (1–3mph): Light wind; rippled surface.
Force 2 (4–7mph): Light breeze; small wavelets.
Force 3 (8–12mph): Gentle breeze; large wavelets, scattered whitecaps.
Force 4 (13–18mph): Moderate breeze; small waves, frequent whitecaps.
Force 5 (19–24mph): Fresh breeze; moderate waves, numerous whitecaps.
Force 6 (25–31mph): Strong breeze; large waves, white foam crests.
Force 7 (32–38mph): Moderate gale; streaky white foam.
Force 8 (39–46mph): Fresh gale; moderate waves.
Force 9 (47–54mph): Strong gale; high waves.
Force 10 (55–63mph): Whole gale; very high waves, curling crests.
Force 11 (64–72mph): Violent storm; extremely high waves, froth and foam, poor visibility.
Force 12 (73+mph): Hurricane; huge waves, thundering white spray, visibility nil.

The beautiful *Sea Cloud* under full sail.

69 passengers and 60 crew members, many of whom have worked aboard the ship for many years. One bonus is the fact that a doctor is available on board at no charge for emergencies or seasickness medication.

A modern interpretation of the original *Sea Cloud*, a second ship, named *Sea Cloud II*, was built and introduced in 2001.

Contemporary sail-cruise ships

To combine sailing with push-button automation, try *Club Med 2* (Club Mediterranée) or *Wind Surf* (Windstar Cruises) – with five tall aluminum masts, they are the world's largest sail-cruise ships – and *Wind Spirit* and *Wind Star* (Windstar Cruises), with four masts. Not a hand touches the sails; they are computer-controlled from the navigation bridge.

The traditional sense of sailing is almost absent in these ocean-going robots, because the computer keeps the ship on an even keel. Also, some people find it hard to get used to the whine of the vessels' generators, which run the lighting and air-conditioning systems 24 hours a day.

From a yachtsman's viewpoint, the sail-to-power ratio is poor. That's why these cruise ships with sails have engine power to get them into and out of port. The *Sea Cloud* and *Star Clipper* ships do it by sail alone, except when there is no wind, which doesn't happen all that often.

On some itineraries, when there's little wind, you could be motor-powered for most of the cruise, with only a few hours under sail. The three Windstar Cruises vessels and one Club Med ship are typically under sail for about 40 percent of the time.

The Windstar ships carry mainly North American passengers, while the Club Med vessel caters mainly to French speakers.

Another slightly smaller vessel is the chic *Le Ponant*. This three-mast ship caters to just 64 French-speaking passengers in elegant, yet casual, high-tech surroundings, advancing the technology of the original Windstar concept. The ship made news in 2008, when its crew was held to ransom by pirates off the Somali coast; no passengers were on board at the time.

When the engine cuts in

So, do you get to cruise under sail most of the time? Not really. Aboard the ships of Sea Cloud Cruises and Star Clippers, because they are real sailing ships, you could be under sail for most of the night when the ships are under way, as long as there is wind, of course, and on the days or part days at sea.

The ship's small engine is used for maneuvering in and out of port. In the Caribbean, for example, the trade winds are good for most of the year, but in the Mediterranean the winds are not so potent.

Aboard the ships of Windstar Cruises, however, the itineraries are so port-intensive that the computer-controlled sails are hardly ever used today – so the experience can be disappointing.

Transatlantic Crossings

You may be facing some unpredictable weather, but there's something romantic and adventurous about this classic ocean voyage.

This should be one of life's essential travel experiences. Crossing the 3,000 miles (4,830km) of the North Atlantic by ship is a great way to avoid the hassles of airports. I have done it 158 times and always enjoy it immensely – and unlike flying, there's no jet lag. Yet the days when ships were built specifically for crossings are almost gone. The only one offering a regularly scheduled service is Cunard's *Queen Mary 2 (QM2)*, built with a thick hull designed to survive the worst weather the North Atlantic has to offer.

It's a leisurely seven-day voyage, on five of which the clocks will be advanced (eastbound) or put back (westbound) by one hour. You can take as many bags as you want, and even your pets – *QM2*'s 24 kennels are overseen by a full-time kennel master, and there is an outdoor walking area. Book well in advance if you want to travel with your dog, however, as numbers are strictly limited.

The 2,691 passenger *QM2* is the largest ocean liner ever built, and a destination on its own. New in 2004, it measures 148,528 gross tons. It has a wide walk-around promenade deck outdoors, and its forward section is under cover from the weather or wind (three times around is 6,102 ft/1,860 m, or 1.1 miles/1.8km).

By comparison, *QM2*'s smaller half-sisters *Queen Elizabeth* and *Queen Victoria* both measure about 90,000 gross tons. The *QE2*, which was retired in 2008, measured 70,327 gross tons – the ill-fated *Titanic* measured a mere 46,328 gross tons. The difference is that *QM2* is a thick-hulled ocean liner, designed to withstand the pressures of the North Atlantic and its unpredictable weather.

The North Atlantic can be as smooth as glass or as rough as old boots, although in my experience it's rare for the weather to be bad for an entire crossing. But when it *is* a bit choppy, its heavy beauty really is mesmerizing – never, ever boring. However, make sure you always use the handrails when you move around, and use the elevators rather than the stairs.

When the ship is under way at speed (above 25 knots – about 30 land miles per hour) on a windy day, a cabin balcony is pretty useless, and the promenade deck is a challenging place to be – if you can even get outside, that is! It can be bitterly cold on deck in winter in the open seas of the Atlantic, so you may never open your balcony door. If you do book a balcony cabin, choose the port side on westbound crossings and the starboard side on eastbound crossings – if the weather is kind and the sun is shining, you'll get the sun. Sometimes, visibility is low (think pea-soup fog), and you'll hear the ship's horn – a powerful, haunting sound – bellowing every two minutes.

Queen Mary 2 leaving New York City.

During the crossing

Once *Queen Mary 2* has left port, and settled down at sea on the second day, the natural rhythm of life slows down, and you begin to understand that time spent at sea, with few distractions, is special indeed, and completely different from any 'normal' cruise. It allows you some well-earned 'me' time – to pamper yourself in the Canyon Ranch Spa, to attend a lecture by a well-known author or other personality, or simply to relax and read a book from the wonderful library on board. Cunard has a list of '101 Things To Do On A *Queen Mary 2* Transatlantic Crossing' – just in case you really do want to be active.

Apart from distinguished guest speakers, *QM2* has a wide variety of leisure facilities, including a superb planetarium (several different shows, for which you'll need to make a reservation) and a 1,000-seat theater. There are acting classes, bridge (the card-playing kind) groups, big-band-style dance sessions, movies, exercise, cooking, and computer classes, so you'll never be bored in mid-ocean. There are now usually three formal (tuxedo) nights and four informal nights during a 7-night crossing, when an outbreak of elegance prevails. The gentlemen dance hosts are always kept busy by the number of solo female passengers who love to go dancing.

One of the ship's most used facilities is its outstanding library and bookshop – it offers around 10,000 books (of which 8,400 are in English and 800 in German, with the rest in Japanese, Spanish, Italian and French) in cabinets that have to be locked by hand – central locking was never part of the ocean liner setup – and is staffed by full-time librarians from maritime library specialists Ocean Books. The bookstore not only sells books, but also Cunard memorabilia and souvenirs.

There's always a cozy chair to curl up on to read, or just admire the sea, and, if the weather's decent, you can even swim outside; this, however, tends to be rare –except in the height of summer – because of the ship's speed and wind speed.

One of the classic things to do is to enjoy the typically British afternoon teatime, complete with cakes, scones, pastries, and finger sandwiches – all served by a rather hurried white-gloved staff – together with tea, and accompanied by live, light classical music.

The problem is that you'll find there simply isn't enough time to do everything, and there's no way you'll ever get bored aboard this ship – the archetypal ocean liner.

You can also get married in mid-Atlantic during a crossing. Cunard started its now immensely popular 'Weddings At Sea' program in 2012. The first couple to be married by the ship's captain was Dr. William De-Luca (from the US) and Kelly Lewis (from the UK). They couldn't decide whether to marry in the UK or the US, so they chose halfway between the two (it was their first crossing, and, indeed, their first-ever vacation at sea). The couple chose Cunard because of the company's 'distinguished history of transatlantic crossings.' Note that only one wedding per day can be arranged, with a time of 11am or 3.30pm. Ceremonies take place only on days at sea, and every detail is planned by an onboard wedding coordinator. The cost starts at $2,500.

A memorable arrival

The day before you arrive in New York, Southampton, or (occasionally) in Hamburg, Germany, the disembarkation procedures will arrive in your suite or cabin. If you are in a hurry to disembark, you can opt to carry your own bags by registering for 'Express Disembarkation.'

Arriving in New York is one of cruising's iconic experiences, but you'll need to be up early. You'll see the lights of Long Island on your starboard side at about 4:30am, while the Verrazzano–Narrows suspension bridge, at the entrance to New York harbor, will be dead ahead. *QM2* usually passes the State of Liberty at about 6am – when a cabin with a balcony on the port side will give you the best views – and then makes a right turn opposite the statue towards the Brooklyn Cruise Terminal. On the occasions when the ship berths at Pier 90 in Manhattan at the Passenger Terminal, it will turn left towards the Hudson River – you'll get the best views of the Manhattan skyline at this point from a cabin with balcony on the starboard side. Arrival always creates a sense of anticipation of what lies ahead, and the feeling that, after a week of being cosseted, you will be thrust back into the fast lane with full force.

Leaving New York/arriving in Southampton

If you sail from Red Hook Point in Brooklyn, the last thing you'll notice before entering the ship is the overhead banner that declares: 'Leaving Brooklyn? Fuhgeddaboudit!' And that, dear reader, is *precisely* what a transatlantic crossing will have you do.

For arrival in Southampton, *QM2* will usually round the Isle of Wight at about 4:30am, and be berthed alongside in Southampton by around 6:30am. Immigration is upon arrival in either New York or Southampton.

Repositioning crossings

Other cruise ships crossing the Atlantic are really little more than repositioning cruises – a way of moving ships that cruise the Mediterranean in summer to the Caribbean in winter, and vice versa, usually in spring and fall. Most of these ships cross the Atlantic using the sunny southern route, departing from southern ports such as Fort Lauderdale, San Juan, or Barbados, and ending the journey in Lisbon, Genoa, or Copenhagen via the Azores or the Canary Islands, off the coast of northern Africa.

These repositioning trips take longer – between eight and 12 days – but they do offer an alternative way of experiencing the romance and adventure of a crossing – with a number of sea days for total relaxation. Note that when the weather is not so good, the outdoor swimming pools will probably be out of use on repositioning crossings.

Cruising Around-the-World

Cruises are a great way to roam the world without having to pack and unpack constantly. But choose carefully: some ships spend very little time in ports.

Since Cunard operated its first world cruise aboard the *Laconia* in 1922, this has become the ultimate classic journey – more a voyage of discovery than a cruise. It is defined as the complete circumnavigation of the earth in a continuous one-way voyage, typically including both the Panama and Suez canals. Ports of call are carefully planned for their interest and diversity, and the entire voyage can last six months or longer.

Galas, themed balls (for example, Cunard's Black & White Ball and Royal Ascot Ball), special social events, top entertainers, and, typically, well-known lecturers are all part of the package. It's a great way of exchanging the northern winter for the southern sun in a grand voyage that is over 32,000 nautical miles long, following in the wake of Ferdinand Magellan, who led his round-the-world voyage in 1519–22, although he himself was killed en route.

Around-the-world cruises generally pursue the sun in a westbound direction, which gives the added bonus of gaining an hour each time a ship goes into the next time zone. Travel in an eastbound direction – between, for example, Europe and Australia – and

Aurora transiting the scenic Panama Canal.

you lose an hour each time. A few ships that include an around-South America voyage will generally travel in a southbound, then westbound, direction.

A world cruise means enjoying stabilized, air-conditioned comfort in luxury cabins, combined with extraordinary sightseeing and excursions on shore and overland. It is all about exchanging familiar environments with new ones, glamorous evening soirées, special social parties, themed balls, and entertainment that ranges from intimate recitals to large-scale shows and headline cabaret specialty acts. Best of all: you need pack and unpack just once during a three-month circumnavigation.

It generally appeals to retirees, anyone who simply wants to escape the winter, and those who delight in roaming the world in search of new experiences, sights, sounds, cultures, and aromas. There'll be lots of sea days, during which your suite or cabin can be a private refuge, so it's worth choosing the best you can afford.

There are four aspects to a good world cruise: itinerary, ship, price, and the cruise line's experience. Some of the most ambitious itineraries are those operated by cruise lines such as Hapag-Lloyd Cruises and Phoenix Reisen (whose itineraries usually feature more than 60 ports of call, compared to the average 35). Staying overnight in several ports of call means that you can plan to meet friends, go out for dinner, and enjoy nights out on the town. But check cruise line websites and brochures and itineraries carefully, because some ships spend surprisingly little time in port.

World cruise segments

If you want to experience all the extra things that around-the-world cruises provide but don't have the three months needed, most lines offer the cruise in several 'segments.' This way you can try the ship and service levels before investing the time and money needed for a full circumnavigation. The most popular length for a segment is 20–30 days.

'Segmenters,' as they are known, typically add on a stay pre- or post-cruise in a destination combining a cruise 'n' stay vacation. In this way, they can visit exotic destinations such as China, the South Pacific, the Indian Ocean, or South America, while also enjoying the elegance, comfort, splendid food, and good company of their cruise ship.

Bear in mind that you get what you pay for. Ships that we have rated at four stars or more will probably include shuttle buses from your ship to town centers; ships rated three stars or less will not.

Ships that roam worldwide during the year offer the most experienced world cruises or segments. In August 2016, for example, *Europa 2* operated a world voyage lasting 337 days, divided into three routes and more than 20 segments,

What's the cost?

Prices for a full world cruise vary depending on the cruise line, ship, and accommodation chosen. The following examples are taken from 2016/17 world cruise brochures. Per person rates are quoted, based on double occupancy (solo-occupancy rates are available on request):

AIDAcara (AIDA Cruises): interior (no-view) cabin from €11,995

Arcadia (P&O Cruises): ocean-view cabin from £10,739

Black Watch (Fred. Olsen Cruise Lines): ocean-view cabin from £11,699

Crystal Serenity (Crystal Cruises): ocean-view cabin from $43,960

Insignia (Oceania Cruises): ocean-view cabin from $44,999

Queen Elizabeth (Cunard): ocean-view cabin from £14,999

Seven Seas Navigator (Regent Seven Seas Cruises): ocean-view cabin from $59,999

Substantial discounts and special incentives are offered by many cruise lines if you book early. The lowest-grade cabins tend to sell out fastest, so book as soon as you can to secure one of these. Some cruise lines quote only a 'from' price as a lead-in rate, and provide the price for the largest suites upon application.

Passengers booking a full world cruise may enjoy a pre-cruise five-star hotel stay and extravagant dinner with the cruise line's top executives, onboard

Europa 2 anchored in Bora Bora.

credit, plus other special events during the cruise (not available to 'segmenters'). Note that some cruise lines reserve the right to add a surcharge if the NYMEX (New York Mercantile Exchange Index) oil price exceeds $70 a barrel – read the fine print in the brochure. Also, the lowest prices may not include the airfare, if any is required.

Some ships include alcoholic drinks and wine in their cruise fares (examples include *Crystal Serenity*, *Seabourn Quest*, *Seven Seas Voyager*, and *Silver Spirit*), but many do not. There will inevitably be the question of gratuities to staff, which are included aboard some ships. Factor in about $15 per person, per day to your budget.

Shore excursions

Part of the excitement of an around-the-world voyage is the anticipation of seeing new destinations, and planning how best to use your time. This is where the expertise of a cruise line's shore-excursion departments and concierges can prove worthwhile.

Aboard some ships, tailor-made excursions are available, as are extras such as arranging private cars with a driver and guide for a few hours or a whole day.

Overland tours lasting from one to five days are sometimes featured. Here, you leave the ship in one port and rejoin in another a few days later – for example, leave the ship in Mumbai, fly to Agra to experience the Taj Mahal, and perhaps ride aboard the Maharajas' Express train, then fly to another port to rejoin the ship. Depending on the 'overland' country, you may need to apply for a visa before your voyage.

Helicopter or seaplane flightseeing tours, typically costing around $300, are always popular.

One challenge is the lack of port information for independent passengers not wishing to join organized excursions. The answer is to do the research yourself. Books in the ship's library should help if you

Around-the-world cruises in late 2017/2018 (only complete circumnavigations are included)							
Ship	Company	Days	Date (start)	Start	End	No. of ports
AIDAcara	AIDA Cruises	116	October 17, 2017	Hamburg	Hamburg	41
Albatros	Phoenix Reisen	101	December, 20 2017	Genoa	Hamburg	43
Amsterdam	Holland America Line	113	January 4, 2018	Ft. Laudedale	Ft. Lauderdale	39
Arcadia	P&O Cruises	100	January 9, 2018	Southampton	Southampton	31
Black Watch	Fred. Olsen Cruise Line	109	January 5, 2018	Southampton	Southampton	33
Columbus	Cruise & Maritime Voyages (CMV)	122	January 5, 2018	London	London	40
Crystal Serenity	Crystal Cruises	112	January 23, 2018	Los Angeles	Rome	45
Europa	Hapag-Lloyd Cruises	149	November 7, 2017	Nice	Dubai	81
Insignia	Oceania Cruises	180	January 3, 2018	Miami	Miami	86
Pacific Princess	Princess Cruises	111	January 5, 2018	Ft. Lauderdale	Ft. Lauderdale	44
Queen Mary 2	Cunard	123	January 7, 2018	Southampton	Southampton	39
Sea Princess	Princess Cruises	107	June 15, 2018	Sydney	Sydney	40
Seven Seas Navigator	Regent Seven Seas Cruises	138	January 8, 2018	Los Angeles	Los Angeles	64
Silver Whisper	Silversea Cruises	122	January 8, 2018	Los Angeles	Rome (Civitavecchia)	60
Viking Sun	Viking Ocean Cruises	141	December 15, 2017	Miami	London	66

haven't done your homework before embarking, as, of course, will information available over the Internet.

Extra baggage

One of the nice things about an around-the-world cruise is that if you buy big or heavy items along the way, the ship can store the item on board for you. If you only take a segment (Southampton to Sydney, say), you may be able to collect the items when the ship completes its voyage at its home port, but not all cruise lines offer this service.

Celebrations at sea

On around-the-world cruises, special dates for English-speaking passengers are usually observed with decorations, dinners, dances, teas, and menus that reflect the occasion. Examples include: Burns Night, Valentine's Day, Australia Day, April Fool's Day, May Day, etc.

Jan 25: Robert Burns Night (Burns Dinner).
Jan 26: Australia's National Constitution Day.
Feb 6: New Zealand (Waitangi) Day.
Feb 14: St. Valentine's Day.
Mar 1: St. David's Day (patron saint of Wales).
Mar 17: St. Patrick's Day (patron saint of Ireland – think green beer).
Apr 1: April Fool's Day (a morning of jokes and tricks).
Apr 23: St. George's Day (patron saint of England).
May 1: May Day (traditional Morris dancing).

Two special ceremonies form part of the passenger participation events on a traditional around-the-world cruise:

Crossing the Equator, when King Neptune (Neptunus Rex, the old man of the sea), his wife Amphitrite, and the Royal Court initiate those crossing the line

for the first time (called pollywogs). An old naval tradition, it is usually conducted at the poolside – with inevitable results.

Crossing the International Date Line, where you gain or lose a day, depending on whether you're traveling eastbound or westbound. The imaginary line, at approximately 180 degrees longitude, isn't straight but zigzags to avoid splitting countries apart. Although it was established with international agreement, there are no formal treaties or conventions. It has confused explorers, navigators, and travelers ever since man began circumnavigating the globe 500 years ago. In Jules Verne's *Around the World in 80 Days* Phileas Fogg and his crew returned to London one day late (or so they thought), but it was the extra day gained by crossing the International Date Line that enabled them to win their wager.

FLAGS AND PENNANTS

Looking at the mast of a cruise ship, you will see several different flags and pennants being used. If you know your flags, then you can read the mast like a book. A ship always flies its own 'house' flag proudly on the mast. When a vessel pulls into port, the national flag of the country being visited is flown in courteous recognition of the host country. Should the ship's captain request a local pilot to assist with maneuvering in and out of channels or ports where a local expert is required to take charge, a blue-and-yellow flag with vertical stripes is flown. A half-red, half-white flag divided vertically shows passengers (and other vessels) that a pilot is on board.

33 Wonderful Cruise Experiences

During the 33-year lifespan of this book, I have been privileged to enjoy some fantastic experiences aboard cruise ships. Here, in no particular order, are 33 wonderful cruise experiences.

Fingal's Cave
Passing within an arm's distance of Fingal's Cave on the uninhabited island of Staffa (one of Scotland's Inner Hebridean Islands), as Felix Mendelssohn's *Hebrides Overture* (inspired by the real molten lava rock cavern) was played on the open back deck of the pocket-sized *Hebridean Princess*. At the time – late one chilly morning in spring– I was sitting wrapped in a tartan blanket under a grey, foreboding sky, enjoying a single malt whisky.

Slice of ice
Watching from the observation deck above the bridge of *Hanseatic*, as the ship sliced slowly through the pack-ice in the incredibly scenic, steep-sided Lemaire Channel in the Antarctic Peninsula.

'Europa's Best'
Tasting some beautiful artisan cuisine prepared by chefs whose restaurants had three Michelin three stars aboard Europa for the annual Europa's Best event in Antwerp. Some of the finest cheese and wine producers from Austria, France, Germany, and Switzerland displayed their wares, too. This culinary heaven can be enjoyed by anyone with a ticket.

The Royal Box
Having breakfast in a 'Royal Box' on deck aboard the boutique ships *SeaDream I* or *SeaDream II* while at sea.

Culinary tour de force
Enjoying freshly sliced tuna and yellowtail sashimi at Nobu Matsuhisa's Silk Road Sushi Bar aboard *Crystal Serenity*. Not only was this a culinary tour de force, but watching the Japanese chefs was entertaining, too.

Amalfi magic
Sitting on the corner balcony of a Club Suite aboard *Azamara Quest*, admiring the beautiful scenery of Sorrento, Italy, with the ship at anchor off the famed coastline and a Limoncello to hand.

Candles in the wind
Dining by candlelight at the aft terrace café of *Aegean Odyssey* while watching the mesmerising patterns created on the water by a full, seemingly orange moon in Southeast Asia.

Noodles in Alaska
Sitting on my balcony, breathing in the fresh air and enjoying room-service steaming hot udon noodles, while transiting Alaska's Inside Passage aboard *Nippon Maru*.

Sydney sights
Being outside on deck watching as *Queen Mary 2* turned majestically in Sydney Harbour and sidled up to Circular Quay, close to the Sydney Harbour Bridge and Opera House. All this with hundreds of spectators.

Blue lagoon nights
Lying down in the padded 'Blue Lagoon' seating area at the stern of the *Sea Cloud*, watching the sails directing this wonderful tall ship and seeing a shooting star pass quickly overhead – a most serene experience.

Shackleton's grave
One Christmas Day, paying homage in Grytviken – the former Norwegian whaling station in South Georgia – with passengers from the expedition ships *Bremen*

Douglas Ward at Shackleton's grave, South Georgia.

The Blue Lagoon thermal hot spring, Iceland.

and *Hanseatic*. We toasted the explorer Sir Ernest Shackleton with Aquavit at his grave.

The green flash
Cruising aboard a *Hurtigruten* ship, near Hammerfest or Honningsvag on the northern coast of Norway in October, and seeing the 'green flash' of the northern lights appear on the horizon, as the sun dipped and disappeared.

Under the stars
Standing on deck at the front of the ship, just before bedtime, in one of the wonderfully comfortable cotton sleep suits provided aboard *SeaDream I* and *SeaDream II*. The rhythm of the ship was lulling me to sleep as it sailed to its next destination.

Spiderman
Sitting in the netting hanging at the bowsprit (front) of the sail-cruise ship (tall ship) *Star Flyer* – an exhilarating experience. On this occasion, the ship was gliding gracefully through the water on a perfect, sun-filled day in the azure blue Caribbean Sea.

Misty morning
Standing on the foredeck of a cruise ship entering Ha Long Bay, a Unesco-protected World Heritage site in the Gulf of Tonkin in Quang Ninh Province in northeastern Vietnam. Go in the early morning, when the mist is heavy, for an ethereal feeling of calmness. The dramatic limestone karsts (stone islands) surrounding the ship loom up from the sea-level cloud of heavy air.

Queen and country
Taking a bath in Cabin 1066 of the *Queen Elizabeth 2* one evening during a transatlantic crossing, listening to Elgar's *Pomp and Circumstance* on the in-cabin broadcast system and thinking: how incredibly British.

Canal move
Watching as steel-wired electric mules (each costing over $2 million) pull your cruise ship into position in one of the lock chambers at Miraflores Locks, in the Panama Canal.

Bird's-eye view
Being aboard a cruise ship sailing into or out of Venice, gliding past St Mark's Square. It's a view of Venice you only get from the deck (or balcony – if yours is on the correct side) of a waterborne vessel.

Steps away
Being aboard a small cruise ship moored alongside the State Hermitage Museum in St. Petersburg, Russia. This takes you literally just a few steps away from the iconic building – one of the largest and oldest museums in the world, with over 3 million items in its collection, including some stunning Fabergé eggs.

Titanic pose
Standing with outstretched arms, just like Kate Winslet in the movie *Titanic*, at the front of *Braemar*, as the ship glided slowly through the Swedish archipelago towards Stockholm.

On top of the world

Standing at 90 degrees north – the geographic North Pole (it's actually an ice flow) – literally looking down the world (the first human set foot there in 1948). I reached the North Pole in 2016 aboard the stunning Russian nuclear-powered icebreaker 50 Years of Victory.

Bathtub cruising

Staring out at the horizon while lying in the bathtub in the 'wet room' (with heated floor) in one of the two Deck 10 Crystal Penthouse suites aboard *Crystal Symphony*, as the ship glided through open water.

33 WAYS TO UPGRADE YOUR CRUISE EXPERIENCE

There are many ways to enhance your cruise and vacation – some of which will add little or no cost, and some may cost more, but add value and comfort. Your cruise booking agent may also be able to obtain additional 'perks' at no additional cost to you. Here are some 33 suggestions for you to consider.

1. Take a digital detox cruise – turn off your mobile phone for a whole cruise, or at least a few days.
2. Go farther afield – take a cruise to an area of the world you haven't yet been to.
3. If you need to fly to get to your ship, consider upgrading from Economy (Coach) Class to Business or First Class.
4. Upgrade your accommodation (if the ship is not full) by paying extra when on board.
5. Be the first to sleep in a brand new bed by booking a maiden voyage aboard a brand new ship.
6. Upgrade your accommodation, if the budget allows. Consider upgrading from an interior (no-view) cabin to one with a window, or a 'virtual' balcony.
7. Consider upgrading from a 'standard' cabin with a window to one with a balcony.
8. If possible, upgrade from a balcony cabin to a suite, as you'll get more 'perks' and better service.
9. Consider upgrading from a 'suite' with just a shower enclosure to a suite, with both a bathtub and a separate shower enclosure.
10. And think about upgrading from standard suite to a grand suite, a penthouse suite, or an 'owner's suite' for even more recognition and more 'perks.'
11. For a more intimate dining experience, reserve a table in one of the extra-cost (à la carte) restaurants.
12. Upgrade your fitness level – have a 'no elevator' day (or two, or more).
13. Upgrade your health by eating lighter, 'heart-healthy' options.
14. If you are a meat eater, have a meat-free day (numerous non-meat choices are available aboard any cruise ship).
15. For a special day, have breakfast in bed – with Champagne.
16. Try a higher-quality wine or Champagne on a special day (birthday, anniversary, or other celebration).
17. Book a culinary lesson aboard a ship with built-in cooking stations, so you can experience 'hands-on' with a professional.
18. Upgrade your drinks package from 'standard' to 'premium' and taste better brands, drinks, and wines.
19. Take a look at your ship at arm's length in a 'glass capsule' aboard *Anthem of the Seas*, *Ovation of the Seas*, or *Quantum of the Seas*.
20. Try a new activity – sign-up for something you'd never considered doing before.
21. Learn something new: for example, how to play a keyboard instrument. You can take part in free hands-on classes aboard *Crystal Serenity* or *Crystal Symphony*.
22. For a better body, book a session or two with a personal trainer.
23. If you've never had one, try a body-pampering treatment (suggestions: a full body massage, a facial, or, if you are traveling with a partner, a couples massage).
24. Book a private (extra-cost) deck night aboard *Azamara Journey* or *Azamara Quest*. The experience involves drinks, a hot tub, and sleeping on deck.
25. If you're married, why not think about renewing your commitment in a Renewal of Vows ceremony?
26. Take a social dance lesson – learn how to do the waltz, foxtrot, quickstep, samba, or tango.
27. Reserve a 'Royal Box' (Champagne and chocolates included) in the Royal Court Theater for the show aboard Cunard's *Queen Elizabeth* or *Queen Victoria*.
28. Take a transatlantic crossing aboard a real ocean liner. *Queen Mary 2* is the only ship built for all weather conditions in the North Atlantic. It's one of the best ways to arrive in a different continent without jet lag.
29. If you are traveling with a baby, take advantage of a night nursery (free aboard Cunard and P&O Cruises ships, but at extra cost aboard most others), so you can have some 'me' time in the evening – and some decent sleep.
30. When you come back from a morning excursion, instead of heading to the self-serve buffet, have a calm room-service lunch.
31. Get real insight into a place you want to visit by booking a private tour with a local guide.
32. Book a post-cruise stay, so that disembarkation day becomes less frenetic and gives you time to adjust to 'normality.'
33. Close up the house and take an around-the-world cruise.

Three-star Michelin chef Dieter Müller plating up.

Burton, Tippi Hedren, Dame Margot Fonteyn, and the great conductor Leopold Stokowski.

Photo opportunity

Being aboard a photo tender arranged by the cruise line (in my case, this was aboard a tall ship) and taking photographs as the tall ship was under full sail and not slowing down. An exhilarating experience that you can still enjoy.

Passing the lava

Being aboard a cruise ship off the north coast of Sicily, where you pass close to Stromboli in action. The almost constantly erupting volcano bursts into life and emits incandescent lava.

Michelin dining

Dining in the intimate Dieter Müller At Sea restaurant aboard Hapag-Lloyd Cruises' *Europa*. Müller sold his own restaurant – which had three Michelin stars – and now operates his own seagoing dining venue for six months each year.

Natural wonders

I was on deck aboard an expedition cruise ship in Antarctic waters when a number of killer whales (orcas) began splashing in the water just off the starboard side aft, making the ship roll. They were so close that I could have touched one of their dorsal fins. A spectacular show of nature.

New Year's Eve pyrotechnics

Being aboard ship supping Champagne while enjoying the magnificently colorful New Year's Eve fireworks display in Funchal, Madeira. A cruise ship offers the very best vantage point for this fantastic display, which lasts around 10 minutes or so and is considered to be one of the most spectacular in the world.

Zip-a-dee-doo-dah

Careening along the zip line strung between rows of cabins high above the deck of *Allure of the Seas, Harmony of the Seas, or Oasis of the Seas*. Quite a surprise to the occupants of some of the interior promenade balcony cabins!

Paw power

Being pulled by a team of huskies in Juneau, Alaska, as we sped past glaciers and ice peaks (taken in combination with a flight to Mendenhall Glacier).

Slipping away

Sitting on the deck of a pocket-sized cruise ship in Glacier Bay, Alaska, watching the blue glacial ice calving, making you rock and roll as it slipped, slid, and crashed into the water within inches of your body.

Melting away

Sitting in a pool of silica- and sulphur-rich geo-thermal water in Iceland's Blue Lagoon – a man-made outlet close to the Svartsengi Power Station and part of the lava field located on the Reykjanes Peninsula. This is offered as part of a tour from your cruise ship.

Surprise, surprise

Meeting someone you never expected to, or thought possible to meet. On cruises over the years, I have been fortunate enough to meet, talk to, and have a drink with some well-known film stars and other personalities including Elizabeth Taylor and Richard

Maiden cruise

Enjoying the anticipation and excitement of a maiden voyage aboard a brand new ship – an experience highly prized among cruise collectors. Just be prepared for the fact that it might not all be smooth sailing, and there might be teething troubles.

Happy ever after

Looking for a partner? I met my future wife aboard a Japanese cruise ship some years ago, and we married several years later. You too, could meet the person of your dreams aboard a cruise ship – it happens all the time.

Life Aboard

This A to Z survey covers the astonishing range of facilities that modern cruise ships offer and tells you how to make the most of them.

Air conditioning

Cabin temperature is regulated by an individually controlled thermostat, so you can adjust it to suit yourself. However, aboard some ships, the cabin air conditioning can't be turned off.

Art auctions

Aboard many large resort ships, art auctions provide cruise line revenue. They are participation events – though 'free Champagne' given to entice customers is usually sparkling wine and not authentic Champagne, while most of the art is rubbish.

Art 'appraisal prices' are done by the art provider, a company that pays a cruise line to be on board. Watch out for 'retail replacement value,' a misleading term used by the art salespeople. Listen for phrases such as 'signed in the stone' – it means that the artists did not sign the work – or *'pochoire'* (a stencil print less valuable than an original etching or lithograph). If the auctioneer tries to sell a piece of art (particularly a 'block' print or woodcut/engraving) with an 'authenticated signature,' don't buy it – when it's delivered to your home and you have it appraised, you'll probably find it's not genuine.

Cashless cruising

You simply settle your account with one payment (by cash or credit card) before disembarking on the last day. An imprint of your credit card is taken at embarkation or when you register online, permitting you to sign for everything. Before the end of the cruise, a detailed statement is delivered to your cabin.

However, not being able to pay in cash for anything can lull you into a false sense of security, because it's easy to overspend. Make a careful note of what you sign for.

Some cruise lines, irritatingly, discontinue their 'cashless' system for the last day of the cruise. Some may add a 'currency conversion service charge' to your credit card account if it is not in the currency of the cruise line.

Comment cards

On the last day of the cruise you will be asked to fill out a 'comment card.' Some lines offer 'incentives' such as a bottle of Champagne. Be truthful, as the form serves as a means of communication between you and the cruise line. Pressure from staff to write 'excellent' for everything is rampant, but, unless you highlight problems you have encountered, things are unlikely to improve.

Disembarkation

This can be the most trying end to any cruise. The cruise director gives an informal talk on customs, immigration, and disembarkation procedures. The night before the ship reaches its destination, you will be given a customs form. Include any duty-free items, whether purchased aboard or ashore. Save the receipts, in case a customs officer asks for them after you disembark.

The night before arrival at your cruise's final destination, place your main baggage outside your cabin on retiring, or before 2am. It will be collected and offloaded on arrival. Leave out fragile items and the clothes you intend to wear for disembarkation and onward travel – it is amazing just how many people pack absolutely everything. Anything left in your cabin will be considered hand luggage.

Before leaving the ship, remember to claim any items placed in your in-cabin safe. Passengers cannot go ashore until all baggage has been offloaded

A beauty treatment aboard a Louis Cruises ship.

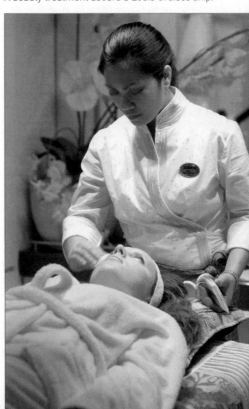

Disembarking from large resort ships can be tedious.

and customs and/or immigration inspections or pre-inspections have been carried out. In most ports, this takes two to three hours after arrival.

On disembarkation day, breakfast will probably be early. It might be better to miss breakfast and sleep later. Even worse than early breakfast is the fact that aboard many ships you will be commanded to leave your cabin early, only to wait in crowded public rooms, sometimes for hours.

Some companies, such as Princess Cruises, offer a more relaxed system that allows you to stay in your cabin as long as you wish, or until your tag color is called, instead of waiting in public areas.

Once off the ship, you identify your baggage on the pier before going through customs inspection. Porters may be there to assist you.

Duty-free liquor

If you buy any 'duty-free' liquor along the way, it will be taken from you at the gangway as you reboard and given back to you the day before you disembark. This is because cruise lines want you to buy your alcohol on board.

Engine room

For insurance and security reasons, visits to the engine room are seldom allowed. Some ships may have a technical information leaflet, with details of what's what in the engine room. Aboard others, a behind-the-scenes video may be shown on the cabin infotainment system. A number of ships do offer 'Behind-the-Scenes' tours, which include the Engine Control Room, at extra cost.

Etiquette onboard

Two points that are sometimes overlooked:
1) If you take a video camera with you, be aware that international copyright laws prohibit you from recording the professional entertainment shows.
2) It is fine to dress in a casual manner onboard ship, but you must not enter a ship's dining room in just a bathing suit, or with bare feet.

Gratuities/tips

Aboard many large resort ships, tipping seems to be mandatory rather than voluntary. Gratuities, typically of around $12 per person (slightly more for occupants of suite-grade or butler-service accommodation), per day, are added automatically to your shipboard account. These may need to be converted to your credit card currency at the prevailing rate.

Be aware that cabin stewards have been known to scroll through their passengers' on-board account on the infotainment system, so they can tell if you have opted out of the automatic gratuity charge!

Gratuities are included in the cruise fare aboard a small number of ships, mainly those at the luxury ('all-inclusive') end of the market, where no extra tipping is permitted – at least in theory. In reality, even when cruise brochures state 'tipping is not required,' gratuities will usually be expected by the staff. Aboard some ships, subtle suggestions are made regarding tips; in others, cruise directors get carried away and dictate rules.

Here are the accepted industry guidelines: dining room waiter, $3–4 per person, per day; assistant waiter (busboy), $1.50–2 per day; cabin steward or stewardess, $3–3.50 per person, per day; butler, $5 per person, per day. Tips are normally given on the last evening of a cruise of up to 14 days' duration. For longer cruises, hand over half the tip halfway through and the rest on your last evening.

Aboard many ships, a gratuity (typically of 15 percent) is automatically added to your bar check, whether you get good service or not, and a gratuity (of 15–18 percent) may be added for spa treatments.

Internet access and cell (mobile) phones

Smartphone/cell phone use aboard ships is common, and most have ship-wide Wi-Fi (at a price). Before you cruise, check with your phone operator for the international roaming rates applicable to your tariff. Calls (at sea) are handled by a marine telecommunications network, which passes on international roaming charges to your phone operator.

Some ships have a room – often part of the library – with Internet-connect computers. The best-wired ships also have strong signals to cabins and public areas, so you can use your own laptop in the privacy of your cabin or on deck (extra charges apply).

Signal strength can vary substantially from hour to hour. The farther north you get, the closer the telecommunications satellite is to the horizon, so signals tend to fade in and out, and waiting for web pages to appear on your computer screen can be frustrating.

Turn off Data Roaming to save charges and Location Services to prevent apps from constantly trying to update your location. Turn off the 'Push' option relating to your e-mail, because some accounts, including Gmail, push the data to your smartphone, incurring charges even if you don't open any e-mails. Turn off the option to synchronize data between devices, because it consumes bandwidth trying to keep your accounts up to date. Better still – have a digital detox and turn your mobile phone off completely!

Launch (shore tender) services

Enclosed or open motor launches ('tenders') are used when your cruise ship is unable to berth at a port or island. In such cases, a regular launch service is operated between ship and shore for the port call. Aboard the large resort ships, you'll need to obtain a tender ticket, usually given out in one of the lounges, unless you are on an organized excursion, which take priority. The procedure can take a long time.

When stepping on or off a tender, extend 'forearm to forearm' to the person who is assisting you. Do not grip their hands because this has the unintentional effect of immobilizing the helper.

Laundry and dry cleaning

Most ships offer a full laundry and pressing (ironing) service. Some ships may also offer dry-cleaning facilities. A detailed list of services, and prices, will be in your cabin. Your steward will collect and deliver your clothes. Some ships have self-service launderettes, well equipped with washers, dryers, and ironing facilities. There may be a charge for washing powder and for the use of the machines.

Tenders transport passengers when a ship can't dock, as seen here aboard *Regatta*.

Library

Some ships have a library offering a selection of books, reference material, and periodicals. Aboard small luxury ships, the library is open 24/7. Aboard the large resort ships, the library may be open only for a few hours a day.

Queen Mary 2, Queen Elizabeth, and *Queen Victoria* have the best libraries.

Aboard the small expedition ships, the library is one of the most important – and most used – facilities, and high-quality reference books on all aspects of nature, marine life, and polar exploration are usually provided.

Lido

This is a deck devoted to swimming pools, hot tubs, showers, and general recreation, often with intrusive 'background' music. Aboard most cruise ships, it also includes a self-serve buffet.

Lost property

Contact the reception desk immediately if you lose or find something aboard the ship.

Mail

You can buy stamps and mail letters at the reception desk. Some ships use the postal privileges and stamps of their flag of registration; others buy local stamps at ports of call. Mail is usually taken ashore by the ship's port agent just before the ship sails.

Medical care

Doctors aboard most cruise ships are required to have current medical licensing, three years of post-medical school clinical practice, certification in emergency medicine, family practice, or internal medicine or experience as a GP or Emergency ward doctor. So, if you have a serious health issue that predates your cruise, or a permanent disability, you need to be upfront about it with your travel agent or the cruise line's reservationist. They may be able to advise you on a ship that best meets your needs.

Anyone with long-term health issues should get prescriptions made up for the whole period of the cruise, because many places will not process prescriptions from other countries. Take out a travel insurance policy that reimburses you for visits to the onboard medical service, but check the small print. These policies often refuse to pay out if you had a condition you didn't mention when you bought the policy. Most medical care on cruise ships is perfectly adequate. Just in case it isn't, the cruise lines have a clause that says they aren't responsible for the malpractice of a ship's doctors.

News/sports bulletins

Most ships have satellite television for world news and sports coverage. On some ships, world news and sports results are printed and delivered, displayed on a bulletin board near the reception desk or in the library, or made accessible via an in-cabin infotainment system. A few ships can even print a full-size version of your favorite newspaper.

Photographs

Professional photographers on board take digital pictures of you during embarkation and throughout the cruise. They cover all the main events and social

Splashaway Bay aboard *Liberty of the Seas*.

No bathing suits in the casual eatery, please!

functions, such as a captain's cocktail party. The pictures can be viewed without any obligation to buy, but the prices may surprise.

Postcards/stationery

Stationery items are typically available from the reception desk, although some cruise lines now charge for them. If you are in suite-grade accommodation, you may be given complimentary stationery personalized with your name and suite number when you embark.

Pre-paid drinks

Most large resort ships offer drinks packages in an effort to 'add value.' However, although these booze-cruise packages mean that you don't need to sign each time you order a drink, they really are a temptation to drink more. Some packages include wine, but it's the cruise line's choice – not yours.

Reception desk

This is also known as the purser's office, guest relations, or information desk. Centrally located, it is the nerve center of the ship for general passenger information and problems. Opening hours – in some ships, 24 hours a day – are posted outside the office and given in the 'daily program,' which is delivered to your cabin.

Religious services

Interdenominational services are conducted on board many ships – usually by the captain or staff captain. Costa Cruises' ships have a small private chapel. Denominational services may also be held by clergy traveling as passengers.

Room service

Beverages and snacks are available at most times. Liquor is normally limited to the opening hours of the ship's bars. Some ships charge for room service.

Sailing time

In each port, sailing and all-aboard times are posted at the gangway. The all-aboard time is usually half an hour before sailing. If you miss the ship, it's entirely your responsibility to get to the next port of call to rejoin the vessel.

Swimming pools

Most ships have swimming pools outdoors; some have pools that can be covered by glass domes in case of inclement weather, while a handful of ships have indoor pools located on the lowest deck. Pools may be closed in port owing to local health regulations or cleaning requirements. Diving is not allowed – pools are shallow.

Parents should note that most ship pools are unsupervised. The main exception to this is Disney Cruise Line, which employs lifeguards. Some ships use excessive chlorine or water-treatment agents, which might cause bathing suits to fade or run.

Telephone calls

Most ships have direct-dial satellite telephones, so you can call from your cabin to anywhere in the

A wine tower aboard *Celebrity Eclipse*.

Television
Programming is obtained from a mixture of (paid) satellite feeds and onboard videos. Some ships lock on to live international news programs such as CNN or BBC World, or to text-only news services. Satellite television reception can sometimes be poor because ships constantly move out of the satellite's narrow beam.

Valuables
Most cabins have a small personal safe, but items of high value should be kept in a safety deposit box (accessible during the cruise) at the reception desk.

Water sports
Some small ships have a water sports platform at the stern or lowered from the side. These ships usually carry windsurfers, water-ski boats, jet skis, water skis, and scuba and snorkel equipment, usually at no extra charge – except for scuba equipment. Make sure you are covered by your travel insurance if you want to partake in water sports.

Wine and liquor
The cost of drinks on board is generally lower than on land, since ships have access to duty-free liquor. Drinks may be ordered in the dining room, at any of the ship's bars, or from room service. There are usually extensive and reasonably priced wine lists in the dining room.

Some ships sell duty-free wine and liquor to drink in your cabin. You can't normally bring these into the dining room or public rooms, nor any duty-free wine or liquor bought in port. These rules protect bar sales, a substantial source of onboard revenue.

world. Ships have an internationally recognized radio call sign, a combination of letters and digits, for example: C6SE7.

To reach a ship from land, dial the International Direct Dial (IDD) code for the country you are calling from, followed by the ship's telephone number.

Anyone without a direct-dial telephone should call the High Seas Operator – in the US, dial 1-800-SEA-CALL. The operator will need the name of the ship, together with the ocean code: Atlantic East is 871; Pacific is 872; Indian Ocean is 873; Atlantic West/Caribbean/US is 874.

DID YOU KNOW...?

...that *Splendour of the Seas* (now *TUI Discovery*) was the first ship to include an iPad in every cabin? It was in 2011.

...that bingo game numbers aboard most ships only use numbers up to 75? On some UK-based cruise lines, however, the bingo numbers go to 99.

...that there is no Deck 13 aboard any ships of Princess Cruises? Good for the superstitious.

...that Royal Caribbean International's *Legend of the Seas* (presently TUI Cruises' *TUI Discovery 2*) was named with the world's largest bottle of Champagne? It had to be specially made, and was a 'Sovereign-size' bottle (the equivalent of 34 bottles) of Moët & Chandon Champagne.

...that the first vessel built exclusively for cruising was Hamburg-America Line's two-funnel *Princessin Victoria Luise*? This luxury yacht even included a private suite for the German Kaiser.

...that the United States Line's *Manhattan* of 1931 was the first ship to have a cocktail named after it?

...that when sailing from England to the Caribbean in 'the old days' a rule of thumb was to sail south until the butter melts, then proceed west?

...that the longest bar aboard any cruise ship can be found aboard *AIDAcara*? It is 195ft (59.5m) long.

...that someone forgot to score the Champagne bottle when Dame Judi Dench named *Carnival Legend* in Harwich, England, on August 21, 2002? On the first two tries, the bottle didn't break. Then Dame Judi took the bottle in her hands and smashed it against the side of the ship. When it broke, the Champagne went all over her, and she was dubbed Dame Judi Drench.

...that from January 2000 until the ship was retired in 2008 octogenarian American Beatrice Muller made Cunard Line's *Queen Elizabeth 2* her permanent home at sea? She preferred life aboard to the daily drudgery of household chores and bills back home and paid a set amount to reside in Cabin 4068.

Cuisine

Anyone determined to eat around the clock could do so aboard many ships, but the health-conscious should exercise restraint, especially at self-service buffets.

The dining rooms and restaurants aboard any cruise ship are the collective lifeblood of the entire ship, cruise, and hospitality experience. Except for the facilities and destinations, it's the food that most people remember and talk about.

Cruise lines love to boast about their food – and often with their celebrity TV chefs – who only sail occasionally for a bit of show. The reality is that most meals aboard most ships are not gourmet affairs. How could they be, when a kitchen has to turn out hundreds of meals at the same time? Most ships simply can't deliver the 'Wow' factor the brochure promises.

Generally speaking, as in most restaurants on land, you get what you pay for. High-quality ingredients cost money, so it's unrealistic to expect low-cost cruises to offer anything other than low-cost, pre-cooked food (most have an overabundance of carbohydrate-rich components such as potato, rice, pasta, and bread).

Most cruise ship cuisine compares favorably with 'banquet' food in a family restaurant. You can expect a selection of palatable and complete meals served properly in comfortable surroundings. Perhaps you will dine by candlelight – well, battery-powered candlelight – which creates some ambience. Menus are typically displayed outside the dining room each day, while they may also be delivered to suite occupants.

The major cruise lines bulk-purchase food items, which means low-quality ingredients and cheaper cuts of meat and fish, perhaps 'enhanced' with preservatives. That said, cruise lines do sometimes upgrade food items – Carnival Cruise Line and Royal Caribbean International, for example, introduced free-range eggs aboard their ships in 2011. The trend now is for several 'alternative' (extra-cost) restaurants.

Food Tip: If you order an omelet, ask for it to be made (in front of you) with real eggs – many companies use the more convenient, but fake, 'liquid egg' mix.

BBQS AND HOT ROCK GRILLS

Some ships – usually the smaller ones – offer barbecues on deck, and also a Hot Rocks Grill. This is for steaks, grilled meats, and seafood presented on a platter that includes a scorchingly hot rock base – so you can cook however little or well you want it done yourself. It makes for a pleasant change, all in a casual pool deck environment. Seabourn and Silversea Cruises pioneered this option.

Where's the (USDA) beef?

Menus, particularly in extra-cost venues, often state that their steaks are made with USDA (United States Department of Agriculture) beef. If this is the case, ask which grade, as there are three main ones: USDA Prime (produced from young, well-fed beef cattle; provides the best-quality meat, with more marbling, meaning more moisture and a better flavor); USDA Choice (some marbling – good for high-quality steak); and USDA Select (leaner, with a rougher texture, and no marbling – adequate for BBQ). Other grades are: Standard, Commercial, Utility, Cutter, and Canner.

Fresh versus frozen

Aboard low-priced cruises, you will typically be served portion-controlled frozen food that has been reheated. Fresh fish and the best cuts of meats cost the cruise lines more, and that cost is reflected in the cruise price. Aboard some ships, the 'fresh' fish – often described as 'Catch of the Day' – has clearly had no contact with the sea for quite some time.

Sushi bars are a fashionable addition to some ships. However, as the kitchen facilities on ships are generally

Choose your steak knife aboard *Mein Schiff 4*.

Colorful and healthy Japanese appetisers.

inadequate to turn out food something as super-fresh as sushi, the only ships with authentic sushi bars and authentic sushi/sashimi are *Asuka II*, *Crystal Serenity*, *MSC Musica*, *MSC Poesia*, and *Nippon Maru*. Note also that many items of 'fresh' fruit may have been treated with 1-MCP (methylcyclopropene) to make them last longer – apples, for example, may be up to a year old.

Bread and pastry items
While there are exceptions, much of the bread baked aboard cruise ships is unappealing, because, with little time for fermentation of natural yeast, it is made instead with instant dough that contains dried yeast from packets. Many baked goods and pastry items are made mostly from refined flours and sugars.

Self-serve buffets
Most ships have self-serve buffets for breakfast and lunch (some also for dinner). But while buffets look fine when they're fresh, they don't after a few minutes of passengers helping themselves. Self-serve buffets have become more user-friendly by increasing the number of 'active cooking' stations and food islands, which help to break up lines created by typical straight-line buffet counters.

Dare to ask for something that's not on the display, however, and any form of human communication ceases and supervisors become invisible. For example: trying to get a freshly cooked four-minute soft-boiled egg at a breakfast buffet is a challenge. I am always met with: 'We've only got the ones in the bowl, sir.' But the 'eight-minute' eggs in the bowl have been sitting there since they were boiled at 6.30am before the buffet opened, and they're still under the infrared heat lamp at 9.30am! Plus, there are typically no eggcups – or small spoons to eat them with!

Nor can you expect to find the following at the large resort ships' breakfast and lunch buffets: warm plates (for 'hot' food items), fish knives, a smoked salmon omelet, soy milk, brown rice, fresh herbs, loose tea, or freshly grated nutmeg for oatmeal or cream of wheat. If you have food allergies, self-serve buffets will present a challenge, but, always, always, ask for help with regard to what's in what.

CELEBRITY CHEFS

Several cruise lines have signed up well-known chefs to devise menus for their alternative dining venues. Celebrity Cruises, for example, worked with three-star Michelin chef Michel Roux from 1989 until 2007. It's worth paying extra because the price is far less than it would be in the celebrity chef's land-based restaurants – there's no extra charge for dining in the Restaurant Dieter Müller aboard *Europa*, for example. Acclaimed chefs have included (in cruise line order): Georges Blanc (Carnival Cruise Line), Elizabeth Blau (Celebrity Cruises), Nobu Matsuhisa (Crystal Cruises), Dieter Müller (Hapag-Lloyd Cruises), Carlo Cracco, Jean-Philippe Maury, and Roy Yamaguchi (MSC Cruises), Geoffrey Zakarian and Jose Garces (Norwegian Cruise Line), Jacques Pépin (Oceania Cruises), Atul Kochhar, James Martin, and Marco Pierre White (P&O Cruises), and Jamie Oliver (Royal Caribbean International).

Most celebrity chefs sail only one or two cruises a year, but Germany's three-star Michelin chef Dieter Müller has set a new benchmark by sailing for up to half a year in order to run his eponymous restaurant aboard Hapag-Lloyd Cruises' *Europa*.

DID YOU KNOW?

The 'menu' (French) or 'bill of fare' (English) was originally never presented at the table. Meals consisted of two main courses, each with a variety of dishes – anything from 10 to 40. The first dishes were usually placed on the table before diners entered (thus the word *entrée*). When these had been consumed, they were removed or relieved by another set of dishes, known as the *relevé*, from the French 'to relieve' (a term no longer used in modern dining).

It was in 1541 that Duke Henry of Brunswick was seen to refer to a long slip of paper, which provided the order of the dishes. By referring to the list he could see what was coming next, and this enabled him to reserve his appetite accordingly. It is presumed that the menu was thus derived from this (or a similar) event.

It was common custom in those days to present a large bill of fare at the end of the table for patrons to read. Only later did the menu become smaller in size. It follows that a number of copies were then made, allowing each diner to have his/her own copy of the menu.

Afternoon tea in *Crystal Symphony*'s Palm Court.

Deli-style (take-away) food

Take away deli-style food can be found in outlets aboard some ships, for those times when you may want to sit somewhere quietly but still have a little pre-wrapped casual snack (think: small ready-made sandwiches, wraps, burritos, salad 'pots' with quinoa or bulgur wheat, for example). This started with the so-called 'café culture' found in coffee and sandwich shops at home.

Examples of companies with small, no extra-cost deli-style outlets for take-away food include P&O Cruises (aboard *Britannia*); Royal Caribbean International (Park Café aboard *Allure of the Seas*, *Harmony of the Seas*, *Oasis of the Seas*, and *Symphony of the Seas*).

Poolside grills

Poolside grills are casual and comfortable, but usually attract long lines – particularly aboard the large resort ships.

Burgers and hot dogs may sound attractive for many passengers, but often there is disappointment. Aboard most large resort ships, it's simply not possible to grill burgers individually due to the large numbers of passengers and long lines. Aboard the smaller ships, however, they can be ordered and individually cooked.

Burgers are typically presented in a display tray for you to collect, and then install your favorite toppings (usually tomato slices, onions, and an iceberg lettuce leaf), with mustard and tomato ketchup available in packets or pump bottles. However, the burgers may have been steamed, and not grilled, before being placed in the display tray, because steaming them keeps them moist. If you like yours grilled, it's best to say so.

As for hot dogs, these may be either grilled or steamed (commercially supplied dogs will be pre-cooked and only need warming), and served in a bread roll. In case you don't eat certain type of meat, you may need to ask someone whether they are made of beef, pork, chicken, or a combination of these.

The common hot dog is typically made from meat trimmings, fat, flavorings (such as salt, garlic, and paprika), bindings, and preservatives (sodium nitrate and sodium erythorbate). A Frankfurter (derived from Frankfurt in Germany, where pork sausages similar to those used in a hot dog, have been made since the 13th century). A Wiener (derived from Vienna) is made from a mixture of pork and beef and placed in a casing.

For anyone on a special diet, alternatives may be available, including vegetarian and vegan burgers, or lobster and shrimp burgers, depending on the ship.

Specialty restaurants

Most new cruise ships have a number of specialty restaurants and dining venues that provide alternatives to the large main dining rooms. Extra-cost specialty restaurants were pioneered in 1936 by RMS *Queen Mary* (Verandah Grill, for first-class passengers only, at a small extra cost, and introduced in modern times by Norwegian Cruise Line in 1988 (The Bistro – an à la carte, extra-cost French dining spot). But it was Star Cruises that introduced *multiple* venues – seven of them – aboard *Star Aquarius* in 1993; some were included in the cruise price, others cost extra. Thus was born 'Freestyle Cruising' – or dine where you want, when you want, and with whom you wish.

These specialist restaurants are smaller, à la carte venues, for which you make a reservation. In return, you get better food, wine selection, service,

The captain giving a toast.

and ambience. Celebrity chefs may add to the mix and are asked to establish their own 'at sea' dining venues, or collaborate on menus for shipboard eateries, although they seldom appear on board.

Some specialty restaurants can also be entertaining, such as the Teppanyaki Grill aboard *Genting Dream*, *MSC Seaside*, and *Norwegian Escape*. Watch while the chefs chop, slice, and flip the food as they cook on an iron griddle next to the seating area. Twiddling and spinning utensils is part of the show!

Chef's Table

An increasingly trendy addition to the culinary side of cruising are pay-extra Chef's Tables, which are typically limited to a maximum 12 participants, featuring multiple fine-dining courses with wine pairings for each course. The food is presented by the Executive Chef – hence the name Chef's Table. You can find such a table aboard the ships of Azamara Club Cruises, for example.

Special diets

Cruise lines tend to cater to general tastes, and cruise ship food tends to be liberally sprinkled with salt, with vegetables often cooked with sauces containing dairy products, salt, and sugar. If you are allergic to ingredients such as nuts or shellfish, want lactose-free, salt-free, low-cholesterol, low-fat or fat-free, gluten-free, or semi-fluid food, or have any other dietary restrictions, let the cruise line know in writing well ahead of time and ask them to confirm that the ship can meet your needs. Once on board, check again with the restaurant manager.

Not all cruise ships cope well with those on vegan or macrobiotic diets who regularly need freshly squeezed juices; many large resort ships use commercial canned or bottled juices containing pre-servatives and may not be able to provide really fresh juices in their bars.

Healthy eating

You can gain weight when cruising, but it's not inevitable. In fact, taking a cruise could be a good reason to get serious about your well-being. Weight- and health-conscious passengers should exercise self-restraint, particularly at self-service buffets.

Many ships' menus include 'heart-healthy' or 'lean and light' options, with calorie-filled sauces replaced by so-called 'spa' cuisine. It may also be wise to choose grilled or poached fish – salmon or sea bass, for example – rather than heavy meat dishes or fried food items.

Quality and variety are directly linked to the per-passenger budget set by each cruise line and are dictated by suppliers, regions, and seasons. Companies operating large resort ships buy fruit at the lowest price, which can translate to unripe bananas, tasteless grapes, and hard-as-nails plums. The smaller, more upscale ships usually carry better-quality ripe fruits as well as the more expensive varieties such as dragon fruit, carambola (starfruit), cherimoya, cactus pear, guava, kumquat, loquat, passion fruit, *physalis* (Cape gooseberry), rambutan, and sharon fruit.

Even some of the world's largest resort ships, such as *Allure of the Seas*, *Harmony of the Seas*, and *Oasis of the Seas*, have calorie-control food items at the Solarum Bistro, where no dish is more than 500 calories. Carnival Cruise Line has a Mongolian barbecue on their buffets, where tofu is a regular feature. Crystal Cruises features more grains and fresh fruits on its buffet lines than is standard on a cruise, and you'll find Ayervedic breakfast items in *Europa 2*'s Yacht Club.

Raw food

In 2011, SeaDream Yacht Club introduced 'raw food' dishes. The cruise line tapped into the Hippocrates Health Institute's Life Transformation Program and introduced a complete additional menu. 'Raw' means that ingredients are raw, organic, enzyme-rich, and vegan: no meat, fish, eggs, or dairy items, and nothing heated above 118 degrees Fahrenheit (48 degrees Celsius), to retain as many micronutrients as possible.

Items include fresh sprout and vegetable juices, plant-based protein foods, and pasta made from spinach leaves and coconut meat. Even desserts are created from raw foods including cashews, almond milk, and coconut butter.

The oatmeal factor

One factor that I have found to be quite consistent across most ships is what I call the 'oatmeal factor': how various cruise ships provide a basic item such as a bowl of oatmeal.

Standard. Hot oatmeal (supermarket brand oats) mixed with water, with little or no chance of obtaining tahini (sesame seed paste) to add taste to the oatmeal. You get it from a soup tureen at the buffet, and put it into a plastic or inexpensive bowl yourself (or it may be served in the dining room; it is eaten with plastic or basic canteen cutlery.

Premium. Hot oatmeal, water, salt, and a little olive oil; served in a higher-quality bowl, by a waiter or waitress, with hotel-quality (or better) cutlery. It's possible that the ship will have tahini, to add taste and creaminess. It's also possible that the waiter/waitress will ask if you'd like hot or cold milk with your oatmeal. There may even be a doily between the oatmeal bowl and base plate.

Luxury. Hot oatmeal (medium or large flakes), water, salt, tahini, a little (extra virgin) olive oil, and nutmeg, with a dash of blended Scotch (whisky); served in a high-quality brand-name bowl (Versace), with base plate and doily, and Hepp- or Robbe & Berking-quality silverware. The waiter/waitress will ask if you'd like hot or cold milk with your oatmeal.

Incomparable. Hot Scottish (large flakes, hand-ground) oatmeal, water, sea salt, tahini, and nutmeg (grated at the table), high-quality cold-pressed olive oil, and a layer of rare single-malt Scotch; served in small-production hand-made china, with base plate and doily, and sterling silver cutlery. The waiter/waitress will ask if you'd like hot or cold milk (or anything else) with your oatmeal.

Service

Aboard many ships today, passengers are often in a hurry (to get to a show or shore excursion) and want service to be as fast as possible. They also don't like seeing empty plates in front of them, and so service speeds up because waiters need to clear the empty plates away as soon as someone has finished eating a particular course ('American Service'). In what is correctly termed 'European Service', however, there should *always* be a pause between courses, not only for conversation, but to let the appetite and digestive tract recover, and also to anticipate the arrival of the next course.

Plate service versus silver service

Plate service. When the food is presented as a complete dish (now the normal presentation), as the chef wants it to look. It works well and means that people seated at a table will be served at the same time and can eat together.

Silver service. When the component parts are brought to the table separately, so that the diner, not the chef, can choose what goes on the plate and in what proportion (best when there is plenty of time, but this is rare aboard today's ships). What some cruise lines class as silver service is actually silver service of vegetables only, with the main item, whether it is fish, fowl, or other meat, already plated.

Note that few large resort ships provide proper fish knives or the correct soup spoons – oval for thin bouillon-style soups and round for creamy soups.

National differences

Different nationalities tend to eat at different times. North Americans and Japanese, for example, tend to dine early (6–7pm), while many Europeans and South Americans prefer to eat much later (at least 8–11pm). Brazilians traditionally like dinner at midnight. During Ramadan, Muslims cannot eat during the daytime, but typically order room-service meals during the night.

Beef, lamb, and pork cuts are different on both sides of the Atlantic, so what you ordered may not be the cut, shape, or size you expected. For example,

---

HEALTHY EATING TIPS

While a ship's self-serve buffet allows you to choose what and how much, there is a tendency for many passengers to overdo it. It's easy to consume more calories than you actually need, so pace yourself. Here are some tips on how to cut down on calories:

Remember that you don't have to order – or eat – every course.

Ask for half-size portions, or children's portions.

Eat some items from the 'heart-healthy,' lighter options, or 'spa' menu, if available.

Eat more fruits and vegetables – some ships have juicers, for freshly squeezed or fresh-pressed items (possibly as part of the spa menu); depending on the ship, there may be an extra cost for this.

It's best not to go to the restaurant when you are 'starving.' Instead, try eating a healthy snack before any heavy meal.

Try not to eat too late in the evening – or too many late-night bites.

Limit your alcohol intake.

DOUGLAS WARD'S TOP RESTAURANTS

If asked to pick a baker's dozen, my choice would probably be (in alphabetical order by restaurant name):

Le Champagne aboard *Silver Spirit*
Le Cordon Bleu aboard *Seven Seas Voyager*
Ocean Grill aboard *Oriana*
Olympic Restaurant aboard *Celebrity Millennium*
Polo Grill aboard *Marina* and *Riviera*
Remy aboard *Disney Dream and Disney Fantasy*
Restaurant Dieter Müller aboard *Europa*
Umi-Uma by Nobu aboard *Crystal Serenity* and *Crystal Symphony*
Surf and Turf aboard *Mein Schiff 3* and *Mein Schiff 4*
Tarragon aboard *Europa 2*
Teppanyaki Grill aboard *Norwegian Escape*
Umihiko aboard *Asuka II*
The Verandah Restaurant aboard *Queen Elizabeth*

Mouth-watering premium-quality Wagyu beef.

there are 15 British cuts of beef, 17 American cuts, and 24 French cuts. There are six American cuts of lamb, eight British cuts, and nine French cuts. There are eight American cuts of pork, 10 British cuts, and 17 French cuts.

A typical day

From morning until night, food is offered to the point of overkill, even aboard the most modest cruise ship. Aboard large resort ships, pizzas, burgers, hot dogs, ice cream, and frozen yogurt are almost always available. If you're still hungry, there's 24-hour room service, which, aboard some large resort ships, may cost extra. Some ships also have extra-charge bistros, cafés, and patisseries.

If you prefer to eat at set times rather than graze, these are the options:

6am: hot coffee and tea on deck for early risers (or late-to-bed types).

Full breakfast: typically with as many as 60 different items, in the main dining room. For a more casual meal, you can serve yourself buffet-style at an indoor/outdoor deck café.

Lunchtime: with service in the dining room, buffet-style at a casual café, or at a grill for hot dogs and burgers, and a pizzeria, where you can watch the cooking.

4pm: afternoon tea, in the British tradition, with finger sandwiches, scones and clotted cream. Typically, this is served in a lounge to the accompaniment of live music (it may even be a 'tea-dance') or recorded classical music.

Dinner: the main event of the evening.

Light bites: typically served in public rooms late at night. These have replaced the traditional midnight buffet.

Gala midnight buffet: this is almost extinct, but if there is one, it is usually on the penultimate evening of a cruise when the chefs pull out all the stops. It

consists of a grand spread with intricate decoration that can take up to 48 hours to prepare.

Seating

Depending on the size of the ship, it may have single, two, or open seatings:

Open seating. You can sit with whomever you wish at any available table, at any time the restaurant is open.

Single seating. This doesn't mean seating for single passengers. It means you can choose when you wish to eat (within dining room hours), but you will have the same table assigned for the whole cruise.

Two seatings. You are assigned (or choose) one of two seatings: early or late.

Some ships operate two seatings for all meals, and some do so only for dinner. Some ships operate a mix of open seating (dine when you want) or fixed dining times, for greater flexibility. Dinner hours may vary when the ship is in port to allow for the timing of shore excursions. Ships that operate in Europe and the Mediterranean or in South America may have later meal times to suit their clientele.

The captain's and senior officers' tables

The captain usually occupies a large table in or near the center of the dining room on 'formal' nights, with senior officers such as the chief engineer and hotel manager hosting adjacent tables. However, the tradition is disappearing, as ship dress codes are now too casual. The table usually seats eight to 12 people picked from the passenger or 'commend' list by the hotel manager. If you are invited to the captain's table (or any senior officer's table), it is gracious to accept.

Dining room and kitchen staff

Although celebrity chefs make the headlines, it's the ship's executive chef who plans the menus, orders the food, organizes and supervises staff, and arranges all the meals.

The restaurant manager, also known as the maître d'hôtel (not to be confused with the ship's hotel manager), is an experienced host, with shrewd percep-

WHERE TO FIND REAL ALE

Most major cruise lines offer mainly branded canned lagers. The best beer from the barrel and bottled beers are stocked by UK-based cruise lines such as Cunard, Fred. Olsen Cruise Lines, P&O Cruises, and Saga Cruises, though the selection is generally unexciting. Many real ales do not travel well. However, AIDA Cruises has a micro-brewery aboard its newest ships (AIDAblu, AIDAmar, AIDAprima, AIDAsol, and AIDAstella), as does Carnival Cruise Line (Carnival Vista, which debuted in 2016).

Remy, an upscale, top-deck restaurant aboard *Disney Dream*.

tions about compatibility. It is his or her responsibility to seat you with suitable companions.

The best waiters are those trained in hotels or catering schools. They provide fine service and quickly learn your likes and dislikes. They normally work aboard the best ships, where dignified professionalism is expected, and living conditions, salary and benefits are good.

Some lines contract the running and staffing of dining rooms to a specialist maritime catering organization. Ships that cruise far from their home country find that professional caterers, such as the Miami-based Apollo Group or Hamburg-based Sea Chefs, do an outstanding job.

Hygiene standards

Galley equipment is in almost constant use, and regular inspections and maintenance help detect potential problems. There is continual cleaning of equipment, utensils, bulkheads, floors, and hands.

Cruise ships sailing from or visiting US ports are subject to in-port sanitation inspections. These are voluntary, not mandatory inspections, carried out by the United States Public Health (USPH) Department of Health and Human Services, under the auspices of the Centers for Disease Control (CDC). Cruise lines pay for thousands of dollars for each inspection.

A tour of the galley proves to be a highlight for some passengers, when a ship's insurance company permits.

In accordance with international standards, all potable water brought on board, or produced by distillation aboard cruise ships, should contain a free chlorine or bromine residual greater than or equal to 0.2ppm (parts per million). This is why drinking water served in dining rooms may taste of chlorine.

How the major cruise lines score on cuisine out of 10				
	Dining room/Cuisine	Buffets/Informal dining	Quality of ingredients	Overall food score
AIDA Cruises	5.6	5.6	6	5.73
Carnival Cruise Line	6.0	6.1	6	6.05
Celebrity Cruises	7.1	7	7	7.0
Costa Cruises	5.7	5.4	6	5.7
Holland America Line	6.3	5.9	6.4	6.2
MSC Cruises	7.2	6.4	7.7	7.1
Norwegian Cruise Line	6.1	6.2	6.1	6.1
Princess Cruises	7.3	6.7	6.8	6.9
Royal Caribbean Intl.	6.5	6.0	6.0	6.1

The Little Mermaid makes an appearance in *The Golden Mickeys*, a revue-style show aboard *Disney Dream*.

Entertainment

The bigger the ship, the bigger the show, with tired old song-and-dance routines now replaced by full-scale Broadway hits and Disney musicals.

Cruise lines with large resort ships have upped the ante lately, competing to attract attention by staging super-lavish, high-tech productions that are licensed versions of Broadway shows, with cruise lines signing partnership deals with musical producers, composers, and songwriters.

Lavish productions: what's playing

Cats (Oasis of the Seas)
Grease (Harmony of the Seas,
Independence of the Seas)
Mamma Mia (Allure of the Seas)
Priscilla Queen of the Desert (Norwegian Epic)
Saturday Night Fever (Liberty of the Seas)

These big theater shows, with impressively large casts, are versions specially adapted to fit a large resort ship's main stage, typically by being cut and finetuned, so that they fit in with the ship's operational schedule – not to mention dinner. The performing standards, energy, and enthusiasm of these big musicals are outstanding – definitely giving the land versions a run for their money.

Other big shows

Disney Cruise Line has other fine stage shows, including *Aladdin: A Musical Spectacular (Disney Fantasy)*, taken from the Disney stable, plus *Believe,* developed specifically for *Disney Dream*. A proven family favorite is *Toy Story – The Musical*. Disney has separate entertainment shows for adults, too.

The good news is you don't pay extra to see the show, except if it's part of a supper club (including dinner). There are also few bad seats in the house, you don't have to find a parking place, or find a restaurant to eat in before or after the show – and there's always a handy bar nearby.

Royal Caribbean International's *Allure of the Seas, Harmony of the Seas,* and *Oasis of the Seas* each have an outdoor 'AquaTheater' (with a part-watery stage), where aquabatics and comedy provide an entertainment spectacular.

THE COST OF STAGING A SHOW

Staging a lavish production show can easily cost $1 million, plus performers' pay, costume cleaning and repair, royalties, and so on. To justify that cost, shows must remain aboard for 18 to 24 months.

Some smaller operators see entertainment as an area for cost-cutting, so you could find yourself entertained by low-budget singers and bands.

Onboard productions

Colorful, 'one-size-fits-all' Las Vegas-style production shows have evolved enormously aboard the large resort ships, as have stages, technical equipment, and facilities. Although they still can't match the budgets of Las Vegas, they can certainly beat many shoreside venues. Most production shows have two things in common: little or no audience contact, and intense volume. With few exceptions, the equation 'volume = ambience' is thoroughly entrenched in the minds of many young audiovisual technicians.

Overall, there's little elegance in most production shows, and all are too long. The after-dinner attention span of most cruise passengers seems to be about 35 minutes, but most production shows run for about 45 to 50 minutes.

The majority of show 'dancing' today consists of stepping in place, while pre-recorded backing tracks are often synthetic and grossly imbalanced.

Some cruise lines have a live showband to back the large-scale shows. The band plays along with a pre-recorded backing track to create an 'enhanced' or larger sound. Some companies, such as Disney Cruise Line, use only a pre-recorded track. This has little 'feel' to it, unlike a live showband that can generate empathy and variation – and provide work for real musicians. Although live music may contain minor im-

A performance of *Grease* aboard *Harmony of the Seas*.

Priscilla Queen of the Desert aboard *Norwegian Epic.*

perfections, which some might regard as 'character-ful', most passengers would prefer it to canned music.

Great expectations

Many passengers, despite having paid comparatively little for their cruise, expect top-notch entertainment and the most dazzling shows with slick special effects, just as one would find in the best venues in Las Vegas, London, or Paris. There are many reasons why the reality is different. Cruise brochures tend to over-hype entertainment. International star acts invariably have an entourage that accompanies them to any venue: their personal manager, their musical director (often a pianist or conductor), a rhythm section with bass player and drummer, and a hairdresser. On land, one-night shows are possible, but aboard ship, an artist can seldom disembark after just one night, especially when it involves moving equipment, costumes, stage props, and baggage. This makes the deal logistically and financially unattractive for all but the largest ships on fixed itineraries, where a marquee-name act would be a draw.

Most entertainers don't like to be away from their 'home base' for long periods, as they rely on reliable phone and Internet access for managing their careers. Nor do they like the long contracts that most ships must offer in order to amortize the high costs.

Entertaining but predictable

So many acts from one cruise ship to the next are interchangeable with each other. Ever wonder why? It relates to the limited appeal of a cruise ship gig. Entertainers aboard ships have to live with their audiences for several days and perhaps weeks – something unheard of on land – as well as work on stages aboard older ships that were not designed for live performances.

Entertainment aboard large resort ships is directed toward family cruising. This is predominantly a fam-

ily audience, so entertainment must appeal to a broad age range. That partly accounts for the frequency of formulaic Cirque du Soleil-style acrobatic routines and rope climbing. The only *real* Cirque du Soleil show (with specially designed showroom) can be found aboard MSC Cruises' *Meraviglia.*

A cruise line with several ships will normally employ an entertainment director and several assistants, and most cruise lines use entertainment agencies that specialize in entertainment for cruise ships. As a result, regular passengers are likely to see the same acts time after time on various ships.

Mistakes do happen. It is no use, for example, booking a juggler who needs a floor-to-ceiling height of 12ft (3.7m) but finds that the ship has a show-lounge with a height of just 7ft (2m) – although I did overhear one cruise director ask if the act 'could juggle sideways'; or a concert pianist when the ship only has an upright honky-tonk piano.

Trying to please everyone

The toughest audience is one of mixed nationalities, each of which will expect entertainers to cater exclusively to their particular linguistic group. Given that cruise lines are now marketing to more international audiences in order to fill ever-larger ships, the problem of finding the right entertainment is far more acute – which is why *Queen Mary 2* is to be envied for the visual appeal of its 20-minute-long *Illuminations* planetarium shows.

Cruise lines operating small ships offer more classical music, guest lecturers, and top authors than seven-day package cruises heading for the sun.

These performers – and ship entertainers generally – need to enjoy socializing. Successful shipboard acts tend to be good mixers, are presentable when in public, do not take drugs or drink excess alcohol, are not late for rehearsals, and must cooperate with the cruise director.

Part of the entertainment experience aboard large resort ships is the glamorous 'production show,' the kind of show you would expect to see in a Las Vegas show palace – think flesh and feathers – with male and female lead singers and Madonna or Marilyn Monroe look-alike dancers, a production manager, lavish backdrops, extravagant sets, grand lighting, special effects, and stunning custom-designed costumes. Unfortunately, most cruise line executives know little or nothing about entertainment, and still favor plumes and huge feather boas paraded by showgirls who step, but don't *dance*. Shows with topless dancers are staged aboard the ships of Hong Kong-based Dream Cruises and Star Cruises.

Book back-to-back seven-day cruises (on alternating eastern and western Caribbean itineraries, for example), and you'll probably find the same two or three production shows and the same acts on the second week of your cruise. The way to avoid seeing everything twice is to pace yourself.

Other entertainment
Most ships organize acts that, while not nationally known 'names,' can provide two or three different shows during a seven-day cruise. These will be singers, illusionists, puppeteers, reality TV show wannabes, hypnotists, and even circus acts, with wide age-range appeal. Also, comedians who perform 'clean' material can find employment year-round on the cruise ship circuit. These popular comics enjoy good accommodation, are mini-stars while on board, and may go from ship to ship on a standard rotation every few days. There are raunchy, late-night 'adults only' comedy acts in some of the ships with younger audiences, but few have enough material for several shows. In general, the larger a ship, the broader the entertainment program will be.

Movies on deck
Showing movies on the open deck has been part of the cruise scene since the 1970s, when they were often classic black-and-white films shown at midnight. In those days, the screens were small, roll-down affairs, and the projectors were set up on makeshift pedestals. The result was often images that vibrated, and sound that quivered.

Speed forward into the 21st century. Most large resort ships now have huge outdoor poolside LED movie screens 300 sq ft (approximately 28 sq m) that cost around $1 million each. The screens are complemented by 50,000- to 80,000-watt sound systems for a complete 'surround the deck' experience.

Princess Cruises started the trend in 2004 aboard *Grand Princess* with its 'Movies Under the Stars' program, but now all companies with large resort ships have them. The experience is reminiscent of the old drive-in movies, the difference being that cruise lines often supply blankets and even popcorn free of charge.

Movies and other presentations are shown day and night. Aboard family-friendly ships, they may include special films for junior cruisers. Big sports events such as the Super Bowl or World Cup soccer are also presented.

Smaller cruise ships, expedition cruise ships, and sail-cruise ships may have little or no entertainment. Aboard those ships, after-dinner conversation, reading, and relaxation become the entertainment of choice.

What's on
Entertainment is listed in the 'daily program' – a mini-newspaper for the following day that is delivered to your suite/cabin each night when your bed is turned down. Any changes (due to bad weather, for example) are announced over the PA system.

FAMOUS CRUISING MOVIES (IN DATE ORDER)

One Way Passage (1932). Bittersweet story about a shipboard romance between a man (William Powell) condemned to be executed and a terminally ill woman (Kay Francis).
The French Line (1954). Life aboard the French Line's *Liberté*, depicted as being frivolous, promiscuous and romantic. Stars Jane Russell, Gilbert Roland, and Arthur Hunnicutt.
An Affair to Remember (1957). Two movie greats (Cary Grant and Deborah Kerr) meet aboard a passenger ship, although most of the movie is actually about the Empire State Building in New York.
A Night to Remember (1958). Another movie about the last night aboard *Titanic*, this movie is dramatically realistic and quite terrifying in parts, and it makes you realize that oceans and seas can be treacherous. The cast includes Kenneth More, Anthony Bushell, Robert Ayres, and Honor Blackman.
The Last Voyage (1960). A movie about (what else) a sinking ship. Instead of effects, a real ship (*Ile de France*) was used in this gripping movie. Robert Stack and Dorothy Malone star.
Carry on Cruising (1962). A classic British comedy about a group of individuals (played by *Carry on* icons Kenneth Williams, Sidney James, and Kenneth Connor), who go cruising, with a heavy emphasis on innuendo and slapstick.
Ship of Fools (1965). A fine cast, including Vivian

Leigh, Simone Signoret, and Lee Marvin, find themselves aboard the same pre-war passenger ship. A splendid example of character study.
The Poseidon Adventure (1972). There are some fine scenes of life upside down aboard a ship on this adventure movie starring Gene Hackman, Ernest Borgnine, Shelley Winters, and Roddy McDowell.
Speed 2: Cruise Control (1997). A madman hijacker takes control of a cruise ship (based on *Seabourn Legend*, whose real captain, Erik Anderssen, and other onboard staff, appeared in the film). The ending is dramatic (shot on the Caribbean island of St. Martin), but the plot is not. The engine room must be enormous, if the film is to be taken seriously! Sandra Bullock, Jason Patric, and Willem Dafoe star.
Titanic (1996). Although you already know the ending, the story and dramatic effects of this movie starring Leonardo DiCaprio and Kate Winslet make it compelling to watch, especially considering its length.
Out to Sea (1997). Starring Jack Lemmon and Walter Matthau this is a playful movie about two 'gentlemen hosts,' who join the cruise staff of a cruise ship in the Caribbean (it's not *quite* like this in real life). The ships used in the movie were Holland America Line's *Westerdam* and *Queen Mary* (the original, now a museum ship and hotel, located in Long Beach, California).

Casinos

Place your bets! Glitzy onboard casinos flash their lights to attract your patronage, and bring Las Vegas-style gaming to open waters. But, watch out, Lady Luck can also bite your wallet.

Shipboard casinos

The word casino comes from the Italian for 'little house,' which referred to a small part of a larger villa used for music, dancing, and socializing. Waterborne gambling started in the mid-1800s aboard Mark Twain-era steamboats on the USA's Mississippi River – when it quickly became a profession – with an estimated 600 to 800 of them plying their trade on the river during the Gold Rush days. Today's ocean-going cruise ships have really taken over (the first recorded casino was aboard the 1906 French ocean liner *La Provence*). So, whether you are a serious gamer or simply want to try your luck on the slot machines, shipboard casinos are now considered a major part of the entertainment, particularly aboard the large resort ships.

Games and rules

The most popular table games include a variety of poker (or video poker) games (Caribbean Stud, Let it Ride, Texas Hold'em, Three Card, etc.). Other table games include blackjack, single-deck blackjack,

Norwegian Breakaway casino.

craps, and roulette. A few ships also have baccarat (including baccarat banque, chemin de fer, and punto banco – the most widely played).

Ships must follow the gaming rules established by the Nevada Gaming Control Board, or other licensed jurisdiction – usually the flag state of the ship. House rules typically include the following provisions:

Only adults are allowed to play the slots or the tables.

Cruise lines must post at every gaming table the minimum and maximum betting limits for each game.

Nothing personal is permitted on the tables.

Opening hours

Unlike casinos on land, most shipboard casinos are not open 24/7. They are always closed in port, with the exceptions of Bermuda, where they are open from 9pm–5am, and Nassau, in the Bahamas, where they stay open from 7pm–3am. Shipboard casinos are typically open once a ship leaves port, but not until it leaves territorial waters – 12 nautical miles away from the coastline (in Alaska it's 3 nautical miles). When a ship passes 24 miles, it is, according to international maritime law, in international waters.

Open all hours

Mobile gaming and wagering was introduced in 2013 by Celebrity Cruises (and in 2015 aboard some of the Carnival Corporation brands), enabling you to play almost anywhere on board – for example when lounging by the pool. You simply download the app prior to cruising (from the App Store for iOS devices, or from Google Play for Android devices).

Payment

Payment for casino credit and chips/tokens can be made in several ways, including by credit card or a pre-loaded 'virtual wallet.' A few ships have cash-only machines, but most operate by touch cards (your cabin card) or tokens. Note that some cruise lines impose a 'service fee' if you charge cash or casino tokens to your cabin charge card (Carnival Cruise Line, for example). Some cruise lines don't allow you to use onboard credit to purchase casino play currency.

Some cruise lines have an app that can be downloaded to your smartphone and then used for playing at the casino once you have loaded and validated your 'virtual wallet' with the casino cashier.

Winnings

Any winnings (and left-over casino chips) must be cashed in on board.

VIP Players Clubs

Some cruise lines reach out to 'high rollers' – those who might play in private clubs or VIP rooms on land, for high stakes. Cruise lines have their own versions of VIP clubs and attract players by giving perks (onboard credit, discounts on future cruises, etc.) and loyalty cards (these are different to a cruise line's loyalty club), just like casinos on land. Examples include most major cruise lines: Carnival Cruise Line (Ocean Players Club); Celebrity Cruises (Blue Chip Club); Norwegian Cruise Line (Casinos at Sea Players Club); and Royal Caribbean International (Club Royale). Typically, a minimum of $5,000 casino credit is required, with a maximum of $100,000. There may be a separate check-in line for VIP club players. High rollers may be invited by a cruise line to travel free or at reduced cost, provided that they participate in various (high-priced) tournaments.

Slots

Slot machines (invented in the 1890s by Charles Fey) bring in more than half of a casino's profits. If you like to play the slots, it may be better to sign up to a cruise line card club. This brings rewards, depending on how much you play. More play equals bigger rewards (including invitations to special events, discounted drinks, etc.). Sometimes, cruise lines offer double or even treble points after midnight. Winnings can be transferred to your card, so you can change machines.

The most popular slot machines are those of the 'reel' type, consisting of a number of spinning wheels that display fixed symbols, but video-display machines are increasing in popularity. Some are of the hybrid type – a mix of reel and video.

Many ships have penny slots, but this could turn out to be much more expensive than the 'lead-in' price (note that penny slot machines typically pay out based on the amount of money that is being bet, and not on the number of times the machine is used).

Tournaments

Shipboard casino and slot tournaments are programmed regularly, with blackjack and slots the most common. You participate by paying a certain amount, and then no more money is spent during the tournament. Some ships provide free (or reduced cost) drinks as an added incentive.

Smoking

Smoking is allowed in some shipboard casinos, depending on the cruise line. There is no smoking in casinos aboard the ships of Celebrity Cruises, Crystal Cruises, Cunard, Oceania Cruises, Regent Seven Seas Cruises, Seabourn, Silversea Cruises, and Windstar Cruises. Some companies, such as Carnival Cruise Line and Royal Caribbean International, have no-smoking sections within the casino, but in health terms this is as effective as having smokers at one end of an aircraft and non-smokers at the other.

Slot machines aboard *Celebrity Equinox*.

Design

Cruise ship casinos have evolved dramatically in terms of design, flow, and noise control. Most ships are designed so that passengers (including children) need to walk through them to reach either the restaurant or showlounge (although they won't be allowed to play the slots). However, aboard ships with multiple passenger room decks this may not be the case – which means it's easier to keep children away from the slot machines.

Both Norwegian Cruise Lines' Norwegian Spirit and Star Cruises' *SuperStar Virgo*, for example, have casino facilities at one end of a main public room deck, behind closed doors, so children cannot walk through – much better.

Which cruise lines don't have casinos?

Examples include Disney Cruise Line, Hapag-Lloyd Cruises, Phoenix Reisen, Saga Cruises, Sea Cloud Cruises, and Viking Ocean Cruises, plus many of the small-ship and expedition cruise lines. Also, Japanese cruise ships cannot pay in cash if you win, so soft toys ('gifts') are awarded instead, as prizes.

A little warning

Casinos are a major source of revenue for many cruise lines. So, if you plan to play, only do so with what you can afford to lose.

The odds

Unlike land-based casinos, shipboard casinos don't need to compete with the casino next door, so don't expect the odds to be good. Note that some ships have blackjack tables with a card-shuffle machine to mix the cards, but this increases the odds in favour of the house.

Excursions Ashore

Escorted tours in ports of call cost extra, but they are often the best way to get a nutshell view of a destination and make the most efficient use of your limited time ashore.

Shore excursions used to be limited to rather cheesy city tours, but today's excursions are extraordinarily varied, from crocodile hunting in the Amazon to kayaking in Alaska, and from elephant riding in Thailand, to flying over Moscow in a MiG jet. Most offer good value, but it's easy to spend more on shore excursions than on buying the cruise.

Shore excursions are offered by cruise lines in order to enhance a destination visit. Booking with a cruise line avoids the hassle of arranging your own excursions, and you'll be covered by the cruise line's insurance just in case things do go wrong. General city tours are designed to give you an overview and show you the highlights in a limited time period – typically about 3 hours. Other excursions provide a mind-boggling array of possibilities, including some that may be exclusive to a particular cruise line – even overland tours are part of the excursions available on longer cruises.

Not all tours are by bus. Some may be by bicycle, boat, car, or mini-van. Some cruise lines also offer private, tailor-made excursions to suit you, a family,

or small group. A private car, with a tour guide who speaks your language, for example, may be a good way for a family to get to know a foreign destination.

To get the most out of your shore visits, doing a little research – particularly if you are visiting foreign countries – will pay dividends. Once on board, attend the shore-excursion lectures, or watch destination and shore-excursion videos on the television in your cabin.

Once your ship reaches a destination, it must be cleared by local officials before you are free to go ashore. In most ports, this is accomplished speedily. Meanwhile, you may be asked to assemble for your organized tours in one of the ship's public rooms. You'll need to carry the ship's identification card with you, to be checked at the gangway, and for when you re-board. Remember to take the ship's telephone number with you, in case of emergencies.

How tiring are excursions?

Most tours will involve some walking; some require extensive walking. Most cruise lines grade their excursions with visual symbols to indicate the level of difficulty, for example in terms of fitness required.

How expensive are they?

For an average three-hour city sightseeing tour, expect to pay $40–100, and for whole-day excursions with lunch, $100–250. Flightseeing or seaplane sightseeing tours will cost $250–350, depending on the location, what is included, and how long they last – the flightseeing itself typically lasts about 30–45 minutes.

What should I take with me?

Only what's necessary; leave any valuables aboard ship, together with any money and credit cards you do not plan to use. Groups of people are often targets for pickpockets in some sightseeing destinations. Also, beware of excursion guides who give you a colored disk to wear for 'identification' – they may be marking you as a 'rich' tourist for local shopkeepers. It's always prudent to wear comfortable rubber-

Playing with stingrays in Nassau.

A TICKET TO RIDE

Many companies with large resort ships charge extra for shuttle buses to take you from the port or other docking area to a local city or town center. The port with the highest charge is Venice, Italy, where the transport is by motorboat between the cruise terminals and St. Mark's Square.

Shopping excursion with Norwegian Cruise Line.

soled shoes, particularly in older ports, where there may be cobblestones or other uneven surfaces.

How can I make a booking?

Several cruise lines allow you to book shore excursions online before you cruise, which means that some popular excursions may sell out before you even get to your ship. So book early.

If you need to cancel a shore excursion, you usually need to do so at least 24 hours before its advertised departure time. Otherwise, refunds are at the discretion of the cruise line, and refunds of pre-paid tickets booked online can take a long time to make and can incur currency-exchange losses.

How to tell which excursions are good?

If it's your first cruise, try to attend the shore-excursion briefing. Read the excursion literature and circle tours that appeal to you, then go to the shore-excursion office and ask any other questions you may have before you book.

Shore excursions are designed for general interest. If you want to see something that isn't described in the excursion literature, skip the excursion. Go on your own or with friends.

Brochure descriptions of shore excursions, often written by personnel who haven't visited the ports of call, can be imprecise. All cruise lines should

10 DESTINATION NIGGLES

These destinations are lovely places, but watch out for the following nuisances.
1. Cagliari, Italy. Poor beaches and staggeringly overpriced shops.
2. Grenada. Intrusive hawkers on Grand Anse and other beaches.
3. Gibraltar. The rock's fine, but that's it – there's nothing else other than duty-free liquor, and some Barbary apes.
4. Naples, Italy. Trying to cross the road from the cruise terminals to town can be a nail-biting experience.
5. Cannes, France. There can be dog muck all over the sidewalks, so tread warily!
6. Portofino, Italy. Several ships disgorging passengers onto the skinniest strip of land in summer.
7. St. Maarten. When six large resort ships are docked at the same time.
8. Ensenada, Mexico. The poor area surrounding the cruise ship docking area.
9. Ocho Rios, Jamaica. Constant hustling to get you to buy something, and the general unsafe feeling.
10. Juneau, Alaska. The tacky souvenir shops are simply overwhelming.

White-water rafting in Costa Rica.

adopt the following definitions in their descriptive literature, lectures, and presentations: the term 'visit' should mean actually entering the place or building concerned; the term 'see' should mean viewing from the outside – as from a bus, for example.

City excursions are basically superficial. To get to know a city intimately, go alone or with a small group. Go by taxi or bus, or explore on foot.

If you don't want to miss the main sightseeing attractions in each port, organized shore excursions provide a good solution. They also allow you to meet fellow passengers with similar interests.

In the Caribbean, many sightseeing tours cover the same ground, regardless of the cruise line you sail with. Choose one and then do something different in the next port. The same is true of the history and archaeology excursions in the Greek islands, where the same ancient gods put in frequent appearances.

What if I lose my ticket?

Report lost or misplaced tickets to the shore excursion manager. Aboard most ships, excursion tickets, once sold, become the sole responsibility of the buyer, and the cruise line isn't generally able to issue replacements.

Are there private excursions?

Most cruise line-organized excursions work on the 'one-size-fits-all' principle. However, a more personalized alternative exists for anyone looking for privately guided tours and land experiences. Tailor-made 'build-your-own' excursions, arranged by a 'travel concierge,' provide private tours of a destination and its environs. These could include lunch or dinner in a hard-to-book top-class restaurant, a visit to a private museum, or other bespoke requirements for small groups.

The right transportation and private guide will be arranged, and all arrangements taken care of – at a cost, of course. A cruise line destination 'expert' will plan an excursion, arrange the right transportation, and attend to all the other details that make the experience more personal. It's all about exclusivity – at a price.

Going ashore independently – and safely

The main advantage of going independently is that you do so at your own pace and see the sights you want to see. If you hire a taxi for sightseeing, negotiate the price in advance, and don't pay until you get back to the ship or to your destination. If you are with friends, hiring a taxi for a full- or half-day sightseeing trip can often work out far cheaper than renting a car – and it's probably safer and more relaxing. Try to find a driver who speaks your language.

Exploring independently is straightforward in the major cruise ports of the Aegean, Alaska, the Bahamas, Bermuda, the Caribbean, the Mexican Riviera, the Canary Islands, the Mediterranean, and the South Pacific's islands. If you don't speak the local language, carry some identification (but not your actual passport, unless required – keep a photocopy with you instead), the name of your ship (and its telephone number, for emergencies), and the area in which it is docked. If the ship is anchored, and you take a launch tender ashore, observe landmarks near the landing place, and write down the location – or take a photo. This will help if you get lost and need to take a taxi back to the launch.

Some small ships provide an identification tag or boarding pass at the reception desk, to be handed in each time you return to the ship. Remember that ships have schedules – and sometimes tides – to meet, and they won't wait for you if you return late. If you are in a launch port and severe weather approaches, the ship's captain could make a decision to depart early to avoid being hemmed in by an approaching storm. Although this is rare, it has happened, especially in the Caribbean. If it does, in the port, locate the ship's agent, who will try to get you back on board.

Planning on going to a quiet, secluded beach to swim? First check with the shore excursion manager, as certain beaches may be considered off-limits because of a dangerous undertow, drug pushers, or persistent hawkers. And don't even think of going diving alone – even if you know the area well.

If you explore independently and need medical help, you could risk missing the ship when it sails. Unless the destination is a familiar one, first-time cruisers are probably safer booking excursions organized by the ship and vetted by the cruise line. Also, if you have a problem during a tour, the cruise line should be able to sort it out on the spot.

The main downside of going it alone is the possibility of delay. If there is a problem with your chosen mode of transport, you could miss the ship as a result. In such a case (it does happen), you are responsible for getting to the ship. This may not be easy if

33 DESTINATION EXCURSIONS TO EXPERIENCE

1. Icy Straight Point, Alaska: Take a trip on the world's longest zipline. With a 1,320ft (402m) vertical drop, the ZipRider transports participants from mountain peak to harbor-side beach at 60mph (97kph).

2. Juneau, Alaska: A flightseeing trip to Mendenhall Glacier, plus an Alaska salmon bake.

3. Skagway, Alaska: The historic White Pass & Yukon Route Railroad train tour.

4. Grand Cayman, The Caribbean: Snorkeling with the stingrays at Stingray City.

5. Jamaica, The Caribbean: Horseback riding on the beach at Montego Bay or Ocho Rios.

6. St. Maarten, The Caribbean: Join the America's Cup Regatta adventure tour and compete in an actual yacht race.

7. Cozumel, Mexico: Children will enjoy a personal dolphin encounter at the Cabo Dolphin Center.

8. Dublin, Ireland: Visit the original Guinness brewery.

9. Edinburgh, Scotland: Take a whisky distillery tour.

10. London, England: Join the London by Night tour. This includes a West End musical or play.

11. Naples, Italy: Take the boat tour to the island of Capri to visit the famous Blue Grotto cave.

12. Nice, France: Enjoy this elegant city, plus the Corniche and the medieval hilltop village of Eze.

13. Palma de Mallorca: Tour the former Carthusian monastery of Valldemossa. Frédéric Chopin and George Sand lived here in 1838.

14. Rome, Italy: Visit the Vatican's Sistine Chapel.

15. Sorrento, Italy: Visit to the ruins of Pompeii, plus the Amalfi Coast and Sorrento.

16. Venice, Italy: Take a romantic trip on a gondola.

17. Reykjavík, Iceland: Take the Ring of Fire tour of the warm geothermal waters of the Blue Lagoon and visit an active volcano.

18. St. Petersburg, Russia: Sign up for a guided walking tour through the Hermitage Museum, or an excursion to the Catherine Palace, summer residence of the tsars.

19. La Coruña, Spain: Pay homage in the city of Santiago de Compostela, home to the shrine of St. James.

20. Aqaba, Jordan: Tour to the 'Rose-Red City' of Petra.

21. Dubai, United Arab Emirates: Take a 4x4 Dune Drive Safari Tour.

22. Mumbai, India: Go on a Buddhist Trail tour to the Kanheri Caves.

23. Hilo, Hawaii: Marvel at the Kilauea Volcano tour in Volcanoes National Park.

24. Key West, USA: Take the Conch Train Tour in Ernest Hemingway's favorite town.

25. Hamilton Island, Australia: Cruise/tour the Great Barrier Reef.

26. Melbourne, Australia: Brave the shark diving in the aquarium tour on the banks of the Yarra River.

27. Singapore: Take the Night Safari tour.

28. Kuala Lumpur, Malaysia: Visit the Petronas Twin Towers and the city's vibrant night markets.

29. Buenos Aires: Take the Steak and Tango night tour.

30. Ushuaia, Argentina: Ride the world's southernmost train.

31. Cape Town, South Africa: Tour of Cape Town and Table Top Mountain.

32. Mombasa, Kenya: Tour of Tsavo National Park, one of Kenya's oldest game parks.

33. Chiang Mai, Thailand: Elephant jungle tour, where you will ride on and bathe these extraordinary animals, and swimming at Mork Fa Waterfall.

Shopping in the center of Fort de France, Martinique.

the next port of call is in another country, and you don't have your passport. You should also be aware that cruise lines do change itineraries occasionally, due to weather, or political or other factors. If you book your own tours, and it's a tender port where the ship has to remain at anchor offshore, you may need to wait until passengers on the ship's organized tours have been offloaded. This can take two or more hours aboard some of the large resort ships.

Allow plenty of time to get back to your ship before sailing time – the ship won't wait. Make sure your travel insurance covers you fully.

Shopping aboard

Many ships have designer brands (clothing items, cosmetics, perfume, watches) on board at duty-free prices, so you don't need to spend time shopping ashore. Some ships have private rooms where you can view expensive jewelry or watches in private. Onboard shops are closed while the ship is in port, however, due to international customs regulations. Good discounts are often offered on the last day of the cruise.

Shopping ashore

Aboard ship, a 'shopping lecturer' will give a presentation about shopping in the various ports of call. Many cruise lines operating in Alaska, the Bahamas, the Caribbean, and the Mexican Riviera engage an outside company that provides the services of a shopping lecturer. Most talks are about designer jewelry and watches – high-ticket items that boost commissions to cruise lines. The shopping lecturers' heavily promote selected shops, goods, and services, authorized by the cruise line, which receives a commission. Shopping maps, with selected stores highlighted, are

usually placed in your cabin, and sometimes include a guarantee of satisfaction valid for 30 days.

During organized shore excursions, be wary of stores recommended by tour guides – they may be receiving commissions from the merchants. Shop around before you purchase. When buying local handicrafts, make sure they have indeed been made locally. Be wary of 'bargain-priced' name brands, as they may be counterfeit. For watches, check the guarantee.

Some of the world's shopping havens put serious temptation in the way of cruise passengers. Top of the list are Hong Kong, Singapore, and Dubai (especially in the Mall of the Emirates – a shopping resort rather than a mall – and the Dubai Mall, with over 1,200 shops, including the only Bloomingdale's outside the US).

Shopping tips

Know in advance just what you are looking for, especially if your time is limited; when time is no problem, browsing can be fun.

When shopping time is included in an excursion, be wary of stores repeatedly recommended by tour guides, as they may be receiving commissions from the merchants.

When shopping for local handicrafts, make sure they have indeed been made locally. It can happen that a so-called local product has in fact been made in Taiwan, Hong Kong, or another Far Eastern country. It pays to check.

Be wary of 'bargain-priced' name brands such as Gucci bags and Rolex or Omega watches – they are probably counterfeit. Check the serial numbers to see whether they are genuine or not. For watches, check the guarantee.

Spas and Wellness Facilities

The 'feel-good factor' is alive and well aboard the latest cruise ships, which offer a growing array of beauty salons and body-pampering treatments.

Land-based health spas have long provided a range of body treatments and services for those who wanted to escape the bustle of everyday life. Responding to the rise in popularity of 'wellness' breaks, today's cruise ships now have elaborate spas to rival those on land, where, for an extra fee, whole days of almost-continuous treatments are on offer. Once the domain of women, spas now cater almost as equally for men.

Many people unaccustomed to spas may find some of the terminology daunting: aromatherapy, hydrotherapy, ionithermie, rasul, thalassotherapy. Spa staff will help you choose the massage or other treatment that best suits you and your needs. Do visit the spa on embarkation day, when staff will be on hand to show you around, and answer your questions. Some cruise lines let you pre-book spa treatments online before your cruise. But take note of prices, which can quickly add up.

Avoid booking massage treatments at a time when the ship is about to leave port (usually in the late afternoon/early evening), because there may be interruptive announcements, plus noise and vibration from the propulsion machinery.

Facilities

Large resort ships have facilities that may include saunas, steam rooms, rasul chamber, several body treatment rooms, thalassotherapy (saltwater) pool, relaxation area, changing/locker rooms, and a beauty salon. Some ships have acupuncture treatment clinics, and some have a built-in juice bar. Some offer a 'couples' experience, complete with 'spa suites' for rent by the day or half-day.

Thermal suites

Thermal suites are private areas that provide a combination of various warm scented rain showers, saunas, steam rooms, and thalassotherapy pools, with relaxation zones offering the promise of ultimate relaxation. Although most ships don't charge for use of the sauna or steam room, some of them do. A number of ships even add a gratuity to a spa day pass, while some ships limit the number of passes available – aboard Cunard's *Queen Elizabeth* and *Queen Victoria*, for example, the limit is 40 persons per day.

Personal spa suites

Each spa suite consists of a large room with floor-to-ceiling windows (with one-way glass), a heated floor, abundant relaxation space, towels, and bathrobes. They may also include a sauna, steam room, shower

enclosure, tiled and heated relaxation loungers, hydraulic massage tables, and a choice of massage oils.

They will also have herbal tea-making facilities and are usually bookable for a couple of hours, a half-day, or a full day.

Pampering treatments

Stress-reducing and relaxation treatments are offered, combined with the use of seawater, which contains minerals, micronutrients, and vitamins. Massages might include Swedish remedial massage, shiatsu, and aromatherapy oils. You can even get a massage on your private balcony aboard some ships.

Having body-pampering treatments aboard a cruise ship can be wonderful, as the ship can provide a serene environment; when enhanced by a massage or facial, the benefits can be even more therapeutic. So, before you actually book your relaxing massage, find out whether the treatment rooms are quiet enough.

Unfortunately, treatments are usually available only until about 8pm, whereas some passengers would welcome being able to have a massage late at

Taking a salt bath aboard *Norwegian Breakaway*.

night before retiring to bed – the problem is that most shipboard spas are run by concessions, with wellbeing treated as a daytime-only activity.

Some of the smaller, more upscale ships also offer 'Spa Days' with a whole day of body-pampering treatments, often termed 'wellness packages.' Expect to pay up to $500 a day *in addition to* the basic cruise fare.

Berlitz Tip: Check the daily program for 'port day specials' and packages that make the prices more palatable.

Fitness centers

Virtual-reality exercise machines are found in the techno-gyms aboard many ships, with state-of-the-art muscle-pumping and body-strengthening equipment, universal stations, treadmills, bicycles, rowing machines, and free weights.

Most fitness centers are open only until early evening, although one exception is the Norwegian Cruise Line, whose gyms are open 24 hours a day. And if you've forgotten your workout clothes, you can probably purchase new items on board.

Typical exercise classes include high-intensity/low-impact aerobics, aquacise (pool-based) classes, interval training, stretch and relax, super body sculpting, fabdominals, sit and be fit, and walk-a-mile.

Group exercycling, kick-boxing, Pilates and yoga classes, body-composition analysis, and sessions with a personal trainer cost extra.

Massage

Having a massage aboard ship can be a good stress-busting experience, although if it's not right it can prove frustrating, and expensive. A whole range of

treatments and styles has evolved from the standard Swedish Remedial Massage.

Here are some favorite massage moments (always taken in the late afternoon or early evening, preferably just before sundown):

Aboard *Celebrity Constellation, Celebrity Infinity, Celebrity Millennium, Celebrity Summit*, on the balcony of a Sky Suite.

Aboard *Royal Clipper*, in a private massage hut on an outside deck.

Aboard *SuperStar Virgo*, on the floor of a junior suite bedroom.

Inside a beach cabana ashore on Castaway Cay or Half Moon Cay in the Bahamas, or as part of a private beach day (*SeaDream I* and *II*) in the British Virgin Islands.

Make appointments for a massage (approximately $2 per minute) as soon as possible, so you can obtain the time and day of your choice. On some ships, massage may be available in your cabin (or on your private balcony), if it's large enough to accommodate a portable massage table.

A gratuity is often added automatically to spa treatments – typically at 15–18 percent. Elixirs of youth, lotions and potions, creams, and scrubs – all are sold by therapists, typically at the end of your treatment, for you to use when you get home. But watch out, as these are expensive items, so beware of falling for subtle and flattering sales talk.

Treatments

Although massage is the most popular shipboard spa treatment, most ships also offer facials, manicures, pedicures, teeth whitening, and acupuncture.

A gym with a view on a Celebrity cruise.

A romantic couples' massage in the Senses Spa & Salon aboard *Disney Magic*.

Most are based on holistic Asian therapies. Some examples include: *mandi lulur*, a scrub made from herbs, essential oils, and rice to soften the skin; and *boreh*, a warm Balinese herb, rice, spice, galangal water, and oil body wrap for detoxification.

The spa will provide towels, robes, and slippers, but it's best to store valuables safely in your cabin prior to your appointment. Some spas offer disposable underwear for body treatments such as a Body Salt Glow or Seaweed Wrap.

Acupuncture. Used to prevent and remedy many maladies, this works by inserting super-fine needles into special points on the skin.

Halotherapy. This detox treatment uses a Himalayan crystal salt bed for deep relaxation and body detoxing. It involves lying on a bed of 290lbs (131.5kg) of Himalayan salt crystals heated from 90 to 104 degrees Fahrenheit (32–40 degrees Celsius), and breathing in the salt-infused air. The salt contains 84 essential minerals as fine particles.

Moxibustion. This is a treatment that involves the insertion of hair-thin needles, dipped into mugwort (*Artemisa capillaris*), into one of the body's many acupuncture points.

Body scrub

This treatment cleanses and softens the skin, and draws out impurities using aromatic oils, creams, lotions, and perhaps sea salt, together with exfoliation (removal of dead skin cells).

Body wrap

Often called a body mask, this treatment typically includes the use of algae and seaweeds applied to the whole body. The body is then covered in aluminum foil and blankets. There are many variations on this theme, using mud from the Dead Sea or the Mediterranean, or sea salt and ginger, or cooling cucumber and aloe, or combinations of herbs and oils that leave you with a warm glow. The aim is to detoxify, firm, and tone the skin, and reduce cellulite.

Facials

Aromatherapy facial. This treatment typically uses aromatic oils such as lavender, sandalwood, and geranium, plus a rejuvenating mask and accompanying creams and essences to 'lift' the skin and facial muscles.

Rejuvenation facial. This is typically a classic French facial, which utilizes the latest skin care products enriched with essential plant and vitamin-rich oils. This facial aims to reduce lines and wrinkles.

Other popular treatments include eye lifting, volcanic mud masks, and manicures.

Rasul chamber

This is a steam chamber (Hammam) that is typically fully tiled, with a domed roof and Moorish decor. You paste yourself or your partner, if you are traveling as a couple, with three types of mud and sit down while gentle steam surrounds you. The various types of mud become heated, and then you're in a mud bath, after which you rub yourself (or perhaps each other) with large crystals of rock salt.

Reflexology

The body's energy meridians exist as reflex points on the soles of the feet. The therapist uses thumb pressure to stimulate these points to improve circulation and restore energy flow throughout the body.

About Face – 'me-time' for your face.

Teeth whitening

This treatment uses one of several methods, including bleaching strips, pen, gel, and laser bleaching. Carbamide peroxide, when mixed with water, forms hydrogen peroxide – the substance most used in teeth-whitening procedures. Power bleaching uses light energy to accelerate the process.

Thalassotherapy

The use of seawater to promote wellbeing and healing dates back to ancient Greece. Today, shipboard spas have whole bath rituals involving water and flower petals, herbs, or mineral salts.

Spa cuisine

Originally designed as low-fat, low-calorie meals for weight loss using grains, greens, and sprouts, spa cuisine now includes whole grains, seasonal fruits and vegetables, and lean proteins – ingredients low in saturated fats and cholesterol, low-fat dairy products, and reduced salt. These foods provide the basis for balanced nutrition and portion sizes, while maintaining some flavor, texture, and taste; foods are typically grilled rather than baked or fried.

Sports facilities

Sports facilities might include basketball, paddle tennis (a sort of downsized tennis court), and electronic golf simulators. Some boutique/small 'luxury' ships offer kayaking, water-skiing, jet skiing, and wake boarding for no extra charge. In reality, however, the water sports equipment is typically only used on one or two days (or part days) during a seven-day cruise.

WHO RUNS THE SPAS?

Aboard most ships, the spa and fitness areas are operated by a specialist concession, although each cruise line may have a separate name for the spa, such as AquaSpa (Celebrity Cruises), The Greenhouse Spa (Holland America Line), Lotus Spa (Princess Cruises), etc.

Aboard the large resort ships, spa staff tends to be young, enthusiastic 'therapists,' who will try hard to sell you own-brand beauty products, for a commission.

Steiner Leisure is the largest concession, operating spas aboard more than 100 ships. The company, founded in London in 1901 by Henry Steiner, began its ambitious growth in 1926, when Herman Steiner got involved in the family beauty salon on his father's death. He opened salons throughout England, became official cosmetician to the late Queen Elizabeth the Queen Mother, and won his first cruise ship contract in 1956.

The company closed its land-based salons in the 1990s, as its cruise ship business burgeoned. It bought Elemis, a lifestyle range of plant-based beauty products, and acquired Mandara Spas, developed in the US alongside its Elemis Spas. In 2010 it bought The Onboard Spa Company.

Other spa concessions include: Blue Ocean (MSC Cruises); Canyon Ranch At Sea (Celebrity Cruises, Cunard, Oceania Cruises, and Regent Seven Seas Cruises); Carita (Ponant); Flair (Louis, Voyages to Antiquity, Thomson); LivNordic (Viking Cruises); and Ocean Spa (Hapag-Lloyd, TUI Cruises).

Living in Luxury

Of the 70-plus cruise lines operating internationally, only a handful provides the kind of stylish ships aboard which the word 'no' is virtually unheard.

One person's luxury is another person's standard. Luxury (elegant, sumptuous) cruises are like the difference between a Bentley automobile and a motor scooter. 'Luxury cruising' should be a flawless combination of ship, facilities, understated decor, culinary excellence, impeccable service – and arriving in style. Unfortunately, the words luxury, luxe, and premium – all used quite interchangeably – have been degraded through constant overuse by marketeers. and advertisers.

Brochure vs reality
The brochure shows a photo of Champagne at embarkation. The reality: it's Prosecco, or another sparkling wine. The brochure shows a photo of a couple having a romantic dinner at a table for two outdoors on deck. The reality: few ships can deliver this.

Little and large
Size is important. Boutique and small ships (characterized by Berlitz as having 50–250 and 251–750 passengers, respectively) can get into ports that larger ships can't. They can also get closer to the center of large cities. For example, in St. Petersburg, Russia, large and mid-size ships (such as those of Crystal Cruises and Regent Seven Seas Cruises) dock about one hour from the city center, while boutique/small ships such as those of Hapag-Lloyd Cruises or Silversea Cruises can dock right next to the Hermitage Museum in the heart of the city.

One area where 'luxury' ships differ least from large resort ships is in shore excursions, particularly in the Caribbean and Alaska, where almost all cruise operators are obliged to use the same local tour operators, and local tour operators treat all cruise passengers the same – as if they are visiting for the first time.

Large resort ships (carrying 2,501–6,500 passengers) simply cannot provide the kind of personal service and attention to detail that the boutique/small ships can. However, the 'Yacht Club' of MSC Cruises and The Haven aboard Norwegian Cruise Line ships are examples of the good levels of personal service that can be provided aboard large resort ships. However, once you leave your 'private living space,' you mix with everyone else, particularly if you want to see a show, have a coffee in the café, disembark at ports of call (think: lines at gangway security checkpoints), or go on organized shore excursions. That's when you appreciate the fact that smaller is better.

These are ships suited to those not seeking the active, family-friendly, and entertainment-driven cruise experiences that large resort ships offer, and they provide facilities and service levels hard to find elsewhere. While they boast about being the best, or boast the awards they receive annually from various bodies (often invited or coerced responses), few provide a true luxury experience.

What are the differences?
Luxury varies by degrees. Although the differences are immediately noticeable when you sail aboard and compare them all, some of the variations in style, service, and – especially staff training – are more subtle. One thing is certain: the word 'no' will be virtually unheard.

Some ships have more public space per passenger. Some definitely have more highly trained service personnel rather than technical staff per passenger. Some have better food and service. Some have entertainment; some don't. Some have more fresh flowers in public areas than others – they're very evident aboard the ships of Hapag-Lloyd Cruises but not aboard Silversea Cruises' ships, for instance (where Prosecco – not Champagne – is provided on embarkation).

Crystal Cruises, for example, has an excellent program of cultural lecturers, professional bridge (the

Butlers at your service in *MSC Divina*'s Yacht Club.

card game, not the navigation bridge) instructors, together with its Yamaha 'Passport to Music' program on each cruise, whereas others (Regent, Seabourn, SeaDream, and Silversea) don't. Hapag-Lloyd has excellent lecturers, and a PGA golf professional aboard every cruise.

Also, the following facilities, services, and approaches are found and experienced aboard the ships of Hapag-Lloyd Cruises, Seabourn, and SeaDream Yacht Club, but not aboard the ships of Crystal Cruises, Regent Seven Seas Cruises, or Silversea Cruises:

Anticipation – more widely practiced by better-trained staff, who are also more adept at passenger recognition (remembering your name and preferences).

Waiters/waitresses escort guests to the dining table and to the dining room exit after meals.

Relaxed embarkation/disembarkation at your leisure.

Cabin stewardesses leave handwritten notes.

There are no announcements, and no background music plays in public rooms, accommodation hallways, or elevators.

The chef invites passengers to accompany him/her on visits to local food markets.

More space, better service

These ships have an excellent amount of open deck and lounging space, and a high passenger space ratio when compared to large resort ships (which are

typically under 35 gross tonnage per passenger), the two SeaDreams being the exception.

In warm-weather areas, the ships of Seabourn and SeaDream Yacht Club all of which have fold-down platforms at the stern, provide jet skis, kayaks, snorkeling gear, windsurfers, and the like, at no extra cost, typically for one day each cruise (the others do not).

Hapag-Lloyd's Europa (space ratio: 70.4) and Europa 2 (space ratio: 83.0) both have a fleet of rigid inflatable craft for in-depth exploration and shore adventures, plus an ice-hardened hull and crew members who understand the *culture* of their passengers. They also have mattresses that are 7ft (2.1m) long.

A good night's sleep

These ships feature premium-quality mattresses and bed linen (all of 100 percent cotton, with a thread count of 300 or more). There's always a little brand-consciousness going on, and some may be better than others.

Crystal Cruises, for example, features Bellora, from Milan (made in India using Egyptian cotton). Silversea Cruises features Egyptian cotton sheets, pillowcases, and duvet covers by Pratesi, founded in 1860, whose custom-made linens come from Tuscany, Italy – the company is known for supplying the Italian and other European aristocracy.

Good pillows are also important for a good night's sleep. You may be able to choose one of several different shapes and fillings. Crystal Cruises' pillow menu, for example, offers a choice of seven, including Side Sleeper Pillow (down or down alternative); Back Sleeper Pillow (down or down alternative); Stomach Sleeper Pillow (down or down alternative); and Body Pillow (down alternative).

---

15 THINGS TO EXPECT

1. Flawless (well, close to) personal service and attention to detail.
2. Genuine Champagne at embarkation (not sparkling wine).
3. Personalized stationery.
4. A crew that anticipates your needs, responds quickly to your requests, and doesn't say 'no' or 'impossible.'
5. No announcements (except for emergencies).
6. No background music in public rooms, hallways, and elevators.
7. High passenger space ratio (35 to 83 gross tons per passenger).
8. High crew to passenger ratio (1.5 to 1.0 or better).
9. The finest-quality bed linens, duvets, towels, and bathrobes.
10. A pillow menu.
11. High-quality toiletries (Aveda, Bulgari, for example).
12. No extra charge for on-demand movies or music.
13. More overnight port stays.
14. Separate gangway for passengers and crew (where possible).
15. Shoeshine service.

CRÈME DE LA CRÈME

These 23 ships (listed alphabetically, by company) belong to 10 cruise lines and are the cream of the cruise industry in terms of style, finesse, staff training, cuisine, service, and hospitality. The ships are fully reviewed in the ratings section of this book, with Berlitz scores awarded for accommodation, food, service, entertainment, and the overall cruise experience.

Crystal Cruises: *Crystal Serenity, Crystal Symphony*
Hapag-Lloyd Cruises: *Europa, Europa 2*
Regent Seven Seas Cruises: *Seven Seas Explorer, Seven Seas Mariner, Seven Seas Voyager*
Sea Cloud Cruises: *Sea Cloud, Sea Cloud II*
Seabourn: *Seabourn Encore, Seabourn Odyssey, Seabourn Ovation, Seabourn Sojourn*
SeaDream Yacht Club: *SeaDream I, SeaDream II*
Silversea Cruises: *Silver Muse, Silver Shadow, Silver Spirit, Silver Whisper, Silver Wind*
Windstar Cruises: *Star Breeze, Star Legend, Star Pride.*

Depending on the cruise line, other choices might include hypoallergenic, hop-filled, or lavender-scented pillows.

A good night's sleep – outside

For something quite different, SeaDream Yacht Club has indulgent 'Balinese Dream Beds' for sleeping under the stars (in a secluded area at the front of the ship on the uppermost open deck), a delightful idea for honeymooners or anyone celebrating a special occasion. Custom-made pajamas are supplied, and you can take them home with you.

Creative cuisine

Fine dining is the highlight of ships in this category and is more of an entertainment feature than these ships' entertainment shows – if there are any. Good company and conversation are crucial. You can expect to find plenty of tables for two, a calm and refined dining atmosphere, open or one-seating dining, by candlelight (when permitted), with high-quality china and silverware, large wine glasses, fresh flowers, a fine wine list, and sommeliers who can discuss fine wines. Service should be unhurried (not like the two-seating ships, where meals tend to be served as speed trials by waiters), well paced, and unobtrusive.

It's really about non-repetitive, highly creative menus, high-quality ingredients, moderate portions, and attractive presentation, with fresh local fish and other items provided (when available) and cooked to order (not in batches), and meat of the highest grade. Caviar, foie gras, black/white truffles and other exotic foods, and fresh vegetables (instead of frozen or canned vegetables) are among the products that feature. Caviar aboard Europa and Europa 2 is typically from farmed sturgeon, and is excellent, while caviar aboard most other ships in this category is from the American farmed hackleback variety of sturgeon, or paddlefish 'caviar' (calling it 'caviar' is really stretching it). The caviar (from Uruguay) aboard the Seabourn ships is decent, however.

Most of the ships provide silver covers for entrées (main courses), creating extra 'wow' effect. Passengers may also be invited to visit local markets with the chef aboard the ships of Hapag-Lloyd Cruises, Seabourn, and SeaDream Yacht Club.

Some luxury ships provide even more special touches. Europa and Europa 2, for example, make their own breakfast preserves and ice cream, as well as fresh-pressed or freshly squeezed juices (most others provide pasteurized juices from concentrate) on board. Europa uses only loose tea (over 30 types), while all the others use teabags of varying quality. All (except Hapag-Lloyd) provide 'free' bottled mineral water.

Lunch and dinner menus may be provided in your suite/cabin in advance, and special orders are often possible. Room-service menus are extensive, and meals can be served in your suite/cabin (either on the balcony or inside on portable or fixed tables). It is

Seven Seas Mariner, Penthouse suite bed.

also possible to have a private dinner setup on deck – wonderful in the right location.

Drinks: included or not?

Crystal Cruises, Regent Seven Seas Cruises, Seabourn, SeaDream Yacht Club, and Silversea Cruises provide wine with dinner (Crystal Cruises, Seabourn, and Silversea also include wine with lunch), although the wines are typically young, and not from first-class houses. Windstar Cruises includes soft drinks and bottled water only (alcoholic beverages cost extra). Real premium brands and classic vintage wines cost extra.

Hapag-Lloyd Cruises charges for all alcoholic beverages (beer and soft drinks are provided in each cabin/suite). Crystal Cruises and Regent Seven Seas Cruise Line provide an all-inclusive product, including gratuities. Crystal, Regent, Seabourn, SeaDream, and Silversea include all drinks, but only standard brands and limited included wines that may not be to your taste. Hapag-Lloyd Cruises doesn't include alcoholic drinks, because those favored by its discerning passengers tend to be far above the level of standard brands carried by the other companies mentioned here (as an example, Hapag-Lloyd Cruises carries about 40 types of premium gins aboard Europa and Europa 2). In addition, this gets around the problem of passengers who don't drink alcohol not liking to subsidize those that do.

Other differences

Crystal Serenity, Crystal Symphony, Europa, Europa 2, Seven Seas Mariner, and Seven Seas Voyager include entertainment featuring multi-cast shows and cabaret acts; Hapag-Lloyd, Seabourn and Silversea Cruises ships also do this, but to a lesser extent. The others do not have entertainment as such, but instead rely on their intimacy and friendliness, and promote after-dinner conversation, or, aboard the ships of Silversea Cruises, individual specialist cabaret acts.

Comparing luxury ships

Ship name	Company (in alphabetical order)	Size	Passenger space ratio	Crew to passenger ratio	Largest suite in sq. ft (sq. m)	Smallest cabin in sq. ft (sq. m)	Water sports toys	Hand-held showers	Personal bathroom products
Crystal Serenity	Crystal Cruises	Mid-size	62.6	1.7	1,345 (125)	226 (21)	No	Yes	Etro
Crystal Symphony	Crystal Cruises	Mid-size	53.1	1.7	982 (91.2)	201 (18.7)	No	Yes	Etro
Europa	Hapag-Lloyd Cruises	Small	70.4	1.5	915 (85)	355 (33)	No	Yes	Own brand
Europa 2	Hapag-Lloyd Cruises	Small	83.0	1.3	1,227 (114)	377 (35)	No	Yes	Own brand
Seven Seas Explorer	Regent Seven Seas Cruises	Small	74.6	1.3	3,875 (360)	301 (28)	No	Yes	Guerlain
Seven Seas Mariner	Regent Seven Seas Cruises	Mid-size	67.9	1.6	1,528 (142)	301 (28)	No	Yes	Canyon Ranch
Seven Seas Voyager	Regent Seven Seas Cruises	Mid-size	59.8	1.6	1,399 (130)	355 (33)	No	Yes	Canyon Ranch
Sea Cloud	Sea Cloud Cruises	Boutique	39.5	1.1	409 (38)	102 (9.5)	No	Yes	Own brand
Sea Cloud II	Sea Cloud Cruises	Boutique	40.9	1.6	323 (30)	215 (20)	No	Yes	Own brand
Seaborn Encore	Seabourn	Small	71.1	1.3	1,438 (133.6)	296 (27.5)	Yes	Yes	Therapies (Molton Brown)
Seabourn Odyssey	Seabourn	Small	71.1	1.3	1,438 (133.6)	296 (27.5)	Yes	Yes	Therapies (Molton Brown)
Seabourn Ovation	Seabourn	Small	71.1	1.3	1,438 (133.6)	296 (27.5)	Yes	Yes	Therapies (Molton Brown)
Seabourn Quest	Seabourn	Small	71.1	1.3	1,438 (133.6)	296 (27.5)	Yes	Yes	Therapies (Molton Brown)
Seabourn Sojourn	Seabourn	Small	71.1	1.3	1,438 (133.6)	296 (27.5)	Yes	Yes	Therapies (Molton Brown)
SeaDream I	SeaDream Yacht Club	Boutique	37.9	1.2	490 (45.5)	195 (18.1)	Yes	Yes	Bulgari
SeaDream II	SeaDream Yacht Club	Boutique	37.9	1.2	490 (45.5)	195 (18.1)	Yes	Yes	Bulgari
Silver Shadow	Silversea Cruises	Small	72.8	1.3	1,435 (133.3)	286 (26.6)	No	No	Bulgari and Ferragamo
Silver Spirit	Silversea Cruises	Small	66.6	1.4	1,615 (150)	312 (29)	No	No	Bulgari and Ferragamo
Silver Whisper	Silversea Cruises	Small	72.8	1.3	1,435 (133.3)	286 (26.6)	No	No	Bulgari and Ferragamo
Silver Wind	Silversea Cruises	Small	57.6	1.4	1,313 (122)	239 (22.2)	No	No	Bulgari and Ferragamo
Star Breeze	Windstar Cruises	Boutique	47.0	1.3	575 (53.4)	277 (25.7)	Yes	Yes	Therapies (Molton Brown)
Star Legend	Windstar Cruises	Boutique	46.9	1.3	576 (53.5)	277 (25.7)	Yes	Yes	Therapies (Molton Brown)
Star Pride	Windstar Cruises	Boutique	47.0	1.3	575 (53.4)	277 (25.7)	Yes	Yes	L'Occitane

The Major Cruise Lines

We compare what the major cruise companies (reviewed in alphabetical order) have to offer when it comes to facilities, service, and ambience.

The major cruise lines are global in scale. The cruise industry may appear diverse, but it is dominated by just three conglomerates, principally the Carnival Corporation, Norwegian Cruise Line Holdings, and Royal Caribbean Cruises Ltd. Just two Carnival Corporation subsidiaries, Holland America Line and Princess Cruises, virtually control large resort-ship cruising in Alaska, where they own hotels, lodges, tour companies, and much land-based transportation (other operators have to buy these services).

What they have in common

All offer one thing: a well-packaged cruise vacation, generally lasting seven days, typically with a mix of days at sea and days in port, plenty of food, reasonable service, large-scale production shows and trendy cabaret acts, plus large casinos, shopping malls, and extensive, busy spa and fitness facilities.

The ships have a lot in common, too. All have art auctions, bingo, horse racing, shopping talks, facilities and programs for children and teens, wedding vows/renewal programs, and Wi-Fi or Internet connect centers. All are dedicated to generating higher revenue returns.

Standing in line for embarkation, disembarkation (and shore tenders, shore excursions, and shuttle buses in ports of call), and for self-serve buffet meals is inevitable aboard large resort ships and the larger mid-size ships. But the ships differ in their characters, facilities, maintenance, space, crew-to-passenger ratio, food and service, and crew training. You'll be escorted to your cabin only if you book Yacht Club-grade accommodation aboard the ships of MSC Cruises. Aboard other lines, staff at the ship-side of the gangway, simply point you in the right direction.

What makes them different

Ships belonging to the major companies may look similar, but they differ not only in their layout, decor, and passenger flow but also in small details. Even towel sizes can vary widely.

Germany-based AIDA Cruises is one of the Carnival brands.

AIDA CRUISES

Ships

AIDAaura (2003), *AIDAbella* (2008), *AIDAblu* (2010), *AIDAcara* (1996), *AIDAdiva* (2007), *AIDAluna* (2009), *AIDAmar* (2012), *AIDAperla* (2017), *AIDAprima* (2016), *AIDAsol* (2011), *AIDAstella* (2013), *AIDAvita* (2002)

About the company

The former East German shipping company Deutsche Seereederei (DSR) and its marketing arm Seetours (Deutsche Seetouristik) were assigned the traditional cruise ship *Arkona* as part of the 1985 East–West integration, which included a contractual agreement with the Treuhandanstalt (the agency that privatized

WHICH CRUISE LINE DOES WHAT BEST

 AIDA Cruises is for youthful German-speaking families who like lively surroundings and bright colors in a club-like resort package. The ships have good entertainment and take care of kids and teens well. The dress code is ultra-casual, and food is more about quantity than quality – unless you pay extra for dining in a 'specialty' restaurant.

 Carnival Cruise Line is for all-round fun, activities, and casinos for the lively, no-sleep-needed youth market. Carnival doesn't sell itself as a 'luxury' or 'premium' cruise line, which it certainly isn't. It delivers exactly the well-packaged cruise vacation its brochures promise. Its ships have good entertainment facilities and features, and some include extra-cost dining spots for the more discerning passenger.

 Celebrity Cruises advertises itself as a 'premium' line offering 'modern luxury.' However, some aspects are definitely not premium – for example, recorded 'music' blaring over pool decks 24 hours a day is not relaxing. Celebrity Cruises is now more akin to Royal Caribbean International, but with a more upmarket wrapper.

 Costa Cruises are all about quasi-Italian style and lively ambience, with a mix of passengers of several nationalities. The swimming pools are full of noisy children in peak holiday periods. Costa provides first-time cruise passengers with a packaged holiday that is a mix of contemporary surroundings and basic fare, accompanied by loud everything. Most passengers are Italian.

Holland America Line has the right touches for seniors and retirees: smiling service staff, lots of flowers, traditions of the past, good cooking demonstrations, and specialty grill venues. The ships are best suited to older couples and solo travelers who like to mingle in a large ship, in an unhurried setting, with fine-quality surroundings. There's plenty of eclectic antique artwork, decent – though not gourmet – food, and service from a smiling crew (many of whom are Indonesian/Filipino), who don't quite have the finesse many expect from a so-called 'premium' product.

 MSC Cruises – a family-owned, Swiss-based company with an Italian heritage – tailors its onboard product mostly to European passengers of all ages (its name, after all, is Mediterranean Shipping Company). The firm displays fine European flair, with a high level of service and hospitality training from a friendly, multilingual crew. It has evolved quickly as the 'new kid on the block.' Of all the major cruise lines, it's also the cleanest. Bed linen and towels are changed every third day, and bathrobes in suites daily, unlike most other brands listed here.

 Norwegian Cruise Line is a really good choice for a first cruise for families with children, with a wide choice of eateries, great entertainment, and friendly service staff. Its ships are best suited to first-time, youthful solo passengers, couples, families with children, and teenagers who want upbeat, color-rich surroundings, plenty of entertainment lounges and bars, and high-tech sophistication – in one programmed, well-packaged vacation.

 Princess Cruises offers consistent product delivery and somewhat restrained decor. Choose Princess Cruises if you enjoy being with families and fellow passengers of mid-50s and upwards, who want a well-organized cruise experience with unpretentious middle-of-the-road cuisine, a good range of entertainment, and an excellent shore excursion program – arguably the best run of any of the major cruise lines. On the down side, several of its ships do now seem somewhat dated.

 Royal Caribbean International is really good for Caribbean itineraries, especially for first-time cruisers and families. The newest ships are stunning, and filled with high-tech gismos, plus entertainment including slightly scaled-down versions of well-known Broadway shows. The ships are for active, young-minded cruisers of all ages who enjoy mingling in a large ship setting with plenty of life. The food is more about quantity than quality – unless you pay extra for dining in a 'specialty' restaurant.

East German enterprises) to build a new ship. It did this in 1996 with the newly built *Aida*, designed to appeal to young, active German-speaking families. The concept was to create a seagoing version of the popular Robinson Clubs – a sort of German Club Med concept. When *Aida* first debuted, there were few passengers, and the company struggled.

In 1998 it was sold to Norwegian Cruise Line, which re-sold it to its original Rostock-based owners. P&O acquired it in 1999, and it is presently a successful multi-ship sub-brand of Carnival Corporation, under the direct control of its Costa Cruises division. AIDA Cruises is known for its self-serve buffet restaurants instead of traditional waiter service.

What is it really like?

The ships have become more sophisticated entertaining venues, and Club Teams (entertainment staff members) interact with passengers throughout the ship. AIDA Cruises has its own training schools in several countries, plus a recognized training academy in Rostock.

The decibel levels are high – it is impossible to escape the noise and loud music, and 'background' music is played in cabin hallways and elevators 24/7.

There are three pricing levels – AIDA Premium, AIDA Vario, and Just AIDA – depending on what you want to be included, plus differences in price according to accommodation size and grade, and itinerary. Opt for the basic, price-driven 'Just Aida' package and the cruise line chooses the ship, itinerary, and accommodation for you – sort of a pot-luck cruise, based on or close to the dates you choose.

CARNIVAL CRUISE LINE

Ships

Carnival Breeze (2012), *Carnival Conquest* (2002), *Carnival Dream* (2009), *Carnival Ecstasy* (1991), *Carnival Elation* (1998), *Carnival Fantasy* (1990), *Carnival Fascination* (1994), *Carnival Freedom* (2007), *Carnival Glory* (2003), *Carnival Horizon* (2018), *Carnival Imagination* (1995), *Carnival Inspiration* (1996), *Carnival Legend* (2002), *Carnival Liberty* (2005), *Carnival Magic* (2011), *Carnival Miracle* (2004), *Carnival Paradise* (1998), *Carnival Pride* (2002), *Carnival Sensation* (1993), *Carnival Spirit* (2001), *Carnival Splendor* (2008), *Carnival Sunshine* (1996), *Carnival Triumph* (1999), *Carnival Valor* (2004), *Carnival Victory* (2000), *Carnival Vista* (2016)

About the company

Israel-born Ted Arison (born Theodore Arisohn), whose ambition was to be a concert pianist, founded Carnival Cruise Line, the world's largest and most successful single cruise line, in 1972, with one ship, *Mardi Gras* (formerly *Empress of Canada*). Carnival wanted to be different, and developed its 'fun ship' concept. It worked, appealing to people of all ages and backgrounds.

The company's first new ship, *Tropicale*, debuted in 1982. In 1984 Carnival started advertising on television, introducing a wider public to the idea of cruising. It introduced the first cruise ship measuring over 100,000 gross tons – *Carnival Destiny* (now named *Carnival Sunshine*) – in 1996.

Today, the Carnival Corporation, parent company of Carnival Cruise Line, is run by Micky Arison, who owns the NBA's Miami Heat basketball team. Over 20 new ships have been introduced since the line was founded in 1972, many of which are now tired and outdated.

What is it really like?

Carnival's fleet of ships is among the oldest of the major cruise companies. The glitzy ships are well suited to multi-generational groups, and for family reunions.

The dress code is ultra-casual – indeed, the waiters are better dressed than most passengers. Carnival is all about 'happy' and 'fun' – cruise directors tell passengers to 'make some noise.' It's all about towels shaped like animals, scheduled participation activities, yelling and screaming, and having fun. But it's an impersonal cruise experience, and solo travelers can get lost in the crowds of couples. Perhaps this doesn't

Enjoying the splash park aboard a Carnival Cruise Line ship.

Carnival Liberty calls at Roatán in Honduras Bay.

matter too much, because this will be a first cruise for many passengers. Repeat customers, however, have a distinct sense of déjà vu, but carry a Gold or Platinum card for better recognition from 'service' staff.

The ships are clean – if you don't look too closely – but maintenance could be better. Open deck space may look adequate when you board, but on days at sea you can expect your plastic deck chair (if you can find one that's free) kissing its neighbor, and probably even tied

to it. There are no cushioned pads, so the sunloungers are uncomfortable to sit on for any length of time.

The decibel level is high: it is impossible to escape the noise and loud music, and 'background' music is played in cabin hallways and elevators 24/7. There are libraries, but with few books, and the bookshelves are locked by 6pm, because you are expected to be out in the (revenue-earning) public areas. If you enjoy casinos, joining Carnival's Ocean Players Club brings benefits, depending on your skill level.

Passenger niggles: Intrusive photographers are almost impossible to escape. There's no listing of the free in-cabin TV movies – only those that are pay-per-view. Non-stop recorded music is intrusive, and *Carnival Capers*, the ship's poorly produced daily program, is mostly devoted to persuading you to spend money.

What is Carnival's 'Ocean Medallion Class?'

It's not a class, but a small device the size of a US$0.25 cent piece (quarter) bristling with antennas that connect to shipboard sensors. The medallion makes it easy for you to pay for onboard purchases (it connects to your credit card details), open your cabin door, and do other things, but it's another thing to wear, whether you hang it around your neck or tuck it into your bathing suit. It contains digital information about you and your preferences. In other words, it's a way that the Carnival Group's cruise lines keep your information – if you change any of your preferences, you'll need to do it digitally – and keep track of you (and take away your privacy). The aim, though, is to delight and surprise you. Naturally, there are endless marketing possibilities for the cruise lines.

For children

Carnival is family-friendly and carries over 700,000 children a year. 'Camp Carnival,' the line's child/

THE BIG PLAYERS: WHO OWNS WHOM

Carnival Corporation

- AIDA Cruises
- Carnival Cruise Line
- Costa Cruises
- Cunard Line
- Holland America Line
- P&O Cruises
  - P&O Cruises (Australia)
- Princess Cruises
- Seabourn

Norwegian Cruise Line Holdings

- Norwegian Cruise Line
- Oceania Cruises
- Regent Seven Seas Cruises

Genting Hong Kong

- Crystal Cruises
- Dream Cruises
- Star Cruises

Royal Caribbean Cruises

- Azamara Club Cruises
- Celebrity Cruises
- Pullmantur Cruises
  - CDF Croisières de France
- Royal Caribbean International

youth program, is well organized. There are five age groups: Toddlers (ages two to five), Juniors (six to eight), Intermediate (nine to 11), Tweens (12–14, Circle C), and Late Teens (15–17, with Club 02). Even the under-twos can be catered to. Soft-drinks packages can be bought for children (adults, too). Note that a babysitting service is not generally available after 10pm.

In 2014 Carnival partnered with children's specialist Dr. Seuss and introduced 'Seuss at Sea,' with immersive family dining (think 'green eggs and ham' for breakfast, served by waiters in Dr. Seuss-inspired uniforms). Characters such as the Cat in the Hat, Thing One and Thing Two, and Sam are in attendance, and there are also special showings of movies such as *The Cat in the Hat* and *How the Grinch Stole Christmas*.

CELEBRITY CRUISES

Ships

Celebrity Constellation (2002), *Celebrity Eclipse (2010)*, *Celebrity Equinox* (2009), *Celebrity Infinity* (2001), *Celebrity Millennium* (2000), *Celebrity Reflection* (2012), *Celebrity Silhouette* (2011), *Celebrity Solstice* (2008), *Celebrity Summit* (2001), *Celebrity Xpedition* (2001)

About the company

Celebrity Cruises was the brainchild of Harry H. Haralambopoulos, and brothers John and Michael Chandris, London-based Greek cargo ship owners and operators of the former Chandris Lines and Chandris Cruises. In 1989, as the cruise industry was gaining momentum, they were determined to create a newer, better cruise line, with new ships, larger, more standard cabins, and greater focus on food and service in the European tradition.

Its image as a 'premium' line is justified because the product delivery on board is superior to (and the price is higher than) that of its parent company, Royal Caribbean International, which bought it in 1997 for $1.3 billion. The ships are recognizable by a large 'X' on the funnel, denoting the third letter from the end of the Greek alphabet, the Greek 'chi' or 'Ch' in English, for Chandris, the founding family.

In 2007 Celebrity Cruises created the sub-brand Azamara Cruises (now Azamara Club Cruises), with two small ships: *Azamara Journey* (2000) and *Azamara Quest* (2000).

What is it really like?

The ships are clean and well maintained. There are always lots of flowers and flower displays.

Celebrity Cruises delivers a well-defined North American cruise experience at a modest price. If the budget allows, book a suite-category cabin for the extra benefits it brings – it's worth it. Strong points include the many European staff, a higher standard of service, and a 'zero announcement policy.' Such touches differentiate Celebrity Cruises from its competitors. Celebrity Cruises also has some of the most eclectic sculptures and original artwork, from Picasso to Warhol, found at sea.

Celebrity Equinox leaves Istanbul.

The ships have more staff than other ships of comparable size and capacity, especially in the housekeeping and food and beverage departments. However, the company has seen fit to take away some items, such as personalized stationery, from some accommodation grades, it has substituted cloth napkins with paper ones, and has reduced the amount and quality of fresh flower displays (although there are still lots).

Sadly, intrusive music is played almost everywhere, and any lounge designated as 'music-free' is typically full of activities and participation events, so it's hard to find a quiet corner to sit and read.

For children

Junior passengers are divided into Shipmates (three to five years), Celebrity Cadets (six to eight years), Ensigns (nine to 11 years), Admiral T's (12–14 years), and Teens (13–17).

On days at sea the program is crammed with things to do, though the emphasis is on revenue-enhancing activities such as art auctions, bingo, and horse racing.

COSTA CRUISES

Ships

Costa Atlantica (2000), Costa Deliziosa (2010), Costa Diadema (2014), Costa Fascinosa (2012), Costa Favolosa (2010), Costa Fortuna (2003), Costa Luminosa (2009), Costa Magica (2004), Costa Mediterranea (2003), Costa neoClassica (1992), Costa neoRiviera (1999), Costa neoRomantica (1993), Costa Pacifica (2009), Costa Serena (2007), Costa Victoria (1996)

About the company

Costa Cruises traces its history back to 1860, when Giacomo Costa started an olive oil business. The first ship, in 1924, transported that oil. After he died in 1924, his sons, Federico, Eugenio, and Enrico, inherited the business. First they bought Ravenna, a cargo ship, to cut transport costs for their olive oil empire. In 1948, Costa's first passenger ship, the Anna 'C', carried passengers in style from Genoa to South America. In 1997, Costa Cruises was bought by the US's Carnival Corporation and UK's Airtours plc. Three years later Carnival took full control.

Costa specializes in cruises for Europeans or passengers with European tastes – particularly Italians – during the summer. It has initiated an aggressive newbuild policy in recent years, in order to modernize the company's aging fleet of different-size ships. The ships operate in three main markets: the Mediterranean, the Caribbean, and South America.

Most ships are well maintained, although there are inconsistencies throughout the fleet. The same is true of cleanliness – some ships are very clean, while others are a little dusty around the edges, as are its shore tenders. The company's safety procedures

Making an entrance down the Grand Foyer aboard a *Celebrity Millennium*-class ship.

CELEBRITY'S CLASSY APPROACH

There really are four 'classes' aboard Celebrity ships: accommodation designated as suites; those in standard (exterior-view) and interior (no-view) cabins; a third that comes between the two, known as Concierge Class; and Aqua (Spa) Class.

Concierge Class brings enhanced facilities including priority embarkation and disembarkation, priority tender tickets, specialty dining, spa reservations, double-bed overlay (no more falling 'between the cracks' for couples). It also offers a choice of four pillows (goose down, isotonic, body, and conformance), throw pillows on sofas, fruit baskets, binocularss golf umbrellas leather telephone notepads, and larger beach towels. Balconies feature better-quality furniture. In the bathrooms expect Frette bathrobes, larger towels, and a flower in a vase.

Aqua Class accommodation occupants get priority access to spa treatments, and special 'uprated' spa amenities.

came under scrutiny when *Costa Concordia* struck rocks and capsized off the Italian island of Giglio in January 2012.

In 2013 the company started a sub-brand called Costa neoCollection, and the ships in this brand (*Costa neoClassica, Costa neoRiviera*, and *Costa neo-Romantica*) now operate only in Asia.

What is it really like?

Costa is noted for its lively 'Italian' ambience. There are few Italian crew members, however, although many officers are Italian. The dress code is casual, even on formal nights. This is a cruise company for those who like to party. If you want quiet, take earplugs – good ones. On European and Mediterranean cruises, most passengers speak Italian, Spanish, French, and German. On Caribbean itineraries, a high percentage of passengers speak Spanish, as the ships carry passengers from Latin American countries in addition to passengers from North America.

Costa ships are best suited to young couples, singles, and families with children who enjoy big-city life, a multicultural social mix, outdoor cafés, constant activity, eating late, and loud entertainment, and are happy with food more notable for quantity than quality. All printed materials (room service folio, menus, etc.) are in six languages: Italian, English, French, German, Portuguese, and Spanish. Announcements are made in at least four languages.

Expect to cruise with a lot of children of all ages if you book for peak holiday period cruises; note that in Europe at certain times (such as Easter) schoolchildren have long vacations. On some European itineraries, passengers embark and disembark in almost every port along the way, which makes for a disjointed cruise experience, with almost no start or end to the cruise. There is little information for passengers who want to be independent in ports of call and not take the ship's organized excursions.

There is extensive smoking on board. No-smoking zones and signs are often ignored to the frustration of non-smoking passengers, and ashtrays are moved at whim; many of the officers and crew also smoke, even when moving through public rooms, so they don't bother to enforce the no-smoking zones.

Cabins tend to be small, but the decor is fresh, and the bathrooms are very practical. Some ships have cabin bathrooms with sliding doors – an excellent alternative to inward-openers that use up space.

Costa neoClassica, Costa neoRiviera, Costa neoRomantica, and *Costa Victoria* have a very European feel. They are lively without being too much, or pastel-toned without being boring, while all the other newer ships have an in-your-face brashness similar to Carnival's ships, with grainy and unflattering digital artwork on walls and panels, and even inside elevators.

For children

Junior passengers are in three groups: Kids Club (ages three to six); Junior Club (seven to 12); and Teen Club (13–17). Programs vary by ship, itinerary, and season. Group babysitting is available 6:30–11pm. During port days, babysitting is available generally 8.30am–12.30pm and 2.30–6.30pm.

Best foot forward beside a Costa funnel.

HOLLAND AMERICA LINE

Ships
Amsterdam (2000), *Eurodam* (2008), *Koningsdam* (2016), *Maasdam* (1993), *Nieuw Amsterdam* (2010), *Nieuw Statendam* (2018), *Noordam* (2006), *Oosterdam* (2003), *Prinsendam* (1988), *Rotterdam* (1997), *Veendam* (1996), *Volendam* (1999), *Westerdam* (2004), *Zaandam* (2000), *Zuiderdam* (2002)

About the company
Holland America Line (HAL) was founded in 1873 as the Netherlands-America Steamship Company, shipping immigrants to the New World from Rotterdam. It moved its headquarters to New York in 1971. It bought into Alaskan hotels and transportation when it acquired Westours in 1983, and is one of the state's biggest employers. In 1989, it was acquired by Carnival Cruise Line, but retained its Seattle-based headquarters.

HAL carries both traditional cruise passengers (senior citizens, alumni groups) and multi-generational families. It tries hard to keep its Dutch connections, with antique artifacts and traditional decor, as

A two-deck dining room is typical aboard Holland America Line ships.

well as Indonesian stewards. It rents a private island, Half Moon Cay, in the Bahamas.

What is it really like?
The brand encompasses basically two types of ship. Younger families with children and grandchildren are best suited to ships such as *Eurodam, Nieuw Amsterdam, Nieuw Statendam, Noordam, Oosterdam, Westerdam*, and *Zuiderdam*, whereas those of senior years – HAL's traditional audience of repeat passengers from alumni groups – are best suited to ships that are smaller and less glitzy (*Amsterdam, Maasdam, Prinsendam, Rotterdam, Veendam*, and *Zaandam*). All ships have teakwood outdoor promenade decks (most rivals have artificial grass or some other form of indoor-outdoor covering). Lifestyle lounge-like Explorations Cafés have been built into its ships.

Holland America Line has its own training school in Jakarta, Indonesia, and pre-trains crew members who have never been to sea before. Many crew members have been promoted to supervisory positions due to new ship introductions, but few have the formal training, professional, or management skills required.

HAL operates many theme-related cruises, and has an extensive program of life-enrichment lecturers, and its 'Culinary Arts' program includes celebrity guest chefs and interactive cooking demos.

HAL has many more smokers than you might expect, depending on ship and itinerary.

Regular coffee is half-decent, but weak. Extra-cost espresso/cappuccino coffees (Dutch) are better, served in proper china, but not quite up to the standard of Celebrity or Costa.

For children
Club HAL: Junior passengers are divided into three age groups: three to eight, nine to 12, and teens. Programming is based on the number of children booked on any given sailing, with children's counselors provided as needed (at least one per 30 children).

MSC CRUISES

Ships
MSC Armonia (2001), *MSC Divina* (2012), *MSC Fantasia* (2008), *MSC Lirica* (2003), *MSC Magnifica* (2010), *MSC Meraviglia* (2017), *MSC Musica* (2006), *MSC Opera* (2004), *MSC Orchestra* (2007), *MSC Poesia* (2008), *MSC Preziosa* (2013), *MSC Seaside* (2017), *MSC Sinfonia* (2005), *MSC Splendida* (2009)

About the company
The HQ of the world's largest privately owned cruise line is in Geneva, Switzerland. It's also home to parent company Mediterranean Shipping Company, the world's second-biggest container shipping company. It started in the cruise business by acquiring Italian company Star Lauro in 1995, with two older ships, *Monterey*

MSC Fantasia's Topsail Lounge.

and *Rhapsody*. It then purchased *Melody*, followed by almost new ships from bankrupt Festival Cruises.

MSC Cruises has grown incredibly fast and is, unusually, owned by a shipping-based family, not a faceless corporation. In 2014, the company 'chopped and stretched' four ships to update them and accommodate more passengers (*MSC Armonia*, *MSC Lirica*, *MSC Opera*, and *MSC Sinfonia*). Then, 2017 saw the addition of two new ships, *MSC Meraviglia* and *MSC Seaside* – really stunning vessels with an array of facilities and family-friendly attractions. With the new ships came a brand rollout that prepared the company for future growth and innovation, and for partnerships with leading brands such as Chicco, Cirque du Soleil, Eataly, Lego, TechnoGym, and Samsung.

What is it really like?

MSC Cruises' ships are suited to adult couples and solo travelers, and families with children. They are good for those who enjoy big-city life, a multinational and multicultural atmosphere, outdoor cafés, and constant activity accompanied by plenty of live music and late nights.

MSC Cruises has four distinct price categories, each including different things, so it's important to choose the right package for your needs and cruise experiences. They are Bella (for a basic, price-driven experience), Fantastica (for greater comfort and flexibility), Wellness (aimed at health and fitness), and Aurea (for more inclusions).

The largest ships (*MSC Divina*, *MSC Fantasia*, *MSC Meraviglia*, *MSC Preziosa*, *MSC Seaside*, and *MSC Splendida*) have an exclusive lounge for Yacht Club-grade passengers, and *MSC Divina*, *MSC Meraviglia*, *MSC Preziosa* and *MSC Seaside* each have a separate dining room for Yacht Club occupants, with open-seating dining, a private sun deck oasis pool, bar, café and sunbathing areas, private access to the well-run Aurea Spa, priority embarkation, and butler service.

Why is the company so successful? It's the software (crew) and attention to the small things.

The ships typically operate in five languages, with embarkation-day announcements in English, French, German, Italian, and Spanish. During the cruise, there are, however, few announcements. Given this multilingual emphasis, production shows and other major entertainment displays are more visual than verbal. For the same reason, the ships don't generally carry lecturers.

Cigar lovers will find a selection of Cuban (including Cohiba, Montecristo, Romeo e Julieta, Partagás), Dominican (Davidoff), and Italian (Toscano) smokes in the cigar lounges.

The decor is decidedly European/Mediterranean, with much understated elegance and really high-quality soft furnishings and other materials such as Italian marble, and Swarovski glass stairways.

For children

Children are divided into three age groups, with facilities to match: Mini Club (ages three to nine); Junior Club (10–13); and Teenagers Club (over 14, a prepaid Teen Card is available). While the facilities and play areas aren't as extensive as those aboard some other major lines, a 'baby parking' service is useful when parents want to go ashore on excursions. MSC Cruises' mascot is Do-Re-Mi – the von Trapp family of *The Sound of Music* fame would no doubt be delighted.

The Ocean Place complex aboard *Norwegian Getaway*.

NORWEGIAN CRUISE LINE

Ships

Norwegian Bliss (2018), *Norwegian Breakaway* (2013), *Norwegian Dawn* (2002), *Norwegian Epic* (2010), *Norwegian Escape* (2015), *Norwegian Gem* (2007), *Norwegian Getaway* (2014), *Norwegian Jade* (2006), *Norwegian Jewel* (2005), *Norwegian Joy* (2017), *Norwegian Pearl* (2006), *Norwegian Spirit* (1998), *Norwegian Star* (2002), *Norwegian Sun* (2001), *Norwegian Sky* (1999), *Pride of America* (2005)

About the company

Norwegian Cruise Line, the originator of contemporary cruising, was founded in 1966 by three Norwegian shipping companies as Klosters Sunward Ferries and was renamed Norwegian Caribbean Line in 1967. It was bought by Star Cruises in 2000, and has been replacing its older, smaller ships with brand new, larger vessels. NCL also operates one ship with a mostly American crew and a base in Hawaii.

Freestyle Cruising is how NCL describes its operation – although it's hard to detect style in the onboard product (I call it American Bistro-style). Its fleet is diverse, so the cruise experience can vary, although this makes for interesting character variation between the various ship categories. There is more standardization aboard the larger, newer ships. The senior officers are the only thing that's Norwegian.

Most standard cabins are extremely small, though they are laid out in a practical manner.

What is it really like?

If this is your first cruise, you should enjoy a good overall vacation in a lively, upbeat setting. The lifestyle is contemporary, fresh, creative, and sporty, with a casualness typical of youthful city dwellers, and with its 'eat when you want' philosophy, the shipboard ambience is ultra-casual. The dress code is, too – indeed, the waiters are probably better dressed than many passengers. The staff members are generally congenial, and you'll find a high percentage of women in cabin and restaurant service departments – more than most major cruise lines.

HOW TO GET HITCHED AT SEA

Princess Cruises has the most extensive wedding program of any of the major lines, with its 'Tie the Knot' wedding packages. The captain can legally marry American couples at sea aboard its Bermuda-registered ships. This is by special dispensation and should be verified when in the planning stage, since it may vary according to where you reside.

The basic wedding at sea package includes a personal wedding coordinator. Live music, a candlelit celebration officiated by the captain, Champagne, fresh floral arrangements, a bridal bouquet, boutonnière, a photographer, and a wedding cake can all be laid on, depending on the cruise line and package, with the wedding do in an exclusive wedding chapel (or other location).

You'll also get keepsake Champagne flutes, and a keepsake wedding certificate. Tuxedo rental is available. Harborside or shoreside packages vary according to the port. For the latest rates, see Princess Cruises' website or your travel agent.

There's plenty of lively music, constant activity, entertainment, and food that's mainstream and acceptable, but nothing more, unless you pay extra to eat in the specialty dining spots. All this is delivered by a smiling, very friendly service staff, who can lack polish, but are obliging. In the latest wheeze to extract revenue, NCL is offering extra-cost 'Backstage Tours.'

For children

Splash Academy and Entourage programs divide children into several age groups: Guppies (ages 6 months to three years); Junior sailors (three to five); First Mates (six to eight); Navigators (nine to 12); and two Teens groups (13–14 and 15–17). The kids and teens clubs were developed in conjunction with UK-based King's Foundation and Camps, a charity that provides quality sports and activity programs. Group babysitting services are also available, at an extra charge. Special price packages are available for soft drinks.

PRINCESS CRUISES

Ships

Caribbean Princess (2004), *Coral Princess* (2002), *Crown Princess* (2006), *Diamond Princess* (2004), *Emerald Princess* (2007), *Golden Princess* (2001), *Grand Princess* (1998), *Island Princess* (2003), *Majestic Princess* (2017), *Pacific Princess* (1999), Regal *Princess* (2014), *Royal Princess* (2013), *Ruby Princess* (2008), *Sapphire Princess* (2005), *Sea Princess* (1998), *Star Princess* (2002), *Sun Princess* (1995)

About the company

Princess Cruises was founded by Stanley McDonald in 1965 with one ship, the former passenger ferry *Princess Patricia,* for cruises along the Mexican Riviera. In 1974, the company was bought by the UK's Peninsular and Oriental Steam Navigation Company (P&O), and in 1988 P&O/Princess Cruises merged with the Italian line Sitmar Cruises. In 2000, Carnival Corporation and Royal Caribbean Cruises fought a protracted battle to buy Princess Cruises. Carnival won.

The company provides comfortable mainstream cruising aboard a fleet of mainly large resort ships (plus one small ship), and its routes cover the world. The ships have a higher-than-average Passenger Space Ratio than competitors Carnival or RCI, and the service is friendly without being showy. In 2010 the company converted to fully digital travel documents (no more ticket document wallets).

What is it really like?

The ships are clean and well maintained, and the open promenade decks of some ships have teak deck lounge chairs, while others are plastic. Only *Coral Princess* and *Island Princess* have full walk-around open promenade decks; aboard the other ships you can't walk completely around the ship without negotiating steps. There is a nice balance of officers, staff, and crew members. Note that there is no Deck 13, which is good news for superstitious passengers.

There are proper cinemas aboard most ships, as well as outdoor poolside mega-screens for showing evening 'movies under the skies.'

Playing air hockey in a Princess Cruises teen centre.

Lines form at peak times at the information office, and for open-seating breakfast and lunch in the main dining rooms. Passengers receive turndown service and a pillow chocolate each night, bathrobes (on request), and toiletry kits (larger ones for suite/mini-suite occupants). All cabins have a hairdryer, which is sensibly located at a vanity desk unit in the lounge area. In 2012, smoking was prohibited in cabins and on cabin balconies.

All Grand-class ships have an adults-only area called 'The Sanctuary,' an extra-cost retreat forward of the mast. It has thickly padded sunloungers both in the sun and in the shade, a swim-against-the-current pool, and two outdoor cabanas for massages. I recommend The Sanctuary as a retreat from the bustle of the rest of the ship. It's worth the extra cost.

Princess's food and entertainment is geared to the North American market, but British and other European nationalities should feel at ease, safe in the knowledge that this is highly organized, packaged cruising, food, and service. There is, however, an increasing emphasis on onboard revenue, so expect to be subjected to daily advertising of art auctions and 'designer' watches.

Princess Cruises' ships are best suited to couples, families with young children and teenagers, and older solo travelers who like to mingle in a large ship setting with sophisticated surroundings and decent entertainment.

Shipboard hospitals have live SeaMed tele-medicine link-ups with specialists at the Cedars-Sinai Medical Center in Los Angeles for emergency help – useful mainly for passengers who reside in the US.

Some balconies can be overlooked from above, as aboard *Ruby Princess*.

Princess Cays is the company's own 'private island' in the Caribbean. It's all yours (along with a couple of thousand other passengers) for a day. However, it's a tender ride away from the ship and getting to it takes time.

If Carnival's ships have the brightest decor imaginable, the decor aboard Princess Cruises' ships is the opposite – bland in places, with much use of neutral tones, calm colors, and pastels.

For children

Children are divided into three age groups: The Treehouse (ages three to seven); The Lodge (eight to 12); and The Beach House (13–17). Princess Cruises has good children's counselors and supervised activities.

ROYAL CARIBBEAN INTERNATIONAL

Ships

Adventure of the Seas (2001), *Allure of the Seas* (2010), *Anthem of the Seas* (2015), *Brilliance of the Seas* (2002), *Empress of the Seas* (1990), *Enchantment of the Seas* (1997), *Explorer of the Seas* (2000), *Freedom of the Seas* (2006), *Grandeur of the Seas* (1996), *Harmony of the Seas* (2016), *Independence of the Seas* (2008), *Jewel of the Seas* (2004), *Liberty of the Seas* (2007), *Mariner of the Seas* (2004), *Navigator of the Seas* (2003), *Oasis of the Seas* (2009), *Ovation of the Seas* (2016), *Quantum of the Seas* (2014), *Radiance of the Seas* (2001), *Rhapsody of the Seas* (1997), *Serenade of the Seas* (2003), *Symphony of the Seas* (2018), *Vision of the Seas* (1998)

About the company

Royal Caribbean Cruise Line (RCI) was founded by three Norwegian shipping company dynasties in 1969: Arne Wilhelmsen, I.M. Skaugen, and Gotaas-Larsen (who was more of a sleeping partner). Its first ship, *Song of Norway*, debuted in 1970, followed by *Nordic Prince* and *Sun Viking*. Royal Caribbean was different from Carnival and NCL in that it launched its cruise operations with brand new ships, whereas the others had only old, pre-owned tonnage. In 1978 the cruise industry's first 'chop-and-stretch' operation enlarged *Song of Norway*, and 1988 saw the debut of the first 'large' cruise ship, *Sovereign of the Seas*.

In 1997, Royal Caribbean International bought Celebrity Cruises for $1.3 billion. In 2007 the company created sister company, Azamara Club Cruises, with two ships (in essence operated by Celebrity Cruises).

What is it really like?

RCI, which has carried over 50 million passengers since its founding in 1970, provides a well-integrated, fine-tuned, and comfortable cruise experience, but there's nothing royal about it except the name. The product is consistent but homogeneous. This is cruising for mainstream America. The ships are innovative, and all have some have really comfortable public rooms, lounges, bars, and fun gimmicks. For example,

Oasis of the Seas' Central Park.

the Bionic Bar aboard *Anthem of the Seas, Harmony of the Seas, Ovation of the Seas,* and *Quantum of the Seas,* where two robots make, mix, and serve drinks.

RCI's largest ships are termed *Oasis*-class, *Freedom*-class, *Quantum*-class, and *Voyager*-class. They differ from other ships in the fleet, mainly in the internal layout, by having a large mall-like high street – a focal point for most passengers. Many public rooms, lounges, and bars are located as adjuncts to the mall. Indeed, they are rather like malls with ships built around them. Also, in placing so much emphasis on 'active' outdoors areas, space has been taken away from the pool areas, leaving little room left just to sit and relax or sunbathe.

The ships in the next group (*Brilliance of the Seas, Jewel of the Seas, Radiance of the Seas,* and *Serenade of the Seas*) have lots of balcony cabins, and glass. *Enchantment of the Seas, Grandeur of the Seas, Rhapsody of the Seas,* and *Vision of the Seas* also have lots of glass in the public areas, but fewer balcony cabins. *Freedom of the Seas* pioneered a concierge lounge available for suite-grade occupants only.

All ships have a rock-climbing wall with several climbing tracks. You'll need to plan what you want to take part in wisely, as almost everything requires you to sign up in advance.

Almost everywhere has intrusive background music, played even in the elevators and passenger hallways. Bars also have very loud music. There are many, many unwelcome and unnecessary announcements for activities that bring revenue, such as art auctions and bingo.

Standing in line for embarkation, the reception desk, disembarkation, for port visits, shore tenders, and for the self-serve buffet stations is an inevitable aspect of cruising aboard most large resort ships. It's often hard to escape the ship's photographers – they're everywhere. Budget extra for all the additional-cost items, and expect to be subjected to a stream of flyers advertising promotions, while frosted drinks in 'souvenir' glasses are pushed to the hilt.

Service personnel are friendly. The elevators talk to you, though 'going up/going down' is informative but monotonous. The signage and illuminated picture displays of decks are all good, particularly aboard the Oasis-class ships. However, there are no cushioned pads for the deck lounge chairs.

Some 'Suite-Class' occupants come with 'Royal Genie' service, a sort of personal butler/concierge who can arrange everything for you.

Interior decor has strong Scandinavian design influences, with some eclectic sculpture and artwork. 'Wayfarer' signage and deck plans are excellent. In 2017, the company reduced the number of cabin categories, and standardized them across all its ships. Well done!

For children

RCI's youth programs include 'My Family Time' dining and extra-cost packages such as a supervised 'Lunch and Play' option. An extra-cost in-cabin babysitting service is available.

Adventure Ocean is RCI's 'edutainment' area, while aboard *Oasis*- and *Freedom*-class ships, there's also The H2O Zone. Children and teens are divided into seven age-appropriate groups: Royal Babies (six to 18 months); Royal Tots (18–36 months); Aquanauts (three to five years); Explorers (six to eight years); Voyagers (nine to 12 years); Navigators (12–14 years); and Teens (15–17 years).

An unlimited soda and juice package for the under-17s is available. There are lots of activities, and children's counselors are found aboard each ship.

The Smaller Cruise Lines

While the major cruise lines dominate the mass market, dozens of smaller companies cater for more specialist tastes and small port experiences.

The international cruise industry comprises around 75 companies. Most major cruise lines are owned and operated by large corporations, with the exception of MSC Cruises, a family firm. Some companies don't actually own their own ships, but charter them from ship-owning and ship-management companies for year-round or seasonal operation (Thomson Cruises, for example).

The following companies are listed in alphabetical order.

Alaskan Dream Cruises

Allen Marine Tours is an operator of local day vessels in Alaska, operating only in Alaska and family-owned by members of the Kaagwaantaan Clans of the Tlingit people. It formed a new micro-cruise company, Alaskan Dream Cruises, in 2010, after buying two Cruise West 78-passenger vessels when Cruise West declared insolvency and ceased operations. *Spirit of Columbia* and *Spirit of Alaska* became *Admiralty Dream* and *Baranhof Dream* in 2011. Another ship, *Chichagof Dream*, (ex-*Nantucket Clipper*), was added in 2016. Gratuities are not included in the cruise fare.

Aurora Expeditions takes passengers to Antarctica.

American Cruise Lines

ACL was originally formed in 1974, at the beginning of American coastal passenger shipping, but it went bankrupt in 1989, the ships were sold off, and the company lay dormant. The original owner, Charles Robertson, a renowned yachtsman who used to race 39-ft (12-m) America's Cup yachts, resurrected it in 2000, and built its own ships in its own small shipyard in Salisbury, Maryland, on the Chesapeake Bay.

ACL's ships (*American Constellation, American Glory, American Spirit, American Star, Independence*) ply the inter-coastal waterways and rivers of the North American East Coast, and provide an up-close, intimate experience for passengers who don't need luxury or much in the way of pampering but do like American history and culture, and service from an all-American college-age staff. The 'D-class' vessels are less than 2,500 gross tonnage, and are subject neither to bureaucratic regulations nor to union rules.

In 2011, the company also started operating paddle-wheelers (replica steamboats) on the Mississippi River, as well as on the Columbia and Snake rivers in the US Pacific Northwest. Gratuities and port charges are extra. The company's sister brand is Pearl Seas Cruises.

Azamara Journey cruising the Norwegian fjords.

Antarpply Expeditions

Based in Ushuaia, Argentina, this company specializes in (comparatively) inexpensive Antarctic expedition cruises including the Falkland Isles, Shetland Isles, and South Georgia, during the austral summer. It has one 'soft' expedition ship, *Ushuaia*, but the quality of its voyages and operation is not as high as that of the better-run, more experienced European companies. Gratuities are not included in the fare.

Aurora Expeditions

This Australian company was founded in 1993 by Australian Mount Everest veteran and geologist Greg Mortimer and adventure travel specialist Margaret Werner. The company, which specializes in small-group expeditions, uses the chartered expedition ship *Polar Pioneer* for its Antarctic expeditions. Other destinations include Papua New Guinea, Australia's Kimberley region, and the Russian Far East, for which it now charters the Russian expedition vessel *Akademik Shokalskiy*. Gratuities are not included in the fare.

Australis

This company, based in Santiago, Chile, operates ships on 'soft' expedition cruises to the Chilean fjords, Patagonia, and Tierra del Fuego – some of the world's most fascinating but hostile environments. It caters increasingly to an international clientele, with Spanish as the official onboard language (English is also spoken). Don't expect high standards aboard its ships, but the service is very friendly, and the organization and operations are extremely good.

The company introduced a brand new ship in 2010, the 210-passenger *Stella Australis*. Its cruises are 'all-inclusive,' with an open bar for beverages, including wine and gratuities. In 2013 the company shortened its name, from Cruceros Australis to Australis.

Azamara Club Cruises

Founded in 2007 this company, formerly Azamara Cruises, is an offshoot of Celebrity Cruises..Having started with little direction, the company was revitalized in 2009–10 by new president Larry Pimentel. It operates two 700-passenger ships, taking people to smaller and less visited ports that the large resort ships can't get into.

Azamara specializes in providing high-quality dining, and the ships offer a floating 'country club' experience. This line is in direct competition with the ships of Oceania Cruises – except that Oceania doesn't charge extra to dine in its specialty restaurants. However, Azamara has longer port stays and more overnight port stays.

The onboard experience is similar to that aboard the ships of parent company Celebrity Cruises (including tacky art auctions), but modified to suit those wanting a more sophisticated cruise experience aboard smaller ships. Its strengths are the food and European-style service; each ship has two extra-charge restaurants in addition to the main dining venues. Included in the fare are gratuities to dining and housekeeping staff, wine with lunch and dinner, coffee and tea 24 hours a day, and shuttle buses in ports of call, where needed. Complimentary standard spirits, wines, and international beers during bar opening hours were introduced in March 2013. One area where Azamara Club Cruises tries to differentiate itself from its competitors is by providing long-stay port days – including several overnight stays – as well as 'AzAmazing Evenings' cultural excursions within its immersive destinations programs. Both the company's ships underwent major refurbishment early in 2016, and now look refreshed, with brighter decor.

Blount Small Ship Adventures

This company was founded in 1966 by the late Luther H. Blount, an engineer and inventor of the American steam trawler, who built his cruise vessels in his own shipyard in Warren, Rhode Island. The firm was established as a family-run venture, and today, as the oldest US-flag cruise line still operating, it is run by Luther's daughter, Nancy Blount.

Cruises are operated like private family outings, using two unpretentious ships that have been specially constructed to operate in close-in coastal areas and inland waterways of the eastern US seaboard, with forays to the Bahamas and Caribbean during the winter. The onboard experience is strictly no-frills cruising in really basic, down-to-earth surroundings that have a 1950s feel.

Its early-to-bed passengers – average age 72 years – are typical of those who don't like glitz or all things trendy. Gratuities are not included in the cruise fare. Blount Small Ship Adventures introduced select beers and house wines with lunch and dinner on cruises in 2013.

Celestyal Cruises

Established in 2014, Celestyal Cruises is a sub-brand of Louis Cruises. It has three all-white ships: the 966-passenger Celestyal Crystal, the 800-passenger Celestyal Nefeli, and the 1,450-passenger Celestyal Olympia. All three ships are dedicated to cruising in the Greek isles, Croatia, and Turkey – destinations with which the company's Cyprus-based parent company (Louis Cruises) has many years of experience, particularly with group travel.

Club Med Cruises

Club Med became renowned for providing hassle-free vacations for the whole family. The first Club Med village was started in 1950 on the Spanish island of Mallorca, but the concept became so popular that it grew to more than 100 vacation villages throughout the world.

Club Med Cruises, an offshoot of the French all-inclusive vacation clubs, introduced its first ocean-going cruise vessel in 1990, the computer-controlled sail-cruise ship *Club Med II* (extensively refurbished in 2008). Aboard the all-inclusive ship, the so-called *gentils organisateurs* serve as both super-cruise staff and 'rah-rah' cheerleaders, carrying out entertainment and activity programs, for the mainly French-speaking passengers. *Club Med II* has a sister ship, Windstar Cruises' *Wind Surf*, which also provides a relaxed onboard experience. Gratuities are included in the fare.

CMV (Cruise and Maritime Voyages)

This UK-based company (with 50 percent owned by Greece's Maritime Group) existed for many years as a sales and marketing organization representing several small cruise lines. It now charters and operates three ships owned by other companies. The firm, some of whose owners originally worked for long-defunct CTC Cruises, specializes in adults-only (16 and over) cruises from regional UK ports, and provides traditional cruise features such as mid-morning bouillon, and captain's welcome and farewell dinners. The onboard product, particularly the food, is at

Crystal Serenity docked in Malta.

Queen Elizabeth and *Queen Mary 2* rendezvous in Sydney.

the lower end of the market. *Magellan* and *Marco Polo* are ships operated for ex-UK cruises. Gratuities are not included in the cruise fare.

Crystal Cruises

Crystal Cruises was founded in 1988 by Nippon Yusen Kaisha (NYK), the world's largest cargo ship and transportation company, with a fleet of more than 700 ships. The American-managed company is based in Century City, Los Angeles. *Crystal Harmony*, the company's first ship, was built in Japan, and debuted in New York in May 1990 to great acclaim. Meanwhile, Crystal Cruises introduced two new ships, *Crystal Symphony* in 1995, and *Crystal Serenity* in 2000, the first built in Finland, the second in France. In 2006 *Crystal Harmony* was transferred to parent company NYK as *Asuka II* for its Asuka Cruise division, for Japanese speakers.

The ships operate worldwide itineraries with flair. Both ships are superbly maintained, and passengers who seek fine food and excellent service in a sophisticated setting should be delighted with their choice of ship and company. There is even an excellent Nobu sushi/sashimi bar aboard *Crystal Serenity*.

Open-seating dining was introduced in January 2011 for the first time, but passengers can still opt for fixed-time dining. In spring 2012 Crystal Cruises adopted all-inclusive pricing, with drinks, wines, and gratuities included in the fare. In 2015 the company was acquired by Genting Hong Kong (owner of Genting Cruise Lines, the parent company of Dream Cruises and Star Cruises and a minor shareholder of Norwegian Cruise Line Holdings Ltd). It introduced Crystal Yacht Cruises (rebranded in 2016 as Crystal Yacht Expedition Cruises) with the introduction of the refurbished *Crystal Esprit*. The company's ambitious expansion plans have since been scaled back some-

what, but there are still three 'Executive-class' ships due for introduction in 2022.

Cunard

Cunard was established in 1839, as the British and North American Royal Mail Steam Packet Company, to carry the Royal Mail and passengers from the Old World to the New. Its first ship, *Britannia*, sailed on its maiden voyage on American Independence Day in 1840. The author Charles Dickens crossed the Atlantic aboard the ship in 1842 together with 62 other passengers, 93 crew members, one cow, and, most important, Her Majesty's mails and dispatches. Since 1840, Cunard has always had ships built to sail across the North Atlantic. From 1850 until the arrival of *QE2* in 1969, all of the line's ships and those of White Star Line (with which Cunard merged in 1934) had several classes. Your luggage label, therefore, declared not only your name but also what you could afford. Today, there's no class distinction, other than by accommodation grade.

Cunard celebrated its 175th anniversary in 2015. One is still reminded of the company's illustrious history. For example, Cunard was the first company to take passengers on regularly scheduled transatlantic crossings. It introduced the first passenger ship to be lit by electricity (*Servia*, 1881) and the first steam turbine engines in an ocean liner (*Carmania*, 1905). The line was the first to have an indoor swimming pool aboard a ship (*Aquitania*, 1914), and it pioneered the around-the-world cruise (*Laconia*, 1922). Cunard long held the record for the largest passenger ship ever built (*Queen Elizabeth*, between 1940 and 1996).

The ships incorporate a lot of maritime history and the grand traditions of ocean liners – as opposed to the other ships, with their tendency toward tacky

Disney takes its brand to Alaska.

high-street trappings. Cunard is also the *only* cruise line that lets you take your dog or cat with you (*Queen Mary 2* transatlantic crossings only).

While Samuel Cunard was from Halifax, Nova Scotia, he established the company in Liverpool. Today, the company is owned by the American Carnival Corporation. The three *Queens* were built in France and Italy, registered in Hamilton, Bermuda, with a home port of Southampton, England. The onboard currency is the US dollar!

Cunard has four distinct accommodation grades, each linked to a specific restaurant: Queens Grill, Princess Grill, Britannia Club, and Britannia.

Cunard has one real ocean liner (*Queen Mary 2*). It provides a regular transatlantic crossing service from April to December, while the company's two other two ships are more about regular cruising, albeit in ocean-liner style. All three are best suited to a wide range of seasoned and well-traveled couples and solo travelers who enjoy the cosmopolitan setting of an ocean liner. Dressing more formally for dinner is encouraged, although – with the exception of the grill rooms – the cuisine is largely of mass-market quality, with many traditional British and French dishes.

Disney Cruise Line

It was Lawrence (Larry) P. Murphy, executive vice-president of the Walt Disney Company, who was the guiding light in the early 1990s behind the expansion of the company into the cruise business. Previously, Disney had flirted with cruising by participating in a licensing agreement with a Florida-based cruise line, the now-defunct Premier Cruise Lines, with three vintage ships based in Port Canaveral. Murphy and other Disney executives explored the possibility of creating their own ships when the licensing agreement ran out. They concluded that pairing with an established cruise line wouldn't work because of Disney's policy of generous spending on the guest experience.

The solution: create a new cruise line, wholly owned and controlled by Disney, and to be known as Disney Cruise Line. The company committed an astonishing $1 billion to the project.

Its two mid-size ships, *Disney Magic* (1998) and *Disney Wonder* (1999), the first cruise ships since the 1950s to be built with two funnels, cater to loyal Disney followers, and everything aboard the ships is Disney – every song, every piece of artwork, every movie and production show – and Mickey's ears adorn the ships' funnels. There's no casino and no library. However, its 'rotation dining' concept proved to be completely Disneylogical; you move, together with your waiter, to each of three identically sized restaurants – each with different decor – in turn.

One new, larger ship, *Disney Dream*, joined the fleet in 2011, and sister ship *Disney Fantasy* arrived in 2012.

Disney, of course, is all about families with children, and the ships cater to both. You can buy a package combining a short stay at a Disney resort and a cruise. Gratuities are not included in the cruise fare. Disney has its own cruise terminal at Port Canaveral, Florida, its design being an imaginative but close copy of the Ocean Terminal in Southampton, UK, frequented by yesteryear's ocean liners but little used today. The terminal and pier were extended in 2010 and connected to a new parking garage. Two new (slightly larger) ships are on order.

Dream Cruises

Owned by Genting Cruise Lines, this brand is a sister company to Star Cruises. Dream Cruises has two ships. The stunning *Genting Dream* started sailing in

November 2016, and she was joined by sister ship *World Dream* in 2017. The company is a much more upscale and advanced version of Star Cruises, and it is aimed specifically at the Asian (and especially, the Chinese) market, with an abundance of bright decor and upbeat, colorful razzle-dazzle shows.

For part of the year, *Genting Dream* offers embarkation in three different countries, including its home port of Hong Kong,

Fred. Olsen Cruise Lines

This Norwegian family-owned and family-run company was founded in Hvitsten, a town on Oslofjord, Norway, in 1848. Today, a fifth-generation Olsen, Anette, owns and runs the company from its headquarters in Suffolk, England. The group also has interests in hotels, aviation, shipbuilding, ferries, and offshore industries. The company specializes in cruises for adults, who are usually retired and of senior years – typically over 65.

Aboard the ships, interior design reflects traditional design features, and dressing for dinner is expected on four nights during a two-week cruise. Many theme cruises, such as gardening and horticulture, and Scottish country dancing, hosted by recognized television celebrities, are regular features. The company welcomes solo passengers as well as couples and delivers a quintessentially 'British' cruise experience, albeit by a mainly Filipino hotel service staff.

The first ship dedicated exclusively to cruising debuted in 1987, and now ships cruise year-round out of UK ports such as Dover, Southampton, Liverpool, Newcastle, Greenock, Leith, Belfast, and Dublin (ideal for anyone based in the UK to join one of the ships without having to fly), with some ships operating fly-cruises from Canary Island ports, or Caribbean ports such as Barbados in winter.

Coffee- and tea-making facilities are provided in each cabin. Smoking is allowed only on the open decks, and nowhere inside the ships. Gratuities are not included in the cruise fare, but are automatically charged to your onboard account. Drink prices are extremely reasonable aboard the ships, where the social scene is courteous, friendly, and warm, and gentlemen hosts are onboard each cruise for unaccompanied women who would like dancing partners.

The National Express bus operator works in conjunction with Fred. Olsen Cruise Lines to provide a Cruiselink service via London's Victoria Coach Station to the UK departure ports of Dover or Southampton.

FTI Cruises

This company, part of the Munich-based FTI Touristik (founded in 1983), bought its only ship from Saga Cruises in 2011 and started its cruise operations in May 2012 for the German-speaking market. The ship, *Berlin,* is known in Germany for low-cost, good-value, well-organized cruising for passengers not expecting luxury.

G Adventures

This Canadian company, based in Toronto, was founded in 1990 as GAP Adventures by Bruce Poon Tip, using funds from his own personal credit cards only. The company has a grassroots approach to travel and operates its own ship – the 140-passenger MS *Expedition – on polar expedition cruises.*

Grand Circle Cruise Line

Ethel Andrus, a retired teacher, wanted to share her vision of helping Americans lead more vital, challenging, and politically active lives. She founded the American Association of Retired Persons (AARP) in 1958. The company has exclusive charters for its small group travel (the company's foundation has donated more than $91 million to cultural, educational, and humanitarian organizations since 1992). For many years, this Boston-based travel company (its brands are Grand Circle Travel, Overseas Adventure Travel, and Grand Circle Cruise Line) has chartered riverships and small ocean-going vessels. The firm has three custom-designed sea-going ships (*Arethusa, Artemis,* and *Athena*) for coastal cruise tours for 50 passengers, and in May 2016 acquired *Tere Moana* from Paul Gauguin Cruises. However, general cruise/travel agents cannot easily book into the company's cruise programs.

Hapag-Lloyd's *Bremen* in the Corinth Canal, Greece.

Aboard *Hebridean Princess*, cruising around Scotland and its islands.

Hapag-Lloyd Cruises

Germany's two most famous ocean-liner companies, the Bremen-based Norddeutscher Lloyd (founded in 1847) and the Hamburg-based Hamburg America Line (founded in the same year), merged in 1970 to become Hapag-Lloyd. The company no longer operates regularly scheduled transatlantic crossings, but promotes instead four ships in three different market segments.

Two small ships are in the specialized expedition cruise market: *Bremen* and *Hanseatic* (operated by Hapag-Lloyd Expedition Cruises, see below); and two (the more formal 400-passenger *Europa* and the more informal 516-passenger *Europa 2* – for international travellers and families with children) are in the luxury market. All provide destination-intensive cruises aimed at the German-speaking market, with an increasing number of dual-language cruises for English-speakers.

The staff on board makes all its own breads, soups, pâtés, jams, and preserves from scratch.

Hapag-Lloyd Cruises hosts the annual Stella Maris International Vocal Competition, which attracts top-notch up-and-coming operatic singers from around the world. A top prize of €15,000 is offered, as well as a Deutsche Grammophon recording contract. The company also sponsors an annual Ocean Sun Festival – for classical/chamber music devotees (concerts are often held ashore as part of the program).

Hapag-Lloyd Expedition Cruises

The company operates two specialist expedition cruise ships, the 164-passenger *Bremen* and the 184-passenger *Hanseatic*. There are occasional dual-language cruises for the English-speaking market, but all the crew members speak English.

Both ships carry a fleet of Zodiac inflatable rubber craft (with environmentally friendly electric motors) for shore landings in the polar region and other destinations with no pier facilities. They have excellent cuisine, proper boot-washing and storage stations, lecture rooms, extensive libraries, and other expedition facilities to suit adventurous itineraries, plus some of the world's best expedition leaders.

Hapag-Lloyd Expedition Cruises is a member of IAATO (International Association of Antarctica Tour Operators), a body committed to the highest standards of responsible tourism to Antarctica and to operating its ships in the most environmentally friendly manner, accompanied by the very best expedition leaders in the business.

Hapag-Lloyd publishes its own excellent handbooks (in both English and German) on expedition regions such as the Arctic, Antarctica, Amazonia, and the South Sea Islands, as well as exclusive maps. Gratuities are not included in the fare.

Two new expedition cruise ships are on order, for delivery in 2019.

Hebridean Island Cruises

The company (formerly Hebridean International Cruises) was set up in 1989 under the Thatcher government's British Enterprise Scheme, and has its headquarters in Skipton, Yorkshire. It is independently owned and operates one all-inclusive boutique ship, *Hebridean Princess,* which conveys the atmosphere of English country-house life – and specializes in cruises for mature adults. Gratuities and all port taxes are included, as are most excursions. The ship offers cruises around the Scottish islands, with occasional sailings to English ports, the Channel Islands, and Norway. Each cabin has coffee- and tea-making facilities. Gratuities are included in the fare. The Queen granted Hebridean Island Cruises a royal warrant in her jubilee year.

Heritage Expeditions

This youth-minded adventure travel company, based in Christchurch, New Zealand, focuses on expedition-style cruising for small groups, specifically to Antarctica, the Sub-Antarctic and Russian Far East. The company was founded in 1985 by biologist Rodney Russ who worked for the New Zealand Wildlife Service for many years. The company's single ship, *Spirit of Enderby* was formerly *Professor Khromov,* a small Russian oceanographic research vessel.

Hurtigruten

The company is an amalgamation of two shipping companies (OVDS and TVDS) and provides year-round service along the Norwegian coast, calling at 34 ports in 11 days. Hurtigruten, formerly known as the Norwegian Coastal Voyage, has also recently developed expedition-style cruises, albeit aboard ships that have been converted for the purpose, rather

than specifically built for expedition cruises. So, as long as you think utilitarian and modest decor, you'll get the idea of life aboard one of the Hurtigruten ships, which are practical rather than beautiful. Even aboard the newest ships, the food and service are fairly basic – there's a lack of green vegetables, for example – but the ships provide a great way to see many, many ports along the coast of Norway in a comfortable manner.

Norway's Crown Princess Mette-Marit was the godmother of the newest ship, *Fram,* a 318-berth expedition-style vessel built for polar and Greenland cruising. The next generation of dual coastal and expedition-style ships (*Roald Amundsen* and *Fridtjof Nansen*) will be delivered in 2018 and 2019, respectively.

Lindblad Expeditions

Lars-Eric Lindblad started the whole concept of expedition cruising with a single ship, *Lindblad Explorer,* in 1969, taking adventurous travelers to remote regions of the world. Today, his son, Sven-Olof Lindblad, runs the company, but with an array of small ships. It's all about nature, wilderness, wildlife, off-the-beaten-path adventures, and learning. Zodiac inflatable craft are used to ferry participants ashore in remote Arctic and Antarctic polar regions.

The ships carry excellent lecturers, who are more academic than entertaining. In partnership with the National Geographic Society, the company operates the wholly owned *National Geographic Endeavour* and *Na-*

Louis Aura in the Mediterranean.

The horseshoe staircase aboard Oceania's *Marina*.

tional Geographic Explorer (both with ice-strengthened hulls), together with two small ships (*National Geographic Sea Bird* and *National Geographic Sea Lion*) for coastal or 'soft' expedition-style cruising in, for example, Alaska. National Geographic photographers take part in all cruises. Zodiac inflatable craft are often used for shore landings, and the ships have extensive libraries. Gratuities are not included in the fare.

The National Geographic Society celebrated its 125th anniversary in 2013, when the company purchased Orion Expedition Cruises, based in Sydney, Australia. Orion Expedition's ship, also called *Orion*, was renamed *National Geographic Orion*, when the ship was transferred from Orion Expeditions to the Lindblad fleet in March 2014. Built in Germany, this ship is a little gem, with handcrafted cabinetry in every cabin, together with marble bathrooms and a health spa and gymnasium. New ships were ordered for delivery in 2017 and 2018.

Louis Cruises

In the 1930s and 1940s, Louis Loizou became the undisputed father of tourism in Cyprus. His venture into sea tourism started with the charter of ships transferring immigrants from Cyprus to other continents. His son, Costakis Loizou, who took over the running of the company after Louis's death in 1971, started organizing short cruises from Cyprus. In 1986 Louis Cruises was officially founded with the acquisition of the company's first fully owned ship, *Princesa Marissa*.

Today, Louis Group owns almost two dozen hotels in the Greek islands and Cyprus, together with a multi-ship fleet of mainly older, small and mid-size ships, which operate principally from Greece and ports in the Mediterranean. Louis has over the years chartered some of its ships to many major UK and

European tour operators. A sub-brand, created in 2014, is Celestyal Cruises.

MOPAS

Osaka Shosen Kaisha was founded in 1884 in Osaka, Japan. In 1964 it merged with Mitsui Steamship, to become Mitsui OSK Passenger Line (MOPAS). It is now one of the oldest and largest shipping companies in the world.

It entered cruise shipping in 1989 with *Fuji Maru*, the first cruise ship in the Japanese-speaking domestic market (now no longer in service). The company specialized in incentive meetings and groups at sea rather than cruising for individuals, but this steadily changed into more cruises for individuals. The firm operates a single ship, the very comfortable *Nippon Maru* (extensively refurbished in 2010), based in Japan for Japanese-speaking passengers. Gratuities are included in the cruise fare.

Noble Caledonia

London-based Noble Caledonia, established in 1991, operates three boutique-size sister ships, *Caledonian Sky*, *Hebridean Sky*, and *Island Sky*, each carrying around 100 passengers. It also sells cruises aboard a wide range of small-ship and expedition cruise companies as well as river cruises. It markets to British passengers of mature years, and operates cruises, generally in sheltered water areas, with cultural-interest themes, and so is not recommended for children.

The company, whose financial partners include Sweden's Salen family, who had been very involved with expedition cruising in the past, has an excellent reputation for well-organized cruises and tours, accompanied by good lecturers. It specializes in itineraries that would be impossible to operate aboard larger ships. A Commodore Club gives repeat passengers advance information about new voyages and special offers. Gratuities are not generally included in the fare, unless otherwise stated in the brochures.

NYK Cruises

Nippon Yusen Kaisha, the world's largest shipping company, owned the well-known, US-based upscale brand Crystal Cruises. It created its own NYK Cruise division – today branded as Asuka Cruise – in 1989 with one Mitsubishi-built ship, *Asuka*, for Japanese-speaking passengers. In 2006, the company sold the original *Asuka* to Germany's Phoenix Reisen, and the former *Crystal Harmony* was transferred from Crystal Cruises to become *Asuka II*. The ship, known for its excellent Japanese and western food, operates an annual around-the-world cruise, plus a wide array of both short and long cruises in the Asia-Pacific region. Coffee- and tea-making facilities are provided in each cabin, as is a large selection of personal toiletries. Gratuities are included in the cruise fare.

Oceania Cruises

The company's ships provide faux English charm in a country-club atmosphere ideal for middle-aged and older couples seeking relaxation. Cruises are usually 10–14 days. Its trademarks are comfortable cabins, warm and attentive service, and fine dining combining French culinary expertise and top-quality ingredients. Breads and other baked goods, such as Poilâne-quality croissants, are excellent.

In 2006, Oceania Cruises was bought by Apollo Management, a private equity company that owns Regent Seven Seas Cruises and 50 percent of Norwegian Cruise Line (NCL). The brand was placed under the umbrella of Apollo's cruise brand, Prestige Cruise Holdings, and now has six ships – *Insignia, Marina, Nautica, Regatta, Riviera,* and *Sirena* – catering to between 684 and 1,250 passengers.

With multiple-choice dining at no extra cost, these ships suit anyone who prefers small and mid-size ships to large resort vessels. Bottled mineral water, soft drinks, and beer are included in the price. Gratuities are added at $10.50 per person, per day, and butler-service suites have an additional charge of $3 per person. Bar drinks and spa treatments have 15–18 percent added.

Oceanwide Expeditions

Founded in 1961 as the Dutch 'Plancius Foundation' to operate cruises around Spitzbergen (Norway), the company changed its name in 1996 to Oceanwide Expeditions in order to offer adventures farther afield. It specializes in small group polar-expedition voyages and active shore visits rather than employing experienced lecturers. It operates two expedition ships, *Ortelius* and *Plancius,* and charters others as needed.

OneOcean Expeditions

Based in Toronto, Canada, this small company was founded by Andrew Prossin. It doesn't own any expedition ships itself, but charters them from the Russian pool of specialist vessels. Environmental responsibility is a key ingredient for its staff, who are all personable and very customer-oriented. The company charters and operates two small sister specialist polar-expedition ships, *Akademik Ioffe* and *Akademik Sergey Vavilov,* on Arctic and Antarctic programs.

Aboard the maiden voyage of P&O Cruises' *Britannia*.

Paul Gauguin was built specifically to operate in French Polynesia.

P&O Cruises

P&O's full name is the Peninsular and Oriental Steam Navigation Company, though none of its ships is powered by steam turbines. Based in Southampton, England, it was founded in 1837, just before Samuel Cunard established his company, and was awarded a UK government contract in 1840 to carry the mail from Gibraltar to Alexandria.

P&O Cruises acquired Princess Cruises in 1974, Swan Hellenic in 1982, and Sitmar Cruises in 1988. In 2000 it demerged from its parent to establish itself as P&O Princess plc. It was bought by the Carnival Corporation in 2003, and celebrated its 175th anniversary on July 3, 2012, when all seven ships assembled in Southampton.

P&O Cruises has always been a traditional British cruise company, never quite matching the quality aboard the Cunard ships, which have more international passengers. With P&O having mainly British captains and navigation officers and Indian/Goanese service staff, the British traditions of unobtrusive service are preserved and well presented. British food favorites provide the real comfort factor in a single-language setting that provides a home from home on ships for families with children, or on adults-only ships.

The company targets British passengers who want to sail from a UK port – except for winter Caribbean cruises from Barbados. But it's also known for having adults-only ships, and so the two products differ widely in their communal spaces. It also makes an effort to provide theme cruises – on antiques, art appreciation, classical music, comedy, cricket, gardening and horticulture, jazz, Scottish dancing, etc.

The ships usually carry ballroom-dance instructors. Bed linen is changed twice a week – not as often as on some lines, such as MSC Cruises, where it is changed every two days. The decor is a mix of British traditional (think comfy, somewhat dated, non-glitzy armchairs, and wood paneling). British artists are featured aboard all ships – *Ventura*, for example, displays works by more than 40 of them.

P&O Cruises (Australia)

Founded in 1932, the Australian division of P&O Cruises provides fun entertainment for the beer-and-bikini brigade and their families, and specializes in cruises in the Pacific and to New Zealand. The line is maturing, though, becoming more of a mainstream operator – particularly so with its latest ships, which are larger, more contemporary hand-me-down vessels (*Pacific Dawn*, *Pacific Jewel*, *Pacific Pearl* from P&O Cruises and Princess Cruises; and *Pacific Aria* and *Pacific Eden* from Holland America Line), from companies that are part of the Carnival Corporation. The ships have open-seating dining and specialty restaurants such as Australian celebrity chef Luke Mangan's 'Salt Grill.' Gratuities are not included in the fare. The company has a new ship on order, due for delivery in 2019.

Paradise Cruise Line

This one-ship company is owned by Celebration Cruise Holdings, which also owned the now-defunct Imperial Majesty Cruise Line, whose reputation suffered from high-pressure telemarketing campaigns. Its *Grand Celebration* (originally built for Carnival Cruise Line in 1987) operates two-night cruises from the Port of Palm Beach, in Florida, to the Bahamas.

Despite the company's claims to 'international gourmet dining,' the ship provides a highly programmed but absolutely basic party getaway cruise with very standard food, and much pressure for revenue from its dining, casino, and shore-excursion operations.

Paul Gauguin Cruises

Created by the Boston-based tour operator Grand Circle Travel, Paul Gauguin Cruises took over the marketing and operation of *Paul Gauguin* in 2009 from Regent Seven Seas Cruises, which had operated the ship since its inception. Also in 2009, the ship was bought by the Tahiti-based investor Richard Bailey and his company Pacific Beachcomber, which owns Polynesian resort hotels (including four InterContinental Hotels). Gratuities are not included in the cruise fare.

Pearl Seas Cruises

Founded in 2007 by Charles Robertson, Pearl Seas Cruises is now a sister company to American Cruise Lines. It has a single ship (a second ship order was canceled), *Pearl Mist*, which was the subject of poor shipbuilding and contract arguments in its early days. *Pearl Mist* was rejected as not fit for purpose by the owner, but she was finally completed and debuted in 2014. The ship's loyalty club is called the Oyster Society.

Phoenix Reisen

Based in Bonn, Germany, the company for many years operated low-budget, tour-operator-style destination-intensive cruises for German speakers. It now has a loyal, widespread audience and more contemporary ships, with better food and service, particularly aboard *Amadea* and *Artania*.

To keep costs down, Phoenix charters its ships for long periods. It is consistently praised for its extremely good itineraries, particularly on world cruises, its pre- and post-cruise programs, and its excellent value for money. The wonderfully comprehensive Phoenix brochure provides photographs of its captains and cruise director, as well as bar lists and drink prices – a refreshing change from the brochures provided by most cruise companies. Single-seating dining is standard, as are low drink prices, and there is no constant pushing for onboard revenue – again different from most rivals.

Phoenix acquired *Artania* (formerly P&O Cruises' *Artemis* and originally *Royal Princess*, named by Princess Diana) in 2011, and also operates the lower-priced *Albatross* (originally *Royal Viking Sea*). Gratuities are included in the fare.

Plantours Cruises

This company, based in Bremen, Germany, provides low-budget cruises for German speakers aboard its single small, chartered cruise ship, *Hamburg*, which was formerly Hapag-Lloyd Cruises' original *Columbus*. The company also sells cruises on the rivers of Europe and Russia. Gratuities are not included in the cruise fare.

Ponant

The company was founded in 1988 by Philippe Videau and Jean-Emmanuel Sauvé. It started life as La

Pacific Pearl, of P&O (Australia), entering Hobart, Tasmania.

The softly lit Horizon Lounge Deck aboard *Seven Seas Voyager*.

Compagnie des Iles du Ponant, and was a subsidiary of the state-owned CMA CGM (Compagnie Maritime d'Affrètement/Compagnie Générale Maritime), until its acquisition by Bridgepoint Capital, a private equity company, in 2012. In 2015, Ponant was acquired by Artemis, the holding company of French billionaire François Pinault and his family.

The cruise company, whose head office is in Marseille, France, operates one boutique-size, high-tech sail-cruise ship, *Le Ponant*. In 2004, the company purchased the Paris-based tour operator Tapis Rouge International, which specializes in upscale travel. Three small ships – *Le Boréal*, introduced in 2010, *L'Austral*, introduced in 2011, and *Le Soléal*, introduced in 2013 – provide more space and more options for passengers, with a fourth *(Le Lyrial)*, introduced in 2015. Four more ships have been ordered, for delivery in 2018 and 2019. Ponant teams with French partners such as Veuve Clicquot, Ladurée, and Alain Ducasse, one of the world's most highly decorated chefs.

Ponant increasingly markets cruises in both English and French to international passengers and onboard announcements are made in both languages. Gratuities are not included.

Poseidon Expeditions

Poseidon Expeditions, the Arctic expedition cruise specialist (founded and owned by Nikolay Saveliev in 2003), the company operates under the strict guidelines of the Association of Arctic Expedition Cruise Operators (AECO), the body committed to minimizing the impact of visits to the Far North. Expeditions to the North Pole (90 degrees North) are operated only at the height of the Arctic summer, in June and July,

aboard the world's most powerful icebreaker – the Russian nuclear-powered *50 Years of Victory* (it can crush ice up to 10ft/3m thick.

This really is a once-in-a-lifetime adventure. Only 10,741 people had visited the North Pole when I went in July 2016.

The company also operates the smaller Sea Spirit – the only non-Russian foreign-flag ship permitted to operate into the territorial waters of Franz Joseph Land in the Arctic Circle from Svalbard without first calling at a mainland Russian port. In 2004 the company achieved the inaugural Northeast Passage via the North Pole. Gratuities are not included in the cruise fare.

Pullmantur Cruises

The cruise division was set up as part of Pullmantur, the Spain-based holiday tour operator founded in 1971. Its cruising division was established in 2000 when it bought *Oceanic* (then known as the Big Red Boat) from the defunct Florida operator Premier Cruise Lines. In 2006, Pullmantur Cruises was bought by Royal Caribbean Cruises; in 2015 it was sold to private equity company Springwater Capital. The company mainly serves the Spanish-speaking market, operating all-inclusive cruises for families with children to the Caribbean and Europe. Gratuities are included in the cruise fare. Pullmantur Cruises has a fleet of four ships (*Horizon, Monarch, Sovereign*, and *Zenith*).

Quark Expeditions

The company was founded in 1991 by Lars Wikander, Mike McDowell, and silent partners the Salen family (formerly of Salen-Lindblad Cruises). Based in Seattle, Washington, Quark specializes in providing up-close-and-personal Arctic and Antarctic expedition cruises.

In 2007, it was sold to the UK's First Choice Holidays (founded in 1973), it merged with Peregrine Shipping, and was then bought, along with First Choice, by German travel company TUI.

Cruising with Quark Expeditions is all about being close to nature, wilderness, wildlife, off-the-beaten-path adventures, and learning, albeit in fairly rustic surroundings and comfort. The company, an associate member of IAATO (International Association of Antarctica Tour Operators), specializes in chartered Russian icebreakers, the most powerful in the world, to provide participants with truly memorable expedition experiences. This is adventure cruising for toughies. Gratuities are not included in the cruise fare.

Regent Seven Seas Cruises

This company has a complicated history. It was born out of Seven Seas Cruises, which was originally based in San Francisco to market the cruise ship *Song of Flower* (belonging to 'K'-Line, a cargo operator based in New Jersey), as well as expedition cruises aboard the chartered *Hanseatic* (then belonging to

Hanseatic Tours). The lyre, logo of that ship, became RSSC's logo.

For many years, the company was part of the Carlson group, and operated as Radisson Seven Seas Cruises. Carlson Hospitality Worldwide ventured into cruising via its Radisson Hotels International division – hence, Radisson Diamond Cruises (when Radisson Diamond joined in 1992). In 1994 Radisson Diamond Cruises and Seven Seas Cruise Line merged to become Radisson Seven Seas Cruises, and in 2007 it became Regent Seven Seas Cruises.

In 2007 the company was bought by US-based investment group Apollo Management, and, together with Oceania Cruises, was placed under the umbrella of its Prestige Cruise Holdings. The company spent $40 million to refurbish its then fleet of three ships in 2009–10.

It operates worldwide itineraries and strives to pay close attention to detail and provide high-quality service aboard its small cruise ships, of which there are now four: *Seven Seas Explorer* (debuted in 2016), *Seven Seas Mariner*, *Seven Seas Navigator*, and *Seven Seas Voyager*.

It provides drinks-inclusive cruising, which means that beverages and gratuities are included in the fare, as are shore excursions – even delicious *illy* coffees are included. Passengers pay extra only for laundry services, beauty services, casino, and other personal items.

Saga Cruises

Saga, based in Folkestone, England, was created by Sidney De Haan as a company offering financial services and holidays to an over-60s clientele. As the company's success grew, it reduced this limitation in 1995 to the over-50s and allowed companions older than 40. Its popular travel flourished because it was good at providing personal attention and had competent staff. Instead of sending passengers to ships operated by other companies, it decided to buy its own ships and market its own product under the Saga Holidays brand.

Saga Shipping (Saga Cruises), the cruising division of Saga Holidays, was set up in 1997 when it purchased *Saga Rose* (formerly *Sagafjord*), followed soon after by *Saga Ruby* (formerly *Vistafjord*), and, in 2010, *Saga Pearl II* (formerly *Astoria*). *Saga Sapphire* (ex-Europa) arrived in 2012.

Another brand, Spirit of Adventure, was added in 2006, and in 2007 Saga merged with Britain's Automobile Association. The 'Adventure' cruise brand ended in November 2013, when *Quest for Adventure* became *Saga Pearl II* again.

The cruise company emphasizes British seamanship and training, and its fleet manages to retain the feel of traditional, elegant, adults-only cruising aboard *Saga Pearl II* and *Saga Sapphire*. Saga Cruises offers open-seating dining, as well as friendly, attentive service from a mainly Filipino hotel service crew, and its ships have many single-occupancy cabins. It takes care of some of the little details that other lines have long forgotten.

All gratuities are included in the fare. Coffee- and tea-making facilities are provided in each cabin aboard *Saga Pearl II*. The company has two new ships on order, for delivery in 2019 and 2021.

Relaxed lifestyle aboard *SeaDream I*.

Scenic

The company was founded in Newcastle, Australia, in 1986 by Glen Moroney, as Scenic Tours. The company began by operating coach tours throughout Australia. In 2008, it began river cruise operations in Europe (mainly for Australasian passengers). It now owns and operates several riverships in Europe, under two brands: Scenic, and Emerald Waterways, The company, which is still Australian owned, changed its name to Scenic in 2015.

The company will branch out into expedition/discovery cruising with its own, custom-designed ship (complete with helicopter), due for delivery in 2018. Expedition cruises are fully inclusive of gratuities and all onboard drinks (a few select premium brands cost extra).

Sea Cloud Cruises

This company was founded in 1979 by a consortium of ship-owners and investors known as the Hansa Treuhand (active in commercial vessel management, engineering, and construction), with headquarters in Hamburg, Germany. It owns and operates two genuine tall ships (cruise-sail vessels), the legendary *Sea Cloud* (built in 1931 for the cereal heiress Marjorie Merriweather Post), and the 1990-built *Sea Cloud II*.

The company has many corporate clients who charter the two sail-cruise ships, while a number of luxury cruise and travel specialist companies sell cruises to individuals. The onboard style and product delivery are something special, with elegant retro

decor and fine food and service. Gratuities are not included in the cruise fare.

Seabourn

Originally founded in 1986 as Signet Cruise Line, the company, then owned by Norwegian industrialist Atle Brynestad, had to change its name in 1988 as a result of a lawsuit brought by a Texas ferry company that had already registered the name Signet Cruise Lines (no ships were ever built for cruising, however).

In 1998, a consortium, which included the Carnival Corporation and Norwegian investors, bought Seabourn Cruise Line and merged its operations into Cunard, which was acquired from Kvaerner. The fleet then included three ships plus *Seabourn Goddess I* and *Seabourn Goddess II* (bought by SeaDream Yacht Cruises in 2002 and named *SeaDream I* and *SeaDream II*) and *Seabourn Sun* (now Holland America Line's *Prinsendam*). The Carnival Corporation acquired 100 percent of Seabourn Cruise Line in 1999.

Three new, larger ships joined the company between 2009 and 2011. All three have an aft watersports platform, as well as a wider number of dining and spa options, and a greater amount of space, for more passengers. Seabourn Cruise Line was briefly rebranded as The Yachts of Seabourn in 2009–10, but then became simply Seabourn. The company is managed from within the headquarters of Holland America Line (also owned by Carnival) in Seattle, US. Gratuities are included in the fare.

In February 2013, the three smaller ships were sold to Xanterra Parks & Resorts, parent company

Seabourn Odyssey's water-sports platform.

of Windstar Cruises. *Seabourn Pride* was delivered in mid-2014; *Seabourn Legend* and *Seabourn Spirit* were delivered in 2015. Seabourn Encore was delivered in 2016, and *Seabourn Ovation* is scheduled for 2018.

Note that quality has been reduced substantially since the management has been taken over by Holland America Line, with various cutbacks reflecting the downgrade – Prosecco is served rather than Champagne, for example, poor canapés and disappointing cheese and meat selections are provided in place of the superior offerings of yesteryear, and reduced dining hours and fixed disembarkation by 8am are now standard. All in all it's a much less upmarket product than previously.

SeaDream Yacht Club

Larry Pimentel, an American, and his Norwegian business partner Atle Brynestad, founder of Seabourn Cruise Line (now called, simply, Seabourn), jointly created the company by buying the former Sea Goddess Cruises' ships. They introduced them in 2002 to an audience anxious for exclusivity, personal pampering, and cuisine prepared to order.

The two ships, *SeaDream I* and *SeaDream II*, have been refreshed several times – although *SeaDream I* is in a better shape than *SeaDream II* – and are often chartered by companies or private individuals who appreciate the refined, elegant, but casual atmosphere on board. The 100-passenger ships operate year-round in the Caribbean and Mediterranean, and provide all-inclusive beverages and open-seating dining at all times, and a high degree of personalized service, all in a cozy, club-like atmosphere, with great attention to detail and personal idiosyncrasies. Brynestad is now the company's chairman and sole owner (Larry Pimentel moved to Azamara Club Cruises). Gratuities are included in the fare.

Serenissima Cruises

Vladimir Esakov, the Russian owner/operator of the rivership *Volga Dream*, purchased the former *MS Andrea* (a Hurtigruten vessel) in 2012, renamed it *Serenissima* and formed Serenissima Cruises to market the ship. The company has a long-standing association with the UK's Noble Caledonia.

Silversea Cruises

Silversea Cruises is a mostly privately owned cruise line. It was founded in 1992 by the Lefebvre d'Ovidio family from Rome (previously co-owners of Sitmar Cruises; 90 percent partners are the Lefebvre d'Ovidios, 10 percent by V-Ships) and is based in Monaco.

Antonio Lefebvre d'Ovidio was a maritime lawyer and professor of maritime law before acquiring and operating cargo ships and ferries in the Adriatic. He took his family into partnership with Boris Vlasov's Vlasov Group (V-Ships) to co-own Sitmar Cruises, until that company merged with Princess Cruises in 1988.

Silversea Cruises has generated tremendous loyalty from its frequent passengers, who view the ships as their own. All Silversea ships have teak verandas and all-inclusive beverages. Open-seating dining prevails at all times, and the company is known for its partnership with the hospitality organization Relais & Châteaux. A new, larger, 540-passenger all-suite luxury ship, *Silver Spirit*, debuted at the end of 2009, while *Silver Whisper* and *Silver Shadow* were refurbished in 2010 and 2011. *Silver Muse* debuted in 2017, with more than a design nod to Hapag-Lloyd's *Europa 2*, but the ship still has the look and feel of a Silversea Cruises product.

Silversea Cruises also has three specialist ships for expedition cruising (*Silver Explorer, Silver Galapagos*, and *Silver Discoverer*, added in 2008, 2013, and 2014, respectively).

Gratuities are included for all ships as part of the company's 'all-inclusive' culture.

SkySea Cruises

This company in the China domestic cruise market is owned by partners Ctrip (which has the world's largest reservations and booking platform in the Chinese language), and Royal Caribbean Cruises, each of which has a 35 percent holding, as well as China's Stone Capital, which holds 30 percent. The ship is the ex-*Celebrity Century*, which debuted in May 2015 as *SkySea Golden Era*, with direct digital (internet) bookings only.

Star Clippers

Swedish-born yachtsman Mikael Krafft founded Star Clippers in 1991 with *Star Flyer* and then *Star Clipper*, both true tall ships. The company went on to build the largest tall ship presently sailing, the five-mast *Royal Clipper*, a truly stunning ship under sail. Friendly service in an extremely laid-back setting, under the romance of sail (when there is enough wind) is what Star Clippers is all about, and the food variety, creativity, and quality are all extremely good. The company's new five-mast ship (*Flying Clipper*) will be added in 2018.

These real tall (sail-cruise) ships sail in the Caribbean, Baltic, and Mediterranean. Gratuities are not included in the fare.

Star Cruises

The company was incorporated in 1993 as a subsidiary of Malaysia's Genting Berhad, set up in 1965 by the late Tan Sri (Dr) Lim Goh Tong as an Asian multinational corporation. Today, Star Cruises comes under the umbrella of Genting Cruise Lines. The group's various businesses include palm oil production, power generation, property development, biotechnology, and oil and gas production, plus leisure activities including resort hotels and casino/entertainment complexes in Malaysia, Manila, and Singapore, and cruise ships. Almost single-handedly, Star Cruises opened up the Asia-Pacific cruise region (except for Japan).

Sea lion with *Silver Galapagos* in the distance.

Genting Hong Kong operates ships dedicated to specific markets. Its brands include Crystal Cruises, Dream Cruises (which started operations in 2016), and Star Cruises.

Gratuities are included in all fares.

Thomson Cruises

Thomson Cruises' first foray into cruising was in 1973 when it chartered two ships, *Calypso* and *Ithaca,* from the Greek-owned Ulysses Line. It was a disaster, and the company withdrew from cruising two years later (Ulysses Line became known as Useless Line).

The company started again in 2002 after seeing rival tour operator Airtours run ships successfully. Thomson Cruises charters its ships, preferring instead to leave ship operations, management, and catering to specialist maritime companies. The company features cruises for the whole family aboard *Thomson Dream, TUI Discovery,* and *TUI Discovery 2* – catering principally to the British market. In 2018 the company is scheduled to add ships from the TUI Cruises fleet. Basic gratuities are included in the price

TUI Cruises

The German-owned TUI Group has several divisions, but started its own cruise line in 2009 with *Mein Schiff 1*, a mid-size ship (formerly *Celebrity Galaxy*) that un-

derwent a huge reconstruction program. *Mein Schiff 2* (formerly *Celebrity Mercury*) was added in 2011. Further new ships followed: *Mein Schiff 3* debuted in 2014, *Mein Schiff 4* in 2015, *Mein Schiff 5* in 2016, and *Mein Schiff 6 in* 2017. Two more ships are under construction, to debut in 2018 and 2019 as the new *Mein Schiff 1* and *Mein Schiff 2*, respectively – they will not be called *Mein Schiff 7* and *8*, as everyone in the industry expected. The original *1* and *2* will transfer out of the fleet as the new models are brought in.

Aboard all TUI Cruises ships, all cabins have an espresso machine, and there is a wide choice of dining venues and food styles, with an emphasis on healthy eating and high-quality ingredients. Much attention is placed on the extensive wellness facilities aboard the ships, which are all geared extensively to family cruising. Gratuities are included in the 'all-inclusive' fare, and the company provides many things that other cruise lines don't, making this an outstanding value-for-money, high-quality cruise line. In other words, TUI Cruises has got it absolutely right.

UnCruise Adventures

This micro-cruise line was founded in 1997 as American Safari Cruises. It was bought in 2008 by Inner-Sea Discoveries, owned by the former chief executive officer of American Safari Cruises, Dan Blanchard. It bought the website and database files of now-defunct Cruise West in order to expand its reach to small-ship enthusiasts, and has a fleet of very small motor yacht-type vessels for six to 86 passengers for expensive cruises in Alaska and the Pacific Northwest. While the vessels are decent, the onboard facilities are few, and the one-seat dining experience is quite casual. However, all beds onboard have Tempur-Pedic mattresses. The advantage of these intimate vessels is that they can take you up close to fascinating parts of Alaska that larger ships can't reach. InnerSea Discoveries changed its name to UnCruise Adventures in 2013. Gratuities are not included.

Venus Cruise

Founded in 1988, Venus Cruise, which was first known as Japan Cruise Line, is owned by four ferry companies: Shin Nihonkai Ferry, Kyowa Shoji, Hankyu Ferry, and Kanko Kisen. Its headquarters are in Osaka, Japan. As Japan Cruise Line, the company at first operated company and incentive charter cruises before branching out into cruises for individuals. The company caters exclusively to Japanese speakers and has a single ship, *Pacific Venus,* which offers cruises in the Asia-Pacific region as well domestic cruises in Japan. Gratuities are included in the cruise fare.

Viking Ocean Cruises

A sister to the long-established Viking River Cruises, this company aims to provide both ocean-going and river cruises to the same passengers and market segment – a unique approach in the cruise industry. The onboard product is aimed squarely at adults who want comfort and some elements of luxe, but no glitz, and at a price that includes many items other cruise lines charge extra for (such as shipwide Wi-Fi). This has proved to be a great success. Its chairman is Torstein Hagen, originally a major shareholder owner of the long-defunct but much-respected Royal Viking Line.

Staying away from large resort ships, the company ordered mid-size ships for 930 passengers. For the ships' size, they offer an impressive array of public rooms and dining options, and modern, uncluttered Scandinavian design. Itineraries are designed so that they stay longer in ports and include overnight stays at some ports, so that passengers can take in the nightlife and cultural attractions of some destinations. The first ship, *Viking Star*, debuted in spring 2015, *Viking Sea in 2016, and Viking Sky in* 2017; *Viking Sun* is scheduled for 2018, and *Viking Spirit* for 2020. The company has established a fine onboard product that seems well placed to grow further in the coming years.

Voyages to Antiquity

Founded in 2007 by Gerry Herrod, who formerly created the now-defunct Ocean Cruise Lines, the company has just one ship, *Aegean Odyssey*, painstakingly converted into a comfortable cruise ship with a fairly handsome profile. The cruises are aimed at British and American passengers who seek educational experiences. Gratuities to dining and housekeeping staff are included, as are most shore excursions and wines with lunch and dinner.

Windstar Cruises

Founded by New York-based Karl Andren in 1984 as Windstar Sail Cruises, the company built high-class sail-cruise ships with computer-controlled sails, outfitting them in a contemporary decor designed by Marc Held. The first ship, *Wind Star*, debuted in 1986 to great acclaim, and was followed by *Wind Spirit* (1988) and *Wind Surf* (1990).

Windstar Cruises was sold to Holland America Line in 1988. The company, with headquarters in Seattle, US, was sold again in 2007 to the Ambassadors Cruise Group, wholly owned by Ambassadors International. It was purchased again in 2011 by Xanterra Parks & Resorts.

In 2014, Windstar took delivery of the former *Seabourn Pride*, renamed *Star Pride,* and, in mid-2015, two more Seabourn ships – *Seabourn Legend* (now *Star Legend)*, and *Seabourn Spirit* (now *Star Breeze)*.

The style is casual and unregimented, but smart, with service by Indonesian and Filipino crew members. The ships carry a variety of water-sports equipment, accessed from a retractable stern platform. Itineraries include off-the-beaten-track ports not frequented by large resort ships. The onboard product is decidedly American ultra-casual, with unfussy bistro-style cuisine, and service that lacks the finesse and the small details that could make it a much better experience overall. Gratuities are not included in the fare.

The main pool on *Viking Star* when the roof is closed.

What To Do If ...

Some practical tips for a good cruise experience, and advice on what to do if you have a problem.

1. Your luggage does not arrive at the ship

If you booked as part of the cruise line's air/sea package, the airline is responsible for locating your luggage and delivering it to the next port. If you arranged your own air transportation, it is wholly *your* problem. Always have easy-to-read name and address tags *inside* as well as *outside* your luggage. Keep track of claim documents, and give the airline an itinerary and list of port agents.

2. You miss the ship

If you miss the ship's departure at the port of embarkation, and you are traveling on an air/sea package, the airline will arrange to get you to the ship, possibly at the next port of call. If you are traveling 'cruise-only,' however, then you are responsible for flights, hotel stays, and transfers.

It is up to you to get back to the ship before the appointed sailing time. Miss the ship and you'll need to get to its next port at your own cost. *Always* take a copy of your passport with you, just in case.

One answer to lack of storage space aboard *Queen Elizabeth*.

Ships have also been known to leave port early because of impending inclement weather conditions or natural disasters. If this happens, the ship's port agent will be there to assist you. Always take the port agent's name and telephone contact details with you.

3. Your cabin is too small

When you book a cruise, you pay for a certain category and cabin grade (low-cost cabins are usually not in good locations), and, generally, you get what you pay for in terms of size.

4. Your cabin has no air conditioning, it is noisy, or there are plumbing problems

If there is anything wrong in your cabin or bathroom, tell your cabin steward or go to the reception desk immediately. Some cabins are located above the ship's laundry, generator, or galley; others may be above the disco. If the ship is full, it will be difficult to change.

5. You have noisy cabin neighbors

First, politely tell your neighbors that you can hear them brushing their hair as the cabin walls are so thin, and would they please not slam the drawers shut at 2am! If that does not work, complain to the hotel manager (via the reception desk).

6. You have a problem with a crew member

Go to the reception desk and explain the problem. Insist on a full written report of the incident, which must be entered into the ship's daily log by the staff captain (deputy captain).

7. You don't like your dining room seating

Many ships operate two seatings for dinner. When you book your cruise, you choose whether you want the first or second seating. The line will make every attempt to please you. If you want second seating and are given first seating, there may be little the restaurant manager can do if the ship is full.

8. You want a table for two and are put at a table for eight

Explain why you are not satisfied to the restaurant manager, who should be able to resolve the situation.

9. You cannot communicate with your waiter

Dining room waiters might be of a nationality and language completely foreign to yours, with limited

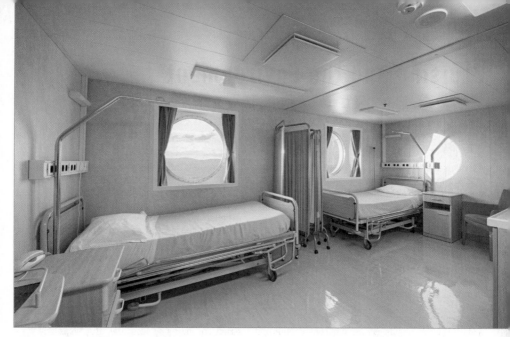

Part of the Medical Center aboard *MSC Musica*.

fluency in your language. This could prove frustrating for a whole cruise. See the restaurant manager, and tell him/her you want a waiter with whom you can communicate.

10. The food is definitely not the gourmet cuisine portrayed in the brochure

If the food is not as described (for example, whole lobster is shown in the brochure, but only cold lobster salad is provided once during the cruise, or the 'fresh squeezed' orange juice on the breakfast menu is anything but), inform the restaurant manager.

11. A large group has taken over the ship

Sometimes, large groups have pre-booked public rooms for meetings. Make your displeasure known to the hotel department immediately. If nothing is resolved, tell your booking agent, and write a follow-up letter to the line when you get home.

12. A port of call is deleted from the itinerary

Read the fine print in the brochure *before* you book. A cruise line is under no obligation to perform the stated itinerary. For whatever reason – political unrest, weather, mechanical problems, safety, etc. – the ship's captain has the ultimate say.

13. You leave personal belongings on a tour bus

If you find you've left something on a tour bus, tell the shore excursion staff. The tour operator will then be contacted to see whether any items have been handed in.

14. You are unwell aboard ship

There will be a qualified doctor (who generally operates as a concession). Medical facilities usually include a small pharmacy. Although there are charges for medical services, almost all cruise lines offer insurance packages that include medical coverage for most eventualities. It is wise to take out this insurance when you book.

15. The ship's laundry ruins your clothes

If any of your clothing is ruined or discolored by the ship's laundry, tell your cabin steward(ess) and register a complaint at the reception desk. Obtain a copy of the complaint, so you can follow up. Unfortunately, you will probably find a disclaimer on the laundry list stating that liability is limited to about $1 per item.

16. You have extra charges on your bill

Check your itemized bill carefully, then go to the reception and ask to be shown the charge slips. Make sure you get a copy of your bill *after* any modifications have been made.

17. You fly internationally to join your cruise

If your cruise begins a long way from your home, it makes sense to fly to your cruise departure point and stay overnight *before* your cruise. You will start the cruise refreshed and adjust better to any time changes.

18. You are unhappy with your cruise experience

If your ship delivers less well than the brochure promises, then let your booking agent and the cruise line know immediately.

Cruising and the Environment

The good: traveling by sea produces an estimated 36 times less carbon dioxide than flying. The bad: that's still not good enough.

Although marine vessels are responsible for almost 3 percent of the world's greenhouse gases, the world's fleet of around 350 oceangoing cruise ships produces just 0.1 percent of those emissions.

Eco diligence

Cruise companies are trying harder than ever to achieve an integrated, industry-wide approach to reduce pollution and noxious air emissions, provide more fuel-efficient ships, and retrofit older ships with more efficient equipment. New ships benefit from improved hydrodynamic hull design. Advanced hull coatings also improve efficiency. Careful handling of solid and liquid waste results in lower fuel consumption and CO_2 emissions. Flue gas from shipboard incinerators is recycled and wastewater treated according to tough eco-friendly standards. Energy recovery (waste-heat recovery) is also incorporated into new ships.

The result is a generous reduction in NOx – the term for a group of highly reactive gases, all of which contain nitrogen and oxygen in varying amounts. Since 2016, new ship engines have had to comply with stricter MARPOL Annex VI Tier III standards. This means using high-efficiency emissions control technology such as selective catalytic converters to further reduce NOx, and greater monitoring and computer control.

Europa 2 is the first cruise ship to be equipped with an SCR-catalytic converter, reducing nitrogen oxides (including nitrogen dioxide) by almost 95 percent. Aboard *Mein Schiff 3, 4, 5,* and *6,* using the combined exhaust after-treatment system – consisting of a scrubber and a catalyser – sulfur emissions were lowered by as much as 99 percent and nitrogen oxide emissions by around 75 percent. Other eco-friendly examples include *MSC Fantasia*-class ships, which use only low-sulfur fuels.

Some ship hulls are treated with 'foul release' paint with fluoropolymers or glass-flake vinyl ester resins – non-toxic substances that help reduce CO_2 emissions by using less fuel. But ships that have switched from heavy fuel oil to low-sulfur fuels have experienced greater fuel pump wear when switching over, thereby adding to maintenance, operational, and replacement costs.

Norwegian Breakaway, which debuted in 2013, was the first cruise ship to take advantage of MARPOL rule MEPC.1/Circ.642 – permitting the recovery and re-use of the HFO fraction of waste oil as fuel for the diesel engines. This is called 'scrubber' technology and is used by several cruise lines to meet the low sulfur emission requirements, effective in January 2015. The ship's waste oil separator system has only

Solar panels aboard *Celebrity Solstice*.

two moving parts and leaves only non-pumpable 'super-dry' solids for landing as dry waste. The separated water, with an oil content of less than 1,000ppm, is pumped to the bilge-water tank as part of an integrated waste oil and bilge-water handling system.

Other measures

Other eco-friendly measures include the use of LED lighting rather than fuel-guzzling halogen lighting and cabin lights and other electrical devices that function only when a cabin key card is in a card device inside the cabin. Motion-activated lighting in closets is now common, as is the replacement of single-use plastic cups by melamine and/or porcelain, the use of permanent dispensers instead of plastic single-use soap/shampoo packs, and the replacement of plastic laundry bags with re-washable cotton bags.

Water-flow reducers can be fitted to faucets (taps) and showers, and paper towels can be made from recycled paper. Using darkness-activated sensors that switch on the ship's external lights at dusk and chilled river rocks that retain low temperatures for buffet items, rather than ice, also helps. Then there are heat-deflecting window coatings and the latest wastewater treatment technology.

Emissions Control Areas

In 2009 the British Isles introduced the first Emissions Control Areas (ECA) around its shores and in the English Channel. They were followed by 10 countries in the Baltic and North Sea region. The International Maritime Organization (IMO) formally established a North American Emission Control Area in August 2012, an area ringing the US/Canada (including Alaska) coast with a 200-mile (320-km) exclusion zone. The IMO's global air emissions standards called for a progressive reduction of SOx – sulfur dioxide – emissions from 3.5 percent in January 2012, to 0.5 percent by January 2020, subject to a review to be completed by 2018.

When the North American Emission Control Area was implemented in August 2012, fuel costs rose 10 percent to 15 percent. When the sulfur limit dropped to 0.1 percent in January 2015 (under MARPOL Annex VI, Reg. 14), those costs rose again. At present, no technological solution exists.

Cold ironing

Plugging a ship into a land-based energy supply capable of running its essential functions while in port only makes sense in areas where electricity can be generated from renewable sources through a national grid, allowing a cruise ship to turn off its generators to reduce emissions.

LNG

Cruise ships are being built with the ability to use LNG (liquefied natural gas) fuel to avoid running the diesel generators in port. (It's worth noting, however, that LNG storage tanks require 3.5 times the space of conventional fuel tanks, so retrofitting existing ships is impractical.) An LNG-based power barge can generate and supply electricity while in port, reducing CO_2 emissions considerably, with almost no SOx, NOx, or particle emissions. This could be a better solution than 'bridge' (interim solution) technology cold ironing, in which power is simply generated in the normal manner and made available to a ship in port.

8 WAYS CRUISE LINES REDUCE THEIR WASTE

Cruise lines reduce their solid waste they generate by purchasing in bulk. Other examples include:

Advanced purification systems treating wastewater.

Ships actively recycleing glass, metals, wood, cardboard, and paper.

Excess heat generated in engine boilers being rerouted to power evaporators used in the process of turning sea water into potable water.

Special high-tech compacters processing garbage (the one aboard Queen Mary 2, for example, is four decks high).

Dry-cleaning machines using non-hazardous detergents formulated with soy, banana, and orange extracts.

Materials printed on board being produced using soy-based inks.

The only solid waste discharged to sea being food waste (considered safe because either animals consume it or natural elements break it down in the water). Some cruise lines use only seafood farmed from sustainable sources.

Ships offloading used cooking oil for recycling to bio-diesel.

WHAT IS MARPOL?

Short for 'Marine Pollution,' the International Convention for the Prevention of Pollution from Ships (MARPOL 73/78 – the dates refer to its adoption) is the convention to which all member countries of the UN specialized agency the International Maritime Organization (IMO) subscribe. It was designed to minimize pollution of the oceans and seas, including dumping, and pollution by oil and exhaust gases, whether by operational or accidental causes. The original MARPOL Convention was signed on February 17, 1973 and modified in 1978, but it did not come into force until October 2, 1983. Presently, some 146 countries, representing 99 percent of the world's shipping tonnage, are signatories to the Convention. Ships flagged under these countries are subject to its requirements, regardless of where they sail.

Cruising and Safety

How likely is an accident at sea? What if there's a fire? Can you fall overboard? How good are medical facilities aboard?

When Costa Cruises' 3,800-passenger *Costa Concordia* capsized off the coast of Tuscany in January 2012 with the loss of 32 lives, questions of safety at sea inevitably arose. But this tragedy was entirely avoidable: if *Costa Concordia*'s captain hadn't deviated from his computer-set course to sail too close to the island of Giglio, it could have been just another uneventful Mediterranean cruise. The company was so fortunate in its crew, who did a wonderful job of evacuating more than 3,000 passengers from the stricken ship, in what were rather chaotic circumstances.

Other losses over the past 25 years include *Jupiter* in 1988 and *Royal Pacific* in 1992, both following collisions; *Explorer*, which struck an iceberg near Antarctica in 2007; and *Sea Diamond*, which foundered on a reef off the Greek island of Santorini in 2007. Given that over 25 million people take a cruise every year, the number of serious incidents is considerably lower than one might expect. After 50 years of sea travel, during which I have experienced

Cabins are checked during a passenger emergency drill.

minor fires and groundings, I know that cruising remains one of the safest forms of transportation. Evacuations are, fortunately, rare events.

Safety measures

New safety procedures have been implemented since the *Costa Concordia* incident in 2012.

All cruise ships built after 2010 with a length of 394ft (120m) or greater, or with three or more main vertical zones, must have two engine rooms, so that if one is flooded or rendered unusable, a ship can safely return to port without requiring evacuation. This requirement came about because of the increasing size of today's cruise ships, and the fact that several ship fires and loss of propulsion/steering have occurred.

Other safety measures include muster drills, bridge procedures, life-jacket availability and location, lifeboat loading drills, recording of passenger nationalities for on-shore emergency-services personnel, and the securing of heavy objects.

International regulations require all crew to undergo basic safety training *before* being allowed to work aboard any cruise ship (on-the-job training is no longer enough). All safety regulations are governed by the international SOLAS Convention, introduced in 1914 in the aftermath of *Titanic*'s sinking in 1912. A mandatory passenger muster drill prior to departure from the port of embarkation is part of the SOLAS Convention. Passengers who don't attend may be disembarked prior to sailing.

All cruise ships built since 1986 must have either totally or partially enclosed lifeboats with diesel engines that can operate even if the lifeboat is inverted.

Since October 1997, cruise ships have had: all stairways enclosed as self-contained fire zones; smoke detectors and smoke alarms fitted in all passenger cabins and public spaces; low-level lighting showing routes of escape; all fire doors controllable from the ship's navigation bridge; all fire doors that can be opened from a remote location; and emergency alarms audible in all cabins.

Since 2002, all ocean-going cruise ships on international voyages now carry voyage data recorders (VDRs), similar to black boxes carried by aircraft, and, since October 2010, SOLAS regulations have prohibited the use of combustible materials in all new cruise ships.

Crew members attend frequent emergency drills, the lifeboat equipment is regularly tested,

Listening to information on safety during a passenger emergency drill.

and fire-detecting devices and alarm and fire-fighting systems are regularly checked. Any passengers spotting fire or smoke are encouraged to use the nearest fire alarm box, alert a member of staff, or contact the bridge.

Take a small flashlight, in case an emergency arises during a blackout or during the night. I have strongly recommended that all ships fit rechargeable flashlights under each passenger bed (a recommendation that was forwarded to the IMO).

Is security good enough?

Cruise lines are subject to stringent international security regulations. Passengers and crew can embark or disembark only by passing through a security checkpoint. Cruise ships maintain zero tolerance for crime or offenses against the person, and trained security professionals are employed aboard all cruise ships.

It is recommended that you keep your cabin locked at all times when you are not there. All new ships have encoded plastic key cards that operate a lock electronically; doors on older ships work with metal keys. Cruise lines do not accept responsibility for any money or valuables left in cabins and suggest that you store them in your in-cabin safe.

You will be issued with a personal boarding pass when you embark. This includes your photo, lifeboat station, restaurant seating, and other pertinent information, and must be shown at the gangway each time you board. You may also be asked for a government-issued photo ID, such as a passport.

Passenger lifeboat drill

A passenger lifeboat drill, announced publicly by the captain, is held for embarking passengers *before* the ship departs the port of embarkation. This rule was adopted by the global cruise industry following the *Costa Concordia* accident and improved on the existing SOLAS regulations, which required a drill to be held within 24 hours of departure.

Attendance is compulsory. Learn your boat station or assembly point and how to get to it in an emergency. Note your exit and escape pathways and learn how to put on your lifejacket correctly. The drill takes no more than 20 minutes and is a good investment – the 600-passenger *Royal Pacific* took fewer than 20 minutes to sink after its collision in 1992.

Assembly stations

An assembly station is where you assemble in an emergency, and is marked by a sign on the evacuation plan on the back of your cabin door. Follow the instructions of crew members, and remain calm. You will be provided with a lifejacket (and with children's lifejackets), if you do not already have one.

Can you accidentally fall overboard?

All cruise ships have railings at least 3ft 7in (1.1m) high to protect you and your children, so rest assured that instances of passengers falling overboard are extremely rare. However, it does occasionally happen, as reports in the press testify – usually the tragic result of reckless behavior.

Medical services

In general, all ships carrying over 50 passengers have medical facilities and at least one doctor. The standard of medical care and of the doctors themselves may vary from company to company. Most shipboard doctors are generalists; there are no cardiologists or neurosurgeons as part of the staff. Doctors are typically employed as outside contractors and charge for their services, including for seasickness shots.

Regrettably, some cruise lines make medical services a low priority, and most shipboard physicians are not certified in trauma treatment or medical evacuation procedures. However, some medical organizations, such as the American College of Emergency Physicians, have a special division for cruise medicine. Most ships catering to North American passengers carry doctors licensed in the US, Canada, or Britain, but doctors aboard many other ships come from a variety of countries and disciplines.

Medical facilities should include an examination room, isolation ward/bed, X-ray machine (to verify fractures), cardiac monitor (EKG) and defibrillator, oxygen-saturation monitor, external pacemaker, oxygen, suction and ventilators, hematology analyzer, culture incubator, and a mobile trolley intensive-care unit.

Existing health problems requiring treatment on board must be reported when you book. Aboard some ships, you may be charged for filling a prescription as well as for the cost of prescribed drugs. There may also be a charge if you have to cancel a shore excursion and need a doctor's letter to prove that you are ill.

Shipboard injury

Slipping, tripping, and falling are the major sources of shipboard injury. Here are some things you can do to minimize the chance of injury.

Aboard many ships, raised thresholds separate a cabin's bathroom from the sleeping area. Mind your step to avoid a stubbed toe or banged head.

Don't hang anything from the fire sprinkler heads on the cabin ceilings.

Fire drill aboard *Hanseatic*.

On older ships, note how the door lock works. In some cases, a key is required on the inside in order for the door to be unlocked. Leave the key in the lock, so that in the event of a real emergency, you don't have to hunt for it.

Aboard older ships, take care not to trip over raised thresholds in doorways leading to the open deck.

Walk with caution when the outer decks are wet. This applies especially to solid steel decks – falling on them is really painful.

Do not throw a lighted cigarette or cigar butt, or knock out your pipe, over the ship's side. They can easily be sucked into an opening in the ship's side or onto an aft open deck area and cause a fire.

Surviving a shipboard fire

Shipboard fires can generate an incredible amount of heat, smoke, and often panic. In the unlikely event that you are in one, try to remain calm and think logically and clearly.

When you first get to your cabin, check the way to the nearest emergency exits. Count the number of cabin doorways and other distinguishing features to the exits in case you have to escape without the benefit of lighting. All ships provide low location lighting systems.

Exit signs are normally located just above your head – this is virtually useless, as smoke and flames rise. Note the location of the nearest fire alarm and know how to use it in case of dense smoke. In future, it is likely that directional sound evacuation beacons will be mandated; these will direct passengers to exits, escape-ways, and other safe areas, and may be better than the present inadequate visual aids.

If you are in your cabin, and there is fire in the passageway outside, put on your lifejacket. If the cabin's door handle is hot, soak a towel in water and use it to turn the handle. If a fire is raging in the passage-

Testing lifeboats aboard *Voyager of the Seas*.

way, cover yourself in wet towels if you decide to go through the flames.

Check the passageway. If there are no flames, walk to the nearest emergency exit or stairway. If there is smoke in the passageway, crawl to the nearest exit. If the exit is blocked, go to an alternate one. It may take considerable effort to open a heavy fire door to the exit. Don't use the elevators.

If there's a fire in your cabin or on the balcony, report it immediately by telephone. Then get out of your cabin, close the door behind you, sound the alarm, and alert your neighbors.

SAFETY MEASURES

Fire control
If anyone sounds the fire alarm, a siren is automatically set off on the bridge. A red panel light will be illuminated on a large plan, indicating the section of the ship that has to be checked, so that the crew can take immediate action.

Ships are sectioned into several zones, each of which can be tightly closed off. In addition, almost all ships have a water-fed sprinkler system that can be activated at the touch of a button, or automatically activated when sprinkler vials are broken by fire-generated heat. New electronic fire-detection systems are being installed aboard ships in order to increase safety further.

Emergency ventilation control
This automatic fire-damper system also has a

manual switch that is activated to stop or control the flow of air to all areas of the ship, in this way reducing the fanning effect on flame and smoke via air-conditioning and fan systems.

Watertight doors
Throughout the ship watertight doors can be closed off, in order to contain the movement of water flooding the vessel. A master switch activates all the doors in a matter of seconds. All watertight doors can be operated electrically and manually, which means that nobody can be trapped in a watertight compartment.

Stabilizers
The ship's two stabilizing fins can be extended, housed, or controlled. They normally operate automatically under the command of a gyroscope located in the engine control room.

Britannia Restaurant aboard *Queen Elizabeth*.

How We Evaluate the Ships

Ships and their facilities count, but just as important are the standards relating to food, service, staff training, and hospitality. This section explains how the Berlitz points system works.

I have been evaluating and rating cruise ships and the onboard product professionally since 1980. I also receive reports from my small team of trained assessors. The Berlitz ratings are conducted with *total objectivity*, from a set of predetermined criteria, using a modus operandi designed to work across the entire spectrum of oceangoing cruise ships, in all segments of the business.

There really is no 'best cruise line in the world' or 'best cruise ship' – only the ship and cruise that is right for you. After all, it's the overall enjoyment of a cruise as a vacation that's important. Therefore, different criteria are applied to ships of different sizes, styles, and market segments throughout the world (vacationers of different nationalities look for different things).

The evaluation and rating of cruise ships is about as contrary to soccer as you can get. In soccer, the goalposts are always in the same place. But with cruise ships, they keep changing, as the industry evolves.

This section includes 300 oceangoing cruise ships in service (or due to enter service) and chosen by the author for inclusion when this book was completed. Note that ships launching in 2018 are not included, as the author will not have had the chance to review them. Almost all except the very latest ships have been carefully evaluated, taking into account up to 400 separate items based on personal cruises, visits, and revisits to ships. In the scoring room, these are channeled into 20 major areas, each with a possible 100 points. The maximum possible score for any ship is therefore 2,000 points.

For user-friendliness and reasons of space on the printed page, scores are further divided into five main sections: Ship, Accommodation, Food, Service, and Cruise Experience.

Cruise lines, ship owners, and operators should note that ratings may be adjusted annually as a result of increased competition, the introduction of newer ships with better facilities, and other market- or passenger-driven factors.

The ratings more reflect the standards of the cruise product (the software: the dining experience, the service, and the hospitality aspects of the cruise), and less the physical plant (the hardware). Thus, although a ship may be the latest, most stunning vessel in the world in terms of design and decor, if the 'software' and actual product delivery are not so good, the scores and ratings will reflect these aspects more clearly.

The stars beside the name of the ship at the top of each page indicate the 'Overall Rating.' The highest number of stars awarded is five stars (★★★★★+), and the lowest is one star. This system has been universally recognized throughout the global hospitality industry for over 30 years. A plus (+) indicates that a ship deserves just that little bit more than the number of stars attained. However, it is the number of points achieved rather than the number of stars attained that perhaps is more meaningful when comparing ships.

The star system
★★★★★+ 1,851–2,000 points
★★★★★ 1,701–1,850 points
★★★★+ 1,551–1,700 points
★★★★ 1,401–1,550 points
★★★+ 1,251–1,400 points
★★★ 1,101–1,250 points
★★+ 951–1,100 points
★★ 801–950 points
★+ 651–800 points
★ 501–650 points

Douglas Ward at work.

WHAT THE RATINGS MEAN

1,851–2,000 points ★★★★★+

You can expect an outstanding, top-class cruise experience – it doesn't get any better than this. It should be truly memorable, and with the highest attention to detail, finesse, and personal service – how important you are made to feel is critical. The decor must be elegant and tasteful, measured by restraint and not flashiness, with fresh flowers and other decorative touches in abundance. The layout of the public rooms might well follow *feng shui* principles.

Any ship with this rating must be just about unsurpassable in the cruise industry, and it has to be very, very special, with service and hospitality levels to match. There must be the highest-quality surroundings, comfort, and service levels, the finest and freshest quality foods, including all breads and rolls baked on board. Highly creative menus, regional cuisine, and dining alternatives should provide maximum choice and variety, and special orders will be part of the dining ritual.

Meals (particularly dinners) are expected to be memorable affairs, correctly served on the finest china, with a choice of wines of suitable character and vintage available, and served in the correct-sized sommelier glasses of the highest quality (Riedel or Schott).

The service staff will take pleasure in providing you with the ultimate personal, yet unobtrusive, attention with the utmost of finesse, and the word 'no' should not be in their vocabulary. This is the very best of the best in terms of refined living at sea, but it is seriously expensive.

1,701–1,850 points ★★★★★

You can expect a truly excellent, memorable cruise experience, with the finesse and attention to detail commensurate with the amount of money paid. The service and hospitality levels will be extremely high from all levels of officers and staff, with strong emphasis on fine hospitality training – all service personnel members must make you feel important.

The food will be at the high level expected from what is virtually the best possible at sea, with service that should be very attentive yet unobtrusive. The cuisine should be memorable, with ample taste. Special orders should never be a problem. There must be a varied selection of wines, which should be served in glasses of the correct size.

Entertainment is expected to be of prime quality and variety. Again, the word 'no' should not be in the vocabulary of any member of staff aboard a ship with this rating. Few things will cost extra on board, and brochures should be more 'truthful' than those for ships with a lower rating.

1,551–1,700 points ★★★★+

You can expect to have a high-quality cruise experience that will be memorable, and just a little short of being excellent in all aspects. Perhaps the personal service and attention to detail could be slightly better, but, nonetheless, this should prove to be a fine all-round cruise experience, in a setting that is extremely clean and comfortable, with few lines (queues) anywhere, a caring attitude from service personnel, and a good standard of entertainment that appeals to a mainstream market.

Balinese day beds aboard *Europa 2*.

The cuisine and service must be carefully balanced, with mostly fresh ingredients and varied menus that should appeal to almost anyone, all served on high-quality china.

This should prove to be an extremely well-rounded cruise experience, probably in a ship that is new or almost new. There will be fewer 'extra-cost' items than ships with a slightly lower rating.

1,401–1,550 points ★★★★

You can expect to have a very good-quality all-round cruise experience, most probably aboard a modern, highly comfortable ship that will provide a good range of facilities and services. The food and service will be quite decent overall, although decidedly not as 'gourmet' and fanciful as the brochures with the always-smiling faces might have you believe.

The service on board will be well organized, if a little robotic and impersonal at times, and only as good as the cruise line's training program allows. You may notice a lot of things cost extra once you are on board, although the typically vague brochure tells you that these things are 'available' or are an 'option.' However, you should have a good time, and your bank account will be only moderately damaged.

1,251–1,400 points ★★★+

You can expect to have a decent-quality cruise experience, aboard a ship where the service levels should be good, but perhaps without the finesse that could be expected from a more upscale environment. The crew aboard any ship achieving this score should reflect a positive attitude towards hospitality, and a willingness to accommodate your needs, up to a point. Staff training will probably be in need of more attention to detail and flexibility.

Food and service levels in the dining venues should be reasonably good, although special or unusual orders might prove more difficult to accommodate. There will probably be a number of extra-cost items you thought were included in the price of your cruise – although the brochure typically is vague and states that the things are 'available' or are an 'option.'

1,101–1,250 points ★★★

You can expect a reasonably decent, middle-of-the-road cruise experience, with a moderate amount of space and quality in furnishings, fixtures, and fittings. The cabins are likely to be a little on the small side. The food and service levels will be quite acceptable, although not at all memorable, and somewhat inflexible with regard to special orders, as almost everything is standardized.

The level of hospitality will be moderate but little more, and the entertainment will probably be weak. This is a good option, however, for those looking for the reasonable comforts of home without pretentious attitudes, and comparatively little damage to their bank statement.

951–1,100 points ★★+

You can expect an average cruise experience in terms of accommodation (typically with cabins that are dimensionally challenged), the quality of the ship's facilities, food, wine list, service, and hospitality levels, in surroundings that are unpretentious. In particular, the food and its service might be disappointing.

There will be little flexibility in the levels of service, hospitality, and staff training and supervision, which will be no better than poor in comparison with that of ships of a higher rating. Thus, the overall experience will be commensurate with the comparatively small amount of money you paid for the cruise.

801–950 points ★★

You can expect to have a cruise experience of modest quality aboard a ship that is probably in need of more attention to maintenance and service levels, not to mention hospitality. The food may be quite lacking in taste, homogenized, and of low quality, and service is likely to be mediocre at best. Staff training is likely to be minimal, and staff turnover may be high. The 'end-of-pier' entertainment could well leave you wanting to read a good book.

651–800 points ★+

You can expect to have only the most basic cruise experience, with little or no attention to detail, from a minimally trained staff that is probably paid low wages and to whom you are just another body. The ship will, in many cases, probably be in need of much maintenance and upgrading, and will probably have few facilities. Dismal entertainment is also likely. On the other hand, the price of a cruise of this rating will probably be alluringly low.

501–650 points ★

You can expect to have a cruise experience that is the bottom of the barrel, with little in terms of hospitality or finesse. Forget about attention to detail – there won't be any. This would equal a stay in the most basic motel on land, with few facilities, a poorly trained, seemingly uncaring staff, and a ship that needs better maintenance.

The low cost of a cruise aboard a ship with this rating should provide a strong clue to the complete absence of any quality, particularly for food, service, and entertainment. You might remember this cruise, but for all the wrong reasons.

Distribution of points

These are the percentage of the total points available that are allocated to each of the main areas evaluated:
The ship: 25 percent
Accommodation: 10 percent
Food: 20 percent
Service: 20 percent
Entertainment: 5 percent
The cruise experience: 20 percent

The categories 'Entertainment' (including lecturers and expedition staff) and 'The cruise experience' may be combined for boutique ships, tall ships, and expedition ships, and adjusted accordingly.

CRITERIA

The ship

Hardware/maintenance/safety. This score reflects the general profile and condition of the ship, its age, exterior paint, decking and caulking; swimming pool and surrounds; deck furniture; shore tenders; and lifeboats and other safety items. It also reflects interior cleanliness (public restrooms, elevators, floor and wall coverings, stairways, passageways, and doorways); food-preparation areas and refrigerators; and garbage handling, compacting, incineration, and waste-disposal facilities.

Outdoor facilities/space. This score reflects the overall open deck space; swimming pools/hot tubs and their surrounds; congestion; number and type of deck lounge chairs (with or without cushioned pads) and other deck furniture; sports facilities; shower enclosures; changing facilities; towels; and quiet (no music) areas.

Interior facilities/space/flow. This score reflects the use of interior public spaces; flow and congestion; ceiling height; lobby, stairways, and hallways; elevators; public restrooms and facilities; signage; lighting, air conditioning, and ventilation.

Decor/furnishings/artwork. This score reflects the overall interior decor and soft furnishings; carpeting (color, pattern, and practicality); chairs (comfort); ceilings and treatments; artwork (paintings, sculptures, and atrium centerpieces); and lighting.

Spa/fitness facilities. This score reflects the spa, wellness, and fitness facilities, including location, accessibility, lighting and flooring materials. Also: fitness machines and fitness programs; sports facilities and equipment; indoor pools; hot tubs; grand baths; hydrotherapy pools; saunas; steam rooms; treatment rooms; changing facilities; jogging and walking tracks; and open promenades.

Accommodation

Cabins: suites and cabins. This score reflects the design and layout, including 'private' balconies and partitions (whether full floor-to-ceiling partition or part partitions). Also: beds/berths, cabinetry, and other fittings; hanging and drawer space, and bedside tables; vanity unit, bathroom facilities, cabinets and other storage for toiletries; lighting, air conditioning, and ventilation; audio-visual facilities; artwork; insulation, noise, and vibration. Suites should not be so designated unless the bedroom is completely separated from the living area.

Also covers cabin service directory of services, interactive TV; paper, postcards, and personalized stationery; telephone information; laundry lists; tea- and coffee-making equipment; flowers; fruit; bathroom personal amenities kits, bathrobes, slippers, and the size and quality of towels.

Cuisine

Cruise lines put maximum emphasis on promising passengers how good their food will be, often to the point of overstatement. There are, of course, at least as many different tastes as there are passengers. As in any good restaurant, you generally get what you pay for.

Dining venues/cuisine. This score reflects the physical structure of dining rooms, layout, seating, and waiter stations; lighting and ambience; table setups; linen, china, and cutlery quality and condition. Also: menus, food quality, culinary creativity, appeal, taste, texture, presentation (garnishes and decorations); tableside cooking (if any); wine list; price range; and service. Alternative dining venues are also checked for menu variety, food and service, ambience, decor, seating, noise levels, china, cutlery, and glassware.

Casual eateries/buffets. This score reflects hot and cold display units and sneeze guards, 'active' stations, tongs and other serving utensils; food displays; temperatures; labeling; deck buffets; decorative elements; and staff communication.

Quality of ingredients. This score reflects taste, consistency, and portion size; grades of meat, fish, and fowl; and the price paid by the cruise line for food per passenger per day.

Tea/coffee/bar snacks. This score reflects the quality and variety of teas and coffees available, including afternoon teas/coffees and their presentation; whether mugs or cups and saucers are used; whether milk is served in the correct open containers or in sealed individual packets; whether self-service or served. It also reflects the quality of cakes, scones, and pastries, bar/lounge snacks, hot and cold canapés, and hors d'oeuvres.

Service

Dining rooms. This score reflects staff professionalism: the maître d'hôtel (restaurant manager), section headwaiters, waiters and assistants (busboys), sommeliers and wine waiters; place settings, cutlery, and glasses; and proper service (serving, taking from the correct side), communication skills, attitude, flair, uniform, appearance, and finesse. Waiters should note whether passengers are right- or left-handed and, when tables are assigned, make sure that cutlery and glasses are placed on the side of preference.

Bars. This score reflects lighting and ambience; seating; noise levels; communication skills; the staff's attitude, personality, and service finesse.

Cabins. This score reflects the cleaning and housekeeping staff, butlers (for top suite passengers), supervisory staff, attention to detail and cleanliness; bedding and bathrobe changes, and language and communication skills.

Balcony cabins at the aft (back) of *Costa Serena*.

Open decks. This score reflects the service for beverages and food items; placement and replacement of towels on deck lounge chairs, and tidiness of any associated deck equipment.

Entertainment

The score reflects the overall entertainment program and its appeal. Also: the physical venue (stage/bandstand); technical support, lighting, backdrop; sound systems; recorded tracks and special effects; production shows (story, plot, cohesion, costumes, quality, choreography, and vocal content); cabaret acts; and bands and solo musicians.

Aboard specialist ships such as those offering expedition cruises, or tall ships (sailing ships such as *Sea Cloud*), where entertainment is not a feature, it relates to the lecture program, library, movies on demand, videos, and use of water-sports items such as jet skis, windsurfers, kayaks, and snorkeling gear, etc.

The cruise experience

Activities program. This score reflects social activities and events; cruise director and staff (visibility and professionalism); special-interest programs; port, shopping, and enrichment lecturers; water-sports equipment, instruction, staff supervision, marina or retractable water-sports platforms, and any enclosed swimming area.

Movies/television program. This score reflects movies in theaters and at poolside screens; picture and sound quality; in-cabin infotainment system, and audio channels.

Hospitality factor. This score reflects the hospitality and professionalism of officers, middle management, cruise staff, and crew; appearance; and communication skills.

Overall product delivery. This score reflects the quality of the overall cruise as a vacation – what the brochure states and promises, and what is delivered

Notes on the rating results

Ship evaluations and ratings have become ever more complex. Although a ship may be the newest, with all the latest facilities, it is the food and service that often disappoint, as well as security lines and issues relating to signing up for activities.

Cruise companies state that food quality is a trade-off against lower prices. However, this implies a downward spiral that affects food quality, service, personnel, training, safety, and maintenance.

Finally, it is the little things that add to points lost on the great scorecard.

What the Descriptions Mean

Each of the following ship reviews is preceded by a panel providing basic data on the ship's size and facilities. Here we explain how to interpret the categories.

Ship size (based on lower bed capacity)

Large resort ship: 2,501–6,500 passengers
Mid-size ship: 751–2,500 passengers
Small ship: 251–750 passengers
Boutique ship: 50–250 passengers

Cruise line

The cruise and the operator may be different if the company that owns the vessel does not routinely market and operate it. Tour operators often charter ships for their exclusive use (for example Thomson Cruises).

Entered service

Where two dates are given, the first is for the ship's maiden (paid) passenger voyage, and the second is the date it began service for the current operator.

Propulsion

The type of propulsion is given (gas turbine, diesel, diesel-electric, or nuclear). The second half denotes the number of propellers or fixed or azimuthing pods.

The favored drivers are eco-friendly diesel-electric or diesel-mechanical propulsion systems that propel ships at speeds of up to 28 knots (32mph). Only Cunard, QM2, with a top speed of more than 30 knots (34.5mph), is faster. LNG-powered ships will debut in 2019.

More than 70 cruise ships are now fitted with the pod propulsion system, first introduced in 1990. It resembles a huge outboard motor fitted below the waterline. It replaces the long-used conventional rudder, shaft, and propeller mechanisms, saves valuable machinery space, and makes stern thrusters redundant.

Royal Caribbean International's *Harmony of the Seas*, the world's largest cruise ship, sails into Southampton, UK.

Lines are inevitable aboard large resort ships.

Pods are compact, self-contained units powered by internal electric propulsion motors. They are turned by the hydraulic motors of the steering gear, and can turn through 360 degrees (azimuthing). This allows even the largest ships to maneuver into tight spaces without help from tugs.

Most ships have two pods, although some have three (*Allure of the Seas*, *Harmony of the Seas*, *Oasis of the Seas*, *Symphony of the Seas*) or even four units (*Queen Mary 2*). Each pod weighs about 170 tons, but the four pods attached to *Queen Mary 2* weigh 250 tons each – more than an empty Boeing 747 jumbo jet; two are fixed, two are of the azimuthing variety. Ships with pod propulsion systems have no noticeable vibration or engine noise aft, unlike ships with conventional propulsion systems.

Some ships have 'Becker' rudders, which is where the main body has a hinged, second part. This second, or aft, section can be pointed in a different direction from the main body; the result is more control over the waterflow.

Passenger capacity

This is based on two lower beds per cabin, including cabins for solo occupancy.

Passenger space ratio (gross tonnage per passenger)

Achieved by dividing the gross tonnage by the number of passengers (lower bed capacity including solo-occupancy cabins).

Passenger to crew ratio

Achieved by dividing the number of (lower-bed) passengers by the number of crew.

Cabin size range

From the smallest cabin to the largest suite (including 'private' balconies), in square feet and square meters and rounded up to the nearest whole number.

Wheelchair-accessible ratings

Cabins designed to accommodate the mobility-limited. There are four accessibility ratings:
Best. This ship is recommended as most suitable for wheelchair passengers.
Good. Reasonably accessible.
Fair. Just about accessible.
None. The ship is not suitable.

About prices

Please note that any price examples given throughout the ship reviews are provided *only* as a guideline and may have changed since publication. Always check with the cruise company, the onboard concession, or your travel booking agent for the latest prices.

The Star Performers

Having reviewed the following 300 cruise ships, Berlitz names the top-rated ships in their size categories for 2018.

Despite constant claims by cruise companies that their ship has been named 'Best Cruise Line' or 'Best Cruise Ship' by this or that magazine or online readers' poll, there really is no such thing – there is only the ship that is right for you. Few operators can really deliver a ship, product, and crew worthy of the highest Berlitz star rating – it's all about excellence, and passion.

For this 2018 edition, just two ships have again achieved the score required for them to be awarded membership in the most exclusive 'five-stars-plus' category:

 *Europa 2*

Hapag-Lloyd Cruises

1,863 points   ★★★★★+

 *Europa*

Hapag-Lloyd Cruises

1,852 points   ★★★★★+

These are both beautiful ships to sail aboard, with an outstanding amount of space per passenger, passageways with high ceilings, a superb range of dining venues and types of cuisine, and attentive, friendly, yet unobtrusive personal service.

However, *Europa* and *Europa 2* really are exclusive, high-priced ships, so we have also included a selection of best cruise ships (sister ships, in some cases, where they are close to identical) in a number of categories, with the winners and runners-up denoted by the star category (listed in order of points scored overall, with the highest-scoring ships first). Entries are listed according their Berlitz score, where applicable, or else in alphabetical order by cruise line or ship's name.

Europa 2's layout.

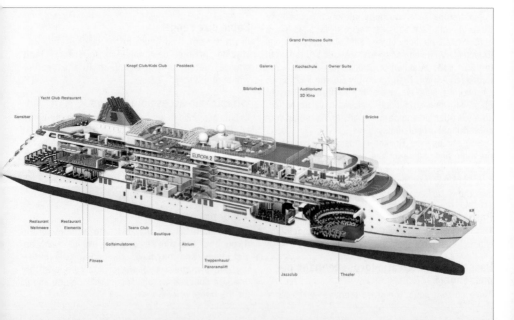

AND THE WINNER IS...

THE TOP 10 LARGE RESORT SHIPS

(2,501–6,500 passengers)

Queen Mary 2. Part transatlantic ocean liner, part cruise ship, this iconic vessel has something for all ages.

Queen Mary 2	**1683** out of 2000	★★★★+
Mein Schiff 6	**1661** out of 2000	★★★★+
Mein Schiff 5	**1659** out of 2000	★★★★+
Mein Schiff 4	**1649** out of 2000	★★★★+
Mein Schiff 3	**1647** out of 2000	★★★★+
Genting Dream	**1585** out of 2000	★★★★+
MSC Meraviglia	**1585** out of 2000	★★★★+
MSC Preziosa	**1548** out of 2000	★★★★
MSC Divina	**1544** out of 2000	★★★★
MSC Fantasia	**1536** out of 2000	★★★★

AND THE WINNER IS...
THE TOP 10 MID-SIZE SHIPS
(751–2,500 passengers)

Viking's premium ships have many elegant touches; enjoy the touchy-feely comforts of home, Nordic history, excellent inclusive value, and unfussy cuisine.

Viking Sun	**1693** out of 2000	★★★★+
Viking Sea	**1692** out of 2000	★★★★+
Viking Sky	**1692** out of 2000	★★★★+
Viking Star	**1692** out of 2000	★★★★+
Crystal Serenity	**1686** out of 2000	★★★★+
Crystal Symphony	**1677** out of 2000	★★★★+
Asuka II	**1662** out of 2000	★★★★+
Riviera	**1601** out of 2000	★★★★+
Marina	**1587** out of 2000	★★★★+
Queen Elizabeth	**1572** out of 2000	★★★★+

AND THE WINNER IS...

THE TOP 10 SMALL SHIPS

(251–750 passengers)

Europa 2. The world's highest scoring ship overflows with contemporary interior design, style, and finesse in food and service for sophisticated international travelers.

Europa 2	**1863** out of 2000	★★★★★+
Europa	**1852** out of 2000	★★★★★+
Silver Muse	**1684** out of 2000	★★★★+
Silver Spirit	**1639** out of 2000	★★★★+
Seabourn Encore	**1633** out of 2000	★★★★+
Seabourn Quest	**1633** out of 2000	★★★★+
Seabourn Odyssey	**1630** out of 2000	★★★★+
Seabourn Sojourn	**1628** out of 2000	★★★★+
Seven Seas Explorer	**1617** out of 2000	★★★★+
Silver Shadow	**1606** out of 2000	★★★★+

AND THE WINNER IS...
THE TOP 10 BOUTIQUE SHIPS
(50–250 passengers)

Hanseatic. This specialist expedition ship is able to combine discovery and exploration with a high degree of comfort, excellent food and service, and some outstanding expedition leaders and lecturers.

Hanseatic	**1716** out of 2000	★★★★★
SeaDream I	**1706** out of 2000	★★★★★
Sea Cloud	**1702** out of 2000	★★★★★
Sea Cloud II	**1701** out of 2000	★★★★★
SeaDream II	**1701** out of 2000	★★★★★
Hebridean Princess	**1669** out of 2000	★★★★+
Caledonian Sky	**1587** out of 2000	★★★★+
Island Sky	**1561** out of 2000	★★★★+
Le Lyrial	**1534** out of 2000	★★★★
Royal Clipper	**1531** out of 2000	★★★★

ADONIA
★★★+

THIS SMALL SHIP IS FOR ADULT-ONLY CRUISING AND IS WELL SUITED TO BRITISH TASTES

Size:	Small Ship	Passenger/Crew Ratio (lower beds):	1.8
Tonnage:	30,277	Cabins (total):	355
Cruise Line:	P&O Cruises	Size Range (sq ft/m):	145.3–968.7/13.5–90.0
Former Names:	Royal Princess, Minerva II, R8	Cabins (for one person):	0
Builder:	Chantiers de l'Atlantique (France)	Cabins with balcony:	258
Entered Service:	Feb 2001/Apr 2017	Cabins (wheelchair accessible):	4
Length (ft/m):	592.0/180.4	Wheelchair accessibility:	Good
Beam (ft/m):	83.5/25.4	Elevators:	4
Propulsion/Propellers:	diesel/2	Casino (gaming tables):	No
Passenger Decks:	9	Swimming Pools:	1
Total Crew:	300	Self-Service Launderette:	Yes
Passengers (lower beds):	710	Library:	Yes
Passenger Space Ratio (lower beds):	42.6	Onboard currency:	UK£

THE SHIP. The ship has an all-white hull and superstructure. There's no walk-around promenade deck, although you can stroll on open decks on the port and starboard sides. The lido (pool) deck has reasonable sunbathing space. Sadly, there are no wooden decks outdoors; they are covered by a sand-colored rubberized material instead.

There may not be marble bathroom fittings or other expensive niceties, but *Adonia* is a pleasant ship, best suited to British couples.

Last in a series of eight almost identical ships originally built for the long-defunct Renaissance Cruises in 2001, *Adonia* is well proportioned, and has the feel of an informal country hotel. The interior decor, designed by Scotsman John McNeece, is a throwback to the heavy hardwood style of the ocean liners of the 1920s and 1930s. It includes detailed ceiling cornices, real and faux wrought-iron staircase railings, wood- and leather-paneled walls, and trompe l'oeil ceilings.

Public rooms are spread over three decks. The reception hall has a staircase with intricate, real wrought-iron railings (a copy of the staircase aboard SS *Titanic*), but these are cleverly painted on plexiglas panels on the stairways on other decks.

Anderson's, the social hub of the ship, is a rather delightful, wood-paneled lounge with a fireplace, a long bar with bar stools, and the feel of a traditional country club.

BERLITZ'S RATINGS		
	Possible	Achieved
Ship	500	341
Accommodation	200	136
Food	400	222
Service	400	256
Entertainment	100	63
Cruise Experience	400	247

OVERALL SCORE 1265 points out of 2000

The Library is a delightful, restful room, designed in the Regency style. It has a fireplace, a high, indented trompe l'oeil ceiling, books, plus comfortable wingback chairs with footstools, and sofas to fall asleep on.

A Crow's Nest Lounge has great views through floor-to-ceiling windows, and comfortable seating. A long bar faces forward, which gives the bartenders the best view. There is a small central bandstand and wooden dance floor forward of the bar.

Although children over eight are allowed on board, there are almost no facilities for them. The ship is staffed and operated by P&O Cruises.

ACCOMMODATION. There are six basic cabin size categories, in many price categories. Some cabins have interconnecting doors, and 18 cabins on Deck 6 have lifeboat-obstructed views. All grades have tea/coffee-making facilities. There are two interior accommodation passageways.

Standard outside-view and interior cabins are compact units, and tight for two. They have twin or queen-size beds, with good under-bed storage, personal safe, a vanity desk with large mirror, and reasonable closet and drawer storage in rich, dark woods.

Balcony cabins have sliding glass doors. Some 14 cabins on Deck 6 have lifeboat-obstructed views. The tiled-floor, plain wall bathrooms are compact, but include a shower stall with a removable hand-held shower unit, wall-mounted hairdryer, cotton towels, toiletries storage shelves, and retractable clothesline.

Six Owner's Suites and four Master Suites provide abundant space and are worth the extra cost. They are located in the forward and aft positions. Particularly nice are those overlooking the stern, on decks 6, 7, and 8. They have extensive balconies that cannot be overlooked. There is an entrance foyer, living room, bedroom (the bed faces the sea), audio unit, bathroom with Jacuzzi tub, and small guest bathroom.

DINING. There are three restaurants, plus a casual self-serve buffet-style venue and an outdoor grill: the Pacific Restaurant, in the aft section, has 338 seats, a raised central section, large ocean-view windows on three sides, and several prime tables overlook the stern. Dining is at assigned tables, in two seatings. The noise level can be high, the result of a single-deck-height ceiling and noisy waiter stations. Curries and other Indian-style dishes are heavily featured, but, overall, the cuisine is just so-so. Adjacent to the restaurant entrance (it forms part of it) is a Club Bar – a cozy, open lounge and bar, with a fireplace.

An L-shaped Ocean Grill has ocean-view windows along one side, and aft. There is a cover charge, and reservations are required.

The Glass House features light, trendy fare, with wine and food pairings by TV personality (and wine expert) Olly Smith – but there's not a decanter in sight.

The Conservatory, with indoor and outdoor seating, is a casual self-serve eatery, while a Poolside Grill is for casual fast food and grilled food items.

ENTERTAINMENT. The Curzon Lounge is a single-level room, with a large bar at the back (the bartender probably has the best views of the stage).

SPA/FITNESS. The Oasis Spa has a fitness room with some muscle-toning equipment, a large hot tub, steam rooms for men and women (but no saunas), treatment rooms, and a beauty salon. A spa concession provides beauty and wellness treatments and exercise classes – some of which may cost extra. On deck are a small swimming pool, two hot tubs, a jogging track, a golf practice net, and shuffleboard courts.

ADVENTURE OF THE SEAS
★★★+

A LARGE SHIP THAT'S BIG ON THINGS TO DO FOR THE WHOLE FAMILY

Size:	Large Resort Ship	Passenger/Crew Ratio (lower beds):	2.7
Tonnage:	137,276	Cabins (total):	1,262
Cruise Line:	Royal Caribbean International	Size Range (sq ft/m):	151.0–1,358.0/14.0–126.1
Former Names:	none	Cabins (for one person):	5
Builder:	Kvaerner Masa-Yards (Finland)	Cabins with balcony:	765
Entered Service:	Nov 2001	Cabins (wheelchair accessible):	26
Length (ft/m):	1,020.6/311.1	Wheelchair accessibility:	Best
Beam (ft/m):	155.5/47.4	Elevators:	14
Propulsion/Propellers:	diesel-electric (75,600kW)/	Casino (gaming tables):	Yes
	3 pods (2 azimuthing, 1 fixed)	Swimming Pools:	3
Passenger Decks:	14	Self-Service Launderette:	No
Total Crew:	1,185	Library:	Yes
Passengers (lower beds):	3,119	Onboard currency:	US$
Passenger Space Ratio (lower beds):	41.4		

THE SHIP. *Adventure of the Seas* (a Voyager-class ship) is a large, floating leisure resort that provides a host of facilities, rather like a small town, yet offers a healthy amount of space per passenger. Outdoor decks have many water park-style activities.

A four-deck-high Royal Promenade (long atrium) is the main interior social and focal point. The length of two American football fields, it rises through 11 decks at both ends. Cafés, shops, and entertainment locations front this winding street and interior 'with-view' bay window cabins look into it from above.

It houses a 'traditional' pub, a Champagne Bar, a Sidewalk Café (for Continental breakfast, all-day pizzas, specialty coffees, and desserts), Sprinkles (for round-the-clock ice cream and yogurt), a sports bar, and several shops – for jewelry, gifts, liquor, cosmetics, and souvenirs. Comedy art has its place here, too, for example in the trompe l'oeil painter climbing up the walls.

Arched across the promenade is a captain's balcony, and in the center of the promenade a stairway connects you to the deck below, with a Schooner Bar (a piano lounge common to all Royal Caribbean International ships) and a flashy Casino Royale, with gaming tables and 300 slot machines.

Other facilities include a regulation-size ice-skating rink (Studio B), with real ice, with 'bleacher' seating for up to 900 and broadcast facilities, and a

BERLITZ'S RATINGS

	Possible	Achieved
Ship	500	366
Accommodation	200	141
Food	400	222
Service	400	268
Entertainment	100	76
Cruise Experience	400	264

OVERALL SCORE 1337 points out of 2000

pleasant two-deck library, open 24 hours a day.

Drinking places include an intimate Champagne Bar and Crown & Anchor Pub. Jazz lovers might like Blue Moon, an intimate room for cool music atop the ship in the Viking Crown Lounge.

Facilities for children and teenagers (in four age groupings) are good and include Adventure Beach, an activity area for all the family with swimming pools, a water slide, and outdoor games areas.

Overall, this is a fine all-round ship for all age groups, but be aware of the extra cost for many optional items (including drinks, drink packages, and excursions).

In late 2017, the ship underwent an extensive $61 million refurbishment, with new cabins added (but no extra elevators), plus dual racer waterslides (Cyclone and Typhoon), a FlowRider surf simulator, Splashaway Bay (children's aqua park), and Chops Grille.

ACCOMMODATION. There is a wide range of cabin price grades, including: interior (no-view) cabins, balcony cabins, and suites. Many cabins are of a similar size, which is good for incentives and large groups, and 300 have interconnecting doors (good for families).

Standard outside-view and interior cabins are of a reasonably adequate size, with just enough facilities to make them comfortable and functional. Twin lower beds convert to queen-size beds, and there is a reasonable amount of closet and drawer space, but the beds take up most of the floor space. Bathrooms are small but functional; shower enclosures are dimensionally challenged, and there is no cabinet for personal toiletries.

Balcony decking is Bolidt – a sort of rubberized sand – and a wood balcony rail. If you have a cabin with a connecting door to another cabin, be aware that you may be able to hear your next-door neighbors. Bathroom toilets are the noisy vacuum type, cabin bath towels are small and skimpy, and room service food menus are simply basic.

Some 138 interior cabins have bay windows with views into the interior Royal Promenade horizontal atrium – a cruise industry first when the ship originally debuted.

Regardless of what cabin grade you choose, all (except for the Royal and Owner's Suites) have twin- or queen-sized beds, infotainment system, telephone, safe, vanity unit, hairdryer, and bathroom. At around 1,146 sq ft (106 sq m), the Royal Suite is the largest private living space, located almost at the top of the Centrum lobby on the port side of Deck 10.

Royal Family Suites. Each of the four Royal Family Suites (two aft on Deck 9, two aft on Deck 8) measures around 574 sq ft/53 sq m.

Owner's Suites. Ten desirable Owner's Suites measuring around 468 sq ft (43 sq m) are in the center of the ship, adjacent to the Centrum lobby on Deck 10.

DINING. The main dining room seats 1,919, on three levels, each named after a famous composer: Mozart, Strauss, and Vivaldi. All share the same menu. A dramatic staircase connects all three levels, and huge, thick support pillars obstruct sight lines from a number of seats.

Two small wings serve private groups: La Cetra and La Notte, each with 58 seats. The place settings, china, and cutlery are of good quality.

'My Time Dining' means choosing either a fixed dining time or any time you want (during opening hours). Main dining room cuisine is all about standardized banquet catering and batch cooking. Menu descriptions sound tempting, but the food, although prepared well enough, is just so-so. Green vegetables are scarce – they're provided basically for decoration – but salad items are plentiful, and the desserts are pretty good. Rice is often used as a source of carbohydrates. Breads and pastry items are reasonably decent (these are thawed and then baked from frozen 'starter' dough), although items such as croissants lack any hint of butter.

Chops Grille (newly added in 2017) is for premium-quality steaks and seafood in a modern bistro-style setting.

Giovanni's Table serves Euro-Italian cuisine. It's open for dinner only, reservations are required, and there's a cover charge.

Casual meals can be taken at:

Windjammer Café: this is a large venue for casual buffet-style, self-help breakfast (this tends to be the busiest time of the day), lunch, and light dinners; it's often difficult to find a table, and, by the time you do, your food could be cold.

Island Grill (inside the Windjammer Café) is for casual dinner (no reservations needed), with a grill and open kitchen.

Johnny Rockets, a retro 1950s all-day, all-night diner-style eatery, has hamburgers, extra-cost malt shakes, and jukebox hits, with both indoor and outdoor seating.

Promenade Café: for Continental breakfast, all-day pizzas, and specialty coffees – provided in paper cups.

ENTERTAINMENT. The 1,350-seat Lyric Theater is a stunning showlounge located forward. It has Art Nouveau-themed decor and spans five decks, with only a few slim pillars and almost no disruption of sight lines. Production shows are presented here by a large cast and live band.

SPA/FITNESS. The ShipShape health spa is reasonably large, and measures 15,000 sq ft (1,400 sq m). It includes an aerobics room, fitness center with muscle-training equipment, treatment rooms, and men's and women's sauna/steam rooms. Another 10,000 sq ft (930 sq m) of space is devoted to a Solarium (with sliding glass-dome roof).

Aft of the funnel is a 32.8ft (10m) rock-climbing wall, with five climbing tracks. Other sports facilities include FlowRider surf simulator, The Perfect Storm (dual waterslides), a full-size basketball court, and a nine-hole, par 26 golf 'course' (Adventure Dunes).

AEGEAN ODYSSEY
★★★+

CULTURAL EXPLORATION AND LEARNING ARE THE BIG DRAW FOR THIS SHIP

Size:	Small Ship	Passenger/Crew Ratio (lower beds):	1.8
Tonnage:	12,094	Cabins (total):	216
Cruise Line:	Voyages to Antiquity	Size Range (sq ft/m):	130.0–550.0/12.0–51.0
Former Names:	Aegean I, Aegean Dolphin,	Cabins (for one person):	26
	Dolphin, Ålkyon, Narcis	Cabins with balcony:	42
Builder:	Santierul N. Galatz (Romania)	Cabins (wheelchair accessible):	2
Entered Service:	1972/May 2010	Wheelchair accessibility:	Fair
Length (ft/m):	460.9/140.5	Elevators:	2
Beam (ft/m):	67.2/20.5	Casino (gaming tables):	No
Propulsion/Propellers:	diesel (10,296kW)/2	Swimming Pools:	1
Passenger Decks:	8	Self-Service Launderette:	No
Total Crew:	200	Library:	Yes
Passengers (lower beds):	408	Onboard currency:	US$
Passenger Space Ratio (lower beds):	29.6		

THE SHIP. This is not a new ship by any stretch of the imagination, but it was tastefully and skillfully converted to provide an extremely comfortable environment. Its profile is quite smart, with a well-shaped funnel that balances a rather angular stern – the result of a $26 million 'chop-and-stretch' operation some years ago. The present operator, Voyages to Antiquity, bought the ship in December 2007, then set about a painstaking refit and refurbishment program that ended up more like a complete rebuild, because the ship now looks much nicer, and has a pleasing profile.

Originally built to carry munitions, the ship's hull is strong. The passenger capacity was significantly reduced – from 650 to 378, with a subsequent increase in the passenger/space ratio – in a well-conceived conversion. As a result, the open deck space, covered in teak, is extremely good, and measures 37,674 sq ft (3,500 sq m) – a lot for a small ship.

The Promenade Deck houses most of the public rooms. There is a forward observation lounge, with many windows providing plenty of natural light. The Charleston Lounge – actually a large lounge with a large dance floor and bar – is quite stunning, and sports a classy black and red decor. The ship also has a good-size library.

Some materials in public rooms are held together by the 'patch-and-fix' method, but subtle, pleasing, warm color combinations – most with earth tones – help to create a spacious, light, and open feel.

BERLITZ'S RATINGS

	Possible	Achieved
Ship	500	313
Accommodation	200	130
Food	400	261
Service	400	273
Entertainment	100	58
Cruise Experience	400	249

OVERALL SCORE 1284 points out of 2000

Gratuities to dining and cabin staff are included in the fare, together with selected wines with dinner (or beer/soft drinks); for non-included drinks, a 12.5 percent service charge is added to bar accounts. Most shore excursions are also included (together with bottled mineral water for the included excursions).

Despite the shakes and rattles of the ship's interior fittings when going at maximum speed, it's the character of the ship, its generous open deck space (and gorgeous thick, highly polished handrails), and an excellent lecture and enrichment program that all help to nudge the final score higher than one might normally expect for a 1970s-built ship.

Aegean Odyssey will appeal to couples and solo travelers looking for a life-enrichment experience in a smart yet somewhat traditional classic ship environment. The credo is based on history, ancient civilizations, and learning, and the main appeal is the quality of the excursions and lecturers.

ACCOMMODATION. There are now many different cabin price grades (six of which are for solo-occupancy cabins), with about half designated as Balcony Class. The accommodation numbering system is nautically incorrect, however, with even-numbered cabins on the starboard side instead of on the port, or left, side of the ship, although the lifeboat numbering is correct. Most cabins have an outside view, with similar sizes and configuration. All have a small refrigerator.

They are reasonably spacious, considering the ship's size, and pleasantly decorated, although closet, drawer, and luggage storage space for two is limited in the lower-grade cabins, particularly for longer cruises. Most bathrooms are partly tiled, with decent storage space for toiletries.

Solo travelers have a choice of 36 single-occupancy cabins (in 6 different grades), most of which are quite spacious.

Two Owner's Suites are located forward on Sun Deck. These are rather nice and have forward ocean views over the bow, and include a narrow balcony on either the port or starboard side. They have a separate bedroom, a walk-in closet, and a bathroom with a tub-shower combination.

DINING. The Marco Polo Restaurant is the main dining room. It is located on the lowest passenger deck (so it's very stable when the ship is at sea). It has a restful color scheme, and a high ceiling. Seating is mostly at large tables – there are no tables for two – in an open-seating arrangement that allows you to dine when you want and with whom you want. The amount of space around each table is good. Port-

holes, rather than windows, are set high up on both sides, and allow some natural light in during the day.

The cuisine is Continental, but the selection of breads, cheeses, and fruit is limited. Meats, fish, and poultry items are not of a high quality, although they are decent enough. For casual meals, self-serve breakfast and lunch buffets are available at the Terrace Café, with indoor-outdoor seating that includes a Tapas Bar each evening ('Tapas on the Terrace'), and daily grilled specialties.

ENTERTAINMENT. The Ambassador Lounge is a single-level showlounge that has a bar at one end, and seating that is mainly in tub-style chairs or old-style banquette seating. The sight lines to the 'stage' from many seats are obstructed, however, because of several support pillars. This room principally serves as a presentation room for the specialist lecturers, and for classical concerts.

SPA/FITNESS. A new indoor wellness centre was built in 2012. It is an attractive facility, and includes a separate men's sauna, women's wet sauna (steam 'pods'), and a changing area for men and women, two body-treatment rooms, plus a beauty salon, and a good-size fitness area.

AIDAAURA
★★★+

THIS UPBEAT, FAMILY-FRIENDLY SHIP IS FOR CASUAL, NO-FRILLS CRUISING

Size:	Mid-size Ship	Passenger/Crew Ratio (lower beds):	3.0
Tonnage:	42,289	Cabins (total):	633
Cruise Line:	AIDA Cruises	Size Range (sq ft/m):	145.3–344.4/13.5–32.0
Former Names:	none	Cabins (for one person):	0
Builder:	Aker MTW (Germany)	Cabins with balcony:	60
Entered Service:	Apr 2003	Cabins (wheelchair accessible):	4
Length (ft/m):	665.5/202.8	Wheelchair accessibility:	Good
Beam (ft/m):	92.2/28.1	Elevators:	6
Propulsion/Propellers:	diesel-electric (27,150kW)/2	Casino (gaming tables):	No
Passenger Decks:	10	Swimming Pools:	2
Total Crew:	389	Self-Service Launderette:	Yes
Passengers (lower beds):	1,266	Library:	Yes
Passenger Space Ratio (lower beds):	33.4	Onboard currency:	Euros

THE SHIP. The ship has a relatively smart profile, with a swept-back funnel and wedge-shaped stern. The bows display the red lips, as well as the blue eyes, of *Aïda* (from Verdi's opera, written in 1871). AIDA Cruises, Germany's largest cruise line, is part of Costa Cruises – itself part of Carnival Corporation.

There are three pricing levels – AIDA Premium, AIDA Vario, and Just AIDA – depending on what is included. The dress code is casual (no ties) at all times, and there are no formal nights. Port taxes and gratuities are included.

This is a family-friendly ship, with a number of bars and lounges, a diverse selection of children's and youth programs, and special Club Team members dedicated to making sure that everyone has a good time. For activities, children are divided into five age groups, each with its own play area.

An AIDA Cruise is for youthful German-speaking couples, solo travelers, and families seeking good value for money in a party-like environment, with decent entertainment. It's all about über-casual cruising for urbanites, with two main self-serve buffet restaurants, tablecloth-free eating, and little contact with relatively few staff.

ACCOMMODATION. There are several grades, from deluxe suites to interior (no-view) cabins, which keeps your cabin choice simple.

BERLITZ'S RATINGS

	Possible	Achieved
Ship	500	350
Accommodation	200	129
Food	400	242
Service	400	269
Entertainment	100	71
Cruise Experience	400	269

OVERALL SCORE 1321 points out of 2000

Contrary to maritime traditions (even-numbered cabins on the port side, odd-numbered cabins on the starboard side), cabin numbers progress numerically (example: 8201–8276 on the port side; 8101–8176 on the starboard side). All grades have two beds (convertible to a queen-size bed); some cabins have interconnecting doors, which is useful for families, with two extra beds/berths for children.

The decor is bright, youthful, minimalist, even whimsical, and accented with multi-patterned fabrics, wood-trimmed cabinetry (with nicely rounded edges), and rattan or wood-look furniture. Beds have duvets and a colorful Arabian-style fabric canopy from headboard to ceiling. Windows have full pull-down blackout blinds (useful in destinations with long daylight hours). Lifeboats may obstruct views in some cabins in the ship's center.

Bathrooms are compact units, with a shower enclosure, small washbasin, and toilet. Only a wall-mounted body wash/shampoo dispenser is provided, so take any other toiletries you need.

Thick, cotton bathrobes are provided for suite-grade accommodation. Only a face cloth and a 'bath' towel are provided; the 'bath' towel is small. A hairdryer is located in the vanity unit. Unusually, nighttime turndown service is not provided (there is no cabin service after 3pm).

Cabins with balconies have an easy-open sliding door, a small drinks table and two small, light chairs.

Balconies on the lowest deck can be overlooked by anyone on a balcony on the decks above. Cabins Nos 5103, 5104, 5105, 5106, 5203, 5204, 5206 (on Deck 5 forward) have an outside view, but are totally obstructed by steel bulkheads that form the front section of the ship.

Suite-grade accommodation has more storage and drawer space, better-quality furniture and furnishings, a larger lounge area, and a slightly larger bathroom with a tub, plus a larger balcony (those at the front and stern of the ship have the best views).

DINING. Two eateries are included in the fare; Markt and Karibik – both are self-serve buffet-style eateries, with open seating at tables for four to eight. Cutlery hangs in a rack (unhygienic because it can be touched by many); there are no soup spoons, only dessert spoons. It's very casual and easy-going mass catering – think food court eating, not formal dining.

It is often challenging to find a seat (unless you go immediately when the venues open), not to mention a clean table. Because these are buffet venues, you sit with different people for each meal – perhaps a good way to make new friends.

Several food islands and active stations cut down on the waiting time for food. There is always a big selection of breads, cheeses, cold cuts, fruits, and make-your-own coffee and teas – with a choice of (low-quality) loose-leaf regular and herbal teas.

Beer is available at the push of a button or a pull of the tap, and table wine – of the sort that would make a good drain cleaner – is provided in carafes set on tables for lunch and dinner. The beverage stations open only during restaurant opening hours, unless you go to the extra-cost coffee bar (Café Mare). Vending machines dispense out-of-hours snacks.

Rossini is a small restaurant, with a more intimate atmosphere. Open for dinner only, it has an à la carte (extra-cost) menu. Reservations are needed, table-cloths are provided, the food is good, and the service is reasonably friendly.

Vinotheque, a wine bar, located in front of the Weide Welt (Wide World) Restaurant, has a premium wine list, and Davidoff cigars (although you can't smoke them at the bar – or anywhere inside the ship).

Pizzeria Mare provides ever-popular pizzas.

ENTERTAINMENT. The Theater (Das Theater) is the venue for shows. Two decks high, it has a raised stage, and amphitheater-style bench seating on all levels. The benches have back rests, and are quite comfortable; sight lines are good from most seats, except for the port and starboard balcony sections, where there are thick safety railings at eye level.

Upbeat high-volume shows are produced by AIDA Cruises' in-house department in a joint venture with SeeLive (Hamburg's Schmidt's Tivoli Theater). Vocals are performed live, to pre-recorded backing tracks that mix recorded live music and synthesized sound.

SPA/FITNESS. The Body and Soul Spa is located forward on Deck 11. Facilities include two saunas (one dry, one wet, both with seats for more than 20 persons, and glass walls that look onto a deck), massage and other treatment rooms, a large relaxation area, plus showers and two 'ice walls' (simply lean into the ice wall for maximum effect). Forward and outside the wellness center is an FKK (Freikoerperkultur) nude-sunbathing deck, on two levels.

Sport biking is part of the line's youthful image, with three different levels of cycling to suit differing fitness levels. 'Sport bikes' (mountain bikes with tough front and rear suspension units) are provided for conducted biking excursions in each port of call. You can also book diving and golfing excursions (golf-theme packages include playing at notable courses in many ports of call), play golf in the electronic golf simulator, try billiards, volleyball, or squash – or go jogging.

AIDABELLA
★★★+

THIS UPBEAT, FAMILY-FRIENDLY SHIP IS GOOD FOR NO-FRILLS CRUISING

Size:	Mid-size Ship	Passenger/Crew Ratio (lower beds):	3.1
Tonnage:	69,203	Cabins (total):	1,025
Cruise Line:	AIDA Cruises	Size Range (sq ft/m):	145.3–473.2/13.5–44
Former Names:	none	Cabins (for one person):	0
Builder:	Meyer Werft (Germany)	Cabins with balcony:	480
Entered Service:	Apr 2008	Cabins (wheelchair accessible):	11
Length (ft/m):	826.7/252.0	Wheelchair accessibility:	Good
Beam (ft/m):	105.6/32.2	Elevators:	10
Propulsion/Propellers:	diesel-electric (36,000 kW)/2	Casino (gaming tables):	Yes
Passenger Decks:	13	Swimming Pools:	3
Total Crew:	646	Self-Service Launderette:	Yes
Passengers (lower beds):	2,050	Library:	Yes
Passenger Space Ratio (lower beds):	33.7	Onboard currency:	Euros

THE SHIP. The ship has a some-what contemporary profile, with a swept-back funnel and wedge-shaped stern. The bows display the red lips and blue eyes, of *Aïda* (from Verdi's opera, written in 1871). AIDA Cruises, Germany's largest cruise line, is part of Costa Cruises, which is itself part of Carnival Corporation.

The open deck space is rather limited, but sunbathing space includes some quiet areas above the navigation bridge. Dip pools and hot tubs, plus seating areas, are provided in a cascading, tiered setting on the pool deck. It's designed to be a 'beach-like' environment, with splash and play areas. Sadly, there is no stroll-around promenade deck, although you can walk outdoors around the funnel area, and partially around Deck 5.

Several decks of public rooms and facilities are positioned above the accommodation decks, and many of the names of the public rooms are common aboard all the ships in the fleet: AIDA Bar, for example, the main social gathering place, where the principal feature is a star-shaped bar (its combined length is among the longest at sea), with many tables for standing drinkers.

There are several other bars and lounges, plus a small casino. There's also a 'no music' observation lounge, and an art gallery. The embarkation entryway is innovative, has a bar/coffee counter and a lookout 'balcony,' and is cheerfully painted to look like a street scene, providing a welcoming environment.

BERLITZ'S RATINGS		
	Possible	Achieved
Ship	500	371
Accommodation	200	133
Food	400	247
Service	400	265
Entertainment	100	72
Cruise Experience	400	275

OVERALL SCORE 1363 points out of 2000

A cruise aboard *AIDAbella* is all about cruising for youthful, laid-back German-speaking families, with a diverse selection of children's and youth programs (and Club Team members dedicated to making sure your kids have a good time). An AIDA cruise isn't cheap, but you do get lots of high-tech, high-energy entertainment, fun activities, with self-serve buffet restaurants, and tablecloth-free eating, although not much contact with the relatively small number of staff.

The dress code is simple: casual (no ties) at all times.

ACCOMMODATION. There are several accommodation grades, from deluxe suites to interior (no-view) cabins.

Contrary to maritime tradition (even-numbered cabins on the port side, odd-numbered cabins on the starboard side – like the lifeboats), cabin numbers progress numerically (example: 8201–8276 on the port side; 8101–8176 on the starboard side). All suites and cabins have two beds (convertible to a queen-size bed). Some cabins also have two extra beds/berths, and some cabins have interconnecting doors – useful for families.

The decor is bright, youthful, minimalist, and slightly whimsical, accented with multi-patterned fabrics, wood-trimmed cabinetry (with nicely rounded edges), and rattan or wood-look furniture. Beds have duvets and a colorful fabric canopy from headboard to ceiling, while windows have full pull-down blackout blinds (useful in destinations with long daylight hours).

The bathrooms are compact, practical units, with a shower enclosure, small washbasin, and small toilet. Only a wall-mounted body wash/shampoo dispenser is provided, so take any conditioner, hand lotion, and other toiletries you may need.

The bathroom does not have a hairdryer, but one is located in the vanity unit in the cabin. Note that the usual night-time turndown service provided aboard most ships is not provided, and there is no cabin service after 3pm.

Cabins with balconies have an easy-to-open sliding door that doesn't impinge on balcony space; a small drinks table and two small, light chairs are provided. Balconies on the lowest deck can be overlooked by anyone on a balcony on the decks above. Balcony cabins have a hammock – for one (slim) person. Some cabins (forward on Deck 5 – Nos 5103, 5104, 5105, 5106, 5203, 5204, 5206) have cabins with an outside view (well, outside light), but they are obstructed by steel bulkheads.

DINING. There are three large self-serve eateries: Markt (Market), Bella Vista (for Italian cuisine), and Weite Welt (Wide World) restaurants, with open seating at tables of four to eight. Cutlery hangs in a rack (unhygienic because it can be touched by many hands); there are no soup spoons, only dessert spoons. Multiple food islands and active stations cut down on the waiting time for food. There is always a good selection of breads, cheeses, cold cuts, fruits, and coffee and teas. The fish section also has its own fish-smoking unit.

Additionally, there's a Buffalo Steakhouse (which serves excellent steaks), an à la carte Rossini Restaurant with waiter and sommelier service, a 12-seat Sushi Bar, a Pizzeria Mare, and a Café Mare.

Push-button beer is available, and table wine is usually provided in carafes on each table for lunch and dinner. Note that the beverage stations open only during restaurant opening hours, unless you go to the extra-cost coffee bar (Café Mare). Vending machines dispense out-of-hours snacks.

ENTERTAINMENT. The Theatrium (theater) is in the ship's center. It is open to the main foyer on three levels (decks 9, 10, and 11), and is topped by a glass dome. Amphitheater-style seating is on three decks (bench seating on the two upper levels has back supports, but not on the lower level), plus standing tables, although sight lines to the raised thrust stage area are poor from many of the seats.

SPA/FITNESS. The Body and Soul wellness/oasis area is located on two decks (connected by a stairway) and encompasses 24,750 sq ft (2,300 sq m). There is also an open-air wellness 'FKK' deck for relaxation/nude sunbathing in an area just forward of the ship's mast. There are saunas and steam rooms, and 14 rooms (most named after places associated with the design theme) for body pampering, plus a fitness room with high-tech machines, neat showers, funky changing rooms, and a tropical garden with real (waxed) palm trees and relaxation loungers. Sport enthusiasts can also play billiards, volleyball or squash – or go jogging.

AIDABLU
★★★+

THIS IS AN UPBEAT, FAMILY-FRIENDLY SHIP FOR NO-FRILLS CRUISING

Size:	Mid-size Ship	Passenger/Crew Ratio (lower beds):	3.1
Tonnage:	71,100	Cabins (total):	1,096
Cruise Line:	AIDA Cruises	Size Range (sq ft/m):	145.3–473.2/13.5–44
Former Names:	none	Cabins (for one person):	0
Builder:	Meyer Werft (Germany)	Cabins with balcony:	491
Entered Service:	Apr 2010	Cabins (wheelchair accessible):	11
Length (ft/m):	831.1/253.3	Wheelchair accessibility:	Good
Beam (ft/m):	105.6/32.2	Elevators:	10
Propulsion/Propellers:	diesel-electric (36,000 kW)/2	Casino (gaming tables):	Yes
Passenger Decks:	14	Swimming Pools:	3
Total Crew:	646	Self-Service Launderette:	Yes
Passengers (lower beds):	2,194	Library:	Yes
Passenger Space Ratio (lower beds):	34.4	Onboard currency:	Euros

THE SHIP. The ship has a fairly contemporary profile, with a swept-back funnel and wedge-shaped stern. The bows display the red lips and blue eyes of *Aïda* (from Verdi's opera, written in 1871). AIDA Cruises, Germany's largest cruise line, is part of Costa Cruises, which is itself part of Carnival Corporation.

The open deck space is somewhat limited, but includes some quiet sunbathing space above the navigation bridge. Dip pools and hot tubs, plus seating areas, are in a cascading, tiered setting on the pool deck, de-signed as a 'beach-like' environment, with splash and play areas. Sadly, there is no stroll-around promenade deck, although you can walk outdoors around the fun-nel area, and partially around Deck 5.

Several decks of public rooms and facilities are positioned above the accommodation decks, and *AIDAblu* has the same names for its public room as all the ships in the fleet: AIDA Bar, for example, the main social gathering place, where the principal fea-ture is a star-shaped bar (it's among the longest at sea), with many tables for standing drinkers.

A small casino has gaming tables and slot ma-chines. There is also a separate aft sports deck, an observation lounge, and an 'art' gallery. The embar-kation entryway has a bar and a lookout 'balcony,' cheerfully painted to look like a street scene in a city like Copenhagen.

A cruise aboard *AIDAblu* is all about cruising for youthful, laid-back German-speaking families with a

BERLITZ'S RATINGS

	Possible	Achieved
Ship	500	371
Accommodation	200	133
Food	400	248
Service	400	265
Entertainment	100	72
Cruise Experience	400	275

OVERALL SCORE 1365 points out of 2000

diverse selection of children's and youth programs (and Club Team members dedicated to making sure that everyone has a good time). An AIDA cruise isn't cheap, but you do get lots of high-tech entertainment, fun activities, plenty of food at the self-serve buffet restaurants, and relaxed, tablecloth-free eating, al-though not much contact with the relatively small number of staff. Port taxes and gratuities are included.

The dress code is simple: casual (no ties) at all times, and all port taxes and gratuities are included.

ACCOMMODATION. There are several price grades, from suites to interior (no-view) cabins, so cabin choice is simple.

Contrary to maritime traditions (even-numbered cabins on the port side, odd-numbered cabins on the starboard side), cabin numbers progress numerical-ly (example: 8201–8276 on the port side; 8101–8176 on the starboard side). All suites and cabins have two beds (convertible to queen-size bed). Some cabins also have two extra beds/berths for children; some cabins have interconnecting doors.

The decor is bright, youthful, rather minimalist, and slightly whimsical. All cabins are accented with multi-patterned fabrics, wood-trimmed cabinetry, and rattan or wood-look furniture. Beds have duvets and a colorful canopy from headboard to ceiling. The windows have full pull-down blackout blinds (useful in destinations with long daylight hours).

Bathrooms are compact, practical units, with a shower enclosure, small washbasin and toilet. Only a wall-mounted body wash/shampoo dispenser is provided, so take your own toiletries if you require more than this.

Thick cotton bathrobes are provided, as are two towels – a face towel and a 'bath' towel, in two different colors. The 'bath' towels are quite small, and the bathroom does not have a hairdryer (it's located in the vanity unit in the cabin). There is also no night-time turndown service.

Cabins with balconies have a sliding door that's easy to open, a small drinks table, and two small, light chairs. Balconies on the lowest deck can be overlooked by anyone on a balcony on the decks above. Some cabins (forward on Deck 5 – Nos 5103, 5104, 5105, 5106, 5203, 5204, 5206) have cabins with an outside 'view' (more like outside light), but they are obstructed by steel bulkheads.

Suite-grade accommodation offers more drawer and storage space, better-quality furniture and furnishings, a larger lounge area, a bathroom with a tub, and a larger balcony (those at the front and stern are the most desirable).

DINING. There are three self-serve eateries: Markt (Market), Bella Vista (for Italian cuisine), and East restaurants. Opening times for lunch and dinner are typically 12.30–2pm and 6.30–9pm respectively. Additionally, there's a Buffalo Steakhouse (which serves excellent steaks), an à la carte Rossini Restaurant with waiter and sommelier service, a Sushi Bar, a Pizzeria Mare, and a Café Mare. These venues are open at set times (there are no 24-hour-a-day outlets, because there is little demand for them), although the Pizzeria typically is open until midnight.

In the three self-serve restaurants, meals are taken when you want them, with open seating at tables of four, six, or eight. Cutlery hangs in a rack, and there are no soup spoons, only dessert spoons.

Multiple food islands and active stations cut down on the waiting time for food. There is always a big selection of breads, cheeses, cold cuts, fruits, and make-your-own coffee and teas – with a choice of more than 30 types of loose-leaf regular and herbal teas. More than 1,200 items of food are offered, and the fish section has its own fish-smoking unit.

Beer is available at the push of a button or a pull of the tap, and table wine is usually provided in carafes on each table for lunch and dinner. Note that the beverage stations open only during restaurant opening hours, unless you go to the extra-cost coffee bar (Café Mare). In case you want something to nibble on, vending machines dispense out-of-hours snacks.

Other dining options. Rossini Restaurant, with mostly high-back seats, is small and intimate. Open for dinner only, it has a set five- or six-course menu, plus daily 'specials,' and à la carte pricing, and reservations are required. Tablecloths are provided, the food is rather good, and service is acceptable.

Buffalo Steakhouse has an open 'display' kitchen, and offers various steak cuts and sizes, plus roast lamb rack. It's like going out to eat in a decent restaurant ashore, although don't expect tablecloths. Wine or any other drinks cost extra.

A 12-seater sushi counter is for Japanese-style sushi and sashimi dishes, at extra cost.

A wine bar, Vinotheque, located in front of the Weide Welt (Wide World) Restaurant, has a list of premium wines, and Davidoff cigars (although you can't smoke them at the bar – or anywhere inside the ship). Worth mentioning is a Brauhaus micro-brewery with good beer at a reasonable price and table-service food in a beer garden setting.

ENTERTAINMENT. The Theatrium (theater) is in the center of the ship. It is open to the main foyer and other public areas, on three levels (decks 9, 10, and 11), and topped by a glass dome. Amphitheater-style seating is on three decks (the bench seating on the two upper levels – but not on the lower level – has back supports), plus standing tables, although sight lines to the raised thrust stage area are less than good from many of the seats.

SPA/FITNESS. The spa, fitness, and sports programming is extensive. The Body and Soul wellness/oasis area is located on two decks (connected by a stairway) and encompasses 24,750 sq ft (2,300 sq m). There is also an open-air wellness 'FKK' deck for relaxation/nude sunbathing in an area forward of the ship's mast.

AIDACARA
★★★+

THIS IS A BUSY, FAMILY-FRIENDLY SHIP FOR FRUGAL CRUISEGOERS

Size:	Mid-size Ship	Passenger/Crew Ratio (lower beds):	3.1
Tonnage:	38,557	Cabins (total):	590
Cruise Line:	AIDA Cruises	Size Range (sq ft/m):	145.3–376.7/13.5–35.0
Former Names:	Aida, Das Clubschiff	Cabins (for one person):	0
Builder:	Kvaerner Masa-Yards (Finland)	Cabins with balcony:	48
Entered Service:	Jun 1996	Cabins (wheelchair accessible):	6
Length (ft/m):	634.1/193.3	Wheelchair accessibility:	Good
Beam (ft/m):	90.5/27.6	Elevators:	5
Propulsion/Propellers:	diesel(21,720kw)/2	Casino (gaming tables):	No
Passenger Decks:	9	Swimming Pools:	1
Total Crew:	370	Self-Service Launderette:	Yes
Passengers (lower beds):	1,180	Library:	Yes
Passenger Space Ratio (lower beds):	32.6	Onboard currency:	Euros

THE SHIP. Despite being over 20 years old, the ship has a relatively modern profile, with a swept-back funnel and wedge-shaped stern. The bows display the red lips and blue eyes of *Aïda* (from Verdi's opera, written in 1871).

Open deck space is quite tight, but places for sunbathing includes a pleasant, quiet section above the navigation bridge. Dip pools and hot tubs, plus seating areas, are arranged in a cascading, tiered setting on the pool deck, designed to be a 'beach-like' environment, with splash and play areas.

Some public rooms and facilities are positioned above the accommodation decks. Public rooms that have become common aboard all the ships include AIDA Bar, the main social gathering place, where the principal feature is a star-shaped bar (whose combined length per ship makes them the longest at sea), with many tables for standing drinkers.

Other facilities include a shore-excursion counter, library, seminar rooms, duty-free shop, several bars and lounges, and eateries.

This ship has a diverse selection of children's and youth programs, and special Club Team members dedicated to making sure that everyone has a good time. For activities, children are divided into five age groups, each with its own play area.

An AIDA Cruise is all about über-casual cruising for youthful German-speaking urbanites including families with children who enjoy a party-like envi-

BERLITZ'S RATINGS	Possible	Achieved
Ship	500	335
Accommodation	200	124
Food	400	238
Service	400	258
Entertainment	100	70
Cruise Experience	400	261

OVERALL SCORE 1286 points out of 2000

ronment, with self-serve buffet restaurants, tablecloth-free eating, and little contact with the relatively few staff. The dress code is simple: casual (no ties) at all times.

ACCOMMODATION. There are several grades, from (more) spacious suites to interior (no-view) cabins.

Contrary to maritime traditions (even-numbered cabins on the port side, odd-numbered cabins on the starboard side), cabin numbers progress numerically (example: 8201–8276 on the port side; 8101–8176 on the starboard side). All have two beds convertible to a queen-size bed. Some also have two extra beds/berths for children, and some have interconnecting doors – useful for families.

The decor is bright, minimalist, and whimsical, accented with multi-patterned fabrics, wood-trimmed cabinetry (with rounded edges), and rattan or wood-look furniture. Beds have duvets and a colorful Arabian-style fabric canopy from the headboard to the ceiling. Windows have full pull-down blackout blinds (useful in destinations with long daylight hours). Lifeboats may obstruct views in some cabins in the ship's center.

The bathrooms are compact, practical units, with a shower enclosure, small washbasin, and toilet. Only a wall-mounted body wash/shampoo dispenser is provided, so take your own toiletries if you require more than this.

Thick cotton bathrobes are provided for suite-grade accommodation only, although non-suite grade passengers can obtain one from the spa. Two towels are provided – a face towel and a 'bath' towel, in two different colors. The 'bath' towels are small, however. Although the bathrooms do not have a hairdryer, one is located in the vanity unit in the cabin. Night-time turndown service is not provided.

Cabins with balconies have an easy-open sliding door, small drinks table, and two small, light chairs. Balconies on the lowest deck can be overlooked from balconies on the decks above.

Suite-grade accommodation offers more space, including more drawer and storage space, better-quality furniture and furnishings, a larger lounge area, a slightly larger bathroom with a tub – and a larger balcony (those at the front and stern are the best).

DINING. Two eateries (for main meals) are included in the cruise fare: the self-serve Markt and Karibik restaurants, with open seating at tables of four to eight. Cutlery hangs in a rack, but there are no soup spoons, only dessert spoons. When the ship is full, it can be challenging to find a seat, not to mention anyone to clean the tables.

The standard of food ranges from adequate to moderately good, with creative displays and presentation.

The many food islands and active stations cut down on the waiting time for food. There is always a big selection of breads, cheeses, cold cuts, fruits, and make-your-own coffee and teas – with a choice of over 30 types of loose-leaf regular and herbal teas.

Beer is available at the push of a button or a pull of the tap, and table wine – of the sort that would make a good drain cleaner – is usually provided in carafes on each table for lunch and dinner. Note that beverage stations open only during restaurant opening hours, unless you go to the extra-cost coffee bar (Café Mare). Vending machines dispense out-of-hours snacks.

The Rossini Restaurant, with mostly high-back seats, is an additional dining venue, with an intimate atmosphere. Open for dinner only, it has à la carte pricing. Reservations are needed, tablecloths are provided, the food is good, and the service is quite friendly.

ENTERTAINMENT. The Theater, the venue for all shows, is two decks high, with a raised stage, and amphitheater-style comfortable bench seating (with back rests) on both levels. Sight lines are good from most seats, except from balcony sections, where they are interrupted by thick safety railings.

SPA/FITNESS. Body and Soul Spa facilities contains two saunas (one dry, one wet, and both with seats for over 20 persons and glass walls that look onto the deck), body-pampering treatment rooms, lounging area, showers, and two 'ice walls' adjacent to the saunas (simply lean into the ice wall for maximum effect). Forward and outside is an 'FKK' (Freikoerperkultur) nude-sunbathing deck, on two levels. A beauty and hair salon is located separately behind the balcony level of the showlounge.

AIDADIVA
★★★+

TRY THIS MID-SIZE FAMILY-FRIENDLY SHIP FOR A GOOD-TIME, CASUAL CRUISE EXPERIENCE

Size:	Mid-size Ship	Passenger/Crew Ratio (lower beds):	3.1
Tonnage:	69,203	Cabins (total):	1,025
Cruise Line:	AIDA Cruises	Size Range (sq ft/m):	145.3–473.2/13.5–44
Former Names:	none	Cabins (for one person):	0
Builder:	Meyer Werft (Germany)	Cabins with balcony:	480
Entered Service:	Apr 2007	Cabins (wheelchair accessible):	11
Length (ft/m):	830.0/253.3	Wheelchair accessibility:	Good
Beam (ft/m):	105.6/32.2	Elevators:	10
Propulsion/Propellers:	diesel-electric (36,000 kW)/2	Casino (gaming tables):	Yes
Passenger Decks:	13	Swimming Pools:	3
Total Crew:	646	Self-Service Launderette:	Yes
Passengers (lower beds):	2,050	Library:	Yes
Passenger Space Ratio (lower beds):	33.7	Onboard currency:	Euros

THE SHIP. The ship has a contemporary profile, swept-back funnel, and wedge-shaped stern, and the red lips painted on the bows and blue eyes of *Aïda* (from Verdi's opera, written in 1871). AIDA Cruises, Germany's largest cruise line, is part of Costa Cruises, itself part of Carnival Corporation.

The open deck space is rather limited, but includes a quiet sunbathing section above the navigation bridge. Dip pools and hot tubs, plus seating areas, are set in a cascading, tiered setting on the pool deck, designed to be a 'beach-like' environment, with splash and play areas. There is no stroll-around promenade deck, but you can walk outdoors around the funnel area, and partially around Deck 5.

Several decks of public rooms and facilities are positioned above the accommodation decks, and *AIDAdiva* shares public room names that are common aboard all the ships in the fleet: AIDA Bar, for example, the main social gathering place, where the principal feature is a large, star-shaped bar, with many tables for standing drinkers. There's also a 'no music' observation lounge, and an 'art' gallery.

Other facilities include a small casino with gaming tables and slot machines, and the embarkation entryway, which has a bar and a lookout 'balcony' and is cheerfully painted to look like a street scene in a city such as Copenhagen. Different from the utilitarian gangway entry areas found aboard most cruise ships, it is a welcoming environment.

BERLITZ'S RATINGS

	Possible	Achieved
Ship	500	365
Accommodation	200	132
Food	400	245
Service	400	266
Entertainment	100	72
Cruise Experience	400	270

OVERALL SCORE 1350 points out of 2000

There are three pricing levels – AIDA Premium, AIDA Vario, and Just AIDA – depending on what you want to be included. Opt for the basic, price-driven 'Just AIDA' package, and the cruise line chooses the ship, itinerary, and accommodation for you – sort of a pot-luck cruise, based on or close to the dates you choose.

The dress code is simple: casual (no ties) at all times. Port taxes and basic gratuities are included.

This is a family-friendly ship, with a diverse selection of children's and youth programs, and special Club Team members dedicated to making sure that everyone has a good time. For activities, children are divided into five age groups, each with its own play area.

An AIDA cruise is for youthful German-speaking couples, solo travelers, and families seeking good value for money in a party-like environment, with decent entertainment. It's all about über-casual cruising for urbanites, with two main self-serve buffet restaurants and laid-back, tablecloth-free eating, and little contact with relatively few staff.

ACCOMMODATION. There are several grades, from deluxe suites to interior (no-view) cabins, depending on the ship.

Contrary to maritime traditions (even-numbered cabins on the port side, odd-numbered cabins on the starboard side), cabin numbers progress numerically (example: 8201–8276 on the port side; 8101–8176 on the starboard side). All suites and cabins have two beds (convertible to a queen-size bed). Some cabins also have two extra beds/berths for children, and some have interconnecting doors – useful for families.

The decor is bright, cheerful, minimalist, and slightly whimsical. All cabins are accented with multi-patterned fabrics, wood-trimmed cabinetry, and rattan or wood-look furniture. Beds have duvets and a colorful canopy from headboard to ceiling, and windows have full pull-down blackout blinds (useful in destinations with long daylight hours).

The bathrooms are compact, with a shower enclosure, small washbasin, and toilet. Only a wall-mounted body wash/shampoo dispenser is provided, so take your own conditioner, hand lotion, and other toiletries you may need.

Thick cotton bathrobes are provided for all passengers, as are two towels – a face towel and a rather small 'bath' towel. The bathroom does not have a hairdryer (it's located in the vanity unit in the cabin). Note that there's no cabin service after 3pm.

Cabins with balconies have an easy-open sliding door, a small drinks table, and two small, light chairs. Balconies on the lowest deck can be overlooked by anyone on a balcony on the decks above. Balcony cabins have a hammock as standard. Some cabins (forward on Deck 5 – Nos 5103, 5104, 5105, 5106, 5203, 5204, 5206) have cabins with an outside view (well, outside light), but they are obstructed by steel bulkheads that form the front section of the ship.

Suite-grade accommodation offers more space, including more drawer and storage space, better-quality furniture and furnishings, a larger lounge area, a slightly larger bathroom with a tub – and a larger balcony (those at the front and stern of the ship are the most desirable).

DINING. There are three self-serve eateries: Markt (Market), Bella Vista (for Italian cuisine), and Weite Welt (Wide World) restaurants. Main meals are taken when you want them, with open seating at tables of four, six, or eight. Cutlery hangs in a rack (a somewhat unhygienic arrangement), but there are no soup spoons, only dessert spoons.

The many food islands and active stations help reduce the waiting time for food. There is always a good selection of breads, cheeses, cold cuts, fruits, and make-your-own coffee and teas.

Beer is available at the push of a button or a pull of the tap, and table wine – of the sort that would make a good drain cleaner – is usually provided in carafes on each table for lunch and dinner. Note that beverage stations open only during restaurant opening hours, unless you go to the extra-cost coffee bar (Café Mare).

Other restaurants include a Buffalo Steakhouse (for excellent steaks), an à la carte Rossini Restaurant with waiter and sommelier service, a Sushi Bar, a Pizzeria Mare, and a Café Mare. These venues are open at set times (there are no 24-hour-a-day outlets, because there is little demand for them), although the Pizzeria is open until late.

The Buffalo Steakhouse has an open 'display' kitchen, and offers various prime steak cuts and sizes, and roast lamb rack. It's like going out to eat in a decent restaurant ashore. Wine or any other drinks cost extra.

The à la carte Rossini Restaurant, with mostly high-back seats, has an intimate atmosphere, and tablecloths. It is open for dinner only, and has a set multi-course menu, plus daily 'specials.' Reservations are needed.

A 12-seater sushi counter is for Japanese-style sushi and sashimi dishes. Pizzeria Mare provides a small selection of ever-popular pizzas.

ENTERTAINMENT. The Theatrium (theater) is in the center of the ship. It is open to the main foyer and other public areas, on three levels (decks 9, 10, and 11), and topped by a glass dome. Amphitheater-style seating is across the three decks (bench seating on the two upper levels has back supports, but not on the lower level), plus there are standing tables, although sight lines to the raised thrust stage area are less than good from many seats.

The shows (each is just 30 minutes long) are produced by AIDA Cruises' in-house department in a joint venture with SeeLive (Hamburg's Schmidt's Tivoli Theater), and consist of around 12 performers. Show vocals are performed live to pre-recorded backing tracks that provide a mix of recorded live music and synthesized sound (there's no live band on stage). The shows are trendy, upbeat, fun, and very entertaining.

SPA/FITNESS. The extensive Body and Soul wellness/oasis area is located on two decks (connected by a stairway) and encompasses some 24,750 sq ft (2,300 sq m). There is also an open-air wellness 'FKK' deck for relaxation/nude sunbathing (atop the ship forward of the ship's mast).

AIDALUNA
★★★+

AN UPBEAT, FAMILY-FRIENDLY, AND CHEERFUL SHIP, BUT THERE'S LITTLE FINESSE

Size:	Mid-size Ship	Passenger/Crew Ratio (lower beds):	3.1
Tonnage:	69,203	Cabins (total):	1,025
Cruise Line:	AIDA Cruises	Size Range (sq ft/m):	145.3 –473.2/13.5–44
Former Names:	none	Cabins (for one person):	0
Builder:	Meyer Werft (Germany)	Cabins with balcony:	480
Entered Service:	Apr 2009	Cabins (wheelchair accessible):	11
Length (ft/m):	831.1/253.3	Wheelchair accessibility:	Good
Beam (ft/m):	105.6/32.2	Elevators:	10
Propulsion/Propellers:	diesel-electric (36,000 kW)/2	Casino (gaming tables):	Yes
Passenger Decks:	13	Swimming Pools:	3
Total Crew:	646	Self-Service Launderette:	Yes
Passengers (lower beds):	2,050	Library:	Yes
Passenger Space Ratio (lower beds):	33.7	Onboard currency:	Euros

THE SHIP. The ship has a modern profile, with a swept-back funnel and wedge-shaped stern. The bows display the red lips and blue eyes of *Aïda* (from Verdi's opera, written in 1871). AIDA Cruises is part of Costa Cruises, itself part of the giant Carnival Corporation.

The open deck space is rather limited, but sunbathing space includes a quiet section above the navigation bridge. Dip pools and hot tubs, plus seating areas, are provided in a cascading, tiered setting on the pool deck, providing a reasonable amount of sunbathing space. It's all designed to be a 'beach-like' environment, with splash and play areas. Sadly, there is no stroll-around promenade deck, although you can walk outdoors around the funnel area, and partially around Deck 5.

Several decks of public rooms and facilities are positioned above the accommodation decks, and *AIDAluna* shares public room names that are common aboard all the AIDA Cruises ships: AIDA Bar, for example, the main social gathering place, where the principal feature is a large, star-shaped bar, with many tables for standing drinkers.

There is a separate aft sports deck, an observation lounge, an art gallery, plus a small casino featuring blackjack, roulette, and poker gaming tables, and a number of slot machines. The embarkation entryway has a bar and a lookout 'balcony,' and is cheerfully painted to look like a waterside street scene. A welcoming environment, it helps to calm tempers

BERLITZ'S RATINGS

	Possible	Achieved
Ship	500	365
Accommodation	200	132
Food	400	245
Service	400	266
Entertainment	100	72
Cruise Experience	400	270

OVERALL SCORE 1350 points out of 2000

after waiting to go through the security check for embarkation or in ports of call.

There are three pricing levels – AIDA Premium, AIDA Vario, and Just AIDA – depending on what you want to be included, plus differences in price according to accommodation size and grade, and itinerary.

The dress code is simple: casual (no ties) at all times, and all port taxes and gratuities are included.

This is a family-friendly ship, with a diverse selection of children's and youth programs, and special Club Team members dedicated to making sure that everyone has a good time. Children are divided into five age groups, each with its own play area.

An AIDA Cruise is all about über-casual cruising for youthful German-speaking urbanites including families with children who enjoy a party-like environment, with self-serve buffet restaurants and tablecloth-free eating, and don't mind little contact with relatively small number of staff.

ACCOMMODATION. There are eight or nine grades, from (more) spacious suites to interior (no-view) cabins, depending on the ship, which keeps your cabin choice simple.

Contrary to maritime traditions (even-numbered cabins on the port side, odd-numbered cabins on the starboard side), cabin numbers progress numerically (example: 8201–8276 on the port side; 8101–8176 on the starboard side). All suites and cabins have two beds (convertible to a queen-size bed). Some cabins also have two extra beds/berths for children, and some cabins have interconnecting doors – useful for families.

The decor is bright, minimalist, and slightly playful, accented with multi-patterned fabrics, wood-trimmed cabinetry (with nicely rounded edges), and rattan or wood-look furniture. Beds have duvets and a colorful Arabian-style headboard-to-ceiling fabric canopy. Windows have full pull-down blackout blinds (useful in destinations with long daylight hours).

The bathrooms are compact, practical units, with shower enclosure, small washbasin, and small toilet. Only a wall-mounted body wash/shampoo dispenser is provided, so take any personal toiletries you may need.

Thick cotton bathrobes are provided, as are a face cloth and a small 'bath' towel. The bathroom does not have a hairdryer, but there is one in the vanity unit in the cabin. Note that the usual night-time turndown service provided aboard most ships is not provided, and there is no cabin service after 3pm.

Cabins with balconies have an easy-open sliding door that doesn't impinge on balcony space, a small drinks table, and two small chairs. Balconies on the lowest deck can be overlooked by anyone on a balcony on the decks above. Balcony cabins have a hammock as standard, although it only accommodates one (slim) person. Some cabins (forward on Deck 5 – Nos 5103, 5104, 5105, 5106, 5203, 5204, 5206) have cabins with an outside view (well, outside light), but they are obstructed by steel bulkheads that form the front section of the ship.

DINING. There are three self-serve main eateries: Markt (Market), Bella Vista (for Italian cuisine), and Weite Welt (Wide World) restaurants, with open seating at tables of four to eight. Cutlery hangs in a rack (not hygienic), and there are no soup spoons, only dessert spoons.

The many food islands and active stations cut down on the waiting time for food. There is always a selection of breads, cheeses, cold cuts, fruits, and make-your-own coffee and teas – with a choice of more than 30 types of loose-leaf regular and herbal teas. The fish section has its own fish-smoking unit, resembling a wine cabinet. It's simply casual and easy-going mass catering, so think food court rather than fine dining.

Beer is available at the push of a button or a pull of the tap, and table wine – of the sort that would make a good drain cleaner – is usually provided in carafes on each table for lunch and dinner.

The beverage stations open only during restaurant opening hours, unless you go to the extra-cost coffee bar. Vending machines dispense out-of-hours snacks.

The à la carte Rossini Restaurant, for which reservations are required, has mostly high-back seats and an intimate atmosphere. It is open for dinner only. Tablecloths are provided, the food is good, and the service is sound.

Buffalo Steakhouse has an open 'display' kitchen, and offers various steak cuts and sizes, and roast lamb rack. It's like going out to eat in a decent restaurant ashore, albeit without tablecloths. Wine or any other drinks cost extra.

There is a 12-stool counter for Japanese-style sushi and sashimi dishes (at extra cost).

A wine bar, Vinotheque, located in front of the Weide Welt (Wide World) Restaurant, has a list of premium wines, and Davidoff cigars (although you can't smoke them at the bar – or anywhere inside the ship).

The Pizzeria Mare provides a small selection of ever-popular pizzas.

ENTERTAINMENT. The Theatrium (theater) is in the ship's center. It is open to the main foyer and other public areas, on three levels (decks 9, 10, and 11), and topped by a glass dome. Amphitheater-style seating is on three decks (bench seating on the two upper levels has back supports, but not on the lower level), and standing tables, although sight lines to the raised thrust stage are poor from many seats.

SPA/FITNESS. The spa, fitness, and sports programming are extensive. The Body and Soul wellness/oasis area is located on two decks (connected by a stairway). There is also an open-air wellness deck for 'FKK' relaxation (nude sunbathing) in an area atop the ship forward of the ship's mast. In keeping with the times, all the treatments are featured in an appealing contemporary setting.

AIDAMAR
★★★+

THIS MID-SIZE FAMILY-FRIENDLY SHIP IS FOR LIVELY, CASUAL CRUISING

Size:	Mid-size Ship	Passenger/Crew Ratio (lower beds):	3.1
Tonnage:	71,304	Cabins (total):	1,097
Cruise Line:	AIDA Cruises	Size Range (sq ft/m):	145.3–473.2/13.5–44
Former Names:	none	Cabins (for one person):	0
Builder:	Meyer Werft (Germany)	Cabins with balcony:	491
Entered Service:	Apr 2012	Cabins (wheelchair accessible):	11
Length (ft/m):	831.1/253.3	Wheelchair accessibility:	Good
Beam (ft/m):	105.6/32.2	Elevators:	10
Propulsion/Propellers:	diesel-electric (36,000 kW)/2	Casino (gaming tables):	Yes
Passenger Decks:	14	Swimming Pools:	3
Total Crew:	646	Self-Service Launderette:	Yes
Passengers (lower beds):	2,194	Library:	Yes
Passenger Space Ratio (lower beds):	34.6	Onboard currency:	Euros

THE SHIP. The vessel's profile is quite well proportioned, with a swept-back funnel and a wedge-shaped stern. The bows display the bright red lips and blue eyes of *Aïda* (from Verdi's opera, written in 1871). AIDA Cruises is part of Costa Cruises, itself part of Carnival Corporation.

The open deck space is rather limited, but sunbathing space includes a quiet section above the navigation bridge. Dip pools and hot tubs, plus seating areas, are provided in a cascading, tiered setting on the pool deck, providing a reasonable amount of sunbathing space. It's all designed to be a 'beach-like' environment, with splash and play areas. Sadly, there is no stroll-around promenade deck, although you can walk outdoors around the funnel area, and partially around Deck 5.

Several decks of public rooms and facilities are positioned above the accommodation decks, and public room names are common to all AIDA Cruises ships: AIDA Bar is the main social gathering place; it features a star-shaped bar (whose combined length makes it among the longest at sea), with many tables for standing drinkers.

A small casino has gaming tables and slot machines. There is a separate aft sports deck, a 'no music' observation lounge, and an art gallery.

This is a family-friendly ship, with a diverse selection of children's and youth programs, and special Club Team members dedicated to making sure

BERLITZ'S RATINGS		
	Possible	Achieved
Ship	500	371
Accommodation	200	133
Food	400	245
Service	400	265
Entertainment	100	72
Cruise Experience	400	275

OVERALL SCORE 1357 points out of 2000

that everyone has a good time. For activities, children are divided into five age groups, each with its own play area.

An AIDA Cruise is all about über-casual cruising for youthful German-speaking urbanites including families with children who enjoy a party-like environment, with self-serve buffet restaurants and table-cloth-free eating, and don't mind little contact with relatively few staff.

ACCOMMODATION. There are several price grades, from deluxe suites to interior (no-view) cabins.

Contrary to maritime traditions (even-numbered cabins on the port side, odd-numbered ones on the starboard side), cabin numbers progress numerically (example: 8201–8276 on the port side; 8101–8176 on the starboard side). All suites and cabins have two beds (convertible to queen-size bed). Some cabins also have two extra beds/berths for children, and some cabins have interconnecting doors – useful for families.

The decor in is bright, youthful, minimalist, and slightly whimsical, and accented with multi-patterned fabrics, wood-trimmed cabinetry (with nicely rounded edges), and rattan or wood-look furniture. Beds have duvets and a colorful Arabian-style fabric canopy from headboard to ceiling. Windows have full pull-down blackout blinds (useful in destinations with long daylight hours).

Bathrooms are compact, practical units, with a shower enclosure, small washbasin, and toilet. As in the most basic hotels and motels, only a wall-mounted body wash/shampoo dispenser is provided, so take your own toiletries if you will require more than this.

Thick cotton bathrobes are provided for all, as are a face towel and a small 'bath' towel. A hairdryer is located in the vanity unit in the cabin. Note that there's no night-time turndown service.

Cabins with balconies have an easy-open sliding door (it doesn't impinge on balcony space), plus a small drinks table and two small chairs. Balconies on the lowest deck can be overlooked by anyone on a balcony on the decks above. Some cabins (forward on Deck 5 – Nos 5103, 5104, 5105, 5106, 5203, 5204, 5206) have cabins with an outside view (well, an outside light), but they are obstructed by steel bulkheads that form the front section of the ship.

DINING. Markt (Market), Bella Vista (for Italian cuisine), and Weite Welt (Wide World) restaurants have open seating at tables of four to eight. Cutlery hangs in a rack, but there are no soup spoons, only dessert spoons.

The standard of food ranges from adequate to quite good, with creative displays and presentation, and table-clearing service that is sometimes efficient, but mostly not. There is a good selection of breads, cheeses, cold cuts, fruits, and make-your-own coffee and teas – with a choice of more than 30 types of loose-leaf regular and herbal teas. The fish section has its own fish-smoking unit, which resembles a wine cabinet.

Beer is at the push of a button or a pull of the tap, and table wine – of the sort that would make a good drain cleaner – is usually provided in carafes on each table for lunch and dinner. Note that the beverage stations open only during restaurant opening hours, unless you go to the extra-cost coffee bar (Café Mare). Vending machines dispense out-of-hours snacks.

Extra-cost dining venues include Rossini Restaurant, open for dinner only, with a set menu plus daily 'specials. Reservations are needed, tablecloths are provided, and the food and service are good.

There's also Buffalo Steakhouse, which has an open 'display' kitchen, and offers various steak cuts and sizes. It's like going out to eat in a restaurant ashore – minus tablecloths.

There's a 12-stool sushi counter for (extra-cost) Japanese-style sushi and sashimi dishes.

A wine bar, Vinotheque, located in front of the Weide Welt (Wide World) Restaurant, has a list of premium wines, and Davidoff cigars (although you can't smoke them at the bar – or anywhere inside the ship). Pizzeria Mare provides a small selection of pizzas. Worth mentioning is a Brauhaus micro-brewery with good beer at a reasonable price and table service food in a beer garden setting.

ENTERTAINMENT. The Theatrium (theater) is in the center of the ship. It is open to the main foyer on three levels and topped by a glass dome. Amphitheater-style seating is on three decks (the bench seating on the two upper levels has back supports, but not on the lower level), plus standing tables, although sight lines to the raised thrust stage area are less than good from many of the seats.

SPA/FITNESS. The Body and Soul wellness/oasis area is located on two decks (connected by a stairway) and encompasses some 24,750 sq ft (2,300 sq m). There is also an open-air wellness deck for 'FKK' relaxation (nude sunbathing) atop the ship forward of the ship's mast. In keeping with the times, all the treatments are provided in an appealing contemporary setting.

AIDAPERLA
★★★★

THIS COLORFUL ULTRA-CASUAL CRUISE SHIP IS FOR YOUTHFUL GERMAN-SPEAKING FAMILIES

Size:	Large Resort Ship	Passenger/Crew Ratio (lower beds):	3.6
Tonnage:	124,000	Cabins (total):	1643
Cruise Line:	AIDA Cruises	Size Range (sq ft/m):	139.9-914.9/13.0-85.0
Former Names:	none	Cabins (for one person):	0
Builder:	Mitsubishi Heavy Industries (Japan)	Cabins with balcony:	1133
Entered Service:	Jul 2017	Cabins (wheelchair accessible):	29
Length (ft/m):	984.2/300.0	Wheelchair accessibility:	Good
Beam (ft/m):	123.3/37.6	Elevators:	18
Propulsion/Propellers:	diesel-electric/ 2 azimuthing pods	Casino (gaming tables):	Yes
Passenger Decks:	18	Swimming Pools:	6
Total Crew:	900	Self-Service Launderette:	Yes
Passengers (lower beds):	3286	Library:	Yes
Passenger Space Ratio (lower beds):	37.7	Onboard currency:	Euros

THE SHIP. When you first step aboard, you may be greeted by Pepper, a 4-ft- (1.2-m-) tall white humanoid robot, who is seaworthy and speaks English, German, and Italian, although he won't take your carry-on luggage. You'll see Pepper(s) around the ship during the cruise, too, as information helpers.

AIDAperla has an unmistakably stark upright bow (unusual for a cruise ship), which is a throwback to the early 20th-century ocean liners. It provides more of a 'cutting-edge' slicing effect through the water, giving greater speed. The cruise line's iconic pursed red lips adorn the bow. This is the first ship in the cruise industry to be fitted with a dual-fuel propulsion system, which includes the possibility to switch to LNG fuel, when available. The ship also has an exhaust-gas treatment system and a Mitsubishi Air Lubrication System.

The outdoor pools, located on Lanai Deck, can be used during the warmer summer season, when the water slide (which starts at the funnel and courses through the colorful Beach Club) and a rock-climbing wall can be used.

A private 'Patio-Bereich' is an adults-only retreat with its own pool, lounge areas, and bar – the first aboard an AIDA ship.

Below the apartment blocks of balcony cabins, just above the safety (lifeboat) deck, alfresco eateries and hot tubs provide the setting for an outdoor lifestyle enjoyed by many. The eateries are not well protected

BERLITZ'S RATINGS

	Possible	Achieved
Ship	500	416
Accommodation	200	143
Food	400	256
Service	400	277
Entertainment	100	77
Cruise Experience	400	289

OVERALL SCORE 1458 points out of 2000

from wind and rain, however, so they may prove to be under-used during cool weather conditions.

Inside, there's a two-decks-high AIDA Beach Club, located aft of the almost mid-ship-placed funnel; this can be covered by a large glass roof, which helps to bring the outside inside during the winter cruises in the cold weather regions of Europe, although it takes away some open deck space.

Other features include glass panoramic elevators and a skywalk. The all-white Champagne Bar is cool. One bar has an ultra-Batman feel to it. There are 17 other bars (both indoor and outdoor, including a Brauhaus, for onboard-brewed beer), a cooking studio, library, biking station, shops, and an art gallery. The bar to try is at the bow – the Splash Bar!

There are three pricing levels – AIDA Premium, AIDA Vario, and Just AIDA – depending on what you want to be included, plus differences in price according to accommodation size and grade, and itinerary.

AIDAperla is all about cruising for youthful, laid-back, German-speaking families with a diverse selection of children's and youth programs and enthusiastic Club Team members dedicated to making sure that everyone has a good time. An AIDA cruise isn't cheap, but you do get lots of high-tech entertainment, fun activities, and plenty of food at the self-serve buffet restaurants (with tablecloth-free eating), although not much contact with the relatively small number of staff. Port taxes and gratuities are included. The dress code is simple: casual (no ties) at all times.

ACCOMMODATION. Modern and minimalist but cheerful, it ranges from small interior (no-view) cabins to large two-bedroom suites, and one owner's suite. Suites range from 344.4–914.9 sq ft (32–85 sq m), but most cabins are much more compact, starting at 139.9 sq ft (13 sq m). Suites have more drawer and storage space, better-quality furniture and furnishings, a larger lounge area, and a slightly larger bathroom with a tub (and a larger balcony) than standard cabins. Those at the front and stern are the most desirable.

Balcony cabins feature beds adjacent to the floor-to ceiling door that slides open.

Thick cotton bathrobes are provided for everyone, as are two towels (a face towel and a 'bath' towel), in two different colors.

DINING. There are several dining and eatery choices for this new ship (13 dining venues and eateries in all – some with waiter service, some at extra cost, some include drinks such as beer and wine), notably the company's self-serve Markt (Market) and Weite Welt (World Wide) restaurants. Here the chairs don't have armrests – they are uncomfortable, so you won't want to stay a long time – like shopping mall food court eateries ashore. The decor is, however, pleasingly bright – yellows and oranges to stimulate the senses (plus a little cream to calm them), with Moroccan-style lampshades hanging from a plain ceiling over tables. The food displays are very attractive, and designed with families in mind. Beer is available at the push of a button or a pull of the tap, and table wine is provided in carafes on each table for lunch and dinner.

There's also Bella Donna Restaurant, and East Restaurant.

French Kiss is a casual French-style brasserie (the first of its type aboard an AIDA Cruises ship),

with red/black chairs and the red lips of Aïda as the decor theme; there's also a Chef's Kitchen (part of the Cooking School), and even a Scharfe Ecke for popular Currywurst.

Restaurant Casa Nova is an elegant (extra-cost) Venetian-inspired venue with elegant surroundings, offering a white tablecloth setting for dinners (although the chairs are not comfortable and lack armrests).

Buffalo Steakhouse has an open 'display' kitchen, and features various prime steak cuts and sizes – Delmonico, New York Strip Loin, Porterhouse, and Filet, plus bison steaks – and roast lamb rack.

Reservations are required in Buffalo Steakhouse, Casa Nova Restaurant, Brasserie French Kiss, and Rossini-Gourmet Restaurant. Drinks are included in: Bella Donna, East Restaurant, French Kiss, Fuego Family Restaurant, Markt Restaurant, Scharfe Ecke, and the Weite Welt Restaurant. Worth a mention is a Brauhaus micro-brewery, with good beer at reasonable prices.

ENTERTAINMENT. The Theatrium acts (no pun intended) as the showlounge; it is located in the ship's center and spans three levels. It has an LED stage backdrop, but no bandstand. Shows are produced by AIDA Cruises' in-house department in a joint venture with SeeLive (Hamburg's Schmidt's Tivoli Theater).

SPA/FITNESS. The ship has an expansive Body and Soul Organic Spa, with multiple body-pampering treatment rooms, extra-cost saunas, steam rooms, thalassotherapy bath, changing rooms, and a beauty salon, plus manicure and pedicure salons. Extra-cost private couples 'wellness suites' are bookable.

Body and Soul sports activities include indoor cycling. Electric bicycles and extra-cost Segways are also available at the Biking Station, and there's a 2,152 sq ft (200 sq m) floating ice-rink on the Sports Deck (winter season only).

AIDAPRIMA
★★★★

STUNNING FAMILY-FRIENDLY SHIP FOR YEAR-ROUND CASUAL CRUISES

Size:	Large Resort Ship	Passenger/Crew Ratio (lower beds):	3.6/1
Tonnage:	124,100	Cabins (total):	1,643
Cruise Line:	AIDA Cruises	Size Range (sq ft/m):	139.9-914.9/13.0-85.0
Former Names:	none	Cabins (for one person):	0
Builder:	Mitsubishi Heavy Industries (Japan)	Cabins with balcony:	1,133
Entered Service:	May 2016	Cabins (wheelchair accessible):	29
Length (ft/m):	984.2/300.0	Wheelchair accessibility:	Good
Beam (ft/m):	123.3/37.6	Elevators:	18
Propulsion/Propellers:	diesel-electric/ 2 azimuthing pods	Casino (gaming tables):	Yes
Passenger Decks:	16	Swimming Pools:	6
Total Crew:	900	Self-Service Launderette:	Yes
Passengers (lower beds):	3,286	Library:	Yes
Passenger Space Ratio (lower beds):	37.7	Onboard currency:	Euros

THE SHIP. When you first step aboard, you'll be greeted by Pepper, a 4-ft- (1.2-m-) tall white humanoid robot, who is seaworthy and speaks English, German, and Italian, although he won't take your carry-on luggage. You'll see Pepper(s) – there are several – around the ship during the cruise, too, as information helpers.

AIDAprima has an unmistakable stark upright bow (unusual for a cruise ship), which is a throwback to the early 20th-century ocean liners. It provides more of a 'cutting-edge' slicing effect through the water, giving greater speed. The cruise line's iconic pursed red lips adorn the bow. This is the first ship in the cruise industry to be fitted with a dual-fuel propulsion system, which includes the possibility to switch to LNG fuel, when available. The ship also has an exhaust-gas treatment system and a Mitsubishi Air Lubrication System.

The outdoor pools, located on Lanai Deck, can be used during the warmer summer season, when the water slide (which starts at the funnel and courses through the colorful Beach Club) and a rock-climbing wall can be used.

The 'Patio-Bereich' is an adults-only retreat with its own pool, lounge areas, and bar – the first aboard an AIDA ship. Below the apartment-blocks of balcony cabins, just above the safety (lifeboat) deck, alfresco eateries and hot tubs provide the setting for an outdoor lifestyle enjoyed by many. Inside, there's a two-decks-high AIDA Beach Club, located aft of the almost

BERLITZ'S RATINGS

	Possible	Achieved
Ship	500	414
Accommodation	200	143
Food	400	256
Service	400	274
Entertainment	100	77
Cruise Experience	400	288

OVERALL SCORE 1452 points out of 2000

mid-ship funnel; this can be covered by a large glass roof, although it takes away some open deck space.

Other features include glass panoramic elevators and a skywalk. The all-white Champagne Bar is cool. One bar has an ultra-Batman feel to it. There are 17 other bars, (both indoor and outdoor, including a Brauhaus, for onboard-brewed beer), a cooking studio, library, biking station, shops, and an art gallery. The bar to try is at the very front of the ship – the Splash Bar!

There are three pricing levels – AIDA Premium, AIDA Vario, and Just AIDA – depending on what you want to be included, plus differences in price according to accommodation size and grade, and itinerary.

A cruise aboard *AIDAperla* is all about cruising for youthful, laid-back, German-speaking families with a diverse selection of children's and youth programs (and Club Team members dedicated to making sure that everyone has a good time). An AIDA cruise isn't cheap, but you do get lots of high-tech entertainment, fun activities, and plenty of food at the self-serve buffet restaurants (tablecloth-free eating), although not much contact with the relatively small number of staff. Port taxes and gratuities are included.

ACCOMMODATION. Modern, colourful, and minimalist best describes it, which ranges from small interior cabins to large two-bedroom suites, and even an owner's suite.

Suites range in size from 344.4–882.6 sq ft (32–82 sq m); most cabins are much more compact, starting at 129.1 sq ft (12 sq m). Suites have more drawer and storage space, better-quality furniture and furnishings, a larger lounge and balcony area, and a slightly larger bathroom with a tub. Those at the front and stern of the ship are the best and most desirable.

Balcony cabins feature beds adjacent to the floor-to ceiling door that slides open.

Thick cotton bathrobes are provided in all accommodation grades, as are two towels – a face towel and a 'bath' towel, in two different colors.

DINING. AIDA Cruises has more dining choices for this ship (13 dining venues and eateries in all – some with waiter service, some at extra cost, some include drinks such as beer and wine), notably the company's self-serve food outlet Markt (Market) Restaurant. Here the chairs don't have armrests – they are uncomfortable, so you won't want to stay a long time – like shopping mall food court eateries ashore. The decor is pleasingly bright – yellows and oranges to stimulate the senses (and cream to calm them), with Moroccan-style lampshades hanging from a plain ceiling over tables. The food displays are attractive; beer is available at the push of a button or a pull of the tap, and table wine is provided in carafes on each table for lunch and dinner.

There's also Bella Donna Restaurant, East Restaurant, and California Grill.

For something different, try French Kiss, a casual French-style brasserie (the first of its type aboard an AIDA Cruises ship), with red/black chairs and the red lips of Aïda as the decor theme; there's also a Chef's Kitchen (part of the Cooking School), and even a Scharfe Ecke for popular Currywurst.

Casa Nova is an extra-cost Venice-inspired restaurant with quasi-elegant surroundings, with a white tablecloth setting (although the chairs are not comfortable and lack armrests).

Buffalo Steakhouse has an open 'display' kitchen, and features various prime steak cuts and sizes.

Reservations are required in Buffalo Steakhouse, Casa Nova Restaurant, Brasserie French Kiss, and Rossini-Gourmet Restaurant. Drinks are included in: Bella Donna, East Restaurant, French Kiss, Fuego Family Restaurant, Markt Restaurant, Scharfe Ecke, and the Weite Welt Restaurant. Worth a mention is a Brauhaus micro-brewery, with good beer at a reasonable price.

ENTERTAINMENT. The Theatrium acts (no pun intended) as the main showlounge; it is located in the center of the ship and spans three levels. It has an LED stage backdrop, but no bandstand. Shows are produced by AIDA Cruises' in-house department in a joint venture with SeeLive (Hamburg's Schmidt's Tivoli Theater).

SPA/FITNESS. The ship has a very expansive Body and Soul Organic Spa, with multiple body-pampering treatment rooms, extra-cost saunas, steam rooms, thalassotherapy bath, changing rooms, and a beauty salon, plus manicure and pedicure salons. Extra-cost private couples 'wellness suites' are bookable.

Body and Soul sports activities include indoor cycling. Electric bicycles and Segways are also available (at extra cost) at the Biking Station, and there's a 2,152 sq ft (200 sq m) floating ice rink on the Sports Deck (winter season only).

AIDASOL
★★★+

THIS CONTEMPORARY, CASUAL, NO-FRILLS CRUISING IS FOR MULTI-GENERATIONAL FAMILIES

Size:	Mid-size Ship	Passenger/Crew Ratio (lower beds):	3.1
Tonnage:	71,304	Cabins (total):	1,097
Cruise Line:	AIDA Cruises	Size Range (sq ft/m):	145.3–473.2/13.5–44
Former Names:	none	Cabins (for one person):	0
Builder:	Meyer Werft (Germany)	Cabins with balcony:	491
Entered Service:	Apr 2011	Cabins (wheelchair accessible):	11
Length (ft/m):	831.1/253.3	Wheelchair accessibility:	Good
Beam (ft/m):	105.6/32.2	Elevators:	10
Propulsion/Propellers:	diesel-electric (36,000 kW)/2	Casino (gaming tables):	Yes
Passenger Decks:	14	Swimming Pools:	3
Total Crew:	646	Self-Service Launderette:	Yes
Passengers (lower beds):	2,194	Library:	Yes
Passenger Space Ratio (lower beds):	34.6	Onboard currency:	Euros

THE SHIP. The ship has a well-proportioned profile with a swept-back funnel. The bows display the bright red lips and blue eyes of *Aïda* (from Verdi's opera). AIDA Cruises, Germany's largest cruise line, is part of Costa Cruises, itself part of Carnival Corporation.

Open deck space is limited. Dip pools and hot tubs, plus seating areas, are in a cascading, tiered setting on the pool deck, providing a reasonable amount of sunbathing space. It's designed to be a 'beach-like' environment, with splash and play areas. Sadly, there is no stroll-around promenade deck, although you can walk outdoors around the funnel area, and partially around Deck 5.

The dress code is simple: casual (no ties) at all times. Port taxes and gratuities are included.

Several decks of public rooms, lounges, and bars are positioned above the accommodation decks, and public room names common to all the ships in the fleet are used. The AIDA Bar is the main social gathering place. It has a star-shaped bar (whose combined length makes it among the longest at sea), and many adjacent tables for standing drinkers. There are several other bars, plus a 'no music' observation lounge, an art gallery, and a small casino with gaming tables and slot machines.

This is a family-friendly ship, with a diverse selection of children's and youth programs, and special Club Team members dedicated to making sure that everyone has a good time. For club purposes, children

BERLITZ'S RATINGS

	Possible	Achieved
Ship	500	371
Accommodation	200	133
Food	400	245
Service	400	264
Entertainment	100	72
Cruise Experience	400	274

OVERALL SCORE 1356 points out of 2000

are divided into five age groups, each with its own play area.

An AIDA Cruise is all about über-casual cruising for youthful German-speaking urbanites including families with children who enjoy a party-like environment, with self-serve buffet restaurants (tablecloth-free eating), and who don't mind little contact with the relatively small number of staff.

ACCOMMODATION. There are several grades, from deluxe suites to interior (no-view) cabins.

Contrary to maritime traditions (even-numbered cabins on the port side, odd-numbered cabins on the starboard side), cabin numbers progress numerically (example: 8201–8276 on the port side; 8101–8176 on the starboard side). All suites and cabins have two beds (convertible to queen-size bed). Some also have two extra beds/berths for children, and some have interconnecting doors – useful for families.

The decor is bright, youthful, and minimalist, and accented with multi-patterned fabrics, wood-trimmed cabinetry (with nicely rounded edges), and rattan or wood-look furniture. Beds have duvets and a colorful Arabian-style fabric canopy goes from the headboard to the ceiling. The windows have full pull-down blackout blinds (useful in destinations with long daylight hours).

Bathrooms are compact, with a shower enclosure, tiny washbasin, and small toilet. Only a wall-mounted body wash/shampoo dispenser is provided, so take any other toiletries you may need.

Thick cotton bathrobes are provided for all, as are two towels – a face towel and a rather small 'bath' towel, in two different colors. The bathroom does not have a hairdryer, but you'll find one in the vanity unit in the cabin. Note that there is no cabin service after 3pm.

Balcony cabins have easy-to-open sliding doors, a small drinks table, and two small chairs. Note that balconies on the lowest deck can be overlooked by anyone on a balcony on the decks above. Balcony cabins have a hammock, although it only accommodates one (slim) person. Some cabins (forward on Deck 5 – Nos 5103, 5104, 5105, 5106, 5203, 5204, 5206) have cabins with an outside view (well, outside light), but they are obstructed by steel bulkheads that form the front section of the ship.

DINING. There are three self-serve eateries: Markt (Market), Bella Vista (for Italian cuisine), and Weite Welt (Wide World) restaurants, with open seating at tables of four to eight. Cutlery hangs in a rack (unhygienic), and there are no soup spoons, only dessert spoons.

There is always a decent selection of breads, cheeses, cold cuts, fruits, and make-your-own coffee and teas – with a choice of more than 30 types of loose-leaf regular and herbal teas. The fish section has its own fish-smoking unit (which resembles a wine cabinet).

Beer is available at the push of a button or a pull of the tap, and table wine – of the sort that would make a good drain cleaner – is usually provided in carafes on each table for lunch and dinner. Beverage stations open only during restaurant opening hours, unless you go to the extra-cost coffee bar (Café Mare). Vending machines dispense out-of-hours snacks.

Rossini Restaurant, with mostly high-back seats, has an intimate atmosphere. It is open for dinner only, and has a set multi-course menu, plus daily 'specials.' There is no cover charge, but charges apply to à la carte menu and to wines. Reservations are needed, tablecloths are provided, the food is very good, and the service is good.

Buffalo Steakhouse has an open 'display' kitchen, and offers various steak cuts and sizes, and roast lamb rack. It's like going out to eat in a decent restaurant ashore – but without tablecloths.

There's a 12-seater sushi counter for extra cost Japanese-style sushi and sashimi dishes.

Vinotheque, a wine bar located in front of the Wei-de Welt (Wide World) Restaurant, has a list of premium wines, and Davidoff cigars (although you can't smoke them anywhere inside the ship).

Pizzeria Mare provides a small selection of ever-popular pizzas. Worth mentioning is a Brauhaus micro-brewery with decent beer at a reasonable price, and table service food in a beer garden setting.

ENTERTAINMENT. Located in the center of the ship, the Theatrium (theater) is open to the main foyer and other public areas, on three levels (decks 9, 10, and 11), and topped by a glass dome. Amphitheater-style seating is on three decks (the bench seating on the two upper levels has back supports, but not on the lower level), plus standing tables, although sight lines to the raised thrust stage area are less than good from many of the seats.

SPA/FITNESS. The spa, fitness, and sports programming are extensive. The Body and Soul wellness/oasis area is located on two decks (connected by a stairway) and encompasses some 24,750 sq ft (2,300 sq m). An open-air wellness deck is for 'FKK' relaxation (nude sunbathing) – forward of the ship's mast.

AIDASTELLA
★★★+

THIS MID-SIZE FAMILY-FRIENDLY RESORT SHIP IS FOR BASIC BUT FUN CRUISING

Size:	Mid-size Ship	Passenger/Crew Ratio (lower beds):	3.1
Tonnage:	71,304	Cabins (total):	1,097
Cruise Line:	AIDA Cruises	Size Range (sq ft/m):	145.3–473.2/13.5–44
Former Names:	none	Cabins (for one person):	0
Builder:	Meyer Werft (Germany)	Cabins with balcony:	722
Entered Service:	Mar 2013	Cabins (wheelchair accessible):	11
Length (ft/m):	831.1/253.3	Wheelchair accessibility:	Good
Beam (ft/m):	105.6/32.2	Elevators:	10
Propulsion/Propellers: diesel-electric (36,000 kW)/2		Casino (gaming tables):	Yes
Passenger Decks:	14	Swimming Pools:	3
Total Crew:	646	Self-Service Launderette:	Yes
Passengers (lower beds):	2,194	Library:	Yes
Passenger Space Ratio (lower beds):	34.6	Onboard currency:	Euros

THE SHIP. The ship has a profile that is quite well proportioned, with a swept-back funnel and wedge-shaped stern. On the bows are the bright red lips and blue eyes of *Aïda* (from Verdi's opera, written in 1871). AIDA Cruises, Germany's largest cruise line, comes under Costa Cruises, itself part of Carnival Corporation.

Open deck space is rather limited, but sunbathing space includes a quiet section above the navigation bridge. Dip pools and hot tubs, plus seating areas, are in a cascading, tiered setting on the pool deck. It's designed to be a 'beach-like' environment, with splash and play areas. Sadly, there is no stroll-around promenade deck, although you *can* walk outdoors around the funnel area, and partially around Deck 5.

The dress code is casual (no ties) at all times. Port taxes and gratuities are included.

Several decks of public rooms and facilities are positioned above the accommodation decks, and *AIDAstella* shares public room names that are common to all AIDA ships. AIDA Bar, the main social gathering place, for example, where the principal feature is a star-shaped bar (its combined length makes it one of the longest at sea), with tables for standing drinkers.

A small casino features blackjack, roulette and poker gaming tables, and slot machines. There are many balcony cabins, a separate aft sports deck, a 'no music' observation lounge, and an art gallery.

BERLITZ'S RATINGS

	Possible	Achieved
Ship	500	371
Accommodation	200	133
Food	400	245
Service	400	265
Entertainment	100	72
Cruise Experience	400	271

OVERALL SCORE 1357 points out of 2000

A cruise aboard *AIDAstella* is all about cruising for youthful, laid-back, German-speaking families with a diverse selection of children's and youth programs (and Club Team members dedicated to making sure that everyone has a good time). An AIDA cruise isn't cheap, but you do get lots of high-tech entertainment, fun activities, and plenty of food at the self-serve buffet restaurants, with tablecloth-free eating, although not much contact with the relatively small number of staff. Port taxes and gratuities are included. The dress code is simple: casual (no ties) at all times.

ACCOMMODATION. There are several cabin grades, from deluxe suites to interior (no-view) cabins.

Contrary to maritime tradition (even-numbered cabins on the port side, odd-numbered cabins on the starboard side), cabin numbers progress numerically (example: 8201–8276 on the port side; 8101–8176 on the starboard side). All have two beds (convertible to a queen-size bed). Some cabins also have two extra beds/berths for children, and some have interconnecting doors – useful for families.

Cabin decor is bright, minimalist, and slightly whimsical. All cabins are accented with multi-patterned fabrics, wood-trimmed cabinetry (with rounded edges), and rattan or wood-look furniture. Each bed has a duvet and a headboard-to-ceiling Arabian-style fabric canopy. Windows have full pull-down blackout blinds (useful in destinations with long daylight hours).

Bathrooms are compact, with a shower enclosure, small washbasin, and toilet. Only a wall-mounted body wash/shampoo dispenser is provided, so take any additional toiletries you may need.

Thick cotton bathrobes are provided, as are two towels – a face towel and a (small) 'bath' towel. The bathroom does not have a hairdryer, but you will find one in the vanity unit in the cabin. Note that the usual night-time turndown service provided aboard most ships is not provided, and there is no cabin service after 3pm.

Cabins with balconies have a one-person hammock, an easy-open sliding door, a small drinks table, and two small, light chairs. Balconies on the lowest deck can be overlooked by anyone on a balcony on the decks above. Some cabins (forward on Deck 5 – Nos 5103, 5104, 5105, 5106, 5203, 5204, 5206) have cabins with an outside view (well, outside light), but they are obstructed by steel bulkheads that form the front section of the ship.

DINING. Markt (Market), Bella Vista (for Italian cuisine), and Weite Welt (Wide World) restaurants offer open seating at tables of four to eight.

There is a selection of breads, cheeses, cold cuts, fruits, and make-your-own coffee and teas – with a choice of more than 30 types of (weak) loose-leaf regular and herbal teas. The fish section has its own fish-smoking unit.

Beer is available at the push of a button or a pull of the tap, and table wine is provided in carafes on tables for lunch and dinner. Beverage stations open only during restaurant opening hours, unless you go to the extra-cost coffee bar (Café Mare). Vending machines dispense out-of-hours snacks.

The Rossini Restaurant, with mostly high-back seats, has an intimate atmosphere. Open for dinner only, it has a set multi-course menu, plus daily 'specials.' There is no cover charge, but the à la carte menu and wines here are at extra cost. Reservations are needed, and tablecloths are provided.

The Buffalo Steakhouse (no tablecloths) has an open 'display' kitchen, and features premium beef and bison steaks, and roast lamb rack. Wine and other drinks cost extra.

There is also a 12-seater sushi counter with stools and two low-slung tables.

A wine bar, Vinotheque, located in front of the Weide Welt (Wide World) Restaurant, features premium wines, and Davidoff cigars (although you can't smoke them at the bar – or anywhere inside the ship).

Pizzeria Mare provides a small selection of basic pizzas. Worth mentioning is a Brauhaus micro-brewery with good beer and table-service food in a beer garden setting.

ENTERTAINMENT. Located in the ship's center, the Theatrium (theater) is open to the main foyer on three levels and topped by a glass dome. Amphitheater-style seating is on three decks; there are back supports to the bench seating on the two upper levels but not on the lower level; there are also some standing tables. However, sight lines to the raised thrust stage are poor from many of the seats.

SPA/FITNESS. The Body and Soul wellness/oasis area is located on two decks (connected by a stairway) and encompasses some 24,750 sq ft (2,300 sq m). An open-air wellness 'FKK' deck is for nude sunbathing (forward of the ship's mast).

AIDAVITA
★★★+

AN UPBEAT, FAMILY-FRIENDLY SHIP FOR VIBRANT, BUSY, CASUAL CRUISING

Size:	Mid-size Ship	Passenger/Crew Ratio (lower beds):	3.0
Tonnage:	42,289	Cabins (total):	633
Cruise Line:	AIDA Cruises	Size Range (sq ft/m):	145.3–344.4/13.5–32.0
Former Names:	none	Cabins (for one person):	0
Builder:	Aker MTW (Germany)	Cabins with balcony:	60
Entered Service:	Apr 2002	Cabins (wheelchair accessible):	4
Length (ft/m):	666.5/202.8	Wheelchair accessibility:	Good
Beam (ft/m):	92.2/28.1	Elevators:	6
Propulsion/Propellers:	diesel-electric/2	Casino (gaming tables):	No
Passenger Decks:	10	Swimming Pools:	2
Total Crew:	389	Self-Service Launderette:	Yes
Passengers (lower beds):	1,266	Library:	Yes
Passenger Space Ratio (lower beds):	33.4	Onboard currency:	Euros

THE SHIP. *AIDAvita* has a smart profile that includes a swept-back funnel and wedge-shaped stern. The bows display the red lips and blue eyes of *Aïda* (from Verdi's opera, written in 1871). AIDA Cruises, Germany's largest cruise line, is part of Costa Cruises, which is itself part of Carnival Corporation. In 2017 the ship underwent a refit that changed some areas and prepared the ship for the company's 'AIDA Selection' program.

Open deck space is tight, but sunbathing space includes a pleasant, quiet section above the bridge. Dip pools and hot tubs, plus seating areas, are in a cascading, tiered setting atop the ship on the pool deck, providing a decent amount of sunbathing space. It's a 'beach-like' environment, with splash and play areas. However, there's no wrap-around outdoor promenade deck.

Several decks of public rooms and facilities are positioned above the accommodation decks, and *AIDAvita* shares public room names common to all the ships in the fleet. AIDA Bar is the main social gathering place; it has a star-shaped bar (whose combined length makes it among the longest at sea), with many tables for standing drinkers.

Other facilities include a shore excursion counter, 'library,' seminar rooms, duty-free shop, several bars and lounges, a small casino with blackjack, roulette, and poker gaming tables, and slot machines.

BERLITZ'S RATINGS

	Possible	Achieved
Ship	500	352
Accommodation	200	132
Food	400	241
Service	400	258
Entertainment	100	70
Cruise Experience	400	271

OVERALL SCORE 1324 points out of 2000

There is an aft sports deck, an observation lounge, and an art gallery. The embarkation entryway has a bar and lookout balcony, and it is painted to look like a city street scene. A welcoming environment, it helps to calm tempers after waiting in a line to go through the security process for embarkation or in ports of call.

The dress code is simple: casual (no ties) at all times. The fees are straightforward too, with port taxes and gratuities are included.

An AIDA cruise is all about über-casual cruising for youthful German-speaking urbanites, including families with children (youngsters are divided into five age groups for club purposes). There's a party-like environment, with self-serve buffet restaurants (tablecloth-free eating), and minimal contact with the relatively small number of staff.

ACCOMMODATION. There are several grades, from so-called deluxe suites to interior (no-view) cabins.

Contrary to maritime traditions (even-numbered cabins on the port side, odd-numbered cabins on the starboard side), cabin numbers progress numerically (example: 8201–8276 on the port side; 8101–8176 on the starboard side). All suites/cabins have two beds (convertible to a queen-size bed). Some cabins have extra beds/berths for children; some have interconnecting doors – practical for families.

Bright, minimalist, and slightly whimsical cabins are accented with multi-patterned fabrics, wood-trimmed cabinetry (with nicely rounded edges), and rattan or wood-look furniture. Beds have duvets and a colorful Arabian-style fabric canopy from headboard to the ceiling. The windows have full pull-down blackout blinds (useful in destinations with long daylight hours). Lifeboats may obstruct views in some cabins in the ship's center.

Bathrooms are compact, with a shower enclosure, small washbasin, and small toilet. Only a wall-mounted body wash/shampoo dispenser is provided, so take any additional toiletries you may need.

Thick cotton bathrobes are provided for suite-grade occupants (non-suite grade passengers can obtain one from the spa). A face towel and a 'bath' towel are provided. A hairdryer is located in the vanity unit in the cabin. Unusually, night-time turndown service is not provided (there is no cabin service after 3pm).

Cabins with balconies have an easy-open sliding door, a small drinks table, and two small chairs. Note that balconies on the lowest deck can be overlooked by anyone on a balcony above. Some cabins (forward on Deck 5 – Nos. 5103, 5104, 5105, 5106, 5203, 5204, 5206) have an outside view (well, outside light), but they are totally obstructed by steel bulkheads forming the front of the ship.

DINING. The Markt and Karibik self-serve buffet-style restaurants have open seating at tables for four to eight. Cutlery hangs in a rack (an unhygienic arrangement), and there are no soup spoons, only dessert spoons. It's very casual and easy-going mass catering, so think food-court eating, not dining.

There is a decent selection of breads, cheeses, cold cuts, fruits, and make-your-own coffee and teas – with over 30 types of loose-leaf regular and herbal teas.

The crew to passenger ratio is poor because there are no waiters as such – just staff for clearing tables.

Beer is at the push of a button or a pull of the tap, and table wine – of the sort that would make a good drain cleaner – is provided in carafes on each table for lunch and dinner. Beverage stations open only during restaurant opening hours, unless you go to the extra-cost coffee bar. Vending machines dispense out-of-hours snacks.

The extra-cost Selection Restaurant has a quiet, intimate atmosphere. It is open for dinner only. Tablecloths are provided.

A wine bar, Vinotheque, has premium wines and Davidoff cigars (smoking is only allowed in designated spaces outdoors).

ENTERTAINMENT. The Theater (Das Theater), the main venue for all shows and most cabaret, is two decks high, with a raised stage, and amphitheater-style bench seating on all levels. Benches have back rests and are quite comfortable, with good sight lines from most seats, except for port and starboard balcony sections, where the view is interrupted by thick safety railings.

SPA/FITNESS. Body and Soul Spa is located forward on Deck 11, and includes two saunas (one dry, one wet, both with seats for over 20 persons, with glass walls that look onto the deck), massage and other treatment rooms, and a large lounging area. There are showers and two 'ice walls' to use when you come out of the saunas (simply lean into the ice wall for maximum effect). Forward and outside the wellness center, is the FKK (Freikoerperkultur) nude-sunbathing deck, on two levels.

ALBATROS
★★★

THIS SHIP IS GOOD FOR LOW-PRICE, NO-FRILLS LONGER CRUISES FOR GERMAN SPEAKERS

Size:	Mid-size Ship	Passenger/Crew Ratio (lower beds):	2.5
Tonnage:	28,078	Cabins (total):	449
Cruise Line:	Phoenix Reisen	Size Range (sq ft/m):	123.7–679.2/11.8–63.1
Former Names:	Crown, Norwegian Star I, Royal	Cabins (for one person):	12
	Odyssey, Royal Viking Sea	Cabins with balcony:	15
Builder:	Wartsila (Finland)	Cabins (wheelchair accessible):	0
Entered Service:	Nov 1973/Apr 2004	Wheelchair accessibility:	Fair
Length (ft/m):	674.2/205.5	Elevators:	5
Beam (ft/m):	82.0/25.0	Casino (gaming tables):	No
Propulsion/Propellers:	diesel (15,840 kW)/2	Swimming Pools:	1
Passenger Decks:	8	Self-Service Launderette:	Yes
Total Crew:	340	Library:	Yes
Passengers (lower beds):	862	Onboard currency:	Euros
Passenger Space Ratio (lower beds):	32.5		

THE SHIP. *Albatros*, originally built for long-distance cruising for the long-defunct Royal Viking Line, was nicely refurbished in 2014. There is plenty of open deck and sunbathing space, although the popular aft pool area can become crowded.

The ship (now over 40 years old) has a good array of public rooms, including several lounges and bars, most of which are elegant in an old-school way, and have high, indented ceilings. The Observation Lounge is a particularly pleasant place to spend time. Wide stairways and foyers give a sense of space, even when the ship is full. The atmosphere is very casual, as is the dress code. A 17 percent gratuity is added to bar accounts, and drink prices are very reasonable. The Phoenix cruise staff is always bright, bubby and friendly, and the shore excursion team is knowledgeable and helpful.

The clientele tends to be mature German-speaking adults and families seeking a low-budget, good-value vacation in a comfortable (although it's not new) ship.

ACCOMMODATION. There are more than 20 price grades, from expansive suites with private balcony to standard outside-view cabins and small interior cabins. A Captain's Suite is located at the front, directly under the navigation bridge, with fine forward-facing views. Nine other Penthouse Suites include a private balcony (with separate bedroom and living area). Most other cabins have an outside view and are quite well appointed, and there is a good amount of storage space; however, some bathrooms in the lower categories have awkward access. All cabins have a TV, bathrobe, and personal safe. Suites and 'comfort cabins' also have a minibar. Occupants of eight (mostly suite) accommodation grades receive 'Phoenix VIP' service.

DINING. The two dining rooms (Mowe and Pelikan) both have high ceilings, and are quite spacious. Dining is in one seating at assigned tables for two to eight. Breakfast and lunch can be taken in the dining room or outdoors at a self-service buffet. Mid-morning bouillon is a Phoenix seagoing tradition, as is a Captain's Dinner (formal night), and a Buffet Magnifique.

The service is friendly and attentive, although there is little finesse, and the food itself (recently upgraded) is quite acceptable (although not as good as *Amadea* or *Artania*). Decent table wines are included for lunch and dinner, but even better-quality wines can also be purchased.

ENTERTAINMENT. The Pacific Lounge is the show-lounge. It seats about 500, but several pillars obstruct the sight lines from some places. Small-scale shows are presented by a small team of resident singers/dancers.

SPA/FITNESS. There are a gymnasium and sauna, two steam rooms, body-treatment rooms, and a beauty salon.

BERLITZ'S RATINGS

	Possible	Achieved
Ship	500	311
Accommodation	200	128
Food	400	214
Service	400	237
Entertainment	100	60
Cruise Experience	400	250

OVERALL SCORE 1200 points out of 2000

ALLURE OF THE SEAS
★★★★

A FINE MEGA-LARGE, FAMILY-FRIENDLY, MULTI-CHOICE SHIP FOR CASUAL CRUISING

Size:	Large Resort Ship	Passenger/Crew Ratio (lower beds):	2.4
Tonnage:	225,282	Cabins (total):	2,704
Cruise Line:	Royal Caribbean International	Size Range (sq ft/m):	150.6–1,523.1/14.0–141.5
Former Names:	none	Cabins (for one person):	0
Builder:	Aker Yards (Finland)	Cabins with balcony:	1,956
Entered Service:	Dec 2010	Cabins (wheelchair accessible):	46
Length (ft/m):	1,181.1/360.0	Wheelchair accessibility:	Good
Beam (ft/m):	216.5/66.0	Elevators:	24
Propulsion/Propellers:	diesel-electric (97,200kW)/	Casino (gaming tables):	Yes
	3 pods (2 azimuthing, 1 fixed)	Swimming Pools:	3
Passenger Decks:	16	Self-Service Launderette:	No
Total Crew:	2,164	Library:	Yes
Passengers (lower beds):	5,408	Onboard currency:	US$
Passenger Space Ratio (lower beds):	41.6		

THE SHIP. When it debuted in 2010, *Allure of the Seas* qualified as the world's largest cruise ship – just 2ins (5cm) longer than sister, *Oasis of the Seas*, the world's first cruise ship measuring over 200,000 tons, which debuted in 2009. However, at time of printing, the 227,700-ton *Harmony of the Seas* was the largest cruise ship in the world (due to be superceded in late 2018 by the 230,000-ton *Symphony of the Seas*).

Allure of the Seas is a real 'Moveable Resort Vacation' for families with children, and a credit to Royal Caribbean International's (RCI's) design team. It provides a fine cruise experience with a wide range of choices for youthful adults and families with children, and is packed with innovative design elements.

Much outdoor and indoor/outdoor space is devoted to aqua-bathing and sports, but there's little space for sunbathing. If all 5,400 passengers want a sunlounger at the same time, forget it! Sun loungers are so tightly packed together that there's little space to put your belongings.

Standout features, however, are the H2O Zone, Central Park, The Boardwalk, and other facilities that young families seek for action-packed cruise vacations. There are several swimming pools, three of which – 'main,' 'beach,' and 'sports' – are high on Deck 15 (Pool and Sports Zone) of the 16 passenger decks, as is the H2O Zone. Two large hot tubs extend over the ship's side (the water for the swimming pools alone weighs 2,300 tons).

BERLITZ'S RATINGS		
	Possible	Achieved
Ship	500	402
Accommodation	200	140
Food	400	234
Service	400	286
Entertainment	100	87
Cruise Experience	400	286

OVERALL SCORE 1435 points out of 2000

There are 37 bars and over 20 places to eat or snack, while public spaces are arranged as seven 'neighborhoods': Central Park, the Boardwalk, the Royal Promenade, the Pool and Sports Zone, Vitality at Sea Spa/Fitness Center, Entertainment Place, and Youth Zone. The most popular are the Boardwalk and Central Park, both open to the air, and the indoor Royal Promenade.

The Boardwalk. An echo of Coney Island, the Boardwalk – which is open to the skies – contains shops and an art gallery. Eateries include a Boardwalk Donut Shop; Johnny Rockets, a burger/milk shake diner; and Sabor, for Mexican-style eats.

Central Park. This is 328ft (100m) long, with real vegetation, including over two dozen trees, almost 12,000 plants, and a vertical 'living' plant wall. Unlike its New York inspiration, it includes, at its lower level, a 'town center.' At night, it's a quiet, serene area. Vintages wine and tapas bar is a chill-out venue, and there are several reservations-required, extra-charge restaurants and eateries. If you are in a Central Park cabin, you'll need to take an elevator to get to the closest pool – it's like going to the top of a building for a dip.

The Royal Promenade is the floating equivalent of a shopping mall, with casual eateries (including extra-cost Starbucks, located at the forward end), shops with all kinds of merchandise, video screens, and changing color lights at every step. It's all a bit surreal – like being in a circus at sea, with something going on every minute. But one thing not to be missed is the 'Move On! Move On!' parade, a delightful circus-like extravaganza that includes characters from DreamWorks Animation's *Madagascar*. Interior-view promenade cabins have balconies that look down onto the action in Central Park. A hydraulic, oval-shaped Rising Tide Bar moves slowly through three decks linking the double-width Royal Promenade with Central Park.

The Pool and Sports Zone forward of the twin funnels is an adventurous fun area for families. Two Flow-Riders (surf simulators) are located atop the ship around the aft exhaust mast, together with basketball courts and golf. There's also a large jogging track. An adults-only open-air solarium and rentable cabanas are part of the outdoor scene.

The Solarium is a welcoming large, light-filled, restful space (shame about the background music). High atop ship, adults can 'escape' the Las Vegas-like atmosphere of other areas. Casino gamers will find roulette (the tables are electronic, with touch buttons), blackjack, craps, Caribbean Stud Poker, and 450 slot machines, plus a player's club and poker room – but this really can be a smoke-filled place, even in the 'no-smoking' area. The casino entrance features a gaming history display.

Sadly, exterior wooden railings have mostly been replaced by fibreglass railings – particularly noticeable on cabin balconies.

Standing in line to make reservations for the main shows can be time-consuming (the reservation booth is in the middle of the Royal Promenade). You could make them online before your cruise – if you can plan ahead (but making changes can be frustrating).

Ordering room service is via the interactive touchscreen television and complicated. Getting reservations in one of the specialty restaurants takes effort (it's easier for suite-grade occupants).

Allure of the Seas operates from the purpose-built Terminal 18 in Port Everglades (Fort Lauderdale), whose restroom facilities are pitiful. In late 2018 the ship moves to the new purpose-built PortMiami terminal, its new year-round base.

Disembarkation. When the two 'flybridge' gangways are working, disembarkation is relatively speedy, but when only one is working, it's not. Disembarkation for non-US citizens can be appallingly slow.

Overall, this stunning ship will provide a fine cruise experience and wide range of choices for youthful families.

ACCOMMODATION. There are a mind-boggling number of accommodation price grades, reflecting the choice of location and size. Suite occupants can access a concierge lounge and associated services. There are many family-friendly cabins, but no solo-occupancy cabins, and the cabin-numbering system is awkward to get used to. Cabin doors open outwards (towards you), as in many European hotels. In many lower-grade rooms, closet access is awkward – often with a small sofa in the way. Most standard cabins are dimensionally tight.

In balcony and non-balcony class standard cabins, the electrical sockets are inconveniently located below the vanity desk, and it's challenging to watch television from the bed.

Wash basins in non-suite grade cabins are low, at just 30.5ins (77.5cm) above the floor, and tiny. Warning – it's easy to hit your head on the mirror above. Small soap bars are provided; shampoo is in a dispenser in the shower enclosures, which have fixed shower heads. Although there is no soap dish or indentation in the washbasin surround, one useful touch is a blue ceiling bathroom nightlight.

Boardwalk cabins are exposed to noise and whatever is happening on the Boardwalk, including rehearsals, bells from the carousel forward (its 18 sculptured wooden animal figures took six weeks to carve), rowdy late-night revelers on the Boardwalk, plus screaming ziplining participants during the day, not to mention loud music from bands playing poolside, and cruise director announcements repeating what's printed in the daily program.

Boardwalk-view balcony-cabin occupants will need to close the curtains for privacy. However, the curved balconies – good for storing luggage to free up space inside the cabin – connect you with the open air. Almost all have sea views aft (just); those close to the aft Aqua Theater can use their balconies for a great view of any shows. The lowest deck of Boardwalk-view cabins has windows but no balcony (actually the view is mainly of the top of things such as the carousel). The best Boardwalk balcony cabins are, in my view, located on decks 8 to 12. For more privacy, however, it might be best to book a sea-facing balcony cabin, not one overlooking the Boardwalk.

Some Family Suite grades have a separate, small room with bunk beds; some, but not all, have curtains to separate them. Some '395' interior balcony cabins have either Central Park or Royal Promenade views from their curved interior balconies (four are wheelchair-accessible), plus 80 cabins with windows (no balconies) and views of Central Park.

Loft Suites. Although ships such as the now-withdrawn *Queen Elizabeth 2*, *Saga Rose*, and *Saga Ruby* had upstairs/downstairs suites, RCI introduced 'loft' suites to the *Oasis*-class ships, with ocean views from floor-to-ceiling, double-height windows. The are 28 Loft Suites – 25 measure 545 sq ft (51 sq m); three others (called Royal Loft Suites) measure 1,524 sq ft (141 sq m); each of them sleeps up to six and has a baby grand piano. Two Sky Loft Suites measure 722 sq ft (67 sq m) and 770 sq ft (72 sq m), and a 737-sq-ft (68-sq-m) Crown Accessible Loft Suite includes an elevator to aid disabled passengers – occupants get "Royal Genie" service (an enhanced personal butler).

DINING. Opus, the main dining room, is big, spanning three decks. It operates in two seatings (early or late) for dinner, although you can also choose 'My Time Dining' and eat at your preferred time. There are tables of all sizes, including some for family reunions.

Menu descriptions make the food sound better than it is, and the selection of breads, rolls, fruit, and cheese is poor. Overall, meals are mostly unmemorable. Lobster and filet mignon (steak) cost extra.

For a change to the main dining room, try one of the alternative dining venues. These are:

150 Central Park: the most exclusive restaurant (extra cost), combining haute-cuisine with interesting design. A kitchen observation window allows passers-by to watch the chefs in action.

Chef's Table: also extra cost, it is available to all and features a six-course meal with wine. It is hosted by the executive chef, but, with just 14 seats, getting a reservation can be difficult.

Giovanni's Table: this casual, rustic Italian-style venue features toasted herb breads, pizzas, salads, pastas, sandwiches, braised meat dishes, and stews.

Izumi Hibachi & Sushi offers Japanese-style cuisine, including a Teppanyaki menu.

Sabor Taquería & Tequila Bar is for modern tastes of Mexico, while Wonderland Imaginative Cuisine features imaginative creations.

Vintage (wine bar) has a decent selection of wines, cheese and tapas (with an à-la-carte item charge).

Central Park Café, a casual deli-style eatery, is an indoor/outdoor food market with line-up counters and limited waiter service. Items include freshly prepared salads, made-to-order sandwiches, panini, crêpes, and soups.

Other Boardwalk snacking spots: Donut Shop (for hot dogs, Wieners, Bratwurst, and other sausages), and an Ice Cream Parlor.

Elsewhere, eateries include Sorrento's Pizzeria; Park Café (for salads and light bites); and a Wipe Out Café.

ENTERTAINMENT. The 1,380-seat main showlounge spans three decks, and stages the musical *Mamma Mia!* – an excellent, 90-minute-long production (performed four times each cruise). Also, *Frozen in Time* is a must-see ice show at the ice-skating rink. There's no charge for any shows, and reservations are not required.

The 750-seat AquaTheater, outside overhanging the ship's stern, has a 6,000-sq-ft (560-sq-m) stage, and is a combination show theatre, sound stage, and event space. There are some fine viewing places high in the aft wings on both sides.

DreamWorks Animation Studios provides interactive shows featuring characters from *Shrek*, *Kung Fu Panda*, *Madagascar*, and *How to Train Your Dragon* – all very entertaining.

SPA/FITNESS. The Vitality at Sea Spa includes a Vitality Café for extra-cost health drinks and snacks. The fitness center includes almost 160 cardio and resistance machines, while an extra-cost thermal suite includes saunas, steam rooms, and heated tiled loungers. Note that you can't just take a sauna for 10 minutes without paying for a one-day pass.

It's not that large. Try not to book a massage when the ship is due to arrive or leave an anchor port – some treatment rooms experience immense vibration when the anchor chain is in use. Steiner Leisure provides the staff and treatments.

Sports facilities include two (Surfrider) surfboard pools, golf putting course, ziplining (screaming mandatory), and an ice-skating rink – it's amazingly popular for kids.

AMADEA
★★★★

A STYLISH, SPACIOUS SHIP WITH FINE FOOD AND SERVICE, FOR GERMAN SPEAKERS

Size:	Small Ship	Passenger/Crew Ratio (lower beds):	2.0
Tonnage:	28,856	Cabins (total):	297
Cruise Line:	Phoenix Reisen	Size Range (sq ft/m):	182.9–649.0/17.0–60.3
Former Names:	*Asuka*	Cabins (for one person):	0
Builder:	Mitsubishi Heavy Industries (Japan)	Cabins with balcony:	122
Entered Service:	Dec 1991/Mar 2006	Cabins (wheelchair accessible):	2
Length (ft/m):	632.5/192.8	Wheelchair accessibility:	Fair
Beam (ft/m):	81.0/24.7	Elevators:	5
Propulsion/Propellers:	diesel (17,300kW)/2	Casino (gaming tables):	No
Passenger Decks:	8	Swimming Pools:	1
Total Crew:	292	Self-Service Launderette:	Yes
Passengers (lower beds):	594	Library:	Yes
Passenger Space Ratio (lower beds):	48.5	Onboard currency:	Euros

THE SHIP. When introduced in 1991 as *Asuka*, this was the first all-new ship specially designed and built in Japan for the domestic market. It was sold to Phoenix Reisen and, as *Amadea*, started cruising for German-speaking passengers in 2006.

A more upscale vessel than other ships in the Phoenix Reisen fleet, the ship has pleasing exterior styling and a contemporary profile, with a large, rounded, but squat funnel. There is a generous amount of open deck and sunbathing space, plus a wide walk-around teakwood promenade deck outdoors, good for strolling.

The 'cake-layer' stacking of the public rooms does hamper passenger flow and makes it a little disjointed, but this is because the public rooms are separated from the accommodation areas. There are many intimate public rooms, plenty of space, and lots of natural light.

The interior decor is understated but elegant, with pleasing color combinations, quality fabrics, and fine soft furnishings. There's some fascinating Japanese artwork, including Noriko Tamura's *Song of the Seasons*, a four-deck-high mural on the wall of the main foyer staircase – in many shades of pink and red.

The relaxing Vista Lounge (an observation lounge and bar) is also used for afternoon tea service.

Harry's Bar is a lounge/bar decorated in the style of a contemporary gentleman's club, with wood-paneled walls and burgundy leather chairs. This popular drinking spot has a light, airy feel. Located in a

BERLITZ'S RATINGS		
	Possible	Achieved
Ship	500	395
Accommodation	200	156
Food	400	319
Service	400	310
Entertainment	100	76
Cruise Experience	400	291

OVERALL SCORE 1547 points out of 2000

quiet area is the ship's library, with deeply comfortable armchairs, and a fireplace with electric fire. Cigar smokers will find the Havanna Club a cozy little hideaway.

The dress code includes a mix of formal and informal nights, while during the day attire is very casual. There is a self-service launderette with eight washing machines – useful for long voyages. Overall, the ship provides an extremely comfortable and serene cruising environment. All gratuities are included.

Amadea is best suited to German-speaking couples, solo travelers, and families with children, who enjoy cruising in very comfortable surroundings aboard a contemporary ship. Because it absorbs people well, there is never any feeling of crowding.

ACCOMMODATION. There are several price categories, although in reality there are just five types of suites and cabins. Three decks (8, 9, and 10) have suites and cabins with a private balcony (but no outside light fitting).

Suites and cabins in all grades have ocean views, although some are slightly obstructed by the ship's gangway when it is in the raised (stowed) position.

In all grades, cherry wood cabinetry, which is in beautiful condition, has nicely rounded edges. Cabin soundproofing is excellent, and there is a good amount of closet and drawer space (including lockable drawers), refrigerator, and personal safe.

Most grades have bathrooms with bathtubs (and cabins available with shower), and all have a tiled floor and bath/shower area. While the suite bathrooms are generously proportioned, the 'standard' bathrooms are practical but small.

Two suites provide the largest accommodation; these are larger versions of the 'A' grade cabins. Each has a separate bedroom, with walk-in closet that includes a luggage deck, and twin beds that convert to a queen-size bed, sofa, two chairs and coffee table, large vanity desk, plenty of drawer space, and large TV. The marble-clad bathroom is large and has a whirlpool tub set alongside large ocean-view windows overlooking the private balcony, and twin washbasins set in a marble surround. There is a living room and separate guest bathroom. The private balcony is quite large and features a tropical plant set in a glass display enclosure.

In 2009, the company added two Spa Junior Suites; each has a private balcony with whirlpool tub, and good closet and drawer space.

The top-grade cabins, which are twice the size and space of the standard ones, are very good living spaces. Nicely decorated and outfitted, they have twin beds (convertible to a queen-size bed), sofa, two chairs and coffee table, large vanity desk, plenty of drawer space, and large color TV. However, when in its twin-bed configuration, the room's feng shui is poor, as one of the beds faces a large mirror at the writing/vanity desk – a negative for some people.

Many cabins have a private balcony with full floor-to-ceiling partition with sliding door (and awkward door handles) and green synthetic turf floor. There is, however, no light outside.

There's also an illuminated walk-in closet with long hanging rail and plenty of drawer space. The bathrooms, partly tiled and generously proportioned, include a plastic, glass-fronted toiletries cabinet, and two washbasins set in a thick marble surround.

DINING. There are two main restaurants, both with open seating for all meals. The Four Seasons has two sections; there are ocean-view windows along one side of the aft section, and along two sides of the forward section. The Amadea Restaurant is located on a higher deck, with ocean-view windows on two sides. The cuisine is the same in both venues. For casual breakfasts and lunches, there's an informal self-serve Lido Café with plenty of outdoor seating, adjacent to a small pool and hot tub.

With this ship, Phoenix Reisen has taken its cuisine and service to a high level by spending more money per passenger per day (this is also reflected in the cruise fare).

ENTERTAINMENT. The Atlantic Lounge is the venue for most entertainment events, including shows, social functions, and lectures. The room spans two decks, with seating on both main and balcony levels, and an extra-large wooden dance floor is provided for social dancing.

SPA/FITNESS. There is a spacious wellness center. It has large ocean-view windows, two baths, one hot tub, two saunas, steam room with wooden floor, several shower enclosures, a changing area with vanity counter, and a gymnasium. There are also five body-pampering treatment rooms, plus a relaxation area. Sports facilities include a golf court, driving cage, and putting green.

AMERICAN CONSTELLATION
NYR

THIS SHIP IS PURPOSE-BUILT FOR INTIMATE INLAND AMERICAN WATERWAYS CRUISING

Size:	Boutique Ship	Passenger/Crew Ratio (lower beds):	3.9
Tonnage:	4,500	Cabins (total):	85
Cruise Line:	American Cruise Lines	Size Range (sq ft/m):	226.0–350.0/20.9–32.5
Former Names:	none	Cabins (for one person):	9
Builder:	Chesapeake Shipbuilding (USA)	Cabins with balcony:	78
Entered Service:	May 2017	Cabins (wheelchair accessible):	2
Length (ft/m):	236.0/71.9	Wheelchair accessibility:	Poor
Beam (ft/m):	56.0/17.0	Elevators:	2
Propulsion/Propellers:	diesel/2	Casino (gaming tables):	No
Passenger Decks:	6	Swimming Pools:	No
Total Crew:	41	Self-Service Launderette:	No
Passengers (lower beds):	161	Library:	Yes
Passenger Space Ratio (lower beds):	27.9	Onboard currency:	US$

THE SHIP. *American Constellation* is a boutique ship designed for senior North American cruisers. More evolutionary than revolutionary, it's a pleasant little club-like ship, built for coastal and inland cruising to destinations – many of which are unreachable by larger cruise ships. The uppermost deck is open behind a forward windbreaker, which is good for views, and there are plenty of sunloungers.

Public rooms include an observation lounge, with views forward and to port and starboard side (complimentary cocktails and hors d'oeuvres are offered before dinner); a library/lounge; a small midships lounge; and an elevator that goes to all decks, including the outdoor sun deck.

The dress code is 'no ties casual.' It is extremely expensive for what you get. There are no additional costs, except for gratuities and port charges, because it's all included (Wi-Fi too).

ACCOMMODATION. There are numerous accommodation price grades, depending on the size, location, and grade you choose. All cabins have twin beds, convertible to a king-size bed, a small desk with chair, satellite-feed flat-screen infotainment system, and Internet access, clothes hanging space, and a modular bathroom with separate shower,

BERLITZ'S RATINGS		
	Possible	Achieved
Ship	500	NYR
Accommodation	200	NYR
Food	400	NYR
Service	400	NYR
Entertainment	100	NYR
Cruise Experience	400	NYR
OVERALL SCORE NYR points out of 2000		

washbasin, and toilet (no cabin has a bathtub), and windows that open. Accommodation/rooms incorrectly designated as suites (23) also have a private balcony each; although narrow, these do have two chairs and a small drinks table.

DINING. The Grand Dining Room – in the aft third of the ship – has large, panoramic picture windows on three sides. Everyone dines at a single open seating. The cuisine is all-American, and it's 'Cruise Local. The company's 'eat local' program includes sourcing produce, fish, and meats as near as possible to each cruise, and supporting local markets and small American businesses. There is no wine list, although basic (young) white and red table wines are included.

Note: on the last morning of each cruise, only Continental breakfast is available (no hot food).

ENTERTAINMENT. There is no formal entertainment, although dinner and after-dinner conversation with fellow passengers in the ship's lounge/bar really becomes the entertainment each evening. Otherwise, take a good book.

SPA/FITNESS. There is a tiny fitness room with a few bicycles and other exercise machines.

AMERICAN STAR
★★+

A SMALL US COASTAL CRUISING SHIP WITH LIMITED FACILITIES

Size:	Boutique Ship	Passenger/Crew Ratio (lower beds):	3.4
Tonnage:	2,000	Cabins (total):	48
Cruise Line:	American Cruise Lines	Size Range (sq ft/m):	204.0–240.0/18.9–22.2
Former Names:	none	Cabins (for one person):	2
Builder:	Chesapeake Shipbuilding (USA)	Cabins with balcony:	27
Entered Service:	Jun 2007	Cabins (wheelchair accessible):	1
Length (ft/m):	220.0/67.0	Wheelchair accessibility:	Fair
Beam (ft/m):	46.0/14.0	Elevators:	1
Propulsion/Propellers:	diesel/2	Casino (gaming tables):	No
Passenger Decks:	4	Swimming Pools:	0
Total Crew:	27	Self-Service Launderette:	No
Passengers (lower beds):	94	Library:	Yes
Passenger Space Ratio (lower beds):	21.2	Onboard currency:	US$

THE SHIP. This is one of five coastal cruise ships in the fleet of American Cruise Lines, which has its own shipyard in Chesapeake, Maryland. *American Star* (sister ships: *American Constellation, American Glory, American Spirit, and Independence*) is built for coastal and inland cruising to destinations unreachable by larger cruise ships. The uppermost deck is open (good for views) behind a forward windbreaker; many sunloungers are provided, and there's a small golf putting green.

Inside, public rooms include an observation lounge, with views forward and to port and starboard side (complimentary cocktails and hors d'oeuvres are offered before dinner); a library/lounge; a small midships lounge; and an elevator that goes to all decks, including the outdoor sun deck.

Cruises are typically of seven to 14 days' duration. The ship docks in town centers, or within walking distance. The dress code is 'no ties casual.' It is extremely expensive for what you get. There are no additional costs, except for gratuities and port charges, because it's all included.

American Star suits mature couples and solo travelers sharing a cabin and wishing to cruise in an all-American environment where the destinations are more important than food, service, or entertainment.

ACCOMMODATION. There are five cabin price grades (four are doubles, one is for solo travelers). All cabins, except those for just one person, have twin

BERLITZ'S RATINGS		
	Possible	Achieved
Ship	500	275
Accommodation	200	122
Food	400	229
Service	400	187
Entertainment	100	40
Cruise Experience	400	147

OVERALL SCORE 1000 points out of 2000

beds, convertible to a king-size bed, or king-size beds, a small desk with chair, satellite-feed flat-screen TV, DVD player and Internet access, clothes hanging space, and a modular bathroom with separate shower, washbasin, and toilet (no cabin has a bathtub), and windows that open. Some types of accommodation incorrectly designated as suites (including 23) also have a private balcony; although narrow, these do have two chairs and a small drinks table.

DINING. The dining salon, in the rear third of the vessel, has large, panoramic picture windows on three sides. Everyone dines at a single open seating. The cuisine is all-American, and its 'Cruise Local. Eat Local.' program includes sourcing produce, fish, and meats as near as possible to each cruise, and supporting local markets and small American businesses. There is no wine list, although basic white and red table wines are included. Note: on the last morning of each cruise, only Continental breakfast is available (no hot food).

ENTERTAINMENT. There is no formal entertainment, although dinner and after-dinner conversation with fellow passengers in the ship's lounge/bar really becomes the entertainment each evening. Otherwise, take a good book.

SPA/FITNESS. There is a tiny fitness room with a few bicycles and other exercise machines.

AMSTERDAM
★★★+

DUTCH-STYLE DECOR AND FRIENDLY SERVICE FOR MATURE CRUISERS

Size:	Mid-size Ship	Passenger/Crew Ratio (lower beds):	2.1
Tonnage:	62,735	Cabins (total):	690
Cruise Line:	Holland America Line	Size Range (sq ft/m):	184.0–1,124.8/17.1–104.5
Former Names:	none	Cabins (for one person):	0
Builder:	Fincantieri (Italy)	Cabins with balcony:	172
Entered Service:	Oct 2000	Cabins (wheelchair accessible):	20
Length (ft/m):	780.8/238.0	Wheelchair accessibility:	Good
Beam (ft/m):	105.8/32.2	Elevators:	12
Propulsion/Propellers:	diesel-electric (37,500kW)/	Casino (gaming tables):	Yes
	2 azimuthing pods	Swimming Pools:	2 (1 w/ sliding glass dome)
Passenger Decks:	12	Self-Service Launderette:	Yes
Total Crew:	650	Library:	Yes
Passengers (lower beds):	1,380	Onboard currency:	US$
Passenger Space Ratio (lower beds):	45.4		

THE SHIP. *Amsterdam*, a close sister ship to *Rotterdam*, has a nicely raked bow, and the familiar interior flow and design style. It is the first ship in the HAL fleet to feature an azimuthing pod propulsion system, with pods powered by a diesel-electric system.

The decor retains much of the traditional ocean liner detailing so loved by frequent passengers, with some use of medium and dark wood paneling. However, some color combinations – particularly for the chairs and soft furnishings – are rather odd. Much of the artwork reflects the line's past, including items depicting the city of Amsterdam's history.

The interior focal point is a three-deck-high atrium, in an oval shape; a whimsical 'Astrolabe' is the centerpiece. Clustered in the lobby are the reception desk, shore-excursion desk, photo shop, and photo gallery.

There are three principal passenger stairways – better than two from the viewpoint of safety, flow, and accessibility. There is a glass-covered pool on the Lido Deck between the mast and the twin funnels, watched over by a sculpture of a brown bear catching salmon.

The casino, in the middle of a major passenger flow on one of the entertainment decks, has gaming tables and slot machines.

HAL provides free ice cream at certain times, plus hot hors d'oeuvres in all bars, but the charge to use the washing machines and dryers in the self-service launderette is irritating.

BERLITZ'S RATINGS		
	Possible	Achieved
Ship	500	378
Accommodation	200	148
Food	400	250
Service	400	268
Entertainment	100	73
Cruise Experience	400	276
OVERALL SCORE 1387 points out of 2000		

Perhaps the ship's best asset is its personable Filipino and Indonesian crew, although communication (in English) can be frustrating at times, particularly in the dining room and buffet areas.

Amsterdam is extremely comfortable, with fine, elegant, and luxurious decorative features. On the negative side, the quality of food and service is poor, and there's a lack of understanding of what it really takes to make a 'luxury' cruise experience, despite what is touted in Holland America Line's (HAL's) brochures.

ACCOMMODATION. This is spread over five decks (some cabins have full or partially obstructed views), in 16 grades: 11 with outside views, and five interior grades (no view). With one deck of suites (and a dedicated, private Concierge Lounge, it's a two-class ship. No cabin is more than 130ft (40m) from a stairway, which makes it very easy to find your way from your cabin to the public rooms. Although 81 percent of cabins have outside views, only 25 percent of those have balconies.

The 'standard' interior and outside-view cabins are tastefully furnished and have twin beds convertible to a queen-size bed – but space is tight for walking between beds and the vanity unit. There is decent closet and drawer space for short cruises. The tiled bathrooms are disappointingly small; the shower tubs are tiny, and storage for toiletries is poor.

The 50 Verandah Suites and four Penthouse Suites on Navigation Deck share a private Concierge Lounge (for making dining arrangements, booking shore excursions, and for other requests; access is via a key card).

Four Penthouse Suites each have a separate steward's entrance, plus a separate bedroom, wet bar, and large bathroom.

DINING. La Fontaine Dining Room seats 747, spans two decks, and has a stained-glass ceiling measuring almost 1,500 sq ft (140 sq m), with a floral motif and fiber-optic lighting. There are tables for two to eight, although few are for two. Both open seating and fixed (assigned tables and times) seating are available, while breakfast and lunch are open seating (you'll be seated by restaurant staff when you enter). Tablecloths, Rosenthal china, and fine cutlery are provided.

With a few exceptions, the cuisine is rather unmemorable, and lacks passion and taste, because it's all about batch cooking. There's a distinct lack of variety of green vegetables, much use of rice, canned fruit, and already sliced and diced cheese. Still, you get friendly service from smiling Indonesian and Filipino stewards, and the plates are attractive.

The 88-seat, extra-cost Pinnacle Grill has better food and presentation than the main dining room. It's open for lunch and dinner, and reservations are required. Its whimsically surreal artwork features scenic landscapes. Pacific Northwest steaks and seafood is featured, with small portions and few vegetables.

Lido Buffet Restaurant is open for casual dinners on all except the last night of each cruise, in an open-seating arrangement. Tables are set with crisp linens, flatware, and standard stemware.

For casual breakfasts and lunches, the Lido Buffet Restaurant provides old-style, stand-in-line, serve-yourself canteen food – adequate for anyone used to TV dinners, but definitely not lavish as the brochures claim. Although the salad items appear adequate when displayed, they are too cold and lack taste. The constant supply of iceberg lettuce doesn't seem to go away, and there is little choice of other, more suitable, lettuces and greens. Each evening, a section opens as Canaletto, featuring popular Italian-style dishes.

Also, a poolside 'Dive-In at the Terrace Grill' features signature burgers (Dive-In sauce), hot dogs, and fries.

The room service menu is really limited, as is food delivery.

ENTERTAINMENT. The 577-seat Queen's Lounge is the venue for all production shows, strong cabaret, and other entertainment. It is two decks high, with main and balcony level seating. The stage has hydraulic lifts and three video screens, and closed-loop system for the hearing-impaired.

While HAL is not known for its fine entertainment (the budgets aren't high enough), what the line does offer is a consistently good, tried-and-tested array of cabaret acts. The production shows, while a decent attempt, fall short on storyline, choreography, and performance, with colorful costuming and lighting hiding the weak spots.

A number of bands, a string ensemble, and solo musicians present live music for dancing and listening in many of the lounges and bars. There's dancing in the Crow's Nest (atop the navigation bridge) and serenading string music in the Explorer's Lounge, among other venues.

SPA/FITNESS. The Ocean Spa is located one deck above the navigation bridge at the very forward part of the ship. It includes a gymnasium with all the latest exercise machines, including an abundance of treadmills. It has forward views over the ship's bows. There's an aerobics exercise area, large beauty salon with ocean-view windows to the port side, several treatment rooms, and men's and women's saunas, steam rooms, and changing areas.

The spa is operated by Steiner, a concession, whose young staff will try to sell you Steiner's own-brand Elemis beauty products. Massage facials, pedicures, and beauty salon treatments cost extra. Some fitness classes are free.

For the sports-minded, two paddle-tennis courts are located at the aft of the Sports Deck.

ANTHEM OF THE SEAS
★★★★

A HIGH-TECH, HIGH-ENERGY, GIZMO-FILLED, FAMILY-FRIENDLY FLOATING RESORT

Size:	Large Resort Ship	Passenger/Crew Ratio (lower beds):	3.2
Tonnage:	168,666	Cabins (total):	2,090
Cruise Line:	Royal Caribbean International	Size Range (sq ft/m):	101.1–799.7/9.4–74.3
Former Names:	none	Cabins (for one person):	34
Builder:	Meyer Werft (Germany)	Cabins with balcony:	1,571
Entered Service:	Mar 2015	Cabins (wheelchair accessible):	34
Length (ft/m):	1,112.2/339.0	Wheelchair accessibility:	Good
Beam (ft/m):	134.5/41.0	Elevators:	16
Propulsion/Propellers:	diesel-electric (41,000kW)/ 2 azimuthing pods	Casino (gaming tables):	Yes
		Swimming Pools:	3
Passenger Decks:	16	Self-Service Launderette:	No
Total Crew:	1,300	Library:	Yes
Passengers (lower beds):	4,180	Onboard currency:	US$
Passenger Space Ratio (lower beds):	40.3		

THE SHIP. *Anthem of the Seas* is the sister ship to *Ovation of the Seas* (2016) and *Quantum of the Seas* (2014). It incorporates all of the latest tech-intensive bling and entertaining features, and then some. The ship's exterior design (built in several huge sections and joined together) looks somewhat like a 'stretched' version of the slender *Celebrity Reflection* and employs the latest in hydrodynamics, hull shape, low emissions, and, importantly, low fuel consumption, and technology. The stern slopes nicely – it looks like it could be the front!

Aft is Two70 – an innovative multi-level venue that is a casual living area by day, and a stunning, high-energy entertainment venue by night, with dynamic robotic screens complementing its huge video wall.

Several novel attractions have been incorporated. North Star – quite the engineering marvel – is a 14-person (including an operator) glass capsule that lifts you off from the ship's uppermost deck for a bird's-eye view of all below you, as it moves around. It's like a posh giant 'cherry picker,' and, with an outreach of almost 135ft (41m), is quite a ride! Located in the front section, just behind the ship's mast, it is complimentary (and wheelchair-accessible), but only operates at sea. A charge applies for booking for weddings and other romantic occasions.

The second stunner is RipCord by iFly – a simulated skydiving experience in a two-storey vertical wind tunnel that lets you experience the thrill of skydiving in a safe, controlled environment. The unit uses a powerful

BERLITZ'S RATINGS		
	Possible	Achieved
Ship	500	414
Accommodation	200	137
Food	400	295
Service	400	279
Entertainment	100	88
Cruise Experience	400	290
OVERALL SCORE 1503 points out of 2000		

air flow to keep you up – like a giant hairdryer underneath you! It is located aft of the ship's funnel housing, and accommodates 13 persons for each 75-minute class, including two 'hovering in the air' experiences, instruction, and gear. You can book both attractions with interactive digital kiosks (adjacent to elevators) and tablets in public areas.

A brain-teasing team challenge can be had in a special puzzle room called Escape from the Future; collectively, the team will need to solve brainteasers within an hour in order to 'get out' – and you thought this was a vacation!

Meanwhile, a SeaPlex complex – located between the two funnels under the North Star – features adrenalin-boosting bumper-car rides, and alternatively acts as a roller-skating rink and basketball court. It's a veritable interactive sporting venue that replaces the ice rinks of most other RCI ships. Other facilities include a rock-climbing wall, and a FlowRider surfing simulator.

Inside, the decor is contemporary, rainbow colorful, and jazzy. The interior focal point is the three-storey-high Royal Esplanade, which includes Michael's Genuine Pub, Sorrento's pizza outlet, a Bionic Bar (no creative mixology – just ice, standard drinks, and no conversation – but it's really a neat feature), Music Hall (a two-deck-high entertainment venue), plus several shops, the Schooner Bar, Boleros (Latin bar), Chops Grille, Izumi (for Japanese-style cuisine), and Wonderland.

This ship will provide a great cruise experience for the whole family, but, be warned: it's all about forward planning and making reservations – lots of them – if you want the best cruise experience. Do look out for 'Gigi' the pink giraffe outside on the starboard side of Deck 15 – you can't miss it – it's 33ft (10m) high.

What this fine resort ship does superbly well is entertain you, and I highly recommended it for a first cruise, because of the excellent range of activities, the entertainment and some good dining and eatery experiences.

Niggles include the high cost for fast Wi-Fi connectivity and for the double bed day 'cabanas' atop the pool deck.

ACCOMMODATION. There are many different accommodation price grades and categories, with the price dependent on size and location. Every cabin has a view, whether real or virtual. 'Virtual' balconies – first introduced aboard *Navigator of the Seas* in 2013 – are a neat feature of the interior cabins; they can provide real-time ocean views, but you *can* turn them off. Optional wristbands (with RFID technology) provide access to your cabin and act as your charge card (you have to take them off in order to give them to the bartender); unfortunately, they are rather uncomfortable to wear.

Several new accommodation categories and types have been introduced aboard this ship. Standard cabins are about 9 percent larger than those aboard the *Oasis*-class ships. Note that suite-grade accommodation occupants can take all their meals in the exclusive Coastal Kitchen.

Loft cabins (including a 975 sq ft/90.5 sq m Owner's Loft) vary in size, but measure about 502 sq ft (46.6 sq m) and are located at the ship's stern.

Inter-connecting family cabins are great for multi-generational groups. The 15 units consist of a junior suite, balcony cabin, and interior studio connected through a shared vestibule. Together they can create 575.8 sq ft (53.5 sq m) of living space with three bedrooms, three bathrooms, and a 216-sq-ft (20-sq-m) balcony.

There are 34 'studio' cabins (12 have real balconies; all have wall beds) for solo occupancy, a first for RCI. As there's no supplement for solo travelers, they have their own price category.

Even the smallest bathroom is well designed, with touches such as a night light, and shower and vanity hooks, while cabins have bedside power outlets, ample storage space, and a USB socket.

Negatives include the fact that tablet-based infotainment systems don't answer questions, and the room service menu for breakfast is poor.

DINING. There are 18 restaurant and eatery choices (there's no single main dining room as such). There are two seatings for dinner (first and second seating), or you can opt for 'My Time Dining' for more flexibility. Overall, meals are rather hit and miss. However, you can have items such as lobster or filet mignon (steak) at an extra cost – and at least they will be cooked individually for you.

Some extra-cost restaurants require reservations, which can prove frustrating; the menus are the same each night, and service can be slow (there are no assistant waiters).

The following are complimentary (with tablecloths for dinner):

The Grande: with 432 seats, the ship's most elegant restaurant (think Southern mansion hospitality) features classic dishes reminiscent of the days of grand ocean liners.

Chic: this 434-seat restaurant features 'contemporary' cuisine and sauces made from scratch.

Silk: this 434-seat restaurant offers pan-Asian cuisine.

American Icon Grill: this 430-seat restaurant serves many of America's favorite 'comfort-food' dishes.'

Extra-cost venues:

Wonderland: based on the real and imagined elements of Fire, Ice, Water, Earth, and Dreams, this surreal 62-seat *Alice in Wonderland*-inspired venue offers food with a quirky touch, including several superb dishes using liquid nitrogen for smoke-infused specialties. It's really worth paying extra for.

Jamie's Italian: it's a 132-seat reservations-required tablecloth-free Euro-Italian bistro – and British celebrity chef Jamie Oliver's first restaurant at sea.

Chops Grille: for premium-quality steaks and grilled seafood.

Chef's Table: this exclusive 16-seat venue (located within Chops Grille) is good for private parties, with wine-and-food pairing the specialty.

Izumi: a 44-seat Japanese-Asian fusion cuisine venue including hot-rock tableside cooking, sashimi, sushi, and sake.

Johnny Rockets: a retro 1950s all-day, all-night diner-style eatery (near the main pool) for hamburgers, extra-cost malt shakes, and jukebox hits (all tables feature a mini-jukebox). A-la-carte pricing applies.

For really casual meals at no extra cost, there's the 860-seat Windjammer Marketplace self-serve, buffet-style eatery. Other casual spots at no extra cost include: The Café at Two70º; SeaPlex Dog House, Sorrento's – for pizza slices and calzones – and Café Promenade.

ENTERTAINMENT. The Royal Theater spans three decks and is the place for 'book' shows and large-scale production shows by a resident troupe of singers and dancers (reservations advised).

There's also entertainment by night at Two70º and in the Music Hall (DJs and theme nights).

SPA/FITNESS. Vitality at Sea Spa facilities include a thermal suite (definitely not worth the extra cost), beauty salon, barber shop, and gymnasium with Technogym equipment. Massage and other body-pampering treatments take place in 19 treatment rooms.

ARCADIA
★★★+

THIS IS A VERY BRITISH, CONTEMPORARY BUT STYLISH ADULTS-ONLY SHIP

Size:	Mid-size Ship	Passenger/Crew Ratio (lower beds):	2.3
Tonnage:	82,972	Cabins (total):	1,000
Cruise Line:	P&O Cruises	Size Range (sq ft/m):	170–516.6/15.7–48
Former Names:	none	Cabins (for one person):	6
Builder:	Fincantieri (Italy)	Cabins with balcony:	684
Entered Service:	Apr 2005	Cabins (wheelchair accessible):	30
Length (ft/m):	936.0/285.3	Wheelchair accessibility:	Good
Beam (ft/m):	105.0/32.0	Elevators:	14
Propulsion/Propellers:	diesel-electric (34,000kW)/	Casino (gaming tables):	Yes
	2 azimuthing pods	Swimming Pools:	2
Passenger Decks:	10	Self-Service Launderette:	Yes
Total Crew:	886	Library:	Yes
Passengers (lower beds):	1,994	Onboard currency:	UK£
Passenger Space Ratio (lower beds):	37.4		

THE SHIP. *Arcadia*, originally intended to be a Holland America Line ship, then Cunard Line's *Queen Victoria*, was transferred instead to P&O Cruises (all three are owned by Carnival Corporation).

Outdoors facilities include a walk-around promenade deck (the ship's forward section is covered), with plenty of sunloungers and cushioned pads. A Lido Deck pool has a moveable glass-domed cover – useful in poor weather. Panoramic exterior glass-wall elevators in the central foyer travel between all 10 passenger decks. Pod propulsion is provided, so there's no vibration.

The layout provides a decent horizontal flow, with most public rooms, shops, bars, and lounges set open-plan style on two principal decks, so finding your way around is relatively easy; the upper public room deck layout is disjointed, however. The interior decor is geared towards the contemporary. It is restrained and lacks the traditional features for which P&O Cruises is known. There are 3,000 works of art, which cost $4 million, by British artists. The decor is restrained, and signage is generally sound.

Facilities include a forward-facing Crow's Nest observation lounge, a florist, a gift shop arcade, a Monte Carlo casino (small for a ship of this size), a library (with leather armchairs and a Waterstones section for paperback sales), a 30-seat boutique screening room, and The Retreat (a good place to meet and chill out). Standout bars include the Spinnaker Bar (with

BERLITZ'S RATINGS

	Possible	Achieved
Ship	500	352
Accommodation	200	132
Food	400	246
Service	400	277
Entertainment	100	68
Cruise Experience	400	261

OVERALL SCORE 1336 points out of 2000

a display of ship models), a 'traditional' English pub (The Rising Sun, with Boddingtons draught beer), plus a bar that overlooks a modest three-deck-high atrium lobby. The ship really lacks a 'soul', however, because there is no central meeting point – no atrium lobby as such to act as a social centre – quite different to *Oceana*, for example.

Arcadia blends time-honored British cruising with contemporary facilities, but is quite different from other more 'traditional' ships in the fleet. It is registered in Bermuda, so UK and US passport holders can be legally married by the ship's captain (always check for the latest requirements). You can also renew your vows in a special, extra-cost ceremony. The ship underwent a refurbishment program in 2013, in which one new suite, and 23 new cabins were added (including 6 for solo travelers) in a new structure aft of the Crow's Nest, plus a new Harrods store (and revitalized shopping area), and an extra-cost East Restaurant, which replaced the former Orchid Restaurant.

Many extra onboard revenue centers have appeared aboard P&O Cruises' ships – such as paying for lectures and thalassotherapy pool use. Smoking is permitted only in designated spots on open decks.

Passenger niggles: there is no room for card games such as bridge; there's pitiful dance floor space; and the embarkation system keeps people waiting in a lounge after check-in and security until boarding card letters are called. The small public toilets are missing touches such as flowers and hand towels; there are no poolside towels (you must take them from your cabin); poolside gala receptions lack atmosphere; and pre-dinner announcements are robotic. The often-noisy air conditioning cannot be turned off in cabins or bathrooms.

Arcadia is good for couples and solo travelers seeking a mid-size, adults-only ship, with entertainment geared to British tastes, an informal setting, and plenty of public rooms to experience.

ACCOMMODATION. While there are plenty of price grades, there are really only five types of accommodation: suites, mini-suites, cabins with private balcony, and twin-bedded cabins either with or without a window.

Cabin doors and elevators also have numbers in Braille. Cabins have duvets, flat-screen infotainment system (the audio channels are also on the television, but you can't turn the picture off), tea/coffee-making sets with Tetley teabags and long-life milk, small refrigerator, vanity/writing desk, personal safe, and a hairdryer; bathrooms have half-size tubs/ showers/washbasins, and toilets. Personal toiletries are provided, with larger bottles and more choice for suite occupants.

Also standard are stylish bed runners, Slumberland 8ins (20cm) sprung mattresses, 10.5 tog duvets (blankets and pillows if you prefer), Egyptian cotton towels and robes, as well as in-cabin toning and fitness facilities for passengers who would prefer to exercise in private.

Niggles include the space-hogging tea/coffee-making set on the small vanity desk in standard cabin grades. Other gripes about standard cabins include: closets with hanging space too narrow for the width of a jacket; lack of drawer space; poor-quality plastic hangers; and no hooks for belts.

In twin-bedded cabin grades (approximately 170 sq ft/16 sq m), when the beds are pushed together, there's little room to maneuver.

Accommodation designated as suites (approximately 516 sq ft/48 sq m, including balcony) and mini-suites (approximately 384 sq ft/36 sq m, including balcony) benefit from more space (some are really just the size of two cabins), including larger bathrooms. So-called 'butler' service is provided, but, unlike most lines with these kinds of grades, bottled water costs extra, as do soft drinks.

DINING. The Meridian Restaurant, located aft, is on two decks, connected by a spiral staircase; it features 11 fine glass fiber-optic ceiling chandeliers created by Neil Wilkin. A podium with grand piano graces the upper level, which is for Freedom Dining. There are two seatings (Club Dining) in the lower level restaurant only, and tables are for two to eight people. Note that glasses for both red and white wines are small.

Other dining options. Ocean Grill, by Marco Pierre White, specializes in prime steaks and seafood – with lots of taste. East Restaurant (on Deck 11) has fine panoramic views, Asian-fusion (spice-heavy) cuisine created by Michelin-starred chef Atul Kochhar, and its own bar. Reservations are required in both venues, and a cover charge applies.

For casual meals and snacks, there's a self-serve 24-hour eatery (The Belvedere), a section of which becomes another dining venue at night, serving Indian cuisine. There's also an open-deck Neptune Grill and Caffè Vivo (indoors, adjacent to the library).

ENTERTAINMENT. The Palladium showlounge has three seating tiers and high-tech staging, lighting, and sound systems. Seating is in both banquette-style and (uncomfortable) individual tub chairs. Sight lines to the stage are generally good.

Late-night party types can dance and scream in The Globe. Classical concerts may also be scheduled occasionally. Professional dance hosts and teachers are usually on board, but ballroom-dance aficionados should note that there are few wooden dance floors.

SPA/FITNESS. The Ocean Spa includes a fitness area with forward ocean views, 10 body-pampering treatment rooms, a thermal suite with a hydrotherapy pool, sauna and steam room, and two small unisex saunas at no charge, but in a location that discourages their use (the extra-cost thermal suite is better). While the tiny sauna is free, there's a charge to use the Aqua Pool. To get from the changing room to the sauna you must walk across a carpeted foyer.

Additionally, The Retreat is a cool space for relaxation, and for calming classes such as tai chi and yoga. The spa is operated by the UK-based Harding Brothers. Sports facilities include a sports court for racquet or football games, a golf driving range, and the traditional shuffleboard and ring toss.

ARTANIA
★★★★

A COMFORTABLE, SPACIOUS SHIP FOR MATURE-AGE, GERMAN-SPEAKING CRUISERS

Size:	Mid-size Ship	Passenger/Crew Ratio (lower beds):	2.2
Tonnage:	44,348	Cabins (total):	588
Cruise Line:	Phoenix Reisen	Size Range (sq ft/m):	182.9–1,124.8/17.0–104.5
Former Names:	Artemis, Royal Princess	Cabins (for one person):	0
Builder:	Wartsila (Finland)	Cabins with balcony:	273
Entered Service:	Nov 1984/Apr 2011	Cabins (wheelchair accessible):	4
Length (ft/m):	754.5/230.0	Wheelchair accessibility:	Good
Beam (ft/m):	95.8/29.2	Elevators:	6
Propulsion/Propellers:	diesel (29,160kW)/2	Casino (gaming tables):	No
Passenger Decks:	9	Swimming Pools:	2
Total Crew:	520	Self-Service Launderette:	Yes
Passengers (lower beds):	1,176	Library:	Yes
Passenger Space Ratio (lower beds):	37.7	Onboard currency:	Euros

THE SHIP. *Artania* has a traditional walk-around teak deck, extensive outdoor deck and sunbathing space, and a wave-action swimming pool.

The interior decor reflects the feeling of space, openness, and light. There are several nicely appointed public rooms, bars, and lounges, plus wide passageways and three spacious stairways.

A Pacific Lounge, set around the funnel base, has fine views and a peaceful environment during the day; each evening it becomes a lively nightclub. Around the central stairway foyer, is the popular Harry's Bar; there's also a Bodega (tavern) for food and drinks. A 7 percent gratuity is added to bar accounts.

Artania should provide a fine experience in spacious, reserved contemporary surroundings, at a decent price. It is best suited to German-speaking couples and solo travelers seeking to cruise in a modern, but unpretentious, mid-size ship.

ACCOMMODATION. All of the cabins have outside views; 270 have private balconies. There are just four accommodation types (including suites), although there are 21 price categories. All of the cabins (most of which have twin beds convertible into a queen-size bed) are comfortable and well appointed.

All cabins have a large shower enclosure, color TV, hairdryer, personal safe, and European two-pin sockets. Also standard are high-quality sprung mattresses, European duvets, and cotton towels.

BERLITZ'S RATINGS		
	Possible	Achieved
Ship	500	382
Accommodation	200	153
Food	400	319
Service	400	308
Entertainment	100	74
Cruise Experience	400	285

OVERALL SCORE 1521 points out of 2000

L'Occitane toiletries are supplied, as are chocolates on your pillow each night. Prompt, attentive room service is provided 24 hours a day.

Some cabins on both Apollo Deck and Orion Deck have full or partial lifeboat- and safety equipment-obstructed views, but some have extra sofa beds fitted, which is good for families during the busy school-holiday periods.

The 12 largest suites are attractive, but, with the exception of the Royal Suite, they are not large, and the balconies are small, although all have teak decking. Suite occupants get an expanded range of toiletries and complimentary mineral water.

DINING. The Vier Jahreszeiten (Four Seasons) restaurant is set low down in the ship, conveniently adjacent to the lobby. One deck above is the Artania Restaurant, with adjacent bar. Casual meals can be taken in the indoor-outdoor Lido Restaurant.

ENTERTAINMENT. The Atlantik Showlounge hosts shows, drama, and cabaret acts. Volume is normally kept to an acceptable level.

SPA/FITNESS. The Artania Spa contains a gym with muscle-toning equipment, saunas and changing rooms. There's also a steam bath, ice-fountain, and salon, plus facilities for table tennis, table soccer, shuffleboard, and darts.

ASTOR
★★★

THE TRADITIONAL STYLE AND RESTFUL DECOR IS COMFORTABLE FOR MATURE-AGE CRUISERS

Size:	Small Ship
Tonnage:	20,606
Cruise Line:	Cruise and Maritime Voyages (CMV)
Former Names:	Fedor Dostoyevskiy, Astor (II)
Builder:	Howaldtswerke Deutsche Werft (Germany)
Entered Service:	Feb 1987/Apr 1997
Length (ft/m):	579.0/176.5
Beam (ft/m):	74.1/22.6
Propulsion/Propellers:	diesel (15,400kW)/2
Passenger Decks:	7
Total Crew:	300
Passengers (lower beds):	590
Passenger Space Ratio (lower beds):	34.9
Passenger/Crew Ratio (lower beds):	1.9
Cabins (total):	288
Size Range (sq ft/m):	140.0–280.0/13.0–26.0
Cabins (for one person):	0
Cabins with balcony:	0
Cabins (wheelchair accessible):	0
Wheelchair accessibility:	Fair
Elevators:	3
Casino (gaming tables):	Yes
Swimming Pools:	2
Self-Service Launderette:	No (ironing room only)
Library:	Yes
Onboard currency:	Euros

THE SHIP. Astor is an attractive, fairly modern, all-white ship with a raked bow, a large square funnel, and a balanced profile. It has been well maintained and refurbished over the years.

Astor was the original name for this ship, the larger of two vessels bearing the same name in the 1980s, built for long-defunct Astor Cruises. The ship features a mix of traditional and modern styling, with restful decor that doesn't jar the senses, although some say it's rather dark. It has teakwood decking, polished wood railings and interior fittings.

There is a good amount of open deck and sunbathing space, there are cushioned pads for the sunloungers, and the exterior handrails are of thick, polished wood. The public rooms are comfortable and varied, most with high ceilings, and include a showlounge, Captain's Club lounge (the most popular room), a library and card room, and two large boutiques. The intimate, wood-paneled Hanse Bar, with German lager on draft, has an outdoor area, too, and is popular as a late-night hangout. There is no crowding anywhere and no annoying background music in hallways or elevators.

The mainly European hotel staff is friendly but not obtrusive.

Some voyages are designated as special-theme cruises. Port taxes, insurance, and gratuities to staff are all included in the fare. Drinks prices are inexpensive compared with land-based prices.

BERLITZ'S RATINGS

	Possible	Achieved
Ship	500	298
Accommodation	200	127
Food	400	212
Service	400	253
Entertainment	100	56
Cruise Experience	400	237

OVERALL SCORE 1183 points out of 2000

Astor is operated under charter to the UK's Cruise & Maritime Voyages, and cruises in Australasian waters during southern-hemisphere summers.

Astor is for couples and solo travelers of mature years and provides a degree of traditional style and comfort in a relaxed environment. It offers a good-value-for-money vacation, with appealing itineraries and destinations, adequate but uninspiring food, and friendly service.

ACCOMMODATION. The accommodation, spanning numerous price categories, is spread over three decks, and comprises 39 suites and 249 outside-view and interior (no-view) cabins. Whichever grade of accommodation is chosen, rosewood cabinetry and plain beige walls are the norm, creating a restful environment. All suites and cabins with outside-view windows have blackout blinds – good for cruises to the land of the midnight sun.

Astor Suite measures approximately 635 sq ft (59 sq m).

Senator Suites measure 516.6 sq ft (48 sq m).

Outside-view and interior cabins measure 139.9 sq ft (13 sq m).

Note that Suite 105 faces the piano in the conference room opposite and is subject to the sound of musical rehearsals.

Outside-view family cabins. These large, four-berth cabins measure 258.3 sq ft (24 sq m) and are good for families.

All grades have a minibar, personal safe, European duvets, 100 percent cotton towels and bathrobe, soap, shampoo, shower cap, sewing kit, and a basket of fruit. The bathroom towels, however, are small. In standard cabins, many day sofas convert to beds. Twin beds cannot be pushed together.

The cabin-service menu is limited; there is an extra charge for sandwiches, and little else is available.

DINING. The Waldorf Dining Room is reasonably elegant, well laid-out, but has two seatings. Service is friendly and unpretentious.

Food quality and presentation are basic, and lack 'wow' factor. In addition to the regular entrées/main courses (typically three of these for dinner), there may also be a pasta dish and a vegetarian specialty dish. The wine list offers (young) wines from several regions, and all at inexpensive to moderate price levels, but the wine glasses are small.

Two small specialty dining venues (one serving Italian cuisine, the other a 'romantic dinner') are reservations-only, extra-cost dining spots for those wanting something a little better. Larger wine glasses are provided.

Casual breakfast and lunch buffets (both in the restaurant and another lounge) are somewhat repetitive, with limited food choice.

ENTERTAINMENT. The Showlounge is a single-level room, but 14 pillars obstruct the sight lines. The venue is best suited to cabaret and mini-concerts. The stage itself is also the dance floor, and cannot be raised for shows. The entertainment possibilities are limited, with vocalists, magicians, and other visual acts providing the bulk of the shows.

SPA/FITNESS. The Wellness Oasis, on the lowest passenger deck, contains a sauna, steam room, solarium, indoor swimming pool, beauty salon, treatment rooms, and changing areas. Massage, facials, manicures, and pedicures are some of the services offered. A separate fitness center, equipped with techno-machinery and exercycles, is located on Bridge Deck. Sports facilities include a basketball court, shuffleboard courts, and a large deck-chess game on an aft deck.

ASTORIA
★★+

THIS RATHER ELDERLY, SMALL SHIP HAS CHARACTER NOT SEEN ABOARD TODAY'S SHIPS

Size:	Small Ship
Tonnage:	16,144
Cruise Line:	Cruise and Maritime Voyages (CMV)
Former Names:	Athena, Caribe, Valtur Prima
Builder:	Varco Chiapella (Italy)
Entered Service:	Feb 1947/Mar 2015
Length (ft/m):	525.2/160.1
Beam (ft/m):	68.8/21.0
Propulsion/Propellers:	diesel/2
Passenger Decks:	7
Total Crew:	280
Passengers (lower beds):	550
Passenger Space Ratio (lower beds):	28.0
Passenger/Crew Ratio (lower beds):	2.0/1
Cabins (total):	277
Size Range (sq ft/m):	129.2-376.7/12.0-35.0
Cabins (for one person):	2
Cabins with balcony:	8
Cabins (wheelchair accessible):	0
Wheelchair accessibility:	None
Elevators:	2
Casino (gaming tables):	Yes
Swimming Pools:	1
Self-Service Launderette:	No
Library:	Yes
Onboard currency:	UK£

THE SHIP. Although it's a dated ship and has had many incarnations, operators and names, this lovingly maintained classic ship, with its dark, strong, riveted hull, funnel placed amidships, and a 'sheer' (longitudinal curvature of the main deck) not seen aboard today's section-built ships, holds a special charm for those not seeking the newest floating resorts. It was a transatlantic liner before being converted into a cruise ship in 1994. It has a large sponson (duck tail-like) stern apron, added to aid stability. It is for adults only, who can expect a comparatively inexpensive cruise in traditional surroundings, with limited facilities and food, and simple entertainment.

However, this is a high-density ship, leaving little space to move around in, and its fixed gangway may be steep, depending on the port and tidal conditions. Outdoors facilities include a walk-around teakwood promenade deck and many real wooden sunloungers are provided, although open deck sunbathing space is extremely limited, and the small swimming pool is really just a dip or plunge pool.

Astoria has non-glitzy but surprisingly modern interiors that are charming in their own way. Most public rooms are located on one deck (Calypso Deck); these include a library, card room, casino (with gaming tables and slot machines), several bars, and a chapel. The ship is operated by CMV under charter from her Lisbon-based owner.

BERLITZ'S RATINGS

	Possible	Achieved
Ship	500	265
Accommodation	200	116
Food	400	209
Service	400	234
Entertainment	100	50
Cruise Experience	400	206

OVERALL SCORE 1080 points out of 2000

ACCOMMODATION. There are numerous accommodation price grades, and the price you pay depends on the size, location, and grade you choose. All cabins have a mini-bar, TV, and safe. Bathrooms have a combination tub/shower, as well as a good amount of space for toiletries. Eight suites each have a small private balcony, and a separate lounge/living area with table and chairs; bathrooms have whirlpool bathtubs with showers, toilet, washbasin, and bidet.

Some cabins (on Promenade Deck) have lifeboat-obstructed views, and some on Mediterranean Deck may pick up noise from the public rooms on the deck above. The largest accommodation is one rather nice Owner's Suite.

DINING. The Olissipo Restaurant has two sections. It is quite attractive, and tables are for two to eight persons. The food quality is in line with the low cost of the cruise.

For basic casual meals, the Lotus Lounge is a self-serve buffet venue.

ENTERTAINMENT. Calypso Show Lounge is the main show lounge, but the views to the stage area are obstructed from many seats. There is a sizeable bar at the back of the room.

SPA/FITNESS. There's a workout room, sauna, steam room, body therapy rooms, and beauty salon.

ASUKA II
★★★★+

AN ELEGANT, SPACIOUS SHIP WITH FINE FOOD, FOR JAPANESE-SPEAKING CRUISERS

Size:	Mid-size Ship	Passenger/Crew Ratio (lower beds):	1.7
Tonnage:	50,142	Cabins (total):	462
Cruise Line:	NYK Cruises	Size Range (sq ft/m):	198.1–949.4/18.4–88.2
Former Names:	Crystal Harmony	Cabins (for one person):	0
Builder:	Mitsubishi Heavy Industries (Japan)	Cabins with balcony:	260
Entered Service:	Jul 1990/May 2006	Cabins (wheelchair accessible):	4
Length (ft/m):	790.5/240.9	Wheelchair accessibility:	Best
Beam (ft/m):	97.1/29.6	Elevators:	8
Propulsion/Propellers:	diesel-electric (32,800kW)/2	Casino (gaming tables):	Yes
Passenger Decks:	8	Swimming Pools:	1
Total Crew:	470	Self-Service Launderette:	Yes
Passengers (lower beds):	800	Library:	Yes
Passenger Space Ratio (lower beds):	52.0	Onboard currency:	Japanese Yen

THE SHIP. Although now over 20 years old, *Asuka II*, formerly *Crystal Harmony*, underwent a four-month-long drydocking and refit in 2005–6, and further refurbishment in 2009. It is a handsome, well-balanced contemporary ship with raked clipper bow, sleek lines, and Nippon Yusen Kaisha (NYK) Line's double red band on the funnel. There is almost no sense of crowding anywhere, and the fact that form follows function means that comfort is built in. There is a wide wraparound teakwood deck for walking, and an abundance of open deck space.

Inside, the layout is completely different from the previous *Asuka* in that there is a horizontal flow through the public rooms, and this better suits the age range of NYK's typical passengers. The design combines open space ship facilities with the intimacy of rooms found aboard many smaller ships. There is a wide assortment of public entertainment lounges and small intimate rooms. Fine-quality fabrics and soft furnishings, china, flatware, and silver are used throughout.

Outstanding are the Vista (observation) Lounge and a tranquil, elegant Palm Court, one of the nicest rooms afloat, while adjacent are an Internet room and a Chashitsu (Japanese 12-tatami mat room). Other public spaces and facilities include the Mariner's Club Lounge (piano bar/lounge), Cigar Bar, Bistro Café, Casino Corner, Mahjong Room with eight tables, Com-

BERLITZ'S RATINGS

	Possible	Achieved
Ship	500	413
Accommodation	200	160
Food	400	338
Service	400	331
Entertainment	100	83
Cruise Experience	400	337

OVERALL SCORE 1662 points out of 2000

pass Room (meeting and activities room), a book/video library, and the Stars karaoke bar. The theater is a dedicated room with high-definition video projection. There is a self-service launderette on each deck – practical for long voyages.

Asuka II is a relaxing, grand hotel afloat – approximately the equivalent of Tokyo's top hotels – and provides abundant choices and flexibility. It has just about everything for the discerning traveler prepared to pay for high style, space, and the comfort and the facilities of a mid-size vessel capable of long voyages. The company pays attention to its repeat passengers, particularly those in Deck 10 penthouses and suites.

Unfortunately, dining is in two seatings, which makes its timing highly structured – there are two shows, because the showlounge can't seat everyone at once. This works well in the Japanese market, however, and you can always choose to eat in a specialty dining venue; overall, though, the arrangement detracts from the otherwise fine setting of the ship and the professionalism of its staff. All gratuities are included.

Asuka II is best suited to Japanese-speaking travelers (typically over 60) seeking a sophisticated ship with high-quality fittings and furnishings, a wide range of public rooms and facilities, and excellent food and service from a well-trained staff. It is the attention to detail that makes this ship so pleasant, such as almost no announcements and little background music.

ACCOMMODATION. There are five categories of suites and cabins (including four Royal Suites with private balcony; 26 Asuka Suites with balcony; 32 suites with balcony; 202 cabins with balcony; 172 cabins without balcony). Regardless of the category, duvets and down pillows are provided, as are lots of other niceties. All cabins have a color TV, mini-refrigerator, personal safe, small couch and coffee table, excellent soundproofing, a refrigerator and minibar, full tea-making set, satellite-linked telephone, hairdryer, and slippers. A full range of toiletries (including Shiseido shampoo, hair rinse, shower cap, soap, cotton pads, razor set, hairbrush, and more) is provided, and cotton towels are plentiful.

Deck 10 penthouses. Four Royal Suites, whose entrance doorway has a door phone and camera, measure 949.4 sq ft (88.2 sq m) and have outstanding ocean-view Japanese-style bathrooms, with quality German fittings including a large overhead shower, jet bathtub, two washbasins, and abundant storage space for toiletries (L'Occitane products are provided).

Other Deck 10 suites. All Deck 10 suites/cabins are attended by social officers, and complimentary in-room dining service is offered.

Deck 9/8/7/5 cabins. Many cabins have a private balcony (in fact, half of all cabins have private balconies, with outside lights) and are extremely comfortable. But they are a little tight for space, with one-way traffic past the bed. Some cabins have lifeboat-obstructed views, so do check the deck plan carefully.

Although well appointed, the bathrooms (except for those in Deck 10 accommodation) are of the 'you first, me next' variety, but they come with generously sized toiletries and amenities, and all have electric 'washlet' high-cleanse toilets.

DINING. The Four Seasons Dining Room is the pleasant main dining room and has a raised central section. It has ample space around each table, well-placed waiter service stations and tables for two to eight.

Dinner is in two seatings, with no set table assignments. Afternoon tea and coffee can be taken in the Vista Lounge.

Umihiko is a Japanese extra-charge restaurant, complete with a wholly authentic sushi bar and live fish tanks for absolutely fresh sashimi. It provides a refined, intimate dining experience with fine ocean views. Reservations are required.

Prego, with 40 seats and ocean views to starboard and aft, is for occupants of the Royal Suites and Asuka Suites. The menu is the same as the main dining room, but with more intensive waiter service.

For casual meals, beverages, and ice cream, the Lido Café has a good self-serve buffet area; it is located high in the ship and has ocean views from large picture windows. There is also a Lido Garden Grill, a large area with wooden tables and chairs, and bar.

Additionally, The Bistro, located on the upper level of the two-deck-high lobby, is a casual spot for coffees and pastries; it has the atmosphere of a European street café.

ENTERTAINMENT. The Galaxy Lounge (showlounge) is a large room on one level, with a sloping floor. The sight lines are good from most seats, although a few pillars obstruct the view from some of them. Both banquette-style and individual seating is provided.

SPA/FITNESS. The Grand Spa includes a large Grand Bath/cleansing center (one for men, one for women), with integral sauna and steam room. Other facilities include five treatment rooms (longevity, water, wind, prosperity, harmony) including one for couples. There's a separate sauna, steam rooms, changing rooms for men and women, a beauty salon, and a relaxation area. Another part of the spa houses the gymnasium, with ocean-view windows on one side.

The Asuka Aveda Salon and Spa offers a wide range of body-pampering treatments using Aveda brand products. The spa also offers a kimono dressing service, which costs ¥12,600 (about $115).

There is an excellent amount of open deck space, including a long swimming pool. Sports facilities include a full-size paddle tennis court, putting green, and golf driving range.

AURORA
★★★+

A TRADITIONAL BRITISH-STYLE SHIP WITH FACILITIES FOR THE WHOLE FAMILY

Size:	Mid-size Ship	Passenger/Crew Ratio (lower beds):	2.2
Tonnage:	76,152	Cabins (total):	934
Cruise Line:	P&O Cruises	Size Range (sq ft/m):	150.6–953.0/14.0–88.5
Former Names:	none	Cabins (for one person):	4
Builder:	Meyer Werft (Germany)	Cabins with balcony:	406
Entered Service:	May 2000	Cabins (wheelchair accessible):	22
Length (ft/m):	885.8/270.0	Wheelchair accessibility:	Good
Beam (ft/m):	105.6/32.2	Elevators:	10
Propulsion/Propellers:	diesel-electric (40,000kW)/2	Casino (gaming tables):	Yes
Passenger Decks:	10	Swimming Pools:	3 (1 w/ sliding glass dome)
Total Crew:	816	Self-Service Launderette:	Yes
Passengers (lower beds):	1,864	Library:	Yes
Passenger Space Ratio (lower beds):	40.7	Onboard currency:	UK£

THE SHIP. *Aurora*, which underwent an extensive make-over in 2014–15, was built specifically for Britain's traditional cruise market. The ship has larger cabins and suites and more dining options and choice of public areas than older sister *Oriana*.

Aurora has a large, glass-domed indoor/outdoor swimming pool – good in all weathers for families with children (*Oriana* doesn't have one). The stern superstructure is nicely rounded, with several tiers that overlook the aft decks, pool, and children's outdoor facilities. There is good sunbathing space and an extra-wide walk-around outdoor promenade deck, with plenty of white plastic sunloungers (cushioned pads are available).

Aurora's focal point is a four-decks-high atrium lobby and a dramatic 35-ft- (10.6-m-) high, Lalique-style fiberglass sculpture of two mythical figures behind a veil of water.

Other features include a virtual-reality games room, 12 lounges/bars (among the nicest are Anderson's – similar to Anderson's aboard *Oriana*, with a fireplace and mahogany paneling), and the Crow's Nest – complete with a one-sided model of former P&O liner *Strathnaver* of 1931 (scrapped in Hong Kong in 1962). A cinema also doubles as a concert and lecture hall.

Aurora is a multi-age, family-friendly mid-size ship that is good for cruises starting and ending in the UK. The vessel has the facilities of a small resort, with food and service that come with a sense of

BERLITZ'S RATINGS

	Possible	Achieved
Ship	500	359
Accommodation	200	143
Food	400	245
Service	400	282
Entertainment	100	69
Cruise Experience	400	265

OVERALL SCORE 1363 points out of 2000

Britishness. At peak holiday times (summer, Christmas, Easter) there could be 400 or more children on board, although the ship absorbs them well.

ACCOMMODATION. There are five main grades in numerous price categories. Included are a couple of two-level penthouses, suites with balconies, mini-suites with balconies, cabins with balconies, standard outside-view cabins, 16 interconnecting family cabins, and interior (no-view) cabins.

All grades provide polished cherry wood laminate cabinetry, full-length mirror, personal safe, refrigerator, television, individually controlled air conditioning, twin beds that convert to a queen-size double bed, sofa, and coffee table. Also standard are stylish bed runners, Slumberland sprung mattresses, duvets, Egyptian cotton towels, and tea/coffee-making facilities with specialty teas (long-life milk is provided). A 110-volt (American) socket is underneath the vanity desk drawer – a difficult-to-access position. Cabins with private balconies have easy-to-open sliding glass floor-to-ceiling doors; the partitions are of the almost full floor-to-ceiling type, so they really are quite private and cannot be overlooked from above.

Cabin insulation could be better, and the magnetic catches in drawers and on closet doors are noisy. Although most doorways are 26ins (66cm) wide, the actual access is 2ins (5cm) less because of the doorframe; however, some doorways are only 21.5ins (55cm) wide.

Standard outside-view/interior cabins measure about 175 sq ft (16.3 sq m).

Outside-view or interior cabins are 150 sq ft (14 sq m) and have two lower beds that are convertible to a queen-size bed; there is closet space, but not many drawers.

Mini-suites measure 325 sq ft (30.2 sq m), while suites are about 445 sq ft (41.3 sq m).

Penthouse Suites: The Library Suite (with a private library) and Piano Suite (with baby grand piano, playable manually or electronically) each measure 953 sq ft (88.5 sq m). Both are duplexes, with the bedroom upstairs and a lounge downstairs.

Note that balcony cabin decking is covered with inelegant blue plastic matting.

There are 22 well-outfiited, wheelchair-accessible cabins – almost all located within easy access to lifts. However, D165 on Deck 8 is located between forward and mid-ships stairways, from where it is difficult to access the public rooms on Deck 8 without first going to the deck below, due to several steps and tight corners. All other wheelchair-accessible cabins are well positioned, and eight have a private balcony.

DINING. The two main dining rooms (each seats about 525) have tables for two, four, six, eight, and 10. The midships Medina has a vaguely Moorish theme, and features 'Freedom dining' – open seating for dinner – with Marco Pierre White dishes on gala evenings, while Alexandria, with windows on three sides, has an Egyptian theme and two seatings for dinner ('Club dining'). Both have more tables for two than in the equiva-lent restaurants aboard close sister ship *Oriana*. The china is Wedgwood; the silverware by Elkington.

The cuisine is straightforward, no-nonsense British food, reasonably well presented on nice china. However, it tends to be rather bland and uninspiring. It is typical of mass-banquet catering with standard fare comparable to that found in a family hotel in a classic English seaside town.

You can also dine in The Glasshouse restaurant/wine bar (selected by Olly Smith); or Sindhu (on the upper deck of the atrium lobby), for an Indian-fusion menu designed by Atul Kochhar. Both are extra-cost venues, for which reservations are required.

Casual, self-serve breakfasts and lunches can be taken from the self-serve buffet in The Orangery, with its fine ocean views. Other casual dining spots include the Sidewalk Café (for fast-food items poolside), The Beach House (for lava-rock sizzle food), a Champagne bar, and Raffles coffee and chocolate bar (minus the ceiling fans).

ENTERTAINMENT. There is a wide variety of mainly British entertainment, from production shows to top British 'name' (and lesser) cabaret acts.

SPA/FITNESS. The Oasis Spa is amidships on Lido Deck – almost at the top of the ship, just forward of the Crystal swimming pool. Facilities include a workout room, with muscle-pumping equipment. There is also a sauna and steam room (both unisex, so take a bathing suit), a beauty salon, a spiral staircase, and a relaxation area overlooking the Riviera pool.

AZAMARA JOURNEY
★★★★+

THIS IS AN INFORMAL SHIP WITH COUNTRY-HOUSE DECOR AND FINE FOOD CHOICES

Size:	Small Ship	Passenger/Crew Ratio (lower beds):	1.6
Tonnage:	30,277	Cabins (total):	338
Cruise Line:	Azamara Club Cruises	Size Range (sq ft/m):	151.0–818.0/14.0–76.0
Former Names:	Blue Star, Blue Dream, R6	Cabins (for one person):	0
Builder:	Chantiers de l'Atlantique (France)	Cabins with balcony:	249
Entered Service:	Feb 2000/May 2007	Cabins (wheelchair accessible):	6
Length (ft/m):	591.8/180.4	Wheelchair accessibility:	Fair
Beam (ft/m):	95.1/29.0	Elevators:	4
Propulsion/Propellers:	diesel (18,600kW)/2	Casino (gaming tables):	Yes
Passenger Decks:	9	Swimming Pools:	1
Total Crew:	407	Self-Service Launderette:	Yes
Passengers (lower beds):	676	Library:	Yes
Passenger Space Ratio (lower beds):	42.7	Onboard currency:	US$

THE SHIP. The ship has a deep blue hull and white superstructure topped by a large, square blue funnel. A lido deck has a small swimming pool flanked by two hot tubs, good sunbathing space, and comfortable sunloungers. Although there is no outdoor walk-around promenade deck, a short jogging track encircles the pool deck (one deck above it). The uppermost outdoors deck includes a golf driving net and shuffleboard court. There are no wooden decks outdoors – the floor is covered instead by a sand-colored rubberized material. Smoking is permitted only in designated spots on the open decks. The interior decor is in good taste, and full of light, contemporary colors.

The public rooms are spread over three decks, and getting around is easy. The reception hall has a staircase with intricate wrought-iron railings. A large observation lounge (The Living Room) is located on an upper deck. It has a long bar with forward views – for the barmen, that is, as passengers sitting at the bar face aft. There's also a bar in each of the restaurant entrances, plus a Martini Bar. There's also a Mosaic Café, a Luxe Casino, and a shop (Boutique C).

The Drawing Room (the ship's library) is a delightful restful room, designed in the Regency style, with a fireplace, a high, indented trompe l'oeil ceiling, and a good selection of books, plus comfortable wingback chairs with footstools, and sofas.

Standard drinks and wines are included (premium brands cost extra). Gratuities to housekeeping and

BERLITZ'S RATINGS	Possible	Achieved
Ship	500	400
Accommodation	200	141
Food	400	299
Service	400	326
Entertainment	100	80
Cruise Experience	400	305
OVERALL SCORE 1551 points out of 2000		

dining staff are included in the fare. Shuttle buses are provided free when needed in ports of call.

Azamara Journey, virtually identical to *Azamara Quest* in features and fittings, best suits mature couples seeking to get away from the crowds aboard a small, contemporary ship with a wide range of bars and lounges, at a slightly lower cost than the luxury lines.

ACCOMMODATION. There are several suite and cabin price grades. The price you pay reflects the size and location of your chosen accommodation. All have so-called butler service (but they are simply betterdressed cabin stewards). The lowest four grades of interior and outside-view cabins are extremely compact units. *Azamara Journey* calls them staterooms, but they are simply cabins – and rather tight for two persons, particularly for cruises of over seven days. The bathrooms are postage-stamp sized, and you'll be fighting with the shower curtain, as well as storage space for toiletries. The standard cabins cannot, in any sense, be considered luxury, and even premium is stretching it a bit.

All cabins have two lower beds convertible to a queen-sized bed, good under-bed storage areas, flat-screen TV, good closet space, thermostat-controlled air conditioning, hairdryer, telephone and voicemail, and 100 percent cotton towels. Most cabins also have a personal safe, and refrigerator with mini bar.

For the extra cost, it's wise to choose a suite or cabin with a balcony. Some cabins have interconnecting doors, while 18 cabins on Deck 6 have lifeboat-obstructed views.

DINING. Discoveries (main dining room) has around 340 seats, a raised central section (conversation at these tables may be difficult, due to its low ceiling height), and open-seating dining. There are large ocean-view windows on three sides, several prime tables overlooking the stern, and a small bandstand for live dinner music. Menus change daily for lunch and dinner, and wine is included. Adjacent to the restaurant is a Martini Bar, with a cozy fireplace.

Aqualina Restaurant is aft on the port side of Deck 10; it has 96 seats and windows along two sides, and features Italian/Mediterranean cuisine. A Tasting Menu, including wine pairing, is available.

Next door is Prime C, which features premium-quality steaks and grilled seafood items. It has 98 seats, windows on two sides, and a set menu, but no tablecloths.

Both Aqualina and Prime C incur a cover charge (included for occupants of top-grade suites).

Windows Café has indoor and outdoor seating (combined, for just over 150, not really enough when cruising in cold areas). It is open for breakfast, lunch, and casual dinners, and incorporates a small Sushi Café.

All dining venues have open-seating dining, although reservations are needed in the Aqualina Restaurant and Prime C, where there are mostly tables for four or six (there are few tables for two). All cappuccino and espresso coffees cost extra.

Mosaic Café features extra-cost Italian coffees, teas, and pastries. Also, a Poolside Grill provides fast-food items (some grilled to order). A self-serve soft ice cream machine is located adjacent to its beverage station. Coffee and tea are free 24 hours a day.

ENTERTAINMENT. Cabaret, located forward, is the venue for most entertainment events.

SPA/FITNESS. The Sanctum spa has a fitness room with high-tech cardiovascular equipment, an extra-cost thalassotherapy pool, steam room, and several body-treatment rooms. An 'Acupuncture at Sea' clinic provides treatments that are operated independently of the spa (as a concession).

AZAMARA QUEST
★★★★+

THIS SMALL SHIP IS REMINISCENT OF AN ELEGANT COUNTRY CLUB

Size:	Small Ship	Passenger/Crew Ratio (lower beds):	2.3
Tonnage:	30,277	Cabins (total):	358
Cruise Line:	Azamara Club Cruises	Size Range (sq ft/m):	156.0–484.3/14.5–45.0
Former Names:	Blue Moon, Delphin Renaissance, R7	Cabins (for one person):	0
Builder:	Chantiers de l'Atlantique (France)	Cabins with balcony:	232
Entered Service:	Oct 2000/Oct 2007	Cabins (wheelchair accessible):	4
Length (ft/m):	591.8/180.4	Wheelchair accessibility:	Fair
Beam (ft/m):	83.3/25.4	Elevators:	4
Propulsion/Propellers:	diesel (18,600kW)/2	Casino (gaming tables):	Yes
Passenger Decks:	9	Swimming Pools:	1
Total Crew:	306	Self-Service Launderette:	Yes
Passengers (lower beds):	716	Library:	Yes
Passenger Space Ratio (lower beds):	42.2	Onboard currency:	US$

THE SHIP. *Azamara Quest* was originally one of a series of eight almost identical ships in the long-defunct Renaissance Cruises fleet (when it was in operation, between 1998 and 2001, it was the cruise industry's only totally no-smoking cruise line). In 2007 it joined Azamara Cruises (renamed Azamara Club Cruises in 2009), and underwent an almost $20 million makeover. The hull is deep blue, while the superstructure is white.

An outdoors lido deck has a swimming pool flanked by two hot tubs and good sunbathing space with wooden sunloungers; one of the aft decks has a thalassotherapy pool. The exterior decks are covered by a rubber and sand-like surface. The uppermost outdoors deck includes a golf driving net and shuffleboard court. The interior decor is elegant, in the style of ocean liner decor of the 1920s.

Standard drinks and wines are included (premium brands cost extra). In 2016, the ship underwent a major refurbishment program that refreshed all accommodation and public areas, with lighter decor that has brightened the interiors.

ACCOMMODATION. There are several suite and cabin price grades. The price reflects the size and location of your chosen accommodation. All have so-called butler service, although they are simply better-dressed cabin stewards. The standard interior and outside-view cabins (the lowest four grades)

BERLITZ'S RATINGS		
	Possible	Achieved
Ship	500	400
Accommodation	200	141
Food	400	299
Service	400	326
Entertainment	100	80
Cruise Experience	400	305

OVERALL SCORE 1551 points out of 2000

are extremely compact units. *Azamara Quest* calls them staterooms, but they are simply cabins – and rather tight for two persons, particularly for cruises longer than seven days. The bathrooms are postage-stamp-sized, and you'll be fighting with the shower curtain and frustrated by the limited storage space for toiletries. The standard cabins cannot, in any sense, be considered luxury, and even premium is stretching it a bit.

All cabins have two lower beds convertible to a (sleep-together) queen-sized bed, good under-bed storage areas, flat-screen TV, good closet space, thermostat-controlled air conditioning, hairdryer, telephone and voicemail, and 100 percent cotton towels. Most cabins also have a personal safe, and refrigerator with minibar.

For the extra cost, it's wise to choose a suite or cabin with a balcony. Some cabins have interconnecting doors while 18 cabins on Deck 6 have lifeboat-obstructed views.

Accommodation sizes are as follows:

Club ocean-view cabins with balcony. Approximate size: 215 sq ft (20 sq m); balcony 38 sq ft (3.5 sq m).

Club Deluxe Veranda cabins. Approximate size: 215 sq ft (20 sq m); balcony 154 sq ft (14 sq m).

Club Continent Suites and superior exterior-view cabins with veranda. Approximate size: 323 sq ft (30 sq m); balcony 57 sq ft (5.3 sq m).

Club Spa Suites. Approximate size: 414 sq ft (38.5 sq m). Veranda 60 sq ft (5.6 sq m).

Club Ocean Suites (Decks 6, 7). In reality these are large cabins, as the sleeping and lounge areas are not divided. Approximate size: 538 sq ft (50 sq m); balcony 173 sq ft (16 sq m).

Club World Owner's Suites with balcony. These are fine, large living spaces in the forward-most and aft-most sections of the ship (much in demand are those overlooking the stern, on decks 6, 7, and 8). Approximate size: 603 sq ft (56 sq m); balcony 215 sq ft (20 sq m).

Suite-grade occupants get priority boarding, tender service, and other perks including free espressos/cappuccinos, bottled water, and silk-wrapped hangers. Note that suites/cabins located at the stern can suffer from vibration when the ship is at or close to full speed, or maneuvering in port.

DINING. Discoveries, the main dining room, has around 340 seats, a raised central section (conversation may be difficult, due to its low ceiling height), and open-seating dining. There are large ocean-view windows on three sides, some with prime tables overlooking the stern. The menu changes daily for lunch and dinner, and wine is included. Adjacent to the restaurant is a Martini Bar, with a cozy fireplace.

Aqualina Restaurant is at the aft of the ship on the port side of Deck 10; it has 96 seats, windows along two sides, and serves Mediterranean cuisine. A Tasting Menu includes wine.

Prime C is located at the aft of the ship on the starboard side of Deck 10, and features premium-quality steaks and grilled seafood items. It has 98 seats, windows along two sides, and a set menu.

Both Aqualina and Prime C incur a cover charge (free for occupants of top-grade suites).

Windows Café has indoor and outdoor seating (combined, for just over 150, not really enough when cruising in cold areas or in the winter months). It is open for breakfast, lunch, and casual dinners, and incorporates a small Sushi Café.

All dining venues have open-seating dining, although reservations are needed in the Aqualina Restaurant and Prime C, where there are mostly tables for four or six (there are few tables for two). Suite-grade occupants get unlimited access. All cappuccino and espresso coffees cost extra.

The Mosaic Café serves Italian coffees, as well as teas and pastries (no extra cost). Additionally, a Poolside Grill provides fast-food items (some items are grilled to order). A self-serve soft ice cream machine is located adjacent to its beverage station. Coffee and tea are free 24 hours a day.

ENTERTAINMENT. Celebrity Cabaret, located forward, is the venue for all main entertainment events, which include a mix of classical concerts, revues, comedy, and drama.

SPA/FITNESS. The Sanctum spa has a gymnasium with high-tech muscle-toning equipment, an extra-cost thalassotherapy pool (outside, forward on deck), and several treatment rooms. An 'Acupuncture at Sea' clinic provides treatments that are operated independently of the spa (but also as a concession).

AZURA
★★★+

THIS LARGE RESORT SHIP WITH SEDATE DECOR REALLY SUITS BRITISH STYLE AND TASTES

Size:	Large Resort Ship	Passenger/Crew Ratio (lower beds):	2.4
Tonnage:	115,055	Cabins (total):	1,557
Cruise Line:	P&O Cruises	Size Range (sq ft/m):	134.5–534.0/12.5–49.6
Former Names:	none	Cabins (for one person):	18
Builder:	Fincantieri (Italy)	Cabins with balcony:	910
Entered Service:	Apr 2010	Cabins (wheelchair accessible):	25
Length (ft/m):	951.4/290.0	Wheelchair accessibility:	Good
Beam (ft/m):	118.1/36.0	Elevators:	12
Propulsion/Propellers:	diesel-electric (42,000kW)/2	Casino (gaming tables):	Yes
Passenger Decks:	14	Swimming Pools:	3
Total Crew:	1,239	Self-Service Launderette:	Yes
Passengers (lower beds):	3,096	Library:	Yes
Passenger Space Ratio (lower beds):	37.2	Onboard currency:	UK£

THE SHIP. *Azura* (like its sister ship *Ventura*) has a flat, upright stern; it looks like a giant hatchback, although its side profile is softer and more balanced. Promenade walking decks are to the port and starboard sides only; it's also narrow in some places, with deck lounge chairs in the way.

There are three main pools: two on the pool deck, one at the stern. There's not a lot of outdoor deck space – unless you pay extra to go into a covered, adults-only zone called The Retreat, located above the spa. It has a faux-grass floor, private cabanas, and personal waiter service, but it costs a lot extra; it is, however, so much quieter that you may feel it's worth it. A large open-air movie screen (SeaScreen) is forward of the funnel by the Aqua Pool.

Inside, a three-deck atrium, with integral dance floor, is the focal social point, rather like a town center. Four large, three-deck-high black granite archways provide 'gateways' to the center. It's the place to see and be seen – as are the specialty dining venues. Also in the atrium is a smallish open-plan library (that isn't at all intimate or good for reading in when noisy events are staged in the atrium), including computers for Internet access. There's also a Java Café for extra-cost coffees, teas, cakes, pastries, and snacks.

Other rooms, bars and lounges include a casino; The Exchange, an urban 'warehouse' bar; the Blue Bar, the ship's social hub; Brodie's, a 'traditional'

BERLITZ'S RATINGS		
	Possible	Achieved
Ship	500	373
Accommodation	200	144
Food	400	246
Service	400	284
Entertainment	100	75
Cruise Experience	400	269

OVERALL SCORE 1391 points out of 2000

British pub (named after Brodie McGhie Willcox, P&O's co-founder); and the Planet Bar, set high in the ship, featuring a video wall.

The upper-deck public room layout means you can't easily go from one end of the ship to the other without first going down, along, and up. Anyone with mobility problems will need to plan their journey and use the most appropriate of three elevator banks.

Gratuities are optional, unless you choose 'Freedom Dining,' when they are automatically applied to your onboard account. Smoking is permitted only in designated spots on the open decks.

Azura is best suited to families with children and adult couples who are seeking a big-ship environment with comfortable, unstuffy surroundings, lots of options, and a distinctly British flavor.

ACCOMMODATION. There are many, many price grades, but really just six types of accommodation: suite with balcony; family suite with balcony; outside-view twin/queen with balcony; outside-view twin/queen; interior cabin, and solo traveler cabin. Although there are more balconies than aboard *Ventura*, more than a third of all cabins have no outside view. Some have extra third/fourth berths that fold down from the ceiling.

Most welcome are the 18 solo-occupancy cabins, a first for P&O Cruises, located in a small port side section. Also available are spa cabins, with added amenities and direct access to the ship's spa, and two large suites for large groups.

While the suites are very small when compared to those of lines such as Celebrity Cruises or Norwegian Cruise Line, they are intelligently laid out, and feel spacious.

Standard in all cabins: bed runners, 10.5 tog duvets, Slumberland 8ins (20cm) sprung mattresses, and Egyptian cotton towels. Tea/coffee-making facilities are adequate, but with UHT, not fresh, milk. Bathrobes are provided only for occupants of certain grades. There are UK three-pin sockets, plus US-style 110-volt sockets for electrical devices.

Open closets provide easy access, but the 'no trust' attached hangers can bang against the wall when the ship is 'moving'. Balcony cabins have wooden railings atop glass dividers, green plastic floors, a couple of small chairs and drinks table, and an outside light. Most cabin bathrooms are small, as are the shower enclosures, with products by The White Company.

Wheelchair-accessible cabins, which have a large, user-friendly shower enclosure, are mostly located in the front section of the ship, but one of the main restaurants is aft. So be prepared for lots of wheeling time, and waiting time at the elevators.

There is no room service breakfast on disembarkation day, when you must vacate your cabin early.

DINING. P&O's marketing blurb claims that there are 10 restaurants. Rubbish! There are five genuine restaurants (Peninsular, Oriental, Meridian, Sindhu, and Seventeen); the others are bistro-style eateries or fast-food joints.

The Peninsular, Oriental, and Meridian restaurants share the same menus. Peninsular and Oriental offer fixed seating dining with assigned tables. In the Meridian restaurant, you can dine when you want, with whomever you want, when open – P&O calls it 'Freedom Dining,' although at peak times there can be a bit of a wait; it's not open for breakfast or lunch. Occasionally, special dinners are served in the main dining rooms, one of which is a Chaîne des Rôtisseurs event.

Wheelchair users should note that breakfast in the fixed dining restaurants typically ends at 9:30am on sea days and 9am on port days. To take breakfast in the self-serve casual eatery, you may need to wheel across the decks containing the forward and midship pools and a sea of deck chairs – not easy. Alternatively, you can order room service breakfast, although this is for cold items only.

The cuisine is straightforward, no-nonsense British food, reasonably well presented on nice Wedg-

wood china. But it tends to be rather bland and uninspiring. It is typical of mass-banquet catering with standard fare comparable to that found in a family hotel in a classic English seaside town.

Sindhu is an Indian-themed restaurant (reservation-only, extra cost). It is overseen by Michelin-star chef Atul Kochhar, whose specialty is British and Indian fusion cuisine. The food is cooked to order, unlike in the three main dining rooms. Table seating includes several alcove-style areas that make it impossible for waiters to serve food correctly without reaching across others at the same table.

For the Glass House, TV wine expert Olly Smith has helped create a 'Select Dining' restaurant and wine bar. The venue offers seafood and grilled items, paired with wines chosen by Smith, although it's rather strange that there are no decanters. You can also, of course, have a glass of wine, without food.

Seventeen is a reservations-only, extra-charge, à la carte restaurant in a quiet setting, with plenty of space around tables for waiters to serve correctly. The venue also features an outdoor terrace for warm-weather areas.

Venezia is a large, casual, self-serve buffet eatery/food court, open almost around the clock, with large indoor-outdoor seating areas. The buffet layout is confined, and can get congested. On the same deck, adjacent to the forward pool, are a poolside grill and pizzeria. In addition, 24-hour room service is available in cabins.

ENTERTAINMENT. The 800-seat Playhouse theater spans two decks and is located at the front of the ship, and is the venue for shows; with two large video screens on either side of the stage; the sight lines are very good from all seats.

The Manhattan Lounge, a multi-function social/entertainment venue, hosts family shows and cabaret acts, and is a late-night disco. Malabar, another night venue, has decor based on the hotels on Marine Drive, Mumbai. Cabaret, live bands, and dancing are featured here. Meanwhile, the Planet Bar, a nightclub and entertainment venue is an activities room by day and a club by night.

SPA/FITNESS. The Oasis Spa – located forward, almost atop the ship – has a gymnasium, aerobics room, beauty salon, separate men's and ladies' sauna and steam rooms (no charge), and 11 treatment rooms. An internal stairway connects to the deck below, which contains an extra-charge Thermal Suite (there's a cost per person, per day, or a composite price per cruise).

BALMORAL
★★★+

A WELL-DESIGNED SHIP WITH A VERY BRITISH AMBIENCE FOR MATURE TRAVELERS

Size:	Mid-size Ship	Passenger/Crew Ratio (lower beds):	3.0
Tonnage:	43,537	Cabins (total):	828
Cruise Line:	Fred. Olsen Cruise Lines	Size Range (sq ft/m):	153.9–613.5/14.3–57.0
Former Names:	Norwegian Crown, Crown Odyssey	Cabins (for one person):	91
Builder:	Meyer Werft (Germany)	Cabins with balcony:	121
Entered Service:	Jun 1988/Jan 2008	Cabins (wheelchair accessible):	9
Length (ft/m):	715.2/218.1	Wheelchair accessibility:	Good
Beam (ft/m):	92.5/28.2	Elevators:	4
Propulsion/Propellers:	diesel (21,330kW)/2	Casino (gaming tables):	Yes
Passenger Decks:	10	Swimming Pools:	2
Total Crew:	471	Self-Service Launderette:	Yes
Passengers (lower beds):	1,747	Library:	Yes
Passenger Space Ratio (lower beds):	24.9	Onboard currency:	UK£

THE SHIP. *Balmoral*, formerly *Norwegian Crown*, is a well-designed and built ship, originally constructed for the long defunct Royal Cruise Line. Norwegian Cruise Line then operated the ship for many years, before it was transferred to Orient Lines in 2000, and then back to Norwegian Cruise Line in September 2003.

Fred. Olsen Cruise Lines bought the ship in 2007 and gave it a major refurbishment, including a 'chop and stretch' operation involving the addition of a 99ft (30.2m) midsection. Although the company's logo includes the Norwegian flag, the ship is registered in the Bahamas.

The ship has a relatively handsome, nicely balanced exterior profile, and one of its plus features is its full, walk-around teak promenade deck outdoors, although it becomes a little narrow in the forward section of the vessel. There are many nicely polished wood railings on balconies and open decks, plus a jogging track on the uppermost deck. Atop the ship is the Observatory Lounge, with fine ocean views, central dance floor, and bar. Out on deck, there is a heated salt-water pool, but little shade, and no glass cover for inclement weather.

The main public room spaces are on Lounge Deck. At the front of the ship is the Neptune Lounge (showlounge), with an integral bar at the back; the raised stage and wood dance floor are surrounded by amphitheater-style seating in banquettes with small drinks tables. To its aft are the shops – a

BERLITZ'S RATINGS

	Possible	Achieved
Ship	500	367
Accommodation	200	142
Food	400	258
Service	400	263
Entertainment	100	64
Cruise Experience	400	269

OVERALL SCORE 1363 points out of 2000

curved staircase connects this deck with the reception lobby on the deck below.

Next is the Braemar Lounge, alongside a lifestyle area that includes an Internet center with good separation for privacy; there are also a library and a separate card room. Aft of the Braemar Lounge is the Morning Light Pub (named after the very first Fred. Olsen ship, *Morning Light*). This venue is more like a lounge than a real pub, although it does have draft beers. Aft is the Palms Café, the ship's casual self-service buffet-style café.

The high lobby has a large gold sculpture in the shape of a globe of the world by the famous Italian sculptor Arnaldo Pomodoro (called *Microcosm, Macrocosm*); it used to revolve.

Balmoral offers a wide range of itineraries, which keeps people coming back to this very comfortable ship; passengers also receive a log of each cruise to take home. Niggles include an inflexible bed layout in some cabins, and dated decor in some older cabins.

Gratuities of £4 (around $5) per passenger, per day, are suggested. The drinks prices are very reasonable, but laundry/dry-cleaning prices are quite high.

Balmoral is best suited to British couples and solo travelers wanting destination-intensive cruising in a ship that has European style and character, a sense of space, comfortable surroundings, decent facilities, and realistic pricing. The mostly Filipino/Thai crew is warm and friendly, and should help make your cruise enjoyable.

ACCOMMODATION. There are several price categories; typically, the higher the deck, the higher the price. Most cabins are of the same size and layout, have blond wood cabinetry and accents, an abundance of mirrors, and closet and drawer space, and are very well equipped. All accommodation grades have a color TV, a hairdryer, music console (plus a button that can be used to turn announcements on or off), personal safe, and private bathroom with shower (many upper-grade cabins have a good-size tub).

All towels are 100 percent cotton, and quite large; a soap and shampoo dispenser is mounted on the shower wall, and a shower cap is provided. Duvets (single) are standard, but blankets and bed linen are available on request, as are double-bed-size duvets. Extra-cost, on-demand movies are available from the in-cabin Infotainment System.

The soundproofing is generally good. Some cabins have interconnecting doors, so that they can make a two-room suite – good for families with children.

The largest cabins are the suites on Highland Deck 10. They are quite spacious.and provide a sleeping area and separate living room, with nicely finished wood cabinetry and a large amount of closet and drawer space, together with a large, white marble-clad bathroom with a full-size tub and integral shower. There is a large private balcony, although some balconies can be overlooked from the deck above.

Nine wheelchair-accessible cabins provide plenty of space to maneuver, and all have a bathroom with roll-in shower. But wheelchair accessibility in some ports on the various itineraries operated by this ship – particularly in Europe – may prove frustrating, and wheelchair-accessible transportation may be limited.

Cabins in the added midsection have attractive, light, airy, contemporary decor. Some on the upper decks (decks 8 and 9) have bathrooms with a verti-cal window with a direct view from the large shower enclosure through the sleeping space to the outside, providing an enhanced feeling of spaciousness. Bathrooms have shower enclosures rather than tub/shower combinations (some have two washbasins), and enough storage space for toiletries.

DINING. The Ballindalloch Restaurant, in the aft section of the ship, has ocean-view windows on port and starboard sides, and operates two sittings. It has comfortable seating at tables for two to eight. However, the waiter stations are exposed and can be extremely noisy; indeed, the noise level in this main restaurant is high, so trying to hold a conversation can be frustrating.

Other dining options. The Avon Restaurant and Spey Restaurant, both named after rivers, are located aft on Highland Deck 10 – the deck that contains the higher-priced suites. The floor-to-ceiling windows provide lots of light. The decor is contemporary and minimalist, and the noise level is low, which makes for comfortable conversation. These venues also operate two seatings.

The 70-seat Palms Café is an alternative, more intimate venue for casual self-serve buffet meals.

All eateries aboard have open seating for breakfast and lunch.

ENTERTAINMENT. The Neptune Lounge is the entertainment venue for shows, cabaret acts, lectures, and some social functions. It is a single-level room with tiered seating levels. Sight lines are generally good, but they could be better.

Revue-style production shows are staged by a resident troupe of singers and dancers.

SPA/FITNESS. There is a reasonably decent – but small – indoor wellness facility, with a fitness room with great ocean views, plenty of gym equipment, and several body-treatment rooms.

BERLIN
★ ★ ★

A SMALL, FAIRLY COMFORTABLE SHIP FOR BASIC 'DESTINATION-A-DAY' CRUISING

Size:	Small Ship	Passenger/Crew Ratio (lower beds):	2.4
Tonnage:	9,570	Cabins (total):	206
Cruise Line:	FTI Cruises	Size Range (sq ft/m):	92.5–191.6/8.6–17.8
Former Names:	FTI Berlin, Spirit of Adventure,	Cabins (for one person):	0
	Berlin, Princess Mahsuri, Berlin	Cabins with balcony:	0
Builder:	Howaldtswerke Deutsche Werft (Germany)	Cabins (wheelchair accessible):	2
Entered Service:	Jun 1980/May 2012	Wheelchair accessibility:	None
Length (ft/m):	457.0/139.3	Elevators:	1
Beam (ft/m):	57.5/17.52	Casino (gaming tables):	No
Propulsion/Propellers:	diesel (7,060kW)/2	Swimming Pools:	2
Passenger Decks:	7	Self-Service Launderette:	Yes
Total Crew:	168	Library:	Yes
Passengers (lower beds):	412	Onboard currency:	Euros
Passenger Space Ratio (lower beds):	23.2		

THE SHIP. Berlin (formerly FTI Berlin), a somewhat angular ship, has an all-white ice-strengthened hull and a profile made more balanced by a thin blue line. It starred for many years in the long-running German TV show Traumschiff (Dream Ship). FTI Cruises bought the ship from previous owners Saga Cruises in 2011.

The interiors are crisp, contemporary, and well appointed, with tasteful European decor and furnishings. The Library occupies an expansive space; Internet access is provided at four computer stations.

The swimming pool, located aft, is just a 'dip' pool. The surrounding open-deck and sunbathing space is cramped, because it's in the same area as the outdoor seating for the Verandah Restaurant. There is only one elevator and it doesn't go to the two topmost decks or to the Spa Aquarius on the lowermost deck. The passenger accommodation hallways are rather narrow.

This ship is best suited to German-speaking couples and solo travelers seeking a vacation in a ship that is unpretentious and provides a reasonable standard.

ACCOMMODATION. There are four types: Superior Suite, Junior Suite, standard outside-view, and standard interior cabins, in 12 price categories. Most of the cabins are small, but comfortable enough for short cruises. There are no balcony cabins. While most cabins have fixed twin beds, more than 60 cabins do have double beds. The bathrooms have showers but no tubs, and storage space for toiletries is very limited. All cabins have a refrigerator and TV/DVD player. Cabins nearest the engine room suffer from more noise.

The largest accommodation is in two Owner's Suites (Rhapsody and Sonata); both have a double bed, lounge area, extra closet and drawer space, larger bathroom, binoculars, and shoe horn/clothes brush.

DINING. The 280-seat main restaurant has large, ocean-view picture windows, and dark wood accents. There are tables for four or six, and dining is in one seating.

Casual breakfasts, lunches and dinners can be taken in the Verandah Restaurant, a self-serve buffet-style venue with both indoor and outdoor seating areas. A variety of well-prepared, attractively presented items is the norm, with of cold cuts, cheeses, bread, and pastry items.

ENTERTAINMENT. The 250-seat Main Lounge is a single-level venue designed for cabaret performances, but used mainly for concerts, lectures, and guest speakers. The Yacht Club Lounge/Bar is the evening/late-night gathering place.

SPA/FITNESS. Spa Aquarius is an indoor health spa; it includes a shallow swimming pool, small fitness area, massage room, sauna, and relaxation room. A beauty salon is adjacent to the Library.

BERLITZ'S RATINGS

	Possible	Achieved
Ship	500	290
Accommodation	200	120
Food	400	248
Service	400	247
Entertainment	100	62
Cruise Experience	400	245

OVERALL SCORE 1212 points out of 2000

BLACK WATCH
★★★+

THIS SHIP PROVIDES REALLY GOOD VALUE FOR MATURE-AGE CRUISERS

Size:	Mid-size Ship	Passenger/Crew Ratio (lower beds):	2.2
Tonnage:	28,613	Cabins (total):	421
Cruise Line:	Fred. Olsen Cruise Lines	Size Range (sq ft/m):	135.6–819.1/12.6–76.1
Former Names:	Star Odyssey, Westward,	Cabins (for one person):	38
	Royal Viking Star	Cabins with balcony:	70
Builder:	Wartsila (Finland)	Cabins (wheelchair accessible):	4
Entered Service:	Jun 1972/Nov 1996	Wheelchair accessibility:	Fair
Length (ft/m):	674.1/205.4	Elevators:	4
Beam (ft/m):	82.6/25.2	Casino (gaming tables):	Yes
Propulsion/Propellers:	diesel (13,400kW)/2	Swimming Pools:	2
Passenger Decks:	8	Self-Service Launderette:	Yes
Total Crew:	350	Library:	Yes
Passengers (lower beds):	804	Onboard currency:	UK£
Passenger Space Ratio (lower beds):	35.5		

THE SHIP. The ship's name is taken from the famous Scottish Black Watch regiment. There is a good amount of open deck and sunbathing space, and a decent health and fitness area high atop the ship, as well as a wide walk-around teakwood promenade deck with windbreaker on the aft part of the deck.

The interior decor is quiet and restful, with wide stairways and foyers, soft lighting and no glitz anywhere, though the artwork is a little drab. In general, good materials, fabrics (including the use of the Black Watch tartan), and soft furnishings give a pleasant ambience and comfortable feeling to the public rooms (most of which are quite spacious, with high ceilings), located on one deck in a user-friendly horizontal layout.

An observation lounge, The Observatory, displays nautical memorabilia and has commanding views. Draft beers are available in all bars, and the whole ship indoors is a smoke-free zone.

There is a good 3D-equipped cinema (few ships today have a dedicated cinema) with a steeply tiered floor.

A popular meeting place is the Morning Light Pub, close to the restaurant, although it becomes overly busy at afternoon tea time. It has a self-help beverage corner for coffees and teas, comfortable chairs, and large ocean-view windows along one side. The Library/Card Room is pleasant, and an adjacent room contains two computer terminals. There is a self-serve launderette, useful on the

BERLITZ'S RATINGS		
	Possible	Achieved
Ship	500	322
Accommodation	200	129
Food	400	252
Service	400	254
Entertainment	100	62
Cruise Experience	400	258

OVERALL SCORE 1277 points out of 2000

longer cruises, with washing machines, dryers, and irons.

Although it is being well maintained, this ship is now over 40 years old, so little problems such as gurgling plumbing, creaking joints, and other idiosyncrasies can occur, and air conditioning may not work well in some cabins. But the ship (refurbished in 2016) still looks good. The company suggests gratuities of £4 (around US$5) per passenger per day.

Black Watch offers a moderate standard of service from a friendly, mostly Filipino staff that provides decent, though not faultless, service. There is ample space per passenger, even when the ship is full. Port taxes are included for UK passengers.

Passenger niggles include: cutbacks in food variety and quality; packets of butter, margarine, and preserves; very poor coffee; long lines at the cramped buffet; poor wine service; and too few staff for the increased passenger numbers after the addition of more cabins.

Black Watch is a comfortable but not luxurious ship best suited to well-dressed, mature-age travelers seeking a British cruise environment. Cruises are well organized, with interesting itineraries and free shuttle buses in many ports of call.

ACCOMMODATION. There are many cabin price categories (plus one Owner's Suite, whose price is not listed in the brochure). These include four solo traveler cabin grades. The range goes from spacious suites with separate bedrooms to small, no-view cabins. While most accommodation options are for two, some can sleep up to five. Some 27 balconies were added to cabins on the Lido Deck in a 2015 refit.

All accommodation grades have hairdryers, duvets, cotton towels, personal safe, mini-fridge, and wall-mounted soap and shampoo dispensers in the bathrooms. Suite-grade occupants also get a cotton bathrobe and cold canapés each evening, plus priority seating in the restaurants.

The suites and cabins on decks 7, 8, and 9 are quiet units. A number of cabins in the aft section of decks 3, 4, and 5 can suffer generator noise, particularly those adjacent to the engine casing. The room service menu is limited.

Outside-view and interior cabins. Spread across decks 3, 4, 5, 7, and 8, all cabins are quite well equipped. Some bathrooms have awkward access.

Deluxe/Bridge/Junior Suites. Each bathroom has a tub and shower (cabin 8019 is the exception, with a shower only).

Marquee Suites. These have a large sleeping area and lounge area with bigger ocean-view picture windows, a refrigerator, more hooks for hanging bathrobes and outerwear, and a bathroom with tub and shower.

Premier Suites. Each of these suites is named after a place: Amalfi (9006), Lindos (9002), and Nice (9004), each measuring 547.7 sq ft (50. 9 sq m); Seville (9001), Singapore (9003), Carmel (9005), Bergen (9007), and Waterford (9009), each measuring 341.7 sq ft (31.7 sq m); and Windsor (9008), measuring 574.8 sq ft (53.4 sq m).

Owner's Suite. This measures 819.1 sq ft (76.1 sq m).

DINING. The 340-seat Glentanar Dining Room has a high ceiling, a white sail-like focal point at its center, and ample space at each table. The chairs have armrests, and are quite comfortable. The Orchid Room is a small offshoot of the dining room, and can be reserved for intimate dining. While breakfast and lunch are typically in an open-seating arrangement, there are two seatings for dinner.

Brigadoon, with 54 seats, is a small, more intimate restaurant with a light, breezy decor.

Fred. Olsen Cruise Lines has above-average cuisine that is attractively presented, with a good range of fish, seafood, meat, and chicken dishes. There's a good selection of cheeses, plus vegetarian options. There is also a decent range of wines, at really moderate prices, but few of the stewards are very knowledgeable about them.

A 80-seat poolside Grill Restaurant costs extra for dinner, but menu items include premium steaks and lobster, and the surroundings are pleasant.

ENTERTAINMENT. The Neptune Lounge seats about 400, but some sight lines are obstructed by pillars. The entertainment consists of small-scale productions presented by resident singers/dancers, and end-of-pier cabaret shows. There is plenty of live music in several lounges, and good old British singalongs.

SPA/FITNESS. Facilities are located at the top and front of the ship, which is inaccessible for wheelchair users. There is a combined gymnasium/aerobics room, plus steam rooms, saunas, and changing rooms. Some fitness classes are free, while some cost extra. Sports facilities include a large paddle tennis court, golf practice nets, shuffleboard, and ring toss.

BOUDICCA
★★★+

AN OLDER-STYLE SHIP WITH A TRADITIONAL BRITISH AMBIENCE AND DECOR

Size:	Mid-size Ship	Passenger Space Ratio (lower beds): 33.8
Tonnage:	28,388	Passenger/Crew Ratio (lower beds): 2.3
Cruise Line:	Fred. Olsen Cruise Lines	Cabins (total): 437
Former Names:	Grand Latino, SuperStar Capricorn,	Size Range (sq ft/m): 135.6–579.1/12.6–53.8
Hyundai Keumgang, SuperStar, Capricorn, Golden Princess,		Cabins (for one person): 35
New Sunward, Birka Queen, Sunward, Royal Viking Sky		Cabins with balcony: 64
Builder:	Wartsila (Finland)	Cabins (wheelchair accessible): 4
Entered Service:	Jun 1973/Feb 2006	Wheelchair accessibility: Fair
Length (ft/m):	674.1/205.4	Elevators: 5
Beam (ft/m):	82.6/25.2	Casino (gaming tables): Yes
Propulsion/Propellers:	diesel (13,400kW)/2	Swimming Pools: 2
Passenger Decks:	8	Self-Service Launderette: Yes
Total Crew:	320	Library: Yes
Passengers (lower beds):	839	Onboard currency: UK£

THE SHIP. Acquired by Fred. Olsen Cruise Lines in 2005, this well-proportioned ship, originally built for long-distance cruising for the now-defunct Royal Viking Line (it was built for one of the three original shipping partners who formed the line – Bergenske Dampskibsselskab), has a sharply raked bow and a sleek appearance. The ship was 'stretched' in 1982 with the addition of a 91ft (28m) midsection.

The outer styling is quite handsome for an early 1970s-built vessel. The single funnel bears the company's starfish logo and balances the profile of this attractive (now contemporary-classic) ship. The name Boudicca comes from the Queen of the Iceni tribe that occupied England's East Anglia, who led a dramatic revolt against the Romans in AD 61; her body is supposedly buried under Platform 10 of King's Cross Station in London.

The ship has a good amount of open deck and sunbathing space; in fact, there is plenty of space everywhere and little sense of crowding because the ship absorbs passengers well. There is a complete walk-around teak promenade deck outdoors.

The interior decor is restful, with a mix of English and Norwegian styles (particularly the artwork) with wide stairways and foyers, good passenger flow, soft lighting, and no glitz. In general, good materials, fabrics, and soft furnishings add to a pleasant ambience and comfortable feeling ex-

BERLITZ'S RATINGS	Possible	Achieved
Ship	500	322
Accommodation	200	129
Food	400	252
Service	400	254
Entertainment	100	62
Cruise Experience	400	258

OVERALL SCORE 1277 points out of 2000

perienced throughout the public rooms, most of which are quite spacious and have high, indented ceilings.

There are lots of (small) public rooms, bars, and lounges, unlike on the newer (larger) ships built today, including a delightful observation lounge, a small casino, card room, large library, and the Secret Garden Lounge.

Boudicca is an extremely comfortable ship in which to cruise, with a moderate standard of food and service from a friendly, mostly Filipino staff, featuring extremely good value for money cruises in a relaxed environment that provides passengers with many of the comforts of home.

Although the ship has benefited from an extensive refit and refurbishment, it is now over 40 years old, which means that little problems such as gurgling plumbing, creaking joints, and other idiosyncrasies can occur, and air conditioning may not be all that it should be. Port taxes are included for UK passengers. Gratuities of £4 ($5) per passenger, per day, are suggested.

Passenger niggles include: cutbacks in food variety and quality; an increased use of packets of butter, margarine, and preserves; the lack of choice of sugar; very poor coffee; long lines at the cramped buffet; and too few wine waiters.

For the ship's mainly British passengers, the National Express coach operator works in conjunction with the cruise line to provide a dedicated service via London's Victoria Coach Station to the departure ports of Dover or Southampton.

Boudicca appeals to British couples and solo travelers seeking a sense of space, comfortable surroundings with decent facilities, and realistic, value-for-money pricing, with British food and entertainment.

ACCOMMODATION.
There is something for every taste and wallet, from spacious family suites to small interior cabins. While most cabins are for two people, some can accommodate a third, fourth, or even a fifth person. There are 20 price categories of cabins (plus one for the Owner's Suite, the price of which isn't listed in the brochure), including four grades of cabin for those traveling solo – these are spread across most of the cabin decks, and not just the lower decks, as is the case with some cruise lines – and three of these have a private balcony. While most cabins have bathtubs, some lower grades have only a shower enclosure.

Some of the quietest cabins are those located just under the navigation bridge, on Lido Deck, as well as those suites and cabins on Bridge Deck. In the refit, a vacuum toilet system was fitted.

All grades have duvets, large cotton bathroom towels, a hairdryer, and a shower wall-mounted soap and shampoo dispenser. Suite-grade occupants also get a cotton bathrobe and cold canapés each evening, and priority seating in the restaurants.

The room service menu is limited and needs improvement, but there is an abundance of food available at most times of the day. All cabins have had a facelift. Only a few suites have private balconies.

DINING.
The main dining room is divided into three venues: Heligan, Tintagel, and Four Seasons; each has a high ceiling, and ample space at each table. Although the decor is reserved, the chairs, which have armrests, are comfortable. Window-side tables for two are the most sought after, naturally.

Breakfast and lunch are in an open-seating arrangement, with two seatings for dinner. Self-service display counters are provided for cold food items for breakfast and lunch.

Fred. Olsen Cruise Lines has above-average cuisine that is attractively presented and includes a good range of fish, seafood, meat, and chicken dishes, plus vegetarian options, and a wide selection of cheeses to suit most British tastes. You'll also find popular British pub standards such as bangers and mash, toad in the hole, and spotted dick. Breakfast buffets tend to be repetitive, although they appear to satisfy most passengers. There is a reasonably decent range of wines, at unpretentious prices.

Coffee and tea are available in the Secret Garden Café (part of the Secret Garden Lounge), just aft of the main dining venues – but, sadly, not round-the-clock, although there are late-night 'supper club' snacks.

Casual self-serve deck buffets are provided outdoors at the Poolside Café. An 80-seat poolside Grill Restaurant costs extra for dinner, but menu items include premium steaks and lobster, and the surroundings are pleasant.

ENTERTAINMENT.
The Neptune Lounge is the venue for shows, cabaret acts, and lectures. It is a large room that seats about 400, although some pillars obstruct sight lines from some seats. The entertainment consists of small-scale shows presented by a small team of resident singers/dancers, and cabaret acts.

There is plenty of live music for social dancing (many of the musicians are Filipino) and listening in several lounges, and good British singalongs are a feature on each cruise.

SPA/FITNESS.
A decent amount of ocean-view space is given to providing health and fitness facilities, which include sauna/steam rooms, gymnasium/aerobics room, changing rooms, while the beauty salon is located in an area without windows.

Some fitness classes are free, while some, such as yoga and kick-boxing, cost extra.

It's best to make appointments early, as treatment time slots go quickly. Sports facilities include golf practice nets, shuffleboard, and ring toss.

BRAEMAR
★★★+

A SMART-LOOKING SHIP WITH DECOR SUITED TO CASUAL CRUISERS

Size:	Mid-size Ship	Passenger/Crew Ratio (lower beds):	2.3
Tonnage:	24,344	Cabins (total):	484
Cruise Line:	Fred. Olsen Cruise Lines	Size Range (sq ft/m):	139.9–349.8/13.0–32.5
Former Names:	Norwegian Dynasty, Crown Majesty,	Cabins (for one person):	38
	Cunard Dynasty, Crown Dynasty	Cabins with balcony:	79
Builder:	Union Navale de Levante (Spain)	Cabins (wheelchair accessible):	4
Entered Service:	Jul 1993/Aug 2001	Wheelchair accessibility:	Fair
Length (ft/m):	639.7/195.0	Elevators:	5
Beam (ft/m):	73.8/22.5	Casino (gaming tables):	Yes
Propulsion/Propellers:	diesel (13,200kW)/2	Swimming Pools:	2
Passenger Decks:	7	Self-Service Launderette:	Yes
Total Crew:	371	Library:	Yes
Passengers (lower beds):	930	Onboard currency:	UK£
Passenger Space Ratio (lower beds):	25.9		

THE SHIP. *Braemar* has attractive exterior styling, and a lot of glass space. There is a good amount of open deck and sunbathing space for its size, and this includes two outdoor bars – one aft and one midships adjacent to the two swimming pools and paddling pool – that have Boddingtons and Stella Artois keg beers. Four open decks, located aft of the funnel, provide good, quiet places to sit and read.

The teak promenade deck is a complete walk-around deck, wrapping around Lounge Deck. Passengers can go right to the ship's bow – good for those Titanic pose photographs. Faux teak floor covering is used on the pool deck, which has two pools; it looks tacky, but works well in warm-weather areas.

Inside, there is a pleasant five-deck-high, glass-walled atrium on the starboard side. Off-center stairways add a sense of spaciousness to a clever interior design that surrounds passengers with light. The interior decor in public spaces is warm and inviting, with contemporary, but not brash, Art Deco color combinations. The artwork is colorful and pleasant, in the Nordic manner.

The Morning Light Club is an open-plan lounge, with its own bar, split by a walkway that leads to the showlounge (forward), a lifestyle lounge (incorporating the library, Internet center, and Café Venus), a card room/arts and crafts centre, and a boutique (midships). Despite being open, it has cozy seating areas and is very comfortable, with a tartan carpet. A

BERLITZ'S RATINGS		
	Possible	Achieved
Ship	500	322
Accommodation	200	128
Food	400	240
Service	400	251
Entertainment	100	62
Cruise Experience	400	266

OVERALL SCORE 1269 points out of 2000

model of the first Fred. Olsen ship named *Braemar* (4,775 gross tonnage) is displayed in the center of the room, as is a large carved wood plaque bearing the name of the Scottish Braemar Castle.

The mostly Filipino staff is attentive, and the hospitality factor is good. The company offers extremely good value for money cruises in a relaxed, welcoming, and laid-back environment.

In 2008, a 102ft (31m) midsection extension was added, providing additional cabins and balcony 'suites.' Facilities added or changed include a second swimming pool and more sunbathing space, an observatory lounge, a new restaurant, and a pub-style bar.

There can be a bit of a wait for shore tenders and for the few elevators aboard this ship. British passengers should note that no suites or cabins have bathtubs.

Passenger niggles include: lines at the cramped self-service buffet; poor wine service (not enough wine waiters); an increase in the use of packets of butter, margarine, and preserves; the lack of choice of sugar; weak coffee; and badly worn bathroom fittings. There is a self-service launderette (£2 for wash and dry) – and the company may charge for shuttle buses in some ports of call.

This smart-looking mid-size ship suits middle-aged and older passengers seeking a casual, un-stuffy environment in a ship with British food and entertainment. It's a refreshing change for those who don't enjoy larger, warehouse-size ships. But it does roll somewhat, probably because of its shallow draft design, meant for warm-weather cruise areas.

ACCOMMODATION. There are several cabin price categories; the higher the deck, the higher the price. All grades have a television and hairdryer (some are awkward to retract from their wall-mount holders), European-style duvets, and large cotton bathroom towels (bathrobes are available upon request in suite-grade cabins). There is no separate audio system in the cabin, but music can be obtained from one of the TV channels, although you'll have to leave the picture on. Suites, however, do have a CD music system.

When Fred. Olsen Cruise Lines bought the ship, it converted a number of cabins from double-occupancy units to solo traveler cabins.

Some cabins suffer from poor soundproofing; passengers in cabins on Deck 4 in particular are disturbed by anyone running or jogging on the promenade deck above. Cabins on the lowest deck (Deck 2) in the ship's center are subject to noise from the adjacent engine room.

DINING. There are two restaurants (Thistle and Grampian: assigned according to your accommodation grade). The Thistle Restaurant is a pleasing and attractive venue, with large ocean-view windows on three sides; its focal point is a large oil painting on a wall behind a buffet food display counter. However, space is tight, and tables are extremely close together, making proper service difficult. There are tables for two, four, six, or eight; the Porsgrund china has a Venus pattern.

There are two seatings for dinner, and an open seating for breakfast and lunch. The menu is varied. Salad items are quite poor and very basic, with little variety, although there is a decent choice of dessert items. For breakfast and lunch the dual food counters are functional, but the layout is not ideal and at peak times they create much congestion. The Grampian Restaurant is located aft at the top of the ship, with fine aft views. Service is attentive (if hurried) in both venues.

Casual breakfasts and luncheons can also be taken in the self-service buffet located in the Palms Café, although these tend to be repetitive. There is indoor and outdoor seating. Although it is the casual dining spot, tablecloths are provided. The indoor flooring is wood, which makes it rather a noisy room, and some tables adjacent to the galley entrance are to be avoided at all costs.

Out on the pool deck, there is a barbecue grill for casual eating – welcome when the ship is in warm-weather areas.

ENTERTAINMENT. The Neptune Showlounge sits longitudinally along one side of the ship, with amphitheater-style seating in several tiers, but its layout is less than ideal for either shows or cocktail parties. There is often congestion between first- and second-seating passengers at the entrance.

Unfortunately, 15 pillars obstruct sight lines to the stage, and the banquet and individual tub chair seating arrangement is quite poor.

The entertainment mainly consists of small-scale production shows and mini-musicals presented by a small troupe of resident singers/dancers, and cabaret acts. They are rather amateurish, but enjoyable.

SPA/FITNESS. The health spa facilities are limited. The spa includes a combined gymnasium/aerobics room, and a separate room for women and men, with sauna, steam room, and small changing area. Spa Rituals treatments are provided by Steiner. Some fitness classes are free; others, such as yoga and kick-boxing, cost extra.

BREMEN
★★★★

A FINE, STRONG EXPEDITION SHIP FOR IN-DEPTH DISCOVERY CRUISES

Size:	Boutique Ship	Passenger/Crew Ratio (lower beds):	1.7
Tonnage:	6,752	Cabins (total):	82
Cruise Line:	Hapag-Lloyd Expedition Cruises	Size Range (sq ft/m):	174.3–322.9/16.2–30.0
Former Names:	*Frontier Spirit*	Cabins (for one person):	0
Builder:	Mitsubishi Heavy Industries (Japan)	Cabins with balcony:	18
Entered Service:	Nov 1990/Nov 1993	Cabins (wheelchair accessible):	2
Length (ft/m):	365.8/111.5	Wheelchair accessibility:	None
Beam (ft/m):	55.7/17.0	Elevators:	2
Propulsion/Propellers:	diesel (4,855kW)/2	Casino (gaming tables):	No
Passenger Decks:	6	Swimming Pools:	1
Total Crew:	94	Self-Service Launderette:	No
Passengers (lower beds):	164	Library:	Yes
Passenger Space Ratio (lower beds):	41.1	Onboard currency:	Euros

THE SHIP. An ageing purpose-built all-white expedition vessel, equipped with 12 Zodiac inflatable craft and a helicopter pad, it has a handsome, wide, squat, contemporary profile and good equipment. Its wide beam provides good stability, and the vessel's long cruising range and ice-hardened hull both allow it access to remote destinations. The ship carries the highest ice classification for passenger vessels.

Sustainable tourism is the norm. Zero-discharge of waste matter is fiercely practiced; this means that absolutely nothing is discharged into the ocean that does not meet with the international conventions on ocean pollution (MARPOL). Equipment for in-depth marine and shore excursions is provided, including a boot-washing station with three water hoses and boot-cleaning brushes.

There is almost a walk-around deck – you have to go up and down steps at the front of the deck to complete the 'walk.' A large open deck aft of the mast provides a good viewing platform that's also useful for sunbathing on warm-weather cruises.

The ship has a decent number of public rooms for its size, including a forward-facing observation lounge/lecture room, and a main lounge (The Club) with a high ceiling, bandstand, dance floor and large bar, and an adjacent library with 12 bookcases (most books are in German).

Bremen is a practical expedition cruise vessel that has been nicely refurbished. Arguably, it is a better ex-

BERLITZ'S RATINGS

	Possible	Achieved
Ship	500	338
Accommodation	200	147
Food	400	308
Service	400	315
Entertainment	100	75
Cruise Experience	400	312

OVERALL SCORE 1495 points out of 2000

pedition vessel than the company's *Hanseatic*, and, although not quite as luxurious in its interiors and appointments, the ship has a loyal following. Its cruises will provide you with a fine educational expedition experience, particularly its Antarctic cruises. All shore landings and tours are included, as is seasickness medication. There are expert lecturers, and a friendly crew. The ship has two microscopes, and a plankton-collection net for in-depth studies.

The onboard ambience is completely casual, cozy, unstuffy (no dressy clothes needed), and very accommodating. Also, there is no music in hallways or on open decks. The reception desk is open 24 hours a day, and there's an 'invitation to the bridge' policy.

On Arctic/Antarctic cruises, parkas (waterproof outdoor jackets) and tough 'snow-grip' boots are supplied, but you should take strong waterproof trousers and thick socks, plus thermal underwear. Each of the fleet of 12 Zodiacs (rubber-inflatable landing craft) is named after a place or ethnic group: Amazon, Antarctic, Asmat, Bora Bora, Cape Horn, Deception, Jan Mayen, Luzon, Pitcairn, San Blas, Spitzbergen, and Ushuaia. On Arctic and Antarctic cruises, it is particularly pleasing to go to the bridge wings late at night to stargaze under pollution-free skies – the watch officers will be pleased to explain star formations.

Special sailings may be under the auspices of various tour operators, although the ship is operated by

Hapag-Lloyd Expedition Cruises. Thus, your fellow expedition voyagers may well be from many different countries. Insurance, port taxes, and all staff gratuities are typically included in the cruise fare, and a logbook is provided at the end of each expedition cruise for all participants – a reminder of what's been seen and done during the course of the adventure.

There's no 'bulbous bow,' which means that the ship can pitch in some more challenging sea conditions; however, it does have stabilizers. The swimming pool is small, as is the open deck space around it, although there are both shaded and open areas. In-cabin announcements cannot be turned off (on cruises in the Arctic and Antarctic regions, announcements are often made at or before 7am on days when shore landings are permitted). Sadly, the ship was not built with good cabin soundproofing.

Hapag-Lloyd publishes its own excellent handbooks, in both English and German, on expedition regions such as the Arctic, Antarctica, Amazonia, and the South Sea Islands, as well as exclusive maps.

ACCOMMODATION. There are just four different configurations. All cabins have an outside view – those on the lowest deck have portholes, while the others have picture windows. All are well equipped for the size of the vessel. Each has wood accenting, a TV and DVD player, telephone, refrigerator (soft drinks are provided free and replenished daily), vanity desk with 220-volt European-style electrical sockets, sitting area with small drinks table, and wireless access.

Cabins have either twin beds (convertible to a queen-size bed, but with individual European cotton duvets) or double bed, according to location, plus bedside reading lights and alarm clock. There is a small indented area for outerwear and rubber boots, while a small drawer above the refrigerator unit provides warmth when needed for such things as wet socks and gloves.

Each cabin has a private bathroom (totally replaced in 2010) with a tiled floor, shower enclosure with curtain, toiletries shelf, washbasin and low-height toilet (vacuum type), a decent amount of under-basin storage space, and an electrical socket for shavers. Large towels and 100 percent cotton bathrobes are provided, as is a range of Crabtree & Evelyn toiletries (shampoo, body lotion, shower gel, soap, and shower cap).

Each cabin has some illuminated closet space (large enough for two weeks for two persons, but tight for longer cruises), although the drawer space is limited – suitcases can be stored under the beds. Some Sun Deck and Bridge Deck cabins also have a small balcony (*Bremen* was the first expedition cruise vessel to have these) with blue plastic, easily cleanable decking, and wooden handrail, but no exterior light. Balconies have two teak chairs and a small drinks table, but are small and narrow, with partial partitions and doors that open outwards onto the balcony, taking up space.

Two Sun Deck suites have a separate lounge area with sofa and coffee table, bedroom with wall clock, large walk-in closet, and marble bathroom with tub and basin.

DINING. The dining room has open seating when operating for mixed German and international passenger cruises, and open seating for breakfast and lunch, with one sitting for dinner (assigned seats) when operated solely as a German-speaking cruise. It is fairly attractive, with pleasing decor and pastel colors; it has big picture windows and 12 pillars placed in inconvenient positions – the result of old shipbuilding techniques.

The food, made with high-quality ingredients, is extremely good. Although the portions are small, the presentation is appealing to the eye – and you can always ask for more. There is an excellent choice of freshly made breads and pastries, and a good selection of cheeses and fruits.

Dinner typically includes a choice of two appetizers, two soups, an in-between course, two entrées (mains), and two or three desserts, plus a cheese board (note that Continental Europeans typically have cheese before dessert). There is always a vegetarian specialty, as well as a healthy-eating option. The service is good, with smartly dressed, bilingual (German- and English-speaking) waiters and waitresses.

As an alternative to the dining room, breakfast and luncheon buffets are available in The Club, or outside on the Lido Deck (weather permitting), where the Starboard Bar/Grill provides grilled food.

ENTERTAINMENT. The Club is the social focus point for gatherings after meals and before expedition landings ashore. There is no formal entertainment as such. At the end of each cruise, the ship's chart is auctioned off one evening to the highest bidder, with profits donated to charity.

SPA/FITNESS. There is a small fitness room, a large sauna, and beauty salon with integral massage table. Out on the open deck is a small swimming pool, which is heated when the ship is sailing in cold-weather regions such as the Arctic or Antarctica.

BRILLIANCE OF THE SEAS
★★★+

THIS SHIP HAS CONTEMPORARY, STYLISH DECOR FOR YOUTHFUL FAMILIES

Size:	Mid-size Ship	Passenger/Crew Ratio (lower beds):	2.5
Tonnage:	90,090	Cabins (total):	1,056
Cruise Line:	Royal Caribbean International	Size Range (sq ft/m):	165.8–1,216.3/15.4–113.0
Former Names:	none	Cabins (for one person):	0
Builder:	Meyer Werft (Germany)	Cabins with balcony:	577
Entered Service:	Jul 2002	Cabins (wheelchair accessible):	24
Length (ft/m):	961.9/293.2	Wheelchair accessibility:	Good
Beam (ft/m):	105.6/32.2	Elevators:	9
Propulsion/Propellers:	gas turbine/2 azimuthing pods	Casino (gaming tables):	Yes
Passenger Decks:	12	Swimming Pools:	2
Total Crew:	869	Self-Service Launderette:	No
Passengers (lower beds):	2,112	Library:	Yes
Passenger Space Ratio (lower beds):	42.6	Onboard currency:	US$

THE SHIP. *Brilliance of the Seas* (a *Radiance*-class ship) is a contemporary vessel, built in 66 blocks and welded together. Along the port side, a central glass wall protrudes, giving great views (balcony cabins occupy the space on the starboard side). A gently rounded stern presents a nicely tiered appearance, giving the ship a well-balanced look. One of two swimming pools can be covered by a glass dome for use in all-weather conditions.

The interior decor is modern and quite elegant, and in 2013 some of the dining options found on the larger ships were added, plus ship-wide Wi-Fi (at extra cost), flat-screen televisions, and finger-touch digital 'Wayfinder' direction screens.

A nine-deck-high atrium lobby (Centrum) is the focal and social meeting point. On its various levels, it houses an R Bar (for creative cocktails), several passenger service counters, art gallery, and Café Latte-tudes (for extra-cost coffee). Close by is the decidedly flashy Casino Royale (for table gaming and slot machines) and other public bars and lounges, and a library.

At the top of the ship a Viking Crown Lounge is set around the ship's funnel; this functions as an observation lounge during the day, and in the evening it's a high-energy dance club.

ACCOMMODATION. A wide range of suites/outside-view and interior (no-view) cabins come in several categories and price groups. Except for the six larg-

BERLITZ'S RATINGS

	Possible	Achieved
Ship	500	357
Accommodation	200	137
Food	400	242
Service	400	278
Entertainment	100	72
Cruise Experience	400	266

OVERALL SCORE 1352 points out of 2000

est suites (called Owner's Suites), which have king-size beds, almost all other cabins have twin beds that convert to queen-size beds. There are 14 wheelchair-accessible cabins, 8 with a private balcony.

All cabins have rich (faux) wood cabinetry, including a vanity desk (with hairdryer), faux silent-close wood drawers, infotainment system, a personal safe, and three-sided bathroom mirrors. Some cabins have ceiling-recessed, pull-down berths for third and fourth persons – although closet and drawer space would be extremely tight for four – and some have interconnecting doors.

Most bathrooms have tiled accenting and a terrazzo-style tiled floor, and a small half-moon shower enclosure, cotton towels, a small cabinet for toiletries, and a shelf.

Occupants of cabins designated as suites get to use a private Concierge Lounge, where priority dining-room reservations, shore excursion bookings, and beauty salon/ spa appointments can be made.

Many 'private' balcony cabins are not particularly private and can be overlooked from the Solarium's port and starboard wings, and from other locations.

DINING. Minstrel, the main dining room, spans two decks (the upper deck level has floor-to-ceiling windows, while the lower deck level has windows). It seats 1,104, and has music of the Middle Ages as its decorative theme. There are tables for two to 10 in two seatings for dinner. Adjacent are two small private dining rooms (Zephyr, with 94 seats, and Lute, with 30 seats).

Choose either one of two seatings or 'My Time Dining' (eat when you want during dining room hours) when you book. Minstrel is closed for lunch on most days, which means scrambling for food and seating in the Windjammer Café – an awful prospect after returning from morning excursions.

The cuisine is typical of mass banquet catering, with food comparable to that found in American family-style restaurants ashore – mostly disappointing and without much taste (a vegetarian menu is available).

Menu descriptions make the food sound better than it is, and the selection of breads and bakery items ('baked' from a frozen 'starter' dough), fruit, and cheese is poor. Overall, meals are rather hit and miss. Also, if you want lobster or a decent filet mignon (steak), you need to pay extra.

Chops Grille Steakhouse (on Deck G) has 95 seats and an open (show) kitchen; it features premium veal chops and steaks (New York Striploin Steak, Filet Mignon, Prime Rib of Beef). There is a per-person cover charge for both, and reservations are required.

Other dining and eatery options include: Giovanni's Table (an Italian trattoria), Izumi (for Asian cuisine), Rita's Cantina (for Mexican-style cuisine), a Chef's Table (for food-and-wine-pairing dinners), and Park Café (a deli-style venue). Some venues incur a cover charge, and some food items have à la carte pricing.

Casual meals (for breakfast, lunch, and dinner) can be taken in the self-serve, buffet-style Windjammer Café, accessed directly from the pool deck. It is impossible to get a hot plate for hot food because the plates are plastic, so things go cold quickly.

ENTERTAINMENT. The Pacifica Theatre (showlounge) is three decks high, has 874 seats, including 24 stations for wheelchairs, and good sight lines from most seats.

The entertainment is always upbeat. There is even background music in all corridors and elevators, and constant music outdoors on the pool deck.

SPA/FITNESS. The Vitality at Sea Spa and Fitness Center includes a 10,176-sq-ft (945-sq-m) solarium with whirlpool and counter-current swimming under a retractable glass roof, a gymnasium with cardiovascular machines, an aerobics room, sauna and steam rooms, and therapy treatment rooms. All are on two of the uppermost decks.

Sports facilities include a 30ft (9m) rock-climbing wall, golf course, jogging track, basketball court, a nine-hole miniature golf course with novel decorative ornaments (Fairways of Brilliance), an indoor/outdoor country club with golf simulator, and an exterior jogging track.

BRITANNIA
★★★★

THIS FLOATING 'SMALL BRITAIN' HAS ALL THE RIGHT FAMILY-FRIENDLY TRIMMINGS

Size:	Large Resort Ship	Passenger/Crew Ratio (lower beds):	2.6
Tonnage:	143,000	Cabins (total):	1,837
Cruise Line:	P&O Cruises	Size Range (sq ft/m):	174.0-387.5/15.0-36.0
Former Names:	none	Cabins (for one person):	18
Builder:	Fincantieri (Italy)	Cabins with balcony:	1,313
Entered Service:	Mar 2015	Cabins (wheelchair accessible):	37
Length (ft/m):	1,082.6/330.0	Wheelchair accessibility:	Best
Beam (ft/m):	125.9/38.4	Elevators:	12
Propulsion/Propellers:	diesel-electric (62,400kW/2	Casino (gaming tables):	Yes
Passenger Decks:	14	Swimming Pools:	3
Total Crew:	1,400	Self-Service Launderette:	Yes
Passengers (lower beds):	3,737	Library:	Yes
Passenger Space Ratio (lower beds):	38.2	Onboard currency:	UK£

THE SHIP. Modeled on the *Royal Princess* platform, *Britannia* – named by Queen Elizabeth II and bearing the same sterling name as her former, slightly smaller Royal Yacht Britannia – is a thoroughly British ship. It incorporates the classic features of ships such as *Aurora* and *Oriana* into a design that is contemporary but not brash. The stern is nicely tiered, and reminiscent of the back of an American Airstream trailer (caravan), but the bow (the front) is extremely short. Sadly, there is no open walk-around promenade deck; there's no Deck 13 either. *Britannia* features a rising sun logo on its two funnels (it's presently the only P&O Cruises ship with two funnels), while along the side of the hull there's no mistaking the Union Jack – at 308.4ft (94m) long, it's a big, bold British statement.

On the open (family-friendly) deck are two main swimming pools (Lido and Riviera) and several hot tubs (close by is a Pizzeria, Lido Grill, and Grab & Go ice cream bar). Some nights may feature sound-and-light shows performed by the ship's resident dance and vocal troupe. To escape the general noise and hubbub of the family-friendly pools and water-splash features, it's worth paying extra to use the adults-only Retreat (just forward of the mast on Deck 17), with its own serenity pool and two hot tubs.

Unusually for P&O Cruises, this ship's interiors were created by a single designer, and the consist-

BERLITZ'S RATINGS		
	Possible	Achieved
Ship	500	408
Accommodation	200	151
Food	400	260
Service	400	286
Entertainment	100	74
Cruise Experience	400	283
OVERALL SCORE 1462 points out of 2000		

ently simple, uncluttered, and tasteful modern design is evident throughout. The interior focal point – and its real social hub – is a spacious and charming three-deck-high atrium lobby, which has curved staircases and four panoramic elevators. Most of the interior decor is restrained. Intended to be a ship for all types of passenger, specific areas have been designed for different age groups and lifestyles.

On the lower level of the atrium (Deck 5) is Market Café, which features some delightful (extra-cost) patisserie items by British-based (French-born) celebrity chef Eric Lanlard as well as coffees, cakes, and pastries, a gelateria, and Blue Bar. Also close by is The Limelight Club (a specialty dining venue that is like a supper club). On the other levels you'll find a range of shops and a comfortable (extra-cost) Java Café.

On the middle level (Deck 6) you'll find Brodies (another rather comfortable place for lounging and drinking – named after Brodie Willcox, co-founder of the Peninsular & Oriental Steam Navigation Company), a fairly small casino (with gaming tables and slot machines, and several shops. On the upper level (Deck 7) is the comfortable Java Café, for extra-cost Costa coffees, and The Glass House extra-cost restaurant.

In all, there are 13 restaurants and eateries, and 13 bars to choose from (one of the favorites will probably be the Blue Bar in the atrium lobby). Atop the ship is the Crow's Nest Bar – a feature aboard P&O ships. Like a large London club, with panoramic views, it's a good meeting place for pre-dinner cocktails and after-dinner lounging; it has a selection of 20 British artisan gins (and more than 70 bottled beers and ales). Adjacent are two meeting rooms, the Marlow Suite (named after a former P&O Cruises managing director), and the Ivory Suite; both are on the port side, while the Library is located on the starboard side.

A constant cause of complaint is the fact that although there are elevators in the center of the ship, there are no stairs between decks 7 and 16 (only at the forward and aft stairways), and waiting for elevators can be very frustrating. The score, therefore, reflects this serious design fault.

ACCOMMODATION. There are five categories: suites; deluxe balcony cabins; outside and balcony cabins; interior (no-view) cabins; single interior cabins and (pleasant) single cabins with balcony; and wheelchair-accessible cabins (roll-in shower only – no bathtubs). All of the outside suites and cabins have private balconies (the best are those on the port and starboard side corners aft – with numbers A726, A727, B725, B726, C736, C737, D738, D739, E742, E743, F730, F731, G732, and G733). The decor is restrained – like that of a boutique hotel, in chocolate, beige, and cream. All shower enclosures are glazed. Suite-grade occupants are given bathrobes, 'butler' service, and chic bathroom toiletries, but note that many suite-grade balconies are disappointingly small and narrow.

All accommodation grades feature a large flat-screen TV for films on demand, as well as products from The White Company, and tea/coffee-making facilities with specialty teas (long-life milk is provided, so if you want fresh milk, ask your room steward). Balcony cabins have rubberized (not wood) decking, sliding glass doors, and low-grade chairs. Note that balcony cabins with a sofa are more comfortable than those without, since they provide seating for a couple together. Cabins for passengers with disabilities are fitted with roll-in showers.

DINING. The three principal dining rooms are Meridian (with classic gray and brown decor), Oriental (with plum, gray, and beige colors), and the Peninsular. Most of the chairs do not have armrests. While Oriental features fixed dining times for dinner, Meridian and Peninsular are for 'Freedom Dining,' so you choose the seating time to suit (early one evening, late the next, for example). Celebrity chef Marco Pierre White has created special dishes to be featured in the main dining rooms on gala evenings.

Epicurean Restaurant (adjacent to Reception on Deck 5) has a setting of understated glamor, and has arguably the best cuisine on board, especially the cheese selection. White individual chairs, however, have only curved half armrests that are uncomfortable.

The Glass House offers trendy light cuisine, with wine and food pairings by TV wine expert Olly Smith – and not a decanter in sight.

Sindhu features British-Indian fusion cuisine, with menus designed by Michelin-starred Atul Kochhar (his other sea-going restaurants are aboard *Azura* and *Ventura*).

The Limelight Club is a rather like a supper club – dinner with a (little) show.

Horizon Restaurant is the main self-serve buffet-style eatery (open 24/7); it has several 'active' stations (for pancakes, omelets, quiches, noodles, for example), plus 'grab and go' sandwiches, filled rolls, and deli-style food – most of which has little taste, because almost nothing is made to order. There's also a grill for fast-food items such as hamburgers and hot dogs, and pizzas at poolside grill stations.

In case you want to hone your culinary skills, a 24-station culinary kitchen – part of the James Martin Cookery Club – can be found aft on Deck 17. Various celebrity chefs (including 'Food Heroes' James Martin, Marco Pierre White, and Atul Kochhar) and other invited chefs may take part and host masterclasses throughout the year.

ENTERTAINMENT. The 936-seat Headline's Theatre is the venue for colorful large-scale productions and top cabaret entertainment. The room has gently tiered seating (with good stage views from almost all seats); an LED stage backdrop provides great sets and lighting effects.

Live Lounge. This room hosts live music, cabaret acts, and comedy, but late at night it morphs into a disco/late-night spot, with bar.

The Crystal Room. This room features a large traditional wooden dance floor, grand piano, and dance hosts to help you dance better or teach you something new.

The Studio. This is a multi-function venue for talks, films, cooking and other demonstrations, recitals, game shows, and conferences.

SPA/FITNESS. Larger than anything (and with more facilities) than on any previous P&O ship, the Oasis Spa is designed to help you relax, be pampered, and achieve serenity and wellbeing. The facility is located forward on the lowest deck (Deck 5), close to the atrium lobby. It includes a thermal suite, thalassotherapy pool, treatment rooms, beauty salon, and a rentable 'private spa villa' for couples, plus a spa shop.

Sports facilities include a 'short' tennis court, and an Arena Sports area that includes a combined football/basketball/cricket court, and other deck games, plus a gymnasium and aerobics room (on Deck 17).

CALEDONIAN SKY
★★★★+

THIS DELIGHTFUL COUNTRY INN AFLOAT IS FOR WELL-SEASONED TRAVELERS

Size:	Boutique Ship
Tonnage:	4,200
Cruise Line:	Noble Caledonia
Former Names:	Sunrise, Hebridean Spirit, Sun Viva 2, MegaStar Capricorn, Renaissance VI
Builder:	Nuovi Cantieri Apuania (Italy)
Entered Service:	Mar 1991/Jul 2012
Length (ft/m):	297.2/90.6
Beam (ft/m):	50.1/15.3
Propulsion/Propellers:	diesel (5,000kW)/2
Passenger Decks:	5
Total Crew:	74
Passengers (lower beds):	114
Passenger Space Ratio (lower beds):	36.8
Passenger/Crew Ratio (lower beds):	1.5
Cabins (total):	57
Size Range (sq ft/m):	215.0–365.9/20.0–34.0
Cabins (for one person):	0
Cabins with balcony:	23
Cabins (wheelchair accessible):	0
Wheelchair accessibility:	None
Elevators:	1
Casino (gaming tables):	No
Swimming Pools:	0
Self-Service Launderette:	No
Library:	Yes
Onboard currency:	UK£

THE SHIP. This vessel has a neat, modern look, coupled with a traditional single funnel and a navigation bridge in a well-rounded half-moon design. It was one of a series of eight similar ships originally built for the long-defunct Renaissance Cruises, and acquired by Noble Caledonia in 2011, after being in the possession of a private Abu Dhabi-based individual for use as his private yacht.

The exterior design has been altered somewhat with the addition of an enclosed lounge deck forward of the funnel. There are teakwood walking decks outdoors, and a good amount of open deck space. All of the deck furniture – the tables and chairs – are made of teak or hardwood, and the sunloungers have thick cushioned pads. All exterior handrails are of beautifully polished wood. There is also a teakwood water sports platform at the stern of the ship. The ship carries 10 Zodiac landing craft for up-close-and-personal coastal excursions or wet landings (where necessary).

You'll find elegant interior design and the touches reminiscent of a small, lavish country house hotel. The lounge has the unmistakable feel of a British traditional drawing room; it includes a large, white Bath stone fireplace with an imitation log fire (safety regulations prohibit a real one) and is the focal point for all social activities and cocktail parties. There is also a good travel library/reading room. Inspector Hercule Poirot would be very much at home here, as it is

BERLITZ'S RATINGS		
	Possible	Achieved
Ship	500	400
Accommodation	200	163
Food	400	318
Service	400	313
Entertainment	100	70
Cruise Experience	400	323

OVERALL SCORE 1587 points out of 2000

rather like a small, exclusive club. The fact that the ship doesn't have photographers and other trappings found aboard larger ships doesn't matter one bit.

The dress code is casual and comfortable, but most passengers tend to dress nicely for dinner. The service is friendly but unobtrusive; the atmosphere is quiet (no music in passageways or elevator) and refined, and the ship is well run by a crew proud to provide the kind of personal service expected by intelligent, well-traveled passengers. In fact, unobtrusive service from a Filipino and East European crew is the hallmark of a cruise aboard this ship. The fare includes gratuities, transfers, and shore excursions, plus house wine, beer, and soft drinks during lunch and dinner.

Although several pillars, needed for structural support, are obstructions in some public rooms and hallways, and the interior decor consists of wood laminates instead of real wood, the ambience is warm.

The ship's itineraries take participants mostly to quiet, off-the-beaten-track ports not often visited by larger cruise ships. Destination lecturers accompany each cruise.

The delightful pocket-sized *Caledonian Sky* is best suited to couples and solo travelers who enjoy learning about the natural sciences, geography, history, etc., and want to be aboard a ship with little or no entertainment – ideal for those who abhor big-ship cruising.

ACCOMMODATION. There are several grades of double or twin-bedded cabins and four grades of cabins for single travelers, priced by grade, size, and location. The cabins are quite spacious, measuring 215–365 sq ft (20–34 sq m), including bathrooms and balconies. All cabins have outside views, and most feature wallpapered walls, lighted closets, full-length mirror, dressing table with three-sided vanity mirrors, tea/coffee-making equipment, large-screen infotainment system, refrigerator/minibar (stocked with fresh milk and mineral water), direct-dial satellite telephone, personal safe, ironing board, and electric trouser press. However, there is no switch to turn announcements off in your cabin. There are two suites that provide lots of extra space, and several other cabins have an additional sofa bed.

The bathrooms are of a decent size, and marble-clad; towels and thick, plush bathrobe are 100 percent cotton, as is the bed linen, but note that there is a small step between bedroom and bathroom.

DINING. The Restaurant has ocean-view portholes, and operates with table assignments in a single seating for dinner, and an open-seating arrangement for breakfast and lunch. It is an elegant and pleasant room, with wood paneling, fine furnishings, subtle lighting, and plenty of space around each table. A mix of chairs with and without armrests is provided. There are many tables for two, but also for four, six, and eight. Breakfast is buffet-style, while lunch and dinner are served.

Fresh ingredients are often bought locally when possible – a welcome change from the mass catering of many ships today, and the desserts are worth saving space for.

Breakfasts and lunches can also be taken outdoors at the alfresco café, particularly when the ship is operating in warm-weather areas. Morning coffee and afternoon tea can be taken in the lounge areas or, weather permitting, on the open decks.

ENTERTAINMENT. The Club Lounge is the room for social gatherings and talks. Passengers particularly like the fact that there is no formal entertainment or forced parlor games – just good company and easy conversation.

SPA/FITNESS. The Asian-style spa, at the aft end of Promenade Deck, is a peaceful place. It contains a hairdressing salon, gymnasium, steam room, shower, and relaxation area.

CARIBBEAN PRINCESS
★★★+

THIS IS A MULTI-CHOICE LARGE RESORT SHIP FOR CASUAL FAMILY CRUISING

Size:	Large Resort Ship	Passenger/Crew Ratio (lower beds):	2.6
Tonnage:	112,894	Cabins (total):	1,557
Cruise Line:	Princess Cruises	Size Range (sq ft/m):	163–1,279/15.1–118.8
Former Names:	none	Cabins (for one person):	0
Builder:	Fincantieri (Italy)	Cabins with balcony:	881
Entered Service:	Apr 2004	Cabins (wheelchair accessible):	25
Length (ft/m):	951.4/290.0	Wheelchair accessibility:	Good
Beam (ft/m):	118.1/36.0	Elevators:	14
Propulsion/Propellers:	diesel-electric (42,000kW)/2	Casino (gaming tables):	Yes
Passenger Decks:	15	Swimming Pools:	3
Total Crew:	1,163	Self-Service Launderette:	Yes
Passengers (lower beds):	3,114	Library:	Yes
Passenger Space Ratio (lower beds):	36.2	Onboard currency:	US$

THE SHIP. *Caribbean Princess* has the same basic profile as its half-sisters *Golden Princess*, *Grand Princess*, and *Star Princess*, but carries 500 more passengers due to an extra accommodation deck (Riviera). Despite the ship's greater capacity, the outdoor deck space remains the same, as do the number of elevators – so there's a longer wait during peak usage.

There is a sheltered faux teak (painted steel) promenade deck, which almost wraps around the ship (three times around is one mile). The outdoor pools have various beach-like surroundings. 'Movies Under the Skies' and major sporting events are shown on a 300-sq-ft (28-sq-m) poolside movie screen.

Unlike the outside decks, there is plenty of space inside, with an array of public rooms – including a casino with gaming table and over 260 slot machines – and several intimate areas. Other facilities include a small library and Internet-connect room, and a wood-paneled Wheelhouse Bar that is finely decorated with memorabilia and ship models tracing part of parent company P&O's history. Atop the stern is a ship-wide glass-walled disco pod with great views from the extreme port and starboard side windows. The passenger flow is generally good, and there is little congestion, except waiting for elevators at peak times.

In a 2017 refit, facilities for kids and teens were reimagined and renamed.

Passenger niggles include the user-unfriendly automated telephone system, the small cabin tow-

BERLITZ'S RATINGS		
	Possible	Achieved
Ship	500	356
Accommodation	200	139
Food	400	288
Service	400	288
Entertainment	100	77
Cruise Experience	400	288

OVERALL SCORE 1399 points out of 2000

els, several extra-cost items such as ice cream, plus the charge (in coins) for the washers and dryers in self-service launderettes.

Overall, however, Princess Cruises delivers a consistently fine, comfortable, well-packaged product, always with a good degree of style, at a competitive price.

ACCOMMODATION. There are six principal types of cabins and configurations: (a) grand suite, (b) suite, (c) mini-suite, (d) outside-view double cabins with balcony, (e) outside-view double cabins, and (f) interior double cabins. There is a bewildering choice of price categories, but the cost depends on two things: size and location.

Even the top-grade suites are small in comparison to similar suites aboard some other ships. Cabin attendants have too many cabins to look after (typically 20), which does not translate to much personal service.

Both interior and outside-view cabins are functional, although almost no drawers are provided. They are quite attractive, with warm, pleasing decor and fine soft furnishing fabrics. Interior cabins measure 163 sq ft (15.1 sq m).

Note that wheelchair-accessible cabins have no mirror for dressing, and no full-length hanging space.

All cabins receive turndown service and chocolates on pillows each night, bathrobes (on request), toiletry kits, and a hairdryer. Bathrooms have tiled floors, and a decent amount of open shelf storage space for toiletries, but the plain walls are unappealing.

Most outside-view cabins on Emerald Deck have views obstructed by lifeboats. There are no cabins for solo travelers.

Some cabins can accommodate a third and fourth person in upper berths; however, the lower beds cannot then be pushed together to make a queen-size bed. Some cabins have interconnecting doors (87 cabins in the 2017 refit). Club Class mini-suites (with exclusive dining) were also introduced.

Suite-grade accommodation occupants receive priority embarkation, disembarkation, and shore-tender ticket privileges. The Grand Suite, aft, is the largest and most lavish.

Note that most balcony accommodation can be overlooked both from the navigation bridge wing and from sections of the discotheque.

DINING. The three main dining rooms are Coral, Island, and Palm. Palm has traditional two seating dining; Coral and Island have 'anytime dining' (you have to wait for a table at peak times). Each dining room is split into multi-tier sections in a non-symmetrical design that breaks quite large spaces into smaller sections for better ambience; each has its own galley. Four elevators go to Fiesta Deck, where the Coral and Island restaurants are located, but only two go to Plaza Deck 5, for the Palm Restaurant. A gratuity is automatically added to all beverage bills, including wines.

Although portions are generous, the food and its presentation are disappointing, and rather standardized. Fish is often disguised with sauces or coatings, the choice of fresh green vegetables is limited, few garnishes are used, and cheese is either pre-sliced or diced. But, this is banquet catering for large numbers. Pasta dishes are acceptable (though voluminous), typically served by section headwaiters, who may also make 'something special just for you' – in search of favorable comments and gratuities.

Extra-cost, reservations-necessary Sabatini's and Crown Grill are open for lunch and dinner on sea days.

Sabatini's is a 132-seat Italian eatery with Tuscan villas and gardens scenes; it is named after Trattoria Sabatini, the historic institution in Florence. Crown Grill, which features premium steaks, chops, and grilled seafood, is located off the main indoor Deck 7 promenade. Seating is mainly in semi-private alcoves, and the restaurant has a show kitchen.

World Fresh Marketplace, with indoor-outdoor seating, is open almost 24 hours a day for casual self-serve buffet meals (on oval plastic plates); it has large ocean-view windows on both sides. At night, two aft, extra-cost sections turn into Planks (for family-style BBQ food) and Steamers (for East Coast-style seafood).

Other casual eateries include a poolside burger bar (Salty Dog Grill), Planks (BBQ), Steamers Seafood, and Slice (pizza bar); extra charges apply for items from the coffee bar/patisserie or the caviar/Champagne bar.

International Café, on Deck 5 in The Plaza, is for coffees and specialty coffees, pastries, light lunches, and cakes, some at no extra cost.

There's 24-hour room service – but some menu items are unavailable during early morning.

ENTERTAINMENT. The Princess Theater spans two decks and has comfortable seating on both main and balcony levels. Colorful production shows are the domain of the resident troupe of singers and dancers.

Club Fusion, located aft, features cabaret, lectures, bingo, and horse racing, while Explorers Lounge hosts cabaret acts and dance bands. Other lounges and bars have live music, and Princess Cruises employs gentleman dance hosts.

SPA/FITNESS. The Lotus Spa is forward on Sun Deck. Facilities include a sauna, steam room, and changing rooms; common facilities include a relaxation/waiting zone, body-pampering treatment rooms, and a gymnasium with muscle-pumping equipment and ocean views.

CARNIVAL BREEZE
★★★

AN ULTRA-FUN, VEGAS-STYLE WATER PARK OF A SHIP FOR THE WHOLE FAMILY

Size:	Large Resort Ship	Passenger/Crew Ratio (lower beds):	2.6
Tonnage:	128,251	Cabins (total):	1,845
Cruise Line:	Carnival Cruise Line	Size Range (sq ft/m):	185.0–430.5/17.1–40.0
Former Names:	none	Cabins (for one person):	0
Builder:	Fincantieri (Italy)	Cabins with balcony:	905
Entered Service:	Jun 2012	Cabins (wheelchair accessible):	35
Length (ft/m):	1,004.0/306.0	Wheelchair accessibility:	Good
Beam (ft/m):	158.0/48.0	Elevators:	20
Propulsion/Propellers:	diesel-electric (75.600kW)/2	Casino (gaming tables):	Yes
Passenger Decks:	13	Swimming Pools:	2
Total Crew:	1,386	Self-Service Launderette:	Yes
Passengers (lower beds):	3,690	Library:	Yes
Passenger Space Ratio (lower beds):	34.7	Onboard currency:	US$

THE SHIP. The ship's profile is quite well balanced, with a rakish (but short) front and rounded stern.

A WaterWorks pool deck has lots of water and sports amusements – including a long orange multi-deck 'Twister Water Slide' and a catch-you-off-guard 'Power Drencher.' There's a Seaside Theater screen for poolside movies and a laser light show, but the general open deck space is small considering the number of passengers carried. Meanwhile, Serenity is an adults-only, extra-charge retreat, with two large hot tubs on deck.

There is a full walk-around open promenade deck lined with deck chairs, and four 'scenic whirlpools' are cantilevered over the water for good views.

On a lower deck, The Ocean Plaza, with around 190 seats, is a comfortable place by day and a trendy entertainment venue by night. Its indoor/outdoor café and live music venue has a bandstand and a large circular dance floor.

The Caribbean-themed interior decor is extremely bright. Many of the public rooms, lounges, bars, and nightspots are located on two main public room/ entertainment decks, which are accessed via an 11-deck-high atrium, whose ground level has a cantilevered bandstand atop a large dance floor.

Jackpot is the colorful lively casino with gaming tables and slots. Other rooms include The Song (Jazz Bar), and Ocean Plaza, quiet during the day, and with live entertainment at night. Internet terminals are

BERLITZ'S RATINGS	Possible	Achieved
Ship	500	344
Accommodation	200	129
Food	400	207
Service	400	251
Entertainment	100	68
Cruise Experience	400	242

OVERALL SCORE 1241 points out of 2000

scattered around the ship, but lack privacy. There's a 232-capacity conference room, while The Library has a bar, board games, but few books.

Carnival Breeze is a big floating playground, carrying almost 5,000 passengers when full. It has lots of facilities for young families with children, who will love the outdoor pool deck and its facilities. However, there's no escape from the incredibly loud rap, rock, and vocal music throughout the ship.

ACCOMMODATION. There are numerous cabin price categories, priced by size, grade and location, from interior (no-view) cabins to much larger 'spa' and balcony suites. Whether you go for high end or low end, all include plush mattresses, good-quality duvets, linens, pillows, and tropical decor (even cabin doors have cabana-style slats to get the mood going. The decor is a mix of light browns and nautical blues, but accommodation deck hallways are bright, even at night. Note that cabins on Deck 12 are subject to lots of noise from kids having fun on the deck above – so forget that afternoon nap.

DINING. There are two main dining rooms: Sapphire (midships) and the smaller Blush (aft), each with main and balcony levels (stairways connect them), and two small restaurant annexes, for small groups. Note that the two main dining rooms are not open for lunch on port days.

Don't even think about a quiet table for two, or a candlelit dinner on deck. This is all about table mates, social talk, lively meals, fast eating, and fast service. Tables do have tablecloths, silverware, and iced water/iced tea whenever you want it. Choose either fixed time dining (6pm or 8.15pm) or flexible dining (during opening hours).

Overall, the food is carbohydrate-rich and non-memorable (it's banquet-style 'batch' production cooking, after all), with simple presentation, few garnishes, and many dishes disguised with gravies and sauces. The selection of fresh green vegetables, bread and bakery items (these are thawed and then baked from frozen 'starter' dough), cheeses, and fruits is limited, and there is heavy use of rice, canned fruit, and jellied desserts.

'Spa Carnival Fare' provides a healthier food option. Vegetarian and children's menus are also available, but they wouldn't get a generous score for their nutritional content.

Fahrenheit 555 Steakhouse (and bar) has an extra-cost à la carte menu, good table settings, china and silverware, leather-bound menus, premium-quality steaks and grilled seafood items.

Lido Marketplace – a copy of the name used aboard (sister company) AIDA Cruises ships – is a large, self-serve buffet facility, with indoor/outdoor seating (lower level) and indoor-only seating (upper level). Designated areas feature different types of ethnic cuisine. The venue includes a Mongolian Wok on the upper level, open for tablecloth-free buffet dinners (no candles). Cucina del Capitano is an Italian extra-charge eatery, also on the upper level, with pasta served at lunch and 'authentic' Italian specialties at night.

On pool deck there's Guy's Burger Joint (for burgers and fries) and BlueIguana Cantina (for Tex-Mex fast-food items including burritos, tacos, and enchiladas). Other eateries include Fat Jimmy's C-Side BBQ (for grilled items such as kielbasa/Polish sausage, grilled chicken breast, and pulled pork sandwiches), and Bonsai Sushi (Carnival's first full-service sushi restaurant), with decor by graffiti artist Erni Vales, and sushi, sashimi, and bento boxes by Carnival.

Kids also get their own restaurant towards the top of the atrium.

ENTERTAINMENT. The 1,964-seat Ovation Show-lounge, located forward, spans three decks, with seating in a horseshoe shape around a large proscenium arch stage. Sight lines are generally good, except from some of the seats at the back of the room. Large-scale production shows, with lots of skimpy costumes and feathers, are typical, together with snappy cabaret acts, all accompanied by a live showband.

The Limelight, aft seats 425, and has a stage, dance floor, and large bar. For late-night raunchy adult comedy, it becomes the Punchline Comedy Club.

For an active movie experience, check out the Thrill 5D Theater, where the seats really move you.

SPA/FITNESS. The expansive 23,750-sq-ft (2,206-sq-m) Cloud 9 Spa is positioned over three decks in the front section of the ship. The uppermost deck includes indoor/outdoor private spa relaxation areas, at extra cost. A spiral staircase connects the two decks.

The spa offers a wide range of treatments, and there are 10 rooms for this. An extra-charge Thermal Suite features the sensory-enhanced soothing heated chambers: Laconium, Tepidarium, Aroma, and Oriental steam baths.

CARNIVAL CONQUEST
★★★

THIS IS A VIVID, FUN-FILLED SHIP FOR ULTRA-CASUAL FAMILY CRUISING

Size:	Large Resort Ship	Passenger/Crew Ratio (lower beds):	2.5
Tonnage:	110,239	Cabins (total):	1,487
Cruise Line:	Carnival Cruise Line	Size Range (sq ft/m):	179.7–482.2/16.7–44.8
Former Names:	none	Cabins (for one person):	0
Builder:	Fincantieri (Italy)	Cabins with balcony:	574
Entered Service:	Dec 2002	Cabins (wheelchair accessible):	25
Length (ft/m):	951.4/290.0	Wheelchair accessibility:	Good
Beam (ft/m):	116.4/35.5	Elevators:	18
Propulsion/Propellers:	diesel-electric (63,400kW)/2	Casino (gaming tables):	Yes
Passenger Decks:	13	Swimming Pools:	2 (1 w/ sliding glass dome)
Total Crew:	1,160	Self-Service Launderette:	Yes
Passengers (lower beds):	2,974	Library:	Yes
Passenger Space Ratio (lower beds):	37.0	Onboard currency:	US$

THE SHIP. *Carnival Conquest* has the same well-balanced profile as close sisters *Carnival Sunshine*, *Carnival Freedom*, *Carnival Glory*, *Carnival Liberty*, *Carnival Triumph*, and *Carnival Victory*.

Amidships on the open deck is a long water slide (200ft/60m long), tiered sunbathing decks positioned between two swimming pools, hot tubs, and a poolside movie screen (Seaside Theater). There are three decks full of lounges, bars, and lots of rooms to enjoy, plus two atriums: the largest, the forward, glass-domed Artists Atrium spans nine decks, while an aft atrium rises through three decks.

The ship's interior decor is all about Impressionist painters such as Degas, Toulouse Lautrec, Gauguin, Cézanne, and others. Murano glass flowers on antiqued brass stems are displayed in several public areas.

Tahiti Casino has numerous gaming tables and over 320 slot machines. There are several nightspots for different musical tastes (except for classical music lovers), such as the Degas Lounge, Vincent's Piano Bar, Henri's Dance Club, and Gauguin's Bar.

Overall, it is a floating playground for the young and young-at-heart, and anyone who enjoys constant stimulation and participation events, together with the three 'Gs' – glitz, glamour, and gambling. This is 'fun' cruising Vegas style – and an all-American fun experience. There may be lines for things such as shore excursions and security control when re-boarding.

BERLITZ'S RATINGS

	Possible	Achieved
Ship	500	338
Accommodation	200	125
Food	400	205
Service	400	247
Entertainment	100	68
Cruise Experience	400	237

OVERALL SCORE 1220 points out of 2000

While the cuisine is just so-so, the real fun begins at sundown when Carnival really excels in sound, lights, and razzle-dazzle shows (think skin and feathers).

Niggles include: a large number of dining room pillars, and utilitarian public toilets. It is impossible to escape from noise and loud music (it's even played in cabin hallways and lifts). You have to carry a credit card to operate the personal safes, which is inconvenient.

The ship underwent an extensive refurbishment program in 2012. This included the installation of a Guy's Burger Joint (in partnership with Guy Fieri of Food Network); a poolside RedFrog Rum Bar (including ThirstyFrog Red – Carnival's private-label draft brew) and BlueIguana Tequila Bar, and a Sports Bar (an interactive venue with video games and a 24/7 sports ticker). Meanwhile, Cherry on Top is a shop full of bins of candy, and novelty gift items.

ACCOMMODATION. There are numerous cabin-price categories, in seven different grades: suites with private balcony; deluxe outside-view cabins with private balcony; outside-view cabins with private balcony; outside-view cabins with window; cabins with a porthole instead of a window; interior cabins; and interior cabins with upper and lower berths.

Five decks of cabins have private balconies – over 150 more than *Carnival Triumph* or *Carnival Victory*, for example. But many are not so private, and can be overlooked.

There are 18 spa cabins, located directly around and behind Spa Carnival, so you can get out of bed and go straight to the treadmill without having to go through any public room.

Most cabins are of good size and have all the basics, although the furniture is rather angular with sharp corners. Three decks of cabins (eight on each deck, each with private balcony) overlook the stern. Most cabins have twin beds, which are convertible to a queen-size bed.

DINING. There are two main dining rooms: the 744-seat Renoir Restaurant, and the larger 1,044-seat Monet Restaurant, both two decks high, and both with a balcony level (larger in the Monet Restaurant). In the Renoir Restaurant, two additional wings (called Cassatt and Pissarro) can accommodate large groups in a private setting.

Don't even think about a quiet table for two, or a candlelit dinner on deck. Dining aboard a Carnival ship is all about table mates, social talk, lively meals, fast eating, and fast service. Tables do have tablecloths, silverware, and iced water/iced tea whenever you want it. Choose either fixed time dining (6pm or 8.15pm) or flexible dining (during opening hours). The main dining rooms are closed for lunch on port days, so you will need to go to the serve-yourself buffet – or order room service.

Overall, the food is quite starchy (it's banquet-style, mass-produced cooking, after all), with simple presentation, few garnishes, and many dishes disguised with gravies and sauces. The selection of fresh green vegetables, bread and bakery items (these are thawed and then baked from frozen 'starter' dough), cheeses, and fruits is limited, and there is heavy use of rice, canned fruit and jellied desserts.

'Spa Carnival Fare' provides a healthier food option. Vegetarian and children's menus are also available, but they wouldn't get a generous score for their nutritional content.

Waiters sing and dance, so think 'foodertainment' rather than food quality. Also, there are no wine waiters, and the wine glasses are small. For something really simple, an 'always available' list of 'Carnival Classics,' includes mahi-mahi (fish), baby back ribs (beef), and grilled chicken.

The Steakhouse is a reservations-only, extra-cost dining spot for steaks and seafood items. Wall murals are in the style of post-Impressionist painter Georges Seurat's Le Cirque (The Circus).

Cézanne Restaurant is a casual self-serve food court-style lido deck eatery, with a capacity for over 1,200, and decor in the style of a 19th-century French café.

Other (complimentary) eateries include: Guy's Burger Joint, a poolside venue for hand-made burgers and fresh-cut fries; BlueIguana Cantina Mexican eatery (for snack food such as tacos and burritos). Poolside watering holes include a BlueIguana Tequila Bar (for Mexican-themed frozen cocktails and Tequila), and a RedFrog Rum Bar.

ENTERTAINMENT. The Toulouse-Lautrec Showlounge is a multi-deck showroom seating 1,400, with a revolving stage, hydraulic orchestra pit, and seating on three levels (the upper levels being tiered through two decks).

SPA/FITNESS. SpaCarnival is a fairly large health, fitness, and spa complex, and accessed from the forward stairway. Facilities include a gymnasium (packed with muscle machines and exercise equipment), treatment area, sauna and steam rooms for men and women, and a beauty salon.

CARNIVAL DREAM
★★★

FUN FOR A FIRST CRUISE, WITH A SPLASH-TASTIC WATER-SLIDE

Size:	Large Resort Ship	Passenger/Crew Ratio (lower beds):	2.6
Tonnage:	128,251	Cabins (total):	1,823
Cruise Line:	Carnival Cruise Line	Size Range (sq ft/m):	185.0–430.5/17.1–40.0
Former Names:	none	Cabins (for one person):	0
Builder:	Fincantieri (Italy)	Cabins with balcony:	887
Entered Service:	Sep 2009	Cabins (wheelchair accessible):	35
Length (ft/m):	1,004.0/306.0	Wheelchair accessibility:	Good
Beam (ft/m):	158.0/48.0	Elevators:	20
Propulsion/Propellers:	diesel-electric (75,600kW)/2	Casino (gaming tables):	Yes
Passenger Decks:	13	Swimming Pools:	2
Total Crew:	1,367	Self-Service Launderette:	Yes
Passengers (lower beds):	3,646	Library:	Yes
Passenger Space Ratio (lower beds):	35.1	Onboard currency:	US$

THE SHIP. *Carnival Dream's* bows are short, but the ship's profile is balanced, with a rakish front and rounded stern. *On deck* attractions include Carnival WaterWorks aqua park, with a long orange multi-deck 'Twister Water Slide' and popular 'Power Drencher' – a big hit with kids. There's also a main pool and large Seaside Theater movie screen. The general open deck space is really poor for the number of passengers carried, so sunbed loungers are packed like sardines.

Meanwhile, Serenity is an adults-only, extra-charge retreat.

Lower down is a full walk-around open promenade deck; it's lined with deck chairs, and it's difficult to navigate through them. Four 'scenic whirlpools,' cantilevered over the water, have sea views. Higher up, Lido Deck 10 offers an open-deck area.

The interior decor is bright (take sunglasses). Most public rooms, lounges, and bars are on Dream Street or Upper Dream Street. The Dream Lobby is the connection point for people and ship functions. Take one of the glass-walled elevators for a neat view. There are three main elevator towers: forward, amidships, and aft.

Many lounges, bars, and nightspots – including a dance club with a twist, offering indoor/outdoor access – are accessible via an 11-deck-high atrium, the ground level of which has a neatly cantilevered bandstand atop a large dance floor. The Page Turner (great name) is the library, although there aren't

BERLITZ'S RATINGS

	Possible	Achieved
Ship	500	347
Accommodation	200	129
Food	400	201
Service	400	251
Entertainment	100	68
Cruise Experience	400	239

OVERALL SCORE 1235 points out of 2000

many books. Jackpot is a colorful casino, with gaming tables and slot machines. Other rooms include The Song (Jazz Bar), and Ocean Plaza, a quiet area during the day, and lively at night. Three dozen Internet terminals are scattered around the ship, but most have no privacy. There's also a 232-capacity conference room, The Chambers.

The indoor/outdoor Ocean Plaza, with around 190 seats, is a comfortable spot for people-watching by day; it's a trendy entertainment venue by night, with dance floor and bandstand.

The ship's layout is disjointed, and prior to second seating there is much congestion on Upper and Lower Dream streets. Passenger niggles highlight the barely warm food in the two main dining rooms, and long lines for self-serve food items in the food court.

Gratuities are automatically charged to your onboard account.

ACCOMMODATION. There are several cabin price categories, and six cabin types. The price depends on the accommodation grade and location you choose. Whether you go for high end or low end, all accommodation includes Carnival's Comfort Bed with plush mattresses, good-quality duvets, linens, and pillows. Straight accommodation deck hallways create the cell-block look, and they are bright, very bright, even at night. There are also lot of interior (no-view) cabins. The cabins to go for are those at the stern: they are quieter and offer great aft ocean views on decks 6, 7, 8, and 9.

Some cabins can accommodate five persons – useful for families. There is a wide selection of balcony cabins and suites, including 'Cove Balcony' cabins that are the closest to the waterline.

Adjacent to the Serenity Spa are 65 'Cloud 9' spa cabins. They include a number of amenities and privileges (all 20 are situated aft of the lower level, with direct access to it).

DINING. There are two main restaurants: the 1,180-seat Crimson (midships) and the smaller 828-seat Scarlet (aft). Each has two levels: main and balcony (stairways connect both levels), with the galley on the lower level. Forward of Crimson are two small annexes, used as private dining venues by small groups. Choose either fixed-time dining (typically 6pm or 8.15pm) or flexible dining (during opening hours). Note that the two main dining rooms are closed for lunch on port days, so you are forced to go to the self-serve buffet. Note also that bakery items are thawed and heated from frozen.

The Gathering is the ship's Lido Deck self-serve buffet facility, with indoor/outdoor seating areas on the lower (main) level, and indoor-only seating on the upper level. The venue includes a Mongolian Wok and Pasta Bar on the upper level. Go off-peak and it's better.

No-cost outdoor eateries include Guy's Pig & Anchor Barbeque Smokehouse (for pork, chicken, and beef); Pizzeria del Capitano (with five types of pizza); BlueIguana (for Mexican-style tacos and burritos).

The Chef's Art Supper Club (and bar) seats 139 and has great views from its aft location high on Spa Deck 12, and an à la carte menu. It has decent table settings, for premium-quality steaks and seafood items. On Promenade Deck you'll find Bonsai Sushi, a tribute-to-sushi venue.

ENTERTAINMENT. The 1,964-seat Encore Showlounge spans three decks at the front of the ship, with seating set in a horseshoe shape around the stage; the sight lines are generally good, except from some of the seats at the back of the lowest level. Large-scale production shows, with lots of feathers and skimpy costumes, are staged, accompanied by a live showband.

The 425-seat Burgundy Lounge, located aft, has a stage, dance floor, and large bar, and is the venue for smutty, no-holds-barred late-night 'adult comedy.' Caliente, a nightclub, provides ultra-loud Latin dance music.

SPA/FITNESS. The expansive 23,750-sq-ft (2,206-sq-m) Cloud 9 Spa is set over three decks in the front of the ship. The uppermost deck includes indoor/outdoor private spa relaxation areas, at extra cost. A spiral staircase connects the two decks.

There are several private rooms for body treatments, including a VIP room, a large massage room for couples, a Rasul mud treatment room, and dry flotation rooms. An extra-charge 'Thermal Suite' has sensory-enhanced soothing herb-scented heated chambers, and Oriental steam baths.

CARNIVAL ECSTASY
★★★

THIS IS A FLOATING FUN PALACE FOR ULTRA-CASUAL FIRST-TIME CRUISERS

Size:	Mid-size Ship	Passenger/Crew Ratio (lower beds):	2.2
Tonnage:	70,526	Cabins (total):	1,026
Cruise Line:	Carnival Cruise Line	Size Range (sq ft/m):	173.2–409.7/16.0–38.0
Former Names:	Ecstasy	Cabins (for one person):	0
Builder:	Kvaerner Masa-Yards (Finland)	Cabins with balcony:	52
Entered Service:	Jun 1991	Cabins (wheelchair accessible):	22
Length (ft/m):	855.8/263.6	Wheelchair accessibility:	Fair
Beam (ft/m):	103.0/31.4	Elevators:	14
Propulsion/Propellers:	diesel-electric (42,240kW)/2	Casino (gaming tables):	Yes
Passenger Decks:	10	Swimming Pools:	3
Total Crew:	920	Self-Service Launderette:	Yes
Passengers (lower beds):	2,056	Library:	Yes
Passenger Space Ratio (lower beds):	34.4	Onboard currency:	US$

THE SHIP. *Carnival Ecstasy* (second in a series of eight almost identical ships in Carnival's *Fantasy*-class) is well over 20 years old and looks tired. Although externally angular, and with inadequate open deck space, this is nonetheless a popular ship – aimed at first-time cruisers. The aft decks tend to be less noisy, since most activities are focused around the main swimming pool. There is no walk-around open promenade deck, although there is a short jogging track. The lifeboats (six double as shore tenders), are positioned high in the ship.

The interior spaces are well utilized, and the general passenger flow is good. The interior design – the work of Miami-based architect Joe Farcus – is clever, functional, and extremely colorful (he calls it 'entertainment architecture'). The design theme is mythical muses and music. You'll find a rather nice Rolls-Royce car (and coffee shop) located on the indoor promenade.

The interior focal point is an 'open' atrium lobby, with a balconied shape recalling some of the world's great opera houses; it spans six decks, and is topped by a large glass dome. The lowest level is where you'll find the purser's desk and shore excursion desk, an Atrium Bar (with live music), and a small sushi bar.

There are public entertainment lounges, bars, and clubs galore, with something for everyone (except quiet space). The public rooms, connected by a double-width City Highlights Boulevard, combine

BERLITZ'S RATINGS		
	Possible	Achieved
Ship	500	299
Accommodation	200	121
Food	400	200
Service	400	247
Entertainment	100	62
Cruise Experience	400	232

OVERALL SCORE 1161 points out of 2000

a colorful mix of classic and garish design elements. Most public rooms and attractions lead off from this boulevard – a sort of shipboard Main Street running between the showlounge (forward) and the Starlight Aft Lounge/nightclub. Gamers and slot players alike will enjoy the action in the Crystal Palace Casino. There is also a fine-looking library and reading room, but few books, and a 1,200-sq-ft (111-sq-m) conference room. From venues such as the Stripes Dance Club/Disco to the Society Cigar Bar, the ship's interior decor will entertain you.

Carnival Ecstasy is for anyone who enjoys constant stimulation and lots of participation events. Because it's a large resort ship, there will be lines for shore excursions, security control when re-boarding, and disembarkation, plus sign-up sheets for fitness equipment. Loud vocal 'music' is everywhere. Shore excursions are booked via the 'Fun Vision' infotainment system, so obtaining advice and suggestions is not easy, the food is basic, and the 'works' in the Art Gallery are tacky.

ACCOMMODATION. There are several types of accommodation and prices, according to facilities, size, and location. Standard outside-view and interior cabins have plain and unmemorable decor, but they do have good storage space, and practical, well-designed bathrooms. However, if you have a queen-bed configuration instead of the standard twin-bed layout, note that one person has to clamber over the bed, which can be a rather ungainly exercise.

Anyone booking an outside suite gets more space, and some rather eclectic decor and furniture.

Room service is available 24 hours a day, although in most cabins, only cold food is available; occupants of suite-grade accommodation have more (both hot and cold) to choose from.

DINING. The two large main dining rooms, Wind Star and Wind Song, are located amidships and aft. They have ocean-view windows and are noisy, but the decor is attractive, although extremely bright. Choose either fixed-time dining (6pm or 8.15pm) or flexible dining (during opening hours).

The food is so-so, presentation is simple, and few garnishes are used. The selection of fresh green vegetables, bread (note that bakery items are thawed and heated from frozen 'starter' dough), cheeses, and fruits is limited, and there is heavy reliance on rice, canned fruit and jellied desserts. There are no wine waiters. The waiters sing and dance, and there are constant parades – so it's more about 'eatertainment' than food quality. Remember, however, that this is standard banquet catering. If you want something simple, there's 'always available' 'Carnival Classics' such as mahi-mahi, baby back ribs, and grilled chicken. Note that both dining rooms are closed for lunch on port days.

The Panorama Bar & Grill features casual self-serve buffet fare, and includes a deli counter and pizzeria. At night, it morphs into the Seaview Bistro, an alternative to the main dining rooms, for pasta, steaks, salads, and desserts. A patisserie offers extra-cost specialty coffees and sweets. A sushi bar is also in the atrium lobby (not authentic sushi, however).

Other (complimentary) eateries include: Guy's Burger Joint, a poolside venue developed with Food Network personality Guy Fieri (for handmade burgers and fresh-cut fries) and BlueIguana Cantina Mexican eatery (for Mexican snack food such as tacos and burritos). Poolside watering holes include a BlueIguana Tequila Bar, and a RedFrog Rum Bar.

There is no specialty (extra-charge) restaurant, as aboard some of the larger ships in the fleet.

ENTERTAINMENT. The 1,010-seat Blue Sapphire Showlounge is the venue for large-scale production shows and major cabaret acts – although 20 pillars obstruct some views. During a typical cruise, there will be several high-energy production shows, with a cast of vocalists and a clutch of dancers, backed by a large live band.

SPA/FITNESS. SpaCarnival is a large, glass-wrapped health, fitness, and spa complex located on the uppermost interior deck, forward of the ship's mast, and is typically open from 6am to 8pm daily. It consists of a gymnasium with ocean-view windows that look out over the bow and the latest in muscle-pumping electronic machines, an aerobics exercise room, men's and women's changing rooms, sauna and steam rooms, beauty salon, and rooms for body treatments. Some fitness classes incur an extra charge. Unfortunately, there are not enough members of staff to keep the area clean and tidy.

Sporty types can also play basketball, volleyball, or table tennis, go jogging, or play mini-golf.

CARNIVAL ELATION
★★★

THIS FLOATING FUN PALACE IS GOOD FOR ULTRA-CASUAL FAMILY CRUISING

Size:	Mid-size Ship
Tonnage:	70,390
Cruise Line:	Carnival Cruise Line
Former Names:	*Elation*
Builder:	Kvaerner Masa-Yards (Finland)
Entered Service:	Mar 1998
Length (ft/m):	855.8/263.6
Beam (ft/m):	103.0/31.4
Propulsion/Propellers:	diesel-electric (42,842kW)/2 azimuthing pods
Passenger Decks:	10
Total Crew:	920
Passengers (lower beds):	2,056
Passenger Space Ratio (lower beds):	34.4
Passenger/Crew Ratio (lower beds):	2.2
Cabins (total):	1,026
Size Range (sq ft/m):	173.2–409.7/16.0–38.0
Cabins (for one person):	0
Cabins with balcony:	152
Cabins (wheelchair accessible):	22
Wheelchair accessibility:	Fair
Elevators:	14
Casino (gaming tables):	Yes
Swimming Pools:	3
Self-Service Launderette:	Yes
Library:	Yes
Onboard currency:	US$

THE SHIP. *Carnival Elation* is an externally angular, but, nonetheless, popular ship for anyone taking their first cruise.

It is one of only two in the series of eight *Fantasy*-class ships (the other is *Carnival Paradise*) with a 'pod' propulsion system, which gives a vibration-free ride, rather than the traditional propeller shaft and rudder system.

The open deck space, however, is really crowded when everyone wants to be out on deck. The aft decks tend to be less noisy whereas all the activities are focused around the main swimming pool and hot tubs (one with a thatched shade). There's also Serenity – an adult-only 'quiet' lounging space on Deck 9 aft. There is no walk-around open promenade deck, although there is a short jogging track atop ship. The lifeboats, six of which double as shore tenders, are positioned high up.

The interior spaces are well utilized. The general passenger flow is busy but good; the interior design – the work of Miami-based architect Joe Farcus – is functional, and extremely colorful. The theme is mythical muses, and composers and their compositions.

The interior focal point is an 'open' atrium lobby, which spans six decks, and is topped by a glass dome. The lowest level houses the purser's desk and shore excursion desk, a popular Atrium Bar (with live music), and a small sushi bar off to one side; it's a good central meeting place.

BERLITZ'S RATINGS		
	Possible	Achieved
Ship	500	299
Accommodation	200	121
Food	400	200
Service	400	250
Entertainment	100	62
Cruise Experience	400	233

OVERALL SCORE 1165 points out of 2000

There are multiple public entertainment lounges, bars, and clubs, connected by the double-width Elation's Way and Promenade, a sort of Main Street between the showlounge (forward) and the Cole Porter lounge/nightclub aft (to be converted into more cabins in a late 2017 refit). There is also a fine-looking library and reading room, but few books, and a 1,200-sq-ft (111-sq-m) conference room.

Carnival Elation offers cruising Splash Vegas style – an all-American experience. The real fun begins at sundown when the ship comes alive. On the down side, expect lines for shore excursions, security control when re-boarding, and disembarkation. There is screaming rap and rock music everywhere, far too many loud, annoying announcements, and a great deal of hustling for drinks.

ACCOMMODATION. There are several accommodation grades, priced according to size, and location. Cabins have simple, plain decor, are marginally comfortable, yet practical, with decent storage space and practical, no-nonsense bathrooms. However, with a queen-bed configuration instead of twin beds, one person has to clamber over the bed – an ungainly exercise.

Outside-view suites have more space. These are mildly attractive, but they are smaller than those aboard ships of a similar size of competing companies. Room service items are available

24/7, although in standard-grade cabins, only cold food is available; occupants of suite-grade accommodation have more items (both hot and cold) to choose from.

DINING. There are two main dining rooms, Imagination and Inspiration (assigned according to your cabin), amidships and aft. They have ocean-view windows and are noisy, but the decor is bright and colorful. Choose either fixed-time dining (6pm or 8.15pm) or flexible dining (during opening hours).

The food is so-so. Presentation is simple, and few garnishes are used. Note that bakery items are thawed and heated from frozen. There are no wine waiters, and the wine glasses are small. Waiters sing and dance, and there are parades – so it's really more 'foodertainment' than food quality. If you want something really simple, there's an 'always available' (when the dining rooms are open) list of 'Carnival Classics.' Note that the two main dining rooms are not open for lunch on port days.

Tiffany's Lido Restaurant features casual self-serve buffet food. A 2017 refit added a Guy's Burger Joint, and a BlueIguana Cantina (for Mexican eats).

ENTERTAINMENT. The Mikado Showlounge is the venue for colourful skin and feather production shows and cabaret acts – although 20 pillars obstruct some views.

SPA/FITNESS. SpaCarnival is a glass-wrapped health, fitness, and spa complex on the uppermost interior deck forward; it is typically open from 6am to 8pm daily. It consists of a gymnasium with ocean-view windows and muscle-pumping machines, an aerobics exercise room, men's and women's changing rooms, sauna and steam rooms, beauty salon, and body treatment rooms. Some fitness classes incur an extra charge.

Sporting types can play basketball or volleyball, or table tennis. There is also a banked jogging track on the deck above the spa, and a mini-golf course.

CARNIVAL FANTASY
★★★

THIS IS ULTRA-CASUAL CRUISING AND ENTERTAINMENT FOR THE WHOLE FAMILY

Size:	Mid-size Ship	Passenger/Crew Ratio (lower beds):	2.2
Tonnage:	70,367	Cabins (total):	1,026
Cruise Line:	Carnival Cruise Line	Size Range (sq ft/m):	173.2–409.7/16.0–38.0
Former Names:	*Fantasy*	Cabins (for one person):	0
Builder:	Kvaerner Masa-Yards (Finland)	Cabins with balcony:	152
Entered Service:	Mar 1990	Cabins (wheelchair accessible):	22
Length (ft/m):	855.8/263.6	Wheelchair accessibility:	Fair
Beam (ft/m):	103.0/31.4	Elevators:	14
Propulsion/Propellers:	diesel-electric (42,240kW)/2	Casino (gaming tables):	Yes
Passenger Decks:	10	Swimming Pools:	3
Total Crew:	920	Self-Service Launderette:	Yes
Passengers (lower beds):	2,056	Library:	Yes
Passenger Space Ratio (lower beds):	34.4	Onboard currency:	US$

THE SHIP. *Carnival Fantasy* is the first (in a series of eight almost identical ships) in the *Fantasy*-class. It has always been a popular ship – good for a first cruise. The ship, which is now over 25 years old and the oldest in the fleet, sports the company's trademark red, white, and blue wing-tipped funnel. The open deck space is inadequate when the ship is full. A Carnival WaterWorks – complete with long (about 300ft/90m) and short water slides with water-burst fountains – a good, active area for children. There's also a Serenity adult-only 'quiet' lounging space outdoors on Deck 9 aft.

There is no walk-around open promenade deck, but there is a short jogging track atop ship. The lifeboats (six double as shore tenders) are positioned high up.

The interior spaces are well utilized. The general passenger flow is good, and the interior design – the work of Miami-based architect Joe Farcus – is clever and extremely colorful; it's inspired by the ancient city of Pompeii.

The interior focal point is a balcony-shaped 'open' atrium lobby. It spans six decks, and is topped by a glass-domed roof. The lowest level houses the purser's desk and shore-excursion desk, a popular Atrium Bar (with live music), and, off to one side, a small sushi bar that is a good meeting place.

The public rooms, connected by double-width Via Marina Promenade – a sort of shipboard Main Street. Gamers and slot players can enjoy the action in the

BERLITZ'S RATINGS		
	Possible	Achieved
Ship	500	299
Accommodation	200	121
Food	400	200
Service	400	246
Entertainment	100	62
Cruise Experience	400	230

OVERALL SCORE 1158 points out of 2000

Club 21 Casino. There is also a nice-looking library and reading room, but few books.

Carnival Fantasy is a floating playground for the young and young-at-heart, and for anyone who enjoys constant stimulation and participation events. Because it's a large resort ship, lines form for security control when re-boarding, at the Purser's Desk, for shore excursions, and for disembarkation.

While the cuisine is just so-so, the vibe gets going at sundown when Carnival really excels in volume, lights, and shows. From venues such as the Electricity Dance Club/Disco to the Majestic Cigar Bar, the ship's bars and lounges will certainly entertain you.

However, there are many annoying revenue announcements, and never-ending hustling to get you to buy ice-filled drinks. Also, there's no escape from the incredibly high-volume music.

ACCOMMODATION. There are several accommodation price grades; you pay for size, and location. Standard outside-view and interior (no-view) cabins have decor that is rather plain and unmemorable. They are adequate and spacious enough and (most have the same size and appointments), with good storage space and practical, no-nonsense bathrooms. However, with a queen-bed configuration instead of a standard twin-bed layout, note that one person has to clamber over the bed to get to the far side.

Anyone booking a suite gets more space, and more eclectic decor and furniture.

Some 50 cabins feature inter-connecting doors, which is good for families with children – so they can be close, but not too close.

Room service items are available 24/7, but in standard-grade cabins only cold food is available, while occupants of suite-grade accommodation have a greater range (both hot and cold) from which to choose.

DINING. The two large main dining rooms, Celebration and Jubilee, are located amidships and aft. Both have ocean-view windows and very bright decor, but they are noisy. Choose either fixed-time dining (6pm or 8.15pm) or flexible dining (during opening hours).

Overall, the food is quite starchy, with simple presentation, few garnishes, and many dishes disguised with gravies and sauces. The selection of fresh green vegetables, breads, cheeses, and fruits is limited (bread is thawed and then baked from frozen 'starter' dough), and there is much use of canned fruit and jellied desserts. The waiters sing and dance, so think 'foodertainment' rather than food quality. For something really simple, an 'always available' list of 'Carnival Classics' includes mahi-mahi (fish), baby back ribs (beef), and grilled chicken. Note that the two main dining rooms are not open for lunch on port days.

The Paris Lido Restaurant features the usual casual self-serve buffet eats. At night, the place morphs into the Seaview Bistro, and is a casual alternative for pasta, steaks, salads, and desserts. Other casual eateries include Guy's Burger Joint (named after TV's Guy Fieri), Blue Iguana (Mexican cantina-style), and Bonsai Sushi. There is no specialty (extra-charge) restaurant, as aboard some ships in the Carnival fleet.

ENTERTAINMENT. The Universe Showlounge is the venue for colourful production shows and major cabaret acts, although 20 pillars obstruct some views. During a typical cruise, there will be several high-energy production shows, with vocalists and a clutch of dancers, backed by a large live band.

SPA/FITNESS. SpaCarnival is a glass-wrapped fitness and spa complex located on the uppermost interior deck. Its gymnasium has ocean views, high-tech muscle-pumping machines, an aerobics room, men's and women's changing rooms, sauna and steam rooms, beauty salon, and rooms for body treatments. Some fitness classes may incur an extra charge.

Sporting types can play basketball, volleyball, table tennis, or mini-golf, or go jogging.

CARNIVAL FASCINATION
★★★

THIS IS A VIBRANT, FLOATING MOVIE SET FOR CASUAL FAMILY CRUISING

Size:	Mid-size Ship
Tonnage:	70,538
Cruise Line:	Carnival Cruise Line
Former Names:	Fascination
Builder:	Kvaerner Masa-Yards (Finland)
Entered Service:	Jul 1994
Length (ft/m):	855.8/263.6
Beam (ft/m):	103.0/31.4
Propulsion/Propellers:	diesel-electric (42,240 kW)/2
Passenger Decks:	10
Total Crew:	920
Passengers (lower beds):	2,056
Passenger Space Ratio (lower beds):	34.4
Passenger/Crew Ratio (lower beds):	2.2
Cabins (total):	1,026
Size Range (sq ft/m):	173.2-409.7/16.0-38.0
Cabins (for one person):	0
Cabins with balcony:	250
Cabins (wheelchair accessible):	22
Wheelchair accessibility:	Fair
Elevators:	14
Casino (gaming tables):	Yes
Swimming Pools:	3
Self-Service Launderette:	Yes
Library:	Yes
Onboard currency:	US$

THE SHIP. Carnival Fascination is the fourth in a series of eight almost identical Fantasy-class ships.

Open deck space is really tight when the ship is full, because it's crammed with Carnival Waterworks, including a long 'Twister' slide that is great for kids. The aft decks, however, tend to be less noisy, because most activities are focused around the main swimming pool and hot tubs (one with a thatched shade). There's also Serenity – an extra-cost adult-only 'quiet' lounging space on Deck 9 aft. While there isn't a walk-around open promenade deck, there is a short jogging track atop ship. The lifeboats, six of which double as shore tenders, are positioned high in the ship.

The interior design – the work of architect Joe Farcus – is clever, functional, and extremely colorful, and includes plenty of neon and glitz. He calls it 'entertainment architecture' and treats every part of a ship as a piece of a giant jigsaw puzzle. The design theme is Hollywood and the movies.

The 'open' atrium lobby has a balconied shape, spans six decks, and is topped by a large domed roof. On the lowest level you'll find the purser's desk, shore excursion desk, a popular Atrium Bar (with live music), and a small sushi bar off to one side; it's a good central meeting place.

There are public entertainment lounges, bars, and clubs galore, with something for everyone (except quiet space). The public rooms, connected by a double-width Via Marina Promenade, combine a colorful mix

BERLITZ'S RATINGS

	Possible	Achieved
Ship	500	299
Accommodation	200	121
Food	400	200
Service	400	250
Entertainment	100	62
Cruise Experience	400	232

OVERALL SCORE 1164 points out of 2000

of classic and contemporary design elements. Most public rooms and attractions lead off from this boulevard, which runs between the showlounge (forward) and the Puttin' on the Ritz aft lounge.

Gamers and slot players alike can grab a piece of the almost non-stop action in the Club 21 Casino. There is also a nice-looking library and reading room, but few books, and there's also a 1,200-sq-ft (111-sq-m) conference room. As for the 'art' in the Art Gallery it's rather tacky, to say the least!

There are great photo opportunities with some 24 life-like beloved movie characters dotted along the Via Marina Boulevard, so you can have your photo taken with stars such as Marilyn Monroe, James Dean, and Lucille Ball (outside the casino). Clark Gable is in the Tara Library, while Humphrey Bogart and Ingrid Bergman are seated at the piano in Bogart's Café; Lena Horne and Sidney Poitier are outside the Beverly Hills Bar, while Katharine Hepburn and Spencer Tracy are inside it.

A Carnival cruise is all about having fun, which begins at sundown with sound, lights, and shows. From venues such as the Diamonds are Forever Dance Club/Disco to the Beverly Hills Cigar Bar, the ship will certainly entertain you.

On the down side, there are many annoying announcements, and a never-ending hustle to get you to buy ice-filled drinks. Also, be warned – super-loud rap and rock music is everywhere.

ACCOMMODATION. There are several grades of accommodation, priced by size, and location. Standard outside-view and interior (no-view) cabins have plain, non-memorable decor. They are fairly comfortable, however, and spacious enough (most are of the same size and appointments), with good storage space and practical bathrooms. However, in a queen-bed instead of a twin-bed configuration, note that one person has to clamber over the bed to get to the far side.

Outside suite occupants receive more space, and some eclectic decor and furniture. These are mildly attractive, but so-so, and they are much smaller than those aboard ships of a similar size of competing companies.

Room service items are available 24/7, but in standard cabins only cold food is available; suite-grade occupants get a greater range of items (both hot and cold) from which to choose.

DINING. The two large main dining rooms, Sensation and Imagination, are located midships and aft. Both have ocean-view windows and attractive, bright decor, but they are noisy. Choose either fixed-time dining (6pm or 8.15pm) or flexible dining (during opening hours).

The food is uninspiring and carbohydrate-heavy (it's banquet-style production catering, after all). The selection of fresh green vegetables, breads, cheeses, and fruits is limited, and there is much use of canned fruit and jellied desserts (bread, rolls and other bakery items are thawed and then baked from frozen 'starter' dough). There are no wine waiters, and the wine glasses are very small.

The waiters sing and dance – so 'service' equates to 'foodertainment.'

A lido café, Tropical Coconut Grove Bar & Grill, features casual self-serve buffet fare, and includes a deli counter and pizzeria. A patisserie offers specialty coffees and sweets (extra charge), and a so-called sushi bar off to one side of the atrium lobby bar on Promenade Deck is open prior to dinner; if you know anything about sushi, don't expect authenticity.

There is no specialty (extra-charge) restaurant, as aboard some of the larger ships in the Carnival fleet.

ENTERTAINMENT. The Palace Showlounge is the venue for large-scale production shows and major cabaret acts; note that pillars (20 in total) obstruct the views from some seats. During a typical cruise, there will be several high-energy production shows, with a cast of singers and dancers, backed by a large live band.

SPA/FITNESS. SpaCarnival is a large, glass-wrapped health, fitness, and spa complex located on the uppermost interior deck, forward of the ship's mast; it is typically open from 6am to 8pm daily. It has a gymnasium with ocean-view windows and good muscle-pumping electronic machines, an aerobics exercise room, men's and women's changing rooms, sauna and steam rooms, beauty salon, and rooms for body treatments. Some fitness classes may incur an extra charge.

Sporting types can play basketball, volleyball, or table tennis. There is also a banked jogging track outdoors on the deck above the spa, and a mini-golf course.

CARNIVAL FREEDOM
★★★

THIS FUN-FILLED, CASUAL CRUISE SHIP REALLY COMES ALIVE AT NIGHT

Size:	Large Resort Ship	Passenger/Crew Ratio (lower beds):	2.5
Tonnage:	110,320	Cabins (total):	1,487
Cruise Line:	Carnival Cruise Line	Size Range (sq ft/m):	179.7–484.2/16.7–44.8
Former Names:	none	Cabins (for one person):	0
Builder:	Fincantieri (Italy)	Cabins with balcony:	574
Entered Service:	Feb 2007	Cabins (wheelchair accessible):	25
Length (ft/m):	951.4/290.0	Wheelchair accessibility:	Good
Beam (ft/m):	105.6/32.2	Elevators:	20
Propulsion/Propellers:	diesel-electric (63,400kW)/2	Casino (gaming tables):	Yes
Passenger Decks:	13	Swimming Pools:	2 (1 w/ sliding glass dome)
Total Crew:	1,150	Self-Service Launderette:	Yes
Passengers (lower beds):	2,974	Library:	Yes
Passenger Space Ratio (lower beds):	37.0	Onboard currency:	US$

THE SHIP. *Carnival Freedom* shares the same generally balanced profile as sisters *Carnival Conquest, Carnival Glory, Carnival Liberty, Carnival Sunshine,* Carnival *Triumph,* Carnival *Valor,* and *Carnival Victory.* Immediately recognizable is the trademark swept-back wingtip funnel.

Carnival's Seaside Theater for movies on an upper outside deck recalls those classic drive-in movie theaters, with seating in tiered rows and the screen in front. Also outside is Serenity, an adult-only quiet spot at the top and front of the ship – a nice escape from all the hubbub on the open decks below.

Inside, the decor is a kaleidoscopic blend of colors (most are a mix of dark and gaudy) to stimulate and excite the senses, and it is dedicated to time and the decades. The deck and public room layout is fairly logical (except for getting from the aft-placed Posh Dining Room to the showlounge, because you have to go up and down a deck or two). Most of the public rooms are located on one deck off a main interior boulevard, above the two main dining rooms (Chic and Posh). Public rooms include the Babylon Casino with gaming tables and over 300 slot machines, a fine Havana Cigar Bar, Monticello Library (sadly, there are few books), Conference Center, Scott's Piano Bar, Swingtime Bar, and a popular Wine Bar, among others.

Carnival Freedom is a large floating playground for the young and young-at-heart, with lots of participa-

BERLITZ'S RATINGS	Possible	Achieved
Ship	500	344
Accommodation	200	125
Food	400	201
Service	400	250
Entertainment	100	66
Cruise Experience	400	237
OVERALL SCORE 1223 points out of 2000		

tion events, together with the three 'Gs' – glitz, glamour, and gambling. This is cruising Splash Vegas style – and a fun, all-American experience. Because it's a large resort ship, expect lines for shore excursions, security control when reboarding, and disembarkation.

While the cuisine is just basic, the fun begins at sundown, with razzle-dazzle shows, and late-night reverie.

Niggles include the many pillars that obstruct passenger flow, particularly in the dining room, where it's difficult for the waiters to serve food properly; the non-stop infomercials on the in-cabin infotainment system (you can, however, turn the system off); the super-loud rap and rock 'music' everywhere; and some rather juvenile cruise directors.

ACCOMMODATION. There are numerous cabin price categories, in several different suite/cabin types, sizes, and grades. These include suites with private balcony; deluxe outside-view cabins with private balcony; outside-view cabins with private balcony; outside-view cabins with window; cabins with a porthole instead of a window; interior cabins; and interior (no-view) cabins with upper and lower berths.

There are five decks of cabins with private balconies. The standard cabins are of modest size, although the furniture is square and angular (no rounded edges). However, there's plenty of drawer space, and space for toiletries in bathrooms. Three decks of cabins (eight on each deck, each with private balcony – they are very pleasant) overlook the stern. Most cabins have twin beds that can be converted to a queen-size bed format.

There is also a group of 18 'spa' cabins, located directly around and behind SpaCarnival; so fitness devotees can get out of bed and go straight to the treadmill without having to go through any of the public rooms first.

DINING. There are two principal dining rooms (Chic, located midships, seating 744; and Posh, aft, seating 1,122). Both are two decks high and have a balcony level (the balcony level in Posh is larger than the one in Chic). There's a choice of either fixed-time dining (6pm or 8.15pm) or flexible dining (during opening hours). Note that they are not open for lunch on port days.

Overall, the food is quite starchy, with simple presentation, few garnishes, and many dishes disguised with gravies and sauces. The selection of fresh green vegetables, breads, cheeses, and fruits is limited (bread is thawed and then baked from frozen 'starter' dough), and there is heavy use of canned fruit and jellied desserts. The waiters sing and dance, so think 'foodertainment' rather than food quality. There are no wine waiters, and wine glasses are really small. For something really simple, an 'always available' list of 'Carnival Classics' includes mahi-mahi (fish), baby back ribs (beef), and grilled chicken.

There are few tables for two, but among my favorites are two tables for two right at the back of the restaurant, with ocean views astern.

The Sun King Supper Club (reservations required) has good table settings, china, and silverware, and features prime dry-aged steaks and grilled seafood items. It's worth paying the cover charge to get a taste of what Carnival can deliver in terms of food that is better quality than the fare from the main dining rooms.

The Freedom Restaurant, a casual self-serve international food court-style lido deck eatery, has two main serving lines. Each night it morphs into Seav-iew Bistro and provides a dress-down alternative for pasta, steaks, salads, and desserts. Other casual eateries include Guy's Burger Joint (named after TV's Guy Fieri), Blue Iguana (for Mexican cantina-style bites) and Seafood Shack.

For a special celebration, try the Chef's Table experience – a multi-course 'dégustation' dinner for up to 12 people. It costs $75 per person and usually takes place in a small, quiet spot such as the Monticello Library, Dynasty Conference room, or other secluded venue.

ENTERTAINMENT. The Victoriana Main Lounge (named after England's Queen Victoria) is the ship's multi-deck showlounge, seating up to 1,400 and staging colorful Las Vegas-style production shows and major cabaret acts. It has a revolving stage, hydraulic orchestra pit, good (but overly loud) sound, and seating on three levels (the upper levels are tiered through two decks); a proscenium arch acts as a scenery loft. The decor is medieval – drinks tables look like shields, and coats of armor and towers with stained-glass windows flank the stage.

An alternative entertainment venue is the aft lounge, with 425 seats, live music, and late-night cabaret acts including smutty adult comedy.

There's also the 100-seat Scott's Piano Bar.

Body-throbbing loud music sensations can be found in the disco, which includes a video wall with live projections from the dance floor.

SPA/FITNESS. SpaCarnival has an area of approximately 13,300 sq ft (1,235 sq m), is located above the navigation bridge, and accessed from the forward stairway. Facilities include a solarium, eight treatment rooms, lecture rooms, sauna and steam rooms for men and women, a beauty parlor, a large gymnasium with floor-to-ceiling windows including forward-facing ocean views, and an aerobics room with instructor-led classes (some at extra cost), for which you'll need to sign up.

CARNIVAL GLORY
★★★

THIS IS AN ULTRA-CASUAL FUN-FILLED SHIP FOR FIRST-TIME CRUISERS

Size:	Large Resort Ship	Passenger/Crew Ratio (lower beds):	2.5
Tonnage:	110,239	Cabins (total):	1,487
Cruise Line:	Carnival Cruise Line	Size Range (sq ft/m):	179.7–482.2/16.7–44.8
Former Names:	none	Cabins (for one person):	0
Builder:	Fincantieri (Italy)	Cabins with balcony:	590
Entered Service:	Jul 2003	Cabins (wheelchair accessible):	25
Length (ft/m):	951.4/290.0	Wheelchair accessibility:	Good
Beam (ft/m):	116.4/35.5	Elevators:	14
Propulsion/Propellers:	diesel-electric (63,400kW)/2	Casino (gaming tables):	Yes
Passenger Decks:	13	Swimming Pools:	2 (1 w/ sliding glass dome)
Total Crew:	1,160	Self-Service Launderette:	Yes
Passengers (lower beds):	2,974	Library:	Yes
Passenger Space Ratio (lower beds):	37.0	Onboard currency:	US$

THE SHIP. There are three decks full of public lounges, bars, and lots of rooms to play in, together with good facilities and programs for children.

A much-needed makeover in 2012 added two half-decks at the front of the ship, extended two other decks at the aft, and added 182 cabins (but no extra elevators), plus several new, and some much revamped, eateries, plus much more. These include an Alchemy Bar – for 'mixologist' (bartender) cocktails; a (music-free) Library Bar; a Sports Bar (interactive, sports ticker results); and an art gallery.

Amidships on the open deck is a water slide (200ft/60m long), plus tiered sunbathing decks between two swimming pools, several hot tubs, and large poolside movie screen (Seaside Theater). For adults to escape the outdoor activities and noise there is Serenity – an extra-cost adults-only relaxation area, located on two decks at the top, forwardmost part of the ship.

The interior decor is a fantasyland of colors, in every hue of the rainbow. Most public rooms are located off the Kaleidoscope Boulevard – the main interior promenade, which is great for strolling and people-watching. The larger of two atriums, Colors Lobby spans nine decks in the forward third of the ship. Check out the interpretative paintings of US flags at the Color Bar. The smaller aft atrium goes through three decks.

Carnival is all about cruising Splash Vegas style – it's a fun, all-American experience. The cuisine is just so-so, but the excitement really begins at sundown

BERLITZ'S RATINGS	Possible	Achieved
Ship	500	340
Accommodation	200	125
Food	400	201
Service	400	247
Entertainment	100	64
Cruise Experience	400	234

OVERALL SCORE 1211 points out of 2000

when Carnival excels in sound, lights, razzle-dazzle shows, and late-night high-volume sounds. There are nightspots and watering holes for just about every musical taste (except classical music), such as the Ivory Club Bar, Ebony Aft Cabaret Lounge, Cinn-a-Bar (Piano Bar), White Heat Dance Club, and Bar Blue.

Niggles: the modifications and additions, while good, have also created a crowded, congested ship. Also, the open deck space is poor considering the large passenger numbers. The pool deck is cluttered, and there are no cushioned pads for the sunloungers. There is constant hustling for drinks. Since it's a large resort ship, there are lines for the likes of shore excursions, security control when re-boarding, disembarkation, and sign-up sheets for fitness equipment. Also, note that ear-splitting rap and rock music is everywhere.

ACCOMMODATION. There are numerous cabin price categories, in seven different grades: suites with private balcony; deluxe outside-view cabins with private balcony; outside-view cabins with private balcony; outside-view cabins with window; cabins with a porthole instead of a window; interior cabins; and interior cabins with upper and lower berths. The price reflects the grade, location, and size.

Several decks of cabins have a private balcony, although many of these are not actually private, as they can be overlooked from various public locations.

During the makeover, a number of Spa-grade cabins were added adjacent to the Carnival Spa and Serenity area; these have all the usual fittings, plus special spa-related extras, and easy access to the spa.

Standard cabins are of an adequate size and are equipped with the basics, although the furniture is angular, and lacks rounded edges. Three decks of cabins (eight on each deck, all with private balcony – these are nice) overlook the stern. Most cabins with twin beds can be converted to a queen-size bed format.

Book one of the Category 11 or 12 suites, and you will get more space and a larger number of perks and privileges.

DINING. The two main dining rooms, Golden and Platinum, are two decks high, with seating on both levels. The decor includes wall coverings featuring a pattern of Japanese bonsai trees. Choose either fixed-time dining (6pm or 8.15pm) or flexible dining (during opening hours).

Overall, the food is quite starchy, with simple presentation, few garnishes, and many dishes disguised with gravies and sauces. The choice of fresh green vegetables, bread and bakery items (these are thawed and then baked from frozen 'starter' dough), cheeses, and fruits is limited, and there is heavy use of canned fruit and jellied desserts. The waiters sing and dance, so think 'foodertainment' rather than food quality. Also, there are no wine waiters, and the wine glasses are small. For something very simple, an 'always available' list of 'Carnival Classics' includes mahi-mahi (fish), baby back ribs (beef), and grilled chicken.

Other (complimentary) eateries include: Guy's Burger Joint, a poolside venue developed with Food Network personality Guy Fieri (for handmade burgers and freshly cut fries) and BlueIguana Cantina Mexican eatery (for Mexican snack food such as tacos and burritos). Poolside watering holes include a BlueIguana Tequila Bar, and a RedFrog Rum Bar.

For something different, try the (extra-cost) Emerald Room Steakhouse, which features large premium-quality steaks and grilled seafood, and has lighting fixtures that look like giant emeralds.

The two-level Red Sail Restaurant is for caual self-serve eats; it includes a Mexican counter for burritos and tacos, a deli, and on the upper level, a fish 'n' chippery (there is seating on both levels).

ENTERTAINMENT. The multi-deck Amber Palace Showlounge seats 1,400. It has a revolving stage, hydraulic orchestra pit, superb sound, and seating on three levels (the upper levels being tiered through two decks). A proscenium arch over the stage acts as a scenery loft.

Jazz lovers could head for the Bar Blue, while the Cinn-A-Bar is a piano bar, with curved aluminum walls – so 'bending' notes should be easy.

SPA/FITNESS. SpaCarnival is a fairly large health, fitness, and spa complex. You'll find it directly above the navigation bridge forward, and accessed from the forward stairway.

Facilities include a gymnasium (packed with muscle machines and exercise equipment), body treatment area, sauna and steam rooms for men and women, and a beauty salon.

CARNIVAL HORIZON
NYR

A SHIP FOR FAMILY FUN AND CARDIO-ACTIVE OUTDOOR FACILITIES

Size:	Large Resort Ship	Passenger/Crew Ratio (lower beds):	2.5
Tonnage:	135,000	Cabins (total):	1,823
Cruise Line:	Carnival Cruise Line	Size Range (sq ft/m):	161.4–344.4/15.0–32.0
Former Names:	none	Cabins (for one person):	0
Builder:	Fincantieri (Italy)	Cabins with balcony:	887
Entered Service:	Mar 2018	Cabins (wheelchair accessible):	35
Length (ft/m):	1,054.7/321.5	Wheelchair accessibility:	Good
Beam (ft/m):	101.7/31.0	Elevators:	16
Propulsion/Propellers:	diesel-electric (62,370kW)/	Casino (gaming tables):	Yes
	2 azimuthing pods	Swimming Pools:	3
Passenger Decks:	13	Self-Service Launderette:	Yes
Total Crew:	1,450	Library:	Yes
Passengers (lower beds):	3,954	Onboard currency:	US$
Passenger Space Ratio (lower beds):	34.1		

THE SHIP. *Carnival Horizon* is a sister ship to *Carnival Vista*. The design is itself old – based mostly on *Carnival Destiny* of 1996. It provides an array of activity-fueled fun for the whole family. This is essentially a ship built around its Waterworks aqua park – plus it has numerous other sporting attractions to keep you occupied. Carnival Horizon is all about the fun of the fair at sea.

So, line up to pedal a bike on the suspended track of Sky Ride – maybe even cycle to the next port! Other attractions include a large Water-Works aqua park, which includes a 445-ft (136m) Kaleid-O-Slide, a twisting, corkscrew-turning waterslide adventure with kaleidoscopic effects (it's a variation on the SkyWalk rope course aboard Carnival Magic); it's an excellent place to keep the kids occupied.

Considering the number of passengers carried, the swimming pools are really small, as is the open deck (sunbathing) space, because of all the sports activity features crammed into the open decks.

An adults-only (extra-cost) Serenity area atop the ship at the front provides a beach-like escape from the noisy family-filled decks below, with hot tubs, sunloungers, a bar, and other 'take a break' facilities, including massage 'huts.'

There is a full walk-around open promenade deck – but it's lined with deck chairs. Also at the aft, two 'scenic whirlpools' are cantilevered over the water (as part of the Havana Outside area), with fine sea views.

BERLITZ'S RATINGS

	Possible	Achieved
Ship	500	NYR
Accommodation	200	NYR
Food	400	NYR
Service	400	NYR
Entertainment	100	NYR
Cruise Experience	400	NYR

OVERALL SCORE NYR points out of 2000

Facilities include a small IMAX Theater (for movies and documentary content), a large Vista Casino (adjacent to the atrium), a Thrill Theater (for a moving 4-D experience), and many other lounges and bars. However, the ship's layout is a little disjointed.

The social center of the ship is the atrium, with LED screens providing mood-changing backdrops. Counters for guest services and shore excursions are just off the atrium; aft of the lobby is Reflections Dining Room.

Most of the public rooms, lounges, bars, and nightspots are located on two main public room/entertainment decks. These can be accessed via an 11-deck-high atrium lobby, with a cantilevered bandstand atop a massive dance floor on the ground level.

The myriad bars include a sports bar, a trendy Havana Bar, Alchemy Bar (for 'mixologist' cocktails, and a RedFrog Pub (with Carnival's own brews – Thirsty-Frog Red, Thirsty Frog Port Hoppin' IPA, Thirsty Frog Caribbean Wheat, and ThirstyFrog Java Stout).

Families with children have lots of hyper-activity sporty areas outdoors, plus play rooms for kids and teens (in several different locations), and plenty of youth counselors to take charge, so parents and minders can get some 'me' time, too.

What Carnival does well is provide almost non-stop excitement, fun and entertainment. While the cuisine is just so-so, the real fun will begin at sundown, when the upbeat kicks in.

ACCOMMODATION. The range of cabin sizes, locations, grades and prices includes 'Family Harbor' – family cabins that can sleep up to five. Whether you go for high end or low end, all include plush mattresses, good-quality duvets, bed linen and pillows. The suites are not large, although they are practically laid out, while some of the standard cabins are fine for two but become crowded for three or more.

All cabins have spy-hole doors, twin beds that can convert into queen-size beds, individually controlled air conditioning, infotainment screen, and telephone. Some cabins can accommodate a third and fourth person, but have little closet space, and only one personal safe. Some Deck 3 cabins have lifeboat-obstructed views. Among the most desirable suites/cabins are on five aft-facing decks, with private balconies overlooking the stern and ship's wash. There's no vibration – a bonus provided by the pod propulsion system.

DINING. Reflections (1,474 seats) and Horizons (702 seats) are main dining rooms, for served meals (breakfast, lunch, and dinner) in early or late seating (note that these restaurants are not open in port). Horizons Restaurant includes some tables aft with fine views (on both main and balcony levels – although the upper level has a low ceiling), plus a bar. You can (at extra cost) also have selections from the steakhouse menu.

Lido Marketplace is the self-serve, buffet-style casual restaurant; close by are other laid-back (free) eateries, including Guy's Burger Joint (yes, that Guy Fieri), Bluelguana Cantina (for Mexican snack food), and Pizzeria del Capitano (where, according to Carnival, you can 'toss it, stretch it, and cheese it'!). There's also Fat Jimmy's C-Side BBQ – oh, and you can get some light bites at The Taste Bar, hot dogs at SeaDogs in SportSquare, sandwiches at the Carnival Deli, and frozen yoghurt at Swirls.

Extra cost dining venues include Fahrenheit 555, an all-American steakhouse (for prime meats and grilled seafood), Bonsai Sushi Restaurant, for Japanese-style cuisine (with both indoor and outdoor seating), and Seafood Shack, a New England-style indoor-outdoor eatery for steamed lobster, crab cakes, and fried shrimp. Plus there's Cucina del Capitano (for Italian-style cuisine), and Ji-Ji Asian Kitchen (for Asian fusion cuisine), both on the upper level of Lido Marketplace. Families with youngsters might like to indulge in a Green Eggs and Ham breakfast, while Chef's Table (for foodies) includes a little showbusiness from the chef for a small number of diners (at extra cost).

ENTERTAINMENT. The Liquid Lounge (showlounge) spans two decks and is the venue for Carnival's Vegas-style production shows (think feathers and skin) and 'A'-list cabaret acts.

A second entertainment lounge is the Limelight Lounge (for adult comedy); a Piano Bar offers lighter fare.

A small IMAX Theater has a three-deck high screen, while adjacent is a multi-dimensional, special-effects experience in the Thrill Theater. Both are located on the interior of the forward section of Upper Promenade Deck. Extra-cost popcorn and movie snacks are available. Adjacent is a video arcade.

SPA/FITNESS. Cloud 9 Spa is on two levels, with treatment rooms, men's and women's infrared saunas and hammam (slow steam and mud room – good for couples), relaxation lounger, fitness center, as well as 'pay more' thermal suites, plus a VIP treatment room for Spa Suite occupants.

Activity/sports facilities include an outdoor Sky-Course suspended ropes course (always fun on a moving ship), Sky Gardens mini-golf course, and a Skycourt (for baseball). The Clubhouse at SportSquare includes mini-bowling, ping-pong, arcade basketball, and video games.

CARNIVAL IMAGINATION
★★★

THIS FUN SHIP IS A GOOD CHOICE FOR HIGH-ENERGY FAMILY CRUISERS

Size:	Mid-size Ship	Passenger/Crew Ratio (lower beds):	2.2
Tonnage:	70,367	Cabins (total):	1,028
Cruise Line:	Carnival Cruise Line	Size Range (sq ft/m):	173.2–409.7/16–38
Former Names:	*Imagination*	Cabins (for one person):	0
Builder:	Kvaerner Masa-Yards (Finland)	Cabins with balcony:	152
Entered Service:	Jul 1995	Cabins (wheelchair accessible):	22
Length (ft/m):	855.0/260.6	Wheelchair accessibility:	Fair
Beam (ft/m):	103.0/31.4	Elevators:	14
Propulsion/Propellers:	diesel-electric (42,240kW)/2	Casino (gaming tables):	Yes
Passenger Decks:	10	Swimming Pools:	3
Total Crew:	920	Self-Service Launderette:	Yes
Passengers (lower beds):	2,056	Library:	Yes
Passenger Space Ratio (lower beds):	34.4	Onboard currency:	US$

THE SHIP. *Carnival Imagination* has a swept-back wing-like funnel above the outdoor pool deck, but the open deck space itself is inadequate when the ship is full and everyone wants to be out on deck. The aft decks used to be less noisy when all the activities were focused around the main swimming pool and hot tubs, but now it has a Carnival WaterWorks – with long (about 300ft/90m) and short water slides and water-burst fountains – it's a very active area. For quiet, adult-only space, pay extra to go to Serenity, on Deck 9 aft.

There is no walk-around open promenade deck, but there is a short jogging track atop ship. The lifeboats, six of which double as shore tenders are positioned high.

The interior spaces are well utilized, but busy. The general passenger flow is good, and the interior design – by Miami-architect Joe Farcus – is clever, functional, and bizarrely colorful. The theme is the legendary symbols of antiquity (think winged deities and beings).

A stylish, 'open' balcony-shaped atrium lobby spans six decks, and is topped by a large glass dome. The lowest level of this focal point houses the purser's desk and shore-excursion desk, a popular Atrium Bar (with live music), and a small sushi bar off to one side.

There are public entertainment lounges, bars, and clubs galore, with something for everyone (except

BERLITZ'S RATINGS

	Possible	Achieved
Ship	500	299
Accommodation	200	121
Food	400	200
Service	400	250
Entertainment	100	62
Cruise Experience	400	229

OVERALL SCORE 1161 points out of 2000

quiet space). The public rooms, connected by a double-width Via Marina Promenade, combine a colorful mix of classic and contemporary design elements. Most public rooms and attractions lead off from this boulevard, which runs between the showlounge (forward) and Xanadu lounge aft. Gamers and slot players alike have almost non-stop action in the El Dorado Casino.

There is also a nice-looking library and reading room, but few books, plus a 1,200-sq-ft (111-sq-m) conference room.

The *sine qua non* of a Carnival cruise is all about fun, which begins at sundown, when the ship excels in lights, volume, and show. *Carnival Imagination* is a floating playground for the young and young-at-heart, and features constant stimulation and lots of participation events. Since it's a large resort ship, there will be lines for the likes of shore excursions, security control when re-boarding, and disembarkation.

Downsides include the many annoying announcements, the never-ending hustling to get you to buy ice-filled drinks, and the ear-splitting rap and rock music.

ACCOMMODATION. There are several grades of accommodation, priced by size, and location. Standard outside-view and interior cabins have clinical, unmemorable decor. They are marginally comfortable (most are of the same size and appointments), with good storage space and practical, well-designed no-nonsense bathrooms. With a queen-bed configuration instead of a twin-bed layout, note that one person has to clamber over the bed – possibly a rather ungainly exercise.

Suite occupants get more space, quirky furniture, and perks, although the suites on this ship are much smaller than those aboard vessels of a similar size of competing companies.

Families have 50 connecting cabins to choose from – good if you have children and want them close by, but not *that* close.

Room service items are available 24 hours a day, although in standard cabins, only cold food is available (there are more choices for suite-grade accommodation).

DINING. The two large main dining rooms, Pride and Spirit, are located amidships and aft. Both have ocean-view windows and bright decor, but they are noisy. Choose either fixed-time dining (6pm or 8.15pm) or flexible dining (during opening hours). Note that they are not open for lunch on port days.

The food is pretty starchy and unmemorable, with simple presentation, and few garnishes. This is bog-standard catering. Many dishes are disguised with gravies and sauces. The selection of fresh green vegetables, bread and bakery items (these are thawed and then baked from frozen 'starter' dough), cheeses, and fruits is limited, and there is heavy use of canned fruit and jellied desserts. The waiters sing and dance, so think 'foodertainment' rather than food quality.

For something simple, a selection of always available (when the dining rooms are open) 'Carnival Classics' includes mahi mahi (fish), baby back ribs (beef), and grilled chicken.

Waiters are almost more about entertaining than serving food with any finesse.

The Horizon Bar & Grill is a Lido cafe, for casual self-serve buffet eats. The venue includes a deli counter and pizzeria. At night, it becomes the Seaview Bistro, for pasta, steaks, salads, and desserts. The food selection, though limited, makes a change from the large, crowded, and noisy main dining rooms.

Other (complimentary) eateries include: Guy's Burger Joint, a poolside venue developed with Food Network personality Guy Fieri (for handmade burgers and freshly cut fries) and BlueIguana Cantina Mexican eatery (for Mexican snack food such as tacos and burritos). Poolside watering holes include a BlueIguana Tequila Bar and a RedFrog Rum Bar.

ENTERTAINMENT. The Universe Showlounge features large-scale production shows and cabaret – although 20 pillars obstruct some views. During a typical cruise, there will be one or two shows, with lead singers and a clutch of dancers, backed by a large live band.

SPA/FITNESS. SpaCarnival is a large, glass-wrapped health, fitness, and spa complex. It is located on the uppermost interior deck, forward of the ship's mast, and is typically open from 6am to 8pm daily. It has a gym with windows that look out over the bows, an aerobics room, changing rooms, sauna and steam rooms, beauty salon, and rooms for body treatments, but not enough staff to keep the area clean and tidy.

Sporty types can play basketball or volleyball, table tennis, go jogging, or play mini-golf.

CARNIVAL INSPIRATION
★★★

THIS ULTRA-COLORFUL SHIP IS GOOD FOR A FIRST CASUAL CRUISE EXPERIENCE

Size:	Mid-size Ship	Passenger/Crew Ratio (lower beds):	2.2
Tonnage:	70,367	Cabins (total):	1,028
Cruise Line:	Carnival Cruise Line	Size Range (sq ft/m):	173.2–409.7/16–38
Former Names:	*Inspiration*	Cabins (for one person):	0
Builder:	Kvaerner Masa-Yards (Finland)	Cabins with balcony:	152
Entered Service:	Apr 1996	Cabins (wheelchair accessible):	22
Length (ft/m):	855.0/260.6	Wheelchair accessibility:	Fair
Beam (ft/m):	103.0/31.4	Elevators:	14
Propulsion/Propellers:	diesel-electric (42,240kW)/2	Casino (gaming tables):	Yes
Passenger Decks:	10	Swimming Pools:	3
Total Crew:	920	Self-Service Launderette:	Yes
Passengers (lower beds):	2,056	Library:	Yes
Passenger Space Ratio (lower beds):	34.4	Onboard currency:	US$

THE SHIP. *Carnival Inspiration* is the sixth in a series of eight almost identical *Fantasy*-class ships. It is ideally suited to anyone taking a first cruise. WaterWorks is the pool deck aqua park; it includes a 334ft (101.8m) Twister water slide, dual Speedway Splash slides, and waterburst fountains, and is a splashtastic (and loud) area for kids. However, the open deck space is quite inadequate when the ship is full and everyone wants to be out on deck. The aft decks tend to be less noisy because activities are focused around the main swimming pool and hot tubs (one has a thatched shade). There's also Serenity – an adult-only 'quiet' (extra-cost; minimum age 21) lounging space on Deck 9 aft. Sadly, there is no walk-around open promenade deck. The lifeboats, six of which double as shore tenders, are positioned high up.

The interior is well designed by Joe Farcus. It's clever, functional, and extremely colorful. The decor theme is the arts (in an Art Nouveau style) and literature, and it includes a colorful mix of classic and contemporary design elements.

The interior focal point (and a good social meeting place) is an 'open' atrium lobby, with a balconied shape (including decoration resembling the necks and heads of violins). It spans six decks, has a marble staircase, and is topped by a glass-domed roof. The purser's desk and shore-excursion desk occupy the lowest level, together with an Atrium Bar with live music.

BERLITZ'S RATINGS	Possible	Achieved
Ship	500	299
Accommodation	200	121
Food	400	200
Service	400	251
Entertainment	100	62
Cruise Experience	400	232

OVERALL SCORE 1165 points out of 2000

There are public entertainment lounges, bars, and clubs galore, with something for everyone (except quiet space). The public rooms, connected by a double-width Inspiration Boulevard, feature many contemporary design elements. Most public rooms and attractions lead off from this boulevard – a sort of shipboard Main Street, which runs between the showlounge (forward) and the Candlelight lounge aft. Gamers and slot players alike can enjoy the almost non-stop action in the Monte Carlo Casino.

The Shakespeare Library is a very nice room (25 of his quotations adorn the oak veneer walls), but, sadly, there are few books. One dazzling room is the Rock and Roll Discotheque, with its guitar-shaped dance floor, video dance club, and dozens of screens.

What's it like? *Carnival Inspiration* is a floating playground for the young, but there will be lines for shore excursions, security control when re-boarding, and disembarkation, as well as sign-up sheets for fitness equipment.

There are many annoying announcements, a never-ending hustle to get you to buy (ice-laden) drinks, and no escape from the ear-splitting rap and rock music everywhere.

ACCOMMODATION. There are several accommodation grades, the price being according to size and location. Standard outside-view and interior cabins have decor that is plain. They are marginally comfortable, yet spacious enough and practical (most are of the same size and appointments), with good storage space and well-designed, no-nonsense bathrooms. However, with a queen-bed configuration instead of a twin-bed layout, one person needs to clamber over the bed.

Choose a suite and you get more space, plus eclectic decor and furniture. The suites are mildly attractive, but they are much smaller than those aboard ships of a similar size of competing companies. A small gift basket of toiletry samples is provided in all grades.

Room service is available 24 hours a day, although in standard cabins, only cold food is available, while suite-grade occupants get both hot and cold items to choose from.

DINING. Two large main dining rooms, Mardi Gras and Carnivale (the names given to Carnival's first two ships), are located amidships and aft, respectively. Both have ocean-view windows and attractive, bright decor, but they are noisy. Choose either fixed-time dining (6pm or 8.15pm) or flexible dining (during opening hours). For something simple, there's an 'always available' (when the dining room is open) list of 'Carnival Classics.' Note that the two main dining rooms may not be open for lunch on port days.

Overall, the food is quite starchy, with simple presentation, few garnishes, and many dishes disguised with gravies and sauces. The selection of fresh green vegetables, breads, cheeses, and fruits is limited (bread and bakery items are thawed and then baked from frozen 'starter' dough), and there is heavy use of canned fruit and jellied desserts. The waiters sing and dance, so think 'foodertainment' rather than food quality. For something really simple, an 'always available' list of 'Carnival Classics' includes mahi-mahi (fish), baby back ribs (beef), and grilled chicken.

This is standard catering, with dishes produced in large batches, and it is difficult to obtain anything unusual or 'off-menu.' A Lido café, called the Brasserie Bar & Grill, features the usual casual self-serve buffet eats, most of which are non-memorable. The venue includes a deli counter and pizzeria.

Other (complimentary) eateries include: Guy's Burger Joint, a poolside venue developed with Food Network personality Guy Fieri (for handmade burgers and freshly cut fries) and BlueIguana Cantina Mexican eatery (for Mexican snack food such as tacos and burritos). Poolside watering holes include a BlueIguana Tequila Bar and a RedFrog Rum Bar.

A patisserie offers specialty coffees and sweets (extra charge), and a sushi bar off to one side of the atrium lobby bar is open prior to dinner only.

ENTERTAINMENT. Paris Main Lounge is the big showlounge – the venue for large-scale production shows and major cabaret acts, although 20 pillars obstruct views from some seats. The resident show troupe includes vocalists and a clutch of dancers, backed by a large live band.

SPA/FITNESS. SpaCarnival is a large, glass-wrapped health, fitness, and spa complex. It is located on the uppermost interior deck, forward of the ship's mast, and is typically open from 6am to 8pm daily. It consists of a gymnasium with ocean-view windows and high-tech muscle-pumping machines, an aerobics room, changing rooms, sauna and steam rooms, beauty salon, and rooms for body treatments. Some fitness classes may incur an extra charge.

Sporting types can play basketball volleyball, table tennis, mini-golf, and go jogging on the banked track on the deck above the spa.

CARNIVAL LEGEND
★★★

THIS IS A CONTEMPORARY SHIP FOR A FUN-FILLED ACTIVE FAMILY CRUISE

Size:	Mid-size Ship	Passenger/Crew Ratio (lower beds):	2.2
Tonnage:	85,942	Cabins (total):	1,062
Cruise Line:	Carnival Cruise Line	Size Range (sq ft/m):	185–490/17.1–45.5
Former Names:	none	Cabins (for one person):	0
Builder:	Kvaerner Masa-Yards (Finland)	Cabins with balcony:	750
Entered Service:	Aug 2002	Cabins (wheelchair accessible):	16
Length (ft/m):	959.6/292.5	Wheelchair accessibility:	Good
Beam (ft/m):	105.6/32.2	Elevators:	15
Propulsion/Propellers:	diesel-electric (62,370kW)/ 2 azimuthing pods	Casino (gaming tables):	Yes
		Swimming Pools:	2
Passenger Decks:	12	Self-Service Launderette:	Yes
Total Crew:	1,030	Library:	Yes
Passengers (lower beds):	2,124	Onboard currency:	US$
Passenger Space Ratio (lower beds):	40.4		

THE SHIP. *Carnival Legend* – sister to *Carnival Miracle*, *Carnival Pride*, and *Carnival Spirit* – shares the same layout and configuration. There's no vibration – a bonus provided by the pod propulsion system. The ship is designed for families with children, and for entertainment, and has been modified to suit Australasian tastes.

The open deck and sunbathing space is not extensive, but there are two swimming pools, one of which can be covered by a sliding glass dome in case of inclement weather. A Water Park and Kids Splash Zone has water wheels, spraying jets, water blasters, pull ropes, two Mini Racer slides, and more (watch out for the giant water bucket), but the really big attraction is Green Thunder, a thrill ride that starts 100ft (30m) above sea level. The floor suddenly drops out of the platform, and you plummet in a near-vertical drop at about 23ft (7m) a second. When you hit the water in the fast water slide, you twist and turn through a transparent tube that extends over the side of the ship. Kids love it. On the negative side, the open deck space is a bit tight when the ship sails to full capacity in warm-weather areas.

For some quiet time, an extra-charge, adults-only area, Sanctuary, which is located aft, has its own bar, pool, hot tub and other facilities.

The interior decor is dedicated to the world's great legends, from the heroes of antiquity to 20th-century jazz masters and athletes – an eclectic mix that somehow works.

BERLITZ'S RATINGS	Possible	Achieved
Ship	500	336
Accommodation	200	125
Food	400	202
Service	400	242
Entertainment	100	63
Cruise Experience	400	239

OVERALL SCORE 1207 points out of 2000

Most bars and lounges are on two entertainment/public room decks, the upper featuring an exterior promenade deck. A walkway, named Hollywood Boulevard, connects many of the major public rooms on Atlantic Deck, one deck above Promenade Deck, which also sports a number of public rooms, including a large Club Merlin Casino (you have to walk though it to get to the main level of the showlounge from the restaurant, which is located aft). In a 2014 makeover, a RedFrog Pub (featuring Carnival's own ThirstyFrog Red draft brew), Bonsai Sushi (a sushi venue with Asian-style decor and food items), and Cherry on Top candy store were added.

The colorful atrium lobby spans eight decks; its wall decorations are best seen from any of the viewing balconies on any deck above the main lobby level. Take a drink from the lobby bar and look upwards – the surroundings are stunning, the focal point being a mural of the Colossus of Rhodes.

The ship's most dramatic room is the Follies Showlounge. Spanning three decks in the forward section, it recalls a 1920s movie palace.

Other facilities include a wedding chapel, a shopping street with boutique stores, a photo gallery, and an observation balcony in the center of the vessel, at the top of the multi-deck atrium.

The real fun begins at sundown, when Carnival turns up the heat with its razzle-dazzle shows, and late-night music.

Niggles include the small reception desk in the atrium lobby, which is often congested. The food is also pretty basic. Many pillars obstruct passenger flow – the ones in the dining room, for example, make it difficult for proper food service by the waiters. Books and computers are cohabitants in the ship's Holmes library/Internet center, but anyone wanting a book has to lean over others who may be using a computer, which is an awkward arrangement. Finally, there's no escape from the incredibly high-volume contemporary music blaring out throughout the ship.

ACCOMMODATION. There are numerous cabin categories, priced by grade, location, and size, including suites (with private balcony), outside-view cabins with private balcony, 68 ocean-view cabins with French doors (pseudo balconies that have doors that open, but no balcony to step onto), and a healthy proportion of standard outside-view to interior (no-view) cabins.

All cabins have spy-hole doors, twin beds that can be converted into queen-size beds, individually controlled air conditioning (it can't be switched off), TV, and telephone. A number of cabins on the lowest deck have lifeboat-obstructed views. Some cabins can accommodate a third and fourth person – useful if you have small children – although they have little closet space and only one personal safe.

Among the most desirable suites and cabins are those on five of the aft-facing decks; these have balconies overlooking the stern and ship's wash.

DINING. This ship has a single, large, two-deck-high, 1,300-seat main dining room, Truffles Restaurant, with seating on both upper and main levels. Its expansive ceiling has large murals of a Royal Copenhagen china pattern, and there are wall-mounted glass cases displaying fine china. Small rooms on both upper and lower levels can be booked for groups of up to 60. Choose either fixed-time dining (6pm or 8.15pm) or flexible dining (during opening hours). Note that the main dining room is not open for lunch on port days.

The food really is pretty starchy (lots of rice and potatoes), with simple presentation, few garnishes, and disguised with gravies and sauces. The selection of fresh green vegetables, bread and bakery items (these are thawed and then baked from frozen 'starter' dough), cheeses, and fruits is limited, and there is heavy use of canned fruit and jellied desserts. The waiters sing and dance, so think 'foodertainment' rather than food quality. Also, there are no wine wait-

ers, and the wine glasses are small. For something really simple, an 'always available' list of 'Carnival Classics' includes mahi-mahi (fish), baby back ribs (beef), and grilled chicken.

The Unicorn Café (Lido restaurant) is a self-serve food court-style buffet-style casual eatery that forms the aft third of Deck 9 (part of it wraps around the upper section of the huge atrium). It includes a central area with a deli sandwich corner, Asian corner, rotisserie, and international (Taste of the Nations) counter. There are salad and dessert counters, and a 24-hour pizzeria counter, with both indoor and outdoor seating. Movement around the buffet area is slow, and you have to stand in line for everything. Each night, the Unicorn Café becomes Seaview Bistro, for serve-yourself dinners (typically 6–9.30pm).

The Steakhouse is an extra-cost dining spot atop the ship, with around 150 seats and a show kitchen, featuring prime steaks and grilled seafood. Reservations are required. The decor features the Greek legend of Jason and the Argonauts (the bar has a large sculpture of the Golden Fleece). Decent table settings, china, and silverware are provided.

ENTERTAINMENT. The four-deck-high, 1,170-seat Follies Showlounge is the main venue for large-scale production shows and cabaret shows. Shows are best seen from the upper three levels. Directly underneath the showlounge is the Firebird lounge and bar.

Almost every lounge/bar, including Billie's Bar (a piano lounge) and Satchmo's Club (a nightclub with bar and dance floor), has live music in the evening. Finally, for the very lively, there's the disco, and, for the unreserved, there's always karaoke!

SPA/FITNESS. SpaCarnival spans two decks above the bridge in the forward part of the ship; it has 13,700 sq ft (1,272 sq m) of space. Lower-level facilities include a solarium, several treatment rooms, sauna and steam rooms for men and women, and a beauty salon. The upper level consists of a gymnasium with floor-to-ceiling ocean-view windows, and an aerobics room.

There are two centrally located swimming pools outdoors: one can be used in inclement weather due to its retractable glass dome. Adjacent are two whirlpool tubs. Another smaller pool is for children. An outdoor jogging track is located around the mast and the forward part of the ship; it doesn't go around the whole ship, but it's long enough for some serious walking.

CARNIVAL LIBERTY
★★★

THIS ULTRA-COLORFUL SHIP SHOULD BE GOOD FOR FIRST-TIME CRUISERS

Size:	Large Resort Ship	Passenger/Crew Ratio (lower beds):	2.5
Tonnage:	110,320	Cabins (total):	1,487
Cruise Line:	Carnival Cruise Lines	Size Range (sq ft/m):	179.7–482.2/16.7–44.8
Former Names:	none	Cabins (for one person):	0
Builder:	Fincantieri (Italy)	Cabins with balcony:	574
Entered Service:	Jul 2005	Cabins (wheelchair accessible):	25
Length (ft/m):	951.4/290.0	Wheelchair accessibility:	Good
Beam (ft/m):	116.4/35.5	Elevators:	18
Propulsion/Propellers:	diesel-electric (63,400kW)/2	Casino (gaming tables):	Yes
Passenger Decks:	13	Swimming Pools:	3 (1 w/ sliding glass dome)
Total Crew:	1,160	Self-Service Launderette:	Yes
Passengers (lower beds):	2,974	Library:	Yes
Passenger Space Ratio (lower beds):	37.0	Onboard currency:	US$

THE SHIP. *Carnival Liberty* shares the same fairly balanced profile as sisters *Carnival Conquest*, *Carnival Freedom*, *Carnival Glory*, *Carnival Sunshine*, *Carnival Triumph*, *Carnival Valor*, and *Carnival Victory*. Amidships on the open deck is a long water slide (200ft/60m long), tiered sunbathing decks and small pool, several hot tubs, and a large Seaside Theater movie screen. An extra-cost Serenity retreat provides quiet sunbathing space and a pool with retractable glass dome, just for adults, aft of the funnel. Inside are three decks full of lounges, 10 bars, and lots of rooms to play in.

The decor in the public rooms, hallways, and atrium adopts a design theme saluting master trades such as ironwork, masonry, pottery, and painting. The layout is logical, so finding your way around is easy. Most public rooms are located off a main boulevard – an interior promenade that is good for strolling and people-watching – particularly from the Jardin Café or Promenade Bar. Other hangouts and drinking places include The Stage (live music/karaoke lounge), the Flower Bar (main lobby), Gloves Bar (sports bar), Paparazzi (wine bar), and The Cabinet.

Carnival Liberty is a floating playground for the young and young-at-heart, and anyone who enjoys constant stimulation and lots of participation events, together with the three 'Gs' – glitz, glamour, and gambling. It's cruising Splash Vegas style – a fun, all-American experience. Because it's a large resort ship, there will be lines for the likes of shore excur-

BERLITZ'S RATINGS		
	Possible	Achieved
Ship	500	337
Accommodation	200	126
Food	400	201
Service	400	241
Entertainment	100	64
Cruise Experience	400	234
OVERALL SCORE 1203 points out of 2000		

sions, security control when re-boarding, and disembarkation, as well as sign-up sheets for fitness equipment.

While the cuisine is just so-so, the real fun begins at sundown, when it excels in terms of sound, lights, razzle-dazzle shows, and late-night high-volume sounds.

Niggles include the many pillars in the dining room, public toilets that are utilitarian and need some cheering up, and a lack of flowers. It is impossible to escape from noise and loud music (it's even played in cabin hallways and lifts), not to mention smokers.

ACCOMMODATION. There are numerous cabin price categories, in seven different grades: suites with private balcony; deluxe outside-view cabins with private balcony; outside-view cabins with private balcony; outside-view cabins with window; cabins with a porthole instead of a window; interior cabins; and interior cabins with upper and lower berths. The price reflects the grade, location, and size. Five decks of cabins have a private balcony, but many are not so private, because they can be overlooked from various public locations.

There are 18 'spa' cabins, located around and behind SpaCarnival, so you can get out of bed and head straight to the treadmill without having to go through any public rooms.

Standard cabins are of good size and have all the basics, although the cabinetry is angular (no rounded corners). Eight balcony cabins on each of three decks overlook the stern (these are very pleasant). Most cabins with twin beds can be converted to a queen-size bed format.

DINING. There are two main dining rooms, Golden Olympian Restaurant, forward, seating 744, and Silver Olympian Restaurant, aft, seating 1,122. Two additional wings (the Persian Room and Satin Room) can accommodate large groups. Choose either fixed-time dining (6pm or 8.15pm) or flexible dining (during opening hours). Note that the main dining room is not open for lunch on port days.

The food is carbohydrate-rich and non-memorable, with simple presentation and few garnishes. Many dishes are disguised with gravies and sauces. The choice of green vegetables, bread and bakery items (these are thawed and then baked from frozen 'starter' dough), cheeses, and fruits is limited, and there is heavy use of canned fruit and jellied desserts. The waiters sing and dance, so think 'food-ertainment' rather than food quality. Also, there are no wine waiters, and the wine glasses are small. For something really simple, an 'always available' list of 'Carnival Classics' includes mahi-mahi (fish), baby back ribs (beef), and grilled chicken.

Two-level Emile's is a casual self-serve international food court-style Lido Deck eatery; Guy's Burger Joint (named after TV's Guy Fieri), Blue Iguana (for Mexican light bites) and Bonsai Sushi are other options, while The Steakhouse is a more intimate setting for (extra-cost) prime meats and seafood.

ENTERTAINMENT. The Venetian Palace Show-lounge is a 1,400-seat multi-deck showroom for large-scale Las Vegas-style production shows and major cabaret acts.

The Victoria Lounge is another, smaller venue, located aft; it seats 425 and typically features live music and late-night cabaret acts, including smutty adult comedy.

The Tattooed Lady Dance Club is a discotheque for the hearing-impaired; it includes a video wall with projections live from the dance floor. There's also the 100-seat Piano Man bar, with keyboard-inspired decor.

SPA/FITNESS. SpaCarnival is a large health, fitness, and spa complex that spans two decks. It is located directly above the navigation bridge and accessed from the forward stairway. The lower level includes a solarium, eight treatment rooms, lecture rooms, sauna and steam rooms for men and women, and a beauty salon. The upper level consists of a large gymnasium with floor-to-ceiling ocean-view windows on three sides, and an aerobics room with instructor-led classes, some at extra cost.

CARNIVAL MAGIC
★★★

THE WHOLE FAMILY SHOULD REALLY ENJOY THIS HIGH-ENERGY FLOATING RESORT

Size:	Large Resort Ship	Passenger/Crew Ratio (lower beds):	2.6
Tonnage:	128,048	Cabins (total):	1,823
Cruise Line:	Carnival Cruise Line	Size Range (sq ft/m):	185.0–430.5/17.1–40.0
Former Names:	none	Cabins (for one person):	0
Builder:	Fincantieri (Italy)	Cabins with balcony:	887
Entered Service:	Jun 2011	Cabins (wheelchair accessible):	35
Length (ft/m):	1,004.0/306.0	Wheelchair accessibility:	Good
Beam (ft/m):	158.0/48.0	Elevators:	20
Propulsion/Propellers:	Diesel-electric (75,600kW)/2	Casino (gaming tables):	Yes
Passenger Decks:	13	Swimming Pools:	2
Total Crew:	1,367	Self-Service Launderette:	Yes
Passengers (lower beds):	3,646	Library:	Yes
Passenger Space Ratio (lower beds):	35.1	Onboard currency:	US$

THE SHIP. *Carnival Magic* is a sister ship to *Carnival Dream*, introduced in 2010 (both are 13 percent larger than earlier close sister *Carnival Splendor*). A standout feature is a long (over 312ft/95m) Twister Water Slide, part of The Water-Works on the pool deck – it's lots of fun for kids. However, there simply isn't enough open deck space for the number of passengers the ship carries, so sunbed loungers are tightly packed together. An extra-charge retreat called Serenity is for adults only.

There is a full walk-around open promenade deck, lined with deck chairs. Four 'scenic hot tubs' are cantilevered over the sea and provide fine views, but they do get crowded, and rowdy. Higher up, Lido Deck 10 offers a good open-deck area, with small pool and a large Seaside Theater LED movie screen and laser light show.

Although the ship's bows are short, its profile is nicely balanced, with a rakish front and a more rounded stern. The ship is based on the original design for *Carnival Sunshine*, and includes some of the design flaws of the *Sunshine*-class, but with a passenger capacity increase of over 1,000. Strangely, the cabin numbering system – even numbers on the starboard (right) side and odd numbers on the port (left) side – goes completely against the maritime tradition that places even-numbered cabins on the port side and odd-numbered cabins starboard (the same as the lifeboats).

BERLITZ'S RATINGS		
	Possible	Achieved
Ship	500	337
Accommodation	200	128
Food	400	150
Service	400	244
Entertainment	100	64
Cruise Experience	400	238
OVERALL SCORE 1161 points out of 2000		

The interior decor is vivid – really vivid. The main lobby is the connection point for ship functions and for meeting people. Take the glass-walled elevators for a neat view, though you may need sunglasses. It's good to see three main elevator towers: forward, amidships, and aft, unlike larger ships such as *Oasis of the Seas*, which, although it carries many more passengers, has only two such towers.

The Ocean Plaza is a comfortable area by day and an entertainment venue by night. The indoor/outdoor café and live music venue has a bandstand where a variety of musical genres are showcased, a large circular dance floor, and around 190 seats. A floor-to-ceiling curved glass wall separates the room, dividing indoor and outdoor seating areas. An adjacent bar offers coffees, ice creams, and pastries. The Page Turner (great name) is the ship's library, while Jackpot is – you guessed it – the colorful, large, lively casino, with abundant gaming tables and slot machines.

Other rooms include The Song (Jazz Bar) and Ocean Plaza (a sort of quiet area during the day, but busy at night with live entertainment); Internet-connect computer terminals are scattered throughout the ship, but few have much privacy. There's also a 232-capacity conference room (The Chambers). This was the first Carnival ship to have a pub, the poolside RedFrog Pub, with its own-label beer, ThirstyFrog Red. Also popular is BlueIguana

Tequila Bar and the Alchemy Bar, both added in a 2016 refurbishment.

So, what's it like? *Carnival Magic* is a floating playground for the party-loving young. The cuisine is not at all memorable, but there's plenty to do for all the family. Because it's a large resort ship, there will be lines for shore excursions, security control when reboarding, and disembarkation, as well as sign-up sheets for fitness equipment. There are many annoying and loud announcements, and a never-ending hustle to get you to buy alcoholic drinks full of ice, and other things.

ACCOMMODATION. There are many different cabin price categories, but just six cabin types. All accommodation includes the Carnival Comfort Bed with good-quality duvets, mattresses, linens, and pillows. However, the straight accommodation deck hallways create rather a cell-block look, and they are bright – very bright – even at night. There are also lot of interior cabins (perhaps those to go for are those at the stern, with great rearward ocean views on decks 6, 7, 8, and 9). There is a wide selection of other balcony cabins and suites, including 'Cove Balcony' cabins (these are the closest to the waterline). Adjacent to the Cloud 9 Spa are 'Cloud 9' spa cabins. They provide a number of 'exclusive' amenities and privileges, and easy access.

DINING. There are two main restaurants: Northern Lights, a 1,180-seat amidships dining room, and a smaller 828-seat aft dining room, Southern Lights. Each has two levels: main and balcony, with the galley on the lower level. Two small restaurant annexes can be reserved as a private dining room. Expect all-singing, all-dancing waiters to entertain you, while you search for the elusive green vegetables. Choose either fixed-time dining (6pm or 8.15pm) or flexible dining (any time between 5.45 and 9.30pm). Note that the two main dining rooms are not open for lunch on port days.

The food really is pretty starchy and non-memorable, with simple presentation and few garnishes. Many dishes are disguised with gravies and sauces. The selection of fresh green vegetables, bread and bakery items (these are thawed and then baked from frozen 'starter' dough), cheeses, and fruits is limited, and there is much use of canned fruit and jellied desserts. The waiters sing and dance, so think 'foodertainment' rather than food quality. Also, there are no wine waiters, and the wine glasses are small. For something really simple, an 'always available' list of 'Carnival Classics' includes mahi-mahi (fish), baby back ribs (beef), and grilled chicken.

Lido Marketplace, the ship's large (but not large enough) self-serve buffet facility, has indoor/outdoor seating areas on the lower (main) level and indoor-only seating on the upper level. A number of designated areas provide different types of ethnic cuisine.

It gets seriously congested – particularly for breakfast – and the food is pretty basic. The venue includes a Mongolian Wok and Pasta Bar on the upper level.

Forward of the buffet venue, adjacent to the 'beach pool' is the Pizzeria del Capitano, expanded in 2016. Other (complimentary) eateries include: Guy's Burger Joint, a poolside venue developed with Food Network personality Guy Fieri (for handmade burgers and freshly cut fries). Aft on the same deck is another Fieri-designed eatery for house-smoked favorites: Guy's Pig & Anchor Bar-B-Que Smokehouse (open at lunchtime on sea days only). There's also Blue Iguana Cantina Mexican eatery (for Mexican snack food such as tacos and burritos). Poolside watering holes include a Blue Iguana Tequila Bar and a RedFrog Rum Bar.

An extra-charge, reservations-required Prime Steakhouse and bar seats 139. Located on Promenade Deck aft, it features an à la carte menu and nice china and silverware. It's worth paying the cover charge to get a taste of what Carnival can deliver. There's a sushi venue, too, called Sushi and More, on Promenade Deck.

ENTERTAINMENT. The 1,964-seat Showtime Theater spans three decks at the front of the ship, with seating in a horseshoe shape around a large proscenium-arched stage. The sight lines are generally good, except from some of the seats at the back of the lowest level. Large-scale production shows with lots of feathers and skimpy costumes are staged, together with snappy cabaret acts, all with a live showband.

The 425-seat Spotlight Lounge, at the aft end of the ship, has a stage, dance floor, and large bar, and is a comedy venue, including late-night 'adult comedy.' Caliente is the ship's loud, Latin nightclub.

SPA/FITNESS. The expansive 23,750-sq-ft (2,206-sq-m) Cloud 9 Spa is a large health and wellness center. The uppermost deck includes indoor/outdoor private spa relaxation areas, at extra cost.

There are 17 treatment rooms, including a VIP room, a large massage room for couples, a Rasul mud treatment room, and two dry flotation rooms. An extra-charge 'Thermal Suite' comes with the typical sensory-enhanced heated chambers: Laconium, Tepidarium, Aroma, and Oriental steam baths. There are two steam rooms, one each for men and women, and a small unisex sauna with a floor-to-ceiling window on its starboard side.

A large contained outdoor SportsSquare for adults is for basketball, football, and volleyball. There's an outdoor weight-training circuit (SkyFitness), and the cutely named Turf on Surf miniature golf course. Perhaps the highlight is SkyCourse, an outdoor ropes course 230ft (70m) long and suspended above the uppermost deck. After all those activities, you'll need a cruise to relax.

CARNIVAL MIRACLE
★★★

THIS FUN-FILLED, FAMILY-FRIENDLY SHIP IS FOR HIGH-ENERGY CRUISING

Size:	Mid-size Ship	Passenger/Crew Ratio (lower beds):	2.2
Tonnage:	85,942	Cabins (total):	1,062
Cruise Line:	Carnival Cruise Line	Size Range (sq ft/m):	185.0–490.0/17.1–45.5
Former Names:	*none*	Cabins (for one person):	0
Builder:	Kvaerner Masa-Yards (Finland)	Cabins with balcony:	750
Entered Service:	Apr 2004	Cabins (wheelchair accessible):	16
Length (ft/m):	959.6/292.5	Wheelchair accessibility:	Good
Beam (ft/m):	105.6/32.2	Elevators:	15
Propulsion/Propellers:	diesel-electric (62,370kW)/ 2 azimuthing pods	Casino (gaming tables):	Yes
		Swimming Pools:	3 (1 w/ sliding glass dome)
Passenger Decks:	13	Self-Service Launderette:	Yes
Total Crew:	961	Library:	Yes
Passengers (lower beds):	2,124	Onboard currency:	US$
Passenger Space Ratio (lower beds):	40.4		

THE SHIP. *Carnival Miracle* is sister to *Carnival Legend, Carnival Pride*, and *Carnival Spirit*. One thing that stands out (apart from Carnival's wing-tipped red, white and blue funnel) is a long Twister Water Slide, part of The WaterWorks on pool deck, which includes multiple water-spray fountains – all good fun for active kids.

Open deck and sunbathing space is not extensive, but there are two small swimming pools (one can be covered by a sliding glass dome when required). An extra-cost, adults-only area, Sanctuary, has its own bar, pool, hot tub, and other facilities. Located at the aft of the ship on Lido Deck, it is for anyone wanting to have a quieter space for sunbathing and relaxation.

Inside, the decor is dedicated to 'fictional icons,' including the Phantom of the Opera, Sherlock Holmes, Philip Marlowe, and Captain Ahab. Bronze statues of Orpheus and Ulysses adorn the swimming pools.

There are two main entertainment/public room decks, the upper with an exterior promenade deck. A walkway, named the Yellow Brick Road, connects many of the major public rooms on Atlantic Deck, one deck above Promenade Deck, which also sports a number of public rooms, including a large Club Merlin Casino that's full of gaming tables and slot machines.

The colorful atrium lobby spans eight decks and has wall decorations best seen from any of the multiple viewing balconies on any deck above the main

BERLITZ'S RATINGS

	Possible	Achieved
Ship	500	339
Accommodation	200	126
Food	400	202
Service	400	241
Entertainment	100	63
Cruise Experience	400	236

OVERALL SCORE 1207 points out of 2000

lobby level. Take a drink from the lobby bar and look upwards – the surroundings are visually stunning, or overpowering, depending on your viewpoint.

Perhaps the most dramatic large room is the Phantom Showlounge, which spans three decks in the forward section. Directly underneath is the Firebird Lounge, which has a bar in its starboard aft section.

Other facilities include a wedding chapel, a shopping street, with boutique stores, a photo gallery, video games room, and an observation balcony in the center of the vessel, at the top of the multi-deck atrium. The large Mr Lucky's Casino invites wishful gamers and slot players.

Niggles include the small reception desk in the atrium lobby, which can become very congested. Many private balconies are not so private and can be overlooked from public locations. You need a credit card to open the personal safe in your cabin – impossible if your credit cards and wallet are inside the safe! In 2015, some facilities were added or changed. These included a RedFrog Pub (it dispenses Carnival's own brew, ThirstyFrog Red), an Alchemy Bar (for vintage pharmacy-inspired cocktails), four new production shows, and *Hasbro, The Game Show* (live versions of favorite games).

Niggles: Many pillars obstruct passenger flow – the ones in the dining room make it difficult for proper food service by the waiters for example. Books and computers cohabit the ship's Holmes library/Internet center, but anyone wanting a book has to lean over others who may be using a computer, which is an awkward arrangement.

Note that in 2018 the ship will be based year-round in Shanghai, for cruises for the Chinese domestic market, and the onboard product will be modified accordingly.

ACCOMMODATION. There are many cabin categories, priced by grade, location, and size. The range of cabins includes suites (with private balcony), outside-view cabins with private balcony, oceanview cabins with French balconies (pseudo balconies that have doors that open, but no balcony to step out onto), and a healthy proportion of standard outside-view to interior cabins.

All cabins have spy-hole doors, twin beds that can be converted into a queen-size bed, individually controlled air conditioning, infotainment system, and telephone. A number of cabins on the lowest deck have lifeboat-obstructed views. Some cabins can accommodate a third and fourth person, but have little closet space, and only one personal safe. Note that audio channels are provided on the infotainment system, but you can't turn the picture off, nor can you turn off the air conditioning in cabins or bathrooms.

Among the most desirable suites and cabins are those on five aft-facing decks, with private balconies overlooking the stern. You might think that these would suffer from vibration, but they don't, thanks to the 'pod' propulsion system.

For extra space, if the budget allows, it's worthwhile booking one of the larger deluxe balcony suites on Deck 6, with private teakwood balcony.

DINING. The Bacchus Dining Room is the 1,300-seat main restaurant; it spans two decks, with seating on both upper and main levels, with large murals on the ceiling of the upper level. The galley is underneath the restaurant, with escalator access. Tables are for two to eight; small rooms on both upper and lower levels can be booked for groups of up to 60. Choose either fixed-time dining (6pm or 8.15pm) or flexible dining (between 5.45pm and 9.30pm). Note that it is not open for lunch on port days.

The food really is carbohydrate-rich and non-memorable (it's mass catering, after all), with simple presentation and few garnishes. Many dishes are disguised with gravies and sauces. The selection of fresh green vegetables, bread and bakery items (these are thawed and then baked from frozen 'starter' dough), cheeses, and fruits is limited, and there is heavy use of rice, canned fruit and jellied desserts. The waiters sing and dance, so think 'foodertainment' rather than food quality. Also, there are no wine waiters, and the wine glasses are small. For something really simple, an 'always available' list of 'Carnival Classics' includes mahi-mahi (fish), baby back ribs (beef), and grilled chicken.

For casual eats, Horatio's Lido Restaurant is an extensive self-serve buffet-style eatery that forms the aft third of Deck 9 (part of it wraps around the upper section of the atrium). Unicorn murals are everywhere. It includes a central area with a deli sandwich corner, Asian corner, rotisserie, salad bar, international counter, a dessert counter, and a 24-hour pizzeria, and has both indoor and outdoor seating. Movement around the buffet area is in a slow-go line.

Nick & Nora's Steakhouse is a more upscale dining spot atop the ship, with just 156 seats and a show kitchen. It is located on two of the uppermost decks of the ship, above Horatio's Lido Restaurant, with good views over the atrium lobby.

ENTERTAINMENT. The 1,170-seat Phantom Showlounge is the principal venue for large-scale production shows and cabaret shows. Spiral stairways at the back of the lounge connect all three levels. Shows are best seen from the upper three levels. Directly underneath the showlounge is the Mad Hatter's Ball Lounge, which has a bar in its starboard aft section.

Almost every lounge/bar, including Sam's Piano Bar, the Jazz Lounge, and Jeeves Lounge, has live music in the evening. Finally, for the very lively, there's a disco; and there's always karaoke.

SPA/FITNESS. SpaCarnival, spanning two decks, is located directly above the navigation bridge in the forward part of the ship and has 13,700 sq ft (1,272 sq m) of space. Lower-level facilities include a solarium, eight treatment rooms, lecture rooms, sauna and steam rooms for men and women, and a beauty parlor. On the upper level there's a large gymnasium with floor-to-ceiling windows on three sides, including forward-facing ocean views, and an aerobics room.

An outdoor jogging track is located around the ship's mast; it doesn't go around the whole ship, but it's long enough for some decent walking.

CARNIVAL PARADISE
★★★

THIS FAMILY-FRIENDLY 'FUN' SHIP IS FINE FOR ULTRA-CASUAL CRUISING

Size:	Mid-size Ship	Passenger/Crew Ratio (lower beds):	2.2
Tonnage:	70,390	Cabins (total):	1,026
Cruise Line:	Carnival Cruise Line	Size Range (sq ft/m):	173.2–409.7/16–38
Former Names:	*Paradise*	Cabins (for one person):	0
Builder:	Kvaerner Masa-Yards (Finland)	Cabins with balcony:	152
Entered Service:	Nov 1998	Cabins (wheelchair accessible):	22
Length (ft/m):	855.0/260.6	Wheelchair accessibility:	Fair
Beam (ft/m):	103.3/31.5	Elevators:	14
Propulsion/Propellers:	diesel-electric (42,842kW)/	Casino (gaming tables):	Yes
	2 azimuthing pods	Swimming Pools:	3
Passenger Decks:	10	Self-Service Launderette:	Yes
Total Crew:	920	Library:	Yes
Passengers (lower beds):	2,052	Onboard currency:	US$
Passenger Space Ratio (lower beds):	34.2		

THE SHIP. *Carnival Paradise* (the last in a series of eight sister ships) provides a vibration-free ride thanks to its pod propulsion system.

While the open deck space is reasonable, it is inadequate when the ship is full and everyone wants to be out on deck. The aft decks tend to be less noisy, whereas all the activities are focused around the main swimming pool and hot tubs (one with a thatched shade).

Serenity is an adults-only 'quiet' lounging space on Deck 9 aft. There is no walk-around open promenade deck. The lifeboats (six double as shore tenders) are positioned high in the ship, rather than lower down, as in newer ships.

The interior design is the work of Miami-based architect Joe Farcus; it's clever, functional, and extremely colorful, with a theme of yesteryear's ocean liners.

The interior focal point is an 'open' atrium lobby, with a balconied shape; styled to impress, it spans six decks and is topped by a large glass dome. The lowest level houses the purser's desk and shore-excursion desk, together with a popular Atrium Bar with live music, and a small sushi bar off to one side; it's a good central meeting place.

There are many public entertainment lounges, bars, and clubs, with something for everyone (except quiet space). Most of these rooms are connected by a double-width Carnival Boulevard Promenade – a sort of shipboard Main Street – which runs between the showlounge (forward) and the Queen Mary Lounge

BERLITZ'S RATINGS		
	Possible	Achieved
Ship	500	300
Accommodation	200	122
Food	400	200
Service	400	247
Entertainment	100	61
Cruise Experience	400	234
OVERALL SCORE 1164 points out of 2000		

aft. Gamers and slot players alike can play in the Majestic Casino, with its gaming tables, and array of slot machines. The Blue Riband library is a pleasant room; although it has only a few books, there are several models of ocean liners. Another dazzling room is the Rock and Roll Discotheque, with its guitar-shaped dance floor, video dance club, and dozens of video monitors.

Carnival Paradise is a floating playground for the young and young-at-heart. This really is cruising Splash Vegas style. Because it's a large resort ship, there will be lines for things such as shore excursions, security control when re-boarding, and disembarkation.

Carnival is not known for its cuisine, but the real fun begins at sundown, when the ship excels in sound, lights, and high-volume shows. Venues from the Rex Dance Club/Disco to the Rotterdam Cigar Bar will certainly keep you occupied.

Niggles include annoying announcements, and the never-ending hustling to get you to spend money. Also, shore excursions are booked via the in-cabin 'Fun Vision' television system, so obtaining personal advice on trips can be difficult.

ACCOMMODATION. There are numerous price grades for accommodation, priced according to size and location. Standard outside-view and interior cabins have simple, unpretentious decor. They are fairly comfortable, and practical (most are of the same size and appointments), with good storage space and no-nonsense bathrooms. With a queen-bed configuration instead of the standard twin-bed layout, note that one person has to clamber over the bed to get in, which can be awkward.

Suites have a little more space, but they are much smaller than those aboard ships of a similar size of competing companies.

Room service is available 24/7, although in standard cabins only cold food is available. Those in suite-grade accommodation are able to choose from a greater range of both hot and cold items.

DINING. The two large main dining rooms, Elation and Destiny, are located amidships and aft. Both have ocean-view windows and attractive, but very bright decor, but they are noisy. Choose either fixed-time dining (6pm or 8.15pm) or flexible dining.

The food is best described as uneventful, with simple presentation and little in the way of garnishes. The selection of fresh green vegetables, bread, rolls (these and other bakery items are first thawed, then baked, from frozen 'starter' dough), cheeses, and fruits is quite unimaginative, and there is too much use of rice, canned fruit, and jellied desserts. There's a decent wine list, but no wine waiters, and the wine glasses are small. The waiters sing and dance, so it's really more about 'eatertainment' than food quality. For something really simple, there's an 'always available' list of 'Carnival Classics' including mahi mahi (fish), baby back ribs (beef), and grilled chicken. Note that the two main dining rooms are not open for lunch on port days.

A Lido café, called the Brasserie Bar & Grill, features the usual casual self-serve buffet eats, most of which are non-memorable. The venue includes a deli counter and pizzeria.

A patisserie offers specialty coffees and sweets (extra charge), and a so-called sushi bar off to one side of the atrium lobby bar on Promenade Deck is open prior to dinner only; the sushi could not be called authentic.

There is no specialty (extra-charge) restaurant, as aboard some of the larger ships in the fleet.

ENTERTAINMENT. The 1,010-seat Normandie Main Lounge is the showlounge, and the venue for large-scale production shows and major cabaret acts – although 20 pillars obstruct some views. During a typical cruise, there will be one or two high-energy production shows, with a cast of two lead singers and a clutch of dancers, backed by a large live band.

SPA/FITNESS. SpaCarnival is a large, glass-wrapped health, fitness, and spa complex. It is located on the uppermost interior deck forward. It includes a fitness room with ocean-view windows, with cardiovascular equipment, an aerobics room, changing rooms, sauna and steam rooms, beauty salon, and rooms for body treatments. Some fitness classes incur an extra charge.

There are also sports facilities for basketball, volleyball, and table tennis, plus a banked jogging track outdoors on the deck above the spa, and a mini-golf course.

CARNIVAL PRIDE
★★★

TRY THIS CASUAL SHIP FOR A FUN-FILLED, CONTEMPORARY FAMILY-FRIENDLY CRUISE

Size:	Mid-size Ship	Passenger/Crew Ratio (lower beds):	2.2
Tonnage:	85,920	Cabins (total):	1,062
Cruise Line:	Carnival Cruise Line	Size Range (sq ft/m):	185.0–490.0/17.1–45.5
Former Names:	none	Cabins (for one person):	0
Builder:	Kvaerner Masa-Yards (Finland)	Cabins with balcony:	750
Entered Service:	Jan 2002	Cabins (wheelchair accessible):	16
Length (ft/m):	959.6/292.5	Wheelchair accessibility:	Good
Beam (ft/m):	105.6/32.2	Elevators:	15
Propulsion/Propellers:	diesel-electric (62,370kW)/	Casino (gaming tables):	Yes
	2 azimuthing pods	Swimming Pools:	3 (1 w/ sliding glass dome)
Passenger Decks:	12	Self-Service Launderette:	Yes
Total Crew:	1,029	Library:	Yes
Passengers (lower beds):	2,124	Onboard currency:	US$
Passenger Space Ratio (lower beds):	40.4		

THE SHIP. *Carnival Pride* is sister to *Carnival Legend, Carnival Miracle,* and *Carnival Spirit,* with the same layout and configuration. Designed for families, the ship has plenty of facilities, so kids should have a great time.

While the open deck and sunbathing space is not extensive, there are two swimming pools: one can be covered by a sliding glass dome when needed, while a smaller pool is for children. An extra-charge, adults-only quiet area, Sanctuary, has its own bar, pool, hot tub, and other facilities, and is located at the aft on Lido Deck.

Inside, the interior decor has an art theme (including nude figures – reproductions from the Renaissance period). Even the elevator doors and interiors contain reproductions (blown-up, grainy photographic copies) of some the great masters such as Gauguin, Matisse, and Jacopo Vignali. It's all a bit of an eclectic mix, but somehow it all just about works.

An interior walkway, the Yellow Brick Road, connects many public rooms on Atlantic Deck, one deck above Promenade Deck, which also has a number of public rooms aft.

The colorful atrium lobby, which spans eight decks, has wall decorations best seen from any of the viewing balconies on any deck above the main lobby level. Take a drink from the lobby bar and look upwards – the surroundings are visually stunning, and include a huge reproduction of Raphael's *Nymph Galatea*.

BERLITZ'S RATINGS

	Possible	Achieved
Ship	500	333
Accommodation	200	124
Food	400	202
Service	400	244
Entertainment	100	62
Cruise Experience	400	240

OVERALL SCORE 1205 points out of 2000

Other facilities include a shopping street with boutique stores, photo gallery, video games room, a wedding chapel, and an observation balcony at the top of the multi-deck atrium. A large Winner's Club Casino (you have to walk though it to get to the main level of the showlounge from the restaurant) invites hopeful gamers and slot players.

Carnival Pride is a floating playground for the young and young-at-heart, and anyone who enjoys lots of participation events plus glitz, glamour, and gambling. This is a fun, all-American experience, but because it's a mid-sized ship, there could be lines for the likes of shore excursions, security control when re-boarding, and disembarkation, as well as sign-up sheets for fitness equipment.

Niggles include many annoying announcements, and constant hustling to get you to buy drinks, jewelry, and trinkets. Also, shore excursions are booked via the in-cabin 'Fun Vision' television system, so obtaining advice and suggestions is not easy. The small reception desk in the atrium lobby is almost always congested. It's hard to escape from noise and loud music (even in cabin hallways and lifts), and there are masses of people walking around day and night. Many private balconies can be overlooked from public locations. You need a credit card to open the personal safe in your cabin – impossible if you want to store all your credit cards and wallet inside it!

ACCOMMODATION. There are many cabin categories, priced by grade, location, and size. The range includes suites (with private balcony), outside-view cabins with private balcony, 68 ocean-view cabins with French doors (pseudo balconies that have doors which open, but no balcony to step out onto), and a healthy proportion of standard outside-view to interior cabins.

All cabins have spy-hole doors, twin beds that can convert into a queen-size bed, individually controlled air conditioning, television, and telephone. A number of cabins on the lowest deck have views that are obstructed by lifeboats. Some cabins can accommodate a third and fourth person, but they have little closet space, and there's only one personal safe.

Among the most desirable suites and cabins are those on five of the aft-facing decks; these have private balconies overlooking the stern. You might think that these units would suffer from vibration, but they don't – a bonus of the pod propulsion system.

For extra space (if the budget allows), it's worthwhile booking one of the larger deluxe balcony suites on Deck 6, with private teakwood balcony.

DINING. The 1,300-seat Normandie Restaurant, the main dining room, has seating on two levels. Choose either fixed-time dining (6pm or 8.15pm) or flexible dining (during restaurant opening hours). Note that the restaurant is not open for lunch on port days.

Overall, the food is quite starchy, with simple presentation, few garnishes, and many dishes disguised with gravies and sauces. The choice of fresh green vegetables, bread and bakery items (these are thawed and then baked from frozen 'starter' dough), cheeses, and fruits is limited, and there is much use of canned fruit and jellied desserts. Waiters sing and dance, so think 'foodertainment' rather than food

quality. Also, there are no wine waiters, and wine glasses are small. For something simple, an 'always available' list of 'Carnival Classics' includes mahi-mahi (fish), baby back ribs (beef), and grilled chicken.

For casual eaters, there's Mermaid's Grill Lido Restaurant – Guy's Burger Joint, Blue Iguana (Mexican fare) and Bonsai Sushi..

There's also David's Steakhouse, an upscale dining spot atop the ship, with just 156 seats and a show kitchen. There are great views over the atrium lobby and fine table settings, with proper china and silverware. Reservations are required and a charge applies.

ENTERTAINMENT. The glamorous 1,170-seat Taj Mahal Showlounge is the venue for large-scale Vegas-style (think feathers and skimpy costumes) productions, and cabaret shows. Spiral stairways at the back of the lounge connect all three levels. Directly underneath the showlounge is the Butterflies lounge and bar.

Almost every lounge/bar, including the Ivory Piano Bar, the Starry Night Jazz Club, and the Florentine Lounge, has live music in the evening. Finally, for the very lively, there's the Beauties Dance Club, a disco with DJs and loud beats; and there's always karaoke.

SPA/FITNESS. SpaCarnival, spanning two decks, is located directly above the navigation bridge. Facilities on the lower level include a solarium, eight treatment rooms, lecture rooms, sauna and steam rooms for men and women, and a beauty parlor. The upper level consists of a large gymnasium with forward-facing ocean views, and an aerobics room.

An outdoor jogging track is located around the ship's mast and the forward third of the ship, close to a basketball court and mini-golf.

CARNIVAL SENSATION
★★★

TRY THIS ULTRA-COLORFUL, CASUAL SHIP FOR A FIRST CRUISE

Size:	Mid-size Ship	Passenger/Crew Ratio (lower beds):	2.2
Tonnage:	70,536	Cabins (total):	1,020
Cruise Line:	Carnival Cruise Line	Size Range (sq ft/m):	173.2–409.7/16.0–38.0
Former Names:	Sensation	Cabins (for one person):	0
Builder:	Kvaerner Masa-Yards (Finland)	Cabins with balcony:	152
Entered Service:	Nov 1993	Cabins (wheelchair accessible):	20
Length (ft/m):	855.0/260.6	Wheelchair accessibility:	Fair
Beam (ft/m):	104.0/31.4	Elevators:	14
Propulsion/Propellers:	diesel-electric (42,240kW)/2	Casino (gaming tables):	Yes
Passenger Decks:	10	Swimming Pools:	3
Total Crew:	920	Self-Service Launderette:	Yes
Passengers (lower beds):	2,040	Library:	Yes
Passenger Space Ratio (lower beds):	34.4	Onboard currency:	US$

THE SHIP. *Carnival Sensation* is the third in a series of eight *Fantasy*-class sister ships (others: *Carnival Ecstasy, Carnival Elation, Carnival Fantasy, Carnival Fascination, Carnival Imagination, Carnival Inspiration,* and *Carnival Paradise*).

Carnival Sensation is well liked and good for families and party-goers taking a first cruise, but the open deck space is inadequate when the ship is full and everyone wants to be out on deck. The aft decks used to be less noisy when all the activities were focused around the main swimming pool and hot tubs, but now that the WaterWorks – with long and short water slides and water-burst fountains – has been added, it's the active area for familes with kids.

Serenity, however, is an extra-charge, quiet, adult-only space on Deck 9 aft.

There is no walk-around open promenade deck, although there is a short jogging track atop ship. The lifeboats, six of which double as shore tenders, are positioned high in the ship.

The interior is well designed, and the general passenger flow is good. It's is all about 'entertainment architecture' and is bright and cheerful throughout. The theme is the arts (in a sort of Art Nouveau style) and literature. It includes a colorful mix of classic and contemporary design elements.

The interior social meeting center is an 'open' atrium lobby, with a balconied shape; it spans six decks, and is topped by a glass domed roof. The low-

BERLITZ'S RATINGS

	Possible	Achieved
Ship	500	300
Accommodation	200	121
Food	400	200
Service	400	245
Entertainment	100	62
Cruise Experience	400	229

OVERALL SCORE 1157 points out of 2000

est level houses the purser's and shore-excursion desks, an Atrium Bar (with live music), plus a small sushi bar off to one side.

There are public entertainment lounges, bars, and clubs galore, with something for everyone (except quiet space). Most public rooms and attractions lead off from Sensation Boulevard – a shipboard Main Street, which runs between the showlounge (forward) and the Plaza Aft lounge, with Joe's Café a popular spot for coffees and teas. For gamers and slot players there's almost non-stop action in the Club Vegas Casino.

The Oak Room Library is a stately reading room, but, sadly, it has few books. Meanwhile, the Kaleidoscope Discotheque, with dozens of video monitors and dance floor, hits you with a dazzling variety of stimulating, electric colors.

This ship is definitely not for anyone seeking a quiet, relaxing cruise. Niggles include the many annoying announcements, and the never-ending hustling to incite you to buy drinks, jewelry, and trinkets. Also, shore excursions are booked via the infotainment system, so obtaining advice and suggestions in person is not easy.

ACCOMMODATION. There are many different accommodation price grades, ranked by facilities, size, and location. The standard outside-view and interior cabins have decor that is rather plain. They are fairly comfortable, and practical (most are of the same size and appointments), with good storage and no-non-sense bathrooms. However, if you have a queen-bed configuration instead of the standard twin-bed lay-out, note that one person has to clamber over the bed to get to the far side – a potentially ungainly exercise.

Suite occupants get more space, and more eclectic decor and furniture. Suites are reasonably attractive, but much smaller than those aboard ships of a similar size of competing companies. Some 50 cabins have interconnecting doors, which is good for families with children.

Room service is available 24 hours a day, although in standard cabins, only cold food is available; those in suite-grade accommodation get a greater range of items (both hot and cold) to choose from.

DINING. The two large main dining rooms, Fantasy and Ecstasy, are located amidships and aft. Both have ocean-view windows and very bright decor, and they are noisy. Choose either fixed-time dining (6pm or 8.15pm) or flexible dining (during opening hours).

The food is not very memorable, with simple presentation and few garnishes used. The selection of fresh green vegetables, bread, rolls (these, and other bakery items are first thawed, the baked, from frozen 'starter' dough), cheeses, and fruits is limited, and there is heavy use of rice, canned fruit, and jellied desserts. The waiters sing, dance, serve wine, and take part in waiter parades – so it's more about 'eatertainment' than food quality.

This is basic catering – with all its attendant standardization and production cooking, which makes it difficult to obtain anything unusual or 'off-menu.' For something simple, there's an 'always available' list of 'Carnival Classics,' including mahi mahi (fish), baby back ribs (beef), and grilled chicken (when the dining rooms are open). The two main dining rooms are not open for lunch on port days.

Other (complimentary) eateries include: the Seaview Bar & Grill (lido café), for self-serve buffet eats; Guy's Burger Joint, a poolside venue developed with Food Network personality Guy Fieri (for handmade burgers and freshly cut fries); and BlueIguana Cantina Mexican eatery (for Mexican snack food such as tacos and burritos). Poolside watering holes include a BlueIguana Tequila Bar and a RedFrog Rum Bar.

A patisserie offers specialty coffees and sweets (extra charge).

There is no specialty (extra-charge) restaurant, as aboard some of the larger ships in the fleet.

ENTERTAINMENT. The Fantasia Lounge is the showlounge, where Vegas-style (think feathers and skimpy costumes) production shows and major cabaret acts entertain the crowds. However, some 20 pillars obstruct the views from several seats.

SPA/FITNESS. SpaCarnival is a large, glass-wrapped health, fitness, and spa complex, located on the uppermost interior deck, forward of the ship's mast. It consists of a gymnasium with ocean-view windows and the latest muscle-pumping equipment, an aerobics exercise room, sauna and steam rooms, beauty salon, and rooms for body treatments. Some fitness classes (such as kick-boxing or yoga) incur an extra charge. A common complaint is that the area is not kept clean and tidy, and used towels are often strewn around the changing rooms.

Other sports for which there are facilities include basketball, volleyball, table tennis, and mini-golf.

CARNIVAL SPIRIT

★★★

GOOD FOR A FUN-FILLED, FAMILY-FRIENDLY CRUISE IN A CONTEMPORARY SETTING

Size:	Mid-size Ship
Tonnage:	85,920
Cruise Line:	Carnival Cruise Line
Former Names:	none
Builder:	Kvaerner Masa-Yards
Entered Service:	Apr 2001
Length (ft/m):	959.6/292.5
Beam (ft/m):	105.6/32.2
Propulsion/Propellers:	diesel-electric (62,370kW)/ 2 azimuthing pods
Passenger Decks:	12
Total Crew:	930
Passengers (lower beds):	2,124
Passenger Space Ratio (lower beds):	40.4
Passenger/Crew Ratio (lower beds):	2.2
Cabins (total):	1,062
Size Range (sq ft/m):	185.0–490.0/17.1–45.5
Cabins (for one person):	0
Cabins with balcony:	750
Cabins (wheelchair accessible):	16
Wheelchair accessibility:	Good
Elevators:	15
Casino (gaming tables):	Yes
Swimming Pools:	3 (1 w/ sliding glass dome)
Self-Service Launderette:	Yes
Library:	Yes
Onboard currency:	US$

THE SHIP. *Carnival Spirit* is a sister to *Carnival Legend*, *Carnival Miracle*, and *Carnival Pride*, with the same layout and configuration.

It's all about active entertainment. Following a 2012 refurbishment before the ship's Australia deployment, much of its outdoor deck space was designated a Water Park and Splash Zone, with water wheels, spraying jets, water blasters, pull ropes, two Mini Racer slides, and more.

Then there's the really big attraction, Green Thunder, a thrill ride that starts 100ft (30m) above sea level. The floor suddenly drops out of the platform, and you plummet in a near-vertical drop at about 23ft (7m) a second. When you hit the water in the fast water slide, you twist and turn through a transparent tube that extends over the side of the ship. Kids will love it, but need to be 42ins (1.1m) tall to be able to experience it. The open deck space is a bit tight when the ship sails at full capacity in warm-weather areas.

An extra-charge, adults-only area, Sanctuary, has its own bar, pool, hot tub, and other facilities. Located at the aft of the ship on Lido Deck, it is a pleasant area for anyone seeking a quieter space for sunbathing and relaxation – and to escape the many children on board during major holidays.

An interior walkway, named the Fashion Boulevard, connects many of the major public rooms on Atlantic Deck, one deck above Promenade Deck, which is also home to a number of public rooms, including a large Louis XIV Casino.

BERLITZ'S RATINGS

	Possible	Achieved
Ship	500	335
Accommodation	200	124
Food	400	202
Service	400	252
Entertainment	100	62
Cruise Experience	400	235

OVERALL SCORE 1210 points out of 2000

The colorful atrium lobby, which spans eight decks, has wall decorations best seen from any of the multiple viewing balconies on any deck above the main lobby level. Take a drink from the lobby bar and look upwards – the surroundings and artwork are visually stunning.

Perhaps the most dramatic room is the Pharaoh's Palace Showlounge, which spans three decks in the forward section. Directly underneath is the Versailles Lounge, which has a bar in its starboard aft section.

Other facilities include a winding shopping street with boutique stores, photo gallery, video games room, wedding chapel, and an observation balcony in the center of the vessel, at the top of the multi-deck atrium. The large Winner's Club Casino has many gaming tables and slot machines.

While the cuisine is just so-so, the real fun begins at sundown, when the ship excels in terms of sound, lights, razzle-dazzle shows, and late-night high-volume sounds.

ACCOMMODATION. There are many different cabin categories, priced by grade, location, and size. The range includes suites (with private balcony), outside-view cabins with private balcony, ocean-view cabins with French doors (pseudo balconies that have doors which open, but no balcony to step out onto), and a healthy proportion of standard outside-view to interior cabins.

Among the most desirable suites and cabins are those on five of the aft-facing decks; these have private balconies overlooking the stern and ship's wash. You might think that these units would suffer from vibration, but they don't – a bonus provided by the pod propulsion system. For extra space, book one of the larger deluxe balcony suites on Deck 6, with private teakwood balcony.

DINING. The Empire Restaurant is the large, two-deck-high, 1,250-seat main restaurant. Small rooms on both upper and lower levels can be closed off for groups of up to 60. Choose either fixed-time dining or flexible dining. The restaurant is not open for lunch on port days.

The food really is pretty starchy and non-memorable (it's mass catering, after all), with simple presentation and few garnishes. Also, many dishes are disguised with gravies and sauces. The selection of fresh green vegetables, bread and bakery items (these are thawed and then baked from frozen 'starter' dough), cheeses, and fruits is limited, and there is heavy use of rice, canned fruit, and jellied desserts. The waiters sing and dance, so think 'food-ertainment' rather than food quality. Also, there are no wine waiters, and the wine glasses are small. For something really simple, an 'always available' list of 'Carnival Classics' includes mahi-mahi (fish), baby back ribs (beef), and grilled chicken.

La Playa Grille Lido Restaurant is the large casual self-serve food court buffet-style eatery on Lido Deck aft. It includes a central area with a deli sandwich corner, Asian corner, rotisserie, salad bar, an international (Taste of the Nations) counter, and a 24-hour pizza counter. Both indoor and outdoor seating is available.

Other (complimentary) eateries include: Guy's Burger Joint, a poolside venue developed with Food Network personality Guy Fieri (for handmade burgers and freshly cut fries). Aft on the same deck is another Fieri-designed eatery for house-smoked favorites – called Guy's Pig & Anchor Bar-B-Que Smokehouse

(open at lunchtime on sea days only). There's also BlueIguana Cantina Mexican eatery (for Mexican snack food such as tacos and burritos). Poolside watering holes include a BlueIguana Tequila Bar and a RedFrog Rum Bar.

Nouveau Steakhouse is a premium (reservations-required) dining spot atop the ship, with 156 seats and a show kitchen. It is located on two of the uppermost decks of the ship, above the Lido Restaurant, in the lower, forward section of the funnel housing, with neat views over the colorful atrium lobby (actually, the four-person tables tucked beneath the overhang of the upper level are cozy and have ocean views). Fine table settings, china, and silverware are provided, a cover charge applies, and reservations are needed.

ENTERTAINMENT. The glamorous 1,167-seat Pharaoh's Palace is the venue for large-scale production shows and cabaret, which are best seen from the upper levels. Directly underneath the show-lounge is the Versailles Lounge and bar.

Almost every lounge/bar, including the Shanghai Piano Bar, the Club Cool Jazz Club, and the Artists' Lobby Lounge, has live music in the evening. Finally, for the very lively, there's the Dancin' Dance Club for thumping music; and there's always karaoke.

SPA/FITNESS. SpaCarnival spans two decks; it is located directly above the navigation bridge and has 13,700 sq ft (1,272 sq m) of space. Facilities on the lower level include a solarium, eight treatment rooms, lecture rooms, sauna and steam rooms for men and women, and a beauty parlor. The upper level consists of a large gymnasium with floor-to-ceiling windows on three sides, including forward-facing ocean views, and an aerobics room with instructor-led classes.

There are two centrally located pools outdoors, one with a retractable glass dome cover. An outdoor jogging track is located around the ship's mast: it doesn't go around the whole ship, but it's long enough for some decent walking.

CARNIVAL SPLENDOR
★★★

THIS FAMILY-FRIENDLY, FUN-FILLED SHIP HAS A GREAT WATERPARK

Size:	Large Resort Ship	Passenger/Crew Ratio (lower beds):	2.5
Tonnage:	113,323	Cabins (total):	1,487
Cruise Line:	Carnival Cruise Line	Size Range (sq ft/m):	179.7–484.2/16.7–44.8
Former Names:	none	Cabins (for one person):	0
Builder:	Fincantieri (Italy)	Cabins with balcony:	574
Entered Service:	Jul 2008	Cabins (wheelchair accessible):	25
Length (ft/m):	951.4/290.0	Wheelchair accessibility:	Good
Beam (ft/m):	105.6/32.2	Elevators:	18
Propulsion/Propellers:	... diesel-electric (63,400kW)/2	Casino (gaming tables):	Yes
Passenger Decks:	13	Swimming Pools:	3
Total Crew:	1,150	Self-Service Launderette:	Yes
Passengers (lower beds):	2,974	Library:	Yes
Passenger Space Ratio (lower beds):	37.0	Onboard currency:	US$

THE SHIP. *Carnival Splendor* shares the same generally balanced profile as sisters *Carnival Conquest, Carnival Freedom, Carnival Glory, Carnival Liberty, Carnival Sunshine, Carnival Triumph, Carnival Valor,* and *Carnival Victory,* although it was originally designated as a ship for Costa Cruises.

The deck and public room layout is fairly logical (although it is a bit disjointed). Most of the public rooms are located on one deck off a main interior boulevard, above a deck that contains the two main dining rooms. The interior decor is basically 50 shades of pink.

Public rooms include a large Royal Flush Casino, with gaming tables and an array of over 300 slot machines.

Recalling the drive-in movie theaters of the 1950s, the Seaside Theater shows movies, and sports features on deck, with seating in tiered rows and the screen facing forward (popcorn obligatory, of course). The ship has bow-to-stern Wi-Fi Internet access (for a fee), and this includes all passenger cabins.

Carnival Splendor is a floating playground for the young and young-at-heart, and anyone who enjoys constant stimulation and lots of participation events, together with the three 'Gs' – glitz, glamour, and gambling. This really is cruising Splash Vegas style – a fun, all-American experience. Because it's a mid-sized ship, there can be lines for shore excursions, security control when re-boarding, dis-

BERLITZ'S RATINGS		
	Possible	Achieved
Ship	500	339
Accommodation	200	127
Food	400	202
Service	400	244
Entertainment	100	62
Cruise Experience	400	235
OVERALL SCORE 1209 points out of 2000		

embarkation, and sign-up sheets for fitness equipment.

The *sine qua non* of a Carnival cruise is all about having fun, which begins at sundown, with sound, lights, razzle-dazzle shows, and late-night high-volume sounds.

Minor niggles include the many pillars obstruct passenger flow, particularly in the dining rooms, making it difficult for the waiters to serve properly, and the food itself (particularly the bakery items), which is just so-so.

Note that in 2019 *Carnival Splendor* will be transferred to P&O Cruises (Australia), and, following a period of refurbishment, the onboard product will be modified to suit Australasian tastes.

ACCOMMODATION. There are many different cabin price categories, in seven suite/cabin types, sizes, and grades. These include suites and 'spa' suites with balcony; deluxe outside-view cabins with private balcony; outside-view cabins with private balcony; outside-view cabins with window; cabins with a porthole instead of a window; interior cabins; and interior cabins with upper and lower berths (good for families with very small children). There are five decks of cabins with private balconies. Note that cabins on Deck 12 are subject to lots of noise from kids having fun on the deck above – so forget that afternoon nap.

Although there is room service, the menu is poor – mainly limited to uninspiring sandwiches.

DINING. There are two main dining rooms, the 744-seat Black Pearl, located amidships, and the 1,122-seat Gold Pearl, located aft. Both are two decks high and include a balcony level – Gold Pearl is the larger of the two balconies. There's a choice of either fixed-time dining (6pm or 8.15pm) or flexible dining (any time between 5.45pm and 9.30pm). There are few tables for two, but my favorites are the two tables for two, right at the back of the Gold Pearl restaurant, with ocean views aft. Note that the two main dining rooms are not open for lunch on port days.

Don't even think about a quiet table for two, or a candlelit dinner on deck. This is all about table mates, social talk, lively meals, fast eating, and fast service. Tables do have tablecloths, silverware, and iced water/iced tea whenever you want it.

Overall, the food is quite starchy, with simple presentation, few garnishes, and many dishes disguised with gravies and sauces. The choice of fresh green vegetables, bread and bakery items (these are thawed and then baked from frozen 'starter' dough), cheeses, and fruits is limited, and there is heavy use of rice, canned fruit and jellied desserts.

'Spa Carnival Fare' provides a healthier food option; vegetarian and children's menus are also available, but they wouldn't get a generous score for their nutritional content.

The extra-cost (reservations-required) Pinnacle Steakhouse has fine table settings, china, and silverware, leather-bound menus, and seats 108. The specialties are USDA dry-aged prime steaks and seafood items.

Lido Restaurant is a casual self-serve international food court-style eatery. Included in this eating mall are a New York-style deli, a 24-hour pizzeria, and a grill for fast foods such as burgers and hot dogs; one section has a tandoori oven for Indian-theme items. The salad bar, however, is poor.

ENTERTAINMENT. The large, multi-deck Spectacular Showlounge seats 1,400, and hosts colorful large-scale entertainment including Vegas-style production shows (all feathers and skimpy costumes) and major cabaret acts. It has a revolving stage, hydraulic orchestra pit, excellent sound, and seating on three levels. The upper levels are tiered through two decks.

An alternative entertainment venue is the El Morocco, a 425-seat lounge located aft; this typically features live music and late-night cabaret acts including smutty adult comedy. Adjacent is the Grand Piano Lounge/Bar.

SPA/FITNESS. The Cloud 9 Spa spans two decks (with a total area of around 40,000 sq ft/3,716 sq m, including the 16 spa suites – or 13,000 sq ft/1,207 sq m, excluding them). Located directly above the navigation bridge in the forward part of the ship, it is accessed from the forward stairway.

Facilities on the lower level include a gymnasium, solarium, a thermal suite (a number of saunas and steam rooms – some infused with herbal aromas), thalassotherapy pool (check out the huge Chinese dogs), and a beauty salon. The upper level houses 17 massage/body treatment rooms, including two VIP suites (one for couples, one configured for wheelchair access), Rasul chamber (Mediterranean mud treatment – best for couples), flotation therapy room, treatment rooms, and outdoor relaxation areas on both port and starboard sides with integrated massage cabana. To use the thermal suite, there's an extra cost.

CARNIVAL SUNSHINE
★★★

THIS VIBRANT SHIP IS GOOD FOR A FIRST-TIME, ACTIVE CRUISE EXPERIENCE

Size:	Large Resort Ship	Passenger/Crew Ratio (lower beds):	2.6
Tonnage:	102,853	Cabins (total):	1,503
Cruise Line:	Carnival Cruise Line	Size Range (sq ft/m):	179.7–482.2/16.7–44.8
Former Names:	Carnival Destiny	Cabins (for one person):	0
Builder:	Fincantieri (Italy)	Cabins with balcony:	418
Entered Service:	Nov 1996	Cabins (wheelchair accessible):	25
Length (ft/m):	892.3/272.0	Wheelchair accessibility:	Good
Beam (ft/m):	116.0/35.3	Elevators:	18
Propulsion/Propellers:	diesel-electric (63,400kW)/2	Casino (gaming tables):	Yes
Passenger Decks:	12	Swimming Pools:	3 (1 w/ sliding glass dome)
Total Crew:	1,150	Self-Service Launderette:	Yes
Passengers (lower beds):	3,006	Library:	Yes
Passenger Space Ratio (lower beds):	34.2	Onboard currency:	US$

THE SHIP. *Carnival Sunshine* (formerly *Carnival Destiny*) was the first cruise ship with a gross tonnage that exceeded 100,000. After a lengthy refurbishment, the ship shouts 'Party, party, party!' It's a good ship for families with children.

The ship – now over 20 years old – has short bows and a distinctive, large, swept-back wing-tipped funnel. Tiered sunbathing decks positioned between small swimming pools, several hot tubs, and a large poolside movie screen have transformed the area.

Also, on the open deck and aft of the funnel is WaterWorks, including a 334ft (101.8m) Twister water slide, and Speedway Splash slide – so you and a competitor race down the Twister to a splashy finish.

The interior decor is a sensory wonderland. There are three decks full of lounges and bars, lots of rooms to play in, and a double-width indoor promenade. A glass-domed rotunda Sunshine Atrium lobby – with bar, two panoramic elevators and dual stairway – is nine decks high. An always-busy Sunshine Casino has ample gaming tables for serious gamers, and over 320 slot machines.

In spring 2013 a much-needed makeover (costing $155 million) lasted almost three months and added two half-decks at the front of the ship, extended two other decks aft, added 182 cabins (but no extra elevators), and several new and other revamped eateries. Public rooms include Piano Bar 88 (named for the 88 keys on a grand piano); Alchemy Bar, for 'mixologist'

BERLITZ'S RATINGS

	Possible	Achieved
Ship	500	332
Accommodation	200	123
Food	400	204
Service	400	247
Entertainment	100	62
Cruise Experience	400	240

OVERALL SCORE 1208 points out of 2000

cocktails; a (music-free) Library Bar; a Sports Bar (interactive, with results on a 24/7 sports ticker); and an art gallery.

What's it like? *Carnival Sunshine* is a floating playground for the young. The cuisine is not at all memorable, but there's plenty to do for all the family. Because it's a large resort ship, there will be lines for shore excursions, security control when re-boarding, and disembarkation, as well as sign-up sheets for fitness equipment. Other downsides include the many annoying announcements and the never-ending hustle to get you to buy alcoholic drinks full of ice and other items.

ACCOMMODATION. There are several accommodation categories (Captain's Suite, Grand Suite, Ocean Suite, Premium Balcony Cabin, Scenic Oceanview Cabin, Oceanview Cabin, Interior Cabin, and Small Interior), and several price grades, depending on size and location. Over half of all cabins have ocean views, and, at 225 sq ft (21 sq m), they are a decent size. Some cabins, spread over four decks, have private balconies with glass rather than steel balustrades for better, unobstructed ocean views; balconies have bright fluorescent lighting. However, there are many, many interior (no-view) cabins.

During the 2013 refit, 95 Cloud 9 Spa Cabins were added over three decks in the front of the ship, adjacent to the Cloud 9 Spa and Serenity adult-only area;

these have all the usual fittings, plus special spa-like extras, and access to the Cloud 9 Spa.

Standard cabins are of an adequate size and come equipped with all the basics, although the furniture is angular (think Ikea flatpack). Three decks of cabins (eight on each deck, each with private balcony) overlook the stern – these are very nice.

Three categories of cabins, both outside and interior, have upper and lower bunk beds, which is useful for families with small children.

Note that the soundproofing between cabins is poor and cabin doors have (non-closable) vents, so any noise from the hallway filters through.

DINING. There are two main restaurants: the Sunrise Forward Dining Room, with windows on two sides; and the Sunrise Aft Dining Room, with windows on three sides). Each is a single deck high and has bright, modern design and decor.

The Sunset dining room has a wall of glass overlooking the stern. There are tables for four, six, and eight and even a few tables for two – nice for honeymooners. Choose either fixed-time dining (6pm or 8.15pm) or flexible dining (during opening hours). Although menu choices look good, the actual cuisine delivered is unmemorable. Still, the waiters try to impress with lots of dancing on tables and other hoopla, telling everyone they're having fun. Note that the two main dining rooms are not open for lunch on port days.

The Carnival is not known for good food. It really is carbohydrate-rich, with simple presentation and few garnishes. Many dishes are disguised with gravies and sauces. The selection of fresh green vegetables, bread and bakery items (these are thawed and then baked from frozen 'starter' dough), cheeses, and fruit is limited, and there is heavy use of rice, canned fruit, and jellied desserts. The waiters sing and dance, so think 'foodertainment' rather than food quality. Also, there are no wine waiters, and the wine glasses are small. For something really simple, an 'always available' list of 'Carnival Classics' includes mahi-mahi (fish), baby back ribs (beef), and grilled chicken.

Fahrenheit 555 Steakhouse is an extra-cost, reservations-required dining spot for fine steaks (arguably worth the extra money) and grilled seafood dishes. There are many tables for two, although they are close together, as well as larger tables, and the seating is comfortable.

For casual eats, Ocean Plaza (Lido Market Place) is an international food court-style self-serve eatery with plenty of food displays (it's a copy of the self-serve Markt Restaurants aboard AIDA Cruises' ships). It includes a 24-hour pizzeria (Pizzeria del Capitano). There's no bar in the venue itself – but there are several on the adjacent pool deck.

A JavaBlue Café with 'comfort' snacks is in the Fun Hub Internet-connect area. A Havana Bar is located within the Market Place, as is a RedFrog Pub, pouring Carnival's own house brew, ThirstyFrog Red. Adjacent, but outside, are: Cucina del Capitano (for Italian cuisine, with made-to-order pasta dishes); the BlueIguana Cantina Mexican-style street eatery (for tacos and burritos); Ji Ji's Asian Kitchen, which features lunchtime stir-fry dishes; a pizzeria; a patisserie (extra charge for pastries); a car-culture-inspired Guy's Burger Joint for fast foods including burgers and hot dogs; and a RedFrog Rum Bar.

For something more unusual, or to celebrate, you can also choose to eat at the Chef's Table (it's reserved for only 12 hungry diners, at $75 each), which includes a look into the galley when it's in full operation, followed by a specially prepared multi-course dinner.

ENTERTAINMENT. The two-level Liquid Lounge – the ship's showlounge, which seats 800 and is the setting for high-energy production legs-and-feathers shows and large-scale cabaret acts – is quite stunning. It has a revolving stage, hydraulic orchestra pit, good sound, and seating on three levels (the upper levels being tiered through two decks). A proscenium arch over the stage acts as a scenery loft.

Other entertainment options include a Hasbro Game Show and the Punchliner Comedy Club presented by George Lopez, and, the Liquid Lounge for those high-volume disco sounds.

SPA/FITNESS. Cloud 9 Spa spans two decks, and encompasses 13,700 sq ft (1,272 sq m). It is located above the navigation bridge, and is accessible via the forward stairway. Lower-level facilities include a solarium, body treatment rooms, sauna and steam rooms for men and women, and a beauty salon; the upper level houses a fitness room with ocean-view windows on three sides, and an aerobics room for instructor-led classes (some at extra cost).

SportSquare is an outdoor recreation area with a suspended ropes course (and some great views).

CARNIVAL TRIUMPH
★★★

THIS IS A FLOATING FUN PALACE FOR ULTRA-CASUAL FAMILY CRUISING

Size:	Large Resort Ship	Passenger/Crew Ratio (lower beds):	2.3
Tonnage:	101,509	Cabins (total):	1,379
Cruise Line:	Carnival Cruise Lin4	Size Range (sq ft/m):	179.7–482.2/16.7–44.8
Former Names:	none	Cabins (for one person):	0
Builder:	Fincantieri (Italy)	Cabins with balcony:	508
Entered Service:	Oct 1999	Cabins (wheelchair accessible):	25
Length (ft/m):	893.0/272.2	Wheelchair accessibility:	Good
Beam (ft/m):	116.0/35.3	Elevators:	18
Propulsion/Propellers:	diesel-electric (34,000kW)/	Casino (gaming tables):	Yes
	2 azimuthing pods	Swimming Pools:	3 (1 w/ sliding glass dome)
Passenger Decks:	13	Self-Service Launderette:	Yes
Total Crew:	1,100	Library:	Yes
Passengers (lower beds):	2,758	Onboard currency:	US$
Passenger Space Ratio (lower beds):	36.8		

THE SHIP. *Carnival Triumph* is a contemporary ship, with extremely short bows (the pointy bit at the front) and swept-wing funnel in red, white, and blue. It is designed specifically for families with children, who probably won't want to leave when the cruise is over. The ship underwent quite an extensive facelift in 2013, which added new facilities and eating options.

Outside on Lido Deck, there is one small pool (with adjacent hot tubs – although the whole area is extremely cluttered and congested), and one aft pool (with retractable glass roof for use in poor weather conditions). Note that there are no cushioned pads for the sunloungers, but there is a large poolside movie screen. Also outside is a long water slide, which travels 200 ft (60m) from just aft of the ship's mast.

Inside, the decor is quite tasteful, and is themed around great European cities including Rome and Paris. The layout is fairly logical and it's quite easy to find one's way around. There are basically three decks full of bars and lounges to enjoy.

The interior focal point is a main (atrium) lobby, which is nine decks high and topped by a glass-domed roof. The lowest deck features a square-shaped bar, facing forward to glass-walled elevators. *Carnival Triumph* is a floating playground for the young, and anyone who enjoys constant stimulation and participation events, together with the three 'Gs' – glitz, glamour, and gambling. The cuisine is not

BERLITZ'S RATINGS

	Possible	Achieved
Ship	500	332
Accommodation	200	124
Food	400	201
Service	400	242
Entertainment	100	61
Cruise Experience	400	235

OVERALL SCORE 1195 points out of 2000

much to write home about, but, hey, this is cruising Splash Vegas style – and it's a fun, all-American experience. Because it's a large resort ship, expect lines for the likes of shore excursions, security control when re-boarding, and disembarkation, plus sign-up sheets for fitness equipment. Getting away from noise is difficult.

ACCOMMODATION. There are numerous price categories, depending on the grade, location and size you choose. Over half of all cabins are outside and measure 225 sq ft (21 sq m). They are spread over four decks and have private balconies extending from the ship's side, with glass rather than steel balustrades for unobstructed ocean views, and bright fluorescent lighting. They are of good size and have all the basics, although the furniture is angular, with no rounded edges. Three decks of cabins – eight per deck, each with private balcony – overlook the stern.

Many cabins have upper and lower bunk beds – good for families with small children. Interactive 'Fun Vision' technology includes movies on demand, for a fee. The bathrooms, which have good-size showers, have good storage space for toiletries.

Book one of the suites, and you get Skipper's Club priority benefits and other perks.

DINING. There are two main dining rooms, one forward (London) with windows on two sides and 706 seats, and the other (Paris) aft with windows on three sides and 1,090 seats. Each spans two decks, and incorporates a dozen domes and chandeliers. Tables are for two to eight. The dining room entrances have comfortable drinking areas for pre-dinner cocktails.

You can choose either fixed-time dining (6pm or 8.15pm), or flexible dining (during opening times). Although the menu choice looks good, the actual cuisine delivered is adequate, nothing more. Note that the two main dining rooms are not open for lunch on port days.

The food really is rather starchy and non-memorable, with simple presentation, few garnishes, and many dishes disguised with gravies and sauces. The selection of fresh green vegetables, bread, and bakery items (these are thawed and then baked from frozen 'starter' dough), cheeses, and fruit is limited, and there is heavy use of rice, canned fruit, and jellied desserts. The waiters sing and dance, so think 'foodertainment' rather than food quality. Also, there are no wine waiters, and the wine glasses are small. For something really simple, an 'always available' list of 'Carnival Classics' includes mahi-mahi (fish), baby back ribs (beef), and grilled chicken.

The Steakhouse is a reservations-required extra-cost venue, featuring prime steaks and grilled seafood. It has fine table settings, china, and silverware, leather-bound menus, and decor set around Scarlett O'Hara, the heroine of Margaret Mitchell's classic novel *Gone With the Wind*.

For ultra-casual eating, go to the Lido Deck self-serve buffet area. There are several sections (the ship's decor theme is, after all, international) including a deli, and an Asian section. Outside on deck and adjacent is a pizzeria, Guy's Burger Joint (for burgers, hand-cut fries, and assorted toppings), and the BlueIguana Cantina. The buffet itself is congested for much of the time, particularly for breakfast (my advice would be to go to one of the main dining rooms for a more relaxed breakfast).

Revamped bars include a poolside RedFrog Rum Bar (where you can also get ThirstyFrog Red – Carnival's private-label draft brew), BlueIguana Tequila Bar (for frozen Mexican-style cocktails and tequila), and a Sports Bar (an interactive venue with video games and a 24/7 sports ticker).

ENTERTAINMENT. The three-level Rome Main Lounge is a stunning room, with a revolving stage, hydraulic orchestra pit, loud sound, and seating on three levels, the upper levels being tiered through two decks. A proscenium arch over the stage acts as a scenery loft.

SPA/FITNESS. SpaCarnival spans two decks, and is located directly above the navigation bridge, and accessed from the forward stairway. Lower-level facilities include a solarium, massage/body treatment rooms, sauna and steam rooms for men and women, and a beauty parlor; the upper level consists of a large gymnasium with floor-to-ceiling windows on three sides, including ocean views, and an aerobics room with instructor-led classes, some at extra cost.

CARNIVAL VALOR
★★★

THIS CASUAL FLOATING FUN PALACE IS A GOOD CHOICE FOR THE WHOLE FAMILY

Size:	Large Resort Ship	Passenger/Crew Ratio (lower beds):	2.3
Tonnage:	110,239	Cabins (total):	1,487
Cruise Line:	Carnival Cruise Line	Size Range (sq ft/m):	179.7–482.2/16.7–44.8
Former Names:	none	Cabins (for one person):	0
Builder:	Fincantieri (Italy)	Cabins with balcony:	574
Entered Service:	Dec 2004	Cabins (wheelchair accessible):	25
Length (ft/m):	951.4/290.0	Wheelchair accessibility:	Good
Beam (ft/m):	116.0/35.3	Elevators:	18
Propulsion/Propellers:	diesel-electric (34,000kW)/2	Casino (gaming tables):	Yes
Passenger Decks:	13	Swimming Pools:	3 (1 w/ sliding glass dome)
Total Crew:	1,160	Self-Service Launderette:	Yes
Passengers (lower beds):	2,974	Library:	Yes
Passenger Space Ratio (lower beds):	37.0	Onboard currency:	US$

THE SHIP. *Carnival Valor* is one of a series of look-alike ships; the others are *Carnival Conquest, Carnival Freedom, Carnival Glory, Carnival Liberty, Carnival Splendor, Carnival Sunshine, Carnival Triumph, Carnival Valor,* and *Carnival Victory.*

Amidships on the open deck, a water slide (200ft/60m) spans two decks and empties onto the pool deck below, which also has a large movie (Seaside Theater) screen. The terraced pool deck is cluttered, particularly at sea when the ship is full, and there are no cushioned pads for the deck chairs. Aft of the funnel an extra-cost Serenity retreat just for adults provides quiet sunbathing space and a pool with retractable glass dome.

Inside are three decks full of lounges, 10 bars, and lots of rooms to play in. Public rooms are given a visual theme, and, on *Carnival Valor,* this is about famous personalities, including the dancer and singer Josephine Baker and the aviator Charles Lindbergh. The layout is fairly logical and easy to navigate.

There is a double-width indoor promenade, and an atrium lobby that spans nine decks, topped by a glass dome. A square-shaped bar sits on the lowest deck of the atrium, and faces forward towards panoramic glass-walled elevators. A sports bar has tables displaying sports memorabilia.

The ship is a floating playground for the young-at-heart and anyone who enjoys taking part in the many participation events, together with glitz, glamour, and gambling (the Shogun Casino is large, and has an abundance of gaming tables and slot machines). Among other attractions are the Iliad Library (nice, but there are few books), Winston's Cigar Bar, One Small Step (disco/nightclub – think loud, loud, loud), the Lindy Hop Piano Bar, and the Paris Hot Bar. The real fun begins at sundown, when Carnival excels in lights, razzle-dazzle shows, and late-night high volume sounds.

On the downside, because it's a large resort ship, you can expect lines for shore excursions, security control when re-boarding, and disembarkation, as well as sign-up sheets for fitness equipment. Getting away from people and noise is also virtually impossible.

ACCOMMODATION. There are numerous price categories, depending on grade, location and size. Over half of all cabins are outside, and, at 225 sq ft (21 sq m), they are among the largest in the standard market. They are spread over four decks and have private balconies extending from the ship's side; these have glass rather than steel balustrades for unobstructed ocean views, as well as bright fluorescent lighting. The standard cabins are of good size and have all the basics, although the furniture is angular, with no rounded edges. Three decks of cabins – eight per deck, each with private balcony – overlook the stern.

There are eight penthouse suites, each with a large private balcony. Although quite decent in their appointments, at only 483 sq ft (44.9 sq m), they are

BERLITZ'S RATINGS

	Possible	Achieved
Ship	500	334
Accommodation	200	124
Food	400	201
Service	400	241
Entertainment	100	61
Cruise Experience	400	236

OVERALL SCORE 1197 points out of 2000

really quite small when compared to the best suites even in smaller ships. In cabins with balconies, the partition between each balcony is open at top and bottom, so you may well hear noise from neighbors.

There are also three cabin categories with upper and lower bunk beds – lower beds are far more preferable (unless you have kids), but this is how the ships absorb hundreds of extra passengers over and above the lower bed capacity.

Interactive 'Fun Vision' technology lets you choose movies on demand, for a fee. Note: the room service menu is poor, as is cabin soundproofing.

DINING. The ship has two main dining rooms, one forward (Lincoln) with windows on two sides and 706 seats, and the other (Washington) aft with windows on three sides and 1,090 seats. Each spans two decks, and features a dozen domes and chandeliers. Washington has two-deck-high glass walls overlooking the stern. Tables are for four, six, and eight. There are even a few tables for two – good for honeymooners who want to be by themselves.

Choose either fixed-time dining (6pm or 8.15pm), or flexible dining (during opening hours). The dining room entrances have comfortable drinking areas for pre-dinner cocktails. Note that the two main dining rooms are not open for lunch on port days.

The food really is pretty starchy and non-memorable (it's mass catering, after all), with simple presentation and few garnishes. Also, many dishes are disguised with sauces. The selection of fresh green vegetables, bread, and bakery items (these are thawed and then baked from frozen 'starter' dough), cheeses, and fruit is limited, and there is heavy use of rice, canned fruit, and jellied desserts. The waiters sing and dance, so think 'foodertainment' rather than food quality. Also, there are no wine waiters, and the wine glasses are small. For something really simple, an 'always available' list of 'Carnival Classics'

includes mahi-mahi (fish), baby back ribs (beef), and grilled chicken.

There are also options for more casual dining. A self-serve buffet-style eatery has seating on two levels. Included are a New York-style deli, a Chinese restaurant with wok preparation, and a 24-hour pizzeria, which typically serves an average of more than 800 pizzas every day.

A (complimentary) Guy's Burger Joint was added in a 2016 refurbishment - the free-of-charge poolside venue was developed in partnership with TV's Food Network personality Guy Fieri for handmade burgers and freshly cut fries.

Scarlett's Steakhouse is a reservations-only, extra-cost dining spot, featuring prime USDA steaks and grilled seafood. It has fine table settings, china, and silverware, as well as leather-bound menus, and a design theme set around Scarlett O'Hara, the heroine of Margaret Mitchell's classic novel *Gone With the Wind*. It's worth the extra cost, if you like really good steaks.

ENTERTAINMENT. The three-level Ivanhoe showlounge is stunning; it has a revolving stage, hydraulic orchestra pit, superb sound, and seating on three levels, the upper levels being tiered through two decks. A proscenium arch over the stage acts as a scenery loft. Aft is a smaller Eagles Lounge, for cabaret and smutty late-night 'comedy.'

SPA/FITNESS. SpaCarnival spans two decks, and measures 13,700 sq ft (1,272 sq m). It is located above the navigation bridge, and accessed from the forward stairway. Facilities on the lower level include a solarium, eight treatment rooms, lecture rooms, sauna and steam rooms for men and women, and a beauty parlor; the upper level consists of a large gymnasium with floor-to-ceiling windows on three sides, including forward-facing ocean views, and an aerobics room with instructor-led classes, some at extra cost.

CARNIVAL VICTORY
★★★

A FUN SHIP FOR A FAMILY-FRIENDLY FIRST CRUISE ADVENTURE

Size:	Large Resort Ship
Tonnage:	101,509
Cruise Line:	Carnival Cruise Line
Former Names:	none
Builder:	Fincantieri (Italy)
Entered Service:	Aug 2000
Length (ft/m):	893.0/272.2
Beam (ft/m):	116.0/35.3
Propulsion/Propellers:	... diesel-electric (34,000kW)/ 2 azimuthing pods
Passenger Decks:	13
Total Crew:	1,100
Passengers (lower beds):	2,758
Passenger Space Ratio (lower beds):	36.8
Passenger/Crew Ratio (lower beds):	2.3
Cabins (total):	1,379
Size Range (sq ft/m):	179.7–482.2/16.7–44.8
Cabins (for one person):	0
Cabins with balcony:	508
Cabins (wheelchair accessible):	25
Wheelchair accessibility:	Good
Elevators:	18
Casino (gaming tables):	Yes
Swimming Pools:	3 (1 w/ sliding glass dome)
Self-Service Launderette:	Yes
Library:	Yes
Onboard currency:	US$

THE SHIP. *Carnival Victory's* sister ships are *Carnival Conquest, Carnival Freedom, Carnival Glory, Carnival Liberty, Carnival Sunshine* (originally named *Carnival Destiny*), *Carnival Valor,* and *Carnival Victory.* The ship has extremely short bows (the front), but still looks balanced overall. From a safety viewpoint, passengers can embark directly into the lifeboats from their secured position without having to wait for them to be lowered, thus saving time in the event of a real emergency.

This is a large, family-friendly resort ship with upper exterior decks full of sports and waterpark attractions (note that sunloungers don't have cushioned pads). The layout is logical and fairly easy to navigate. The theme of the interior decor is the oceans of the world, with seahorses, corals, and shells proliferating.

There are three decks full of lounges, 10 bars, and lots of rooms to explore and play in (including an expansive South China Sea Club Casino, with gaming tables and slot machines). There is a double-width indoor promenade, with statues of Neptune at both ends, and a glass-domed rotunda atrium lobby spans nine decks. On the lowest level is a square-shaped bar, which faces glass-walled panorama elevators.

Niggles include standing in lines for shore excursions, security control when re-boarding, and disembarkation, and well as for filling in sign-up sheets for fitness equipment.

BERLITZ'S RATINGS

	Possible	Achieved
Ship	500	329
Accommodation	200	124
Food	400	201
Service	400	238
Entertainment	100	61
Cruise Experience	400	234

OVERALL SCORE 1187 points out of 2000

Don't go for the cuisine because it's really not that good. The real fun on this ship begins at sundown when lights, razzle-dazzle shows, and late-night high volume sounds abound.

ACCOMMODATION. The price you pay depends on the grade, location and size you choose. Over half of all cabins have outside views and, at 225 sq ft (21 sq m), are quite large.

Standard cabins are of decent size and have all the basics, although the furniture is angular, and the decor is bland; the bathrooms, however, are quite practical. Soundproofing could be better.

Cabins with balconies (those overlooking the stern are really nice) have glass rather than steel balustrades for unobstructed ocean views, and bright lighting. Note that the partition between each balcony is open at top and bottom, so you will hear noise from neighbors.

Eight penthouse suites each measure only 483 sq ft (44.9 sq m), and are small when compared to the suites aboard the competitor's ships.

DINING. There are two main dining rooms, the Atlantic (forward) with windows on two sides and 706 seats, and the Pacific (aft) with windows on three sides and 1,090 seats. Each spans two decks, and features a dozen domes and chandeliers. Tables are for four to eight, and even a few tables for two. The dining room entrances have comfortable drinking areas.

Choose either fixed-time dining (6pm or 8.15pm) or flexible dining (during opening hours. Although the menu choice looks good, the actual cuisine delivered is adequate, but quite unmemorable. Note that the two main dining rooms are not open for lunch on port days.

The food really is pretty starchy and non-memorable (it's mass catering, after all), with simple presentation and few garnishes. Many dishes are disguised with gravies and sauces. The choice of fresh green vegetables, bread and bakery items (these are thawed and then baked from frozen 'starter' dough), cheeses, and fruit is limited, and there is heavy use of rice, canned fruit, and jellied desserts. The waiters sing and dance, so think 'foodertainment' rather than food quality. Also, there are no wine waiters, and the wine glasses are small. For something really simple, an 'always available' list of 'Carnival Classics' includes mahi-mahi (fish), baby back ribs (beef), and grilled chicken.

A casual 'international' self-serve buffet-style eatery (the Mediterranean Lido Restaurant) has seating on two levels. It includes a deli (for sandwiches and wraps), a Yangtze Wok, a Mississippi BBQ, a Seafood Shack, and a pizzeria (Pizzeria Arno), which often provides over 800 pizzas every day.

The one reservations-only, extra-cost dining spot is The Steakhouse. It features prime USDA steaks and grilled seafood items (perhaps worth paying extra for, if the budget allows). It has fine table settings, china, and silverware, as well as leather-bound menus, and a design theme set around Scarlett O'Hara, the heroine of Margaret Mitchell's classic novel *Gone With the Wind*.

ENTERTAINMENT. The three-level Caribbean Main Lounge (showlounge) is stunning; it has a revolving stage, hydraulic orchestra pit, and seating on three levels, the upper levels being tiered through two decks. A proscenium arch over the stage acts as a scenery loft. Other entertainment spots include the Club Arctic (disco), Adriatic Aft Lounge (for cabaret and late-night adult-only 'comedy'), and the Irish Sea Piano Bar (good for singalongs).

SPA/FITNESS. SpaCarnival spans two decks, with 13,700 sq ft (1,272 sq m), and is located directly above the navigation bridge. Flower-level facilities include a solarium, body treatment rooms, sauna and steam rooms for men and women, and a beauty parlor; the upper level consists of a large fitness area with ocean-view windows, and an aerobics room with instructor-led classes, some at extra cost.

CARNIVAL VISTA
★★★+

A SHIP FOR FAMILY FUN ENTERTAINMENT AND CARDIO-ACTIVE OUTDOOR FACILITIES

Size:	Large Resort Ship	Passenger/Crew Ratio (lower beds):	2.7
Tonnage:	135,000	Cabins (total):	2,000
Cruise Line:	Carnival Cruise Line	Size Range (sq ft/m):	161.4–344.4/15.0–32.0
Former Names:	none	Cabins (for one person):	0
Builder:	Meyer Werft (Germany)	Cabins with balcony:	887
Entered Service:	May 2016	Cabins (wheelchair accessible):	35
Length (ft/m):	1,054.7/321.5	Wheelchair accessibility:	Good
Beam (ft/m):	101.7/31.0	Elevators:	16
Propulsion/Propellers:	diesel-electric/ 2 azimuthing pods	Casino (gaming tables):	Yes
		Swimming Pools:	3
Passenger Decks:	15	Self-Service Launderette:	Yes
Total Crew:	1,450	Library:	Yes
Passengers (lower beds):	4,000	Onboard currency:	US$
Passenger Space Ratio (lower beds):	33.7		

THE SHIP. Although its design is quite old – based mostly on *Carnival Destiny* of 1996 – this (*Carnival Breeze*-plus) ship nevertheless provides an array of activity-fuelled fun for the whole family. *Carnival Vista* is all about the fun of the fair at sea.

So, line up to get on your bike to pedal the suspended track of Sky Ride – maybe cycle yourself to the next port! Other attractions include a large WaterWorks aqua park, which features a 445-ft (136m) Kaleid-O-Slide, a twisting, corkscrew-turning waterslide adventure with kaleidoscopic effects (a variation on the SkyWalk rope course aboard *Carnival Magic*), and an excellent place to keep the kids occupied.

Considering the number of passengers carried, the swimming pools are disappointingly small, as is the open deck space, because of all the activity features crammed in. However, there's usually no shortage of available sun loungers.

The ship has a full walk-around open promenade deck, but it's lined with deck chairs. Also at the aft, two 'scenic whirlpools' are cantilevered over the water (as part of the Havana Outside area), with fine sea views.

Inside, facilities include an IMAX Theater (for blockbuster movies and documentary content), a large Vista Casino (adjacent to the atrium), a Thrill Theater (for a 4D moving experience), and many other lounges and bars, although the ship's layout is a little disjointed.

The main social center of the ship is the atrium, with large LED screens to provide mood-changing

BERLITZ'S RATINGS		
	Possible	Achieved
Ship	500	368
Accommodation	200	133
Food	400	202
Service	400	251
Entertainment	100	68
Cruise Experience	400	251
OVERALL SCORE 1275 points out of 2000		

backdrops. Counters for guest services and shore excursions are just off the atrium, while aft of the lobby is the Reflections Dining Room.

Many of the public rooms, lounges, bars, and nightspots are located on two main public room/ entertainment decks. These can be accessed via an 11-deck-high atrium lobby, with a cantilevered bandstand atop a massive dance floor on the ground level.

The myriad bars include a sports bar, a trendy Havana Bar, Alchemy Bar (for 'mixologist' cocktails, and a RedFrog Pub (with Carnival's own brews: the ThirstyFrog Red; ThirstyFrog Port Hoppin' IPA; ThirstyFrog Caribbean Wheat; and ThirstyFrog Java Stout).

An adults-only (extra-cost) Serenity area atop the ship at the front provides a beach-like escape from the noisy family-filled decks below, with hot tubs, sunloungers, a bar, and other facilities, including massage 'huts.'

Families with children are well catered for, not only with hyper-activity sporty areas outdoors, but also play rooms for kids and teens (in several different locations), and plenty of youth counselors to take charge, so parents and carers can get some 'me' time, too.

What Carnival does well is to provide lots of almost non-stop excitement, and entertainment fun, and this ship provides the right setting for it all. While the cuisine is pretty uninspiring, the real fun begins at sundown, when the entertainment kicks in.

ACCOMMODATION. The range of cabin sizes, locations, grades and prices includes 'Family Harbor' – family cabins that can sleep up to five. Whether you go for high end or low end, all include plush mattresses, and good-quality duvets, bed linen, and pillows. The suites are not large, although they are laid out practically, while some of the standard cabins are fine for two but crowded for three or more (there's only one personal safe).

All cabins have spy-hole doors, twin beds that can convert into queen-size beds, controllable air conditioning, infotainment set, and telephone. Some cabins can accommodate a third and fourth person, but they have limited closet space. A number of cabins on Deck 3 have lifeboat-obstructed views.

Among the most desirable are those on five of the aft-facing decks; these have private balconies overlooking the stern and ship's wash. There's no vibration, a bonus provided by the pod propulsion system.

CUISINE. The two main dining rooms – Horizons and Reflections – are for served meals (breakfast, lunch, and dinner) in two seatings. Horizons Restaurant has some tables at the stern with fine views (on both main and balcony levels – although the upper level has a low ceiling), plus a bar. You can (at extra cost) also have selections from the steakhouse menu.

Don't even think about a quiet table for two, or a candlelight dinner on deck. This is all about table mates, social talk, lively meals, fast eating, and fast service. Tables do have tablecloths, silverware, and iced water/iced tea whenever you want it. Choose either fixed time dining (6pm or 8.15pm) or flexible dining (during opening hours).

Overall, the food is carbohydrate-rich and non-memorable (it's mass catering, after all), with simple presentation, few garnishes, and many dishes disguised with gravies and sauces. The selection of fresh green vegetables, bread and bakery items (these are thawed and then baked from frozen 'starter' dough), cheeses, and fruit is limited, and there is heavy use of rice, canned fruit and jellied desserts.

'Spa Carnival Fare' provides a healthier food option; vegetarian and children's menus are also available, but they wouldn't get a generous score for their nutritional content.

Lido Marketplace is a self-serve, buffet-style casual restaurant, while close by are other laid-back eateries (no extra cost), including Guy's Burger Joint (named after restaurateur Guy Fieri), Blueiguana Cantina (for Mexican snack burritos and tacos), and Pizzeria del Capitano. There's also Fat Jimmy's C-Side BBQ – oh, and you can get some light bites at The Taste Bar, hot dogs at SeaDogs in SportSquare, sandwiches at the Carnival Deli, and frozen yoghurt at Swirls.

Extra-cost dining spots include: Fahrenheit 555, an all-American steakhouse (for prime meats and grilled seafood); Bonsai Sushi Restaurant, for Japanese-style cuisine (with both indoor and outdoor seating); and Seafood Shack, a New England-style indoor-outdoor eatery for steamed lobster, crab cakes, and fried shrimp. Plus there's Cucina del Capitano (for Italian-style cuisine), and Ji-Ji Asian Kitchen (for Asian fusion cuisine), both on the upper level of Lido Marketplace. Families with youngsters might like to indulge in a Green Eggs and Ham breakfast (extra cost), while Chef's Table (for foodies) includes a little showbusiness from the chef for a small number of diners (also at extra cost).

ENTERTAINMENT. Liquid Lounge, the show-lounge, spans two decks and is the venue for Vegas-style production shows (all feathers and skimpy costumes) and 'A'-list cabaret acts.

A second entertainment lounge is the Limelight Lounge (for adult comedy), while a Piano Bar offers a gentler tone.

An IMAX Theater has a three-deck high screen, while adjacent is a multi-dimensional, special-effects experience in the Thrill Theater. Both are located on the interior of the forward section of Upper Promenade Deck. Extra-cost popcorn and movie snacks are available, of course. Next door is a video arcade.

SPA/FITNESS. The Cloud 9 Spa is on two levels, with treatment rooms, men's and women's infrared saunas and hammam (slow steam and mud room – good for couples), relaxation lounger, fitness center, and 'pay more' thermal suites, plus a VIP treatment room for Spa Suite occupants.

Activity/sports facilities include an outdoor Sky-Course suspended ropes course (always fun on a moving ship), Sky Gardens mini-golf course, and a Skycourt (for baseball). The Clubhouse at SportSquare includes mini-bowling, ping-pong, arcade basketball, and video games.

CELEBRITY CONSTELLATION
★★★★

THIS SHIP'S UNDERSTATED DECOR PROVIDES A STYLISH SETTING FOR FAMILIES

Size:	Mid-size Ship	Passenger/Crew Ratio (lower beds):	2.0
Tonnage:	90,940	Cabins (total):	1,085
Cruise Line:	Celebrity Cruises	Size Range (sq ft/m):	165.1–2,530.0/15.34–235.0
Former Names:	*Constellation*	Cabins (for one person):	0
Builder:	Chantiers de l'Atlantique (France)	Cabins with balcony:	569
Entered Service:	May 2002	Cabins (wheelchair accessible):	26
Length (ft/m):	964.5/294.0	Wheelchair accessibility:	Best
Beam (ft/m):	105.6/32.2	Elevators:	12
Propulsion/Propellers:	gas turbine/2 azimuthing pods	Casino (gaming tables):	Yes
Passenger Decks:	11	Swimming Pools:	3 (1 w/ sliding glass dome)
Total Crew:	999	Self-Service Launderette:	No
Passengers (lower beds):	2,170	Library:	Yes
Passenger Space Ratio (lower beds):	44.6	Onboard currency:	US$

THE SHIP. *Celebrity Constellation* is sister to *Celebrity Infinity*, *Celebrity Millennium*, and *Celebrity Summit*. Unfortunately, there is no walkaround promenade deck outdoors.

Inside, the decor is of understated elegance, with high-quality materials, including lots of wood, glass, and marble.

A four-deck-high atrium, with a separately enclosed room for shore excursions, houses the reception desk and financial services. Four glass-walled elevators travel through 10 passenger decks, including the tender stations.

Standout bars include the Martini Bar with frosted countertop, and a Cellar-Masters wine bar.

A cruise aboard a mid-sized ship provides a good range of choices. Travel in one of the suites, and you get better service levels.

ACCOMMODATION. There are many price grades from which to choose, depending on your preference for the size and location – and your budget. These range from standard interior (no view) and outside-view cabins (with or without balcony) to spacious suite grades Aqua, Concierge, Royal, Celebrity, and Penthouse. There are also wheelchair-accessible cabins (all with wheel-in showers), positioned close to the elevators.

If you choose a balcony cabin on one of the upper decks, note that it could be shaded under the pool deck, which extends over the ship's side – and by many balconies (no good for private sunbathing). Some suites

BERLITZ'S RATINGS

	Possible	Achieved
Ship	500	362
Accommodation	200	153
Food	400	264
Service	400	21
Entertainment	100	74
Cruise Experience	400	273

OVERALL SCORE 1418 points out of 2000

have extremely large balconies – check the deck plan before choosing. Note that a charge for room service applies between 11pm and 6am.

DINING. The 1,198-seat San Marco Restaurant is the main dining room. Two decks high, it has a grand connecting staircase and a huge glass wall with aft sea views (electrically operated blinds provide different backdrops). There are two seatings for dinner (open seating for breakfast and lunch), at tables for two to 10. The table settings are good, with quality linen, china, and glassware, but staff training could be better.

The cuisine represents a good range of traditional and modern culinary influences, but overall it's fairly decent although not inspiring. There are too many sauces and little use of garnishes. For better-quality food, it might be worth paying extra to eat in the specialty venues, where you get better cuts of meat and food cooked to order instead of the standardized batch cooking provided in the main dining room.

The regular (free) coffee is weak and poor. Espresso/cappuccino coffees in the dining room incur a charge, because they are treated as a bar item. For better-quality coffee, it's worth paying extra in Café al Bacio.

Suite occupants dine in the exclusive Luminae restaurant, with tableside preparation of signature dishes, an eclectic menu, and a choice of over 400 wines.

Blu, located on the port side on upper level entrance of the San Marco dining room, is provided exclusively for occupants of Aqua-class accommodation.

Qsine is an extra-cost, reservations-required, tablecloth-free 'fun-food' restaurant, with trendy digital food and wine menus that include cute foodie video snaps. It's all about quirky multi-flavored, multi-colored, small-bite items that tease the taste buds. The food is presented in many unusual ways – even on sticks – rather like 'lollipop' cuisine.

In addition, there's a Burger Bar just aft of the mast, above the pool deck.

Tuscan Grill is an extra-cost, reservations-required venue for Italian-style cuisine, while QSine (an extra-cost dining venue with iPad menus) has tasty food and quirky presentation.

The Seaside Café & Grill (with around 750 seats) is a casual self-serve buffet area with tablecloths in the evening. Reservations are needed, but there's no additional charge.

Café al Bacio & Gelateria, on the uppermost (third) level of the atrium lobby, is for (extra-cost) coffees, pastries, cakes, and ice creams.

Sushi on Five features extra-cost sushi and cooked items including noodle and hot pot dishes.

ENTERTAINMENT. The 900-seat Celebrity Theater is the venue for production shows and major cabaret acts. Spanning three decks, it is located forward, with seating on the main level and two balcony levels.

SPA/FITNESS. SpaClub measures 24,219 sq ft (2,250 sq m) and is operated by Canyon Ranch. Facilities include a large thalassotherapy pool under a solarium glass dome, complete with health bar for light breakfast and lunch items and freshly squeezed fruit and vegetable juices.

CELEBRITY ECLIPSE
★★★★

THIS LARGE, STYLISH PREMIUM SHIP IS GOOD FOR FAMILY-FRIENDLY CRUISING

Size:	Large Resort Ship	Passenger/Crew Ratio (lower beds):	2.3
Tonnage:	121,878	Cabins (total):	1,426
Cruise Line:	Celebrity Cruises	Size Range (sq ft/m):	182.9–1,668.4/17.0–155.0
Former Names:	none	Cabins (for one person):	0
Builder:	Meyer Werft (Germany)	Cabins with balcony:	1,216
Entered Service:	Jun 2010	Cabins (wheelchair accessible):	30
Length (ft/m):	1,033.4/315.0	Wheelchair accessibility:	Best
Beam (ft/m):	120.7/36.8	Elevators:	12
Propulsion/Propellers:	diesel (67,200kW)/ 2 azimuthing pods	Casino (gaming tables):	Yes
		Swimming Pools:	3
Passenger Decks:	14	Self-Service Launderette:	No
Total Crew:	1,210	Library:	Yes
Passengers (lower beds):	2,852	Onboard currency:	US$
Passenger Space Ratio (lower beds):	42.7		

THE SHIP. This slimline ship is a sister to *Celebrity Equinox* (2009), *Celebrity Reflection* (2012), *Celebrity Silhouette* (2011), and *Celebrity Solstice* (2008). *It* has a steeply raked stern, which includes a mega-yacht-style ducktail platform above the ship's propulsion pods; it is attractive, and nicely balances the ship's contemporary profile.

Behind the two smallish funnels is a real grass outdoor area, the Lawn Club. This is the authentic stuff – not green fake turf – and it seems to like the salty air. The club is open to all, so you can putt, play croquet or bocce ball (like bowling or French boules), picnic on the grass, or perhaps sleep on it. Several pool and water-play areas are found on Resort Deck: one in a glass-roofed solarium, a sports pool, a family pool, and a wet zone. The deck space around the two pools, however, isn't large enough for the number of passengers carried.

The interior spaces are well designed, with most of the entertainment rooms positioned forward, and dining venues located in the aft section. There's a wine bar with a sommelier; a cocktail lounge that reflects the jazz age of the 1930s and '40s; a bar with the look of an ocean-going yacht; Quasar, a bar with designs from the 1960s and '70s and large screens that create a nightly light show synchronized to music; and an observation lounge with a dance floor.

Celebrity's signature Martini Bar, with its frosted bar and more than 100 varieties of vodka as well as

BERLITZ'S RATINGS		
	Possible	Achieved
Ship	500	392
Accommodation	200	159
Food	400	267
Service	400	301
Entertainment	100	77
Cruise Experience	400	287

OVERALL SCORE 1483 points out of 2000

martinis, has a small alcove called Crush with an ice-filled table where you can participate in caviar and vodka tasting, or host a private party. It's noisy and congested.

An innovative Hot Glass Show, housed in an outdoor studio on the open deck as part of the Lawn Club and created in collaboration with Corning Museum of Glass, includes demonstrations and a narrated performance of glass-blowing. Resident glass-blowing artists also host workshops.

An Apple 'iLounge' is equipped with 26 Apple MacBook Pro work stations (you can also buy Apple products). Also, the elevator call buttons are located in a floor-stand 'pod' and, when the elevator arrives, a glass panel above it turns from blue to pink.

Gratuities are automatically charged to your onboard account.

ACCOMMODATION. This is both practical and comfortable. There are numerous price grades, depending on size and location.

In non-suite-grade cabins there is little space between the bed and the wall, but all accommodation includes twin beds convertible to a queen- or king-size bed with premium bedding, sitting area, and vanity desk with hairdryer, but little drawer space. Although closets have good hanging space, other storage space is limited. Bathrooms have a shower enclosure, toilet, and *tiny* washbasin. A charge of $3.95 for room service applies between 11pm and 6am.

Note that cabins 1551–1597 on the port side and 1556–1602 on the starboard side on Penthouse Deck (Deck 11) suffer from 'aircraft carrier' syndrome because they are directly under the overhanging Resort Deck. They have little exposure to sun or light, so sunbathing is out of the question. Many thick supporting struts ruin the view from these cabins, which are otherwise pleasant enough.

Other accommodation grades are: Veranda; Family Veranda; Concierge; Ocean View; and Interior (noview) cabins. Suite-grade categories are: Aqua; Sky; Celebrity; Royal; and Penthouse. Suites have much more space, plus larger balconies with good-quality sunloungers, and more personal amenities.

DINING. Moonlight Sonata is the 1,430-seat two-deck main dining room (included in the cruise price). It has ocean views on the port and starboard sides, and to the stern (aft). The design is stunning and contemporary. At the forward end, a two-deck-high wine tower provides an eye-catching focal point.

Suite-class occupants can dine in the more exclusive Luminae restaurant, with tableside preparation of signature dishes, an eclectic menu, and a selection of over 400 wines.

Blu is a 130-seat specialty restaurant just for the occupants of Aqua-class cabins. The room has a pleasing, but rather cool, blue decor.

The following dining spots provide an alternative to the main dining room, good for special occasions or just for something different.

Murano is an extra-cost, reservations-required venue offering high-quality traditional dining with a French flair and fine table settings, including large Riedel wine glasses. Food and service are very good.

The Tuscan Grille is an extra-cost venue that serves Kobe beef and premium-quality steaks. Its entrance has beautifully curved arches – it's like walking into a high-tech winery. There are fine views from huge aft-view windows.

Qsine is an extra-cost, 90-seat, reservations-required venue, tablecloth-free 'fun-food' restaurant, with trendy interactive iPad food and wine menus that include cute foodie video snaps. The food consists of

multi-flavored, multi-colored, quirky small-bite items to tease your taste buds. The food is presented in some unusual ways – even on sticks. It's a quirky experience.

For snacks and less ambitious meals, the options are:

Sushi on Five features extra-cost sushi and cooked items including noodle and hot pot dishes.

Café al Bacio & Gelateria is a coffeehouse serving Lavazza Italian coffee. It is on one side of the main lobby, but it's small and lines quickly form at peak times. The seating is mostly in large, very comfortable armchairs.

Oceanview Café and Grill, a large, tray-free, casual self-serve buffet venue, which includes a number of food islands, and good signage. However, it's impossible to get a warm plate for so-called hot food items.

The AquaSpa Café is for light, healthier options (solarium fare), but the selections are not exactly thrilling.

The Mast Bar Grill and Bar is an outside venue offering fast food.

ENTERTAINMENT. The 1,115-seat Eclipse Theater (the main showlounge) stages three circus-themed production shows featuring acrobatics.

Colorful theme nights are held in the Observation Lounge (whose bland daytime decor comes alive at night thanks to mood lighting effects). The 200-seat Celebrity Central hosts stand-up comedy, cooking demonstrations, enrichment lectures, and feature films. Quasar is a high-volume nightclub.

An Entertainment Court showcases street performers, psychics, and caricaturists, and is in the center of the ship. There's also a big-band-era cocktail lounge with live jazz-styled music, set adjacent to the Murano, the specialty restaurant.

SPA/FITNESS. The Canyon Ranch SpaClub is laid out over two decks. A large fitness center includes kinesis (pulleys against gravity) workout equipment, plus all the familiar gym machinery.

An extra-cost, unisex thermal suite features several steam and shower mist rooms and a glacial ice fountain, plus a calming relaxation area with heated tiled beds, and an acupuncture center.

CELEBRITY EQUINOX
★★★★

THIS LARGE SHIP OFFERS CONTEMPORARY STYLE TO THOSE WHO LIKE TO TRAVEL WELL

Size:	Large Resort Ship	Passenger/Crew Ratio (lower beds):	2.3
Tonnage:	122,000	Cabins (total):	1,426
Cruise Line:	Celebrity Cruises	Size Range (sq ft/m):	182.9–1,668.4/17.0–155.0
Former Names:	none	Cabins (for one person):	0
Builder:	Meyer Werft (Germany)	Cabins with balcony:	1,216
Entered Service:	Aug 2009	Cabins (wheelchair accessible):	30
Length (ft/m):	1,033.4/315.0	Wheelchair accessibility:	Best
Beam (ft/m):	120.7/36.8	Elevators:	12
Propulsion/Propellers:	diesel (67,200kW)/ 2 azimuthing pods	Casino (gaming tables):	Yes
		Swimming Pools:	3
Passenger Decks:	14	Self-Service Launderette:	No
Total Crew:	1,210	Library:	Yes
Passengers (lower beds):	2,852	Onboard currency:	US$
Passenger Space Ratio (lower beds):	42.7		

THE SHIP. This is a sister ship to *Celebrity Eclipse, Celebrity Reflection, Celebrity Silhouette,* and *Celebrity Solstice.* The steeply sloping stern, with its mega-yacht-style ducktail platform above the propulsion pods, is attractive, and balances the ship's contemporary profile, while the bows are rounded to accommodate a helipad.

Between the two slim funnels (set one behind the other) is a grass outdoor area, the Lawn Club, with real grass that seems to like the salty air. The Lawn Club is open to all, so you can go putting, play croquet or bocce ball (like bowling or boules), or have a picnic on the grass.

There are several pool and water-play areas on Resort Deck: one in a solarium (with glass roof), a sports pool, a family pool, and a wet zone. However, the deck space around the two pools is not large enough for the number of passengers carried.

The interior decor is elegant, yet contemporary. Attractions include a Gastropub; a cocktail lounge with jazz; a bar with the look of an ocean-going yacht; Quasar, a bar with large screens that create a nightly light show synchronized to music; and an observation lounge with dance floor.

Celebrity's signature Martini Bar, with its frosted bar, includes a small alcove called Crush with an ice-filled table for caviar and vodka tastings.

Fortunes Casino has 16 gaming tables and 200 slot machines. There's a two-deck library, but the books on the upper shelves are impossible to reach.

BERLITZ'S RATINGS	Possible	Achieved
Ship	500	392
Accommodation	200	159
Food	400	267
Service	400	302
Entertainment	100	77
Cruise Experience	400	287
OVERALL SCORE 1484 points out of 2000		

An innovative Hot Glass Show, created in collaboration with Corning Museum of Glass, includes demonstrations and a narrated performance of glass-blowing, housed in an outdoor studio on the open deck as part of the Lawn Club.

Passenger niggles include poor drawer space in cabins; inadequate children's facilities and staff; congestion when you exit the showlounge; and noise in all areas of the lobby when the Martini Bar is busy.

Good points include the elevator call buttons located in a floor-stand 'pod'; when an elevator arrives, a glass panel above it turns from blue to pink. Also, the ship has a good collection of designer chairs and sunloungers in various locations.

The ship sails year-round in the Caribbean. Gratuities are charged to your onboard account. A refurbishment in 2014 added more branded merchandise for shops, changed Cellar Masters into a Gastrobar featuring more than 40 craft beers and 'comfort food,' and online@Celebrity into the Celebrity iLounge (a computer room equipped with Apple Macs).

ACCOMMODATION. The accommodation is both practical and comfortable. There are numerous price grades, depending on size and location. In non-suite-grade cabins there is little space between the bed and the wall, but all include twin beds convertible to a queen- or king-size bed with premium bedding, sitting area, and vanity desk with hairdryer, but little drawer space. Although closets have good hanging space, other storage space is limited. Bathrooms have a shower enclosure, toilet, and tiny washbasin. A charge of $3.95 for room service applies between 11pm and 6am.

Note that cabins 1551–1597 on the port side and 1556–1602 on the starboard side on Penthouse Deck (Deck 11) suffer from 'aircraft carrier' syndrome because they are directly under the overhanging Resort Deck. They have little exposure to sun or light, so sunbathing is out of the question. Many thick supporting struts ruin the view from these cabins, which are otherwise pleasant enough.

Other accommodation grades are named Veranda, Family Veranda, Concierge, Ocean View, and Interior (no-view) cabins. Suite-grade categories are: Aqua; Sky; Celebrity; Royal; and Penthouse. Suites have much more space, larger balconies with good-quality sunloungers, and more personal amenities than standard cabins.

DINING. Silhouette, the ship's balconied main dining room (included in the cruise price), has ocean views on the port and starboard sides. The contemporary design is stunning. At the forward end, a two-deck-high wine tower provides an eye-catching focal point. As for the food, it's a bit of a let down – the decreased quality is all too obvious to repeat Celebrity passengers.

Suite occupants can dine in the exclusive setting of Luminae, a restaurant with tableside preparation of signature dishes, an eclectic menu, and a selection of over 400 wines. Blu is a 128-seat specialty restaurant designated just for the occupants of Aqua-class cabins. The room has pleasing, but rather cold, blue decor.

Murano is an extra-cost, reservations-required venue offering high-quality traditional dining with a French flair and exquisite table settings, including large Riedel wine glasses. Food and service are good.

The Tuscan Grille, an extra-cost venue, features Kobe beef and premium quality steaks, and has beau-tifully curved archways – reminiscent of walking into a high-tech winery. There are great views from huge aft-view windows.

QSine is an extra-cost, reservations-required quirky fine-dining venue, with iPad menus.

Sushi on Five features extra-cost sushi and cooked items including noodle and hot pot dishes.

The Café al Bacio & Gelateria coffee lounge serves Lavazza Italian coffee. It is on one side of the main lobby, but it's small and lines form at peak times. The seating is mostly in large, very comfortable armchairs.

Oceanview Café and Grill is the expansive, tray-free, casual self-serve buffet venue. There are food islands rather than those awful straight buffet counters, and good signage. However, it's impossible to get a warm plate for so-called hot food items, and condiments are hard to find.

The AquaSpa Café is for light, healthier options (solarium fare), but the selections are bland and boring.

The Mast Bar Grill and Bar is an outside venue offering fast food.

ENTERTAINMENT. The 1,115-seat Equinox Theater, the ship's showlounge, has a main level and two balconied sections positioned amphitheater-style around a stage with music lofts on either side.

Colorful theme nights are held in the Sky Observation Lounge, where the daytime decor comes alive at night thanks to mood lighting. The 200-seat Celebrity Central hosts comedy, cooking demonstrations, enrichment lectures, and feature films. The Ensemble Lounge big-band-era cocktail lounge has live jazz, next to the Murano restaurant.

SPA/FITNESS. This is a large, two-deck Canyon Ranch SpaClub at Sea. The fitness center includes kinesis (pulleys against gravity) and cardio-vascular machinery. An extra-cost, unisex thermal suite has steam and shower mist rooms, and a glacial ice fountain, plus a calming relaxation area with heated tiled beds, and an acupuncture center.

CELEBRITY INFINITY
★★★★

THIS FAMILY-FRIENDLY, MODERN RESORT SHIP HAS PLENTY OF STYLE

Size: .... Mid-size Ship	Passenger/Crew Ratio (lower beds): 2.1
Tonnage: 90,940	Cabins (total): 1,085
Cruise Line: ....Celebrity Cruises	Size Range (sq ft/m): 165.1–2,530.0/15.34–235.0
Former Names: .... Infinity	Cabins (for one person): 0
Builder: .... Chantiers de l'Atlantique (France)	Cabins with balcony: 606
Entered Service: .... Mar 2001	Cabins (wheelchair accessible): 26
Length (ft/m): 964.5/294.0	(17 with private balcony)
Beam (ft/m): 105.6/32.2	Wheelchair accessibility: .... Best
Propulsion/Propellers: .... gas turbine (39,000kW)/	Elevators: 12
2 azimuthing pods	Casino (gaming tables): .... Yes
Passenger Decks: 11	Swimming Pools: .... 3 (1 w/ sliding glass dome)
Total Crew: 999	Self-Service Launderette: .... No
Passengers (lower beds): 2,170	Library: .... Yes
Passenger Space Ratio (lower beds): 41.9	Onboard currency: .... US$

THE SHIP. *Celebrity Infinity* is a sister ship to *Celebrity Constellation*, *Celebrity Millennium*, and *Celebrity Summit*. Famous mega-yacht designer Jon Bannenberg created the exterior.

The atrium is the interior focal point; three decks high, it houses the reception desk, tour desk, and bank. Four glass-walled elevators travel through the ship's exterior (port) side, connecting the atrium with another seven decks, thus traveling through 10 passenger decks, including the tender stations – a nice ride.

Michael's Club (which was a cigar smoker's haven, when the ship was new) is now a pleasant, comfortable lounge for suite-grade occupants only.

Gaming sports include the ship's overly large Fortunes Casino, with blackjack, roulette, and slot machines, and lots of bright lights and action.

The ship provides a wide range of choices and possibilities. Travel in one of the suites and you will receive the highest level of personal service, while cruising in non-suite accommodation is much like any ship. It all depends how much you are willing (and able) to pay. The two-seating dining and two shows nightly detract from an otherwise excellent product. A 15 percent gratuity is added to bar and wine accounts. Note that a charge of $3.95 for room service applies between 11pm and 6am.

ACCOMMODATION. There are many price grades from which to choose, depending on your preference

BERLITZ'S RATINGS		
	Possible	Achieved
Ship	500	362
Accommodation	200	157
Food	400	285
Service	400	289
Entertainment	100	74
Cruise Experience	400	280

OVERALL SCORE 1416 points out of 2000

for the size and location. These include Standard Interior (no view) and Outside View Cabins (with or without balcony) to spacious suite grades named Aqua, Concierge, Royal, Celebrity, and Penthouse. There are also wheelchair-accessible cabins (all with wheel-in showers), positioned close to elevators.

All accommodation grades are very comfortable, but suites, naturally, have more space. If you choose a balcony cabin on one of the upper decks, note that it could be shaded under the pool deck, which extends over the ship's side – and by many balconies (so, not good for private sunbathing).

DINING. The 1,170-seat Thellis Restaurant is the main dining room. It is two decks high; a grand staircase connects the two levels. A huge glass wall overlooks the sea at the stern (electrically operated shades provide several different backdrops), and a musicians' gallery on the upper level. There are two seatings for dinner (open seating for breakfast and lunch), at tables for two to 10. The dining room, like all large dining halls, can be extremely noisy. Menu variety is good, the food has taste, and it is attractively presented and served in an orchestrated fashion with European traditions and training. Full service in-cabin dining is also available for all meals, including dinner.

Suite occupants can dine in the exclusive setting of 'Luminae,' which features tableside preparation of signature dishes, an eclectic menu, and a selection of over 400 wines.

Blu, located on the port side of the upper level entrance of The Thellis dining room, is exclusively for the use of occupants of Aqua-class accommodation.

The former United States Restaurant, adjacent to the main lobby, is now the Tuscan Grille. The extra-cost, reservations-required venue features Kobe beef and premium-quality steaks, and includes a dine-in wine cellar and a demonstration galley.

QSine, with menus and wine list on iPads, is another extra-cost, fine-dining venue (added in 2011, it replaced the former Conservatory); reservations are required.

Las Olas Café and Grill is a casual self-serve buffet area, with six principal serving lines, and seating for 754; there is also a grill and pizza bar.

For Champagne and caviar lovers, not to mention Martinis, Carlisle's is the place to see and be seen.

Café al Bacio & Gelateria, on the third level of the atrium lobby, is the place to go for (extra-cost) coffees, pastries, cakes, and ice creams, in a trendy setting.

Sushi on Five features extra-cost sushi and cooked items including noodle and hot pot dishes.

ENTERTAINMENT. The 900-seat Celebrity Theater is the venue for production shows and major cabaret acts. Spanning three decks in height, it is located in the forward part of the ship; seating is on main, and two balcony levels, and the large stage has a full fly loft behind its proscenium.

SPA/FITNESS. The Canyon Ranch SpaClub at Sea measures 24,219 sq ft (2,250 sq m). It includes a large thalassotherapy pool under a solarium glass dome, complete with health bar for light breakfast and lunch items and freshly squeezed fruit and vegetable juices.

CELEBRITY MILLENNIUM
★★★★

THIS MID-SIZE, FAMILY-FRIENDLY SHIP HAS A TOUCH OF CLASS

Size:	Mid-size Ship	Passenger/Crew Ratio (lower beds):	2.1
Tonnage:	90,940	Cabins (total):	1,079
Cruise Line:	Celebrity Cruises	Size Range (sq ft/m):	170.0–2,350.0/15.7–235.0
Former Names:	*Millennium*	Cabins (for one person):	0
Builder:	Chantiers de l'Atlantique (France)	Cabins with balcony:	606
Entered Service:	Jun 2000	Cabins (wheelchair accessible):	26
Length (ft/m):	964.5/294.0	Wheelchair accessibility:	Best
Beam (ft/m):	105.6/32.2	Elevators:	12
Propulsion/Propellers:	gas turbine (39,000kW)/ 2 azimuthing pods	Casino (gaming tables):	Yes
		Swimming Pools:	3 (1 w/ sliding glass dome)
Passenger Decks:	11	Self-Service Launderette:	No
Total Crew:	999	Library:	Yes
Passengers (lower beds):	2,158	Onboard currency:	US$
Passenger Space Ratio (lower beds):	42.1		

THE SHIP. *Celebrity Millennium* is a sister ship to *Celebrity Constellation*, *Celebrity Infinity*, and *Celebrity Summit*. Sadly, there is no walkaround wooden promenade deck outdoors. There are cushioned pads for poolside deck lounge chairs only, but not for chairs on other outside decks. Passenger participation activities are mostly amateurish.

The interiors exude understated elegance, with high-class decor and materials (wood, glass, and marble) and a four-deck-high atrium. It houses the reception desk, tour operator's desk, and bank. Four glass-walled elevators travel through 10 decks (including tender stations).

Located directly in front of the main funnel, and with glass walls overlooking the ship's side, is a 70-person-capacity sports bar, Extreme; somehow, however, it just doesn't belong. Gaming sports include the ship's overly large Fortunes Casino.

AquaClass veranda cabins and Blu, a Mediterranean-themed specialty restaurant exclusively for Aqua-Class passengers, were added in a 'Solsticizing' of the ship in 2012. Also added were a Celebrity iLounge (for Apple products, computer classes, and Internet connection); a Martini Bar with a frosted bar top; a Cellar-Masters wine bar; QSine, an extra-cost fine-dining venue with iPad menus; and a Bistro on Five crêperie.

Celebrity Millennium delivers a well-defined North American cruise vacation at a relatively modest price. A zero-announcement policy means there is little intrusion.

BERLITZ'S RATINGS	Possible	Achieved
Ship	500	362
Accommodation	200	157
Food	400	285
Service	400	215
Entertainment	100	74
Cruise Experience	400	281
OVERALL SCORE 1415 points out of 2000		

ACCOMMODATION. Choose from either suite-grade or non-suite-grade accommodation, depending on your preference for the size and location. These include standard interior (no-view) and outside-view cabins (with or without balcony) to spacious suite grades named Aqua, Concierge, Royal, Celebrity, and Penthouse. There are also wheelchair-accessible cabins (all with wheel-in showers), positioned close to elevators.

All accommodation grades are comfortable; suites, naturally, have more space. If you choose a balcony cabin on one of the upper decks, note that it could be shaded under the pool deck, which extends over the ship's side – and by many balconies (so, not good for private sunbathing). Some suites have extremely large balconies (always check the deck plan before choosing). Note that a charge of $3.95 for room service applies between 11pm and 6am.

DINING. The 1,224-seat Metropolitan Restaurant is the main dining room. Two decks high, it has a grand staircase connecting the two levels, a huge glass wall aft overlooking the sea, and a small 'musicians' gallery' on the upper level. There are two dinner seatings (open seating for breakfast and lunch), at tables for two to 10. Menu variety is good, the food has taste, and it is attractively presented. Full service in-cabin dining is also available, with dinner menu items from the Metropolitan Restaurant.

Suite occupants dine in Luminae, a restaurant with tableside preparation of signature dishes, an eclectic menu, and a selection of over 400 wines.

Blu, located on the port side of the upper level entrance of the Metropolitan dining room, is exclusively for the use of occupants of Aqua-class accommodation.

Celebrity Cruises created its first 'alternative' restaurant aboard this ship. The Olympic Restaurant is named after White Star Line's transatlantic ocean liner (sister ship to *Titanic*, *Olympic* sailed between 1911 and 1935). Adjacent to the atrium lobby, its dining lounge contains figured French walnut wood paneling from the à la carte dining room of the SS *Olympic*, which was decorated in Louis XVI splendor.

Classic French cuisine and good service are provided. This is, indeed, a room for a very leisurely dinner. The wine list is extensive and includes an additional list of rare vintage wines. However, with just 134 seats, it's best to make reservations early (a cover charge applies). There's also a dine-in wine cellar and a demonstration galley.

QSine, which features its menus and wine list on iPads, is an extra-cost, fine-dining venue (added in 2010); reservations are required.

Ocean Café is a self-serve 754-seat buffet-style eatery. At the aft end of the Ocean Buffet, a separate pasta bar, sushi counter, grill/rotisserie, and pizza station provide freshly made items. Pizzas are made on board from pizza dough and do not come ready made for reheating, as with many cruise lines. There is also an outdoor grill, adjacent to the swimming pool, for fast-food items.

Café al Bacio & Gelateria, located on the third level of the atrium lobby, is the place to see and be seen, for extra-cost coffees, pastries, cakes, and ice cream all in a comfortable setting.

Sushi on Five features extra-cost sushi and cooked items including noodle and hot pot dishes.

ENTERTAINMENT. The 900-seat Celebrity Theater is a three-deck-high showlounge for production shows and major cabaret acts. It is located forward, with seating on all levels. The stage is equipped with a full fly loft behind its proscenium.

SPA/FITNESS. Canyon Ranch SpaClub at Sea measures 24,219 sq ft (2,250 sq m). It features a large thalassotherapy pool under a solarium dome; a health bar provides light breakfast and lunch items and freshly squeezed fruit and vegetable juices.

CELEBRITY REFLECTION
★★★★

A PREMIUM-QUALITY SHIP FOR FAMILY-FRIENDLY CRUISING IN STYLE

Size:	Large Resort Ship	Passenger/Crew Ratio (lower beds):	2.3
Tonnage:	125,366	Cabins (total):	1,523
Cruise Line:	Celebrity Cruises	Size Range (sq ft/m):	182.9–1,668.4/17.0–155.0
Former Names:	none	Cabins (for one person):	0
Builder:	Meyer Werft (Germany)	Cabins with balcony:	1,216
Entered Service:	Oct 2012	Cabins (wheelchair accessible):	30
Length (ft/m):	1,047.2/319.2	Wheelchair accessibility:	Best
Beam (ft/m):	120.7/36.8	Elevators:	12
Propulsion/Propellers:	diesel (70,500kW)/ 2 azimuthing pods	Casino (gaming tables):	Yes
		Swimming Pools:	3
Passenger Decks:	14	Self-Service Launderette:	No
Total Crew:	1,271	Library:	Yes
Passengers (lower beds):	3,046	Onboard currency:	US$
Passenger Space Ratio (lower beds):	41.1		

THE SHIP. *Celebrity Reflection* has a steeply sloping stern with a mega-yacht-style ducktail platform above the propulsion pods. It's attractive, and nicely balanced (the hull is 2ft (0.6m) wider, and has an additional deck, although the ship's superstructure is the same width, than *Celebrity Silhouette*).

Behind the funnels, the ship recreates the great outdoors with a Lawn Club, with real grass. You can go putting, play croquet or bocce ball (similar to boules), picnic on the grass, or walk barefoot. On the open deck, 'The Alcoves' are extra-cost 'private' Wi-Fi-equipped cabanas.

Celebrity Reflection is similar to *Celebrity Silhouette*, but with an additional deck. With a larger number of passengers (but the same number of elevators), the passenger/space ratio is therefore reduced. The ship's name is positioned directly under the navigation bridge and not forward on the bows (for space reasons), and the rounded bows accommodate a helicopter winch pad.

Several pool and water-play areas are on Resort Deck: one under a glass-roofed solarium (with Aqua Café for light healthy bites). There's a sports pool, a family pool, and a wet zone. The open deck and sunning space around the main pool, however, isn't large enough for the number of passengers carried, although there are several other outdoor areas, including a music-free Solstice Deck high atop the ship – a nice space in which to relax.

BERLITZ'S RATINGS	Possible	Achieved
Ship	500	396
Accommodation	200	160
Food	400	267
Service	400	301
Entertainment	100	80
Cruise Experience	400	289

OVERALL SCORE 1493 points out of 2000

The interior spaces are well designed, and the passenger flow is good; most of the entertainment rooms are positioned forward, while dining venues are located in the aft of the ship.

Celebrity's signature Martini Bar has a frosted bar and carries over 100 varieties of vodka, as well as Martinis. It's lively (noisy) and can get congested, but it can be a lot of fun, as can the Molecular Bar, with its special mixologist concoctions, including fruits and ingredients, aided by liquid nitrogen.

Cellar Masters, which is hosted by a sommelier, provides a cozy space for drinking wines. Its wine list is extensive, and drinks are served in Riedel glasses. The room has several hideaway alcoves.

A two-deck library is a delightful open-ended space (operated on an 'honor' system – so you can check out a book 24/7), though books on the upper of 12 shelves are just for show.

Fortunes Casino is a non-smoking gaming room with multiple tables for serious players, and 235 slot machines. It is open sided, so anyone passing is subject to noise from the slot machines.

Elevator call buttons are in a floor-stand 'pod,' and, when an elevator arrives, a glass panel above it turns from blue to pink, which is fun. Also notable is a collection of designer chairs and sunloungers in various locations, although some are on the impractical side of comfort.

Public rooms include an Art Studio, for the budding artist in you (classes and projects are at extra cost). Have a look along the 'dining walkway,' where several specialty restaurants are located. Two pieces of art stand out: one is a delightful optical illusion, by Anthony James, featuring seemingly never-ending (kiln-dried) birch trees, set within glass-sided, mirrored boxes); the other is a fascinating video art piece that tells a story about a man, his flashlight, a forest, and things that happen – I won't tell you more – you'll simply have to experience it for yourself.

Passenger niggles include lack of usable drawer space in standard-grade cabins; congestion when exiting the showlounge after a show; and the noise level in all areas of the lobby (which has a marble dance floor), particularly when the Martini Bar on the deck above is busy.

Gratuities are automatically charged to your on-board account.

ACCOMMODATION. The accommodation is both practical and comfortable. There are numerous price grades, depending on size and location. In non-suite-grade cabins there is little space between the bed and the wall, but all include twin beds convertible to a queen- or king-size bed with premium bedding, sitting area, and vanity desk with hairdryer, but little drawer space. Although closets have good hanging space, other storage space is limited. Bathrooms have a shower enclosure, toilet, and tiny washbasin. A charge for room service now applies between 11pm and 6am.

Note that cabins 1551–1597 on the port side and 1556–1602 on the starboard side on Penthouse Deck (Deck 12) suffer from 'aircraft carrier' syndrome because they are directly under the overhanging Resort Deck. They have little exposure to sun or light, so sunbathing is out. Thick supporting struts ruin the view from these cabins, which are otherwise pleasant enough.

Other accommodation grades are named Veranda, Family Veranda, Concierge, Ocean View, and Interior cabins (no view). Suite-grade categories are: Aqua, Sky, Celebrity, Royal, and Penthouse. Suites have more space and larger balconies with good-quality sunloungers, and more personal amenities than standard cabins.

DINING. Meals in Opus, the ship's expansive two-level, 1,454-seat principal dining room, are included in the cruise price. It has ocean views on the port and starboard sides, and two seating times, and anyone choosing 'Celebrity Select Dining' is usually assigned to the upper level, which helps to keep the dining room running smoothly. The design is contemporary, and, despite its size, it's very comfortable. A two-deck-high wine tower – located towards the aft of the room is a great focal point.

Celebrity Cruises features cuisine that is creative, trendy, and slightly more health-oriented (ie less re-liance on salt and food modifiers) than that of many of its competitors. If you like to eat in different venues instead of the main dining room, different dining packages are available, so you can 'dine around.' These venues provide options that are good for something different (including the self-serve casual eatery, Oceanview Café).

Murano is an extra-cost, 72-seat, reservations-required dinner venue (with tablecloths), offering high-quality traditional dining with a real French flair and fine table settings, including large Riedel wine glasses. The food, its preparation and presentation, and the service are excellent.

Suite occupants can dine in the exclusive setting of Luminae, a restaurant with tableside preparation of signature dishes, an eclectic menu, and a selection of over 400 wines.

Blu is a 156-seat specialty restaurant, with tablecloths, designated exclusively for occupants of Aqua-class cabins, with cool ice white decor; the cuisine focuses slightly more on nicely presented healthy combinations.

Tuscan Grille is a 146-seat, extra-cost informal restaurant (no tablecloths), for both traditional and trendy fare with an Italian focus, but includes Kobe beef, premium-quality steaks, and seafood. Its entrance is barrel-shaped, with curved archways – it's like walking into a high-tech winery. Large aft-facing windows offer a great view.

Qsine is an extra-cost, 92-seat reservations-required, tablecloth-free 'fun-food' restaurant, with trendy digital food and wine menus that include cute foodie video snaps. The food consists of multi-flavored, multi-colored, quirky small-bite items that provide you with a selection to tease your taste buds. The food is presented in many unusual ways – even on sticks – sort of 'lollipop' or 'circus' cuisine.

A wine-tasting and enjoyment lounge, the 72-seat Cellar Masters features several alcoves for intimate discussions about wine. A wide choice is available, and a sommelier will make suggestions (about wine).

Sushi on Five features extra-cost sushi and cooked items including noodle and hot pot dishes.

Café al Bacio & Gelateria is a coffeehouse serving (extra-cost) Lavazza Italian coffees, teas, and herbal infusions. It is on one side of the main lobby, with seating mostly in large, comfortable armchairs.

For something different, there's the Lawn Club Grill, a patio-style, glass-covered, outdoor lean-to-style venue that overlooks the lawn and cabanas (reservable). It's the place to go for beautifully grilled steaks, lamb chops, and seafood dishes. You can even grill the food to your liking – with a chef at your side, of course, just in case you burn your fingers!

Close by is The Porch, another enclosed venue, on the starboard side, with 48 seats, for paninis and light bites throughout the day (including breakfast, with delightful fruit muffins and pastry items).

Oceanview Café and Grill is an expansive, tray-free, casual self-serve buffet venue. A number of food 'islands' help to prevent lines, and the flow is good; the signage is clear and concise. A wide variety of food items is available, and plates are available at each of the 'islands' and cooking stations (such as 'Eggs and More' for breakfast). However, it *is* challenging to get a warm plate for hot food items.

The AquaSpa Café is for lighter options – low-salt solarium dishes, including a choice of salad items – and even a few sprouts, together with grilled items such as salmon and chicken, all attractively presented.

The Mast Bar Grill, an outside venue above the main pool deck, provides comfort fast-food items including burgers.

Try the Elegant Champagne High Tea in Murano. Presented once each cruise (usually on a sea day), it comes with a choice of seven teas and tisanes, a three-tier stand full of finger sandwiches and pastry items, plus scones and real clotted cream, and a glass of Perrier Jouet Champagne.

ENTERTAINMENT. The 1,160-seat Reflection Theater (showlounge) has a main level and two bal-conied sections set amphitheater-style around the stage.

Colorful nights are held in the Sky Observation Lounge, where the minimalist decor (relaxing by day) comes alive at night with mood lighting.

Meanwhile, Celebrity Central hosts adult-only stand-up comedy, cooking demonstrations, enrichment lectures, and feature films.

Ensemble Lounge is a big-band-era-style cocktail lounge with live jazz-styled music, and is located close to specialty restaurant, Murano.

SPA/FITNESS. The Canyon Ranch SpaClub at Sea is laid out over two decks. A large fitness center includes kinesis equipment, plus all the familiar muscle-pumping machinery.

An extra-cost (free to occupants of AquaSpa-grade accommodation) unisex thermal suite contains several steam and shower mist rooms, and a glacial ice fountain, plus a calming relaxation area with heated tiled beds.

Additionally a small fitness 'suite' (for two), each with a selection of cardio-vascular machines, treadmills, etc., can be rented, so you can exercise in privacy.

CELEBRITY SILHOUETTE
★★★★

THIS PREMIUM LARGE SHIP HAS CONTEMPORARY DECOR AND STYLE

Size:	Large Resort Ship	Passenger/Crew Ratio (lower beds):	2.3
Tonnage:	122,210	Cabins (total):	1,443
Cruise Line:	Celebrity Cruises	Size Range (sq ft/m):	182.9–1,668.4/17.0–155.0
Former Names:	none	Cabins (for one person):	0
Builder:	Meyer Werft (Germany)	Cabins with balcony:	1,216
Entered Service:	Jul 2011	Cabins (wheelchair accessible):	30
Length (ft/m):	1,047.2/319.2	Wheelchair accessibility:	Best
Beam (ft/m):	120.7/36.8	Elevators:	12
Propulsion/Propellers:	diesel (70,500kW)/	Casino (gaming tables):	Yes
	2 azimuthing pods	Swimming Pools:	3
Passenger Decks:	14	Self-Service Launderette:	No
Total Crew:	1,210	Library:	Yes
Passengers (lower beds):	2,886	Onboard currency:	US$
Passenger Space Ratio (lower beds):	42.3		

THE SHIP. *Celebrity Silhouette* looks sleek, with its two slim funnels. Behind them is the great outdoors and Lawn Club, an area with real Bermudan grass. You can putt, play croquet or bocce ball (similar to boules), picnic on the grass, and enjoy walking around barefoot. Part of the Lawn Club is an interactive Lawn Club Grill, while The Porch is a 48-seat eatery overlooking the lawn, for complimentary breakfast and lunches, plus specialty coffees, wine, and beer (at extra cost).

Near the Lawn Club entrance is an Art Studio, for demonstrations and classes on various topics. Some are free, some cost extra.

Resort Deck has several water-play areas, one within a glass-roofed solarium. However, deck space around the two pools is small considering the number of passengers carried. For open deck privacy, try 'The Alcoves'; these are garden cabanas for two to four persons, positioned on the lawn (naturally, they cost extra).

Michael's Club, an intimate lounge with classic English leather club chairs and a handsome fireplace, is for suite-grade occupants only.

Most entertainment rooms are positioned forward, with dining venues located aft. There's a wine bar; a jazz-age cocktail lounge; a bar with the look of an ocean-going yacht; Quasar, a bar with a nightly light show synchronized to music; and an observation lounge with a dance floor.

BERLITZ'S RATINGS		
	Possible	Achieved
Ship	500	391
Accommodation	200	161
Food	400	267
Service	400	301
Entertainment	100	78
Cruise Experience	400	287
OVERALL SCORE 1483 points out of 2000		

The two-deck library is a delightful open-ended space. The card room – located in the center of the ship – has no ocean-view windows to distract players, but it attracts noise from adjacent areas, so it's almost useless as a serious card playing room. Fortunes Casino (non-smoking) has gaming tables and slot machines.

Celebrity's signature Martini Bar carries over 100 varieties of vodka, as well as Martinis. There's also a small alcove called Crush with an ice-filled table where you can participate in caviar- and vodka-tasting, or host a private party. It's noisy and congested, but can be a lot of fun.

Passenger niggles include lack of usable drawer space in cabins; inadequate children's facilities and staff during school holidays; congestion when you exit the showlounge; and noise in all areas of the lobby when the Martini Bar is busy.

Gratuities are charged to your onboard account.

ACCOMMODATION. The accommodation is both practical and comfortable. There are numerous price grades, depending on size and location.

In non-suite-grade cabins there is little space between the bed and the wall, but all accommodation includes twin beds convertible to a queen- or king-size bed with premium bedding, sitting area, and vanity desk with hairdryer, but little drawer space. Although closets have good hanging space, other storage space is limited. Bathrooms have a shower enclosure, toilet, and tiny washbasin. A charge for room service applies between 11pm and 6am.

Note that cabins 1551–1597 on the port side and 1556–1602 on the starboard side on Penthouse Deck (Deck 11) suffer from 'aircraft carrier' syndrome because they are directly under the overhanging Resort Deck. They have little exposure to sun or light, so sunbathing is out of the question. Many thick supporting struts ruin the view from these cabins, which are otherwise pleasant enough.

Other cabin accommodation grades are: Veranda; Family Veranda; Concierge; Ocean View; and Interior (no view). Suite-grade categories are: Aqua; Sky; Celebrity; Royal; and Penthouse. Suites have much more space, plus larger balconies with good-quality sunloungers, and more personal amenities than standard cabins.

DINING. Eating at Grand Cuvée, the ship's 1,430-seat main dining room, is included in the cruise price. It is spread over two decks, with ocean views on the port and starboard sides and at the stern, and its contemporary design is stunning. Towards the aft section, a two-deck-high wine tower provides a focal point.

Suite occupants can dine in the exclusive setting of Luminae, a restaurant offering tableside preparation of signature dishes, an eclectic menu, and a selection of over 400 wines.

Blu is a 128-seat specialty restaurant, with tablecloths, exclusively for Aqua-class cabin occupants. It has pleasing but rather cool decor.

Murano is an extra-cost, reservations-required, 70-seat dinner venue (with tablecloths), offering high-quality traditional dining with a French flair and gorgeous table settings. The cuisine and service are extremely good.

Tuscan Grille is an extra-cost, tablecloth-free venue, for Italian cuisine, Kobe beef and premium-quality steaks. It has nicely curved archways – like a high-tech winery. Large aft-facing windows offer a great view.

Qsine is a 90-seat 'fun-food' venue. The food consists of multi-flavored, multi-colored, quirky small-bite items. The food is presented in quirky fashion – even on sticks – sort of 'lollipop' cuisine.

Sushi on Five features extra-cost sushi and cooked items including noodle and hot pot dishes. Close by is Café al Bacio & Gelateria, a coffeehouse featuring Lavazza Italian coffee.

Oceanview Café and Grill is a casual, tray-free self-serve buffet venue with a number of food islands and decent signage.

AquaSpa Café is for light, healthier options (solarium fare).

The Mast Bar Grill and Bar is an outside fast-food venue.

ENTERTAINMENT. Celebrity Theater is a three-deck-high, 900-seat venue for production shows and major cabaret acts.

Theme nights are held in the Observation Lounge (whose daytime bland and minimalist decor comes alive at night), while 200-seat Celebrity Central hosts comedy, cooking demonstrations, lectures, and films.

An Entertainment Court showcases street performers, psychics, and caricaturists; it's in the center of the ship, linked to Quasar, a high-pulse, high-volume nightclub, while Ensemble Lounge is a big-band-era cocktail lounge with live music.

SPA/FITNESS. Canyon Ranch SpaClub at Sea measures 24,219 sq ft (2,250 sq m). It includes a large thalassotherapy pool under a solarium glass dome, with health bar for light food and fresh squeezed juices.

Facilities include 25 treatment rooms, including one for wheelchair passengers. There's also an aerobics room, a gymnasium, large men's and women's saunas with a sizable ocean-view window, and a beauty salon.

An extra-cost (free to occupants of Aqua-grade accommodation) unisex thermal suite contains several steam and shower mist rooms and a glacial ice fountain, plus a calming relaxation area with heated tiled beds.

CELEBRITY SOLSTICE
★★★★

THIS SHIP HAS REALLY ELEGANT, UNDERSTATED DECOR IN A SEMI-PREMIUM SETTING

Size:	Large Resort Ship	Passenger/Crew Ratio (lower beds):	2.3
Tonnage:	121,878	Cabins (total):	1,426
Cruise Line:	Celebrity Cruises	Size Range (sq ft/m):	182.9–1,668.4/17.0–155.0
Former Names:	none	Cabins (for one person):	0
Builder:	Meyer Werft (Germany)	Cabins with balcony:	1,216
Entered Service:	Nov 2008	Cabins (wheelchair accessible):	30
Length (ft/m):	1,033.4/315.0	Wheelchair accessibility:	Best
Beam (ft/m):	120.7/36.8	Elevators:	12
Propulsion/Propellers:	diesel (67,200kW)/ 2 azimuthing pods	Casino (gaming tables):	Yes
Passenger Decks:	14	Swimming Pools:	3
Total Crew:	1,210	Self-Service Launderette:	No
Passengers (lower beds):	2,852	Library:	Yes
Passenger Space Ratio (lower beds):	42.7	Onboard currency:	US$

THE SHIP. *Celebrity Solstice* is a sleek-looking ship, with two slim funnels. The vessel has a steeply sloping stern, which includes a mega-yacht-style ducktail platform above the propulsion pods, and is quite attractive. The ship's name is positioned directly under the navigation bridge and not forward on the bows (for space reasons). An unusual feature is an outdoor grass area (Lawn Club); it's open to all, so you can go putting, play croquet or bocce ball, or have a picnic on the grass, or walk barefoot.

Several pool and water-play areas are on Resort Deck; one within a glass-roofed solarium, a sports pool, a family pool, and a fun wet zone. The deck space around the two pools, however, isn't large enough for the number of passengers carried.

The interior spaces are well designed, and the decor is elegant yet contemporary. Most of the entertainment rooms are positioned forward, with dining venues mostly located aft.

There's a wine bar with a sommelier; a pre-dinner cocktail lounge that reflects the jazz age of the 1930s; a bar with the look of an ocean-going yacht; Quasar, a retro bar with large screens that create a nightly light show synchronized to music; and an observation lounge with a dance floor.

Celebrity's signature Martini Bar has over 100 varieties of vodka, as well as Martinis. There's also a small alcove called Crush with an ice-filled table where you can participate in caviar- and vodka-

BERLITZ'S RATINGS		
	Possible	Achieved
Ship	500	392
Accommodation	200	161
Food	400	267
Service	400	300
Entertainment	100	78
Cruise Experience	400	287

OVERALL SCORE 1485 points out of 2000

tasting, or host a private party. It's noisy and congested, but can be a lot of fun.

A two-deck library is a delightful open-ended space, though books on the upper shelves are impossible to reach. The card room – located in the center of the ship, with no ocean-view windows to distract players – is open to noise from adjacent areas, so it's useless as a serious card playing room. Fortunes Casino (non-smoking) has 16 gaming tables and 200 slot machines.

A Hot Glass Show, housed in an outdoor studio on the open deck as part of the Lawn Club and created in collaboration with Corning Museum of Glass, includes a novel glass-blowing show.

Public rooms include an Art Studio, for your artistic needs. Meanwhile The Alcoves are extra-cost 'private' Wi-Fi-equipped cabanas on deck ($149 per day on sea days and $99 on port days).

Passenger niggles include lack of usable drawer space in cabins; inadequate children's facilities and staff during school holidays; congestion when you exit the showlounge; and noise in the lobby when the Martini Bar is busy.

Gratuities are automatically charged to your onboard account.

ACCOMMODATION. The accommodation is both practical and comfortable. There are numerous price grades, depending on size and location.

In non-suite-grade cabins there is little space between the bed and the wall, but all rooms include twin beds convertible to a queen- or king-size bed with premium bedding, sitting area, and vanity desk with hairdryer, but little drawer space. Although closets have good hanging space, other storage space is limited. Bathrooms have a shower enclosure, toilet, and tiny washbasin. A charge of $3.95 for room service applies between 11pm and 6am.

Note that cabins 1551–1597 on the port side and 1556–1602 on the starboard side on Penthouse Deck (Deck 11) suffer from 'aircraft carrier' syndrome because they are directly under the overhanging Resort Deck. They have little exposure to sun or light, so sunbathing is out of the question. Many thick supporting struts ruin the view from these cabins, which are otherwise pleasant enough.

Other accommodation grades are: Veranda; Family Veranda; Concierge; Ocean View; and Interior cabins (no view). Suite-grade categories are: Aqua; Sky; Celebrity; Royal; and Penthouse. Suites have much more space, plus larger balconies with good-quality sunloungers, and more personal amenities than standard cabins.

DINING. Grand Epernay, the principal dining room (included in the cruise price), is located towards the aft, and has ocean views on both sides. The design is contemporary; however, the almost-backless tub-style chairs are uncomfortable. At the forward end, a two-deck-high wine tower provides a fine talking point. The food is disappointing; the decreased quality all too obvious to repeat Celebrity passengers.

Suite occupants can dine in the exclusive setting of Luminae, a restaurant with tableside preparation of signature dishes, an eclectic menu, and a selection of over 400 wines.

Blu is a 130-seat specialty restaurant designated for occupants of Aqua-class cabins. The room has pleasing (but rather cold) blue decor. The ambience is cool.

Murano is an extra-cost, reservations-required venue offering high-quality traditional dining with a French flair and fine table settings.

The Tuscan Grille, an extra-cost, reservations-required venue, serves Kobe beef and premium quality steaks.

Silk Harvest is a Southeast Asian extra-cost dining venue serving unmemorable pan-Asian fusion cuisine.

Sushi on Five features extra-cost sushi and cooked items including noodle and hot pot dishes.

Café al Bacio & Gelateria, situated on one side of the main lobby, is a small coffeehouse serving Lavazza Italian coffee; lines quickly form at peak times.

Oceanview Café and Grill is the expansive, trayless, casual self-serve buffet venue. It has a number of food islands rather than those awful straight buffet counters. The signage is reasonable, but condiments are hard to find.

The AquaSpa Café is for light, healthier options (solarium fare), but the selections need improvement.

ENTERTAINMENT. The 1,115-seat Solstice Theatre, the main showlounge, stages custom-designed, circus-themed production shows. Meanwhile, colorful theme nights take place in the Observation Lounge. The 200-seat Celebrity Central hosts comedy, cooking demonstrations, enrichment lectures, and feature films. Quasar is a high-pulse, high-volume nightclub. An Entertainment Court showcases street performers. The Ensemble Lounge is a big-band-era cocktail lounge with live jazz.

SPA/FITNESS. The large Canton Ranch SpaClub at Sea is laid out over two decks. A large fitness center includes kinesis (pulleys against gravity) workout equipment, plus all the familiar muscle-pumping cardio-vascular machinery. An extra-cost, unisex thermal suite features several steam and shower mist rooms with fragrances such as chamomile, eucalyptus, and mint, and a glacial ice fountain, plus a calming relaxation area with heated tiled beds, and an acupuncture center.

CELEBRITY SUMMIT
★★★★

A PREMIUM-QUALITY MID-SIZE SHIP THAT IS GOOD FOR FAMILY-FRIENDLY CRUISING

Size:	Mid-size Ship	Passenger/Crew Ratio (lower beds):	2.1
Tonnage:	90,940	Cabins (total):	1,079
Cruise Line:	Celebrity Cruises	Size Range (sq ft/m):	165.1–2,530.0/15.34–235.0
Former Names:	*Summit*	Cabins (for one person):	0
Builder:	Chantiers de l'Atlantique (France)	Cabins with balcony:	606
Entered Service:	Oct 2001	Cabins (wheelchair accessible):	26 (17 with private balcony)
Length (ft/m):	964.5/294.0		
Beam (ft/m):	105.6/32.2	Wheelchair accessibility:	Best
Propulsion/Propellers:	gas turbine (39,000kW)/ 2 azimuthing pods	Elevators:	12
		Casino (gaming tables):	Yes
Passenger Decks:	11	Swimming Pools:	3 (1 w/ sliding glass dome)
Total Crew:	999	Self-Service Launderette:	No
Passengers (lower beds):	2,158	Library:	Yes
Passenger Space Ratio (lower beds):	42.1	Onboard currency:	US$

THE SHIP. *Celebrity Summit* is a sister ship to *Celebrity Constellation*, *Celebrity Infinity*, and *Celebrity Millennium*. Mega-yacht designer Jon Bannenberg was responsible for the exterior, with its royal blue-and-white hull. In early 2012, the ship underwent a 'Solsticizing' program, which meant more cabins, more facilities, and more dining options to match the newer ships in the fleet; no extra elevators were added, however.

Inside, the ship has a similar standard of decor and materials to other ships in this group, and public rooms that are user-friendly. An atrium spans three decks and houses the reception desk, tour operator's desk, and bank. Four glass-walled elevators travel through the ship's exterior (port) side, connecting the atrium with another seven decks, traveling through 10 decks, including the tender stations – a nice ride.

Facilities include a combination Cinema/Conference Center, an expansive shopping arcade with oodles of of retail store space (with designer labels such as Fendi, Fossil, Hugo Boss, and Versace), a lavish four-deck-high showlounge with high-tech sound and lighting, a two-level library (one level for English-language books; a second for other languages and reference material), card room, music-listening room, and an observation lounge/discotheque with fine views.

Michael's Club, formerly a cigar smoker's haven,

BERLITZ'S RATINGS		
	Possible	Achieved
Ship	500	362
Accommodation	200	153
Food	400	263
Service	400	287
Entertainment	100	74
Cruise Experience	400	273
OVERALL SCORE 1412 points out of 2000		

is now a lounge for suite-grade occupants only; it has large leather chairs and a fireplace. An Internet café has almost 20 computers and extra-cost Internet connectivity.

Gaming sports include the ship's overly large Fortunes Casino, with lots of bright lights and action. Families with children will appreciate the Fun Factory (for younger children) and The Tower (for teenagers). Children's counselors and youth activities staff provide a wide range of supervised activities.

ACCOMMODATION. There are many price grades from which to choose, depending on your preference for the size and location – and your budget. These include standard interior cabins (no view) and outside-view cabins (with or without balcony) to spacious suite grades named Aqua, Concierge, Royal, Celebrity, and Penthouse. There are also wheelchair-accessible cabins (all with wheel-in showers), positioned close to elevators.

All accommodation grades are very comfortable, but the suites, naturally, have more space. If you choose a balcony cabin on one of the upper decks, note that it could be shaded under the pool deck, which extends over the ship's side – and by many balconies (not good for private sunbathing). Some suites have extremely large balconies – always check the deck plan before choosing. Note that a charge for room service applies between 11pm and 6am.

DINING. The Cosmopolitan Restaurant is a 1,170-seat main dining room. It is two decks high with a grand staircase connecting the two levels, a huge glass wall overlooking the sea aft (electrically operated shades provide several different backdrops), and a musicians' gallery on the upper level. As a tribute to the French Line ship *Normandie*, a statue (called *La Normandie*) that was created by Léon-Georges Baudry and once overlooked the ship's grand staircase (and for the past approximate half a century graced Miami's Fontainebleau Hotel) was bought for $250,000 and can now be seen here.

There are two seatings for dinner (open seating for breakfast and lunch), at tables for two to 10. Suite occupants dine in the exclusive setting of Luminae, a restaurant featuring tableside preparation of signature dishes, an eclectic menu, and a selection of over 400 wines.

Blu, located on the port side of the upper level entrance to the Cosmopolitan dining room, is exclusively for the use of occupants of Aqua-class accommodation.

The former Normandie Restaurant is now the Tuscan Grille. This extra-cost, reservations-required venue features Kobe beef and premium-quality steaks. It includes a dine-in wine cellar and a demonstration galley.

QSine, which has iPad menus and wine list, is another extra-cost dining venue; reservations are required.

There are several other options in more casual settings.

The Waterfall Café and Grill is a casual self-serve buffet area, with six serving lines, and seating for 754; there is also a grill and pizza bar. For Champagne and caviar lovers, and for Martinis, Carlisle's is the place to see and be seen.

Café al Bacio & Gelateria, on the third level of the atrium lobby, is the place for (extra-cost) coffees, pastries, cakes, and ice cream, in a trendy setting.

Sushi on Five features extra-cost sushi and cooked items including noodle and hot pot dishes.

ENTERTAINMENT. The 900-seat Celebrity Theater is the three-deck-high venue for production shows and major cabaret acts. It is located forward, with seating on main, and two balcony levels. The large stage is equipped with a full fly loft behind its traditional proscenium.

SPA/FITNESS. A large Canyon Ranch SpaClub at Sea measures 24,219 sq ft (2,250 sq m). It has a large thalassotherapy pool under a solarium dome, complete with health bar for fresh squeezed fruit and vegetable juices.

CELEBRITY XPEDITION
★★★+

A COMFORTABLE SHIP FOR EXPERIENCING THE GALÁPAGOS ISLANDS

Size:	Boutique Ship	Passenger/Crew Ratio (lower beds):	1.4
Tonnage:	2,842	Cabins (total):	45
Cruise Line:	Celebrity Cruises	Size Range (sq ft/m):	156.0–460.0/14.5–42.7
Former Names:	Sun Bay	Cabins (for one person):	0
Builder:	Cassens-Werft (Germany)	Cabins with balcony:	8
Entered Service:	Jun 2001/Jun 2004	Cabins (wheelchair accessible):	0
Length (ft/m):	290.3/88.5	Wheelchair accessibility:	None
Beam (ft/m):	45.9/14.0	Elevators:	0
Propulsion/Propellers:	diesel (3,000kW)/2	Casino (gaming tables):	No
Passenger Decks:	4	Swimming Pools:	No
Total Crew:	64	Self-Service Launderette:	No
Passengers (lower beds):	90	Library:	Yes
Passenger Space Ratio (lower beds):	31.5	Onboard currency:	US$

THE SHIP. This was the first specialist boutique ship for Celebrity Cruises and it is like a small private club for Galápagos ecotourism. It will suit mature adults who want an intimate and casual cruise experience, and, of course, to see the famous Galápagos Islands.

There is a surprisingly good amount of open deck space – much of it with teakwood decking, as well as teak sunloungers and patio furniture. Although there is no swimming pool, there is a whirlpool tub. Stabilizers were installed in 2004.

All accommodation is located in the forward half, with the public rooms aft. The ambience is unhurried, yet subtly elegant. Except for the dining room, which can double as a conference room, there is only one public room: the main lounge, complete with bar, dance floor, and bandstand.

Shore excursions by Zodiac inflatable boats are in small groups led by Ecuadorian guides. On your return, waiters greet you with refreshing drinks and towels. Included in the fare: excursions, gratuities to shipboard staff, beverages including house wine, Champagne, liquor, beer, and soda.

ACCOMMODATION. There are four price categories in two cabin types: nine Suites measuring 247 sq ft (23 sq m); 34 Comfort Cabins, 172 sq ft (16 sq m); and three Comfort Cabins, 156 sq ft (14.5 sq m). All suites and cabins have twin beds (four comfort cabins

BERLITZ'S RATINGS

	Possible	Achieved
Ship	500	331
Accommodation	200	140
Food	400	241
Service	400	274
Entertainment	100	50
Cruise Experience	400	227

OVERALL SCORE 1263 points out of 2000

have double beds), TV, sofa, drinks table, vanity desk with hairdryer, minibar/refrigerator, and personal safe. Bathrooms all have a good-size shower enclosure (there are no tubs) with soap/shampoo dispenser and white marble-clad walls.

The largest accommodation is in nine suites, each with a private balcony. One suite has forward-facing views and a sloping ceiling with character. Balcony partitions are almost private; the balcony deck is teak covered. Two of the suites can be joined together. One bedroom has two pull-down Murphy beds.

DINING. The Darwin Dining Room operates on an open-seating basis. A self-serve buffet offers salads, cold cuts, and cheeses. House wines and beer are included in the fare; a few better wines can be bought. The cuisine depends on local suppliers; fish seafood and fruits are good, but vegetables are inconsistent. The casual, self-serve Seagull Buffet is just behind the main lounge, with teak tables and chairs.

ENTERTAINMENT. After-dinner conversation with fellow passengers is the main entertainment.

SPA/FITNESS. There is a small fitness room, and adjacent unisex sauna located inside on the uppermost deck, while a small beauty salon is located on the lowest deck.

CELESTYAL CRISTAL
★★★

A CASUAL SHIP WITH FRIENDLY CREW FOR PORT-INTENSIVE CRUISES

Size:	Mid-size Ship	Passenger/Crew Ratio (lower beds):	2.4
Tonnage:	25,611	Cabins (total):	483
Cruise Line:	Celestyal Cruises	Size Range (sq ft/m):	107.6–462.8/10.0–43.0
Former Names:	Louis Crystal, Silja Opera, SuperStar	Cabins (for one person):	0
	Taurus, Leeward, Sally Albatross, Viking Saga	Cabins with balcony:	53
Builder:	Wartsila (Finland)	Cabins (wheelchair accessible):	6
Entered Service:	1980/Jul 2007	Wheelchair accessibility:	None
Length (ft/m):	530.5/161.7	Elevators:	4
Beam (ft/m):	100.0/30.5	Casino (gaming tables):	Yes
Propulsion/Propellers:	diesel (19,120kW)/2	Swimming Pools:	1 (indoors)
Passenger Decks:	7	Self-Service Launderette:	No
Total Crew:	400	Library:	Yes
Passengers (lower beds):	966	Onboard currency:	Euros
Passenger Space Ratio (lower beds):	26.5		

THE SHIP. *Celestyal Cristal* has a smart wedge-shaped profile with a squared-off stern and short, stubby bows. It benefits from a good, walk-around teak promenade deck. The pool deck is very cramped, although the pool itself can be covered by a sliding glass dome. There is no forward-facing observation lounge atop the ship. There is a reasonable array of public rooms, lounges, bars, including a casino with both gaming tables and slot machines, a convenience store, duty-free shop, and internet center (Wi-Fi costs extra).

Celestyal Cristal should appeal to anyone seeking to cruise the Greek Islands in a modicum of comfort, and at a very modest price. The dress code is casual throughout, with no formal nights. The ship operates 3-, 4- and 7-day cruises (many of them with themes including history, wine, food, and health). Drinks-inclusive packages are available. Note that gratuities are not included in the fare.

ACCOMMODATION. There are three suite categories (Imperial, Balcony, and Junior), and a mix of several outside-view cabins (some of which have balconies) and interior cabins in 19 price grades.

The top-grade suites have neatly angled private balconies and provide a decent amount of space for short cruises; the bathrooms have a tub, separate shower, and good storage facilities for toiletries. Most of the standard cabins and bathrooms are really

BERLITZ'S RATINGS		
	Possible	Achieved
Ship	500	322
Accommodation	200	133
Food	400	230
Service	400	246
Entertainment	100	62
Cruise Experience	400	243

OVERALL SCORE 1236 points out of 2000

very small, and in need of updating and better soundproofing. Also, note that some cabins have views obstructed, by safety equipment.

DINING. Olympus Restaurant is the main dining room, but there are also a number of other dining spots and casual eateries. There are two seatings for dinner on most nights (typically an open seating for the first night), and open seating for breakfast and lunch. Seating and table assignments for dinner are made by the maître d' during embarkation.

Celestyal Cruises (a sub-brand of Louis Cruises) specializes in Greek regional cuisine. All tables are laid with crisp white linen. Spa and vegetarian dishes are available on lunch and dinner menus.

Amalthia is an L-shaped self-serve buffet restaurant for casual meals and snacks, with some excellent views aft. Other casual eateries include Aura and Leda Casual Dining venues, both located aft of the swimming pool.

ENTERTAINMENT. The Muses Lounge is the ship's showlounge; it spans two decks and has decent sight lines.

SPA/FITNESS. Sana Beauty facilities include a beauty salon, fitness room, and men's and women's saunas and steam rooms. Wellness and beauty treatments are available.

CELESTYAL NEFELI
★★★

A SMART-LOOKING SHIP BEST SUITED TO SMALL ISLAND CRUISING

Size:	Mid-size Ship	Passenger/Crew Ratio (lower beds):	1.4
Tonnage:	19,093	Cabins (total):	400
Cruise Line:	Celestyal Cruises	Size Range (sq ft/m):	139.9–377.8/13.0–35.0
Former Names:	*Gemini, Cunard Crown Jewel*	Cabins (for one person):	0
Builder:	Union Navale de Levante (Spain)	Cabins with balcony:	20
Entered Service:	Aug 1992/Feb 2016	Cabins (wheelchair accessible):	4
Length (ft/m):	537.4/163.8	Wheelchair accessibility:	Fair
Beam (ft/m):	73.8/22.5	Elevators:	4
Propulsion/Propellers:	diesels/2	Casino (gaming tables):	Yes
Passenger Decks:	7	Swimming Pools:	1
Total Crew:	560	Self-Service Launderette:	No
Passengers (lower beds):	800	Library:	Yes
Passenger Space Ratio (lower beds):	23.8	Onboard currency:	Euros

THE SHIP. The all-white *Celestyal Nefeli* (the name means goddess of hospitality and nymph of the clouds) has attractive exterior styling, and a lot of glass space (plenty of connection with the sea). There is a good amount of open deck and sunbathing space for its size, and this includes two outdoor bars – one aft and one amidships adjacent to the swimming pool. Four open decks provide good, quiet places to sit and read. There is a complete walk-around deck, made of teak. You can go right to the ship's bow – good for those *Titanic*-pose photographs. Inside, there is a pleasant five-deck-high, glass-walled atrium on the starboard side.

Public rooms include a large lounge, library/Internet-connect room, card room, karaoke room, children's center, video games arcade, and several bars. The Star Club has gaming tables and an array of slot machines.

This is a casual ship with a modern look. It does get a little congested in some places, but overall it's a very pleasant ship for inter-island cruising.

ACCOMMODATION. There are several cabin price categories; the higher the deck, the higher the cost. All grades have a television and hairdryer (some are awkward to retract from their wall-mount holders), European-style duvets, and large cotton bathroom towels (bathrobes are available upon request in suite-grade cabins).

BERLITZ'S RATINGS	Possible	Achieved
Ship	500	309
Accommodation	200	128
Food	400	230
Service	400	246
Entertainment	100	62
Cruise Experience	400	241
OVERALL SCORE 1216 points out of 2000		

Note that some cabins suffer from poor soundproofing; passengers in cabins on Deck 4 in particular are disturbed by anyone running or jogging on the promenade deck above. Cabins on the lowest deck (Deck 2) in the ship's center are subject to noise from the adjacent engine room.

DINING. The Ocean Palace Restaurant is a pleasant venue for main meals. However, space is tight, and the tables are extremely close together, making proper service difficult at some tables. There are tables for two to eight. Celestyal Cruises specializes in Greek regional cuisine, as well as some international favorites. All tables are laid with crisp white linen. Spa and vegetarian dishes are available on lunch and dinner menus.

Mariner's Buffet is a self-serve food court-style eatery. It has both indoor and outdoor seating (overlooking the stern), but the food display area is small.

ENTERTAINMENT. The Galaxy of the Stars (showlounge) sits longitudinally along one side of the ship, with amphitheater-style seating in several tiers, but its layout is less than ideal for either shows or cocktail parties.

SPA/FITNESS. There is a beauty salon, a combined fitness and aerobics room, plus a separate room for women and men, with sauna, steam room, and small changing area.

CELESTYAL OLYMPIA
★★★

A COMFORTABLE FAMILY-FRIENDLY SHIP FOR CASUAL CRUISING

Size:	Mid-size Ship	Passenger/Crew Ratio (lower beds):	2.6
Tonnage:	37,773	Cabins (total):	725
Cruise Line:	Celestyal Cruises	Size Range (sq ft/m):	118.4–425.1/11.0–39.5
Former Names:	Louis Olympia, Thomson Destiny,	Cabins (for one person):	0
	Sunbird, Song of America	Cabins with balcony:	9
Builder:	Wartsila (Finland)	Cabins (wheelchair accessible):	0
Entered Service:	Dec 1982/May 2012	Wheelchair accessibility:	Fair
Length (ft/m):	705.0/214.8	Elevators:	7
Beam (ft/m):	93.1/28.4	Casino (gaming tables):	Yes
Propulsion/Propellers:	diesel (16,480kW)/2	Swimming Pools:	2
Passenger Decks:	11	Self-Service Launderette:	No
Total Crew:	540	Library:	Yes
Passengers (lower beds):	1,450	Onboard currency:	Euros
Passenger Space Ratio (lower beds):	26.0		

THE SHIP. Originally built for Royal Caribbean International, the all-white ship is smart looking, with nicely rounded lines, sharply raked bow, and a single funnel with a cantilevered, wraparound lounge – a fine place from which to observe the world around and below you.

There's a decent amount of open deck and sunbathing space, but it gets crowded when the ship sails full, which is most of the time. There are some nicely polished wooden decks and rails and two swimming pools – the aft one is designated for children, the forward one for adults.

The interior decor is bright and breezy. There's a good array of public rooms, most with high ceilings. All are located one deck above the dining room and include the main showlounge, casino, and nightclub. There's also a small conference center for meetings, as well as an Internet café with several computer terminals.

There are no cushioned pads for the sunloungers. Standing in line for embarkation, disembarkation, shore tenders, and for self-serve buffet meals is an inevitable aspect of cruising aboard all large ships. Passenger niggles include the dated look of the ship's interiors.

Celestyal Olympia is best suited to adult couples and solo travelers taking their first or second cruise, and families with children, all seeking a modern but not glitzy ship with a wide array of public lounges and bars, a middle-of-the-road lifestyle, and decent

BERLITZ'S RATINGS		
	Possible	Achieved
Ship	500	310
Accommodation	200	118
Food	400	242
Service	400	246
Entertainment	100	62
Cruise Experience	400	256

OVERALL SCORE 1234 points out of 2000

food and service. It operates in the Greek Islands and Mediterranean.

The best part of cruising aboard Celestyal Olympia lies in the destinations, and not the ship – although it is perfectly comfortable, and Celestyal Cruises provides a consistent, well-tuned, and well-packaged product.

ACCOMMODATION. This is provided in several categories and price bands: interior cabins (parallel or L-shaped bed arrangement), outside-view cabins (parallel or L-shaped bed arrangement), deluxe cabins (with parallel twin beds that can convert to a queen-size bed), suites, and Grand Suites.

Most cabins are of a similar size – dimensionally challenged when compared to today's newer ships – and insulation between them is poor. The cabins also have mediocre closets and little storage space, yet somehow everyone seems to manage. They are just about adequate for a one-week cruise, as you'll require only a small selection of mainly casual clothes. You'll probably need to store your shoes and luggage under the bed.

Most bathrooms contain a washbasin, toilet, and shower, with very little space for toiletries. Although they are reasonably cheerful, the shower enclosure is small, and has a curtain that you might end up fighting with.

In some cabins, twin beds are fixed in a parallel mode – some are moveable and can be made into a queen-size bed – while others may be in an L-shape. In almost all cabins there is a threshold of about 9ins (23cm) at the bathroom door to step over.

You can get more space and a larger cabin if you book one of the 21 slightly more expensive deluxe-grade cabins on Promenade Deck. These have twin beds that convert to a queen-size bed, set diagonally into a sleeping area adjacent to outside-view windows. There's more drawer space, more closet space, and the bathroom has a half-size tub and shower combination. Bathrobes are also provided. The largest of these deluxe-grade cabins is Cabin 7000.

For even more exclusivity, you can book one of nine suites. All are located in a private area, have fine wood paneling and trim, and come with additional space and better, more personalized service.

The additional space includes a lounge area with sofa (this converts to a double bed – making it ideal for families with children), coffee table and two chairs, a vanity desk, combination TV/DVD, an abundance of drawers, illuminated closets with both hanging space and several shelves, excellent storage space, king-size bed, and bathrobes. The bathroom is completely tiled and has a full-size enamel tub (rare in ships today) with shower, pink granite-look washbasin, and plenty of storage space for toiletries.

Suite occupants also get a semi-private balcony – with a door that is extremely heavy and hard to open – with drinks table and two teak chairs. Book one of the two Grand Suites, and you'll get even more room – plus views over the bows and a larger balcony (these can be overlooked from the open deck above, however), more floor space, and a walk-in closet. Missing are a bedside telephone and a bathroom telephone.

Note that the accommodation deck hallways are very narrow on some decks.

DINING. The Seven Seas Restaurant, a large room, consists of a central main section and two long, slim wings – the Magellan Room and Galileo Room – with large, ocean-view windows. The low ceiling creates a high level of ambient noise. There are two seatings. There are tables for two (only 14 of them), four, six, or eight, and window tables are for two or six.

If you enjoy eating out adventurously, you could be disappointed. The menus are standard, and deviation is difficult. Bottled water costs extra. There is an adequate wine list. Wine prices are quite modest, as are the prices for most alcoholic drinks.

For casual, self-serve breakfasts and lunches, the Veranda Café is the alternative choice, although the tables and seats outdoors are of metal and plastic, and the buffets are basic and old-fashioned. The low cruise fare dictates the use of plastic cups and plastic stirrers – teaspoons are unheard of. At night you can 'dine' under the steel-and-canvas canopy, where the café becomes a pleasant, outdoors alternative to the dining room – and includes waiter service.

The excellent Italian illy coffee brand is featured aboard this ship, together with a selection of fine teas, in several bars and lounges.

ENTERTAINMENT. The Can Can Lounge, the venue for all entertainment events and social functions, has a stage and hardwood dance floor. It is a single-level room, designed more for cabaret acts than for large-scale production shows. The revue-style shows are typical of the end-of-pier variety type, with an energetic, well-meaning cast of young people who also double as cruise staff during the day, together with some professional cabaret acts.

Another, smaller room, the Oklahoma Lounge, has a stage and dance floor, and is often used to present late-night comedy and other acts.

SPA/FITNESS. Although the Sana Spa facilities are not exactly generous, they include a gymnasium, sauna (but no steam room), changing rooms for men and women, and a beauty salon. You can book a massage, aromatherapy facial, manicure, and pedicure, among other treatments. Sports facilities include basketball, badminton, and table tennis.

CLUB MED 2
★★★+

THE SHIP'S FRENCH AMBIENCE AND STYLE PUTS WIND IN YOUR SAILS

Size:	Small Ship	Passenger/Crew Ratio (lower beds):	1.9
Tonnage:	14,983	Cabins (total):	197
Cruise Line:	Club Med Cruises	Size Range (sq ft/m):	193.8–322/18–30
Former Names:	none	Cabins (for one person):	0
Builder:	Ateliers et Chantiers du Havre	Cabins with balcony:	0
Entered Service:	Dec 1992	Cabins (wheelchair accessible):	0
Length (ft/m):	613.8/187.1	Wheelchair accessibility:	None
Beam (ft/m):	65.6/20.0	Elevators:	2
Propulsion/Propellers:	diesel (9,120kW)/2	Casino (gaming tables):	No
Passenger Decks:	8	Swimming Pools:	2
Total Crew:	200	Self-Service Launderette:	No
Passengers (lower beds):	394	Library:	Yes
Passenger Space Ratio (lower beds):	38.0	Onboard currency:	Euros

THE SHIP. *Club Med 2* is one of a pair of the world's largest high-tech sail-cruisers (the other is *Wind Surf*), part-cruise ship, part-yacht. Five huge masts rise 221ft (67.4m) above sea level; they carry seven triangular, self-furling Dacron sails with a total surface area of 26,881 sq ft (2,497 sq m). No human hands touch the sails, as everything is controlled by computer from the bridge. This also keeps the ship on an even keel via the movement of a hydraulic ballast system, so there is no rolling over 6°. The ship was refurbished in 2008, when 10 new cabins were added.

An array of water-sports facilities is provided (all except scuba gear are included in the cruise fare), and equipment on the aft marina platform includes 12 windsurfers, three sailboats, two water-ski boats, several kayaks, 20 single scuba tanks, snorkels, and four motorized water-sports boats. There are two small saltwater swimming pools (really 'dip' pools).

Inside, facilities include a main lounge, meeting room, and an extra-charge golf simulator, plus a fitness and beauty center, and piano bar. No gratuities are expected.

This ship appeals best to youthful French-speaking couples and solo travelers who want contemporary facilities and water sports in a casual but chic setting that's different from 'normal' cruise ships, with good food and service, and little or no entertainment.

BERLITZ'S RATINGS		
	Possible	Achieved
Ship	500	341
Accommodation	200	136
Food	400	242
Service	400	251
Entertainment	100	60
Cruise Experience	400	243
OVERALL SCORE 1273 points out of 2000		

ACCOMMODATION. There are five suites and 192 standard cabins, all of equal size. All cabins are nicely equipped and very comfortable, and have an inviting decor that includes much blond wood cabinetry. They have a minibar/refrigerator, 24-hour room service (but you pay for food), a safe, television, plenty of storage space, bathrobes, and a hairdryer. There are six four-person cabins, and some 35 doubles are fitted with an extra Pullman berth.

DINING. The two main dining rooms are Le Mediterranée and Le Magellan. Both have tables for two, four, six, or eight. There is open seating, so you can sit with whom you wish. The Grand Bleu Restaurant has a delightful open terrace for informal meals. Complimentary wines and beers are available with lunch and dinner; there is also an à la carte wine list, at a price. Afternoon tea is a delight. The cuisine provides French, Continental, and Japanese specialties, and the creativity and presentation are good.

ENTERTAINMENT. Apart from occasional cabaret acts, there is live music each evening.

SPA/FITNESS. The Health Spa has a sauna, beauty salon, and treatment rooms for massage, facials, and body wraps. There is also a decent fitness room and a beauty salon, but spa facilities are split over three separate decks.

COLUMBUS
★★★

A DATED BUT VERY FRIENDLY SHIP FOR MATURE-AGE TRAVELERS

Size:	Mid-size Ship	Passenger/Crew Ratio (lower beds):	3.1
Tonnage:	63,786	Cabins (total):	775
Cruise Line:	Cruise and Maritime Voyages	Size Range (sq ft/m):	182.9–398.2/17.0–37.0
Former Names:	Pacific Pearl, Ocean Village, Arcadia,	Cabins (for one person):	0
	Star Princess, FairMajesty	Cabins with balcony:	64
Builder:	Chantiers de l'Atlantique (France)	Cabins (wheelchair accessible):	8
Entered Service:	Mar 1989/Apr 2017	Wheelchair accessibility:	Good
Length (ft/m):	810.3/247.0	Elevators:	9
Beam (ft/m):	105.6/32.2	Casino (gaming tables):	Yes
Propulsion/Propellers:	diesel-electric (42,000kW)/2	Swimming Pools:	3
Passenger Decks:	12	Self-Service Launderette:	Yes
Total Crew:	514	Library:	Yes
Passengers (lower beds):	1,550	Onboard currency:	UK£
Passenger Space Ratio (lower beds):	41.5		

THE SHIP. *Columbus* (some UK cruisegoers may remember it as *Ocean Village* – one of her former names) is best suited to mature couples, and solo travelers who like to cruise in an older mid-size ship and are happy with food that offers quantity rather than quality, all at an attractive price. The ship's passenger capacity was reduced from the original, which means there's more space per person.

The ship was originally designed and built as *FairMajesty* for Sitmar Cruises, and was formerly operating in Australasian waters between 2010 and 2017.

Columbus is well proportioned, with decent open deck and sunbathing space. On the open leisure deck are two pools, one with sloping steps, the other with vertical steps (one has a sit-in 'splash' bar). An Oasis (quiet zone) with day beds and a hot tub is aft on Deck 8. There's no full walk-around promenade deck outdoors, but open port and starboard walking areas stretch partly along the sides. There is, however, a walking track on the uppermost open deck. The interiors are quite pleasant, with much attention paid to lighting. There are also a few items that have a link with the past, such as the Art Deco stainless-steel balustrades and soulless stainless-steel elevators.

The interior focal point is a three-deck-high atrium lobby and a multi-deck dual staircase. There are seven lounges and bars. Highlights include The Dome, an observation lounge, which sits atop the ship, for-

BERLITZ'S RATINGS		
	Possible	Achieved
Ship	500	316
Accommodation	200	124
Food	400	212
Service	400	237
Entertainment	100	56
Cruise Experience	400	230

OVERALL SCORE 1175 points out of 2000

ward of the mast. It is a lounge for cocktails, but at night it turns into a night-spot, with a sunken, circular wooden dance floor. There's also a casino, card room, and a craft center. Most public rooms have ceilings higher than the average for modern-day cruise ships.

For retail therapy, several shops are clustered around the second and third levels of the atrium lobby.

ACCOMMODATION. There are four basic types: mini-suites; outsides with balcony; outside-view; and interior. They come in 20 different price grades, depending on location and size.

Most outside-view/interior cabins have twin beds that can, in most cases, be put together to form a queen-size bed. All have a good amount of storage, including wooden drawer units, plus some under-bed space for luggage, and a walk-in closet. Sound insulation between cabins could be better, though (TV sound late at night can be irritating). Decent-quality bed linen, duvets, and pillows are provided. Note that Cabins 8120–8157 and 9138–9149 have lifeboat and safety equipment-obstructed views.

The modular design bathrooms have good-size shower enclosures and a retractable clothesline. Only mini-suites have bathtubs, as the ship was originally built for North American passengers, who tend to prefer showers. However, shower heads are fixed to the wall, denying you the ease of a flexible shower hose.

Mini-suites have a small private balcony, walk-in closet, masses of storage space, and wood-floored bathroom with bathtub and shower.

DINING. The Waterfront (main restaurant) seats 800-plus, with open seating. It has ocean-view windows, sit-down tablecloth dining, and tables for two to eight. It has a high ceiling, and seating sections help divide the room into comfortable spaces.

The food is straightforward, unfussy, and geared to British tastes, with little use of garnishes. For more intimate dining and (extra-cost) food cooked to order, try the Grill specialty venue, which has an open kitchen.

Plantation is a self-serve buffet venue, open for breakfast, lunch, and dinner. It's typically slow-going along straight buffet lines, so patience is needed. Tea and coffee are provided at the beverage stations.

The Café, for coffees, hot chocolate, and snacks, is adjacent to the forward swimming pool. Charlie's, a neat little coffee bistro, located on the lowest lobby level opposite the reception desk, is for extra-cost coffees, teas, pastries, and snacks. The pool has an ice cream bar.

ENTERTAINMENT. The Palladium Showlounge is a horseshoe-shaped showlounge with main and balcony levels, with a bar at the back on the main level. It has adequate sight lines from most of the banquette-style seating, but sight lines from the upper-level front-row seats are obstructed by a safety rail.

Although the ship isn't young and doesn't have the latest bells and whistles, the stage has a good LED lighting backdrop. Entertainment includes production shows and cabaret. There is also live music in several lounges and bars.

SPA/FITNESS. The Thermal spa facilities – located on the lowest deck – include a beauty salon, workout room, and a thermal/relax area that includes a unisex sauna, steam room, herbal showers, and two body-shaped tiled hot beds.

CORAL PRINCESS
★★★+

THIS IS A COMFORTABLE MID-SIZE SHIP FOR MATURE-AGE CRUISERS

Size:	Mid-size Ship	Passenger/Crew Ratio (lower beds):	2.1
Tonnage:	91,627	Cabins (total):	987
Cruise Line:	Princess Cruises	Size Range (sq ft/m):	156–470.0/14.4–43.6
Former Names:	none	Cabins (for one person):	0
Builder:	Chantiers de l'Atlantique (France)	Cabins with balcony:	727
Entered Service:	Dec 2002	Cabins (wheelchair accessible):	20
Length (ft/m):	964.5/294.0	Wheelchair accessibility:	Good
Beam (ft/m):	105.6/32.2	Elevators:	14
Propulsion/Propellers:	gas turbine + diesel (40,000kW)/2	Casino (gaming tables):	Yes
		Swimming Pools:	2
Passenger Decks:	11	Self-Service Launderette:	Yes
Total Crew:	900	Library:	Yes
Passengers (lower beds):	1,974	Onboard currency:	US$
Passenger Space Ratio (lower beds):	46.4		

THE SHIP. *Coral Princess* (sister to *Island Princess*) has an instantly recognizable funnel due to two jet engine-like pods high up on its structure, but these really are mainly for decoration. Four diesel engines provide the generating power.

The layout is quite user-friendly and less disjointed than on many ships of a similar size. The interior layout is similar to that of the *Grand*-class ships, but with two decks of public rooms, lounges, and bars instead of just one. Sensibly, it has three major stair towers. *Coral Princess* has a walk-around open promenade deck, a feature appreciated by many. An adults-only 'Sanctuary' area is available as an extra-cost quiet zone, with comfortable padded sunloungers. There's a large 'Movies Under the Stars' screen in a second pool area forward of the funnel.

The ship has a Wedding Chapel, from which a live web-cam can relay ceremonies via the Internet. The ship's captain can legally marry (American) couples, thanks to the ship's registry and a special dispensation – though this may depend on where you live – to be verified when in the planning stage. The Wedding Chapel can also host renewal of vows ceremonies, for a fee.

Also, at the forward end of decks 10 and 11, doors open onto an observation terrace.

Niggles include the fact that the forward elevators go between decks 15 and 7, so you need to change elevators to get down to the dining rooms on Deck

BERLITZ'S RATINGS

	Possible	Achieved
Ship	500	348
Accommodation	200	136
Food	400	247
Service	400	287
Entertainment	100	76
Cruise Experience	400	286

OVERALL SCORE 1380 points out of 2000

5. Also unpopular are the user-unfriendly automated telephone system, the small cabin towels, having to pay extra for items such as ice cream, and needing change for the washers and dryers in the self-service launderettes.

Overall, however, Princess Cruises delivers a consistently fine, comfortable, well-packaged product, always with a good degree of style, at a competitive price.

ACCOMMODATION. With many different price categories, there's a wide choice: 16 suites with balcony (470 sq ft/43.6 sq m); 184 mini-suites with balcony (285–302 sq ft/26.5–28 sq m); eight mini-suites without balcony (300 sq ft/27.8 sq m); 527 outside-view cabins with balcony (217–232 sq ft/ 20–21.5 sq m); 144 standard outside-view cabins (162 sq ft/15 sq m); plus 108 interior cabins (156 sq ft/14.5 sq m). There are 20 wheelchair-accessible cabins (217–374 sq ft/20–34.7 sq m). All measurements are approximate. Almost all outside-view cabins have private balconies. Some cabins can accommodate a third, or third and fourth person, which is good for families with children. Some cabins on Emerald Deck (Deck 8) have a view obstructed by lifeboats.

Suites are located on either Deck 9 or Deck 10, but none has an aft view. There are also four Premium Suites, located sensibly in the ship's center, adjacent to a bank of six elevators. Six other suites, called Verandah Suites, are located further aft.

Nearly all accommodation is equipped with a refrigerator, personal safe, interactive TV, hairdryer, satellite-dial telephone, and twin beds that convert to a queen-size bed. All cabins have a bathroom with shower enclosure and toilet. Suites and mini-suites (there are several price categories) come with a bathtub, separate shower enclosure, and two TV sets.

Cabin attendants have many cabins to look after – typically 20 – which does not translate to fine personal service.

DINING. The two main dining rooms, Bordeaux and Provence, are located forward, on the two lowest passenger decks. Both are almost identical in design and layout. The ceilings are quite low and make the rooms appear confined. They have plenty of intimate alcoves, and tables are for two to eight. There are two seatings for dinner (or you can opt for 'Anytime Dining' in the Bordeaux Restaurant), while breakfast and lunch are on an open-seating basis. You may have to wait at peak times.

Although portions are generous, the food and its presentation are disappointing and standardized – it's mass catering, after all. Fish is often disguised with sauces or coatings, the choice of fresh green vegetables is limited, few garnishes are used, and cheese is either pre-sliced or diced. Pasta dishes are acceptable (though voluminous).

Horizon Court, a casual eatery that is open almost 24 hours, is located in the forward section of Lido Deck, with superb ocean views. Several self-serve counters provide breakfast and lunch buffets, and offer bistro-style casual dinners in the evening. The venue is a bit short on seating, however.

There are two specialty dining rooms: Sabatini's and the Bayou Café. Both cost extra. Sabatini's is an Italian eatery, with colorful tiled Mediterranean-style decor; it is named after Trattoria Sabatini, the historic institution in Florence. It has Italian-style pizzas and pastas, and Italian-style entrées (mains) – all served with flair. The food is both creative and tasty, with seriously sized portions. Sabatini's is by reservation only, and there's a cover charge.

Bayou Café (reservations required) is open for lunch and dinner and has a cover charge (this includes a Hurricane cocktail). It evokes the charm of New Orleans' French Quarter, with wrought-iron decoration, and features Cajun/Creole cuisine. The venue has a small stage with baby grand piano.

ENTERTAINMENT. The Princess Theater is two decks high and, unusually, has much more seating in the upper level than on the main floor. Productions are colorful, glamorous affairs with well-designed costumes and good lighting.

A second entertainment lounge (Universe Lounge) is used for cabaret-style shows. It also has two levels – a first for a Princess Cruises ship – and three separate stages, enabling non-stop entertainment without constant set-ups. The room, with a full kitchen set, is also used for cooking demonstrations and other life-enrichment participation activities. There is a good mix of music in the various bars and lounges.

SPA/FITNESS. The Lotus Spa is located aft on one of the uppermost decks. It contains men's and women's saunas, steam rooms, changing rooms, relaxation area, beauty salon, body-treatment rooms, and an aerobics exercise room and gymnasium with ocean views and high-tech muscle-pumping equipment.

Sports enthusiasts will find a nine-hole golf putting course, two computerized golf simulators, and a sports court.

COSTA ATLANTICA
★★★+

A CONTEMPORARY ITALIAN SHIP WITH LOUD VOLUME EVERYWHERE

Size:	Mid-size Ship	Passenger/Crew Ratio (lower beds):	2.3
Tonnage:	85,700	Cabins (total):	1,056
Cruise Line:	Costa Cruises	Size Range (sq ft/m):	161.4–387.5/15.0–36.0
Former Names:	none	Cabins (for one person):	0
Builder:	Kverner Masa-Yards (Finland)	Cabins with balcony:	742
Entered Service:	Jul 2000	Cabins (wheelchair accessible):	8
Length (ft/m):	959.6/292.5	Wheelchair accessibility:	Good
Beam (ft/m):	105.6/32.2	Elevators:	12
Propulsion/Propellers:	diesel-electric (34,000kW)/ 2 azimuthing pods	Casino (gaming tables):	Yes
Passenger Decks:	12	Swimming Pools:	2 (1 w/ sliding glass dome)
Total Crew:	920	Self-Service Launderette:	No
Passengers (lower beds):	2,112	Library:	Yes
Passenger Space Ratio (lower beds):	40.5	Onboard currency:	Euros

THE SHIP. *Costa Atlantica* is a sister ship to *Costa Mediterranea*. It has two centrally located swimming pools outdoors, one with a retractable glass dome cover that can be used in poor weather conditions. A bar abridges two adjacent hot tubs. There's also a smaller pool for children, and a winding water slide spanning two decks in height.

The deck names are inspired by Federico Fellini movies (Roma Deck, Le Notte di Cabiria, La Voce della Luna, La Strada, Luci del Varietà). One deck is named after a Fellini TV movie, *Ginger and Fred*. This ship is designed to wow the trendy as well as pay homage to many of Italy's great art and past masters. The interior design is brash – a mix of classical Italy and contemporary features, with huge splashes of red and gold – to suit Chinese tastes. Good points include the fact that there are several floor spaces for dancing, and a wide range of bars and lounges for socializing.

The colorful lobby spans eight decks. Take a drink from the lobby bar and look upwards – the surroundings are visually stunning.

A small chapel is located forward of the uppermost level. Other facilities include a winding shopping street with boutique stores, plus a shop that sells Caffè Florian products, a photo gallery, a video games room, an observation balcony, a casino, a library with Internet access, and a card room (with a striking red and gold decor).

BERLITZ'S RATINGS	Possible	Achieved
Ship	500	348
Accommodation	200	130
Food	400	222
Service	400	246
Entertainment	100	61
Cruise Experience	400	246

OVERALL SCORE 1253 points out of 2000

Costa Atlantica is for young (and young-at-heart) couples and families with children. Note that the ship is now based year-round in Shanghai, China. The cuisine has been modified to accommodate Chinese preferences; announcements are made in Mandarin, while all signage is in Italian, and Mandarin. The passengers (mostly Chinese) are offered constant activity accompanied by Italian ambience, and loud entertainment.

Niggles! Several pillars obstruct passenger flow and sight lines throughout the ship. The fit and finish of some interior decoration is quite poor, and the decor is a bit overdone.

ACCOMMODATION. There are many different price categories, and a healthy (78 percent) proportion of outside-view to interior cabins. All cabins (now decorated with bright reds to appeal to the Chinese market) have twin beds that can convert into queen-size ones, air conditioning (but it can't be turned off), infotainment system, telephone, personal safe, and vanity desk with built-in hairdryer (but you'll need to hold down the on button continuously). Many cabins have views obstructed by lifeboats on Deck 4 (Roma Deck), the lowest accommodation deck, as well as some cabins on Deck 5. Some cabins have additional pull-down (Pullman-style) berths that are hidden in the ceiling when not in use. There is too much use of fluorescent lighting, and soundproofing could be better. Bathrooms are simple, modular units that have shower enclosures with soap dispensers. Some bathroom fixtures – bath and shower taps in particular – are frustrating to use at first.

Some of the most desirable suites and cabins are those with private balconies on five aft-facing decks (decks 4, 5, 6, 7, and 8) with views overlooking the stern and ship's wash. Other cabins with private balconies will find the balconies not so private – the partition between one balcony and the next is not a full partition – so you will be able to hear your neighbors.

However, balconies all have good views through glass and wood-topped railings, and the deck is made of teak. The largest suites are really small when compared with suites aboard other ships of a similar size. However, they do at least offer more space to move around in, and a slightly better bathroom.

DINING. The 1,320-seat Tiziano Dining Room is in the aft section of the ship on two levels, with a spiral stairway between them. There are two seatings, with tables for two to eight. Themed evenings are a part of the Costa Cruises tradition, and three different window blinds help create a different feel. However, artwork is placed at table height, so the room seems closed in. Some tables have a less-than-comfortable view of the harsh lighting of the escalators between the galley and the two decks of the dining room. This cuisine is traditional cruise fare that is best described as banquet-style food, now modified to include Chinese tastes and preferences. There are no sommeliers, so the waiters (who are young) serve the wine (which is also young). Note that table water is not provided – you are expected to purchase it.

The extra-cost, reservations-required 125-seat dinner venue, Ristorante Club Atlantica has a cover charge (suite-grade occupants get a free pass for one evening). It's a smaller, quieter venue, and the food, though nothing special is cooked to order and is decidedly better than in the main dining room.

Casual breakfast and luncheon self-serve buffet-style meals can be taken in the Botticelli Buffet Restaurant, adjacent to the swimming pools, with seating both indoors and outdoors. A grill (for hamburgers and hot dogs) and a pasta bar are conveniently adjacent to the second pool, while indoors is the Napoli Pizzeria. Excellent (illy brand) cappuccino and espresso coffees are always available in various bars around the ship, served in the right-sized china cups.

One place to see and be seen is in Caffè Florian – a replica of the famous indoor/outdoor café that opened in 1720 in Venice's St Mark's Square. There are four separate salons (Sala delle Stagioni, Sala del Senato, Sala Liberty, and Sala degli Uomini Illustri) and the same fascinating mosaic, marble, and wood floors, opulent ceiling art, and special lampshades. Even the espresso/cappuccino machine is a duplicate of the one found in the real thing. The only problem is that the chairs are much too small.

ENTERTAINMENT. A three-deck-high, 949-seat showlounge (Caruso Theater) is an imposing room. Spiral stairways at the back connect all levels. Stage shows are best seen from the upper levels, from where the sight lines are reasonably good.

Directly underneath is the Coral Lounge, with its own bar. An onboard resident troupe of singers and dancers provides the cast members for colorful, high-energy production shows. A number of bands and small musical units provide a variety of live music in many lounges and bars, and there is also a discotheque.

SPA/FITNESS. The Ischia Spa spans two decks. Facilities include a solarium, eight treatment rooms, lecture rooms, sauna and steam rooms for men and women, and a beauty parlor. A large gymnasium has floor-to-ceiling windows on three sides, including forward-facing ocean views, and an aerobics room with instructor-led classes. There is a jogging track outdoors.

The spa is operated by Steiner, a specialist concession, whose young staff will try to sell you Steiner's own-brand Elemis beauty products. Some fitness classes are free, while some (yoga, for example) cost extra.

Massages (including exotic massages such as Aroma Stone massage, and other wellbeing massages), facials, pedicures, and beauty salon treatments are at extra cost.

COSTA DELIZIOSA
★★★+

IT'S ITALY AFLOAT ABOARD THIS CASUAL, VERY CONTEMPORARY, BRIGHT SHIP

Size:	Mid-size Ship
Tonnage:	92,700
Cruise Line:	Costa Cruises
Former Names:	none
Builder:	Fincantieri (Italy)
Entered Service:	Mar 2010
Length (ft/m):	958.0/292.0
Beam (ft/m):	111.5/34.0
Propulsion/Propellers:	diesel-electric (42,000kW)/ 2 azimuthing pods
Passenger Decks:	13
Total Crew:	1,050
Passengers (lower beds):	2,260
Passenger Space Ratio (lower beds):	41.0/32.7

Passenger/Crew Ratio (lower beds):	2.1
Cabins (total):	1,130
Size Range (sq ft/m):	134.5–534.0/12.5–49.6
Cabins (for one person):	0
Cabins with balcony:	772
Cabins (wheelchair accessible):	12
Wheelchair accessibility:	Good
Elevators:	12
Casino (gaming tables):	Yes
Swimming Pools:	2 (1 w/ sliding glass dome)
Self-Service Launderette:	No
Library:	Yes
Onboard currency:	Euros

THE SHIP. *Costa Deliziosa* has a nicely balanced profile and a single large funnel in the Costa colors of yellow and blue. The ship, sister to *Costa Luminosa*, was named in Dubai, the first new cruise ship to be named in an Arab city (a bottle of fig juice, instead of Champagne, was used for the ceremony). A two-deck midships Lido area swimming pool can be covered with a sliding glass roof in poor weather. A large 194-sq-ft (18-sq-m) poolside movie screen often plays lots of Costa Cruises commercials as well as feature films.

The interior decor, which includes marble and gold, pays tribute to the senses, although sensory overkill might be a better description; in any event, it's a lot of overdone bling, although it's also amazing that the incredible mix of colors somehow just seem to go together. The focal point (and always a good meeting place) is the atrium lobby, which features a large sculpture, *Sphere*, by Arnaldo Pomodoro.

The public rooms include 11 bars (one of the largest is Grand Bar Mirabilis), a large casino (Casino Gaius, for table gaming and slot machines), lots of lounges and entertainment venues to enjoy, including a piano bar (Excite), card room, a small screening room (Cinema Etoiles – a 4D cinema highlights sound and lighting effects, with scent pumped in to heighten the experience), a cigar lounge (Tabac Blonde), and a shopping arcade (Galleria Shops).

Although Costa Cruises is noted for its 'Italian' style, ambience and spirit, there are actually few

BERLITZ'S RATINGS

	Possible	Achieved
Ship	500	375
Accommodation	200	135
Food	400	230
Service	400	251
Entertainment	100	64
Cruise Experience	400	256

OVERALL SCORE 1311 points out of 2000

Italian crew members on board. Although many officers are Italian, most of the crew members, particularly the dining room and housekeeping staff, are from the Philippines. But the lifestyle on board is perceived to be Italian – lively, noisy, with lots of love for life and a love of all things casual, even on so-called formal nights.

All printed material – room service folio, menus, etc. – is typically in six languages. During peak European school holiday periods, particularly Christmas and Easter, expect to be cruising with a lot of children of all ages.

Most passengers will be Italian, with a sprinkling of other nationalities.

As aboard other Costa ships, note that for embarkation, few staff members are on duty at the gangway when you arrive; they merely point you in the direction of your deck, or to the ship's elevators, and do not escort you to your cabin. Also, note that 'wallpaper' music is played 24 hours a day in all accommodation hallways and elevators, so you may well hear it if you are a light sleeper. Expect lots of announcements – especially for revenue activities such as art auctions, bingo, horse racing – and much hustling for drinks.

Gratuities are charged to your onboard account.

ACCOMMODATION. About 68 percent of all accommodation suites and cabins have an ocean view, and there are 772 balcony cabins. Four suites and 52 Samsara Spa cabins are adjacent to (and considered part of) the designated wellness area. Samsara suite/cabin occupants get unlimited access to the spa plus two treatments and fitness or meditation lessons as part of their package, and they can dine in one of the two Samsara restaurants.

A pillow menu, with five choices, is available to suite-grade occupants, who also get bathrobes, better amenities, a shaving mirror, and walk-in closets. Background music is played 24 hours a day in all hallways and elevators, so you may well be aware of it if you are a light sleeper.

DINING. The 1,264-seat Albatros Restaurant is the ship's large, main dining hall. It is located aft and you eat at one of two seatings for dinner, at tables for two to eight assigned according to your accommodation grade.

The cuisine is Continental European, with many regional Italian dishes and considerable emphasis on starchy foods, particularly pasta: 50 pasta dishes per cruise (buffalo mozzarella cheese is made on board). Except for the pasta dishes and cream sauces, however, the presentation and food quality are unmemorable, and the subject of negative passenger comments. Green vegetables are hard to come by, and rice is used as a plate-filler. Breads and bakery items are decent enough (but made from frozen 'starter' dough), but desserts are of supermarket quality and lack taste. There is heavy use of canned fruit and jellied desserts and packeted jam, butter, etc.

There are no sommeliers, so the waiters, who are young, serve the wine, which is also young. Note that table water is not provided – you are expected to purchase it.

A reservations-required, 68-seat Samsara Restaurant is adjacent; it is a smaller, quieter, and more intimate venue than the main dining venue, and features healthier food with reduced calories, fat, and salt content. The venue is open for lunch and dinner to anyone in Samsara-grade accommodation, and to anyone else for dinner only at an extra daily or weekly charge.

The Restaurant Club Deliziosa is an extra-cost, reservations-required venue with 182 seats. It features an open show kitchen. The food is cooked à la minute, and so it is fresher than the batch cooking of the main dining room, and it looks (and is) much more appetizing.

Buffet Muscadins is the self-serve casual eatery, but its disjointed layout invites congestion. While there appears to be a decent choice of food, it is extremely repetitive (particularly for breakfast), and a major source of passenger complaints. Also, after it closes in the afternoon, only slices of pizza are available.

One event not to be missed, however, is an 'Elegant Teatime,' during which rather nice cakes and sandwiches are served, together with a choice of teas or tisanes, in one of the lounges.

Espresso/cappuccinos coffees (illy brand) are available in the Atrium Bar – a good place to sit and be seen, and to observe others.

ENTERTAINMENT. The Theater Duse, with over 800 seats, spans three decks (with seating on all three levels) and is the ship's main showlounge, with the latest computer-controlled lighting and high-volume sound equipment. High-energy production shows are performed here, with Costa's own song and dance troupe.

SPA/FITNESS. The Samsara Spa area occupies some 37,674 sq ft (3,500 sq m) of space, and spans two decks in height. Facilities include a large fitness room (with all the techno gym muscle-pumping equipment), separate saunas, steam rooms, UVB solarium, changing rooms for men and women, and 10 private massage/body-treatment rooms. Two VIP treatment rooms, available to couples as a half-day rental, are located on the upper level.

The facilities are staffed and operated by Steiner Leisure, a specialist spa/beauty concession. Some fitness classes are free, while some, such as Pathway to Yoga, and Pathway to Pilates, cost extra. It's wise to make any treatment appointments early as time slots can go quickly.

You can buy a day pass in order to use the sauna/steam rooms, thermal suite and relaxation area, at a cost of €35 per person. However, there's an additional free (no charge) sauna for men and women, but to access it you must walk through an active fitness area, maybe with your bathrobe on, which is not ideal.

For the sports-minded, a Grand Prix Formula One simulator is housed in a glass enclosure close to the spa. A golf simulator provides a choice of 37 18-hole courses.

COSTA DIADEMA
★★★+

THIS SPARKLY, FAMILY-FRIENDLY ITALIAN SHIP IS MORE WATER TAXI THAN CRUISE SHIP

Size:	Large Resort Ship	Passenger/Crew Ratio (lower beds):	2.9
Tonnage:	132,500	Cabins (total):	1,854
Cruise Line:	Costa Cruises	Size Range (sq ft/m):	125.9–554.3/11.7–51.5
Former Names:	none	Cabins (for one person):	0
Builder:	Fincantieri (Italy)	Cabins with balcony:	913
Entered Service:	Nov 2013	Cabins (wheelchair accessible):	8
Length (ft/m):	1,003.9/306.0	Wheelchair accessibility:	Good
Beam (ft/m):	122.0/37.2	Elevators:	19
Propulsion/Propellers:	diesel-electric (42,000kW)/2	Casino (gaming tables):	Yes
Passenger Decks:	14	Swimming Pools:	2 (1 w/ sliding glass dome)
Total Crew:	1,253	Self-Service Launderette:	No
Passengers (lower beds):	3,708	Library:	Yes
Passenger Space Ratio (lower beds):	35.7	Onboard currency:	Euros

THE SHIP. *Costa Diadema* is the newest, largest, and grandest ship in the growing Costa Cruises fleet of family-friendly ships, and the company's flagship. When you step aboard, you'll be greeted by a 4ft (1.2m) white humanoid robot named 'Pepper,' who is seaworthy, and speaks English, German, and Italian, but he won't carry your carry-on luggage. You'll see Pepper(s) – there are several of them – dotted around the ship during the cruise, acting as information helpers.

The ship (whose name means 'tiara') has a well-proportioned profile with a rounded front, bolt-upright Costa yellow funnel, and nicely tiered aft decks. The lifeboats are mounted lower down; this position gives a sense of balance to the ship's towering superstructure. *Costa Diadema* is equipped with a cold ironing facility, allowing it to plug into shore-side electric power, and all solid waste is collected for recycling. All exterior decks are covered in a rubberized material (no teak anywhere), but the railings are made of hardwood. A nice feature is the outdoor 1,640-ft (500-m) walk-around promenade deck.

The interior decor is best decribed as glowing, very bright, and ultra-bold. The central focal point is an (enlarged) atrium lobby (Atrio Eliodoro), with four panoramic elevators. Look upwards from the floor of the lobby and you'll see the inner part of the multi-deck atrium studded with diamonds – well, blue diamond-look lighting (you'll find it on the ceilings of other public areas, too). In fact, you'll see diamonds

BERLITZ'S RATINGS		
	Possible	Achieved
Ship	500	378
Accommodation	200	135
Food	400	230
Service	400	252
Entertainment	100	64
Cruise Experience	400	253
OVERALL SCORE 1312 points out of 2000		

in the artworks throughout the ship. The reception and the shore-excursion desk (called the Costa Travel Office) are located to one side, while comfortable seating is set around the lobby and adjacent areas.

There are seven restaurants and eateries (four of these are at extra cost) and 15 bars to enjoy including the Birreria La Flamma (a pub with several draft beers/lagers).

A whole shopping street awaits you in the form of the Portobello Market Piazza – filled with designer stores within its 11,840-sq-ft (1,100-sq-m) area. Other public rooms include a 4D racing-car experience, and a chapel – a Costa Cruises must-have.

Niggles include the fact that, in common with many large resort ships today, there is little open space on the upper decks, so be prepared to hunt for seating around the main swimming pool/water park area. You'll need to take a towel from your cabin, as they are not provided at the pool. Note that passengers embark and disembark at each port of call, so a cruise is more like a water taxi; this means there is little communication between staff and passengers. This is also a high-density ship, with the lowest number of crew per passengers of all the ships in the Costa Cruises fleet. This is all about casual cruising for a youthful clientele who enjoy the Italian flair for life.

ACCOMMODATION. The accommodation configuration consists of 12 Grand Suites, 49 Suites, 14

Mini-Suites, 795 Balcony Cabins, 110 Cove Balcony Cabins, 240 Oceanview Cabins, and 666 Interior Cabins. The Grand Suites are not true suites (there's no completely separate bedroom), and are small when compared to many other ships; they measure 554.3 sq ft (51.5 sq m), including balcony. Some 130 of the suites/cabins are designated Samsara Spa-grade accommodation, whose occupants eat in the intimate Samsara Restaurant.

Suites have larger bathrooms (some with a tub/shower), while many cabins have a shower curtain, instead of a proper glazed door, and a shower head that is fixed (no flexible shower hose except in high-grade accommodation).

DINING. Restaurant Sissi is the cavernous main dining room; located aft, it is two decks high, with bright decor. Seating, which is allocated according to your accommodation grade and location, is at banquettes and individual chairs without armrests.

A second dining room, the single-deck-height Scudo Rosso Restaurant, is located in the center of the ship.

If you expect to be served by jovial Italian waiters, you'll be disappointed – although the restaurant managers might be Italian. Few tables for two are available, most being for four, six, or eight.

The cuisine is Continental European, with many regional Italian dishes and considerable emphasis on starchy food, particularly pasta: 50 pasta dishes per cruise (buffalo mozzarella cheese is made on board). The food is banquet-style catering, and, except for pasta dishes and cream sauces, its presentation and quality are unmemorable, and the subject of negative passenger comments. Green vegetables are hard to come by, and rice is used as a plate-filler. Breads and bakery items are decent enough (but made from frozen 'starter' dough), but desserts are of supermarket quality and lack taste. There is heavy use of canned fruit and jellied desserts and packeted jam, butter, etc.

There's a wine list, but no wine waiters (table waiters serve both food and wine). Almost all wines are young, and the glasses are small. Note that table water is not provided – you are expected to purchase it.

If you opt for one of the specialty restaurants, note that charges apply.

All ships have self-serve lido buffets with basic items. The regular coffee is decent and quite strong, but the extra-cost (illy) coffee is excellent.

The Samsara Restaurant is a smaller, more intimate venue for occupants of Samsara-grade accommodation. The cuisine focuses more on healthy items, with reduced calories and less fat and salt.

The self-serve Corona Blu Restaurant (a buffet on the Lido Deck) has tacky (AIDA-style), unhygienic cutlery stands on tables.

Costa has introduced some more ethnic-centric eating areas (some at extra cost), such as a Vinoteca, Proseccheria (a Bavarian Bierkeller), a Japanese Tavola Teppanyaki Grill, an extra-cost pizzeria (it's in the Piazza, so it's called the Pizzeria in Piazza Pizza – now there's a mouthful!), and a Gelateria. Club Diadema restaurant is an extra-cost, reservations-required dining spot, and delivers more upscale cuisine. It's worth it if you are celebrating something special, or for something a little different to the noisy main dining room.

ENTERTAINMENT. The Emerald Theater – the ship's showlounge – is spread over three decks and has over 1,500 seats (with tables for drinks), many of which have upright backs, a large stage with proscenium arch, and the latest in LED lighting technology. Costa Cruises' revue-style shows – performed by a troupe of resident onboard singers/dancers – are all about color, lights, high-energy action, and volume.

A Country Rock Club is something new for Costa Cruises; it's an upbeat venue for listening to country-rock crossover music.

SPA/FITNESS. Measuring some 8,395 sq ft (780 sq m), Samsara Spa is a large facility, spread over three decks. It includes a large gymnasium with the latest in muscle-training equipment, saunas, steam rooms, a thermal area, and several massage/body-treatment rooms. VIP treatment rooms are also available to couples for half-day rentals. You'll need to purchase a day pass in order to use the sauna/steam rooms, thermal suite, and relaxation area. Some fitness classes are free, while others cost extra.

COSTA FASCINOSA
★★★+

UPBEAT ITALIAN DECOR AND STYLE, FOR TRENDY FAMILY CRUISING ABOARD THIS SHIP

Size:	Large Resort Ship	Passenger/Crew Ratio (lower beds):	2.7
Tonnage:	114,500	Cabins (total):	1,508
Cruise Line:	Costa Cruises	Size Range (sq ft/m):	179.7–482.2/16.7–44.8
Former Names:	none	Cabins (for one person):	0
Builder:	Fincantieri (Italy)	Cabins with balcony:	650
Entered Service:	May 2012	Cabins (wheelchair accessible):	12
Length (ft/m):	952.0/290.2	Wheelchair accessibility:	Good
Beam (ft/m):	116.4/35.5	Elevators:	14
Propulsion/Propellers:	diesel-electric (75,600kW)/2	Casino (gaming tables):	Yes
Passenger Decks:	13	Swimming Pools:	2
Total Crew:	1,090	Self-Service Launderette:	No
Passengers (lower beds):	3,016	Library:	Yes
Passenger Space Ratio (lower beds):	38.0	Onboard currency:	Euros

THE SHIP. With an instantly recognizable single, large yellow funnel, *Costa Fascinosa* is a sister to *Costa Favolosa*, *Costa Fortuna*, *Costa Magica*, *Costa Pacifica*, and *Costa Serena*. On the open decks, two pool areas can be covered with retractable glass domes – useful for inclement weather conditions; one pool has a long water slide, much liked by children; there is also a large poolside movie screen. However, the open deck space is pretty cramped when the ship is full, and the plastic sunloungers are crammed together and do not have cushioned pads.

With three decks packed with 13 bars and lounges and other public rooms, there's a place for all tastes. The decor throughout is on the wild side. The focal social point is a three-deck-high atrium lobby, with four glass panoramic elevators providing a neat view over the lobby bar – a good place for an espresso/cappuccino and people-watching. The Casino is large and very colorful, but the slot machines occupy a separate area from the gaming tables, so serious gamers can concentrate. Other public rooms include a small library, an Internet-connection center, 4D cinema, card room, art gallery, and video game room, plus a chapel – a standard aboard all Costa Cruises' ships.

Families like Costa Cruises for its perceived 'Italian' style, ambience and spirit, and most passengers will be Italian, with a sprinkling of other European nationals. However, you won't find many Italian hotel

BERLITZ'S RATINGS		
	Possible	Achieved
Ship	500	371
Accommodation	200	134
Food	400	230
Service	400	249
Entertainment	100	64
Cruise Experience	400	251
OVERALL SCORE 1299 points out of 2000		

service staff on board – although many of the officers are Italian, most crew members, particularly the dining room and housekeeping staff, are from the Philippines. But the lifestyle on board is perceived to be Italian – lively, noisy, with lots of love for life and a love of all things casual, even on so-called formal nights. Note that during peak European school holiday periods, especially during Christmas and Easter, you can expect to be cruising with a lot of children of all ages.

Printed material such as the cabin service folio and menus, are provided in six languages – Italian, English, French, German, Portuguese, and Spanish – and announcements are also made in several languages.

As aboard other Costa ships, few staff members are on duty at the gangway when you arrive for embarkation; they merely point you in the direction of your deck, or to the ship's elevators and do not escort you to your cabin.

However, Costa Cruises does a good job of providing first-time cruise passengers (particularly families with children) with a packaged seagoing vacation that's a mix of sophistication and noisy chaos.

ACCOMMODATION. There are many accommodation price grades, from two-bed interior cabins to grand suites with private balcony, although in reality there are only three different sizes: suites with 'private' balcony – which are really not particularly large in comparison with some other large ships; two- or four-bed outside-view cabins; and two- or four-bed interior cabins. Fortunately, no cabins have lifeboat-obstructed views, and, in most cabins, twin beds can be changed to a double/queen-bed configuration.

Eight Grand Suites, in the center of the ship on one of the uppermost decks, comprise the largest accommodation.

Some 103 Samsara Spa Suite occupants get unlimited spa access, two treatments, plus fitness or meditation lessons, and meal in one of two designated Samsara restaurants.

Suite-grade occupants get bathrobes and better amenities, shaving mirror, a pillow menu, and walk-in closets – although the hangers are plastic. Note that music is played 24/7 in accommodation hallways and elevators, so you may well hear it if you are a light sleeper.

DINING. There are two principal dining rooms, Il Gattopardo and Otto e Mezzo. One is aft, the other in the ship's center. Tables for two to eight are allocated according to your accommodation grade and location, in one of two seating times.

If you expect to be served by jovial Italian waiters, you'll be disappointed – although the restaurant managers might be Italian. Few tables for two are available, most being for four, six, or eight.

The cuisine is Continental European, with many regional Italian dishes and considerable emphasis on starches, particularly pasta: 50 pasta dishes per cruise (buffalo mozzarella cheese is made on board). The food is banquet-style catering. Except for pasta dishes and cream sauces, presentation and food quality are unmemorable, and the subject of negative passenger comments. Green vegetables are hard to come by, and rice is used as a plate-filler. Breads and bakery items are decent enough (but made from frozen 'starter' dough), but desserts are of supermarket quality and lack taste. There is heavy use of canned fruit and jellied desserts and packeted jam, butter, etc.

There's a wine list, but no wine waiters (table waiters serve both food and wine). Almost all wines are young, and glasses are small. Note that table water is not provided – you are expected to purchase it.

If you opt for one of the specialty restaurants, note that charges apply.

All ships have self-serve lido buffets with basic items. The regular coffee is decent and quite strong, but the extra-cost (illy) coffee is excellent.

Two Samsara restaurants – open for lunch and dinner to those in Samsara-grade suites and cabins, and to anyone else for dinner only at an extra charge – have separate entrances. While the two main restaurants offer traditional cruise fare, these 'spa cuisine' spots feature healthier food – reduced calories, fat, and salt.

A reservations-required, extra-cost restaurant, Club Fascinosa, has fine table settings, leather-bound menus, and decent food.

For really casual meals, the self-serve, buffet-style eatery, Tulipano Nero, is open for breakfast, lunch, afternoon pizzas, and coffee or tea at any time. A balcony level provides additional seating, but you'll need to carry your own plates because there are no trays. The food is extremely repetitive, and a major source of passenger complaints.

ENTERTAINMENT. The Fascinosa Showlounge seats over 800. It's three decks high and is the venue for all production shows and large-scale cabaret acts, with a revolving stage, hydraulic orchestra pit, good sound, and seating on three levels, the upper levels being tiered through two decks.

High-energy revue-style shows are performed by a small troupe of resident onboard singers/dancers, with fast-moving action and busy lighting and costume changes.

SPA/FITNESS. The Samsara Spa is a large facility occupying some 64,585 sq ft (6,000 sq m) of space, including relaxation areas, spread over two decks. It has a large fitness room, plus separate saunas, steam rooms, UVB solarium, and changing rooms for men and women, and 10 rooms for body treatments. Two VIP treatment rooms, available to couples for half-day rentals, are located on the upper level.

The Spa/fitness facilities are staffed and operated by Steiner Leisure, a specialist spa/beauty concession. Some fitness classes are free, while some, such as Pathway to Yoga, Pathway to Pilates, and Pathway to Meditation, cost extra. It's wise to make appointments early, as time slots can go quickly.

You can buy a day pass in order to use the sauna/steam rooms, thermal suite and relaxation area, at a cost of €35 per person. However, there's an additional no-charge sauna for men and women, but to access it you must walk through an active fitness area, maybe with your bathrobe on, which is not ideal.

COSTA FAVOLOSA
★★★+

THIS SHIP HAS RATHER UPBEAT ITALIAN DECOR AND STYLE, FOR FAMILY CRUISING

Size:	Large Resort Ship	Passenger/Crew Ratio (lower beds):	2.7
Tonnage:	114,500	Cabins (total):	1,506
Cruise Line:	Costa Cruises	Size Range (sq ft/m):	179.7–482.2/16.7–44.8
Former Names:	none	Cabins (for one person):	0
Builder:	Fincantieri (Italy)	Cabins with balcony:	579
Entered Service:	Jul 2011	Cabins (wheelchair accessible):	12
Length (ft/m):	952.0/290.2	Wheelchair accessibility:	Good
Beam (ft/m):	116.4/35.5	Elevators:	14
Propulsion/Propellers:	diesel-electric (75,600kW)/2	Casino (gaming tables):	Yes
Passenger Decks:	13	Swimming Pools:	2
Total Crew:	1,110	Self-Service Launderette:	No
Passengers (lower beds):	3,012	Library:	Yes
Passenger Space Ratio (lower beds):	38.0	Onboard currency:	Euros

THE SHIP. Displaying a single, large funnel, *Costa Favolosa* is a close sister to *Costa Serena*. Two pool areas can be covered with retractable glass domes – useful in case of bad weather – and one has a long water slide, which is great for kids. There is a large poolside movie screen and, on one of the upper decks, a Grand Prix simulator. However, the open deck space can be pretty cramped when the ship is full, so the sunloungers, which don't have cushioned pads, will be crammed together.

There are three decks full of bars and lounges plus many other public rooms. A glass-domed rotunda atrium lobby is nine decks high, with excellent upward views from the lobby bar, as well as from its four glass panoramic elevators.

The Casino is large and glitzy; lot machines occupy a separate area to gaming tables, so serious gamers can concentrate. There's also a small library, an Internet center, card room, art gallery, 4D cinema (Belphegor), and a video game room, plus a small chapel – a standard aboard all Costa Cruises' ships.

Although Costa Cruises is noted for its 'Italian' style, ambience and spirit, there are few Italian crew members on board. Although many officers are Italian, most of the crew members, particularly the dining room and housekeeping staff, are from the Philippines. But the lifestyle on board is perceived to be Italian – lively, noisy, with lots of love for life and a love of all things casual, even on so-called formal nights.

BERLITZ'S RATINGS		
	Possible	Achieved
Ship	500	371
Accommodation	200	134
Food	400	230
Service	400	248
Entertainment	100	64
Cruise Experience	400	250

OVERALL SCORE 1297 points out of 2000

All printed material – room service folio, menus, etc. – will typically be in six languages: Italian, English, French, German, Portuguese, and Spanish. During peak European school holiday periods, particularly Christmas and Easter, you can expect to be cruising with a lot of children of all ages.

A Costa cruise is good if you like a lively atmosphere. The company does a good job of providing first-time cruise passengers (particularly families with children) with a packaged seagoing vacation that is a mix of sophistication and chaos. Most passengers are Italian, with a sprinkling of other European nationals.

As aboard other Costa ships, note that for embarkation, few staff members are on duty at the gangway when you arrive; they merely point you in the direction of your deck, or to the ship's elevators and do not escort you to your cabin. Also, note that 'wallpaper' music is played 24 hours a day in all accommodation hallways and elevators, so you may well hear it if you are a light sleeper.

ACCOMMODATION. There are numerous accommodation price grades, from two-bed interior cabins (no view) to grand suites with private balcony, although in reality there are only three different sizes: suites with 'private' balcony – these are really not particularly large in comparison with some other large ships; two- or four-bed outside-view cabins; and two- or four-bed interior cabins. Fortunately, no cabins have views obstructed by lifeboats or other safety equipment views, and, in most cabins, twin beds can be changed to a double/queen-bed configuration.

Two Grand Suites comprise the largest accommodation, and include a large balcony with hot tub. They have a queen-size bed and larger living area with vanity desk; the bathrooms have a tub and two washbasins.

Twelve Samsara Spa Suites are located just aft of the spa itself, although 99 cabins, including these 12, are designated as Samsara-grade. Occupants of this grade get unlimited access to the spa plus two treatments and fitness or meditation lessons as part of their package, and can dine in one of two Samsara restaurants. All Samsara-designated accommodation grades have an Oriental decorative theme, and special Samsara bathroom personal amenities.

A pillow menu, with five choices, has been introduced in suite-grade accommodation. Only suite grades get bathrobes and better amenities, shaving mirror, and walk-in closets – although the hangers are still plastic.

DINING. There are two main dining rooms, Duke of Burgundy and Duke of Orleans. One is aft, while the other is in the ship's center. Tables for two to eight are allocated according to your accommodation grade and location, in one of two seating times. These dining rooms offer traditional cruise fare that is best described as banquet-style food.

Two 100-seat Samsara restaurants are for healthier food, with reduced calories, fat, and salt content. These venues are open for lunch and dinner to anyone in Samsara-grade accommodation, and to others for dinner only at an extra charge.

If you expect to be served by jovial Italian waiters, you'll be disappointed – although the restaurant managers might be Italian. Few tables for two are available, most being for four, six, or eight.

The cuisine is Continental European, with many regional Italian dishes and considerable emphasis on starchy food, particularly pasta: 50 pasta dishes per cruise (buffalo mozzarella cheese is made on board). Except for pasta dishes and cream sauces, the presentation and food quality are unmemorable, and the subject of negative passenger comments. Green vegetables are hard to come by, and rice is used as a plate-filler. Breads and bakery items are decent enough (but made from frozen 'starter' dough), but desserts are of supermarket quality and lack taste. There is much use of canned fruit and jellied desserts, and packeted jam, butter, etc.

There's a wine list, but no wine waiters (table waiters serve both food and wine). Almost all wines are young, and the glasses are small. Note that table water is not provided – you are expected to purchase it.

If you opt for one of the specialty restaurants, note that charges apply.

All ships have self-serve lido buffets with basic items. The regular coffee is decent and quite strong, but the extra-cost (illy) coffee is excellent.

The intimate Favolosa Club Restaurant sits under a huge glass dome and Murano-glass decorative elements. Fine table settings, china, silverware and leather-bound menus are provided. There's a cover charge and reservations are required.

The self-service Ca' d'Oro food court-style buffet restaurant offers breakfast, lunch, afternoon pizzas, and coffee and tea at any time. A balcony level provides additional seating, but you'll need to carry your own food plates since there are no trays. The food in this venue is extremely repetitive, and a major source of passenger complaints.

ENTERTAINMENT. The Favolosa showlounge, seating more than 800, has LED backdrop technology. Three decks high, it is decorated in a Baroque style, with warm colors and a Murano-glass chandelier. It is the venue for all production shows and cabaret acts, is stunningly glitzy, and has a revolving stage, hydraulic orchestra pit, superb sound, and seating on three levels – the upper levels are tiered through two decks.

Revue-style shows are performed by a small troupe of resident singers and dancers. Their fast-moving action, busy lighting and costume changes all add up to a high-energy performance.

SPA/FITNESS. The Samsara Spa is a large facility that occupies 23,186 sq ft (2,154 sq m), spread over two decks. It includes a large fitness room, separate saunas, steam rooms, UVB solarium, changing rooms for men and women, and 10 rooms for body treatments. Two VIP treatment rooms, available to couples as a half-day rental, are located on the upper level.

The Spa/fitness facilities are staffed and operated by Steiner Leisure, a specialist concession. Some fitness classes are free, while some cost extra.

You can buy a day pass in order to use the sauna/steam rooms, thermal suite, and relaxation area. However, there's an additional no-charge sauna for men and women, but to access it you must walk through an active fitness area, maybe with your bathrobe on, which some people might not be comfortable with.

COSTA FORTUNA
★★★+

A LARGE, COLORFUL FAMILY-FRIENDLY ITALIAN-STYLE FLOATING RESORT

Size:	Large Resort Ship	Passenger/Crew Ratio (lower beds):	2.5
Tonnage:	102,587	Cabins (total):	1,358
Cruise Line:	Costa Cruises	Size Range (sq ft/m):	179.7–482.2/16.7–44.8
Former Names:	none	Cabins (for one person):	0
Builder:	Cantieri Sestri Navale (Italy)	Cabins with balcony:	522
Entered Service:	Nov 2003	Cabins (wheelchair accessible):	8
Length (ft/m):	892.3/272.0	Wheelchair accessibility:	Good
Beam (ft/m):	124.6/38.0	Elevators:	14
Propulsion/Propellers:	diesel-electric (34,000kW)/ 2 azimuthing pods	Casino (gaming tables):	Yes
		Swimming Pools:	2
Passenger Decks:	13	Self-Service Launderette:	No
Total Crew:	1,068	Library:	Yes
Passengers (lower beds):	2,716	Onboard currency:	Euros
Passenger Space Ratio (lower beds):	37.7		

THE SHIP. The ship's name is an interesting one: in Greek mythology, Fortuna is the daughter of Poseidon (God of the sea). The name is also associated with the Temple Fortuna, located along one of Pompeii's conserved streets.

The aft decks are well tiered, with cut-off quarters that make the ship's stern look a little less square than it otherwise would. There are three pools, one of which can be covered by a sliding glass dome in case of inclement weather, while one pool (Barcelona Pool) features a long water slide. There is not a lot of open deck space considering the number of passengers carried, so sunloungers tend to be crammed together (there's a lack of small tables for drinks – or for somewhere to place those small items you always take to the pool), and they lack cushioned pads.

The interior decor focuses on the Italian passenger ships of yesteryear, so much of the finishing detail replicates the Art Deco interiors fitted aboard ocean liners such as the *Conte de Savoia*, *Michelangelo*, *Neptunia*, *Rafaello*, *Rex*, etc., although in the kind of contemporary colors not associated with such ships, whose interiors were rather subdued.

The deck names are those of major cities in Europe and North and South America (Barcelona, Buenos Aires, Caracas, Lisbon, Genoa, Miami). The passenger flow is generally good, with few congestion points.

There are three decks full of lounges, and 11 bars to enjoy, and almost all have espresso coffee machines – a must for Italians – featuring the illy brand. The interior focal point is a nine-deck high, glass-domed atrium lobby: it houses a Costa Bar on the lower level, a bank of four glass-walled (panoramic) elevators, and, in a tribute to ship buffs, 26 models of Italian ships past and present are glued upside down on the ceiling – it's a bit of a strange feeling to look at them and then look down at your feet. The lowest three decks connect the public rooms, the upper levels being mainly for accommodation (plus the pool deck).

For gamers, Neptunia 1932 Casino is the place to go (if you want to get from the center to the aft lounges you have to walk through it). There's also a chapel – standard aboard Costa ships – and a small library that's really a a token gesture, an Internet center, card room, art gallery, and video games room.

Costa Fortuna – now over 10 years old – was built to impress trendy city-dwellers. It absorbs passengers quite well, with a good passenger/space ratio. As aboard other Costa ships, note that for embarkation, few staff members are on duty at the gangway when you arrive; they merely point you in the direction of your deck, or to the ship's elevators and do not escort you to your cabin. Also, note that 'wallpaper' music is played 24 hours a day in all accommodation hallways and elevators, so you may well hear it if you are a light sleeper. Other niggles include the drinks package and its rules.

BERLITZ'S RATINGS		
	Possible	Achieved
Ship	500	368
Accommodation	200	134
Food	400	230
Service	400	249
Entertainment	100	63
Cruise Experience	400	251
OVERALL SCORE 1295 points out of 2000		

Although Costa Cruises is noted for its Italian style, ambience and spirit, there are few Italian crew members on board. Although many officers are Italian, most of the crew members, particularly the dining room and housekeeping staff, are from the Philippines. But the lifestyle on board is perceived to be Italian – lively, noisy, with lots of love for life and a love of all things casual, even on so-called formal nights.

All printed material – room service folio, menus, etc. – will typically be in six languages: Italian, English, French, German, Portuguese, and Spanish. During peak periods (European school holidays, particularly Christmas and Easter), you can expect to be cruising with a lot of children of all ages.

ACCOMMODATION. There are 15 price grades, from two-bed interior cabins to grand suites with private balcony, although in reality there are only three different sizes: suites with balcony, two- or four-bed outside-view cabins (some 335 of which have portholes rather than windows), and two- or four-bed interior cabins. There are also two cabins for solo travelers. In an example of good design, no cabins have lifeboat-obstructed views; this is something not easy to design in large ships such as this.

The largest accommodation can be found in eight Grand Suites, located in the center of the ship on one of the higher decks. They have a queen-size bed; bathrooms have a tub and two washbasins.

Note that 12 of the best (outside-view) wheelchair-accessible cabins are ludicrously located a long way from elevators; eight others are, however, located close to the elevators.

DINING. There are two dining rooms: the 1,046-seat Michelangelo 1965 Restaurant (aft), whose ceiling features frescoes by the Old Masters, and the 664-seat Rafaello 1965 Restaurant (midships); both are two decks high and each has two seatings for dinner, which is typically scheduled at 7pm and 9pm on European cruises.

If you expect to be served by jovial Italian waiters, you'll be disappointed – although the restaurant managers might be Italian. Few tables for two are available, most being for four, six, or eight.

The cuisine is Continental European, with many regional Italian dishes and considerable emphasis on starchy food, particularly pasta: 50 pasta dishes per cruise (buffalo mozzarella cheese is made on board). The food is banquet-style catering. Except for the pasta dishes and cream sauces, the presentation and food quality are unmemorable, and the subject of negative passenger comments. Green vegetables are hard to come by, and rice is used as a plate-filler. Breads and bakery items are decent enough (but made from frozen 'starter' dough), but desserts are of supermarket quality and lack taste. There is heavy use of canned fruit and jellied desserts and packeted jam, butter, etc.

There's a wine list, but no wine waiters (table waiters serve both food and wine). Almost all the wines are young, and the glasses are small. Note that table water is not provided – you are expected to purchase it.

If you opt for one of the specialty restaurants, note that charges apply.

All ships have self-serve lido buffets with basic items. The regular coffee is decent and quite strong, but the extra-cost (illy) coffee is excellent.

Conte Grande 1927 Club is an intimate, upscale 94-seat dining venue under a huge glass dome – if the lights were turned out, you might be able to see the stars. In its show kitchen, chefs can be seen preparing your food. Fine table settings, china, silverware, and leather-bound menus are used. Reservations are required, and a cover charge applies.

The Cristoforo Columbus 1954 Buffet Restaurant is a self-serve eatery for breakfast, lunch, and afternoon pizzas, and for beverages at any time. The food in this venue is repetitive, and a major source of passenger complaints.

ENTERTAINMENT. The Rex 1932 Theater spans three decks in the ship's forward-most section. It is a stunning setting for all production shows and large-scale cabaret acts, and has a revolving stage, hydraulic orchestra pit, excellent (but usually loud) sound system, and seating on three levels – the upper levels being tiered through two decks.

Typical fare consists of revue-style shows performed by a small troupe of resident singers/dancers, with fast-moving action and busy lighting and costume changes that all add up to a high-energy performance.

SPA/FITNESS. Facilities in the two-deck high Saturnia Spa 1927, which measures about 14,424 sq ft (1,340 sq m), include a large solarium, eight private massage/ treatment rooms, sauna and steam rooms for men and women, and a beauty parlor. A gym has floor-to-ceiling windows on three sides, including forward-facing ocean views, and there's an aerobics section with instructor-led classes.

The spa/fitness facilities are staffed and operated by Steiner Leisure, a specialist spa/beauty concession. Some fitness classes are free; others cost extra. Make appointments early, as time slots can go quickly. If you like being near the spa, note that there are 18 two-bed cabins with ocean-view windows, located adjacent (just aft of it).

COSTA LUMINOSA
★★★+

THIS SHIP HAS BOLD DECOR AND BIG-SHIP FACILITIES THAT ARE GOOD FOR FAMILIES

Size:	Mid-size Ship
Tonnage:	92,700
Cruise Line:	Costa Cruises
Former Names:	none
Builder:	Fincantieri (Italy)
Entered Service:	Jun 2009
Length (ft/m):	958.0/292.0
Beam (ft/m):	111.5/34.0
Propulsion/Propellers:	diesel-electric (42,000kW)/ 2 azimuthing pods
Passenger Decks:	13
Total Crew:	1,050
Passengers (lower beds):	2,260
Passenger Space Ratio (lower beds):	41.0
Passenger/Crew Ratio (lower beds):	2.1
Cabins (total):	1,130
Size Range (sq ft/m):	134.5–534.0/12.5–49.6
Cabins (for one person):	0
Cabins with balcony:	772
Cabins (wheelchair accessible):	12
Wheelchair accessibility:	Good
Elevators:	12
Casino (gaming tables):	Yes
Swimming Pools:	2
Self-Service Launderette:	No
Library:	Yes
Onboard currency:	Euros

THE SHIP. *Costa Luminosa is a sister ship to Costa Deliziosa.* The ship's two-deck midships Lido area swimming pool can be covered with a sliding glass roof. There's also a large 194-sq-ft (18-sq-m) poolside movie screen.

The interior decor, which includes marble, wood, and mother of pearl, pays tribute to light and lighting – hence the name *Costa Luminosa* – so it feels like you are cruising in a stunning special-effects bubble, with reflections everywhere.

Public rooms include 11 bars, a large Casino Vega (with gaming tables and slot machines), and lots of lounges and entertainment venues. Sony PlayStation fans can enjoy PlayStation World. PlayStations are also available in cabins, on the pool-deck movie screen, and in the children's and teens' clubs. A 4D cinema highlights sound and lighting effects, with scent pumped in to heighten the experience. One thing you can't miss is a fascinating – and rather large, at 11ft long (3.4m) – *Reclining Woman 2004* bronze sculpture by Fernando Botero, in the Atria Supernova, the atrium lobby. Weighing 2,000lbs (907kg), the suntanned, rather voluminous woman is depicted staring into the atrium space, with her legs in a dynamic position of movement.

Although Costa Cruises is noted for its Italian style, ambience, and spirit, there are few Italian crew members on board. Although many officers are Italian, most of the service crew, particularly the dining room

BERLITZ'S RATINGS

	Possible	Achieved
Ship	500	372
Accommodation	200	134
Food	400	229
Service	400	251
Entertainment	100	64
Cruise Experience	400	249

OVERALL SCORE 1299 points out of 2000

and housekeeping staff, are from the Philippines. But the lifestyle on board is perceived to be Italian – lively, noisy, with lots of love for life and a love of all things casual, even on so-called formal nights.

All printed material – room service folio, menus, etc. – is usually available in six languages: Italian, English, French, German, Portuguese, and Spanish. During the European school holidays, particularly Christmas and Easter, you can expect to be cruising with a lot of children of all ages.

As aboard other Costa ships, note that for embarkation, few staff members are on duty at the gangway when you arrive; they merely point you in the direction of your deck, or to the ship's elevators and do not escort you to your cabin. Also, note that 'wallpaper' music is played 24 hours a day in all accommodation hallways and elevators – you may well hear it, if you are a light sleeper.

ACCOMMODATION. There are numerous price grades. About 68 percent of all accommodation suites and cabins have an ocean view. Four suites and 52 Samsara Spa cabins are located adjacent to (and considered part of) the designated wellness area. As part of their package, Samsara accommodation occupants get unlimited access to the spa plus two treatments and fitness or meditation lessons, Samsara bathroom amenities, and can dine in one of the two Samsara restaurants.

A pillow menu, with five choices, is available to suite-grade occupants, who also get bathrobes, better amenities than standard-grade cabin occupants, a shaving mirror, and walk-in closets – although the hangers are plastic.

All cabins have twin beds that can convert into a queen-size one, air conditioning, television, telephone, vanity desk with built-in hairdryer, infotainment system, personal safe, and one closet that has moveable shelves –providing useful space for storing luggage. Some cabins have views obstructed by lifeboats – on decks 4 and 5. Some cabins have pull-down Pullman berths that are fully hidden in the ceiling when not in use.

Some of the most desirable suites and cabins are on aft-facing decks 4, 5, 6, 7, and 8, with private balconies and views overlooking the stern. In most other cabins with balconies are not as private – the partition between adjacent cabins is not a full partition, so you may be able to hear your neighbors. However, these balcony occupants all have good views through glass and wood-topped railings, and the deck is made of teak.

Penthouse Suites are the largest type of accommodation, although they are small when compared with suites aboard other ships of a similar size.

DINING. The Taurus Restaurant is the large, main restaurant. It is located at the aft of the ship. There are two seatings, with assigned tables for two to eight, according to your chosen accommodation grade. Dinner on European cruises is typically scheduled at 7pm and 9pm. Some tables have an unwelcome view of the harsh lighting of the escalators between the galley and the two decks of the dining room. Also, a number of support pillars provide something of an obstacle course for the waiters. If you expect to be served by jovial Italian waiters, you'll be disappointed – although the restaurant managers might be Italian. Few tables for two are available, most being for four, six, or eight.

The cuisine is Continental European, with many regional Italian dishes and considerable emphasis on starchy food, particularly pasta: 50 pasta dishes per cruise (buffalo mozzarella cheese is made on board). The food is banquet-style catering. Except for the pasta dishes and cream sauces, the presentation and food quality are unmemorable, and the subject of negative passenger comments. Green vegetables are hard to come by, and rice is used as a plate-filler. Breads and bakery items are decent enough (but made from frozen 'starter' dough), but desserts are of supermarket quality and lack taste. There is heavy use of canned fruit and jellied desserts and packeted jams, butter, etc.

There's a wine list, but no wine waiters (table waiters serve both food and wine). Almost all the wines are young, and the glasses are small. Note that table water is not provided – you are expected to purchase it.

If you opt for one of the specialty restaurants, note that charges apply.

All ships have self-serve lido buffets with basic items. The regular coffee is decent and quite strong, but the extra-cost (illy) coffee is excellent.

A Samsara Restaurant is for occupants of the Samsara-grade cabins, and is located adjacent to the Taurus Restaurant; because it's small, it provides a quieter environment in which to dine. Healthier food with reduced calories, fat, and salt content is featured.

The Club Restaurant is a reservations-only, intimate restaurant that features à la carte dining with a pristine show kitchen as part of the venue. The food is cooked to order and is therefore better than food in the main dining room. It's a good idea to go for a meal in this venue, particularly to celebrate a special occasion.

The Andromeda Buffet is the self-serve casual eatery. While there appears to be a decent choice of food, it is extremely repetitive (particularly for breakfast), and is a major source of passenger complaints. Its layout invites congestion because of some narrow passageways between the indoor seating and the food dispensing areas.

ENTERTAINMENT. The Phoenix Theater, with over 800 seats, spans three decks and is the ship's main showlounge. It appears as if it is illuminated by a rainbow of effects, using the latest computer-controlled lighting. Typical fare consists of revue-style shows performed by a small troupe of resident onboard singers/dancers, with fast-moving action and busy lighting and costume changes that all add up to a high-energy performance.

SPA/FITNESS. This area contains 37,700 sq ft (3,500 sq m) of Samsara Spa space. Included are a Venus beauty salon, saunas for men and women, several private treatment rooms, a fitness center, and a relaxation area.

The spa/fitness facilities are staffed and operated by Steiner Leisure, a specialist spa/beauty concession. Some fitness classes are free, while some cost extra. It's wise to make appointments early, as time slots can go quickly.

Close by, a Grand Prix Formula One simulator is housed in a glass enclosure. For tee-time, a golf simulator provides a choice of several 18-hole courses. Other sporting facilities include a roller-skating track.

COSTA MAGICA
★★★+

THIS IS A FAMILY-FRIENDLY LARGE SHIP WITH ULTRA-BRIGHT ITALIAN DECOR

Size:	Large Resort Ship	Passenger/Crew Ratio (lower beds):	2.5
Tonnage:	102,587	Cabins (total):	1,359
Cruise Line:	Costa Cruises	Size Range (sq ft/m):	179.7–482.2/16.7–44.8
Former Names:	none	Cabins (for one person):	0
Builder:	Fincantieri (Italy)	Cabins with balcony:	522
Entered Service:	Nov 2004	Cabins (wheelchair accessible):	8
Length (ft/m):	893.3/272.3	Wheelchair accessibility:	Good
Beam (ft/m):	124.6/38	Elevators:	14
Propulsion/Propellers:	diesel-electric (34,000kW)/ 2 azimuthing pods	Casino (gaming tables):	Yes
		Swimming Pools:	2
Passenger Decks:	13	Self-Service Launderette:	No
Total Crew:	1,068	Library:	Yes
Passengers (lower beds):	2,718	Onboard currency:	Euros
Passenger Space Ratio (lower beds):	37.7		

THE SHIP. *Costa Magica* (sister to *Costa Fortuna*) has a balanced all-white profile topped by a single large yellow funnel. The ship's aft decks are nicely tiered. There is not a lot of open deck space considering the number of passengers carried, so sunloungers on the open decks must be crammed tightly together; unfortunately they don't have cushioned pads, and there are no small drinks tables. The aft swimming pool can be covered by a retractable glass dome when required. The forwardmost pool has a water slide, which kids love.

Decks are named after famous Italian artists. The decor is quite chic, and not overly glitzy. There are three decks of lounges and bars to choose from, including a very pleasant Piano Bar Capo Colonna. A nine-deck-high, glass-domed atrium lobby houses a Costa Bar on its lowest level (you'll find extra-cost illy-brand coffees here), and panoramic elevators provide atrium views. In the Sicilia Casino, some 65 sculptured soldier puppets oversee the venue, which also has gaming tables and slot machines. The ship is designed for upbeat and active families with children. It is very Italian, and there are lots of loud announcements.

While a variety of nationalities are carried, most of the passengers are Italian, so the ship is lively but quite noisy, with lots of children running around, particularly during the main European school holidays.

All printed material – room service folio, menus, etc. – will typically be in six languages: Italian, Eng-

BERLITZ'S RATINGS		
	Possible	Achieved
Ship	500	367
Accommodation	200	134
Food	400	229
Service	400	246
Entertainment	100	63
Cruise Experience	400	245

OVERALL SCORE 1284 points out of 2000

lish, French, German, Portuguese, and Spanish.

Note that for embarkation, few staff members are on duty at the gangway when you arrive; they merely point you in the direction of your deck, or to the ship's elevators and do not escort you to your cabin. Also, note that 'wallpaper' music is played 24 hours a day in all accommodation hallways and elevators, so you may hear it if you are a light sleeper. Expect lots of announcements in several languages, especially for revenue activities such as art auctions, bingo, and horse racing – and much hustling for drinks. Gratuities are charged to your onboard account. Although Costa Cruises is noted for its Italian style, ambience, and spirit, there are few Italian crew members on board. Although many officers are Italian, most of the crew members, particularly the dining room and housekeeping staff, are from the Philippines. But the lifestyle on board is perceived to be Italian – lively, noisy, with lots of love for life and a love of all things casual, even on so-called formal nights.

ACCOMMODATION. There are numerous price grades, and accommodation ranges from two-bed interior cabins to grand suites with private balcony. There are also two solo-occupancy cabins (unusual for a large ship). No cabins have lifeboat-obstructed views, due to the smart design.

The largest accommodation comes in the form of eight Grand Suites, in the ship's center on Perugino

Deck 7. These feature a queen-size bed, while the bathrooms have a tub, two washbasins, and ample storage space for personal toiletry items. Note that 12 of the most desirable (outside-view) wheelchair-accessible cabins are located a long way from elevators, which is something of a design error.

DINING. The two main dining rooms are Costa Smeralda Restaurant (aft) and the Portofino Restaurant (midships); both span two decks and feature two seatings for dinner (typically scheduled at 7pm and 9pm on European cruises) at assigned tables. If you expect to be served by jovial Italian waiters, you'll be disappointed – although the restaurant managers might be Italian. Few tables for two are available, most being for four, six, or eight.

The cuisine is Continental European, with many regional Italian dishes and considerable emphasis on starchy food, particularly pasta: 50 pasta dishes per cruise (buffalo mozzarella cheese is made on board). The food is banquet-style catering. Except for the pasta dishes and cream sauces, the presentation and food quality are unmemorable, and the subject of negative passenger comments. Green vegetables are hard to come by, and rice is used as a plate-filler. Breads and bakery items are decent enough (but made from frozen 'starter' dough), but desserts are of supermarket quality and lack taste. There is heavy use of canned fruit and jellied desserts, and packeted jams, butter, etc.

There's a wine list, but no wine waiters (table waiters serve both food and wine). Almost all the wines are young, and the glasses are small. Note that table water is not provided – you are expected to purchase it.

If you opt for one of the specialty restaurants, note that charges apply.

All ships have self-serve lido buffets with basic items. The regular coffee is decent and quite strong, but the extra-cost (illy) coffee is excellent.

Club Vincenza is a more intimate dining venue, with seating for around 150 under a large glass dome. There is a cover charge, and reservations are required, but it's worth the effort to sample what Costa can do when food is cooked to order and presented freshly, with classy china and silverware, and enough space around the tables for decent service.

The Bellagio Buffet Restaurant is a self-serve eatery for breakfast, lunch, afternoon pizzas, and beverages at just about any time. The food here is extremely repetitive, however.

ENTERTAINMENT. The Urbino Theater spans three decks in the forward-most section of the ship. It is the setting for all production shows and large-scale cabaret acts, is quite stunning, and has a revolving stage, hydraulic orchestra pit, good (loud) sound, and seating on three levels. In the ship's aft section is the Salon Capri – a dancing lounge and nightclub – always popular with Europeans.

SPA/FITNESS. Facilities in the two-deck high Saturnia Spa, with about 14,000 sq ft (1,300 sq m) of space, include a large solarium, eight treatment rooms, sauna and steam rooms for men and women, and a beauty parlor.

COSTA MEDITERRANEA
★★★+

THIS SHIP HAS UPBEAT ITALIAN DECOR AND STYLE, FOR FAMILIES OF ANY AGE

Size:	Mid-size Ship	Passenger/Crew Ratio (lower beds):	2.2
Tonnage:	85,700	Cabins (total):	1,056
Cruise Line:	Costa Cruises	Size Range (sq ft/m):	161.4–387.5/15.0–36.0
Former Names:	none	Cabins (for one person):	0
Builder:	Kvaerner Masa-Yards (Finland)	Cabins with balcony:	742
Entered Service:	May 2003	Cabins (wheelchair accessible):	8
Length (ft/m):	959.6/292.5	Wheelchair accessibility:	Good
Beam (ft/m):	105.6/32.2	Elevators:	12
Propulsion/Propellers:	diesel-electric (34,000kW)/	Casino (gaming tables):	Yes
	2 azimuthing pods	Swimming Pools:	3 (1 w/ sliding glass dome)
Passenger Decks:	11	Self-Service Launderette:	No
Total Crew:	920	Library:	Yes
Passengers (lower beds):	2,112	Onboard currency:	Euros
Passenger Space Ratio (lower beds):	40.5		

THE SHIP. *Costa Mediterranea is a sister ship to Costa Atlantica.* There are two centrally located swimming pools outdoors, one with a retractable glass dome – so it can be covered in poor weather conditions or when it's cold. Two hot tubs are adjacent. Another smaller pool is for children. There is a winding water slide spanning two decks in height, starting on a platform bridge well aft of the funnel.

BERLITZ'S RATINGS		
	Possible	Achieved
Ship	500	353
Accommodation	200	130
Food	400	227
Service	400	248
Entertainment	100	63
Cruise Experience	400	247
OVERALL SCORE 1268 points out of 2000		

The interior design is bold and brash – a mix of Classical Italy and contemporary features. There is good passenger flow, several spaces for dancing, and a range of bars and lounges for socializing. The interior focal point is a dramatic eight-deck atrium lobby, with two grand stairways. It features a stunning wall decoration, which consists of two huge paintings and *Danza*, a 25-piece wall sculpture by Gigi Rigamonti – best seen from any of the multiple viewing balconies on the decks above the main lobby-floor level. The squid-shaped wall-lighting sconces are neat, too.

The decor itself is inspired by many Italian palaces (some well known, many less so) and by a love of art and architecture. It is extremely upbeat, bright, glitzy, and quite in your face.

A small chapel is located forward of the uppermost level. Other facilities include a winding shopping street with fashionable brands such as Fendi, Fossil, and Paul & Shark Yachting. There's also a photo gallery, video games room, observation balcony, a large Grand Canal Casino with gaming tables, as well as an array of slot machines – and a rarely open library with Internet access but not many books. Printed material such as room service folio and menus are in six languages (Italian, English, French, German, Portuguese, Spanish).

The ship best appeals to young and young-at-heart couples and solo travelers, plus families with children, who enjoy big-city life and loud entertainment, and want an international passenger mix. Expect lots of announcements – especially for revenue activities such as art auctions, bingo, and horse racing – and much hustling for drinks.

ACCOMMODATION. There are several different price grades; this includes a healthy 78 percent proportion of outside-view to interior cabins. All cabins have twin beds that convert into a queen-size bed, individually controlled air conditioning, TV set, and telephone. Some cabins have views obstructed by lifeboats – on Deck 4 (Roma Deck), the lowest of the accommodation decks, as well as some cabins on Deck 5. Some cabins have pull-down Pullman berths that are fully hidden in the ceiling when not in use.

There is too much use of fluorescent lighting in the suites and cabins, and the soundproofing could be better. Some of the bathroom fixtures such as the bath and shower taps can be frustrating to use at first.

Some of the most desirable suites and cabins are those with private balconies on the five aft-facing decks (decks 4, 5, 6, 7, and 8) with views overlooking the stern and ship's wash. Those in other cabins with 'private' balconies will find the balconies not so private – the partition between them is not a full partition, so you'll be able to hear your neighbors (and smell their smoke, if they are smokers).

However, these balcony occupants all have good views through glass and wood-topped railings, and the deck is teak. The cabins are well laid out, typically with twin beds that convert to a queen-size one, vanity desk (with built-in hairdryer), large television, personal safe, and one closet with moveable shelves – to provide more space for storing luggage. However, the lighting is fluorescent and too harsh. The bedside control is for a master switch only – other lights cannot be controlled.

The bathrooms are simple, modular units (a little on the bland, minimalist side), with shower enclosures with soap dispensers; there is a good amount of storage space for personal toiletries.

The largest suites are the Penthouse Suites, although they are small when compared with suites aboard other ships of a similar size. At least they do offer more space to move around in, and a slightly larger, better bathroom.

In 2008, some 44 cabins were converted to become Samsara Spa cabins. Occupants get special spa amenities and access to the spa. You pay a little extra for these cabins, but you get more, and it may be worth it if you want to focus your vacation on wellness.

DINING. The 1,320-seat Ristorante degli Argentiere, the ship's main dining room, is a very large venue. It is located in the aft section of the ship on two levels with a spiral stairway between them. There are two seatings, with assigned tables for two, four, six, or eight. Dinner on European cruises is typically scheduled at 7pm and 9pm. Some tables have a less-than-comfortable view of the harsh lighting of the escalators between the galley and the two decks of the dining room. Also, a number of support pillars provide a bit of an obstacle course. If you expect to be served by jovial Italian waiters, you'll be disappointed – although the restaurant managers might be Italian. Few tables for two are available, most being for four, six, or eight.

The cuisine is Continental European, with many regional Italian dishes and considerable emphasis on starchy food, particularly pasta: 50 pasta dishes per cruise (buffalo mozzarella cheese is made on board). The food is banquet-style catering. Except for the pasta dishes and cream sauces, the presentation and food quality are unmemorable, and the subject of negative passenger comments. Green vegetables are hard to come by, and rice is used as a plate-filler. Breads and bakery items are decent enough (but made from frozen 'starter' dough), but desserts are of supermarket quality and lack taste. There is heavy use of canned fruit and jellied desserts and packeted jam, butter, etc. There's a wine list, but no wine waiters (table waiters serve both food and wine). Almost all the wines

are young, and the glasses are small. Note that table water is not provided – you are expected to purchase it.

If you opt for one of the specialty restaurants, note that charges apply.

All ships have self-serve lido buffets with basic items. The regular coffee is decent and quite strong, but the extra-cost (illy) coffee is excellent.

The Club Medusa is a more upscale dining spot that spans two of the uppermost decks under a large glass dome that is adjacent to the ship's funnel. It seats around 125 and has a menu by Zeffirino, a well-respected restaurant in Genoa. An open kitchen provides a view into the cooking area, so you can watch the chefs preparing their masterpieces. Fine table settings, china, and silverware are used, and the menus are leather-bound. Reservations are needed and there's a cover charge, although you may think it's worth it in order to have dinner in a setting that's quieter and much more refined than the main dining room.

The Perla del Lago Buffet is an extensive eatery forming the aft third of Deck 9, with part of it wrapping around the upper section of the multi-deck atrium. It includes a central area with several small buffet counters; there are salad counters, a dessert counter, and a 24-hour Posillipo Pizzeria counter, all creating a large eatery with both indoor and outdoor seating. Movement around the buffet area is slow. Venture outdoors and you'll find a grill for burgers and hot dogs, and a pasta bar, both conveniently located adjacent to the second of two swimming pools on the Lido Deck.

The place most people will want to see and be seen is the ultra-casual Oriental Café; it features four separate 'salons,' which provide intimate spaces for drinks, conversation, and people-watching.

ENTERTAINMENT. The 949-seat Osiris Theater is the venue for the Vegas-style production shows and major cabaret acts. It spans three decks, with seating on all three levels. Sight lines to the stage are, however, a little better from the second and third levels. Curving stairways at the back of the show-lounge connect all levels.

SPA/FITNESS. Located directly above the navigation bridge in the forward part of the ship (accessed by the forward stairway elevators), the expansive Ischia Spa spans two decks and has around 13,700 sq ft (1,272 sq m) of space. Lower-level facilities include a solarium, eight private treatment rooms, sauna and steam rooms for men and women, and a beauty parlor. The upper level has a large gymnasium with floor-to-ceiling windows on three sides, and an aerobics room with instructor-led classes (some, such as yoga, may cost extra).

There's a jogging track outdoors, around the ship's mast and the forward third of the ship, as well as a multi-purpose court for basketball, volleyball, and deck tennis.

COSTA NEOCLASSICA
★★★

THIS ELEGANT ITALIAN-STYLE SHIP IS GOOD FOR MATURE-AGE PASSENGERS

Size:	Mid-size Ship	Passenger/Crew Ratio (lower beds):	2.0
Tonnage:	52,950	Cabins (total):	654
Cruise Line:	Costa Cruises	Size Range (sq ft/m):	185.1–430.5/17.2–40.0
Former Names:	Costa Classica	Cabins (for one person):	0
Builder:	Fincantieri (Italy)	Cabins with balcony:	10
Entered Service:	Jan 1992	Cabins (wheelchair accessible):	6 (interior)
Length (ft/m):	718.5/220.6	Wheelchair accessibility:	Good
Beam (ft/m):	98.4/30.80	Elevators:	8
Propulsion/Propellers:	diesel (22,800kW)/2	Casino (gaming tables):	Yes
Passenger Decks:	10	Swimming Pools:	2
Total Crew:	650	Self-Service Launderette:	No
Passengers (lower beds):	1,308	Library:	Yes
Passenger Space Ratio (lower beds):	40.4	Onboard currency:	Euros

THE SHIP. Costa neoClassica (in December 2014 its name was changed from Costa Classica) is an all-white ship, now over 20 years old, with a slab-sided unflattering profile, topped by an unmistakable trio of tall yellow funnels. Lifeboats positioned in an upper location make the high-sided ship look ungainly.

The interior design, however, incorporates much use of circles – large portholes instead of windows can be found in cabins on lower decks, and in the dining room, self-serve buffet area, coffee bar (for illy-brand espressos and cappuccinos), and discotheque, for example. There is an excellent range of public rooms, lounges, and bars.

Some fascinating artwork includes six hermaphrodite statues in one lounge. The multi-level atrium is stark, angular, and cold. The marble-covered staircases look pleasant, but they are uncarpeted and a little dangerous if water or drinks are spilled on them when the ship is moving.

Perhaps the interior is best described as an innovative design project that almost works. A forward observation lounge/nightclub sits atop ship like a lump of cheese, and, unfortunately, fails to work well as a nightclub. Internet access is available from one of several computer terminals in an Internet café.

This ship, which brought Costa into the mainstream of cruising Italian-style, has a fairly modern design and styling best described as befitting European tastes. It attracts a multinational group of

BERLITZ'S RATINGS		
	Possible	Achieved
Ship	500	323
Accommodation	200	130
Food	400	214
Service	400	258
Entertainment	100	60
Cruise Experience	400	235

OVERALL SCORE 1220 points out of 2000

mature but young-at-heart couples and solo travelers who enjoy big-city life with constant activity and lots of bustle.

Although Costa Cruises is noted for its Italian style, ambience and spirit, there are few Italian crew members. Most of the crew, particularly the dining room and housekeeping staff, are from the Philippines. But the lifestyle on board is perceived to be Italian – lively, noisy, with lots of love for life and a love of all things casual, even on so-called formal nights.

Note that all printed material – room service folio, menus, etc. – will typically be in six languages: Italian, English, French, German, Portuguese, and Spanish. During peak European school holidays, particularly Christmas and Easter, you can expect to be cruising with a lot of children of all ages.

Gratuities are charged to your onboard account.

As aboard other Costa ships, few staff members are on duty at the gangway when you arrive for embarkation; they merely point you in the direction of your deck, or to the ship's elevators and do not escort you to your cabin. Also, note that 'wallpaper' music is played 24 hours a day in all accommodation hallways and elevators, so you may well hear it if you are a light sleeper.

Niggles include the fact that there is no walk-around promenade deck outdoors. The ship's rather slow service speed (19.5 knots) means that itineraries have to be carefully chosen, as the ship cannot compete with the newer ships with faster speeds. Also, the air-conditioning system in the Tivoli Dining Room is noisy. There are also too many loud, repetitious, and irritating multilingual announcements.

ACCOMMODATION. There are several categories, including 10 suites. The cabins are fairly standard in size, shape, and facilities, with a higher price being asked for the ones on the highest decks. All suites and cabins have twin lower beds, color TV set, telephone, illy coffee-pod machine, and Elemis toiletries.

Suites. The 10 suites, located in the center of Portofino Deck, have a private rounded balcony, marble-clad bathroom with Jacuzzi tub, and separate shower enclosure. There is plenty of space in the living and sleeping areas, and for storing luggage.

Standard outside-view/interior cabins. In general, the cabins are of a fairly generous size, and are laid out in a practical manner. They have cherry wood-veneered cabinetry and accenting, and include a vanity desk unit with a large mirror. There are useful (unusual, for a cruise ship) sliding doors to the bathroom and closets, but the cabin soundproofing is poor. The soft furnishings are of good quality, but the room-service menu is disappointing. The suites have more space – although they are not large by any means – and hand-woven bedspreads.

Some cabins have one or two extra pull-down (Pullman-style) berths – good for families with small children.

DINING. The Tivoli Dining Room has an indented, clean white ceiling. Open seating is the norm for all meals, and there are now more tables for two and four (plus some larger tables) than before. Changeable wall panels help create a European Renaissance atmosphere, albeit at the expense of blocking off windows – but during dinner, it's dark outside anyway unless you're in the far North.

The cuisine is traditional cruise fare that is best described as banquet-style food. Note that there are no real sommeliers, so the young waiters serve the (mostly Italian) wine, which is also young. They also dance at the tables during the cruise – it's a little bit of show business that you get caught up in, whether you like it or not. Note that table water is not provided – you are expected to purchase it.

For casual outdoor eating, the Alfresco Café has teak decking and traditional canvas sailcloth awning. Breakfast and luncheon buffets are repetitious and uncreative, and the source of many passenger complaints. However, after a recent refit, the venue presents its new 'green' image.

Excellent (extra-cost) Italian illy-brand coffees are always available in various bars around the ship, served in the right-sized china cups.

ENTERTAINMENT. The Colosseo Theater, the main showlounge, has an interesting amphitheater-like design. However, the seats are bolt upright, and quite uncomfortable for any length of time. A Galileo disco is located atop the ship, for the young-at-heart (with robust hearing).

SPA/FITNESS. The Caracalla Spa, on one of the uppermost decks, contains a gymnasium with good forward-facing views over the ship's bows and high-tech muscle-pump machines, an aerobics exercise area, two hot tubs, Roman bath, health bar, sauna and steam rooms, and beauty salon. The spa is operated by Steiner, a specialist concession, whose young staff will try to sell you Steiner's own-brand Elemis beauty products.

Some fitness classes are free, while some, such as yoga and kick-boxing, cost extra. Massage, facials, pedicures, and beauty treatments cost extra. It's best to make appointments as early as possible, as time slots can go quickly.

COSTA NEORIVIERA
★★★

THIS FAMILY-FRIENDLY, ULTRA-CASUAL SHIP IS DATED

Size:	Mid-size Ship	Passenger/Crew Ratio (lower beds):	2.0
Tonnage:	48,200	Cabins (total):	624
Cruise Line:	Costa neoCollection	Size Range (sq ft/m):	139.9–236.8/13.0–22.0
Former Names:	*Grand Mistral, Mistral*	Cabins (for one person):	0
Builder:	Chantiers de l'Atlantique (France)	Cabins with balcony:	90
Entered Service:	Jul 1999/Nov 2013	Cabins (wheelchair accessible):	2
Length (ft/m):	709.9/216.4	Wheelchair accessibility:	Fair
Beam (ft/m):	94.6/28.8	Elevators:	6
Propulsion/Propellers:	diesel-electric (31,680kW)/2	Casino (gaming tables):	Yes
Passenger Decks:	8	Swimming Pools:	2
Total Crew:	600	Self-Service Launderette:	No
Passengers (lower beds):	1,248	Library:	Yes
Passenger Space Ratio (lower beds):	38.6	Onboard currency:	Euros

THE SHIP. *Costa neoRiviera* (formerly *Grand Mistral*) is part of a new sub-brand of Costa Cruises, called Costa neoCollection – a strange name – which operates slower, longer cruises than Costa's other brands. The vessel's profile is similar to that of most new cruise ships, although the built-up stern makes it look bulky and is less than handsome.

The lido deck surrounding the small outdoor swimming pool has two whirlpool tubs, and a large canvas-covered bandstand. There is no full walk-around promenade deck outdoors, although there is a partial walking deck on port and starboard sides under the lifeboats, plus an oval jogging track atop ship.

The interior layout and general passenger flow is good, as are the 'you are here' deck signs, and the ship absorbs passengers quite well. It is light and cheerful without being glitzy in any way – there's not even a hint of colored neon – and there's much use of blond/cherry wood paneling and rich, textured soft furnishings.

Public rooms include six lounges and bars, with names inspired by European places or establishments such as Sainte Maxime Casino, Saint Paul de Vence Lounge, the San Marco Lounge, plus a Library (Biblioteca Conca dei Marini, with real writing desks, something most ships no longer have).

Atop the ship is an observation lounge with a twist – it faces aft, instead of forward; it doubles as a

BERLITZ'S RATINGS

	Possible	Achieved
Ship	500	333
Accommodation	200	128
Food	400	223
Service	400	256
Entertainment	100	58
Cruise Experience	400	236

OVERALL SCORE 1234 points out of 2000

disco for the late nighters. There's a video games room for teens, and a small children's center (Squok Club). A conference center provides facilities for meetings.

Costa neoRiviera is best suited to mature couples, solo travelers, and families with children – those who enjoy big-city life and outdoor cafés, constant activity accompanied by lots of noise, late nights, loud entertainment, and food that focuses on seasonal and regional cuisine.

Although Costa Cruises is noted for its Italian style, ambience, and spirit, there are few Italian crew members on board. Most of the crew, particularly the dining room and housekeeping staff, is from the Philippines. But the lifestyle on board is perceived to be Italian – lively, noisy, with lots of love for life. Gratuities are charged to your onboard account.

ACCOMMODATION. There are three basic cabin types, in several different price grades. These include 80 'suites' (each with a private balcony, although partitions are of the partial, and not the full type), ocean-view standard cabins, and interior standard cabins. The price you pay will depend on grade, size, and location.

Note that cabins on Deck 10 are subject to noise from the Lido Deck above. Good planning and layout means that no outside-view cabins have lifeboat-obstructed views, but there are many, many interior (no-view) cabins. The cabin numbering system goes against maritime tradition, where even-numbered cabins are on the port side and odd-numbered cabins on the starboard; on this ship, the opposite is the case.

All cabins have twin beds that convert to a queen-size unit, bold, colorful bedspreads (with blankets and sheets, not duvets), a personal safe, a flat-screen television, and a good amount of closet and drawer space for a one-week cruise. The bathrooms, although not large, do have a good-size shower enclosure, and there is a decent amount of stowage space for toiletries.

Accommodation designated as suites – which are really only larger cabins and not suites, as there is no separation of lounge and sleeping space – have more space, larger (walk-in) closets, more drawers and better storage space, plus a two-person sofa, coffee table and additional armchair, vanity desk, floor-to-ceiling mirrors, and hairdryer; bathrooms have a tub/shower combination.

Six Grand Suites are well-designed units that have a separate bedroom with flat-screen TV, bedside tables, vanity desk, floor-to-ceiling windows, and door to balcony; the lounge has an audio-visual center, sofa, dining table, and lots of space, plus a balcony door. A large bathroom has contemporary styling, two washbasins, dark hardwood storage cabinets, Jacuzzi tub, separate shower enclosure (hand-held shower), and bathrobes.

In addition, there are two interior wheelchair-accessible cabins for the handicapped, which provide more spacious interiors than standard cabins.

DINING. There are two dining rooms (and two seatings for meals, with dinner at 6.30pm and 9pm), which can be configured in several different ways. Both have ocean-view windows. The principal 612-seat Restaurant Cetara has round tables for two, four, six, or eight, and a small podium with baby grand piano.

Restaurant Saint Tropez, a second dining venue seating 274 in chairs with no armrests, is on a different deck. Smaller and more intimate, it is for pas-

sengers occupying Deck 10 accommodation; it has tables for two, four, or six, and ocean-view windows.

The food is quite sound, and, with varied menus and decent presentation, should prove a highlight for most passengers. The wine list features a fair variety of standard wines at reasonable prices, but almost all are young. Note that table water is not provided – you are expected to purchase it, and there are no sommeliers, with the normal waiters serving any wines purchased.

The casual Vernazza Buffet is for alfresco self-serve breakfasts and lunches; it has ocean-view windows, but the flow is awkward and cramped. Additionally, there's an outdoor pool bar pizzeria and a grilled food counter (for burgers and hot dogs). Also, there's a pleasant little coffee bar (Café Eze – for excellent illy coffees) on the upper level of the two-deck high lobby, which, unfortunately, has lifeboat-restricted ocean views.

ENTERTAINMENT. The Teatro Ravello, the showlounge, spans two decks, has a sloping floor, and good sight lines from most seats (the seating is in banquettes), and there is a small balcony level at the rear. Sadly, the designer forgot to include space for a live band (so all shows are performed to pre-recorded backing tracks), and the lighting facilities are anything but high-tech. Entertainment is, without doubt, a weak link in the chain for passengers.

SPA/FITNESS. The Santai Spa health/fitness facilities, located forward of the mast, are quite decent. Included is a gymnasium with high-tech muscle-pump equipment, lifecycles, and rowing machines and a view over the bow of the ship through floor-to-ceiling windows.

Other facilities include a thalassotherapy room, and beauty salon, six rooms for massage and other body treatments, as well as a sauna each for men and women, plus an aerobics exercise room. It's best to make appointments early, as the best time slots can go fairly quickly.

COSTA NEOROMANTICA
★★★

THIS ELEGANT ITALIAN-STYLE SHIP IS FOR MATURE-AGE CRUISERS

Size:	Mid-size Ship	Passenger/Crew Ratio (lower beds):	2.3
Tonnage:	57,150	Cabins (total):	789
Cruise Line:	Costa neoCollection	Size Range (sq ft/m):	185.1–430.5/17.2–40.0
Former Names:	*Costa Romantica*	Cabins (for one person):	0
Builder:	Fincantieri (Italy)	Cabins with balcony:	74
Entered Service:	Nov 1993/Nov 1993	Cabins (wheelchair accessible):	6
Length (ft/m):	718.5/220.6	Wheelchair accessibility:	Good
Beam (ft/m):	98.4/30.8	Elevators:	8
Propulsion/Propellers:	diesel (22,800kW)/2	Casino (gaming tables):	Yes
Passenger Decks:	10	Swimming Pools:	2
Total Crew:	662	Self-Service Launderette:	No
Passengers (lower beds):	1,578	Library:	Yes
Passenger Space Ratio (lower beds):	36.2	Onboard currency:	Euros

THE SHIP. *Costa neoRomantica* (a play on the ship's original name of *Costa Romantica*) is now 25 years old – the oldest ship in the fleet. Although not handsome, it is easily recognizable by its cluster of three upright yellow funnels. There is, however, no walk-around promenade deck outdoors, so contact with the sea is minimal, although there's some good open space on several of the upper decks.

In 2011–12, the ship was given an extensive €90 million renewal program that added more public rooms, two half-deck extensions, 111 new cabins, 120 suites and cabins with balcony, wine and cheese bar, a chocolate confectionary bar, new Pizzeria Capri (with its black-and-white tiled decor), a cabaret lounge and nightclub, and LED lighting. However, no additional elevators were installed for the additional passenger numbers, the swimming pool remains very small, and the layout and flow are disjointed.

Facilities also include a Monte Carlo Lido indoor/outdoor bar; Vienna cabaret lounge; Piazza Italia Grand Bar (arguably the best place to see and be seen); an atrium (with minimalist design features); a neoRomantica Club Restaurant; Casino Excelsior; and a Caffeteria that is part of the Via Condotti shopping area. Out on the pool deck (Lido Saint-Tropez) several 'private' cabanas, adjacent to the pool, can be rented.

Although Costa Cruises is noted for its Italian style, ambience, and spirit, there are few Italian crew

BERLITZ'S RATINGS

	Possible	Achieved
Ship	500	328
Accommodation	200	130
Food	400	220
Service	400	257
Entertainment	100	60
Cruise Experience	400	235

OVERALL SCORE 1230 points out of 2000

members on board. Although many officers are Italian, most of of the crew, particularly the dining room and housekeeping staff, is from the Philippines. But the lifestyle on board is perceived to be Italian – lively, noisy, with lots of love for life and a love of all things casual, even on so-called formal nights.

All printed material – room service folio, menus, etc. – will typically be in six languages: Italian, English, French, German, Portuguese, and Spanish. During peak European school holidays, particularly Christmas and Easter, you can expect to be cruising with a lot of children of all ages.

As aboard other Costa ships, few staff members are on duty at the gangway during embarkation; they merely point you in the direction of your deck, or to the ship's elevators and do not escort you to your cabin. Also, note that 'wallpaper' music is played 24 hours a day in accommodation hallways and elevators, so you may well hear it if you are a light sleeper. Gratuities are automatically charged to your onboard account.

Since April 2017 the ship has been based year-round in China, following a multi-million 'Mandarinization' to suit Asian tastes and preferences.

ACCOMMODATION. There are several different price categories. These include 16 suites, 10 of which have a private semicircular balcony, while six suites command views over the ship's bows. The other cabins are fairly standard in size, shape, and facilities; the ones on the highest decks cost more.

There's a whole wedge of cabins with half-moon-shaped balconies, as well as normal balconies, in the mid-section of the ship.

Samsara Suites/Cabins. Occupants of these 6 suites and 50 cabins have access to the Samsara Spa and its facilities, located at the front of the ship. Samsara accommodation provides organic cotton bed linen, purifying shower filter, and a selection of Ayurvedic teas.

Suites/Mini-Suites. The suites (with floor-to-ceiling windows) and mini-suites are quite pleasant, except for the rounded balconies of the suites on Madrid Deck, where a solid steel half-wall blocks the view. A sliding door separates the bedroom from the living room, and bathrooms are of a decent size. Cherry wood walls and cabinetry help make these suites warm and attractive.

The six suites at the forward section of Monte Carlo Deck are the largest, with large glass windows with commanding forward views, but no balconies.

All other cabins are of a moderately generous size, and all have nicely finished cherry wood cabinetry and walls. However, the cabin bathrooms and shower enclosures are quite small. There are a number of triple and quad cabins, ideal for families with children. The company's in-cabin food service menu is extremely basic.

DINING. The 738-seat Botticelli Restaurant is of a fine design. There are tables for two to eight persons, and open-seating ('My Time') for all meals. Romantic candlelight dining is typically featured on 'formal' night. Traditional cruise fare is served, and best described as banquet-style food. Note that there are no sommeliers, so the waiters serve the wine. They also dance in the restaurant – an example of Costa Cruises' penchant for show business. Note that table water is not provided – you are expected to purchase it.

The 72-seat Samsara Restaurant is for occupants of Samsara-grade accommodation. The restaurant is located at the aft of the ship on the port side of Vienna Deck. The cuisine is more health-oriented, and the venue is quieter and more intimate than the main dining room.

The 90-seat Club neoRomantica Restaurant is an extra-cost, reservations-required, à la carte venue. While the banquette seating is unbecoming of 'fine' dining, this is still a rather pleasant and cozy spot for an intimate dinner, and it features contemporary French and Italian fare that is worth the extra cost.

For casual meals and snacks, the self-serve Giardino Buffet is a small, cramped buffet. The buffet food items are very much standard fare (repetitive breakfast items are a major source of passenger complaints), with the exception of some good commercial pasta dishes.

Pizzeria Capri has something unusual for any cruise ship – a real wood-burning oven – used for making proper Neapolitan-style pizzas (the venue makes 15 different ones).

Enoteco Verona is a wine and cheese bar that features more than 100 different wines, and 80 cheeses from around the world. Italian coffee machines are provided in all bars (coffees are at extra cost, however), so there's never a shortage of espressos and cappuccinos and the like.

ENTERTAINMENT. The Cabaret Vienna is the ship's main showlounge. It is an interesting amphitheater-like design that spans two decks, with seating on both levels. However, the seats are quite upright and uncomfortable, and 10 large pillars obstruct the sight lines from many seats. Typical fare consists of revue-style shows performed by a small troupe of resident singers/dancers, with fast-moving action and busy lighting and costume changes that all add up to a high-energy performance.

SPA/FITNESS. A Samsara Spa spans two decks in the forward section of the ship. It contains a gymnasium with some high-tech muscle-pump machines, an aerobics exercise area, thalassotherapy pool, Turkish baths, health bar, sauna and steam rooms, a solarium, and a beauty salon. Occupants of the 56 adjacent Samsara Spa cabins also dine at the health-conscious, intimate Samsara Restaurant.

The spa/fitness facilities are staffed and operated by Steiner Leisure, a specialist spa/beauty concession. Some fitness classes are free, while some, such as Pathway to Yoga, Pathway to Pilates, and Pathway to Meditation, cost extra. It's wise to make appointments early, as time slots can go quickly.

COSTA PACIFICA
★★★+

THIS IS A COLORFUL, FAMILY-FRIENDLY ITALIAN-STYLE SHIP FOR CASUAL CRUISING

Size:	Large Resort Ship	Passenger/Crew Ratio (lower beds):	2.7
Tonnage:	114,500	Cabins (total):	1,506
Cruise Line:	Costa Cruises	Size Range (sq ft/m):	179.7–482.2/16.7–44.8
Former Names:	none	Cabins (for one person):	0
Builder:	Fincantieri (Italy)	Cabins with balcony:	579
Entered Service:	Apr 2009	Cabins (wheelchair accessible):	12
Length (ft/m):	952.0/290.0	Wheelchair accessibility:	Good
Beam (ft/m):	116.4/35.5	Elevators:	14
Propulsion/Propellers:	diesel-electric (34,000kW)/ azimuthing pods	Casino (gaming tables):	Yes
		Swimming Pools:	2
Passenger Decks:	13	Self-Service Launderette:	No
Total Crew:	1,110	Library:	Yes
Passengers (lower beds):	3,012	Onboard currency:	Euros
Passenger Space Ratio (lower beds):	38.0		

THE SHIP. Sporting a single, large funnel, *Costa Pacifica* is a sister to the popular *Costa Serena*, which now operates short Asia cruises from its year-round base in Shanghai, China. Two pool areas can be covered with retractable glass domes – good in case of poor weather – and one of the pools has a water slide that's great for kids. There is also a huge screen for poolside movies. A Grand Prix simulator is positioned on one of the upper decks.

However, the open deck space is cramped when the ship is full, so sunloungers tend to be crammed together, and they don't have cushioned pads.

There are three decks full of bars and lounges plus many other public rooms. The glass-domed atrium lobby is nine decks high, with great upward views from the lobby bar, as well as from its four glass panoramic elevators. The passenger flow inside is quite good, and the ship absorbs passengers reasonably well. It also provides a decent passenger/space ratio, which means that it won't feel too crowded. The ship has a musical design theme featuring 'greatest hits.' The lobby, for example, is covered in musical symbols and instruments.

Facilities include the Flamingo Casino, which is large and glitzy, but always lively and entertaining; slot machines occupy a separate area from gaming tables, so that serious gamers can concentrate. There's also a very small library, an Internet-connection center, card room, art gallery, and video game room, together with several other bars and lounges. A chapel is a standard

BERLITZ'S RATINGS		
	Possible	Achieved
Ship	500	369
Accommodation	200	134
Food	400	229
Service	400	250
Entertainment	100	63
Cruise Experience	400	248

OVERALL SCORE 1293 points out of 2000

aboard all Costa ships.

Costa Cruises are great for families with children, who are are divided into three age groups for the purpose of groups onboard. Kids even have their own swimming pool in an area called Lido La Bamba, while other facilities include playrooms and video games rooms.

Although Costa Cruises is noted for its Italian style, ambience and spirit, there are few Italian crew members on board its ships. Most of the crew – particularly the dining room and housekeeping staff – is from the Philippines. The lifestyle on board is, however, perceived to be Italian – lively, noisy, and embracing a casual lifestyle – even on so-called formal nights. Most passengers will be Italian, with a sprinkling of other European nationals.

Printed material such as room service folio and menus will typically be in six languages (Italian, English, French, German, Portuguese, and Spanish). During peak European school holidays, particularly Christmas and Easter, expect to be cruising with a lot of children of all ages. Sony PlayStation fans can enjoy PlayStation World. PlayStations are also available in cabins, in the children's and teens' clubs, and can be used with the poolside movie screen.

As aboard other Costa ships, few staff members are on duty at the gangway when you embark; they merely point you in the direction of your deck, or to the ship's elevators and do not escort you to your cabin. Gratuities are automatically added to your onboard account.

Costa provides a well-packaged cruise holiday, especially to first-timers as well as to families with kids.

ACCOMMODATION. There are numerous price grades, from two-bed interior cabins to grand suites with private balcony, although in reality there are only three different sizes: suites with 'private' balcony (which are not large when compared with many other large ships), two- or four-bed outside-view cabins, and two- or four-bed interior cabins. No cabins have views obstructed by lifeboats or other safety equipment, and, in all cabins, twin beds can be changed to a double/queen-bed configuration.

A total of eight Grand Suites comprise the largest accommodation. These are in the center of the ship on one of the uppermost decks. They have a queen-size bed and larger living area with vanity desk; the bathrooms have a tub and two washbasins.

If you like wellness treatments, 12 Samsara Spa Suites are located just aft of the spa – although 91 cabins, including the suites, are designated as Samsara-grade. Samsara suite/cabin occupants get unlimited access to the spa plus two treatments and fitness or meditation lessons as part of their package, and dine in one of the two Samsara restaurants. All Samsara-designated accommodation grades have an Oriental decorative theme, and special Samsara bathroom amenities.

A pillow menu, with five choices, is available in all suite accommodation grades. Only suite grades get bathrobes and better amenities, shaving mirror, and walk-in closets – although the hangers are plastic. Music is played 24 hours a day in all hallways and elevators, so you may well hear it, if you are a light sleeper.

DINING. There are two main dining rooms (the 1,036-seat New York, New York, and the 752-seat My Way), allocated according to your accommodation grade and location. There are two seatings in each for dinner. If you expect to be served by jovial Italian waiters, you'll be disappointed – although the restaurant managers might be Italian. Few tables for two are available, most being for four, six, or eight.

The cuisine is Continental European, with many regional Italian dishes and considerable emphasis on starchy food, particularly pasta: 50 pasta dishes per cruise (buffalo mozzarella cheese is made on board). The food is banquet-style catering. Except for the pasta dishes and cream sauces, the presentation and food quality are unmemorable, and the subject of negative passenger comments. Green vegetables are hard to come by, and rice is used as a plate-filler. Breads and bakery items are decent enough (but made from frozen 'starter' dough), but desserts are of supermarket quality and lack taste. There is heavy use of canned fruit, jellied desserts ,and packeted jam, butter, etc.

There's a wine list, but no wine waiters (table waiters serve both food and wine). Almost all the wines are young, and the glasses are small. Note that table

water is not provided – you are expected to purchase it. If you opt for one of the specialty restaurants, note that charges apply.

All ships have self-serve lido buffets with basic items. The regular coffee is decent and quite strong, but the extra-cost (illy) coffee is excellent.

Two 84-seat Samsara restaurants have separate entrances, located adjacent to the My Way restaurant. Unlike the main restaurants that offer traditional cruise fare, these provide more health-conscious fare – this means reduced calories and less fat and salt in the cooking. These dining venues are open for lunch and dinner for occupants of Samsara-grade suites and cabins, and to anyone else (for dinner only) for an extra charge.

The 118-seat Club Restaurant Blue Moon (reservations required) is an elegant, intimate venue with seating under a huge glass dome. Fine table settings, china, silverware, and leather-bound menus are provided. A cover charge applies, for service and a gratuity.

La Paloma Buffet Restaurant is a self-serve eatery for breakfast, lunch, afternoon pizzas, and coffee and tea at any time. A balcony level provides additional seating. You'll need to carry your own food plates – there are no trays.

ENTERTAINMENT. The Stardust Theater seats more than 800 and utilizes the latest in LED technology. It is three decks high and is decorated in a Baroque style, with warm colors and a Murano-glass chandelier. It is the venue for all production shows and large-scale cabaret acts, is quite stunningly glitzy, and has a revolving stage, hydraulic orchestra pit, superb sound, and seating on three levels (the upper levels are tiered through two decks).

Typical fare consists of revue-style shows performed by a small troupe of resident onboard singers/dancers, with fast-moving action and busy lighting and costume changes that all add up to a high-energy performance.

SPA/FITNESS. The Samsara Spa is a large facility that occupies 23,186 sq ft (2,154 sq m) of space, spread over two decks. It includes a large fitness room, separate saunas, steam rooms, UVB solarium, changing rooms for men and women, and 10 treatment rooms. On the upper level, two VIP treatment rooms are available to couples for half-day rentals.

The spa/fitness facilities are staffed and operated by Steiner Leisure, a specialist spa/beauty concession. Some fitness classes are free; others, such as Pathway to Yoga, and Pathway to Pilates, cost extra. Make appointments early, as time slots can go quickly.

You can buy a day pass in order to use the sauna/steam rooms, thermal suite, and relaxation area, at a cost of €35 per person. However, there's an additional no-charge sauna for men and women, but to access it you must walk through an active fitness area, perhaps wearing your bathrobe – not ideal

COSTA SERENA
★★★+

THIS SHIP HAS REALLY UPBEAT ITALIAN DECOR AND STYLE, FOR FAMILY CRUISING

Size:	Large Resort Ship	Passenger/Crew Ratio (lower beds):	2.7
Tonnage:	114,147	Cabins (total):	1,500
Cruise Line:	Costa Cruises	Size Range (sq ft/m):	482.2–179.7/44.8–16.7
Former Names:	none	Cabins (for one person):	0
Builder:	Fincantieri (Italy)	Cabins with balcony:	575
Entered Service:	May 2007	Cabins (wheelchair accessible):	12
Length (ft/m):	952.0/290.2	Wheelchair accessibility:	Good
Beam (ft/m):	116.4/35.5	Elevators:	14
Propulsion/Propellers: ... diesel-electric (34,000kW)/	2 azimuthing pods	Casino (gaming tables):	Yes
		Swimming Pools:	2
Passenger Decks:	13	Self-Service Launderette:	No
Total Crew:	1,090	Library:	Yes
Passengers (lower beds):	3,000	Onboard currency:	Euros
Passenger Space Ratio (lower beds):	38.0		

THE SHIP. *Costa Serena* absorbs passengers well and won't feel too crowded, except on the open decks. The delightful interior design is themed around the heavens and astrology. In April 2015 *Costa Serena* started sailing year-round from Shanghai, China, with mostly Chinese passengers (and announcements in Mandarin).

There are three decks full of bars and lounges plus lots of other public rooms. This ship has a nine-deck-high glass-domed atrium lobby with four panoramic elevators providing great views. The Casino is large and glitzy, but always lively and entertaining. There's also a very small library, an Internet-connect center, card room, art gallery, and video game room, together with several other bars and lounges, plus a chapel.

Costa Cruises does a good job of providing first-time cruise passengers with a well-packaged holiday that is a mix of sophistication and basic fare. Gratuities are automatically charged to your onboard account.

ACCOMMODATION. There are numerous price grades, although in reality there are only three different sizes: suites with balcony, two- or four-bed outside-view cabins, and two- or four-bed interior cabins. Eight Grand Suites comprise the largest accommodation.

DINING. There are two main dining rooms: the 1,125-seat Ceres, located aft, and the 775-seat

BERLITZ'S RATINGS		
	Possible	Achieved
Ship	500	369
Accommodation	200	134
Food	400	228
Service	400	250
Entertainment	100	63
Cruise Experience	400	249
OVERALL SCORE 1293 points out of 2000		

Vesta, amidships. Tables for two to eight are allocated according to your accommodation grade and location, in one of two seating times. If you expect to be served by jovial Italian waiters, you'll be disappointed – although the restaurant managers might be Italian. Few tables for two are available, most being for four, six, or eight.

The cuisine is Continental European, with many regional Italian dishes and considerable emphasis on starchy food, particularly pasta: 50 pasta dishes per cruise (buffalo mozzarella cheese is made on board). The food is banquet-style catering. Except for the pasta dishes and cream sauces, the presentation and food quality are unmemorable, and the subject of negative passenger comments. Green vegetables are hard to come by, and rice is used as a plate-filler. Breads and bakery items are decent enough (but made from frozen 'starter' dough), but desserts are of supermarket quality and lack taste. There is heavy use of canned fruit, jellied desserts, and packeted jam, butter, etc.

There's a wine list, but no wine waiters (table waiters serve both food and wine). Almost all the wines are young, and the glasses are small. Note that table water is not provided – you are expected to purchase it.

If you opt for one of the specialty restaurants, note that charges apply.

All ships have self-serve lido buffets with basic items. The regular coffee is decent and quite strong, but the extra-cost (illy) coffee is excellent.

Two 84-seat Samsara Restaurants are for those seeking spa food with reduced calories, fat, and salt. Menu creations are under the direction of dietary consultant and Michelin-starred chef Ettore Bocchia. This venue is open for lunch and dinner to those in Samsara-grade suites and cabins, and to anyone else for dinner only at an extra daily or weekly charge.

Other dining options. The 90-seat Bacco Club Restaurant is an upscale, intimate, extra-cost, reservations-required restaurant. The Promotea Buffet Restaurant is a self-serve eatery, with repetitive food (a source of complaints). The Caffeteria is the place to go for excellent (extra-cost) illy-brand Italian coffees and pastries.

ENTERTAINMENT. The three-deck-high 1,287-seat Giove Theater is the venue for all production shows and large-scale cabaret acts. Typically, it presents revue-style shows.

SPA/FITNESS. Samsara Spa occupies 23,186 sq ft (2,154 sq m) of space, spread over two decks. It includes a fitness room, saunas, steam rooms, UVB solarium, changing rooms, and treatment rooms.

COSTA VICTORIA
★★★

SEDATE DECOR IN A COZY ITALIAN SETTING FOR CRUISES IN ASIA

Size:	Mid-size Ship	Passenger/Crew Ratio (lower beds):	2.4
Tonnage:	75,200	Cabins (total):	964
Cruise Line:	Costa Cruises	Size Range (sq ft/m):	120.0–430.5/11.1–40.0
Former Names:	none	Cabins (for one person):	0
Builder:	Bremer Vulkan (Germany)	Cabins with balcony:	246
Entered Service:	Jul 1996	Cabins (wheelchair accessible):	6
Length (ft/m):	823.0/251.0	Wheelchair accessibility:	Good
Beam (ft/m):	105.5/32.2	Elevators:	12
Propulsion/Propellers:	diesel (30,000kW)/2	Casino (gaming tables):	Yes
Passenger Decks:	10	Swimming Pools:	3
Total Crew:	800	Self-Service Launderette:	Yes
Passengers (lower beds):	1,928	Library:	Yes
Passenger Space Ratio (lower beds):	39.0	Onboard currency:	Euros

THE SHIP. *Costa Victoria* – now over 20 years old – does have an outdoor walk-around promenade deck, although it tends to be full of sunloungers. Where this ship differs from many other ships is in its distinct interior decor, with a decidedly Italian influence, and quite cozy feeling.

A seven-deck-high 'planetarium' atrium is the ship's focal point. The uppermost level of the atrium is the deck where two outdoor swimming pools are located, together with four blocks of showers, a grill, and an ice cream bar. Also notable is a four-deck-high observation lounge with a glass elevator.

ACCOMMODATION. There are several different price categories. Six Panorama Suites (each with third/fourth Pullman berths in tiny compartments, like those on a train) and 14 mini-suites are the largest.

All cabins have wood cabinetry, mini-bar/refrigerator, and electric blackout window blinds, but the storage space is very limited. The ocean-view cabins have large picture windows. Bathrooms are small but quite well appointed.

DINING. This ship has two main dining rooms: the 594-seat Sinfonia Restaurant and the 506-seat Fan-

BERLITZ'S RATINGS		
	Possible	Achieved
Ship	500	310
Accommodation	200	126
Food	400	210
Service	400	246
Entertainment	100	58
Cruise Experience	400	239

OVERALL SCORE 1189 points out of 2000

tasia Restaurant. Some tables have a less-than-comfortable view of harsh lighting of the escalators between the galley and the two decks of the restaurant. Also, a number of support pillars provide an obstacle course for the waiters. Note that table water is not provided (you are expected to purchase it).

Ristorante Magnifico by Zeffirino (reservations only, service charge added). Suite occupants receive a free pass for one evening.

Buffet Bolero is a self-serve cafeteria for casual eats, although the food displays and variety are poor (and a source of passenger complaints). Outdoors is a Pizzeria and Tavernetta, while extra-cost illy-brand coffees are available at various bars.

ENTERTAINMENT. The entertainment consists of revue-style shows performed by a small troupe of resident onboard singers/dancers in the Festival Theatre.

SPA/FITNESS. The congested spa/fitness area, on a lower deck, is much too small for the size of the ship. It has a beauty salon, tiny indoor swimming pool, treatment rooms, sauna, and steam room, but cramped changing areas. Sporting facilities include a covered walking/jogging track and a tennis court.

CROWN PRINCESS
★★★★

THIS SHIP HAS COMFORTABLE, SEDATE DECOR FOR MATURE-AGE CRUISERS

Size:	Large Resort Ship	Passenger/Crew Ratio (lower beds):	2.6
Tonnage:	116,000	Cabins (total):	1,557
Cruise Line:	Princess Cruises	Size Range (sq ft/m):	163–1,279/15.1–118.8
Former Names:	none	Cabins (for one person):	0
Builder:	Fincantieri (Italy)	Cabins with balcony:	881
Entered Service:	May 2006	Cabins (wheelchair accessible):	25
Length (ft/m):	951.4/290.0	Wheelchair accessibility:	Best
Beam (ft/m):	118.1/36.0	Elevators:	14
Propulsion/Propellers:	diesel-electric/	Casino (gaming tables):	Yes
	2 azimuthing pods	Swimming Pools:	3
Passenger Decks:	15	Self-Service Launderette:	Yes
Total Crew:	1,163	Library:	Yes
Passengers (lower beds):	3,114	Onboard currency:	US$
Passenger Space Ratio (lower beds):	37.2		

THE SHIP. If you are not used to large ships, it may take some time to find your way around, despite the company's claim that it offers passengers a 'small ship feel, big ship choice.' One nice feature is The Sanctuary, an extra-cost adults-only retreat located forward on the uppermost deck.

Outdoors, there is a sheltered teakwood promenade deck, which almost wraps around, and a walkway that leads to the enclosed bow of the ship. The outdoor pools have quasi-beach-like surroundings, while 'Movies Under the Skies' and major sporting events are shown on a large movie screen located at the pool in front of the large funnel. Just aft of the funnel is Skywalkers nightclub/disco.

The interior decor is attractive, with lots of earth tones (some say it's bland), and an extensive collection of artworks.

Facilities include a decent library/computer room. Ship lovers should enjoy the wood-paneled Wheelhouse Bar, finely decorated with memorabilia and ship models tracing part of parent company P&O's history. A large Gatsby's Casino has gaming tables and more than 260 slot machines, while a Wedding Chapel with a live web-cam is used to relay ceremonies via the Internet (the ship's captain can legally marry American couples, thanks to the ship's Bermuda registry and a special dispensation).

Gratuities are automatically charged to your onboard account (gratuities for children are at the same daily rate).

BERLITZ'S RATINGS	Possible	Achieved
Ship	500	363
Accommodation	200	139
Food	400	247
Service	400	289
Entertainment	100	76
Cruise Experience	400	288
OVERALL SCORE 1402 points out of 2000		

Passenger niggles include the user-unfriendly automated telephone system, the small cabin towels, several extra-cost items such as ice cream, and the charge (coins are needed) for the washers and dryers in self-service launderettes.

Overall, Princess Cruises delivers a consistently fine, comfortable, well-packaged product, always with a good degree of style, at a competitive price.

ACCOMMODATION. There are six principal types of cabins and configurations: (a) grand suite, (b) suite, (c) mini-suite, (d) outside-view double cabins with balcony, (e) outside-view double cabins, and (f) interior double cabins. These come in a bewildering choice of over 30 different brochure price categories.

Some 28 wheelchair-accessible cabins measure 250–385 sq ft (23.2–35.8 sq m); surprisingly, there is no mirror for dressing, and no full-length hanging space.

Cabin bath towels are small, and drawer space is limited. There are no butlers, even for top-grade suites. Cabin attendants have many cabins to look after (typically 20), which does not translate to fine personal service. All cabins receive toiletry kits and include a hairdryer.

Most outside-view cabins on Emerald Deck have views obstructed by lifeboats. There are no cabins for solo travelers. There is 24-hour room service, but some items on the room service menu are not available during early morning hours.

Some cabins can accommodate a third and fourth person in upper berths. However, in some cabins, the lower beds cannot then be pushed together to make a queen-size bed.

Almost all balcony suites and cabins can be overlooked both from the navigation bridge wing, as well as from the port and starboard sections of the ship's discotheque – high above the ship at the stern. Cabins with balconies on Dolphin, Caribe, and Baja decks can also be overlooked. Eight balcony cabins located forward on Emerald Deck may be the least desirable accommodation, as the balconies do not extend to the side of the ship and can be passed by walkers and gawkers on the adjacent walkway. Passengers occupying some of the most expensive suites with balconies at the ship's stern may experience vibration during maneuvers.

DINING. Of the three principal formal dining rooms (Botticelli, Da Vinci, and Michelangelo), one has traditional two-seating dining, while the other two offer 'anytime dining.' All are divided into multi-tier sections in a non-symmetrical design breaking what are quite large spaces into smaller sections. While six elevators go to Fiesta Deck, where two of the restaurants are located, only four go to Plaza Deck 5, where the Michelangelo Restaurant is located – this can lengthen waits at peak times, particularly for those in wheelchairs.

Although portions are generous, the food and its presentation are disappointing, and standardized. Fish is often disguised with sauces or coating, the choice of fresh green vegetables is limited, few garnishes are used, and cheese is either pre-sliced or diced. But, this is banquet catering, which means batch cooking and large quantities. Pasta dishes are acceptable (though voluminous), typically served by section headwaiters, who may also make 'something special just for you' – in search of favorable comments.

Extra-cost, reservations required Sabatini's and Crown Grill are both are open on days at sea. Sa-

batini's has Italian-style pizzas and pastas, with a variety of sauces, as well as Italian-style entrées (mains) – all provided with flair and entertainment by the waiters.

The 160-seat Crown Grill is a steakhouse, for premium-quality steaks, grilled meat, and seafood items; note that there's a cover charge. It is in a wide promenade area, to tempt you as you pass by, and it's worth the extra cost to get food cooked to order.

Casual eateries include a poolside hamburger grill and pizzeria. Some items cost extra at the International Café coffee bar/patisserie in the atrium lobby.

Vines, in the atrium lobby, features sushi and cheese at no extra charge, and extra-cost wine. Other casual meals can be taken in the Horizon Court, open 24 hours a day, with ocean views.

For something different, however, you could try a private dinner on your balcony ('Ultimate Balcony Dinner'), an all-inclusive evening featuring cocktails, fresh flowers, Champagne, and a deluxe four-course meal including Caribbean lobster tail; or an 'Ultimate Balcony Breakfast.'

ENTERTAINMENT. The Princess Theater spans two decks and has comfortable seating on both main and balcony levels. It has $3 million worth of sound and light equipment, plus a nine-piece showband and a resident troupe of almost 20 singers and dancers.

Club Fusion, a second (aft) entertainment lounge, features cabaret acts at night, and lectures, bingo, and horse racing by day. Explorers, a third entertainment lounge, can also host cabaret acts and dance bands. A variety of other lounges and bars have live music, and a number of male dance hosts act as partners for women traveling alone.

SPA/FITNESS. Steiner Leisure operates the Lotus Spa, which has separate saunas, steam rooms, and changing rooms for men and women. There's also a mixed-gender relaxation/waiting zone, body-pampering treatment rooms, and a gymnasium with great ocean views and the latest high-tech equipment. Some fitness classes are free, while others cost extra.

CRYSTAL ESPRIT
★★★★

THIS PREMIUM SHIP IS FOR DISCERNING MATURE-AGE SMALL GROUP TRAVELERS

Size:	Boutique Ship	Passenger/Crew Ratio (lower beds):	0.6
Tonnage:	3,300	Cabins (total):	31
Cruise Line:	Crystal Yacht Cruises	Size Range (sq ft/m):	226.0-516.6/21.0-48.0
Former Names:	*Megastar Aries, Aurora I, Lady Sarah*	Cabins (for one person):	0
Builder:	Flender Werft (Germany)	Cabins with balcony:	0
Entered Service:	1990/Dec 2015	Cabins (wheelchair accessible):	0
Length (ft/m):	269.6/82.2	Wheelchair accessibility:	None
Beam (ft/m):	45.9/14.0	Elevators:	8
Propulsion/Propellers:	diesel/2	Casino (gaming tables):	Yes
Passenger Decks:	4	Swimming Pools:	1
Total Crew:	91	Self-Service Launderette:	Yes
Passengers (lower beds):	62	Library:	Yes
Passenger Space Ratio (lower beds):	53.2	Onboard currency:	US$

THE SHIP. *Crystal Esprit* has had several past lives (it was originally built for long-defunct Windsor Line but operated for many years by Star Cruises for private charters). Although it has profile that is less than handsome, the interiors were tastefully refurbished in 2015, which help to turn it into a premium pocket-sized ship for well-educated travelers seeking a small village feel rather than a big-city feel.

A small aft 'marina' includes water-sports equipment (kayaks, water skis, jet skis, wakeboard, scuba and snorkeling gear), fishing rods, and a two-person submersible (a 30-minute trip costs $600). Two Zodiac inflatable craft are for close-in trips, while several bicycles are carried for passenger use ashore.

Cove is a small main lounge at the ship's front, with comfortable seating for social gatherings. Other facilities include an outdoor Sunset Bar, pool deck grill (for fast-food items), a 'dip' pool, and a self-service laundry room.

Overall, *Crystal Esprit* is a very comfortable little 'yachtie'-style ship, but there's no elevator (stairs only). Almost everything is included – except a lot of space – and a submersible trip.

ACCOMMODATION. There are five accommodation price grades, and, although the company calls them 'suites,' they are definitely not – except for one Owner's Suite, measuring 516.6 sq ft (48 sq m). All

BERLITZ'S RATINGS		
	Possible	Achieved
Ship	500	341
Accommodation	200	142
Food	400	290
Service	400	308
Entertainment	100	60
Cruise Experience	400	265

OVERALL SCORE 1406 points out of 2000

other cabins measure either 226 or 279.8 sq ft (21 or 26 sq m). The price you pay depends on the location, and grade you choose (none has a balcony, because the ship is too low to the waterline). Six cabins (Nos. 301–303, 203–306 and 205–207) have an interconnecting door. All accommodation is practical, and comes with lots of personal comfort items (cotton bathrobe, slippers, hairdryer, infotainment system, and ETRO personal toiletry items). But not even the Owner's Suite has a bathtub, although all have showers and two washbasins.

DINING. The Yacht Club (indoor) Restaurant is the main dining room; it's intimate, although the ceiling is low. The cuisine is based on specialties from the region the ship is in. Also, a Compass Room acts as a wine-tasting room, and can be booked for private parties.

The Patio Café is for casual bistro bites outside on deck.

ENTERTAINMENT. This is a pocket-size ship, so entertainment is minimal, although there is some live music.

SPA/FITNESS. Spa facilities consists only of a small beauty salon and body treatment area. A workout room (with exercise equipment), and two hot tubs are on a different deck.

CRYSTAL SERENITY
★★★★+

THIS ELEGANT, SPACIOUS SHIP HAS VERY GOOD FOOD, SERVICE, AND STYLE

Size:	Mid-size Ship	Passenger/Crew Ratio (lower beds):	1.7
Tonnage:	68,870	Cabins (total):	545
Cruise Line:	Crystal Cruises	Size Range (sq ft/m):	226–1,345.5/21–125
Former Names:	none	Cabins (for one person):	0
Builder:	Chantiers de l'Atlantique (France)	Cabins with balcony:	465
Entered Service:	Jun 2003	Cabins (wheelchair accessible):	8
Length (ft/m):	820.2/250.0	Wheelchair accessibility:	Best
Beam (ft/m):	111.5/34.0	Elevators:	8
Propulsion/Propellers:	diesel/2 azimuthing pods	Casino (gaming tables):	Yes
Passenger Decks:	9	Swimming Pools:	2 (1 w/ sliding glass dome)
Total Crew:	650	Self-Service Launderette:	Yes
Passengers (lower beds):	1,090	Library:	Yes
Passenger Space Ratio (lower beds):	62.6	Onboard currency:	US$

THE SHIP. *Crystal Serenity* is the slightly larger, but still mid-size, close sister ship to *Crystal Symphony*, with a similar look and profile. There is an excellent amount of open deck, sunbathing space, and sports facilities. There is no sense of crowding anywhere, although the self-service buffet can get very busy. There is also a really wide walk-around teakwood deck for walking, and it's pleasingly uncluttered by sunloungers.

Elegant public rooms include the Palm Court, evoking images of a Colonial-style grand hotel lounge; the Avenue Saloon, a favorite watering hole of late-nighters and a throwback to traditional gentlemen's clubs; the Connoisseur Club, for cigar and cognac enthusiasts; and the Stardust Club, a lounge/nightclub. There are shops, a private jewelry room, a computer-learning center with 24 terminals, and an Internet center. There's also the Vintage Room, a private dining room, where 12 invited diners can enjoy exclusive vintages, paired with food, in special wine-tasting dinners. Another feature is a Yamaha keyboard-learning center for the excellent 'Passport to Music' program, which gives you a chance to learn how to play a keyboard instrument (and you get to take home a manual, so you can carry on learning); the program is free – great value indeed.

The 'inclusive' *Crystal Serenity* is best suited to sophisticated travelers, typically over 50, who seek

BERLITZ'S RATINGS

	Possible	Achieved
Ship	500	424
Accommodation	200	164
Food	400	339
Service	400	337
Entertainment	100	83
Cruise Experience	400	339

OVERALL SCORE 1686 points out of 2000

contemporary ship surroundings, with fine-quality fittings and furnishings, a wide range of public rooms and facilities, and excellent food and service from a well-trained staff. This ship has just about everything for its target clientele (including a laid-back California lifestyle), plus an excellent array of guest lecturers.

ACCOMMODATION. This consists of cabins from large to smaller, but no matter what accommodation you choose, all types have duvets, down pillows, a refrigerator and mini-bar, flat-screen infotainment TV (close-captioned videos are available for the hearing-impaired), data laptop socket, satellite-linked telephone, and hairdryer. There's a range of Aveda toiletries (suite-grade occupants get personalized stationery on request, plus a larger list of 'inclusive' brands to choose from), a plush cotton bathrobe, and plenty of good-sized towels. A slight niggle is that the air conditioning in bathrooms and walk-in closets is quite noisy and cannot be turned off.

The accommodation includes: Crystal Penthouse suites with balcony; penthouse suites with balcony; Seabreeze penthouse suites with balcony; superior outside-view cabins with balcony; outside-view cabins with balcony; and outside-view cabins without balcony. Wheelchair-accessible accommodation is also available over several different grades and locations.

The best accommodation is on decks 11 and 10; all other accommodation is located on decks 7, 8, and 9. Each room has an electronic 'Do Not Disturb'/doorbell system. Butlers provide service in deck 10 and 11 suites, where room service arrives on silver trays. Afternoon-tea trolley service and evening hors d'oeuvres are delivered in butler-grade suites.

DINING. There is one main dining room – the open-seating Waterside Restaurant – and two specialty, reservations-required venues. Waterside is quite elegant, with a crisp, clean style that includes plenty of space around each table. It is well laid-out and has a raised, circular central section, although it is noisy at times and not conducive to a fine-dining experience. There are tables for two, many positioned adjacent to ocean-view windows, and for four to eight.

Prego is for Italian food from a menu created by Piero Selvaggio; it offers Italian wines, and the service has flair.

Umi Uma by Nobu is for Asian-California fusion food, with a semi-separate sushi bar with counter stools, and chefs trained by Los Angeles-based Japanese super-chef Nobuyuki 'Nobu' Matsuhisa.

The Bistro, located on the upper level of the two-deck-high lobby, is the casual spot for coffees and pastries, with the atmosphere of a European street café.

For informal eats, the Marketplace has an extensive self-serve buffet area. It's high up in the ship, with great views from its large picture windows.

For casual meals, Silk features regional cuisine and family-style service, and four vertical 'living walls' of greenery. There's also an ice cream/frozen yoghurt counter (no extra charge), and a Chinese street food zone (for steamed dumplings).

ENTERTAINMENT. The Galaxy Lounge (show-lounge) has a high ceiling, with a sloping floor for good sight lines from almost all seats (both banquette and individual seating is provided). The stage, lighting, and sound equipment are all first rate.

SPA/FITNESS. Crystal Spa is located aft on an uppermost deck. Facilities include men's and women's changing rooms with sauna (with a large porthole-shaped window), steam rooms, gymnasium with high-tech muscle-pumping equipment, an aerobics exercise area, and a reception/relaxation area.

CRYSTAL SYMPHONY
★★★★+

THIS HIGHLY COMFORTABLE SHIP HAS ELEGANT, REFINED DECOR AND STYLE

Size:	Mid-size Ship
Tonnage:	51,044
Cruise Line:	Crystal Cruises
Former Names:	none
Builder:	Masa-Yards (Finland)
Entered Service:	Mar 1995
Length (ft/m):	777.8/237.1
Beam (ft/m):	98.0/30.2
Propulsion/Propellers:	diesel-electric (33,880kW)/2
Passenger Decks:	8
Total Crew:	545
Passengers (lower beds):	960
Passenger Space Ratio (lower beds):	53.1
Passenger/Crew Ratio (lower beds):	1.7
Cabins (total):	480
Size Range (sq ft/m):	201.2–981.7/18.7–91.2
Cabins (for one person):	0
Cabins with balcony:	276
Cabins (wheelchair accessible):	7
Wheelchair accessibility:	Best
Elevators:	8
Casino (gaming tables):	Yes
Swimming Pools:	2 (1 w/ sliding glass dome)
Self-Service Launderette:	Yes
Library:	Yes
Onboard currency:	US$

THE SHIP. *Crystal Symphony* has a nicely raked clipper bow and well-balanced lines. While some might not like the 'apartment-block' look of its exterior, it is the contemporary, fashionable look. This ship has an excellent amount of open deck, sunbathing space, and sports facilities, and a nice long swimming pool. There is no sense of crowding anywhere. It combines big-ship facilities with the intimacy of rooms found aboard many small vessels. There is a wide walk-around teakwood deck for strolling – pleasantly uncluttered by lounge chairs. The ship has, over the years, had a number of refurbishments that have brought it up to date.

The Palm Court, an observation lounge with forward-facing views over the ship's bows, is tranquil; one of the nicest rooms afloat, it is larger than its equivalent aboard *Crystal Serenity*.

There is an excellent library, combined with a business center. The cinema has high-definition video projection and headsets for the hearing-impaired. Useful self-service launderettes are provided on each deck.

Connoisseurs Club, adjacent to the Avenue Saloon, features fine premium brands of liquor, and cigars. The Computer Learning Center, with more than 20 stations, is popular; private lessons are available here, but they're expensive.

The ship achieves a high rating because of its fine facilities, space, service, and crew. It is the extra at-

BERLITZ'S RATINGS

	Possible	Achieved
Ship	500	419
Accommodation	200	163
Food	400	339
Service	400	337
Entertainment	100	83
Cruise Experience	400	336

OVERALL SCORE 1677 points out of 2000

tention to detail that really counts. Crystal Cruises also provides impressive lecturers, and the 'Passport to Music' keyboard-learning center is excellent. The passenger mix is approximately 85 percent North American, and 15 percent other nationalities.

In March 2012, *Crystal Symphony* became an 'all-inclusive' ship, with gratuities to staff, wines for lunch and dinner, and bar drinks included – so, no more signing for drinks, which makes for a more relaxed cruise experience. Except for the Connoisseur Lounge (cigar lounge), there's no smoking anywhere inside the ship.

Crystal Symphony is best suited to discerning adult travelers, typically over 50, who seek contemporary (but not brash) ship surroundings, with fine-quality fittings and furnishings, a wide range of public rooms and facilities, and excellent food and service. This is announcement-free cruising in a well-tuned, very well-run, service-oriented ship.

ACCOMMODATION. There are eight categories, with the most expensive suites located on the highest accommodation deck (Deck 10). There are two Crystal Penthouses with large private balcony; Penthouse Suites with balcony; Seabreeze Penthouse Suites with balcony; cabins with balcony; and cabins without balcony. Some cabins have obstructed views. Except for the suites on Deck 10, most other cabin bathrooms are compact, but they are still comfortable. Some have interconnecting doors, which is good for families with children.

Duvets and down pillows are provided for all occupants, as are many other niceties, including a data socket for computer connection, a refrigerator and minibar, infotainment system, satellite-linked telephone, hairdryer, a range of Aveda toiletries a plush cotton bathrobe and plenty of good-sized cotton towels. Suite-grades get a wider choice of drinks and personalized stationery on request. Excellent in-cabin infotainment programming is provided, including close-captioned videos for the use of the hearing-impaired.

Five butlers provide the best in personal service in the top-grade suites on Deck 10. Afternoon tea and evening hors d'oeuvres are standard, and any food arrives on silver trays.

DINING. The open-seating Waterside restaurant is quite elegant, with crisp design and plenty of space around each table. The food, which is of a high standard, is always attractively presented and well served – it's a mix of plate service and silver service. European dishes are predominantly featured, but in an American style. The menus include a selection of meat, fish, and vegetarian dishes. Off-menu orders are also possible.

Kosher meals are also available (frozen when brought on board); Kosher pots, pans, and utensils are sterilized in saltwater, and all plates used during service are hand-washed.

Overall, the food is really good for the size of ship, and, with the choice of the two specialty dining spots, receives high praise. Dessert flambé specialties can be made at your table each day by the headwaiters.

Prego is a 75-seat restaurant, featuring fine Italian cuisine created by Piero Selvaggio, with good Italian wines, and service with flair.

Umi Uma by Nobu is for Asian fusion cuisine by Nobu Matsuhisa-trained chefs.

Afternoon tea in the Palm Court is a pleasant, civilized daily event, but do try the Mozart Teatime, for which the waiters all dress in period costume.

For informal eats, the Lido Café has great views from its windows and a good selection of items in several sections. There is also Trident Bar & Grill, plus an ice cream/frozen yoghurt counter (no extra charge). A Chinese street food zone has favorites such as steamed dumplings.

ENTERTAINMENT. The Galaxy Lounge has a high ceiling, but it's on one level with a tiered floor for good visibility. A few pillars obstruct sight lines from some seats. Both banquette and individual seating is provided. The stage, lighting, and sound equipment are all excellent.

The shows are elegant, with excellent costuming and scenery, but they are too long, and too familiar to Crystal Cruises' many repeat passengers. On the plus side, the cabaret acts are of a good caliber, and constantly changing. The bands are also good, and there's plenty of music for social dancing. The ship also provides male dance hosts for solo female travelers.

SPA/FITNESS. Facilities include one room for yoga and Pilates, an aerobics/exercise room, plus sauna and steam rooms for men and women. There are seven treatment rooms and a beauty salon.

DEUTSCHLAND
★★★★

AN APPEALING SHIP WITH VERY TRADITIONAL GERMANIC STYLE AND GRACE

Size:	Small Ship	Passenger/Crew Ratio (lower beds):	2.0
Tonnage:	22,400	Cabins (total):	294
Cruise Line:	Phoenix Reisen	Size Range (sq ft/m):	129.1–365.9/12.0–34.0
Former Names:	none	Cabins (for one person):	36
Builder:	Howaldswerke Deutsche Werft (Germany)	Cabins with balcony:	2
Entered Service:	May 1998	Cabins (wheelchair accessible):	1
Length (ft/m):	574.1/175.0	Wheelchair accessibility:	Fair
Beam (ft/m):	75.4/23.0	Elevators:	3
Propulsion/Propellers:	diesel (12,300kW)/2	Casino (gaming tables):	No
Passenger Decks:	7	Swimming Pools:	1 (+1 indoors)
Total Crew:	270	Self-Service Launderette:	No
Passengers (lower beds):	552	Library:	Yes
Passenger Space Ratio (lower beds):	40.8	Onboard currency:	Euros

THE SHIP. *Deutschland*, now over 25 years old but in good condition, has an angular, low-in-the-water profile that is not particularly handsome, and a large, single, squat, traditional funnel. The ship, built in sections by four shipyards, was assembled in Kiel, Germany. It is well maintained and kept clean.

Although there is no walk-around promenade deck outdoors as such – it's full of chairs around the central section where a swimming pool is located – you can walk along some of the open space, although there are windbreakers to negotiate. There are also port and starboard midship walking decks under the inboard lifeboats. There is a decent amount of open deck and sunbathing space for a ship of this size, including three aft decks for open-air lovers, and real teakwood deck chairs with thick royal blue cushioned pads.

The Lido Deck has sides covered by canvas shading and white support pillars – like the ones you would find on seaside piers in England – as a setting for the outdoor swimming pool. This is a self-contained deck that has not only the pool but also the casual Lido Buffet restaurant and Lido Terrasse Café. One could spend all day outdoors on this deck without having to dress to go indoors to eat. There is also a small waterfall aft of the pool.

The ship is laid out in a classic symmetrical pattern, and the interior decor has been successfully designed to re-create the atmosphere of 1920s

BERLITZ'S RATINGS

	Possible	Achieved
Ship	500	495
Accommodation	200	138
Food	400	295
Service	400	275
Entertainment	100	63
Cruise Experience	400	255

OVERALL SCORE 1521 points out of 2000

ocean liners. The ship is finely decorated throughout (some might say overly so), with rich, dark woods and intricate brass and wrought-iron staircases that remind one of old-style gentleman's clubs. There is so much detail in the decoration work, and especially in the ornate ceilings, and cleaning it all is labor-intensive. There are a number of real statues, which don't fit well aboard a cruise ship, but there are also many works of art on display.

There's a good range of public rooms and spaces, although these have been possible only by making the cabins smaller than one would expect of a ship of this size. The ship has an interesting, eclectic decor from different periods, as well as a wide assortment of cabin sizes, configurations, and grades.

There are two favorite drinking places: Zum Alten Fritz (Old Fritz) Bar, with dark wood interiors and Belle Epoque ambience; and the Lili Marleen Salon, adjacent to the Berlin Restaurant, with mahogany channeled ceiling. Another nice public room is the Lido Terrace, which would have made a superb observation lounge had the designers extended it to the forward extremes of the deck. It is reminiscent of the winter gardens aboard the early transatlantic liners, and a delightful place to read or take afternoon tea.

The friendliness of the staff is good. Although the ship absorbs passengers well, the space ratio is poor. The onboard product is generally sound, with decent food and attentive service. While the interiors are very attractive, the vessel does not come close to ships such as *Europa*, *Europa 2*, *Silver Shadow*, and *Silver Whisper*, with their much larger suites/cabins, open-seating dining (except *Europa*, which has open seating for breakfast and lunch, and assigned tables for dinner), and their abundance of cabins with private balconies. Just two suites have private balconies; most other cabins are very small when compared to other ships in the premium sector of the international market. Smoking is permitted only on open decks.

During the summer *Deutschland* is operated by Phoenix Reisen, while during the winter the ship is called *World Odyssey* and operates under charter to Semester at Sea (for university students).

Overall, *Deutschland* is a fine, traditional ship best suited to German-speaking couples and solo travelers of mature years looking for a very comfortable cruise ship with appealing itineraries and destinations, good food, and attentive service.

ACCOMMODATION. There are several price categories (the higher the deck, the higher the cost). There are 18 outside-view (small) suites, 189 outside-view doubles, 17 outside-view single cabins; 12 interior doubles, and 50 interior solo-occupancy cabins.

While most cabins are disappointingly small, all are furnished in fancy bird's-eye maple, and all ceilings are one-piece units, unlike the metal strip ceilings of most cruise ships, and they come with molded coving and ornamentation. The closet and drawer space is quite generous, and the attention to detail is good. All cabins have a TV set, direct-dial satellite telephone, minibar/refrigerator, and real cabin keys (not plastic cards) are provided. Many cabins have only one electrical outlet.

The bathrooms are nicely appointed, with pink marble washbasin, gold anodized fittings, gilt-edged mirrors, hairdryer, and ample space for personal toiletries. Both 110 and 230 volt power outlets are provided. Bathrobes are provided for all passengers.

Accommodation designated as suites (there are two grades) is more spacious than a standard cabin, and includes a living area with couch, coffee table, and two chairs; the bathroom has a full-size tub (all other cabins have showers only). The Executive Suites and Owner's Suites are located in the center of the ship; each has a small private balcony. There is one wheelchair-accessible cabin (8042).

DINING. Berlin, the 300-seat main restaurant, is a homely room. All the chairs have armrests, although space for serving at window-side tables is limited, and the hard chair backs are not really very comfortable.

There are tables for two, four, six, or eight, and two seatings for dinner. Two cold buffet bars for cold cuts of meat, cheese, and salad items – either your waiter can obtain the food for you or you can choose it yourself – are featured for breakfast and lunch. Overall, the cuisine is quite creative, with several courses, small portions of nouvelle cuisine, and a wide variety of choice and good taste. The place settings are extensive.

The Restaurant Vierjahreszeiten (Four Seasons), with 104 seats, is an intimate dining room, principally for suite occupants and for à la carte dining, for which a reservation is necessary. There is much detailing and ornamentation in the decor, and the ornate ceiling lamps and indented ceiling coving create an elegant ambience that is relatively intimate. There are tables for two, four, or six.

There is also a small private dining room, the Chancellor Room, with a large oval table seating 10 to 12 – ideal for special occasions and celebrations.

An extensive wine list includes a fine selection of wines from Germany and Austria, although wines choices from other countries are limited. Eating in this restaurant takes considerably longer than in the Berlin Restaurant, and is best for those seeking an evening of fine dining and conversation.

The Lido Restaurant is for casual dining. It has large ocean-view windows on two sides and a centrally located, multi-section self-serve buffet station. Additionally, there is a Lido Terrasse, at the stern, with windows on three sides. It is set on two slightly different levels, houses the ship's library, and has statuary and a relaxing, garden conservatory-like setting. This room also has a bar, plus elegant tea and coffee service.

ENTERTAINMENT. The Kaisersaal (Emperor's Saloon) is the main showlounge. It is a galleried period room with red velveteen chairs and more like a ballroom than showlounge. It is reminiscent of a small opera house and has a beautiful, huge central chandelier. However, sight lines are obstructed from some seats on both seating levels by many large marble-effect pillars.

SPA/FITNESS. The main spa area is on Deck 3. It includes a small indoor swimming pool with a statue of a female diver at one end, sauna, solarium, thalassotherapy baths, and massage/body-therapy rooms; there is also a dialysis station. Deck 6 has a fitness/sport center with a few exercise machines, a sauna with a sea view, and a steam room. A beauty salon is on Deck 7.

DIAMOND PRINCESS
★★★★

THIS LARGE, COMFORTABLE RESORT SHIP IS GOOD FOR CRUISERS OF ANY AGE

Size:	Large Resort Ship	Passenger/Crew Ratio (lower beds):	2.4
Tonnage:	115,875	Cabins (total):	1,351
Cruise Line:	Princess Cruises	Size Range (sq ft/m):	168–1,329.3/15.6–123.5
Former Names:	none	Cabins (for one person):	0
Builder:	Mitsubishi Heavy Industries (Japan)	Cabins with balcony:	750
Entered Service:	Feb 2004	Cabins (wheelchair accessible):	28
Length (ft/m):	951.4/290.0	Wheelchair accessibility:	Good
Beam (ft/m):	123.0/37.5	Elevators:	14
Propulsion/Propellers:	diesel-electric (42,000kW)/2	Casino (gaming tables):	Yes
Passenger Decks:	13	Swimming Pools:	3
Total Crew:	1,100	Self-Service Launderette:	Yes
Passengers (lower beds):	2,702	Library:	Yes
Passenger Space Ratio (lower beds):	42.8	Onboard currency:	US$

THE SHIP. *Diamond Princess*, sister to *Sapphire Princess* (both built in Japan), has an instantly recognizable funnel due to two jet engine-like pods that sit high up on its structure (these are mainly for decoration).

Four areas focus on swimming pools. One has a large poolside movie screen, and another is two decks high and is covered by a retractable glass dome, itself an extension of the funnel housing. One pool lies within The Sanctuary – an adults-only, extra-cost (it's worth it) relaxation area. There's also a children's pool. The passenger flow has been well thought-out aboard this ship, and works with little congestion. There is plenty of space inside the ship (but there are also plenty of passengers) and a wide array of public rooms, with many 'intimate' – this being a relative word – spaces and places to enjoy.

The decor is quietly attractive, with lots of earth tones. The interior focal point is a piazza-style atrium lobby, with Vines (wine bar), an International Café (for coffee, pastries, panini sandwiches, etc.) library/Internet-connect center, and Alfredo's sit-down pizzeria.

A Wedding Chapel has a web-cam that can relay ceremonies via the Internet. The ship's captain can legally marry American couples, due to the ship's Bermuda registry and a special dispensation (which should be verified when in the planning stage, according to where you reside). Princess Cruises offers three wedding packages – Pearl, Emerald, Diamond; the fee includes registration and official marriage

certificate. The Hearts & Minds chapel is useful for renewal of vows ceremonies.

The large Grand Casino has gaming tables, over 260 slot machines. Linked slot machines provide a combined payout.

Other facilities include a library/computer room and a card room. Ship lovers should enjoy the wood-paneled Wheelhouse Bar, housing memorabilia and ship models tracing part of parent company P&O's history. Aft of the International Dining Room is the Wake View Bar, with a spiral stairway leading down to a great viewing spot for watching the ship's wake; it is reached from the back of Club Fusion, on Promenade Deck. Skywalkers Nightclub is set around the base of the funnel structure and has a view overlooking the aft-facing cascading decks and children's pool.

There are many extra-charge items such as ice cream and freshly squeezed orange juice. There's an hourly charge for group babysitting services and a charge for use of the washers and dryers in the self-service launderettes.

In 2014 the ship underwent a $30 million refit that included the addition of 14 cabins, and the installation of the Izumi Japanese baths on Deck 15.

Diamond Princess operates cruises from Yokohama during the summer, with extra Japanese-speaking staff employed in key positions. The ship operates in Australasian waters during the Northern Hemisphere winter (Australia's summer).

Passenger niggles include the user-unfriendly automated telephone system, the small cabin towels, the extra cost for items such as ice cream, and the (coins-needed) charge for the washers and dryers in self-service launderettes.

Overall, however, Princess Cruises delivers a consistently fine, comfortable, well-packaged product, always with a good degree of style, at a competitive price.

ACCOMMODATION. All cabins receive turndown service and pillow chocolates each night, as well as bathrobes on request and toiletry kits (larger for suite/mini-suite occupants). A hairdryer is located at the vanity desk unit in the lounge area. The tiled bathrooms have a decent amount of open shelf storage space for toiletries.

Many outside cabins on Emerald Deck have views obstructed by the lifeboats. There are no cabins for solo travelers. Your name is typically placed outside your suite or cabin – making it simple for delivery service personnel, but limiting your privacy. There is 24-hour room service, but some items on the room service menu are not available during early morning hours. Most balcony suites and cabins can be overlooked from the navigation bridge wing. Cabins with balconies on Baja, Caribe, and Dolphin decks are also overlooked by passengers on balconies on the deck above.

Note that the bath towels are small, and drawer space is limited. The top-grade suites are not really large in comparison to similar suites aboard some other ships of a similar size.

DINING. There are five principal dining rooms with themed decor and cuisine: International; Santa Fe; Savoy; Vivaldi; and Pacific Moon. These offer a mix of two seatings, assigned according to your cabin grade and location, and 'anytime dining,' where you choose when and with whom you want to eat ('anytime' is not available in the International Dining Room).

The main dining rooms are split into sections in a non-symmetrical design that breaks the large spaces into many smaller sections, for more intimate ambience and less noise pollution. Specially designed dinnerware and good-quality linens and silverware include Dudson of England (dinnerware), Frette Egyptian cotton table linens, and Hepp silverware.

Although portions are generous, the food and its presentation are very standardized. Fish is often disguised by sauces or a coating, the choice of fresh green vegetables is limited, few garnishes are used, and cheese is either pre-sliced or diced. But, this is banquet catering, with its attendant 'batch' cooking. Pasta dishes are acceptable (though voluminous), typically served by section headwaiters, who may also make 'something special just for you.' If you like desserts, do try the sundaes.

Sabatini's (on Deck 7) is an informal Italian-style eatery (reservations needed) featuring Italian-style pizzas and pastas with a variety of sauces, and entrées (mains), all cooked to order and presented with flair by the waiters.

Next door is Kai Sushi – a 66-seat restaurant (added in 2014) with its own integral sushi bar. The venue features extra-cost, à la carte sushi (maki sushi, nigiri sushi, and sashimi), and matcha (green tea) ice cream, a noodle bar, regional tea tastings, and a special sake menu.

Sterling Steakhouse (on the starboard side aft of the Horizon Court on Deck 14) is an extra-cost (reservations-required) venue for prime steaks and grilled meats and seafood items, with everything cooked to order, but it's nothing special.

A poolside burger grill and a pizza bar (no additional charge) are eateries for casual bites, while extra charges will apply if you order items to eat at the Lobby bar/patisserie.

Other casual meals can be taken in the Horizon Court, open 24 hours a day, with large ocean-view on port and starboard sides and direct access to the two main swimming pools and Lido Deck. There is little presentation finesse, and oval-shaped plastic plates, not trays, are provided.

ENTERTAINMENT. The Princess Theater spans two decks and has comfortable seating on both main and balcony levels. Princess Cruises prides itself on its glamorous production shows, performed by its resident troupe of singers/dancers.

A second entertainment lounge, Club Fusion, presents cabaret acts at night, lectures, bingo, and other activities during the day. A third entertainment lounge can also host cabaret acts and dance bands. Many other lounges and bars have live music, and a number of male dance hosts act as partners for women traveling alone.

SPA/FITNESS. The Lotus Spa complex (on Deck 15 forward), with Japanese-style decor, surrounds a lap pool – you can have a massage or other spa treatment in an ocean-view treatment room. Facilities include a beauty salon, men's and women's saunas and changing rooms, and an aerobics room and gymnasium.

Izumi, a delightful 8,800-sq-ft (817.5-sq-m) onsen-style (with a daily charge) Japanese grand bath and garden area on Deck 15 aft, includes gender-separated indoor and outdoor cypress baths, stone baths with adjacent utase-yu hot water cascades, and saunas.

Activities such as yoga, group exercise bicycling, and kick-boxing classes cost extra. For exercise, there is a good sheltered faux teak promenade deck (it's actually painted steel), which almost wraps around the ship (three times around equals one mile).

DISNEY DREAM
★★★★

THIS IS THE ULTIMATE FAMILY-FRIENDLY FLOATING THEME PARK FOR ALL AGES

Size:	Mid-size Ship	Passenger/Crew Ratio (lower beds):	1.7
Tonnage:	129,690	Cabins (total):	1,250
Cruise Line:	Disney Cruise Line	Size Range (sq ft/m):	169–1,781/15.7–165.5
Former Names:	none	Cabins (for one person):	0
Builder:	Meyer Werft (Germany)	Cabins with balcony:	901
Entered Service:	Jan 2011	Cabins (wheelchair accessible):	37
Length (ft/m):	1,113.8/339.5	Wheelchair accessibility:	Good
Beam (ft/m):	120.7/36.8	Elevators:	14
Propulsion/Propellers:	diesel-electric (42,000kW)/2	Casino (gaming tables):	No
Passenger Decks:	14	Swimming Pools:	3
Total Crew:	1,458	Self-Service Launderette:	No
Passengers (lower beds):	2,500	Library:	No
Passenger Space Ratio (lower beds):	51.8	Onboard currency:	US$

THE SHIP. Made of pieces of steel and pixie dust, the ship's exterior is about 40 percent larger than the first two Disney ships, *Disney Magic* and *Disney Wonder*. It also has two extra decks, although the design is similar – a tribute to the grand ocean liners of the 1930s. On as all Disney ships, there are two large funnels. The bows have handsome gold scrollwork more typically seen adorning yesteryear's tall ships (the stern is reminiscent of one of those lovely Airstream trailers). The ship's exterior colors are also those of Mickey himself: red, white, yellow, and black. The lifeboats are yellow, and not the normal orange, by special dispensation.

The biggest outdoor 'wow' factor is definitely going to be the AquaDuck, a 765ft (233m) shipboard 'watercoaster' spanning four decks in height – two-and-a-half times the length of a football field. It's pure Disney, really splash-tastic, and beyond anything aboard any other cruise ship dedicated to family cruising.

Disney whimsy and Art Deco style are the hallmarks of the stunning interior decor, too. In the main three-deck-high lobby stands a bronze statue of none other than Admiral Donald (Duck). The decor is enhanced by original paintings, statues, and woodwork all bearing the characteristic Disney attention to detail.

Most public rooms have high ceilings, and the Art Deco theme of the old ocean liners or New York's Radio City Music Hall has been tastefully carried out.

BERLITZ'S RATINGS		
	Possible	Achieved
Ship	500	406
Accommodation	200	153
Food	400	212
Service	400	269
Entertainment	100	88
Cruise Experience	400	314
OVERALL SCORE 1442 points out of 2000		

Have a look at the stainless-steel/pewter Disney detailing on the handrails and balustrades in the atrium lobby. Other facilities include a digital photo kiosk.

Grown-ups can inhabit their own area of the ship – away from the kids. Known as The District, it includes five different adults-only venues, including Evolution (a lounge with dance floor and bar), a cozy Skyline Lounge, Pink, 687 Lounge, and District Lounge. There's also a centrally located Concierge Lounge, for occupants of accommodation designated as Concierge Class, all on Deck 12, plus a dedicated private sundeck for Concierge-class occupants.

Other venues include: Mickey's Mainsail, Sea Treasure, Whitecaps, and Whozits and Whatsits (retail shops); District Bar, Pink Champagne Bar, Skyline Bar, Waves Bar, Bon Voyage, Meridian Bar, 687 (sports bar), Currents Bar, and Arr-cade. The best place for a quiet drink, however, is in the ship's delightful Observation Bar.

During the winter, *Disney Dream* sails on three- and four-day cruises to the Bahamas as part of a seven-night vacation package that includes a three- or four-day stay at a Walt Disney World resort hotel in Orlando; the cruise then forms the second half of the vacation. The ship calls at Castaway Cay, Disney's excellent private beach island, whose facilities are constantly being enhanced. American Express cardholders get special treatment and extra goodies.

Members of Disney's Vacation Club can exchange points for cruises.

Disney Dream is ideal for families with children or grandchildren. Couples and solo travelers are also welcome, though there are few activities for couples in the daytime, and just enough entertainment at night. You will, however, need to be a real Disney fan, as everything revolves around Disney characters and the family theme. Gratuities are extra (about $12 per person, per day), and 15 percent is added to all bar/drinks purchases.

ACCOMMODATION. There are nine types of suites and cabins, but many more price grades, depending on the size and location of the accommodation.

Interior cabins have a virtual porthole that gives you the feeling that you are in an outside cabin. It's done with high-definition cameras positioned on the outside decks to feed live video to each virtual porthole. You almost expect one or more Disney characters to pop by.

All bathrooms have round tubs with a pull-down seat and hand-held shower hose – practically perfect for washing babies and small children. Bed frames have been elevated so that luggage can easily be stored underneath.

The largest accommodation can be found in the Concierge Royal Suite (1,781 sq ft/165 sq m, including balcony), with hot tub. It can sleep five and has one master bedroom with a large walk-in closet, a living room (with one additional pull-down wall double bed and one pull-down single bed), two bathrooms (one has two washbasins), dining room, media library, pantry, and wet bar, plus a large balcony. These suites are located in the best possible position in the ship, with great ocean views.

If you opt for one of the 21 Concierge Class suites, you'll get higher-quality bed linen (Frette 300-thread count Egyptian cotton), feather and down duvets, cotton bathrobe, and H2O Plus bath and spa products.

DINING. There are three main dining rooms, each with a different decor. Passengers rotate through all three, together with their regular waiter (server in Disney-speak).

Expect to see the surfer-dude sea turtle from *Finding Nemo* swimming around Animator's Palate, making special appearances and interacting with passengers; the room transforms into a coral reef during dinner. It's all about 'foodertainment,' which Disney does well, but the noise level can sometimes be a little intense.

Royal Palace has decor inspired by the classic Disney films *Cinderella*, *Snow White and the Seven Dwarfs*, *Beauty and the Beast*, and *Sleeping Beauty*.

The Enchanted Garden is a whimsical main dining room inspired by the gardens of Versailles, in France, and the lighting magically transforms from day to night (the central glass panel ceiling is almost covered in what can only be magical foliage).

Cabanas is open to all. At night, it becomes another restaurant where meals from the main dining room menu are available in an even more casual setting, but with waiter service.

For something different, Remy is an upscale French-style restaurant with menus created by Michelin-starred French chef Arnaud Lallement from L'Assiette Champenoise, close to Reims in France, in conjunction with Scott Hunnel from Victoria & Albert's at Walt Disney World. An extra-cost, reservations-only venue, it offers leisurely European-style dining – ideal for an evening out (without the kids, of course), but at $75 a head for dinner (plus wine) it's not cheap. The design is rather ratty, too (think Disney's Ratatouille); in fact, rats are everywhere in the 'fine-dining' venue – though not on your plate. A new seasonal tasting menu was added in 2015.

Palo is an Italian-cuisine themed adults-only restaurant, with items cooked to order. On days at sea, high tea is also served here. Note that there's a cover charge.

ENTERTAINMENT. Live shows are presented at the Walt Disney Theater, the ship's 1,340-seat showlounge. It has a star-studded ceiling and proscenium arch stage.

Beauty and the Beast is one of the shows being presented, along with other Disney favorites.

The Buena Vista Theater – which is not to be confused with the Walt Disney Theater – is the ship's movie house, with 399 seats.

There's live evening entertainment on deck including a Pirate Night, with visual and lighting effects, and live fireworks. Everyone's favorite Disney characters will be on board in many different locations, so make sure you have your camera with you (there are lots of photo opportunities).

SPA/FITNESS. Senses Spa and Salon has 17 treatment rooms and private outdoor verandahs. An area called Rainforest offers steam heat, misty showers, and hydrotherapy for relaxation. Teens can also have specially tailored spa treatments in their own chill-out zone.

DISNEY FANTASY
★★★★

THIS IS AN EXCELLENT FAMILY-FRIENDLY, VERY CASUAL, FLOATING THEME PARK

Size:	Mid-size Ship	Passenger/Crew Ratio (lower beds):	1.7
Tonnage:	129,690	Cabins (total):	1,250
Cruise Line:	Disney Cruise Line	Size Range (sq ft/m):	169–1,781/15.7–165.5
Former Names:	none	Cabins (for one person):	0
Builder:	Meyer Werft (Germany)	Cabins with balcony:	901
Entered Service:	Apr 2012	Cabins (wheelchair accessible):	37
Length (ft/m):	1,113.8/339.5	Wheelchair accessibility:	Good
Beam (ft/m):	120.7/36.8	Elevators:	14
Propulsion/Propellers:	diesel-electric (42,000kW)/2	Casino (gaming tables):	No
Passenger Decks:	14	Swimming Pools:	3
Total Crew:	1,458	Self-Service Launderette:	No
Passengers (lower beds):	2,500	Library:	No
Passenger Space Ratio (lower beds):	51.8	Onboard currency:	US$

THE SHIP. Made of pieces of steel and pixie dust, the ship's exterior is about 40 percent larger than the first two Disney ships, *Disney Magic* and *Disney Wonder*. It also has two extra decks, although the design is similar – a tribute to the grand ocean liners of the 1930s. On as all Disney ships, there are two large funnels. The bows have handsome gold scrollwork more typically seen adorning yesteryear's tall ships (the stern is reminiscent of one of those lovely Airstream trailers). The ship's exterior colors (red, white, and black) are also those of Mickey himself. The lifeboats are yellow, and not the normal orange, by special dispensation.

No doubt the biggest outdoor 'wow' factor is Aqua-Duck, a 765ft (233m) AquaDuck shipboard 'watercoaster' spanning four decks in height – two-and-a-half times the length of a football field.

Disney whimsy and Art Deco style are the hallmarks of the stunning interior decor, too. In the main three-deck-high lobby stands a bronze statue of none other than Admiral Donald (Duck). A chandelier is the atrium's focal point. The Art Nouveau decor is enhanced by original paintings, statues, and woodwork all bearing the characteristic Disney attention to detail.

Most public rooms have high ceilings, and the Art Nouveau theme has been tastefully carried out. All the artwork in public areas comes from Disney films or animation features.

BERLITZ'S RATINGS

	Possible	Achieved
Ship	500	405
Accommodation	200	153
Food	400	212
Service	400	269
Entertainment	100	88
Cruise Experience	400	316

OVERALL SCORE 1443 points out of 2000

Grown-ups inhabit their own area of the ship, in an area known as The District. It includes five different adults-only venues, including The Tube (lounge with dance floor and bar), a cozy Skyline Lounge, O'Gill's Pub, La Piazza, and Ooh La La. There's also a centrally located Concierge Lounge, for occupants of accommodation designated as Concierge Class, all on Deck 12, plus a dedicated private sundeck for Concierge-class occupants.

Other venues include: Mickey's Mainsail, Sea Treasure, Whitecaps, and Whozits and Whatsits (retail shops); District Bar, Pink Champagne Bar, Skyline Bar, Waves Bar, Bon Voyage, Meridian Bar, 687 (sports bar), Currents Bar, and Arr-cade. The best place for a quiet drink, however, is in the Observation Bar.

Disney has its own private island, Castaway Cay, where the facilities are constantly being enhanced. American Express cardholders get special treatment and extra goodies.

At Port Canaveral, the Disney terminal was inspired by the original Ocean Terminal in Southampton, England, from which the famous ocean liners *Queen Elizabeth*, *Queen Mary*, and the ill-fated *Titanic* once sailed.

Disney Fantasy is ideal for families with children or grandchildren. Couples and solo travelers are also welcome, though there are few activities for couples in the daytime, and enough entertainment at night.

Gratuities are extra and 15 percent is added to all bar/drinks purchases.

ACCOMMODATION. There are nine types of suites and cabins, but many more price grades, depending on size and location.

Interior cabins have a virtual porthole that gives you the feeling that you are in an outside cabin, done with high-definition cameras positioned on the outside decks to feed live video to each virtual porthole. You almost expect one or more Disney characters to pop by.

One feature that's different to *Disney Magic* and *Disney Wonder* is that all bathrooms have round tubs with a pull-down seat and hand-held shower hose – brilliant for washing small children. Bed frames have been elevated, so that luggage can easily be stored underneath.

The largest accommodation is the Concierge Royal Suite (1,781 sq ft/165 sq m, including balcony with hot tub). It can sleep five and has one master bedroom with a large walk-in closet, a living room (with an additional pull-down wall double bed and a pull-down single bed), two bathrooms (one has two washbasins), dining room, pantry, and wet bar. These suites are in the best position in the ship, with great ocean views.

If you opt for one of the 21 Concierge Class suites, you'll get higher-quality bed linen (Frette 300-thread count Egyptian cotton), feather and down duvets, cotton bathrobe, and H2O Plus bath and spa products.

DINING. There are three main dining rooms, each with a different decor. Passengers rotate through all three, together with their regular waiter (server in Disney-speak).

Expect to see the surfer-dude sea turtle from *Finding Nemo* swimming around Animator's Palate, making special appearances and interacting with passengers; the room transforms into a coral reef during dinner. It's all about 'foodertainment,' which Disney does well, but the noise level can sometimes be a little intense.

Royal Court has decor inspired by the classic Disney films *Cinderella*, *Snow White and the Seven Dwarfs*, *Beauty and the Beast*, and *Sleeping Beauty*.

The Enchanted Garden is a whimsical main dining room inspired by the gardens of Versailles, in France, and the lighting magically transforms from day to night (the central glass panel ceiling is almost covered in what can only be magical foliage).

Cabanas, which is open to all, is an alternative place for enjoying food (evening only) from the main dining room menu. It's a more casual setting but offers waiter service.

As a change from the big, lively dining rooms, try Remy. It's an upscale French-style restaurant with menus created by Michelin-starred French chef Arnaud Lallement from L'Assiette Champenoise, close to Reims in France, in conjunction with Scott Hunnel from Victoria & Albert's at Walt Disney World. An extra-cost, reservations-only venue, it offers leisurely European-style dining – ideal for an evening out without the kids, but at $75 a head for dinner (plus wine) it's not cheap. The design is rather ratty, too (think Disney's Ratatouille); in fact, rats are everywhere in the 'fine-dining' venue – though not on your plate. A new seasonal tasting menu was added in 2015.

Palo is an Italian-cuisine themed adults-only restaurant, with items cooked to order. On days at sea, high tea is also served here, and there's a cover charge.

ENTERTAINMENT. Live shows are presented at the Walt Disney Theater, the ship's 1,340-seat showlounge, which has a star-studded ceiling and proscenium arch stage.

Villains Tonight, which premiered in 2010 aboard *Disney Dream* and features the baddies in Disney's films, is one of the shows, together with other Disney favorites.

The Buena Vista Theater – which is not to be confused with the Walt Disney Theater – is the ship's movie house, with 399 seats.

There's live evening entertainment on deck including a Pirate Night, with visual and lighting effects, and live fireworks. Everyone's favorite Disney characters will be on board in many different locations (including some of the Star Wars characters as holographic models), so do have your camera with you (there are lots of photo opportunities).

SPA/FITNESS. Senses Spa and Salon has 17 treatment rooms and private outdoor verandahs. An area called Rainforest features steam heat, misty showers, and hydrotherapy for relaxation. Teens can also have specially tailored spa treatments in their own chill-out zone.

DISNEY MAGIC
★★★+

ULTRA FAMILY-FRIENDLY CRUISING IN A CASUAL THEME PARK SETTING

Size:	Mid-size Ship	Passenger/Crew Ratio (lower beds):	1.8
Tonnage:	83,338	Cabins (total):	875
Cruise Line:	Disney Cruise Line	Size Range (sq ft/m):	180.8–968.7/16.8–90.0
Former Names:	none	Cabins (for one person):	0
Builder:	Fincantieri (Italy)	Cabins with balcony:	388
Entered Service:	Jul 1998	Cabins (wheelchair accessible):	12
Length (ft/m):	964.5/294.0	Wheelchair accessibility:	Good
Beam (ft/m):	105.7/32.2	Elevators:	12
Propulsion/Propellers:	diesel-electric (38,000kW)/2	Casino (gaming tables):	No
Passenger Decks:	11	Swimming Pools:	3
Total Crew:	945	Self-Service Launderette:	Yes
Passengers (lower beds):	1,750	Library:	No
Passenger Space Ratio (lower beds):	47.6	Onboard currency:	US$

THE SHIP. Disney Cruise Line's first ship's profile is sleek, and combines streamlining with tradition and nostalgia, a black hull, and two red-and-black funnels reminiscent of the ocean liners of yesteryear – *Disney Magic* was the first cruise ship built with two funnels since the 1950s. The forward funnel is a dummy containing various public spaces, including a teen center, Aloft.

There are two outdoor pools: one pool for adults only (in theory), and one for families (with a massive poolside movie screen). In a 2013 makeover, a super-popular AquaDunk water-slide experience was added.

Inside, it's all about Disney. Most public rooms have high ceilings, and the Art Deco theme of the old ocean liners or New York's Radio City Music Hall has been tastefully carried out. Check out the stainless-steel/pewter Disney detailing on the handrails and balustrades in the three-deck-high lobby – it provides a real photo opportunity, with a 6ft (1.8m) bronze statue of Mickey Mouse in the role of a ship's helmsman.

A highlight for most is a day spent on Disney's private island, Castaway Cay in the Bahamas. It is an excellent private island, with its own pier for the ship to dock alongside. Water-sports equipment – floats, paddle-boats, kayaks, hobie cats, aqua fins, aqua trikes, and snorkels – can be rented.

Disney Magic is a seagoing Never-Never Land. In reality, it provides a highly programed, well-organ-ized, and regimented onboard experience, with registrations and reservations needed for almost everything. Children of all ages (minimum 12 weeks old) should have a great time.

Take mainly casual clothing (although there are two 'formal' nights on seven-day cruises). Gratuities are extra, suggested at about $12 per person, per day, and 15 percent is added to all bar/beverage/wine and 18 percent for spa accounts.

ACCOMMODATION. There are just six different cabin layouts, in several price grades; the price will depend on the grade, size, and location chosen, and is linked to the resort accommodation for those taking a combined resort/cruise vacation. Spread over six decks, all types have been designed for practicality and have space-efficient layouts.

Most cabins have common features such as a neat vertical steamer trunk for clothes storage, illuminated closets, a hairdryer located at a vanity desk or in the bathroom, and bathrobes for all passengers. Many cabins have third and fourth pull-down berths that rise and are totally hidden in the ceiling when not in use, but the standard interior and outside cabins, while acceptable for two, are extremely tight with three or four. Some cabins can also accommodate a fifth person. Cabins with refrigerators can have them stocked, at extra cost, with one of several drinks/soft drinks packages.

BERLITZ'S RATINGS		
	Possible	Achieved
Ship	500	378
Accommodation	200	144
Food	400	203
Service	400	265
Entertainment	100	86
Cruise Experience	400	305
OVERALL SCORE 1381 points out of 2000		

Bathrooms, although compact due to the fact that the toilet is separate, are really functional units, designed with split-use facilities so that more than one person can use them at the same time – good for families. Many have bathtubs, which are really shower tubs.

Accommodation designated as suites offers much more space, and extra goodies including CD and DVD players, big-screen TVs, and extra beds (useful for larger families). Some suites are beneath the pool deck, teen lounge, or informal café, so there could be noise as the ceiling insulation is poor – although cabin-to-cabin insulation is good.

Wheelchair-bound passengers have a variety of cabin sizes and configurations, including suites with a private balcony (unfortunately you can't get a wheelchair through the balcony's sliding door) and over-sized bathrooms with excellent roll-in showers, and good closet and drawer space. Almost the entire vessel is accessible. For the sight-impaired, cabin numbers and elevator buttons are braille-encoded.

DINING. There are three main dining rooms – non-smoking, of course – each with over 400 seats, two seatings, and unique themes. Lumiere's (in the center of the ship on Deck 3) has Beauty and the Beast; Parrot Cay (Deck 4) has a tacky, pseudo-Caribbean theme; also on Deck 4 aft, with great ocean views over the stern, is Animator's Palate, the most visual of the three, with food and electronic art that makes the evening decor change from black and white to full color (this author's signature is on a hidden wall panel in this venue – it was done in the shipyard at Disney Cruise Line's invitation).

You eat in all three dining rooms in rotation – twice per seven-day cruise – and move with your assigned waiter and assistant waiter to each dining room in turn, thus providing the variety of different decor and different menus. It's a great concept – and unique in the cruise industry. As you will have the same waiter in each of the three restaurants, any gratuities go only to 'your' waiter. Parrot Cay and Lumiere's have open seating for breakfast and lunch, but the lunch menu is pitiful.

Palo is a 140-seat reservations-only alternative restaurant with a small cover/gratuity charge, serving Italian cuisine. It has a 270-degree view and is for adults only; the cuisine is cooked to order, and the wine list is good, although prices are high. Make your reservations as soon as you board or you will miss out on the ship's only decent food. Afternoon High Tea is presented here, on days at sea.

Topsider's (incorporating Beach Blanket Buffet) is an indoor/outdoor café serving low-quality self-serve breakfast and lunch buffets with limited choice and presentation, and a buffet dinner, consisting mostly of fried foods, for children. But the venue is often overcrowded at lunchtime, so it may be better to go to the Parrot Cay dining room, which offers breakfast and lunch buffet, too. A poolside Goofy's Galley has grilled panini and wraps, and complimentary soft drinks.

Scoops, an ice cream and frozen yogurt bar, opens infrequently; other fast-food outlets include Pluto's for hamburgers and hot dogs, and Pinocchio's, which is open all day but not in the evening, for basic pizza and sandwiches.

On one night, there is also an outdoor self-serve Tropicalifragilisticexpialidocious buffet.

A casual Outlook Café, installed in 2010, has fine views from Deck 10, just forward of the first funnel housing. Vegetarians and those looking for light cuisine will be underwhelmed by the lack of green vegetables. Guest chefs from Walt Disney World Resort prepare signature dishes each cruise, and also host cooking demonstrations.

ENTERTAINMENT. The entertainment and activities programs for families and children are extremely good. There are three big stage shows in the stunning 977-seat showlounge, presenting original Disney musicals and the latest comedy productions, bring together a cast of Disney baddies from many Disney films. Sadly, there is no live orchestra, although the lighting, staging, and technical effects are excellent. There is also a Disney-themed Trivia Game Show.

SPA/FITNESS. The Vista Spa is the ship's fitness/wellbeing complex, measuring 10,700 sq ft (994 sq m). The fitness/workout room, with high-tech Cybex muscle-toning equipment, has ocean-view windows overlooking the navigation bridge one deck below. There are 11 rooms for spa/beauty treatments – but note that the pounding from the basketball court on the sports deck directly overhead makes spa treatments less than relaxing.

DISNEY WONDER
★★★+

THIS IS GOOD, THEME-PARK, CASUAL CRUISING FOR THE WHOLE FAMILY

Size:	Mid-size Ship	Passenger/Crew Ratio (lower beds):	1.8
Tonnage:	85,000	Cabins (total):	875
Cruise Line:	Disney Cruise Line	Size Range (sq ft/m):	180.8–968.7/16.8–90.0
Former Names:	none	Cabins (for one person):	0
Builder:	Fincantieri (Italy)	Cabins with balcony:	388
Entered Service:	Aug 1999	Cabins (wheelchair accessible):	12
Length (ft/m):	964.5/294.0	Wheelchair accessibility:	Good
Beam (ft/m):	105.7/32.2	Elevators:	12
Propulsion/Propellers:	diesel-electric (38,000kW)/2	Casino (gaming tables):	No
Passenger Decks:	11	Swimming Pools:	3
Total Crew:	945	Self-Service Launderette:	Yes
Passengers (lower beds):	1,750	Library:	No
Passenger Space Ratio (lower beds):	48.5	Onboard currency:	US$

THE SHIP. *Disney Wonder* is the second of an identical pair of ships (the first was the 1998-built *Disney Magic*). The ship's profile is sleek, and combines streamlining with tradition and nostalgia, a black hull and two red-and-black funnels designed to remind you of the ocean liners of yesteryear – *Disney Magic* was the first cruise ship built with two funnels since the 1950s. One funnel is a dummy containing various public spaces, including a teen center.

There are three outdoor pools: one pool for adults only (in theory), one for families (with a large poolside movie screen), and one for children, with Mickey's face and ears painted into the bottom.

Inside, the ship is quite stunning. Most public rooms have high ceilings, and the Art Deco theme of the old ocean liners or New York's Radio City Music Hall has been tastefully carried out. Look at the stainless-steel/pewter Disney detailing on the handrails and balustrades in the three-deck-high lobby.

Apart from the ports of call, the highlight for most is a day spent on Disney's private island, Castaway Cay in the Bahamas. It is an outstanding private island for families.

Disney Wonder is a seagoing Never-Never Land. In reality, the ship provides a highly programed, well-organized, strictly timed, and regimented cruise experience, with registration and reservations necessary for almost everything. But for children of all ages (minimum 12 weeks old), it's hard to beat Dis-

BERLITZ'S RATINGS

	Possible	Achieved
Ship	500	380
Accommodation	200	144
Food	400	203
Service	400	265
Entertainment	100	86
Cruise Experience	400	308

OVERALL SCORE 1386 points out of 2000

ney's family entertainment. There's also an adults-only entertainment area called 'After Hours' that includes a nightspot called Azure and Cadillac Lounge piano lounge with retro car design decor and seating, and the Crown and Fin bar.

Take just casual clothing. Gratuities are extra (suggested at $12 per person per day); 15 percent is added to all bar/beverage/wine and 18 percent for spa accounts.

In a 2016 refurbishment, Disney Wonder gained a new restaurant – Tiana's Place, a revamped British pub, a Twist and Spout waterslide, a Dory's Reef splash zone, and an Aqualab play area.

ACCOMMODATION. There are 12 grades, but just six different cabin layouts; the price will depend on the grade, size, and location chosen, and are linked to the resort accommodation for those taking a combined resort/cruise vacation. Spread over six decks, all suites and cabins have been designed for practicality and have space-efficient layouts.

Most cabins have common features such as a neat vertical steamer trunk for clothes storage, illuminated closets, a hairdryer located at a vanity desk or in the bathroom, and bathrobes for all passengers. Many cabins have third and fourth pull-down berths that rise and are totally hidden in the ceiling when not in use, but the standard interior and outside cabins, while acceptable for two, are extremely tight with three or four. Some cabins can also accommodate a fifth person. The cabin decor is practical, creative, and colorful, with lots of neat styling touches. Cabins with refrigerators can have them stocked, at extra cost, with one of several drinks/soft drinks packages.

Bathrooms, although compact due to the fact that the toilet is separate, are really functional units, designed with split-use facilities, so that more than one person can use them at the same time – good for families. Many have bathtubs, which are really shower tubs.

Accommodation designated as suites offers much more space, and extra goodies such as CD and DVD players, big-screen TVs, and extra beds (useful for larger families). Some suites are beneath the pool deck, teen lounge, or informal café, so there could be noise as the ceiling insulation is poor – although cabin-to-cabin insulation is good.

The two largest suites, the Walter E. Disney Suite and the Roy O. Disney Suite, are located beside the central bank of elevators. These are luxurious living spaces, each with two bedrooms, and all the Disney trimmings you'd expect.

Wheelchair-bound passengers have a variety of cabin sizes and configurations, including suites with a private balcony – unfortunately you can't get a wheelchair through the balcony's sliding door – and extra-large bathrooms with excellent roll-in showers, and good closet and drawer space. Almost all the vessel is accessible. For the sight-impaired, cabin numbers and elevator buttons are braille-encoded.

A 24-hour room service is available, and suites also get 'concierge service.' But the room service and cabin breakfast menu are limited. A 15 percent service charge applies to beverage deliveries, including tea and coffee.

DINING. There are has three main dining rooms, all non-smoking, each with over 400 seats, two seatings, and unique themes. Lumiere's (in the center of the ship on Deck 3) has Beauty and the Beast; Tiana's (supper club on Deck 4) has a New Orleans jazz-and-blues theme, with live music; also on Deck 4 aft, with great ocean views over the stern, is Animator's Palate, the most visual of the three with food and electronic art that makes the evening decor change from black and white to full-color.

You will eat in all three dining rooms in rotation – twice per seven-day cruise – and move with your assigned waiter and assistant waiter to each dining room in turn, thus providing the variety of different decor and different menus. It's a great concept – and

unique in the cruise industry. As you will have the same waiter in each of the three restaurants, any gratuities go only to 'your' waiter. Parrot Cay and Lumiere's have open seating for breakfast and lunch, but the lunch menu is pitiful.

Palo is a 140-seat reservations-only, extra-cost restaurant, for Italian cuisine. It has a 270-degree view and is for adults only; the cuisine is cooked to order, and the wine list is good, although prices are high. Make reservations as soon as you board or you will miss out on the ship's only decent food. Afternoon High Tea is presented here, on days at sea.

Cabanas is a large indoor/outdoor self-serve eatery breakfast and lunch buffets with limited choice and presentation, and a buffet dinner, consisting mostly of fried foods, for children. A poolside Goofy's Galley has grilled paninis, wraps, and complimentary soft drinks.

Scoops, an ice cream and frozen yogurt bar, opens infrequently; other fast-food outlets include Boiler Bar, for hamburgers and hot dogs, and Pinocchio's, which is open all day but not in the evening, for basic pizza and sandwiches.

One night features an outdoor self-serve Tropicalifragilisticexpialidocious buffet.

A casual Outlook Café, installed in 2010, has good views from Deck 10, just forward of the first funnel housing. Vegetarians and those looking for light cuisine will be underwhelmed by the lack of green vegetables. Guest chefs from Walt Disney World Resort prepare signature dishes and host cooking demonstrations.

ENTERTAINMENT. The entertainment and activities programs for families and children are superb. There are three large-scale stage shows in the stunning 977-seat showlounge, presenting original Disney musicals and comedy productions, bringing together a cast of Disney baddies from many Disney films. Sadly, there is no live orchestra, although the lighting, staging, and technical effects are excellent. There is also a Disney-themed Trivia Game Show.

SPA/FITNESS. The Senses Spa & Salon is a fitness/wellbeing complex measuring 10,700 sq ft (994 sq m). The fitness/workout room, with high-tech Cybex muscle-toning equipment, has ocean-view windows overlooking the navigation bridge one deck below. There are 13 rooms for spa/beauty treatments – but note that the pounding from the basketball court on the sports deck directly overhead makes spa treatments less than relaxing.

EMERALD PRINCESS
★★★★

THIS IS A CASUAL, VERY COMFORTABLE, FAMILY-ORIENTED LARGE RESORT SHIP

Size:	Large Resort Ship	Passenger/Crew Ratio (lower beds):	2.5
Tonnage:	113,561	Cabins (total):	1,557
Cruise Line:	Princess Cruises	Size Range (sq ft/m):	163–1,279/15.1–118.8
Former Names:	none	Cabins (for one person):	0
Builder:	Fincantieri (Italy)	Cabins with balcony:	881
Entered Service:	May 2007	Cabins (wheelchair accessible):	25
Length (ft/m):	951.4/290.0	Wheelchair accessibility:	Good
Beam (ft/m):	118.1/36.0	Elevators:	14
Propulsion/Propellers:	diesel-electric (42,000kW)/2	Casino (gaming tables):	Yes
Passenger Decks:	15	Swimming Pools:	3
Total Crew:	1,200	Self-Service Launderette:	Yes
Passengers (lower beds):	3,114	Library:	Yes
Passenger Space Ratio (lower beds):	36.2	Onboard currency:	US$

THE SHIP. *Emerald Princess* has the same profile as sister *Crown Princess* (similar to half-sisters *Diamond, Golden, Grand, Ruby, Sapphire,* and *Star Princess*). Although the ship takes over 500 more passengers than the half-sisters, outdoor deck space remains the same, as do the number of elevators, so waiting time increases at peak periods. The Passenger Space Ratio is also considerably reduced.

BERLITZ'S RATINGS	Possible	Achieved
Ship	500	363
Accommodation	200	139
Food	400	248
Service	400	285
Entertainment	100	79
Cruise Experience	400	290

OVERALL SCORE 1404 points out of 2000

An extra-cost adults-only retreat (The Sanctuary), located forward on the uppermost deck, provides a 'private' place to relax and unwind. There are attendants to provide chilled face towels, and light bites are available; there are also two outdoor cabanas for massages.

The ship has a sheltered faux teak (actually painted steel) promenade deck, which almost wraps around (three times round equals 1 mile/1.6km) and a walkway that goes to the enclosed, protected bow of the ship. The outdoor pools have various beach-like surroundings. Movies Under the Skies and major sporting events are shown on a 300-sq-ft (28-sq-m) movie screen at the pool in front of the large funnel structure.

Inside is a wide array of public rooms, with some 'intimate' (this being a relative term) spaces and places to play.

Aft of the funnel housing is a ship-wide glass-walled disco called Skywalkers, with fine views from port and starboard side windows (it would make a great penthouse).

The interior decor is attractive, with lots of earth tones. An extensive collection of artworks complements the interior design and colors well. If you see something you like, you may be able to purchase it.

The ship also has a Hearts & Minds wedding chapel, with a live web-cam to relay ceremonies via the Internet. The captain can legally marry (American) couples, thanks to the ship's Bermuda registry. But getting married and taking close family members and entourage with you on your honeymoon may prove expensive.

Gamers should enjoy the large Gatsby's Casino, with more than 260 slot machines, and gaming tables.

Other features include a small library, and a decent Internet-connect room. Ship lovers should enjoy the wood-paneled Wheelhouse Bar (a good place for cocktails and beer), finely decorated with memorabilia and ship models tracing part of parent company P&O's history. A sports bar has two billiard tables, and several television screens.

The ship is a fine resort playground in which to roam when you are not ashore, and Princess Cruises consistently delivers a well-packaged cruise, always with a good degree of style, at an attractive, highly competitive price. With many choices and 'small' rooms to enjoy, the ship has been well designed, and you should have an enjoyable time.

As with any large resort ship it takes time to find your way around, despite the company's claim that it offers passengers a 'small ship feel, big ship choice.' There are several points of congestion, particularly outside the shops, when bazaar tables are set up outside on the upper level of the atrium lobby.

Passenger niggles include the user-unfriendly automated telephone system, the small cabin towels, the extra cost for items such as ice cream, and the (coins-needed) charge for the washers and dryers in self-service launderettes.

ACCOMMODATION. There are six main types of cabins and configurations: (a) grand suite, (b) suite, (c) mini-suite, (d) outside-view double cabins with balcony, (e) outside-view double cabins, and (f) interior double cabins. These come in many price categories (the choice is bewildering), depending on size and location. Some 100 cabins have interconnecting doors (good for families).

DINING. Of the three main dining rooms – Botticelli, Da Vinci, and Michelangelo – one has two-seating dining and the other two have 'anytime dining' that allows you to choose when and with whom you want to eat. All three are split into multi-tier sections in a non-symmetrical design.

While four elevators go to the deck where two of the restaurants are located, only two go to Plaza Deck 5, where the Michelangelo Dining Room is located – this causes waiting problems at peak times, particularly for anyone in a wheelchair.

High-quality linens and silverware, Frette Egyptian cotton table linens, and Hepp silverware are provided in the main dining rooms. Note that 15 percent is added to all beverage bills, including wines.

Although portions are generous, the food and its presentation are disappointing, and standardized. Fish is often disguised by sauces or coatings, the choice of fresh green vegetables is limited, few garnishes are used, and cheese is either pre-sliced or diced. But, this is banquet catering, with all its attendant standardization and 'batch' cooking. Pasta dishes are acceptable (though voluminous), typically served by section headwaiters, who may also make 'something special just for you' – in search of favorable comments. If you like desserts, order a sundae at dinner (most other items are just so-so).

There are two extra-cost, reservations-required venues. The first, SHARE by Curtis Stone, is located on a high deck aft of the funnel, and features a six-course degustation menu. The extra -cost, reservations-required Crown Grill, located aft on Promenade Deck, features premium-quality American steaks and seafood.

Other eateries include a poolside burger grill and pizza bar (no additional charge). Extra charges apply if you order items to eat at the International Café (a coffee bar/patisserie) or in Vines seafood/wine bar in the atrium lobby. Other casual meals can be taken in the Horizon Court (open 24 hours a day). It has large ocean-view on port and starboard sides and direct access to the two principal swimming pools and Lido Deck. Although there is a wide variety of food, there is no presentation finesse, as plastic plates are provided.

ENTERTAINMENT. The 800-seat Princess Theater spans two decks, and has comfortable seating on both main and balcony levels. It has $3 million worth of sound and light equipment, plus a nine-piece band and a resident troupe of singers and dancers.

A second entertainment lounge, Club Fusion, is located aft, for cabaret acts and karaoke contests at night, and lectures, bingo, and horse racing during the day. Explorer's Lounge, a third entertainment lounge, can also host cabaret acts and live music.

A number of other lounges and bars feature live music, including a string quartet, and 'street performers' in the main atrium lobby.

SPA/FITNESS. The Lotus Spa, located forward on one of the uppermost decks (Sun Deck), has separate facilities for men and women, including a sauna, steam room, and changing rooms; common facilities include a relaxation/waiting zone, body-pampering treatment rooms, and a gymnasium packed with cardio-vascular equipment. Some fitness classes are free, while others cost extra.

EMPRESS OF THE SEAS
★★+

THIS IS A DATED BUT FAMILY-FRIENDLY SHIP FOR ULTRA-CASUAL GETAWAYS

Size:	Mid-size Ship	Passenger/Crew Ratio (lower beds):	2.3
Tonnage:	48,563 tons	Cabins (total):	800
Cruise Line:	Royal Caribbean International	Size Range (sq ft/m):	117.0–818/10.8–76
Former Names:	Empress, Empress of the Seas, Nordic Empress	Cabins (for one person):	0
		Cabins with balcony:	69
Builder:	Chantiers de l'Atlantique (France)	Cabins (wheelchair accessible):	4
Entered Service:	Jun 1990/May 2008	Wheelchair accessibility:	Fair
Length (ft/m):	692.2/211.0	Elevators:	7
Beam (ft/m):	100.7/30.7	Casino (gaming tables):	Yes
Propulsion/Propellers:	diesel (16,200kW)/2	Swimming Pools:	1
Passenger Decks:	9	Self-Service Launderette:	No
Total Crew:	685	Library:	No
Passengers (lower beds):	1,600	Onboard currency:	US$
Passenger Space Ratio (lower beds):	30.2		

THE SHIP. Now over 25 years old (the oldest in the fleet), the all-white *Empress of the Seas* has a somewhat boxy profile. The swimming pool is tiny for the number of passengers carried (this is a very high-density ship), and there's little open deck space, so the unpadded sun-loungers are crammed tight. There is, however, a walk-around outdoor promenade deck. Wrapped around the funnel, the Viking Crown Lounge is a nice place for drinks and good ocean views.

Inside, a nine-deck-high atrium is the social meeting place. Most public rooms are on two decks, including a Schooner Bar, shops, aft lounge, library, card room, plus facilities for children and teens at Adventure Ocean near the pool. A three-level Casino Royale has gaming tables and slot machines.

You'll be overwhelmed by the public spaces, but underwhelmed by the size of the cabins. However, for short cruises it's adequate if you pack lightly. The ship underwent a refurbishment in 2016, following a number of years being operated by Pullmantur Cruises. It is now back in the RCI fold.

ACCOMMODATION. From interior (no-view) cabins to larger suites; the price you pay depends on the location and size. All have twin beds that convert to a

BERLITZ'S RATINGS

	Possible	Achieved
Ship	500	376
Accommodation	200	107
Food	400	187
Service	400	214
Entertainment	100	48
Cruise Experience	400	196

OVERALL SCORE 1028 points out of 2000

queen-size configuration, and tiny bathrooms.

DINING. The Miramar Restaurant is two decks high, but it really is a noisy room. There are two seatings, at tables for four to 10. The cuisine is typical of mass banquet catering, and pretty unmemorable.

Chops Grille is an extra-charge venue, with dishes available à la carte; reservations are required. Its intimacy makes it more inviting, with a number of tables for two.

For self-serve, food court-style casual meals, Windjammer Buffet provides an alternative to the Miramar Restaurant.

ENTERTAINMENT. The two-level Royal Theatre has poor sight lines in the upper lateral balconies, and the sight lines from the front rows of the balcony are ruined by railings. The entertainment throughout is upbeat – in fact, it is difficult to get away from music (it's everywhere – even in the elevators).

SPA/FITNESS. Vitality Spa facilities include saunas and a beauty salon. A fitness facility is in another location. For sports fans, there's an outdoor rock-climbing wall at the aft of the ship.

ENCHANTMENT OF THE SEAS
★★★+

A FINE SHIP WITH ELEGANT DECOR, FOR ACTIVE FAMILIES

Size:	Mid-size Ship	Passenger/Crew Ratio (lower beds):	2.6
Tonnage:	81,500	Cabins (total):	1,126
Cruise Line:	Royal Caribbean International	Size Range (sq ft/m):	158.2–1,267.0/14.7–117.7
Former Names:	none	Cabins (for one person):	0
Builder:	Kvaerner Masa-Yards (Finland)	Cabins with balcony:	248
Entered Service:	Jul 1997	Cabins (wheelchair accessible):	20
Length (ft/m):	990.1/301.8	Wheelchair accessibility:	Good
Beam (ft/m):	105.6/32.2	Elevators:	9
Propulsion/Propellers:	diesel-electric (50,400kW)/2	Casino (gaming tables):	Yes
Passenger Decks:	11	Swimming Pools:	3 (1 w/ sliding glass dome)
Total Crew:	840	Self-Service Launderette:	No
Passengers (lower beds):	2,252	Library:	Yes
Passenger Space Ratio (lower beds):	36.1	Onboard currency:	US$

THE SHIP. *Enchantment of the Seas* (a *Vision*-class ship) has a fairly sleek profile, with a single funnel located well aft – almost a throwback to the designs of the 1950s, and a nicely rounded stern. There is a walk-around promenade deck outdoors, but no cushioned pads for the plastic sunloungers.

A Viking Crown Lounge, a trademark lounge aboard many Royal Caribbean International ships, sits between the funnel and mast at the top of the atrium lobby, and overlooks the forward section of the pool deck, accessible from a stairway off the central atrium.

In 2005, a $60 million 'chop-and-stretch' exercise added a 72.8ft (22.2m) mid-section, increasing its overall length to 990.1ft (301.8m) and upping its gross tonnage. It added 151 passenger cabins, including two 'family' cabins that can sleep six. The pool deck was given more space plus soaring 'suspension' bridges. Special lifts were provided for the two pools, as was a new Splash Deck (kids love the 64 water jets). While not as large as some of the newer ships in the fleet, *Enchantment of the Seas* is best suited to couples and families with children who don't need all the latest bells and whistles, but want to cruise with up-to-date facilities, and multiple dining choices. Between 2011 and 2014 the company added some of the dining options found on the larger ships, and enhanced the overall onboard experience. Finger-touch digital 'Wayfinder' direction screens make getting around easy.

BERLITZ'S RATINGS

	Possible	Achieved
Ship	500	369
Accommodation	200	137
Food	400	239
Service	400	262
Entertainment	100	75
Cruise Experience	400	264

OVERALL SCORE 1346 points out of 2000

The principal interior focal point (and the social hub of the ship) is a seven-deck-high Centrum (atrium lobby). On its various levels, it houses an R Bar (for some creative cocktails), several passenger-service counters, an art gallery, and Café Latte-tudes (for coffee). Aerial entertainment happens in the Centrum, too. Close by is the decidedly flashy Casino Royale (for table gaming and slot machines – and interesting exhibits under several glass floor panels), the popular Schooner Bar, with its nautical-theme decor and maritime art, Boleros (for Latin sounds and dancing), Centrum shops, and the library.

The varied collection of artworks includes several sculptures, principally by British artists; much of it is on the themes of classical music, ballet, and theater, and huge murals of opera scenes adorn several stairways. There is a good use of tropical plants throughout the public rooms, which helps to counteract the plain, clinical pastel wall colors.

This company provides a well-organized but rather homogenous cruise experience, with the same decades-old passenger participation activities and events.

ACCOMMODATION. There are multiple price grades, with location and grade perhaps the most important determining factors, given that so many of the cabins are of the same or very similar size. All suite and cabin grades are provided with a hairdryer. Room service offers only the most basic menu.

Most of the standard cabins have twin beds that convert to a queen-size one, ample closet space for a week-long cruise, and a good amount of drawer space, although under-bed storage space is limited. Bathrooms have nine mirrors. The plastic buckets, provided for Champagne/wine, are rather tacky.

DINING. The 1,365-seat My Fair Lady Dining Room spreads over two decks, connected by a grand, sweeping staircase. When you book, choose one of two seatings, or 'My Time Dining' (eat when you want, during dining hours). The food is not as good as the menu makes it sound, and the selection of breads, rolls, fruit, and cheese is poor. Overall, meals are rather hit and miss – in fact it's unmemorable. Also, if you want lobster or a decent filet mignon (steak) you'll need to pay extra.

The extra-cost, reservations-required Chops Grille Steakhouse is an à la carte venue serving prime steaks and veal chops. Aft is the Park Café: an indoor/outdoor deli for salads, sandwiches, soups, and pastries.

Casual, self-serve meals can be taken in the 790-seat casual Windjammer Marketplace. It has a great expanse of ocean-view glass windows, the decor is bright and cheerful, and buffet 'islands' contain food from around the world.

ENTERTAINMENT. The 875-seat Orpheum Theater (the main showlounge) is a grand room at the forward section. This is where the big production shows are staged, and major cabaret acts are presented.

A second showlounge, the 575-seat Carousel Lounge, is located aft, and is for smaller shows and adult cabarets, including late-night adults-only comedy. A variety of other lounges and bars have almost constant live music; in fact, there's no bar without music for a quiet drink. There's even background music in all corridors and elevators, and constant music outdoors on the pool deck. If you want a quiet relaxing holiday, choose another ship.

SPA/FITNESS. Vitality at Sea Spa is aft of the funnel and spans two decks. Facilities include a gymnasium (with some techno- and cardio muscle-pumping machines), aerobics room, sauna and steam rooms, a beauty salon, and 13 private massage/body treatment rooms, including a massage room for couples.

The Spa and fitness facilities are staffed and operated by Steiner Leisure, a specialist spa/beauty concession. Some fitness classes are free, while some cost extra.

EURODAM
★★★+

A SPACIOUS MID-SIZED SHIP WITH DUTCH-STYLE INTERIOR DECOR

Size:	Mid-size Ship	Passenger/Crew Ratio (lower beds):	2.2
Tonnage:	86,273	Cabins (total):	1,052
Cruise Line:	Holland America Line	Size Range (sq ft/m):	170.0–1,318.6/15.7–122.5
Former Names:	none	Cabins (for one person):	0
Builder:	Fincantieri (Italy)	Cabins with balcony:	708
Entered Service:	Jul 2008	Cabins (wheelchair accessible):	30
Length (ft/m):	935.0/285.0	Wheelchair accessibility:	Good
Beam (ft/m):	105.6/32.2	Elevators:	14
Propulsion/Propellers:	diesel-electric (34,000kW)/	Casino (gaming tables):	Yes
	2 azimuthing pods	Swimming Pools:	2 (1 w/ sliding glass dome)
Passenger Decks:	12	Self-Service Launderette:	No
Total Crew:	929	Library:	Yes
Passengers (lower beds):	2,104	Onboard currency:	US$
Passenger Space Ratio (lower beds):	41.0		

THE SHIP. *Eurodam* has two funnels, positioned close together – one behind the other instead of side by side. This design is the result of the machinery configuration, because the ship has, in effect, two engine rooms – one with three diesels, and one with two diesels. A pod propulsion system is provided.

There are 22 rent-by-the-day cabanas, with goodies such as Champagne, chocolate strawberries, an iPod pre-stocked with music, bathrobes, fresh fruit, and chilled towels. These are designed for two adults and two children, so they may not be the promised 'quiet' spaces, after all. They are located in an area on observation deck and around the Lido Pool.

There is an exterior teak promenade deck, although it doesn't wrap-around the front section, plus real teak steamer-style sunloungers.

There are two swimming pools outdoors, one of which has a retractable glass roof.

The ship has a bright interior decor designed to appeal to younger, more vibrant, multi-generational holidaymakers. In keeping with the traditions of Holland America Line (HAL), a collection of artwork highlighting the former Dutch East Indies is featured.

The small lobby spans three decks. Adjacent are interior and glass-walled elevators with fine ocean views through 11 decks. The information desk (on the lobby's lowest level) is small and somewhat removed from the main passenger flow on the two decks above it.

BERLITZ'S RATINGS

	Possible	Achieved
Ship	500	364
Accommodation	200	144
Food	400	233
Service	400	254
Entertainment	100	67
Cruise Experience	400	266

OVERALL SCORE 1328 points out of 2000

There are two decks of public rooms. Perhaps the most dramatic is the showlounge, spanning four decks in the forward section. Other facilities include a winding shopping street with several boutique stores, card room, an art gallery, photo gallery, and several meeting rooms; a casino is large and equipped with gaming tables and slot machines. One of the most popular public rooms is Explorations – a combination coffee bar (drinks are at extra cost), lounge, library, and Internet center, all in one attractive, open 'lifestyle' environment, adjacent to a Crow's Nest Lounge.

Other facilities include a Queen's Lounge, which doubles as a lecture room, a Culinary Arts Center (for cooking demonstrations and classes), and a number of bars and lounges, including a small movie-screening room.

Gratuities are automatically added to your onboard account. Passenger niggles include noisy cabin air conditioning (the flow can't be turned off, the only regulation being for temperature control), and the many pillars that obstruct passenger flow and lines of sight throughout the ship.

ACCOMMODATION. There are numerous price categories, with grades from interior (no view) cabins to fairly spacious suites, including spa 'suites' adjacent to The Retreat, an extra-cost relaxation area.

All accommodation grades have plush Mariner's Dream beds, waffle/terry cloth robes, Egyptian cotton towels, flat-panel infotainment systems, make-up mirrors with halo lighting, massage shower heads, large hairdryers, and fruit baskets. Suites receive fresh flowers.

Some cabins have interconnecting doors. Some balconies have solid steel lower sections instead of glass, so your view is a little restricted when seated.

Some cabins accommodating a third and fourth person have little closet space, and only one personal safe. Occupants of suites have exclusive use of the Neptune Lounge and concierge service, priority embarkation and disembarkation, and other benefits. In many of the suites/cabins with private balconies, the balconies can be overlooked from various public locations.

Standard outside cabins measure 197 sq ft (18 sq m). Interior cabins (no view) are slightly smaller, at 183 sq ft (17 sq m). Deluxe Verandah Suites measure 563 sq ft (52 sq m). Verandah Suites: these are actually cabins, not suites, and measure 284 sq ft (26 sq m). Penthouse Verandah Suites offer the largest accommodation and measure 1,318 sq ft (122 sq m), including balcony.

DINING. The Rembrandt Dining Room – a stunning bi-level room – is at the stern. Both open seating (you may have to wait some time for a table) and fixed (assigned tables and times) seating is available.

With a few exceptions, the cuisine is rather unmemorable and is missing passion and taste. There's a distinct lack of variety of green vegetables, too great a use of rice, canned fruit, and already sliced and diced cheese. Still, you get friendly service from the Indonesian and Filipino stewards, and the plates are nice.

'Lighter-option' meals are always available. HAL can also provide kosher meals, although these are prepared ashore, frozen, and brought to your table sealed in their original containers.

A 130-seat Pinnacle Grill is a more upscale, more intimate restaurant, with higher-quality ingredients and better presentation than in the larger main dining room. It is on Lower Promenade Deck and fronts onto the second level of the atrium lobby. Pacific Northwest cuisine is featured, including premium-quality steaks. There are fine table settings, china and silverware, and leather-bound menus. The wine bar offers mostly American varietals. Reservations are required, and there's a cover charge (the steaks are worth it).

There's also Tamarind, a 144-seat pan-Asian (fusion cuisine) restaurant; there's no charge for lunch, but there is a cover charge for dinner.

For casual eats, there's an extensive self-serve food court-style Lido Market. It includes a pizzeria/Italian specialties counter, a salad bar, Asian stir-fry counter, deli sandwiches, and desserts. Movement through the buffet area can be very slow. In the evenings, part of one side of this venue is turned into an extra-cost Canaletto Restaurant – a quasi-Italian informal eatery with waiter service.

Also, a poolside 'Dive-In at the Terrace Grill' features multi-choice signature burgers (and special Dive-In sauce), hot dogs, and fries.

ENTERTAINMENT. Theater-style seating is provided in the Mainstage showlounge, the venue for colourful Vegas-style revues and major cabaret shows. Stage shows are best seen from the two levels, from where the sight lines are quite good.

SPA/FITNESS. The Greenhouse Spa includes a thermal suite, hydropool, several private rooms for body treatments, and a large fitness center. Sports enthusiasts can enjoy a basketball court and a volleyball court.

EUROPA
★★★★★+

A TRULY SOPHISTICATED, TOP-CLASS SHIP FOR ELEGANT, FORMAL CRUISING

Size:	Small Ship	Passenger/Crew Ratio (lower beds):	1.4
Tonnage:	28,890	Cabins (total):	204
Cruise Line:	Hapag-Lloyd Cruises	Size Range (sq ft/m):	355.2-914.9/33.0-85.0
Former Names:	none	Cabins (for one person):	0
Builder:	Kvaerner Masa-Yards (Finland)	Cabins with balcony:	168
Entered Service:	Sep 1999	Cabins (wheelchair accessible):	2
Length (ft/m):	651.5/198.6	Wheelchair accessibility:	Good
Beam (ft/m):	78.7/24.0	Elevators:	4
Propulsion/Propellers:	diesel-electric (21,600kW)/ 2 azimuthing pods	Casino (gaming tables):	No
		Swimming Pools:	1 (1 w/ sliding glass dome)
Passenger Decks:	7	Self-Service Launderette:	No
Total Crew:	280	Library:	Yes
Passengers (lower beds):	408	Onboard currency:	Euros
Passenger Space Ratio (lower beds):	70.4		

THE SHIP. This sleek-looking ship has a gracefully shaped stern topped by Hapag-Lloyd's signature orange-and-blue funnel. It is very stable at sea, with no vibration or noise – thanks partly to its pod propulsion and excellent build quality. Some 14 Zodiac landing craft for close-up coastal shore excursions and boot-washing areas are provided, as are over 20 bicycles free for use ashore, offloaded on to the dock in each port (where possible).

There is an outdoor walking/jogging area with rubberized deck (plus a walk-around teak promenade deck), and a small 'FKK' (Freikörperkultur) deck for nude sunbathing. Sunloungers have thick cushioned pads.

There is a long, rectangular swimming pool, which is half indoors and half outdoors. While not the widest, it is longer than pools aboard many other cruise ships (measurements are 56.7 x 16.8ft/17.3 x 5.12m). Movies can be screened poolside, and themed social events are held here on selected evenings.

Most of *Europa's* hotel service crew understand the culture and can talk in depth about German, Swiss, and Austrian life.

Europa, one of the world's most spacious purpose-built cruise ships, offers formal cruising (more formal than Europa 2, for example – despite the similarity in name, this is a very different ship), and painstakingly accomplished service. The space per person is high, there is never a hint of a line, and

BERLITZ'S RATINGS		
	Possible	Achieved
Ship	500	471
Accommodation	200	183
Food	400	373
Service	400	360
Entertainment	100	91
Cruise Experience	400	373

OVERALL SCORE 1852 points out of 2000

both restaurant and showlounge can seat a full complement of passengers. Only the best-quality soft furnishings are used, blending traditional with modern designs and materials. Most public rooms and hallways have extremely high ceilings, providing an enhanced sense of space and grandeur, with no hint of glitz. The interior focal point is a seven-deck-high central atrium, with two glass-walled elevators (operated by 'piccolos' on embarkation day). The lower level features a white Steinway grand piano and Piano Bar, reception desk, concierge and shore-excursion desks. It's a cozy, open space for parties, particularly on 'formal' nights, when passengers dress appropriately. Tucked away in one corner is a business center.

Several public rooms are located along a curved 'street' leading aft from the atrium, including Gatsby's – a speakeasy-style place to meet, chat, and be entertained, with superbly crafted vintage cocktails, half-moon-shaped bar, small stage, and wooden dance floor..

What was originally designed as a casino is now a multi-function space for small cocktail parties; it also serves as a high-class art gallery showcasing German artists.

Supremely comfortable, the sidewalk Havana Bar cigar lounge is a clubby room (with cigar-colored armchairs and, on one wall, a huge photograph of Che Guevara), with three large glass-fronted, conditioned humidor cabinets, and an extensive range of cigars (from 102mm to 232mm) of top, mostly Cuban brands. It also serves a fine range of armagnacs, calvados, cognacs, and Cuban beer, while a wall-mounted digital jukebox has a push-button selection of songs and instrumental music. Do try an Irish Coffee, correctly made with the glass rotated while sugar is blended with the alcohol, then heated gently over a candle. Adjacent is the ship's jeweler/clothing boutique (Wempe).

On a higher deck, Club Belvedere is a lovely room, with a curved bar; afternoon tea (with a choice of over 30 mostly loose-leaf teas) takes place here, as do intimate music recitals. There is a superb selection of cakes, made fresh daily.

The library, home to an illuminated globe of the world and numerous bookcases, is open 24/7. Opposite is a small cinema/meeting/function room.

For passengers dependent on wheelchairs, a special ramp is provided from the outdoor lido/pool deck down to where the lifeboats are located; only three other ships have such a ramp (*Asuka II*, *Crystal Serenity*, and *Crystal Symphony*).

Europa is arguably the most luxurious of the smaller, more formal cruise ships, and for the German-speaking market (the crew also speaks English) nothing else comes close. The tradition of indulgent cruising is taken to the highest level, with superb food and culinary diversity, a wide range of creature comforts, and wonderful flowers. A drydocking stint, scheduled for late 2017, will substantially change some areas, including the enlargement of the Ocean Spa, larger spa suites, and substantial refreshing of many areas.

ACCOMMODATION. This is in five configurations and several price categories, and consists of all-outside-view suites: two Penthouse Grand Suites (Hapag and Lloyd) and 10 Penthouse Deluxe Suites (Bach, Beethoven, Brahms, Handel, Haydn, Lehár, Mozart, Schubert, Strauss, Wagner; each suite contains a large framed picture of the relevant composer), 156 suites with private balcony, 36 standard suites, two suites (with private balcony) for passengers with disabilities, and eight suites with interconnecting doors.

Almost all suites have a private balcony with wide teak deck and lighting, and a smoked glass screen topped by a teak rail. Twelve suites overlooking the stern are among the most sought-after accommodation – six on each of two decks, including a balcony with canvas 'ceiling' for shade and privacy.

All suites have a wooden floor entryway, a sleeping area with twin beds convertible to a queen-size bed, and bedside tables with lamps and two drawers. There is a lounge area with curtain divider and bird's-eye maple wood cabinetry, with rounded edges. Facilities include a refrigerator/mini-bar (beer and soft drinks are supplied at no extra charge), writing/vanity desk, and couch with large table. An illuminated

walk-in closet provides ample hanging space, six drawers, personal safe, umbrella, shoehorn, and clothes brush. European duvets are also provided.

All passengers receive a practical shoulder travel bag, an insulated lunch bag for shore excursions, and keycard holder.

An infotainment system includes 24 hours per day video and audio on-demand, a large flat-screen television, Internet connection via a wireless keyboard, and a data socket.

All suites have a 100 percent air-circulation system, and excellent soundproofing.

The white/gray/sea green marble-tiled bathrooms are well designed, and include two good-size cabinets for toiletries. Each has a full bathtub plus an integral shower, retractable clothesline, and separate glazed shower enclosure. Thick cotton bathrobes are provided, as are slippers and an array of personal amenities.

Deck 10 Suites. There are two Penthouse Grand suites, and 10 Penthouse Deluxe suites, all with electronically adjustable beds and coffee machines. A teakwood entrance hall opens into a spacious living room with dining table and four chairs, stocked drinks cabinet with refrigerator and complimentary bar set-up, laundry and ironing service, priority spa reservations, pre-dinner canapés daily, handmade chocolates, petit-fours, and other niceties. Balconies have teakwood decking, and white canvas ceiling shades. For the ultimate in exclusivity, two Penthouse Grand (1001 and 1002) suites have huge bathrooms (each with a private sauna, angled bathtubs, and heated floor), and extensive forward views from their prime location, with a large wrap-around balcony; they also have larger walk-in closets (with a window), large flat-screen infotainment screens, Robbe & Berking silver Champagne goblets, and Bulgari bathroom amenities. Well-trained butlers provide the highest level of unobtrusive Western European service.

Four 'spa suites' incorporate a large private teak-decked balcony; twin or queen-size bed; walk-in closet; dark wood cabinetry housing a refrigerator stocked with fruit juices and different mineral waters; and bar set-up. There's a flat-screen infotainment system, and storage space (including a jewelry drawer) with pull-around doors, a writing/vanity desk, and floor-to-ceiling windows. Decor colors are warm reds, yellow, and gold. There is a large window between the living/sleeping area and the bathroom, with its Asian-style decor, Jacuzzi bath with underwater lighting, separate large shower enclosure with rain shower, a toilet, gold, thick-glass washbasin, and hairdryer. Special teas and other services are provided by spa personnel.

Disabled suites (Deck 7) have one electronically operated bed with hydraulic elevator, one regular bed, and a closet with drawers (replacing the walk-in closet in all other suites). Bathrooms have a roll-in shower, fittings at the right height, several grab handles, and an emergency call-for-help button. Wheelchair-accessible public toilets are provided on the main restaurant/entertainment deck.

DINING. With so many separate food ingredients carried, the executive chef produces menus that don't repeat even for around-the-world voyages. The cuisine is outstanding, and always full of surprises. Seasonal and regional ingredients and totally fresh fish and seafood are standard. Plated presentation of food is provided for entrées with silver service for additional vegetables. Portion size is sensible, and never overwhelming. There are four restaurants.

Europa Restaurant is a beautiful, high-ceilinged formal dining room. Tables are assigned for dinner only (breakfast and lunch are open seating), so you keep your waiter throughout each cruise. There are tables for two to eight. For correct service, there is a *chef de rang* and an assistant waiter system, with the assistant waiter acting as runner.

On sea days, an additional Gourmet Breakfast menu includes items such as beef tartare, smoked tuna carpaccio with wasabi cream, and other specialties rarely found aboard cruise ships today. A Cuisine Légère menu features light, healthy, but tasty spa cuisine.

Table settings include Dibbern china, Robbe & Berking silverware, and Riedel wine glasses. The cuisine includes German favorites and regional dishes from around the world. Top-grade caviar is on the dinner menu at least once each week, and available on request, at extra cost.

An extensive wine list includes a wide selection of vintage French wines, as well as a well-balanced selection of Austrian, German, and Swiss wines.

In a cruise industry first, three Michelin-starred chef Dieter Müller has his Dieter Müller at Sea Restaurant, a pocket-sized 26-seat intimate restaurant featuring a five-course menu (three for lunch). The menu changes three times during a world cruise, and seasonally during the rest of the year. Müller participates in about half of *Europa*'s annual program. The restaurant – a haven for lovers of haute cuisine – is open for dinner nightly and for lunch on sea days, at no extra charge.

Venezia, a second specialty restaurant, is admired for its fine Italian cuisine, notably its range of olive oils and grappa, and its antipasti trolley. It is open for lunch and dinner, at no extra charge.

Both venues are adjacent to the main restaurant, and provide the setting for intimate dining experiences (reservations required).

Lido Café is the casual eatery for serve-yourself breakfasts (the ship even makes its own preserves), luncheons, and dinners, with indoor and outdoor seating (under heat lamps, when needed) and adjacent indoor/outdoor bar. Themed evening dining is also featured, with skilled waiter service. There is a wide variety of food, and many lunch buffets host popular themes and fresh local specialties.

Above the Lido Café is the popular indoor/outdoor chill-out late-night spot Sansibar, with great aft-facing views, and some excellent drinks.

Europa is known for its real German sausages, available in Gatsby's and at a typical Bavarian Frühschoppen (featured once each cruise in the Lido Café). Nautical tradition is maintained with bouillon service each sea day, and other daily niceties include fresh waffles and ice cream poolside.

ENTERTAINMENT. The Europa Lounge, with its rich red decor, is a traditional showlounge with a sloping floor, a U-shaped seating configuration, and a proper raised stage, although several pillars obstruct sight lines. Its intellectual entertainment program is tailored to the theme of the cruise – and includes a constant supply of high-quality classical and contemporary musical artistes, cabaret acts, and expert lecturers.

The ship carries a main showband, plus small musical units for live music for listening and dancing to. Most classical concerts and recitals take place in the Belvedere Lounge, with its dropped central circular wood floor.

SPA/FITNESS. Ocean Spa has a wide range of beauty services and treatments, and full-day spa packages.

Facilities include a steam room and sauna (mixed), two shower enclosures and foot-washing stations, relaxation room, men's and women's changing/dressing rooms, and beauty salon. Treatment rooms have music menus, so you can choose what music you wish to hear (if any). The gymnasium includes a 'miha bodytec' training machine and personal trainer.

An electronic golf simulator room complements a golf driving range; a PGA golf pro is carried on all cruises, and shuffleboard courts are on the open deck.

EUROPA 2
★★★★★+

A STUNNINGLY ELEGANT, SPACIOUS, INFORMAL SHIP FOR STYLISH INTERNATIONAL TRAVELERS

Size:	Small Ship	Passenger/Crew Ratio (lower beds):	1.3
Tonnage:	42,830	Cabins (total):	258
Cruise Line:	Hapag-Lloyd Cruises	Size Range (sq ft/m):	376.7–1,227.1/35.0–114.0
Former Names:	none	Cabins (for one person):	0
Builder:	STX France	Cabins with balcony:	258
Entered Service:	May 2013	Cabins (wheelchair accessible):	2
Length (ft/m):	739.5/225.4	Wheelchair accessibility:	Best
Beam (ft/m):	87.5/26.7	Elevators:	4
Propulsion/Propellers:	diesel-electric (24,000kW)/	Casino (gaming tables):	No
	2 azimuthing pods	Swimming Pools:	1 (1 w/ sliding glass dome)
Passenger Decks:	8	Self-Service Launderette:	No
Total Crew:	370	Library:	Yes
Passengers (lower beds):	516	Onboard currency:	Euros
Passenger Space Ratio (lower beds):	83.0		

THE SHIP. *Europa 2* has a sleek profile and appearance, balanced by Hapag-Lloyd's signature orange-and-blue funnel. Look down from an upper aft deck and you'll see a fine rounded stern.

Spaciousness, natural light, and contemporary style are evident everywhere. There is a complete walk-around deck – an unusual feature for a ship of this size. Teak decking is everywhere (no artificial turf anywhere), as are teak handrails on all balconies and outdoor stairways.

The two-level pool deck is a stunning space, with a 49-ft (15-m) rectangular heated pool, and a large moveable glass roof that can cover the area as needed (when closed the area is like a cozy winter garden). Five Balinese sleep beds inhabit the aft upper level (another seven can be found on the secluded open aft deck), contemporary sun beds and drinks tables, bar and separate food bar (homemade waffles in the afternoon, ice cream, etc.), and removable movie screen.

A fleet of 12 Zodiacs – all named after Hamburg suburbs – is carried for landings in small harbors and isolated bays, and there are 20 bicycles for passenger use (at no charge).

Europa 2 is beautifully appointed, with a high-quality fit and finish. The interior designers have created both contemporary and slightly edgy in a ship that includes some traditional Hapag-Lloyd characteristics from yesteryear, such as indented handrails in the

BERLITZ'S RATINGS

	Possible	Achieved
Ship	500	476
Accommodation	200	185
Food	400	373
Service	400	362
Entertainment	100	92
Cruise Experience	400	375

OVERALL SCORE 1863 points out of 2000

main stairways, yet is completely different to the more formal *Europa*. There's even an outstanding museum-quality art collection.

The atrium lobby has chic gray, black and chrome decor, armchair-style seating, a long bar, and a specially commissioned gray Steinway grand piano. A high ceiling sets it all off, together with what look like four large gray-and-black distillery still-like features, and a reception desk. A glass viewing wall in the centre on both sides of the main elevator foyer provides multi-deck contact with the outside, and lets natural outside light flood in, providing a connection with the sea (isn't this why people go cruising, after all)? Adjacent is a large, upscale Wempe boutique and jewelry store, and, along the walls, some rather expensive pieces of art (including some by Gerhard Richter).

There are seven restaurants, two lounges, and six bars – some with familiar names carried over from the tradition of *Europa*.

The Collins cigar lounge has three large glass-fronted, temperature-controlled cigar cabinets and a bar with a wide range of armagnacs, calvados, cognacs, all poured tableside, plus Cuban beer, a collection of over 40 premium and trendy multi-country artisan gins.

Sansibar is a sea-going outpost of the fashionable seafood/wine restaurant on the north German island of Sylt. It has indoor-outdoor seating aft, a bar, a dance floor, and an à la carte menu, tapas-style nibbles, special wines, and a great club-like atmosphere. It's an 'in' place to be late at night, and it also offers a 'late riser's' breakfast.

Other standout public rooms include Club 2, a trendy venue with dance floor; it features live jazz, soul music, and other artistic presentations, and at night is like a speakeasy, with superb mood lighting.

There's also an auditorium with a stage for presentations as well as 3D movies, a Miele Culinary Arts School, and Beleveedere, a 'lifestyle' lounge with integral library, bar – the place for afternoon tea and superb cakes, sandwiches, and patisserie items.

Europa 2 and *Europa* are vastly different ships – and cater to a very different set of passengers. *Europa 2* has even more delightful dining venues than its sister ship, and the ship's focus is definitely on cuisine, modern lifestyle, and wellness.

There's no traditional captain's dinner, because the ship is aimed at a more youthful clientele seeking high quality in a relaxed but refined setting, although senior officers often dine with passengers in various venues. Details really matter here, however: examples include leather-covered tissue boxes and different-sized spoons for small or large coffees in your suite.

Europa 2 offers the benchmark in contemporary cruising. It exudes discreet quality at every turn (no bling), truly impressive culinary diversity, unobtrusive service with a smile at its very best, an outstanding wellness spa, and flowers everywhere.

The ship operates in English and German, and is aimed at youthful, sophisticated, cosmopolitan travelers and their families – with three areas for kids and teens: a Knopf Club (a new 'Cap'n Knopf' bear was created specially by Steiff and is only available aboard *Europa 2*) for toddlers aged 2–3; a Kids' Club for 4- to 10-year-olds; and a Teens' Club for 11 to 15s, with iPod chairs, table football, and a chill-out area. Special (parent-free) shore excursions for children are also available. For something different, teens could try the chocolate massage in the spa. The kid's pool dinner party is really special.

ACCOMMODATION. There are several price categories and eight accommodation grades (sizes given include balcony). From the smallest to the largest, they are: 141 Ocean Suites measuring 376.7 sq ft (34 sq m); 16 Spa Suites measuring 560 sq ft (52 sq m); 24 Grand Suites measuring 559.7 sq m (52 sq m), including two for the disabled; 59 Ocean Suites and seven Family Apartments measuring 581 sq ft (54 sq m); two Grand Penthouses measuring 947 sq ft (88 sq m); and two Owner's Suites measuring 1,227 sq ft (114 sq m).

Even the smallest balcony measures 75.3 sq ft (7 sq m), and all except the Family Apartments have Jacuzzi bathtubs. All Penthouse Deck suite occupants can choose their favorite bottles of spirits at no extra cost; these suites also come with butler service.

Two Owner's Suites are truly luxurious apartments (like a villa, with hotel attached), with double-width balconies, and a beautiful piece of butterfly art by Damien Hirst. The standout feature is a large ocean-view wet room with steam sauna, large 'rain' shower with built-in chromo-therapy lighting, and a separate hand-held shower hose, a separate circular whirlpool tub large enough for four, window-side daybed, two large washbasins, and floor-to-ceiling windows. The spacious living area has walk-in closets to die for, a fully stocked refrigerator, large dining table and chair set, and an Eames lounge chair. There are multiple TV sets, including one integrated in a bathroom mirror adjacent to the wet room.

Spa Suites have a rain-shower/steam sauna combination, whirlpool bathtub, and a large window between sleeping/living area and bathroom (with a wooden blind for complete privacy), and separate toilet. There's also an infotainment screen within the bathroom mirror.

Two suites for the disabled each have a large bathroom with roll-in shower, three washbasins, and an integrated 'mirror' TV.

Facilities in even the smallest standard suite are excellent; the layout is well designed and practical, and the overall decor is relaxing, in brown, beige, and cream, and with custom-made deep-pile carpets. Beds have a torsion arrangement (variable from hard to soft, while both head and body/foot sections can be raised electrically. One neat feature is a push-button bedside lighting panel with four mood settings.

A wide choice of large-size, daily newspapers is available (at extra cost except for occupants of Penthouse Deck 10 suites, which also have multi-way electric beds); all accommodation grades feature a Nespresso coffee machine and associated items. Other features include an anti-rattle 'butler's pantry'-like refrigerator/minibar cabinet (beer and soft drinks are included) with several 'quiet-close' storage trays for glasses, cups, and other bar amenities. There's also a writing/vanity desk, and couch with large table in a separate lounge area, and door-touch keycard holder.

An integrated infotainment system includes 24/7 video and audio on-demand, and internet connection via a wireless keyboard or tablet. A data socket is provided for digital devices.

DINING. *Europa 2* really is all about an elegant, but utterly relaxed, lifestyle and a wide choice of dining experiences and culinary adventures, including selections from Michael Hoffman's celebrated vegetarian and vegan dishes (different choices in each restaurant). Open-seating in all restaurants makes it easy for families with children to choose when to eat, and reservations are not needed in any restaurant for lunch. Dibbern china and Schott Zwiesel glassware are provided. Impressively (and unusually for a ship of this size), some 40 percent of all tables are for two – the others are for four, six or eight. What makes most of the ship's double-deck height restaurants special is their decor, individuality, and the different cuisines featured.

Weltmeere (Worldwide): This 266-seat restaurant (with huge, whimsical, pink 'octopus' tentacle-like glass chandeliers) features international culinary favorites, and the contemporary chairs have armrests. Open for breakfast and dinner.

Yachtclub: this 276-seat (142 indoor and 134 outdoor seats) restaurant is open for breakfast, lunch, and dinner. It includes a self-serve multi-section buffet (including an Ayurvedic 'bio-food' section), rotisserie, and two active cooking stations – plus a wonderful manual Berkel meat-slicing machine for wafer-thin cold cuts. Outside there's a Pasta Bar (several types of pasta are made on board, as are six different sauces daily), and a separate Grill Bar (featuring several types of fish). A canvas-like canopy incorporates heaters for cool-weather conditions.

Tarragon: this chic, tile-floored 44-seat French-style bistro features tableside carving (the steak tartare – prepared tableside – is exceptional, and you choose the accompanying ingredients), regional/seasonal food, and a focus on fresh herbs. It is open for dinner (and on selected days for lunch). Reservations are required for dinner.

Serenissima: this popular 56-seat Italian restaurant has open seating for lunch and dinner (reservations are required for dinner). Large white columns add to the sense of grandeur, and the chandeliers are stunning.

Elements: a reservations-required 48-seat pan-Asian restaurant, for lunch and dinner.

Sakura is a 58-seat sushi restaurant (part of the Yacht Club, for dinner), featuring Japanese cuisine and incorporating a sit-up sushi counter. Reservations are required.

Hapag-Lloyd Cruises has long been known for its culinary creativity and extremely high quality of food and service. This ship won't disappoint those seeking the best.

Sansibar is a trendy indoor-outdoor venue with special drinks, wines, and items from its namesake restaurant on the island of Sylt, Germany. It features special wines, has an à la carte late-riser's breakfast, and constantly changing tapas-style eats. It has a dance floor, and is the late-night disco-style venue, and the place to see and be seen.

ENTERTAINMENT. The Theater is a two-level showlounge, with good sightlines from almost all seats. It has LED lighting for show backdrops, and a thrust stage for cabaret acts, or concerts. Multi-faceted entertainment is provided by the company's own production team, each designed to be highly visual to accommodate the bi-lingual, international clientele.

For live music, Club 2 is a standout for the cool stuff; its bar has a long drinks list. Meanwhile light classical and chamber concerts take place in various other venues.

SPA/FITNESS. The Ocean Spa is to die for; it is a real center of serenity and calm. It is the largest wellness and spa zone for this size of ship, with indoor and outdoor areas measuring 10,764 sq ft (1,000 sq m) that do justice to the trend for combining holidays and wellbeing.

Facilities (all are mixed gender except for the changing rooms) include: a beauty salon; eight massage/body-treatment rooms; a steam room; three dry saunas (Finnish, Herbal, and Bio, two of which look aft) with different temperatures; two foot-washing stations (with different temperatures); two relaxation rooms (one with three hot, tiled beds); men's and women's changing/dressing rooms; showers; and two Dr. Kneipp basins for foot baths and water walks.

There are two electronic golf simulators – Europa 2 is the first ship to combine a state-of-the-art golf-simulator with full-body video analysis – and there's also a golf driving range and a storage room for golf clubs.

EXPEDITION
★★+

THIS SHIP IS QUITE SUITABLE FOR NO-FRILLS DISCOVERY CRUISING

Size:	Boutique Ship	Passenger/Crew Ratio (lower beds):	1.9
Tonnage:	3,960	Cabins (total):	60
Cruise Line:	G Adventures	Size Range (sq ft/m):	161.4-322.9/15.0-30.0
Former Names:	*Alandsfarjan, Tiger, Kattegat*	Cabins (for one person):	0
Builder:	HesingorSkibsverft (Denmark)	Cabins with balcony:	0
Entered Service:	Jul 1972/Oct 2009	Cabins (wheelchair accessible):	0
Length (ft/m):	341.2/104.0	Wheelchair accessibility:	None
Beam (ft/m):	62.0/18.9	Elevators:	0
Propulsion/Propellers:	diesel/2	Casino (gaming tables):	No
Passenger Decks:	5	Swimming Pools:	0
Total Crew:	69	Self-Service Launderette:	No
Passengers (lower beds):	120	Library:	Yes
Passenger Space Ratio (lower beds):	33.0	Onboard currency:	US$

THE SHIP. Built and operated as a car-passenger ferry from 1972 until it was converted into an expedition cruise ship in 2008, the little ship has raw character.

It is best suited to adventurous, hardy couples and solo travelers who enjoy being outdoors with nature and wildlife in one of the most interesting regions on earth, and for whom the ship is secondary – to act purely a means of transportation and accommodation.

The ship has outside (forward) viewing platforms, a fitness room, a large mud room (for boot washing – boots are provided), a small sauna (adjacent to the mud room), a small library with a selection of books on the polar region, a computer room and a small gift shop. A lecture room (main lounge) has seating for all participants, and there's also a bar – called the Polar Bear Pub.

A small fleet of zodiacs is carried for shore landings. There's also a lecture room, which accommodates all passengers at once. Note that the height of ceilings is low, so anyone considered tall will need to be careful to avoid the sprinklers.

The interior decor is ultra-plain and basic, which

BERLITZ'S RATINGS		
	Possible	Achieved
Ship	500	255
Accommodation	200	111
Food	400	198
Service	400	235
Entertainment	100	50
Cruise Experience	400	210

OVERALL SCORE 1059 points out of 2000

is acceptable for this type of in-your-face nature and expedition-style of cruising.

ACCOMMODATION. There are several cabin price grades. The price you pay depends on the size and location you choose, although, frankly, most cabins are of the same or similar measurements. Note that (for anyone who is tall) the cabin beds may prove to be rather short.

DINING. The dining room operates a one-seating arrangement. Food is hearty fare (think lots of carbohydrates to keep you warm, plus meat and fish dishes). Fruits, vegetables, and international cheeses tend to be in limited supply. Self-serve buffet selections for breakfast and lunch are pretty basic. A barbeque grill is featured on an outer aft deck, for use in appropriate conditions.

ENTERTAINMENT. This consists of recaps and after-dinner conversation with fellow voyage participants.

SPA/FITNESS. The only facility is a small sauna.

EXPLORER OF THE SEAS
★★★+

THIS LARGE RESORT SHIP WILL ENTERTAIN THE WHOLE FAMILY IN COMFORT

Size:	Large Resort Ship	Passenger/Crew Ratio (lower beds):	2.6
Tonnage:	137,308	Cabins (total):	1,557
Cruise Line:	Royal Caribbean International	Size Range (sq ft/m):	151.0–1,358.0/14.0–126.1
Former Names:	none	Cabins (for one person):	0
Builder:	Kvaerner Masa-Yards (Finland)	Cabins with balcony:	757
Entered Service:	Oct 2000	Cabins (wheelchair accessible):	26
Length (ft/m):	1,020.6/311.1	Wheelchair accessibility:	Best
Beam (ft/m):	155.5/47.4	Elevators:	14
Propulsion/Propellers:	diesel-electric (75,600kW)/	Casino (gaming tables):	Yes
	3 pods (2 azimuthing, 1 fixed)	Swimming Pools:	3
Passenger Decks:	14	Self-Service Launderette:	No
Total Crew:	1,181	Library:	Yes
Passengers (lower beds):	3,114	Onboard currency:	US$
Passenger Space Ratio (lower beds):	44.0		

THE SHIP. *Explorer of the Seas* (a *Voyager*-class ship) is a large, family-friendly resort at sea that provides an abundance of facilities and options, but has a healthy amount of space per passenger. One neat feature is an outdoors observation deck at the bows (good for photos, if you face aft, with most of the ship behind you).

A four-deck-high Royal Promenade, 394ft (120m) long, is the main interior focal point. Two American football fields long, it has two internal lobbies that rise up to 11 decks high. Eateries, shops, and entertainment locations line the street, and interior 'with-view' cabins look onto it from above. Entertaining street parades take place here. Reception and shore-excursion counters are aft, as is an ATM machine. Look up: you'll see a large moving, asteroid-like sculpture (constantly growing and contracting).

Arched across the promenade is a captain's balcony. A central promenade stairway connects to the deck below, where you'll find Schooner Bar (a piano lounge that's a feature of all RCI ships), the colorful Casino Royale, and several shops.

Studio B is an ice-skating rink, with seating for up to 900, although slim pillars obstruct clear-view arena stage sight lines. If ice-skating in the Caribbean doesn't appeal (it has actually become extremely popular), perhaps you'd like to do some reading in the two-deck library, open 24 hours a day.

Drinking places include an Aquarium Bar, with 50 tons of glass and water in four large aquariums (no

BERLITZ'S RATINGS		
	Possible	Achieved
Ship	500	379
Accommodation	200	132
Food	400	222
Service	400	266
Entertainment	100	74
Cruise Experience	400	261

OVERALL SCORE 1334 points out of 2000

swimming!), a Champagne Bar, a Crown & Kettle Pub, a Café Promenade (for Continental breakfast, pizzas, coffee, and desserts), Weekend Warrior (a sports bar), and a Connoisseur Club (for cigars and cognacs). Jazz fans can head to Dizzy's, an intimate room within the Viking Crown Lounge, or the Schooner Bar piano lounge. Golfers might also enjoy the 19th Hole, a golf bar, as they play the Explorer Links.

Passenger gripes include small cabin bath towels and noisy (vacuum) toilets; there are also few quiet places to sit and read – almost everywhere there is intrusive background music (particularly on the pool deck). And if you have a cabin with an interconnecting door to another cabin, be aware that you'll be able to hear everything your next-door neighbors say and do.

In 2015, the ship underwent an extensive refurbishment, which added a greater number of dining options, a Flowrider surf simulator, 'virtual' balconies for interior cabins, and a 3D cinema.

Facilities for children and teenagers (in four age groupings) are extensive and include Adventure Beach, an area for all the family, with swimming pools, a water slide, and outdoor game areas.

Overall, it's a good all-round ship for all age groups, but be aware of the many extra costs for optional items (drinks, drink packages, excursions, etc.).

ACCOMMODATION. There are numerous cabin categories, in four major groupings: premium ocean-view suites and cabins, promenade-view (interior-view) cabins, ocean-view cabins, and interior cabins (with no view). Many cabins are of a similar size – good for incentives and large groups – and 300 have interconnecting doors, which works well for families.

Most cabins are of a reasonably adequate size, with just enough facilities to make them comfortable and functional. Twin lower beds convert to a queen-size bed, and there is a reasonable amount of closet and drawer space, although the beds take up most of the space. The bathrooms are compact, with dimensionally challenged shower enclosures and no cabinet for personal toiletries, but they do at least have a proper shower enclosure, not a shower curtain.

All cabins have interactive TV and pay-per-view movies. Cabins with 'private' balconies aren't so private, because the partitions are only partial.

Some 138 interior cabins have bay windows looking into the central shopping plaza – and into your neighbor's cabin, unless you keep the curtains closed. All cabins (except the Royal Suite and Owner's Suite) have twin beds convertible to a queen-size one, plus a TV set, radio and telephone, personal safe, vanity unit, minibar, hairdryer, and bathroom.

The largest accommodation is the Royal Suite, on the port side, measuring 1,146 sq ft (106 sq m), followed by the Owner's Suites, measuring 468 sq ft (43 sq m), and the Royal Family Suites, each measuring 574 sq ft (53 sq m) and located at the stern, with fine views over the ship's wake.

DINING. The huge Sapphire Dining Room has three levels, all of which offer the same menu.

Place settings, china, and cutlery are of good quality. Choose one of two seatings, or My Time Dining (eat when you want during dining room hours). The food in the main dining room is pretty standard mass-catered fare. The menu descriptions sound tempting, but the food, although prepared well, is just so-so. Vegetarian and children's menus are also available. Note that there are no wine waiters.

Most meat dishes are disguised with gravies or heavy sauce reductions; rice is often used as a source of carbohydrates. Green vegetables are scarce, but basic salad items are plentiful, and desserts are very decent. Breads and pastry items are plentiful (though these are thawed and then baked from frozen 'starter' dough), but croissants lack any hint of butter.

Other dining venues and eateries (most at an extra cost) include: Chops Grille (open for lunch and dinner, for prime steaks, other meats, and grilled seafood items); Giovanni's Table (for lunch and dinner; Italian classics served family-style); Izumi Asian Cuisine (for lunch and dinner; includes a sushi bar and sizzling hot-rock cooked items); Chef's Table (open for dinner only, this 'private' experience is co-hosted by the executive chef and sommelier and features a multi-course dinner with wine pairing); and Park Café (for breakfast, lunch and dinner, this indoor/outdoor deli is for salads, sandwiches, soups, and pastries).

Johnny Rockets, a retro 1950s all-day, diner-style eatery, has hamburgers, malt shakes (at extra cost), and jukebox hits, with both indoor and outdoor seating.

Promenade Café: for Continental breakfasts, all-day pizzas, and specialty coffees (in paper cups).

Sprinkles, located on the Royal Promenade, is for round-the-clock ice cream and yogurt, pastries, and coffee.

For casual, self-serve meals, the large Windjammer Cafe has several sections. It is open almost round-the-clock.

ENTERTAINMENT. The stunning 1,350-seat Palace showlounge spans five decks, with only a few slim pillars and almost no disruption of sight lines – an example of fine design and shipbuilding.

Strong cabaret acts perform in the main showlounge, while others perform in Maharaja's Lounge, also the venue for adult-only late-night comedy. The best shows are the Ice Spectaculars.

SPA/FITNESS. The Vitality at Seas Spa measures 15,000 sq ft (1,400 sq m), and includes an aerobics room, workout center, treatment rooms, and men's and women's sauna/steam rooms. Another 10,000 sq ft (930 sq m) of space features a Solarium (with sliding glass-dome roof) to relax in after you've exercised.

Aft of the funnel is a 33ft (10m) rock-climbing wall, with five climbing tracks. Other sports facilities include a roller-blading track, a dive-and-snorkel shop (equipment rentals available), a full-size basketball court, and a nine-hole, par-26 golf 'course.'

FIFTY YEARS OF VICTORY
★★★★

NUCLEAR-POWERED, THIS IS THE ULTIMATE NORTH POLE AND ARCTIC EXPEDITION SHIP

Size:	Boutique Ship	Passenger/Crew Ratio (lower beds):	0.9
Tonnage:	23,439	Cabins (total):	66
Cruise Line:	Various expedition operators	Size Range (sq ft/m):	148.5–367.0/13.8–34.1
Former Names:	*Ural*	Cabins (for one person):	0
Builder:	Baltic Works, St Petersburg (Russia)	Cabins with balcony:	0
Entered Service:	Jul 2009	Cabins (wheelchair accessible):	0
Length (ft/m):	523.6/159.6	Wheelchair accessibility:	None
Beam (ft/m):	98.4/30.0	Elevators:	1
Propulsion/Propellers:	nuclear reactors (2)/	Casino (gaming tables):	0
	3 propulsion motors (75,000 hp)	Swimming Pools:	1
Passenger Decks:	6	Self-Service Launderette:	Yes
Total Crew:	140	Library:	Yes
Passengers (lower beds):	132	Onboard currency:	US$
Passenger Space Ratio (lower beds):	177.5		

THE SHIP. An advanced vessel of the *Arktika*-class of icebreaking ships, *Fifty Years of Victory* is an outstanding polar expedition cruise ship that carries adventurous, hardy outdoors types of mature years. It is powered by two nuclear reactors, providing 75,000hp, and carries enough fuel to power it for four years. Experienced lecturers are carried on each sailing.

This dramatic, incredibly impressive vessel (*Let Pobedy* in Russian) is the world's largest and most powerful icebreaker, capable of breaking through ice up to 8ft (2.4m) thick. While the noise created by the ice-crushing capability of this marine machine is intense, it is all part of the great adventure.

There are more crew members than passengers, giving a most impressive passenger/space ratio. The ship is comfortable, and it carries a fleet of Zodiac inflatable landing craft, as well as two helicopters for passenger use, and expedition leaders. The crew is experienced in challenging conditions.

Fifty Years of Victory typically leaves from its northern Russian base city of Murmansk before heading across the Barents Sea. Approaching the North Pole – 90° north and 1,000 miles (1,600km) from the closest tree – aboard a Russian icebreaker is the ultimate prize of a true Arctic Expedition voyage. It's really one of the most spectacular voyages to be made by ship.

A library is stocked with books about polar exploration, nature, and wildlife. Because there are so few voyages to the North Pole, places sell out quickly.

BERLITZ'S RATINGS		
	Possible	Achieved
Ship	500	362
Accommodation	200	143
Food	400	260
Service	400	273
Entertainment	100	80
Cruise Experience	400	306
OVERALL SCORE 1424 points out of 2000		

Yellow parkas and rubber boots are provided, but you should take waterproof trousers and thermal wear.

Gratuities to the staff are at your discretion, but a suggestion is about $10 per day, per person. Note that the ship will be withdrawn from service after the 2018 Arctic season.

ACCOMMODATION. There are two 'suite' grades and three cabin grades. The suites have a spacious bedroom and separate lounge room, while the bathroom has a tub. Suites also have a coffee-making machine, and fresh fruit is replenished daily. All suites/cabins have windows that open. Each has private bathroom facilities (with shower, except the suites with bathtub), TV/DVD player, and a decent amount of storage space. Only two cabins (46 and 48) have obstructed views.

DINING. The dining room operates in a single open seating, so you sit with whomever you wish. Expect the food to be carbohydrate-rich, hearty fare that will provide the energy you need for the adventures ahead.

ENTERTAINMENT. There isn't any as such: conversation among all participants is the main event each day, as well as evening recaps and wildlife spotting.

SPA/FITNESS. Facilities include a sauna, fitness center, basketball, and indoor volleyball court. There is a small 'dip' pool at the stern, underneath the helicopter deck.

FLYING CLIPPER
NYR

THIS SAIL-CRUISE SHIP WILL GIVE YOU AN EXTRAORDINARY WIND-IN-YOUR-HAIR EXPERIENCE

Size:	Small Ship	Passenger/Crew Ratio (lower beds):	2.1
Tonnage:	8,770	Cabins (total):	150
Cruise Line:	Star Clippers	Size Range (sq ft/m):	141.0–586.6/13.1–54.5
Former Names:	none	Cabins (for one person):	0
Builder:	Star Clippers	Cabins with balcony:	34
Entered Service:	Spring 2018	Cabins (wheelchair accessible):	0
Length (ft/m):	532.2/162.22	Wheelchair accessibility:	None
Beam (ft/m):	60.6/18.5	Elevators:	0
Propulsion/Propellers:	sail power + diesel/2	Casino (gaming tables):	No
Passenger Decks:	4	Swimming Pools:	3
Total Crew:	140	Self-Service Launderette:	No
Passengers (lower beds):	300	Library:	Yes
Passenger Space Ratio (lower beds):	29.2	Onboard currency:	Euros

THE SHIP. *Flying Clipper* is the world's largest square rigger and the largest real 'tall ship' of its kind today. Built as almost a replica of the famed *France II*, the sail-cruise ship has five masts, and 35 sails totaling more than 68,350 sq ft (6,350 sq m). It is decidedly impressive.

Building it was the culmination of a lifelong dream of Swedish yachtsman Michael Krafft. His passion for sailing is indisputably embedded within this great sail-cruise ship.

The ship is simply exhilarating when the ship is moving under sail. One neat chill-out pleasure is to lie in the netting at the front of the ship's bows, watching the bow's wake as it streams along the ship's sides.

An aft marina platform can be lowered (at anchor), so that passengers can use surfboards, sailing dinghies, take a ride on the banana boat, or go waterskiing or swimming. Snorkeling gear is available free, but there is a charge for scuba gear. You will be asked to sign a waiver if you use the watersports equipment.

The dress code is always casual (shorts and casual tops are the order of the day – yachting wear), with no ties needed ever.

Flying Clipper is all about an interpretation of the 'Golden Age of Sail' and would be an excellent choice for anyone who would probably not consider a 'normal' cruise ship, but who enjoys sailing and the thrill of ocean and wind, but wants a package that includes

BERLITZ'S RATINGS	Possible	Achieved
Ship	500	NYR
Accommodation	200	NYR
Food	400	NYR
Service	400	NYR
Entertainment	100	NYR
Cruise Experience	400	NYR

OVERALL SCORE NYR points out of 2000

accommodation, food, like-minded companions, and interesting destinations, and not the bother of owning or chartering their own yacht.

You may be allowed to climb to special lookout points aloft, and on the bridge at any time – but you are not allowed in the galley or engine room.

ACCOMMODATION. There are numerous accommodation price grades. Pricing depends on the size, location, and grade you choose. From the smallest interior cabin (no view) to the largest suites (four Owner's Suites), the decor has a very nautical theme.

DINING. The restaurant spans two decks, has 'grand hotel'-style decor, and seats all passengers at one seating. Breakfast and lunch are self-serve buffets, but dinner is served by waiters. The wine list consists of young wines, and prices are pretty high.

Entertainment. Depending on the itinerary and region, passengers may gather for 'captain's story time,' normally held on an open deck area adjacent to the bridge, or in the bar – which, incidentally, has a collection of single malt whiskies. The captain may explain sailing maneuvers when changing the rigging or directing the ship as it sails into port, and note the important events of the day.

SPA/FITNESS. There is a fitness room and treatment rooms for massages, facials, etc.

FRAM
★★★

EXPEDITION-STYLE CRUISING IN A MODERN, BUT MINIMALIST SHIP

Size:	Small Ship	Passenger/Crew Ratio (lower beds):	3.3
Tonnage:	11,647	Cabins (total):	127
Cruise Line:	Hurtigruten	Size Range (sq ft/m):	113.0–415.5/10.5–38.6
Former Names:	none	Cabins (for one person):	0
Builder:	Fincantieri (Italy)	Cabins with balcony:	6
Entered Service:	Apr 2007	Cabins (wheelchair accessible):	2
Length (ft/m):	374.0/114.0	Wheelchair accessibility:	Fair
Beam (ft/m):	66.2/20.2	Elevators:	2
Propulsion/Propellers:	diesel (4.6MW)/2	Casino (gaming tables):	No
Passenger Decks:	6	Swimming Pools:	0
Total Crew:	75	Self-Service Launderette:	No
Passengers (lower beds):	254	Library:	No
Passenger Space Ratio (lower beds):	45.8	Onboard currency:	Norwegian krona

THE SHIP. Designed to operate in polar waters, *Fram* sails from Reykjavík, Iceland, operating Greenland and Spitzbergen cruises from May through September, and winter cruises to Antarctica. It suits mature adults who like exploring independently.

The ship's design reflects Norwegian and Greenlandic culture, using an extensive mix of wool, leather, and oak. The interior decor is decidedly Inuit. The few public rooms include the Quilac observation lounge, an Internet café, board room, and a small shop. There is no walk-around promenade deck. Hurtigruten doesn't have a great culture of hospitality and service, so many passengers feel they are traveling with a transportation company rather than a cruise line. The crew to passenger ratio is really low, and service training is poor, so there's little attention to detail.

In Antarctica, the ship is a fairly capable expedition vessel, but it can still get stuck in heavy pack-ice. An Expedition Leader organizes everything to do with a specific voyage. Expedition specialists provide daily lectures. Boots are provided; they come in European sizes – so it helps to know yours before you go.

Life on board is very relaxed, so formal attire is never needed. Smoking is allowed only on the open deck – and not at all when *Fram* is in port. The ship operates in Norwegian and English. There are no safety deposit boxes. Hurtigruten operates a no-tipping-required policy. All in all, the ship should provide a fine expedition-style experience in a modicum of comfort.

BERLITZ'S RATINGS		
	Possible	Achieved
Ship	500	328
Accommodation	200	126
Food	400	228
Service	400	237
Entertainment	100	67
Cruise Experience	400	259

OVERALL SCORE 1245 points out of 2000

ACCOMMODATION. There are 13 price categories (too many), according to size and location. The good thing is that no cabins have obstructed views. The largest accommodation is one Owner's Suite, which consists of a bedroom, living room, and bathroom with Jacuzzi tub. Six cabins at the aft of the ship, overlooking the stern and the ship's wake, have a shared balcony. There are several price grades for the standard cabins, which typically have one bed and a sofa that converts to a fold-down bed, or two pull-down sofa beds; there's little room and only a few shelves (these cabins are really only good for daytrippers).

DINING. Restaurant Imaq, the main dining room, is located aft and connects to the main lobby via an arcade. Local cuisine and recipes, including bison meat and fresh fish, are featured. However, several meals are of the self-help buffet variety only. An extra-charge bistro and self-serve buffet is available for snacks. Dessert items are particularly good. Alcohol prices are very high.

ENTERTAINMENT. There isn't any. Guides and lecturers organize talks and informative briefings based on the cruise area.

SPA/FITNESS. Saunas are located one deck above the exercise area; there's also a small, well-equipped exercise room.

FREEDOM OF THE SEAS
★★★+

THIS IS A LARGE FLOATING THEME PARK – GOOD FOR THE WHOLE FAMILY

Size:	Large Resort Ship	Passenger/Crew Ratio (lower beds):	2.7
Tonnage:	154,407	Cabins (total):	1,817
Cruise Line:	Royal Caribbean International	Size Range (sq ft/m):	153.0–2,025.0/14.2–188.1
Former Names:	none	Cabins (for one person):	0
Builder:	Kvaerner Masa-Yards (Finland)	Cabins with balcony:	842
Entered Service:	Jun 2006	Cabins (wheelchair accessible):	32
Length (ft/m):	1,112.2/339.0	Wheelchair accessibility:	Best
Beam (ft/m):	183.7/56.0	Elevators:	14
Propulsion/Propellers:	diesel-electric (75,600kW)/	Casino (gaming tables):	Yes
	3 pods (2 azimuthing, 1 fixed) (42,000kW)	Swimming Pools:	2
Passenger Decks:	15	Self-Service Launderette:	No
Total Crew:	1,360	Library:	Yes
Passengers (lower beds):	3,701	Onboard currency:	US$
Passenger Space Ratio (lower beds):	41.7		

THE SHIP. *Freedom of the Seas* (with sisters *Independence of the Seas* and *Liberty of the Seas*) is an extension of the popular *Voyager*-class of ships, introduced in 1999. For this ship, the length and beam were extended, enabling an increase in cabins and passenger capacity, and a combined pool area 43 percent larger than the *Voyager*-class – but with 500 more passengers (and, after a 2015 refit, another 134 passengers), yet the same number of elevators. The ship is the length of 37 London double-decker buses.

The 'wow' factor (particularly for younger cruisers) is its connection with water, including its 40 x 32ft (12.2 x 9.7m) Flowrider body/board surfing zone aft. This wave simulator creates a wall of water, flowing at 35,000 gallons per minute.

There's also an H2O Zone forward of the funnel, an interactive water-themed play area with a pool fed by a waterfall, two hot tubs, water cannons, spray fountains, water jets, and ground gushers; at night, it all morphs into a colorfully lit Sculpture Garden. Twin central pools consist of a main and a sports pool, with grandstand-style seating and competitive games.

There are multiple bars and lounges, and a whole promenade of shops and munching and drinking spots along an indoor mall-like environment called the Royal Promenade. It is four decks high, and some interior-facing cabins have great views into it. It is home to fashion, jewelry and perfume shops, a gen-

BERLITZ'S RATINGS		
	Possible	Achieved
Ship	500	365
Accommodation	200	132
Food	400	235
Service	400	278
Entertainment	100	73
Cruise Experience	400	261

OVERALL SCORE 1344 points out of 2000

eral store, logo shop, Promenade Café, Ben & Jerry's ice cream outlet, a Book Nook, a 'classic' barber shop (A Close Shave), a pizzeria, and a Bull and Bear (English pub).

The forward section of it leads into a large nightclub – Star Lounge – usually for late-night adult-only comedy. One deck down from the Royal Promenade you'll find a large Casino Royale (gaming tables and slot machines), The Crypt disco, Schooner Bar (piano bar), Boleros (Latin hangout), and a photo gallery, while forwardmost is the Arcadia Theatre.

A lively large resort ship, with tasteful decor, *Freedom of the Seas* is a good ship for young, active families with children, as long as you don't mind lines when signing up for popular activities (the Flowrider surf area, rock-climbing wall, and full-size boxing ring, for example).

ACCOMMODATION. There is a wide range of suites and cabins in several categories and price grades, from a Presidential Family Suite that can sleep up to 14 to twin-bed two-person interior cabins without a view, and interior cabins with bay windows that look into the Royal Promenade. The price you pay depends on the size, grade, and location. There are many family-friendly cabins, good for reunions, but no solo-occupancy cabins. All outside-view cabins have even numbers; all interior cabins have odd numbers.

DINING. The large main dining room is set on three levels, each with a theme and different name – Leonardo, Isaac, and Galileo – all have the same menus and food. A dramatic staircase connects the three levels, but huge support pillars obstruct the sight lines from many seats.

Choose one of two seatings, or My Time Dining (to eat when you want during dining-room hours). The cuisine in the main dining room is all about standardized banquet catering, with food cooked in batches. Menu descriptions sound tempting, but the food, although prepared well, is just so-so. Vegetarian and children's menus are also available. Note that there are no wine waiters.

Most meat dishes are disguised with gravies or heavy sauce reductions; rice is often used as a source of carbohydrates. Green vegetables are scarce, but basic salad items are plentiful, and the desserts are very decent. Breads and pastry items are plentiful (though these are thawed and then baked from frozen 'starter' dough), but croissants lack any hint of butter.

Other dining venues and eateries (some of which cost extra, but the food is mostly cooked to order) include favorites such as Chops Grille Steakhouse (for premium veal chops, steaks ,and seafood items) and Portofino (for Italian-American cuisine). Reservations (make them through the digital system – and as early as possible to avoid disappointment) are required; note that menus do not change. Additional extra-cost eateries include Sabor (for 'authentic' Mexican specialty cuisine) and Giovanni's Table (for Italian cuisine). There's also Johnny Rockets, a retro 1950s all-day, all-night, extra-cost diner-style eatery that serves burgers, hot dogs, and other fast-food items, plus malt shakes and sodas. It has indoor and outdoor seating. Indoor tables have a mini-jukebox (dimes are provided for you to make your selection of vintage records). The waitresses are all-singing and all-dancing. There's a cover charge.

No reservations are needed for venues including: Promenade Café (Continental breakfast, sandwiches, and coffees); Cupcake Cupboard (for fairy cakes); Sorrento's (pizzas and Italian cakes); Sprinkles Ice Cream Parlor (for round-the-clock ice cream and yoghurt, pastries, and coffee); and Windjammer Café (a large, sprawling venue for casual buffet-style, self-help meals – part of this, Jade 'Restaurant,' does Asian-themed food).

ENTERTAINMENT. The 1,350-seat Arcadia Theater spans three decks (five if you count the orchestra pit and scenery storage space). It is a well-designed showlounge, with only a small number of pillars disrupting the sight lines to the stage.

SPA/FITNESS. The large Steiner-operated Vitality at Sea Spa and Fitness Center includes a large aerobics room, fitness center, several treatment rooms, men's and women's sauna/steam rooms, and relaxation areas. Some exercise classes are free, but some cost extra.

GENTING DREAM
★★★★+

THIS FAMILY-FRIENDLY SHIP IS FOR ASIA CRUISING IN HIGH-TECH SURROUNDINGS

Size:	Large Resort Ship		Passenger/Crew Ratio (lower beds):	1.6/1
Tonnage:	151,300		Cabins (total):	1,680
Cruise Line:	Dream Cruises		Size Range (sq ft/m):	150.6–1,969.8/14.0–183.0
Former Names:	none		Cabins (for one person):	0
Builder:	Meyer Werft (Germany)		Cabins with balcony:	1,188
Entered Service:	Nov 2016		Cabins (wheelchair accessible):	32
Length (ft/m):	1,100.0/335.3		Wheelchair accessibility:	Good
Beam (ft/m):	130.2/39.7		Elevators:	16
Propulsion/Propellers:	diesel-electric/ 2 azimuthing pods		Casino (gaming tables):	Yes
Passenger Decks:	18		Swimming Pools:	2
Total Crew:	2,030		Self-Service Launderette:	No
Passengers (lower beds):	3,360		Library:	Yes
Passenger Space Ratio (lower beds):	45.0		Onboard currency:	CNY (RMB)

THE SHIP. This is the first of two stunning large resort ships for Dream Cruises (a 'premium' brand created in 2015, it is owned by Genting Hong Kong, owner of Crystal Cruises and Star Cruises). *Genting Dream* has really extensive facilities and entertainment features for the whole family. Its smooth lines and profile are similar to those of Norwegian Cruise Line's *Norwegian Escape*, in terms of exterior design and styling (but with the lifeboats hanging out from the ship's side). The attention-getting hull (conceived by Chinese Pop artist Jacky Tsai, and featuring a story involving a mermaid and an astronaut) is painted in flamboyant red and gold. The superstructure glows with LED lighting at night.

There is a complete, 2,000-ft- (610-m-) long walk-around outside promenade deck (with indoor-outdoor seaside eateries), multiple pools (including a private, extra-cost adults-only pool and relaxation area), and, in the ship's center (adjacent to the main pool), the Wet 'n' Wild Water Park, which includes six water slides for children and teens to enjoy. Zouk Beach and bar, music lounge, and a sports bar are located aft of the funnel.

Inside, the decor is ultra-upbeat, with an abundance of bright colors that work extremely well for Asians. There are numerous bars, lounges, karaoke and Mahjong rooms, large duty-free shopping street, as well as a large Genting Casino filled with gaming tables and slot machines (and private gaming rooms),

BERLITZ'S RATINGS		
	Possible	Achieved
Ship	500	422
Accommodation	200	155
Food	400	315
Service	400	290
Entertainment	100	86
Cruise Experience	400	422

OVERALL SCORE 1585 points out of 2000

Resorts World Casino, Resorts World Premium Club, and Maxim's – for card games. Other facilities include a business center, meeting rooms, a shopping street, and numerous bars and lounges. Also, the ship has a special street night 'market' complete with hawker stalls that feature Asian delicacies.

Genting Dream has three homeports: Guangzhou (Nansha Port), Hong Kong, and Sanya, which means that there really is no beginning or end to a cruise, just a rotating itinerary, although Singapore will be the home port from December 2017. Overall, this ship has all the right ingredients for Asia cruises for Asians, served mostly by Asians, who understand the cultures of the region better than the western cruise lines.

ACCOMMODATION. There are numerous accommodation grades. From the smallest interior (no-view) cabin (measuring 150 sq ft/14 sq m) to the largest suite (142 Dream Suites), which measures 1,970 sq ft/183 sq m and is spread over two decks, the price you pay depends on the size, location, and grade you choose.

The more you pay, the more you get – for occupants of Dream Palace, a private-access VIP area located in a section at the front of the ship above the navigation bridge (similar to but more expansive than MSC Cruises' Yacht Club and Norwegian Cruise Line's The Haven). Dream Suite occupants have access to a private outdoor pool, hot tubs, relaxation area, and cabanas, Horizons Lounge (observation lounge), and a private club for gaming (so there's no need to go downstairs to the busier Resorts World and other casino areas).

Over 100 family-friendly cabins have interconnecting doors, so parents can take their young ones and feel comfortable.

DINING. With an abundance of dining, eatery and drinking options, the ship can cater to just about any taste and dietary and ethnic persuasion. Main dining venues include a large bi-level Windows, located aft, with ocean views from its huge dining hall windows (a window table is definitely one to have). A second 'main' dining room is Genting Palace.

The culinary emphasis is, naturally, on the Asia-Pacific region, including the Chinese lunchtime favorite – dim-sum (whose meaning, literally, is 'to touch the heart').

Noted Australian chef Mark Best has his first restaurant at sea, whose 'Bistro' menu's focuses on small producer Australian beef, lamb, river fish and the freshest seafood.

Some other venues (indoor and outdoor) include:

Silk Road: à la carte Chinese regional and provincial cuisine in a tablecloth setting.

Blue Lagoon: the venue for tuck-in Chinese street (finger) food and clay pot cuisine.

Umi-Uma: a Japanese restaurant with Teppanyaki grills, and sushi bar.

Positano: an Italian eatery to remind you of the Amalfi coast.

Genting Palace: another venue featuring Chinese (Cantonese) dishes.

Makan Makan: for south-east Asian cuisine, including Chinese and Malaysian specialties.

World Buffet: this is an international food court-style area with self-serve food from various display counters and active cooking stations, while adjacent and outside is a pool bar and grill.

Bread Box and Tiffin Café: a 'see and be seen' venue for coffees/teas and light bites.

Drinking places include a Red Lion Pub, Johnny Walker bar (with a wall full of decorative bottles of JW and a special Dream Cruises JW whisky), a Martini bar, Bar City, Boba Cha, Bar 360, and several other bars.

ENTERTAINMENT. The multi-deck 1,000-seat Zodiac Theater is the main showlounge. It features glamorous production shows (including acrobatics) and major cabaret acts.

Silk Road is an extra-cost bordello-look nightclub with topless Burlesque show. Adjacent are several (bookable, extra-cost) Karaoke rooms.

SPA/FITNESS. The Crystal Life Spa has two sections (East, and Aeris West), one for Asians (for whom ambience and 'flow-through' are more important than the range of treatments offered), and one for Westerners. The spa – the largest at sea – has its own eatery (Aeris Spa Café), for 'healthy' food and drinks (some of which are at extra cost). *Genting Dream* also has an MRI scanner (it was the first cruise ship to carry one). Sports facilities in various locations include a bowling alley, basketball court, a climbing wall, and an extensive Dreamcatcher rope-climbing course.

GOLDEN PRINCESS
★★★+

A COMFORTABLE, INFORMAL, FAMILY-FRIENDLY LARGE RESORT SHIP

Size:	Large Resort Ship	Passenger/Crew Ratio (lower beds):	2.1
Tonnage:	108,865	Cabins (total):	1,312
Cruise Line:	Princess Cruises	Size Range (sq ft/m):	161.4–764.2/15.0–71.0
Former Names:	none	Cabins (for one person):	0
Builder:	Fincantieri (Italy)	Cabins with balcony:	720
Entered Service:	May 2001	Cabins (wheelchair accessible):	28
Length (ft/m):	951.4/290.0	Wheelchair accessibility:	Best
Beam (ft/m):	118.1/36.0	Elevators:	14
Propulsion/Propellers:	diesel-electric (42,000kW)/2	Casino (gaming tables):	Yes
Passenger Decks:	13	Swimming Pools:	3
Total Crew:	1,100	Self-Service Launderette:	Yes
Passengers (lower beds):	2,624	Library:	Yes
Passenger Space Ratio (lower beds):	41.4	Onboard currency:	US$

THE SHIP. *Golden Princess*, sister to *Grand Princess* and *Star Princess*, has a racy 'spoiler' at the stern that is an observation lounge with aft-facing views by day, and a discotheque by night. The ship has a rather flared snub-nosed bow and a galleon-like transom stern.

There is a good sheltered faux teak promenade deck – it's actually painted steel – which almost wraps around (three times round is equal to 1 mile/1.6km) and a walkway that goes to the enclosed bow. The outdoor pools have various beach-like surroundings, plus a large poolside movie screen. One lap pool has a pumped 'current' to swim against.

The Sanctuary is adult passengers only; it has plush padded lounge chairs, two private massage cabanas, and Serenity Stewards.

There is plenty of space inside the ship and a wide array of public rooms. The passenger flow is good, with minimal congestion. The decor is mildly attractive, with many earth tones.

The main lobby, La Piazza, often has live entertainment; an International Café for (extra-cost) coffees, fresh cookies, pastries, panini, and tapas; and Vines, a wine bar.

There is a Wedding Chapel, with a web-cam to relay ceremonies via the Internet. The ship's captain can legally marry (American) couples, thanks to the ship's Bermuda registry (this should, however, be verified when in the planning stage; it may vary according to where you reside).

BERLITZ'S RATINGS	Possible	Achieved
Ship	500	334
Accommodation	200	129
Food	400	247
Service	400	265
Entertainment	100	74
Cruise Experience	400	271
OVERALL SCORE 1320 points out of 2000		

A large casino, on Deck 7, has over 260 slot machines, plus gaming tables. A wood-paneled Wheelhouse Bar is decorated with memorabilia and ship models tracing part of parent company P&O's history.

Passenger niggles include the user-unfriendly automated telephone system, the small cabin towels, the extra cost for items such as ice cream, and the (coins-needed) charge for the washers and dryers in self-service launderettes.

Overall, however, Princess Cruises delivers a consistently fine, comfortable, well-packaged product, always with a good degree of style, at a competitive price.

ACCOMMODATION. There are six main cabin types, from small interior (no-view) cabins to the largest suite (the Grand Suite – B748), at the stern, but a bewildering number of price categories. The price depends on grade, size, and location.

Anyone occupying the best suites will receive greater attention, including priority embarkation and disembarkation. But some of the most expensive accommodation has balconies that can be overlooked, so there is no privacy (suites C401, 402, 409, 410, 414, 415, 420, 421, 422, 423, 424, and 425 on Caribe Deck in particular). Also, the extremely large suites D105 and D106 (Dolphin Deck) have balconies that can be seen from above.

Standard interior and outside-view cabins (the outside ones come either with or without private balcony) are of a functional, practical, design, although almost no drawers are provided. They are attractive, with warm, pleasing decor and decent soft furnishings.

Two family suites consist of two suites with an interconnecting door, plus a large balcony. These can sleep up to 10 (if at least four are children), or up to eight adults.

Note that the views from most outside cabins on Emerald Deck are obstructed by lifeboats. Some cabins can accommodate a third and fourth person in upper berths, but the lower beds are fixed and cannot then be pushed together

Cabins with balconies on Dolphin, Caribe, and Baja decks are overlooked by passengers on balconies on the deck above; they are, therefore, not at all private. However, perhaps the least desirable balcony cabins are the eight located forward on Emerald Deck, as the balconies don't extend to the side of the ship and can be passed by walkers and gawkers on an adjacent walkway (so occupants need to keep their curtains closed most of the time). Cabin attendants have many cabins to look after (typically 20), which cannot translate to fine personal service. Other niggles include the limited drawer space.

DINING. For 'formal' meals there are three principal dining rooms (Bernini, Canaletto, and Donatello). There are two seatings in one restaurant, and the others have 'anytime dining,' where you choose your time and companions. The dining rooms are split into multi-tier sections in a non-symmetrical design that breaks what are large spaces into many smaller sections. Each dining room has its own galley. While four elevators go to Fiesta Deck for Canaletto and Donatello, only two go to Plaza Deck 5 for Bernini, which can mean long wait problems at peak times, particularly for anyone in a wheelchair. Note that 15 percent is added to all beverage bills, including wines, coffees, etc.

Although portions are generous, the food and its presentation are disappointing, and standardized. Fish is often disguised by sauces or coatings, the choice of fresh green vegetables is limited, few

garnishes are used, and cheese is either pre-sliced or diced. But, this is banquet catering, with all its attendant standardization and cooking in batches. Pasta dishes are acceptable (though voluminous), typically served by section headwaiters, who may also make 'something special just for you.' If you like desserts, order a sundae at dinner (most other items are just so-so).

There are two extra-cost, reservations- required dining venues: Sabatini's and Crown Grill. Sabatini's features Italian-style pizzas and pastas, with a variety of sauces, as well as Italian-style entrées (mains), including tiger prawns and lobster tail. Sabatini's is by reservation only and open for lunch or dinner on sea days only. Crown Grill has a viewable galley, and features premium-quality steaks and grilled seafood items. It's worth it for food cooked to order.

Poolside burger grill and pizza bars offer casual bites. Other casual meals can be taken in the 24-hour Horizon Court, with large ocean-view windows and direct access to the two main swimming pools and Lido Deck, and outdoor seating. Plastic plates are provided instead of trays.

ENTERTAINMENT. The 748-seat Princess Theater spans two decks and has comfortable seating on both levels. Princess Cruises prides itself on its glamorous, all-American production shows, always with live music.

Vista Lounge is a second entertainment venue and multi-function room. It presents cabaret acts at night, and lectures, bingo, and horse racing during the day.

Explorers is a third entertainment lounge for cabaret acts and live bands; it has a decent-sized dance floor.

Many other lounges and bars have live music, and there are male dance hosts as partners for women traveling alone.

SPA/FITNESS. The Lotus Spa is a complex that surrounds one of the swimming pools at the forward end of the ship. It comprises a large fitness room with all the high-tech workout machinery, an aerobics room, sauna and steam rooms, beauty salon, treatment rooms, and a relaxation area.

GRAND CELEBRATION
★★+

THIS FAMILY-FRIENDLY SHIP IS FOR LOW-COST PARTY CRUISES TO THE BAHAMAS

Size:	Mid-size Ship	Passenger/Crew Ratio (lower beds):	2.4
Tonnage:	47,262	Cabins (total):	751
Cruise Line:	Bahamas Paradise Cruise Line	Size Range (sq ft/m):	184.0/17.1
Former Names:	*Grand Celebration, Celebration*	Cabins (for one person):	0
Builder:	Kockums (Sweden)	Cabins with balcony:	10
Entered Service:	Mar 1987/Jun 2008	Cabins (wheelchair accessible):	14
Length (ft/m):	732.6/223.3	Wheelchair accessibility:	Fair
Beam (ft/m):	92.5/28.2	Elevators:	8
Propulsion/Propellers:	diesel (23,520kW)/2	Casino (gaming tables):	Yes
Passenger Decks:	10	Swimming Pools:	3
Total Crew:	620	Self-Service Launderette:	Yes
Passengers (lower beds):	1,502	Library:	No
Passenger Space Ratio (lower beds):	31.4	Onboard currency:	US$

THE SHIP. *Grand Celebration*, now 30 years old, is really a large water-taxi to the Bahamas. It also has extremely short bows and a swept-back, wing-tipped blue funnel just aft of the ship's center. The swimming pools are very small, and the open deck space is extremely limited, which makes it feel crowded.

It has a double-width indoor promenade and a good selection of public rooms, including a large (Paradice – cute spelling!) casino, and several lounges and bars. There is no walk-around open promenade deck.

ACCOMMODATION. There are several accommodation grades, and several price categories: suite with balcony; junior suite with balcony; outside-view; and interior cabins. The cabins are quite standard, are of fairly generous proportions, except for the interior cabins, which are very small. A 24-hour room service menu is provided. The best living spaces are in 10 suites, each of which has much more space than a standard cabin, plus its own private balcony, a larger bathroom and more closet, drawer, and storage space.

DINING. There are two dining rooms: the 550 seat Restaurant Vistahermosa and the 450-seat Res-

BERLITZ'S RATINGS		
	Possible	Achieved
Ship	500	262
Accommodation	200	108
Food	400	171
Service	400	213
Entertainment	100	52
Cruise Experience	400	206

OVERALL SCORE 1012 points out of 2000

taurant Riazor. They are cramped when full, and extremely noisy. There are tables for four, six, or eight, but none for two. The decor is bright and extremely colorful. Dining is in two seatings. Meals for vegetarians and special children's menus are available.

Food presentation is simple, and few garnishes are used. Some meat and fowl dishes are disguised with gravies and sauces. There is much use of canned fruit and jellied desserts. This is strictly banquet catering, with all its standardization and production cooking. For casual meals, there's the 280-seat, self-serve Buffet Triana.

ENTERTAINMENT. Gran Teatro Mirasierra is the venue for high energy, high volume shows. Almost every lounge/bar onboard has live bands and musical units, so there's always plenty of live music in the evening.

SPA/FITNESS. The Indulgence Spa is located on the ship's uppermost deck. It has a gymnasium with muscle-pumping equipment, men's and women's changing rooms, and saunas. The beauty salon is elsewhere. Massages, facials, pedicures, and beauty treatments cost extra.

GRAND PRINCESS
★★★+

A MULTI-CHOICE LARGE RESORT SHIP FOR INFORMAL FAMILY CRUISING

Size:	Large Resort Ship	Passenger/Crew Ratio (lower beds):	2.3
Tonnage:	108,806	Cabins (total):	1,300
Cruise Line:	Princess Cruises	Size Range (sq ft/m):	161.4–764.2/15.0–71.0
Former Names:	none	Cabins (for one person):	0
Builder:	Fincantieri (Italy)	Cabins with balcony:	710
Entered Service:	May 1998	Cabins (wheelchair accessible):	28
Length (ft/m):	951.4/290.0	Wheelchair accessibility:	Best
Beam (ft/m):	118.1/36.0	Elevators:	14
Propulsion/Propellers:	diesel-electric (42,000kW)/2	Casino (gaming tables):	Yes
Passenger Decks:	13	Swimming Pools:	3
Total Crew:	1,100	Self-Service Launderette:	Yes
Passengers (lower beds):	2,600	Library:	Yes
Passenger Space Ratio (lower beds):	41.8	Onboard currency:	US$

THE SHIP. *Grand Princess* was first in a series of *Grand*-class ships, whose interior design and configuration evolved with each new ship in the series. Now looking quite tired in places (it's almost 20 years old), it has a flared dolphin-like bow and a galleon-like transom stern. There is a sheltered faux teak promenade deck – it's actually painted steel – which almost wraps around, and a walkway that goes to the enclosed, protected bow.

Unlike the outside decks, there is plenty of space inside the ship and a decent array of public rooms, with some 'intimate' (this being a relative word) spaces. The decor is attractive, with lots of earth tones.

Four areas center on swimming pools, which have various beach-like surroundings; one 'lap' pool has a pumped 'current' to swim against. One pool is two decks high and can be covered by a retractable glass dome.

Facilities include a Piazza Atrium (a good place to sit, watch, and meet others), with an integral International Café, Vines wine bar (including tapas and sushi items and wines for purchase); and Leaves Tea Lounge and Library. There's a Wedding Chapel with a web-cam to relay ceremonies via the Internet – the ship's captain can legally marry US citizens, due to the ship's Bermuda registry.

A motion-based 'virtual reality' room has enclosed motion-based rides. There is a library/computer room, and a separate card room. Youngsters

BERLITZ'S RATINGS	Possible	Achieved
Ship	500	332
Accommodation	200	129
Food	400	247
Service	400	263
Entertainment	100	74
Cruise Experience	400	270

OVERALL SCORE 1315 points out of 2000

have a two-deck-high playroom, teen room, and trained counselors. Gamblers should enjoy the large casino, with gaming tables and over 260 slot machines. A wood-paneled Wheelhouse Bar is decorated with memorabilia and ship models tracing part of the history of sister company P&O.

Gratuities are automatically charged to your account, and tips for children are at the same rate. If you want to pay less than the automatic rate, you need to go to the reception desk.

Passenger niggles include the user-unfriendly automated telephone system, the small cabin towels, the extra cost for items such as ice cream, and the (coins-needed) charge for the washers and dryers in self-service launderettes.

Overall, however, Princess Cruises delivers a consistently fine, comfortable, well-packaged product, always with a good degree of style, at a competitive price.

ACCOMMODATION. There are six types of cabins and configurations, from the smallest interior cabin(no view) to the largest (the Grand Suite), in a bewildering choice of price categories. Many balcony cabins overhang the ship's lower hull section.

There are two family suites, consisting of two suites with an interconnecting door, plus a large balcony. They can sleep up to 10 (if at least four are children), or up to eight adults.

Most outside cabins on Emerald Deck have views obstructed by lifeboats. Sadly, there are no cabins for solo travelers. Your name is placed outside your suite or cabin – making it simple for delivery service personnel but compromising privacy. Some 609 cabins can accommodate a third and fourth person in upper berths – but in such cabins, the lower beds cannot then be pushed together to make a queen-size one.

Perhaps the least desirable balcony cabins are eight located forward on Emerald Deck (E101–121), whose balconies do not extend to the side of the ship, so they can be passed by walkers and gawkers on the adjacent Upper Promenade walkway. Passengers occupying some the most expensive suites aft may experience some vibration during certain ship maneuvers.

Cabin attendants have many cabins to look after (typically 20), which cannot translate to fine personal service.

DINING. There are three main dining rooms, each with its own galley: Botticelli (504 seats), Da Vinci (486), and Michelangelo (486). There are two seatings in one restaurant; the others have 'Anytime Dining' where you choose when, and with whom, you want to eat. All three split into multi-tier sections in a non-symmetrical design. Four elevators go to Fiesta Deck for the Botticelli and Da Vinci restaurants, but only two go to Plaza Deck 5 for Michelangelo – this can cause long waits at peak times, especially for wheelchair users.

Although portions are generous, the food and its presentation are disappointing, and standardized. Fish is often disguised by crumb or batter coatings, the choice of fresh green vegetables is limited, and few garnishes are used. But, this is big-ship banquet catering, with all its attendant standardization and cooking in batches. Pasta dishes are acceptable (though voluminous), typically served by section

headwaiters, who may also make 'something special just for you' – in search of favorable comments and gratuities. If you like desserts, order a sundae at dinner (most other items are just so-so). Other, extra-cost, reservations required dining venues include Sabatini's, a reservations-required Italian eatery, with colorful tiled Mediterranean-style decor. It features Italian-style pizzas and pasta with a variety of sauces, and Italian-style entrées (mains).

Crown Grill steakhouse – for premium American steaks and seafood, with plenty of space around diners' tables.

A poolside burger grill and a pizza bar (no charge) are additional eateries for casual bites. Extra charges apply if you order items to eat at the coffee bar/ patisserie, or the caviar/ Champagne bar.

Other casual eats can be taken in the self-serve Horizon Court buffet – open almost around the clock. Note that plastic plates are used (there are no trays).

ENTERTAINMENT. The 748-seat Princess Theater spans two decks and has comfortable seating on both main and balcony levels. Princess Cruises has long been known and liked for its traditional colourful Hollywood-style (rather than Vegas-style) production shows.

The Vista Lounge, a second entertainment lounge, presents cabaret acts by night, and lectures by day. Explorers, a third lounge, can also host cabaret acts and dance bands. Just aft of the funnel is the One5 nightclub.

SPA/FITNESS. The Lotus Spa complex surrounds one of the swimming pools at the forward end. It comprises a large gymnasium with all the usual equipment, an aerobics room, sauna and steam rooms, salon, ocean-view treatment rooms, and a relaxation area. It is operated by Steiner Leisure.

GRANDE MARINER
★★

A US COASTAL CRUISE SHIP WITH BASIC FOOD AND FEW FACILITIES

Size:	Boutique Ship	Passenger/Crew Ratio (lower beds):	5.8
Tonnage:	99	Cabins (total):	50
Cruise Line:	Blount Small Ship Adventures	Size Range (sq ft/m):	72.0–96.0/6.6–8.9
Former Names:	none	Cabins (for one person):	9
Builder:	Blount Industries (USA)	Cabins with balcony:	0
Entered Service:	Jun 1998	Cabins (wheelchair accessible):	0
Length (ft/m):	183.0/55.7	Wheelchair accessibility:	None
Beam (ft/m):	40.0/12.1	Elevators:	0
Propulsion/Propellers:	diesel (1,044kW)/2	Casino (gaming tables):	No
Passenger Decks:	3	Swimming Pools:	0
Total Crew:	17	Self-Service Launderette:	No
Passengers (lower beds):	91	Library:	Yes
Passenger Space Ratio (lower beds):	0.99	Onboard currency:	US$

THE SHIP. *Grande Mariner* is the second of two almost identical Blount-built vessels. Like sister ship *Grande Caribe* (not featured in *Cruising and Cruise Ships 2018*), it has stabilizers. During emergency drill, passengers are taught how to use fire extinguishers – a useful piece of training.

The ship's shallow draft enables it to cruise into off-the-beaten-path destinations well out of reach of larger ships. It also has a retractable navigation bridge, which is practical for those low bridges along inland waterways. An underwater video camera allows passengers, while seated in comfort in the lounge, to view on large-screen TV monitors what a scuba diver might see underneath the ship. Underwater lights, which attract fish and other marine life, are fitted. There are two 24-passenger launches, one of which is a glass-bottomed boat, and snorkeling equipment.

There is one lounge/bar, located on a different deck to the dining room. The style is casual – no jackets or ties. An electric stairway chairlift is provided for those with restricted mobility.

This pocket-sized ship is for mature-age couples and solo travelers who enjoy nature and wildlife up close, who wouldn't dream of cruising in the mainstream sense aboard large ships, and who don't necessarily require a high standard of service. It's a basic, no-glitz vessel, providing an all-American cruise experience, albeit at a high price. It is not one for children. Gratuities (high at the suggested $10–15

BERLITZ'S RATINGS	Possible	Achieved
Ship	500	160
Accommodation	200	67
Food	400	190
Service	400	196
Entertainment	100	35
Cruise Experience	400	192

OVERALL SCORE 840 points out of 2000

per person, per day) are pooled and shared by all the staff.

ACCOMMODATION. The cabins are all extremely small, relatively utilitarian units, with very little closet space but just enough drawers. The very small bathrooms have vacuum toilets. The twin beds convert to a queen-size bed, with good storage space underneath. There is no room service menu, and only soap is supplied – bring your own toiletries. Each cabin has its own air conditioner. Refreshingly, there are no cabin keys. Be prepared for noise from the generators.

DINING. The dining room seats all passengers in one open seating, so you eat with whomever you wish, making new friends each day – it is also good for small groups. The tables convert to card tables for use between meals. Passengers should bring their own alcohol, as the company doesn't sell it aboard ship. There is an effervescent, young American team of wait staff, although there is little finesse.

A hand-held bell is rung to summon passengers to the dining room.

ENTERTAINMENT. There is no formal entertainment, so conversation with fellow passengers in the ship's lounge/bar becomes the diversion each evening. If that isn't appealing, take a good book.

SPA/FITNESS. There are no facilities.

GRANDEUR OF THE SEAS
★★★+

A FAMILY-FRIENDLY, CASUAL MID-SIZE SHIP WITH MULTIPLE-CHOICE DINING

Size:	Mid-size Ship	Passenger/Crew Ratio (lower beds):	2.5
Tonnage:	73,817	Cabins (total):	975
Cruise Line:	Royal Caribbean International	Size Range (sq ft/m):	158.2–1,267.0/14.7–117.7
Former Names:	none	Cabins (for one person):	0
Builder:	Kvaerner Masa-Yards (Finland)	Cabins with balcony:	212
Entered Service:	Dec 1996	Cabins (wheelchair accessible):	14
Length (ft/m):	916.0/279.6	Wheelchair accessibility:	Good
Beam (ft/m):	105.6/32.2	Elevators:	9
Propulsion/Propellers:	diesel-electric (50,400kW)/2	Casino (gaming tables):	Yes
Passenger Decks:	11	Swimming Pools:	2 (1 w/ sliding glass dome)
Total Crew:	760	Self-Service Launderette:	No
Passengers (lower beds):	1,950	Library:	Yes
Passenger Space Ratio (lower beds):	37.8	Onboard currency:	US$

THE SHIP. *Grandeur of the Seas* (a *Vision-class ship*) has an attractive shape, with a single funnel located well aft – almost a throwback to some ship designs used in the 1950s – and a nicely rounded stern. A Viking Crown Lounge, a trademark of former Royal Caribbean International (RCI) ships, sits between the funnel and mast at the top of the atrium lobby, and overlooks the forward section of the swimming pool deck, with access provided from stairway off the central atrium. This, together with the forward mast, provides three distinct focal points of the ship's exterior profile. There is a walk-around promenade deck outdoors, but there are no cushioned pads for the tacky plastic sunloungers.

Grandeur of the Seas is best suited to couples and families with children that want to have multiple dining choices for more convenience.

The ship features a varied collection of artworks including several sculptures, principally by British artists, with classical music, ballet, and theater themes. Huge murals of opera scenes adorn several stairways.

A seven-deck high atrium lobby, called the Centrum, is the social focal point within the ship. On its various levels it houses an R Bar (for some creative cocktails), several passenger-service counters, an art gallery, Casino Royale (for table gaming and slot machines – and viewing the theatrical glass-covered underfloor exhibits), the popular Schooner

BERLITZ'S RATINGS		
	Possible	Achieved
Ship	500	337
Accommodation	200	129
Food	400	239
Service	400	259
Entertainment	100	75
Cruise Experience	400	260

OVERALL SCORE 1299 points out of 2000

Bar, with its nautical-theme decor and maritime art, Café Lattetudes (for coffee), and a library. Aerial entertainment happens in the Centrum, too.

There is a good use of tropical plants throughout the public rooms, which helps counteract the otherwise rather plain and clinical pastel wall colors.

Niggles include charges for shuttle buses in many ports of call; the high cost of bottled water; and receipts that provide an extra line 'for additional gratuity,' when a gratuity has already been added.

ACCOMMODATION. There are numerous price grades, including several grades of suites, the largest of which is the Royal Suite. Many cabins are of the same, or similar, size, well appointed, and with pleasing decor, best described as Scandinavian Modern, with wood and color accenting. There are, however, a huge number of interior cabins (no view).

All cabins have twin beds that convert to a queen-size one, decent closet space for a week-long cruise, and a good amount of drawer space, although under-bed storage space is not good for large suitcases. Bathrooms have nine mirrors. Plastic buckets are provided for Champagne or wine and are really tacky; a hairdryer is also provided.

Room service offers only a basic menu, and no hot items for breakfast.

DINING. The 1,171-seat Great Gatsby Dining Room is spread over two decks, with both levels connected by a grand, sweeping staircase. When you book, choose one of the two seatings for dinner or 'My Time Dining' – so you can eat when you want, during dining room hours. A neat Champagne terrace bar sits forward of the lower level of the two-deck-high dining room.

Menu descriptions make the food sound good, but this is really about catering on a large scale. The selection of breads, rolls, fruit, and cheese is poor. Overall, meals are rather hit and miss – in fact it's unmemorable. Also, lobster or a decent filet mignon (steak) cost extra.

The large (790-seat), glass-walled Windjammer Café is a casual, eatery for self-serve breakfast, lunch and dinner buffet items. Note that there are no cups and saucers for tea – only paper cups or plastic mugs, and only plastic plates are provided (so hot food doesn't stay hot long).

For decent (extra-cost) Seattle's Best espressos/cappuccinos, head for Cafe Latte-tudes on Deck 6.

Other eateries (some at extra cost) include: Giovanni's Table, an Italian trattoria (a service charge applies); Izumi (located in a delightful spot just forward of the funnel) for pan-Asian cuisine including hot-rock cooking (service charge and à la carte menu pricing apply); Park Café outdoor market; Chops Grille steakhouse; and Chef's Table, an exclusive hosted event (it is located on the starboard side aft, within the dining room) with a five-course, wine-paired menu (worth it for celebrating a birthday or special event, perhaps).

ENTERTAINMENT. The 875-seat Palladium Theater is the main showlounge. Located at the forward part of the ship, it is used for big production shows. It has excellent sight lines from 98 percent of the seats.

Another showlounge, the 575-seat South Pacific Lounge, is used for smaller shows and cabaret acts, including smutty late-night adult-only comedy.

SPA/FITNESS. The Vitality at Sea spa is aft of the funnel and spans two decks. Facilities include a gymnasium with all the latest muscle-pumping exercise machines, aerobics exercise room, sauna and steam rooms, a beauty salon, and a clutch of private massage/body treatment rooms. The spa is staffed and operated by specialist Steiner Leisure.

There's also a rock-climbing wall with several separate climbing tracks located outdoors at the aft end of the funnel, just behind the spa. A jogging track (outside on Deck 10) takes you around most of the ship.

HAMBURG
★★★

THIS SMALL SHIP IS FOR PORT-INTENSIVE CRUISING FOR GERMAN-SPEAKERS

Size:	Small Ship	Passenger/Crew Ratio (lower beds):	2.4
Tonnage:	14,903	Cabins (total):	205
Cruise Line:	Plantours Cruises	Size Range (sq ft/m):	139.9–339.0/13.0–31.5
Former Names:	*Columbus*	Cabins (for one person):	2
Builder:	MTW Schiffswerft (Germany)	Cabins with balcony:	2
Entered Service:	Jul 1997/Jun 2012	Cabins (wheelchair accessible):	2
Length (ft/m):	472.8/144.1	Wheelchair accessibility:	Fair
Beam (ft/m):	70.5/21.5	Elevators:	2
Propulsion/Propellers:	diesel (10,560kW)/2	Casino (gaming tables):	No
Passenger Decks:	6	Swimming Pools:	1
Total Crew:	170	Self-Service Launderette:	No
Passengers (lower beds):	408	Library:	Yes
Passenger Space Ratio (lower beds):	36.5	Onboard currency:	Euros

THE SHIP. *Hamburg* has an ice-strengthened hull, useful for cold-weather cruise areas. While it's a comfortable, trendy ship, the swimming pool is small – it's really a 'plunge' pool – as is the open deck space, and there is no walk-around promenade deck outdoors.

The delightful Palm Garden doubles as an observation lounge and has four Internet-connect computers. Shipwide Wi-Fi is also available. The fit and finish of the interiors is a little utilitarian.

This ship will appeal to youthful-minded German-speaking couples and solo travelers seeking good value for money on a first cruise, aboard a ship with contemporary, comfortable, and unpretentious surroundings, and good itineraries, at a very modest price.

ACCOMMODATION. The standard cabins are really small. All but 10 cabins have lower berths. Except for two forward-facing suites, there are only two balcony cabins, and no room service except for accommodation designated as suites. There are several single-occupancy cabins. Note that 16 cabins on Deck 4 have lifeboat-obstructed views. The cabin decor is bright and upbeat, and there's a good amount of closet and shelf space. All cabins have a mini-bar/refrigerator, flat-screen TV, personal safe, and hairdryer.

There are eight suites, each at least double the size of a standard cabin and each with a curtained partition between its lounge and sleeping areas. Two

BERLITZ'S RATINGS		
	Possible	Achieved
Ship	500	313
Accommodation	200	127
Food	400	240
Service	400	255
Entertainment	100	57
Cruise Experience	400	244
OVERALL SCORE 1236 points out of 2000		

suites at the bows each have a narrow private verandah, a bedroom and lounge area separated by a curtain, two TV sets, and an excellent amount of storage space.

DINING. There's one large main dining room, at the stern, with large ocean-view windows on three sides. All passengers can be seated in a single seating, at assigned tables, although breakfast is open seating. There are just two tables for two, but other tables can accommodate up to 16. The unstuffy cuisine is good, though the choice is small. Themed dinners make dining a treat. Breakfast and lunch can also be taken in the bright, but casual, setting of the self-serve Palm Garden, which doubles as a comfortable observation lounge. Light dinners can also be taken there; a small dance floor adds another dimension.

ENTERTAINMENT. The showlounge is a single-level H-shaped room, with banquette and individual seating in tub chairs, and a bar, which is located at the back of the room. Because the apron stage is in the center of the room, the sight lines from many seats aren't good.

SPA/FITNESS. A fitness room is located forward on the uppermost deck of the ship. There's a sauna on the lowest passenger deck, next to the beauty salon. Massage and facial treatments are available.

HANSEATIC
★★★★★

A DELIGHTFUL SMALL AND STYLISH EXPEDITION SHIP FOR DISCOVERY CRUISES

Size:	Boutique Ship	Passenger/Crew Ratio (lower beds):	1.5
Tonnage:	8,378	Cabins (total):	92
Cruise Line:	Hapag-Lloyd Expedition Cruises	Size Range (sq ft/m):	231.4–470.3/21.5–43.7
Former Names:	Society Adventurer	Cabins (for one person):	0
Builder:	Rauma Yards (Finland)	Cabins with balcony:	0
Entered Service:	Mar 1993	Cabins (wheelchair accessible):	2
Length (ft/m):	402.9/122.8	Wheelchair accessibility:	None
Beam (ft/m):	59.1/18.0	Elevators:	2
Propulsion/Propellers:	diesel (5,880kW)/2	Casino (gaming tables):	0
Passenger Decks:	7	Swimming Pools:	1
Total Crew:	122	Self-Service Launderette:	No
Passengers (lower beds):	184	Library:	Yes
Passenger Space Ratio (lower beds):	45.5	Onboard currency:	Euros

THE SHIP. *Hanseatic*, operated by Hapag-Lloyd Expedition Cruises, was designed for worldwide expedition-style cruises in contemporary, but quite luxurious, surroundings. It is extremely environmentally friendly, and is one of few ships that allow you to tour the engine room. It has a fully enclosed bridge and an ice-hardened hull with the highest passenger vessel ice classification, plus a helicopter pad and the very latest in high-tech navigation equipment.

A fleet of 14 Zodiac inflatable craft (with environmentally friendy electric motors), each named for a famous explorer, is used for in-depth shore landings; one is named David Fletcher, after the expedition leader who spent 16 years working with the British Antarctic Expedition – he loves being aboard *Hanseatic*. These craft provide the ship with tremendous flexibility in itineraries, with excellent possibilities for up-close wildlife viewing in natural habitats. Rubber boots, parkas, boot-washing stations, and storage rooms are provided. For warmer climes, a Bike Box, with 10 bicycles for passenger use at no charge, is offloaded in each port the ship is alongside, where possible.

Inside, the ship is equipped with fine-quality luxury fittings and soft furnishings, and exudes a microclimate of good taste. There is a choice of several public rooms – most located aft, with accommodation forward. All are well furnished and decorated, and all have high ceilings, which help to make the ship feel much larger than its actual size. The library/observation lounge provides a good selection of hardback books in English and German, including many geographical, travel, wildlife, and archaeology titles; it has a sunken bar, and a warm, inviting atmosphere, and two Internet-access computer stations. A large lecture hall, with excellent audio-visual facilities, on a lower deck, can accommodate almost all passengers.

The passenger count is generally kept to about 150, which means plenty of comfort, no lines, and lots of space. In passageways and suites/cabins, 400 large, framed, black-and-white photographs depict wildlife and expedition experiences. Bouillon is always served at 11am.

Safety is paramount, particularly in Antarctica, and here the ship excels with professionalism, pride, and skilled seamanship. Most of each day is taken up with being ashore, and evenings consist mainly of dinner and daily recaps. Lectures, briefings, and the amount of information provided about the itinerary, ports of call, and expedition landings are excellent. Well-qualified lecturers and naturalists accompany each cruise, and a discreet crew and service staff are hallmarks of this ship.

Hanseatic operates in two languages, English and German, though many staff members speak several languages; the ship caters well to both sets of passengers. All port taxes, insurance, staff gratuities, and Zodiac trips are included. A relaxed ambience and informal dress code prevail.

BERLITZ'S RATINGS

	Possible	Achieved
Ship	500	421
Accommodation	200	172
Food	400	348
Service	400	344
Entertainment	100	85
Cruise Experience	400	346

OVERALL SCORE 1716 points out of 2000

Hapag-Lloyd publishes its own excellent handbooks (in both English and German) on expedition regions such as the Arctic, Antarctica, Amazonia, and the South Sea Islands, as well as exclusive maps.

All in all, *Hanseatic* provides destination-intensive, nature cruises and expeditions in elegant but unstuffy surroundings at a suitably handsome price that includes good food and service. In fact it really is all about seeing and experiencing nature – in comfort – and safety. It is at its best in the Arctic and Antarctic, but passengers should be wary of the difficult conditions for shore landings in these areas.

There are few negatives. The ship is marketed mainly to German and English speakers, so other nationalities may find it hard to integrate.

ACCOMMODATION. There are no bad cabins, and accommodation is priced in seven grades. The all-outside cabins, located in the forward section, are large and very well equipped, and include a separate lounge area next to a large picture window (which has a pull-down blackout blind as well as curtains).

All furniture is in warm woods such as beech, and everything has rounded edges. Wood trim accents the ceiling perimeter, and acts as a divider between bed and lounge areas. Each cabin has a minibar, flat-screen interactive TV with Internet access, when available, and wireless keyboard. A complete infotainment system includes movies and audio tracks on demand at no extra charge. There's a separate bedside three-channel radio, two locking drawers, a retro alarm clock, and plenty of closet and drawer space, as well as two separate cupboards and hooks for all-weather outerwear. One useful feature of all cabins is a blue night/safety light, nicely hidden in each bathroom. A privacy curtain between the cabin door and the sleeping area of the cabin would be useful – you can be seen from the hallway when the cabin door is opened.

All cabin bathrooms have a large shower enclosure with curved glass wall, toiletries cabinets, hairdryer, and bathrobe. There are only two types of cabins; 34 have double beds, others have twin beds. The bath-size towels are large, bed linens and pillowcases are 100 percent cotton, and individual cotton-filled duvets are provided. Laundry, dry cleaning, and pressing services are available.

Suites and cabins on Bridge Deck have impeccable butler service and in-cabin dining privileges, plus stationery and a larger flat-screen TV. Free soft drinks in the refrigerator are replenished daily, but all liquor costs extra. Bulgari and Crabtree & Evelyn bathroom products are provided.

DINING. The 186-seat Marco Polo restaurant is elegant, warm, and welcoming, with large picture windows on two sides as well as aft. There is one seating for dinner, and open seating for breakfast and lunch, although many passengers like to be seated at their 'regular' table. On embarkation day, waiters introduce themselves after the meal, so hungry passengers won't be delayed by small talk.

The cuisine and service are absolutely first-rate, but they are slightly more informal than, for example, aboard the larger *Europa*, which is at or close to the same price level. Top-quality ingredients are always used, and most items are bought fresh when available. In some ports, passengers can go shopping with the chef to source local, regional ingredients and fresh fish.

The meals are very creative and nicely presented, each being appealing to the eye as well as to the palate. There is always an outstanding selection of breads, cheeses, desserts, and pastry items. In the Arctic or Antarctic, table setups are often minimal, due to possible movement of the ship – stabilizers can't be used in much of the Antarctic – so cutlery is provided and changed for each course. Three types of sugar are presented when coffee or tea is ordered – it should never be placed on the table during meal service.

Other dining. An alternative dining spot is the Bistro Lemaire, with 74 seats and leather-topped tables indoors, as well as copious seating at outdoor tables. An informal, open-seating, self-serve (or waiter service) buffet-style eatery by day, it changes into a second dining room at night, with themed dinners and barbeques featuring region-specific food. Reservations are required – you make them in the morning of the day you want to dine there – but there is no extra charge and no tipping.

The Bistro features several different breakfast themes: the well-named Zodiac breakfast (quick and easy before Zodiac landing); Small Hanseatic Breakfast; Big Hanseatic Breakfast; Gourmet Breakfast; and Healthy Breakfast. Each cruise also includes a full Viennese teatime, as well as a daily teatime with a selection of cakes, pastries, and finger sandwiches befitting a Viennese coffeehouse.

ENTERTAINMENT. There is no showlounge as such, although there is a lecture room. Entertainment is certainly not a priority aboard this ship, since the itinerary and destinations are the main show. There is no formal entertainment – except on some summer cruises, when a small classical music ensemble might be on board – nor does the ship normally carry a band.

SPA/FITNESS. The spa facilities include a decent-size gymnasium (with up-to-date cardio-vascular and muscle-toning equipment, treadmills, and exercycles) and sauna, all located forward on the Sun Deck in an area that also includes a solarium and hot tub. There's also a cosmetics/make-up room. Massage is available in a rather clinical room within the medical facility, on a lower deck.

HARMONY OF THE SEAS
★★★★

THIS ULTRA-LARGE RESORT SHIP IS IDEAL FOR HIGH-ENERGY FAMILIES

Size:	Large Resort Ship	Passenger/Crew Ratio (lower beds):	2.2
Tonnage:	226,693	Cabins (total):	2,747
Cruise Line:	Royal Caribbean International	Size Range (sq ft/m):	96.8–2,389.6/9.0–222.0
Former Names:	none	Cabins (for one person):	15
Builder:	STX France (France)	Cabins with balcony:	2,000
Entered Service:	May 2016	Cabins (wheelchair accessible):	46
Length (ft/m):	1,187.9/362.1	Wheelchair accessibility:	Best
Beam (ft/m):	234.5/71.5	Elevators:	24
Propulsion/Propellers:	diesel-electric/3 pods	Casino (gaming tables):	Yes
	(2 azimuthing, 1 fixed)	Swimming Pools:	3
Passenger Decks:	16	Self-Service Launderette:	No
Total Crew:	2,394	Library:	Yes
Passengers (lower beds):	5,496	Onboard currency:	US$
Passenger Space Ratio (lower beds):	41.3		

THE SHIP. Longer by 7ft (2.1m) than the first two *Oasis*-class ships (*Allure of the Seas* and *Oasis of the Seas*, which, when built, were the largest cruise ships in the world), at time of printing Harmony of the Seas was still officially the largest resort ship in the world – although it was due to be superseded from April 2018 by *Symphony of the Seas*. It is absolutely stunning for families with children. It is a benchmark for self-contained resorts with propellers (and 20 percent more efficient than its two sister ships, with 38 more cabins). No matter what your entertainment and activity interests are, this ship should really turn you on – and then some. Neat fact: there are four bow thrusters, each with more power than 7 Ferraris.

It includes some of the high-tech whiz-kid gismos and gadgets, and stimulating features that have become standard aboard new ships. While the uppermost exterior decks have quite a lot of space, there's little room for sunbathing quietly or reading a book on deck (unless you occupy suite-grade accommodation, in which case there is the adults-only Suite Sundeck, located forward). Much of the open deck space is taken up by Splashaway Bay – a water park that includes 'The Perfect Storm,' mind-numbing waterslides (called The Abyss – this is a scream-inducing 13-second ride through 10 decks that you won't forget in a hurry), fountains, water cannons, and sports activities. Sadly, there's not a hint of teak decking or wood-topped railings.

BERLITZ'S RATINGS

	Possible	Achieved
Ship	500	403
Accommodation	200	140
Food	400	234
Service	400	286
Entertainment	100	87
Cruise Experience	400	286

OVERALL SCORE 1436 points out of 2000

As aboard the *Oasis*-class ships, the inner 'city' is divided into seven neighborhoods: Central Park (with its Rising Tide Bar, Dazzles, a Trellis Bar, Chops Grille, and 150 Central Park, plus 10,587 plants and 52 real trees); The Boardwalk (for Starbucks, the Boardwalk Dog House, Johnny Rockets, Sabor (for Mexican food), and a children's carousel); the Royal Promenade (where you'll find the Boot and Bonnet Pub, Sorrento's, Boleros, and the Bionic Bar – with bartenders you can't talk to, although you can order a wide variety of cocktails from the brands and ingredients provided... and you'll still have to tip); the Pool and Sports Zone; Entertainment Place; Youth Zone; plus a Vitality at Sea Spa and Fitness Center. The most popular strolling areas are the Boardwalk and Central Park, both open to the air, and the indoor Royal Promenade (look out for the huge 'head').

In all, there are around three dozen bars/lounges, and more than 20 restaurants, cafés, and other eateries to experience, although some are dedicated exclusively to Pinnacle members, certain suite accommodation grades, and SeaPass gold card holders. It's all part of the 'pay more, get more' system of class distinction, like anywhere else. There's also a large casino, with gaming tables (plus a player's club and poker room) and slot machines.

WOWbands (you wear them on your wrist), using RFID technology, can provide access to your accommodation (a 'normal' key card is also provided) and make on-board reservations and purchases easy. Super-high-speed Internet enables video streaming, Skyping, and social-media sharing (at a hefty price).

The wow factor aboard this ship come in the entertainment (particularly the big theater shows), and not just the waterslides and sports facilities, which are really good for kids of any age) rather than the food. Book any of the extra-cost dining venues as soon as possible, because availability is limited.

ACCOMMODATION. From the smallest cabin (for solo occupancy) to the largest (Presidential Suite), there is a wide range of cabins and larger suites to suit all tastes, including Royal Family Suites, Loft Suites, and family cabins. Choosing the right one for your needs is not easy! Some 15 Studio category cabins are designed for solo occupancy (new for RCI), while over 690 have a third/fourth bed – good for families with small children. Some 76 Interior cabins have virtual balconies (this feature can be turned off). All cabins have a mini-bar.

On the down side, the cabin-numbering system is hard to get used to. Also, cabin doors open outwards (towards you), as in many European hotels. In many lower grade rooms, closet access is awkward, as most are dimensionally challenged and quite tight – but just manageable for a week.

All suite-class accommodation and balcony cabins have floor-to-ceiling sliding glass doors, and different (better) amenities than standard class, and the six most expensive suite grades have access to a private sunning deck and can eat in the Coastal Kitchen restaurant.

CUISINE. Opus, the cavernous main restaurant, spans decks 3 to 5 and is in three sections: Silk, The Grande, and American Icon Grill. It operates in two seatings (early or late) for dinner (or you can choose 'My Time Dining' and eat at your preferred time). There are tables of all sizes, including some for family reunions.

The meals are of a very acceptable standard for such a large ship, although this is banquet-style food featuring pre-decided portions for meat and fish. There are few green vegetables, and lots of potato – often used as a base for main courses. The selection of bread, cheese, and ripe fruit could be better. Overall, it's decent, though.

Other free dining/eating venue options include:

Central Park Café – for deli-style sandwiches, salad items, paninis, crêpes, and hearty soups.

Windjammer Marketplace is an extremely large self-serve casual food court/buffet-style eatery, with several different sections featuring different food types, salad bar, etc. It can be extremely crowded due to the number of passengers carried, but the layout of the various food islands and sections is good.

Other snacking spots include: Boardwalk Dog House, Rita's Cantina (quasi-Mexican fare), Starbucks, Solarium Bistro, and Vitality Café.

The following restaurants are at extra cost:

150 Central Park – for the best, most exclusive, cooked-to-order cuisine.

Chops Grille – a 'signature' steakhouse featuring large, premium-quality steaks and other grilled food items (open for dinner, reservations required).

Izumi Hibachi and Sushi – for Japanese-style dishes.

Jamie's Italian – a tablecloth-free Euro-Italian bistro-style trattoria with rustic decor; open for lunch and dinner (reservations are required, and there's a cover charge for dinner).

Johnny Rockets (diner-style – for burgers and ice cream shakes).

Sabor Taqueria – for Mexican-style cantina food.

Vintages – a nice, sociable wine bar with cheese and tapas (at à la carte prices).

Wonderland – a funky two-deck-high venue (with decor and seating inspired by Alice in Wonderland) for quirky small-portion molecular cuisine (fussy, but lacking substance).

ENTERTAINMENT. The 1,380-seat Royal Theater (main showlounge) spans three decks. Reservations for shows can be made up to three months ahead (there is no charge). The hit musical *Grease* is the star, together with *Columbus, The Musical* (an RCI original).

The Ice Skating Rink (on Deck 4) has seats for about 900, and the shows are dazzlingly top-notch.

Adult-only (smutty) comedy is featured in 'The Attic Comedy Club.'

A 750-seat Aqua Theater, located outside at the ship's stern with a 6,000-sq-ft (557-sq-m) stage, is a stunning combination show theatre, sound stage, and events space (some great viewing places can be found high in the aft wings of the ship on both sides). The stern has some 'overhang,' to accommodate the venue.

There's also a delightful, intimate venue called Jazz on 4 (because it's on Deck 4) for (relatively) quiet evenings with live jazz ensembles.

SPA/FITNESS. Set low down forward on decks 5 and 6, the Steiner Leisure-operated Vitality at Sea Spa includes a large fitness center (cardio and resistance equipment) and beauty salon, while an extra-cost Thermal Suite pass allows you access to men's and women's saunas, steam rooms, and heated, tiled relaxation loungers, plus a 60-seat Vitality Café for extra-cost 'health' drinks and snacks.

Other highlights include two Flowriders for body surfing, a zipline that careers over The Boardwalk (and its inner balcony cabins), and three waterslides that career over Central Park. There's also a Sports Pool, Harmony Dunes (mini-golf), a Sports Court, two rock-climbing walls (aft), and an ice skating rink.

HEBRIDEAN PRINCESS
★★★★+

THIS CHARMING ENGLISH COUNTRY INN AFLOAT IS THE REAL MCCOY

Size:	Boutique Ship
Tonnage:	2,112
Cruise Line:	Hebridean Island Cruises
Former Names:	*Columba*
Builder:	Hall Russell (Scotland)
Entered Service:	1964/May 1989
Length (ft/m):	235.0/71.6
Beam (ft/m):	46.0/14.0
Propulsion/Propellers:	diesel (1,790kW)/2
Passenger Decks:	5
Total Crew:	38
Passengers (lower beds):	50
Passenger Space Ratio (lower beds):	42.2
Passenger/Crew Ratio (lower beds):	1.3
Cabins (total):	30
Size Range (sq ft/m):	144.0–340.0/13.4–31.6
Cabins (for one person):	10
Cabins with balcony:	4
Cabins (wheelchair accessible):	0
Wheelchair accessibility:	None
Elevators:	0
Casino (gaming tables):	No
Swimming Pools:	0
Self-Service Launderette:	No
Library:	Yes
Onboard currency:	UK£

THE SHIP. Small and old can be chic and comfortable. *Hebridean Princess*, originally one of three Scottish ferries built for David MacBrayne Ltd – although actually then owned by the British government – was skillfully converted into a gem of a cruise ship in order to operate island-hopping itineraries in Scotland, together with the occasional jaunt to Norway and an occasional sailing around the UK coast. It was renamed in 1989 by the Duchess of York, and underwent a facelift in 2015.

BERLITZ'S RATINGS		
	Possible	Achieved
Ship	500	407
Accommodation	200	169
Food	400	349
Service	400	342
Entertainment	100	84
Cruise Experience	400	318
OVERALL SCORE 1669 points out of 2000		

This little ship has a warm, totally cosseted, traditional Scottish country house ambience and a stately home service that's unobtrusive but always at hand when you need it. It suits mature-age adult couples and solo travelers who enjoy learning about the natural sciences, geography, history, gardening, art, architecture, and enjoy a very small ship with almost no entertainment.

There is an outdoors deck for occasional sunbathing and alfresco meals, as well as a bar where occasional formal cocktail parties are held when weather conditions are right. There is no walk-around promenade deck, although there is an open deck atop ship. The ship carries two Zodiac inflatable runabouts (*Calgary* and *Kiloran*) and two shore tenders (*Sanda* and *Shona*).

Use of the ship's small boats, speedboat, a dozen or so bicycles, and fishing gear are included in the price, as are entrance fees to gardens, castles, other attractions, and the occasional coach tour, depending on the itinerary. The destination-intensive cruises have very creative itineraries, and there's plenty to do, despite the lack of big-ship features. Specialist guides, who give daily talks about the destinations to be visited, accompany all cruises.

What passengers appreciate is the fact that the ship does not have photographers or some of the trappings found aboard larger ships. They also love the fact that there is no bingo, art auctions, or parlor games.

The principal public room inside the ship is the charming Tiree Lounge, which has a real brick-walled inglenook fireplace, plus a very cozy bar with a wide variety of whiskies – the selection of single malts is excellent – and cognacs for connoisseurs. Naturally, the ship specializes in Scottish spirits.

Agatha Christie's Inspector Hercule Poirot would be very much at home here, particularly in the Tiree Lounge. Who needs megaships when you can take a retro-cruise aboard this little gem? Direct bookings are accepted.

Hebridean Princess has UK officers and an excellent Lithuanian service crew; all are discreet and provide unobtrusive service. This little ship remains one of the world's best-kept travel secrets, although Queen Elizabeth II chartered the vessel for a family-only celebration of her 80th birthday in 2006, and again for a family holiday in 2010, which raised its profile.

A roughly polished gem, it is especially popular with single passengers. More than half the passengers are repeaters. Children under nine are not accepted. Despite the shortcomings of the ship itself, it's the food that rates highly.

If you cruise from Oban, you can be met at Glasgow station (or airport) and taken to/from the ship by private motor coach. Passengers are piped aboard at embarkation by a Scottish bagpiper – a neat touch. All drinks (except premium brands, which incur a small charge), soft drinks, and bottled Scottish mineral water are included in the fare, as are gratuities – the company requests that no additional gratuities be given.

Although this vessel is strong, it does have structural limitations and noisy engines that cause some vibration. However, the engines do not run at night because the ship anchors before bedtime, providing soul-renewing tranquility – except for the sound of a single generator. The ship doesn't have an elevator, so anyone with walking disabilities may find it challenging – and there may be several tender ports on each itinerary. It is often cold and very wet in the Scottish highlands and islands, so take plenty of warm clothing for layering.

ACCOMMODATION. All cabins have different names – there are no numbers, and, refreshingly, no door keys, although cabins can be locked from the inside. The older cabins feature delightfully eclectic curtains, sweeping drapes over the beds, and lots of cushions. One third of the cabins were refurbished for 2017, using smart woollen plaid fabric from Mulberry as a base fabric to create what the line calls a 'comfortable contemporary twist,' although the traditional look is still maintained. They come in a wide range of configurations (some with single, some with double, some with twin beds), including four with a private balcony – a private and self-indulgent bonus.

All cabins have a private bathroom with bath or shower. All have a refrigerator, ironing board with iron, trouser press, brass clock, and tea/coffee-making set – there's something magical about getting up in the morning, making fresh tea in your cabin using mineral water and organic teas, and sitting outside on a protected balcony watching Scotland's islands come and go. All seems right with the world.

Cabins have Victorian-style bathroom fittings, many of which are gold-plated, and some have brass cabin portholes or windows that actually open. Three of the newest cabins are outfitted in real Scottish Baronial style. All towels and bathrobes are 100 percent cotton, as is the bed linen. Some cabins in the front of the ship are subject to noise from the anchor being weighed each morning.

Each cabin has Villeroy & Boch china, fairtrade coffee, organic teas, and fresh milk – not the irradiated long-life milk or chemical milk found aboard many ships these days.

DINING. The Columba Restaurant has ocean-view windows and tables laid with crisp white linen and classic white Schönwald china. There is a single seating at assigned tables. Some chairs have armrests, while some do not. While days are casual, dinner means jackets and ties, and formal attire typically twice per cruise.

The cuisine is extremely creative, and at times outstanding – and about the same quality and presentation as *SeaDream I* and *SeaDream II*. Menus offer just one meat choice and one fish dish (a different fish each day), plus an alternative, casual option. Fresh ingredients are sourced and purchased locally, supporting Scottish suppliers – a welcome change from the mass catering of most ships. Although there are no flambé items – the galley has electric, not gas, ranges – what is created is beautifully presented and of the highest standard. Just remember to save space for the desserts.

The breakfast menu is standard each day, although you can always ask for any favorites, and each day there's a specialty item, plus a help-yourself buffet table. Try the porridge and a 'wee dram' (Scotch whisky – single malt, of course) – it's lovely on a cold morning, and it sets you up for the whole day.

Not to be missed is the exclusive theatrical treat 'a tasting o' haggis wi' bashed neeps an champit tatties,' (haggis with mashed swede and potatoes), accompanied by bagpipe music and an 'address to the haggis' ceremony, traditionally given by the captain. Although there is waiter service for most things, there is also a good buffet table display during breakfast and luncheon. Wines are provided at lunch and dinner, although an additional connoisseur's list is available for those seeking fine vintage wines. Highly personal and attentive service from an attentive staff completes the picture.

ENTERTAINMENT. The Tiree Lounge is the equivalent of a main lounge aboard this very small ship. Dinner is the entertainment of the evening. Occasionally, there might be after-dinner drinks, poetry readings, and an occasional storyteller, but little else (passengers neither expect nor need it).

SPA/FITNESS. There is no spa, as the ship is too small. The only concessions to fitness are an exercycle and treadmill.

HEBRIDEAN SKY
★★★★

FOR LIFE ENRICHMENT IN A COMFORTABLE SMALL-SHIP ENVIRONMENT

Size:	Boutique Ship	Passenger Space Ratio (lower beds):	37.5
Tonnage:	4,280	Passenger/Crew Ratio (lower beds):	1.6
Cruise Line:	Noble Caledonia	Cabins (total):	53
Former Names:	Sea	Size Range (sq ft/m):	234.6–353.0/21.8–32.8
Explorer, Corinthian II, Island Sun, Sun, Renaissance VII,		Cabins (for one person):	0
Regina Renaissance, Renaissance VII		Cabins with balcony:	4
Builder:	Nuovi Cantieri Appaunia (Italy)	Cabins (wheelchair accessible):	0
Entered Service:	Dec 1991/May 2016	Wheelchair accessibility:	None
Length (ft/m):	297.2/90.6	Elevators:	1
Beam (ft/m):	50.1/15.3	Casino (gaming tables):	No
Propulsion/Propellers:	diesel (5,000kW)/2	Swimming Pools:	0
Passenger Decks:	5	Self-Service Launderette:	No
Total Crew:	66	Library:	Yes
Passengers (lower beds):	115	Onboard currency:	UK£

THE SHIP. *Hebridean Sky* has a smart profile and handsome styling, with twin flared funnels and a 'ducktail' (or sponson) stern to provide fairly decent stability and seagoing comfort. Purchased by Noble Caledonia in 2014, it has a narrow teak walk-around promenade deck outdoors, and a decent amount of open deck space.

The interior design is elegant, with polished wood-finish paneling throughout. There is also a very small book and video library. Although *Hebridean Sky* is not up to the standard of a Seabourn or Silversea ship, it will provide a good cruise experience at a moderate cost. Gratuities are appreciated but not required.

This intimate little ship is very comfortable and inviting, and operates in regions devoid of large cruise ships. It suits mature adults who like to discover small ports in a relaxed lifestyle combined with good food and service, and itineraries that enable you to get away from it all, but in comfort.

ACCOMMODATION. The cabins are quite spacious and combine highly polished imitation rosewood paneling with lots of mirrors and hand-crafted Italian furniture, lighted walk-in closets, and vanity mirrors. In fact, there are a lot of mirrored surfaces in the decor, as well as just about everything you need, including a TV set and DVD

BERLITZ'S RATINGS

	Possible	Achieved
Ship	500	352
Accommodation	200	156
Food	400	303
Service	400	287
Entertainment	100	60
Cruise Experience	400	271

OVERALL SCORE 1429 points out of 2000

player, a refrigerator, and free soft drinks and bottled water. The beds are fixed, so there's no under-bed storage space.

The bathrooms are extremely compact; they have real teakwood floors and marble vanities, and shower enclosures. None have tubs, not even the Owner's Suite. Cabins with balconies have glass panels topped with a polished wood railing.

DINING. The dining room operates in an open-seating arrangement, so you sit where you like, with whom you like, and at what time you like. It is small but quite smart, with tables for two, four, six, and eight. The meals are self-service, buffet-style cold foods for breakfast and lunch, with hot foods chosen from a table menu and served properly, and sit-down service for dinner. The food quality, choice, and presentation are all very good.

ENTERTAINMENT. There is no formal entertainment in the main lounge, the venue for all social activities. However, six pillars obstruct the sight lines to the small stage area, so it's not easy to see the speaker/lecturer.

SPA/FITNESS. Sports-related facilities include an aft platform, and Zodiacs for close-in coastal visits.

HORIZON
★★★+

THIS IS A FAMILY-FRIENDLY CASUAL SHIP FOR SPANISH-SPEAKERS

Size: .... Mid-size Ship	Passenger/Crew Ratio (lower beds): 2.0
Tonnage: 47,427	Cabins (total): 721
Cruise Line: .... CDF Croisieres de France	Size Range (sq ft/m): 172.2–500.5/16–46.5
Former Names: ... *Pacific Dream, Island Star, Horizon*	Cabins (for one person): 0
Builder: .... Meyer Werft (Germany)	Cabins with balcony: 68
Entered Service: .... May 1990/Apr 2012	Cabins (wheelchair accessible): 4
Length (ft/m): 682.4/208.0	Wheelchair accessibility: .... Good
Beam (ft/m): 95.1/29.0	Elevators: 7
Propulsion/Propellers: .... diesel (19,960kW)/2	Casino (gaming tables): .... Yes
Passenger Decks: 10	Swimming Pools: 2
Total Crew: 620	Self-Service Launderette: .... No
Passengers (lower beds): 1,442	Library: .... Yes
Passenger Space Ratio (lower beds): 32.8	Onboard currency: .... Euros

THE SHIP. *Horizon* was originally built for and owned and operated by Celebrity Cruises. Although now around 25 years old, it still has a fairly contemporary, though angular, profile that looks powerful thanks to its blue hull (the hull itself was designed by mega-yacht designer Jon Bannenberg).

The exterior pool deck features one large pool and another for children, plus a couple of hot tubs, and in-built shower enclosures.

Inside, there is a similar interior layout to its sister ship, Pullmantur Cruises' *Zenith*, with decor that is quite restrained, even elegant. The feeling is one of uncluttered surroundings, and the ship features some interesting artwork. Soothing, pastel colors and high-quality soft furnishings are used throughout the interiors. The decks are named after colors (cobalt, turquoise, indigo, etc.).

An elegant Art Deco-style hotel-like lobby, reminiscent of Miami Beach hotels, has a two-deck-high ceiling and a spacious feel, and is the contact point for the reception desk, shore excursions, and onboard accounts counters.

The principal deck that houses many of the public entertainment rooms (located two decks above the lobby), has a double-width indoor promenade, which is good for strolling and people-watching. There is a decent-size library. Other facilities include the Zephyr Lounge Bar; a Piano Bar; a Café Moka; and an Internet center. The large, elegantly appointed Monte

BERLITZ'S RATINGS		
	Possible	Achieved
Ship	500	335
Accommodation	200	131
Food	400	222
Service	400	261
Entertainment	100	61
Cruise Experience	400	251

OVERALL SCORE 1261 points out of 2000

Carlo Casino has its own bar. 'Inclusive' drinks packages are available at an additional cost per day.

This ship is quite well suited to young (and young-at-heart) French-speaking couples, solo travelers, and families with children of all ages who want a first cruise experience in a smart ship, with plenty of public rooms, a lively atmosphere, and a French cruise experience. Expect to find an abundance of children during the peak holiday periods, when the passenger mix becomes younger.

Passenger niggles include lines for embarkation, disembarkation, shore tenders, and for self-serve buffet meals. The doors to the public restrooms and the outdoor decks are very heavy. The public restrooms are clinical and need some refreshing. There are no cushioned pads for the poolside sunloungers.

ACCOMMODATION. There are several price grades, including outside-view suites and cabins, and interior cabins. Note that many of the outside-view cabins on the safety equipment deck have lifeboat-obstructed views. The standard maritime cabin numbering system (even numbers port side, odd numbers starboard side) is reversed on this ship.

Standard cabins. The outside-view and interior cabins have good-quality fittings with wood accenting. They are tastefully decorated and of average size, with an excellent amount of closet and drawer space. All have twin beds that convert to a queen-size bed, and a good amount of closet and drawer space. The cabin soundproofing is quite good although this depends on location – some cabins are located opposite crew access doors, which can be noisy. The bathrooms have a generous shower area, and a small range of toiletries is provided, although towels are small, as is storage space for toiletries. The lowest priced outside-view cabins have a porthole – all others have picture windows.

Royal Suites. The largest accommodation is in two Royal Suites midships on Deck 10, and forward on Deck 11. These have a large private balcony, separate bedroom and lounge, a dining area with glass dining table, plus infotainment system. The bathroom is also large and has a whirlpool tub with integral shower.

Another 20 suites, also on Atlantic Deck, are tastefully furnished, although they are really just larger cabins, not suites. They have generous drawer and other storage space, and a sleeping area (with European duvets on the beds), plus a lounge area, and decent bathrooms. All accommodation designated as suites suffers from noise generated on the swimming pool deck directly above.

DINING. The main dining room features a raised section in its center. It has several tables for two, as well as for four, six, or eight (in banquettes), although the chairs don't have armrests. There are two seatings for dinner and open seating for breakfast and lunch, at tables for two to 10. The cuisine, its presentation, and service are so-so.

For informal meals, the Marché Gourmand has a traditional single-line self-service buffet for breakfast and lunch, and includes a pasta station, rotisserie, and pizza ovens. At peak times, the buffet is simply too small, too crowded, and noisy. It is also open (as Bistro Gourmand) for casual dinner between 6.30pm and 11pm.

The Terrace and Grill, located outdoors adjacent to the Bistro, serves typical fast-food items such as burgers and hot dogs.

ENTERTAINMENT. The two-level Broadway Theater, with main and balcony levels, has good sight lines from almost all seats, although the railing at the front of the balcony level impedes sight lines. It has a large stage for this size of ship.

The shows consist of a troupe of showgirl dancers, plus cabaret acts including singers, magicians, and comedians, among others, and are geared to the family audience carried on most cruises. There is also plenty of live – and loud – music for dancing to in various bars and lounges, plus the Saphir Dance Club (disco). Participation activities tend to be quite amateurish.

SPA/FITNESS. The Salle de Fitness is located high in the ship, just aft of the funnel. It has a gymnasium with ocean-view windows and high-tech muscle-pumping equipment, an exercise area, several therapy rooms including a Rasul (mud treatment) room, and men's/women's saunas.

INDEPENDENCE
★★+

THIS VERY SMALL, PERSONAL US COASTAL SHIP IS FOR MATURE-AGE CRUISERS

Size:	Boutique Ship	Passenger/Crew Ratio (lower beds):	3.5
Tonnage:	2,300	Cabins (total):	52
Cruise Line:	American Cruise Lines	Size Range (sq ft/m):	204.0–240.0/18.9–22.2
Former Names:	none	Cabins (for one person):	7
Builder:	Chesapeake Shipbuilding (USA)	Cabins with balcony:	40
Entered Service:	Jun 2010	Cabins (wheelchair accessible):	1
Length (ft/m):	223.0/67.9	Wheelchair accessibility:	None
Beam (ft/m):	51.0/15.5	Elevators:	1
Propulsion/Propellers:	diesel/2	Casino (gaming tables):	No
Passenger Decks:	4	Swimming Pools:	0
Total Crew:	27	Self-Service Launderette:	No
Passengers (lower beds):	97	Library:	Yes
Passenger Space Ratio (lower beds):	23.7	Onboard currency:	US$

THE SHIP. *Independence* is the fourth vessel in this cruise line's growing fleet (sister ships: *American Glory, American Spirit,* and *American Star*). The company builds the ships in its own shipyard in Chesapeake, Maryland. *Independence* is built specifically for coastal and inland cruising, in a casual, unregimented setting, to destinations unreachable by large cruise ships.

The uppermost deck is open – good for views – behind a forward windbreaker; plenty of sun-loungers are provided, as is a small golf putting green.

The public rooms include an observation lounge, with views forward and to port and starboard side; a library/lounge; a small midships lounge; and an elevator that goes to all decks, including the outdoor sun deck.

The ship docks in the center, or within walking distance, of most towns and ports. The dress code is 'no ties casual.' There are no additional costs, except for gratuities and port charges, because it's all included – quite different from big-ship cruising. This ship is for couples and solo travelers of mature years sharing a cabin and wishing to cruise in an all-American environment, with destinations more important than food, service, or entertainment. It is extremely expensive for what you get – although this is a fairly new ship, and the cabins are larger and marginally better equipped than those in comparable ships.

ACCOMMODATION. There are five cabin price grades: four are for doubles, while one is for singles.

BERLITZ'S RATINGS		
	Possible	Achieved
Ship	500	279
Accommodation	200	127
Food	400	211
Service	400	180
Entertainment	100	10
Cruise Experience	400	145

OVERALL SCORE 952 points out of 2000

All cabins have twin beds that convert to a king-size bed, a small desk with chair, flat-screen television, DVD player, and hanging space for clothes. All also have Internet access, a private (modular) bathroom with separate shower, washbasin and toilet (no cabin has a bathtub), windows that open, and satellite-feed TV sets. Rooms incorrectly designated as suites (23) have private balconies; although narrow, these do have two chairs and a small drinks table.

DINING. The dining salon, in the latter third of the vessel, has large, panoramic picture windows on three sides. Everyone eats in a single open seating, so you can get to know your fellow passengers. The cuisine is mainstream American: simple, honest food highlighting regional specialties. The choice of soups, appetizers, and entrées (mains) is limited. There is no wine list, although basic white and red American table wines are included. On the last morning of each cruise, Continental breakfast only is available.

ENTERTAINMENT. Dinner and after-dinner conversation with fellow passengers in the ship's lounge/bar form the entertainment each evening. Alternatively, take a good book.

SPA/FITNESS. There is a tiny fitness room with a few bicycles and other exercise machines.

INDEPENDENCE OF THE SEAS
★★★+

THIS SHIP HAS EXCELLENT FAMILY-FRIENDLY FACILITIES AND PLENTY OF ENTERTAINMENT

Size:	Large Resort Ship	Passenger/Crew Ratio (lower beds):	2.6
Tonnage:	154,407	Cabins (total):	1,817
Cruise Line:	Royal Caribbean International	Size Range (sq ft/m):	149.0–2,025.0/13.8–188.1
Former Names:	none	Cabins (for one person):	0
Builder:	Kvaerner Masa-Yards (Finland)	Cabins with balcony:	842
Entered Service:	May 2008	Cabins (wheelchair accessible):	32
Length (ft/m):	1,112.2/339.0	Wheelchair accessibility:	Good
Beam (ft/m):	184.0/56.0	Elevators:	14
Propulsion/Propellers:	diesel-electric (75,600kW)/	Casino (gaming tables):	Yes
	3 pods (2 azimuthing, 1 fixed)	Swimming Pools:	2
Passenger Decks:	15	Self-Service Launderette:	No
Total Crew:	1,397	Library:	Yes
Passengers (lower beds):	3,634	Onboard currency:	US$
Passenger Space Ratio (lower beds):	42.0		

THE SHIP. This *Freedom*-class ship is essentially split into three separate areas, rather like Disney's cruise ships: adults-only, family, and main.

The ship's 'wow' factor (particularly for children) is its connection with water in the design of a dramatic water theme park afloat. By day, an H2O Zone (in the center of the pool deck, has an interactive water-themed play area for families that includes water cannons and spray fountains, water jets and ground gushers; by night the 'water park' turns into a colorfully lit sculpture garden. Adjacent is a sports pool – with grandstand-style seating – for the likes of jousting contests and other sports-related pool games, plus a main pool.

There are 16 bars and lounges to enjoy, plus a whole street of shops and food/ drink spots along an indoor mall-like environment called the Royal Promenade. This is four decks high, and some cabins have great views into it. It is home to fashion, jewelry and perfume shops, a general store, logo shop, Promenade Café, Ben & Jerry's ice cream outlet, a Book Nook, a 'classic' barber shop called A Clean Shave (for a razor shave experience), a pizzeria, and an English pub – the Dog & Badger. Look out for stilt walkers and inflatable elephants when the circus is in town (promenades will be announced in the daily program).

One deck below the Royal Promenade is a large Casino Royale (full of gaming tables and slot machines), plus The Raven disco, Schooner Bar (piano bar),

BERLITZ'S RATINGS		
	Possible	Achieved
Ship	500	366
Accommodation	200	132
Food	400	235
Service	400	284
Entertainment	100	75
Cruise Experience	400	268

OVERALL SCORE 1360 points out of 2000

Boleros Lounge (a Latin hangout), and a photo gallery and shop, while the forward section leads into the three-deck-high Alhambra Theatre.

A regulation-size ice-skating rink (Studio B) has real, not fake, ice, with 'bleachers'-style seating, and broadcast facilities. Outstanding Ice Follies shows are presented here, but note that a number of slim pillars obstruct clear-view arena stage sight lines.

Almost at the top of the ship is RCI's trademark Viking Crown Lounge, the Olive or Twist jazz lounge, and a Wedding Chapel (this is actually one deck above). Other facilities include a cigar smoker's lounge, conference center, a concierge lounge (for suite occupants only), and a comfortable 3,600-book library – located at the aft end of the Royal Promenade, on Deck 7.

Overall, this is a good all-round ship for all age groups, but be aware of the many extra costs for optional items (including drinks and drink packages and excursions).

ACCOMMODATION. There is a wide range of suites and cabins in several categories and different price grades, from a Presidential Family Suite that can sleep up to 14 to twin-bed two-person interior cabins, and interior cabins with bay windows that look into an interior shopping/strolling atrium promenade. The price you pay depends on the size, grade, and location you choose. There are many family-friendly cabins, good for reunions, but no solo-occupancy cabins. All outside-view cabins have even numbers; all interior cabins have odd numbers.

Interior cabins. These no-view cabins measure 160 sq ft (14.9 sq m), and sleep two (some rooms sleep three or four).

Interior (promenade-view) cabins. These cabins, on three decks, are interior cabins, but with bay windows that allow occupants to look into the Royal Promenade. They sleep two.

Deluxe ocean-view cabins. These measure 173 sq ft (16 sq m) plus balcony: 46 sq ft (4.3 sq m). They sleep two (some rooms sleep three or four).

Superior ocean-view cabins. These measure 202 sq ft (18.8 sq m) plus balcony: 42 sq ft (3.9 sq m). They sleep two (some rooms sleep three or four).

Family ocean-view cabin. Located at the front of the ship, it has two twin beds (convertible to queen-size), sofa and/or Pullman beds, sitting area, and bathroom with shower. Accommodates six, and has round windows measuring 48ins (122cm). Size: 265 sq ft (4.6 sq m).

Junior Suites. These sleep up to four, and measure 277 sq ft (25.7 sq m) plus balcony: 65 sq ft (6 sq m).

Grand Suite. Sleeps up to four. Size: 381 sq ft (35.4 sq m) plus balcony: 89 sq ft (8.3 sq m).

Royal Suite. Sleeps up to four (and includes a black baby grand piano). Size: 1,406 sq ft (130.6 sq m) plus balcony: 377 sq ft (35 sq m).

Owner's Suite. Sleeps up to five. Size: 506 sq ft (47 sq m) plus balcony: 131 sq ft (12 sq m).

Presidential Family Suites. These comprise five rooms, and can accommodate eight to 14. They are located aft, at the opposite end of the ship to the show-lounge. Size: 1,215 sq ft (113 sq m) plus balcony: 810 sq ft (75 sq m). They are pleasant, but nothing special – they actually feel cramped and the ceilings are plain – but they could be good value for a large family.

DINING. The large Shakespeare-themed main dining room is on three levels, each with a different name (King Lear, Macbeth, and Romeo and Juliet); all levels have the same menus and food. A dramatic staircase connects all three, but large support pillars obstruct many sight lines. When you book, choose one of two seatings, or 'My Time Dining' (eat when you want, during dining-room hours). Tables are for four to 12 persons, and have good-quality place settings, china, and cutlery.

Overall, meals are rather hit and miss. Also, if you want lobster or a decent filet mignon (steak) you will be asked to pay extra.

Other places for a pitstop include:

Promenade Café: for Continental breakfast, all-day pizzas (Sorrento's), sandwiches, and coffee in paper cups or plastic mugs.

Windjammer Café: this large, sprawling venue is for casual buffet-style, self-help breakfast (the busiest time of the day), lunch, and light dinners; it can be difficult to find a table and by the time you do your food could be cold. The venue bears the brunt of many passenger complaints regarding lukewarm food, and complacent staff.

Jade 'Restaurant' (actually a section of the Windjammer Café) is the spot for casual Asian-themed food.

Giovanni's Table: a Euro-Italian venue, open for dinner only. Reservations are required, and a there's a cover charge. It has a set menu.

Chops Grille: an intimate restaurant for steaks and seafood. There's a cover charge (worth it for freshly cooked items) and reservations are required.

Johnny Rockets: a retro 1950s all-day, all-night diner-style eatery (with cover charge) featuring burgers, hot dogs, and other fast food, plus malt shakes. There is indoor and outdoor seating. All indoor tables have a mini-jukebox; dimes are provided for you to make your selection of vintage records.

Sprinkles: for round-the-clock ice cream and yoghurt, pastries, and coffee.

ENTERTAINMENT. The 1,350-seat Alhambra Theater – a stunning showlounge – is located forward. It spans five decks in height, with only a few slim pillars and almost no disruption of sight lines. The venue has a hydraulic orchestra pit and huge stage area, together with sonic-boom loud sound, and good lighting equipment.

SPA/FITNESS. Independence Day Spa includes an aerobics room, workout room, several rooms for body treatments, men's and women's sauna/steam rooms, and relaxation areas. Some basic exercise classes are free, but the good ones (such as yoga) cost extra.

INSIGNIA
★★★★

THIS COMPACT, CONTEMPORARY SHIP IS GOOD FOR WORLDWIDE CRUISING

Size:	Small Ship	Passenger/Crew Ratio (lower beds):	1.7
Tonnage:	30,277	Cabins (total):	342
Cruise Line:	Oceania Cruises	Size Range (sq ft/m):	145.3–968.7/13.5–90.0
Former Names:	Columbus 2, Insignia, R One	Cabins (for one person):	0
Builder:	Chantiers de l'Atlantique	Cabins with balcony:	232
Entered Service:	Jul 1998/Apr 2014	Cabins (wheelchair accessible):	3
Length (ft/m):	593.7/181.0	Wheelchair accessibility:	Good
Beam (ft/m):	83.5/25.5	Elevators:	4
Propulsion/Propellers:	diesel (18,600kW)/2	Casino (gaming tables):	Yes
Passenger Decks:	9	Swimming Pools:	1
Total Crew:	386	Self-Service Launderette:	Yes
Passengers (lower beds):	684	Library:	Yes
Passenger Space Ratio (lower beds):	44.2	Onboard currency:	US$

THE SHIP. *Insignia* started life as one of a series of almost identical ships built for the now-defunct Renaissance Cruises. The all-white ship has a large, square funnel, and a very pleasant lido and pool deck outdoors, with teak overlaid decking and high-quality lounge chairs. In 2014, the ship underwent a refurbishment program that included the addition of Barista's coffee bar (for *illy* coffees), installed new bathrooms in the Owner's Suites and Vista Suites, and updated the decor in all other cabins. Also added were a miniature golf course, shuffleboard courts, and other deck games.

There is, however, no walk-around promenade deck outdoors.

The decor is a stroll through the ocean liners of the 1920s. It's all in fine taste, though a bit fake in places, with detailed ceiling cornices, both real and faux wrought-iron staircase balustrades, leather-paneled walls, trompe l'oeil ceilings, and rich carpeting in the hallways.

The public rooms are spread over three decks. The reception hall has a staircase that is a scaled-down version of *Titanic*'s First-class staircase. A Horizon Lounge is located high atop ship; it's a bar with forward ocean views (at least for the barman), lots of seating, and a dance floor.

There are plenty of bars, including one in each restaurant entrance. Perhaps the nicest is Martinis, a lovely room, with an inviting marble fireplace, sofas, individual armchairs, and a dance floor.

BERLITZ'S RATINGS		
	Possible	Achieved
Ship	500	382
Accommodation	200	139
Food	400	302
Service	400	289
Entertainment	100	71
Cruise Experience	400	293
OVERALL SCORE 1476 points out of 2000		

The Library is a stunning Regency-style room, with a fireplace, a high, indented, trompe l'oeil ceiling, and a decent selection of books, plus comfortable wingback chairs with footstools, and sofas you could sleep on.

There may not be marble bathroom fittings, but the value for money is good. Note that a whopping 18 percent gratuity is added to bar purchases. The dress code is informal.

Overall, this ship is suitable for couples who like good food and style, but want informality, and interesting itineraries at a price well below what the luxury ships charge, in an informal setting that approaches elegant, and with almost no announcements.

ACCOMMODATION. There are nine cabin categories and price grades. The standard interior and outside-view cabins (the lowest four grades) are compact – tight for two persons, particularly for longer cruises. They have twin beds or a queen-size bed, with good under-bed storage areas, personal safe, vanity desk with large mirror, good closet and drawer space, dark wood furniture, cotton bathrobe and towels, slippers, clothes brush, and shoehorn.

Suite occupants get Bulgari bathroom amenities, complimentary shoeshine, cashmere throw blanket, bottle of Champagne on arrival, hand-held hairdryer, and priority restaurant reservations.

Owner's Suites (6). Measuring 968.7 sq ft (90 sq m), these are the most spacious accommodation. They are outstanding, decadent living spaces located aft on decks 6, 7, and 8. The bed faces the sea through floor-to-ceiling windows and sliding glass door.

Vista Suites (4). Measuring 785.7 sq ft (73 sq m), these are located forward on decks 5 and 6. They have extensive teak-floor private balconies that can't be overlooked from the decks above.

Penthouse Suites (52). These measure about 322.9 sq ft (30 sq m). They are not really suites, but large cabins, because the bedrooms aren't separate from the living areas.

Cabins with balcony. Cabins with private balconies (about 216 sq ft/20 sq m) comprise about two-thirds of all cabins. They have partial balcony partitions and sliding glass doors, and 14 cabins on Deck 6 have lifeboat-obstructed views and no balcony.

Outside-view and interior cabins. These measure around 160–165 sq ft (14.9–15.3 sq m) with twin beds convertible to a queen-size bed.

DINING. Flexibility and choice are what the dining is about. There are four restaurants:

Grand Dining Room has around 320 seats, open seating, and a raised central section. There are large ocean-view windows on three sides, with prime tables overlooking the stern. The chairs are comfortable and have armrests.

Toscana Italian Restaurant has 96 seats, windows along two sides, and a set menu (reservations required).

Polo Grill has 98 seats and windows along two sides; it features prime steaks and seafood (reservations required).

The Lido Café self-serve buffet has indoor and outdoor seating, and is open for breakfast, lunch, and casual dinners (including Tapas on the Terrace). It has a small pizzeria and grill.

Unlike other same-size ships in the same class, there's no extra charge for these eateries.

There is also a Poolside Grill outdoors. On days at sea, afternoon teatime is presented in the Horizon Lounge, with formally dressed staff, cake display trolleys, and a selection of different teas.

ENTERTAINMENT. The Insignia Lounge presents entertainment, cabaret, lectures, and some social events. There is also live music in several bars and lounges.

SPA/FITNESS. A Lido Deck has a swimming pool and good sunbathing space, plus a thalassotherapy tub. A jogging track encircles the swimming pool deck (one deck above). The uppermost outdoors deck includes a golf driving net and shuffleboard court. The Canyon Ranch SpaClub consists of a beauty salon, three treatment rooms, men's and women's changing rooms, steam room (but no sauna), and a good range of body treatments. An 18 percent gratuity is added for spa and beauty treatments and services.

ISLAND PRINCESS
★★★+

THIS IS A VERY COMFORTABLE CONTEMPORARY SHIP FOR MATURE-AGE CRUISERS

Size: .... Mid-size Ship	Passenger/Crew Ratio (lower beds): 2.1
Tonnage: 91,627	Cabins (total): 987
Cruise Line: .... Princess Cruises	Size Range (sq ft/m): 156–470.0/14.4–43.6
Former Names: .... *none*	Cabins (for one person): 0
Builder: .... Chantiers de l'Atlantique (France)	Cabins with balcony: 727
Entered Service: .... Jun 2003	Cabins (wheelchair accessible): 20
Length (ft/m): 964.5/294.0	Wheelchair accessibility: .... Good
Beam (ft/m): 105.6/32.2	Elevators: 14
Propulsion/Propellers: .... gas turbine + diesel	Casino (gaming tables): .... Yes
(40,000kW)/2	Swimming Pools: 2
Passenger Decks: 11	Self-Service Launderette: .... Yes
Total Crew: 900	Library: .... Yes
Passengers (lower beds): 1,974	Onboard currency: .... US$
Passenger Space Ratio (lower beds): 46.4	

THE SHIP. *Island Princess* has an instantly recognizable funnel due to two jet engine-like pods that sit high up on its structure, but these really are mainly for decoration. Four diesel engines provide the generating power. Electrical power is provided by a combination of four diesel and one gas turbine (CODAG) unit; the diesel engines are located in the engine room, while the gas turbine unit is located in the ship's funnel housing. The ship also has three bow thrusters and three stern thrusters.

There are has two decks full of public rooms, lounges, and bars instead of just one. Sensibly, there are three major stair towers for passengers, with plenty of elevators for easy access.

A large 'Movies Under the Stars' screen is located in the second of two pool areas on the open deck just forward of the funnel. Adults using the 'Sanctuary' area have their own splash pool. Walkers will like the ship's full walk-around exterior promenade deck.

Despite the ship's size, it's actually easy to find one's way around quickly – due to good design and its practical layout. Facilities include a flower shop where you can order flowers and Godiva chocolates for cabin delivery – nice for a birthday or anniversary – plus a pleasant cigar and cognac lounge (Churchill Lounge), and a Martini bar (Crooners). The casino has a London theme, and both gaming tables and slot machines.

An AOL Internet Café is conveniently located on the top level of the four-deck-high lobby. Adjacent

BERLITZ'S RATINGS

	Possible	Achieved
Ship	500	346
Accommodation	200	136
Food	400	247
Service	400	290
Entertainment	100	76
Cruise Experience	400	281

OVERALL SCORE 1376 points out of 2000

is the Wedding Chapel, with a live web-cam to relay ceremonies via the Internet. The captain can legally marry American couples, thanks to the ship's registry and a special dispensation. The Wedding Chapel can host renewal of vows ceremonies, for a fee.

This ship has lots of nooks and crannies – so you can hide away and just read a book if you want to. Also, at the forward end of decks 10 and 11, doors open onto an observation terrace. There are also several self-service launderettes.

Niggles include the fact that the forward elevators go between decks 15 and 7, but you need to change elevators to get down to the dining rooms on Deck 5 (strangely, the 'panoramic' elevators go only between decks 5 and 8; passengers find this a trifle confusing, but it's all about the way the layout has to work – from a designer's point of view, that is).

Passenger niggles include the user-unfriendly automated telephone system, the small cabin towels, the extra cost for items such as ice cream, and the (coins-needed) charge for the washers and dryers in self-service launderettes.

Overall, however, Princess Cruises delivers a consistently fine, comfortable, well-packaged product, always with a good degree of style, at a competitive price.

ACCOMMODATION. There are numerous price categories, in six types: suites with balcony (470 sq ft/43.7 sq m); mini-suites with balcony (285–302 sq ft/26.5–28 sq m); mini-suites without balcony (300 sq ft/27.9 sq m); outside-view cabins with balcony (217–232 sq ft/ 20.2–21.6 sq m); standard outside-view cabins (162 sq ft/15 sq m); interior (no view) cabins (156 sq ft/14.5 sq m). Wheelchair-accessible cabins measure 217–374 sq ft/20.2–34.7 sq m. some cabins have an extra bed for a third person.

All accommodation grades have a refrigerator, personal safe, infotainment system, hairdryer, satellite-dial telephone, twin or queen-sized beds (with premium-quality bedding), and pillow chocolates each night. All have bathroom with shower enclosure and toilet (suites have a bathtub and separate shower enclosure). Note that most ocean view cabins on Emerald Deck 8 have views obstructed by lifeboats.

DINING. The two, almost-identical, main dining rooms, Bordeaux and Provence, are in the forward section of the ship, on the two lowest passenger decks. They have quite low ceilings, plenty of intimate alcoves and cozy dining spots, and tables for two, four, six, or eight. There are two seatings for dinner (or you can opt for 'Anytime' Dining in the Bordeaux Restaurant), while breakfast and lunch are on an open-seating basis; you may have to wait for some while at peak times.

Although portions are generous, the food and its presentation are disappointing, and standardized. Fish is often disguised by a crumb or batter coating, the choice of fresh green vegetables is limited, few garnishes are used, and cheese is already sliced and diced. But, this is banquet-style catering, which means standardization and cooking in batches. Pasta dishes are acceptable (though voluminous), typically served by section headwaiters, who may also make 'something special just for you.'

There are two extra-charge, reservations-required restaurants: Sabatini's and the Bayou Café. Sabatini's, with colorful tiled Mediterranean-style decor, features Italian-style pizzas and pastas, with a variety of sauces, as well as Italian-style entrées. The food is both creative and tasty.

Bayou Café, open for lunch and dinner, has a cover charge that includes a Hurricane cocktail. It evokes the charm of New Orleans' French Quarter, with wrought-iron decoration, and features Cajun/Creole cuisine. The venue has a small stage, with a baby grand piano; live jazz is part of the evening dining scenario.

Horizon Court, a casual, almost 24-hour eatery, is in the forward section of Lido Deck with superb ocean views. Self-serve counters provide food for breakfast and lunch buffets, and bistro-style casual dinners are available each evening. Sadly, there's just not enough seating for the number of passengers using the facility.

Also, La Pâtisserie, in the reception lobby, is a coffee, cakes, and pastries spot and good for informal meetings. There's also a pizzeria, burger grill, and an ice cream bar (extra charge for the ice cream).

ENTERTAINMENT. The Princess Theater is two decks high, and, unusually, there is much more seating on the upper level than on the main floor below. Princess Cruises prides itself on its colorful Hollywood-style production shows.

A second entertainment venue, the Universe Lounge, is more for cabaret-style features. It also has two levels, and three separate stages, enabling non-stop entertainment to be provided without constant set-ups. Some 50 of the room's seats are equipped with a built-in laptop computer. The room is also used for cooking demonstrations (it has a full kitchen set), and other participation activities.

Princess Cruises always provides plenty of live music in bars and lounges, with a wide mix of light classical, jazz, and dance music, from solo entertaining pianists to showbands, and volume is normally kept to an acceptable level.

Those craving education can learn aboard ship with the ScholarShip@Sea program, which includes about 20 courses per cruise (six on any given day at sea). Although all introductory classes are free, fees apply if you want to continue any chosen subject in a smaller setting. There are four core subjects: culinary arts, visual/creative arts, photography, and computer technology. A full culinary demonstration kitchen set is built into the Universe Lounge (it's also used for wine tastings), and there's a pottery studio with kiln.

SPA/FITNESS. The Lotus Spa is located aft on one of the ship's uppermost decks. It contains men's and women's saunas, steam rooms, changing rooms, relaxation area, beauty salon, aerobics exercise room, and gymnasium with aft-facing ocean views, with high-tech muscle-pumping, cardiovascular equipment. There are several large rooms for individual treatments.

Sports enthusiasts will find a nine-hole golf putting course, two computerized golf simulators, and a sports court.

ISLAND SKY
★★★★+

A DELIGHTFUL, VERY COMFORTABLE SHIP FOR LIFE-ENRICHMENT CRUISES

Size:	Boutique Ship	Passenger/Crew Ratio (lower beds):	1.7
Tonnage:	4,280	Cabins (total):	59
Cruise Line:	Noble Caledonia	Size Range (sq ft/m):	234.6–353.0/21.8–32.8
Former Names:	Sky, Renai II, Renaissance VIII	Cabins (for one person):	0
Builder:	Nuovi Cantieri Appaunia (Italy)	Cabins with balcony:	4
Entered Service:	Dec 1991/May 2004	Cabins (wheelchair accessible):	0
Length (ft/m):	297.2/90.6	Wheelchair accessibility:	None
Beam (ft/m):	50.1/15.3	Elevators:	1
Propulsion/Propellers:	diesel (5000kW)/2	Casino (gaming tables):	No
Passenger Decks:	5	Swimming Pools:	0
Total Crew:	66	Self-Service Launderette:	No
Passengers (lower beds):	122	Library:	Yes
Passenger Space Ratio (lower beds):	35.0	Onboard currency:	UK£

THE SHIP. *Island Sky* has contemporary mega-yacht looks and handsome styling, with twin flared funnels that give it a smart profile, and a 'ducktail' (sponson) stern that provides stability and seagoing comfort. This ship was originally built as one of a series of eight similar ships for the now-defunct Renaissance Cruises. It was completely refurbished in 2010.

There is a narrow teak walk-around promenade deck outdoors, and a reasonable amount of open deck and sunbathing space. The ship has a fleet of Zodiac inflatables for shore landings.

Inside, the interior design is elegant, with polished wood-finish paneling throughout. There is a very small library with two Internet-connect workstations. Gratuities are included, as are house wine, beer, and soft drinks during lunch and dinner.

This comfortable, intimate ship operates in areas devoid of large cruise ships. Although not quite matching the standard of Seabourn or Silversea ships, it provides a fine cruise experience at a moderate cost. It suits seasoned travelers who like a relaxed lifestyle, good food and service, and an itinerary that promises to get away from it all, but in comfort.

ACCOMMODATION. The spacious cabins combine highly polished imitation rosewood paneling

BERLITZ'S RATINGS		
	Possible	Achieved
Ship	500	392
Accommodation	200	161
Food	400	317
Service	400	307
Entertainment	100	70
Cruise Experience	400	314
OVERALL SCORE 1561 points out of 2000		

with lots of mirrors and hand-crafted furniture, illuminated walk-in closets, three-sided vanity mirrors – in fact, there are a lot of mirrored surfaces in the decor – and just about everything you need, including a refrigerator, a TV set and DVD player, and Wi-Fi access. The bathrooms are extremely compact; they have real teakwood floors and marble vanities, and shower enclosures, but none have tubs, not even the Owner's Suite. All were replaced in the 2010 refit.

DINING. The dining room operates with open seating for all meals. Small, but quite smart, it has tables for two, four, six, and eight. You sit where you like, with whom you like, and at what time you like. The meals are self-service, buffet-style foods for breakfast and lunch, with hot foods chosen from a table menu and served properly. The dining room operation works well. The food quality, choice, and presentation are all very decent.

ENTERTAINMENT. There is no formal entertainment in the main lounge, the venue for all social activities. Six pillars obstruct sight lines to the small stage area.

SPA/FITNESS. Facilities include an aft platform, and Zodiac inflatable craft.

JEWEL OF THE SEAS
★★★+

THIS MID-SIZED SHIP IS A GOOD CHOICE FOR FAMILY-FRIENDLY CASUAL CRUISING

Size:	Mid-size Ship	Passenger/Crew Ratio (lower beds):	2.4
Tonnage:	90,090	Cabins (total):	1,055
Cruise Line:	Royal Caribbean International	Size Range (sq ft/m):	165.8–1,216.3/15.4–113.0
Former Names:	none	Cabins (for one person):	0
Builder:	Meyer Werft (Germany)	Cabins with balcony:	577
Entered Service:	Jun 2004	Cabins (wheelchair accessible):	14
Length (ft/m):	961.9/293.2	Wheelchair accessibility:	Good
Beam (ft/m):	105.6/32.2	Elevators:	9
Propulsion/Propellers:	gas turbine (39,000kW)/ 2 azimuthing pods	Casino (gaming tables):	Yes
		Swimming Pools:	2
Passenger Decks:	12	Self-Service Launderette:	No
Total Crew:	858	Library:	Yes
Passengers (lower beds):	2,110	Onboard currency:	US$
Passenger Space Ratio (lower beds):	42.9		

THE SHIP. *Jewel of the Seas* (a *Radiance*-class ship) is contemporary, with a two-deck-high Viking Crown Lounge in the forward section of the funnel. It functions as an observation lounge during the daytime, with views forward over the swimming pool. In the evening, the space morphs into a high-energy dance club, as well as a more intimate and relaxed entertainment venue for softer mood music and 'black box' theater.

The ship's gently rounded stern has nicely tiered decks, giving it a well-balanced look. In the front of the ship is a helipad/viewing platform. Pod propulsion power is provided.

Inside, the decor is modern, elegant, bright, and cheerful. The artwork is eclectic and provides a spectrum and a half of color works. The interior focal point is a nine-deck-high atrium lobby with glass-walled elevators that travel through 12 decks, face the sea, and provide a link with nature and the ocean. The Centrum, as the atrium is called, has several public rooms connected to it: desks for guest relations and shore excursions, a lobby bar, a Champagne bar, a small library, Royal Caribbean Online (an Internet center with 12 computers), a Concierge Club, and a Crown & Anchor Lounge. A great view can be had of the atrium by looking down through the flat glass dome high above it.

Other facilities include a Schooner Bar that houses maritime art in an integral art gallery, and a rather large, noisy, and colorful Casino Royale (with

BERLITZ'S RATINGS		
	Possible	Achieved
Ship	500	379
Accommodation	200	137
Food	400	242
Service	400	270
Entertainment	100	72
Cruise Experience	400	261

OVERALL SCORE 1361 points out of 2000

gaming tables and slot machines). There's also a small dedicated screening room for movies (with space for two wheelchairs), as well as a 194-seat conference center, and a business center.

This ship also contains a Viking Crown Lounge, a large structure set around the base of the ship's funnel. The very comfortable *Jewel of the Seas* offers more space, more comfortable public areas and several more intimate spaces, slightly larger cabins, and more dining options than most of the larger ships in the Royal Caribbean International fleet. A 15 percent gratuity is automatically added to all bar and spa bills.

This ship is best suited to young-minded adult couples, solo travelers, and families with children of all ages, who like to mingle in a mid-sized ship setting with plenty of city-like life and high-energy entertainment. The food is acceptable, stressing quantity rather than quality, unless you pay extra to dine in the specialty restaurant.

Niggles? There are no cushioned pads for sunloungers, and the deck towels are quite thin and small. It is virtually impossible to escape background music anywhere (it's even played in the hallway outside your cabin).

ACCOMMODATION. There's a wide range of suites and standard outside-view and interior cabins to suit different tastes, requirements, and depth of wallet, in 10 different categories and numerous price groups. There are 14 wheelchair-accessible cabins, eight of which have a private balcony.

Apart from six Owner's Suites, which have king-size beds, almost all other cabins have twin beds that convert to a queen-size bed. All cabins have rich but faux wood cabinetry, including a vanity desk with hairdryer, faux wood drawers that close silently (hooray), television, personal safe, and three-sided mirrors. Some cabins have ceiling-recessed, pull-down third and fourth berths, although closet and drawer space would be extremely tight. Some cabins have interconnecting doors, allowing families with children to cruise together in adjacent cabins. Audio channels are available through the TV set, so you can't switch off its picture while listening. Data ports are provided in all cabins.

Many 'private' balcony cabins aren't very private, as they can be overlooked by anyone standing in the port and starboard wings of the Solarium, and from other locations.

Most cabin bathrooms have tiled accenting and a terrazzo-style tiled floor, and a (rather small) shower enclosure in a half-moon shape, Egyptian cotton towels, a small cabinet for toiletries, and a small shelf. There is little space to stow toiletries for two or more.

The largest accommodation consists of a family suite with two bedrooms. One bedroom has twin beds that convert to a queen-size bed, while a second has two lower beds and two upper Pullman berths, a combination that can sleep up to eight persons – this would be suitable for large families.

Occupants of accommodation designated as suites also get the use of a private Concierge Lounge, where priority dining-room reservations, shore-excursion bookings, and beauty salon/spa appointments can be made.

DINING. Tides – the main dining room – spans two decks; the upper deck level has floor-to-ceiling windows, while the lower deck level has picture windows. It is a fine, but inevitably noisy dining hall and eight huge, thick pillars obstruct the sight lines. It seats 1,222, and the decor has a cascading water theme. There are tables for two to 10, in two seatings for dinner. Two small private dining rooms (Illusions and Mirage) are located off the main dining room. There is an adequate wine list, with moderate prices.

Menu descriptions make the food sound better than it is, and the selection of breads, rolls, fruit, and cheese is poor. Overall, meals are rather hit and miss

– in fact it's unmemorable. Additionally, if you want lobster or a decent filet mignon (steak), you will be asked to pay extra.

Extra-cost venues include Giovanni's Table, with 112 seats and offering Italian cuisine, and Chops Grille Steakhouse, with 95 seats and an open 'show' kitchen – it serves premium meats in the form of chops and steaks. Both have food that is of a better quality than in the main dining room. They are typically open 6–11pm. There is a cover charge, and reservations are required.

Casual breakfasts, lunches, and dinners can be taken in the self-serve, buffet-style Windjammer Café, which can be accessed directly from the pool deck. It has about 400 seats, and 'islands' for specific food types, and indoor and outdoor seating. Additionally, there is Seaview Café, open for lunch and dinner. You can choose from the self-serve buffet, or from the menu for casual, fast-food seafood items including fish sandwiches, fish 'n' chips, as well as non-seafood items such as burgers and hot dogs.

ENTERTAINMENT. Facilities include the three-level Coral Theater, the showlounge, with 874 seats, including 24 wheelchair stations. The sight lines are good from most seats due to steep tiers. A second entertainment venue is the Safari Club, which hosts cabaret shows, late-night adult comedy, and dancing to live music. All the ship's entertainment is upbeat – so much so that it's virtually impossible to get away from music and noise.

SPA/FITNESS. The Day Spa health and fitness facilities have themed decor, and include a 10,176-sq-ft (945-sq-m) solarium with whirlpool and counter current swimming under a retractable glass roof, a gymnasium with many cardiovascular machines, a 50-person aerobics room, sauna and steam rooms, and private massage/body treatment rooms. The facility is staffed and operated by Steiner Leisure.

For the sports-oriented, there are activities galore – including a 30ft (9m) -high rock-climbing wall with five separate climbing tracks. It's free, and all safety gear is included, but you'll need to sign up.

Other sports facilities include a nine-hole miniature golf course, and an indoor/outdoor country club with golf simulator, a jogging track, and basketball court. Want to play pool? You can, thanks to two special tables whose gyroscopic technology adjusts to the movement of the ship.

KAPITAN KHLEBNIKOV
★★★

THIS RUGGED SHIP IS BUILT FOR POLAR EXPLORATION IN BASIC COMFORT

Size: ....Boutique Ship	Passenger/Crew Ratio (lower beds): 1.7
Tonnage: 12,228	Cabins (total): 51
Cruise Line: .... Quark Expeditions	Size Range (sq ft/m): 150.6-269.1/14.0-25.0
Former Names: .... none	Cabins (for one person): 0
Builder: .... Wartsila (Finland)	Cabins with balcony: 0
Entered Service: 1981	Cabins (wheelchair accessible): 0
Length (ft/m): 401.9/122.5	Wheelchair accessibility: .... None
Beam (ft/m): 86.9/26.5	Elevators: 1
Propulsion/Propellers: diesel-electric/2	Casino (gaming tables): .... No
Passenger Decks: 6	Swimming Pools: 0
Total Crew: 60	Self-Service Launderette: .... No
Passengers (lower beds): 102	Library: .... Yes
Passenger Space Ratio (lower beds): 120.4	Onboard currency: .... US$

THE SHIP. *Kapitan Khlebnikov* is a true polar-class icebreaker that was designed and built to take the rigors of northern Siberia. It is extremely reliable and well equipped for Arctic expedition voyages (particularly the Northwest Passage). The ship has an extremely thick hull, its diesel-electric powerplant delivers 24,000 hp, and the bow looks like an inverted whale head. It really is a tough vessel that can plough through ice several feet thick. In 1997 it became the first passenger ship to circumnavigate Antarctica. There's plenty of open deck space for viewing, and the vessel has an open bridge policy.

The interior decor is spartan, but then this is a real, classic working ice-breaker with an ice-experienced crew. Communal facilities include a lecture room that seats all participants. There is always a team of expert naturalists and lecturers, because the voyages are all about nature, wildlife, and other specialisms.

ACCOMMODATION. Cabins are spread over four decks. The cruise price depends on the size, location,

BERLITZ'S RATINGS		
	Possible	Achieved
Ship	500	279
Accommodation	200	118
Food	400	219
Service	400	253
Entertainment	100	50
Cruise Experience	400	234
OVERALL SCORE 1153 points out of 2000		

and grade you choose. From largest to smallest, they are nothing special, but each has two lower beds (one is a fixed bed, the other a convertible sofa bed, either in a twin or L-shaped format), large closets, storage for outerwear and boots, and portholes that actually open. The bathrooms are practical units, but storage space for personal toiletry items is tight. Four suites simply have a little more space.

DINING. The open seating dining room is plain and unpretentious, but quite comfortable. The food is hearty fare, with an emphasis on fish and potatoes. Fruits, vegetables, and international cheeses tend to be in limited supply. Quark Expeditions has its own catering team on board.

ENTERTAINMENT. This consists of recaps and after-dinner conversation with fellow travelers.

SPA/FITNESS. There is a workout room with some fairly basic equipment; there's also a tiny (heated) pool, and a sauna.

KONINGSDAM
★★★★

FAMILY-FRIENDLY SHIP WITH A GOOD MIX OF MODERN AND DUTCH TRADITIONAL DECOR

Size:	Large Resort Ship	Passenger/Crew Ratio (lower beds):	2.5
Tonnage:	99,500	Cabins (total):	1,331
Cruise Line:	Holland America Line	Size Range (sq ft/m):	127.0–1,291.1/11.7–120.0
Former Names:	none	Cabins (for one person):	12
Builder:	Fincantieri (Italy)	Cabins with balcony:	912
Entered Service:	May 2016	Cabins (wheelchair accessible):	27
Length (ft/m):	983.5/299.8	Wheelchair accessibility:	Good
Beam (ft/m):	114.8/35.0	Elevators:	12
Propulsion/Propellers:	diesel/2 azimuthing pods	Casino (gaming tables):	Yes
Passenger Decks:	12	Swimming Pools:	3 (1 w/ sliding glass dome)
Total Crew:	1,025	Self-Service Launderette:	No
Passengers (lower beds):	2,650	Library:	Yes
Passenger Space Ratio (lower beds):	37.7	Onboard currency:	US$

THE SHIP. The first of what Holland America Line calls its *Pinnacle*-class ships is a natural extension of the company's fleet, and includes a few more up-to-date features while maintaining the company's Dutch heritage.

The exterior profile (black hull and white upper part) is not exactly handsome, due to extra decks added forward and above the navigation bridge, but the single large funnel tries hard to balance the upper structure. The ship's name honors the first Dutch king in more than a century – King Willem-Alexander. It's the company's largest ship to date, although it is really an extension of the Vista class of ships – for example, the company's previous new build, *Nieuw Amsterdam*.

There is a complete walk-around exterior teak promenade deck, with hardwood steamer-style sun-loungers, and a jogging track is located in the forward third of the ship and around its mast. Exterior glass elevators, mounted midships on both the port and starboard sides, provide fine ocean views from any one of 10 decks. One of the two centrally located swimming pools outdoors can be used in inclement weather thanks to a retractable sliding glass roof. Two hot tubs, adjacent to the pools, are bridged by a bar. There's also a small pool for children.

The interior focus is the three-deck-high atrium lobby. Decks are named after famous composers, including Beethoven and Gershwin.

BERLITZ'S RATINGS		
	Possible	Achieved
Ship	500	407
Accommodation	200	155
Food	400	257
Service	400	286
Entertainment	100	73
Cruise Experience	400	295

OVERALL SCORE 1473 points out of 2000

Facilities (spread over two decks) include the Queen's Lounge (it's also a lecture and demonstration room); a Culinary Arts Center (for cooking demonstrations and classes), a large casino with gaming tables and slot machines; and a Crow's Nest – an observation lounge that includes a library and Explorations Café (extra cost).

Other facilities include a shopping street, card room, art gallery, photo gallery, and four small meeting rooms. The ship doesn't have rock-climbing walls, rope walks, and other gimmicky features. Holland America Line is known for its slower, more relaxed pace of living, and delivers a decent onboard experience, although the dining experience just doesn't cut it.

ACCOMMODATION. There are a mind-boggling 35 price categories for seven accommodation grades, from small cabins for solo travelers to grand suites. Some 32 family-together cabins (222–231 sq ft/20.6–21.4 sq m) are a newish feature for HAL, in a bid to provide better accommodation for families with children. Also of note are 12 single-occupancy cabins (127–172 sq ft/11.8–16 sq m), although they are all the way forward on the lowest deck. There's also a Grand Pinnacle suite (1,290 sq ft/119.8 sq m); two Neptune Spa suites and 43 Neptune suites ranging from 465–855 sq ft (43.1–79.4 sq m); 14 Signature suites (up to 400 sq ft/37.2 sq m); and Vista suites (260–356 sq ft/24.2–33.1 sq m).

Neptune and Pinnacle suite-grade occupants can access to the Neptune Lounge.

DINING. The Dining Room is on two levels, with two seatings (dining at set times). The decor is pure Americana, in white and cream – like a throwback to the steamboat era. The focal point is a wine tower spanning two decks, but the large restaurant is not helped by many slim, straight, and curved pillars (although this could be described as being part of its decorative 'charm').

With a few exceptions, the cuisine is rather unmemorable, and is disappointing taste-wise, because it's all about cooking for the masses. There's a distinct lack of variety of green vegetables, and too much use of rice, canned fruit, and ready-prepared cheese. Still, you get friendly service from smiling Indonesian and Filipino stewards, and the plates are nice.

HAL can provide Kosher meals (if requested when you book), although these are prepared ashore, then frozen, and brought to your table sealed in their original containers.

Extra-cost (reservations required) venues include:

Pinnacle Grill, for premium steaks and grilled seafood items – part of the line's focus on 'Pacific Northwest' cuisine.

Tamarind, for Asian 'fusion' cuisine; it includes a sushi bar.

Sel de Mer, a French-style seafood brasserie.

Culinary Arts Center – open for dinner; the venue is more bistro than restaurant.

For pastries and coffee, Grand Dutch Café is on the third level of the atrium, opposite the Front Office (reception desk).

For casual eating, there is an extensive Lido Café, a self-serve, buffet-style eatery that wraps around the funnel, with indoor-outdoor seating and ocean views. It includes several sections including a salad bar, Asian stir-fry and sushi section, deli sandwiches, and a separate dessert buffet, although lines can form for made-to-order items such as omelets for breakfast and pasta for lunch. Each evening, Canaletto – formed from a large section of the venue – serves Italian-style cuisine.

ENTERTAINMENT. Spanning two decks is the 'circular' World Stage main showlounge, which features a 270-degree LED screen that acts as a surround stage backdrop. It's a sort of 'theater in the round' within the showlounge.

SPA/FITNESS. The Greenhouse Spa is a good-sized, two-decks-high facility, located above the navigation bridge. It includes a solarium, hydrotherapy pool, and unisex thermal suite (with steam rooms and aromatic steam rooms), a beauty salon, private massage/body-treatment rooms (including one for couples), and a large fitness room with floor-to-ceiling windows and ocean views, and muscle-toning equipment.

L'AUSTRAL
★★★★

A CONTEMPORARY SHIP WITH STYLE TO SUIT FRENCH SPEAKERS

Size:	Small Ship	Passenger/Crew Ratio (lower beds):	1.5
Tonnage:	10,944	Cabins (total):	132
Cruise Line:	Ponant	Size Range (sq ft/m):	226.0–581.2/21.0–54.0
Former Names:	none	Cabins (for one person):	0
Builder:	Fincantieri (Italy)	Cabins with balcony:	125
Entered Service:	May 2011	Cabins (wheelchair accessible):	3
Length (ft/m):	465.8/142.0	Wheelchair accessibility:	Fair
Beam (ft/m):	9.0/18.0	Elevators:	3
Propulsion/Propellers:	diesel-electric (4,600kW)/2	Casino (gaming tables):	No
Passenger Decks:	6	Swimming Pools:	1
Total Crew:	140	Self-Service Launderette:	No
Passengers (lower beds):	264	Library:	Yes
Passenger Space Ratio (lower beds):	41.4	Onboard currency:	Euros

THE SHIP. One of four almost identical sister ships (the others are Le Boréal, Le Lyrial, and Le Soléal) catering to French speakers, L'Austral (South Wind) is a gem of contemporary, uncluttered design and chic details. With a dark gray hull and sleek white superstructure, it looks like a large private yacht rather than a traditional cruise ship. The passenger/space ratio, a healthy 53.5, decreases if the 40 deluxe cabins that convert into 20 larger suites are all occupied by two persons.

L'Austral has a smart 'sponson' skirt built-in at the stern for operational stability, and carries a fleet of 12 Zodiac landing craft for soft expedition voyages. For Antarctic voyages, passenger numbers are kept to a maximum of 199. The ship does not, however, have boot storage lockers.

There is some sunbathing space outdoors forward of the funnel and around the small pool – aft of the casual eatery one deck below – together with one shower enclosure. Aft of the funnel is an outdoor bar (Copernico) and grill, but seating is limited.

Almost all public rooms are aft, with accommodation located forward; the elevators go to all decks except the uppermost one (Deck 7). The decor is minimalist and super-yacht chic – relaxing and pleasant, with lots of browns and creams and a splash of red here and there. Glitz is entirely absent, although there are many reflective surfaces, and the overall feeling of the decor is cool rather than warm.

BERLITZ'S RATINGS		
	Possible	Achieved
Ship	500	399
Accommodation	200	155
Food	400	289
Service	400	301
Entertainment	100	74
Cruise Experience	400	299
OVERALL SCORE 1517 points out of 2000		

The focal point is the main lobby, with a central, circular seating and tiled floor surround; its small central section spans two decks. The other flooring is wood, which can be noisy. The lower decks of the main stairway are made of faux gray wood, while the upper decks are carpeted – a strange combination that somehow works.

L'Austral is best suited to young-minded couples and solo travelers who enjoy sophisticated facilities in a relaxed but chic, premium, yacht-like environment quite different from most cruise ships, with good food and decent service.

This is all-inclusive cruising – except for spa treatments – with drinks, table wine for lunch and dinner, bottled mineral water, port charges, and Zodiac excursions on expedition-style cruises all included in the fare. The crew is English- and French-speaking, with many hotel service staff from Asia. How delightful – cruise tickets are provided in a proper document pouch and sent to you.

Passenger niggles? There's no outside walking or jogging deck. The interior stairways are a quite steep and have short steps. The restaurant is noisy. The entertainment system is not user-friendly, and Internet connection is slow and expensive. Overall, it's difficult for French-speaking and non-French-speaking passengers to mix.

ACCOMMODATION. Of the 132 suites/cabins, there are three Prestige Suites with 301 sq ft plus a 54-sq-ft balcony (28 plus 5 sq m). Forty of the 94 deluxe cabins – 200 sq ft plus a 43-sq-ft balcony (18.6 plus 4 sq m) – can be combined into 20 larger suites, each with two bathrooms, and separate living area and bedroom. All cabinetry is made in elegant dark woods. A real plus is that there are no interior (no-view) cabins – all cabins have a view of the outside – and cabin insulation is good.

Each deluxe and standard cabin has a large ocean-view window, two beds that convert to a queen-size bed, and a long vanity desk with good lighting. Facilities include a TV set, DVD player, refrigerator, and personal safe. The marble-appointed bathrooms have large, rather heavy hand-held shower hoses. Amenities include a minibar, personal safe, hairdryer, bathrobe, and French bathroom products. Wi-Fi costs extra.

All other cabins have good-size beds, although the corners of the bed frames are square, so, be careful when passing between the bed and the storage units – these are quite large, with two deep drawers. Other facilities include refrigerator, television, wall mirror, good-size wardrobe-style closet (armoire) with personal safe, and a vanity desk with drawer and a small shelf.

The small cabin bathrooms (the entrance door is only 20.5ins/52cm wide) also have a sliding partition window that enables you to see through the cabin to the ocean, and a deep, half-size tub/shower combination. The lip between floor and bathroom is just over 6ins (15cm) high. L'Occitane products are provided.

There are no shelves for toiletries, but there are two drawers under the washbasin – although they are not very practical. A separate cubicle houses the vacuum toilet. Balconies have faux wood decking and a fine (real) wood handrail, although solid paneling obstructs views when seated and makes the cabin seem dark – glass panels would have been nicer; the balconies are also narrow. The closet space is quite good, although the doors, with excellent white leather handles, are wide – at 31ins (79cm), they are wider than the cabin door, and can't be opened without first closing the bathroom and toilet doors that are directly opposite.

Good-quality bed linen, overlays, and cushions are provided, although there is no choice of pillows.

DINING. The main restaurant is chic but not pretentious. It accommodates all passengers in an open-seating arrangement and has two integral wine display cabinets (not temperature-controlled). The chairs are square and have thin armrests and low backs – but they look good. And the food? While appetizers and entrées (mains) are reasonably good, but certainly nothing special, the cakes and desserts are delightful.

A casual indoor/outdoor Grill (although there is no actual grill) has seating for up to 130, with self-serve buffet set-up for breakfast and lunch, and a 'fast grill' dinner in an alfresco setting. But the layout is disjointed, and the port and starboard sides are separated by two elevators. There are two main buffet display units (one for cold food, one for hot), a separate table set-up for bread, and an active cooking station (eggs for breakfast, pasta dishes at lunchtime).

Veuve Clicquot is the Champagne chosen by Ponant, a perfect example of French *savoir-faire*, and premium selections include Brut Carte Jaune, Rosé, and La Grande Dame varieties.

ENTERTAINMENT. French Line, the show-lounge/lecture hall, has amphitheater-style seating for 260, and a raised stage suited to concerts and cabaret. The production shows are weak, repetitive, and loud. The venue is also used for expert specialist lecturers, and expedition-style recaps. Two large pillars obstruct the sight lines from several seats.

SPA/FITNESS. The Yacht Spa facilities include a fitness room with starboard-side ocean views, adjacent kinetic wall, and a steam room, but there's no changing room. A wide range of massage and other body treatments are provided by Carita of Paris, which staffs and oversees the facility.

LE BOREAL
★★★★

THIS SMALL SHIP EXUDES FRENCH AMBIENCE AND SUPER-YACHT STYLE

Size:	Small Ship	Passenger/Crew Ratio (lower beds):	1.5
Tonnage:	10,700	Cabins (total):	132
Cruise Line:	Ponant	Size Range (sq ft/m):	226.0–581.2/21.0–54.0
Former Names:	none	Cabins (for one person):	0
Builder:	Fincantieri (Italy)	Cabins with balcony:	124
Entered Service:	May 2010	Cabins (wheelchair accessible):	3
Length (ft/m):	465.8/142.0	Wheelchair accessibility:	Fair
Beam (ft/m):	9.0/18.0	Elevators:	3
Propulsion/Propellers:	diesel-electric (4,600kW)/2	Casino (gaming tables):	No
Passenger Decks:	6	Swimming Pools:	1
Total Crew:	140	Self-Service Launderette:	No
Passengers (lower beds):	264	Library:	Yes
Passenger Space Ratio (lower beds):	41.4	Onboard currency:	Euros

THE SHIP. One of four almost identical new ships catering to French speakers, *Le Boréal* (North Wind) is a gem of contemporary design – chic and uncluttered. The ship has a smart 'sponson' skirt built-in at the stern for operational stability, and carries a fleet of 12 Zodiac landing craft for soft expedition voyages.

There is some sunbathing space outdoors forward of the funnel and around the small pool – aft of the casual eatery one deck below – together with one shower enclosure. Aft of the funnel is an outdoor bar/grill, but not much seating.

Almost all public rooms are aft, with accommodation located forward; the elevators go to all decks except the uppermost one (Deck 7). The decor is minimalist and super-yacht chic – relaxing and pleasant, with lots of browns and creams and a splash of red here and there. Glitz is entirely absent, although there are many reflective surfaces, and the overall feeling of the decor is cool rather than warm.

The focal point is the main lobby, with a central, circular seating and tiled floor surround; its small central section spans two decks. The other flooring is wood, which can be noisy. The lower decks of the main stairway are made of faux gray wood, while the upper decks are carpeted – a strange combination that somehow works.

Le Boréal is best suited to young-minded couples and solo travelers who want some contemporary, sophisticated facilities and a chic yet relaxed yacht-like

BERLITZ'S RATINGS

	Possible	Achieved
Ship	500	399
Accommodation	200	155
Food	400	289
Service	400	301
Entertainment	100	74
Cruise Experience	400	299

OVERALL SCORE 1517 points out of 2000

environment quite different to most cruise ships, with very good food and decent service. The ship is often chartered or part-chartered by 'premium' travel organizers, such as Abercrombie & Kent, Gohagan, and Tauck, who prefer smaller ships.

This is all-inclusive cruising – except for spa treatments – with drinks, table wine for lunch and dinner, bottled mineral water, port charges, and Zodiac excursions on expedition-style cruises all included in the fare. The crew is English- and French-speaking, with many hotel service staff from Asia. It's refreshing to note that cruise tickets and documents are provided in a proper ticket pouch and sent to you – so, there's no digital frustration, but much anticipation.

Passenger niggles? There's no outside walking or jogging deck. The interior stairways are a quite steep and have short steps. The restaurant is noisy. The entertainment system is not user-friendly, and Internet connection is slow and expensive. Overall, it's difficult for French-speaking and non-French-speaking passengers to mix.

ACCOMMODATION. Of the 132 suites/cabins, there are three Prestige Suites with 301 sq ft plus a 54-sq-ft balcony (28 plus 5 sq m). Forty of the 94 deluxe cabins – 200 sq ft plus a 43-sq-ft balcony (18.6 plus 4 sq m) – can be combined into 20 larger suites, each with two bathrooms, and separate living area and bedroom. All cabinetry is made in elegant dark woods. A real plus is that there are no interior (no-view) cabins – every cabin has an outside view, and the cabin insulation is good.

Each deluxe and standard cabin has a large ocean-view window, two beds that convert to a queen-size bed, and a long vanity desk with good lighting. Facilities include a TV set, DVD player, refrigerator, and personal safe. The marble-appointed bathrooms have heavy hand-held shower hoses. Amenities include a minibar, personal safe, hairdryer, bathrobe, and French bathroom products. Wi-Fi costs extra.

All other cabins have good-size beds, although the corners of the bed frames are square, so you need to be careful when passing between the bed and adjacent storage units – these are quite large, with two deep drawers. Other facilities include a refrigerator, television, wall mirror, good-size wardrobe-style closet (armoire) with personal safe, and a vanity desk with drawer and a small shelf.

The small cabin bathrooms (the entrance door is only 20.5ins/52cm wide) also have a sliding partition window that enables you to see through the cabin to the ocean, and a deep, half-size tub/shower combination. The lip between floor and bathroom is just over 6ins (15cm) high. L'Occitane products are provided.

There are no shelves for toiletries, but there are two drawers under the washbasin – although they are not really practical in use. A separate cubicle houses the vacuum toilet. Balconies have faux wood decking and a fine (real) wood handrail, although solid paneling obstructs views when seated and makes the cabin seem dark – glass panels would have been nicer; the balconies are also very narrow. The closet space is quite good, although the doors, with excellent white leather handles, are wide – at 31ins (79cm), they are wider than the cabin door, and can't be opened without first closing the bathroom and toilet doors, which are directly opposite. Good-quality bed linen, overlays, and cushions are provided, although there is no choice of pillows.

DINING. The main restaurant, La Licorne, is chic but not pretentious. It accommodates all passengers in an open-seating arrangement and has two integral wine display cabinets (not temperature-controlled). The chairs are rather square and have very thin armrests and low backs – but they certainly look good. And the food? While appetizers and entrées (mains) are reasonably good but nothing special, the cakes and desserts are delightful.

La Boussole, an indoor/outdoor Grill (though there's no actual grill), has casual seating for up to 130, with a self-serve buffet set-up for breakfast and lunch, and a 'fast grill' dinner in an alfresco setting. However, the layout is quite disjointed, and the port and starboard sides are separated by two elevators. There are two main buffet display units – one for cold food, one for hot – and a separate table set-up for bread, and an active cooking station (eggs for breakfast, pasta at lunchtime).

ENTERTAINMENT. French Line, the show lounge/lecture hall, has amphitheater-style seating for 260, and a raised stage suited to concerts and cabaret presentations. The production shows are weak, repetitive, and loud. The venue is also used for expert specialist lecturers and expedition-style recaps. Two large pillars obstruct the sight lines from several seats, however.

SPA/FITNESS. The Yacht Spa facilities include a fitness room with starboard-side ocean views, adjacent kinetic wall, and a steam room, but no changing room. A wide range of massage and body treatments are provided by Carita of Paris, which staffs and operates the facility.

LE CHAMPLAIN
NYR

THIS SHIP HAS FRENCH CHIC AND STYLE FOR EXPLORING THE MORE REMOTE REGIONS

Size:	Boutique Ship	Passenger/Crew Ratio (lower beds):	1.6
Tonnage:	10,000	Cabins (total):	92
Cruise Line:	Ponant	Size Range (sq ft/m):	247.5-807.3/23.0-75.0
Former Names:	none	Cabins (for one person):	4
Builder:	Vard (Norway)	Cabins with balcony:	92
Entered Service:	Summer 2018	Cabins (wheelchair accessible):	0
Length (ft/m):	429.7/131.0	Wheelchair accessibility:	Fair
Beam (ft/m):	59.0/18.0	Elevators:	3
Propulsion/Propellers:	diesel-electric/	Casino (gaming tables):	No
	2 azimuthing pods	Swimming Pools:	1
Passenger Decks:	6	Self-Service Launderette:	No
Total Crew:	110	Library:	Yes
Passengers (lower beds):	180	Onboard currency:	Euros
Passenger Space Ratio (lower beds):	1.6		

THE SHIP. *Le Champlain* is named after the French explorer Samuel de Champlain. It is designed primarily to take you to some of the more remote areas of the planet in contemporary comfort. The shape is similar to the larger general-purpose yacht-style Ponant cruise ships, but with an open (trawler) stern that provides access to the marine equipment and acts as a landing platform.

This expedition-style ship has some premium contemporary touches in its interiors. What's really impressive – and different – is seating under the sea! It's in an underwater lounge called the 'Blue Eye.'

The interior design itself is functional, but the ship feels a little closed-in, due to the low ceiling heights. Public rooms include a Panoramic Lounge, Main Lounge (which seats all passengers at once), a Theatre/Lecture Room, and the aforementioned 'Blue Eye' lounge.

This ship is really for anyone looking for sophisticated contemporary facilities in a relaxed but chic, French, yacht-like environment – quite different

BERLITZ'S RATINGS		
	Possible	Achieved
Ship	500	NYR
Accommodation	200	NYR
Food	400	NYR
Service	400	NYR
Entertainment	100	NYR
Cruise Experience	400	NYR

OVERALL SCORE NYR points out of 2000

to most large cruise ships – with decent food, and friendly, casual service.

ACCOMMODATION. There are numerous accommodation price grades. The price you pay depends on the size, location, and grade you choose. From the smallest interior (no-view) cabin to the largest suite, all are comfortable, and many have balconies.

DINING. The restaurant, located aft, is cheerful, and has both indoor and outdoor seating.

ENTERTAINMENT. Movies are shown in the theater.

SPA/FITNESS. The Yacht Spa facilities include a fitness room with starboard-side ocean views, a kinetic wall, and a steam room with shower, but no changing room. A range of massage and body treatments are provided by Sothys, whose staff operates the facility.

LE LAPÉROUSE
NYR

THIS SHIP HAS FRENCH CHIC FOR DISCOVERING DESTINATIONS IN STYLISH COMFORT

Size:	Boutique Ship	Passenger/Crew Ratio (lower beds):	1.6
Tonnage:	10,000	Cabins (total):	92
Cruise Line:	Ponant	Size Range (sq ft/m):	247.5–807.3/23.0–75.0
Former Names:	none	Cabins (for one person):	4
Builder:	Vard (Norway)	Cabins with balcony:	92
Entered Service:	Summer 2018	Cabins (wheelchair accessible):	0
Length (ft/m):	429.7/131.0	Wheelchair accessibility:	Fair
Beam (ft/m):	59.0/18.0	Elevators:	3
Propulsion/Propellers:	diesel-electric/ 2 azimuthing pods	Casino (gaming tables):	No
		Swimming Pools:	1
Passenger Decks:	6	Self-Service Launderette:	No
Total Crew:	110	Library:	Yes
Passengers (lower beds):	180	Onboard currency:	Euros
Passenger Space Ratio (lower beds):	1.6		

THE SHIP. Le Laperouse (sister to Le Champlain) is designed to take you to some the more remote areas of the planet in comfort. The shape is similar to the larger general-purpose 'yacht'-style Ponant ships, but with an open (trawler) stern that provides access to the marine equipment and acts as a landing platform.

This expedition-style ship has some premium contemporary touches in its interiors. What's really impressive – and different – is seating under the sea! It's in an underwater lounge called the 'Blue Eye.'

The interior design is quite practical, but the ship feels a little closed-in and cramped due to the low ceiling heights. Public rooms include a Panorama Lounge, Main Lounge, a Theatre/Lecture Room, and the aforementioned 'Blue Eye' lounge.

If you are looking for sophisticated facilities in a relaxed but chic, French, yacht-like environment – quite different to most large cruise ships – with decent food, and friendly, informal service, then Le

BERLITZ'S RATINGS		
	Possible	Achieved
Ship	500	NYR
Accommodation	200	NYR
Food	400	NYR
Service	400	NYR
Entertainment	100	NYR
Cruise Experience	400	NYR
OVERALL SCORE NYR points out of 2000		

Laperouse should fit the bill.

ACCOMMODATION. There are numerous accommodation price grades. The price you pay depends on the size, location, and grade you choose. From the smallest interior cabin(no view) to the largest suite, all are comfortable, and many have balconies.

DINING. The restaurant, located aft, is cheerful, and has both indoor and outdoor seating.

ENTERTAINMENT. Movies are shown in the theater.

SPA/FITNESS. The Yacht Spa facilities include a fitness room with starboard-side ocean views, a kinetic wall, and a steam room with shower, but no changing room. A range of massage and body treatments are provided by Sothys, whose staff operates the facility.

LE LYRIAL
★★★★

THIS IS A SMALL, CHIC CONTEMPORARY YACHT-LIKE, VERY FRENCH SHIP

Size:	Small Ship	Passenger/Crew Ratio (lower beds):	1.5
Tonnage:	10,944	Cabins (total):	122
Cruise Line:	Ponant	Size Range (sq ft/m):	226.0–710.4/21.0–66.0
Former Names:	none	Cabins (for one person):	0
Builder:	Fincantieri (Italy)	Cabins with balcony:	122
Entered Service:	Apr 2015	Cabins (wheelchair accessible):	3
Length (ft/m):	465.8/142.0	Wheelchair accessibility:	Fair
Beam (ft/m):	9.0/18.0	Elevators:	3
Propulsion/Propellers:	diesel-electric/2	Casino (gaming tables):	No
Passenger Decks:	6	Swimming Pools:	1
Total Crew:	140	Self-Service Launderette:	No
Passengers (lower beds):	244	Library:	Yes
Passenger Space Ratio (lower beds):	44.8	Onboard currency:	Euros

THE SHIP. *Le Lyrial* (its name refers to the Lyra constellation in the northern hemisphere) has a smart 'sponson' skirt built-in at the stern for operational stability, and a fleet of 12 Zodiac landing craft is carried for shore landings and viewing excursions during soft expedition and nature cruises. The hull is the color of gray slate.

There is some sunbathing space outdoors forward of the funnel and around the small pool – aft of the deck below – together with a shower enclosure. Aft of the funnel is an outdoor bar/grill, but there's really not enough seating if the ship operates in warm-weather areas.

It's trendy and uncluttered, with contemporary mega-yacht chic decor, and, although it carries a few less passengers, it's the same size as sister ships *L'Austral*, *Le Boréal*, and *Le Soleil*. So, it is classed as a Boutique ship, and not a small ship. Almost all public rooms are aft, with accommodation located forward; the elevators go to all decks except the uppermost one (Deck 7). The decor is minimalist and super-yacht chic – relaxing and pleasant, with lots of blue and white. Glitz is absent, although there are many reflective surfaces, and the overall 'feel' of the decor is cool rather than warm.

The focal point is the two-deck high main lobby, which has a central, circular seating area, although its design is not exactly warm.

BERLITZ'S RATINGS

	Possible	Achieved
Ship	500	408
Accommodation	200	158
Food	400	291
Service	400	299
Entertainment	100	75
Cruise Experience	400	299

OVERALL SCORE 1534 points out of 2000

This is all-inclusive cruising with drinks, table wine for lunch and dinner, bottled mineral water, port charges, and Zodiac excursions on 'expedition-style' cruises all included in the fare; spa treatments cost extra, however. Note, however, that the cruise line chooses the drinks and wine – not you.

It is very refreshing (retro) to know that cruise tickets and documents are provided in a proper ticket pouch and sent to you, so, there's no digital frustration, but much anticipation.

The crew is English- and French-speaking, with many hotel service staff from Asia. However, there's no outside walking or jogging deck. The interior stairways are a quite steep and have short steps.

Le Lyrial is best suited to young-minded couples and solo travelers who are looking for sophisticated facilities in a relaxed but chic French yacht-like environment that is quite different to most large cruise ships, with decent food, and informal service. The ship can also be chartered or part-chartered by 'premium' travel organizers who prefer smaller ships.

ACCOMMODATION. There are 122 suites/cabins (10 fewer than the earlier sister ships).

The largest accommodation includes: eight suites of 484.3 sq ft (45 sq m), including an 86.1 sq ft (8 sq m) balcony; one larger Owner's Suite measuring 721.2 sq ft (67 sq m), including a 21.5 sq ft (2 sq m) balcony); and a Grand Deluxe Suite of 581.2 sq ft (54 sq m), including a 96.8 sq ft (9 sq m) balcony).

The cabin cabinetry is crafted in elegant woods. A real plus is that there are no interior (no-view) cabins – each cabin has an outside view, plus good-quality bed linen, overlays, cushions, refrigerator, personal safe, television, wall mirror, L'Occitane bathroom products, and good soundproofing. However, note that the step into the bathroom is high, at 6.5ins (16.5 cm).

CUISINE. The main restaurant is chic but not overly pretentious. It accommodates all passengers in an open-seating arrangement and has an integral wine display cabinet. The chairs are quite square and have thin armrests and low backs – but they look good.

An indoor/outdoor Grill (though there's no grill) has casual seating for up to 130, with self-serve buffet setup for breakfast and lunch, and a 'fast grill' dinner in an alfresco setting. But the layout is rather disjointed, and the port and starboard sides are sep-arated by two elevators. There are two main buffet display units – one for cold food, one for hot – and a separate table setup for bread and an active cooking station (eggs for breakfast, pasta at lunchtime).

ENTERTAINMENT. The show lounge/lecture hall has amphitheater-style seating for all passengers, and a raised stage suited to concerts, other shows and cabaret presentations. It's also used for specialist lecturers and expedition-style recaps. Two large pillars obstruct the sight lines from several seats, however.

SPA/FITNESS. The Yacht Spa facilities include a fitness room with port-side ocean views, adjacent kinetic wall, and a steam room with shower (there's no separate shower aboard L'Austral, Le Boreal, or Le Soleil), although isn't a changing room. A range of massage and body treatments are provided by Sothys, which staffs and oversees the facility.

LE PONANT
★★★+

CHIC DECOR AND RELAXED, YACHT-STYLE CRUISING FOR FRENCH-SPEAKERS

Size:	Boutique Ship	Passenger/Crew Ratio (lower beds):	2.1
Tonnage:	1,489	Cabins (total):	32
Cruise Line:	Ponant	Size Range (sq ft/m):	145.3–164.6/13.5–15.3
Former Names:	none	Cabins (for one person):	0
Builder:	SFCN (France)	Cabins with balcony:	0
Entered Service:	Jun 2009	Cabins (wheelchair accessible):	0
Length (ft/m):	288.7/88.0	Wheelchair accessibility:	None
Beam (ft/m):	39.3/12.0	Elevators:	No
Propulsion/Propellers:	diesel/sail power/1	Casino (gaming tables):	No
Passenger Decks:	3	Swimming Pools:	0
Total Crew:	32	Self-Service Launderette:	No
Passengers (lower beds):	64	Library:	Yes
Passenger Space Ratio (lower beds):	23.2	Onboard currency:	Euros

THE SHIP. Ultra sleek, and very efficiently designed, this contemporary sail-cruise ship has three masts that rise 54.7ft (16.7m) above the water line, and electronic winches that assist in the furling and unfurling of the sails. The total sail area measures approximately 16,140 sq ft (1,500 sq m). This captivating ship has plenty of room on its open decks for sunbathing. Although they have padded cushions, the off-white plastic sunloungers are still not at all elegant.

The interior design is clean, stylish, functional, and high-tech. Three public lounges have pastel decor, soft colors, and great flair. One price fits all. The ship is marketed mainly to young, sophisticated French-speaking passengers who love yachting and the sea. The company has four mega-yacht cruise ships.

Gratuities are 'not required', but they are expected. It's refreshing to find that cruise tickets and documents are provided in a proper ticket pouch and sent to you (so, there's no digital frustration, but much anticipation).

ACCOMMODATION. There are five cabins on Antigua Deck (the open deck) and 27 on Marie-Galante Deck (the lowest one). Crisp, clean blond woods and pristine white cabins have twin beds that convert to a double. There's a minibar, personal safe, and a bathroom. All cabins have portholes,

BERLITZ'S RATINGS		
	Possible	Achieved
Ship	500	348
Accommodation	200	148
Food	400	267
Service	400	282
Entertainment	100	70
Cruise Experience	400	217

OVERALL SCORE 1332 points out of 2000

artwork, and a refrigerator. There is limited storage, however, and few drawers – they are also very small. The cabin bathrooms are quite small, but efficient.

DINING. The lovely Karukéra dining room has an open-seating policy. There is fresh fish daily, when available, and dinner is always treated as a true gastronomic affair. Free wines are included for lunch and dinner, and the cuisine is, naturally, classic French. That Gallic inclination also means the selection of cheeses, breads, and breakfast croissants is good. There are free cappuccinos and espressos. For casual breakfasts and luncheons, there is a charming outdoor café under a canvas sailcloth awning.

ENTERTAINMENT. There is no professional entertainment as such, although occasionally the crew may put on a little soirée. Dinner is the main event each evening, and, being a French product, dinner can provide several hours of entertainment in itself.

SPA/FITNESS. There is no spa, fitness room, sauna, or steam room. However, for recreation, there are water-sports facilities, and these include an aft marina platform from which you can swim. There is also windsurfing, water-ski boating, and scuba and snorkel equipment. Scuba diving costs extra, charged per dive.

LE SOLEAL
★★★★

FRENCH AMBIENCE AND SMALL MEGA-YACHT PREMIUM CHIC ABOARD THIS SHIP

Size:	Small Ship	Passenger/Crew Ratio (lower beds):	1.5
Tonnage:	10,944	Cabins (total):	132
Cruise Line:	Ponant	Size Range (sq ft/m):	226.0–581.2/21.0–54.0
Former Names:	none	Cabins (for one person):	0
Builder:	Fincantieri (Italy)	Cabins with balcony:	125
Entered Service:	Jul 2013	Cabins (wheelchair accessible):	3
Length (ft/m):	465.8/142.0	Wheelchair accessibility:	Fair
Beam (ft/m):	9.0/18.0	Elevators:	3
Propulsion/Propellers:	diesel-electric (4,600kW)/2	Casino (gaming tables):	No
Passenger Decks:	6	Swimming Pools:	1
Total Crew:	140	Self-Service Launderette:	No
Passengers (lower beds):	264	Library:	Yes
Passenger Space Ratio (lower beds):	41.4	Onboard currency:	Euros

THE SHIP. One of four almost identical sister ships catering mainly to French speakers, Le Soléal is contemporary, chic, and uncluttered. With a dark gray hull and sleek white superstructure, the ship looks more like a large private yacht than a traditional cruise ship.

The ship has a smart 'sponson' skirt built in at the stern – this is for operational stability – and carries a fleet of 12 Zodiac landing craft for soft expedition voyages. There is some sunbathing space outdoors forward of the funnel and around the small pool – aft of a casual eatery located one deck below – together with a shower enclosure.

Almost all the public rooms are located in the aft section, with accommodation located forward; the elevators go to all decks except the uppermost one (Deck 7). The decor is minimalist and super-yacht chic – relaxing and pleasant, with lots of browns and creams and a splash of red here and there. However, there are many reflective surfaces, and the overall feeling of the decor is cool rather than warm and cosseting.

The focal point of the interior is the main lobby, with a central, circular seating and tiled floor surround; its small central section spans two decks. The other flooring is wood, which can be noisy. The lower decks of the main stairway are made of faux gray wood, while the upper decks are carpeted – a strange combination that somehow works.

Le Soléal is geared to young-minded couples and solo travelers who want semi-sophisticated facilities

BERLITZ'S RATINGS		
	Possible	Achieved
Ship	500	400
Accommodation	200	155
Food	400	290
Service	400	301
Entertainment	100	74
Cruise Experience	400	302
OVERALL SCORE 1522 points out of 2000		

in a relaxed but stylish yacht-like environment quite different from most cruise ships, and are happy with reasonably good food and service. The ship is often chartered or part-chartered by 'premium' travel organizers, such as Abercrombie & Kent, Gohagan, and Tauck, who prefer smaller ships.

This is all-inclusive cruising – except for spa treatments – with drinks, table wine for lunch and dinner, bottled mineral water, port charges, and Zodiac excursions on expedition-style cruises included in the fare. The crew is English- and French-speaking, with many hotel service staff from Asia. It is, however, refreshing to note that cruise tickets and documents are provided in a proper ticket pouch and sent to you.

Passenger niggles? There's no outside walking or jogging deck. The interior stairways are a quite steep and have short steps. The restaurant is noisy. The entertainment system is not user-friendly, and the Internet connection is slow and expensive. Overall, it's difficult for French-speaking and non-French-speaking passengers to mix.

ACCOMMODATION. Of the 132 suites/cabins, there are three Prestige Suites with 301 sq ft plus a 54-sq-ft balcony (28 plus 5 sq m). Forty of the 94 deluxe cabins – 200 sq ft plus a 43-sq-ft balcony (18.6 plus 4 sq m) – can be combined into 20 larger suites, each with two bathrooms, and separate living area and bedroom. All cabinetry is made in elegant dark woods. A real plus is that there are no interior cabins, which means that every cabin has an outside view. Cabin insulation is also good, so you shouldn't hear your neighbor.

The deluxe and standard cabins have a large ocean-view window, two beds that convert to a queen-size one, and a long vanity desk with good lighting. Facilities include a TV set, DVD player, refrigerator, and personal safe. The bathrooms are marble-appointed, but they have very heavy hand-held shower hoses. Amenities include a minibar, personal safe, hairdryer, bathrobe, and French (L'Occitane) bathroom products. Wi-Fi costs extra.

All other cabins have good-size beds, although the corners of the bed frames are square, so be careful when passing between bed and an adjacent storage unit – it's quite large, with two deep drawers. Other facilities include a refrigerator, television, wall mirror, good-size wardrobe-style closet (armoire) with personal safe, and a vanity desk with drawer and a small shelf.

The small cabin bathrooms (the entrance door is only 20.5ins/52cm wide) also have a sliding partition window that enables you to see through the cabin to the ocean, and a deep, half-size tub/shower combination. The lip between floor and bathroom is just over 6ins (15cm) high.

There are no shelves for toiletries, but there are two drawers under the washbasin – although they are not very practical. A separate cubicle houses the vacuum toilet. Balconies have faux wood decking and a fine (real) wood handrail, although solid paneling obstructs views when seated and makes the cabin seem dark – glass panels would have been nicer; the balconies are also narrow. The closet space is decent enough, although the doors, with nice white leather handles, are wide – at 31ins (79cm), they are wider than the cabin door, and can't be opened without first closing the bathroom and toilet doors that are directly opposite.

Good-quality bed linen, overlays, and cushions are provided, although there is no choice of pillows.

DINING. The main restaurant is chic but not pretentious – or even warm. It accommodates all passengers in an open-seating arrangement and has two integral wine-display cabinets. The chairs are rather square and have very thin armrests and low backs – but they look good. And the food? While the appetizers and entrées (mains) are reasonably good but nothing special, the cakes and desserts are delightful.

An indoor/outdoor Grill has casual seating for up to 130, with self-serve buffet set-up for breakfast and lunch, and a 'fast grill' dinner in an alfresco setting. The layout is disjointed, and port and starboard sides are separated by two elevators. There are two main buffet display units – one for cold food, one for hot, plus a separate table set-up for bread and an active cooking station (eggs for breakfast, pasta at lunch-time, for example).

ENTERTAINMENT. The showlounge, which doubles as a lecture hall, has amphitheater-style seating for 260, and a raised stage for concerts and cabaret-style entertainment. The production shows are weak, repetitive, and loud, but they do have a sort of French flair about them. The venue is also used for expedition-style recaps and lectures, but two large pillars obstruct the sight lines from several seats.

SPA/FITNESS. The Yacht Spa facilities include a fitness room with starboard-side ocean views, adjacent kinetic wall, and a steam room, but there is no changing room. A wide range of massage and body treatments are provided by Carita of Paris, which staffs and oversees the facility.

LIBERTY OF THE SEAS
★★★+

A LARGE RESORT SHIP FOR CASUAL, BUT ACTIVE CRUISING FOR THE WHOLE FAMILY

Size:	Large Resort Ship	Passenger/Crew Ratio (lower beds):	2.6
Tonnage:	154,407	Cabins (total):	1,815
Cruise Line:	Royal Caribbean International	Size Range (sq ft/m):	149.0–2,025.0/13.8–188.1
Former Names:	none	Cabins (for one person):	0
Builder:	Kvaerner Masa-Yards (Finland)	Cabins with balcony:	842
Entered Service:	May 2007	Cabins (wheelchair accessible):	32
Length (ft/m):	1,112.2/339.0	Wheelchair accessibility:	Best
Beam (ft/m):	184.0/56.0	Elevators:	14
Propulsion/Propellers:	diesel-electric (75,600kW)/3	Casino (gaming tables):	Yes
	pods (2 azimuthing, 1 fixed)	Swimming Pools:	2
Passenger Decks:	15	Self-Service Launderette:	No
Total Crew:	1,397	Library:	Yes
Passengers (lower beds):	3,630	Onboard currency:	US$
Passenger Space Ratio (lower beds):	42.0		

THE SHIP. *Liberty of the Seas* (a *Freedom*-class ship) – a large resort at sea – is a really good choice for families with children. The ship's 'pod' propulsion system virtually eliminates vibration. The outer decks are full of water features for the whole family. Splashaway Bay is a water-themed play area for families, with water cannons, geysers, and more (above it is a large movie screen).

The water and sports facilities are good for adults, too. Aft is a boomerang-style water slide, called Tidal Wave, and two racer slides (Cyclone and Typhoon), all adjacent to a Flowrider surf simulator. Two 16-person hot tubs are cantilevered 12ft (3.7m) over the ship's sides in an adults-only Solarium area.

There are 16 bars and lounges to enjoy, plus a promenade of shops, munching and drinking spots along the Royal Promenade. One deck down from the Royal Promenade is a large Casino Royale, The Catacombs disco, Schooner Bar, Boleros Lounge, and a photo gallery and shop, while the forward section leads into the three-deck-high Platinum Theater.

A regulation-size ice-skating rink (Studio B) has real ice, with bleachers seating. Outstanding Ice Follies shows are presented here, but note that a number of slim pillars obstruct clear-view arena stage sight lines. Adjacent is the On Air broadcast studio.

Almost at the top of the ship is the company's trademark Viking Crown Lounge, the Olive or Twist jazz lounge, and a Wedding Chapel. Other facilities in-

BERLITZ'S RATINGS		
	Possible	Achieved
Ship	500	368
Accommodation	200	132
Food	400	235
Service	400	283
Entertainment	100	74
Cruise Experience	400	266

OVERALL SCORE 1358 points out of 2000

clude a cigar-smoker's lounge, conference center, a concierge lounge (for suite occupants only), and a comfortable 3,600-book library.

Liberty of the Seas is an exciting and very comfortable ship, with contemporary decor. However, there are only four banks of elevators (two forward and two aft) totaling 14, so if you have a cabin in the center of the ship, you'll need to walk in order to travel vertically between decks; and there are only two major passenger stairways – one forward, one aft. More cabins were added in a 2015 refit, but no extra elevators.

Niggles include the high cost for internet connectivity, the constant push to sell you ice-laden drinks, lines for the security check when reboarding in ports, the poor quality of food at the Windjammer Buffet, the lack of green vegetables in main dining room food, and poor cheese and fruit choices.

ACCOMMODATION. There is a wide range of cabins in 14 categories and 21 price grades. There are many family-friendly cabins, which are good for family reunions.

All cabins have a private bathroom (with tub and shower, or shower only), vanity desk with hairdryer, mini-bar, safe, flat-screen infotainment system, iPod dock, radio, and satellite telephone. A room service menu is provided. Suite occupants have access to a Concierge Lounge, for personal service – this saves standing in line at the reception desk.

Interior (no-view) cabin (there are many of these): sleep two (some rooms sleep three or four). Size: 152 sq ft (14.1 sq m).

Family ocean-view cabin: located at the front of the ship. Accommodates six and has round windows measuring 48ins (122cm). Size: 265 sq ft (24.6 sq m).

Promenade family cabin: size: 300 sq ft (27.9 sq m).

Promenade cabins: interior, but overlooking the Royal Promenade, with bay windows. Size: 149 sq ft (13.8 sq m).

Deluxe ocean-view cabin: these measuere 173 sq ft (16 sq m) plus balcony: 46 sq ft (4.3 sq m).

Superior ocean-view cabins: sleep two (some rooms sleep three or four) and measure 202 sq ft (18.8 sq m) plus balcony: 42 sq ft (3.9 sq m).

Junior Suites: sleep up to four and measure 285.2 sq ft (26.5 sq m) plus balcony: 101 sq ft (9.4 sq m).

Grand Suites: sleep up to four and measure 381 sq ft (35.4 sq m) plus balcony: 89 sq ft (8.3 sq m).

Owner's Suites: sleep up to five and measure 506 sq ft (47 sq m) plus balcony: 131 sq ft (12.2 sq m).

Royal Family Suites: sleep up to 6 and measure 588 sq ft (54.6 sq m) plus Balcony: 234 sq ft (21.7 sq m).

Royal Suite: measures 1,406 sq ft (130.6 sq m) plus balcony: 377 sq ft (35 sq m).

Presidential Family Suite: sleeps up to 14 (at a pinch) and measures 1,215 sq ft (112.9 sq m) plus balcony: 810 sq ft (75.3 sq m).

DINING. The main dining room is large and is set on three levels, each with a different name: Botticelli, Michelangelo, and Rembrandt. A dramatic staircase connects all three, but huge support pillars obstruct the sight lines. When you book, choose one of two seatings, or 'My Time Dining' (be prepared to wait for a table at peak times). Tables are for four to 12.

The place settings, porcelain, and cutlery are of good quality. The menu descriptions make the food sound better than it is, however, and the selection of breads, rolls, fruit, and cheese is poor. Overall, meals are rather hit and miss, depending on your taste, and nothing is really memorable. That's because this is catering on a large scale. Also, if you want lobster or a decent filet mignon (steak), you will be asked to pay extra.

Other eateries include: Sabor (for modern tastes of Mexico); Giovanni's Table (open for lunch and din-

ner, a trattoria featuring Italian classics served family-style); Izumi Asian Cuisine (open for lunch and dinner, includes a sushi bar and sizzling hot-rock cooked items); Chef's Table (open for dinner only, this 'private' experience features a wine pairing dinner); and Park Café (open for all meals, this indoor/outdoor deli is for salads, sandwiches, soups, and pastries). All except Park Café incur a cover charge.

There's also:

Café Promenade: for Continental breakfast, all-day pizzas (Sorrento's), sandwiches, and coffees (in paper cups).

Windjammer Café: this is a really large, sprawling venue for casual buffet-style, self-help breakfast (this tends to be the busiest time of the day), lunch, and light dinners; it's often difficult to find a table and by the time you do, your food could be cold.

Chops Grille: an intimate restaurant for steaks and seafood; a cover charge applies.

Johnny Rockets: a retro 1950s all-day, all-night diner-style eatery for burgers, hot dogs, other fast-food items, and malt shakes; there is both indoor and outdoor seating (indoor tables have a mini-jukebox). There's a cover charge.

Sprinkles: for round-the-clock ice cream and yoghurt, pastries, and coffee.

ENTERTAINMENT. The Platinum Theater is a well-designed showlounge located forward, with only a few slim pillars and almost no disruption of sight lines. It has a hydraulic orchestra pit and huge stage areas, as well as superb lighting equipment.

A performance not to be missed is the Greatest Show at Sea Parade – a 15-minute extravaganza that bumbles along the Royal Promenade; it replicates the parade of stars and animals at a circus of yesteryear. This is when it's really good to have one of those interior-view atrium cabins. Otherwise, get a position early along the Royal Promenade.

SPA/FITNESS. The Steiner-operated Day Spa is large. It includes a large aerobics room, fitness center, treatment rooms, and sauna/steam rooms and relaxation areas. Some basic exercise classes are free, but others cost extra. Active types can go body-boarding, boxing in the full-size boxing ring, go rock-climbing, in-line skating, jog, putt, swim, surf, play in the golf simulators or on the mini-golf course (Liberty Dunes).

MAASDAM
★★★

THIS SHIP HAS DUTCH-STYLE DECOR FOR MATURE-AGE TRAVELERS

Size:	Mid-size Ship	Passenger/Crew Ratio (lower beds):	2.2
Tonnage:	55,451	Cabins (total):	632
Cruise Line:	Holland America Line	Size Range (sq ft/m):	186.2–1,124.8/17.3–104.5
Former Names:	none	Cabins (for one person):	0
Builder:	Fincantieri (Italy)	Cabins with balcony:	150
Entered Service:	Dec 1993/Dec 1993	Cabins (wheelchair accessible):	6
Length (ft/m):	719.3/219.3	Wheelchair accessibility:	Good
Beam (ft/m):	101.0/30.8	Elevators:	8
Propulsion/Propellers:	diesel-electric (34,560kW)/2	Casino (gaming tables):	Yes
Passenger Decks:	10	Swimming Pools:	2 (1 w/ sliding glass dome)
Total Crew:	557	Self-Service Launderette:	Yes
Passengers (lower beds):	1,266	Library:	Yes
Passenger Space Ratio (lower beds):	43.8	Onboard currency:	US$

THE SHIP. *Maasdam* (now over 25 years old and well worn) is one of four almost identical ships, along with *Ryndam* (now *Pacific Eden*), *Statendam* (now *Pacific Aria*), and *Veendam*. Although the exterior styling is angular (some say boxy – the funnel certainly is), it is softened and balanced somewhat by its black hull. There is a full walk-around teak promenade deck outdoors – excellent for strolling, and no sign of synthetic turf. The sunloungers on the exterior promenade deck are wood, and have comfortable cushioned pads; those at the swimming pool on Lido Deck are of white plastic. There is good passenger flow throughout the public areas.

The interior has an asymmetrical layout, which helps to reduce congestion. Most public rooms are concentrated on two decks, Promenade Deck and Upper Promenade Deck, which creates a spacious feel. In general, the decor is restrained, with contemporary materials combined with traditional woods and ceramics. There is, thankfully, little glitz anywhere.

Some $2 million worth of artwork represents HAL's fine Dutch heritage. Several oil paintings of the line's former ships by Stephen Card (a former ship's captain) adorn the stairway landings. Also noticeable are the fine flower arrangements in the public areas and foyers – used to to brighten the decor. Atop the ship, with forward-facing views that wrap around the sides, is a Crow's Nest Lounge. By day, a pleasant observation lounge, with ocean-view windows, it turns

BERLITZ'S RATINGS		
	Possible	Achieved
Ship	500	297
Accommodation	200	125
Food	400	228
Service	400	267
Entertainment	100	60
Cruise Experience	400	240

OVERALL SCORE 1240 points out of 2000

into a nightclub with extremely variable lighting in the evenings.

The atrium foyer is three decks high, although its light-catching green glass sculpted centerpiece (*Totem* by Luciano Vistosi, composed of almost 2,000 pieces of glass) makes it look crowded, leaving little room in front of the front office. A hydraulic glass roof covers the reasonably sized swimming pool/hot tubs and central Lido area, whose focal point is a large dolphin sculpture.

This ship has a relaxing Leyden Library, a card room, an Explorer's Lounge (for afternoon tea and after-dinner coffee), a Piano Bar, and a casino featuring gaming tables and slot machines. However, note that part of the casino is open, and passers-by can be subject to cigarette smoke (yes, smoking is still permitted), which non-smokers may well find unpleasant.

HAL's many repeat passengers seem to enjoy the fact that social dancing is always on the menu.

HAL continues its strong maritime traditions and keeps its vessels clean and tidy, but the food and service components let the rest of the cruise experience down.

Other niggles? A pointless escalator travels between two of the lower decks, one of which was originally planned for embarkation. The charge to use the washing machines and dryers in the self-service launderette is petty, particularly for suite occupants, who pay a higher price for their cruise. The men's urinals in public restrooms are unusually high. The ship is now looking decidedly tired and past its sell-by date.

ACCOMMODATION. The accommodation ranges from small interior (no-view) cabins to a Penthouse Suite, in multiple price categories. Interior and outside standard cabins have twin beds convertible to a queen-size bed, with sofa and coffee table. Drawer space is generally good, but closet space is very tight, particularly for long cruises, although adequate for a seven-night cruise. Bathrobes are provided for all, as are hairdryers, and a small range of toiletries. The bathrooms are quite well laid out, but the bathtubs are really just shower tubs.

DINING. The Rotterdam Dining Room, spanning two decks, is aft. It has a grand staircase, panoramic views on three sides, and a music balcony. Both open seating and assigned seating are available, while breakfast and lunch are only open seating – you'll be taken to your table by restaurant staff, when you enter. The waiter stations are noisy for anyone seated near them.

With a few exceptions, the cuisine is quite unmemorable, and is missing anything approaching passion and taste. There's a distinct lack of variety of green vegetables, too heavy a use of rice, canned fruit, and already sliced and diced cheese. Still, you get friendly service from the Indonesian and Filipino stewards.

A 66-seat, extra-cost Pinnacle Grill is located just forward of the balcony level of the main dining room on the starboard side. It features Pacific Northwest cuisine (prime steaks and seafood), and reservations

are needed. A Bulgari show plate, Rosenthal china, Riedel wine glasses, and Frette table linen are provided. It's is a better, more relaxed dining experience than the main dining room and worth the extra cost, if your budget allows.

The Lido Buffet is open for casual dinners on all except the last night of each cruise. It's open seating, and the tables are set with crisp linens, flatware, and stemware. A set menu includes a choice of entreés (mains). It is also open for breakfasts and lunches. Again, there is much use of canned fruits and items in packets. The beverage station, which is similar to those found in family outlets in the United States, is poor. Additionally, a poolside 'Dive-In at the Terrace Grill' features burgers, hot dogs, and fries.

Passengers have to use the Lido Buffet on days when the dining room is closed for lunch, depending on the itinerary.

ENTERTAINMENT. The Showroom at Sea, located forward, spans two decks, with banquette seating on both main and upper levels. The ceiling is low, and the sight lines from the balcony level are quite poor. The production shows are passé, but individual cabaret acts are sometimes good.

SPA/FITNESS. The Ocean Spa is located one deck below the navigation bridge. It has ocean views and includes a gymnasium with all the latest muscle-pumping exercise machines. There's also a beauty salon with ocean-view windows to the port side, several treatment rooms, and men's and women's sauna, steam room, and changing areas.

MAGELLAN
★★★

AN INFORMAL, COLORFUL, ADULTS-ONLY SHIP FOR BRITISH CRUISERS

Size:	Mid-size Ship	Passenger/Crew Ratio (lower beds):	2.2
Tonnage:	46,052	Cabins (total):	726
Cruise Line:	Cruise and Maritime Voyages	Size Range (sq ft/m):	189.2–420.0/17.0–39.0
Former Names:	Grand Holiday, Holiday	Cabins (for one person):	0
Builder:	Aalborg Vaerft (Denmark)	Cabins with balcony:	10
Entered Service:	Jul 1985/Jun 2015	Cabins (wheelchair accessible):	15
Length (ft/m):	726.0/221.3	Wheelchair accessibility:	None
Beam (ft/m):	92.4/28.1	Elevators:	8
Propulsion/Propellers:	diesel (22,360kW)/2	Casino (gaming tables):	Yes
Passenger Decks:	9	Swimming Pools:	3
Total Crew:	660	Self-Service Launderette:	No
Passengers (lower beds):	1,452	Library:	Yes
Passenger Space Ratio (lower beds):	31.7	Onboard currency:	UK£

THE SHIP. *Magellan* (formerly *Grand Holiday*) is a rather boxy-looking, all-white vessel, although CMV has managed to soften its looks with a bow to stern stripe. It does, however, have a distinctive swept-back wing-tipped funnel.

The salt-water swimming pools are quite small, as are the hot tubs, but the open deck and sunning space atop ship is decent. There is an exterior walking area, although it doesn't wrap around the front of the ship. There are numerous public rooms (with British names such as Hampton's, Kensington, etc.) on two main entertainment decks, and these flow from a wide indoor promenade. Unusually, the Neptune Observation Bar is aft.

This ship is best suited to British mature-age adults seeking a low-cost cruise experience. The good: the staff escort to your cabin when you embark; the staff are friendly; and the decor is appealingly non-glitzy. The not-so-good: there is no walk-around promenade deck outdoors, although the outdoor space itself is reasonably good; a lot of chairs in the two restaurants have no armrests; many of the low-back tub chairs have no back support. Note also that the cabin walls are paper thin. Also, the air conditioning tends to be overly cold throughout the ship.

ACCOMMODATION. There are just four cabin categories: Suite with balcony; Junior Suite with balcony; exterior cabins; and interior (no-view) cabins, in 15 different price grades. The standard outside and interior

BERLITZ'S RATINGS		
	Possible	Achieved
Ship	500	294
Accommodation	200	121
Food	400	212
Service	400	237
Entertainment	100	56
Cruise Experience	400	228

OVERALL SCORE 1148 points out of 2000

cabins are plain but functional units and they provide all the basics including a small vanity/writing desk. TV sets are typically placed high in one corner and are not easy to see. The bathrooms are practical, with decent-size shower enclosures.

DINING. There are two main restaurants: Kensington (in the center) and Waldorf (aft – with some nice ocean-view tables at the back). Both have low ceilings and raised center sections, and feel cramped. This is banquet-style catering, so standardization and cooking on a large scale is the norm. Several traditional British favorite dishes are on offer. The wine list is very limited; there are no wine waiters.

Raffles Bistro is a self-serve buffet area that provides all the basics (except service and enough seats), although its layout is old in style, which makes the venue seem more like a canteen than a bistro. Still, it's adequate for a quick meal.

ENTERTAINMENT. The Magellan Show Lounge is the venue for colorful, low-cost production shows and cabaret acts, bu pillars obstruct the views from several seats. Most lounges and bars also have live music.

SPA/FITNESS. The Jade Wellness Center is located on an upper deck, but the fitness room is on a different deck. Some fitness classes are free, while some may cost extra. Book early for massages, facials, or other beauty treatments, because time slots go quickly.

MAJESTIC PRINCESS
★★★★

THIS MULTI-CHOICE, FAMILY-FRIENDLY RESORT SHIP HAS CONTEMPORARY ASIAN STYLING

Size:	Large Resort Ship	Passenger/Crew Ratio (lower beds):	2.6/1
Tonnage:	142,229	Cabins (total):	1,780
Cruise Line:	Princess Cruises	Size Range (sq ft/m):	163–1,279/15.1–118.8
Former Names:	none	Cabins (for one person):	0
Builder:	Fincantieri (Italy)	Cabins with balcony:	1,438
Entered Service:	Apr 2017	Cabins (wheelchair accessible):	36
Length (ft/m):	1,082.6/330.0	Wheelchair accessibility:	Best
Beam (ft/m):	126.3/38.6	Elevators:	14
Propulsion/Propellers:	diesel-electric/2	Casino (gaming tables):	Yes
Passenger Decks:	17	Swimming Pools:	2
Total Crew:	1,346	Self-Service Launderette:	Yes
Passengers (lower beds):	3,560	Library:	Yes
Passenger Space Ratio (lower beds):	39.9	Onboard currency:	US$

THE SHIP. Although large, the ship's profile, which is tailored somewhat for the Asian/Chinese market (at least for its first season), has a decent balance. In terms of practical design, the lifeboats are located outside the main public room areas, so they don't impair the view from balcony cabins. There is a complete walk-around promenade deck.

An over-the-water SeaWalk, an open deck glass-bottomed enclosed walkway (first introduced in 2013 aboard *Royal Princess*) on the starboard side extends almost 30ft (9.2m) beyond the vessel's edge and forms part of a lounge/bar venue. This is the place to view the sea 128ft (39m) below, so you *can* 'walk' on water (well, over it).

There are two principal stair towers and elevator banks, plus four panoramic-view elevators in a third, central bank (these elevators do not go between decks 7 and 16 – stairways are only at the forward and aft elevator banks).

The interior decor includes an abundance of bright colors to suit Chinese tastes. This ship features a large amount of space dedicated to gaming, including VIP and private gaming rooms (for high rollers).

The Piazza Atrium is the ship's multi-faceted, multi-level social and dining hub, with a horseshoe-shaped flowing stairway and four panoramic elevators. The base level includes the Harmony Chinese Restaurant and the large International Café.

BERLITZ'S RATINGS		
	Possible	Achieved
Ship	500	401
Accommodation	200	139
Food	400	268
Service	400	294
Entertainment	100	82
Cruise Experience	400	298
OVERALL SCORE 1482 points out of 2000		

Princess Cruises delivers a consistent, well-packaged cruise vacation, with a range of entertainment options, at an attractive price. One downside (and a serious design flaw) is the lack of a central stairway above two of the main restaurants, which leads to severe crowding of the adjacent elevators.

ACCOMMODATION. There are six main types of accommodation and numerous price grades: (a) Grand Suite; (b) suites with balcony; (c) mini-suites with balcony; (d) deluxe outside-view balcony cabins; (e) outside-view cabins with balcony; and (f) interior cabins (no view). Pricing depends on two things: size and location. Outside-view cabins account for about 81 percent of all accommodation, and all have a small balcony; those located at the stern are the quietest and most sought-after. Some of the most sought-after suites are located aft, occupying the corner (port and starboard) positions.

All accommodation grades share energy-efficient key card-controlled lighting. All cabins have beds with upholstered headboards, wall-mounted flat-screen TV sets, 220v electrical socket, turndown service, bathrobes (on request, unless you are in suite-grade accommodation), and toiletries. A hairdryer is provided, sensibly located at the vanity desk unit. Bathrooms have good shelf storage space for toiletries, and all have hand-held, flexi-hose showers, and decent shower enclosures.

DINING. There are three 'formal' main dining rooms (Allegro, Concerto, and Symphony), assigned according to your accommodation grade. The Harmony Chinese Restaurant, located off The Piazza (atrium) features Cantonese cuisine with menus designed by Richard Chen. Other restaurants and eateries clustered around various levels of The Piazza include Alfredo's Pizzeria (named for Princess Cruises' executive chef Alfredo Marzi), the International Café (for extra-cost coffees and teas), and Vines Wine Bar (for wines and tapas).

Elsewhere, there's the Crown Grill, serving extra-cost steaks and seafood. For casual meals, there's a large self-serve buffet venue, World Fresh Marketplace, which offers food by theme and features active cooking stations.

ENTERTAINMENT. The Princess Theater, the main showlounge, is a two-deck-high venue for the large-scale production shows that Princess Cruises is renowned for. There's also a 'Princess Live' auditorium for and other small-audience entertainment features.

SPA/FITNESS. Lotus Spa is located forward on the lower atrium level. Separate facilities for men and women include a sauna, steam room, and changing rooms; common facilities include a relaxation/waiting zone, body-pampering treatment rooms, and a gymnasium with the latest high-tech, muscle-pumping cardio-vascular equipment. Some fitness classes are free, while others cost extra. Children and teens have their own fitness rooms adjacent to their age-related facilities.

Spa operator Steiner Leisure runs the Lotus Spa. You can make online reservations for any spa treatments before your cruise, which could be a great time-saver, as long as you can plan ahead.

MAJESTY OF THE SEAS
★★+

THIS OLDER BUT NICELY REVITALIZED SHIP IS ADEQUATE FOR SHORT CRUISES

Size:	Mid-size Ship
Tonnage:	73,941
Cruise Line:	Royal Caribbean International
Former Names:	none
Builder:	Chantiers de l'Atlantique (France)
Entered Service:	Apr 1992
Length (ft/m):	879.9/268.2
Beam (ft/m):	105.9/32.3
Propulsion/Propellers:	diesel/2
Passenger Decks:	11
Total Crew:	827
Passengers (lower beds):	2,380
Passenger Space Ratio (lower beds):	30.8
Passenger/Crew Ratio (lower beds):	2.8
Cabins (total):	1,190
Size Range (sq ft/m):	118.4–670.0/11.0–62.2
Cabins (for one person):	0
Cabins with balcony:	63
Cabins (wheelchair accessible):	4
Wheelchair accessibility:	Fair
Elevators:	11
Casino (gaming tables):	Yes
Swimming Pools:	2
Self-Service Launderette:	No
Library:	Yes
Onboard currency:	US$

THE SHIP. When first introduced, together with sisters *Monarch of the Seas* and *Sovereign of the Seas* – both now operated by *Pullmantur Cruises*, *Majesty of the Seas* was an innovative ship. In May 2018, *Majesty of the Seas* will also be moved from the RCI fleet to the Pullmantur Cruises fleet.

The company's trademark Viking Crown lounge and bar surrounds the funnel and provides a great view, but it is lacking in soul and tired. The open deck space is very cramped when full, although there appears to be plenty of it.

The ship underwent an extensive revitalization in 2016, when cabins were refreshed and more eateries were introduced. But perhaps the biggest change was the addition of three waterslides (named Cyclone, Supercell, and Typhoon) to the AquaPark outdoors on the lido deck, together with water cannons and 'drench' bucket.

The interior layout is a little awkward to get used to at first, because it was designed (cleverly, actually) in a vertical stack, with most public rooms located aft, and accommodation forward. There's an impressive array of spacious and elegant public rooms, although the decor is from the Ikea school of interior design.

A pleasant five-deck-high Centrum lobby has cascading stairways and two glass-walled elevators. There is a two-level showlounge and a selection of shops, albeit with lots of tacky merchandise. Casino gamers will find gaming tables and an array of slot machines in the expansive Casino Royale.

BERLITZ'S RATINGS	Possible	Achieved
Ship	500	273
Accommodation	200	104
Food	400	204
Service	400	233
Entertainment	100	56
Cruise Experience	400	219

OVERALL SCORE 1089 points out of 2000

Other public rooms include a library (good for quiet relaxation, with a decent selection of books), Boleros (Latin) Lounge, Schooner Bar (a nautical-themed hangout). An Internet center has 10 workstations, and the high-speed Internet access (called Voom) is free.

There's a decent range of children's and teens' programs (teens have their own chill-out room – adults not allowed) and youth counselors.

Because the public rooms are mostly located aft, with accommodation in the forward section, there is often a long wait for elevators, particularly at peak times after dinner, shows, and talks (at least the restrooms are quite welcoming).

This ship provides well-orchestrated short cruises (three- and four-day Bahamas cruises) year-round from Port Canaveral. The dress code is very casual. You will probably be overwhelmed by the public spaces, and underwhelmed by the size of the cabins. Note that there is constant background music in all corridors and elevators, as well as outdoors on the lido (pool) deck.

ACCOMMODATION. There are numerous accommodation price grades. From the smallest interior (no-view) cabin to the largest suite, the price you pay depends on the size, location, and grade you choose.

Standard outside-view and interior cabins are extremely small, although an arched window treatment and colorful soft furnishings give an illusion of more space. Almost all cabins have twin beds convertible to a queen-size or double-bed configuration, together with moveable bedside tables, and flat-screen TV sets. The cabins have very little closet and drawer space – you will need some luggage engineering to stow your cases. So, pack only minimal clothing – all you really need for a short cruise. All cabins have a bathroom with shower enclosure, toilet, and washbasin. All are provided with good mattresses, and duvets.

Suite-grade occupants get much more space, a queen-sized bed, larger bathroom, and priority reservations and attention.

DINING. There are two main dining rooms: Moonlight, with 675 seats, located on the lowest level of the atrium (Centrum) lobby, and Starlight, one deck higher, with 697 seats. When you book, choose early or late seating, or 'My Time Dining' (eat when you want, during dining room hours), at tables for two to eight. The dining operation is well orchestrated, with emphasis on highly programmed, extremely hurried service that many find insensitive.

For casual breakfasts and lunches, Windjammer Marketplace is split into various areas including American, Asian, Latin, and Mediterranean fare. Compass Deli is a bar where you can 'build' your own sandwich.

Themed specialty (extra-cost) dining spots include: Giovanni's Table (for Italian trattoria-style favorites); Izumi (for Japanese-style cuisine); and Sabor (for modern tastes of Mexico).

Johnny Rockets is a 1950s retro diner for fast foods such as burgers, hot dogs, sodas, and shakes, located on an upper deck section of the Windjammer Marketplace (a cover charge applies). At no extra cost, there is Sorrento's for American-Italian pizzas.

The lobby level Café Latte-tudes features Starbucks brand coffees (extra cost) in paper cups, plus free desserts and pastries. And for ice cream lovers, there's Freeze Ice Cream.

ENTERTAINMENT. A Chorus Line is the ship's showlounge, with 1,027 seats. It has both main and balcony levels, with banquette seating, but many pillars prevent good sight lines from many side seats on the lower level.

The production shows are extremely colorful spectaculars with high-energy hype, presentation, and glitz. They are fast-moving, razzle-dazzle shows that rely on lighting and special effects, with choreography that's more stepping in place than dancing. Strong cabaret acts are also presented here.

SPA/FITNESS. The Vitality at Sea Spa has a workout room with aft views and muscle-pumping equipment, an aerobics studio (classes are offered), a beauty salon, a sauna, and body-pampering treatment rooms. The facilities are quite adequate for the short cruises that this ship presently operates.

For sporty types, there is a rock-climbing wall with several separate climbing tracks. It is located outdoors aft of the funnel, as is a basketball court – and a shuffleboard.

MARCO POLO
★★+

A COMFORTABLE, CLASSIC, BUT MODEST SHIP FOR FRUGAL CRUISERS

Size:	Mid-size Ship	Passenger/Crew Ratio (lower beds):	2.3
Tonnage:	22,080	Cabins (total):	425
Cruise Line:	Cruise and Maritime Voyages	Size Range (sq ft/m):	93.0–484.0/8.6–44.9
Former Names:	Aleksandr Pushkin	Cabins (for one person):	0
Builder:	VEB Mathias Thesen Werft (Germany)	Cabins with balcony:	0
Entered Service:	Apr 1966/Apr 2008	Cabins (wheelchair accessible):	2
Length (ft/m):	578.4/176.2	Wheelchair accessibility:	Fair
Beam (ft/m):	77.4/23.6	Elevators:	4
Propulsion/Propellers:	diesel(14,444kW)/2	Casino (gaming tables):	No
Passenger Decks:	8	Swimming Pools:	1
Total Crew:	356	Self-Service Launderette:	No
Passengers (lower beds):	848	Library:	Yes
Passenger Space Ratio (lower beds):	26.0	Onboard currency:	UK£

THE SHIP. Growing old gracefully (but now past its sell by date), *Marco Polo* was built as one of five sister ships for the Russian/Ukrainian cruise fleet. Originally designed in 1966 to re-open the Leningrad to Montréal transatlantic route (inoperative since 1949), it has a 'real ship' profile, an extremely strong ice-strengthened hull, huge storage spaces for long voyages, and lovely thick, polished exterior wood railings.

The ship passed to Norwegian Cruise Line in 1998, and has been operated by CMV for several years, but, in May 2018, it will be withdrawn from service.

Marco Polo adults-only cruises from the UK (although during school vacation periods anyone 16 and over becomes an eligible passenger), with Tilbury (London International Cruise Terminal) as its home port.

Marco Polo has the latest navigational aids and biological waste treatment center, and carries 10 Zodiac landing craft for in-depth shore trips in eco-sensitive areas. With its strong hull and deep draft, it rides well in any unkind sea conditions. There are two large, forward-facing open-deck viewing areas, and its teakwood-decked aft swimming pool/Lido Deck area is kept in good condition. Joggers and walkers can circle around the ship – not on the promenade deck, but one deck above, although this goes past vast air intakes that are noisy, and the walkway is narrow.

BERLITZ'S RATINGS

	Possible	Achieved
Ship	500	264
Accommodation	200	114
Food	400	197
Service	400	223
Entertainment	100	56
Cruise Experience	400	213

OVERALL SCORE 1067 points out of 2000

When you walk aboard, you feel a warm, welcoming, homely ambience. There is a wide range of public rooms, most of which are arranged on one deck. A sense of spaciousness pervades, as most rooms have high ceilings. The interior decor is quite tasteful, with careful use of mirrored surfaces and colors that do not clash but aren't boring. Subdued lighting helps maintain an air of calmness.

This ship operates well-planned destination-intensive cruises (mostly taken up by couples and solo travelers of mature years) and offers really good value for money in very comfortable, unpretentious but tasteful surroundings, while an accommodating crew helps to make a cruise a pleasant, no-hassle experience. Gratuities are automatically applied to your onboard account.

Niggles? There is no observation lounge with forward-facing views over the bows. There are many raised thresholds, so you need to be on your guard when walking through the ship – particularly when negotiating the exterior stairways.

ACCOMMODATION. The cabins, which come in various price grades, depending on location and size, are a profusion of different sizes and configurations. All are pleasingly decorated, practical units with good, solid, rich wood cabinetry, wood and mirror-fronted closets, adequate drawer and storage space, TV, thin cotton bathrobe (upper grades only), and bathroom-mounted hairdryer and non-vacuum, non-noisy toilets. Carpets, curtains, and bedspreads are all nicely color-coordinated. Weak points include poor sound insulation between cabins – you can probably hear your neighbors brushing their hair – and the fact that the bathrooms are quite small.

The largest accommodation is found in two suites: Dynasty and Mandarin, on Columbus Deck, but other suites have superior locations with forward-facing views over the ship's bow.

Also quite comfortable are the superior deluxe ocean-view cabins that have two lower beds, some of which can be converted to a queen-size bed.

Some cabins have lifeboat-obstructed views. It is advisable to avoid cabins 310/312, as these are located close to the engine room doorway, and the noise level is considerable. No cabins have a balcony – the ship was built for long-distance ocean/sea crossings before they became popular.

DINING. The Waldorf, in the ship's center, is nicely decorated in soft pastel colors. It functions well, but it has a low ceiling, is noisy, and the tables are close together. There are two seatings, with tables for two to 10, and good place settings/china. The food itself is of a modest standard, and presentation, quality, and taste that begs improvement. The (mostly young) wines and prices are reasonable.

Marco's Restaurant is for informal self-serve breakfasts and lunches – there is seating inside as well as outdoors around the ship's single, aft swimming pool. On most evenings, it also becomes an alternative dining spot for about 75 people.

ENTERTAINMENT. The Marco Polo Lounge is the venue for shows and lectures. A single-level room, it has banquette seating and fairly decent sight lines, although several pillars obstruct the view from some seats. Entertainment is low key and low budget, and consists of cabaret acts such as singers, magicians, and comedians. There's live music (and some dancing) in several bars and cocktail lounges.

SPA/FITNESS. This is an older ship that was built when spa and wellbeing facilities were not really standard features onboard. A Health Spa, operated by Mandara, was added in a later refit. It is located aft on Upper Deck, and contains a small gymnasium with a few treadmills, exercycles, and some muscle-toning equipment. There's also a beauty salon, a sauna, changing facilities, and treatment rooms for massages, facials, and other body-pampering treatments.

MARINA
★★★★+

THIS SHIP PROVIDES PREMIUM COUNTRY CLUB STYLE FOR MATURE-AGE CRUISERS

Size:	Mid-size Ship	Passenger/Crew Ratio (lower beds):	1.5
Tonnage:	66,084	Cabins (total):	629
Cruise Line:	Oceania Cruises	Size Range (sq ft/m):	172.2–2,000/16.0–185.0
Former Names:	none	Cabins (for one person):	0
Builder:	Fincantieri (Italy)	Cabins with balcony:	593
Entered Service:	Jan 2011	Cabins (wheelchair accessible):	6
Length (ft/m):	776.5/236.7	Wheelchair accessibility:	Good
Beam (ft/m):	105.3/32.1	Elevators:	6
Propulsion/Propellers:	diesel-electric/2	Casino (gaming tables):	Yes
Passenger Decks:	11	Swimming Pools:	1
Total Crew:	800	Self-Service Launderette:	Yes
Passengers (lower beds):	1,258	Library:	Yes
Passenger Space Ratio (lower beds):	52.5	Onboard currency:	US$

THE SHIP. Built in 55 blocks, *Marina* is the first new build for this growing small cruise line. Its profile is quite handsome, with a nicely rounded front and topped by a swept-back funnel. Able to cruise at a speed 25 percent faster than the other three ships in the fleet, it can operate cruises over longer distances.

Oceania Cruises has been careful to try to keep the warm and tasteful 'country house' decor style for which it has become known – the smaller ships were styled by the Scottish interior designer John McNeece – together with an uncomplicated layout that's easy to master quickly.

The interior focal point is the stunning wrought-iron and Lalique glass horseshoe-shaped staircase in the main lobby. Public rooms include nine bars and lounges. There is a 2,000-book library, set on the port side of the funnel housing. The Monte Carlo Casino has its own soft lavender-colored Casino Bar.

The Culinary Center, a cooking demonstration kitchen with 24 workstations run in conjunction with the US-based *Bon Appétit* magazine, incurs a fee for each of several cookery classes, but at least you get to eat your creations. An Artist's Loft hosts constantly changing artists – bring your own paintbrushes. If you like art, look for the genuine Picassos on board; there are 16 of them, including six in the casino.

The dress code is country club – no pajamas or track suits, but no ties, either. Note that a gratuity of 18 percent is added to bar and spa accounts.

BERLITZ'S RATINGS		
	Possible	Achieved
Ship	500	420
Accommodation	200	166
Food	400	310
Service	400	304
Entertainment	100	77
Cruise Experience	400	310
OVERALL SCORE 1587 points out of 2000		

Marina is really comfortable, although you will need to walk a little more than on many cruise ships. It will suit mature-age adults who appreciate quality and style, with plenty of space, plus excellent cuisine and service, in an informal setting with realistic pricing.

In 2012, some of the modifications made when building its close sister *Riviera* were incorporated in its first drydocking. These include better lighting and deeper drawers in suites and cabins, teak decking, plus hand-held shower hoses in suites with bathtubs, and chandeliers in public rooms. Overall, a cruise aboard Marina is a very nice experience.

ACCOMMODATION. There are several price categories, including four suite grades: Owner's Suite; Oceania Suite; Vista Suite; and Penthouse Suite. There are four cabin grades: concierge-level veranda cabin; veranda cabin; deluxe ocean-view cabin; and interior cabin. Price depends on size and location, but all have one thing in common – a good-size bathroom with tub, and separate (but small) shower enclosure, plus two toiletry cabinets.

Around 96 percent of all the accommodation onboard has teak-decked balconies. There's no tie rack in the closets, because the dress code is casual. The decor includes chocolate brown, cream, and white – earthy colors that don't jar the senses. All suites and cabins have dark wood cabinetry with rounded edges.

Standard veranda cabins measure 282 sq ft (26 sq m). Veranda and Concierge-level cabins have a sitting area and teak balcony with faux wicker furniture. Concierge-level grades receive L'Occitane toiletries.

Penthouse Suites measure 420 sq ft (39 sq m) with living/dining room separate from the sleeping area, walk-in closet, and bathroom with a double vanity.

Oceania Suites measure about 1,030 sq ft (96 sq m). Vista Suites range from 1,200 to 1,500 sq ft (111–139 sq m).

At more than 2,000 sq ft (186 sq m), the Owner's Suite spans the ship's entire beam. It is decked out in furniture, fabrics, lighting, and bedding from the Ralph Lauren Home collection, with design by New York-based Tocar, Inc. It is outfitted with a Yamaha baby grand piano, private fitness room, laptop computers, Bose audio system, and a teak-decked balcony with Jacuzzi tub.

Suite-category occupants receive Champagne on arrival, 1,000-thread-count bed linen, 42ins (107cm) plasma TV sets, Hermès and Clarins bath products, butler service, en-suite delivery from any of the ship's restaurants, and priority check-in, early embarkation, and priority luggage delivery. Amenities include Tranquility beds, Wi-Fi laptop computer, refrigerated mini-bar with unlimited free soft drinks and bottled water replenished daily, personal safe, writing desk, cotton bathrobes, slippers, and marble and granite bathroom.

Occupants of Owner's, Vista, Oceania, and Penthouse suites can enjoy in-suite course-by-course dining from any restaurant menu, making private dining possible as a change to being in the restaurants.

Some grades get access to an Executive Lounge or Concierge Lounge. These are great little hideaways, with sofas, Internet-connect computers, Continental breakfast items, soft drinks, and magazines. Self-service launderettes are on each accommodation deck, which is useful for long voyages.

DINING. Six open-seating dining venues provide ample choice, enough even for long cruises, although banquette seating in some venues does not evoke the image of premium dining as much as individual seating does. Also, it would be hard to describe some of the specialty dining venues as intimate. This is, however, a foodie's ship, with really high-quality ingredients and effectively fancy presentation. Particularly notable are the delicious breads, rolls, croissants, and brioches – all made on board from French flour and Isigny butter. The Grand Dining Room has 566 seats, and a delightful domed, or raised, central ceiling. Versace bone china, Christofle silver, and fine linens are used. Canyon Ranch Spa dishes are available for all meals.

French celebrity chef Jacques Pépin, Oceania's executive culinary director, has his first sea-going restaurant, Jacques, with 124 seats. It has antique oak flooring, antique flatware, and Lalique glassware, and offers fine dining in an elegant but informal setting, with roast free-range meats, nine classic French dessert items, and a choice of AOC cheeses.

Polo Grill, with 134 seats, serves steaks and seafood, including Oceania's signature 32oz (900g) bone-in King's Cut prime rib. The setting is classic traditional steakhouse, with dark wood paneling and classic white tablecloths, although the tables are a little close together.

The 124-seat Toscana features Italian-style cuisine, served on Versace china.

Privée, with seating for up to 10 in a private setting, invites exclusivity for its seven-course dégustation menu.

La Réserve offers a choice of two seven-course small-portion dégustation menus (Discovery and Explorer), paired with wines. With just 24 seats, it's really intimate.

The Terrace Café is the casual self-serve buffet-style venue; outdoors, as an extension of the café, is Tapas on the Terrace – it's good for light bites, although the ceiling is low, and it can be very noisy.

Red Ginger is a specialty restaurant featuring 'classic and contemporary' Asian cuisine; the setting is visually refined, with ebony and dark wood finishes, but the banquette-style seating lets the venue down. Your waiter will ask you to choose your chopsticks from a lacquered presentation box.

The poolside Waves Grill, shaded from the sun, serves Angus beef burgers, fishburgers, veggie burgers, Reuben sandwiches, seafood, and other fast food, cooked to order.

Baristas coffee bar overlooks the pool deck and has excellent (and free) illy coffee. However, in the bars the tonic mixed with gin and vodka is too sweet and of inferior quality.

ENTERTAINMENT. The 600-seat Marina Lounge spans two decks, with tiered amphitheater-style seating. It's more cabaret-style entertainment than big production shows, in keeping with the cruise line's traditions, which suits the passenger clientele just fine.

SPA/FITNESS. The Canyon Ranch SpaClub provides wellness and personal spa treatments. The facility includes a fitness center, beauty salon, several treatment rooms, thalassotherapy pool, and sauna and steam rooms. A jogging track is located aft of the funnel, above two of the specialty restaurants.

MARINER OF THE SEAS
★★★+

THIS LARGE RESORT SHIP IS FOR ENERGETIC, FAMILY-FRIENDLY, CASUAL CRUISING

Size:	Large Resort Ship	Passenger/Crew Ratio (lower beds):	2.6
Tonnage:	137,276	Cabins (total):	1,557
Cruise Line:	Royal Caribbean International	Size Range (sq ft/m):	151.0–1,358.0/14.0–126.1
Former Names:	none	Cabins (for one person):	0
Builder:	Kvaerner Masa-Yards (Finland)	Cabins with balcony:	765
Entered Service:	Nov 2004	Cabins (wheelchair accessible):	26
Length (ft/m):	1,020.6/311.1	Wheelchair accessibility:	Best
Beam (ft/m):	155.5/47.4	Elevators:	14
Propulsion/Propellers:	diesel-electric (75,600kW)/	Casino (gaming tables):	Yes
	3 pods (2 azimuthing, 1 fixed)	Swimming Pools:	3
Passenger Decks:	14	Self-Service Launderette:	No
Total Crew:	1,185	Library:	Yes
Passengers (lower beds):	3,114	Onboard currency:	US$
Passenger Space Ratio (lower beds):	44.0		

THE SHIP. *Mariner of the Seas* (a *Voyager*-class ship) is a large, floating leisure resort. It has a healthy passenger/space ratio and extensive facilities such as a regulation-size ice-skating rink.

A four-deck-high Royal Promenade, 394ft (120m) long and the main interior focal point, is a good place to hang out or to arrange to meet someone. It has two internal lobbies that rise through 11 decks. Casual eateries, shops, and entertainment locations front this winding street and interior 'with-view' cabins look into it from above. The guest reception and shore excursion counters are located at the aft end of the promenade, as is an ATM machine.

Arched across the promenade is a captain's balcony. A stairway in the center of the promenade connects you to the deck below, where you'll find Schooner Bar and the colorful Casino Royale. Several shops line the Royal Promenade, including a jewelry store, gift shop, and liquor store.

There is a regulation-size ice-skating rink (Studio B), with real ice, and stadium-style seating for up to 900, plus high-tech broadcast facilities. Ice Follies shows are also presented here. Slim pillars obstruct clear-view arena stage sightlines, however. You can also read in the two-deck library, open 24 hours a day.

Drinking places include an intimate Champagne Bar, Wig & Gavel Pub, a Sidewalk Café, Sprinkles, a sports bar, and a Connoisseur Club. Jazz fans might like the intimate Jazz Club. Golfers might also enjoy

BERLITZ'S RATINGS		
	Possible	Achieved
Ship	500	376
Accommodation	200	132
Food	400	223
Service	400	258
Entertainment	100	73
Cruise Experience	400	259
OVERALL SCORE 1321 points out of 2000		

the 19th Hole, a golf bar, as they play the Explorer Links.

A TV studio is adjacent to rooms useable for trade show exhibit space, with a 400-seat conference center and a multimedia screening room seating 60. You can tie the knot in the Skylight Chapel, which has wheelchair access via an electric stairlift.

Facilities for children and teenagers (in four age groupings) are quite extensive, and include Adventure Beach, an area for all the family, with swimming pools, a waterslide, and outdoor game areas.

Passenger niggles: small cabin bath towels and noisy (vacuum) toilets, and few quiet places to sit and read – almost everywhere has intrusive background music. If you have a cabin with an interconnecting door to another cabin, you'll be able to hear everything they do.

Overall, this is a good all-round ship for all age groups, but be aware of the many extra costs for optional items, including drinks and excursions.

ACCOMMODATION. There is a wide range of cabin price grades, in four major groupings. Premium ocean-view suites and cabins, interior (atrium-view) cabins, ocean-view cabins, and interior cabins. Many cabins are of a similar size, and 300 have interconnecting doors.

The standard outside-view and interior (no-view) cabin are of a reasonably adequate size, with just enough facilities to make them comfortable and functional. Twin lower beds convert to queen-size ones, and there is a reasonable amount of closet and drawer space, but the bed(s) take up most of the space. Bathrooms are small but functional; shower enclosures are dimensionally challenged, and there is no cabinet for personal toiletries. Overall, they're cramped.

Some accommodation grades have a refrigerator/mini-bar, although there is no space left because it is crammed with 'take-and-pay' items.

Cabins with 'private balconies' aren't so private. The balcony decking is made of Bolidt – a sort of rubberized sand – and not wood, though the balcony rail is of wood. Cabin bath towels are small and skimpy. Room service offers a really basic menu.

Some 138 interior cabins have bay windows that look into the Royal Promenade. However, you need to keep the curtains closed in the bay windows, because you can be seen easily from adjacent bay windows.

Suites include:

A Royal Suite, measuring 1,146 sq ft (106 sq m), is the largest private living space. It is located almost at the top of the Centrum lobby on the port side on Deck 10.

Four Royal Family Suites (two aft on Deck 9, two aft on Deck 8), each measuring around 574 sq ft (53 sq m) have two bedrooms, and large balconies with views over the ship's stern.

Ten slightly smaller but still desirable Owner's Suites (around 468 sq ft/43 sq m) are in the center of the ship, on both port and starboard sides, adjacent to the Centrum lobby on Deck 10. There's also a private balcony, although it's small.

DINING. The main dining room, with a seating capacity of 1,919, is set on three levels: Rhapsody in Blue, Top Hat and Tails, and Sound of Music, all offering exactly the same menus and food. A dramatic staircase connects all three levels, but huge, fat support pillars obstruct the sight lines from many seats. When you book, choose one of two seatings, or 'My Time Dining'. Tables are for 4 to 12 people. The place settings, porcelain, and cutlery are of good quality.

Dining options for casual and informal meals include: Promenade Café: for Continental breakfast, all-day pizzas, and specialty coffees (only available in paper cups). Windjammer Café: this is a really large, sprawling venue for casual buffet-style, self-help breakfast (the busiest time of the day), lunch, and light dinners (but not on the last night of the cruise); it's often difficult to find a table and by the time you do your food could be cold. Giovanni's Table (for Italian cuisine) and Chop's Grille (for premium steaks and seafood items) are extra-cost venues, and reservations are required. Johnny Rockets, a retro 1950s eatery, has burgers, malt shakes (at extra cost), and jukebox hits, with both indoor and outdoor seating. Sprinkles, located on the Royal Promenade, is for round-the-clock ice cream and yogurt, pastries, and coffee.

ENTERTAINMENT. The 1,350-seat Savoy Showlounge is a stunning room that could well be the equal of many showrooms on land. It has a hydraulic orchestra pit and a huge stage area, and superb lighting equipment. *Mariner of the Seas* also has an array of cabaret acts. The best shows of all are the Ice Spectaculars. Note that RCI's entertainment is always upbeat. There is even background music in all corridors and elevators, and constant music outdoors on the pool deck.

SPA/FITNESS. The Vitality at Sea Spa is reasonably large, and measures 15,000 sq ft (1,400 sq m). It includes an aerobics room, fitness center, treatment rooms, and sauna/steam rooms. Another 10,000 sq ft (930 sq m) of space is devoted to a Solarium (with sliding glass-dome roof) to relax in.

On the back of the funnel is a 32.8ft (10m) rock-climbing wall, with five climbing tracks. It gives you a great buzz being 200ft (60m) above the ocean while the ship is moving. Other facilities include a roller-blading track, a full-size basketball court, and a nine-hole, par 26 golf course. A dive-and-snorkel shop provides equipment for rental, and diving classes.

MEIN SCHIFF 1
★★★★

THIS SHIP HAS CONTEMPORARY STYLE FOR CASUAL, FAMILY-FRIENDLY CRUISING

Size:	Mid-size Ship	Passenger/Crew Ratio (lower beds):	2.4
Tonnage:	77,713	Cabins (total):	962
Cruise Line:	TUI Cruises	Size Range (sq ft/m):	172.2–1,054/16.0–98.0
Former Names:	Celebrity Galaxy, Galaxy	Cabins (for one person):	0
Builder:	Meyer Werft (Germany)	Cabins with balcony:	430
Entered Service:	Dec 1996/May 2009	Cabins (wheelchair accessible):	8
Length (ft/m):	865.8/263.9	Wheelchair accessibility:	Good
Beam (ft/m):	105.6/32.2	Elevators:	10
Propulsion/Propellers:	diesel (31,500kW)/2	Casino (gaming tables):	Yes
Passenger Decks:	10	Swimming Pools:	2
Total Crew:	780	Self-Service Launderette:	No
Passengers (lower beds):	1,924	Library:	Yes
Passenger Space Ratio (lower beds):	40.3	Onboard currency:	Euros

THE SHIP. *Mein Schiff 1*, originally built for Celebrity Cruises, was transferred in 2009 to then-newcomer TUI Cruises (part of TUI Travel – Europe's largest tour operator) for German-speaking passengers, in a joint venture with Royal Caribbean Cruises, parent of Royal Caribbean International. The ship is moving to Thomson Cruises and will be renamed *TUI Explorer* in May 2018.

This all-inclusive mid-size ship has just about all you need for an enjoyable and rewarding cruise experience, and provides competition for AIDA Cruises, whose ships lack a traditional dining room and have few service staff. TUI Cruises has got the onboard product just right, with multiple dining and eating choices. With 10 bars, four restaurants, six bistros, and good facilities for families, *Mein Schiff 1* is a high-value, full-service cruise product.

The ship has good tender-loading platforms. But, although there are more than 4.5 acres (1.8 hectares) of space on the open decks, it can be cramped when the ship is full. Nice touches include the two-person cabanas on an upper, outside deck; available at extra cost, they have great ocean views, and are insulated from the life that goes on around the ship.

Inside, a four-deck-high main foyer houses the reception desk and shore-excursion station. There's a small cinema, which doubles as a conference and meeting center with audio-visual technology including simultaneous translation and headsets for the hearing-impaired.

BERLITZ'S RATINGS	Possible	Achieved
Ship	500	373
Accommodation	200	148
Food	400	280
Service	400	299
Entertainment	100	70
Cruise Experience	400	287

OVERALL SCORE 1457 points out of 2000

Relaxation is a key element of the product, and *Mein Schiff 1* has individual hammocks in various locations, including on cabin balconies. Additionally, 'Meditation Islands' are installed on deck.

Overall, Mein Schiff 1 is for German-speaking families with children who want to cruise aboard a ship with a contemporary environment, good itineraries and food, and European-style service from a well-trained crew that delivers a product that's surprisingly good. Making it even more user-friendly for families is the 'inclusive' pricing (but excluding the extra-cost restaurants Richards Feines Essen, Blaue Welt Sushi Bar, and the Surf 'n' Turf Steakhouse, excursions and spa treatments). The dress code is smart casual.

ACCOMMODATION. There are several price grades, depending on the size and location of your living space, but the accommodation is comfortable. Every cabin has its own Nespresso coffee machine, with two free coffee pods (additional packets cost €1 each). All accommodation grades are designated no-smoking.

All the standard outside-view/interior (no-view) cabins are of a good size – larger than those aboard the ships of AIDA Cruises, for example – and come nicely furnished with twin beds that convert to a queen-size unit. The bathrooms have generous-size showers, hairdryers, and space for personal toiletries. Baby-monitoring telephones are provided.

There are no dedicated cabins for solo travelers.

Most of the Deck 10 suites/cabins are of generous proportions and have balconies with full floor-to-ceiling partitions and large flat-screen infotainment screens.

Two Penthouse Suites, located amidships, are the largest accommodation on offer. Each has its own butler's pantry, and an interconnecting door for linking to the suite next door.

Most suites with balconies have floor-to-ceiling windows and sliding balcony doors, while a few have outward opening doors. Suite occupants get special cards to open their doors, plus several extra perks, including access to a private 100-seat concierge lounge/bar and social venue (the 'X' Lounge) atop the ship, with great ocean views.

DINING. Restaurants and bistros range from self-serve buffet style to service, with a focus on healthy eating. There is no pre-defined seating, so you can dine when you want, and with whomever you want – good for multi-generational families. The emphasis is on healthy food, including power food, brain food, soul food, and even erotic food.

The Atlantik Restaurant is a large two-level dining hall – reminiscent of the dining halls aboard 1930s ocean liners – with a grand staircase that flows between both levels and perimeter alcoves that provide intimate dining spaces. Tables are for two to 10.

Richards Feines Essen (Gourmet Restaurant) is an à la carte, reservations-only venue, with a calming, restful wood-laden interior, where high-quality fine dining and service are offered.

The extra-cost (reservations-required) Surf 'n' Turf Steakhouse features premium steaks and grilled seafood, with aged beef commanding different price points.

In a venue covered by a retractable glass dome, in the aft section of the ship, three eateries, combined with a communal bar, provide different food experiences: Bistro La Vela for Italian cuisine, including an 'active' pasta cooking station, and pizza; Gosch Sylt, for fresh fish and seafood; and the fashionable Tapas y Mas, for tapas and other tasting dishes.

Other dining spots include: La Vida Sana, for wellness cuisine; Blaue Welt (Blue World) Sushi Bar, on the upper level of the atrium; Vino, a wine-tasting bar; and a coffee lounge set around the atrium lobby, for specialty coffees and pastries.

For informal breakfasts and lunches, the two-level self-serve Anckelmannsplatz Buffet – the name comes from the road on which TUI Cruises Hamburg offices are located – is the place to go. It has several serving counters and 'active' food islands, warm, wood-accented decor, and eight bay windows. There are also two poolside grills – one located adjacent to the midships pools, the other wedged into an area aft of the swimming pool/hot tub cluster.

ENTERTAINMENT. The Theater is a 927-seat showlounge spanning two decks, with seating on both main and cantilevered balcony levels. There are good sight lines from all seats. It has a revolving stage, 'hard' curtain, and large fly tower.

SPA/FITNESS. The Spa and More, located at the front, one deck above the navigation bridge, has 18,299 sq ft (1,700 sq m) of space. It includes a large fitness/exercise area with the latest machines and exercise bikes, beauty salon, thalassotherapy pool, seven treatment rooms, and a Rasul room for Mediterranean mud and gentle steam bathing. Private 'spa suites' with fine, relaxing views are located above the ship's navigation bridge and can be rented for the morning, afternoon, or the whole day. Atop the ship at the front is a 'FKK' (Freikörperkultur) deck for nude sunbathing.

MEIN SCHIFF 2
★★★★

A STYLISH PREMIUM MID-SIZE SHIP THAT IS GOOD FOR THE WHOLE FAMILY

Size:	Mid-size Ship	Passenger/Crew Ratio (lower beds):	2.4
Tonnage:	77,713	Cabins (total):	956
Cruise Line:	TUI Cruises	Size Range (sq ft/m):	172.2–1,054.0/16.0–98.0
Former Names:	Celebrity Mercury, Mercury	Cabins (for one person):	0
Builder:	Meyer Werft (Germany)	Cabins with balcony:	220
Entered Service:	Nov 1997/May 2011	Cabins (wheelchair accessible):	8
Length (ft/m):	865.8/263.9	Wheelchair accessibility:	Good
Beam (ft/m):	105.6/32.2	Elevators:	10
Propulsion/Propellers:	diesel (31,500kW)/2	Casino (gaming tables):	Yes
Passenger Decks:	10	Swimming Pools:	3 (1 w/ sliding glass dome)
Total Crew:	780	Self-Service Launderette:	No
Passengers (lower beds):	1,912	Library:	Yes
Passenger Space Ratio (lower beds):	40.6	Onboard currency:	Euros

THE SHIP. Mein Schiff 2, originally built as Mercury for Celebrity Cruises, was transferred in 2011 to TUI Cruises (part of TUI Travel, Europe's largest tour operator) specifically for German-speaking passengers, in a joint venture with Royal Caribbean Cruises, parent of Royal Caribbean International. The ship underwent a major conversion at that time. In 2019, it is expected that Mein Schiff 2 will be moved to the UK's Thomson Cruises fleet to become TUI Explorer 2.

This all-inclusive mid-size ship has just about all you need for an enjoyable and rewarding cruise experience. There are 10 bars, four restaurants, six bistros, and good facilities for families with children.

The ship has good tender-loading platforms. Although there are more than 4.5 acres (1.8 hectares) of space on the open decks, it can, however, become crowded when the ship is full. Charming two-person cabanas can be rented on an upper, outside deck, with great ocean views, but insulated from shipboard life.

Inside, a four-deck-high main foyer houses the reception desk and shore excursion station. There's a small cinema, which doubles as a conference and meeting center, with the latest audio-visual technology, including simultaneous translation and headsets for the hearing-impaired. There's a large shopping center, including ultra-smart shops such as Swarovski, while cigar smokers will appreciate the private club-like cigar lounge and bar.

BERLITZ'S RATINGS

	Possible	Achieved
Ship	500	373
Accommodation	200	148
Food	400	280
Service	400	299
Entertainment	100	70
Cruise Experience	400	287

OVERALL SCORE 1457 points out of 2000

The interior decor is at once contemporary in style, but with many restful colors and combinations throughout and nothing garish – except, perhaps, for the starkly contrasting wallcovering of blood-red capillaries in the Blue World Bar.

Mein Schiff 2 has individual hammocks in various outdoor locations, including on some suite-grade balconies. 'Meditation Islands' are also installed on the open deck: the ship's rail is fitted with mini-balconies, equipped with special blinds, and created as spaces for private relaxation.

This vessel is for German-speaking families with children (the latter should look out for Captain Sharky), who want to cruise aboard a ship with a contemporary environment, good itineraries, great food, and European-style service from a well-trained crew that delivers a cruise that's fresh and surprisingly good. Making it even more user-friendly for families is the all-inclusive pricing, though this excludes spa treatments, excursions, and the extra-cost restaurants: Richards Feines Essen, Blaue Welt Sushi Bar, and Surf 'n' Turf Steakhouse. The dress code is smart casual.

ACCOMMODATION. There are several price grades, depending on the size and location of your living space, but the accommodation is very comfortable. Every cabin has its own Nespresso coffee machine, which comes with two free coffee pods (any additional packets cost €1 each, although they are free in suites). All accommodation grades are designated no-smoking.

Standard outside-view/interior cabins. These are of a decent size,and furnished with twin beds that convert to a queen-size unit. The bathrooms are spacious and have generous-size showers, hairdryers, and space for toiletries. Baby-monitoring telephones and personal safes are provided in all cabins. A box containing three crystal-mineral stones provides special filtration for the ship's own water.

Most of the Deck 10 suites and cabins are generously proportioned, nicely equipped, and have balconies with full or almost-full floor-to-ceiling partitions. They have large flat-screen TV sets, a wall clock, floor-to-ceiling mirrors, a well-stocked mini-bar, a marble-topped vanity/writing desk, excellent closet and drawer space, and large shower enclosure. Suite occupants get newspapers, chocolates, Champagne, and access to the exclusive X Lounge. Look out for the phrase 'Wood Thrust Into Brine' in large letters above the bar – you'll have to look up to see it.

Two Penthouse Suites, located amidships, are the largest. Each has its own butler's pantry, and an interconnecting door to link it to the next-door suite.

Most suites with private balconies have floor-to-ceiling windows and sliding doors to large balconies – 12 have balconies measuring 258.3 sq ft (24 sq m), with a hammock, two sunloungers and a dining table, and a few have outward opening doors. Suite-grade accommodation have European duvets on the beds instead of sheets and blankets. A balcony massage service is also available. Suite occupants get special cards to open their doors, plus priority service throughout the ship and for embarkation and disembarkation, free cappuccinos and espressos, welcome Champagne, flowers, and picnic baskets as required. Suite occupants also have keycard access to a private, 100-seat concierge lounge/bar and social venue (the 'X' Lounge), with a selection of cold food, including some decent caviar for breakfast.

DINING. Restaurants and bistros range from self-serve buffet style to service. There is no pre-defined seating. The emphasis is on healthy food, including power food, brain food, soul food, erotic food, and fresh fish. The Atlantik Restaurant is a lovely, two-level Art Deco grand dining hall with a grand staircase. Tables are for two to 10.

Richards Feines Essen (Gourmet Restaurant), a specialty dining venue, is à la carte and reservations only, with a restful wood-laden interior and high-quality fine dining and service. A dégustation menu and three specialty vegetarian menus are also available, and the wine list is extensive.

Surf 'n' Turf Steakhouse features premium steaks and grilled seafood, with aged beef, displayed in a 'proving' or maturing cabinet – a cruise industry first.

In an area covered by a retractable glass dome in the aft section of the ship, three eateries and a communal bar provide very different food experiences (all included in the cruise price): Bistro La Vela for Italian cuisine, including an 'active' pasta-cooking station with your choice of six pastas, and freshly made pizza; Gosch Sylt for fresh fish and seafood, with daily specials (it's hugely popular, so make a reservation early); and Tapas y Mas for tapas and other tasting dishes. This venue is a most popular place to meet the fashionable set, with both indoor and outdoor seating and bar.

There's also Blaue Welt (Blue World) Sushi Bar, on the upper level of the atrium; Vino, a wine-tasting bar specializing in Austrian and German wines; Cliff 24, a 24-hour poolside grill with different food items throughout the day; and the TUI Bar, a coffee lounge set around the atrium lobby for specialty coffees and pastries, and a separate praline chocolate counter.

For informal breakfasts and lunches, the two-level self-serve Anckelmannsplatz Buffet is the place to go. There are several serving counters and 'active' food islands. There are also two poolside grills – one adjacent to the midships pools, the other wedged into an area aft of the swimming pool/hot tub cluster.

ENTERTAINMENT. The Theater is a 927-seat showlounge spanning two decks, with seating on both main and cantilevered balcony levels. There are good sight lines from all seats. The large-scale production shows are excellent.

SPA/FITNESS. The Spa and More, located at the front of the ship one deck above the navigation bridge, has 18,299 sq ft (1,700 sq m) of space. It includes a large exercise area with the machines and cycles, a beauty salon, thalassotherapy pool, 15 treatment rooms, a Rasul chamber for mud and steam bathing, and a sauna.

Private 'spa suites,' bookable for an hour or two, or a half- or full-day, are extremely large, and include a steam/shower cabinet, thalassotherapy bath, two hydraulic massage/relaxation tables, relaxation seating, and great floor-to-ceiling windows. A balcony adjacent to the sauna is designated as an 'FKK' (Freikörperkultur) deck for nude sunbathing.

MEIN SCHIFF 3
★★★★+

THIS STYLISH SHIP HAS IT ALL FOR YOUTHFUL GERMAN-SPEAKING FAMILIES

Size:	Large Resort Ship	Passenger/Crew Ratio (lower beds):	2.5
Tonnage:	99,300	Cabins (total):	1,250
Cruise Line:	TUI Cruises	Size Range (sq ft/m):	182.9–581.2/17.0–54.0
Former Names:	none	Cabins (for one person):	0
Builder:	STX Europe (Finland)	Cabins with balcony:	1,033
Entered Service:	May 2014	Cabins (wheelchair accessible):	10
Length (ft/m):	967.8/295.0	Wheelchair accessibility:	Good
Beam (ft/m):	118.1/36.0	Elevators:	10
Propulsion/Propellers:	diesel-electric (28,000kW)/2	Casino (gaming tables):	Yes
Passenger Decks:	12	Swimming Pools:	3 (1 w/sliding glass dome)
Total Crew:	1,000	Self-Service Launderette:	No
Passengers (lower beds):	2,506	Library:	Yes
Passenger Space Ratio (lower beds):	39.7	Onboard currency:	Euros

THE SHIP. Mein Schiff 3 is aimed at German-speaking families. Larger than Mein Schiff 1 and Mein Schiff 2, this ship incorporates the best of the previous two ships, and has added more facilities and tailored the design to its passengers' needs. Its new-generation propulsion system is stunningly quiet in operation, with absolutely no vibration anywhere.

A superb 82ft (25m) lap pool (long by cruise ship standards and half the length of an Olympic-sized pool) is featured outdoors, together with a large-scale movie screen and sports area for basketball and volleyball, while a second, indoor, pool and adjacent hot tubs provide plenty of choice for families with children.

High up on Deck 14 is what's known as the Blue Balcony, a 118.4-sq-ft (11-sq-m) glass-floored platform some 121.3ft (37m) above the sea, which gives the sensation of floating over the ocean.

Public rooms are plentiful, and include a superb music academy-style concert hall (auditorium), which has been designed to the highest acoustic specifications.

What makes a cruise aboard Mein Schiff 3 really user-friendly for families is the inclusive pricing, though this excludes spa treatments, excursions, and the extra-cost restaurants: Richards Feines Essen, Blaue Welt Sushi Bar, Gosch Sylt, and a Surf 'n' Turf Steakhouse, among others. The dress code is smart casual. But the real diamond in the crown is

BERLITZ'S RATINGS

	Possible	Achieved
Ship	500	435
Accommodation	200	161
Food	400	324
Service	400	327
Entertainment	100	82
Cruise Experience	400	318

OVERALL SCORE 1647 points out of 2000

the two-deck-high glass enclosure, which houses two restaurants – with great views over the ship's stern – and an outstanding barista-style coffee lounge.

Mein Schiff 3 has a really comforting feel, and boasts a number of outstanding passenger-friendly features, including: the joint-longest swimming pool of any cruise ship; an ocean-connect museum (I call it an 'oceano-quarium'); water-dispenser units on each accommodation deck (special quartz crystals are provided in each cabin to add to the water pitcher for negative ion purification); vertical walls of living plants; a large meat-ageing (proving) cabinet adjacent to the Surf 'n' Turf Restaurant; smartphone food ordering for waiters (sent electronically to the kitchen, so the waiter is always at his/her station to attend to passengers); a Nespresso coffee machine in every cabin; large spa and wellness facilities; a large choice of (included and extra-cost) dining venues and eateries; and a completely enclosed shore-excursion information and booking lounge. Plus there's Captain Sharky to appeal to the kids.

ACCOMMODATION. About 82 percent of all cabins feature private balconies, and each one features a hammock. Likewise, every cabin comes with a Nespresso coffee machine.

Combination balcony cabins allow for interconnecting balconies, and a 'holiday home' package provides a *Mein Schiff 3* chef to prepare a barbeque on the balcony grill.

Spa accommodation is located near the spa and part of a package that includes a massage for two in one of the most extensive wellness spa environments at sea.

A Captain's Suite, at 581.2 sq ft (54 sq m), is the largest suite aboard ship; appropriately, it's located near the navigation bridge. Meanwhile, each of the spacious Sea & Sky Suites has its own large 312 sq ft (29 sq m) roof terrace and private sunbathing and shaded areas, including a large hammock and upscale sunbeds. Premium veranda cabins offer large, diagonal terraces. Family-friendly suites sleep up to 6 (they come in three different types). One example measures about 452 sq ft (42 sq m), but there's also a huge balcony measuring 506 sq ft (47 sq m). The total adds up to a delightfully large 958 sq ft (89 sq m). All come with Xbox game consoles.

DINING. With a choice of 11 dining venues, there really is plenty of choice. The Atlantik Restaurant is the ship's main restaurant. It is divided into three sections, and focuses on three styles of food: Classic – for dishes such as steak with roasted shallots and a chili-chocolate reduction; Mediterranean – for choices including homemade pasta, grilled fish, and lamb with Provençal herbs; and Eurasian – for items such as sweet-and-sour vegetables with fried jasmine rice. Five-course menus include antipasti, homemade pasta, grilled fish, and Asian dishes, and are part of the inclusive offering.

Aft is a 1,798-sq-ft (167-sq-m) multifaceted glass structure, nicknamed the 'diamond' and spanning two decks. Inside it are two restaurants: Richards Feines Essen for fine dining and the Surf 'n' Turf Steakhouse, which features a superb glass-enclosed meat dry-ageing cabinet.

Hanami (it means flower-watching – particularly cherry blossom) is a Japanese restaurant (try the shabu-shabu beef), which incorporates a sushi bar.

The venue offers sushi creations and other specialties of Japanese cuisine, at an additional cost.

A real bakery, an adjunct of the self-serve buffet restaurant Anckelmannsplatz, features freshly baked crispy rolls, paninis, and cakes all day long. Already appearing aboard *Mein Schiff 1* and *Mein Schiff 2*, the popular informal Gosch Sylt now has about 130 seats aboard *Mein Schiff 3* (versus 88 seats aboard *Mein Schiff 1* and *Mein Schiff 2*), and offers fresh fish and well-prepared seafood dishes, with daily specials listed on a blackboard.

The Day & Night Bistro provides regional and international snacks, including Currywurst, around the clock, while in a modern coffee lounge a barista brews international coffees and presents *Mein Schiff*'s own hand-crafted pralines and chocolates.

ENTERTAINMENT. The Theater is the ship's showlounge. It is a three-deck venue with 949 seats, and features colorful, razzle-dazzle production shows and major cabaret acts.

What is really innovative, however, is a stunning concert hall/movie theater called Klanghaus, which was developed in conjunction with renowned acoustics experts from leading opera houses and concert halls. It provides a really fine setting for live classical and jazz concerts, theatrical readings, lectures, and movies with surround sound.

Numerous bands, small musical units, and solo musical entertainers provide live music in several of the lounge venues throughout the ship.

SPA/FITNESS. The Spa and Meer wellness and fitness facilities are really extensive, and include a large (mixed-gender) sauna, steam rooms, and several body-pampering treatment rooms. They also include a private (rentable) spa room for couples, with integral sauna, massage tables, shower, and relaxation areas. Sports facilities include a large arena in the aft section of the ship for volleyball, basketball, and football.

MEIN SCHIFF 4
★★★★+

THIS IS LAID-BACK CRUISING IN STYLE FOR GERMAN-SPEAKING FAMILIES

Size:	Large Resort Ship	Passenger/Crew Ratio (lower beds):	2.5
Tonnage:	99,300	Cabins (total):	1,250
Cruise Line:	TUI Cruises	Size Range (sq ft/m):	182.9–581.2/17.0–54.0
Former Names:	none	Cabins (for one person):	0
Builder:	Meyer Turku (Finland)	Cabins with balcony:	1,033
Entered Service:	May 2015	Cabins (wheelchair accessible):	10
Length (ft/m):	967.8/295.0	Wheelchair accessibility:	Good
Beam (ft/m):	118.1/36.0	Elevators:	10
Propulsion/Propellers:	diesel-electric/2	Casino (gaming tables):	Yes
Passenger Decks:	12	Swimming Pools:	3 (1 w/sliding glass dome)
Total Crew:	1,000	Self-Service Launderette:	No
Passengers (lower beds):	2,506	Library:	Yes
Passenger Space Ratio (lower beds):	39.7	Onboard currency:	Euros

THE SHIP. *Mein Schiff 4*, the sister ship to *Mein Schiff 3*, is for youthful German-speaking families. Its latest-generation propulsion system is extremely quiet in operation, with no vibration anywhere. The premium ship features a wide choice of dining venues, has an excellent spa, and, for younger cruisers, there's an enthusiastic team of children's activity hosts (kids should keep a lookout for Captain Sharky).

BERLITZ'S RATINGS		
	Possible	Achieved
Ship	500	436
Accommodation	200	161
Food	400	324
Service	400	328
Entertainment	100	82
Cruise Experience	400	318

OVERALL SCORE 1649 points out of 2000

A superb 82ft (25m) lap pool (long by cruise ship standards and half the length of an Olympic-sized pool) is outdoors (check out the meerkats), and a second, indoor, pool and adjacent hot tubs provide plenty of choice for families with children.

High on Deck 14 is 'Blue Balcony,' a 118-sq-ft (11-sq-m) glass-floored platform 121ft (37m) above the sea, giving the sensation of floating over the ocean.

There are numerous public rooms; these include a superb music academy-style concert hall (auditorium), designed to the highest acoustic specifications.

What makes a cruise aboard *Mein Schiff 4* really user-friendly for families is the all-inclusive pricing, though this excludes spa treatments, excursions, and the extra-cost restaurants: Richards Feines Essen, Blaue Welt Sushi Bar, Gosch Sylt, and a Surf 'n' Turf Steakhouse, among others. The dress code is smart casual. But the diamond in the crown, and with fine views over the ship's stern, is the two-deck high glass enclosure, which houses two different restaurants and a fine barista coffee lounge.

Mein Schiff 4, in keeping with sister *Mein Schiff 3*, feels comfortable and spacious. Its features include: the joint-longest swimming pool of any cruise ship; water-dispenser units on each accommodation deck (special quartz crystals are provided to add to the water pitcher for negative ion purification); vertical walls of living plants; a large meat-ageing (proving) cabinet adjacent to the Surf 'n' Turf Steakhouse; and a Nespresso coffee machine in every cabin. The spa and wellness facilities are large and well run. With its included (and extra-cost) dining venues and eatery choices, this ship really delivers laid-back cruising with style.

ACCOMMODATION. The cabins are well designed, practically laid out, and the interactive infotainment system is excellent. Also, each comes with a Nespresso coffee machine, hairdryer, several personal amenities, and a decent amount of storage space (and much more in the larger categories and suites).

Combination balcony cabins allow for interconnecting balconies, and a 'holiday home' package provides a chef to prepare a barbeque on the balcony grill.

Spa accommodation is located adjacent to the spa and is available as part of a package that includes a massage for two in what is one of the most extensive wellness spa environments at sea.

A Captain's Suite, at 581 sq ft (54 sq m), is the largest suite; it is located near the navigation bridge. Meanwhile, each of the spacious Sea & Sky Suites has its own large 312 sq ft (29 sq m) roof terrace and private sunbathing (including a large hammock, upscale sunbeds, and shaded areas). Premium veranda cabins offer large, diagonal terraces, and there are three suite categories. Family-friendly suites sleep up to 6 (they come in three different types). One example measures about 452 sq ft (42 sq m), but there's also a huge balcony measuring 506 sq ft (47 sq m). The total adds up to a very large 958 sq ft (89 sq m). All come with Xbox game consoles.

DINING. With 11 dining venues (some at extra cost), there really is abundant choice. The largest is the Atlantik Restaurant, which is included in the cruise fare. It is divided into three sections, each with a slightly different menu: Classic – for dishes such as steak with roasted shallots and a chili-chocolate reduction; Mediterranean – for choices including homemade pasta; and Brasserie – for French-style grilled fish and meat dishes and herbs from Provence. Some dining venues have both indoor and outdoor seating – slightly different from *Mein Schiff 3*. Smartphones are provided to waiters for orders (digitally sent to the kitchen, so the waiter is always at his station to attend to you).

Aft is a 1,798-sq-ft (167-sq-m) multifaceted glass structure (nicknamed the 'diamond'), which spans two decks. Inside you'll find a spacious coffee and chocolate lounge and two restaurants: Richards Feines Essen for haute cuisine, and the Surf 'n' Turf Steakhouse, which features a superb glass-enclosed meat dry-ageing cabinet.

Hanami (it means flower-watching – particularly cherry blossom) is a Japanese restaurant (try the shabu-shabu beef), which incorporates a sushi bar. The venue offers sushi creations and other specialties of Japanese cuisine at an additional cost.

A real bakery, an adjunct of the self-serve buffet restaurant Anckelmannsplatz, features freshly baked bread, rolls, paninis, cakes, and pastry items (including gluten-free selections). You can also buy specially packaged artisan bread to take home).

Gosch Sylt has about 130 seats and features fresh fish and well-prepared seafood dishes, with daily specials, such as supremely tasty oysters from the German island of Sylt itself, and lobster, all listed on a blackboard.

A Day & Night Bistro provides regional and international snacks, including Currywurst, around the clock, while in the coffee lounge at the stern, baristas brew superb international coffees and present *Mein Schiff*'s own hand-crafted pralines and chocolates, which are made in front of you.

For something different, I recommend booking one of the three private barbeque stations (each seats up to six – excellent for a family, or for two or three couples); these are located outdoors on a small section of an aft deck (exclusive to *Mein Schiff 4*). They come with a superb selection of seafood and meat items, cooked right in front of you by a private chef (it's exclusive and great value).

ENTERTAINMENT. The Theater is the ship's showlounge. A three-deck venue with 949 seats, it features colorful, razzle-dazzle production shows and major cabaret acts.

What is really innovative, however, is the Klanghaus, a stunning small concert hall/movie theater developed in conjunction with renowned acoustics experts. It provides a really fine setting for live classical and jazz concerts, theatrical readings, lectures, and movies with surround sound.

Numerous bands, small musical units, and solo musical entertainers provide live music in several of the lounge venues throughout the ship.

SPA/FITNESS. The Spa and Meer wellness and fitness facilities are really extensive, and include a large (mixed-gender) sauna, steam rooms, and several body-pampering treatment rooms. They also include a private (rentable) spa room for couples, with integral sauna, massage tables, shower, and relaxation areas.

Sports facilities include a large arena in the aft section of the ship for volleyball, basketball, football, and stadium-style seating (look out for the big sunglasses). Sport bikes are also carried for excursions.

MEIN SCHIFF 5
★★★★+

THIS FAMILY-FRIENDLY SHIP HAS SOME FINE FACILITIES AND A BUCKETFUL OF STYLE

Size:	Large Resort Ship	Passenger/Crew Ratio (lower beds):	2.5
Tonnage:	99,980	Cabins (total):	1,276
Cruise Line:	TUI Cruises	Size Range (sq ft/m):	182.9–581.2/17.0–54.0
Former Names:	none	Cabins (for one person):	0
Builder:	Meyer Turku (Finland)	Cabins with balcony:	1,033
Entered Service:	June 2016	Cabins (wheelchair accessible):	10
Length (ft/m):	967.8/295.0	Wheelchair accessibility:	Good
Beam (ft/m):	118.1/36.0	Elevators:	10
Propulsion/Propellers:	diesel-electric/2	Casino (gaming tables):	Yes
Passenger Decks:	12	Swimming Pools:	3
Total Crew:	1,000	Self-Service Launderette:	No
Passengers (lower beds):	2,506	Library:	Yes
Passenger Space Ratio (lower beds):	39.1	Onboard currency:	Euros

THE SHIP. *Mein Schiff 5* is a close sister ship to *Mein Schiff 3* and *Mein Schiff 4*, but with 16 more cabins. It is strongly recommended for youthful German-speaking families. The ship features a wide choice of dining venues, has an excellent spa, and, for younger cruisers, there's an enthusiastic team of children's activity hosts (kids should keep a lookout for Captain Sharky). Also, the propulsion system is extremely quiet, with no vibration anywhere.

An outstanding 82ft (25m) lap pool (long by cruise ship standards and half the length of an 'Olympic'-sized pool) is outdoors – together with a large movie screen and sports area for basketball and volleyball, while a second, indoor, pool and adjacent hot tubs provide plenty of choice.

High on Deck 14 (aft) is 'Blue Balcony,' a 118-sq-ft (11-sq-m) glass-floored platform 121ft (37m) above the sea, giving a sensation of 'floating' over the water.

There are numerous public rooms (in a slightly different arrangement from on *Mein Schiff 3* and *Mein Schiff 4*); these include a superb Studio auditorium, designed to a high acoustic specification, a shore-excursion information and booking lounge, and shops selling upscale items.

What makes a cruise aboard *Mein Schiff 5* really user-friendly for families is the inclusive nature of the pricing, though this excludes spa treatments, excursions, and the extra-cost restaurants: Hanami Restaurant and Sushi Bar, Gosch Sylt, Surf 'n' Turf

BERLITZ'S RATINGS		
	Possible	Achieved
Ship	500	442
Accommodation	200	163
Food	400	324
Service	400	328
Entertainment	100	82
Cruise Experience	400	320

OVERALL SCORE 1659 points out of 2000

Steakhouse, and Schmankerl Osteria (for Austrian cuisine). The diamond in the crown is a two-deck-high glass enclosure, which houses three different restaurants – with fine views over the ship's stern.

This is a very comfortable ship, with a laid-back feel, and little sense of crowding anywhere, except the pool deck on a sunny day. It boasts a number of outstanding passenger-friendly features, including water-dispenser units on each accommodation deck (special quartz crystals are provided in each cabin to add to the water pitcher for negative ion purification); a large dry-ageing meat (proving) cabinet adjacent to the Surf 'n' Turf Restaurant; and smartphone food ordering for waiters – sent electronically to the galley (kitchen), so the waiter stays at his station to attend to you. The dress code is smart casual.

ACCOMMODATION. There are numerous accommodation price grades; the price depends on the size, location, and grade you choose. Strangely, even-numbered cabins are on the starboard side – contrary to nautical tradition, with even-numbered lifeboats on the port side.

All accommodation grades have a Nespresso coffee machine, hairdryer, and personal bathroom amenities. Also, note that all doors open outwards, not inwards.

From the smallest to the largest, there's something for all needs, including three types of family-friendly suites that can sleep up to six. One example measures about 452 sq ft (42 sq m), plus an extensive balcony of 506 sq ft (47 sq m), totaling 958 sq ft (89 sq m).

Premium veranda cabins offer large, diagonal terraces, and there are three suite categories. Each of the spacious Sea & Sky Suites has its own large 312 sq ft (29 sq m) roof terrace, and private lounging/sunbathing space (including a large hammock, upscale sunbeds, and shaded areas). A Captain's Suite, at 581 sq ft (54 sq m), is the largest; it is located near the navigation bridge.

DINING. With a total of 12 dining venues (some at extra cost), there is plenty of choice. Atlantik, the main restaurant, is included in the cruise fare. It is divided into three, each with a different menu: Classic (for dishes such as steak with roasted shallots and a chili-chocolate reduction); Mediterranean (for choices including homemade pasta); and Brasserie (for French-style grilled fish and lamb with Provençal herbs, etc.).

Aft of the ship, a 1,798-sq-ft (167-sq-m) multi-faceted glass structure (nicknamed the 'diamond') spans two decks. It contains three restaurants: Schmankerl (for Austrian regional specialties); Hanami, which means flower-watching (particularly cherry blossom), for pan-Asian cuisine and incorporating a sushi bar with sit-up stools; and Surf 'n' Turf Steakhouse, which features a large glass-enclosed meat dry-ageing display cabinet with various cuts of beef, and an open-view kitchen.

Gosch Sylt has about 130 seats and features fresh fish and all kinds of well-prepared seafood dishes, plus daily specials (including fresh oysters from the German island of Sylt, and lobster), which are listed on a blackboard.

Day & Night Bistro provides regional and international snacks, including Currywurst, around the clock, while in a modern coffee lounge baristas brew an array of superb international specialist coffees and also the ship's own hand-crafted pralines and truffle chocolates.

Osteria is for hand-made pizzas, pasta, and other Italian culinary favorites.

A real bakery, an adjunct of the self-serve food court-style buffet restaurant Anckelmannsplatz, features freshly baked bread, rolls, paninis, cakes, and pastry items (including gluten-free selections). You can also buy artisan bread – specially baked and packaged on the last day of the cruise – to take home).

ENTERTAINMENT. The Theater is a three-deck-high showlounge with approximately 950 seats. It's used for colorful, trendy production shows and major cabaret acts.

What is really innovative is the Klanghaus concert hall/movie theater, developed in conjunction with renowned acoustics experts. It provides an outstanding setting for live classical and jazz concerts, theatrical readings, lectures, and movies with surround sound.

Numerous bands, small musical units, and solo musical entertainers provide live music in several of the lounges.

SPA/FITNESS. The Spa and Meer wellness and fitness facilities are extensive, and include a large (mixed-gender) sauna, steam rooms, and numerous body-pampering treatment rooms (including a private (rentable) spa room for couples, with integral sauna, massage tables, shower, and relaxation areas), a double-sided vertical wall of living plants, and juice/tea bar.

Sports facilities include a large arena in the aft section of the ship for volleyball, basketball, and football. Sport bikes are also carried.

MEIN SCHIFF 6
★★★★+

THIS FAMILY-FRIENDLY CASUAL SHIP FEATURES CONTEMPORARY STYLE AND GREAT FOOD

Size:	Large Resort Ship	Passenger/Crew Ratio (lower beds):	2.5/1
Tonnage:	99,800	Cabins (total):	1,276
Cruise Line:	TUI Cruises	Size Range (sq ft/m):	182.9–581.2/17.0–54.0
Former Names:	none	Cabins (for one person):	0
Builder:	Meyer Turku (Finland)	Cabins with balcony:	1,033
Entered Service:	Jun 2017	Cabins (wheelchair accessible):	10
Length (ft/m):	967.8/295.0	Wheelchair accessibility:	Good
Beam (ft/m):	118.1/36.0	Elevators:	10
Propulsion/Propellers:	diesel-electric/2	Casino (gaming tables):	Yes
Passenger Decks:	12	Swimming Pools:	3
Total Crew:	1,000	Self-Service Launderette:	No
Passengers (lower beds):	2,552	Library:	Yes
Passenger Space Ratio (lower beds):	39.1	Onboard currency:	Euros

THE SHIP. *Mein Schiff 6*, a sister ship to *Mein Schiff 5*, is for youthful German-speaking families. The propulsion system is extremely quiet, with no vibration anywhere. It has choice of dining venues, an excellent spa, and younger cruisers will have an enthusiastic team of children's activity hosts to look after and entertain them (kids should keep a lookout for Captain Sharky).

An outstanding 82ft (25m) lap pool (long by cruise ship standards and half the length of an Olympic-sized pool) is outdoors – together with a large movie screen and sports area for basketball and volleyball, while a second, indoor, pool and adjacent hot tubs provide plenty of choice.

High on Deck 14 aft is 'Blue Balcony,' a 118-sq-ft (11-sq-m) glass-floored platform 121ft (37m) above the sea, giving a sensation of floating over the water.

There are numerous public rooms; these include a fine Studio auditorium designed to a high acoustic specification (for classical concerts and cultural presentations), a shore-excursion information and booking lounge, and shops selling upscale items.

What makes a cruise aboard *Mein Schiff 6* really user-friendly for families is the inclusive nature of the pricing, though this excludes spa treatments, excursions, and the extra-cost restaurants: Hanami Restaurant and Sushi Bar, Gosch Sylt, Surf 'n' Turf Steakhouse, and Schmankerl Osteria (for Austrian cuisine). But the diamond in the crown is a two-deck-high glass enclosure, which houses three different

BERLITZ'S RATINGS		
	Possible	Achieved
Ship	500	442
Accommodation	200	163
Food	400	324
Service	400	328
Entertainment	100	82
Cruise Experience	400	322
OVERALL SCORE 1661 points out of 2000		

restaurants and has fine views over the ship's stern.

Like *Mein Schiff 5*, this is a very comfortable, laid-back ship, with almost no sense of crowding anywhere – except perhaps for the pool deck on a sunny day. It has a number of proven passenger-friendly features, including water-dispenser units on each accommodation deck (special quartz crystals are provided in each cabin to add to the water pitcher for negative ion purification); a large dry-ageing meat (proving) cabinet adjacent to the Surf 'n' Turf Restaurant; and smartphone food ordering for waiters – sent electronically to the galley (kitchen), so the waiter stays at his station to attend to you.

ACCOMMODATION. There are numerous accommodation price grades, with the price dependent on the size, location, and grade you choose. Strangely, even-numbered cabins are on the starboard side – contrary to nautical tradition – with even-numbered lifeboats on the port side.

All accommodation grades have a Nespresso coffee machine, hairdryer, and personal bathroom amenities. Also, note that all doors open outwards, not inwards.

From the smallest to the largest, there's something for all needs, including three types of family-friendly suites that can sleep up to six. One example measures about 452 sq ft (42 sq m), plus an extensive balcony of 506 sq ft (47 sq m), totaling 958 sq ft (89 sq m).

Premium veranda cabins offer large, diagonal terraces, and there are three suite categories. Each of the spacious Sea & Sky Suites has its own large 312 sq ft (29 sq m) roof terrace, and private lounging/sunbathing space (including a large hammock, upscale sunbeds, and shaded areas). A Captain's Suite, at 581 sq ft (54 sq m), is the largest; it is located near the navigation bridge.

DINING. With a total of 12 dining venues and eateries (some at extra cost), there is plenty of choice. Atlantik, the main restaurant, is included in the cruise fare. It is divided into three sections, each with a different menu: Classic (for dishes such as steak with roasted shallots and a chili-chocolate reduction); Mediterranean (for choices including homemade pasta); and Brasserie (French-style grilled fish and lamb with Provençal herbs, etc.).

Aft, a 1,798-sq-ft (167-sq-m) multifaceted glass structure (nicknamed the 'diamond') spans two decks. Within it are three restaurants: Schmankerl (for authentic Austrian regional specialties in the setting of a real Austrian tavern); Hanami – it means flower-watching – particularly cherry blossom (for pan-Asian cuisine – do try the beef shabu-shabu); and Surf 'n' Turf Steakhouse, which features a large glass-enclosed meat dry-ageing display cabinet various steak cuts, an open-view kitchen, and a choice of several different steak knives.

The casual restaurant Gosch Sylt has about 130 seats aboard this ship, and features fresh fish and well-prepared seafood dishes, with daily specials (including fresh oysters from the German island of Sylt, and lobster) listed on a blackboard.

Osteria is for hand-made pizzas, pasta, and other Italian culinary favorites.

A real bakery, an adjunct of the self-serve buffet restaurant Anckelmannsplatz, features freshly baked bread, rolls, paninis, cakes, and pastry items (including gluten-free selections). You can also buy artisan bread – specially baked and packaged on the last day of the cruise – to take home).

Day & Night Bistro provides regional and international snacks, including Currywurst, around the clock, while in a delightful coffee lounge baristas brew an array of superb international specialist coffees and chocolatiers also create the ship's own hand-crafted pralines and truffle chocolates.

ENTERTAINMENT. The Theater is the showlounge. It's a three-deck-high venue with approximately 950 seats, and features colorful, very trendy production shows and major cabaret acts.

What is really innovative is the Klanghaus concert hall/movie theater, developed in conjunction with renowned acoustics experts. It provides an outstanding setting for live classical and jazz concerts, theatrical readings, lectures, and movies with surround sound.

Numerous bands, small musical units, and solo musical entertainers provide live music in several of the lounges.

SPA/FITNESS. The Spa and Meer wellness and fitness facilities are extensive, and include a large (mixed-gender) sauna, steam rooms, and numerous body-pampering treatment rooms (including a private (rentable) spa room for couples, with integral sauna, massage tables, shower, and relaxation areas), a double-sided vertical wall of living plants, and juice/tea bar.

Sports facilities include a large arena in the aft of the ship for volleyball, basketball, and football. Sport bikes are also carried.

MONARCH
★★+

A MID-SIZED FAMILY-FRIENDLY SHIP, GOOD FOR A FIRST CRUISE EXPERIENCE

Size:	Mid-size Ship
Tonnage:	73,937
Cruise Line:	Pullmantur Cruises
Former Names:	Monarch of the Seas
Builder:	Chantiers de l'Atlantique (France)
Entered Service:	Nov 1991/Apr 2013
Length (ft/m):	879.9/268.2
Beam (ft/m):	105.9/32.3
Propulsion/Propellers:	diesel (21,844kW)/2
Passenger Decks:	11
Total Crew:	858
Passengers (lower beds):	2,384
Passenger Space Ratio (lower beds):	31.0
Passenger/Crew Ratio (lower beds):	2.8
Cabins (total):	1,192
Size Range (sq ft/m):	118.4–670.0/11.0–62.2
Cabins (for one person):	0
Cabins with balcony:	62
Cabins (wheelchair accessible):	4
Wheelchair accessibility:	Fair
Elevators:	11
Casino (gaming tables):	Yes
Swimming Pools:	2
Self-Service Launderette:	No
Library:	Yes
Onboard currency:	Euros

THE SHIP. Monarch is almost identical in size and appearance to sister ship Sovereign, but actually has a slightly improved internal layout and better features in the public rooms. The ship, whose hull is painted a deep blue, has a lounge and a bar that is wrapped around the blue funnel and provides a stunning view – it's a great place to sit and enjoy a decent coffee from one of its 320-plus seats. Despite it being expansive, the open deck space itself is very cramped when the ship is full. There is a basketball court aft for sports lovers.

The interior layout is designed in a vertical stack, with most public rooms located aft, and the accommodation forward. There's a good array of spacious and elegant public rooms to play in, although the decor brings to mind the IKEA school of interior design. A spacious five-deck-high Centrum lobby has cascading stairways and two glass-walled elevators. You may be overwhelmed by the public spaces, but underwhelmed by the size of the cabins.

The ship has a good array of spacious, smart public rooms, including a conference room, library, and card players' room, plus a Monte Carlo Casino for the more serious gamers, as well as shops and an Internet-connect center. The decor is accented with wood paneling, and some bright color splashes. Children and teens are well catered for, and there's a whole team of youth activity staff, together with a range of rooms for children and teens, including a chill-out

BERLITZ'S RATINGS

	Possible	Achieved
Ship	500	271
Accommodation	200	104
Food	400	202
Service	400	233
Entertainment	100	56
Cruise Experience	400	223

OVERALL SCORE 1089 points out of 2000

lounge and an open aft sundeck with a dance floor.

The dress code is ultra-casual. All gratuities and port taxes are included in the cruise fare.

Passengers can embark at Panama's Colón, Colombia's Cartagena, or Venezuela's La Guaira on a seven-night year-round itinerary that also includes Aruba and Curaçao. Although Pullmantur Cruises markets this ship in Europe, it focuses more on Latin America, where it provides a visa-free alternative for many nationalities. This provides an opportunity for South Americans to cruise the Caribbean in their winter. This ship provides the basics for a somewhat impersonal, short cruise experience for Spanish-speaking families. The range of facilities is decent enough, and you can expect highly programmed service from a reasonably attentive young staff.

Note that it's difficult to get away from music and noise. There's even background music in all corridors and elevators, and constant music outdoors on the pool deck. If you want a quiet relaxing holiday, choose another ship.

ACCOMMODATION. There are numerous categories, priced by grade, size, and location. Note that there are no cabins with private balconies.

The standard outside-view and interior cabins are very small, although an arched window treatment and colorful soft furnishings give the illusion of more space. Almost all cabins have twin beds that convert to a queen-size or double bed configuration, together with moveable bedside tables. However, when in a queen-bed configuration, the bed is flush against the wall, with access from one side only. All standard cabins have very little closet and drawer space. You should, therefore, pack only minimal clothing (all you really need for a short cruise). All cabins have a private bathroom, with a shower enclosure, toilet, and washbasin.

Thirteen suites on Bridge Deck are fairly large and nicely furnished (the largest is the Royal Suite), with separate living and sleeping spaces. These provide more space, with better service and more perks than standard-grade accommodation.

DINING. The two large dining rooms, Claude's and Vincent's, are located off the Centrum lobby. There are tables for four, six, or eight, but none for two. There are two seatings, and the dining operation is well orchestrated, with emphasis on well-timed, well-organized service. The cuisine is typical of mass banquet catering that offers standard fare comparable to that found in family-style eateries ashore. While menu descriptions are tempting, the actual food may be somewhat disappointing and unmemorable. Many items are pre-prepared ashore to keep costs down.

A decent selection of light meals is provided, and a vegetarian choice is also available. The selection of breads, rolls, and pastry items is good. The wine list is not extensive, but the prices are moderate.

For casual breakfasts and lunches, the Café is the place to go, although there are often long lines at peak times. On the aft of the upper level of the venue is a pizzeria.

ENTERTAINMENT. Entertainment across the ship is upbeat. The Sound of Music is the principal showlounge; it has both main and balcony levels, with banquette seating, although sight lines from many of the balcony seats are poor.

A smaller entertainment venue, the April in Paris Lounge, is where cabaret acts, including late-night adult comedy are featured, as well as music for dancing.

SPA/FITNESS. The Spa del Mar features a gymnasium with aft-facing views and a selection of muscle-pumping equipment. There is also an aerobics studio, and classes are offered in a variety of keep-fit regimens, a beauty salon, and a sauna, as well as treatment rooms for pampering massages and facials. While the facilities aren't extensive, they're adequate.

For the sports-inclined, there is activity galore, including a rock-climbing wall with several separate climbing tracks. It is located outdoors aft of the blue funnel and wrap-around panoramic lounge.

MSC ARMONIA
★★★+

THIS IS A COMFORTABLE MID-SIZED SHIP FOR PAN-EUROPEAN CRUISERS

Size:	Mid-size Ship	Passenger/Crew Ratio (lower beds):	2.7
Tonnage:	65,542	Cabins (total):	976
Cruise Line:	MSC Cruises	Size Range (sq ft/m):	139.9–236.8/13.0–22.0
Former Names:	European Vision	Cabins (for one person):	0
Builder:	Chantiers de l'Atlantique (France)	Cabins with balcony:	224
Entered Service:	Jun 2001/May 2004	Cabins (wheelchair accessible):	2
Length (ft/m):	902.2/275.0	Wheelchair accessibility:	Good
Beam (ft/m):	95.1/29.0	Elevators:	9
Propulsion/Propellers:	diesel-electric (31,680kW)/ 2 azimuthing pods	Casino (gaming tables):	Yes
		Swimming Pools:	2
Passenger Decks:	10	Self-Service Launderette:	No
Total Crew:	721	Library:	Yes
Passengers (lower beds):	1,952	Onboard currency:	Euros
Passenger Space Ratio (lower beds):	33.5		

THE SHIP. As *European Vision*, the ship began its working life auspiciously, having been used to accommodate the leaders and staff of the G8 summit in 2001. When its owner, Festival Cruises, ceased operations in 2004, it was bought by MSC Cruises (a Swiss-based company with Italian roots) and renamed *MSC Armonia*. The exterior deck space is barely adequate for the number of passengers carried. The Lido Deck surrounding the outdoor swimming pool also has whirlpool tubs and a large bandstand is set in raised canvas-covered pods. All sunloungers have cushioned pads.

In August 2014 a 'chop-and-stretch' operation added an 82ft (25m) mid-section, almost 200 additional cabins, more public rooms, entertainment facilities and shops (but no additional elevators), a greater amount of exterior deck space, and a large waterpark for children. Families with children will also find special kids' areas equipped with Chicco® and LEGO® products, and an energetic multilingual youth activity team.

Inside, the layout and passenger flow became slightly disjointed after the 'stretch.' The decor is modern European and includes crisp, clean lines and minimalist furniture. The interior colors are good; nothing jars the senses, but rather calms them.

Facilities include Amadeus, a nightclub; Ambassador, a cigar-smoking room, and the Red Bar, a piano lounge. There is an extensive Internet café, and

BERLITZ'S RATINGS

	Possible	Achieved
Ship	500	367
Accommodation	200	153
Food	400	238
Service	400	288
Entertainment	100	60
Cruise Experience	400	267

OVERALL SCORE 1373 points out of 2000

an English pub, the White Lion. The Lido Casino has gaming tables plus an array of slot machines.

Announcements are made in several languages.

Wheelchair-bound passengers should note that there is no access to the uppermost forward and aft decks, but access throughout most of the interior is good. The passenger hallways are a little narrow on some accommodation decks to pass when housekeeping carts are in place.

MSC Armonia will suit those keen to travel with an international mix of passengers. It is best for adult couples and solo travelers, and families with children, who enjoy constant activity accompanied by lots of noise, late nights, and entertainment that is loud.

ACCOMMODATION. There are numerous categories, with the price depending on the grade, size, and location you choose. These include 132 'suites' with private balcony (whose partitions are only of the partial and not the full type), outside-view cabins, and interior (no-view) cabins.

Suite-grade accommodation – not true suites, as there's no separate bedroom and lounge – have more room than standard cabins, a larger lounge area, walk-in closet, wall-to-wall vanity counter, a bathroom with combination tub and shower, toilet, and private balcony with light. Bathrobes are provided. However, except in accommodation of the highest category, the bathrooms are plain, with white plastic washbasins and white walls, small shower enclosures, and mirrors that steam up.

Even the smallest interior cabins are acceptable, however, with enough space between two lower beds. All grades of accommodation have a TV, mini-bar/refrigerator, personal safe cleverly positioned behind a vanity desk mirror, hairdryer, and bathroom with shower and toilet. But standard grade cabins, at a modest 140 sq ft (13 sq m), are really small when compared to those in many other ships.

DINING. The principal dining room, the 610-seat Marco Polo Restaurant, has two sittings for dinner, and an open seating (meaning you can arrive for dinner whenever you like, during dining hours) for breakfast and lunch. During an open seating, you may well be seated with others with whom you may not necessarily be able to communicate very easily, given the wide mix of nationalities and languages on board.

MSC Cruises highlights regional Italian cuisine and wines, with dining room menus that feature food from Calabria, Piedmont, Lazio, Puglia, and Sicily. Items that are always available include spaghetti (with a tomato sauce freshly made each day), chicken breast, salmon fillet, and vegetables of the day. All pizza dough is made on board, and risotto is a daily signature item, as is fresh pasta. Several varieties of Italian breads such as bruschetta, focaccia, and panettone are provided. Light 'always available' meals and vegetarian dishes are also provided.

The wine list has quite a wide variety of wines at fairly reasonable prices, although most of the wines are very young.

La Pergola the most formal restaurant, features stylish Italian cuisine. It is assigned to all passengers occupying suite-grade accommodation, although others can dine in it too, on a reservations-only basis.

Il Girasole, on the starboard side aft, adjacent to the ship's funnel, is a grill area for fast food. La Brasserie is a casual, self-serve buffet eatery, and includes a sit-down, casual dinner each evening with waiter service. Café San Marco, on the upper, second level of the main lobby, serves extra-cost Segafredo coffee, and pastry items.

ENTERTAINMENT. Teatro La Fenice, which is two decks high, is the venue for production shows, cabaret acts, and other theatrical presentations. It is a well-designed room, except for the fact that no space was allocated for a live showband – productions are performed to pre-recorded backing tracks. The sight lines from most seats are good, and four entrances allow easy access and exit.

Other shows consist of singers, magicians, mimes, and comedy jugglers. A number of bands and small musical units provide live music for dancing or listening.

SPA/FITNESS. The Atlantica Spa has numerous body-pampering treatments, a gymnasium with ocean views, and high-tech, muscle-toning and strengthening equipment. A thermal suite has different kinds of steam rooms combined with aromatherapy infusions such as chamomile and eucalyptus, and a Rasul chamber provides a combination of two or three kinds of application mud and gentle steam shower. The spa, operated by the Italian concession OceanView, offers a wide range of wellbeing treatments. Gratuities to spa staff are at your discretion.

For active types, there's a simulated climbing wall outdoors aft of the ship's funnel, as well as a volleyball/basketball court, and mini-golf.

MSC DIVINA
★★★★

A HIGHLY COMFORTABLE, LARGE FAMILY-FRIENDLY, MULTI-CHOICE RESORT SHIP

Size:	Large Resort Ship	Passenger/Crew Ratio (lower beds):	2.5
Tonnage:	139,400 tons	Cabins (total):	1,751
Cruise Line:	MSC Cruises	Size Range (sq ft/m):	148.5–568.3/13.8–52.8
Former Names:	none	Cabins (for one person):	0
Builder:	STX France	Cabins with balcony:	1,125
Entered Service:	Jun 2012	Cabins (wheelchair accessible):	45
Length (ft/m):	1,093.5/333.3	Wheelchair accessibility:	Good
Beam (ft/m):	124.6/38.0	Elevators:	17
Propulsion/Propellers:	diesel-electric (40,000kW)/2	Casino (gaming tables):	Yes
Passenger Decks:	13	Swimming Pools:	3
Total Crew:	1,388	Self-Service Launderette:	No
Passengers (lower beds):	3,502	Library:	Yes
Passenger Space Ratio (lower beds):	39.8	Onboard currency:	Euros

THE SHIP. *MSC Divina* is sister to *MSC Preziosa*, and features green-technology engines. Its exclusive area, the MSC Yacht Club, includes a large Top-Sail Lounge (an observation/lifestyle lounge and social meeting place), private sunbathing deck with integral dip pool, two hot tubs, concierge services, and bar/snack bar. Yacht Club-grade occupants are escorted to their cabins by their butlers on embarkation. Housekeeping staff point passengers in the right direction but no longer escort them to their cabins.

The interior decor is quite stunning. There are basically two decks full of public lounges, bars, and eateries, including a large two-deck-high theater-style showlounge, a nightclub/disco, library, card room, an Internet center, virtual-reality center, shopping gallery, and large casino. Drinking places include a large number of lounges and bars, most with live music. One lounge in the aft section is for adults only, as is an aft swimming pool and relaxation deck. The Golden Jazz Bar is a must (the walls are 'stoned'). Additionally, there are conference and small group meeting facilities.

The ship's interior focal point is a gorgeous three-decks-high atrium lobby with shimmering Swarovski crystal stairways and elegant, Art Deco-influenced decor. Reception and financial-services desks are located on the lower level, which also has a stage and seating in oversized armchairs.

BERLITZ'S RATINGS

	Possible	Achieved
Ship	500	419
Accommodation	200	162
Food	400	276
Service	400	308
Entertainment	100	78
Cruise Experience	400	301

OVERALL SCORE 1544 points out of 2000

You can drive an F1 Ferrari racing car in a simulator, and experience seat-of-your-pants rides in a 4D theater.

This large, elegantly attired resort ship has a trendy infinity pool and 'beach' zone, and will appeal to young adult couples, solo travelers, and families with children and teens.

Niggles include the fact that all the lounges 'flow' into each other, and music from each one bleeds into the adjacent room. Men should note that the public restrooms have cubicles (there are no urinals).

ACCOMMODATION. There are nine types of accommodation, in numerous cabin price grades. Included are two Royal Suites, three Executive/Family Suites, and a mix of outside-view (with or without balconies) and interior cabins. The price you pay depends on the grade, size, and location you choose.

The 'Yacht Club' exclusive (ship within a ship) accommodation consists of 67 'suites,' in a key-operated access only area of the ship. It comes with butler service, interactive TV, mini-bar, personal safe, hairdryer, and satellite-link telephone. Number 16007 is the Sophia Loren Suite, in rich reds, specially designed lamps, and stunning photos of her great movie roles, together with a replica of the dressing table that Ms Loren uses in her home.

DINING. There are two main restaurants. The two-level Black Crab has 626 seats on one level and 529 on the other, and assigned tables and seating for dinner. The second is the 766-seat Villa Rossa Restaurant.

MSC Cruises highlights regional Italian cuisine and wines, with dining room menus that feature food from Calabria, Piedmont, Lazio, Puglia, and Sicily. Items that are always available include spaghetti (with a tomato sauce freshly made each day), chicken breast, salmon fillet, and vegetables of the day. However, the company has tailored its cuisine to North American tastes, and included some down-home favorites, produced with Italian flair.

All pizza dough is made on board, and risotto is a daily signature item, as is fresh pasta. Several varieties of Italian breads such as bruschetta, focaccia, and panettone are provided.

Occupants of Yacht Club accommodation grades eat in Le Muse, a private, quite intimate restaurant that overlooks an aft infinity pool area. The service here is less hurried and much more personalized.

Other options include the bistro-style, extra-cost Eataly, which is a sea-going version of a chain of the same name. It has ultra-clean white decor. The portions (especially the steaks) are impressively large, and everything is cooked to order.

Lido-style self-serve buffet cafeterias (Calumet and Manitou – named after peace pipes and spirits of the indigenous American Indians; each has about 400 seats) are for breakfasts and lunches, and served, casual dinners. The buffets are open for up to 20 hours daily, so there's always something to eat whenever you're hungry.

Additional foodie-type places include La Cantina di Bacco (a wine bar and pizzeria), Piazza del Doge (for Italian pastries, coffees, and huge selection of gelato), an Italia Bar for coffees (Lavazza is featured, always served in proper china cups) and pastries, and Galaxy (an à la carte eatery located as part of the disco, it overlooks the entire mid-ship pool deck, and is good for a late-riser's brunch (featuring several trendy tapas-style dishes, steaks, and seafood).

A Sports and Bowling Diner features a classic American food experience (including sandwiches and burgers).

ENTERTAINMENT. The 1,603-seat Pantheon Theater is spread over two decks. Because passengers really are multinational, the entertainment shows are highly visual, including dancing and acrobatics, and are performed to recorded music. A number of bands and small musical groups provide live music for dancing or listening in most lounges and bars.

SPA/FITNESS. The large Aurea Spa and Wellbeing Center houses a beauty salon, numerous body-treatment rooms (with Balinese therapists and 21 types of massage), a bar (for fruit drinks and smoothies), relaxation room, solarium, and a gymnasium with great ocean views. A thermal suite contains two steam rooms and four saunas combined with herbal aromatherapy infusions. This is the first cruise ship to have a halotherapy (Himalayan salt crystal) bed for body detoxing. There's also a Shu Uemura Art of Hair Cabin. Gratuities to spa staff are at your discretion.

Sports facilities include basketball, tennis court, volleyball, a power-walking track, bowling, and shuffleboard.

MSC FANTASIA
★★★★

THIS SHIP HAS COMFORT, SPACE, AND A MEDITERRANEAN LIFESTYLE FOR FAMILIES

Size:	Large Resort Ship	Passenger/Crew Ratio (lower beds):	2.5
Tonnage:	137,936	Cabins (total):	1,637
Cruise Line:	MSC Cruises	Size Range (sq ft/m):	161.4–699.6/15–65
Former Names:	none	Cabins (for one person):	0
Builder:	STX Europe (France)	Cabins with balcony:	1,260
Entered Service:	Dec 2008	Cabins (wheelchair accessible):	43
Length (ft/m):	1,093.5/333.3	Wheelchair accessibility:	Best
Beam (ft/m):	124.3/37.9	Elevators:	14
Propulsion/Propellers:	diesel-electric (40,000kW)/2	Casino (gaming tables):	Yes
Passenger Decks:	13	Swimming Pools:	3 (1 w/sliding glass dome)
Total Crew:	1,325	Self-Service Launderette:	No
Passengers (lower beds):	3,274	Library:	Yes
Passenger Space Ratio (lower beds):	442.1	Onboard currency:	Euros

THE SHIP. Built in 67 blocks, some more than 600 tons, *MSC Fantasia* is one of the largest ships built for a European cruise company. It is about 33ft (10m) longer than the Eiffel Tower is high, and the propulsion power is the equivalent of 120 Ferraris. There are four swimming pools, one of which can be covered by a glass dome.

The interior design is an enlargement and extension of MSC's smaller *Musica-* and *Orchestra-*class ships, but with the addition of an exclusive area called the MSC Yacht Club for occupants of the 99 suites. This 'club' includes a Top-Sail Lounge, private sunbathing with integral dip pool, two hot tubs, and concierge services such as making dining reservations, and booking excursions and spa treatments.

If your wallet allows, it's worth paying extra to stay in one of the 'suites' in the Yacht Club accommodation. You'll get silver-tray room service by a team of well-trained butlers, a reserved (quieter) section of the Il Cerchio d'Oro restaurant, plus keycard access to a members-only sundeck sanctuary area that includes its own bar and food counters, a small dip pool, two hot tubs, and expansive open but sheltered lounging deck. It's a world away from the hustle and bustle of the main pool decks and solarium on the decks below.

The interior decor is quite stunning. There are basically two decks full of public lounges, bars, and eateries, including a large two-deck-high theater-style

BERLITZ'S RATINGS

	Possible	Achieved
Ship	500	413
Accommodation	200	162
Food	400	273
Service	400	306
Entertainment	100	77
Cruise Experience	400	305

OVERALL SCORE 1536 points out of 2000

showlounge, a nightclub/disco, library, card room, an Internet center, virtual-reality center, shopping gallery, and large casino (inhabited by many people who can smoke at the bar). There's a big city-like environment in the shopping areas. The Monte Carlo Casino features blackjack, poker, and roulette games, plus an array of slot machines.

Drinking places include a pub-like venue and several comfortable lounges with live music. Note that 15 percent is added to all drinks/beverage orders. A neat mini-golf course is on the port side of the funnel, and a walking and jogging track encircles the two swimming pools.

This ship appeals to young adult couples, solo travelers, and families with children and teens – anyone who enjoys big ships, a big-city lifestyle, and a mix of nationalities, mostly European. You can drive an F1 Ferrari racing car in a simulator, and experience hair-raising, seat-of-your pants rides in a 4D theater. Note that only Yacht Club-grade occupants are escorted to their cabins by their butlers. Housekeeping staff point passengers in the right direction, but no longer escort them to their cabins.

Niggles include the fact that all the lounges flow into each other, and music from each one bleeds into any adjacent room.

ACCOMMODATION. Eighty percent of cabins have an outside view, and 95 percent of these have a balcony – a standard balcony cabin will measure almost 172 sq ft (16 sq m), plus bathroom and balcony. There are 72 suites in a MSC Yacht Club VIP section; each measures 312 sq ft (29 sq m) and comes with full butler service. The price you pay depends on the grade, size, and location you choose.

In a 2011 refit, 28 Aurea Suites were created with direct access to the Aurea Spa. The spa suites come with amenities and 'extras,' including a non-alcoholic cocktail at the Aurea Spa Bar, unlimited access to the Thermal Suite (sauna and steam room) and a private consultation with the spa doctor. Also included in the price are a Balinese massage, a facial relax treatment using skin-firming cream, and a solarium session for full-body tanning.

A black marble floor leads to a magnificent Swarovski glass staircase that connects the concierge facilities between decks 15 and 16 under a glass-domed ceiling.

DINING. There are four dining venues. The two-deck-high Red Velvet, the main restaurant, is in the aft section. It has a ship-wide balcony level, with a stairway to connect its two levels.

MSC Cruises highlights regional Italian cuisine and wines, with menus that feature food from Calabria, Piedmont, Lazio, Puglia, and Sicily. Items that are always available include spaghetti (with a tomato sauce freshly made each day), chicken breast, salmon fillet, and vegetables of the day. All pizza dough is made on board, and risotto is a daily signature item, as is fresh pasta. Several varieties of Italian breads such as bruschetta, focaccia, and panettone are provided. Light 'always available' and vegetarian dishes are also provided.

Il Cerchio d'Oro is a single-level specialty restaurant, with a different menu each evening devoted to a different region of Italy. The Murano chandeliers are quite lovely, and definitely worth admiring.

L'Etoile is a classic French restaurant, with decor reminiscent of the Belle Epoque era. Menus focus either on the sea, the countryside, or the kitchen garden, and change seasonally. There's also an extra-charge Tex-Mex restaurant, El Sombrero, serving large portions of burritos, fajitas, enchiladas, tacos, tortillas, and more, together with a choice of several Mexican beers.

Casual breakfasts, lunches, and sit-down, served, but casual, dinners can be taken in the large self-serve L'Africana Café, a self-serve buffet-style eatery that is open 20 hours daily.

A casual spot that's good for people-watching is the Il Cappuccino coffee bar. Located two decks above the main reception area, it serves Lavazza and Segafredo coffee, as well as fine chocolate delicacies.

La Cantina Toscana is a neat wine bar that pairs wines with food from several regions of Italy, in a setting that includes alcove seating.

A Sports and Bowling Diner features a classic American food experience (including sandwiches and burgers).

ENTERTAINMENT. L'Avanguardia, the main showlounge, has 1,603 seats, and facilities that rival almost any to be found on land. Shows are highly visual, due to the multi-national passenger make-up. Additionally, live music is performed in most lounges by small musical groups and solo musicians.

SPA/FITNESS. The Aurea Spa has a beauty salon, several treatment rooms, and a gymnasium with great ocean views. A thermal suite contains different kinds of steam rooms combined with herbal aromatherapy infusions, in a calming Asia-themed environment. The spa is operated by OceanView, a specialist spa provider. Gratuities are not included, but left to your discretion.

Sports facilities include deck quoits, shuffleboard courts, a large tennis/basketball court, mini-golf, and a jogging track.

MSC LIRICA
★★★+

THIS IS A STRETCHED, EURO-STYLE, INFORMAL, FAMILY-FRIENDLY SHIP

Size:	Mid-size Ship
Tonnage:	65,542
Cruise Line:	MSC Cruises
Former Names:	none
Builder:	Chantiers de l'Atlantique (France)
Entered Service:	Mar 2003
Length (ft/m):	902.2/275.0
Beam (ft/m):	95.1/29.0
Propulsion/Propellers:	diesel (31,680kW)/2 azimuthing pods
Passenger Decks:	10
Total Crew:	721
Passengers (lower beds):	1,976
Passenger Space Ratio (lower beds):	33.1
Passenger/Crew Ratio (lower beds):	2.7
Cabins (total):	988
Size Range (sq ft/m):	139.9–302.0/13.0–28.0
Cabins (for one person):	0
Cabins with balcony:	224
Cabins (wheelchair accessible):	4
Wheelchair accessibility:	Good
Elevators:	9
Casino (gaming tables):	Yes
Swimming Pools:	2
Self-Service Launderette:	No
Library:	Yes
Onboard currency:	Euros

THE SHIP. *MSC Lirica*, sister to *MSC Opera*, was the first of a pair of new-builds for Mediterranean Shipping Cruises (MSC), a Swiss-based company with Italian roots. The ship's deep blue funnel is quite sleek; it has a swept-back design. The ship is fitted with an azimuthing pod propulsion system.

In 2015 the ship underwent a 'chop-and-stretch' operation, which added an 82ft (25m) mid-section, almost 200 additional cabins, more public rooms, entertainment facilities, new shops (but no additional elevators), a greater amount of exterior deck space, plus a large waterpark for children. Families with children will also find special kids' areas equipped with Chicco® and LEGO® products, and an energetic multilingual youth activity team.

Inside, the layout (and passenger flow) is quite good with the exception of some congestion points – typically when first seating passengers exit the dining room and second seating passengers are waiting to enter.

An abundance of real woods and marble are used extensively in the interiors, and the standard of the fit and finish reflects MSC's commitment to high quality.

Facilities include a large main showlounge, a nightclub/disco, multiple lounges and bars, an Internet center, a virtual-reality center, a children's club, and a shopping gallery named Rodeo Drive with stores that have an integrated bar and entertainment area, where you can conveniently shop,

BERLITZ'S RATINGS

	Possible	Achieved
Ship	500	378
Accommodation	200	150
Food	400	236
Service	400	299
Entertainment	100	60
Cruise Experience	400	269

OVERALL SCORE 1392 points out of 2000

drink, and be entertained all in one place. The Las Vegas Casino offers blackjack, poker, and roulette games, together with an array of slot machines. There is also a card room, but the integral library is small and disappointing, and there are no hardback books.

The ship is designed to accommodate families with children, who have their own play center, youth counselors, and activity programs. Anyone wheelchair-bound should note that there is no access to the uppermost forward and aft decks, although access throughout most of the interior is very good and there are also several wheelchair-accessible public restrooms. But passenger hallways are a little narrow on some decks, when housekeeping carts are in place.

MSC Lirica is best suited to young adult couples, solo travelers, and families with children who enjoy big-ship surroundings and facilities, and passengers of different nationalities and languages (mostly European). The decor has many Italian influences, including clean lines, minimalism in furniture design, and an eclectic collection of colors and soft furnishings that somehow work well together without any hint of garishness.

Some things that passengers find irritating: the ship's photographers always seem to be in your face; the telephone numbering system to reach such places as the information bureau (2224) and hospital (2360) are not easy to remember – single digit numbers would be better. Gratuities are extra, even though bar drinks already includes a 15 percent service charge added to all drinks/beverage orders.

ACCOMMODATION. There are several different price levels for accommodation, depending on grade and location: one suite category including 132 'suites' with private balcony, five outside-view cabin grades, and five interior cabin grades.

All cabins have a mini-bar and personal safe, satellite-linked television, several audio channels, and 24-hour room service. While tea and coffee are complimentary, snacks from room service incur a delivery charge.

Accommodation designated as suites (they are not true suites, as there is no separate bedroom and lounge) offers more room, a larger lounge area, walk-in closet, wall-to-wall vanity counter, a bathroom with combination tub and shower, toilet, and semi-private balcony with a light but partitions that are partial, not full. The bathrobes are 100 percent cotton. However, the suite bathrooms are very plain, with white plastic washbasins and white walls, and mirrors that steam up.

Some cabins on Scarlatti Deck have views obstructed by lifeboats, while those on Deck 10 aft (10105–10159) can be subject to late-night noise from the disco on the deck above.

DINING. There are two dining rooms: La Bussola Restaurant, and the smaller, slightly more intimate L'Ippocampo Restaurant, located one deck above. Both have ocean-view picture windows at the aft end of the ship. There are tables are for two to eight.

La Pergola is the most formal restaurant, offering stylish Italian cuisine. It is assigned to passengers in accommodation designated as suites, although other passengers can dine in it, too, on a reservations-only basis. The food and service are superior to that in the main dining rooms.

Jereme Leung, well known for his contemporary interpretation of Chinese cuisine, has created menus aimed at Chinese passengers.

Casual, self-serve buffets for breakfast and lunch can be taken in Le Bistrot Buffet. For fast foods, there is also a La Pergola grill and pizzeria, located outside adjacent to the swimming pool and ship's funnel.

Coffee Corner, located on the upper, second level of the main lobby, is the place for Lavazza coffees, and pastry items – as well as for people-watching throughout the day and evening. Although there are windows, the view is not of the ocean, but of the stowed gangways and associated equipment.

ENTERTAINMENT. The Broadway Theater, the main showlounge, is located in the forward section. It has tiered seating set in a sloping floor, and sight lines are good from most seats. The room can also serve as a venue for large social functions. There is no separate bandstand, and the shows work with recorded music, with little consistency in orchestration and sound balance.

The Lirica Lounge, one deck above the showlounge, is the place for social dancing, with live music. For the young and lively set, there is The Blue Club, the ship's throbbing, ear-melting disco.

Additionally, live music is provided in most lounges by small groups and solo musicians.

SPA/FITNESS. The Lirica Health Center is located one deck above the navigation bridge at the forward end of the ship. The complex has a beauty salon, several private massage/bodytreatment rooms, plus a fitness center with ocean views and an array of cardio-vascular equipment. There's also a thermal suite, containing different kinds of steam rooms combined with aromatherapy infusions, available at extra cost.

The spa is operated by the Italian company OceanView, with European hairstylists and Balinese massage and body-treatment staff. Gratuities to spa staff are not included, but left to your discretion.

MSC MAGNIFICA
★★★★

THIS IS A LARGE, FAMILY-FRIENDLY SHIP WITH STYLISH, BRIGHT DECOR

Size:	Large Resort Ship
Tonnage:	95,128
Cruise Line:	MSC Cruises
Former Names:	none
Builder:	Aker Yards (France)
Entered Service:	Mar 2010
Length (ft/m):	963.9/293.8
Beam (ft/m):	105.6/32.2
Propulsion/Propellers:	diesel (31,680kW)/2
Passenger Decks:	13
Total Crew:	1,038
Passengers (lower beds):	2,518
Passenger Space Ratio (lower beds):	37.0
Passenger/Crew Ratio (lower beds):	2.4
Cabins (total):	1,259
Size Range (sq ft/m):	150.6–301.3/14.0–28.0
Cabins (for one person):	0
Cabins with balcony:	827
Cabins (wheelchair accessible):	17
Wheelchair accessibility:	Good
Elevators:	13
Casino (gaming tables):	Yes
Swimming Pools:	2
Self-Service Launderette:	No
Library:	Yes
Onboard currency:	Euros

THE SHIP. *MSC Magnifica* is one of a quartet of the same class, the others being *MSC Musica*, *MSC Poesia*, and *MSC Orchestra*. The ship sports a dark blue funnel, which has a swept-back design that balances an otherwise large-ship profile. The hull itself has large circular porthole-style windows instead of square or rectangular ones. The vessel is powered by diesel motors driving electric generators to provide power to two conventional propellers.

This large resort ship is designed to accommodate families with children, who have their own play center, video games room, youth counselors, and activity programs. The interior layout and passenger flow are quite good, and decks are named after Mediterranean destinations such as Capri, Positano, Portovenere, and Ischia. The focal point is a main three-deck-high lobby; it has a water-feature backdrop and a crystal (glass) piano on a small stage that appears to float on a pond.

The decor has an abundance of Italian and general Mediterranean influences, including clean lines, minimalism in furniture design, and a collection of colors, soft furnishings, and fabrics that work well together. Real wood and marble have been used extensively, and the high quality reflects the commitment that MSC Cruises (a Swiss-based company with Italian roots) has in the vessel's future. Some of the artwork is quite whimsical, but it suits the ship's contemporary design.

BERLITZ'S RATINGS		
	Possible	Achieved
Ship	500	403
Accommodation	200	155
Food	400	242
Service	400	298
Entertainment	100	62
Cruise Experience	400	291

OVERALL SCORE 1451 points out of 2000

Facilities include a large main showlounge (Royal Theater), a nightclub, Atlantic City Casino, a disco that incorporates two bowling lanes, numerous lounges and bars (including L'Olimpiade sports/wine/food bar), a library, a card room, an Internet center, a 4D virtual-reality center, children's club, and a dedicated cigar lounge (Cuba Lounge) with specialized smoke extraction and stocking a selection of Cuban, Dominican, and Italian smokes.

One of the most popular venues is the Tiger Lounge/Bar. It features animal-themed decor and sumptuous but heavy chairs, and a long curvy bar. A shopping area, which includes an electronics store, is well integrated with bars and entertainment offerings in the main lobby, so you can shop, drink, and be entertained all in one convenient area.

Drinking places include a pub-like venue as well as several comfortable lounges with live music. Note that 15 percent is added to all bar drink prices. Although access throughout most of the interior is very good, wheelchair-bound passengers should note that accommodation hallways are narrow on some decks for you to pass when housekeeping carts are in place. Sadly, there is no walk-around open promenade deck.

ACCOMMODATION. There are numerous different price levels, depending on grade and location. Included are 18 'suites' with private balcony, mini-suites, outside-view cabins, and interior cabins. Contrary to nautical convention, the cabin numbering system has even numbered cabins on the starboard side, and odd numbered cabins on the port side.

All cabins have high-quality Italian bed linen (400-count cotton for suites, 300-count cotton for all other cabins), a mini-bar, safe, satellite flat-screen TV, several audio channels, and 24-hour room service. Continental breakfast is complimentary in cabins from 7.30am to 10am, and snacks are available from room service at extra cost at any other time.

Accommodation designated as 'suites' (they are not true suites, as there is no separate bedroom and lounge) also has more space, although less than on suites on some other major cruise lines. Suites have a larger lounge area, walk-in closet, vanity desk with drawer-mounted hairdryer, a bathroom with combination tub and shower, toilet, and semi-private balcony with light. The partitions between each balcony are of the partial, not full, type. The bathrobes and towels are 100 percent cotton, and a pillow menu with a choice of five pillows is available.

Views from many cabins on Camogli Deck are obstructed by lifeboats. Some of the most popular cabins are those at the aft section of the ship, with views over the stern from the balcony cabins. The 17 cabins for the disabled are spacious and well equipped.

DINING. There are two principal dining rooms: L'Edera and Quattro Venti. Both are located aft, on different decks, with large ocean-view picture windows. There are two seatings for meals, at assigned tables for two to eight. Seating is both banquette-style and in individual chairs, although the chairs are slim and do not have armrests.

MSC Cruises highlights regional Italian cuisine and wines, with menus that feature food from Calabria, Piedmont, Lazio, Puglia, and Sicily. Items that are always available include spaghetti (with a tomato sauce freshly made each day), chicken breast, salmon fillet, and vegetables of the day. All pizza dough is made on board, and risotto is a daily signature item, as is fresh pasta. Several varieties of Italian breads such as bruschetta, focaccia, and panettone are provided. Light 'always available' and vegetarian dishes are also provided.

Casual, self-serve buffets for breakfast and lunch are set out in the Sahara Cafeteria (open 20 hours every day), where you can also enjoy sit-down and be served dinners in a laid-back setting each evening. There's also a pool deck fast-food eatery for burgers. Segafredo-brand coffees, and pastries, are available in several bars adjacent to the mid-ships atrium lobby.

Enclosed in the ship's center, Shanghai is a Chinese extra-cost, reservations-required restaurant with high-temperature wok cooking, dim sum, and other Chinese and Asian specialties available à la carte. The food embraces four main cuisines – Beijing, Cantonese, Shanghai, and Szechuan – and there's Tsing Tao beer.

L'Oesi is a reservation-required, extra-charge, à la carte dining spot that, by day, forms the aft section of the Sahara Cafeteria, complete with Moroccan-style decor. Dinners are cooked to order from the adjacent galley.

A Sports Bar is the venue for light-bite snack foods (examples: chicken breast and rocket salad; eggs stuffed with salmon roe; smoked salmon rosettes; assorted sole rolls – all at a small additional cost).

Silver trays full of late-night snacks are taken throughout the ship by waiters, and, on some days, special late-night desserts, such as flambé items, are showcased in various lounges. Ice cream is made on board.

ENTERTAINMENT. The Royal Theater is the large, principal showlounge, and the tiered seating spans three decks in the forward section of the ship, with good sight lines from most of the plush, comfortable seats. The room can also serve as a venue for large groups or social functions. All the large-scale production shows are performed to prerecorded music – there is no showband.

L'Amethista Lounge is the place for social dancing and functions such as cooking demonstrations, with live music provided by a band. For the young and lively crowd, there's the ear-blasting T32 disco. With its floor-to-ceiling windows, it is a quiet, pleasant place to relax and read during sea days.

Additionally, big-screen movies are shown on a mega-screen above the forward pool, just behind the ship's mast. Live music is provided in most bars and lounges.

SPA/FITNESS. The Aurea Spa is one deck above the navigation bridge at the forward end of the ship. The complex has a beauty salon, several treatment rooms offering massage and other body-pampering treatments, and a gymnasium with forward ocean views and an array of muscle-toning and strengthening equipment. There's also a Middle East-themed thermal suite, containing steam rooms and saunas with aromatherapy infusions, and a relaxation/hot tub room; there's an extra charge for using these facilities. Note that gratuities to staff are not included, but left to your discretion.

Sports facilities include table tennis, a tennis court, mini-golf course, golf practice net, two shuffleboard courts, and a jogging track.

MSC MERAVIGLIA
★★★★+

THIS STUNNING, FAMILY-FRIENDLY, ULTRA-STYLISH SHIP HAS GREAT WOW FACTORS

Size:	Large Resort Ship
Tonnage:	171,598
Cruise Line:	MSC Cruises
Former Names:	none
Builder:	STX (France)
Entered Service:	Jun 2017
Length (ft/m):	1,033.4/315.0
Beam (ft/m):	141.0/43.0
Propulsion/Propellers:	diesel-electric/ 2 azimuthing pods
Passenger Decks:	14
Total Crew:	1,540
Passengers (lower beds):	4,500
Passenger Space Ratio (lower beds):	38.2
Passenger/Crew Ratio (lower beds):	2.9/1
Cabins (total):	2,244
Size Range (sq ft/m):	172.2–699.6/16.0–65.0
Cabins (for one person):	0
Cabins with balcony:	1,401
Cabins (wheelchair accessible):	47
Wheelchair accessibility:	Good
Elevators:	16
Casino (gaming tables):	Yes
Swimming Pools:	2
Self-Service Launderette:	No
Library:	Yes
Onboard currency:	Euros

THE SHIP. *MSC Meraviglia* is an absolutely stunning ship, with a large indoor atrium, and outdoors sports and waterpark facilities. The ship will appeal to young-at-heart adult couples, solo travelers, and families with children and teens enjoying an urban lifestyle, with a mix of mostly European nationalities and style.

Standout features include real Cirque du Soleil shows (custom designed for MSC Cruises) and an Aqua Park aft and atop ship with five slides and water entertainment features for children. Above it all is an 'Adventure Trail' ropes course with bridges, towers, climb-through spaces – all subject to water attacks from the water park below.

Inside, a two-deck-high Promenade 'Village' has an extremely impressive LED-screen domed ceiling showing constantly changing digital scenes. The indoor area, which leads off from an expansive multi-deck atrium, is home to a parade of shops, restaurants, and bars. One bar (Champagne Bar) features a wide variety of Champagnes and sparkling wine, plus caviar, oysters, and crab. There's also a good English pub.

There are many excellent offerings on board for children and teens, including five clubs. Other facilities include numerous bars and lounges, and a casino (with gaming tables and slot machines).

An exclusive key-card access area called the MSC Yacht Club is like a 'ship within a ship' of 'suite-grade'

BERLITZ'S RATINGS	Possible	Achieved
Ship	500	430
Accommodation	200	162
Food	400	280
Service	400	309
Entertainment	100	856
Cruise Experience	400	3148

OVERALL SCORE 1585 points out of 2000

accommodation, with larger bathrooms and duplex suites. Exclusive facilities include a large observation/lifestyle lounge (with great views) and social meeting place, a dedicated restaurant, plus private sunbathing with integral dip pool, hot tubs, and concierge services for making dining reservations, booking excursions and spa treatments, and arranging private parties.

The schedule calls for passenger embarkation from three countries: Italy (Genoa), France (Marseille), and Spain (Barcelona).

ACCOMMODATION. There are numerous accommodation price grades and name designations (such as Fantastica Cabins), which come with different inclusions (such as discounts on fitness classes, 24-hour room service, etc.). The price you pay depends on the size, location, and grade you choose. From the smallest to the largest, all have two lower beds (convertible to a twin or double format) personal safe, and mini-bar/fridge. Some cabins have interconnecting doors to make larger family cabins. Some are Duplex Suites (with upper and lower sections).

All Yacht Club grade accommodation has a Nespresso coffee machine and larger bathroom with bathtub, and its occupants eat in a dedicated restaurant.

DINING. The Restaurant (there are two, one on each of two different decks) has both 'Fixed Time' (you have the same waiter for the whole cruise) and 'Flexi Time' (you have a different waiter each day) dining options.

MSC Cruises highlights regional Italian cuisine and wines, with dining room menus that feature food from Calabria, Piedmont, Lazio, Puglia, and Sicily. Items that are always available include spaghetti (with a tomato sauce freshly made each day), chicken breast, salmon fillet, and vegetables of the day. All pizza dough is made on board, and risotto is a daily signature item, as is fresh pasta. Several varieties of Italian breads such as bruschetta, focaccia, and panettone are provided. Light 'always available' and vegetarian dishes are also provided.

MSC Cruises has been paying more attention to its cuisine, and Michelin-starred Italian celebrity chef Carlo Cracco has developed special dishes for Gala, Christmas and New Year menus, and developed a cooking experience for the DoReMi kids club.

For casual eating, a self-serve Buffet Restaurant is large. It is open 20 hours a day for breakfasts and lunches, and waiter-served dinners in a relaxed setting. A bakery corner provides freshly baked breads and rolls throughout the day.

Butcher's Cut is MSC's answer to the all-American steakhouse experience, with extra-cost king-sized steaks and grilled seafood items.

Eataly is for tastes of Italy the 'slow-food' way. A popular Turin-based chain (founded in 2007 by Oscar Farinetti), the bistro-style venue places its emphasis on local artisanal producers, food education, accessibility and affordability, and sustainable sourcing and production.

Award-winning French chocolatier's Jean-Philippe Chocolat & Café features an open chocolate atelier. Meanwhile, extra-cost Segafredo coffees are available in several locations.

ENTERTAINMENT. A Cirque du Soleil-designed multi-level showlounge (it cost a whopping €20 million) has excellent sightlines from almost all seats in its amphitheater-style setting. The stunning, colourful acrobatic shows are provided by a real Cirque du Soleil troupe as part of a joint venture with MSC Cruises, featuring a dinner-and-show package.

A second entertainment venue, called The Lounge, has a stage (mainly for cabaret-style shows and other presentations), and a dance floor; it is adjacent to a 5D cinema. A number of bars and small lounges have live music.

Atop ship is an observation lounge called the Piano Lounge, with great views.

SPA/FITNESS. The Aurea Spa is certainly large. Facilities include several body-treatment rooms, saunas and steam rooms for men and women, a large workout room full of high-tech Technogym cardiovascular equipment, and a beauty salon.

MSC MUSICA
★★★★

THIS SHIP EXUDES LIVELY ITALIAN DECOR AND GOOD STYLE FOR FAMILY CRUISING

Size:	Large Resort Ship	Passenger/Crew Ratio (lower beds):	2.6
Tonnage:	92,409	Cabins (total):	1,275
Cruise Line:	MSC Cruises	Size Range (sq ft/m):	150.6–301.3/14.0–28.0
Former Names:	none	Cabins (for one person):	0
Builder:	Aker Yards (France)	Cabins with balcony:	827
Entered Service:	Jul 2006	Cabins (wheelchair accessible):	17
Length (ft/m):	963.9/293.8	Wheelchair accessibility:	Good
Beam (ft/m):	105.6/32.2	Elevators:	13
Propulsion/Propellers:	diesel (31,680kW)/2	Casino (gaming tables):	Yes
Passenger Decks:	13	Swimming Pools:	2
Total Crew:	987	Self-Service Launderette:	No
Passengers (lower beds):	2,550	Library:	Yes
Passenger Space Ratio (lower beds):	36.2	Onboard currency:	Euros

THE SHIP. *MSC Musica* suits young adult couples, solo travelers, and families with children of all ages who enjoy big-ship surroundings and a big-city lifestyle, with different multilingual (mostly European) nationalities. Youngsters have their own play center, video games room, youth counselors, and activity programs.

The ship's sleek, deep blue funnel features a swept-back design with the MSC logo in gold. The overall profile is quite well balanced. The hull has large circular porthole-style windows instead of square or rectangular windows. The ship is powered by diesel motors driving electric generators that provide power to two conventional propellers.

Real wood and marble are used extensively in the interiors, reflecting the commitment that MSC Cruises (a Swiss-based company with Italian roots) has in the cruise industry.

The interior focal point is a main three-deck-high lobby, with a water-feature backdrop and a crystal (glass) piano on a small stage that appears to float on a pond. Other principal facilities include a large main show lounge, a nightclub, disco, numerous lounges and bars (including a wine bar), library, card room, an Internet center, virtual-reality center, children's club, and cigar lounge with specialized smoke extraction and a selection of Cuban, Dominican, and Italian (Toscana) smokes.

A shopping gallery has an integrated bar and entertainment area that flows through the main lobby,

BERLITZ'S RATINGS

	Possible	Achieved
Ship	500	396
Accommodation	200	155
Food	400	242
Service	400	298
Entertainment	100	61
Cruise Experience	400	289

OVERALL SCORE 1441 points out of 2000

which is not only convenient, with everything all in the one place, but also has something of a city feel. The expansive San Remo Casino has blackjack, poker, and roulette games, and an array of slot machines for entertainment.

Drinking places include a publike venue as well as several comfortable lounges with live music. A gratuity of 15 percent is added to all drinks/beverage orders. Some of the artwork is whimsical, but fishermen will appreciate the stuffed head from a blue marlin caught by Pierfrancesco Vago, chairman of MSC Cruises, in 2004; it weighs 588lbs (267kg) and stands at the Blue Marlin Bar on the pool deck. And do check out the 'restroom with a view' – the toilets have a great ocean view, if you leave the door open.

Although access throughout most of the interior of the ship is very good, anyone who is wheelchair-dependent should note that the passenger hallways are narrow on some decks. There is no walk-around open promenade deck.

Although the interior layout (and passenger flow) is good, congestion occurs when first-seating passengers exit the two main dining rooms, as diners on the second seating are waiting to enter.

ACCOMMODATION. There are several price levels, depending on grade and location. There are suites with private balcony, mini-suites, outside-view cabins, and interior (no-view) cabins. Contrary to nautical convention, the cabin-numbering system has even-numbered cabins on the starboard side, and odd-numbered cabins on the port side.

All cabins have a mini-bar and personal safe, satellite flat-screen TV with audio channels, and 24-hour room service. Continental breakfast is complimentary from 7.30 to 10am, but room service costs extra at any other time.

Accommodation designated as 'suites' – they are not true suites, as there is no separate bedroom and lounge – is more roomy than standard accommodation, although suites are small compared to those on some other cruise lines. They have a larger lounge area, walk-in closet, vanity desk with drawer-mounted hairdryer, and a bathroom with combination tub and shower. There is a semi-private balcony with light, but the partitions between each balcony are partial, not full. The suite bathrooms are plain, with white plastic washbasins and white walls, and mirrors that steam up.

Many cabins on Forte Deck have views obstructed by lifeboats. Cabins on the uppermost accommodation deck (Cantata Deck) are subject to the noise of sunloungers being dragged across the deck above when it is set up or cleaned early in the morning. Some of the most popular cabins are those with aft views from the balcony cabins (on Virtuoso, Adagio, Intermezzo, and Forte decks). The 17 cabins for the disabled are spacious and well equipped.

DINING. There are two main dining rooms, L'Oleandro and Le Maxim's, both located aft, with large ocean-view picture windows. There are two seatings for meals, and tables are for two to eight. Seating is both banquette-style and in individual chairs; the chairs are slim and lack armrests.

MSC Cruises highlights regional Italian cuisine and wines, with dining room menus that feature food from Calabria, Piedmont, Lazio, Puglia, and Sicily. Items that are always available include spaghetti (with a tomato sauce freshly made each day), chicken breast, salmon fillet, and vegetables of the day. All pizza dough is made on board, and risotto is a daily signature item, as is fresh pasta. Several varieties of Italian breads such as bruschetta, focaccia, and panettone are provided. Light 'always available' and vegetarian dishes are also provided.

Passengers occupying accommodation designated as suites and deluxe grades are typically assigned the best tables in the quietest sections of Le Maxim's restaurant, which is quieter than L'Oleandro.

Gli Archi Cafeteria (a section of which forms the reservations-only Il Giardino) is for casual, self-serve breakfast and lunch buffets and for sit-down, served, but casual dinners each evening. It's actually open for 20 hours daily, so there's always something available. There's also an outside fast-food eatery on the pool deck for burgers and other grilled food items.

Several bars adjacent to the midships atrium lobby, serve extra-cost Segafredo Italian coffees, and tea and pastries.

Il Giardino is an à la carte dining spot that costs extra and requires reservations.

Kaito is a Japanese sushi bar with counter and table seating and a menu that has a fine array of extra-cost à la carte sashimi pieces, nigiri and temaki sushi and maki rolls, tempura and teriyaki items, and a choice of several types of cold or hot sake, and Japanese beer. Reservations are needed.

Enoteca Wine Bar, a very creative wine bar, provides a selection of famous regional Italian cheeses, hams, honey, and wines in a relaxing and entertaining bistro-style setting.

Silver trays full of late-night snacks are taken throughout the ship by waiters, and, on some days, special late-night desserts, such as flambé items, are showcased in various lounges such as the Il Tucano Lounge. The ship makes ice cream freshly on board.

ENTERTAINMENT. Teatro La Scala, the principal showlounge, is in the ship's forward section. It has tiered seating on two levels, and sight lines are good from most of the plush, comfortable seats. The room also serves as a venue for large groups or social functions.

High-quality entertainment has not, to date, been a priority for MSC Cruises. Production shows and the variety acts could be better. However, due to the multi-national passenger mix, almost all entertainment needs to be visual rather than vocal. There is no space for a showband, so all shows are performed to pre-recorded tracks.

Il Tucano Lounge, aft of the showlounge, is the place for social dancing and functions such as cooking demonstrations, with live music provided by a band. Another nightclub, the Crystal Lounge, provides music for social dancing. The young and lively crowd have the ear-splitting G32 disco; with its floor-to-ceiling windows, it is a quiet, pleasant place to relax and read by day.

Big-screen movies are shown on a large screen above the forward pool, just behind the ship's mast.

SPA/FITNESS. The Aloha Beauty Farm is located above the navigation bridge at the forward end of the ship. The complex has a beauty salon, several body-treatment rooms, and a gymnasium with forward ocean views and an array of high-tech, muscle-toning, and strengthening equipment. There's also an extra-cost Middle East-themed thermal suite, with steam rooms, saunas with aromatherapy infusions, and a relaxation/hot tub room.

Sports facilities include table tennis, a tennis court, mini-golf course, golf practice net, two shuffleboard courts, and a walking/ jogging track.

MSC OPERA
★★★+

THIS MID-SIZED FAMILY-FRIENDLY SHIP HAS EUROPEAN STYLE AND FLAIR

Size:	Mid-size Ship	Passenger/Crew Ratio (lower beds):	2.9
Tonnage:	65,000	Cabins (total):	1,071
Cruise Line:	MSC Cruises	Size Range (sq ft/m):	139.9–302.0/13.0–28.0
Former Names:	none	Cabins (for one person):	0
Builder:	Chantiers de l'Atlantique (France)	Cabins with balcony:	232
Entered Service:	Mar 2004	Cabins (wheelchair accessible):	4
Length (ft/m):	902.2/275.0	Wheelchair accessibility:	Good
Beam (ft/m):	95.1/29.0	Elevators:	9
Propulsion/Propellers:	diesel (31,680kW)/ 2 azimuthing pods	Casino (gaming tables):	Yes
		Swimming Pools:	2
Passenger Decks:	10	Self-Service Launderette:	No
Total Crew:	721	Library:	Yes
Passengers (lower beds):	2,142	Onboard currency:	Euros
Passenger Space Ratio (lower beds):	30.3		

THE SHIP. *MSC Opera* suits young adult couples, solo travelers, and families with tots, children, and teens who enjoy big-ship surroundings and a noisy, big-city lifestyle, with different nationalities and languages, mostly European. The ship is well set up for children, who have their own play center, video games room, youth counselors, and activity programs.

The ship's deep blue funnel is quite sleek, and features a swept-back design with the MSC logo.

Between May and July 2015 the ship underwent a 'chop-and-stretch' operation, which added an 82ft (25m) mid-section, almost 200 additional cabins, more public rooms, entertainment facilities and new shops (but no additional elevators), and more exterior deck space, which houses a large water-park for children. Families with children will also find special kids' areas equipped with Chicco® and LEGO® products, and an energetic multilingual youth activity team.

All decks are named after well-known operas. The interior layout and passenger flow are quite good, except for a couple of points of congestion, typically when the first seating exits the dining room and passengers on second seating are waiting to enter. The decor has many Italian and other Mediterranean influences, including clean lines, minimalist furniture, and a collection of colors, soft furnishings, and fabrics that work well together,

BERLITZ'S RATINGS		
	Possible	Achieved
Ship	500	378
Accommodation	200	155
Food	400	238
Service	400	295
Entertainment	100	60
Cruise Experience	400	273
OVERALL SCORE 1399 points out of 2000		

and without any hint of garishness. Real wood and marble have been used extensively in the interiors, and the fit and finish are good.

Facilities include the ship's main showlounge, a nightclub/disco, several lounges and bars, an Internet center with 10 terminals, a virtual-reality center, a children's club, and the Via Condotti shopping gallery with shops, integrated bar, and entertainment area – so that you can shop, drink, and be entertained conveniently all in the one place. The Monte Carlo Casino provides blackjack, poker, and roulette games, together with an array of slot machines. There is also a card room, but the integral library is small, uncared for, and disappointing, and there are no hardback books.

Drinking places include the Sotto Vento Pub (under the showlounge) and the La Cabala lounge. A 15 percent gratuity s added to all drinks/beverage orders.

Anyone who is wheelchair-dependent should note that there is no access to the uppermost forward and aft decks, although access throughout most of the interior of the ship is very good, and there are several wheelchair-accessible public restrooms. In passenger hallways it can be a squeeze to get past housekeeping carts at certain hours.

Minor niggles include: the in-your-face photographers; constant music in every lounge; and all the standing in line for embarkation, disembarkation, shore tenders, and for self-serve buffet meals that is unfortunately an inevitable aspect of cruising aboard all similarly sized ships. There is no forward observation lounge.

ACCOMMODATION. There are several different price levels, depending on grade and location: one suite category including 172 'suites' with private balcony, five outside-view cabin grades, and five interior cabin grades. The cabin-numbering system has even-numbered cabins on the starboard side, and odd-numbered cabins on the port side – contrary to nautical convention.

All cabins have a minibar and personal safe, satellite TV, several audio channels, and 24-hour room service. Tea and coffee are complimentary, but snacks delivered by room service cost extra.

Accommodation designated as suites – they are not true suites, as there is no separate bedroom and lounge – has more room, a larger lounge area, walk-in closet, wall-to-wall vanity counter, a bathroom with combination tub and shower, toilet, and semi-private balcony with a light but partitions between each balcony that are partial, not full. Cotton bathrobes are provided. The suite bathrooms are very plain, with white plastic washbasins and white walls, and mirrors that steam up.

Some cabins on Othello Deck and Rigoletto Deck have views obstructed by lifeboats, while those on Turandot Deck aft (10192–10241) may be subject to late-night and early-morning noise from the cafeteria on the deck above. Cabins on the uppermost accommodation deck are subject to deck chairs and tables being dragged across the deck, when it is set up or cleaned early in the morning.

DINING. There is one principal dining room, La Caravella Restaurant, with ocean-view picture windows in the aft section of the ship. There are two seatings for meals, in keeping with other ships in the MSC Cruises (a Swiss-based company with Italian roots) fleet, and tables are for two to eight.

MSC Cruises highlights regional Italian cuisine and wines, with menus that feature food from Calabria, Piedmont, Lazio, Puglia, and Sicily. Items that are always available include spaghetti (with a tomato sauce freshly made each day), chicken breast, salmon fillet, and vegetables of the day. All pizza dough is made on board, and risotto is a daily signature item, as is fresh pasta fresh. Several varieties of Italian breads such as bruschetta, focaccia, and panettone are provided. Light 'always available' and vegetarian dishes are also provided.

L'Approdo Restaurant is assigned to all passengers occupying accommodation designated as suites, although other passengers can dine in it, too,

on a reservations-only basis. As you might expect, the food and service are superior to that in the main dining room.

Casual, self-serve buffets for breakfast and lunch can be taken in Le Vele Cafeteria, although the serving lines on both port and starboard sides are quite cramped, and the food is quite basic, or at the pool deck outside the fast-food eatery, with grill and pizzeria. Le Vele is also open for sit-down, served, but casual, dinners each evening – it's actually open for 20 hours a day – so even in the middle of the night you can find something to eat. Extra-cost Segafredo coffees and pastries are featured in the Aroma Café, on the upper level of the two-deck-high atrium lobby, but annoying videos constantly play on TV sets in the forward section of the area.

ENTERTAINMENT. The 713-seat Teatro dell'Opera is the main showlounge, located in the forward section of the ship. It has tiered seating set in a sloping floor, and the sight lines are good from most seats, which are plush and comfortable. The venue is also used for large social functions. There is no separate bandstand, and the shows use recorded music, so there's little consistency in orchestration and sound balance.

High-quality entertainment has not, to date, been a priority for MSC Cruises. As a result, production shows and variety acts tend to be amateurish at best when compared to those on some other major cruise lines.

The Opera Lounge, one deck above the showlounge, is used extensively for social dancing, and features a live band. Meanwhile, for the young and lively set, there is the Byblos Discotheque, the ship's ear-splitting club. A number of bands and musical groups provide live music in the various bars and lounges.

SPA/FITNESS. The Opera Health Center is one deck above the navigation bridge at the forward end of the ship. The complex has a beauty salon, several treatment rooms offering massage and other body-pampering treatments, as well as a gymnasium with ocean views and an array of high-tech, muscle-toning, and strengthening equipment. There's also a thermal suite, containing different kinds of steam rooms combined with aromatherapy infusions, at extra cost.

The health center is operated by the excellent Italian company OceanView, with European hairstylists and Balinese massage and body-treatment staff. Gratuities are not included, and are at your discretion.

Outside on deck, sports fans will appreciate a neat eight-hole mini-golf course that wraps around the funnel, while a walking/jogging track encircles the two swimming pools in the center of the ship.

MSC ORCHESTRA
★★★★

THIS LARGE, COMFORTABLE, FAMILY-FRIENDLY SHIP HAS ELEGANT, CHIC DECOR

Size:	Large Resort Ship	Passenger/Crew Ratio (lower beds):	2.6
Tonnage:	92,409	Cabins (total):	1,275
Cruise Line:	MSC Cruises	Size Range (sq ft/m):	150.6–301.3/14.0–28.0
Former Names:	none	Cabins (for one person):	0
Builder:	Aker Yards (France)	Cabins with balcony:	827
Entered Service:	May 2007	Cabins (wheelchair accessible):	17
Length (ft/m):	963.9/293.8	Wheelchair accessibility:	Good
Beam (ft/m):	105.6/32.2	Elevators:	13
Propulsion/Propellers:	diesel-electric (40,4000kW)/2	Casino (gaming tables):	Yes
Passenger Decks:	13	Swimming Pools:	2
Total Crew:	987	Self-Service Launderette:	No
Passengers (lower beds):	2,550	Library:	Yes
Passenger Space Ratio (lower beds):	36.2	Onboard currency:	Euros

THE SHIP. *MSC Orchestra* will suit young adult couples, solo travelers, and families with tots, children, and teens who enjoy big-ship surroundings and a big-city lifestyle, with different nationalities and languages, mostly European. Children have their own meeting and play centers, video games room, youth counselors, and fun programs.

The ship's deep blue funnel is sleek, and has a swept-back design with the MSC logo in gold lettering. The overall profile is quite well balanced. The hull has large circular porthole-style windows instead of square or rectangular windows.

MSC Orchestra is a sister to *MSC Musica* and *MSC Poesia*, though the fabrics and furnishings used in the interiors are nicer and softer. Among the numerous lounges and bars, the Out of Africa Savannah Lounge is stunning. A delightful four-piece classical ensemble regularly performs in the atrium lobby.

Plenty of real wood and marble have been used in the interiors, and the high quality reflects the commitment that MSC Cruises (a Swiss-based company with Italian roots) has in the vessel's future.

The focal point is a three-deck-high lobby, with a water-feature backdrop and a crystal piano on a small stage that appears to float on a pond. Other facilities include a large main show lounge, a nightclub, disco, numerous lounges and bars (including a wine bar), library, card room, an Internet center, virtual-reality center, children's club, and cigar lounge

BERLITZ'S RATINGS		
	Possible	Achieved
Ship	500	398
Accommodation	200	155
Food	400	241
Service	400	298
Entertainment	100	62
Cruise Experience	400	291
OVERALL SCORE 1445 points out of 2000		

with specialized smoke extraction and a selection of Cuban, Dominican, and Italian (Toscana) smokes.

A shopping gallery has an integrated bar and entertainment area that flows through the main lobby, so that you can shop, drink, and be entertained all in one place. The expansive San Remo Casino has table games and an array of slot machines.

Drinking places include a pub-like venue as well as several comfortable lounges with live music. A 15 percent gratuity is added to all drinks/beverage orders. Some of the artwork is whimsical. And, speaking of whimsical, check out the 'restrooms with a view' – the men's/ladies' toilets adjacent to the forward pool deck bar have a great ocean view, and you can even watch the passing scenery while sitting on the toilet – if you leave the door open.

The decor has many Italian influences. There are clean lines and minimalist furniture, combined with a wide range of colors, soft furnishings, and fabrics that work well together, although it's a little more garish than one would expect.

Anyone who is wheelchair-bound should note that the accommodation hallways are narrow on some decks. Note that there is no walk-around open promenade deck.

Although the interior layout and passenger flow is good, congestion occurs when first seating exits the two main dining rooms and second seating passengers are waiting to enter.

The MSC Cruises crew does its best to provide good service to a multi-national clientele, and the ship exudes a noticeable feel-good factor.

ACCOMMODATION. There are several price levels, depending on grade and location. There are suites with private balcony, mini-suites, outside-view cabins, and interior (no-view) cabins. Contrary to nautical convention, the cabin-numbering system has even-numbered cabins on the starboard side, and odd-numbered cabins on the port side.

All cabins have a mini-bar and personal safe, satellite flat-screen TV with audio channels, and 24-hour room service. Continental breakfast is complimentary from 7.30 to 10am, but snacks from room service cost extra at any other time.

Accommodation designated as 'suites' – not true suites, as there is no separate bedroom and lounge – is bigger than standard cabins, although suites are small compared to those on some on other cruise lines. Suites have a larger lounge area, walk-in closet, vanity desk with drawer-mounted hairdryer, and a bathroom with combination tub and shower. There is a semi-private balcony with light, but the partitions between each balcony are of the partial type. The suite bathrooms are plain, with white plastic washbasins and white walls, and mirrors that steam up.

Many cabins on Forte Deck have views obstructed by lifeboats. Cabins on the uppermost accommodation deck (Cantata Deck) may be subject to the noise of sunloungers being dragged across the deck above when it is set up or cleaned early in the morning. Some of the most popular cabins are those at the aft end of the ship, with views over the ship's stern from the balcony cabins (on Virtuoso, Adagio, Intermezzo, and Forte decks). The 17 cabins for the disabled are spacious and well equipped.

DINING. There are two main dining rooms, Villa Borghese Restaurant and L'Ibiscus, located in the aft section of the ship, and with large ocean-view picture windows. There are two seatings for dinner, and open seating for breakfast and lunch. Tables are for two to eight, as well as some alcove banquette-style seats. Anyone occupying upper-grade accommodation typically gets the better tables in quieter areas.

MSC Cruises highlights regional Italian cuisine and wines, with menus that feature food from Calabria, Piedmont, Lazio, Puglia, and Sicily. Items that are always available include spaghetti (with a to-mato sauce freshly made each day), chicken breast, salmon fillet, and vegetables of the day. All pizza dough is made on board, and risotto is a daily signature item, as is fresh pasta. Several varieties of Italian breads such as bruschetta, focaccia, and panettone are provided. Light 'always available' meals and vegetarian dishes are also provided.

Shanghai Chinese Restaurant makes a change from the main restaurants. This was the first real Chinese restaurant aboard any cruise ship – mainly because of the challenges of providing high-temperature wok and deep fryer preparation. Dim sum steamed dishes are also served, typically for lunch. The food embraces four main cuisines – Beijing, Cantonese, Shanghai, and Szechuan – and there's Tsing Tao beer.

The Four Seasons Restaurant offers extra-cost, à la carte Italian cuisine in a garden-style setting with fine china, and a menu reflecting regional and seasonal fare. Food is cooked to order, so it tends to taste better than the meals in the main dining room. Reservations are required, and there's a cover charge.

La Piazzetta Café is open 20 hours a day for casual, self-serve buffet-style breakfasts and for sit-down, served dinners in a relaxed environment.

ENTERTAINMENT. Covent Garden is the ship's stunning large showlounge. The Opera Lounge, one deck above, is the place for social dancing, with live music. The G32 disco is for the more energetic. A large poolside movie screen provides moviegoers with more choices. All the activities are provided by energetic multilingual cruise staff. Also, live music is provided in almost all bars and lounges.

SPA/FITNESS. The Orchestra Health Center, operated by the Italian company OceanView, includes a beauty salon, several treatment rooms offering massage and other body-pampering treatments, and a fitness center with ocean views and high-tech muscle-toning equipment.

There's also a thermal suite, containing different kinds of steam rooms combined with aromatherapy infusions, at extra cost. There's a neat juice and smoothie bar opposite the reception desk. Gratuities are at your discretion.

Additional sports facilities include deck quoits, shuffleboard courts, tennis and basketball courts, mini-golf, and a jogging track.

MSC POESIA
★★★★

THIS IS A DELIGHTFUL, LARGE, INFORMAL, AND COMFORTABLE FAMILY-FRIENDLY SHIP

Size:	Large Resort Ship	Passenger/Crew Ratio (lower beds):	2.6
Tonnage:	92,490	Cabins (total):	1,275
Cruise Line:	MSC Cruises	Size Range (sq ft/m):	150.6–301.3/14.0–28.0
Former Names:	none	Cabins (for one person):	0
Builder:	Fincantieri (Italy)	Cabins with balcony:	827
Entered Service:	Oct 2008	Cabins (wheelchair accessible):	17
Length (ft/m):	963.9/293.8	Wheelchair accessibility:	Good
Beam (ft/m):	105.6/32.2	Elevators:	13
Propulsion/Propellers:	diesel (58,000kW)/2	Casino (gaming tables):	Yes
Passenger Decks:	13	Swimming Pools:	2
Total Crew:	987	Self-Service Launderette:	No
Passengers (lower beds):	2,550	Library:	Yes
Passenger Space Ratio (lower beds):	36.2	Onboard currency:	Euros

THE SHIP. *MSC Poesia* will suit young adult couples, solo travelers, and families with tots, children, and teens who enjoy big-ship surroundings and a noisy, big-city lifestyle, with many different nationalities and languages, mostly European. The ship is designed to accommodate families with children, who have their own play centers, video games room, and youth counselors, and plenty of activity programs.

The vessel is a sister ship to *MSC Musica* and *MSC Orchestra, with* a sleek, deep blue funnel and swept-back design with the MSC logo. The hull has large circular porthole-style windows instead of square or rectangular windows. From a technical viewpoint, the ship is powered by diesel motors driving electric generators to provide power to two conventional propellers.

The interior layout and passenger flow are good – with the exception of a couple of points of congestion, typically when the first seating exits the two main dining rooms, and passengers on the second seating are waiting to enter.

The interior focal point is a main three-deck-high lobby, which has a grand water-feature backdrop and a crystal (glass) piano on a small stage that appears to float on a pond. Other facilities include a large main showlounge, a nightclub, disco, numerous lounges and bars – including a wine bar – library, card room, Internet center, virtual-reality center, children's club, and cigar lounge with specialized

BERLITZ'S RATINGS

	Possible	Achieved
Ship	500	398
Accommodation	200	155
Food	400	241
Service	400	298
Entertainment	100	62
Cruise Experience	400	292

OVERALL SCORE 1446 points out of 2000

smoke extraction and a selection of Cuban, Dominican, and Italian (Toscana) smokes.

The musically themed decor has many Italian influences, including clean lines, minimalism in furniture design, and a collection of colors, soft furnishings, and fabrics that work well together, although it's a little more garish than one would expect.

Real wood and marble have been used extensively in the interiors, and the high quality reflects the commitment that Switzerland-based MSC Cruises has in the vessel's future.

A shopping gallery, including an electronics store, has an integrated bar and entertainment area that flows through the main lobby, so you can conveniently shop, drink, and be entertained all in the one place. An expansive Casino Royale has several gaming tables, and an array of slot machines.

Drinking places include several comfortable lounges – all with live music. A 15 percent gratuity is added to all drinks/beverage orders. Some of the artwork is whimsical. Do check out the 'restroom with a view' – the men's/ladies' toilets adjacent to the Blue Marlin pool deck bar have a great ocean view, and you can even watch the passing scenery while sitting on the toilet, if you leave the door open.

Although access throughout most of the interior of the ship is good, wheelchair-bound passengers should note that the passenger hallways are a little narrow on some decks for you to pass when housekeeping carts are in place. There is no walk-around open promenade deck.

ACCOMMODATION. There are several price levels, depending on grade and location. Included are 18 'suites' with private balcony, mini-suites, outside-view cabins, and interior cabins. Contrary to nautical convention, the cabin-numbering system has even-numbered cabins on the starboard side, and odd-numbered cabins on the port side.

All cabins have a mini-bar and personal safe, satellite flat-screen TV with audio channels, and 24-hour room service. Continental breakfast is complimentary from 7.30 to 10am; snacks from room service cost extra at any other time.

Accommodation designated as 'suites' – not true suites, as there is no separate bedroom and lounge – also has more room, although these suites are small compared to those on some on other cruise lines. They have a larger lounge area, walk-in closet, vanity desk with drawer-mounted hairdryer, and a bathroom with combination tub and shower. There is a semi-private balcony with light, but the partitions between each balcony are of the partial, not full, type. The suite bathrooms are plain, with white plastic washbasins and white walls, and mirrors that steam up.

Many cabins on Forte Deck have views obstructed by lifeboats. Cabins on the uppermost accommodation deck (Cantata Deck) may be subject to the noise of sunloungers being dragged across the deck above when it is set up or cleaned early in the morning. Some of the most popular cabins are those at the aft end of the ship, with views over the ship's stern from the balcony cabins on four of the aft decks. The 17 cabins for the disabled are spacious and well equipped.

DINING. There are two principal dining rooms, both of them located aft (on different decks), with large ocean-view picture windows. There are two seatings for meals, as aboard other ships in the MSC Cruises fleet, and tables are for two to eight; seating is both banquette-style and in individual armless chairs.

MSC Cruises highlights regional Italian cuisine and wines, with dining room menus that feature food from Calabria, Piedmont, Lazio, Puglia, and Sicily. Items that are always available include spaghetti (with a tomato sauce freshly made each day), chicken breast, salmon fillet, and vegetables of the day. All pizza dough is made on board, and risotto is a daily signature item, as is fresh pasta. Several varieties of Italian breads such as bruschetta, focaccia, and panettone are provided. Light 'always available' meals and vegetarian dishes are also provided.

Kaito is a delightful, extra-cost Japanese restaurant, with a sushi bar and an extensive à la carte menu. Reservations are needed, but the cuisine is worth the extra cost.

A Tex-Mex Restaurant is an extra-cost, à la carte dining spot, for which reservations are necessary.

The Wine Bar (Enoteca) provides a selection of famous regional cheeses, hams, and a variety of wines in a bistro-style setting that is relaxing and entertaining.

The Villa Pompeiana Cafeteria is for casual, self-serve buffets for breakfast and lunch and for sit-down, served, but casual, dinners (it's actually open for 20 hours a day, so there's always something available to eat, even in the middle of the night). Outside, there's a fast-food eatery on the pool deck for burgers and other grilled fast-food items. Extra-cost Segafredo Italian coffees, together with a variety of teas and pastry items, are also available in several bars adjacent to the atrium midships lobby.

Silver trays full of late-night snacks are taken throughout the ship by waiters, and, on some days, special late-night desserts, such as flambé items, are showcased in various lounges.

ENTERTAINMENT. Teatro Carlo Felice is the ship's principal showlounge; it is in the forward section of the ship, with tiered seating on two levels, and the sight lines are good from most of the plush, comfortable seats. The room can also be a venue for large group meetings or social functions. There is no showband, so all shows are performed to pre-recorded music tracks.

Almost all the entertainment is more visual than vocal, owing to the multi-national passenger mix,

Another large lounge (Zebra Bar), aft of the show-lounge, is the place for social dancing and functions such as cooking demonstrations. Live music is provided by a band (as it is across various bars and lounges across the ship).

Big-screen movies are shown on a large screen above the forward pool, just behind the ship's mast.

SPA/FITNESS. The Poesia Health Center is run by OceanView, an Italian spa specialist. The complex features a beauty salon, several treatment rooms offering massage and other body-pampering treatments, and a gymnasium with forward ocean views and an array of high-tech, muscle-toning, and strengthening equipment. There's also a Middle East-themed thermal suite, containing steam rooms and saunas with aromatherapy infusions, and a relaxation/hot tub room; it costs extra to use these facilities.

Sports facilities include table tennis, a tennis court, mini-golf course, golf practice net, two shuffleboard courts, and a jogging track. A mini-golf course is on the port side of the funnel, while a walking/jogging track encircles an upper level above the two swimming pools.

MSC PREZIOSA
★★★★

A FINE, LARGE, FAMILY-FRIENDLY SHIP DESIGNED WITH EUROPEANS IN MIND

Size:	Large Resort Ship
Tonnage:	139,400
Cruise Line:	MSC Cruises
Former Names:	none
Builder:	STX France
Entered Service:	Mar 2013
Length (ft/m):	1,093.5/333.3
Beam (ft/m):	124.6/38.0
Propulsion/Propellers:	diesel-electric (40,000kW)/2
Passenger Decks:	13
Total Crew:	1,370
Passengers (lower beds):	3,502
Passenger Space Ratio (lower beds):	39.8
Passenger/Crew Ratio (lower beds):	2.5
Cabins (total):	1,751
Size Range (sq ft/m):	148.5–568.3/13.8–52.8
Cabins (for one person):	0
Cabins with balcony:	1,125
Cabins (wheelchair accessible):	45
Wheelchair accessibility:	Good
Elevators:	16
Casino (gaming tables):	Yes
Swimming Pools:	3 (1 w/sliding glass dome)
Self-Service Launderette:	No
Library:	Yes
Onboard currency:	Euros

THE SHIP. This large resort ship, a close sister to *MSC Divina, MSC Fantasia,* and *MSC Splendida,* will appeal to young-at-heart adult couples, solo travelers, and families with children and teens enjoying an urban lifestyle, with a mix of mostly European nationalities and style.

MSC Preziosa was originally ordered by the Libyan government-owned shipping company GNMTC (the contract was signed by Captain Hannibal Muammar Gaddafi – fifth-eldest son of Colonel Gaddafi) before Switzerland-based cruise line MSC Cruises acquired the hull and configured the ship as the fourth in its *Fantasia*-class. It has the very latest in green-technology engines.

Outside on the expansive main pool deck, there is a main swimming pool, together with a whole Aqua Park with raised sections, hot tubs, and numerous water features. Slightly forward of the pool deck is a family swimming pool; it's open well into the late evening, and can be covered by a sliding glass dome in case of inclement weather.

Facilities for all passengers include a large three-deck-high theater-style showlounge, a nightclub/disco, library, card room, an Internet center, a 4D virtual-reality center, multi-deck shopping gallery, a large Millennium Star Casino with gaming tables and an array of slot machines and a nicely-shaped stairway, and, in the aft section, an 'infinity' pool that overlooks the stern, and 'beach club' area. Drinking places include numer-

BERLITZ'S RATINGS

	Possible	Achieved
Ship	500	416
Accommodation	200	162
Food	400	278
Service	400	308
Entertainment	100	78
Cruise Experience	400	308

OVERALL SCORE 1548 points out of 2000

ous lounges and bars (including a trendy 'Green Sax' jazz lounge/bar), most with live music. One lounge in the aft section of the ship is for adults only.

An area called the MSC Yacht Club – an exclusive community of 'suite-grade' accommodation, including a Top-Sail Lounge – has a large observation/lifestyle lounge (like a private club) and social meeting place, private sunbathing with integral dip pool, hot tubs, and concierge services for making dining reservations, booking excursions and spa treatments, and arranging private parties. A marble floor leads to a shiny Swarovski glass staircase that connects the concierge facilities between decks 15 and 16 under a glass-domed ceiling.

ACCOMMODATION. If the budget allows, it's worth paying extra to stay in one of the 'suites' in the Yacht Club accommodation. You'll get silver-tray room service by a team of impressive, well-trained butlers. The suites have a minibar, interactive TV, personal safe, hairdryer, and satellite-link telephone.

DINING. There are two main restaurants: Golden Lobster, on Deck 5, and L'Arabesque, on Deck 6. There are two seatings for dinner, and open seating for breakfast and lunch. Tables are for two, four, six, or eight, and include some cozy alcove banquette seating (although it's challenging for waiters to serve these alcove tables properly). Both restaurants feature Mediterranean cuisine.

Occupants of Yacht Club-grade accommodation have their own intimate La Palmeraie Restaurant, with North African decor, Moroccan-style arches, and hanging brass lamps. Dining is in an open-seating arrangement.

A 115-seat Eataly Restaurant – a specialty eatery (together with a 30-seat Ristorante Italia) – provides tastes of Italy, the 'slow food' way, with a choice of 18 items. A popular Turin-based chain (founded by Oscar Farinetti), Eataly places its major emphasis on local artisanal producers, food education, accessibility and affordability, and sustainable sourcing and production. The chairs in the Ristorante Italia section of the Eataly Restaurant, however, are see-through plastic, and grossly uncomfortable.

The Galaxy Restaurant is an extra-charge venue that sits high above the main pool, and has great views. It has a trendy vibe (it forms part of the disco), and the food – Mediterranean fusion fare, including steaks and seafood items – is good.

Casual serve-yourself buffet-style meals can be taken in the huge Inca and Maya buffet venue (open 20 hours daily) for breakfasts and lunches, and waiter-served dinners in a relaxed, but always busy, setting. A bakery corner provides freshly baked breads and rolls throughout the day.

A Sports and Bowling Diner features a classic American food experience, including sandwiches and burgers. Meanwhile, Segafredo Italian (extra-cost) coffees are available in several locations.

ENTERTAINMENT. The 1,600-seat Platinum Theater is a vast showlounge – it's really more like a concert theatre and auditorium. It is spread over three decks, and there are good sight lines from almost all seats except for a few rows at the back on port and starboard sides. It is a well-designed room, except for the fact that no space is allocated for a live showband.

The shows concentrate more on visual entertainment such as mime, magic, dancing, and acrobatics, because the clientele is so multinational. Productions are performed with recorded music (known as a 'click-track'), and introductions are done at breakneck speed by the multilingual cruise director.

There is live music in almost all the other lounge/bar venues – one of the most popular of which is the Golden Jazz Bar.

SPA/FITNESS. The Aurea Wellbeing Center is large and houses a beauty salon, body-pampering treatment rooms, and a gymnasium with great ocean views. A thermal suite contains different kinds of steam rooms combined with herbal aromatherapy infusions, in a calming Asia-themed environment. Features include a Shu Uemura Art of Hair cabin, a vintage barbershop, and a Himalayan salt crystal 'bed.' The spa is operated by OceanView, a specialist spa provider, and most of the therapists are from Bali.

Sports facilities include deck quoits, shuffleboard courts, large tennis/basketball court, mini-golf, and a jogging track.

MSC SEASIDE
NYR

THIS REALLY IS MIAMI BEACH AT SEA FOR FAMILY-IMMERSIVE RESORT CRUISING

Size:	Large Resort Ship	Passenger/Crew Ratio (lower beds):	2.9
Tonnage:	160,000	Cabins (total):	2,067
Cruise Line:	MSC Cruises	Size Range (sq ft/m):	129.1–968.7/12.0–90.0
Former Names:	None	Cabins (for one person):	0
Builder:	Fincantieri (Italy)	Cabins with balcony:	1,519
Entered Service:	Nov 2017	Cabins (wheelchair accessible):	54
Length (ft/m):	1,059.7/323.0	Wheelchair accessibility:	Good
Beam (ft/m):	134.5/41.0	Elevators:	18
Propulsion/Propellers:	diesel-electric/2	Casino (gaming tables):	Yes
Passenger Decks:	13	Swimming Pools:	3 (1 w/sliding glass dome)
Total Crew:	1,413	Self-Service Launderette:	No
Passengers (lower beds):	4,134	Library:	Yes
Passenger Space Ratio (lower beds):	37.2	Onboard currency:	US$

THE SHIP. MSC Seaside is really quite a handsome vessel, with a refreshing beach-resort look aft. It has a sleek, streamlined, and contemporary funnel that, unusually, is almost in the center of the ship. It has been specifically tailored for total family-immersive cruising.

The outstanding design (it's like an enhancement of the Oasis of the Seas class of ships but with much more open access) has created a most intelligent use of the aft of the ship, giving it a combination of an upscale Miami Beach apartment and beach club look, including panoramic glass elevators to connect the promenade deck with the upper deck Aqua Park non-stop). A 360-degree walk-round outdoor promenade deck has a number of indoor/outdoor restaurants and eateries and is destined to be the 'strolling to be seen' area. One of several pools can be covered by a retractable glass dome for use in inclement (or chilly) weather.

Atop ship and aft of the funnel, an Aqua Park play area is full of spray cannons, water-stream jets, tipping buckets, and more. It also features five large waterslides (between 367 and 525ft long (112–160m), including two for side by side races down (the Duelling High-Speed Aqua Tubes), with internal game controllers; players are challenged to match colored strobe lights along the route. There's also a 'Himalayan Bridge' walking (ropes) course.

Inside, the layout makes it easy to find one's way around, and, because of the ship's 'open-flow' de-

BERLITZ'S RATINGS		
	Possible	Achieved
Ship	500	NYR
Accommodation	200	NYR
Food	400	NYR
Service	400	NYR
Entertainment	100	NYR
Cruise Experience	400	NYR

OVERALL SCORE NYR points out of 2000

sign, public rooms flow seamlessly from one to another. Almost all the public rooms, bars and lounges for socializing (including a casino with gaming tables and slot machines), plus hangouts for coffee and chocolate, a 5D cinema, and a shopping arcade (with some very well-known luxury designer brands) are located on decks 5, 6, 7, and 8 (with accommodation decks above). Facilities for children and teens are excellent, and MSC Cruises has excellent counselors and programs.

MSC Seaside is based year-round in Miami, for follow-the-sun Caribbean cruises, and the onboard currency is the US dollar.

ACCOMMODATION. There are many, many accommodation price grades; the price depends on the size, location, and grade you choose. From the smallest to the largest, they are comfortable, well-laid out, with ample closet and drawer space. All bathrooms have glazed shower enclosures, shelves for personal toiletries, and towels of a decent size.

Yacht Club ('ship within a ship') accommodation occupants have a gorgeous exclusive observation lounge, reception area, concierge desk, and a small library area. All Yacht Club accommodation grades have a Nespresso coffee machine, and all dine in a dedicated restaurant, located directly above the Yacht Club (observation) lounge, which also incorporates a small dance floor and food area.

DINING. The two main restaurants have many tables for two, as well as tables for four-eight persons. MSC Cruises has certainly been paying more attention to its cuisine recently, in an effort to appeal to a more international clientele. Michelin-starred Italian celebrity chef Carlo Cracco has developed special dishes for the Gala, Christmas, and New Year menus for the company, and introduced a cooking experience for the DoReMi kids club.

MSC Cruises highlights regional Italian cuisine and wines, with menus that feature food from Calabria, Piedmont, Lazio, Puglia, and Sicily. Items that are always available include spaghetti (with a tomato sauce freshly made each day), chicken breast, salmon fillet, and vegetables of the day. All pizza dough is made on board, and risotto is a daily signature item, as is fresh pasta. Several varieties of Italian breads such as bruschetta, focaccia, and panettone are provided. Light 'always available' and vegetarian dishes are also provided.

A dedicated restaurant is provided for occupants of Yacht Club accommodation. It is located at the front of the ship, with great views, and direct access from the Yacht Club lounge one deck below.

Several extra-cost restaurants are positioned close to the Yacht Club accommodation (forward). These include a Mediterranean Steakhouse (for premium quality steaks and grilled food items cooked to order), a Fish/Seafood Restaurant, Asian Market Kitchen by Roy Yamaguchi (for à la carte pan-Asian cuisine and including two large Teppanyaki grills), and an adjacent sushi bar – on Deck 16.

A large self-serve food-court style buffet area is located low and aft, and is conveniently accessible to the aft 'beach' and outdoor promenade area on Deck 8; it includes a French-style crêperie and a 'gourmet' ice cream parlor (both of these are by the famous chocolatier and pastry chef Jean-Philippe Maury).

Extra-cost Lavazza coffees are available in several bars and lounges, and all are served in proper china cups.

ENTERTAINMENT. The stunning two-deck high amphitheatre-style showlounge seats 934, and is like a theatre-in-the-round, with very comfortable seating and excellent sightlines. It has been custom designed by, and is dedicated to presenting real Cirque du Soleil shows (to recorded, timed show-backing music).

A Comedy Club, located in the ship's center near the atrium lobby, provides an entertainment alternative.

SPA/FITNESS. Located on a lower deck, the Aurea Spa is extensive (it also includes an outdoor section). Facilities include a large workout room (full of Technogym cardiovascular equipment), saunas, steam and relaxation rooms for men and women, a large beauty salon, and several body-pampering treatment rooms. Sports facilities include a tennis/basketball court, and a bowling alley.

MSC SINFONIA
★★★+

THIS IS A EURO-STYLE, INFORMAL, FAMILY-FRIENDLY MID-SIZED SHIP

Size:	Mid-size Ship	Passenger/Crew Ratio (lower beds):	2.7
Tonnage:	65,542	Cabins (total):	876
Cruise Line:	MSC Cruises	Size Range (sq ft/m):	139.9–236.8/13–22
Former Names:	European Stars	Cabins (for one person):	0
Builder:	Chantiers de l'Atlantique (France)	Cabins with balcony:	224
Entered Service:	Apr 2002/Mar 2005	Cabins (wheelchair accessible):	2
Length (ft/m):	902.0/275.0	Wheelchair accessibility:	Good
Beam (ft/m):	95.1/29.0	Elevators:	9
Propulsion/Propellers:	diesel (31,680kW)/2 azimuthing pods	Casino (gaming tables):	Yes
		Swimming Pools:	2
Passenger Decks:	10	Self-Service Launderette:	No
Total Crew:	721	Library:	Yes
Passengers (lower beds):	1,952	Onboard currency:	Euros
Passenger Space Ratio (lower beds):	33.5		

THE SHIP. *MSC Sinfonia*, a sister ship to *MSC Armonia*, is best for adult couples and solo travelers, and families with children, who enjoy lots of activity, accompanied by lots of noise and late nights, in a setting that exudes Mediterranean family values. The international mix of passengers adds to the overall ambience of the cruise experience.

The exterior deck space is barely adequate for the number of passengers carried. The Lido Deck surrounding the outdoor swimming pool also has whirlpool tubs and a bandstand. All sunloungers have cushioned pads.

In 2015, the ship underwent a 'chop-and-stretch' operation, which added an 82ft (25m) mid-section, almost 200 additional cabins, more public rooms, entertainment facilities and new shops (but no additional elevators), and more exterior deck space, which houses a large waterpark for children. Families with children will also find special kids' areas equipped with Chicco® and LEGO® products, and an energetic multilingual youth activity team.

The interior decor is modern European, with crisp, clean lines, and minimalist furniture design – including some chairs that look interesting but are totally impractical. However, the interior colors are good; nothing jars the senses, but rather calms them, unlike the effect aboard many ships.

Standing in line for embarkation, disembarkation, shore tenders, and self-serve buffet meals is an inevitable aspect of cruising aboard ships of a similar

BERLITZ'S RATINGS

	Possible	Achieved
Ship	500	373
Accommodation	200	149
Food	400	238
Service	400	289
Entertainment	100	55
Cruise Experience	400	267

OVERALL SCORE 1371 points out of 2000

size. Announcements are made in several languages.

Wheelchair-dependent passengers should note that there is no access to the uppermost forward and aft decks, although access throughout most of the interior is good. Also, passenger hallways are a little narrow on some accommodation decks to pass when housekeeping carts are in place.

The company keeps prices low by providing air transportation that may be at inconvenient times, or that involves long journeys by bus. In other words, be prepared for a little discomfort in getting to and from your cruise in exchange for low cruise rates. Note that 15 percent is added to all drinks and beverage orders.

ACCOMMODATION. There are numerous categories, with the price depending on the grade, size, and location you choose. These include 'suites' with private balcony (with partial partitions only, not full ones), outside-view cabins, and interior (no-view) cabins.

Suite-grade accommodation (they are not true suites, as there's no separate bedroom and lounge) has more room, a larger lounge area, a walk-in closet, a wall-to-wall vanity counter, a bathroom with combination tub and shower, and toilet, and a private balcony with light. Bathrobes are provided. However, except for the highest category, the bathrooms are very plain, with white plastic washbasins and white walls, small shower enclosures, and mirrors that steam up.

Standard grade cabins, at a modest 140 sq ft (13 sq m), are quite small when compared to those on many other ships, but they are reasonably comfortable, with plenty of space between two lower beds. All grades of accommodation have a TV, minibar/refrigerator, personal safe cleverly positioned behind a vanity desk mirror, hairdryer, and bathroom with shower and toilet.

DINING. There are two main dining rooms, the 610-seat Il Galeone Restaurant and the Il Covo Restaurant; both have two seatings and share the same menu. The cuisine is reasonably sound, and, with varied menus and good presentation, should prove a highlight for most passengers. The wine list has a wide variety of wines at fairly reasonable prices, although almost all are very young.

MSC Cruises highlights regional Italian cuisine and wines, with dining room menus that feature food from Calabria, Piedmont, Lazio, Puglia, and Sicily. Items that are always available include spaghetti (with a tomato sauce freshly made each day), chicken breast, salmon fillet, and vegetables of the day. All pizza dough is made on board, and risotto is a daily signature item, as is fresh pasta. Several varieties of Italian breads such as bruschetta, focaccia, and panettone are provided. Light 'always available' meals and vegetarian dishes are also provided.

La Terrazza is a casual, self-serve buffet eatery that is open 20 hours a day, including sit-down, waiter-served dinners in a very relaxed setting. The selections are very standardized and could be better. Café del Mare, adjacent to one of two swimming pools and the ship's funnel, is a grill area for burgers and other fast-food items.

Extra-cost Segafredo Italian coffee and pastries are available in Le Baroque Café, set around the upper level of the two-deck-high atrium lobby. It's a good location for people-watching, but annoying music videos are constantly played on TV monitors in the forward sections.

ENTERTAINMENT. The two-deck-high Teatro San Carlo is the showlounge, for production shows, cabaret acts, plays, and other theatrical presentations. Entertainment consists mainly of visual shows, because of the mix of nationalities carried onboard. Other shows consist of singers, magicians, mime artists, and comedy jugglers.

The ship carries a number of bands and small musical units that provide live music for dancing or listening to in various lounges and bars throughout the ship.

SPA/FITNESS. The spa features a gymnasium with ocean views, and high-tech, muscle-toning equipment. A thermal suite has multiple steam rooms with aromatherapy infusions such as chamomile and eucalyptus, and a Rasul chamber with two or three kinds of application mud and a gentle steam shower. The spa, operated by the Italian concession OceanView, offers a wide range of body-pampering wellbeing treatments.

For active types there's a simulated climbing wall outdoors aft of the ship's funnel, as well as a volleyball/basketball court, and mini-golf.

MSC SPLENDIDA
★★★★

A LARGE, FAMILY-FRIENDLY SHIP WITH TASTEFUL, ELEGANT DECOR AND STYLE

Size:	Large Resort Ship	Passenger/Crew Ratio (lower beds):	2.4
Tonnage:	137,936	Cabins (total):	1,637
Cruise Line:	MSC Cruises	Size Range (sq ft/m):	161.4–699.6/15–65
Former Names:	none	Cabins (for one person):	0
Builder:	Aker Yards (France)	Cabins with balcony:	1,260
Entered Service:	Jul 2009	Cabins (wheelchair accessible):	43
Length (ft/m):	1,093.5/333.3	Wheelchair accessibility:	Good
Beam (ft/m):	124.6/38.0	Elevators:	14
Propulsion/Propellers:	diesel (40,000kW)/2	Casino (gaming tables):	Yes
Passenger Decks:	13	Swimming Pools:	3 (1 w/sliding glass dome)
Total Crew:	1,313	Self-Service Launderette:	No
Passengers (lower beds):	3,274	Library:	Yes
Passenger Space Ratio (lower beds):	42.1	Onboard currency:	Euros

THE SHIP. *MSC Splendida* will appeal to young adult couples, solo travelers, and families with children and teens who enjoy big ships with a mix of nationalities, mostly European. Children appreciate Virtual World's five white-knuckle 4D rides in a 10-seat thrill room. It all feels rather like a European city center, and is full of large and small rooms, nooks and crannies, and places to play in.

A sister ship to *MSC Fantasia*, *MSC Splendida* is a stunning ship, and one of the largest ships built for a European cruise company. It is about 33ft (10m) longer than the Eiffel Tower is high, and the propulsion power is the equivalent of 120 Ferraris. There are four swimming pools, one of which can be covered by a glass dome.

The interior includes an exclusive area called the MSC Yacht Club for the occupants of some 99 suites. This 'club' includes a Top-Sail Lounge (with butler service, canapés, and bite-sized food items), private sunbathing with an integral dip pool, two hot tubs, and concierge services for making dining reservations, and booking excursions and spa treatments.

If your budget allows, it's worth paying extra to stay in Yacht Club accommodation. You'll get silver-tray room service from a butler, a reserved (quieter) section of the Villa Verde Restaurant, and keycard access to a members-only sundeck sanctuary area that includes its own bar and food counters, a small dip pool, two hot tubs, and an open but sheltered lounging deck.

BERLITZ'S RATINGS

	Possible	Achieved
Ship	500	410
Accommodation	200	161
Food	400	273
Service	400	306
Entertainment	100	77
Cruise Experience	400	305

OVERALL SCORE 1532 points out of 2000

It's a world away from the hustle and bustle of the main pool decks and solarium on the decks below.

The ship's interior decor is stunning. There are basically two decks full of public lounges and bars (most with live music), and eateries, including a large two-deck-high theater-style showlounge (The Strand), a nightclub/disco (The Aft Lounge), library, card room, an Internet center, virtual-reality center, extensive shopping gallery (that has the feel of a city), and large casino (inhabited by many who can smoke at the bar). The Royal Palm Casino features gaming tables plus an array of slot machines.

The ship is well designed to accommodate families with children. A 15 percent gratuity is added to all drinks/beverage orders.

Niggles include the fact that all the lounges flow into each other, and so the music from each one bleeds into the adjacent room. Note that only Yacht Club-grade occupants are escorted to their cabins by butlers. Men should note that the public restrooms have cubicles (there are no urinals).

ACCOMMODATION. Eighty percent of the cabins are outsides, and 95 percent of these have a balcony – the standard balcony cabin is almost 172 sq ft (16 sq m), plus bathroom and balcony. If the budget allows, it's worth paying extra to stay in one of the 72 'suites' (each 312 sq ft/29 sq m) in the Yacht Club area at the top, front end of the ship.

Spa Suites include unlimited access to the sauna and steam room, a private consultation with the spa doctor, a Balinese massage, a facial relax treatment, and a solarium session.

The Yacht Club has its own serene concierge lounge, small library, and reception desk. A Swarovski glass stairway leads to the Yacht Club suites, and private elevator accesses the Aurea Spa, located one deck below. The lounge has its own galley and dedicated chef.

DINING. La Reggia, the main restaurant spans two decks; it has two seatings for dinner, and open seating for breakfast and lunch. Tables are for two to eight, plus there's some alcove banquette seating on both the main and balcony levels. A second restaurant, the single-level Villa Verde, is for occupants of suite-grade accommodation and features panoramic windows at the stern of the ship.

MSC Cruises highlights regional Italian cuisine and wines, with menus that feature food from Calabria, Piedmont, Lazio, Puglia, and Sicily. Items that are always available include spaghetti (with a tomato sauce freshly made each day), chicken breast, salmon fillet, and vegetables of the day. All pizza dough is made on board, and risotto is a daily signature item, as is fresh pasta. Several varieties of Italian breads such as bruschetta, focaccia, and panettone are provided. Light 'always available' and vegetarian dishes are also provided.

L'Olivo, an Italian/Mediterranean extra-cost, à la carte venue, is located in a smaller, more intimate setting aft, overlooking a small pool and relaxation area. The food is cooked to order, and dining here is a pleasant, less hurried experience. Reservations are required.

Santa Fe is an extra-cost, L-shaped Tex-Mex restaurant with food items cooked to order.

Bora Bora Cafeteria is a large casual self-serve lido buffet-style eatery. It is open 20 hours a day, for breakfast and lunch, and for sit-down, casual, waiter-served dinners each evening.

Extra-cost Lavazza coffees are available in several locations on the ship.

ENTERTAINMENT. The Strand Theater has plush seating in tiers for as many as 1,700, and good sight lines. Because of the multi-national background of passengers, the shows concentrate on more visual entertainment such as mime, magic, dancing, and acrobatics, and are performed with recorded music – there is no orchestra pit. Live music for dancing and listening to is provided by a number of bands and soloists throughout the ship.

SPA/FITNESS. The Aurea Spa (16,000 sq ft/1,485 sq m) has a beauty salon, well-equipped treatment rooms, and a large gymnasium with ocean views. Included is a large thermal suite, and saunas. The decor is welcoming and restful. The spa is run by OceanView. Gratuities to spa staff are at your own discretion. Sports facilities include deck quoits, large tennis/basketball court, mini-golf, and a jogging track.

NATIONAL GEOGRAPHIC ENDEAVOUR
★★+

A VERY SMALL OLDER, RUGGED SHIP, FOR NATURE AND WILDLIFE CRUISES

Size:	Boutique Ship	Passenger/Crew Ratio (lower beds):	1.7
Tonnage:	3,132	Cabins (total):	62
Cruise Line:	Lindblad Expeditions	Size Range (sq ft/m):	191.6–269.1/17.8–25.0
Former Names:	*Caledonian Star, North Star, Lindmar, Marburg*	Cabins (for one person):	14
		Cabins with balcony:	0
Builder:	A.G. Weser Seebeckwerft (Germany)	Cabins (wheelchair accessible):	0
Entered Service:	1966/Jun 2009	Wheelchair accessibility:	None
Length (ft/m):	292.6/89.20	Elevators:	0
Beam (ft/m):	45.9/14.0	Casino (gaming tables):	No
Propulsion/Propellers:	diesel (3,236kW)/1	Swimming Pools:	1
Passenger Decks:	6	Self-Service Launderette:	No
Total Crew:	64	Library:	Yes
Passengers (lower beds):	113	Onboard currency:	US$
Passenger Space Ratio (lower beds):	27.7		

THE SHIP. Renamed in 2005, the former *Endeavour* was built as a factory fishing trawler for North Sea service. Today, *National Geographic Endeavour* is a tidy and well-cared-for discovery-style cruise vessel operating 'soft' expedition cruises. There is an open-bridge policy for all passengers. It carries 10 Zodiac landing craft for excursions, and has a helicopter pad and an enclosed shore tender. A steep aft stairway leads down to the landing craft platform. This small ship has a reasonable number of public rooms and facilities, including a lecture room/lounge/bar/library, where videos are also stocked for in-cabin use. There's a good book selection.

This likeable, homey ship runs well-organized, destination-intensive cruises, at a very reasonable price. It attracts loyal repeat passengers who don't want to sail aboard ships that look like apartment blocks. The itineraries include Antarctica, where this ship has been operating since 1998.

The interior stairways are steep, as is the exterior stairway to the Zodiac embarkation points. Noise from the diesel engines can be irksome, particularly on the lower decks. Gratuities are at your discretion.

National Geographic Endeavour and its type of soft exploration cruising are best suited to adventurous, hardy types who enjoy being with nature and wildlife in some of the world's most extraordinary settings, but cosseted aboard a small, modestly comfortable

BERLITZ'S RATINGS

	Possible	Achieved
Ship	500	199
Accommodation	200	94
Food	400	194
Service	400	216
Entertainment	100	60
Cruise Experience	400	209

OVERALL SCORE 972 points out of 2000

ship. Specialized lecturers accompanying each cruise make this a real life-enriching experience.

ACCOMMODATION. There are five categories of cabins: one for suites and four for non-suites. All cabins have outside views and are compact, but reasonably comfortable; they are decorated in warm, muted tones. All cabins have a mini-bar/refrigerator, video player, and a decent amount of closet and drawer space – though it's tight for long voyages. The bathrooms are small, with little space for storing toiletries. Four 'suites' are basically double the size of a standard cabin, and have a wood partition separating the bedroom and lounge area. The bathroom is still little, however.

DINING. The open-seating dining room is small and charming, but the low-back chairs are not comfortable. The cuisine is reasonably high quality, with fresh ingredients, but not a lot of choice. Salad items lack variety, as do international cheeses. Service is attentive and friendly.

ENTERTAINMENT. The main lounge is the venue for lectures, slide shows, and occasional film presentations. There are no shows.

SPA/FITNESS. There is a small fitness room and a tiny sauna.

NATIONAL GEOGRAPHIC EXPLORER
★★+

A STURDY LITTLE SHIP FOR UP-CLOSE NATURE AND WILDLIFE CRUISES

Size:	Boutique Ship	Passenger/Crew Ratio (lower beds):	2.1
Tonnage:	6,471	Cabins (total):	81
Cruise Line:	Lindblad Expeditions	Size Range (sq ft/m):	n/a
Former Names:	*Lyngen, Midnatsol II, Midnatsol*	Cabins (for one person):	14
Builder:	Ulstein Hatlo (Norway)	Cabins with balcony:	13
Entered Service:	1982/Jun 2008	Cabins (wheelchair accessible):	1
Length (ft/m):	367.4/112.0	Wheelchair accessibility:	None
Beam (ft/m):	54.1/16.5	Elevators:	1
Propulsion/Propellers:	diesel/2	Casino (gaming tables):	No
Passenger Decks:	6	Swimming Pools:	0
Total Crew:	70	Self-Service Launderette:	No
Passengers (lower beds):	148	Library:	Yes
Passenger Space Ratio (lower beds):	43.7	Onboard currency:	US$

THE SHIP. Originally built as *Midnatsol* for Hurtigruten, the ship was purchased by Lindblad Expeditions in 2007 and extensively refitted for expedition-style cruising, with some really good facilities and expedition equipment.

The ship has an ice-strengthened hull and is quite stable due to the stabilizers, so movement is minimized. Twin funnel uptakes are located almost at the very stern – an unusual design. There is little outdoor deck space, but it's not needed in cold-weather areas.

The main facilities include a lecture room and bistro bar with espresso machine adjacent to the restaurant, and boot-washing stations. This ship best suits hardy, adventurous types who enjoy being with nature and wildlife in some of the most extraordinary, and occasionally inhospitable, places on earth, cosseted aboard a small but comfortable ship.

The dress code is completely casual; layered clothing and sturdy outerwear is recommended. Gratuities to staff are not included in the price.

ACCOMMODATION. The price you pay depends on size and location. The cabins are small, as are the bathrooms, although they are nicely designed, practical units. Some have queen-size beds, others have twin beds (some can be pushed together, some are fixed). There are several cabins for single

BERLITZ'S RATINGS		
	Possible	Achieved
Ship	500	265
Accommodation	200	110
Food	400	195
Service	400	232
Entertainment	100	60
Cruise Experience	400	215

OVERALL SCORE 1077 points out of 2000

occupancy. The tiled bathrooms have shower enclosures and small shelves for toiletries. Suites have two washbasins, premium bedding, and feather-fluffy duvets.

There is a decent supply of electrical outlets and an ethernet connection for laptops. Closet doors are of the sliding type instead of the outward-opening type, to minimize noise and banging when the ship is in tough weather conditions. Naturally, a National Geographic Atlas is provided.

DINING. There is one main dining room, as well as areas for self-serve buffet-style food. The food is hearty and fairly healthy, although you should not expect to find fresh greens in some of the more out-of-the-way areas.

ENTERTAINMENT. Lectures, briefings, and recaps, plus after-dinner conversation with fellow participants are the main entertainment – if you're not too tired after exhausting days of landings and other adventures.

SPA/FITNESS. There are two body-treatment rooms – with skylights, for wildlife-inspired wellness, facials, and massage, including a special 'ice-bear massage,' as well as a fitness/workout room.

NATIONAL GEOGRAPHIC ORION
★★★★

MATURE TRAVELERS SHOULD ENJOY THIS 'SOFT' ADVENTURE SHIP

Size:	Boutique Ship	Passenger/Crew Ratio (lower beds):	1.4
Tonnage:	4,050	Cabins (total):	53
Cruise Line:	Lindblad Expeditions	Size Range (sq ft/m):	175.0–345.0/16.3–32.1
Former Names:	Orion	Cabins (for one person):	0
Builder:	Cassens-Werft (Germany)	Cabins with balcony:	9
Entered Service:	Nov 2003/Mar 2014	Cabins (wheelchair accessible):	0
Length (ft/m):	337.0/102.7	Wheelchair accessibility:	None
Beam (ft/m):	46.0/14.0	Elevators:	1
Propulsion/Propellers:	diesel/1	Casino (gaming tables):	No
Passenger Decks:	5	Swimming Pools:	0
Total Crew:	75	Self-Service Launderette:	No
Passengers (lower beds):	106	Library:	Yes
Passenger Space Ratio (lower beds):	38.2	Onboard currency:	Australian $

THE SHIP. This pocket-sized ship with its dark blue hull topped by a yellow/gold line is enjoyed by mature couples and single travelers who like discovering small hidden gems that large cruise ships cannot visit.

The former *Orion* (Orion Expedition Cruises) was acquired in 2013 by Lindblad Expeditions. It was renamed *National Geographic Orion*, and transferred to the new operator in March 2014, when it became part of Lindblad Expeditions/National Geographic. More snorkeling gear and enough diving gear for 24 diving program participants was added, together with an ROV (remote-operated vehicle) able to descend up to 1,000ft (305m).

National Geographic Orion (according to one myth, Neptune was Orion's father, while Queen Euryale of the Amazon – sister of Medusa – was his mother) features nature- and wildlife-rich expedition-style cruises in high-quality surroundings, in the company of other like-minded travelers. It has all the comforts of home, as well as specialist equipment for expedition cruising. Although small, it has stabilizers, bow and stern thrusters for maximum maneuverability, and a fleet of 14 heavy-duty Zodiac inflatable landing craft and a fishing boat, BeeKay. There is also an aft marina platform for swimming off.

There is no swimming pool, nor is one needed, but a hot tub is set amid an open deck, together with a bar and a small rock garden/water feature. All out-

BERLITZ'S RATINGS		
	Possible	Achieved
Ship	500	376
Accommodation	200	149
Food	400	298
Service	400	294
Entertainment	100	77
Cruise Experience	400	304

OVERALL SCORE 1498 points out of 2000

door tables, chairs, and real steamer-style sunloungers are made of tropical hardwood.

The interior decor is warm and inviting, providing a cozy, cosseting, yet contemporary environment. Public rooms include an observation lounge and library (plus a nautical chart table and a self-serve beverage station), which opens onto a walk-around open promenade deck; it also connects with the small Health Spa.

Other public rooms include The Lounge (main lounge), the Observation Lounge, a boutique, and a dedicated Theater with surround-sound system for lectures and movies. National Geographic provides stunning photographic images of the oceans as part of the artwork. Typically, an expedition leader and marine biology lecturers are carried on each expedition.

The reception desk is manned 24 hours a day, and there's an Internet-connect computer. Some rooms are clustered around a glass-walled atrium and the single elevator. A 'mud room,' complete with boot-washing stations, is adjacent to a Zodiac/tender loading platform on the port side.

This is about as far away from big cruise ships as you can get, with well-planned itineraries to some extraordinary areas, including Antarctica. If you want memorable moments in soft adventure travel, wrapped in the comfort of some contemporary surroundings and good food, this ship would make a good choice.

ACCOMMODATION. There are four suite grades, and two cabin grades; the facilities in all of them are very good. All have twin beds that convert to a queen-size bed, a TV infotainment system, a mini-refrigerator, ample closet space, a good-sized vanity desk, and a small personal safe.

The marble-clad bathroom (with glazed shower enclosure) has a small toiletries cabinet, single washbasin, and a large shower enclosure, with a retractable clothesline. Toiletries are by Escada. All the cabinetry was custom-made, and the bathrooms were fitted individually, which is rare in today's modular-fit world.

There are 13 suites, nine with a small 'French' balcony (meaning you can open the door, but you cannot step outside), four Owner's Suites, six Balcony Suites, two Deluxe Suites, and one odd-shaped but delightful Junior Suite. These have more space, and some share a narrow communal balcony (meaning there is no partition between them), as well as having a sofa, glass drinks table, and good-size vanity desk. Only the four Owner's Suites have a bathtub; all other suites/cabins have large shower enclosures.

DINING. The Restaurant has ocean-view picture windows, artwork based on the astrological signs, and operates one open seating. Its low ceiling, however, makes it rather noisy.

The cuisine is quite good and varied, and the wine selection is adequate. While portions are not large, they are colorful and creative. Place settings include Bauscher china and Hepp silverware.

The Outdoor Café, an open deck aft of the Leda Lounge, serves as an alfresco dining spot for casual breakfasts, lunches, and occasional barbeque dinners.

Continental breakfast and afternoon tea are also available in the Galaxy Lounge. Espressos and cappuccinos are available at no extra charge in two lounges/bars and restaurant, and there are typically delicious brownies on the bar counter.

The Filipino service staff members are friendly and communicate well with passengers.

ENTERTAINMENT. There is no formal entertainment, although the ship may carry an occasional entertaining pianist. Each evening, lecturers provide daily recaps and fascinating, in-depth talks on marine or plant biology.

SPA/FITNESS. There's a workout center, sauna, shower enclosure, and a private treatment room (for massages). A beauty salon is located two decks below.

The ship carries a range of personal beauty products used on board and also for sale; creams, oils, and other ingredients are mixed by the therapist and tailored to your own needs.

NATIONAL GEOGRAPHIC QUEST
NYR

THIS SHIP IS FOR CASUAL SMALL GROUP UP-CLOSE AND PERSONAL CRUISING

Size:	Boutique Ship	Passenger/Crew Ratio (lower beds):	2.8
Tonnage:	1,800	Cabins (total):	50
Cruise Line:	Lindblad Expeditions	Size Range (sq ft/m):	136.0-187.0/3.3-17.3
Former Names:	none	Cabins (for one person):	0
Builder:	Nichols Boat Brothers Builders (USA)	Cabins with balcony:	22
Entered Service:	Jul 2017	Cabins (wheelchair accessible):	0
Length (ft/m):	238.0/72.5	Wheelchair accessibility:	Poor
Beam (ft/m):	101.7/31.0	Elevators:	0
Propulsion/Propellers:	diesel/2	Casino (gaming tables):	No
Passenger Decks:	4	Swimming Pools:	0
Total Crew:	35	Self-Service Launderette:	No
Passengers (lower beds):	100	Library:	Yes
Passenger Space Ratio (lower beds):	18.0	Onboard currency:	US$

THE SHIP. *National Geographic Quest* was designed and built for cruising in North American coastal waters, and in the tropical waters of Central America. It has a number of Zodiac craft for shore landings when needed, two loading platforms, and a dedicated mud room for expedition gear.

The decor is minimalist, yet comfortable.

Facilities include a lecture room, a lounge/bar, and a dining room.

Lindblad Expeditions does a fine job of providing nature-related lecturers and youthful, friendly staff.

Note that gratuities are not included in the fare.

BERLITZ'S RATINGS

	Possible	Achieved
Ship	500	NYR
Accommodation	200	NYR
Food	400	NYR
Service	400	NYR
Entertainment	100	NYR
Cruise Experience	400	NYR

OVERALL SCORE NYR points out of 2000

ACCOMMODATION. The price you pay depends on the size, location, and grade you choose. Four cabins have interconnecting door. Naturally, a National Geographic Atlas is provided.

DINING. The dining room, where all passengers eat together in one seating, is located aft.

ENTERTAINMENT. Briefings, recaps, and after-dinner conversation form the entertainment, not forgetting a good book or two.

SPA/FITNESS. A tiny fitness room has some basic exercise equipment.

NAUTICA
★★★★

THIS PREMIUM SHIP HAS TRADITIONAL DECOR, FOR MATURE-AGE CRUISERS

Size:	Small Ship	Passenger/Crew Ratio (lower beds):	1.7
Tonnage:	30,277	Cabins (total):	342
Cruise Line:	Oceania Cruises	Size Range (sq ft/m):	145.3–968.7/13.5–90.0
Former Names:	R Five	Cabins (for one person):	0
Builder:	Chantiers de l'Atlantique	Cabins with balcony:	232
Entered Service:	Dec 1998/Nov 2005	Cabins (wheelchair accessible):	3
Length (ft/m):	593.7/181.0	Wheelchair accessibility:	Good
Beam (ft/m):	83.5/25.5	Elevators:	4
Propulsion/Propellers:	diesel (18,600kW)/2	Casino (gaming tables):	Yes
Passenger Decks:	9	Swimming Pools:	1
Total Crew:	386	Self-Service Launderette:	Yes
Passengers (lower beds):	684	Library:	Yes
Passenger Space Ratio (lower beds):	44.2	Onboard currency:	US$

THE SHIP. *Nautica*, almost identical to *Insignia* and *Regatta*, is all-white, with a large square funnel and a pleasant Lido and Pool Deck outdoors, with teak overlaid decking and high-quality lounge chairs. It is best suited to couples who like good food and style, but want informality and interesting itineraries.

In 2014, the ship underwent a refurbishment program that included the addition of Barista's coffee bar (for illy coffees), new bathrooms for the Owner's Suites and Vista Suites, and updated decor in all other cabins. The interior decor is a delightful throwback to the ocean liners of the 1920s and 1930s, with dark woods and warm colors, all in good taste, if a little fake in places. It includes detailed ceiling cornices, both real and faux, wrought-iron staircase railings, leather-paneled walls, trompe l'oeil ceilings, and rich carpeting in hallways with an Oriental rug-look center section.

Public rooms are spread over three decks. The lobby has a staircase with intricate wrought-iron railings. A large observation lounge, the Horizon Bar, is high atop ship.

There are plenty of bars, including one in each restaurant entrance. Perhaps the nicest is the casino bar/lounge, a lovely room that includes a Martini bar. It has an inviting marble fireplace, comfortable sofas, and individual chairs.

The Library is a grand Regency-style room, with a fireplace, a high, indented, trompe l'oeil ceiling, and

BERLITZ'S RATINGS

	Possible	Achieved
Ship	500	377
Accommodation	200	145
Food	400	305
Service	400	292
Entertainment	100	71
Cruise Experience	400	296

OVERALL SCORE 1482 points out of 2000

an excellent selection of books, plus very comfortable wingback chairs.

Gratuities are automatically added to your onboard account. Accommodation designated as suites pay more, for the butler. An 18 percent gratuity is added to bar and spa accounts.

ACCOMMODATION. There are six cabin categories, and several price grades, including three suite-price grades, five outside-view cabin grades, and two interior cabin grades. All of the standard interior and outside-view cabins – the lowest four grades – are very compact units, with twin beds or a queen-size bed, with good under-bed storage areas, personal safe, vanity desk with large mirror, good closet and drawer space in rich, dark woods, cotton bathrobe and towels, slippers, clothes brush, and shoehorn.

About 100 cabins qualify as 'Concierge Level' accommodation, and occupants get extra goodies such as enhanced bathroom amenities, complimentary shoeshine, tote bag, cashmere throw blanket, bottle of Champagne on arrival, hairdryer, priority restaurant reservations, priority embarkation, and dedicated check-in desk.

Owner's Suites. There are six of these, measuring 962 sq ft (89.4 sq m). The most spacious accommodation, they are fine, large living spaces located aft overlooking the stern on decks 6, 7, and 8. They are, however, subject to movement and vibration.

Vista Suites. There are four, each measuring around 786 sq ft (73 sq m), located forward on decks 5 and 6.

Penthouse Suites. There are 52 of these – though they are not suites at all, but large cabins (the bedrooms aren't separate from the living areas). They measure around 323 sq ft (30 sq m).

Cabins with balcony. Cabins with private balconies (around 216 sq ft/20 sq m) comprise about two-thirds of all cabins. They have partial, not full, balcony partitions and sliding glass doors, and 14 cabins on Deck 6 have lifeboat-obstructed views and no balcony.

Outside-view and interior cabins. These measure around 160–165 sq ft (14.9–15.3 sq m). Some suites/cabins located at the stern may suffer from vibration and noise, particularly when the ship is proceeding at, or close to, full speed, or maneuvering in port.

DINING. There are four different restaurants:

The Grand Dining Room has around 340 seats and a raised central section, but the noise level is very high when the dining room is full, due to the low ceiling. Being located aft, it has large ocean-view windows on three sides – prime tables overlook the stern. The chairs are comfortable and have armrests. The menus change daily for lunch and dinner.

Toscana Italian Restaurant has 96 seats, windows along two sides, and a set menu plus daily chef's specials (reservations required).

Polo Grill has 98 seats, windows along two sides, and a set menu including prime steaks and seafood (reservations required).

The self-serve Terrace Café has indoor and outdoor seating. It is open for breakfast, lunch, and casual dinners, with tapas (Tapas on the Terrace) and other Mediterranean food, and it incorporates a small pizzeria and grill. There are basic salads, a meat-carving station, and a reasonable selection of cheeses.

All restaurants have open-seating dining, so you can dine when you want, with whom you wish. Reservations are needed in Toscana Restaurant and Polo Grill, but there's no extra charge; there are mostly tables for four or six, and few for two. There is also a Poolside Grill Bar. All cappuccino and espresso coffees cost extra.

The food and service staff is provided by a respected maritime catering company with an interest in Oceania Cruises. This is a foodie's ship, with high-quality ingredients. Particularly notable are the breads, rolls, croissants, and brioches – made on board from French flour and Isigny butter.

On sea days, an elegant tea is presented in the Horizon Lounge, with formally dressed staff, cake trolleys, and an excellent array of cakes and scones. Sadly, teabags – not loose tea – prevail.

ENTERTAINMENT. The Nautica Lounge has entertainment, lectures, and some social events. There is little entertainment because of the intensive nature of the itineraries. However, there is live music in several bars and lounges.

SPA/FITNESS. The Lido Deck has a swimming pool, and good sunbathing space, plus a thalassotherapy tub. A jogging track circles the swimming pool deck, but one deck above. The uppermost outdoors deck includes a golf driving net and shuffleboard court. The Canyon Ranch SpaClub consists of a beauty salon, three treatment rooms, men's and women's changing rooms, and steam room (but no sauna). An 18 percent gratuity applies to massages and treatments.

NAVIGATOR OF THE SEAS
★★★+

THIS IS A COLORFUL, FUN-FILLED LARGE RESORT SHIP FOR FAMILY CRUISING

Size:	Large Resort Ship	Passenger/Crew Ratio (lower beds):	2.6
Tonnage:	137,276	Cabins (total):	1,643
Cruise Line:	Royal Caribbean International	Size Range (sq ft/m):	151.0–1,358.0/14.0–126.1
Former Names:	none	Cabins (for one person):	0
Builder:	Kvaerner Masa-Yards (Finland)	Cabins with balcony:	779
Entered Service:	Dec 2002	Cabins (wheelchair accessible):	26
Length (ft/m):	1,020.6/311.1	Wheelchair accessibility:	Best
Beam (ft/m):	155.5/47.4	Elevators:	14
Propulsion/Propellers:	diesel-electric (75,600kW)/3	Casino (gaming tables):	41
	pods (2 azimuthing, 1 fixed)	Swimming Pools:	3
Passenger Decks:	14	Self-Service Launderette:	No
Total Crew:	1,185	Library:	Yes
Passengers (lower beds):	3,286	Onboard currency:	US$
Passenger Space Ratio (lower beds):	44.0		

THE SHIP. *Navigator of the Seas* (a *Voyager*-class ship) provides a host of facilities (rather like a small town), with lots of entertainment for all ages, with a healthy amount of space per passenger. The food focuses on quantity rather than quality, unless you are prepared to pay extra in a specialty restaurant.

The first ship in the Royal Caribbean International (RCI) fleet to receive 'virtual balconies' for all interior (no-view) cabins – a neat feature installed during a 2013/14 revitalization, which also added 81 cabins, but no extra elevators; a digital photo kiosk was also added, meaning no more photo walls, or lines.

A stunning four-deck-high Royal Promenade is the main interior focal point; it's a fun place to hang out or meet friends. The length of two American football fields, it has two 11-deck-high internal lobbies. Cafés, shops, and entertainment locations line this 'street,' and interior 'with-view' cabins look into it from above (it's an imaginative piece of design work).

The horizontal atrium includes Two Poets (a 'traditional' pub), a Champagne Bar, a Sidewalk Café (for Continental breakfast, all-day pizzas, specialty coffees, and desserts), Ben & Jerry's (for round-the-clock ice cream and yoghurt), a sports bar, several shops – for jewelry, gifts, liquor, perfumes, wine, and souvenirs – and Boleros (for Latin music and nightlife). Guest reception and shore-excursion counters

BERLITZ'S RATINGS

	Possible	Achieved
Ship	500	366
Accommodation	200	137
Food	400	223
Service	400	257
Entertainment	100	73
Cruise Experience	400	259

OVERALL SCORE 1315 points out of 2000

are located at the aft end of the promenade, as is an ATM machine. At times, street entertainers appear, and parades are staged; at other times it's difficult to walk through the area, as it can be filled to the brim with tacky shopping items.

Arched across the promenade is a captain's balcony, and in the center of the promenade a stairway connects you to the deck below, where you'll find the Schooner Bar (a lounge common to all RCI ships) and a flashy Casino Royale. Gaming facilities include gaming tables and 300 slot machines.

There's a regulation-size ice-skating rink (Studio B), with real ice, with bleacher seating for up to 900, and the latest in broadcast facilities. A fine two-deck library is open 24 hours a day.

Other drinking places include the intimate Connoisseur Club – for cigars and cognacs. There is a TV studio (Studio B) with high-tech broadcast facilities, located adjacent to rooms that can be used for trade show exhibit space, with a conference center seating 400 and a multimedia 60-seat screening room.

Facilities for children and teenagers (in four age groupings) are quite extensive, and include Adventure Beach, an area for all the family, with swimming pools, a waterslide, and outdoor game areas.

Overall, this is a good all-round ship for all age groups, but be aware of the many extra costs for optional items (including drinks and drink packages and excursions).

ACCOMMODATION. There is a wide range of cabin price grades, in four major groupings: premium ocean-view suites and cabins; interior (atrium-view) cabins; ocean-view cabins; and interior cabins (which now have 'virtual balconies' projected on a formerly blank wall – a really neat feature). Many cabins are of a similar size (good for incentives and large groups), and 300 have interconnecting doors (good for families). Some 138 interior cabins have bay windows that look into the Royal Promenade.

Regardless of which cabin grade you choose, all except for the Royal Suite and Owner's Suite have twin beds that convert to a queen-size unit, infotainment system, radio and telephone, personal safe, vanity unit, hairdryer, and bathroom. However, you'll need to keep the curtains closed in the bay windows if you are scantily clad, as you can be seen easily from adjacent bay windows.

Standard outside-view and interior cabins are of a reasonably adequate size, with just enough facilities to make them comfortable and functional. Twin lower beds convert to queen-size beds, and there is a reasonable amount of closet and drawer space, but the bed(s) take up most of the space. Bathrooms are small but functional; the shower enclosures are dimensionally challenged, and there is no cabinet for personal toiletries. Overall, they're cramped.

DINING. The Sapphire (main dining room) has a total capacity of 1,889. It consists of three levels (a dramatic stairway connects them all), but the menu is the same on all three. Huge, fat support pillars obstruct sight lines from a number of seats.

Choose one of two seatings – or 'My Time Dining' (eat when you want during dining room hours). Tables are for four to 12. Place settings, china, and cutlery are of good quality. Two small private wings serve small groups: La Cetra and La Notte, each with 58 seats.

The main dining room cuisine is all about standardized banquet catering and batches cooking. The menu descriptions sound tempting, but the food, although prepared well, is just so-so. Vegetarian and children's menus are also available. Note that there are no wine waiters.

Most meat dishes are disguised with sauce reductions, and rice is often used as a source of carbohydrates. Green vegetables are scarce, but basic salad items are plentiful, and the desserts are very decent. Breads and pastry items are plentiful (though these are thawed and then baked from frozen 'starter' dough), but the croissants lack any hint of butter.

Other dining venues and eateries (some of which cost extra, but the food is mostly cooked to order) include favorites such as Chops Grille Steakhouse (for premium veal chops, steaks, and seafood items) and Portofino (for Italian-American cuisine). Reservations (make them through the digital system) are required; note that menus do not change.

Other eateries include Sabor, for extra-cost Mexican-style cuisine, and Giovanni's Table, a popular Italian family-style eatery.

Johnny Rockets, a retro 1950s all-day, all-night diner-style eatery, has hamburgers, malt shakes (at extra cost), and jukebox hits, with both indoor and outdoor seating.

Windjammer Café is a really large, sprawling venue for casual buffet-style, self-help (always busy) breakfast, lunch, and light dinners. It's often difficult to find a table, and, by the time you do, your food could be cold.

The Island Grill (a section of Windjammer Café), for casual dinners (no reservations needed), has an open kitchen.

Promenade Café is for Continental breakfast, all-day pizzas, and specialty coffees, which are provided in paper cups.

ENTERTAINMENT. The 1,350-seat Metropolis Theater is a stunning showlounge, located at the forward end of the ship. It has Art Nouveau-themed decor, and spans three decks, with only a few slim pillars, and good sight lines from most seats. Production shows are presented here by a large cast and a live band, plus an array of up-and-coming cabaret acts and late-night adults-only comedy.

SPA/FITNESS. The ShipShape health spa is reasonably large, and measures 15,000 sq ft (1,400 sq m). It includes an aerobics room, fitness center (with stairmasters, treadmills, exercise bikes, weight machines, and free weights), treatment rooms, and men's and women's sauna/steam rooms. Another 10,000 sq ft (930 sq m) of space is devoted to a Solarium (with sliding glass-dome roof).

NIEUW AMSTERDAM
★★★+

THIS SHIP FEATURES DUTCH DECOR, TRADITIONS, AND COMFORT FOR ENTIRE FAMILIES

Size:	Mid-size Ship	Passenger Space Ratio (lower beds):	41.1
Tonnage:	86,700	Passenger/Crew Ratio (lower beds):	2.2
Cruise Line:	Holland America Line	Cabins (total):	1,053
Former Names:	none	Size Range (sq ft/m):	170.0–1,318.6/15.7–122.5
Builder:	Fincantieri (Italy)	Cabins (for one person):	0
Entered Service:	Jul 2010	Cabins with balcony:	708
Length (ft/m):	935.0/285.0	Cabins (wheelchair accessible):	30
Beam (ft/m):	105.6/32.2	Wheelchair accessibility:	Good
Propulsion/Propellers:	diesel-electric (34,000kW)/	Elevators:	14
	2	Casino (gaming tables):	Yes
	azimuthing pods	Swimming Pools:	2 (1 w/sliding glass dome)
Passenger Decks:	12	Self-Service Launderette:	No
Total Crew:	929	Library:	Yes
Passengers (lower beds):	2,106	Onboard currency:	US$

THE SHIP. *Nieuw Amsterdam* is close sister to *Eurodam, Noordam, Oosterdam, Westerdam,* and *Zuiderdam.* It is named after the Dutch name for New York City, and the interior design reflects the great metropolis. It has two upright 'dustbin lid' funnels in a close-knit configuration. The twin working funnels are the result of the machinery configuration; the ship has, in effect, two engine rooms – one with three diesels, and one with two diesels and a gas turbine. There's a pod propulsion system, so there's no vibration.

There is a complete walk-around exterior teak promenade deck, with teak steamer-style sunloungers. A jogging track outdoors is located around the mast and the forward third of the ship. Exterior glass elevators, mounted midships on both the port and starboard sides, provide fine ocean views from any one of 10 decks. One of the two centrally located swimming pools outdoors can be used in inclement weather because of a retractable sliding glass roof. Two hot tubs, adjacent to the swimming pools, are abridged by a bar. There's also a small swimming pool for children.

There are two entertainment/public room decks, the most dramatic space being a showlounge spanning four decks in the forward section. Other facilities include a winding shopping street with several boutique stores and logo shops, a card room, an art gallery, photo gallery, and several small meeting rooms. The large casino is equipped with an array of gaming

BERLITZ'S RATINGS		
	Possible	Achieved
Ship	500	373
Accommodation	200	144
Food	400	244
Service	400	274
Entertainment	100	70
Cruise Experience	400	276

OVERALL SCORE 1381 points out of 2000

tables and slot machines, and you have to walk through it to get from the restaurant to the showlounge.

Explorations – perhaps the most popular public room – is a combination of a coffee bar (where coffees and other drinks cost extra), lounge, extensive library, and Internet-connect center, all within an attractive, open 'lifestyle' environment. It's popular for relaxation and reading, although noise from the coffee machine can interrupt concentration.

On other decks (lower down), you'll find the Queen's Lounge, which is part lecture room and part Culinary Arts Center and bar, where culinary demonstrations and cooking classes are held. There are also a number of other bars and lounges, including an Explorer's Lounge (live string and piano music is appropriate for cocktails in the evenings, when warm hors d'oeuvres are provided). The ship also has a small movie-screening room.

The information desk in the lobby is small and somewhat removed from the main passenger flow on the two decks above it. Many pillars obstruct the passenger flow and lines of sight throughout the ship. There are no self-service launderettes – something that families with children tend to miss, although special laundry packages are available.

Gratuities are automatically added to your onboard account. Passenger niggles? These include noisy cabin air conditioning, as the flow can't be regulated or turned off.

ACCOMMODATION. There are many price categories. The views from some cabins on the lowest accommodation deck (Main Deck) are obstructed by lifeboats. Some cabins that can accommodate a third and fourth person have very little closet space, and only one personal safe. Occupants of suites get exclusive use of the Neptune Lounge and concierge service, priority embarkation and disembarkation, and other benefits. In many of the suites/cabins with private balconies, the balconies are not so private and can be overlooked from various public locations.

Standard outside cabins measure (197 sq ft/18.3 sq m). Interior (no-view) cabins are slightly smaller (183 sq ft/17 sq m).

Penthouse Verandah Suites measure 318 sq ft/29.5 sq m). Deluxe Verandah Suites measure 563 sq ft (52.3 sq m). Verandah Suites measure 284 sq ft (26.3 sq m).

DINING. The 1,045-seat Manhattan Dining Room spans two decks at the stern, with seating at tables for two, four, six, or eight on both main and balcony levels. It provides a traditional HAL dining experience, with friendly service from smiling Indonesian and Filipino stewards. Both open seating and assigned seating are available for dinner, while breakfast and lunch are open seating – you'll be seated by restaurant staff when you enter.

HAL can provide Kosher meals (if requested when you book), although these are prepared ashore, then frozen, and brought to your table sealed in their original containers.

The extra-cost, reservations-required 148-seat Pinnacle Grill is a more intimate venue than the main dining room, with higher-quality ingredients and better presentation. On Lower Promenade Deck, it fronts onto the second level of the atrium lobby; tables along its outer section are open to it and can suffer from noise from the Atrium Bar one deck below, though these tables are good for those who like to see and be seen. Pacific Northwest food is featured, including premium-quality steaks and seafood. The wine list includes a range of fine wines from around the world. Another (extra-cost, reservations-required) option is Tamarind, which features Southeast Asian cuisine.

For casual eating, there is a large, self-serve Lido Café, an eatery that wraps around the funnel, with indoor-outdoor seating and ocean views. It includes several sections including a salad bar, Asian stir-fry and sushi section, deli sandwiches, and a separate dessert buffet, although lines can form for made-to-order items such as omelets for breakfast and pasta for lunch.

Also, a poolside 'Dive-In at the Terrace Grill' features multi-choice signature burgers (with special Dive-In sauce), hot dogs, and fries. On certain days, barbeques and other culinary specialties are available poolside.

ENTERTAINMENT. The 867-seat Mainstage Lounge is the venue for Vegas-style revues and major cabaret shows. The main floor level includes a bar in its aft section. Spiral stairways at the back of the showlounge connect all levels. Stage shows are best seen from the upper levels, from where the sight lines are quite good.

SPA/FITNESS. The Greenhouse Spa, a two-deck-high facility, is located above the navigation bridge. It includes a solarium, hydrotherapy pool, and a unisex thermal suite – incorporating a laconium (gentle sauna), hammam (mild steam), and chamomile grotto (small aromatic steam room).

There is a beauty salon, several private massage/treatment rooms (including one for couples), and a large gymnasium with floor-to-ceiling windows on three sides and forward-facing ocean views, and the latest high-tech muscle-toning equipment. There's also a basketball court, volleyball court, and a golf simulator.

NIPPON MARU
★★★★

THIS SHIP FEATURES MODERN, COMFORTABLE STYLING FOR JAPANESE-SPEAKING CRUISERS

Size:	Small Ship
Tonnage:	22,472
Cruise Line:	Mitsui OSK Passenger Line
Former Names:	none
Builder:	Mitsubishi Heavy Industries
Entered Service:	Sep 1990
Length (ft/m):	546.7/166.6
Beam (ft/m):	78.7/24.0
Propulsion/Propellers:	diesel (15,740kW)/2
Passenger Decks:	7
Total Crew:	230
Passengers (lower beds):	408
Passenger Space Ratio (lower beds):	55.0
Passenger/Crew Ratio (lower beds):	2.5
Cabins (total):	204
Size Range (sq ft/m):	150.6–430.5/14.0–40.0
Cabins (for one person):	6
Cabins with balcony:	27
Cabins (wheelchair accessible):	2
Wheelchair accessibility:	Fair
Elevators:	5
Casino (gaming tables):	Yes
Swimming Pools:	1
Self-Service Launderette:	Yes
Library:	Yes
Onboard currency:	Japanese Yen

THE SHIP. *Nippon Maru* is really for Japanese-speaking couples and solo travelers who want very comfortable surroundings combined with decent food and good service, all at a reasonable cost.

The interior's focal point is an atrium lobby that spans six decks. Public rooms include a show-lounge, piano lounge, a 54-seat screening room/lecture room (Mermaid Theater), a gaming corner with giveaways rather than cash prizes, and a Chashitsu tatami room within the Horizon Lounge. The Neptune Bar has probably the most extensive assortment of Scotch whiskies (including many rare single malts) at sea.

ACCOMMODATION. The newer suites, on Deck 6, are large and have a separate sleeping and living areas. A sofa, two chairs, and coffee table occupy one section of the lounge; there is also a writing desk with Nespresso machine and tea-making facilities. The two beds can be pushed together. The bathroom includes a 'washlet,' (a toilet with a built-in water spray for washing – very popular in Japan), but the step into the bathroom is high, at 8ins (20cm). Slippers and bathrobes are provided. Nine suites include two with huge balconies. Suites and deluxe-grade cabins are nicely decorated, and the living area has a table and two chairs, and two beds; there's also a personal computer.

BERLITZ'S RATINGS		
	Possible	Achieved
Ship	500	371
Accommodation	200	147
Food	400	306
Service	400	301
Entertainment	100	78
Cruise Experience	400	285

OVERALL SCORE 1488 points out of 2000

All standard cabins have blond wood cabinetry and good drawer space. Many have a third (or third and fourth) pull-down upper Pullman berth. Tea-making sets are provided, as is a good range of personal toiletry items.

DINING. The Mizuho dining room, which seats around 320, serves both traditional Japanese cuisine and Western dishes. There is one open seating. The ship is known for its high-quality food. A premium dining room, Kasuga, is for suite- and deluxe-grade occupants only; adjacent is the excellent Shiosai sushi bar – always with some very high-quality sashimi and sushi and a good selection of sakés.

ENTERTAINMENT. The two-deck-high Dolphin Hall has a proscenium-arched stage, wooden dance floor, and seating on both the main and balcony levels. There's social dancing, with gentlemen hosts available as partners, and a rich program of lecturers and musicians.

SPA/FITNESS. The Terraké Spa includes beauty and nail-treatment rooms, three body-treatment rooms, and a small fitness room. There's a traditional Japanese Grand Bath (one for women, one for men, open until 1am), with washing stations and a sauna. Adjacent is a sports-massage room.

NOORDAM
★★★+

A FAMILY-FRIENDLY SHIP WITH TRADITIONAL DUTCH DECOR

Size:	Mid-size Ship	Passenger/Crew Ratio (lower beds):	2.3
Tonnage:	82,318	Cabins (total):	959
Cruise Line:	Holland America Line	Size Range (sq ft/m):	170.0–1,318.6/15.7–122.5
Former Names:	none	Cabins (for one person):	0
Builder:	Fincantieri (Italy)	Cabins with balcony:	641
Entered Service:	Feb 2006	Cabins (wheelchair accessible):	28
Length (ft/m):	935.0/285.0	Wheelchair accessibility:	Good
Beam (ft/m):	105.6/32.2	Elevators:	14
Propulsion/Propellers:	diesel-electric (34,000kW)/ 2 azimuthing pods	Casino (gaming tables):	Yes
		Swimming Pools:	2 (1 w/sliding glass dome)
Passenger Decks:	11	Self-Service Launderette:	No
Total Crew:	820	Library:	Yes
Passengers (lower beds):	1,924	Onboard currency:	US$
Passenger Space Ratio (lower beds):	42.7		

THE SHIP. *Noordam* is one of the *Vista*-class ships in the Holland America Line (HAL) fleet, designed to appeal to multi-generational holidaymakers. The twin working funnels are the result of the slightly unusual machinery configuration; the ship has, in effect, two engine rooms. A pod propulsion system is provided, so there's no vibration.

There is a complete walk-around exterior teak promenade deck, with teak steamer-style sunloungers. A jogging track outdoors is located around the mast and the forward third of the ship. Exterior glass elevators provide fine ocean views from any one of 10 decks. One of two swimming pools outdoors has a retractable sliding glass roof. Two hot tubs, adjacent to the swimming pools, are abridged by a bar. There's also a small swimming pool for children.

The intimate lobby – the ship's central spot – spans three decks, and is topped by a rotating Waterford Crystal globe of the world. Adjacent are interior and glass-walled elevators with exterior views. The information desk (on the lobby's lowest level) is small and somewhat removed from the main passenger flow on the two decks above it.

The interior decor is bright in many areas, and the ceilings are particularly noticeable. A collection of artwork is a standard feature, and the pieces reflect the history of the former Dutch East Indies.

There are two whole entertainment/public room decks, the most dramatic space being a showlounge

BERLITZ'S RATINGS

	Possible	Achieved
Ship	500	371
Accommodation	200	144
Food	400	244
Service	400	273
Entertainment	100	69
Cruise Experience	400	276

OVERALL SCORE 1377 points out of 2000

spanning four decks in the forward section. Other facilities include a winding shopping street with several boutique stores and logo shops, card room, an art gallery, photo gallery, and several small meeting rooms. The large casino has gaming tables and slot machines, and you have to walk through it to get from the restaurant to the showlounge.

Explorations is a combination of a coffee bar (where coffees and other drinks cost extra), lounge, extensive library, and Internet center – it's a popular area for relaxation and reading, although noise from the coffee machine can interrupt concentration.

On other decks (lower down), you'll find the Queen's Lounge and bar, which acts as a lecture room a Culinary Arts Center, where cooking demonstrations and cooking classes are held.

Gratuities are automatically added to your onboard account. Passenger niggles? Noisy cabin air conditioning – the flow can't be regulated or turned off, the only regulation being for temperature control. Also, several pillars obstruct passenger flow and lines of sight throughout the ship. There are no self-service launderettes, although special laundry packages are available.

ACCOMMODATION. There are numerous price categories: 16 outside view and eight interior. The views from some cabins on the lowest accommodation deck (Main Deck) are obstructed by lifeboats.

Some cabins that can accommodate a third and fourth person have very little closet space, and only one personal safe. Occupants of suites get exclusive use of the Neptune Lounge and concierge service, priority embarkation and disembarkation, and other benefits. In many of the suites/cabins with private balconies, the balconies are not particularly private and can be overlooked from various public locations.

Penthouse Verandah Suites (2). These offer the largest accommodation (1,318 sq ft/122 sq m, including balcony). Deluxe Verandah Suites (60). These suites measure 563 sq ft (52.3 sq m). Verandah Suites (100). Actually they are cabins, not suites, and measure 284 sq ft (26.4 sq m). Outside-view cabins. Standard outside cabins measure 197 sq ft (18.3 sq m). Interior cabins. At 183 sq ft (17 sq m) these are just slightly smaller than the outside-view ones.

DINING. Located aft, the 1,045-seat Vista Dining Room is two decks high, with seating at tables for two to eight on both main and balcony levels. It provides a traditional HAL dining experience, with friendly service from Indonesian and Filipino stewards. Both open seating and assigned seating are available for dinner, while breakfast and lunch are open seating – you'll be taken to a table by restaurant staff when you enter.

With a few exceptions, the cuisine is not very memorable, and is missing passion and taste, because it's all about mass catering (batch cooking). There's a distinct lack of variety of green vegetables, too heavy a use of rice, canned fruit, and already sliced and diced cheese. Still, you get friendly service, and the plates are nice.

Kosher meals are also available (if requested when you book), although these are prepared ashore, then frozen, and brought to your table sealed in their original containers.

The extra-cost (reservations-required) 148-seat Pinnacle Grill is a more intimate venue, with better-quality ingredients and presentation. It fronts onto the second level of the atrium lobby on Lower Promenade Deck. However, tables along its outer section are open to it and can suffer from noise from the Atrium Bar one deck below. Pacific Northwest cuisine (particularly seafood and prime-quality steaks) is featured. The wine list includes bottles from around the world.

The Lido Café is a casual self-serve eatery that wraps around the funnel, with indoor-outdoor seating. Several sections include a salad bar, stir-fry and sushi section, deli sandwiches, and a dessert buffet, although lines can form for made-to-order items. Also, a poolside 'Dive-In at the Terrace Grill' features multi-choice burgers (with special Dive-In sauce), hot dogs, and fries.

ENTERTAINMENT. The 867-seat Vista Lounge is for Las Vegas-style revues and major cabaret shows. The main floor level has a bar in its starboard aft section. Spiral stairways at the back of the lounge connect all levels. Shows are best seen from the upper levels, from where the sight lines are decent.

SPA/FITNESS. The Greenhouse Spa, a two-decks-high facility, is located directly above the navigation bridge. It includes a solarium, hydrotherapy pool, unisex thermal suite – a unisex area incorporating sauna and steam rooms) – plus a beauty salon, several private massage/therapy rooms (including one for couples) for body-pampering treatments, and a large gym with ocean views, and high-tech muscle-toning equipment. Other sports facilities include a basketball court, volleyball court, and a golf simulator.

NORWEGIAN BLISS
NYR

AN ÜBER-CASUAL, ENTERTAINMENT-FILLED PLAYGROUND FOR THE ENTIRE FAMILY

Size:	Large Resort Ship	Passenger/Crew Ratio (lower beds):	2.2/1
Tonnage:	167,800	Cabins (total):	1,850
Cruise Line:	Norwegian Cruise Line	Size Range (sq ft/m):	96.8–1,087.1/9.0–101.0
Former Names:	none	Cabins (for one person):	82
Builder:	Meyer Werft (Germany)	Cabins with balcony:	1,571
Entered Service:	Spring 2018	Cabins (wheelchair accessible):	47
Length (ft/m):	1,066.2/325.0	Wheelchair accessibility:	Good
Beam (ft/m):	178.8/54.5	Elevators:	16
Propulsion/Propellers:	diesel-electric/ 2 azimuthing pods	Casino (gaming tables):	Yes
Passenger Decks:	15	Swimming Pools:	5
Total Crew:	1,731	Self-Service Launderette:	No
Passengers (lower beds):	3,850	Library:	No
Passenger Space Ratio (lower beds):	43.8	Onboard currency:	US$

THE SHIP. *Norwegian Bliss* is a large resort ship for urbanites – for families, single parents, and solo travelers, with a mountain of entertainment choices, in an environment that is a pure playground for active cruising.

Norwegian Bliss (close sister to *Norwegian Getaway*) has hull artwork designed by marine life artist Robert Wyland, featuring cruising with whales.

Norwegian Bliss is cool, with a nod towards Alaska. It has some really good outdoor features for active types (including a superb jungle-like rope trek high above the aft decks). There are extensive pool deck facilities including an Aqua Park with multiple water slides and a rock-climbing wall and rope walk (more for adult kids). Aft is a large movie screen with amphitheater-style seating. Despite the ship's size, open deck space for sunbathing is minimal, because of the exclusive Haven area in the forward section, where suites-only occupants have their own sunbathing space, bar, pool, hot tubs, and beach club-like area. The rest of the ship shares multiple pools and water-fun exterior decks, designed for families and children.

Most of the public rooms, shops, entertainment spots, the casino, and a number of the bars and themed dining venues are located on decks 6, 7, and 8 – in a three-deck indoor-outdoor complex (678 Ocean Place).

'Waterfront' boardwalk-style outdoor areas with bars and eateries bring you more in contact with the sea. They form part of the outdoor experience, and

BERLITZ'S RATINGS	Possible	Achieved
Ship	500	NYR
Accommodation	200	NYR
Food	400	NYR
Service	400	NYR
Entertainment	100	NYR
Cruise Experience	400	NYR
OVERALL SCORE NYR points out of 2000		

are away from the hubbub of the family-friendly sun/sports action deck atop the ship.

Careful planning and time management will be needed to make the most of all this ship has to offer. It's worth spending time to decide what you want to get out of your cruise vacation before you board the ship, which sort of negates the freestyle aspect of a large resort ship cruise. You'll be sharing the ship with about 4,000 others, so there's no doubt it will be a lively travel experience.

Gratuities are automatically charged to your onboard account, or you can pre-pay online. Bar purchases and spa treatments incur an 18 percent gratuity. Overall, unless you are happy to settle for the most basic food, you'll need to pay extra to eat in one or more restaurants and eateries not included. It's all the extras that make a cruise aboard *Norwegian Bliss* a rather expensive vacation. Note that some public room and eatery names were not available at the time of going to press.

ACCOMMODATION. There is an almost endless variety of accommodation grades and suite/cabin types, shapes, and sleeping capacities, from small interior (no-view) cabins to two bedroom Villa suites.

The more exclusive accommodation is located in a two-deck-high section called The Haven – really a 'ship within a ship.' It consists of suites, a private restaurant, cocktail bar, and concierge desk (for making dining, entertainment, and spa reservations), a private pool, changing areas, hot tubs, gym, saunas, private massage rooms, and sun deck with bar. Occupants have private access to the spa and fitness center, butler service, and in-suite, white-tablecloth dining service. Suite occupants get a platinum key card, which gives better recognition in the rest of the ship – who said the class system was dead?

Other accommodation includes Spa mini-suite rooms and Spa balcony cabins, all with easy access to the adjacent spa and its facilities. While most outside-view cabins have a balcony, some have only windows, but all have flat-screen televisions, satellite-linked telephone, and private bathroom. There are also many Family 'suites' with ocean views, and many cabins with interconnecting doors.

Balcony suites/cabins have rich wood-look paneling with warm tones. Each has a queen-size bed (or twins), with a pillow-top mattress. There's a lighted recess above the bed for books, magazines, tablets, mobiles, or other items. Each room has a sofa bed with additional storage. A 26ins (66cm) flat-screen television is mounted on the wall and tilts for viewing from the sofa or the bed. Underneath the television is another recessed nook to hold cruise information, books, and magazines. A built-in vanity area has shelving and decent storage space. There's also a full-size closet with sliding doors. The cabins are energy-efficient, with key-card access to control lighting in the room.

The balcony bathroom features clean design, with generous space. An enclosed under-washbasin vanity hides the trash bin. A private shower with a shaving bar for women completes the picture. Mini-suite bathrooms get a rain shower plus a hand-held shower hose.

There are 59 studio (single-occupancy) interior-only cabins. They are colorful, trendy, and minimally designed, but small, especially the closet space. Still this is a neat way to cruise solo – just don't bring many clothes. Many interior cabins also have one or two additional upper berths, while the lower beds are twins that convert to a queen-size bed – good for families with young children.

Note that cabin doors open *outwards* (towards you) rather than inwards, as is more traditional. Also, when music is being played late at night in the lobby, cabins located above it may suffer from volume levels that are quite intrusive, despite some generally good soundproofing.

Note that room service incurs a 'convenience' per order charge (free for occupants of The Haven).

DINING. Freestyle Dining means no assigned dining rooms, tables, or seats, so you can choose which restaurant to eat in, at what time, and with whom. In practice, the wealth of choices means that you'll need to make reservations wherever you choose to eat, so be prepared for a little planning and waiting

– just like on land. To see a show in the evening, your dining time will really be dictated by the time of the show, which rather limits your choice.

There are three main dining rooms. Other dining venues include Cagney's Steakhouse (an open-kitchen classic American steakhouse; excellent for meat-eaters) and Moderno Churrascaria (a Brazilian-style steakhouse with tableside carved meat service by passadores, plus a salad bar); these are located one deck above, with a view into the Tropicana Room.

The Waterfront is a boardwalk-style outdoor area with bars and eateries. These include La Cucina (Italian family food with a focus on Tuscany), or, for alfresco eating, Maltings, and the à la carte Tapas Bar.

Other venues include Le Bistro, for classic French-style cuisine; a 96-seat Teppanyaki restaurant with 12 flat-top grills and a lot of show and noise; a Supper Club (for set dinner and show); Bayamo by Jose Garces (for Mexican cuisine); and an Asian fusion restaurant (including a sushi bar). All cost extra, and reservations are required.

Casual eateries, at no extra cost, include O'Sheehan's Neighborhood Bar & Grill, an always-open fast-food joint, with a screen for sporting events, two bowling lanes, and interactive games, and the Atrium Café and Bar, for extra-cost (Lavazza brand) coffees and pastries. Perhaps in a tribute to Man v. Food (the US food reality television show), the Dolce Gelato Bar signature item is extra-cost sundaes, with multiple scoops of ice cream in up to three flavors topped with 'everything under the sun.'

The Garden Café is an extremely large, self-serve buffet, with indoor and outdoor seating. It's open round the clock. Many different counters provide themed and ethnic food varieties, and there's a special section for kids.

ENTERTAINMENT. The two-deck-high Escape Theater, located at the front of the ship, is a stunning showlounge, for featuring the line's signature productions, while smaller shows are presented in the Manhattan Room, and the Supper Club.

SPA/FITNESS. The Mandara Spa and fitness center, spread over two decks, houses a large gymnasium, with high-tech cardiovascular exercise equipment. The complex includes an extra-cost thermal suite (herbal rainshowers, a snow grotto, saunas and steam rooms, and relaxation area with hot-tile beds), a beauty salon, and multiple body-treatment rooms, including massage rooms for couples. The fitness room has Technogym fitness and cardio equipment, which is linked to Apple devices.

A Sports Complex includes Aqua Park's multiple thrilling water slides, a multi-elevated rope course (with over than 40 elements), The Plank (a platform extending over the ship's side), a rock-climbing wall, a spider-web-like enclosed spiral climbing cage, a bungee trampoline, and a bocce ball court.

NORWEGIAN BREAKAWAY
★★★★

ÜBER-CASUAL, MULTI-CHOICE FLOATING PLAYGROUND FOR THE WHOLE FAMILY

Size:	Large Resort Ship	Passenger/Crew Ratio (lower beds):	2.4
Tonnage:	144,017	Cabins (total):	1,994
Cruise Line:	Norwegian Cruise Line	Size Range (sq ft/m):	96.8–1,022.6/9.0–95.0
Former Names:	none	Cabins (for one person):	59
Builder:	Meyer Werft (Germany)	Cabins with balcony:	1,252
Entered Service:	Apr 2013	Cabins (wheelchair accessible):	40
Length (ft/m):	1,066.2/325.0	Wheelchair accessibility:	Good
Beam (ft/m):	133.0/40.5	Elevators:	16
Propulsion/Propellers:	diesel-electric (79,800kW)/2 azimuthing pods	Casino (gaming tables):	Yes
Passenger Decks:	15	Swimming Pools:	5
Total Crew:	1,651	Self-Service Launderette:	No
Passengers (lower beds):	4,028	Library:	No
Passenger Space Ratio (lower beds):	35.7	Onboard currency:	US$

THE SHIP. *Norwegian Breakaway* is for young, trendy, edgy urbanites. It provides families with children, single parents, couples, and solo travelers with a mountain of entertainment choices, in an environment that is a pure playground for an active, entertaining cruise vacation.

It has a more streamlined and a better, more balanced profile than the slightly larger *Norwegian Epic*, with a less boxy look to its front upper forward section. The colorful, signature artwork on the lower front section of the hull depicting the city of New York was created by Peter Max, the popular American-based illustrator and graphic artist.

Families with children really enjoy the pool-deck facilities such as the Aqua Park, with five huge water slides, a large rock-climbing wall and rappelling wall, and a rope and scaffold-like walking course – with a small section that extends over the side. Aft is a large movie screen with amphitheater-style seating in an adults-only area called Spice H20.

Despite the ship's size, however, the open deck space for sunbathing is rather tight, and made smaller by the exclusive 'Haven' area in the forward section, whose suites-only occupants are given enough sunbathing space, bar, pool, and hot tubs, all in a beach-club-like setting. The rest of the ship shares multiple pools and water-fun exterior decks, designed for families and children.

Lower down, on an outdoor promenade deck, a 'Waterfront' boardwalk-style outdoor area with bar

BERLITZ'S RATINGS		
	Possible	Achieved
Ship	500	395
Accommodation	200	149
Food	400	247
Service	400	275
Entertainment	100	86
Cruise Experience	400	286
OVERALL SCORE 1438 points out of 2000		

and eateries brings you more in contact with the sea. It forms part of the outdoor experience, and away from the hubbub of the family-friendly sun/sports action deck.

Inside, the decor is decidedly more traditional and provides a more restful, relaxed feel and ambience – although this is all relative, and it's still rather upbeat and jazzy.

Careful planning and time management will be needed to make the most of this large resort ship and all it has to offer. It's really worth spending time to decide what you want to get out of your cruise vacation before you board the ship, which sort of negates the freestyle aspect of a large resort ship cruise, although it is still all about choice.

Most of the public rooms, shops, entertainment spots, the large casino (gaming tables and slots), and a number of the 12 bars and 17 themed dining venues are located on decks 6, 7, and 8 – a three-deck area complex called 678 Ocean Place.

A venue that proved popular aboard other Norwegian Cruise Line (NCL) ships is Bliss Ultra Lounge, a decadent venue (think late-night SoHo, minus the edginess).

The ship's home port is New York. Indeed, *Norwegian Breakaway* is the largest cruise ship ever to homeport in the Big Apple. Gratuities (called a 'service charge') are charged to your onboard account, or you can prepay online. Bar purchases incur a 15 percent gratuity; spa treatments are an eye-popping 18 percent.

ACCOMMODATION. *Norwegian Breakaway* has a traditional, practical bathroom layout for its 'standard' cabins, which have ample storage space and a clean design, with compact, but comfortable sleeping and living areas.

More exclusive accommodation is located in a two-deck-high section called The Haven – a 'ship within a ship.' It consists of 42 suites on Decks 15 and 16 forward, with a private restaurant, a cocktail bar, and a concierge desk area for relaxing, and making reservations for dining, entertainment, and the spa. There is a private pool, changing areas, two hot tubs, gym, saunas, two private massage rooms, and sun deck with bar. Occupants get butler service, and in-suite, white-tablecloth dining service. Suite occupants get a platinum key card and priority reservations for all the restaurants, spa, and entertainment venues.

The top suites within The Haven are two contemporary, apartment-style Deluxe Owner's Suites, with an elegant living room and dining area with wet bar. The bedroom has a king-size bed that faces floor-to-ceiling windows and a large wraparound balcony. The bathroom has a large bathtub, two washbasins, and a shower. Deluxe Owner's Suites can be joined to Owner's Suites to create a grand suite that can sleep up to eight.

The 21 two-bedroom Family Villas have two bathrooms and two bedrooms. The living room and dining area includes a single sofa bed, writing desk, and bar. The master bedroom has a king-size bed, floor-to-ceiling windows, and a private balcony. The master bath includes an oversize oval tub that looks out to the sea. The second bedroom includes a double sofa bed and bathroom.

Also in The Haven are Courtyard Penthouses, with a king-size bed, living and dining area, a single sofa bed, writing desk, and ample storage spaces. On other (non-Haven) decks are eight aft-facing penthouses and 10 forward-facing penthouses.

Other accommodation includes Spa mini-suite rooms and Spa balcony cabins, all with easy access to the adjacent spa and its facilities. While most outside-view cabins have a balcony, some have only windows, but all have flat-screen televisions, satellite-linked telephone, and private bathroom. There are also 42 Family 'suites' with ocean views.

Balcony suites/cabins have rich wood-look paneling with warm tones and accent colors. Each has a king-size bed that can convert into twins, with a pillow-top mattress set against a chestnut leather headboard cushioned and tufted to make reading and sitting up in bed more comfortable. There's an illuminated recess above the bed for books, magazines, tablet computers, or electronic reading devices. Each room has a sofa bed with additional storage. A built-in 26ins (66cm) flat-screen television is mounted on the wall and tilts, so that it can be seen from the sofa or the bed. Underneath the television is another recessed nook to hold cruise information, books, and magazines. A vanity area has shelving and abundant storage space. LED lighting surrounds the perimeter of the ceiling to give the room warmth. There is also a full-size closet that is easily accessible with sliding doors. The cabins are energy-efficient, and key card access controls the lighting.

The bathroom features a contemporary, clean design, with rich-wood shelves to help reduce clutter and keep everything within easy reach. There's an enclosed vanity unit underneath the washbasin to hide the trash bin, and more storage space. The built-in washbasin is generous in size and has an easy-to-use faucet. A private shower with a shaving bar for women completes the picture. Mini-suite bathrooms have a rainshower plus a hand-held shower hose.

There are 59 studio (solo-occupancy) cabins. They are colorful, hip, trendy, and capsule-hotel small, with minimalist design – especially for closet space. Still this is a neat way to cruise on your own – just don't bring too much luggage.

The many interior cabins also have one or two additional upper berths, while the lower beds are twins that convert to a queen-size bed – good for families with young children.

Note that room service (other than coffee/tea and Continental breakfast) incurs a 'convenience' charge of $7.95 per order (except for occupants of The Haven, for whom it is free).

DINING. There are many food-themed restaurants (including the largest venues, Savor and Taste), dining venues, and casual eateries from which to choose.

Norwegian Cruise Line has championed more choices in dining than any other cruise line. 'Freestyle Dining' is good in that you can try different types of cuisine, in different settings, when you want. In practice, however, it means you need to make reservations, which can prove frustrating at times. This takes a little planning and, often, waiting. Food in the main dining rooms is poor to average (with few vegetables and garnishes, and an over use of rice, but it is much better in some of the extra-cost venues. Wall-based touch-screen reservations systems work well, so you can see instantly how long you may have to wait if your chosen restaurant is fully booked.

The Manhattan Room is the equivalent of a main restaurant, and is included in the fare; it is large, with an integral dance floor and large ocean-view windows aft. Other dining venues (Cagney's Steakhouse and Moderno Churrascaria – good for meat-lovers) are located one deck above, with a view into the Manhattan Room.

Because the lifeboats hang over the side of the ship's hull, and not inboard as is usual, the promenade deck has become an oceanfront extension of the eateries on the *inside*, creating a New York sidewalk-style experience, called The Waterfront.

Inside, 678 Ocean Place (meaning decks 6, 7, and 8) connects with several interior extra-cost dining venues as well as an extensive Breakaway Casino, cigar-smoking room, and several entertainment venues. These include Moderno Churrascaria, a Brazilian-style steakhouse with tableside carved-meat service by 'passadores,' and a salad bar; Cagney's Steakhouse, a classic American steakhouse, with open kitchen; La Cucina, for Italian family food with a focus on Tuscany, with inside seating; or for alfresco eating on The Waterfront, Maltings (bar) and Ocean Blu by Geoffrey Zakarian – NCL's first à la carte all-seafood and raw bar/eatery, designed and overseen by the popular Food Network chef. The ingredients and techniques that he employs in his land-based establishments are featured here.

Other venues include Le Bistro, for classic French-style cuisine; a 96-seat Teppanyaki restaurant with 12 flat-top grills and a lot of show, plus a Japanese rock garden with bamboo plants and bonsai trees; and Cirque Dreams and Dinner, a big-top, circus-like dining spot with a Cirque Dreams and Dinner show (a lively, action-filled supper club). All are extra-cost, and reservations are required.

Casual eateries, at no extra cost, include O'Sheehan's Neighborhood Bar & Grill, a sports bar and popular fast-food joint, with a big screen for sporting events, miniature bowling alley, pool and air hockey tables, and interactive games; the Atrium Café and Bar (for coffees and pastries), and Shang-hai's Noodle Bar (for Chinese-style noodle dishes). The Ice Cream Bar signature item is a ship-specific sundae (Breakaway Sundae or Getaway Sundae), with nine scoops of ice cream in up to three flavors, topped with 'everything under the sun.'

Garden Café is a large, self-serve buffet, with indoor and outdoor seating. It's open round the clock, with different counters providing themed food varieties; there's a special section for kids, too.

ENTERTAINMENT. The two-deck-high Breakaway Theater, located at the front, is a fine large showlounge, where all the major production shows and mainline cabaret acts are presented.

Spiegel Tent is a two-deck-high domed Cirque-like space, combining an extra-cost show with dinner, similar to the Teatro ZinZanni dinner theater in Seattle. It's a mix of in-your-face street theater, acrobatics, and Berlin-style 'foodertainment,' with lots of clowning and satire during a two-hour show.

Dinner with entertainment is featured in the Manhattan Room. The Fat Cats Jazz & Blues Club is an intimate room that's often standing room only (when live jazz is on), while Howl at the Moon features a piano duel.

SPA/FITNESS. The spa and fitness center is spread over two decks and houses a warehouse-size gymnasium. The complex includes an extra-cost thermal suite (herbal rain showers, saunas and steam rooms, and relaxation area with hot-tile beds), a salt room, a beauty salon, and multiple body-treatment rooms, including massage rooms for couples.

NORWEGIAN DAWN

★★★+

THIS CASUAL MID-SIZE SHIP IS FOR LIVELY, FAMILY-FRIENDLY CRUISING

Size: .... Mid-size Ship	Passenger/Crew Ratio (lower beds): 2.3
Tonnage: 91,740	Cabins (total): 1,238
Cruise Line: .... Norwegian Cruise Line	Size Range (sq ft/m): 142.0–5,350.0/13.2–497.0
Former Names: .... none	Cabins (for one person): 0
Builder: .... Meyer Werft (Germany)	Cabins with balcony: 511
Entered Service: .... Oct 2002	Cabins (wheelchair accessible): 20
Length (ft/m): 964.9/294.1	Wheelchair accessibility: .... Best
Beam (ft/m): 105.6/32.2	Elevators: 12
Propulsion/Propellers: diesel-electric/2 azimuthing pods	Casino (gaming tables): .... Yes
	Swimming Pools: 3
Passenger Decks: 11	Self-Service Launderette: .... No
Total Crew: 1,069	Library: .... Yes
Passengers (lower beds): 2,476	Onboard currency: .... US$
Passenger Space Ratio (lower beds): 36.7	

THE SHIP. *Norwegian Dawn*, sister to *Norwegian Star*, was built in 64 sections and has a pod propulsion system, so there's no vibration. In 2011, some 58 additional suites/cabins were added, making the ship more crowded.

Facilities include a large Dawn Club Casino gaming area, a large library, a 1,150-seat showlounge, and a large retail shopping complex (Tradewinds).

Plenty of choices, including many dining options, add up to an attractive vacation package suitable for families with children – in a contemporary floating leisure center that provides ample facilities for you to have an enjoyable time. Despite the company's name, Norwegian Cruise Line (NCL), there's almost nothing Norwegian about it.

A non-changeable per-person service charge is automatically added to your account daily for staff gratuities; a service charge also applies to bar and spa charges.

ACCOMMODATION. Although the suites and junior suites are quite spacious, the standard interior and outside-view cabins are small compared to those of other cruise lines such as Carnival or Celebrity. The bathrooms, however, are decently sized, with large shower enclosures. There are many different price grades. All accommodation was refreshed during a 2016 refurbishment.

Many cabins have third- and fourth-person pull-

BERLITZ'S RATINGS		
	Possible	Achieved
Ship	500	356
Accommodation	200	145
Food	400	238
Service	400	268
Entertainment	100	67
Cruise Experience	400	269

OVERALL SCORE 1343 points out of 2000

down berths or trundle beds.

A small room service menu is available; non-food items cost extra, and a per-order service charge is added to your account. Bottled water is placed in each cabin, but it's chargeable if opened.

Mini-Suites are just larger cabins than the standards and each measure 229 sq ft (21 sq m).

Romance Suites each measure 288 sq ft (27 sq m).

Penthouse Suites each measure 366 sq ft (34 sq m). Penthouse Suites on Deck 11 can connect to a children's cabin with double sofa bed and a pull-down Pullman-style bed, separate bathroom, and shower enclosure.

Owner's Suites are located in the front of the ship; each measures 750 sq ft (70 sq m). Two are nestled under the enclosed navigation bridge wings on Deck 11, and the other two are in the equivalent space on the deck below. If you don't need the entertaining space of the Garden Villas, these suites are delightful living spaces. Each can also be interconnected to a Penthouse Suite and balcony cabin, which is useful for large families, when parents value privacy.

Garden Villas (Horizon and Vista) provide the largest living spaces. They are atop the ship in a pod just forward of the funnel, overlooking the main pool/recreation deck. They are stunning and have huge glass walls and landscaped private roof gardens for outdoor dining – with whirlpool tubs and huge private sunbathing areas. Each has three bedrooms and bathrooms, a large living room, private elevator, and stairway access. Each measures 5,350 sq ft (497 sq m); they can be combined to create a double-size 'house' measuring 10,700 sq ft (994 sq m), with a garden, and butler service.

Closet space in some of the smaller units is tight. Some suites have extras including a trouser press, and a larger range of personal toiletries.

DINING. With Freestyle Dining, you can choose which restaurant to eat in, at what time, and with whom (no assigned dining rooms, tables, or seats). While this is fine in theory, in practice it means that you need to make reservations for a specific time, so 'freestyle dining' actually turns out to be programmed dining.

There are three main dining rooms, plus several themed eateries, giving a wide choice (some cost extra and require advance reservations). Two entire decks are filled with 10 restaurants and eateries. NCL's dress code states that 'jeans, T-shirts, tank tops, and bare feet are not permitted in restaurants.'

Venetian: the first main dining room (seats 472) offers traditional dining. It is aft, with good views over the stern (at least in the daytime), although 14 pillars means obstructed views from some seats. The room has a baby grand piano. Quieter tables are in the two wings in the forward section near the entrance/steps.

Aqua: the second main dining room seats 344.

Other Eateries include:

Bamboo (a Taste of Asia) is a Japanese/Thai/Chinese restaurant, with 140 seats, a sit-up conveyor-belt style sushi/sashimi bar, sake bar, show galley, and a separate room with a Teppanyaki grill.

Le Bistro is a French restaurant with 72 seats, serving nouvelle cuisine. The decor includes four Impressionist paintings on loan from the private collection of the chairman of Genting Hong Kong. There's a cover charge and also a line for you to add an extra gratuity – cheeky. But it's the best food on board and worth the extra cost.

Cagney's Steak House incorporates a show kitchen and serves excellent (large) US prime steaks and seafood. Reservations are required, and a cover charge applies.

Moderno Churrascaria is for Argentine-style meats presented at your table by attendants in gaucho uniforms.

Garden Café is an indoor/outdoor self-serve buffet. It includes 'action stations' with made-to-order omelets, waffles, fruit, soups, ethnic specialties, and pasta.

There's also Los Lobos, for Mexican fare.

Other eating/drinking spots include O'Sheehan's (sports eatery and bar); the Pearly Kings (English pub for draft beer and perhaps a game of darts); Havanas, a cigar and cognac lounge; Java, an atrium lobby café and bar (hot and frozen coffees, teas, and pastries); a Beer Garden (grilled foods); a Gelato Bar (ice cream); and a Gym and Spa Bar (health food snacks and drinks).

ENTERTAINMENT. The 1,037-seat Stardust Theater is the venue for colorful Vegas-style production shows and major cabaret acts. It is designed in the style of an opera house, spans three decks, and has a steeply tiered main floor and port and starboard balconies. High-energy, razzle-dazzle shows feature extensive use of pyrotechnics, lasers, and other fancy lighting.

SPA/FITNESS. Wellness devotees should enjoy the two-deck-high spa complex, operated by the Steiner-owned Mandara Spa. Located at the stern, it has large ocean-view windows on three sides. There are many facilities and services, almost all at extra cost, including Thai massage in the spa, outdoors on deck, in your cabin, or on your balcony.

NORWEGIAN EPIC
★★★★

THIS IS AN EPIC-SIZED, FAMILY-FRIENDLY, MULTIPLE-CHOICE RESORT SHIP

Size:	Large Resort Ship
Tonnage:	155,873
Cruise Line:	Norwegian Cruise Line
Former Names:	none
Builder:	STX Europe (France)
Entered Service:	Jun 2010
Length (ft/m):	1,080.7/329.4
Beam (ft/m):	133.0/40.5
Propulsion/Propellers:	diesel-electric (79,800kW)/ 2 azimuthing pods
Passenger Decks:	15
Total Crew:	1,730
Passengers (lower beds):	4,200
Passenger Space Ratio (lower beds):	37.1
Passenger/Crew Ratio (lower beds):	2.4
Cabins (total):	2,100
Size Range (sq ft/m):	850.3–100.1/79–9.3
Cabins (for one person):	128
Cabins with balcony:	1,415
Cabins (wheelchair accessible):	42
Wheelchair accessibility:	Good
Elevators:	16
Casino (gaming tables):	Yes
Swimming Pools:	5
Self-Service Launderette:	No
Library:	Yes
Onboard currency:	US$

THE SHIP. Norwegian Epic is a blast for youthful adults and kids alike. It's all about lifestyle – bistro eateries, lots of dining choices, color and noise, the perceived über-chic South Beach nightlife at sea, stuffed with entertainment. It is an example of 'all-exclusive' cruising – a throwback to the days when First Class, Cabin Class, and Tourist Class meant passengers could not access certain areas of the ship (the 'pay more, get more' philosophy).

BERLITZ'S RATINGS	Possible	Achieved
Ship	500	379
Accommodation	200	145
Food	400	245
Service	400	273
Entertainment	100	85
Cruise Experience	400	279

OVERALL SCORE 1406 points out of 2000

Its profile is not particularly handsome because several decks above the navigation bridge make it look really top-heavy, like a square lump of cheese. But the two side-by-side funnels – between which is a 60-ft- (18-m-) wide rock-climbing wall – bring some semblance of balance. The ship is about 30 percent wider than the Norwegian Jewel-class ships.

The pool deck has an Aqua Park, with three major water slides – one involves inner tubes that give you a spin before spitting you out into a big bowl, reminiscent of a washing machine. Aft is a large movie screen with amphitheater-style seating, and a nightclub within an area called Spice H2O, which also includes a sun deck. However, despite the ship's size, the open deck space for sunbathing is extremely small and cramped – much diminished by the 'exclusive' Courtyard block in the forward section, whose occupants do have enough sunbathing space.

The three lowest passenger decks house the main entertainment venues, restaurants and other dining venues, show lounges, and a large casino. Some spaces open to two or three decks in height to create an illusion of space – like mini-atriums – but the overall flow is disjointed and invites congestion, particularly around a casino walk-through area. A dramatic three-deck-high chandelier in the lobby is the largest at sea.

Two escalators do nothing to diminish congestion – they even encourage gridlock at peak times. Sandwiched between these three lower entertainment decks and the upper entertainment decks are seven decks mainly comprised of accommodation. Something new for Norwegian Cruise Line (NCL) is a bridge-viewing room, just behind the navigation bridge.

NCL extracts more money with a number of 'exclusive' experiences, including a members-only POSH Beach Club, above the more exclusive Courtyard area atop the ship. This has a Miami South Beach vibe and includes four pay-extra experiences: (1) POSH Vive, 6–9am, when you can participate in yoga classes and treatments in private cabanas; (2) POSH Rehab until noon, so you can recover from a hard night, with Bloody Marys and chill-out music; (3) POSH Sol, noon–6pm, when you can lounge on day beds and enjoy a beach-themed atmosphere; and (4) Pure POSH, echoing Caesars Palace hotel in Las Vegas, where you can drink and dance under the stars.

Other ship features include a novel Ice Bar, a chill-out hangout inspired by the original ice bars and ice hotels of Scandinavia. In this frozen chamber of iced vodka, the centerpiece is a giant ice cube that glows and changes color. The Ice Bar accommodates 25 passengers, who are given fur coats, gloves, and hats because the room's temperature does not rise above −8°C (around 17°F). Naturally, there's a cover charge, but it includes two drinks. Svedka vodka and Canada's Inniskillin ice wine are featured.

Then there's Halo, an über-bar, where garden and courtyard villa occupants, who pay a premium for much better accommodation, have exclusive access, although other passengers can use it by paying a cover charge. This bar sits at the top of the ship on Deck 16 and showcases art and jewelry, 'modeled' by shop staff.

Spice H2O is a tiered pool, stage, and movie screen complex for adults only, at the stern. It's a smaller version of the Aqua Theater aboard Royal Caribbean International's *Oasis*-class ships. With all-day-long music and a huge screen, different themes prevail: (1) Sunny Spice 8am–11am, including spicy drinks and breakfast; (2) Daytime Aqua Spice with sun and water and Chinese take-away food; (3) Evening Sunset Spice, with a perfect sunset every day; and (4) All Spice at night, offering a show of aqua ballet and dancing. A Beyond the Velvet Rope package for all clubs is available at extra cost.

It's a big ship, but elevators are only forward and aft (none in the middle), which is tough for mobility-limited passengers. Yet *Norwegian Epic* has more elevators than the much larger *Oasis of the Seas*.

A 'ship within a ship' two-deck complex provides a private courtyard/pool area, men's and women's steam rooms, concierge lounge, and private dining rooms and lounge for those willing to pay more for exclusivity.

Niggles include cigarette smokers in the casino, a walk-through area.

The ship sails on alternating seven-day eastern and western Caribbean itineraries during the winter season, and operates Mediterranean cruises in summer.

A non-changeable per person service charge is automatically added to your account daily; 15 percent is also added for bar charges, and a whopping 18 percent for spa treatments.

ACCOMMODATION. There are many different accommodation price levels and accommodation grades. In true nautical tradition, even-numbered cabins are on the port side (red carpet), with odd-numbered cabins on the starboard side (blue carpet).

The Courtyard Suites (decks 16 and 17) are located in the 'block of cheese' in the forward section called The Haven, above the navigation bridge. There are six courtyard 'villas' – two face forward, while the rest overlook the central pool section, although none has a private balcony. Occupants have access to a four-deck gated-community style grouping of facilities, including a Concierge Lounge, private courtyard and pool, his-and-her steam rooms, and private sunbathing areas – so no need to go to the rest of the ship underneath you, except to disembark or go out to the entertainment decks to play, or escape.

All outside-view suites/cabins have a 'private' balcony, 'wave' shape curved walls for a contemporary look, LED lighting, backlit domed ceiling, comfortable sofa seating (except standard cabins), vanity desk, and mini-bar. A palette of soft, warm colors in each cabin melds beautifully with walnut- and rosewood-colored veneers and stark white surfaces. See-through (no-privacy) bathrooms have a separate toilet; tub or tub/shower combination, and separate vanity washbasin (few people like the see-through toilet).

Although they are about the same size as current standard industry cabins, there's an efficient use of space, achieved by separating the toilet and shower unit to either side of the entryway, and by curving the bulkheads and furniture to give the cabins a more open, wavy, and contemporary feel. However, space at the foot of the bed is poor. Also, you'll need to grab a towel before you step into the shower, because they are in a different location – adjacent to a tiny washbasin.

Eight Spa Suites have private key-card entry to the adjacent Mandara Spa, and complimentary 24-hour access to the inner Thermal Spa. These have more space and larger balconies.

Solo travelers can try one of the 128 studio cabins, many of which interconnect – reminiscent of a capsule hotel. A small window looks out into the passageway. On decks 11 and 12, these are priced for single occupancy, although they can be occupied by two persons (and two toothbrushes only), since there is a double bed. They measure 100 sq ft (9.3 sq m) and occupants have access to a common lounge with hostess, and free espressos/cappuccinos. In interior (no-view) cabins and studio categories, the bed faces the cabin door, so there's no privacy.

DINING. Norwegian Cruise Line has championed more choices in dining than any other cruise line. 'Freestyle Dining' is good in that you can try different types of cuisine, in different settings, when you want. In practice, however, it means you need to make reservations, which can prove frustrating at times. This takes a little planning and, often, waiting. Food in the main dining rooms is poor to average (with few vegetables and garnishes, and an over use of rice as a carbohydrate source), but it can be much better in the extra-cost venues.

Several different food outlets have been created in numerous locations – many are included in the cruise fare, the others require a per-person cover or à la carte charge. Because gratuities are automatically added to your account, if you change dining venues, there's no need to think about tips.

Cagney's Steakhouse & Churrascaria (skewered meats presented by tableside 'gauchos') has 276 seats and a central self-help salad bar.

Taste, on Deck 5, is touted as a European retro-chic restaurant with brick detailing and floor-to-ceiling velvet curtains. The menu includes traditional and contemporary cuisine for breakfast, lunch, and dinner.

The Manhattan Room, located aft, is two decks high and reminiscent of an elegant Art Deco supper club, with dance floor and live Celebrity Look-Alike shows. It's the closest thing to a main dining room and has a spectacular glass window wall aft.

La Cucina is from Tuscany. It's at the front of the ship, providing great ocean views, one deck above the navigation bridge.

The 124-seat Le Bistro serves French cuisine; there has been a Le Bistro aboard all NCL ships since the first one was installed aboard the now-scrapped *Norway*.

Multiple Asian-themed venues include Shanghai's for Chinese dishes and noodle bar specialties with an open kitchen and 133 seats; the 20-seat Wasabi for sushi and sakes; and a showy, food-chopping Teppanyaki Grill, with 115 seats.

The Epic Club and Courtyard Grill, in the Courtyard Villas complex, is exclusive to suite and villa occupants and split between an elegant, private club-style restaurant with a large wine display and a casual outdoor area for breakfast and lunch. It can accommodate 127.

O'Sheehan's neighborhood-style sports bar and grill is open 24 hours (no extra charge). It is adjacent to a bowling alley, though I'm not sure why – it disturbs the ambience.

Café Jardin (Garden Café) is a large self-serve buffet, with 728 seats; it is like an English country garden conservatory – but with a French name and ocean views. It includes 'action' stations, where chefs prepare pasta and other items. The outdoor seating area, the Great Outdoors, looks over the Aqua Park.

A section for children, the Kids Café, has low-height tables and seats.

ENTERTAINMENT. The two-deck-high Epic Theater, at the front of the ship, presents hit show Priscilla Queen of the Desert, plus major production shows and mainline cabaret acts. Another entertainment venue, the Bliss Ultra Lounge, is a decadent venue that includes a bowling alley – there's another one in Sheehan's on the deck above. This is where late-night comedy and some cabaret acts are presented.

Spiegel Tent is a two-deck-high Cirque-like space, combining a show (a cover charge applies) with dinner, similar to the Teatro ZinZanni dinner theater in San Francisco and Seattle. It's a mix of in-your-face street theater, acrobatics, and Berlin-style 'foodertainment,' with lots of clowning and satire during the two-hour show.

The Cavern Club (named after the club where The Beatles started out) is home ground for rock 'n' roll lovers.

As part of NCL's creative Check In, Rock Out program, guitar enthusiasts can, for a daily fee, rent a real Gibson guitar and a set of headphones to play in the comfort of their cabin.

SPA/FITNESS. The Smile Spa and Pulse Fitness Center complex is possibly the largest at sea (31,000 sq ft/2,880 sq m). Operated by the Steiner-owned Mandara Spa, it is in the center of the ship, and some of the 24 treatment rooms have no view. The Fitness Center has port-side ocean views; the aerobics room has no view.

Sports facilities include six bowling lanes in two venues (O'Sheehan's Neighborhood Bar & Grill and Bliss Ultra Lounge), a full-size basketball court, volleyball, soccer, dodge ball, a batting cage, bungee trampoline, a 24-ft- (7.3-m-) tall climbing cage called the spider web, and an abseiling wall. Walkers should note that 2.2 laps around the walking track equals 1 mile (1.6km).

NORWEGIAN ESCAPE
★★★★

A MULTI-CHOICE, ÜBER-CASUAL PLAYGROUND THAT WORKS FOR THE ENTIRE FAMILY

Size:	Large Resort Ship
Tonnage:	164,600
Cruise Line:	Norwegian Cruise Line
Former Names:	none
Builder:	Meyer Werft (Germany)
Entered Service:	Oct 2015
Length (ft/m):	1,097.7/334.6
Beam (ft/m):	136.1/41.5
Propulsion/Propellers:	diesel-electric/
	2 azimuthing pods
Passenger Decks:	15
Total Crew:	1,651
Passengers (lower beds):	4,266
Passenger Space Ratio (lower beds):	38.5

Passenger/Crew Ratio (lower beds):	2.5
Cabins (total):	2,174
Size Range (sq ft/m):	96.8–1,090.0/9.0–101.0
Cabins (for one person):	82
Cabins with balcony:	1,571
Cabins (wheelchair accessible):	47
Wheelchair accessibility:	Good
Elevators:	16
Casino (gaming tables):	Yes
Swimming Pools:	5
Self-Service Launderette:	No
Library:	Yes
Onboard currency:	US$

THE SHIP. *Norwegian Escape* is a large resort ship for young and trendy urbanites – and perhaps the best ship in the fleet. Families with children, single parents, couples, and solo travelers have a mountain of entertainment choices, in an environment that is a pure playground for an active, feature-filled cruise.

Norwegian Escape (close sister to *Norwegian Breakaway* and *Norwegian Getaway*) has a more streamlined, balanced profile than its slightly larger sibling ship, *Norwegian Epic*, with less of a boxy look to its forward section, and a small, squat funnel, plus a better Passenger Space Ratio (more space per passenger). The hull artwork is designed by marine wildlife artist and champion of ocean conservation, Guy Harvey, featuring an underwater scene of marine wildlife.

Norwegian Escape is cool, but the ambience is South Beach in heat, with all the hype and volume to prove it. It has some really good outdoor features for active types (including a superb jungle-like rope trek high above the aft decks). Families with children can enjoy extensive pool deck facilities including the Aqua Park (it's larger than on Norwegian Breakaway, Norwegian Epic, and Norwegian Getaway), with multiple water slides and a rock-climbing wall and rope walk (more for adult kids). Aft is a large movie screen with amphitheater-style seating. But, despite the ship's size, the open deck space for sunbathing is really tight, made smaller by the exclusive Haven area in the forward section, whose

BERLITZ'S RATINGS

	Possible	Achieved
Ship	500	405
Accommodation	200	150
Food	400	254
Service	400	284
Entertainment	100	86
Cruise Experience	400	294

OVERALL SCORE 1473 points out of 2000

suites-only occupants are given their own sunbathing space, bar, pool, hot tubs, and beach club-like setting. The rest of the ship shares multiple pools and water-fun exterior decks, designed for families and children. Still, the pool deck is where all the family action takes place, particularly on sea days.

Most of the public rooms, shops, entertainment spots, the casino, and a number of the bars and themed dining venues are located on decks 6, 7, and 8 – a three-deck indoor-outdoor complex called 678 Ocean Place. This includes Tobacco Road, named for a Miami icon that closed in 2014 after 102 years in business. Elements of the original Tobacco Road include the original iconic neon sign, memorabilia, and photographs that showcase Miami's history and happenings over the past century.

'Waterfront' boardwalk-style outdoor areas with bars and eateries bring you closer to the sea. They form part of the outdoor experience, and are away from the hubbub of the family-friendly sun/sports action deck atop the ship.

Careful planning and time management will be needed to make the most of all this ship has to offer, which sort of negates the freestyle aspect of a large resort ship cruise. You'll be sharing the ship with about 4,000 others, so there's no doubt it will be a lively travel experience.

Norwegian Escape's year-round homeport is Miami. Gratuities are automatically charged to your onboard account, or you can pre-pay online. Bar purchases and spa treatments incur an 18 percent gratuity. Overall, unless you are happy to settle for the most basic food, you'll need to pay extra to eat in one or more restaurants and eateries not included in the cruise fare. It's all the extras that make a cruise aboard *Norwegian Escape* a rather expensive vacation.

ACCOMMODATION. There is an almost endless variety of accommodation grades and suite/cabin types, shapes, and sleeping capacities, from small interior (no-view) cabins to two bedroom Villa suites.

The more exclusive accommodation is located in a two-deck-high section called The Haven – really a 'ship within a ship.' It consists of 42 suites on decks 15 and 16 forward, and includes a private restaurant, cocktail bar, and concierge desk for relaxing, drinking, and making dining, entertainment, and spa reservations. The area has a private pool, changing areas, hot tubs, gym, saunas, private massage rooms, and sun deck with bar. The Haven occupants have private access to the spa, butler service, and in-suite, white-tablecloth dining service. Suite occupants get a platinum key card, which gives better recognition in the rest of the ship – who said the 'class' system was dead?

The top suites within The Haven are two Deluxe Owner's Suites, including an extra-spacious wraparound private balcony. Deluxe Owner's Suites can be joined to Owner's Suites, creating one grand suite that can sleep up to eight.

Two-bedroom Family Villas have two bathrooms and two bedrooms. Also in The Haven are Courtyard Penthouses. On other (non-Haven) decks throughout the ship are eight aft-facing penthouses and 10 forward-facing penthouses.

Other accommodation includes Spa mini-suite rooms and Spa balcony cabins, all with easy access to the adjacent spa and its facilities. While most outside-view cabins have a balcony, some have only windows, but all have flat-screen televisions, satellite-linked telephone, and private bathroom. There are also many Family 'suites' with ocean views.

Balcony suites/cabins have rich wood-look paneling with warm tones. Each has a queen-size bed (or twins), with a pillow-top mattress. There's an illuminated recess above the bed for books, magazines, tablets, mobiles, or other items. Each room has a sofa bed with additional storage. A built-in 26ins (66cm) flat-screen television is mounted on the wall and tilts for viewing from the sofa or the bed. Underneath the television is another recessed nook to hold cruise information, books, and magazines. A built-in vanity area has shelving and decent storage space. There's also a full-size closet with sliding doors. The cabins are energy-efficient, with key card access to control lighting in the room.

The balcony bathroom features a contemporary, clean design, with generous and comfortable space.

An enclosed under-washbasin vanity hides the trash bin. A private shower with a shaving bar for women completes the picture. Mini-suite bathrooms get a rainshower plus a hand-held shower hose.

There are 59 studio (single-occupancy) interior-only cabins. They are colorful, trendy, and minimalist in design, but small – especially the closet space. Still this is a neat way to cruise solo – just don't bring many clothes.

Many interior cabins also have one or two additional upper berths, while lower beds are twins that convert to a queen-size bed – good for families with young children.

Note that cabin doors open *outwards* (towards you) rather than inwards, as is more traditional. Also, when music is being played late at night in the lobby, cabins located above it may suffer from volume levels that are quite intrusive, despite some generally good soundproofing.

Room service incurs a 'convenience' charge of $7.95 per order (free for The Haven accommodation occupants).

DINING. Freestyle Dining means no assigned dining rooms, tables or seats, so you can choose which restaurant to eat in, at what time, and with whom. In practice, the wealth of choices means that you'll need to make reservations wherever you choose to eat, so be prepared for a bit of planning and waiting – just like you would ashore. If you want to see a show in the evening, then your dining time will really be dictated by the time of the show, which rather limits your choice.

Norwegian Cruise Line has championed more choices in dining than any other cruise line. 'Freestyle Dining' is good in that you can try different types of cuisine, in different settings, when you want. In practice, however, it means you need to make reservations, which can prove frustrating at times. This takes a little planning and, often, waiting. Food in the main dining rooms is poor to average (with few vegetables and garnishes, and an over use of rice as a carbohydrate source), but it is much better in the extra-cost venues.

There are three main dining rooms: Savor, Taste, and the Manhattan Room. Other dining venues include Cagney's Steakhouse (an open-kitchen classic American steakhouse) and Moderno Churrascaria (a Brazilian-style steakhouse with tableside carved meat service by passadores, plus a salad bar), which are located one deck above, with a view into the Tropicana Room.

The Waterfront is a boardwalk-style outdoor area with bars and eateries. These include La Cucina (Italian family food with a focus on Tuscany), and, for alfresco eating, there's Maltings, and Pinchos Tapas Bar (à la carte).

Other venues include Le Bistro, for classic French-style cuisine; a 96-seat Teppanyaki restaurant with

12 flat-top grills and a lot of show and noise; the Supper Club (for set dinner and show); Bayamo by Jose Garces (for Mexican cuisine); and Food Republic, for Asian fusion cuisine (including a sushi bar). All are extra-cost, and reservations are required.

Casual eateries, at no extra cost, include O'Sheehan's Neighborhood Bar & Grill, an always-open fast-food joint, with a screen for sporting events, two bowling lanes, and interactive games; Margaritaville – a Jimmy Buffet-themed outdoor eatery; and the Atrium Café and Bar, for extra-cost (Lavazza) coffees, and pastries. Perhaps in a tribute to Man v. Food (the US reality television show), the Dolce Gelato Bar signature item is a ship-specific extra-cost sundae (Breakaway Sundae or Getaway Sundae), with multiple scoops of ice cream in up to three flavors topped with 'everything under the sun.'

The Garden Café is a large, self-serve buffet, with indoor and outdoor seating. It's open round the clock. Many different counters provide themed and ethnic food varieties, and there's a special section for kids.

ENTERTAINMENT. The two-deck-high Escape Theater, located at the front of the ship, is a stunning showlounge, for featuring the line's signature productions, while smaller shows are presented in the Manhattan Room, and the Supper Club.

SPA/FITNESS. The Mandara Spa and fitness center, spread over two decks, houses a large gymnasium, with high-tech cardiovascular exercise equipment, an extra-cost thermal suite (herbal rainshowers, a snow grotto, saunas and steam rooms, and relaxation area with hot-tile beds), a beauty salon, and multiple body-treatment rooms, including massage rooms for couples. The fitness room has Technogym fitness and cardio equipment, which is linked to Apple devices.

A Sports Complex includes Aqua Park's multiple thrilling water slides, a multi-elevated rope course (with over than 40 elements), The Plank (a platform extending over the ship's side), a rock-climbing wall, a spider-web-like enclosed spiral climbing cage, a bungee trampoline, and a bocce ball court.

NORWEGIAN GEM
★★★+

A FAMILY-FRIENDLY MID-SIZE SHIP WITH MULTIPLE EATING VENUE CHOICES

Size:	Mid-size Ship	Passenger/Crew Ratio (lower beds):	2.1
Tonnage:	93,530	Cabins (total):	1,197
Cruise Line:	Norwegian Cruise Line	Size Range (sq ft/m):	142.0–4,390.0/13.2–407.8
Former Names:	none	Cabins (for one person):	0
Builder:	Meyer Werft (Germany)	Cabins with balcony:	540
Entered Service:	Oct 2007	Cabins (wheelchair accessible):	27
Length (ft/m):	964.8/294.1	Wheelchair accessibility:	Good
Beam (ft/m):	105.6/32.2	Elevators:	12
Propulsion/Propellers:	diesel-electric/ 2 azimuthing pods	Casino (gaming tables):	Yes
		Swimming Pools:	2
Passenger Decks:	12	Self-Service Launderette:	Yes
Total Crew:	1,126	Library:	Yes
Passengers (lower beds):	2,394	Onboard currency:	US$
Passenger Space Ratio (lower beds):	39.0		

THE SHIP. A multitude of choices, including many dining options, add up to a very attractive vacation package, highly suitable for families with children, in a floating leisure center that provides ample facilities for enjoyment.

The design and layout of *Norwegian Gem* is similar to that of *Norwegian Pearl*, and there is a pod propulsion system for vibration-free cruising. The white hull has a colorful string of gems along its sides as a design. There are plenty of deck lounge chairs – more than the total of passengers. Water slides are included for the adult swimming pools. Children have their own pools at the ship's stern.

Inside the ship is an entertaining mix of bright, warm colors and decor that you probably wouldn't have in your home, and yet somehow they all work well.

The dress code is ultra-casual: no jacket and tie needed, although you are welcome to dress formally – but jeans are probably essential. Although service levels and finesse may be inconsistent, the level of hospitality aboard Norwegian Cruise Line (NCL) ships is good. There's plenty of lively music, constant activity, entertainment, and food that is mainstream and acceptable but nothing more – even when you pay extra to eat in the specialty dining spots.

There are 11 bars (including a 24-hour 'pub') and lounges, including Bar Central, four specialty bars: a Martini bar, a Champagne and wine bar, a beer and whiskey bar, and a cigar lounge; these interconnect

BERLITZ'S RATINGS

	Possible	Achieved
Ship	500	357
Accommodation	200	145
Food	400	238
Service	400	269
Entertainment	100	66
Cruise Experience	400	269

OVERALL SCORE 1344 points out of 2000

with the lobby, yet have distinct personalities. The lobby houses a Java Bar, plus a two-deck-high movie screen, typically used to show sports events and Wii activities. One neat room is the Bliss Ultra Lounge & Night Club, at the aft end of the ship; it houses a V-shaped sports bar and lounge complex, including a bowling alley with four real bowling lanes – the cost is $5 per person, including special playing shoes, and it is limited to six persons per lane. The lounge doesn't have many seats, but it does have a couple of decadent beds.

The casino has plenty of gaming tables, slot machines, noise, and smoke. So, if you walk through the casino to get from the showlounge to other public rooms, you'll be subject to cigarette smoke.

The ship has many revenue centers designed to help you part with even more money than you paid for your cruise ticket. Expect to be subjected to a stream of flyers advertising art auctions, 'designer' watches, gold and silver chain by the inch, and other promotions – and the cruise director's long program announcements three times a day.

A per person service charge that can't be changed is automatically added to your account daily; 15 percent is also added for bar charges, and a whopping 18 percent for spa treatments.

ACCOMMODATION. There are many, many different price grades, from small interior cabins to lavish suites in a private courtyard setting.

Although they are nicely furnished and quite well equipped, the standard outside-view and interior cabins are quite small, particularly when occupied by three or four people. A small room service menu is available – all non-food items cost extra, and a service charge is automatically added to your account. Bottled water is placed in each cabin, but you will be charged if you open the bottle.

The following suites (from largest to smallest), part of The Haven, are also available:

Two Courtyard Villas/Garden Villas, each measuring 4,390 sq ft (408 sq m), and 10 Courtyard Villas share a private courtyard with its own small pool, hot tub, and small fitness room, and butler service. These units enjoy exclusivity – rather like living in a gated community – where others cannot live unless they pay the asking price.

Deluxe Owner's Suites. The Black Pearl and Golden Pearl suites have stunning ocean views, and consist of a master bedroom, a dining/lounge area, a decent-size balcony, and access to a private courtyard.

Penthouse Suites. Located at the front of the ship, they have a partly private balcony under the navigation bridge.

DINING. There are two main dining rooms: the 304-seat Grand Pacific, with minimalist decor; and the 558-seat Magenta Restaurant. There are several other themed eating spots, giving a wide range of choice; some cost extra, and require advance reservations, particularly for dinner. All are part of NCL's Freestyle Dining – there are no assigned dining rooms, tables, or seats, so you'll need to plan your meals and times accordingly.

With 17 video screens located around the ship, you can check how busy each dining spot is and make a booking and find out whether, or how long, you'll need to wait for a table; pagers are also available, so you can go bar-hopping while you wait for a table in your chosen venue. The system generally works well, with colored bars to indicate whether a restaurant is 'full,' 'moderately busy,' or 'empty.' This has cut down the frustration of waiting a long time for a table, although on formal nights, when you may want to see the pro-

duction shows, congestion certainly does occur. Note that NCL's dress code states that 'jeans, T-shirts, tank tops, and bare feet are not permitted in restaurants.'

Additional dining options, some of which cost extra, include Cagney's Steak House (for steaks from 5oz to 48oz and grilled seafood); Blue Lagoon (for trendy fast-food street snacks); Moderno Churrascaria (for Argentinian-style grilled meats); Le Bistro for classic French cuisine; Orchid Garden (an Asian-style eatery with sushi bar and Teppanyaki grill, where the chef puts on a display in front of you); La Cucina Italian Restaurant; O'Sheehan's Neighborhood Bar & Grill; Garden Café, a large self-serve buffet-style restaurant, for casual meals; Kids' Café; and Java Café, for extra-cost Lavazza coffee, in the lobby.

ENTERTAINMENT. The 1,042-seat Stardust Theater is the venue for colorful Las Vegas-style production shows and major cabaret acts. It is designed in the style of an opera house, spans three decks, and has a steeply tiered main floor and port and starboard balconies.

All the high-energy production shows are ably performed by the Jean Ann Ryan Company.

SPA/FITNESS. Wellness devotees should enjoy the two-deck-high Yin-Yang Health Spa complex, open until 10pm and operated by Mandara Spa (owned by Steiner Leisure). It is located in the front of the ship, with large ocean-view windows on three sides. There are many facilities and services to pamper you, and 18 treatment rooms. There's also a 37ft (11m) indoor lap pool, hydrotherapy pool, two sit-in deep tubs, aromatherapy and wellness centers, and mud-treatment room.

The Body Waves fitness and exercise rooms are within the spa and have Cybex muscle-pumping equipment. Most classes, such as Pathway to Yoga, Body Cycling Class, and others, cost extra.

Recreational sports facilities include a jogging track, golf driving range, and basketball and volleyball courts, as well as several levels of sunbathing decks, plus four bowling lanes, and a funnel-mounted rock-climbing wall.

NORWEGIAN GETAWAY
★★★★

THIS IS A MULTI-CHOICE, SUPER-CASUAL FLOATING PLAYGROUND FOR THE FAMILY

Size:	Large Resort Ship	Passenger/Crew Ratio (lower beds):	2.4
Tonnage:	145,655	Cabins (total):	1,994
Cruise Line:	Norwegian Cruise Line	Size Range (sq ft/m):	96.8–1,022.6/9.0–95.0
Former Names:	none	Cabins (for one person):	59
Builder:	Meyer Werft (Germany)	Cabins with balcony:	1,252
Entered Service:	Apr 2013	Cabins (wheelchair accessible):	40
Length (ft/m):	1,066.2/325.0	Wheelchair accessibility:	Good
Beam (ft/m):	133.0/40.5	Elevators:	16
Propulsion/Propellers:	diesel-electric (79,800MW)/2	Casino (gaming tables):	Yes
Passenger Decks:	15	Swimming Pools:	5
Total Crew:	1,595	Self-Service Launderette:	No
Passengers (lower beds):	3,929	Library:	Yes
Passenger Space Ratio (lower beds):	37	Onboard currency:	US$

THE SHIP. *Norwegian Getaway* (sister to *Norwegian Breakaway*) has a more streamlined, balanced profile than its slightly larger close-sister ship, *Norwegian Epic*, with a less boxy look to its forward section. Miami artist and muralist David 'Lebo' Le Batard provided the artwork on the hull, which depicts a whimsical mermaid holding the sun above the waves.

Norwegian Getaway is a cool ship, but the ambience is pure South Beach in terms of heat, with all the hype and volume to prove it, as well as some really great outdoor features for active types. Families with children have extensive pool deck facilities including the Aqua Park, with multiple water slides and a rock-climbing wall and, rope walk (more for adult kids). Aft is a large movie screen with amphitheater-style seating. But, despite the ship's size, the open deck space for sunbathing is rather tight, and made smaller by the exclusive Haven area in the forward section, whose suites-only occupants have their own sunbathing space, a bar, pool, and hot tubs. The rest of the ship shares multiple pools and water-fun exterior decks, designed for families and children – the kids will love it (little ones should look for Sponge Bob in the wading pool).

Lower down, on an outdoor promenade deck, a 'Waterfront' boardwalk-style outdoor area with bar and eateries brings you more in contact with the sea. It forms part of the outdoor experience, away from the

BERLITZ'S RATINGS		
	Possible	Achieved
Ship	500	397
Accommodation	200	149
Food	400	247
Service	400	272
Entertainment	100	87
Cruise Experience	400	289

OVERALL SCORE 1441 points out of 2000

hubbub of the family-friendly sun/sports action deck atop the ship.

Inside, the decor is decidedly more traditional and provides a more restful, relaxed feel and ambience – although this is all relative and still rather upbeat. Careful planning and time management will be needed to make the most of this large resort ship and all it has to offer. So it's worth spending time to decide what you want to get out of your cruise vacation before you board the ship – which sort of negates the freestyle aspect of a large resort ship cruise. You'll be sharing the ship with about 4,000 others, so there's no doubt it will be a lively travel experience.

Most of the public rooms, shops, entertainment spots, the casino, and a number of the bars and themed dining venues are located on decks 6, 7, and 8 – a three-deck indoor-outdoor complex called 678 Ocean Place.

Norwegian Getaway really is a ship for young and trendy urbanites. It provides families with children, single parents, couples, and solo travelers with a mountain of entertainment choices, in an environment that is a pure, lively playground for an active, entertaining cruise vacation.

The ambience on board is lively, and invites plenty of social interaction. *Norwegian Getaway*'s homeport is Miami. Gratuities are charged to your onboard account, or you can pre-pay online. Bar purchases incur a 15 percent gratuity; spa treatments are 18 percent.

ACCOMMODATION. There is an almost endless variety of accommodation grades and suite/cabin types, shapes, and sleeping capacities, so you'll need to decide what you are looking for, or are comfortable with.

Aboard this ship, cabin doors open *outwards* (towards you) rather than inwards, as is more traditional. Also, note that when music is being played late at night in the lobby, cabins located above it can suffer from intrusive volume levels, despite the generally good soundproofing.

The many interior (no-view) cabins also have one or two additional upper berths, while the lower beds are twins that convert to a queen-size unit – possibly good for families with young children. Note that room service incurs a per-order 'convenience' charge.

There are 59 studio (solo-occupancy) interior-only cabins (none has a sea view). They are colorful, trendy, and small, with a minimalist design – especially the closet space. Still this is a neat way to cruise on your own – just don't bring many clothes.

Balcony suites/cabins have rich wood-look paneling with warm tones. Each balcony cabin has a queen-size bed that can be made into twins, with a pillow-top mattress set against a chestnut leather headboard cushioned and tufted to make reading and sitting up in bed more comfortable. There's a lighted recess above the bed for books, magazines, mobiles, tablets, or electronic reading devices. Each room has a sofa bed with additional storage. A built-in flat-screen television is mounted on the wall and tilts for viewing from the sofa or the bed. Underneath the television is another recessed nook for cruise information, books, and magazines. A built-in vanity area has shelving and decent storage space. There's also a full-size closet with sliding doors. The cabins are energy-efficient, using key card access to control lighting in the room.

Bathrooms feature a contemporary, clean design. An enclosed vanity unit underneath the (generously sized) washbasin hides the trash bin. A private shower with a shaving bar for women completes the picture. Mini-suite bathrooms have a rainshower plus a hand-held shower hose.

More exclusive accommodation is located in a two-deck-high section called The Haven – a 'ship within a ship.' It consists of 42 suites on decks 15 and 16 forward. This area includes a private restaurant, a cocktail bar, and a concierge desk where passengers can relax, and make reservations. There is a pool (with a deep end for swimming and a shallow area for relaxing), changing areas, two hot tubs, gym, saunas, two private massage rooms, and sun deck with bar. The Haven's occupants have private access to the spa and fitness center, butler service, and in-suite, white-tablecloth dining service. Suite occupants also get a different key card, which presumably gives better recognition in the rest of the ship – who said the 'class' system was dead?

The top suites within The Haven are two Deluxe Owner's Suites, with a contemporary skyscraper apartment look – including an elegant living room and dining area with wet bar. Deluxe Owner's Suites can be joined to the Owner's Suites, creating one grand suite that can sleep up to eight.

The two-bedroom Family Villas have two bathrooms as well as two bedrooms. The separate living room and dining area includes a single sofa bed, writing desk, and bar.

Also in The Haven are Courtyard Penthouses, with a king-size bed, living and dining area, a single sofa bed, writing desk, and ample storage spaces. On other (non-Haven) decks throughout the ship are eight aft-facing penthouses and 10 forward-facing penthouses.

Spa mini-suite rooms and Spa balcony cabins all have easy access to the adjacent spa. While most outside-view cabins have a balcony, some have only windows, but all have flat-screen televisions, satellite-linked telephone, and private bathroom. There are also 42 Family 'suites' with ocean views.

DINING. Freestyle Dining means no assigned dining rooms, tables or seats, so you can choose which restaurant to eat in, at what time, and with whom. In practice, however, it means you need to make reservations, which can prove frustrating at times. This takes a little planning and, often, waiting. Food in the main dining rooms is poor to average (with few vegetables and garnishes, and an over use of rice as a carbohydrate source), but is much better in the extra cost venues.

The Tropicana Room is a large restaurant (included in the fare), with an integral dance floor (for shows and dancing during dinner) and large ocean-view windows aft. Other dining venues (Cagney's Steakhouse and Moderno Churrascaria – a Brazilian-style steakhouse with meat carved at your table by 'passadores,' and with a salad bar) are located one deck above, with views into the Tropicana Room.

The Waterfront is a boardwalk-style outdoor area with bar and eateries, while Geoffrey Zakarian's 678 Ocean Place (meaning decks 6, 7, and 8) connects it with several interior extra-cost dining venues as well as the extensive Getaway Casino, a cigar-smoking room, and several entertainment and dining venues. These include: Moderno Churrascaria; La Cucina, for Italian family food with a focus on Tuscany, with inside seating; or, for alfresco eating on The Waterfront, Ocean Blu (designed and overseen by US TV's Food Network's Geoffrey Zakarian). The celebrity chef uses fresh-as-possible ingredients and techniques that he employs in his land-based establishments.

Other venues include Le Bistro, for classic French-style cuisine; a 96-seat Teppanyaki restaurant with 12 flat-top grills and a lot of knife show and noise; and The Illusionarium – a combination magic show with dinner.

Casual eateries (no extra cost) include O'Sheehan's Neighborhood Bar & Grill, a sports bar and popular always-open fast-food joint, with a big screen for sporting events, miniature bowling alley, pool and air hockey tables, and interactive games; the Atrium Café and Bar, for coffees, pastries, and music; and Shanghai's Noodle Bar, for Chinese-style noodle dishes. The Ice Cream Bar signature item is a ship-specific extra-cost sundae (Breakaway Sundae or Getaway Sundae), with nine scoops of ice cream in up to three flavors topped with 'everything under the sun.' There's also Wasabi, an à la carte sushi bar.

The Garden Café is an extremely large, self-serve buffet, with indoor and outdoor seating. It's open almost round the clock. Many different counters provide themed and ethnic food varieties, and there's a special section for kids

ENTERTAINMENT. Two-deck-high Getaway Theater, located at the front of the ship, is a stunning showlounge for major production shows and mainline cabaret acts. A specially produced version of seven-time Tony-award nominated *Legally Blonde* is one of the highlights, while *Burn the Floor* is an excellent, fast-paced and exciting Latin dance show (it is presented in the Tropicana Room).

Really cool: The Illusionarium and its Grand Master Magic Show with Dinner. It's presented in a cir-cular room with a large dome (think South Beach meets handcuffs and magic wand). The show is the result of collaboration between NCL's entertainment department and Broadway director/choreographer Patricia Wilcox, Tony Award-winning scenic designer David Gallo, and veteran magician Jeff Hobson. Its design is inspired by the science fiction of Jules Verne, the artistry of legendary magicians such as Houdini, and by the supernatural. Whether you can get your water changed into wine remains to be seen.

Also, Grammy Experience at Sea is a small venue featuring headline-name musical artists.

SPA/FITNESS. The spa and fitness center, spread over two decks, houses a warehouse-size gymnasium. The complex includes an extra-cost thermal suite (herbal rain showers, saunas and steam rooms, relaxation area with hot-tile beds), a beauty salon, and multiple body-treatment rooms, including massage rooms for couples.

The Sports Complex includes Aqua Park's five thrilling water slides, a multi-elevated rope course (there are more than 40 elements), The Plank (a platform extending over the ship's side), rock-climbing wall, a spider-web-like enclosed spiral climbing cage, bungee trampoline, and a nine-hole miniature golf course.

NORWEGIAN JADE
★★★+

GOOD ENTERTAINMENT AND A CASUAL LIFESTYLE FOR THE WHOLE FAMILY

Size:	Mid-size Ship	Passenger/Crew Ratio (lower beds):	2.2
Tonnage:	93,558	Cabins (total):	1,233
Cruise Line:	Norwegian Cruise Line	Size Range (sq ft/m):	142.0–4,390.0/13.2–407.8
Former Names:	*Pride of Hawaii*	Cabins (for one person):	0
Builder:	Meyer Werft (Germany)	Cabins with balcony:	763
Entered Service:	May 2006/Mar 2008	Cabins (wheelchair accessible):	27
Length (ft/m):	964.8/294.1	Wheelchair accessibility:	Good
Beam (ft/m):	105.6/32.2	Elevators:	12
Propulsion/Propellers:	diesel-electric (40,000kW)/	Casino (gaming tables):	Yes
	2 azimuthing pods	Swimming Pools:	2
Passenger Decks:	12	Self-Service Launderette:	No
Total Crew:	1,076	Library:	Yes
Passengers (lower beds):	2,466	Onboard currency:	US$
Passenger Space Ratio (lower beds):	37.9		

THE SHIP. Built from 67 blocks, this is a sister ship to *Norwegian Jewel*. After service as *Pride of Hawaii*, it underwent a small transformation, gained a casino, and became *Norwegian Jade* for cruising in Europe and the Caribbean – though some interior decor elements from the ship's former life in Hawaii (the scheme is decidedly bright and cheerful) remain. The ship was set to undergo a refurbishment at time of printing. Because the ship has a pod propulsion system, it's quiet, and vibration is minimal.

The ship's interior focal gathering place is Bar Central – three specialty bars (Magnum's Champagne/Wine Bar, Mixers' Martini/Cocktail Bar, and Tankard's Beer/Whiskey Bar) that are connected but have distinct personalities. They are on the deck above the reception lobby. All told, there are a dozen bars and lounges. Other facilities include a casino, three meeting rooms, a chapel, card room, bridge viewing room, and the SS *United States* Library with original photography and material about America's last ocean liner.

The dress code is casual. The ship has many revenue centers designed to help you part with more of your money. You can expect to be subjected to a stream of flyers advertising daily art auctions, 'designer' watches, and many other promotions including poolside 'inch of gold' sales outlets.

A non-negotiable per person service charge is automatically added to your account daily; 15 percent is also added for bar charges.

BERLITZ'S RATINGS		
	Possible	Achieved
Ship	500	356
Accommodation	200	145
Food	400	238
Service	400	269
Entertainment	100	66
Cruise Experience	400	267
OVERALL SCORE 1341 points out of 2000		

Norwegian Jade best suits youthful adult couples, solo travelers, and families with children and teenagers who want upbeat surroundings, good facilities, a wide range of entertainment lounges and bars, and high-tech sophistication – all in a neat, highly programmed and well-packaged cruise. Although the initial fare seems very reasonable, the extra costs and charges can soon mount up.

Passenger niggles include waiting to use the interactive dining reservation screens in the public areas; and lines for breakfast in the main dining spots, particularly before the shore excursions start.

ACCOMMODATION. There are many, many different price grades, determined by size and location. Although they are nicely furnished and quite well equipped, the standard outside-view and interior cabins are quite small, particularly when occupied by three or four people.

A small room service menu is available; all non-food items cost extra, and a 15 percent service charge is added to your account. Bottled water is placed in each cabin, but it is chargeable if you open the bottle.

Garden Villas. Two multi-room villas have great views over the pool deck and ocean. Each has a roof terrace and private garden, with open-air dining, hot tub, and private sunning and relaxation areas. Each measures approximately 4,390 sq ft (408 sq m), the ultimate in living space, exclusivity and privacy.

Courtyard Villas (up to 660 sq ft/61 sq m) share a private courtyard, small pool, hot tub, massage bed, and fitness room – all in a distinctly Asian setting. Owner's Suites. These five units measure approximately 1,195 sq ft (111 sq m). Penthouse Suites. These measure up to 600 sq ft (56 sq m). All villas and suites have a private balcony, walk-in closet, rich cherry wood cabinetry, tea/coffee/espresso/cappuccino makers, plus butler and concierge service.

DINING. Freestyle Dining has no assigned dining rooms, tables, or seats, so you can choose which restaurant to eat in, at what time, and with whom. In reality, this means you have to make reservations for a specific time, so 'freestyle dining' turns out to be programmed dining. Ten restaurants and eateries are spread over two entire decks. Some are included in the cruise fare, others cost extra.

The two main restaurants, included in the cruise fare, are Alizar (310 seats) and Grand Pacific (486 seats). Specialty dining venues include Cagney's Steak House, Blue Lagoon (a casual eatery serving American food), Le Bistro (a classic French restaurant (check out the beautiful, genuine, Van Gogh painting), the neighbourhood 24-hour O'Sheehans Bar and Grill (for pub-style eats), and Pit Stop (for poolside American diner fare).

Others eateries include a Moderno Churrascaria (a Brazilian style steakhouse with adjacent self-help salad bar), Jasmine Garden (with sushi counter, sake bar, and Teppanyaki Grill for grilled food and knife show), La Cucina (for Italian fare). Self-serve buffet-style meals can be taken in the ultra-casual Garden Café and its outdoor section, while extra-cost Lavazza coffees can be found in the Aloha Café.

You can make reservations through the Freestyle Dining information system; plasma screens showing waiting times for the various venues are located in high-traffic areas.

ENTERTAINMENT. The 1,042-seat Stardust Theater is the venue for colorful Las Vegas-style production shows and major cabaret acts. It is designed in the style of an opera house, spans three decks, and has a steeply tiered main floor and port and starboard balconies.

Bands and solo entertaining musicians provide live music for listening and dancing to in several lounges and bars. Throughout the ship, loud music prevails. In Spinnakers Lounge, a nightclub located high atop the ship with great ocean views on three sides, a Pachanga Party (a Miami South Beach rave) is held during each cruise.

SPA/FITNESS. The two-deck-high Yin and Yang health spa complex, operated by the Steiner-owned Mandara Spa, is at the stern, with ocean-view windows on three sides. There are many facilities and services, almost all costing extra. In addition, there is a 37ft (11m) indoor lap pool, hydrotherapy pool, two sit-in deep tubs, aroma-therapy and wellness centers, and mud-treatment rooms, including one for couples. Spa treatments incur an 18 percent gratuity.

The fitness and exercise rooms, with Cybex muscle-pumping equipment, are located not within the spa, but at the top of the glass-domed atrium lobby. Included is a room for exercycle classes.

Recreational sports facilities include a jogging track, two golf driving nets (there's a golf pro shop, too), basketball and volleyball courts, paddle tennis, mini-golf, oversize chess, and several sunbathing decks.

NORWEGIAN JEWEL
★★★+

A CASUAL MID-SIZE SHIP FOR LIVELY, FAMILY-FRIENDLY CRUISING AND ENTERTAINMENT

Size:	Mid-size Ship	Passenger/Crew Ratio (lower beds):	2.1
Tonnage:	93,502	Cabins (total):	1,188
Cruise Line:	Norwegian Cruise Line	Size Range (sq ft/m):	142.0–4,390.0/13.2–407.8
Former Names:	none	Cabins (for one person):	0
Builder:	Meyer Werft (Germany)	Cabins with balcony:	540
Entered Service:	Aug 2005	Cabins (wheelchair accessible):	27
Length (ft/m):	964.8/294.1	Wheelchair accessibility:	Good
Beam (ft/m):	105.6/32.2	Elevators:	12
Propulsion/Propellers:	diesel-electric (40,000kw)/ 2 azimuthing pods	Casino (gaming tables):	Yes
		Swimming Pools:	2
Passenger Decks:	12	Self-Service Launderette:	No
Total Crew:	1,089	Library:	Yes
Passengers (lower beds):	2,376	Onboard currency:	US$
Passenger Space Ratio (lower beds):	39.3		

THE SHIP. *Norwegian Jewel*, assembled from 67 blocks, has a basic design and layout similar to that of *Norwegian Gem* and *Norwegian Pearl*, and a pod propulsion system. The white hull has a colorful, funky design on its sides featuring sparkling jewels. There are plenty of sunloungers – in fact, more than the number of passengers carried. Waterslides are included for the adult swimming pools. Children have their own pools at the stern, out of sight of adult areas.

Inside the ship, you'll be met by an eclectic mix of colors and decor that you probably wouldn't have in your home, and yet somehow it works extremely well in this mid-size ship designed to attract the young and active.

There are 13 bars and lounges, including Bar Central, three specialty bars that are connected but have distinct personalities. Shakers Martini and Cocktail Bar is a 1960s-inspired lounge; Magnum's Champagne and Wine Bar recalls Paris of the 1920s and the liner *Normandie*; and Maltings Beer and Whiskey Pub is a contemporary bar with artwork themed around whiskey and beer production.

Despite the company's name, there's little that's Norwegian about this product, except perhaps for some senior officers. There's plenty of lively music, constant activity, entertainment, and food that is mainstream and acceptable but nothing more, unless you pay extra to eat in the specialty dining spots.

BERLITZ'S RATINGS		
	Possible	Achieved
Ship	500	352
Accommodation	200	145
Food	400	238
Service	400	269
Entertainment	100	66
Cruise Experience	400	267

OVERALL SCORE 1337 points out of 2000

All this is delivered by a smiling, friendly service staff that lacks polish but is willing.

A multitude of choices, including many dining options, add up to a very attractive vacation package, highly suitable for families with children, in a floating leisure center that provides ample facilities for enjoyment. However, the ship is full of revenue centers designed to part you from your cash. Expect to be subjected to a stream of flyers advertising daily art auctions, 'designer' watches, and 'inch of gold/silver.' The initial cruise fare is reasonable, but extra costs soon mount up, if you want to sample more than the basics. A mandatory per-person service charge is added to your account daily; 15 percent is also added for bar charges, and a whopping 18 percent for spa treatments.

ACCOMMODATION. There are numerous accommodation price grades, so there's something for all tastes, from small interior cabins to lavish Penthouse Suites in a private courtyard setting – part of the exclusive Haven complex. Although they are nicely furnished and quite well equipped, the standard outside-view and interior cabins are quite small, particularly when occupied by three or four people.

A small room service menu is available, and a service charge is added to your account. Bottled water is placed in each cabin, but you will be charged if you open the bottle.

Two Garden Villas (each measures 4,390 sq ft/408 sq m), and 10 Courtyard Villas share a private courtyard with a small pool, hot tub, massage bed, and fitness room. They also share a private concierge lounge with the two largest villas, as well as butler and concierge service. These units enjoy exclusivity – rather like accommodation in a gated community – where others cannot live unless they pay the asking price. The two are duplex apartments, with a spiral stairway between upper and lower quarters.

DINING. The ship's freestyle dining has no assigned dining rooms, tables or seats, so you can choose which restaurant to eat in, at what time, and with whom. In reality, this means you have to make reservations for a specific time, so 'freestyle dining' turns out to be programmed dining. Ten restaurants and eateries are spread over two entire decks. Some are included in the cruise fare, others cost extra.

There are two main dining rooms: the 552-seat Tsar's Palace, designed to look like the interior of Catherine the Great's St Petersburg palace in Russia, and the 310-seat Azura. There are also a number of other themed eating establishments, giving a wide range of choice, though some cost extra and require advance reservations.

Computer screens around the ship enable you to check how long you'll have to wait for a table at each dining spot. Pagers are available, so you can go bar-hopping while you wait for a table. The system works well, although on formal nights when you may want to see the show, congestion can occur. Note: Norwegian Cruise Line's dress code states: 'jeans, T-shirts, tank tops, and bare feet are not permitted in restaurants.'

Established favorites include: Cagney's Steakhouse (for fine steaks and seafood); Moderno Churrascaria (a Brazilian-style steakhouse for meat and seafood dishes); and Le Bistro (for fine classic French cuisine). In a 2014 refit, O'Sheehan's Neighborhood Bar and Grill was added, for homey pub food and beer.

Chin Chin is an Asian eatery with a Teppanyaki Grill and sushi counter adjacent. La Cucina Italian Restaurant has a long wooden table running through the room to create the ambience of a Tuscan farmhouse.

The Garden Café is a large self-serve buffet-style eatery; it incorporates an ice cream bar, and Kid's Café, with its own kid-height counter, located opposite the children's play areas. For coffee, head to the Atrium Café in the lobby, and taste some of Buddy Valasco's cupcakes in Carlo's Bakery, adjacent.

ENTERTAINMENT. The Stardust Theater, seating 1,037, is for colorful large-scale production shows and cabaret acts. It is designed in the style of an opera house, spans three decks, and has a steeply tiered main floor and port and starboard balconies.

A number of bands and solo entertaining musicians provide live music for listening and dancing in lounges and bars. In Spinnakers Lounge, a nightclub, a Pachanga Party is held each cruise (a Miami South Beach rave).

SPA/FITNESS. Wellness devotees should enjoy the two-deck-high Bora Bora health spa complex, operated by the Hawaii-based Mandara Spa, located in the front of the ship with large ocean-view windows on three sides. There are many facilities and services to pamper you, almost all at extra charge, including Thai massage in the spa, outdoors on deck, in your cabin or on your private balcony.

In addition, there is a 37ft (11m) indoor lap pool, hydrotherapy pool, two sit-in deep tubs, aromatherapy and wellness centers, and mud-treatment rooms. There are 15 treatment rooms in all, including one specifically designed for couples, and heated tile loungers in a relaxation area.

The fitness and exercise rooms, with the latest Cybex muscle-pumping equipment, are located not within the spa, but at the top of the glass-domed atrium lobby. Included is a room for exercycle classes. Some classes, such as Pathway to Yoga, Body Cycling Class, and Body Beat Class (cardio kick-boxing), cost extra.

Recreational sports facilities include a jogging track, golf driving range, basketball and volleyball courts, as well as four levels of sunbathing decks.

NORWEGIAN JOY
★★★★

THIS FAMILY-FRIENDLY, ÜBER-CASUAL SHIP IS TOTALLY DEDICATED TO CHINESE TASTES

Size:	Large Resort Ship	Passenger/Crew Ratio (lower beds):	2.2/1
Tonnage:	168,800	Cabins (total):	1,925
Cruise Line:	Norwegian Cruise Line	Size Range (sq ft/m):	96.8–1,087.1/9.0–101.0
Former Names:	none	Cabins (for one person):	0
Builder:	Meyer Werft (Germany)	Cabins with balcony:	1,571
Entered Service:	Jun 2017	Cabins (wheelchair accessible):	47
Length (ft/m):	1,068.5/325.7	Wheelchair accessibility:	Good
Beam (ft/m):	178.8/54.5	Elevators:	16
Propulsion/Propellers:	diesel-electric/ 2 azimuthing pods	Casino (gaming tables):	Yes
		Swimming Pools:	5
Passenger Decks:	15	Self-Service Launderette:	No
Total Crew:	1,731	Library:	No
Passengers (lower beds):	3,850	Onboard currency:	RMB
Passenger Space Ratio (lower beds):	43.8		

THE SHIP. Shanghai-based *Norwegian Joy* (喜悦号 or Xĭ Yuè Hào – the characters mean 'inner joy') really is a large floating resort for young and trendy Chinese urbanites. Families with children, single parents, couples, and solo travelers have a mountain of dining, sports, and entertainment choices, in an environment that is a pure playground for an active, feature-filled cruise experience. All signage is in both English and Mandarin.

Immediately noticeable is the novel artwork on the ship's hull, provided by renowned Chinese artist Tan Ping; its theme is the mythical bird, the phoenix. Also, in a cruise industry first, in partnership with Scuderia Ferrari watches there's a real open-air track for go karting, where you can reach speeds of up to 20mph (32kph), just forward of the ship's low-slung funnels. Meanwhile, an an activity-driven Aqua Park has multiple thrilling water slides, a multi-elevated rope course, and many other facilities for sporting activity. The ship's lifeboats are inboard, rather than hanging over the side.

Despite the ship's size, the open deck space is actually quite small, and made smaller by the exclusive Haven area in the forward section, whose suites-only occupants (pay more, get more) are given their own sunbathing space, bar, pool, hot tubs, and beach-club-like setting.

Most public rooms, shops, entertainment spots, the casino, and a number of the bars and themed

BERLITZ'S RATINGS

	Possible	Achieved
Ship	500	406
Accommodation	200	150
Food	400	252
Service	400	286
Entertainment	100	83
Cruise Experience	400	295

OVERALL SCORE 1472 points out of 2000

dining venues are located on decks 6, 7, and 8 – a three-deck indoor-outdoor complex. Here, the 'Waterfront' boardwalk-style outdoor areas with bars and eateries bring you more in contact with the sea. They form part of the outdoor experience, and take you away from the hubbub of the family-friendly sun/sports action deck atop the ship.

One neat area is the Galaxy Pavilion, with its hang-gliding simulator, racing-car simulator, and several virtual-reality experiences, including hovercraft bumper cars.

Some planning and time management will be needed to make the most of all this ship has to offer, which sort of negates the freestyle aspect of a large resort ship. You'll be sharing the ship with almost 4,000 others, so be prepared for a really lively cruise experience.

ACCOMMODATION. There is an almost endless variety of accommodation grades and suite/cabin types, shapes, and sleeping capacities, from small interior (no-view) cabins to two bedroom Villa suites. The price you pay depends on the size, location, and grade you choose.

Note that the cabin doors open outwards (towards you) rather than inwards, as is more traditional. Also, when music is being played late at night in the lobby, cabins located above it may suffer from volume levels that are quite intrusive, despite some generally good soundproofing. Room service breakfasts incur a per-order 'convenience' charge (free for occupants of The Haven accommodation).

Instead of solo-occupancy Studio cabins, this ship has two-bedroom interior (no-view) suites (with virtual balcony). Occupants have access to a dedicated concierge for making dining, entertainment, and spa reservations.

The Haven accommodation is located in a two-deck-high section and consists of many large suites. The area has a private pool, changing areas, hot tubs, gym, saunas, private massage rooms, and sun deck with bar. Occupants have private access to the spa and fitness center, butler service, in-suite, white-tablecloth dining service, and access to a private VIP (high stakes) gambling room.

The Haven has four Deluxe Owner's Suites, including an extra-spacious wraparound private balcony. Deluxe Owner's Suites can be joined to the Owner's Suites, creating one grand suite that can sleep up to eight. Two-bedroom Family Villas have two bathrooms and two bedrooms. Also in The Haven are Courtyard Penthouses. On other (non-Haven) decks throughout the ship are eight aft-facing penthouses and 10 forward-facing penthouses.

Concierge-grade suites (located above The Haven in a separate complex) are something new for the cruise line; these feature larger balconies, a concierge lounge and bar, and a better level of personal service.

DINING. Freestyle Dining means no assigned dining rooms, tables or seats, so you can choose which restaurant to eat in, at what time, and with whom. In reality, the wealth of choices means that you'll need to make reservations in whichever venue you want to eat, so you'll need to be prepared for a bit of planning and waiting – just like you would ashore.

There are 29 dining venues and eateries (nine of which are complimentary), including some fleet-wide favorites: Cagney's Steakhouse (for premium-grade steaks), La Cucina (for Italian fare), Le Bistro (for French cuisine), and Manhattan (a large two-deck-high dining spot with Chinese and Western cuisine and entertainment). Extra-cost venues include a Supper Club (dinner and show), Neptune's (for premium seafood), Grand Tea Room (for traditional, elegant teatime), and a Noodle Bar (for noodles and dim sum).

ENTERTAINMENT. The two-deck-high Joy Theater, located at the front of the ship, is a stunning showlounge, for featuring the line's signature productions, while smaller dinner shows are presented in the large Manhattan Room, and the (extra-cost) Supper Club.

SPA/FITNESS. The Spa and fitness center, spread over two decks, houses a large gymnasium, with high-tech cardiovascular exercise equipment. The complex includes an extra-cost thermal suite (herbal rainshowers, a snow grotto, saunas and steam rooms, and relaxation area with hot-tile beds), a beauty salon, and multiple body-treatment rooms, including massage rooms for couples. The fitness room has Technogym fitness and cardio equipment, which is linked to Apple devices.

NORWEGIAN PEARL
★★★+

A CASUAL, FAMILY-FRIENDLY SHIP WITH MULTI-CHOICE DINING OPTIONS

Size:	Mid-size Ship	Passenger/Crew Ratio (lower beds):	2.2
Tonnage:	93,530	Cabins (total):	1,197
Cruise Line:	Norwegian Cruise Line	Size Range (sq ft/m):	142.0–4,390.0/13.2–407.8
Former Names:	none	Cabins (for one person):	0
Builder:	Meyer Werft (Germany)	Cabins with balcony:	540
Entered Service:	Dec 2006	Cabins (wheelchair accessible):	27
Length (ft/m):	964.8/294.1	Wheelchair accessibility:	Good
Beam (ft/m):	105.6/32.2	Elevators:	12
Propulsion/Propellers:	diesel-electric (39,000kW)/ 2 azimuthing pods	Casino (gaming tables):	Yes
		Swimming Pools:	2
Passenger Decks:	12	Self-Service Launderette:	No
Total Crew:	1,087	Library:	Yes
Passengers (lower beds):	2,394	Onboard currency:	US$
Passenger Space Ratio (lower beds):	39.0		

THE SHIP. The ship's white hull has a colorful, funky design on its sides featuring sparkling jewels. There are plenty of sunloungers – in fact, more than the number of passengers carried. Waterslides are included for the adult swimming pools. Children have their own pools at the stern, out of sight of adult areas.

Inside, you'll be met by an eclectic mix of colors and decor that you probably wouldn't have in your home, and yet somehow it works extremely well in this mid-sized ship designed for the young and active.

There are 13 bars and lounges, including Shakers Martini and Cocktail Bar (a 1960s-inspired lounge); Magnum's Champagne and Wine Bar recalls Paris of the 1920s and the liner *Normandie*; and Maltings Beer and Whiskey Pub, a contemporary bar with artwork themed around whiskey and beer production.

Despite the company's name, there's little that's Norwegian about it, except for some senior officers. There's plenty of lively music, constant activity, entertainment, and food that is mainstream and acceptable but nothing more, unless you pay extra to eat in the specialty dining spots. All this is delivered by a smiling, friendly service staff that lacks polish but is willing.

Plenty of choices, including many dining options, add up to an attractive vacation package that is highly suitable for families with children, in a floating leisure center that provides ample facilities for enjoyment. The ship is, however, full of revenue centers

BERLITZ'S RATINGS		
	Possible	Achieved
Ship	500	353
Accommodation	200	145
Food	400	238
Service	400	269
Entertainment	100	66
Cruise Experience	400	268
OVERALL SCORE 1339 points out of 2000		

designed to part you from your cash. Expect to be subjected to a stream of flyers advertising art auctions, 'designer' watches, and 'inch of gold/silver.'

The initial cruise fare is reasonable, but extra costs soon mount up if you want to sample more than the basics. A mandatory per person service charge is added to your account daily; 15 percent is also added for bar charges, and a whopping 18 percent for spa treatments.

ACCOMMODATION. There are numerous accommodation price grades, so there's something for all tastes, from small interior cabins to lavish Penthouse Suites in a private courtyard setting – part of The Haven complex. Although they are nicely furnished and quite well equipped, the standard outside-view and interior cabins are quite small, particularly when occupied by three or four people.

A small room service menu is available, and a service charge is added to your account. Bottled water is placed in each cabin, but you will be charged if you open the bottle.

Two Garden Villas (each measures 4,390 sq ft/408 sq m), and 10 Courtyard Villas share a private courtyard with a small pool, hot tub, massage bed, and fitness room. They also share a private concierge lounge with the two largest villas, as well as butler service. These units are like accommodation in a gated community – where others cannot live unless they pay the asking price. The two largest are duplex apartments, with a spiral stairway between the upper and lower quarters.

Two deluxe Owner's Suites have stunning ocean views, a master bedroom with king-size bed, a dining/lounge area, a decent-size balcony, and access to a private courtyard.

DINING. Freestyle Dining has no assigned dining rooms, tables or seats, so you can choose which restaurant to eat in, at what time, and with whom. In reality, this means you have to make reservations for a specific time, so 'freestyle dining' turns out to be programmed dining. Some restaurants and eateries are included in the cruise fare, others cost extra.

The two principal dining rooms are the 304-seat Indigo, with its minimalist decor, and the 558-seat Summer Palace, plus several other themed eating spots. Video screens around the ship enable you to check how long you'll have to wait for a table at each dining spot. Norwegian Cruise Line's dress code states that 'jeans, T-shirts, tank tops, and bare feet are not permitted in restaurants.'

Other dining options (some cost extra) include Cagney's Steakhouse (for premium steaks and seafood); Moderno Churrascaria (for Argentinian-style meats and seafood); Le Bistro (for fine French cuisine); Mambo's (for tapas/Latin fare); Lotus Garden (an Asian eatery featuring a Teppanyaki Grill and sushi counter); O'Sheehan's Neighborhood Bar & Grill (for pub-style eats); while La Cucina Italian Restaurant has a long wooden table running through the room to create the ambience of a Tuscan farmhouse.

For casual (self-serve) buffet-style eating, there's the Great Outdoors, while the Garden Café incorporates an ice cream bar, and Kid's Café, with its own kid-height counter (located opposite the children's play areas). Java Café, in the lobby is for extra-cost coffees.

ENTERTAINMENT. The 1,037-seat Stardust Theater is the showlounge for colorful production shows and major cabaret acts. It is designed in the style of an opera house, spans three decks, and has a steeply tiered main floor and port and starboard balconies.

A number of bands and solo entertaining musicians provide live music for listening and dancing in lounges and bars.

SPA/FITNESS. Bodywaves is the name of the spa/fitness center. It is operated by the Hawaii-based Mandara Spa (Steiner Leisure), located in the front of the ship with large ocean-view windows on three sides. There are lots of facilities and services to pamper you, almost all at extra charge, including Thai massage in the spa, outdoors on deck, in your cabin or on your private balcony.

In addition, there is a 37ft (11m) indoor lap pool, hydrotherapy pool, two sit-in deep tubs, aromatherapy and wellness centers, mud-treatment rooms, and 15 private massage/body-treatment rooms including one for couples.

The fitness and exercise rooms, with the latest muscle-pumping equipment, are located not within the spa, but at the top of the glass-domed atrium lobby. Included is a room for exercycle classes. Some classes, such as Pathway to Yoga, Body Cycling Class, and Body Beat Class, cost extra.

Additional facilities include a jogging track, golf driving range, basketball and volleyball courts, as well as four levels of sunbathing decks.

NORWEGIAN SKY
★★★+

A MULTI-CHOICE SHIP GEARED TO CASUAL, UPBEAT, FAMILY-FRIENDLY CRUISING

Size:	Mid-size Ship	Passenger/Crew Ratio (lower beds):	2.1
Tonnage:	77,104	Cabins (total):	1,001
Cruise Line:	Norwegian Cruise Line	Size Range (sq ft/m):	120.5–488.6/11.2–45.4
Former Names:	Pride of Aloha, Norwegian Sky	Cabins (for one person):	0
Builder:	Lloyd Werft (Germany)	Cabins with balcony:	252
Entered Service:	Aug 1999/Jun 2008	Cabins (wheelchair accessible):	6
Length (ft/m):	853.0/260.0	Wheelchair accessibility:	Good
Beam (ft/m):	105.8/32.2	Elevators:	12
Propulsion/Propellers:	diesel-electric (50,000kW)/2	Casino (gaming tables):	Yes
Passenger Decks:	12	Swimming Pools:	2
Total Crew:	914	Self-Service Launderette:	No
Passengers (lower beds):	2,002	Library:	Yes
Passenger Space Ratio (lower beds):	38.5	Onboard currency:	US$

THE SHIP. In 2004 *Norwegian Sky* was 'Hawaiianized' and morphed into *Pride of Aloha* for Norwegian Cruise Line's (NCL's) Hawaii cruise operation; however, it was withdrawn from that market in 2008 and transferred to NCL for short cruises. The interior decor reflects its operating area, and the focal point is an eight-deck-high atrium lobby, with spiral sculptures and rainbow-colored sails.

Public rooms include a shopping arcade, children's playroom, Internet center with 14 terminals and coffee available from an adjacent bar, several lounges and bars, small conference room, the Mark Twain library, and Captain Cook's for cigars and cognac. Those with a black belt in shopping may seek out the Black Pearl Gem Shop.

Norwegian Sky, a resort at sea, caters well to a multi-generational clientele, with lots of choices for dining and entertainment. It provides a fine, comfortable base from which to explore. Niggles? The hustling for passengers to attend art auctions is aggressive and annoying, as is the constant bombardment for revenue activities and the daily junk mail that arrives at one's cabin door. There are many announcements – particularly annoying are those that state what is already written in the daily program. There is little connection to the sea from many public rooms. Passenger hallways are quite plain.

A per-person service charge you can't change is added to your account daily; 15 percent is also added

BERLITZ'S RATINGS

	Possible	Achieved
Ship	500	353
Accommodation	200	145
Food	400	238
Service	400	265
Entertainment	100	74
Cruise Experience	400	267

OVERALL SCORE 1342 points out of 2000

for bar charges, and a whopping 18 percent for spa treatments.

ACCOMMODATION. There are numerous price categories, from the smallest interior (no-view) cabins to the largest suites. The price you pay depends on size, grade, and location.

All standard cabins have two lower beds that convert to a queen-size bed, a small lounge area with sofa and table, and a decent amount of closet space, but very little drawer space, and the cabins themselves are disappointingly small. However, each is decorated in bright Hawaiian style, with an explosion of floral themes and vibrant colors.

Over 200 outside-view cabins have their own private balcony. Each cabin has a small vanity/writing desk, color TV, safe, climate control, and a laptop computer connection socket. Audio can be obtained only through the TV set. Bottled water is placed in each cabin – but your account will be charged if you open it.

The largest accommodation comes in the form of four Owner's Suites. Each has a hot tub, large teak table, two chairs, and two sunloungers outside on a huge, private, forward-facing teakwood-floor balcony just under the ship's navigation bridge, with floor-to-ceiling windows. Each suite has a separate lounge and bedroom.

There are 10 Junior Suites, each with a private teak-decked balcony, in a secluded position overlooking the ship's aft. They have almost the same facilities as the Owner's Suites, except for the outdoor hot tub, and less space.

DINING. Freestyle Dining has no assigned dining rooms, tables or seats, so you can choose which restaurant to eat in, at what time, and with whom. In reality, this means you have to make reservations for a specific time, so 'freestyle dining' turns out to be programmed dining.

The main dining rooms – Palace Restaurant, with 510 seats, and Crossings Restaurant, with 556 seats – have tables for four, six, or eight and an open-seating arrangement. The cuisine in both includes regional specialties. However, it's best to have dinner in one of the specialty restaurants, as the food in these two large dining rooms is just so-so.

A smaller eatery, the 83-seat Plantation Club Restaurant, is an à la carte, light-eating option, serving 'healthy' spa dishes and tapas. It has half-moon-shaped alcoves and several tables for two. The wine list is quite decent and well arranged, with moderate prices, although you won't find many good vintage wines. The cutlery is very ordinary, and there are no fish knives.

For classic and nouvelle French cuisine, the 102-seat Bistro has an à la carte menu. The decor is inspired by royal and aristocratic gardens. For premium steaks and lamb chops, there's Cagney's Restaurant, with 84 seats, intimate seating alcoves, and good food, at extra cost.

Other eateries include Pacific Heights, a casual Pacific Rim/Asian Fusion eatery that has steaks plus local fish and seafood. Casual, self-serve buffet-style meals can be taken in the Garden Café.

ENTERTAINMENT. The 1,000-seat, two-deck-high (main and balcony levels) Stardust Theater is the venue for production shows and major cabaret acts, although the sight lines are quite poor from some seats. A number of bands and solo entertaining musicians provide live music for listening and dancing in several lounges and bars.

SPA/FITNESS. Body Waves is the health/fitness spa; it includes an exercise studio, a fitness room, and several treatment rooms. It is operated by Mandara Spa, headquartered in Honolulu but owned by Steiner Leisure. A sizeable gratuity is added to spa treatments.

Sports fans will appreciate the large basketball/volleyball court, baseball-batting cage, golf-driving net, platform tennis, shuffleboard, and table tennis facilities. A sports bar, with baseball and surfing themes, has live satellite television coverage of sports events and major games on TV screens. Joggers can take advantage of a walk-around indoor/outdoor jogging track.

NORWEGIAN SPIRIT
★★★+

THIS IS A MID-SIZED SHIP THAT PROVIDES A CASUAL, LIVELY, ACTIVE VACATION

Size:	Mid-size Ship	Passenger/Crew Ratio (lower beds):	2.0
Tonnage:	75,338	Cabins (total):	988
Cruise Line:	Norwegian Cruise Line	Size Range (sq ft/m):	150.6–638.3/14.0–59.3
Former Names:	*SuperStar Leo*	Cabins (for one person):	0
Builder:	Meyer Werft (Germany)	Cabins with balcony:	374
Entered Service:	Oct 1998/May 2004	Cabins (wheelchair accessible):	4
Length (ft/m):	879.2/268.0	Wheelchair accessibility:	Good
Beam (ft/m):	105.6/32.2	Elevators:	9
Propulsion/Propellers:	2 diesels (50,400kW)/2	Casino (gaming tables):	Yes
Passenger Decks:	10	Swimming Pools:	2
Total Crew:	948	Self-Service Launderette:	No
Passengers (lower beds):	1,976	Library:	Yes
Passenger Space Ratio (lower beds):	38.1	Onboard currency:	US$

THE SHIP. A full walk-around promenade deck outdoors is good for strolling and has lots of space, including a whole area devoted to children's outdoor activities and pool. Inside, there are two indoor boulevards and a stunning, two-deck-high central atrium lobby with three glass-walled lifts and ample space to peruse the shops and cafés that line its inner sanctum. The lobby itself is modeled after the lobby of Hong Kong's Hyatt Hotel, with little clutter from the usual run of desks found aboard other cruise ships.

The interior design theme revolves around art, architecture, history, and literature. The ship has a mix of both Eastern and Western design and decor details. Three stairways are each carpeted in a different color, which helps new passengers find their way around.

A 450-seat room atop the ship functions as an observation lounge during the day and a nightclub at night, with live music. From it, a spiral stairway takes you down to a navigation bridge viewing area, where you can see the captain and bridge officers at work.

There is a business and conference center – good for small groups – and a writing room, and a smoking room for those who enjoy cigars and cognac. A shopping concourse is set around the second level of the lobby.

The casino complex is at the forward end of the atrium boulevard on Deck 7 (not between show-lounge and restaurant as in most Western ships).

BERLITZ'S RATINGS		
	Possible	Achieved
Ship	500	353
Accommodation	200	145
Food	400	238
Service	400	269
Entertainment	100	66
Cruise Experience	400	267

OVERALL SCORE 1338 points out of 2000

This includes Maharajah's, a brightly lit casino, with gaming tables and slot machines.

The dress code is extremely casual – no jacket and tie needed. With many dining choices, some of which cost extra, to accommodate different tastes and styles, your cruise and dining experience will largely depend on how much you are prepared to spend.

Norwegian Spirit is quite a stunning ship that features a wide choice of dining venues. Delivering a consistently good product depends, however, on the quality of the service staff. Watch out for the many extra-cost items in addition to the extra-charge dining spots.

Note that a non-changeable per person service charge is added to your account daily; 15 percent is also added for bar charges, and a whopping 18 percent for spa treatments.

ACCOMMODATION. Three whole decks of cabins have private balconies, while two-thirds of all cabins have an outside view. Both the standard outside-view and interior cabins really are very small – particularly given that all cabins have extra berths for a third/fourth person – although the bathrooms have a good-size shower enclosure. So, take only the least amount of clothing you can manage with. All cabins have a personal safe, cotton towels, and cotton duvets. In cabins with balconies, the balconies are extremely narrow, and the cabins themselves are very small – the ship was originally constructed for three-and four-day cruises.

Choose one of the six largest Executive Suites (named Hong Kong, Malaysia, Shanghai, Singapore, Thailand, and Tokyo) and you'll have an excellent amount of private living space, with separate lounge and bedroom with a large en-suite bathroom with gorgeous mosaic tiled floors, kidney bean-shaped whirlpool tubs, dual washbasins, separate shower enclosures with floor-to-ceiling ocean-view windows, and separate toilets with glass doors. The Singapore and Hong Kong suites and the Malaysia and Thailand suites can be combined to form a double suite – useful for families with children. Butler service and a concierge come with the territory.

Twelve Zodiac Suites, each named after an astrological sign, are the second largest type of accommodation, and also have a butler and concierge. Each has a separate lounge, bedroom, bathroom, and an interconnecting door to an ocean-view cabin with private balcony – again, good for families. All cabinetry features richly lacquered woods. The bedrooms are small but have a queen-size bed; there is a decent amount of drawer space, although the closet space is limited because it contains two personal safes.

A small room service menu is available; all non-food items cost extra, and a service charge and a gratuity are added to your account.

DINING. There are eight places to eat, two at extra cost, so you need to plan where you want to eat well in advance or you may be disappointed.

Windows Restaurant: the equivalent of a main dining room, it seats 632 in two seatings, is two decks high at the aft-most section, and has huge cathedral-style windows set in three sections overlooking the ship's stern and wake. Waiter stations are tucked neatly away in side wings, which help to keep down noise levels.

Other dining options (some cost extra) include:

The Garden Room Restaurant: this venue has 268 seats.

Raffles Terrace Café is a large self-serve buffet restaurant with indoor/outdoor seating for 400 and pseudo-Raffles Hotel-like decor, with rattan chairs, overhead fans, etc.

Moderno Churrascaria: a Brazilian steakhouse with 'passadores' serving skewered meats table-side. Reservations are required, and there's a cover charge.

Taipan: a Chinese Restaurant, with traditional Hong Kong-themed decor and items such as dim sum made from fresh, not frozen, ingredients. Cover charge applicable, and reservations needed.

Shogun Asian Restaurant: a Japanese restaurant and sushi bar, for sashimi, sushi, and tempura. A section can be closed off to make the Samurai Room, with 22 seats, while a traditional Tatami Room has seats for eight. There's also a Teppanyaki grill, with 10 seats, where the chef cooks in front of you and displays his knife-juggling skills.

Maxim's: a small à la carte restaurant with ocean-view windows; fine cuisine in the classic French style. Cover charge applicable, reservations necessary.

Blue Lagoon Café: a small, casual café for cooked-to-order savory fast food. Adjacent is a street bar called The Bund.

In addition, The Café, in the atrium lobby, is a patisserie serving several types of coffees, teas, cakes, and pastries, at extra cost.

ENTERTAINMENT. The Stardust Theater, with just under 1,000 seats, is the showlounge; it is two decks high, with a main and balcony levels. There are almost no support columns to obstruct the sight lines, and a revolving stage for review-style shows. The venue is also used as a large-screen cinema, and has excellent surround sound.

SPA/FITNESS. The Roman Spa and Fitness Center is on one of the uppermost decks, just forward of the Tivoli Pool. It has a gymnasium full of high-tech muscle-toning equipment, and aerobics exercise room, hair and beauty salon, and saunas, steam rooms, and changing rooms for men and women, as well as several treatment rooms, and aqua-swim pools that provide counter-flow jets for swimming against the current. The spa facility is operated by the Hawaii-based Mandara Spa, which is owned by Steiner Leisure.

The fitness and exercise rooms, with the latest Cybex muscle-pumping equipment, are located not within the spa, but at the top of the glass-domed atrium lobby. Included is a room for exercycle classes. Sports facilities include a jogging track, golf driving range, basketball and tennis courts, and there are four levels of sunbathing decks.

NORWEGIAN STAR
★★★+

A FINE FAMILY-FRIENDLY, MULTI-CHOICE SHIP FOR ACTIVE TYPES

Size:	Mid-size Ship	Passenger/Crew Ratio (lower beds):	2.1
Tonnage:	91,740	Cabins (total):	1,174
Cruise Line:	Norwegian Cruise Line	Size Range (sq ft/m):	142.0–5,350.0/13.2–497.0
Former Names:	none	Cabins (for one person):	0
Builder:	Meyer Werft (Germany)	Cabins with balcony:	410
Entered Service:	Dec 2001	Cabins (wheelchair accessible):	20
Length (ft/m):	964.9/294.1	Wheelchair accessibility:	Best
Beam (ft/m):	105.6/32.2	Elevators:	12
Propulsion/Propellers:	diesel-electric (39,000kW)/	Casino (gaming tables):	Yes
	2 azimuthing pods	Swimming Pools:	3
Passenger Decks:	12	Self-Service Launderette:	No
Total Crew:	1,083	Library:	Yes
Passengers (lower beds):	2,348	Onboard currency:	US$
Passenger Space Ratio (lower beds):	39		

THE SHIP. *Norwegian Star*, a sister ship to *Norwegian Dawn*, has a pod propulsion system. A large structure located forward of the funnel houses a children's play center, and, one deck above, the two outstanding 'villa' suites. The hull is adorned with a decal consisting of a burst of colorful stars and streamers.

There are plenty of sunloungers. Water slides are included for the adult swimming pools, while children have their own pools at the ship's stern.

Facilities include an Internet café, a showlounge with main floor and two balcony levels, 3,000-book library, card room, writing and study room, business center, karaoke lounge, conference and meeting rooms, a large retail shopping complex, and a casino.

With so many dining choices, some cost extra. The dress code is very casual – no jacket and tie needed, although you are welcome to dress formally if you wish. Although service levels and finesse are sometimes inconsistent, the level of hospitality is very good. But the hustling for passengers to attend art auctions is aggressive and annoying. Reaching room service tends to be an exercise in frustration.

A mandatory per-person service charge is added to your account daily; 15 percent is also added for bar charges.

ACCOMMODATION. With many price grades, there is something for everyone. There are 36 suites, including two of the largest aboard any cruise ship,

BERLITZ'S RATINGS		
	Possible	Achieved
Ship	500	360
Accommodation	200	145
Food	400	239
Service	400	266
Entertainment	100	67
Cruise Experience	400	269

OVERALL SCORE 1346 points out of 2000

balcony-class standard cabins, outside-view cabins (no balcony), interior cabins, and 20 wheelchair-accessible cabins. Suites and cabins with private balconies have easy-to-use sliding glass doors.

All have a hairdryer, tea- and coffee-making sets, and rich cherry wood cabinetry, and a bathroom with a sliding door and a separate toilet, and shower enclosure and washbasin compartments. There is plenty of wood accenting in all accommodation, including wood frames surrounding balcony doors.

The largest accommodation is in two huge Garden Villas (Vista and Horizon), located high atop the ship in a pod that is located forward of the ship's funnel, and overlooks the main swimming pool. Each measures 5,350 sq ft (497 sq m) and can be combined to create a huge, double-size 'house.' These villas have huge glass walls and landscaped private roof gardens (one has a Japanese-style garden, the other a Thai-style garden) for outdoor dining (with whirlpool tubs, naturally), and huge private sunbathing areas that are completely shielded.

Each of these villas has three bedrooms, one with a sliding glass door that leads to the garden, and bathrooms. One bathroom has a large corner tub, and two washbasins set in front of large glass walls that overlook the side of the ship as well as the swimming pool, although most of the view is of the overlarge water slide, and a large living room with Yamaha baby grand piano, glass dining table, and eight chairs. These units have their own private elevator and stairway access.

There are many suites (the smallest measures 290 sq ft/27 sq m) in several different configurations. Some overlook the stern, while others are in the forward part of the ship. All are lavishly furnished, although closet space in some of the smaller units is tight.

Although the suites and junior suites are quite spacious, the standard interior and outside-view cabins are very small when compared to those of other major cruise lines such as Carnival or Celebrity, particularly when occupied by three or four people. The bathrooms, however, are of quite a decent size and have large shower enclosures. Some cabins have interconnecting doors – good for families with children – and many cabins have third- and fourth-person pull-down berths or trundle beds.

A small room service menu is available; all non-food items cost extra, and a 15 percent service charge are added to your account. Bottled water is placed in each cabin, but a charge is made if you open the bottle.

DINING. Norwegian Cruise Line has championed more choices in dining than any other cruise line. Its 'Freestyle Dining' is good in that you can try different types of cuisine, in different settings, when you want. In practice, however, it means you need to make reservations. This takes a little planning and, often, involves waiting around. Food in the main dining rooms is poor to average (with few vegetables and garnishes, and an over use of rice as a carbohydrate source), but it can be much better in the extra-cost venues on the ship.

Versailles is a large (375-seat), ornate dining room, located aft and decorated in brilliant red and gold. It offers traditional six-course dining and has excellent views through windows that span two decks.

Aqua is a second large (374-seat), contemporary-styled dining room, offering lighter cuisine. It has an open galley, where you can view the preparation of pastries and desserts.

Cagney's Steakhouse: for (extra-cost, but well worth it) prime USDA steaks and grilled seafood items.

Moderno Churrascaria: a Brazilian-style steakhouse for meat and seafood dishes. Adjacent is a Sugar Cane Mohito Bar.

Ginza Asian Restaurant: this includes a sit-up sushi bar (complete with moving sushi belt), à la carte Japanese Hot Rock Ishiyaki cuisine, the adjacent Teppanyaki Grill (for lots of show and go), and a Noodle bar for Chinese noodles, wok-fried dishes, and dim sum.

Le Bistro: a French restaurant, with 66 seats, serving nouvelle cuisine and six courses.

Market Café: a large indoor/outdoor self-serve buffet eatery, with almost 400ft (122m) of buffet counter space. 'Action Stations' has made-to-order omelets, waffles, fruit, soups, ethnic specialties, and pasta dishes. Outside on deck is Topsiders Grill, for burgers and hot dogs.

O'Sheehans Neighborhood Bar and Grill: for down-home comfort food and drinks.

La Cucina: for casual family-style Italian cuisine.

Other spots include the Red Lion, an English pub for draft beer and a game of darts; Havana Club cigar and cognac lounge; Atrium Café, a lobby bar-café for hot and frozen coffees, teas, and pastries; Bier Garten, a beer garden serving grilled foods; Spinkles, an ice cream bar; and Gatsby's wine bar.

ENTERTAINMENT. The Stardust Theater, seating 1,037, is the venue for colorful Las Vegas-style production shows and major cabaret acts. Two or three production shows are presented in a typical seven-day cruise, all ably performed by Jean Ann Ryan Productions.

A number of bands and solo entertainers provide live music for listening and dancing to in several lounges and bars.

SPA/FITNESS. The two-deck-high Barong health spa complex, operated by the Steiner-owned Mandara Spa, is at the stern, with large ocean-view windows on three sides. A sizeable gratuity is automatically added for spa and beauty treatments.

The many facilities and services, almost all cost extra, include Thai massage. There is an indoor lap pool measuring 37ft (11m), a hydrotherapy pool, aromatherapy and wellness centers, several treatment rooms, and a juice bar.

The fitness and exercise rooms, with the latest equipment, are at the top of the atrium lobby. Recreational sports facilities include a jogging track, golf driving range, basketball and volleyball courts, as well as four levels of sunbathing decks.

NORWEGIAN SUN
★★★+

THIS IS ULTRA-CASUAL CRUISING ABOARD A FAMILY-FRIENDLY, MID-SIZE SHIP

Size:	Mid-size Ship	Passenger/Crew Ratio (lower beds):	2.1
Tonnage:	78,309	Cabins (total):	968
Cruise Line:	Norwegian Cruise Line	Size Range (sq ft/m):	120.5–488.6/11.2–45.4
Former Names:	none	Cabins (for one person):	0
Builder:	Lloyd Werft (Germany)	Cabins with balcony:	252
Entered Service:	Nov 2001	Cabins (wheelchair accessible):	6
Length (ft/m):	853.0/260.0	Wheelchair accessibility:	Good
Beam (ft/m):	105.8/32.2	Elevators:	12
Propulsion/Propellers:	diesel-electric (50,000kW)/2	Casino (gaming tables):	Yes
Passenger Decks:	12	Swimming Pools:	2
Total Crew:	916	Self-Service Launderette:	No
Passengers (lower beds):	1,936	Library:	Yes
Passenger Space Ratio (lower beds):	40.4	Onboard currency:	US$

THE SHIP. *Norwegian Sun* is a close sister ship to *Norwegian Sky*, but with an extra deck of balcony cabins, and additional cabins to accommodate the extra 200 crew needed for the Freestyle dining concept. The outdoor space is quite good, especially with its wide pool deck, with two swimming pools and four Jacuzzi tubs, and plenty of sunloungers, albeit arranged in camping-style rows.

A separate cabaret venue, Dazzles Lounge, has an extremely long bar. A large casino operates 24 hours a day. There's a shopping arcade, children's playroom, and a video arcade. Other facilities include a small conference room, library and beauty salon, a lounge for smoking cigars and drinking cognac, and an Internet café. You can expect to be subjected to a stream of flyers advertising daily art auctions, 'designer' watches, and other promotions, while 'artworks' for auction are strewn throughout the ship.

What this offers is plenty of bars and lounges to play in, and multiple dining and snacking options. But the food in the large dining rooms is not memorable, and the ship is full of revenue centers, designed to help you part you from your money.

A mandatory per person service charge is added to your account daily; 15 percent is also added for bar charges, and a whopping 18 percent for spa treatments.

ACCOMMODATION. There are many, many different price categories, depending on size and location.

BERLITZ'S RATINGS

	Possible	Achieved
Ship	500	357
Accommodation	200	145
Food	400	238
Service	400	265
Entertainment	100	74
Cruise Experience	400	268

OVERALL SCORE 1347 points out of 2000

The standard interior and outside-view cabins are very small when compared to those of other major cruise lines. All standard outside-view and interior cabins have common facilities, such as two lower beds that can convert to a queen-size bed, a small lounge area with sofa and table, and a decent amount of closet and drawer space, although the cabins themselves are disappointingly small. Over 200 outside-view cabins have a private balcony. All cabins have tea-/coffee-making sets, a safe, satellite-linked telephone, and bathroom with bath or shower.

The largest accommodation? Two Owner's Suites, each with a hot tub, large teak table, two chairs and two sunloungers outside on a huge, private, forward-facing teak-floor balcony, located just under the navigation bridge, with floor-to-ceiling windows. There are also two Honeymoon/Anniversary Suites, each with a separate lounge and bedroom

DINING. Freestyle Dining lets you choose which restaurant you would like to eat in, at what time, and with whom. Apart from two large dining rooms, there are a number of other themed eating establishments – although it is wise to plan in advance, particularly for dinner. Some incur an extra charge. The dress code states that: 'jeans, T-shirts, tank tops and bare feet are not permitted in restaurants.'

The two main dining rooms – the 564-seat Four Seasons Dining Room and the 604-seat Seven Seas

Dining Room – have tables for two, four, six, or eight. Sandwiched between the two (rather like a train carriage) is a third, 84-seat Italian Restaurant, Il Adagio, available for dining à la carte (extra charge, reservations required), with tables for two or four by the windows. Reservations are necessary.

Overall, the food is decent, but it lacks quality in terms of taste and presentation, although the menus make the dishes sound good. There's a reasonably decent selection of breads, rolls, cheeses, and fruits. The wine list is quite good and moderately priced, though the glasses are small.

Most dining venues are located on one of the uppermost decks, with great views from large picture windows, and include:

Le Bistro: a 90-seat dining spot for French-style meals, including tableside cooking. Reservations required.

Las Ramblas: a Spanish/Mexican style eatery serving tapas (light snack items).

Ginza: a Japanese Restaurant, with a sushi bar and a Teppanyaki grill (show cooking in a U-shaped setting where you sit around the chef). Reservations required.

East Meets West: a Pacific Rim Fusion Restaurant, featuring California/Hawaii/Asian cuisine à la carte. Reservations are necessary for dinner.

Moderno Churrascaria: Brazilian steakhouse and salad bar, with tableside meat carving. Reservations required.

Garden Café: a busy 24-hour restaurant indoor/outdoor self-serve buffet-style eatery with fast foods and salads.

There is no formal afternoon tea, although you can make your own at beverage stations (but it's difficult to get fresh milk, as non-dairy creamers are typically supplied). The service is, on the whole, adequate, nothing more.

ENTERTAINMENT. The Stardust Theater is a two-level showlounge with more than 1,000 seats and a large proscenium arch-topped stage. However, the sight lines are obstructed in a number of seats by several slim pillars. Two or three production shows are presented in a typical seven-day cruise (all ably performed by Jean Ann Ryan Productions). These are very colorful, high-energy, high-volume razzle-dazzle shows with extensive use of pyrotechnics, lasers, and color-mover lighting.

The ship carries a number of bands and solo entertaining musicians. These provide live music for listening and dancing in several of the lounges and bars, including the loud Dazzles, home to musical groups.

SPA/FITNESS. Bodywaves, at the top of the atrium, is a large health/fitness spa (including an aerobics room and separate gymnasium), several treatment rooms, and men's and women's saunas/steam rooms and changing rooms.

There is an indoor-outdoor jogging track, a large basketball/volleyball court, baseball batting cage, golf driving range, platform tennis, shuffleboard and table tennis facilities, and sports bar with 24-hour live satellite TV coverage of sports events and major games.

OASIS OF THE SEAS
★★★★

THIS HUGE FLOATING RESORT HAS ACTIVITIES GALORE FOR FAMILIES WITH BOUNDLESS ENERGY

Size:	Large Resort Ship	Passenger/Crew Ratio (lower beds):	2.4
Tonnage:	222,900	Cabins (total):	2,704
Cruise Line:	Royal Caribbean International	Size Range (sq ft/m):	150.6–1,523.1/14.0–141.5
Former Names:	none	Cabins (for one person):	0
Builder:	Aker Yards (Finland)	Cabins with balcony:	1,956
Entered Service:	Dec 2009	Cabins (wheelchair accessible):	46
Length (ft/m):	1,181.1/360.0	Wheelchair accessibility:	Good
Beam (ft/m):	216.5/66.0	Elevators:	24
Propulsion/Propellers:	diesel-electric (97,200kWW)/ 3 pods (2 azimuthing, 1 fixed)	Casino (gaming tables):	Yes
		Swimming Pools:	3
Passenger Decks:	16	Self-Service Launderette:	No
Total Crew:	2,164	Library:	Yes
Passengers (lower beds):	5,408	Onboard currency:	US$
Passenger Space Ratio (lower beds):	41.6		

THE SHIP. *Oasis of the Seas*, the world's first cruise ship measuring over 200,000 tons – essentially a large block of apartments sitting on a white hull – was a benchmark for all floating self-contained resorts. It is no longer the world's largest cruise ship – at time of printing, its sister ships *Allure of the Seas* and *Harmony of the Seas* had overtaken it, with Royal Caribbean International's *Symphony of the Seas* set to take the title of world's largest cruise ship from April 2018.

Still, this a stunning ship and a credit to its design team. There is a lot of outdoor and indoor/outdoor space for aqua-bathing and sports, although there's little actual space for sunbathing. There are several swimming pools, and an H2O Zone. Two large hot tubs hang over the ship's side.

Public spaces are arranged as seven 'neighborhoods': Central Park, the Boardwalk, the Royal Promenade, the Pool and Sports Zone, Vitality at Sea Spa/Fitness Center, Entertainment Place, and Youth Zone. The most popular are the Boardwalk and Central Park, both open to the air, and the indoor Royal Promenade.

The Boardwalk. With a design reminiscent of New York's Coney Island, the Boardwalk is home to trendy shops.

Eateries include the Boardwalk Donut Shop; Johnny Rockets, a burger/milk shake diner with juke-boxes; and Sabor (Mexican eats).

BERLITZ'S RATINGS

	Possible	Achieved
Ship	500	400
Accommodation	200	140
Food	400	234
Service	400	285
Entertainment	100	87
Cruise Experience	400	284

OVERALL SCORE 1440 points out of 2000

Central Park. This space is 328ft (100m) long, and has 27 real trees and almost 12,000 plants, including a vertical 'living' plant wall. Unlike its New York inspiration, it includes, at its lower level, a 'town center' (including a Tiffany & Co. store). At night, it's a quiet, serene area – good for couples. Vintages wine (and tapas) bar is a good chill-out place. There are several reservations-required, extra-charge dining venues; arguably the nicest is 150 Central Park, while Chops Grille and Giovanni's Table are also popular. Anyone in a Central Park cabin will need to take the elevator to get to the closest pool.

Central Park and the Boardwalk are open to the elements, so you might consider taking an umbrella, just in case it rains in the sunny Caribbean!

Royal Promenade. This is like shopping mall afloat, with casual food eateries (including a Starbucks at the forward end), shops with all kinds of merchandise, and changing color lights everywhere. Don't miss the 'Move On! Move On!' parade, a superb circus-like extravaganza including characters from DreamWorks' *Madagascar*. A hydraulic, oval-shaped Rising Tide Bar moves slowly through three floors and links the double-width Royal Promenade with Central Park.

The Pool and Sports Zone. Forward of the twin funnels is this fun area for families. An adults-only open-air solarium and rentable cabanas are part of the outdoor scene today (there are several). Two

FlowRiders are located atop the ship around the aft exhaust mast, as are basketball courts and mini-golf. The ship also has a really long jogging track.

The Solarium. This is a most welcoming large, light-filled, and restful (despite the background music) space. High up, it is frequented by few children – so adults can 'escape' the Vegas-like atmosphere of much of the ship.

In the casino, the roulette tables are all electronic and operated by touch buttons. There are also 450 slot machines, plus a player's club and poker room – but this really can be a smoke-filled place, even in the 'no-smoking' area.

The Caribbean itinerary includes a 'private' beach day at Labadee, the company's leased island. RCI built its own 800ft (244m) pier, making it simple for you to access the ship and beach several times during the day-long stay. Do try the zipline – it's long, and a real blast. Other fun things: an alpine coaster, a beach club with 20 private cabanas, a large artisans' market, and a Haitian Cultural Center.

Passenger niggles: Finding a sunlounger and, if you do, the space to store your things (they're so tightly packed together that there's little room for belongings). Exterior wooden railings have mostly been replaced by fiberglass ones – particularly noticeable on the balconies.

Oasis of the Seas operates from a purpose-built $75 million Terminal 18 in Port Everglades (Fort Lauderdale). If the two 'flybridge' gangways are working, disembarkation is relatively speedy, but, when only one is working, a line forms in the Royal Promenade, in which case it's better to sit somewhere until the line gets shorter. Disembarkation for non-US citizens can be appallingly slow.

The super-large *Oasis of the Seas* provides a fine all-round cruise and a wide range of choices for young adults and families with children. It's packed with innovative design elements, including a dramatic Central Park, a real park at sea. As might be expected, service is best in suite-class accommodation.

ACCOMMODATION. There are numerous accommodation price grades, reflecting the choice of location and size. Suite occupants get access to a concierge lounge and associated services. There are many family-friendly cabins, good for family reunions, but no solo-occupancy cabins. The cabin-numbering system is awkward to get used to. Note that cabin doors open outwards (towards you), as in many European hotels. In many of the lower grade accommodation, closet access is awkward – often with small sofas in the way. Most cabins feel extremely small, given the size of the ship. All cabins have an iPod dock.

Occupants of standard cabins (balcony and non-balcony class) should note that electrical sockets are located below the vanity desk unit in a user-unfriendly position. Also, it's difficult to watch television from the bed.

Washbasins in non-suite-grade cabins are tiny and low, at just 30.5ins (77.5cm) above floor level. Be careful – it's easy to hit your head on the mirror above. Small soap bars are provided, with shampoo provided in a dispenser in the shower enclosure. The shower head is fixed. Although there is no soap dish or indentation in the washbasin surround for soap, useful touches include a blue ceiling bathroom nightlight.

Cabins are exposed to noise and whatever is happening on the Boardwalk, including rehearsals and sports activities in the Aqua Theater aft, bells from the carousel (whose animal figures took six weeks to carve), rowdy revelers late at night, plus screaming ziplining participants high above during the day, loud music from bands playing at one of the pools, and exceedingly loud announcements by the cruise director repeating what's already printed in the daily program.

Boardwalk-view balcony cabin occupants need to close their curtains for privacy at times. However, the curved balconies – good for storing luggage to free up space inside the cabin – connect you with the open air and provide a community feeling, as you look across at balconies on the opposite side. Almost all have a sea view aft (just); those close to the aft Aqua Theater can use their balconies for a great view of any shows or events. Boardwalk-level cabins have windows but no balcony – and actually the view is mainly of the top of things such as the carousel or beach hut-like structures. The best Boardwalk balcony cabins are, in my view, located above on decks 8–12, but, for more privacy, book a sea-facing balcony cabin, not one overlooking the Boardwalk.

Some interior balcony cabins have either Central Park or Royal Promenade views from their curved interior balconies (four are wheelchair-accessible), plus 80 cabins with windows (no balconies) and Central Park views. But you'll need to keep your curtains closed for privacy, which rather defeats the object. Noise could be generated along the inner promenades, particularly late at night along with street parades and non-stop music.

Loft Suites. Although a few ships, such as the now-withdrawn QE2, *Saga Rose*, and *Saga Ruby*, had upstairs/downstairs suites, RCI introduced its version ('loft' suites) to the *Oasis*-class ships. These offer great views, with floor-to-ceiling, double-height windows, a lower living area plus a large balcony with sun chairs, and a stairway that connects to the sleeping area, which overlooks the living area. There are 28 Loft Suites; 25 of them measure 545 sq ft (51 sq m), while three more spacious ones measure 1,524 sq ft (141 sq m). Each sleeps up to six and has a baby grand piano, indoor and outdoor dining areas, a wet bar, and an 843-sq-ft (78.3-sq-m) balcony with flat-screen TV, and Jacuzzi. Two large Sky Loft Suites measure 722 sq ft (67 sq m) and 770 sq ft (71 sq m), and a 737-sq-ft (68-sq-m) Crown Accessible Loft Suite includes an elevator to aid disabled passengers.

DINING. Spanning three decks, Opus, the main dining room is cavernous. It has two seatings (early or late) for dinner, or you can choose 'My Time Dining' and eat at your preferred time. There are tables of all sizes, including some for family reunions.

Main dining room cuisine is all about standardized banquet catering and batch cooking. The menu descriptions sound tempting, but the food, although prepared well, is just so-so. Vegetarian and children's menus are also available. Note that there are no wine waiters.

Most meat dishes have heavy sauce reductions, and rice is overused as a source of carbohydrates. Green vegetables are scarce, but basic salad items are plentiful; the desserts are very decent. Breads and pastry items are also plentiful (though these are thawed and then baked from frozen 'starter' dough), but the croissants lack any hint of butter.

Other dining venues and eateries (some of which cost extra, but the food is mostly cooked to order) include favorites such as Chops Grille Steakhouse (for premium veal chops, steaks and seafood items) and Portofino (for Italian-American cuisine). Reservations (make them through the digital system) are required; note that menus do not change.

Others eateries include: 150 Central Park: the most exclusive restaurant combines cutting-edge cuisine with interesting design. An observation window into the kitchen allows passers-by to watch the chefs in action, preparing the multi-course tasting menu (open for dinner only).

Chef's Table, on the upper level of the Concierge Lounge, offers a multi-course meal with wine. It is hosted by the executive chef, but there are just 14 seats, so getting a reservation is difficult.

Giovanni's Table is a casual Italian dining spot with a rustic feel. It features toasted herb breads, pizzas, salads, pastas, sandwiches, braised meat dishes, and stews.

Izumi Hibachi & Sushi features Japanese-style cuisine, including a Teppanyaki menu (a show grill featuring cooks with acrobatic knives).

Sabor Taqueria & Tequila Bar is for modern tastes of Mexico.

Vintage is a wine bar with a robust selection of wines, accompanied by cheese and tapas (with a per-item charge).

Central Park Café, a casual dining spot with a high level of variety and flexibility, is an indoor/outdoor food market with line-up counters and limited waiter service. Items include freshly prepared salads, made-to-order sandwiches, paninis, crêpes, and hearty soups.

Other Boardwalk spots for snacking include: Boardwalk Dog House (for hot dogs, wieners, bratwurst, and sausages), the Donut Shop, and Ice Cream Shoppe.

Elsewhere, eateries include Sorrento's Pizzeria; Park Café (for salads and light bites); and Wipe Out Café.

For the sweet toothed, there's a 1940s-style Cupcake Shop. For lighter, more health-conscious fare, there's a self-serve section in the Solarium Bistro for breakfast and lunch – it's usually quieter, too.

Windjammer Café is the (free) casual, self-serve eatery common to all RCI ships. No trays are provided – just oval plates; because they're plastic, it's impossible to get a hot plate. If you are disabled or have mobility difficulties, do ask for help. Unfortunately, the venue is simply too small to handle the number of diners invading it at peak times – my advice is to try some of the other eateries to avoid the overcrowding. The food varies from quite acceptable to less so – fresh fruit tends to be hard and unripe. It's best to arrive early, when the food has just been cooked and displayed. Although there's a decent enough variety, the quality of some of the meat is poor, and the food is often overcooked.

Regular coffee is free in many venues, but espressos and cappuccinos (in paper cups) in Starbucks cost extra.

Check with RCI's website or your travel provider for the latest cover charges.

ENTERTAINMENT. The 1,380-seat main showlounge (Opal Theater), spread over three decks, stages the popular musical *Cats*, an excellent, 90-minute-long production, just like a Broadway show, while *Frozen in Time* is a stunning, must-see ice show at the ice-skating rink.

The 750-seat Aqua Theater, located outside at the ship's stern with a 6,000-sq-ft (557-sq-m) stage, is a stunning combination show theatre, sound stage, and events space (some great viewing places can be found high in the aft wings of the ship on both sides). The ship's stern has some 'overhang,' to accommodate the venue. A DreamWorks Animation aquatic acrobatic and dive show is also presented.

SPA/FITNESS. The Vitality at Sea Spa includes a Vitality Café for extra-cost health drinks and snacks. Its fitness center includes 158 cardio and resistance machines, while an extra-cost thermal suite includes saunas, steam rooms, and heated, tiled loungers. You can't just take a sauna for 10 minutes without paying for a one-day pass, however.

OCEAN DIAMOND
★★+

FOR 'SOFT' DISCOVERY CRUISING ABOARD A SMALL, VERY DATED SHIP

Size:	Boutique Ship	Passenger/Crew Ratio (lower beds):	1.4
Tonnage:	8,282	Cabins (total):	113
Cruise Line:	Quark Expeditions	Size Range (sq ft/m):	183.0–398.0/17.0–37.0
Former Names:	Le Diamant, Song of Flower, Explorer Starship	Cabins (for one person):	19
		Cabins with balcony:	10
Builder:	KMV (Norway)	Cabins (wheelchair accessible):	0
Entered Service:	1986/2012	Wheelchair accessibility:	None
Length (ft/m):	407.4/124.2	Elevators:	2
Beam (ft/m):	52.4/16.0	Casino (gaming tables):	Yes
Propulsion/Propellers:	diesel (5,500kW)/2 (CP)	Swimming Pools:	1
Passenger Decks:	6	Self-Service Launderette:	No
Total Crew:	144	Library:	Yes
Passengers (lower beds):	207	Onboard currency:	US$
Passenger Space Ratio (lower beds):	40		

THE SHIP. This vessel was originally built as the ro-ro vessel *Begonia* in 1974 and converted for cruising in 1986. Operated for many years by Radisson Seven Seas Cruises (now Regent Seven Seas Cruises), the ship was acquired in 2011 by a ship holding company, who chartered it to Quark Expeditions. It was modified to operate 'soft' expedition cruises and has tall twin funnels (with a platform between them) that give a somewhat squat profile. If only the foredeck and bow could be a little longer, the ship would look less ungainly. There is, however, a fairly decent amount of sheltered open-deck space.

The interior decor is warm, with pastel colors accented by splashes of color. Good-quality soft furnishings and fabrics make the ship feel chic and comfortable. The crew is caring and tries hard to make you feel at home during your cruise adventure.

BERLITZ'S RATINGS		
	Possible	Achieved
Ship	500	263
Accommodation	200	117
Food	400	214
Service	400	228
Entertainment	100	50
Cruise Experience	400	227

OVERALL SCORE 1099 points out of 2000

ACCOMMODATION. There are 10 fairly comfortable suites. All other accommodation grades are nicely equipped, but dated. However, all come with a good amount of closet and drawer space. Some cabins have bathtubs, but they are tiny – deep shower tubs would be a better description.

DINING. The dining room is quite charming and has warm colors, a welcoming ambience, and one seating, with no assigned tables. Tables are for two to six (some are subject to vibration at times).

ENTERTAINMENT. The well-tiered main lounge is ideal as a comfortable lecture hall, and there are good sight lines from almost all the banquette-style seats.

SPA/FITNESS. The health spa facility is compact and short on space, but is adequate, and includes a beauty salon and sauna.

OCEAN ENDEAVOUR
★★★

THIS STURDY SHIP IS ALL ABOUT NO-FRILLS DISCOVERY CRUISING FOR ADULTS

Size:	Boutique Ship
Tonnage:	12,907
Cruise Line:	One Ocean Expeditions
Former Names:	*Francesca, Konstantin, Simonov*
Builder:	Stettin Shipyard (Poland)
Entered Service:	1982/2016
Length (ft/m):	449.4/137.0
Beam (ft/m):	68.8/21.0
Propulsion/Propellers:	diesel/2
Passenger Decks:	6
Total Crew:	124
Passengers (lower beds):	198
Passenger Space Ratio (lower beds):	65.1
Passenger/Crew Ratio (lower beds):	1.5
Cabins (total):	99
Size Range (sq ft/m):	96.8–322.9/9.0–30.0
Cabins (for one person):	25
Cabins with balcony:	0
Cabins (wheelchair accessible):	0
Wheelchair accessibility:	None
Elevators:	0
Casino (gaming tables):	No
Swimming Pools:	1
Self-Service Launderette:	No
Library:	Yes
Onboard currency:	US$

THE SHIP. *Ocean Endeavour* is well engineered to visit the Polar Regions. However, it is a little over-sized to get really up close and per-sonal, even though it carries sev-eral zodiac inflatable landing craft and other expedition equipment, as well as water-sports items. The many thick and thin pillars in the public rooms are annoying – a result of the ship having been de-signed and built as a ferry.

There are several public rooms, but many of the chairs are of the low-back tub type. Some public are-as lack carpeting and can be noisy. Overall, however, the ship is comfortable, but quite basic.

The evenings consist of recaps and after-dinner conversation with fellow voyage participants. Note that there are extra charges for kayaking and stand-up paddleboarding.

ACCOMMODATION. There are several accom-modation price grades; the price you pay depends on the size, location, and grade you choose. From larg-est to the smallest (96.8 sq ft/9 sq m) to the largest (322.9 sq ft/30 sq m), each has its own washroom. Cabins are for one, two, or three persons, depend-ing on the category. All, however, are really basic,

BERLITZ'S RATINGS

	Possible	Achieved
Ship	500	278
Accommodation	200	112
Food	400	218
Service	400	230
Entertainment	100	50
Cruise Experience	400	232

OVERALL SCORE 1120 points out of 2000

and many have additional old-style pull-down berths (and ladders), with very little storage space for clothes and personal items. Note that the cabin beds may be rather short for anyone tall.

DINING. The Polaris Restaurant is a moderately attractive room that has mostly tables for four persons. Large windows provide plenty of natural light, and all chairs have armrests. Thick pillars break up the large room, which accommodates all passengers in a single seating. The food is hearty stuff, but there are few green vegetables, and the self-serve buffet selections for breakfast and lunch are pretty basic fare. Wine is provided during dinner, but the glasses are small.

ENTERTAINMENT. This consists of recaps and after-dinner conversation in one of the three loung-es, with one's fellow adventure participants.

SPA/FITNESS. There is a simple day spa (Mare), a small fitness/workout room (with a few machines), and, close by on the same deck, one sauna each for men and women.

OCEANA
★★★+

THIS SHIP IS FOR FAMILY-FRIENDLY CRUISING IN A COMFORTABLE ENVIRONMENT

Size:	Mid-size Ship	Passenger/Crew Ratio (lower beds):	2.2
Tonnage:	77,499	Cabins (total):	975
Cruise Line:	P&O Cruises	Size Range (sq ft/m):	158.2–610.3/14.7–56.7
Former Names:	Ocean Princess	Cabins (for one person):	0
Builder:	Fincantieri (Italy)	Cabins with balcony:	410
Entered Service:	Feb 2000/Nov 2002	Cabins (wheelchair accessible):	19
Length (ft/m):	857.2/261.3	Wheelchair accessibility:	Good
Beam (ft/m):	105.6/32.2	Elevators:	11
Propulsion/Propellers:	diesel-electric (28,000kW)/2	Casino (gaming tables):	Yes
Passenger Decks:	10	Swimming Pools:	4
Total Crew:	850	Self-Service Launderette:	Yes
Passengers (lower beds):	1,950	Library:	Yes
Passenger Space Ratio (lower beds):	39.7	Onboard currency:	UK£

THE SHIP. *Oceana* is all about British-ness and will be comfortingly familiar for families with children who want to travel and take their British traditions and food with them. It is suited to adults of all ages and families with children of all ages, and offers good value for money.

The all-white *Oceana* has a pleasing profile and is well balanced by its large funnel, which contains a deck tennis/basketball/volleyball court in its sheltered aft base. There is 93,000 sq ft (8,640 sq m) of open deck space and a wide, teakwood walk-around promenade deck. The pool deck is cluttered with white plastic chairs, which lack cushioned pads.

There is a good range of public rooms, lounges, and bars. The interior focal and social meeting point is a four-deck-high atrium lobby with winding, double stairways and two panoramic glass-walled lifts (the Captain's cocktail party is held here).

The Monte Carlo Club Casino, while large, is out of the main passenger flow. The most traditional room is the Yacht and Compass Bar, decorated in the style of a turn-of-the-century wood-paneled gentleman's club.

In the quest for increased onboard revenue, even birthday cakes are an extra-cost item, as are espressos and cappuccinos (unauthentic ones, made from instant coffee, are available in the dining rooms), ice cream and bottled water – items that can add up to a considerable amount. Expect to be subjected to flyers advertising daily art auctions, 'designer' watches, and other promotions. Gratuities are automatically charged

BERLITZ'S RATINGS		
	Possible	Achieved
Ship	500	344
Accommodation	200	128
Food	400	238
Service	400	270
Entertainment	100	68
Cruise Experience	400	259

OVERALL SCORE 1307 points out of 2000

to your onboard account. *Oceana* is based in Dubai during the the winter.

ACCOMMODATION. There are many different cabin grades, designated as: suites with private balcony; mini-suites with private balcony; outside-view twin-bedded cabin with balcony; outside-view twin bedded cabin; and interior twin-bedded cabins. Although the standard outside-view and interior cabins are a little small, they are well designed and functional in layout, and are decorated in earth tones accentuated by colorful bedspreads.

Many outside-view cabins have private (narrow) balconies, although the balcony partition is not of the floor-to-ceiling type, so you can hear your neighbors clearly. Balconies have no lights. Many cabins have third- and fourth-person upper bunk beds – good for families with children – and all cabins have useful tea- and coffee-making facilities.

There is a reasonable amount of closet and abundant drawer and other storage space in all cabins; although adequate for a seven-night cruise, it could prove to be quite tight for longer. A refrigerator is also provided, and each night a chocolate will appear on your pillow. Bathrooms are small but practical. Fortunately, the shower enclosure is a decent size, and there's a small amount of shelving for your toiletries, genuine glasses, and a hairdryer.

Also standard in all cabins: Slumberland 8ins (20cm) sprung mattresses, 10.5-tog duvets (blankets and pillows, if you prefer), Egyptian cotton towels, and tea/coffee-making facilities with specialty teas (long-life milk is provided).

The largest accommodation is in six suites, two on each of three decks at the aft of the ship, with a private balcony giving great views over the stern. Each of these suites – Orcades, Orion, Orissa, Orontes, Oronsay, and Orsova (all P&O ships of yesteryear) has a large balcony, marble-clad bathrooms a Jacuzzi tub, and separate shower enclosure. The bedroom has wood accenting and detailing, indented ceilings, and TV sets in both bedroom and lounge areas, which also have a dining room table and four chairs.

DINING. There are two principal asymmetrically designed dining rooms, Adriatic and Ligurian, each seating about 500, located just off the two lower levels of the four-deck-high atrium lobby. One has open seating, and the other has two seatings. Each has its own galley, and is split into multi-tier sections, creating a feeling of intimacy, although there is much noise from waiter stations. Open-seating breakfast and lunch are provided; dinner is in two seatings.

The cuisine is decidedly British – sometimes adventurous, but always with plenty of curry dishes and other standard British comfort-food dishes. Don't expect exquisite dining – this is unpretentious British hotel catering that is attractive and tasty, with some excellent gravies and sauces to accompany meals, and desserts that are always decent. The wine list is quite reasonable. A statement in the onboard cruise folder states that P&O Cruises does not knowingly purchase genetically modified foods, though it makes no mention of all those commercial American cereals provided.

The Plaza, a self-serve buffet, is located above the navigation bridge, with great views. At night, it morphs into an informal dinner setting with sit-down waiter service.

Outdoors on deck, Horizon Grill has fast-food items for those who want to stay in their sunbathing attire.

For other informal eats, there is Café Jardin, with a Frankie's Bar & Grill-style menu serving Italian-inspired dishes; it is on the uppermost level of the atrium lobby.

Explorer's is for extra-cost 'premium' coffees, teas, and pastries, and Magnums is a Champagne/caviar bar.

ENTERTAINMENT. There are two showlounges – Footlights Theatre and Starlights – one forward, and one aft. Footlights is a 550-seat showlounge, for drama productions and movies. Starlights is a 480-seat cabaret-style lounge with bar.

A resident group of actors, singers, and dancers, who provide theater-style presentations including cut-down versions of well-known musicals. In addition, the ship features an array of cabaret acts who regularly travel the cruise ship circuit.

SPA/FITNESS. The Ocean Spa facilities are contained in a glass-walled complex on one of the highest decks aft and include a gymnasium, with high-tech muscle-pumping equipment, a combination aerobics/exercise-class room, sauna, steam room, and several treatment rooms.

The spa is operated by UK concession Harding Brothers.

One swimming pool is 'suspended' aft between two decks – it forms part of the spa complex. Two other (small) pools are located in the ship's center. Sports facilities include basketball, volleyball, badminton, and paddle tennis. Joggers can exercise on a walk-around open promenade deck. There's an electronic golf simulator – no need to bring your own clubs.

OOSTERDAM
★★★+

THIS IS A CONTEMPORARY, FAMILY-FRIENDLY SHIP WITH TRENDY DUTCH DECOR

Size:	Mid-sized Ship	Passenger/Crew Ratio (lower beds):	2.3
Tonnage:	82,305	Cabins (total):	924
Cruise Line:	Holland America Line	Size Range (sq ft/m):	185.0–1,318.6/17.1–122.5
Former Names:	none	Cabins (for one person):	0
Builder:	Fincantieri (Italy)	Cabins with balcony:	623
Entered Service:	Aug 2003	Cabins (wheelchair accessible):	28
Length (ft/m):	935.0/285.0	Wheelchair accessibility:	Good
Beam (ft/m):	105.6/32.2	Elevators:	14
Propulsion/Propellers:	diesel-electric (35,240kW)/	Casino (gaming tables):	Yes
	2 azimuthing pods	Swimming Pools:	2 (1 w/sliding glass door)
Passenger Decks:	11	Self-Service Launderette:	No
Total Crew:	800	Library:	Yes
Passengers (lower beds):	1,918	Onboard currency:	US$
Passenger Space Ratio (lower beds):	42.9		

THE SHIP. *Oosterdam* is one of a series of ships, designed for younger, vibrant, multi-generational, family-oriented cruisers.

Twin working funnels are the result of the slightly unusual machinery configuration with, in effect, two engine rooms – one with three diesels, and one with two diesels and a gas turbine.

There's a complete walk-around exterior teak promenade deck, with teak steamer-style sunloungers. An outdoor jogging track is laid around the mast and forward third of the ship. Exterior midships glass elevators on both port and starboard sides, provide ocean views. There are two centrally located swimming pools outdoors; one can be used in poor weather thanks to its retractable sliding glass roof. Two whirlpool tubs, adjacent, are abridged by a bar. A small pool is available for children.

The ship offers a range of public rooms with a comfortable, intimate atmosphere. In keeping with Holland America Line traditions, there's a collection of Dutch artworks and artifacts.

The intimate lobby spans just three decks, but it is topped by a beautiful, rotating Waterford crystal globe of the world. The interior decor is bright, yet comfortable. The ceilings are particularly noticeable in the public rooms. The cast-aluminum elevator doors are interesting – the design inspired by the Art Deco designs from New York's Chrysler Building.

There are two decks of entertainment/public rooms. A winding shopping street has several boutiques, and

BERLITZ'S RATINGS		
	Possible	Achieved
Ship	500	361
Accommodation	200	144
Food	400	233
Service	400	254
Entertainment	100	67
Cruise Experience	400	266

OVERALL SCORE 1325 points out of 2000

includes an Internet center, library, card room, art gallery, photo gallery, and several small meetings rooms. A casino (with gaming tables and slot machines) is large, but you have to walk through it to get from the restaurant to the showlounge. Ice cream is free at certain hours, and warm hors d'oeuvres are provided in all bars.

On other decks, you'll find the Queen's Lounge lecture room and the Culinary Arts Center, as well as bars and lounges including an Explorer's Lounge (lifestyle/coffee lounge), and a small movie-screening room.

The lobby reception area is small and removed from the main passenger flow on the two decks above it. Many pillars obstruct passenger flow and lines of sight throughout the ship. There are no self-service launderettes – something that families with children will miss, although special laundry packages are available.

ACCOMMODATION. There are many price categories. Lifeboats obstruct the view from some cabins on Main Deck. Some cabins can accommodate a third and fourth person but have little closet space, and only one personal safe. Suite occupants get exclusive use of the Neptune Lounge and concierge, priority embarkation and disembarkation, and other benefits. In many of the suites/cabins with private balconies the balconies are not so private and can be overlooked from various public locations.

Outside-view cabins. Standard outside cabins measure 197 sq ft (18 sq m). Interior (no-view) cabins are slightly smaller (183 sq ft/17 sq m).

Niggles include noisy air conditioning – the flow in cabins and bathrooms can't be turned off, and the only regulation is for temperature control.

Other grades include Penthouse Verandah Suites, which measure 1,318 sq ft (122 sq m). Deluxe Verandah Suites measure 563 sq ft (52 sq m). Verandah Suites are actually cabins, not suites, and measure 284 sq ft (26 sq m).

DINING. The 1,045-seat Vista Dining Room is aft. It spans two decks and is a stunning room, with seating on both levels. Both open seating, and fixed seating are available for dinner, while breakfast and lunch are open-seating (restaurant staff seat you when you enter). There are tables for two to eight. The waiter stations can be noisy for anyone seated adjacent to them.

With a few exceptions, the cuisine is rather unmemorable, because it's all about batch cooking for large numbers. There's a distinct lack of variety of green vegetables, too much use of rice, canned fruit, and already sliced and diced cheese. Still, you get friendly service from smiling Indonesian and Filipino stewards, and the plates are nice.

'Lighter option' meals are always available for the nutrition- and weight-conscious. Kosher meals are also available; these are prepared ashore, frozen, and brought to your table sealed in their original containers.

The 130-seat Pinnacle Grill has higher-quality ingredients and better presentation than in the main dining room. Pacific Northwest cuisine is featured, including premium-quality steaks. There are fine table settings, china, and silverware, and leather-bound menus. A wine bar offers mostly American wines. Reservations are needed, and there's a cover charge.

For casual eating, Lido Café is a self-serve buffet-style eatery that wraps around the funnel housing and extends aft, with fine views over the multi-deck atrium. Movement through the buffet area can be slow at peak times. Each evening, one side is turned into an extra-cost, 72-seat Canaletto Restaurant – a quasi-Italian informal eatery with waiter service.

Also, a poolside 'Dive-In at the Terrace Grill' features multi-choice signature burgers (with Dive-In sauce), hot dogs, and fries, and, on certain days, barbeques may be featured.

An extra-cost Windsurf Café in the atrium lobby (open most of the day) has coffee, pastries, snack foods, deli sandwiches, and, in the evenings, liqueur coffees.

ENTERTAINMENT. The 867-seat Vista Lounge is the venue for Vegas-style revues and cabaret shows. The main-floor level has a bar in its starboard aft section. Spiral stairways at the back of the lounge connect all levels. Stage shows are best seen from the upper levels, which have good sight lines.

SPA/FITNESS. The Greenhouse Spa is a two-deck-high facility, located directly above the navigation bridge. It includes a solarium, a hydrotherapy pool, and a unisex thermal suite, incorporating a laconium, hammam, and chamomile grotto. There is also a salon, several private massage/body-treatment rooms including one for couples, and a fitness room with floor-to-ceiling windows. Sports enthusiasts can enjoy a basketball court, volleyball court, and golf simulator.

ORIANA
★★★+

THIS SHIP OFFERS BRITISH DECOR, STYLE, AND FOOD FOR ADULTS-ONLY CRUISING

Size:	Mid-size Ship	Passenger/Crew Ratio (lower beds):	2.4
Tonnage:	69,153	Cabins (total):	936
Cruise Line:	P&O Cruises	Size Range (sq ft/m):	150.6–500.5/14.0–46.5
Former Names:	none	Cabins (for one person):	2
Builder:	Meyer Werft (Germany)	Cabins with balcony:	118
Entered Service:	Apr 1995	Cabins (wheelchair accessible):	8
Length (ft/m):	853.0/260.0	Wheelchair accessibility:	Good
Beam (ft/m):	105.6/32.2	Elevators:	10
Propulsion/Propellers:	diesel (47,750kW)/2	Casino (gaming tables):	Yes
Passenger Decks:	10	Swimming Pools:	3
Total Crew:	760	Self-Service Launderette:	Yes
Passengers (lower beds):	1,870	Library:	Yes
Passenger Space Ratio (lower beds):	36.9	Onboard currency:	UK£

THE SHIP. Although now over 20 years old, *Oriana, with its blue funnel,* has a feeling of timeless elegance. There's a good amount of outdoor space, with enough (white plastic) sunloungers for all, and an extra-wide, traditional walk-around outdoor promenade deck. The stern superstructure is rounded, and several tiers overlook a pool and hot tub. In 2011, *Oriana* changed from a ship for family cruising to adults-only – and, as such, is better suited to longer cruises. The former children's playrooms were converted into additional cabins. Vibration at the stern still persists (it has been a problem for years).

Inside, the design provides good horizontal passenger flow and wide passageways, with decor that is gentle and welcoming. Of note are some fine, detailed ceiling treatments. The interior focal point is a four-deck-high atrium. It is quite elegant but not glitzy, and is topped by a dome of Tiffany glass. The many public rooms provide plenty of choice.

The L-shaped Anderson's Lounge – named after Arthur Anderson, co-founder of the Peninsular Steam Navigation Company in the 1830s – contains an attractive series of 19th-century marine paintings and is decorated in the manner of a fine London club.

Atop the ship and forward is the Crow's Nest, a U-shaped observation lounge with a small wing for small group privacy. A long bar includes a model of *Oriana* and others in a glass case. Two small stages are set into the forward port and starboard

BERLITZ'S RATINGS	Possible	Achieved
Ship	500	349
Accommodation	200	136
Food	400	245
Service	400	280
Entertainment	100	69
Cruise Experience	400	264

OVERALL SCORE 1343 points out of 2000

sections, each with a wooden dance floor. The library has inlaid wood tables and bookcases crafted by Viscount Linley's company, and some comfortable chairs. By the second day of any cruise, the library will have been almost stripped of books by word-hungry passengers. Adjacent is Thackeray's, a reading/writing room named after the novelist William Makepeace Thackeray, a P&O passenger in 1844. Lord's Tavern, decorated with cricket memorabilia, is a sporting place to pitch a beverage or two, or partake in a singalong. There's also a small casino with table games and slot machines, and, unusually for a mid-sized ship today, not only a small cinema/lecture room but also a decent-sized room for card players.

The carpeting throughout was replaced in 2016 and is of a high quality, much of it custom designed. Some fine pieces of sculpture add the feeling of a floating museum, and original artworks by all-British artists include several tapestries and sculptures.

Occasional theme cruises cover areas such as antiques, art appreciation, classical music, comedy, cricket, gardening, motoring, popular fiction, and Scottish dancing.

Most cabin stewards and dining-room personnel are from India, and provide service with a warm smile. However, in the quest for increased onboard revenue, even birthday cakes cost extra, as do proper espressos and cappuccinos – fakes, made from instant coffee, are available in the dining rooms. Ice cream and bottled water also cost extra.

Anyone cruising aboard *Oriana* will get a well-organized cruise experience. It suits mature adults seeking to cruise aboard a mid-sized vessel with the facilities of a small resort.

ACCOMMODATION. There are various categories, from interior (no-view) cabins to small suites, priced according to size and location.

Standard interior cabins and outside-view cabins are well equipped, but compact. There is much use of rich, warm limed oak or cherry wood, which makes even the least-expensive interior cabin inviting. All have good closet and drawer space, small refrigerator, full-length mirror, and blackout curtains (essential for North Cape cruises), premium Slumberland mattresses, duvets, and high-quality bedding. Some can accommodate a third or fourth person, so sharing with friends can make for an economical cruise. Cabin soundproofing could be better, however.

The modest-size standard cabin bathrooms have mirror-fronted cabinets, soft lighting, and wall-mounted hairdryers. High-quality toiletries are by The White Company; suite occupants get larger bottles of these.

There are a number of cabins for solo travelers. (Anyone sharing a cabin should note that only one personal safe is provided in most twin-bedded cabins.)

The few balcony cabins (called 'outside deluxe') measure 210 sq ft (19.5 sq m), and have ample closet and drawer space. The bathrooms are really dated, and have a very small, plain washbasin. One would expect marble or granite units in these grades.

There are also eight suites, each measuring 500 sq ft (46 sq m), with butler service.

DINING. There are two main restaurants: Peninsular (located amidships, for 'Freedom' dining) and Oriental (aft, for 'Club' dining; note that it can only be reached by the aft stairway). Both are moderately handsome, with tables for two to eight. In the aft dining room, however, the noise level is high at many tables – this is because of the room's position above the propellers, and vibration at almost any speed. Meals are mostly of the 'Middle-England' variety, and the presentation generally lacks creativity. Curries and other Indian-style dishes are heavily featured, particularly on luncheon menus. Afternoon tea is disappointing. The typical menu cycle is 14 days, and anyone on a long voyage may find it quite repetitive.

An adjacent Tiffany's Bar serves as a pre-dinner anteroom for drinks.

The Conservatory is for casual self-serve breakfast and luncheon buffets, and 24-hour self-serve beverage stands, although the selection of teas is poor, and the coffee is … well, let's not talk about that.

The 50-seat Beach House (evenings only) has ocean views from its upper-level location at the aft portside section of the buffet venue (mainly with outdoor seating).

ENTERTAINMENT. The well-designed Theatre Royal has a sloping floor and good sight lines from almost all seats. The fare is mainly British, from production shows staged by a resident company to top British 'names' and lesser artists. A second, smaller multi-function venue (Pacific Lounge) is for late-night comedy and cabaret, and for daytime lectures. However, pillars obstruct the stage from a number of seats.

Ballroom dance fans will appreciate the four good-sized wood dance floors aboard his ship. A professional dance couple hosts and teaches (social dancing time is always included in the programming).

SPA/FITNESS. The Oasis Spa is reasonably large, and the gymnasium has high-tech muscle-toning equipment. There's also a fairly big unisex sauna, a steam room each for men and women, several massage/body-treatment rooms, an aerobics room with wood floor, and a relaxation area with hot tub.

ORTELIUS
★★+

THIS SHIP IS EXTREMELY WELL-BUILT FOR EXPEDITION-STYLE CRUISING

Size:	Boutique Ship	Passenger/Crew Ratio (lower beds):	2.4
Tonnage:	4,575	Cabins (total):	58
Cruise Line:	Oceanwide Expeditions	Size Range (sq ft/m):	N/A
Former Names:	*Marina Svetaeva*	Cabins (for one person):	0
Builder:	Gdynia Shipyard (Poland)	Cabins with balcony:	0
Entered Service:	1989/Dec 2011	Cabins (wheelchair accessible):	0
Length (ft/m):	299.2/91.2	Wheelchair accessibility:	None
Beam (ft/m):	57.7/17.6	Elevators:	0
Propulsion/Propellers:	diesel/2	Casino (gaming tables):	No
Passenger Decks:	3	Swimming Pools:	0
Total Crew:	47	Self-Service Launderette:	No
Passengers (lower beds):	116	Library:	Yes
Passenger Space Ratio (lower beds):	39.4	Onboard currency:	US$

THE SHIP. This ice-strengthened ship was originally built for the Russian Academy of Science as a research vessel capable of navigating in ice-laden waters. Ortelius carries 11 zodiacs (9 are for use, and two are kept as reserve units) for shore landings, as well as two small helicopters (a helipad and hangar were added in 2007).

The ship is strong and well equipped for up-close-and-personal Polar discovery cruises. It also carries kayaks and scuba equipment (usage incurs an extra cost).

Although the interior decor is very plain and utilitarian, remember that this is an expedition ship. Nightly recaps, board games, books, and after-dinner conversation provide the entertainment.

ACCOMMODATION. There are six cabin categories and price grades, depending on the size, location (some have windows, those on the lowest deck have portholes), and grade you choose (some cabins have a double bed, but most of the fixed twin bed variety, and four cabins have two beds and two

BERLITZ'S RATINGS		
	Possible	Achieved
Ship	500	230
Accommodation	200	90
Food	400	210
Service	400	191
Entertainment	100	45
Cruise Experience	400	200

OVERALL SCORE 966 points out of 2000

upper berths. From the smallest to the largest, they are all rather minimalist in terms of creature comforts and decor (the beds have wooden surrounds; they are short, too), but they are adequate for sleeping in. The bathrooms are basic, but functional, but storage space for personal toiletries is limited.

DINING. Two dining rooms together accommodate all passengers in a single seating. They are plain but cozy (think rustic canteen-style). All tables have 'storm' edges, and seat six. The cuisine is best described as hearty comfort food (think meat and potatoes). Green vegetables and salad items are few and far between. Self-serve buffet selections for breakfast are pretty basic, to say the least.

ENTERTAINMENT. This consists of recaps and after-dinner conversation.

SPA/FITNESS. There are no facilities.

OVATION OF THE SEAS
★★★★

A HIGH-TECH, HIGH-ENERGY, BLING-FILLED CRUISE SHIP FOR THE WHOLE FAMILY

Size:	Large Resort Ship	Passenger/Crew Ratio (lower beds):	3.2
Tonnage:	168,666	Cabins (total):	2,090
Cruise Line:	Royal Caribbean International	Size Range (sq ft/m):	101.1–799.7/9.4–74.3
Former Names:	none	Cabins (for one person):	34
Builder:	Meyer Werft (Germany)	Cabins with balcony:	1,571
Entered Service:	May 2016	Cabins (wheelchair accessible):	34
Length (ft/m):	112.2/339.0	Wheelchair accessibility:	Good
Beam (ft/m):	134.5/41.0	Elevators:	16
Propulsion/Propellers:	diesel-electric/ 2 azimuthing pods	Casino (gaming tables):	Yes
Passenger Decks:	16	Swimming Pools:	3
Total Crew:	1,300	Self-Service Launderette:	No
Passengers (lower beds):	4,180	Library:	Yes
Passenger Space Ratio (lower beds):	40.3	Onboard currency:	US$

THE SHIP. *Ovation of the Seas* is a sister ship to *Anthem of the Seas* and *Quantum of the Seas* – a trilogy of innovative ships designed to create the 'wow' factor for families with children and technology fans.

The ship, which is based in Tianjin, China, and partly customized for the Asian market, features several high-tech attractions, such as North Star, a large cherry-picker-like glass pod for 14 persons including the operator – it lifts you off the ship for a stunning bird's-eye view. Located in the front section, just behind the ship's mast, it is wheelchair-accessible but only operates at sea.

Also neat is RipCord by iFly, a simulated skydiving experience in a two-storey vertical wind tunnel – for a taste of skydiving in a safe, controlled environment. The unit uses a powerful air flow to keep you up – rather like a giant hairdryer underneath you. Located aft of the ship's funnel it can accommodate 13 persons in each class; a turn in it includes two 'hovering in the air' experiences, instruction, and gear. Both attractions are bookable at interactive digital kiosks (adjacent to elevators) and tablets in public areas.

SeaPlex sports complex – located between the two funnels under the North Star – features adrenalin-boosting bumper car rides. It also has a court for basketball, volleyball, dodge ball, table tennis, a rock-climbing wall, and trapeze, plus SeaPlex Dog House (fast-food eatery). Outside, perched atop the SeaPlex is Mama and Baby (a giant art installation of a panda

BERLITZ'S RATINGS		
	Possible	Achieved
Ship	500	411
Accommodation	200	137
Food	400	289
Service	400	272
Entertainment	100	88
Cruise Experience	400	280

OVERALL SCORE 1477 points out of 2000

and its baby), providing a subtle link with the World Wildlife Fund.

Two70° is an innovative multi-level venue at the stern that provides a casual living area by day and at night becomes a foot-stomping, high-energy entertainment venue, with multiple dynamic robotic screens.

The decor is contemporary, but restrained and not really glitzy. There are some delightful Asian touches throughout (about $3.1 million has been spent on art pieces), including some interesting East-meets-West pieces – lookout for 'the 'gold finger' at Wonderland, and some eclectic white keyhole chairs. The multi-deck-high silk-effect sash-aying 'tapestry' that adorns the Royal Esplanade (indoor promenade – the focal point and social meeting 'street') is a delight, as is the kinetic ceiling sculpture called Sky Wave.

The Royal Esplanade includes Michael's Genuine Pub, Sorrento's pizza outlet, a Bionic Bar, Music Hall (a two-deck-high entertainment venue), several brand-name shops, a Schooner Bar, Boleros (Latin bar), the Music Hall, and a large Casino Royale – with gaming tables (including Chinese table games) and slot machines. A separate, super-exclusive room (by invitation only) is set aside for high-stake players. DreamWorks Animation characters will be on board too, including Po (from the Kung Fu Panda movies) – good for photo opportunities.

Ovation of the Seas provides an active cruise experience for the whole family (young ones absolutely love the facilities and programs aboard this ship), but, be warned: it's important to make reservations for the various restaurants and eateries if you want to be sure not to miss out on the different experiences. High-speed Wi-Fi is extremely expensive, but at least all cabins come equipped with one or more USB sockets for charging digital items. As on most large resort ships, if you stay in a suite-grade accommodation, you will receive more privileges and perks. If you don't, you'll be just one the crowd.

ACCOMMODATION. There are many different accommodation price grades and categories, with the price dependent on size (from grand loft-style suites with large wet rooms – to tiny studio cabins) and location. Every cabin has a real or virtual view. 'Virtual' balconies – first introduced aboard *Navigator of the Seas* in 2013 – are a neat feature of the interior cabins; they can provide real-time ocean views, but you *can* turn them off if you wish.

Standard cabins (the majority) are about 9 percent larger than those aboard the Oasis-class ships. Note that most cabin doors open outwards into the hallway, and not inwards into the cabin.

Loft cabins (including a 975 sq ft/90.5 sq m Owner's Loft) vary in size and configuration, but measure about 502 sq ft (46.6 sq m) and are located aft.

Inter-connecting family cabins are great for multi-generational groups. Some 15 units consist of a junior suite, balcony cabin, and interior studio, linked through a shared vestibule. Together they create 575.8 sq ft (53.5 sq m) of living space with three bedrooms, three bathrooms, and a 216-sq-ft (20-sq-m) balcony.

There are 34 'studio' cabins (12 have real balconies; all have wall beds) for solo occupancy. These cabins have their own pricing, as there are no supplements for solo occupancy.

Even the smallest bathroom is quite practical, with touches such as a night light, bedside power outlets, ample storage space, and shower and vanity hooks.

Negatives: tablet-based infotainment systems don't answer questions, and the breakfast room-service menu is poor.

DINING. There are 18 restaurant and eatery choices (there's no single main dining room as such). Suite occupants can eat in Coastal Kitchen (a private section of the Windjammer Marketplace).

Menu descriptions make the food sound better than it is, however, and the selection of breads, rolls, fruit, and cheese is limited. Overall, meals are rather hit and miss.

Some extra-cost restaurants require reservations. Note that the menus are the same each night in most extra-cost restaurants, and service can be slow (there are no assistant waiters). Dining 'packages' are available for purchase – these include costs for 3, 4, or 5 nights.

The following are complimentary (with tablecloths for dinner):

The Grande: with around 430 seats, the elegant Southern mansion-style hospitality restaurant features classic dishes reminiscent of the days of the grand ocean liners of yesteryear.

Chic: this 434-seat restaurant serves 'contemporary' cuisine and sauces made from scratch.

Silk: this restaurant features pan-Asian cuisine, including a touch of spice.

American Icon Grill: this 430-seat restaurant does many of America's favorite 'comfort food' dishes.'

Extra-cost venues, with either a cover charge or à la carte pricing, include:

Wonderland: based on the (real and imagined) elements of Fire, Ice, Water, Earth, and Dreams, this surreal 62-seat Alice in Wonderland-inspired venue features food with a quirky touch, using ingredients such as Japanese bonito flakes.

Jamie's Italian: it's a 132-seat reservations-required tablecloth-free Euro-Italian bistro – British celebrity chef Jamie Oliver's second restaurant at sea.

Chops Grille: for premium-quality steaks and grilled seafood (but an additional cost for dry-aged steaks and lobster, on top of the cover charge).

Chef's Table: this exclusive 16-seat venue (located within Chops Grille) can be booked for private parties, with wine-and-food pairing the specialty.

Izumi: a 44-seat Japanese-Asian fusion cuisine venue including hot-rock tableside cooking, sashimi, sushi, and sake.

Kung Fu Panda's Noodle Bar (located on the pool deck): this is the venue for some bold flavors, and traditional Chinese desserts (it replaces Johnny Rocket's aboard *Anthem of the Seas* and *Quantum of the Seas*). Look out for Po!

For casual meals at no extra cost, the 860-seat Windjammer Marketplace is a self-serve buffet-style eatery. Other casual (included) spots include: The Café at Two70°; SeaPlex Dog House; Sorrento's – for pizza slices and calzones; and Café Promenade.

ENTERTAINMENT. The Royal Theater spans three decks and seats 1,299. It is the principal showlounge for large-scale production shows and cabaret by a resident troupe of singers and dancers (reservations advised). During the day, on sea days, the venue acts as a large movie theatre.

Music Hall is a two-deck-high venue (with pool tables on the lower deck) for live shows that feature tribute acts from the rock scene.

SPA/FITNESS. The Vitality at Sea Spa facilities include: a thermal suite (extra cost), beauty salon, barber shop, and gymnasium with Technogym equipment. Massage and other body-pampering treatments take place in 19 treatment rooms, including one for acupuncture and two bookable, private treatment rooms for couples.

PACIFIC ARIA
★★★+

THIS FAMILY-FRIENDLY SHIP HAS TRENDY DECOR AND FOOD FOR AUSTRALASIANS

Size:	Mid-size Ship	Passenger/Crew Ratio (lower beds):	2.2
Tonnage:	55,819	Cabins (total):	630
Cruise Line:	P&O Cruises (Australia)	Size Range (sq ft/m):	186.2–1,124.8/17.3–104.5
Former Names:	Ryndam	Cabins (for one person):	0
Builder:	Fincantieri (Italy)	Cabins with balcony:	150
Entered Service:	Jan 1993/Nov 2015	Cabins (wheelchair accessible):	6
Length (ft/m):	719.4/219.3	Wheelchair accessibility:	Good
Beam (ft/m):	101.0/30.8	Elevators:	8
Propulsion/Propellers:	diesel-electric (34,560kW)/2	Casino (gaming tables):	Yes
Passenger Decks:	10	Swimming Pools:	2 (1 w/sliding glass dome)
Total Crew:	560	Self-Service Launderette:	Yes
Passengers (lower beds):	1,260	Library:	Yes
Passenger Space Ratio (lower beds):	44.3	Onboard currency:	Australian $

THE SHIP. This ship formerly sailed for Holland America Line and was refurbished and 'Aussified' for its new role. Those in the know may find it strange to see P&O on a white funnel, and might notice the dark hull leftover from the vessel's HAL days.

The exterior styling is quite angular, but the ship does have a full walk-around teakwood Promenade Deck outdoors – excellent for strolling and watching the water. A hydraulic glass roof covers the swimming pool, whirlpools, and central Lido area. Aft is The Oasis, a quiet area for (adult-only) relaxation, with its own small (dip) pool.

Inside, an asymmetrical layout helps to reduce bottlenecks and congestion. Most public rooms are on two decks, which creates a spacious feel. Atop the ship, with forward-facing views that wrap around the sides, is The Dome, an observation lounge with oceanview windows; by night it's a trendy nightspot.

The ship has a large, relaxing library and Internet-connect center. There's also a room for card games, a Mix Lounge for relaxing in and afternoon tea, an intimate Piano Bar, an indoor cinema, and a casino with gaming tables and slots.

ACCOMMODATION. There are 23 cabin price grades (a lot for this size of ship), but only 24 percent of all cabins have a balcony. The accommodation ranges from small interior cabins (with very little storage space) to cabins with balcony, to a large Penthouse Suite.

BERLITZ'S RATINGS

	Possible	Achieved
Ship	500	312
Accommodation	200	127
Food	400	242
Service	400	264
Entertainment	100	64
Cruise Experience	400	249

OVERALL SCORE 1258 points out of 2000

Occupants of suite-grade accommodation also get use of a Nespresso coffee machine and iPod docking station pre-loaded with music, plus priority reservations for specialty dining venues, spa treatment bookings, and shore excursions.

DINING. The Waterfront restaurant, located aft, features open seating, with tables for two to 10, but the waiter stations are noisy for anyone seated near them. The food is large-scale catering, but it's decent enough.

Other dining spots include: Angelo's, for Italian cuisine; Salt Grill by Luke Mangan (worth the extra cost for items cooked to order, and for the fresh oysters) and the adjacent bar; plus Dragon Lady for extra-cost Asian-fusion. For more casual eating, head to The Pantry, an array of food court-style outlets.

ENTERTAINMENT. The Marquee Theater is the showlounge; it spans two decks, with banquette-style seating. It is basically a well-designed room, but the sight lines from the balcony level are poor. Production shows are presented in the evening, with bingo games and trivia quizzes in the daytime.

SPA/FITNESS. The Spa includes a gym with all the latest exercise machines, aerobics area, a beauty salon, treatment rooms, and men's and women's sauna, steam room, and changing areas. The Edge features a high-adrenalin program that offers 20 different activities.

PACIFIC DAWN
★★★+

THIS DATED MID-SIZE SHIP IS A GOOD CHOICE FOR FAMILY-FRIENDLY CRUISING

Size:	Mid-size Ship	Passenger/Crew Ratio (lower beds):	2.2
Tonnage:	70,285	Cabins (total):	798
Cruise Line:	P&O Cruises (Australia)	Size Range (sq ft/m):	193.7–592.0/18.0–55.0
Former Names:	Regal Princess	Cabins (for one person):	0
Builder:	Fincantieri Navali (Italy)	Cabins with balcony:	148
Entered Service:	Aug 1991/Nov 2007	Cabins (wheelchair accessible):	13
Length (ft/m):	811.0/247.2	Wheelchair accessibility:	Fair
Beam (ft/m):	105.6/32.2	Elevators:	9
Propulsion/Propellers:	diesel (24,000kW)/2	Casino (gaming tables):	Yes
Passenger Decks:	11	Swimming Pools:	2
Total Crew:	725	Self-Service Launderette:	Yes
Passengers (lower beds):	1,596	Library:	Yes
Passenger Space Ratio (lower beds):	44.0	Onboard currency:	Australian $

THE SHIP. *Pacific Dawn* has all the right facilities to provide a pleasant cruise in comfortable, but somewhat dated, surroundings. A new waterpark was added in a 2017 refit, so sunbathing space is a bit tight when the ship is full.

There is no walk-around promenade deck outdoors – the only walking space being along the sides of the ship. Inside, the understated decor of soft pastel shades is highlighted by colorful artwork. A striking, elegant three-deck-high atrium has a grand staircase with fountain sculpture. The Dome, an observation dome set high atop the ship, houses a multi-purpose lounge/comedy club with live music.

ACCOMMODATION. There are numerous different price grades, ranked by location and size. In a recent refit, some 282 cabins had upper berths fitted to accommodate two adults and two children. In general, the cabins are well designed, with large bathrooms and good soundproofing. All cabins have walk-in closets, refrigerator, personal safe, and TV. Twin beds convert to queen-size beds in standard cabins. Lifeboats obstruct the view from the outside-view cabins for disabled passengers.

The 14 most expensive suites, each with a private balcony, are well equipped, and storage space is generous, adequate even for long cruises.

DINING. The Waterfront Restaurant has open seat-

BERLITZ'S RATINGS		
	Possible	Achieved
Ship	500	318
Accommodation	200	134
Food	400	243
Service	400	265
Entertainment	100	68
Cruise Experience	400	260

OVERALL SCORE 1288 points out of 2000

ing for all meals. The food tastes good thanks to the use of fresh produce. An 'always available' selection is combined with multiple daily additions; vegetable and potato side orders are always provided.

For more intimate dining, with food prepared to order, try the specialty venue Salt Grill by Australian chef Luke Mangan. The fish specialties include barramundi and fresh oysters. There's a cover charge, and reservations are required. The downside is the intrusive background music.

Other eateries include Nick and Toni's (for Mediterranean-inspired cuisine) and Shell and Bones (for seafood).

The Pantry replaces the ship's former self-serve buffet. There is a Trattoria (nominal fee) for informal meals; this is popular at lunchtime and in the afternoons. There's also an extra-cost patisserie, Charlie's Bar, in the spacious lobby.

ENTERTAINMENT. The Marquee Showlounge spans two decks. There's plenty of live music for the bars and lounges, with a wide mix of classical, jazz, and dance, from solo pianists to showbands. Several times each cruise, a stunning laser light and sound show is presented in the atrium.

SPA/FITNESS. The Aqua Spa and fitness center has a gymnasium, exercise room, steam room, and sauna.

PACIFIC EDEN
★★★+

A GOOD MID-SIZE, FAMILY-FRIENDLY SHIP AIMED AT AUSTRALASIANS

Size:	Mid-size Ship	Passenger/Crew Ratio (lower beds):	2.2
Tonnage:	55,819	Cabins (total):	630
Cruise Line:	P&O Cruises Australia	Size Range (sq ft/m):	186.2–1,124.8/17.3–104.5
Former Names:	*Statendam*	Cabins (for one person):	0
Builder:	Fincantieri (Italy)	Cabins with balcony:	150
Entered Service:	Nov 1994/Nov 2015	Cabins (wheelchair accessible):	6
Length (ft/m):	719.3/219.3	Wheelchair accessibility:	Fair
Beam (ft/m):	101.0/30.8	Elevators:	8
Propulsion/Propellers:	diesel-electric (34,560kW)/2	Casino (gaming tables):	Yes
Passenger Decks:	10	Swimming Pools:	2 (1 w/sliding glass dome)
Total Crew:	560	Self-Service Launderette:	Yes
Passengers (lower beds):	1,260	Library:	Yes
Passenger Space Ratio (lower beds):	44.3	Onboard currency:	Australian $

THE SHIP. *Pacific Eden* formerly sailed for Holland America Line and was refurbished and 'Aussified' for its new role Down Under. The ship's exterior styling is pretty boxy, but there is a full walk-around teakwood Promenade Deck outdoors – good for strolling and whale-watchingA hydraulic glass roof covers the swimming pool and whirlpools and central Lido area. Aft is The Oasis, a quiet area for (adult-only) relaxation, with its own small (dip) pool.

Inside, an asymmetrical layout helps to reduce bottlenecks and congestion. Most public rooms are concentrated on two decks, which creates a spacious feel. Atop the ship, with forward-facing views that wrap around the sides, The Dome is an observation lounge with ocean-view windows by day; by night it's a trendy nightspot. The atrium foyer is three decks high, although its sculptured centerpiece, *Fountain of the Sirens*, makes it a bit crowded, and leaves little room in front of the reception desk.

The ship has a decent-sized library, and Internet-connect center. There's also a room for card games, a Mix Lounge for relaxing in and afternoon tea, an intimate Piano Bar, indoor cinema (and culinary center), and a casino with gaming tables and slots. Children and teens have their own areas, but they are not expansive.

ACCOMMODATION. There are many cabin price grades; just under a quarter of all cabins have a balcony. Cabins range from small interior cabins (with very little

BERLITZ'S RATINGS		
	Possible	Achieved
Ship	500	318
Accommodation	200	127
Food	400	242
Service	400	264
Entertainment	100	64
Cruise Experience	400	251

OVERALL SCORE 1260 points out of 2000

storage space) to a seriously large Penthouse Suite. All benefit from shoeshine, express ironing, laundry, bathrobes and slippers, pillow menu, and yoga mat. Occupants of suite-grade accommodation also get use of a Nespresso coffee machine and iPod docking station pre-loaded with music, plus priority reservations.

DINING. The Waterfront restaurant is at the aft of the ship. It features open seating, with tables for two to 10. Other dining venues and eateries include: Angelo's (named for Italian photographer Angelo Frontoni), for Italian cuisine; the specialty venue Salt Grill by Luke Mangan (worth the extra cost for food that is cooked to order); or Dragon Lady for extra-cost Asian-fusion cuisine. For more casual eating, head to The Pantry, which provides an array of self-serve outlets, similar to a food court.

ENTERTAINMENT. The Marquee Theater is the showlounge; it spans two decks, and has banquette-style seating. It is basically a well-designed room, but the sight lines from the balcony level are quite poor. Production shows are presented in the evening, with bingo games and trivia quizzes in the daytime.

SPA/FITNESS. The Spa includes a workout room with high-tech machines, ocean views, an aerobics area, beauty salon, treatment rooms, and men's and women's sauna and steam rooms. The Edge features a high-adrenalin program with 20 different activities.

PACIFIC EXPLORER
★★★+

THIS MID-SIZE SHIP HAS STYLISH DECOR FOR AUSTRALASIAN FAMILIES

Size:	Mid-size Ship
Tonnage:	77,499
Cruise Line:	P&O Cruises Australia
Former Names:	*Dawn Princess*
Builder:	Fincantieri (Italy)
Entered Service:	May 1997/Jun 2017
Length (ft/m):	857.2/261.3
Beam (ft/m):	105.6/32.2
Propulsion/Propellers:	diesel-electric/2
Passenger Decks:	10
Total Crew:	924
Passengers (lower beds):	1,950
Passenger Space Ratio (lower beds):	39.7
Passenger/Crew Ratio (lower beds):	2.1
Cabins (total):	975
Size Range (sq ft/m):	135.0–635.0/12.5–59.0
Cabins (for one person):	0
Cabins with balcony:	446
Cabins (wheelchair accessible):	19
Wheelchair accessibility:	Good
Elevators:	11
Casino (gaming tables):	Yes
Swimming Pools:	3
Self-Service Launderette:	Yes
Library:	Yes
Onboard currency:	Australian $

THE SHIP. *Pacific Explorer* has a fairly stylish profile balanced by a large funnel. There is a wide, teak walk-around outdoor promenade deck and 93,000 sq ft (8,640 sq m) of space, plus two large waterslides in a mega-waterpark (great for kids – but watch out for the 'flying fox'), a large poolside movie screen, and an adults-only (extra-cost) Sanctuary relaxation area.

The interiors have attractive decor, appealing colors, and artwork. There are a number of dead ends in the interior layout, so it's not as user-friendly as a ship this size should be. The interior focal point is a four-deck-high atrium lobby with winding, double stairways, two panoramic glass-walled elevators, and a dance floor.

There are numerous public rooms, bars and lounges, including a library, casino (with gaming tables and slot machines), Internet-connect center, shops (Atrium Boutiques), photo gallery, café, and art gallery (plus so-called 'art' auctions). One bar is decorated in the style of a late 19th-century gentleman's club, with dance floor and comfortable seating. The focal point is a large ship model, *Kenya*, from the P&O collection archives.

Niggles include the fact that cruising aboard ships such as this has become increasingly about extra on-board revenue; also, the swimming pools are small, given the number of passengers. As aboard most ships, if you live in the top suites, you'll be well cared for; if not, you'll just be one of a crowd.

BERLITZ'S RATINGS

	Possible	Achieved
Ship	500	353
Accommodation	200	145
Food	400	243
Service	400	275
Entertainment	100	68
Cruise Experience	400	272

OVERALL SCORE 1356 points out of 2000

ACCOMMODATION. There are many, many different cabin price grades. Although the standard interior (no view) and outside view cabins are small, they are well designed and functional in layout; they are decorated in earth tones, accentuated by splashes of color from the bedspreads. Proportionately, there are a lot of interior (no view) cabins. Many outside-view cabins are quite well soundproofed. Note that the balcony partition on cabins with private balconies are not the floor-to-ceiling type, so you can hear your neighbors clearly, or smell their smoke (if they smoke). The balconies are very narrow, only just large enough for two small chairs, and there is no outdoor light fitting. All cabins have reasonable closet and abundant drawer and shelf space, and a refrigerator. The bathrooms are really tight spaces, only appropriate for one person at a time. However, they do have a decent shower enclosure, a small amount of shelving for toiletries, a hairdryer, and a bathrobe.

The largest accommodation comes in the form of six suites, two on each of three decks located aft. There are also wheelchair-accessible cabins, which measure 213–305 sq ft (19.7–28.2 sq m); these consist of seven outside-view and 12 interior cabins.

DINING. The two main dining rooms (both simply called Restaurant) are of asymmetrical design, and each has about 500 seats. They are located adjacent to the two lower levels of the atrium lobby. Each is split into multi-tier sections, which helps to create a feeling of intimacy, although there is noise from the waiter stations adjacent to many tables. Breakfast and lunch are provided in an open-seating arrangement, while dinner is in two seatings (at 5.45pm and 7.45pm). Note that there are no wine waiters.

Other restaurants/eateries include the popular Salt Grill by Luke Mangan (think: sardines in a tin on a plate) in a great location overlooking the pool area.

The Black Circus is an extra-cost, reservations-required supper club with cabaret entertainment.

The Pantry is a casual self-serve food court-style eatery (it includes Nic and Toni's for Mediterranean specialties), while poolside there's a lobster and burger bar.

ENTERTAINMENT. There are two showlounges, both theatre and cabaret style. The main one, Marquee Theater, has a sloping floor, with aisle-style seating (as found in shoreside movie theaters) that is well tiered, and with good sight lines to the raised stage from most of the 500 seats.

A second showlounge, Vista Lounge, located aft is for cabaret, lectures, and other presentations.

SPA/FITNESS. A glass-walled health spa complex located high atop the ship includes a gymnasium with the latest high-tech machines. One swimming pool is 'suspended' aft between two decks. There are two other pools, although they are not large for the size of the ship.

Sports facilities are located in an open-air sports deck positioned inside the funnel and adaptable for basketball, volleyball, badminton, or paddle tennis. Joggers can exercise on the walk-around open Promenade Deck.

PACIFIC JEWEL
★★★+

A MID-SIZE SHIP FOR ACTIVE FAMILY-FRIENDLY AUSSIE CRUISING

Size:.. Mid-size Ship	Passenger/Crew Ratio (lower beds):...................... 2.6
Tonnage: 70,310	Cabins (total): 837
Cruise Line: .... P&O Cruises (Australia)	Size Range (sq ft/m): 193.7–398.2/18.0–37.0
Former Names: *Ocean Village Two, AIDAblu, A'RosaBlu,*	Cabins (for one person):................................. 0
Crown Princess	Cabins with balcony:.................................... 198
Builder: .... Fincantieri Navali (Italy)	Cabins (wheelchair accessible): 10
Entered Service: .... Jul 1990/Dec 2009	Wheelchair accessibility: .... Fair
Length (ft/m): 805.7/245.6	Elevators: 9
Beam (ft/m): 105.8/32.2	Casino (gaming tables): .... Yes
Propulsion/Propellers: diesel-electric (24,000kW)/2	Swimming Pools: 2
Passenger Decks: 11	Self-Service Launderette:.................................. Yes
Total Crew: 621	Library: .... Yes
Passengers (lower beds): 1,674	Onboard currency: ....Australian $
Passenger Space Ratio (lower beds): 42	

THE SHIP. *Pacific Jewel* is best suited to young Australian couples, single travelers, families, and single-parent families with children seeking a good-value-for-money first cruise in a casual, mid-sized ship setting, with appealing itineraries and destinations and a range of fun-filled activities. The young, vibrant staff members make passengers feel welcome.

Originally ordered by Sitmar Cruises, this ship debuted in 1990 as *Crown Princess* but has since assumed many identities. It was moved to the A'Rosa Cruises brand and, as *A'Rosa Blu*, began operating cruises for the German-speaking family market in 2002. Two years later, it was refitted and renamed *AIDAblu* for AIDA Cruises, then became *Ocean Village Two* for the UK's Ocean Village brand. In 2009 it turned into *Pacific Jewel*, specifically for the Australian market.

It has a dolphin-like upper front structure made of lightweight aluminum alloy, originally designed to keep the weight down in line with stability requirements. It was designed by Renzo Piano, the renowned Italian architect behind the Centre Georges Pompidou in Paris and Japan's Kansai International Airport, Osaka. A large swept-back funnel, also made from aluminum alloy, is placed aft.

Facilities are in line with the tastes of young, active Aussie families and single travelers. The interior layout is a bit disjointed, however. Some innovative and elegant styling is mixed with traditional features

BERLITZ'S RATINGS		
	Possible	Achieved
Ship	500	322
Accommodation	200	139
Food	400	243
Service	400	264
Entertainment	100	67
Cruise Experience	400	258

OVERALL SCORE 1293 points out of 2000

and a reasonably spacious interior layout. An understated decor of soft pastel shades is highlighted by splashes of color, as well as some colorful artwork.

The oval-shaped atrium lobby is three decks high and has a grand staircase as its focal point; it provides a good meeting and gathering point. Shops, bars, and lounges span out from the lobby on three decks. Other facilities include an Internet café, Mix Bar, and Charlie's Bar. Child-free areas include Oasis, a sunbathing quiet zone aft on Deck 10, and the Aqua Spa and Health Center.

There is no decent outdoor or indoor forward observation viewpoint, and no walk-around promenade deck outdoors, the only walking space being along the port and starboard sides of the ship. In fact, there's little contact with the outdoors, and sunbathing space is quite limited. Other niggles include the many support pillars throughout the public rooms; these obstruct sight lines and impede passenger flow.

P&O Cruises (Australia) scrapped automatic tipping from October 2010, so tips are at your discretion. P&O provides good value for money, particularly when compared to most land-based resorts in Australia. Some cruises have special themes, such as food and wine. The onboard product is playful and casual, and its delivery is highly targeted to the Australasian lifestyle. The crew are extremely friendly, and service is better than you can find in many parts of Australia.

ACCOMMODATION. There are many different price categories, including mini-suites with private balconies, outside-view cabins, interior cabins, and cabins for the disabled. Generally, accommodation on the higher decks will cost more because, aboard ship, location is everything. Occupants of mini-suites (there are 36) get more space, a larger bathroom, and premium bathroom amenities.

Single-parent families comprise an increasing number of today's cruise passengers, so a good number of two-bed cabins also have a third (or third/fourth) pull-down berth that would suit their needs well.

In general, the well-designed cabins have large bathrooms as well as decent soundproofing. Walk-in closets, refrigerator, personal safe, and color TV are provided in all of them. Twin beds convert to queen-size beds in most cabins. Bathrobes and toiletries are provided. Views from the outside-view cabins for the disabled are obstructed by lifeboats, as are those from some other cabins on the same deck (Deck 8).

The most expensive suites have a private balcony, and are quite well laid out to a practical design. The bedroom is separated from the living room by a heavy wooden door; there are TV sets in both rooms, and closet and drawer space are generous.

DINING. There are two principal restaurants, several decks apart: Plantation and The Waterfront. There are a few tables for two, but most are for four to eight. Plantation is open 24 hours a day, while The Waterfront is open for breakfasts, lunches, and dinner at times given in the daily program. There's a neat table for 10 persons in the Wine Room (within The Waterfront) for use as a Chef's Table, complete with a dégustation menu.

The Waterfront's menu is really varied and caters to the multicultural, multi-ethnic passenger mix. The food has good taste, thanks to the use of fresh Australian produce and meat and other items of Australian origin. It is perhaps best described as modern Australian fare. An 'always available' selection is combined with multiple daily additions, plus vegetable and potato side orders ('sides' in Aussie-English).

For something a little more special, extra-charge full service dining is available in the intimate bistro-style restaurant, Salt Grill by Luke Mangan (think: Sydney crab omelet with miso mustard broth); it's

worth the extra cost for food that is cooked to order. It is located forward of the main pools, on the starboard side, and a cover charge applies.

La Luna, a small, casual deck restaurant adjacent to the aft pool and funnel, serves Asian-style cuisine.

For coffee, tea, chocolate, and sweet snacks during the day, and drinks in the evening, Charlie's Bar is an extra-cost patisserie/bar on the lower level of the spacious lobby.

ENTERTAINMENT. The Marquee Theatre, the venue for main entertainment events, spans two decks, with seating on both main and balcony levels. Several support pillars obstruct sight lines from a number of seats. There's plenty of colorful entertainment, including a song and dance troupe, and a good stable of Aussie cabaret acts. A high-energy acrobatic-and-dance deck show is provided for warm nights under the stars, on a stage and acrobatic archway fitted during one of the ship's refits.

Connexions (lounge/bar) is an adults-only comedy venue that doubles as a karaoke and live music venue. Also, if you like country and western music, hoedowns, and line dancing, you'll find your tastes are catered for.

SPA/FITNESS. The Aqua Spa and Health Club, an extensive wellness center, spans two decks and measures almost 14,000 sq ft (1,300 sq m); a staircase connects two levels. Located at the top of the ship at the forward stairway, it occupies the space in the 'dolphin head' section. With its curved surfaces, walking the treadmills or exercycling and facing out to sea (albeit on the port side) makes you feel you're doing so in the upper deck of a Boeing 747.

Panoramic saunas and hammam steam room are on the lower level; a seven-day pass for the sauna and steam rooms costs extra. The reception area has a waterfall and cypress trees, and there are 11 treatment rooms for facials, massages (including hot stones and couples massage), manicure and pedicure, dry float and hydrobath. There is also a solarium, and a four-person relaxation room. It's a very nice spa facility.

The spa is operated by a specialist concession. Some exercise classes and health talks are free; others may incur a charge.

PACIFIC PRINCESS
★★★+

THIS SHIP HAS ENGLISH COUNTRY HOUSE DECOR AND STYLE FOR MATURE-AGE CRUISERS

Size:	Small Ship	Passenger/Crew Ratio (lower beds):	1.8
Tonnage:	30,277	Cabins (total):	344
Cruise Line:	Princess Cruises	Size Range (sq ft/m):	145.3–968.7/13.5–90.0
Former Names:	R Three	Cabins (for one person):	0
Builder:	Chantiers de l'Atlantique (France)	Cabins with balcony:	232
Entered Service:	Aug 1999/Nov 2002	Cabins (wheelchair accessible):	3
Length (ft/m):	593.7/181.0	Wheelchair accessibility:	Good
Beam (ft/m):	83.5/25.5	Elevators:	4
Propulsion/Propellers:	diesel-electric (18,600kW)/2	Casino (gaming tables):	Yes
Passenger Decks:	9	Swimming Pools:	1
Total Crew:	373	Self-Service Launderette:	Yes
Passengers (lower beds):	688	Library:	Yes
Passenger Space Ratio (lower beds):	44.1	Onboard currency:	US$

THE SHIP. *Pacific Princess* is a decent choice for mature adults who seek value for money aboard a comfortable small ship with plenty of dining choices and limited entertainment.

The ship (the smallest in the fleet) has an all-white hull, which makes it appear larger than it is – and a large, square-ish funnel. A Lido Deck has a swimming pool and good sunbathing space, while one of the aft decks has a thalassotherapy pool. A jogging track circles the swimming pool deck, but one deck above. The uppermost outdoors deck includes a golf driving net and shuffleboard court.

Although there is no walk-around promenade deck outdoors, there is a small jogging track around the upper perimeter of the swimming pool, and on port and starboard side decks by the lifeboats. Instead of wooden decks outdoors, these are covered by Bolidt, a sand-colored rubberized material. Room service is extremely limited. Stairways, although carpeted, are tinny. In order to keep the prices low, often the air routing to get to/from your ship is not the most direct.

The interior decor is quite stunning and elegant, a throwback to ship decor of the ocean liners of the 1920s and '30s, executed in fine taste. This includes detailed ceiling cornices, both real and faux wrought-iron staircase railings, leather- and cherry wood-paneled wall, trompe l'oeil ceilings, and rich carpeting in hallways with an Oriental rug-look cent-

BERLITZ'S RATINGS

	Possible	Achieved
Ship	500	341
Accommodation	200	141
Food	400	247
Service	400	287
Entertainment	100	71
Cruise Experience	400	272

OVERALL SCORE 1359 points out of 2000

er section. The overall feel echoes that of an old-world country club. The staircase in the main, two-deck-high foyer recalls the staircase in the 1997 movie *Titanic*.

The public rooms are spread over three decks. The reception hall has a staircase with intricate wrought-iron railings. The Nightclub, with forward-facing views, sits high in the ship and has some Polynesian-inspired decor and furniture.

There are plenty of bars – including one in the entrance to each restaurant. Perhaps the nicest of all bars and lounges are in the casino bar/lounge that is a beautiful room reminiscent of London's grand hotels and understated gaming clubs. It has an inviting marble fireplace – in fact, there are three such fireplaces aboard – and comfortable sofas and individual chairs. There is also a large Card Room, which incorporates an Internet center with eight stations.

The Library is a lovely, grand Regency-style room, with a fireplace, a high, indented, trompe l'oeil ceiling, and a decent selection of books, plus very comfortable wingback chairs with footstools, and sofas you could sleep on; it's the most relaxing room aboard. There's very little entertainment, but it is not needed in the cruise areas featured. *Pacific Princess* is much more about relaxation than the larger Princess ships.

As with all Princess Cruises ships, 15 percent is added to all bar and spa accounts – most drink prices are moderate, but beer prices are high. A standard gratuity is automatically added to onboard accounts – to reduce the amount, you'll need to go to the reception desk.

There is a charge – tokens must be obtained from the reception desk – for using the machines in the self-service launderette. A change machine in the launderette itself would be more user-friendly.

ACCOMMODATION. There is a variety of about eight different cabin types to choose from, with prices linked to grade, location and size.

All of the standard interior cabins (no view) and outside-view cabins are extremely compact, and tight for two persons – especially for cruises longer than seven days. Cabins have twin beds or a queen-size bed, with good under-bed storage areas. The bathrooms have tiled floors and plain walls, and are compact, standard units; they include a shower enclosure with a removable, strong hand-held shower unit, hairdryer, (small) cotton towels, storage shelves for toiletries, and a retractable clothesline.

Note that the suites/cabins that have private balconies (66 percent of all suites/cabins, or 73 percent of all outside-view suites/cabins) have partial, and not full, balcony partitions, and sliding glass doors. Thanks to good design and layout, only 14 cabins on Deck 6 have lifeboat-obstructed views. The balcony floor is covered in thick plastic matting – teak would be nicer – and it has some awful plastic furniture.

Accommodation units designated as mini-suites are in reality simply larger cabins than the standard varieties, as the sleeping and lounge areas are not divided. While not overly large, the bathrooms have a good-size tub and ample space for storing toiletries. The living area has a refrigerated mini-bar, lounge area with breakfast table, and a balcony with two plastic chairs and a table.

The most spacious accommodation are 10 Owner's Suites. These are fine, large living spaces in the forward-most and aft-most sections of the accommodation decks. Particularly nice are those that overlook the stern, on decks 6, 7, and 8. They have bigger balconies that really are private and cannot be overlooked by anyone from the decks above. There is an entrance foyer, living room, bedroom, CD player, bathroom with Jacuzzi tub, and small guest bathroom. The bed faces the sea, which can be seen through the floor-to-ceiling windows and sliding glass door.

Note that all suites/cabins located at the stern may suffer from vibration and noise, particularly when the ship is proceeding at or close to full speed, or maneuvering in port.

DINING. There are four different dining spots – three restaurants and one casual self-serve buffet:

The Club Restaurant has 338 seats, all with armrests. There are large ocean-view windows on three sides, and some prime tables that overlook the stern, as well as a small bandstand for occasional live dinner music. However, the noise level can be high because of the single-deck-height ceiling.

Although portions are generous, the food and its presentation are not really memorable. Fish is often disguised by a crumb or batter coating, the choice of fresh green vegetables is limited, few garnishes are used, and cheese is already sliced and diced. But, this is banquet-style catering, which means standardization and cooking in batches. Pasta dishes are acceptable (though voluminous), typically served by section headwaiters, who may also make 'something special just for you' – in search of favorable comments and gratuities. If you like desserts, order a sundae at dinner (most other items are just so-so).

Extra-cost, reservations-required Sabatini's Trattoria has 96 seats (all with armrests), windows along two sides, and a set 'Bellissima' dégustation menu.

Extra-cost, reservations-required Sterling Steakhouse is an 'American steak house' with a good selection of prime steaks and other meats and seafood. It has 98 comfortable seats (with armrests), and windows along two sides. It has a set menu, together with added daily chef's specials.

The serve-yourself Lido Café is open for breakfast, lunch, and casual dinners. The buffet restaurant is open almost 24 hours a day. In addition, there is a Poolside Grill and Bar for fast food.

ENTERTAINMENT. The 345-seat Cabaret Lounge, in the forward part of the ship on Deck 5, is the main venue for entertainment events and some social functions. The single-level room has a stage, and circular hardwood dance floor with adjacent banquette and individual tub chair seating, and raised sections on the port and starboard sides. It is not a large room, and not really designed for production shows, so cabaret acts and local entertainment form the main focus. Mini-revue style shows with colorful costumes are presented by a troupe of resident singer/dancers. Art auctions and bingo take place almost daily.

SPA/FITNESS. Facilities, which are located in the forward part of the ship on a high deck (Deck 9), include a workout room with ocean-view windows, high-tech muscle-toning equipment, and treadmills. There are steam rooms but no sauna, changing areas for men and women, and a beauty salon with ocean-view windows.

The spa is operated by Steiner, whose retail products are also sold here. Some fitness classes are free, while some cost extra, as do massage, facials, pedicures, and beauty treatments.

PACIFIC VENUS
★★★+

THIS SHIP HAS COMFORTABLE DECOR AND DECENT STYLE FOR JAPANESE CRUISERS

Size:	Small Ship	Passenger/Crew Ratio (lower beds):	2.1
Tonnage:	26,518	Cabins (total):	238
Cruise Line:	Venus Cruise	Size Range (sq ft/m):	164.6–699.6/15.3–65.0
Former Names:	none	Cabins (for one person):	0
Builder:	Ishikawajima Heavy Industries (Japan)	Cabins with balcony:	20
Entered Service:	Apr 1998	Cabins (wheelchair accessible):	1
Length (ft/m):	601.7/183.4	Wheelchair accessibility:	Fair
Beam (ft/m):	82.0/25.0	Elevators:	4
Propulsion/Propellers:	diesel (13,636kW)/2	Casino (gaming tables):	Yes
Passenger Decks:	7	Swimming Pools:	1
Total Crew:	220	Self-Service Launderette:	Yes
Passengers (lower beds):	476	Library:	Yes
Passenger Space Ratio (lower beds):	55.7	Onboard currency:	Japanese yen

THE SHIP. The company Venus Cruise is part of Japan Cruise Line, which is itself part of SHK Line Group, a joint venture between the Shin Nihonkai, Hankyu, and Kampu ferry companies, which operate more than 20 ferries. There is a decent amount of open deck space aft of the funnel – good for deck sports – while protected sunbathing space is provided around a small swimming pool. All sunloungers have cushioned pads. The open walking promenade decks are rubber-coated steel – hardwood would be more desirable.

The base of the funnel is the site of a day/night lounge, which overlooks the pool; this is slightly reminiscent of Royal Caribbean International's funnel-wrapped Viking Crown lounges aboard its earlier ships. There is plenty of space per passenger. The decor is clean and fresh, with much use of pastel colors and blond woods, giving the interiors a feeling of warmth.

The dining rooms are located off Deck 7, which has a double-width indoor promenade, with high ceiling height. A three-deck-high atrium has a crystal chandelier as its focal point, and a white baby grand piano sits on its lower level, close to the Reception Desk.

There are special rooms for meetings and conference organizers, for use when the ship is chartered. A piano salon has colorful low-back chairs, and a large main hall has a finely sculptured high ceil-

BERLITZ'S RATINGS		
	Possible	Achieved
Ship	500	330
Accommodation	200	134
Food	400	258
Service	400	276
Entertainment	100	62
Cruise Experience	400	262
OVERALL SCORE 1322 points out of 2000		

ing and over 700 moveable seats. There's a 350-seat main lounge for cabaret shows and ballroom dancing, a small movie theater, and a library/writing room and card room. A casino gaming area is located as part of the Top Lounge set at the front of the funnel. Winners receive prizes instead of cash, under Japanese law. There's also a smoking room, Chashitsu (tatami mat) room, karaoke room (for rent), card room/Mahjong room, free self-service launderettes on each accommodation deck, and two (credit card/coin) public telephone booths.

Overall, this company provides a well-packaged cruise in a ship that has a comfortable, serene environment. The dress code is relaxed, and no tipping is allowed.

The ship has two classes: Salon Class and Standard Class. Salon Class passengers pay more, but get suite-grade accommodation, eat in a private dining room, and are given extra perks and services, including a welcome embarkation basket, more toiletries, and priority tickets for shows and shore tenders.

Pacific Venus is best suited to Japanese-speaking couples and solo travelers of mature years who appreciate very comfortable surroundings and good food and service, all at a relatively moderate cost. The ship is often operated under charter to travel organizations, so drinks aren't always included in the fare; when operated by Venus Cruise, alcoholic drinks are not included.

ACCOMMODATION. There are five types: Royal Suites, suites, deluxe cabins, state cabins (in four price grades), and standard cabins. All are located from the uppermost to lowermost decks, respectively. All suites and cabins have an outside view, but few cabins have a private balcony.

The four Royal Suites (Archaic, Elegant, Modern, and Noble) are decorated in two different styles – one contemporary, one in a more traditional Japanese style. Each has a private balcony (with a drinks table and two chairs) with sliding door, an expansive lounge with large sofa and plush armchairs, coffee table, window-side chairs and drinks table, floor-to-ceiling windows, and a large flat-screen TV set, with separate DVD unit. The bedroom has twin beds or a queen-size one, vanity/writing desk, and a large walk-in closet with personal safe. Also provided are high-quality binoculars, camera tripod, humidifier, tea/coffee-making set, and free mini-bar set-up. The large bathroom has ocean-view windows, Jacuzzi tub, a separate shower enclosure, and his/her washbasins.

Sixteen other suites have private balconies (with teak table and two chairs), a good-size living area with vanity/writing desk, dining table, chair and curved sofa, separate sleeping area, and bathroom with deep tub slightly larger than the Royal Suites, and single large washbasin. There is ample illuminated closet and drawer space (two locking drawers instead of a personal safe), and a DVD unit.

Some 20 deluxe cabins have large picture windows fronted by a large, curtained arch, a sleeping area with twin or queen beds, plus a daytime sofa that converts into a third bed.

So-called 'state' cabins, many with upper berths for third passengers, are in three price levels, and have decor that is best described as basic, with reasonable closet space but very little drawer space.

Standard cabins, however, are really plain, but can accommodate three persons – useful for families – although the drawer and storage space is a bit tight.

All accommodation grades have a tea set with electric kettle, TV set, telephone, and stocked mini-bar/refrigerator – all items included in the cruise price. Bathrooms have a hairdryer and lots of Shiseido toiletries, particularly in the suites. All room service menu items cost extra – this is typical of all Japanese cruise ships – except for Salon Class suite-grade accommodation. All passengers receive a yukata (a Japanese-style light cotton robe). Suite occupants also get a plush bathrobe, and all accommodation grades have electric, automatic toilets (washlets) with heated seats.

DINING. The Primavera Restaurant is located aft, with ocean views on three sides, and a high ceiling. Passengers dine in one seating, at tables for six, 10, or 12. The food consists of both Japanese and Western items; the menu is varied, and the food is attractively presented. For breakfast and lunch it includes a self-serve buffet, while dinner is typically a fully served set meal.

A separate, intimate 42-seat restaurant, Grand Siècle, is reserved for occupants of suite-grade (Salon Class) accommodation; it is tastefully decorated in Regency style, with fine wood-paneling and a detailed, indented ceiling. It has mostly tables for two (with plenty of space for correct service), better-quality chopsticks, nori seaweed, and better-quality fine china. Cold and hot towels are provided.

ENTERTAINMENT. Le Pacific Main Lounge is the venue for all shipboard entertainment and also functions as a lecture and activities room during the day. It is a single-level room with seating clustered around a thrust stage, so that entertainers are in the very midst of their audience.

On most cruises, special featured entertainers such as singers, instrumentalists, storytellers, and dance champions are brought on board from ashore.

SPA/FITNESS. Spa facilities comprise men's and women's Grand Baths, which include two bathing pools and health/cleansing stations. There are ocean-view windows, a steam room, a gymnasium with ocean-view windows (in a different location just aft of the funnel), and a sauna.

Japanese massage is available, as are hairdressing and barber services in the small salon, located on the lowest passenger-accessible deck of the ship.

PAUL GAUGUIN
★★★★

AN ELEGANT, COOL SHIP FOR CHIC WARM-WEATHER ISLAND CRUISING

Size:	Small Ship	Passenger/Crew Ratio (lower beds):	1.5
Tonnage:	19,200	Cabins (total):	166
Cruise Line:	Paul Gauguin Cruises	Size Range (sq ft/m):	200.0–588.0/18.5–54.6
Former Names:	none	Cabins (for one person):	0
Builder:	Chantiers de l'Atlantique (France)	Cabins with balcony:	89
Entered Service:	Jan 1998/Jan 2010	Cabins (wheelchair accessible):	1
Length (ft/m):	513.4/156.5	Wheelchair accessibility:	Fair
Beam (ft/m):	72.1/22.0	Elevators:	4
Propulsion/Propellers:	diesel-electric (9,000kW)/2	Casino (gaming tables):	Yes
Passenger Decks:	7	Swimming Pools:	1
Total Crew:	215	Self-Service Launderette:	No
Passengers (lower beds):	332	Library:	Yes
Passenger Space Ratio (lower beds):	57.8	Onboard currency:	US$

THE SHIP. Built by a French company specifically to operate in shallow waters, *Paul Gauguin* is now under long-term charter to Pacific Beachcombers of Tahiti, who also own the Intercontinental Tahiti, Intercontinental Bora Bora Le Moana, Intercontinental Bora Bora, and Intercontinental Moorea. The ship cruises around French Polynesia and the South Pacific, and, while it could carry many more passengers in terms of its size, it is forbidden to do so by French law. It has a well-balanced, all-white profile, and a single funnel.

Paul Gauguin is suited to couples and solo travelers seeking out-of-the ordinary itineraries, good regional cuisine and service, and plenty of scuba and snorkeling opportunities. It suits those who are happy with almost no evening entertainment. Where the ship really shines is in its variety of water-sports equipment, and its shallow draft that allows it to navigate and anchor in lovely little places that larger ships couldn't possibly reach.

The ship also has a retractable aft marina platform, and carries two water-skiing boats and two inflatable craft for water sports. Windsurfers, kayaks, plus scuba and snorkeling gear, and dive helmets are available for your use; all except scuba gear are included in the cruise fare. Islands, beaches, and water sports are what *Paul Gauguin* is good at. Perhaps the best island experience is in Bora Bora. Its shallow draft means there could be some movement, as

BERLITZ'S RATINGS		
	Possible	Achieved
Ship	500	371
Accommodation	200	160
Food	400	297
Service	400	311
Entertainment	100	70
Cruise Experience	400	275

OVERALL SCORE 1484 points out of 2000

the ship is a little high-sided for its size.

Inside, there is a pleasant array of public rooms, and both the artwork and the decor have a real French Polynesia look and feel. The interior colors are quite restful, although a trifle bland, but the new deck and direction signage has been improved, and the ship was refreshed during a 2011 refurbishment. The tub chairs in some of the public rooms are uncomfortable.

Expert lecturers on Tahiti and Gauguin accompany each cruise, and a Fare (pronounced *foray*) Tahiti Gallery features books, film, and other materials on the unique art, history, and culture of the islands. Three original Gauguin sketches are displayed under protective glass.

The dress code is totally relaxed – every day. The standard itinerary means the ship docks only in Papeete, and shore tenders are used in all other ports. There is little entertainment (and little needed), as the ship stays overnight in several ports. The high crew-to-passenger ratio translates to a high level of personalized service.

The ship has become a favorite of travelers to these climes, and the quiet, refined atmosphere on board gives it a clubby feel, with passengers getting to know each other easily. Wi-Fi spots are provided, but Internet charges are high. Le Casino has blackjack and roulette tables, while slot players will find 13 machines in an adjacent area.

A cruise aboard *Paul Gauguin* is all about connecting with French Polynesia, and the ship carries lecturers to inform you about the life, history, and sea life of the region.

All in all, the ship will provide you with a delightful, intimate cruise and product that most will really enjoy. Gratuities are included. Soft drinks and mineral water are included in the cruise price. Note that if you fly out to Tahiti a day or so before the cruise and stay in a hotel, bugs (insects) are a problem encountered by many travelers, so it is wise to take some insect repellent.

ACCOMMODATION. There are eight suite/cabin grades, priced according to location and size. The outside-view cabins, half of which have private balconies, are nicely equipped, although they are all strictly rectangular. Most have large windows, except those on the lowest accommodation deck, which have portholes. Each has a queen-size bed, or twin-size beds convertible to a queen, and wood-accented cabinetry with rounded edges. A minibar/refrigerator stocked with complimentary soft drinks, a DVD player, personal safe, hairdryer, and umbrellas are standard. A selection of L'Occitane toiletries is provided.

The marble-look bathrooms are large and pleasing and have a tub as well as a separate shower enclosure. All passengers are provided with 100 percent cotton bathrobes and cotton slippers. The two largest suites have a private balcony at the front and side of the vessel. Although there's a decent amount of in-cabin space, with a beautiful long vanity unit and plenty of drawer space, the bathrooms are disappointingly small and plain, and too similar to all other standard cabin bathrooms. Butler service is provided in all accommodation designated as Owner's Suite, Grand Suites, and ocean-view 'A' and 'B' category suites.

DINING. L'Etoile, the main dining room, is open for dinner only, while La Veranda, an alternative dining spot, serves breakfast, lunch, and dinner. Both have open seating, which means you can choose when you want to dine and with whom. This provides a good opportunity to meet new people for dinner each evening. The chairs have armrests, making it more comfortable for a leisurely mealtime. The dining operation is well orchestrated, with cuisine and service of a reasonably high standard. Select wines and liquor are included in the fare, while the limited selection of premium wines costs extra.

The 134-seat La Veranda Restaurant is one deck above L'Etoile, and has both indoor and outdoor seating. This is a self-serve buffet venue for breakfast and lunch. The breakfast buffets tend to be extremely repetitive (especially the boxed cereals), and lunch buffets are often a disappointment; there is, however, a decent selection of olive oils and sauces made on board. At night, the venue provides better, more creative fare in very pleasant surroundings (reservations are required, but there's no extra charge, and the capacity is limited to 75 persons). La Veranda provides dinner by reservation, with alternating French and Italian menus; the French menus are provided by Jean-Pierre Vigato, chef of the Michelin-starred Apicius, in Paris.

Located outdoors (but covered), Le Grill provides informal café fare on deck aft of the pool, with up 100 seats. Each evening it becomes Pacific Grill and serves Polynesian cuisine; although reservations are required, there is no extra charge.

For something different, it is possible to have dinner on the Marina platform on certain nights (when it's calm, of course).

ENTERTAINMENT. Le Grand Salon is the venue for shows and cabaret acts. It is a single-level room, and seating is a combination of banquettes and individual tub chairs. Sight lines are quite good from most seats, although there are some obstructions. Don't expect lavish production shows (there aren't any), as the main entertainment consists of local Polynesian shows brought on board from ashore, plus the odd cabaret act. A piano lounge was added in a 2006 refit.

SPA/FITNESS. The Deep Nature Spa, on Deck 6 in the ship's center, is the wellbeing space. It includes a fitness centre with muscle-pumping and body-toning equipment (in a windowless room), a steam room, several treatment rooms, changing area (very small), and beauty salon. Spa/beauty services and staff are provided by Algotherm. There is no sauna, but use of the steam room is complimentary. Body-pampering treatments include various massages, aromatherapy facials, manicures, pedicures, and hairdressing services.

PEARL MIST
★★★+

THIS SMALL SHIP SPECIALIZES IN US COASTAL AREA CRUISES

Size:	Boutique Ship	Passenger/Crew Ratio (lower beds):	3.4
Tonnage:	5,600	Cabins (total):	108
Cruise Line:	Pearl Seas Cruises	Size Range (sq ft/m):	302.0–580.0/28.0–53.8
Former Names:	none	Cabins (for one person):	10
Builder:	Irving Shipbuilding (Canada)	Cabins with balcony:	108
Entered Service:	Jun 2014	Cabins (wheelchair accessible):	4
Length (ft/m):	335.0/102.1	Wheelchair accessibility:	Fair
Beam (ft/m):	56.0/17.0	Elevators:	1
Propulsion/Propellers:	diesel (4,700kW)/2	Casino (gaming tables):	No
Passenger Decks:	6	Swimming Pools:	0
Total Crew:	60	Self-Service Launderette:	No
Passengers (lower beds):	206	Library:	Yes
Passenger Space Ratio (lower beds):	27.1	Onboard currency:	US$

THE SHIP. Pearl Seas Cruises is an offshore outgrowth of the all-American company, American Cruise Lines, based in Connecticut. But don't confuse the US's Pearl Seas Cruises with Australia's Pearl Sea Cruises.

Pearl Mist is designed to be a much more comfortable and upscale ship than the smaller *American Glory, American Spirit,* and *American Star.* It has greater speed, the latest navigational technology and propulsion equipment, and better onboard facilities and service. It is meant to appeal to passengers who enjoy discovering ports in the company of like-minded people, away from the hunting grounds of crowded large resort ships.

Public rooms include two principal lounges, the Pacific Lounge, and the Atlantic Lounge; one is above, and the other is below the navigation bridge. Other public rooms include a small Coral Lounge located just behind the mast; a library, and two small midship lounges – one named Caribbean Lounge. A single elevator goes to all decks, including the outdoor sun deck. Shipwide Wi-Fi is complimentary, but Internet access is patchy.

The ship cruises in the east coast waters of the US and Canada during the summer season and in the Caribbean during the winter season, from St Martin. Gratuities are not included. Niggles: there is no laundry; some cabins (particularly aft) are extremely noisy; and there are no personal safes.

Pearl Mist is best suited to couples and solo travel-

BERLITZ'S RATINGS		
	Possible	Achieved
Ship	500	361
Accommodation	200	148
Food	400	264
Service	400	285
Entertainment	100	67
Cruise Experience	400	266
OVERALL SCORE 1391 points out of 2000		

ers of mature years who want to cruise in an all-American environment aboard a very small ship where the destinations are a more important consideration than food, service, or entertainment.

ACCOMMODATION. There are seven cabin price grades, but all accommodation grades offer outside-view suites/cabins with private balcony (although the balcony is quite slender). All cabins feature twin beds that convert to a king-sized bed, and have high-quality bed linens; bathrooms have a walk-in shower. Some cabins can be interconnected, so a couple (partners or friends traveling together, for example) can have a bathroom each.

DINING. The single dining room, which is aft, accommodates all passengers at a set time in an open seating, so you can sit where and with whom you want. Complimentary cocktails and hors d'oeuvres are offered before dinner in the lounges.

ENTERTAINMENT. The Main Lounge is the venue for evening entertainment, lectures, and recaps, plus any entertainment that is brought on board from ashore in the various ports of call. However, it doesn't accommodate all passengers at once.

SPA/FITNESS. The small spa has a beauty salon. There is also one hot tub on deck.

PRIDE OF AMERICA
★★★

A FAMILY-FRIENDLY RESORT SHIP FOR AROUND THE HAWAIIAN ISLANDS

Size:	Mid-size Ship	Passenger Space Ratio (lower beds):	36.7
Tonnage:	80,439	Passenger/Crew Ratio (lower beds):	2.3
Cruise Line:	Norwegian Cruise Line	Cabins (total):	1,171
Former Names:	none	Size Range (sq ft/m):	129.1–1,377.8/12.0–128.0
Builder:	Ingalls Shipbuilding (USA)/Lloyd Werft (Germany)	Cabins (for one person):	4
		Cabins with balcony:	785
Entered Service:	Jul 2005	Cabins (wheelchair accessible):	21
Length (ft/m):	920.3/280.5	Wheelchair accessibility:	Good
Beam (ft/m):	106.6/32.2	Elevators:	10
Propulsion/Propellers:	diesel-electric (32,000kW)/ 2 azimuthing pods	Casino (gaming tables):	Yes
		Swimming Pools:	2
Passenger Decks:	11	Self-Service Launderette:	No
Total Crew:	940	Library:	Yes
Passengers (lower beds):	2,186	Onboard currency:	US$

THE SHIP. *Pride of America* sails on inter-island cruises, focusing on Hawaii's islands. The 85,850-sq-ft (7,975-sq-m) open deck space includes a sunbathing/pool deck inspired by Miami's South Beach – think Ocean Drive/Lincoln Mall.

The interior is modeled after a 'Best of America' theme, with public rooms named after famous Americans. Facilities include the Capitol Atrium (a lobby spanning eight decks and said to be inspired by the Capitol Building and White House), a large casino (with gaming tables and slot machines), a conservatory with tropical landscaped garden, SoHo Art Gallery (for displaying 'art' and holding auctions), Washington Library (with six internet-connect computer terminals), and a Newbury Shopping Center.

Six meeting rooms range in size from boardrooms for 10 to an auditorium for up to 250. The ship has a mainly Hawaiian crew.

A non-changeable, daily service charge (as distinct from a gratuity) is added to your onboard account and pooled for all crew and provides payment when they are on vacation. In addition, a 15 percent gratuity plus Hawaii's sales tax (because of the ship's US registry) is added to all bar (and 18 percent for spa treatment) accounts.

Although the islands are pleasant enough, a cruise aboard this ship might well test your patience, since most of the all-American crew simply don't cut it. That said, the ship is still popular with couples, solo travelers, and families with children and teenagers who want contemporary, upbeat surroundings, in a well-packaged cruise, with constant music, participation activity, and entertainment.

ACCOMMODATION. About 75 percent of all cabins have ocean views. Outside-view cabins have either a window or porthole, depending on location, twin beds convertible into a queen-size bed.

There are also family-friendly interconnecting cabins (some can sleep up to six); many cabins have third/fourth upper berths. Some suites have king-size beds, while most cabins have twin beds convertible to a queen-size bed. Butler and concierge service is provided for suite-grade occupants, who also get Lavazza espresso makers, Elemis bath products, private dining for breakfast and lunch, and other perks. A number of cabins are wheelchair-accessible, with some equipped for the hearing-impaired.

Grand Suites have around 1,400 sq ft (130 sq m) of living space. Owner's Suites measure around 870 sq ft (80 sq m), these are named after Deluxe Penthouse Suites measure around 735 sq ft (68 sq m).

Penthouse Suites measure 504–585 sq ft (47–55 sq m).

Family Suites measure around 360 sq ft (34 sq m). Another four family 'suites,' measuring 330–380 sq

BERLITZ'S RATINGS

	Possible	Achieved
Ship	500	346
Accommodation	200	139
Food	400	211
Service	400	209
Entertainment	100	68
Cruise Experience	400	242

OVERALL SCORE 1215 points out of 2000

ft (30.5–35 sq m), have an interconnecting door between two cabins; there are thus two bathrooms.

DINING. Freestyle Cruising means you get a choice of several restaurants and casual eateries. Choose from two main dining rooms, and six other à la carte and casual venues (some cost extra).

Main restaurants include the 628-seat Skyline Restaurant – with decor inspired by the skyscrapers of the 1930s – and the 496-seat Liberty Dining Room, with two seatings.

The extra-cost 106-seat Lazy J Texas Steak House is a contemporary steak house with Texas decor – the artwork includes Houston Space Center, Texas Rangers, and Dallas Cowboys.

East Meets West is an intimate 32-seat Pacific Rim/Asian Fusion restaurant with sushi/sashimi bar and a grill room with two Teppanyaki tables (showmanship food is prepared in front of you). Jefferson's Bistro, seating 104, is a 'signature' restaurant, with an à la carte menu of classic and French nouvelle cuisine. The decor is inspired by Thomas Jefferson's home in Monticello – Jefferson was the US ambassador to France from 1785 to 1789, before becoming America's third president.

Little Italy, a casual Italian eatery, features pasta, pizza, and other light Italian fare. It has 116 seats.

Cadillac Diner accommodates 70 indoors and 36 outdoors, and is open 24 hours a day, with quirky Cadillac-shaped seats and a video jukebox. It's for fast food: burgers and hot dogs, fish and chips, pot pies, and wok dishes.

Moderno Churrascaria is a Brazilian steakhouse, for meat delivered on a skewer by service staff dressed 'gaucho' style.

Cagney's Steak House is for prime American steaks and grilled seafood. A cover charge applies to both venues and reservations are required.

Aloha Café/Kids Café is an indoor/outdoor self-serve buffet-style eatery with a Hawaiian theme. A section for children has counter tops at just the right height, as well as chairs and tables that have been shrunk to a child-friendly size.

Other eateries and bars include the Napa Wine Bar (wines by the glass), Pink's Champagne and Cigar Bar (inspired by Hawaii's Pink Palace Hotel on Waikiki Beach), the Gold Rush saloon (pub with karaoke, plus a darts board and bar billiards), and a John Adams Coffee Bar. Outdoor eateries and drinking places include the Key West Bar and Grill, and the Waikiki Bar.

ENTERTAINMENT. The Hollywood Theater seats 840 and stages large-scale production and local Hawaiian shows. A 590-seat Mardi Gras cabaret lounge, located above the showlounge, has features cabaret and late-night (smutty) comedy.

SPA/FITNESS. The Mandara Spa is decorated with artefacts from New Mexico, and the decor uses natural stone and wood.

While some fitness classes are free, others cost extra. Massage facials, pedicures, and beauty treatments also cost extra.

PRINSENDAM
★★★+

THIS VERY COMFORTABLE, BUT NOW QUITE DATED SHIP HAS A PREMIUM AMBIENCE

Size:	Mid-size Ship	Passenger/Crew Ratio (lower beds):	1.8
Tonnage:	38,100	Cabins (total):	419
Cruise Line:	Holland America Line	Size Range (sq ft/m):	137.7–723.3/12.8–67.2
Former Names:	Seabourn Sun, Royal Viking Sun	Cabins (for one person):	3
Builder:	Wartsila (Finland)	Cabins with balcony:	166
Entered Service:	Dec 1988/May 2002	Cabins (wheelchair accessible):	10
Length (ft/m):	674.2/205.5	Wheelchair accessibility:	Best
Beam (ft/m):	91.8/28.0	Elevators:	4
Propulsion/Propellers:	diesel (21,120kW)/2	Casino (gaming tables):	Yes
Passenger Decks:	9	Swimming Pools:	2
Total Crew:	443	Self-Service Launderette:	Yes
Passengers (lower beds):	835	Library:	Yes
Passenger Space Ratio (lower beds):	45.6	Onboard currency:	US$

THE SHIP. *Prinsendam* is a well-designed ship with sleek lines, a sharply raked bow, and a well-rounded profile, with lots of floor-to-ceiling glass. Having started life as *Royal Viking Sun*, it was bought by Seabourn Cruise Line in 1998 and refitted as *Seabourn Sun*. In 2002, it was transferred to HAL as *Prinsendam*, and the color of the hull was changed from all white to dark blue, with a white superstructure.

This ship is best suited to older adult couples and solo travelers who like to mingle in a mid-size ship operating longer cruises, in an unhurried setting with some eclectic, antique artwork, good food, and service from a smiling crew. It is a very comfortable vessel – smaller than other Holland America Line (HAL) ships, but more refined.

Wide teakwood decks provide excellent walking areas including a decent walk-around promenade deck outdoors, but there's no jogging track. The swimming pool, outdoors on Lido Deck, is small, but it is quite adequate; the deck above has a croquet court and golf driving range. The interior layout is quite spacious – it is even more ideal when no more than 600 passengers are aboard. Impressive public rooms and tasteful decor reign. Two handrails – one of wood, one of chrome – are provided on all stairways, which is a thoughtful touch.

The Crow's Nest, the forward observation lounge, is an elegant, contemporary (at least in decor) space. Pebble Beach is the name of the electronic

BERLITZ'S RATINGS

	Possible	Achieved
Ship	500	331
Accommodation	200	145
Food	400	240
Service	400	272
Entertainment	100	63
Cruise Experience	400	266

OVERALL SCORE 1317 points out of 2000

golf simulator room, complete with wet bar, with play possible on 11 virtual courses.

The Erasmus Library is well organized, although it's simply too small for long-distance cruising.

The Oak Room is the ship's cigar/pipe smoker's lounge; it has a marble fireplace, which sadly cannot be used due to United States Coast Guard regulations.

Whether by intention or not, the ship has a two-class feeling, with passengers in 'upstairs' Penthouse Suites and 'A' grade staterooms gravitating to the quieter Crow's Nest lounge, particularly at night, while other passengers go to the main entertainment deck.

The wide range of facilities includes a concierge, self-service launderettes (useful on long voyages), a varied guest lecture program, 24-hour information office, and true 24-hour cabin service. This ship operates mainly long-distance cruises in great comfort, and free shuttle buses are provided in almost all ports of call.

While *Prinsendam* isn't perfect, the few design flaws (for example: poorly designed bar service counters) are minor points. The elegant decorative features include Dutch artwork and memorabilia. Added benefits include a fine health spa facility, spacious, wide teakwood decks and many teak sunloungers.

There are only four elevators, so anyone with walking disabilities may have to wait for some time during periods of peak usage, such as before meals. This spacious ship shows signs of wear and tear in some areas, particularly in the accommodation passageways, despite recent refurbishments. The library is difficult for anyone in a wheelchair to enter. The shore tenders are thoughtfully air conditioned.

ACCOMMODATION. There are several accommodation grades, ranging from Penthouse Verandah Suites to standard interior cabins. All suites and cabins have undergone some degree of refurbishment since the ship was taken over by HAL in 2002.

The Penthouse Verandah Suite measures 723 sq ft (67 sq m) and is a desirable living space, although not as large as on similarly sized ships. It is light and airy, with two bathrooms, one of which has a large whirlpool tub with ocean views, and anodized gold bathroom fittings.

Deluxe Verandah Suites, located in the forward section, have large balconies. If you choose one of these suites, it might be best on the starboard side, where they are located in a private hallway, while those on the port side (including the Penthouse Verandah Suite) are set along a public hallway. Ten suites on Lido Deck are positioned along private port and starboard side hallways.

Passengers in Penthouse and Deluxe Verandah Suites have a private concierge lounge.

Other cabin grades are of generous proportions and nicely equipped. About 38 percent have a small, private balcony. All cabins have walk-in closets, lockable drawers, full-length mirrors, hairdryers, ample cotton towels, and flat-screen infotainment systems. A few cabins have third berths, while some have interconnecting doors – good for couples who want two bathrooms and more space, or for families with children.

In all accommodation grades, passengers receive a basket of fresh fruit, fluffy cotton bathrobes, and a HAL signature tote bag. Filipino and Indonesian cabin stewards and stewardesses provide unobtrusive personal service.

Four well-equipped, L-shaped cabins for the disabled are quite well designed, fairly large, and equipped with special wheel-in bathrooms with shower facilities and closets.

DINING. La Fontaine Dining Room wraps around the aft end of Lower Promenade Deck and has extensive ocean-view windows; along the starboard side is a second, smaller and quieter section. There is plenty of space around tables. A good number of window-side tables are for two persons, although there are also tables for four, six, or eight. Crystal glasses, Rosenthal china, and fine cutlery are provided.

There are two seatings for dinner, at assigned tables, and an open-seating arrangement for breakfast and lunch – you'll be seated by restaurant staff, when you enter. On most port days the restaurant is closed at lunchtime, which means using the self-serve buffet or ordering room service.

With a few exceptions, the cuisine is rather unmemorable because it's all about batch cooking. There's a distinct lack of variety of green vegetables, and too much rice, canned fruit, and already sliced and diced cheese. Still, you get friendly service from Indonesian and Filipino stewards, and the plates are nice.

A small, quiet dining spot on the port side is the Pinnacle Dining Room, with 48 seats, wood-paneled decor that increases the feeling of intimacy and privacy, and fine ocean views. Table settings include Bulgari china, Riedel glassware, and Frette table linens. The venue specializes in fine steaks and seafood. Seating preference is given to suite occupants. Reservations are required, and there is a cover charge. There is a well-chosen wine list, although there's a great deal of emphasis on California wines, with prices that are quite high.

There is also a Lido Restaurant, for decent casual dining and self-serve buffet-style meals. At night, this eatery becomes the Canaletto (named after the Venetian artist).

Also, a Lido Deck poolside 'Dive-In at the Terrace Grill' features signature burgers, hot dogs and fries, and, on certain days, barbecues and other culinary treats may be featured.

ENTERTAINMENT. The Queen's Showlounge is an amphitheater-style room, with a tiered floor, and both banquette and individual seating. While HAL isn't known for fine entertainment, what it does offer is a consistently good, tried-and-tested array of cabaret acts. There are also male 'dance hosts,' who act as partners for women traveling alone.

SPA/FITNESS. The Greenhouse Health Spa includes six treatment rooms with integral showers, a Rasul chamber (for mud and gentle steam heat), a gymnasium with views over the stern, and separate sauna, steam room, and changing rooms for men and women. The spa is operated by specialist concession Steiner Leisure.

QUANTUM OF THE SEAS
★★★★

A HIGH-ENERGY, STATE-OF-THE-ART, GIZMO-FILLED FAMILY-FRIENDLY FLOATING RESORT

Size:	Large Resort Ship	Passenger/Crew Ratio (lower beds):	3.2
Tonnage:	168,666	Cabins (total):	2,090
Cruise Line:	Royal Caribbean International	Size Range (sq ft/m):	101.1-799.7/9.4-74.3
Former Names:	none	Cabins (for one person):	34
Builder:	Meyer Werft (Germany)	Cabins with balcony:	1,571
Entered Service:	Oct 2014	Cabins (wheelchair accessible):	34
Length (ft/m):	1,145.0/348.0	Wheelchair accessibility:	Good
Beam (ft/m):	134.5/41.0	Elevators:	16
Propulsion/Propellers:	diesel-electric (41,000kW)/	Casino (gaming tables):	Yes
	2 azimuthing pods	Swimming Pools:	3
Passenger Decks:	16	Self-Service Launderette:	No
Total Crew:	1,300	Library:	Yes
Passengers (lower beds):	4,180	Onboard currency:	US$
Passenger Space Ratio (lower beds):	40.3		

THE SHIP. *Quantum of the Seas*, a new class and type of smart ship for popular Royal Caribbean International (RCI), has a slender profile – it was actually built in several huge sections and joined together. The ship is based in Tianjin (the port for Beijing), China, and the whole family will love it because it incorporates the very latest tech-intensive and creative features, and then some. You can even go flying aboard this ship! It's a lot of Royal Caribbean wow in an all-weather environment.

The ship employs the latest in hydrodynamics, hull shape, low emissions, and, importantly, low fuel consumption, and technology. The stern (back of the ship) slopes nicely – it looks like it could be the front! It contains the impressive Two70º – an innovative multi-level venue that is a casual living area by day and a stunning, high-energy entertainment venue by night, with dynamic robotic screens complementing its huge video wall.

Several exciting features have been incorporated. North Star – quite the engineering marvel – is a 13-person (plus operator) glass capsule that lifts you off from the ship's uppermost deck and provides a bird's-eye view of all below you (including the sea) as it moves around. It's like a posh giant 'cherry picker' with attitude – and, lifting you almost 300ft (91m) above sea level (with an outreach of almost 135ft (41m), is quite a ride! Located in the front section of the ship, just behind the mast, it is complimentary

BERLITZ'S RATINGS

	Possible	Achieved
Ship	500	412
Accommodation	200	140
Food	400	292
Service	400	274
Entertainment	100	85
Cruise Experience	400	283

OVERALL SCORE 1486 points out of 2000

(and wheelchair-accessible), but only operates at sea. A charge applies for booking for weddings and other romantic occasions.

The second stunner is RipCord by iFly – an extra-cost simulated sky-diving experience in a two-storey vertical wind tunnel that lets you experience the thrill of skydiving in a safe, controlled environment. The unit uses a powerful air flow to keep you up in the air and free-flying – like a giant hairdryer underneath you! It is located aft of the ship's funnel housing, and accommodates 13 persons for each 75-minute class, including two 'hovering in the air' experiences, instruction, and gear. You can book both attractions with interactive digital kiosks (adjacent to elevators) and tablets in public areas. Look out for Felicia, the magenta-colored bear located outside on the starboard side of Deck 15 aft.

Meanwhile, a SeaPlex complex – located just underneath the North Star offers a circus 'school' and adrenalin-boosting bumper-car rides, and acts as a roller-skating rink and basketball court. It's a veritable active interactive sporting venue that replaces the ice rinks of other large RCI ships. Other features include a rock-climbing wall, and a FlowRider surfing simulator.

The decor is stunningly colorful, contemporary, and jazzy. The interior focal point is the three-storey-high Royal Esplanade, which includes Michael's Genuine Pub, Sorrento's pizza outlet, a Bionic Bar, a two-deck-high entertainment venue called Music Hall, plus lots of shops, the Schooner Bar, Boleros

(Latin bar), Izumi (for Japanese-style cuisine), and the American Icon Grill. This where the action is day and night – note that it can be noisy.

Since mid-2015 *Quantum of the Seas* has been based year-round in Shanghai, China, and the principal language is Mandarin.

ACCOMMODATION. There are many different price grades and categories for accommodation. The price you pay depends on the size and location you choose. Fortunately, every cabin aboard this ship has a view – whether real or virtual. 'Virtual' balconies were first introduced aboard *Navigator of the Seas* in a 2013 refit and are a really neat feature of interior (no-view) cabins; they can provide real-time ocean views, but you *can* turn them off, if you prefer. Although these cost more than standard interior cabins, they're worth it. Wristband RFID technology provides access to your cabin, and acts as your charge card, but it's not comfortable to wear.

Several new accommodation categories and types have been introduced aboard this ship. Standard cabins are about 9 percent larger than those aboard the Oasis-class ships. Note that if you book suite-grade accommodation, you can eat all your meals in the exclusive Coastal Kitchen.

Loft cabins (including a 975 sq ft/90.5 sq m Owner's Loft) vary in size and configuration, but measure approximately 502 sq ft (46.6 sq m) and are located at the ship's stern, with great views of where you've been.

Inter-connecting family cabins are really good for multi-generational groups, and highly sought after. The 15 units consist of a junior suite, balcony cabin, and interior studio, connected through a shared vestibule. Together they can create 575.8 sq ft (53.5 sq m) of living space with three bedrooms, three bathrooms, and a 216-sq-ft (20-sq-m) balcony.

There are studio cabins (12 have real balconies) for solo occupancy, a first for RCI. As there's no supplement, they are priced in a new category for solo travelers.

Even the smallest bathroom is well designed, with thoughtful touches such as a night light, and shower and vanity hooks, while cabins have bedside power outlets, and ample storage space.

DINING. There are 18 restaurant and eatery choices (there's no designated main dining room as such), part of what the line calls Dynamic Dining. This means that you need to make reservations in some venues, just like eating ashore – a concept first introduced by Star Cruises.

The following are complimentary, and all have tablecloths at dinner:

The Grande: with 432 seats, the ship's most elegant restaurant (think Southern mansion hospitality), featuring classic dishes reminiscent of the days of the grand ocean liners of yesteryear.

Chic: this 434-seat restaurant features 'contemporary' cuisine and sauces made from scratch.

Silk: this 434-seat restaurant features pan-Asian cuisine.

American Icon Grille: this 430-seat restaurant features many of America's favorite 'comfort food' dishes including New England clam chowder, Southern buttermilk fried chicken, and New Orleans gumbo.

Extra-cost dining venues include the following:

Wonderland: based on the (real and imagined) elements Fire, Ice, Water, Earth, and Dreams, this surreal 62-seat Alice in Wonderland-inspired venue offers food with a quirky touch (such as the oddly shaped 'hoodie' chairs), thanks to ingredients including Japanese bonito flakes. I can just imagine the Mad Hatter's Tea Party here.

Jamie's Italian: it's a 132-seat reservations-required tablecloth-free Euro-Italian restaurant – and British celebrity chef Jamie Oliver's first restaurant at sea.

Chops Grille: for premium-quality steaks and grilled seafood (plus an integral Chef's Table).

Chef's Table: this exclusive 16-seat venue is good for private parties, with wine-and-food pairing the specialty.

Izumi: a 44-seat Japanese-Asian fusion cuisine venue including hot-rock tableside cooking, sashimi, sushi, and sake. The lantern lights fit perfectly into the decor.

Johnny Rockets: a retro 1950s all-day, all-night diner-style eatery (near the main pool) for hamburgers, extra-cost malt shakes, and jukebox hits (all tables feature a mini-jukebox). À la carte pricing applies.

For ultra-casual meals at no extra cost, the 860-seat Windjammer Marketplace is a self-serve buffet-style eatery. Other casual spots at no extra cost include: The Café @ Two70°; SeaPlex Dog House; Sorrento's – for pizza slices and calzones; and Café Promenade.

ENTERTAINMENT. The Royal Theater spans three decks and is the principal showlounge for 'booked' shows and large-scale production shows by a resident troupe of singers and dancers.

Two70° is a stunning, multi-level, glass-walled 'living' room spanning almost three decks in height at the ship's stern (in many other ships this would probably be a main dining room). It includes a food-court-style marketplace, and sit-down eateries, including The Café @ Two70°. By night, the big venue morphs into the entertainment house, with Robo-screens and Bionic Bar featuring high-tech wizardry.

Music Hall is two-decks high a rock-'n'-roll joint, outfitted with all the right paraphernalia, and will feature DJs and theme nights.

SPA/FITNESS. The Vitality at Sea Spa facilities include a thermal suite (extra cost), beauty salon, barber shop, and gymnasium with Technogym equipment. Massage and other body-pampering treatments take place in 19 treatment rooms.

QUEEN ELIZABETH
★★★★+

THIS SHIP HAS A DELIGHTFUL INTERIOR DECOR THAT REPRESENTS GREAT BRITISH HERITAGE

Size:	Mid-size Ship	Passenger/Crew Ratio (lower beds):	2.0
Tonnage:	90,900	Cabins (total):	1,046
Cruise Line:	Cunard	Size Range (sq ft/m): 152.0–1,493 sq.ft/14.0–138.5	
Former Names:	none	Cabins (for one person):	9
Builder:	Fincantieri (Italy)	Cabins with balcony:	820
Entered Service:	Oct 2010	Cabins (wheelchair accessible):	20
Length (ft/m):	964.5/294.0	Wheelchair accessibility:	Good
Beam (ft/m):	105.9/32.3	Elevators:	12
Propulsion/Propellers: diesel-electric (64,000kW)/		Casino (gaming tables):	Yes
	2 azimuthing pods	Swimming Pools:	2
Passenger Decks:	12	Self-Service Launderette:	Yes
Total Crew:	1,005	Library:	Yes
Passengers (lower beds):	2,101	Onboard currency:	US$
Passenger Space Ratio (lower beds):	43.2		

THE SHIP. *Queen Elizabeth*, a cruise ship that longs to be an ocean liner, suits mature adults and solo travelers, and families with children. It's pitched at traditionalists who like to dress more formally for dinner, and sail with a sense of style. Note that Berlitz's Ratings scores are the averages for both Grill Class and Britannia Class.

The ship, named in the company's 170th year (the company began operations in 1840), is the second-largest Cunarder ordered in that long history. Although Cunard purports to offer a resolutely British experience, the marketing hype is undermined by the use of US dollars as the onboard currency, and trying to find British service staff is challenging. The Cunard red funnel is instantly recognizable.

Once inside, the ship feels instantly comfortable, rather like a mini-*QE2*. It has less somber colors than *Queen Victoria*, commendably little glitzy brass or chrome surfaces, and more of the look and feel of an ocean liner, including some gorgeous carpeting. The decor is classic and timeless.

Features include a majestic three-deck-high Grand Lobby with a sweeping staircase, sculpted balconies, and elegant decorative touches, and an adjacent Cunarders' Galleria floating museum, with memorabilia displayed in glass cabinets. The original Asprey silver model of *QE2* is in the Yacht Club, and there's a nice model of the original *Queen Elizabeth* in a cabinet on the upper level of the atrium.

BERLITZ'S RATINGS

	Possible	Achieved
Ship	500	416
Accommodation	200	145
Food	400	300
Service	400	315
Entertainment	100	81
Cruise Experience	400	315

OVERALL SCORE 1572 points out of 2000

The Royal Arcade is a cluster of shops, selling goods connected with traditional and modern-day Britain, all set in an arcade-like environment; they include Hackett, Penhaligon's, and Aspinal of London.

The Library is a stunning two-deck-high wood-paneled book facility serviced by full-time librarians, although there are few chairs in which to sit and read. Few ships today have such a fine library. There's also a bookshop selling maritime-related books, memorabilia, maps, and stationery.

Gratuities – called a Hotel and Dining charge, depending on your accommodation grade – are added to your onboard account daily.

Queen Elizabeth provides an elegant setting for a traditional cruise experience, with a wide choice of public rooms, bars, and lounges, and a mostly attentive staff. But, in the final analysis, the finesse is missing, and the ship's Princess Cruises-style cabins are below the standard expected.

ACCOMMODATION. There are three class categories of accommodation: Queens Grill; Princess Grill; and Britannia Club and Britannia Restaurant grade. So, it's all about location, location, location. Yet however much or little you pay, passengers all embark and disembark via the same gangway. Note that the air conditioning cannot be turned off in cabins or bathrooms.

All accommodation grades have both British three-pin (240-volt) sockets and American (110-volt) and European-style two-pin (220-volt) sockets. Penhaligon's toiletries are supplied to all passengers, and a hairdryer is stored in the vanity desk units. Some cabins have nicely indented ceilings with suffused lighting.

Standard cabins (Grades C/D) are small, but functional, although the cabinetry is austere and lacks character. There's a lack of drawer space in a cabin supposedly designed for two persons – it's noticeable on long voyages; additional drawers are located under the bed, but these may prove challenging for some to use. The premium mattresses are excellent – as is the bed linen. European duvets are standard. The bathrooms are rather bland, like those found aboard the ships of Princess Cruises, with small washbasins, and little storage space for toiletries.

The largest accommodation is in four Grand Suites: 1,918–2,131 sq ft (178–197 sq m), named Bisset, Charles, Illingworth, and Rostron (all former Cunard captains). These are located aft, with great ocean views from private wrap-around balconies. In-suite dining from the Queens Grill menus is available.

DINING. The 878-seat Britannia Restaurant – the name is taken from a former Cunard ship of 1914–50 – is located aft. It is two decks high, with seating on both levels (stairways link both levels), and two seatings for dinner. An adjacent restaurant houses Britannia Club passengers, who get single-seat dining.

Exclusive dining (Queens Grill, Princess Grill). As with its sister ships, the *Queen Elizabeth* has two special Grill Class-only restaurants. These have a single-seating arrangement, providing a more intimate and exclusive dining experience than can be found in the two-seating main Britannia Restaurant.

The 142-seat Queens Grill (on the starboard side), with single-seating dining, is for those in suites and the top accommodation grades, and provides the best cuisine and service aboard the ship. The beloved Cunard Grill experience includes alfresco dining in The Courtyard, a courtyard terrace protected from the wind, and access for Grill Class passengers only to an exclusive lounge and bar to their own upper terrace deck.

The 132-seat Princess Grill (on the port side), with single-seating dining, is for passengers in middle-class accommodation grades.

The Verandah Restaurant is a beautiful à la carte specialty dining venue with a bar, and is available to all passengers. It is located on the second level of the three-deck high lobby. The decor and ambience recreate the Verandah Grill restaurant aboard the original *Queen Elizabeth* and *Queen Mary*. The classic French cuisine is exceptionally good and makes for a fine dining experience. Reservations are require for lunch or dinner, with à la carte pricing.

The Lido Café (on Deck 9) has panoramic views, indoor/outdoor seating for approximately 470, and operates a standard multi-line self-serve buffet arrangement. It's a bit downmarket for what is supposed to be a stylish ship. At night, the venue is transformed into three distinct flavors: Asado (South American Grill); Aztec (Mexican cuisine); and Jasmine (Asian cuisine), each with a small cover charge.

For excellent Italian coffees from Luigi (the name given to the coffee machine), teas, and light bites, there's Café Carinthia, one deck above the purser's desk and adjacent to the popular Veuve Clicquot Champagne bar.

For traditional British comfort food, the Golden Lion Pub offers fish and chips, steak and mushroom pie, a ploughman's lunch, and, of course, bangers (sausages) and mash, plus, there's a wide range of draft beers and lagers.

ENTERTAINMENT. The 830-seat, three-deck-high Royal Court Theatre is designed in the style of a classic opera house. It has 20 private boxes that can be reserved by anyone for special nights, and a special package includes Champagne, chocolates, and a ticket printed with name and box number – in the tradition of a real London West End theatre. There's a lounge for pre-show drinks.

SPA/FITNESS. The Cunard Royal Spa includes a beauty salon, large gymnasium with high-tech muscle-pumping equipment and great ocean views; an aerobics area; separate changing rooms for men and women, each with its own ocean-view sauna; a Thermal Area with sauna and steam rooms (extra-cost day passes are available, if you don't book a treatment, or at a lower per-day cost for a multi-use pass); several body-treatment rooms; a Rasul chamber for private hammam-style mud/steam bathing; and a relaxation area. A gratuity is added to all spa treatment prices.

QUEEN MARY 2
★★★★+

A REAL STURDY OCEAN LINER BUILT SPECIFICALLY FOR TRANSATLANTIC CROSSINGS

Size:	Large Resort Ship	Passenger/Crew Ratio (lower beds):	2.1
Tonnage:	151,400	Cabins (total):	1,360
Cruise Line:	Cunard	Size Range (sq ft/m):	194.0–2,249.7/18.0–209
Former Names:	none	Cabins (for one person):	0
Builder:	Chantiers de l'Atlantique (France)	Cabins with balcony:	953
Entered Service:	Jan 2004	Cabins (wheelchair accessible):	30
Length (ft/m):	1,131.8/345.0	Wheelchair accessibility:	Best
Beam (ft/m):	134.5/41.0	Elevators:	22
Propulsion/Propellers: gas turbine + diesel-electric		Casino (gaming tables):	Yes
(103,000kW)/4 pods (2 azimuthing, 2 fixed)		Swimming Pools:	2
Passenger Decks:	12	Self-Service Launderette:	Yes
Total Crew:	1,250	Library:	Yes
Passengers (lower beds):	2,705	Onboard currency:	US$
Passenger Space Ratio (lower beds):	55.9		

THE SHIP. RMS *Queen Mary 2*, designated a Royal Mail Ship by the British Post Office, is the largest ocean liner ever built in terms of gross tonnage, length, and beam, though not in terms of passengers carried. A powerful propulsion system allows it to go backwards faster than many cruise ships can go forwards. It was the first new ship to be built for Cunard since 1969. In addition to its scheduled transatlantic crossings, *QM2* operates an annual round-the-world cruise, and other, shorter cruises.

Almost everything about the liner is British in style, but with some American decor input and accents; even the four tender stations have London names: Belgravia, Chelsea, Kensington, and Knightsbridge. There is a wide walk-around promenade deck outdoors (the forward section is under cover from the weather). Three times around is 6,102ft (1,860m), or about 1.2 miles (1.9km). Teak 'steamer' chairs adorn the walk-around deck, with plenty of room for walkers to pass. However, plastic sunloungers are provided on some other open decks.

Here's a deck-by-deck look at the facilities and public rooms, starting at the lowest deck and working our way upward, forward to aft:

Deck 2: Illuminations (and integral planetarium), Royal Court Theatre, lower level of the six-deck-high atrium lobby, purser's desk, Video Arcade, Empire Casino, Golden Lion Pub, and lower level of the Britannia Restaurant.

BERLITZ'S RATINGS		
	Possible	Achieved
Ship	500	430
Accommodation	200	174
Food	400	320
Service	400	335
Entertainment	100	86
Cruise Experience	400	338

OVERALL SCORE 1683 points out of 2000

Deck 3: upper level of Illuminations and Royal Court Theatre, second level of the six-deck-high atrium lobby, Mayfair shops, Sir Samuel's, The Chart Room, Champagne Bar, upper level of the Britannia Restaurant, the Queens Room, and G32 nightclub.

Decks 4/Deck 5/Deck 6: accommodation and the third, fourth, and fifth levels of the six-deck-high atrium lobby; at the aft end of Deck 6 are facilities for children, including an outdoor pool (Minnows Pool).

Deck 7: Canyon Ranch Spa, Carinthia Lounge, the sixth and uppermost level of the six-deck-high atrium lobby, Kings Court Buffet, Queens Grill Lounge, Queens Grill, and Princess Grill dining salons.

Deck 8 (forward): upper level of the Canyon Ranch Spa, and the Library and Bookshop. The center section has accommodation. In the aft section is The Verandah Restaurant, plus a Terrace Bar, and an outdoor swimming pool.

Deck 9 (forward): Commodore Club, Boardroom, and Cigar Lounge (Churchills). The rest of the deck has accommodation and a Concierge Club for suite occupants.

Deck 10: accommodation only.

Deck 11 (forward): outdoor observation area. The rest of the deck comprises accommodation. The aft section outdoors has a hot tub and sunbathing space.

Deck 12 (forward): accommodation. The midsection has an indoor/outdoor pool with sliding glass roof, and golf areas (Fairways), located just aft of the public restrooms. Aft is a Boardwalk Café, kennels, and shuffleboard courts.

Deck 13: Sports Centre, Regatta Bar, a splash pool, and extensive outdoor sunbathing space.

There are 14 lounges, clubs, and bars. An observation lounge, the delightful Commodore Club, has commanding views forward over the bows; light jazz is played in this room, which is connected to the Boardroom, and Cigar Lounge. Other drinking places include a Golden Lion Pub (pub lunches are served here, too), Sir Samuel's (wine bar), a nautically themed cocktail bar (The Chart Room), and a Champagne/Coffee Bar. Outdoor bars include the Regatta Bar and Terrace Bar. The G32 nightclub, which has a main and mezzanine level, is at the aft end of the ship, away from passenger cabins; it is named after the number designated to the ship by its French builder.

Illuminations, the first and only full-scale planetarium at sea, is a stunning multi-purpose show-lounge that also functions as a 473-seat grand cinema and broadcast studio. As a planetarium, it has tiered seating rows, and you sit in a special area with 150 reclining seats, under a dome, which is 38ft (11.5m) in diameter and almost 20ft (6m) deep – this forms the setting for the night sky. It's worth reserving a seat for at least one of the seven outstanding 20-minute programs (with narration by Hollywood stars including Harrison Ford, Sigourney Weaver, and Tom Hanks). The venue also screens 3D movies.

There are five swimming pools, including one that can be enclosed under a retractable glass roof. A large area of open sunning space includes a sports bar at one end. The ship's Library and Bookshop is the world's largest floating library and the most popular public room on transatlantic crossings. It has 10,000 books in several languages, in 150 cabinets. It is a delightful facility, but there are few chairs, and the adjacent bookshop is poor. Children have their own spaces, with a dedicated play area, and qualified nannies.

Queen Mary 2 (QM2) offers the pleasures of crossing the North Atlantic comfortably on a regular schedule. It is really suited to couples and solo travelers who enjoy the cosmopolitan setting of a floating city with an unequaled maritime heritage. It's also for anyone who can't contemplate sailing without their dog or cat – it's the only liner with kennels. (Note that if you want to take your cat, you need to reserve two kennels – one is for the litter box.)

Scores given are averaged for all accommodation grades.

ACCOMMODATION. Although there are four separate categories – Queens Grill, Princess Grill, Britannia Club, and Britannia – QM2 really operates as a two-class ship (Grill Class and Britannia Class); the restaurant to which you are assigned depends on your accommodation grade. You even get a different cabin breakfast menu in all accommodation grades, plus a tea/coffee-making set.

All grades have a flat-screen infotainment system, European duvets, a mini-fridge, safe, and hand-held hairdryer. All bathrooms have Penhaligon's toiletries. Other features include digital video on demand (English-, French-, and German-language movies are available), music on demand with 3,000 titles, and audiobooks on demand. One channel covers Cunard's eventful history since 1840.

Beware of cabins on deck 6 located under the Kings Court – they can be subject to noise from the casual eatery on the deck above, where almost constant trolley movement creates noise.

From the smallest to the largest, they are as follows:

Standard outside-view/interior cabins. These measure 194 sq ft (18 sq m).

Atrium-view cabins. These 12 interior cabins measure 194 sq ft (18 sq m). They look into the six-deck-high atrium lobby.

Deluxe/premium balcony cabins. These measure 248 sq ft (23 sq m).

Junior Suites (Grade P1/P2). These measure 381 sq ft (35 sq m).

Suites (Grade Q5/Q6). These measure 506 sq ft (47 sq m).

Penthouse Suites (Grade Q4). Penthouse Suites measure 758 sq ft (70 sq m).

Queen Anne/Queen Victoria Suites (Grade Q3). These suites measure 796.5 sq ft (74 sq m) and have outstanding views over the ship's long bows.

Queen Elizabeth/Queen Mary Suites (Grade Q2). Measuring 1,194 sq ft (111 sq m), these are located just under the navigation bridge, with good views over the ship's long bows. Each suite has the convenience of private elevator access.

Duplex apartments (Grade Q2). There are three of these: Buckingham and Windsor (each 1,291 sq ft/120 sq m), and Holyrood (1,566 sq ft/145 sq m).

Balmoral/Sandringham Duplexes (Grade Q1). The largest stand-alone accommodation, these measure 2,249 sq ft (209 sq m) and have excellent views along the the ship's exterior length.

Wheelchair-accessible cabins. These are in various categories. All have pull-down rails in the closet, above-bed emergency pull-cord, and large, well-equipped bathrooms with roll-in showers and handrails. Braille signs and tactile room signs are provided. Eight wheelchair-accessible elevators service the dining areas. Also, 36 cabins accommodate deaf or hearing-impaired passengers.

DINING. There are 10 dining rooms and eateries (and seven galleys to service them), and all dining venues have ocean-view windows. The wines and Champagnes have been selected by Michael Broadbent, one of the world's top wine experts.

Britannia Restaurant. This main dining room seats 1,347 and spans the ship's beam. Almost three decks high, it has two grand sweeping staircases, so you can make your entry in style. Breakfast and lunch are open seating, while dinner is in two seatings, all with crisp linen and fine china. Vegetarian options are included on all lunch and dinner menus. One downside of open seating for breakfast or lunch is that each time you'll probably have a different waiter, who won't know your preferences. Also, if you are seated on the lower level underneath the balcony formed along the sides of the upper level, you may feel enclosed in an inferior space. It's better to get a table in the central well or on the upper level.

Queens Grill/Princess Grill. There are two Grill dining salons: the 200-seat Queens Grill and the 178-seat Princess Grill. Which you dine in depends on your accommodation grade and fare. Both are located aft and have, in theory, fine ocean-view windows – although walkers passing by on the exterior promenade deck can be distracting in the daytime. Canyon Ranch SpaClub recommendations and vegetarian options are provided on all lunch and dinner menus.

The Verandah Restaurant. This reservations-only venue carries on the tradition of extra-tariff restaurants first seen aboard the original *Queen Mary* and *Queen Elizabeth*. The room has intimate detailing and overlooks the Pool Terrace, for alfresco dining.

Kings Court. This revamped, informal, open-plan eatery offers self-serve breakfast and lunch. Breakfasts are repetitive, but include British traditional standards such as eggs, bacon, kippers, and fried tomatoes. Lunch menus change daily, and include several popular Indian dishes. At night, decorated screens transform sections of the venue into extra-cost dining areas.

Comfort foods are available in the outdoors Boardwalk Café, weather permitting, while pub lovers can find traditional British fare in the popular Golden Lion Pub. The multi-use Carinthia Lounge is for extra-cost coffees and light items for breakfast and lunch; it includes a patisserie, and is a good venue for socializing, with some evening entertainment.

Note: You can also order from the restaurant menus and have breakfast, lunch, and dinner served in your own suite or cabin.

ENTERTAINMENT. The Royal Court Theatre, a lovely venue, has tiered seating for 1,094, though some sight lines are less than ideal. It stages West End-style productions and hosts headline entertainers and cabaret acts. The Royal Academy of Dramatic Art (RADA) supplies a company of actors to give Shakespearean performances, lead acting workshops, and take part in street-theater performances.

Images of movie stars and notable celebrities who have sailed aboard the Cunard 'Queens' can be seen together with famous former Cunard ocean liners, in a superb display (you can see everything on a self-guided tour) called Maritime Quest.

SPA/FITNESS. Health Spa and Beauty Services are provided in a 20,000-sq-ft (1,858-sq-m) Canyon Ranch SpaClub, arranged on two decks. There's a thalassotherapy pool, whirlpool, and thermal suite (at extra cost, but waived if you buy a treatment). There are 20 treatment rooms. Sports facilities include an electronic golf simulator, giant chess board, and a paddle-tennis court.

QUEEN VICTORIA
★★★★+

A PRETEND OCEAN LINER THAT REALLY SUITS TRADITIONAL BRITISH TASTES

Size:	Mid-size Ship	Passenger/Crew Ratio (lower beds):	2.2
Tonnage:	90,049	Cabins (total):	1,046
Cruise Line:	Cunard	Size Range (sq ft/m):	143.0–2,131.3/13.2–198.0
Former Names:	none	Cabins (for one person):	9
Builder:	Fincantieri (Italy)	Cabins with balcony:	718
Entered Service:	Dec 2007	Cabins (wheelchair accessible):	20
Length (ft/m):	964.5/294.0	Wheelchair accessibility:	Good
Beam (ft/m):	105.9/32.3	Elevators:	12
Propulsion/Propellers:	diesel-electric (64,00kW)/ 2 azimuthing pods	Casino (gaming tables):	Yes
		Swimming Pools:	2
Passenger Decks:	12	Self-Service Launderette:	Yes
Total Crew:	1,001	Library:	Yes
Passengers (lower beds):	2,083	Onboard currency:	US$
Passenger Space Ratio (lower beds):	44.5		

THE SHIP. *Queen Victoria*, which underwent a $40 million refit in 2017, will appeal to any Anglophile, because Cunard is still a British experience. (To some extent, this is marketing hype, since British members of staff are rather thin on the ground nowadays.)

Basically a stretched, modified platform and layout as the *Vista* series of ships (examples include: *Arcadia*, *Carnival Legend*, *Costa Atlantica*, and *Oosterdam*), the Cunard version has an additional passenger deck, a specially strengthened hull lengthened by 36ft (11m), giving the ship more of an 'ocean liner' feel. It also has a more traditional interior layout reminiscent of yesteryear's ocean liners.

The interior decor is 'traditional' in Cunard-speak, with many public rooms finely decorated in Edwardian/Victorian styles, with wrought-iron balustrades on staircases and in some bars. A three-deck-high Grand Lobby has a sweeping staircase and sculpted balconies. The Cunardia museum's glass cabinets display models of former Cunard ships, old menus, and daily programs.

The Royal Arcade houses a cluster of seven shops, including Harrods, Royal Doulton, and Wedgwood, set in an arcade-like environment.

Other public areas worth mentioning include the following:

The Library, a stunning two-deck-high wood-paneled 6,000-book facility but with few chairs; its upper level has Internet-connect computer terminals.

BERLITZ'S RATINGS		
	Possible	Achieved
Ship	500	412
Accommodation	200	145
Food	400	299
Service	400	313
Entertainment	100	81
Cruise Experience	400	316

OVERALL SCORE 1566 points out of 2000

A Golden Lion Pub is a must aboard a Cunarder, and this one lies along the starboard side. It's a good gathering place for karaoke, singalong, and quiz enthusiasts, plus it provides tasty pub food.

The Commodore Club acts as a large observation lounge; adjacent on the starboard side is Churchill's Cigar Lounge, for cigar-smokers.

Chart Room Bar has some Cunard memorabilia displays.

Hemispheres, aft of the mast and adjacent to the Commodore Club, overlooks the wood-decked Pavilion Pool; this is the high-volume disco and themed nightclub.

There's also a casino on the port side of the lower level of the Royal Court.

A grand conservatory-style Winter Gardens has a moveable glass wall to an open-air swimming pool. Rattan furniture and ceiling fans help to conjure up the area's colonial theme.

Queen Victoria, a very comfortable, likeable cruise ship posing as an ocean liner, is best suited to a couples and solo travelers who enjoy traditional British ocean liner-style decor, world-wide itineraries, and dressing for dinner. A per-person, per-day gratuity is charged to your onboard account, and a 15 percent gratuity is added to all bar and wine accounts. Gratuities, called a 'Hotel and Dining' charge, are automatically added to your account daily. The onboard currency is the US dollar – another reason to take the Britishness claims with a pinch of salt.

Sadly, there's no help with hand luggage at embarkation. Quality has decreased in little things such as toilet paper and facial tissues – do they think no one notices? The variety of cheese is very limited now (even in Grill Class venues). Other niggles include many staff touting for extra gratuities, lack of attention to detail, dispensers in the Lido buffet for condiments such as mustard, ketchup, and mayonnaise.

ACCOMMODATION.

There are numerous price grades and different types of accommodation, ranging from ample but basic to opulent. Nine cabins for solo-occupancy were added in 2015, and in 2017 43 Britannia Club-grade cabins were added to the range.

All accommodation grades have both British three-pin (240-volt) sockets and American (110-volt) and European-style two-pin (220-volt) sockets. Penhaligon's toiletries are supplied to all passengers, and a hairdryer is stored in the vanity desk units. Some cabins have nicely indented ceilings with suffused lighting. However, the flat-screen TV sets are small – not good for watching movies at bedtime.

The regular cabins (Grades C/D) are small, but functional, although completely lacking in 'wow' factor. The cabinetry is a bit austere and lacking in character. There is a distinct lack of drawer space in a cabin supposedly designed for two persons; it's noticeable on long voyages, and additional drawers located under the bed have proved challenging for some to use. The premium mattresses are, however, excellent, as is the bed linen; European duvets are standard. The bathrooms are stunningly bland, with small washbasins, little storage space for toiletries, cold, tiled floors, and wall-mounted shower heads.

DINING.

Cunard is respected for its cuisine and service, with a wide variety of well-prepared and presented dishes. The Britannia Restaurant – the name is taken from a former Cunard ocean liner of 1914–50 (not from P&O Cruises' *Britannia*) – is located in the aft section. It is two decks high, with seating on both the main level (two seatings for dinner, but open seating for breakfast and lunch) and balcony level. A

horseshoe-shaped stairway links both levels. While lower-level diners have a good sea view through large picture windows, balcony diners get a promenade view. Waterford Wedgwood china is used, and there's a wide range of wines (and prices).

Queens Grill and Princess Grill, two Grill Class-only restaurants, with a single-seating arrangement, provide more exclusive dining. On the port side, the 142-seat Queens Grill is for passengers in suites and top-category accommodation grades, and provides the best cuisine and service aboard. On the starboard side, the 132-seat Princess Grill is for passengers in middle-class accommodation grades.

The Cunard Grill experience also includes alfresco dining in a seldom-used courtyard terrace (The Courtyard), suitably protected from the wind, and exclusive access to an upper terrace deck, with dedicated staff, as well as the Grills' lounge and bar.

A Britannia Club Restaurant was added in a 2017 refit, for the exclusive use of Britannia Club-class occupants.

A 100-seat, reservations-required, extra-cost Verandah Restaurant focuses on classic French cuisine. It is on the second level of the three-deck-high lobby.

The Lido Café, on Deck 11, has good panoramic views, indoor/outdoor seating for 468, and offers a fairly standard multi-line self-serve buffet arrangement.

For traditional British pub food, the Golden Lion Pub serves fish and chips, steak and mushroom pie, ploughman's lunch, and bangers (sausages) and mash – particularly good at lunchtime – with a nice draft pint of bitter, naturally.

Excellent extra-cost *illy* coffee and Godiva chocolates are available on the second level of the lobby.

ENTERTAINMENT.

The 830-seat, three-deck-high Royal Court Theatre is designed in the style of a classic opera house, complete with royal boxes.

SPA/FITNESS.

The Cunard Royal Spa has features including a beauty salon, large gymnasium and several body-treatment rooms, but young staff with poor communication skills.

RADIANCE OF THE SEAS
★★★+

THIS MID-SIZE, FAMILY-FRIENDLY SHIP IS FOR CASUAL CRUISING

Size:	Mid-size Ship
Tonnage:	90,090
Cruise Line:	Royal Caribbean International
Former Names:	none
Builder:	Meyer Werft (Germany)
Entered Service:	Apr 2001
Length (ft/m):	961.9/293.2
Beam (ft/m):	105.6/32.2
Propulsion/Propellers:	Gas turbine (40,000kW)/2 azimuthing pods
Passenger Decks:	12
Total Crew:	858
Passengers (lower beds):	2,146
Passenger Space Ratio (lower beds):	42.0
Passenger/Crew Ratio (lower beds):	2.5
Cabins (total):	1,072
Size Range (sq ft/m):	165.8–1,216.3/15.4–113.0
Cabins (for one person):	0
Cabins with balcony:	578
Cabins (wheelchair accessible):	14
Wheelchair accessibility:	Good
Elevators:	9
Casino (gaming tables):	Yes
Swimming Pools:	2
Self-Service Launderette:	No
Library:	Yes
Onboard currency:	US$

THE SHIP. *Radiance of the Seas* was the first RCI ship to use gas and steam turbine power instead of the more conventional diesel or diesel-electric combination. Pod propulsion is provided. At the very front of the ship is a helipad, which also acts as a viewing platform for passengers.

This is a modern-looking ship, with a two-deck-high walk-around structure in the forward section of the funnel. Along the ship's starboard side, a central glass wall protrudes, giving great views – cabins with balconies occupy the space directly opposite on the port side. The gently rounded stern has nicely tiered decks. One of two swimming pools can be covered by a glass dome for use as an indoor/outdoor pool.

Inside, the decor is contemporary, yet elegant, bright, and cheerful. A nine-deck-high atrium lobby has glass-walled elevators that travel through 12 decks, face the sea, and provide a link with nature and the ocean, while a finger-touch digital 'way-finder' system helps you find your way around. The Centrum (city center), as the atrium is called, is the social hub of the ship. It is nine decks high, and has many public rooms and facilities connected to it: the business services desks, a Lobby Bar, Champagne Bar, Schooner Bar (the nautical-themed bar, with maritime art), Café Latte-tudes (for extra-cost coffees), Royal Caribbean Online (with a dozen Internet-connect computers), the flashy Casino Royale (for casino gamers and slot machine fans; it has a

BERLITZ'S RATINGS		
	Possible	Achieved
Ship	500	338
Accommodation	200	128
Food	400	237
Service	400	279
Entertainment	100	74
Cruise Experience	400	267

OVERALL SCORE 1323 points out of 2000

French Art Nouveau decorative theme and sports 11 crystal chandeliers), a Quill and Compass Pub, Concierge Lounge, and a Crown & Anchor Lounge. There's also a 194-seat conference center, and a business center. The Viking Crown Lounge (a trademark aboard all RCI ships) is a large structure set around the base of the ship's funnel. It functions as an observation lounge during the daytime, with views forward over the swimming pool.

Shipwide Wi-Fi is available for a fee. More Internet-access terminals are located in Books 'n' Coffee, a bookshop with coffee and pastries, located in an extensive area of shops.

The artwork is eclectic, providing a spectrum of color. It ranges from Jenny M. Hansen's *A Vulnerable Moment* glass sculpture to David Buckland's *Industrial and Russian Constructionism 1920s* in photographic images on glass and painted canvas, to a huge, multi-deck-high, contemporary bicycle-cum-paddle-wheel sculpture design suspended in the atrium.

Radiance of the Seas offers a decent amount of space, comfortable public areas, and slightly larger cabins than some Royal Caribbean International (RCI) ships for younger, active travelers. A grand amount of glass provides extensive views of the ocean. While the ship is delightful in many ways, the operation does suffer from a lack of well-trained service staff.

ACCOMMODATION. There is a wide range of suites and standard outside-view and interior cabins in 10 different categories and numerous price groups.

Apart from the largest suites (six Owner's Suites), which have king-size beds, almost all other cabins have twin beds that convert to a queen-size bed. All cabins have rich (but faux) wood cabinetry, including a vanity desk with hairdryer, faux wood silent-close drawers, flat-screen television, personal safe, and three-sided mirrors. Some cabins have ceiling-recessed, pull-down berths for third and fourth persons, although closet and drawer space would be extremely tight for four persons, even if two were small children; some have interconnecting doors, so families with children can cruise together in separate but adjacent cabins. Audio channels are available through the TV set, so the picture cannot be turned off while you are listening to an audio channel.

Many bathrooms have a terrazzo-style tiled floor, and a small shower enclosure in a half-moon shape, Egyptian cotton towels, a cabinet for toiletries, and a shelf. In reality, there is little space to stow toiletries for two (or more).

The largest accommodation consists of a family suite with two bedrooms. One bedroom has twin beds that convert to queen-size bed, while a second has two lower beds and two upper Pullman berths, a combination that can sleep up to eight persons. Many of the 'private' balcony cabins aren't very private, as they can be overlooked.

DINING. Cascades, the main dining room, spans two decks. The upper level has floor-to-ceiling windows, while the lower deck level has picture windows. It is a delightful, but noisy, dining hall, although eight thick pillars obstruct sight lines. It seats 1,110, and has cascading water-themed decor, and a large glass mural. There are tables for two to 10. A small private dining room (the 30-seat Tides) is located adjacent. When you book, choose one of two seatings, or 'My Time Dining,' so you can eat when you want, during dining room hours.

The cuisine is typical of mass banquet catering that offers standard fare comparable to that found in American family-style restaurants ashore. Overall, meals are rather non-memorable. Also, if you want lobster or a decent filet mignon (steak), you will need to pay extra.

The following are optional dining venues/eateries:

Boardwalk Dog House, for hot dogs, wieners, brats, sausages, and a variety of toppings to split a long bun (open for lunch and dinner, no cost).

Giovanni's Table, an extra-cost trattoria with Italian classics served family-style (open for lunch and dinner). Reservations are required.

Izumi features a sushi bar with hot-rock cooking (open for lunch and dinner). A cover charge applies, and there's additional à la carte menu item pricing. Reservations are required.

Park Café, an indoor/outdoor market for salads, sandwiches, soups, and pastries (open for breakfast, lunch and dinner; no added cost, but reservations are required).

Rita's Cantina, a casual (extra-cost, reservations-required) indoor/outdoor eatery, for families by day, and adults by night, for Mexican cuisine.

Chef's Table, a private experience co-hosted by the executive chef and sommelier for a multi-course wine-pairing dinner. A cover charge applies, and reservations are required.

Samba Grill, an extra-cost Brazilian churrascaria (steakhouse), for a variety of meats, chicken, and seafood brought to the table ready to slice and serve upon request (open for dinner only, and reservations are required).

For casual eats, the place to go is the expansive Windjammer Café, a self-serve venue, similar to a food court.

ENTERTAINMENT. The three-level Aurora Theater has 874 seats, including 24 stations for wheelchairs, and good sight lines from most seats; it's the venue for large-scale shows and cabaret acts. The Colony Club hosts casual cabaret shows, including late-night adult comedy, and has live music for dancing. The entertainment throughout is lively and upbeat. Sadly, 'background' music pervades all corridors and elevators; there's also constant intrusive music on the pool deck.

SPA/FITNESS. The Day Spa fitness and spa facilities have themed decor, and include a gymnasium with numerous cardiovascular machines, a large aerobics room, sauna and steam rooms, and body-pampering treatment rooms. All are located on two of the uppermost decks, forward of the mast, with access from the forward stairway.

A climate-controlled 10,176-sq-ft (945-sq-m) indoor/outdoor Solarium has a sliding glass roof that can be closed in cool or inclement weather.

Sports facilities include a 30ft (9m) rock-climbing wall with five separate climbing tracks, an exterior jogging track, a nine-hole miniature golf course with novel 17th-century decorative ornaments, and an indoor/outdoor country club with golf simulator, a jogging track, and basketball court. There are two specially stabilized pool tables (within the Bombay Billiard Club).

REGAL PRINCESS
★★★★

THIS LARGE, MULTI-CHOICE FAMILY-FRIENDLY RESORT SHIP HAS STYLE

Size:	Large Resort Ship	Passenger/Crew Ratio (lower beds):	2.6
Tonnage:	142,229	Cabins (total):	1,780
Cruise Line:	Princess Cruises	Size Range (sq ft/m):	161.4–554.3/15–51.5
Former Names:	none	Cabins (for one person):	0
Builder:	Fincantieri (Italy)	Cabins with balcony:	1,438
Entered Service:	May 2014	Cabins (wheelchair accessible):	36
Length (ft/m):	1,082.6/330.0	Wheelchair accessibility:	Best
Beam (ft/m):	126.3/38.5	Elevators:	14
Propulsion/Propellers:	diesel-electric (52,000kW)/2	Casino (gaming tables):	Yes
Passenger Decks:	17	Swimming Pools:	2
Total Crew:	1,346	Self-Service Launderette:	Yes
Passengers (lower beds):	3,560	Library:	Yes
Passenger Space Ratio (lower beds):	39.9	Onboard currency:	US$

THE SHIP. *Regal Princess* is a sister to *Royal Princess*, which debuted in 2013. Although large, the ship's profile is quite well balanced – an enhancement of the older *Grand*-class ships. In terms of practical design, the lifeboats are located outside the main public room areas, so they don't impair the view from balcony cabins. The ship features a complete (well, sort of) walk-around promenade deck.

An over-the-water SeaWalk, an open deck glass-bottomed enclosed walkway (first introduced in 2013 aboard sister ship *Royal Princess*) on the starboard side extends almost 30ft (9.1m) beyond the vessel's edge and forms part of a lounge/bar venue. This is the place to go for dramatic (downward) views, including to the sea 128ft (39m) below, so you *can* 'walk' on water (or, at least, over it). On the ship's port side is a SeaView bar.

There are two principal stair towers and elevator banks, plus some panoramic-view elevators in a third, central bank (these elevators do not go between decks 7 and 16 – a serious design omission because stairs are only at the forward and aft elevator banks). The interior decor is warm and attractive, with an abundance of earth tones that suit both American and European tastes. One of the line's hallmark venues, the Piazza Atrium, was significantly expanded compared to the older ships in the fleet. This area is the ship's multi-faceted so-

BERLITZ'S RATINGS		
	Possible	Achieved
Ship	500	401
Accommodation	200	139
Food	400	268
Service	400	294
Entertainment	100	82
Cruise Experience	400	304

OVERALL SCORE 1480 points out of 2000

cial hub and combines a specialty dining venue, light meals, snack-food items, pastries, beverages, entertainment, shopping, and guest services. It is larger than aboard any other Princess Cruises ship (except sister ships *Majestic Princess* and *Royal Princess*), and has a horseshoe-shaped flowing stairway and lots of mood lighting effects.

The base level includes an International Café, for coffees, teas, panini, and pastries (and to see and be seen); Sabatini's, a Tuscan specialty extra-cost restaurant (located just off the atrium itself), with both regular and à la carte menus; and a gift shop. Upstairs, level two includes Alfredo's Pizzeria, Bellini's (a bar serving Bellini drinks), a photo gallery, the reception desk, and a counter for shore excursions. On the third level, Crooners Bar features entertaining pianists. The Piazza Atrium is all about food, entertainment, and passenger services, and is the social nerve center of the ship.

Passenger niggles include the user-unfriendly automated telephone system, the small cabin towels, having to pay extra for items such as ice cream, and the charge (coins needed) for the washers and dryers in the self-service launderettes.

Overall, however, Princess Cruises delivers a consistently fine, comfortable, well-packaged product, always with a good degree of style, at a competitive price.

ACCOMMODATION. There are six main types of accommodation in many price grades: (a) Grand Suite; (b) suites with balcony; (c) mini-suites with balcony; (d) deluxe outside-view balcony cabins; (e) outside-view cabins with balcony; and (f) interior cabins. Pricing depends on two things: size and location. Outside-view cabins account for about 81 percent of all accommodation, and all have a balcony; those located at the stern are the quietest and most sought-after. Some of the most sought-after suites are located aft, occupying the corner (port and starboard) positions. Each accommodation deck houses a self-service launderette.

All accommodation grades share energy-efficient lighting and key card readers that automatically turn off lights when occupants leave. All cabins get beds with upholstered headboards, wall-mounted TV sets, additional 220v electrical socket, turndown service and heart-shaped chocolates on pillows each night, bathrobes (on request, unless you are in suite-grade accommodation), and toiletries. A hairdryer is provided, sensibly located at the vanity desk unit in the living area. Bathrooms have decent open-shelf storage space for toiletries, and all bathrooms have hand-held, flexi-hose showers, and large shower enclosures.

Suite and mini-suite grade occupants have a concierge lounge (towards the aft on Deck 14) – useful for making dining, spa, and shore-excursion reservations. They also get more amenities and larger TV sets, while suite bathrooms have two washbasins.

Be aware that the balconies of cabins on Marina Deck 15 can be seen by anyone on the overhanging Skywalk on the deck above, so choose your cabin wisely.

DINING. There are three 'formal' main dining rooms. You can choose either traditional two-seating dining (typically 6pm and 8.15pm for dinner), or 'anytime dining,' which allows you to choose when and with whom you want to eat.

Although portions are generous, the food and its presentation are disappointing, and simply standardized. Fish is often disguised by a crumb or batter coating, the choice of fresh green vegetables is limited, few garnishes are used, and cheese is already sliced and diced. But, this is big-ship banquet catering, with all its attendant standardization. Pasta dishes are acceptable (though voluminous), typically served by section headwaiters, who may also make 'something special just for you' – in search of favorable comments and gratuities. If you like desserts, order a sundae at dinner (most other items are just so-so).

Extra-cost, reservations-required Sabatini's, located adjacent to Vines Wine Bar on the lower atrium level, is an Italian restaurant with Tuscan decor. Named after Trattoria Sabatini, in Florence, it serves Italian-style pasta dishes with a choice of sauces, as well as Italian-style entrées (mains) all presented with flair and entertainment by energetic waiters. There's both a table-d'hôte and an à la carte menu. This venue also hosts Italian wine tastings.

Ocean Terrace, located on the atrium's second level is a seafood bar. International Café, on the atrium's lowest level is for extra-cost coffees, pastries, panini, and more. Vines Wine Bar, adjacent to Sabatini's, is for a glass of extra-cost wine, and for tapas. This is a pleasant area to while away a late afternoon, trying out new wines.

Crown Grill is an extra-cost, à la carte dining venue, adjacent to the Wheelhouse Bar, on the uppermost level of the three-deck-high atrium, and is the place to go for steaks and seafood.

For casual eats the self-serve buffet venue (Horizon Court) seats 900 indoors and 350 outdoors. There are multiple 'active' cooking stations and themed sections (Mediterranean, Asian, Italian, etc.); there's also a deli section. At night, the Horizon Bistro (aft) section is for casual dinners. Certain nights feature special themes and foods, such as British pub food or Brazilian churrascaria (for meat). Rotisseries, carvings, hibachi grill, and other active cooking station items are all part of the scenario.

The ship's bakery (well, part of it) comes out of the galley and into a separate area of the Horizon Court. Called the Horizon Bistro Pastry Shop, it offers freshly baked bread, croissants and other pastry items, and waffles.

ENTERTAINMENT. The Princess Theater, the showlounge, is a two-deck-high venue for the large-scale production shows for which Princess Cruises is renowned. There's also a 'Princess Live' auditorium for stand-up comedy and other small-audience entertainment features. Aft on the same deck is a Vista Lounge; this has a large dance floor. The ship carries a number of gentlemen dance hosts on each cruise for female passengers without partners.

SPA/FITNESS. The Lotus Spa is located forward on the lower level of the atrium, so it doesn't take away premium outdoor-view real estate space. Separate facilities for men and women include a sauna, steam room, and changing rooms; common facilities include a relaxation/waiting zone, body-pampering treatment rooms, and a gymnasium packed with the latest high-tech, muscle-pumping equipment. Some fitness classes are free, while others cost extra. Children and teens have their own fitness rooms adjacent to their age-related facilities.

Spa operator Steiner Leisure is in charge of the Lotus Spa. You can make online reservations for any spa treatments before your cruise, which could be a great time-saver.

REGATTA
★★★★

THIS IS AN INFORMAL SHIP WITH COUNTRY CLUB DECOR FOR MATURE-AGE CRUISERS

Size:	Small Ship	Passenger/Crew Ratio (lower beds):	1.7
Tonnage:	30,277	Cabins (total):	342
Cruise Line:	Oceania Cruises	Size Range (sq ft/m):	145.3–968.7/13.5–90.0
Former Names:	R Two	Cabins (for one person):	0
Builder:	Chantiers de l'Atlantique	Cabins with balcony:	232
Entered Service:	Dec 1998/Dec 2003	Cabins (wheelchair accessible):	3
Length (ft/m):	593.7/181.0	Wheelchair accessibility:	Good
Beam (ft/m):	83.5/25.5	Elevators:	4
Propulsion/Propellers:	diesel (18,600kW)/2	Casino (gaming tables):	Yes
Passenger Decks:	9	Swimming Pools:	1
Total Crew:	386	Self-Service Launderette:	Yes
Passengers (lower beds):	684	Library:	Yes
Passenger Space Ratio (lower beds):	44.2	Onboard currency:	US$

THE SHIP. *Regatta* was originally one of eight almost identical ships built for the now-defunct Renaissance Cruises. The uniform color (all white) of the exterior and large, square funnel help to balance the ship's high sides. Teak overlaid decking and high-quality lounge chairs help create a very comfortable Lido and Pool Deck.

In 2014, the ship underwent a refurbishment program that included the addition of Barista's coffee bar (for illy coffees), installed completely new bathrooms for the Owner's Suites and Vista Suites, and updated the decor in all other cabins. Also added were a miniature golf course, shuffleboard courts, and other deck games.

There is no walk-around promenade deck outdoors as such – there is, however, a small jogging/walking track, above the swimming pool.

The stunningly elegant interior decor is a throwback to the ocean liners of the 1920s and 1930s, with dark woods and warm colors, all carried out in fine taste – if a bit faux in places. It feels like an old-world country club.

The public rooms are spread over three decks. The reception hall has a staircase with intricate wrought-iron railings. A large observation lounge, the Horizon Bar, is located high atop ship. There are plenty of bars, including one in each of the restaurant entrances. Perhaps the nicest is the casino bar/lounge, a beautiful room reminiscent of London's grand ho-

BERLITZ'S RATINGS		
	Possible	Achieved
Ship	500	378
Accommodation	200	145
Food	400	298
Service	400	291
Entertainment	100	71
Cruise Experience	400	294
OVERALL SCORE 1477 points out of 2000		

tels. It has an inviting marble fireplace, sofas, and chairs.

The Library is a grand Regency-style room, with a fireplace, a high, indented, trompe l'oeil ceiling, and excellent selection of books, plus very comfortable wingback chairs with footstools, and sofas you could sleep on.

The dress code is 'smart casual.' Gratuities are added at $10.50 per person, per day, and accommodation designated as suites have an extra $3 per person charge for the butler. A rather large gratuity of 18 percent is added to bar and spa accounts.

Oceania Cruises is a young company that aims to provide a high level of food and service in an informal setting that's elegant yet comfortable. *Regatta* suits couples who like really good food and style, but want informality and not formal nights on board, as well as interesting itineraries, all at a reasonable price.

Passenger niggles include all the inventive extra charges that can be incurred. What's really nice is the fact that there are almost no intrusive announcements.

ACCOMMODATION. There are six cabin categories, and 10 price grades (three suite price grades; five outside-view cabin grades; two interior cabin grades). All of the standard interior and outside-view cabins (the lowest four grades) are extremely tight for two people, particularly for cruises longer than five days. They have twin beds or a queen-size bed, with good under-bed storage areas, personal safe, vanity desk with large mirror, good closet and drawer space in rich, dark woods, 100 percent cotton bathrobe and towels, slippers, clothes brush, and shoehorn.

Certain cabin categories (about 100 of them) qualify as Concierge Level accommodation, and occupants get extra goodies such as enhanced bathroom amenities, complimentary shoeshine, tote bag, cashmere throw blanket, bottle of Champagne on arrival, a hand-held hairdryer, priority restaurant reservations, and priority embarkation.

Outside-view and interior (no-view) cabins measure around 160–165 sq ft (14.9–15.3 sq m) and have twin beds that convert to a queen-size unit, and a bathroom with a shower enclosure with a strong, removable hand-held shower unit, hairdryer, storage shelves for toiletries, retractable clothesline, washbasin, and toilet. Although not large, they are quite comfortable, with a decent amount of storage space.

Cabins with balcony measure around 216 sq ft (20 sq m) and comprise about two-thirds of all cabins (14 cabins on Deck 6 have lifeboat-obstructed views).

Penthouse Suites are actually large cabins rather than suites, as the bedrooms aren't separate from the living areas, and measure around 323 sq ft (30 sq m).

Vista Suites measure around 786 sq ft (73 sq m), and are located forward on decks 5 and 6. The bed faces the sea, which is visible through the floor-to-ceiling windows and sliding glass door.

Owner's Suites each measure around 962 sq ft (89 sq m), which makes these fine living spaces the most spacious accommodation on board. Located aft and overlooking the stern on decks 6, 7, and 8, they are subject to more movement and some vibration. The bed faces the sea, which can be seen through the floor-to-ceiling windows and sliding glass door.

DINING. Flexibility and choice are what the dining facilities aboard Oceania Cruises ships are all about. There are four different restaurants:

The Grand Dining Room has around 340 seats, and a raised central section, but the problem is the noise level – because of the low ceiling height, it's atrocious when the dining room is full. Being located at the stern, there are large ocean-view windows on three sides, and prime tables overlook the stern. The chairs are comfortable, with armrests. Menus change daily for lunch and dinner.

Toscana Italian Restaurant has 96 seats, windows along two sides, and a set menu plus daily chef's specials.

The cozy Polo Grill has 98 seats, windows along two sides and a set menu including prime steaks and seafood.

The Terrace Café has both indoor and outdoor seating. It is open for breakfast, lunch, and casual dinners, with some fine tapas and other Mediterranean dishes. As the self-serve buffet restaurant, it incorporates a small pizzeria and grill.

A poolside Waves Grill serves fish burgers, veggie burgers, and Reuben sandwiches, as well as Angus beef burgers, and hot dogs.

All restaurants have open-seating dining, so you can dine when you want, with whom you wish. Reservations are needed in the Toscana Restaurant and Polo Grill (but there's no extra charge), where there are mostly tables for four or six, and few tables for two. There is a Poolside Grill Bar.

The food and service staff is provided by a respected maritime catering company that also has an interest in Oceania Cruises. This is definitely a foodie's ship, with really high-quality ingredients. Particularly notable are the delicious breads, rolls, croissants, and brioches – all made on board from French flour and Isigny butter.

On sea days, afternoon tea is presented in the Horizon Lounge, with formally dressed staff, cake trolleys, and an array of cake and scones.

ENTERTAINMENT. The Regatta Lounge has entertainment, lectures, some social events, and a mix of production shows and cabaret acts.

SPA/FITNESS. A Lido Deck has a swimming pool, and good sunbathing space, plus a thalassotherapy tub. The uppermost outdoors deck includes a golf driving net and shuffleboard court. Canyon Ranch SpaClub consists of a beauty salon, three treatment rooms, changing rooms, and steam room (but no sauna). Note that an 18 percent 'gratuity' is added to your spa account.

RHAPSODY OF THE SEAS
★★★+

THIS MODERN SHIP IS GOOD FOR CASUAL, FAMILY-FRIENDLY VACATIONS

Size:	Mid-size Ship	Passenger/Crew Ratio (lower beds):	2.6
Tonnage:	78,491	Cabins (total):	1,000
Cruise Line:	Royal Caribbean International	Size Range (sq ft/m):	135.0–1,270.1/12.5–118.0
Former Names:	none	Cabins (for one person):	0
Builder:	Chantiers de l'Atlantique (France)	Cabins with balcony:	229
Entered Service:	May 1997	Cabins (wheelchair accessible):	14
Length (ft/m):	915.3/279.0	Wheelchair accessibility:	Good
Beam (ft/m):	105.6/32.2	Elevators:	9
Propulsion/Propellers:	diesel-electric (50,400kW)/2	Casino (gaming tables):	Yes
Passenger Decks:	11	Swimming Pools:	2
Total Crew:	765	Self-Service Launderette:	No
Passengers (lower beds):	2,000	Library:	Yes
Passenger Space Ratio (lower beds):	39.2	Onboard currency:	US$

THE SHIP. This all-white (*Vision*-class) ship has a nicely rounded stern and a single, slim funnel aft. There is a reasonable amount of outdoor walking space, although this tends to be cluttered with sun-loungers.

The ship shares design features that make many, but not all, Royal Caribbean International (RCI) ships identifiable, including a domed Viking Crown Lounge, above the atrium lobby. The artwork is upbeat and colorful, with a musical theme. There's a wide range of interesting public rooms, lounges, and bars, and the interiors have been cleverly designed to avoid congestion and aid flow into revenue areas.

The seven-deck high atrium lobby – called the Centrum – is the interior focal and social hub of the ship. It houses an R Bar (for cocktails), several service counters, an art gallery, and Café Latte-tudes (for coffee). Close by is the superbly flashy Casino Royale (with gaming tables and slot machines), and the company's signature Schooner Bar, with nautical-theme decor.

Ship-wide Wi-Fi is provided (a charge applies), as is a digital direction-finding system, electronic mustering, and an outdoor poolside movie screen. Cabin iPads contain content about the ship's amenities and activities. Ship enthusiasts will like the chair fabric in the Shall We Dance Lounge, with its large aft-facing windows, and the glass case-enclosed mechanical sculptures.

BERLITZ'S RATINGS

	Possible	Achieved
Ship	500	338
Accommodation	200	129
Food	400	257
Service	400	250
Entertainment	100	63
Cruise Experience	400	270

OVERALL SCORE 1307 points out of 2000

ACCOMMODATION. There are numerous accommodation grades, priced by size and location. The standard interior and exterior-view cabins are very small but have just enough functional facilities to make them acceptable for a one-week cruise (longer might prove confining). The decor is bright and cheerful, although the ceilings are plain; the soft furnishings make this home away from home look like the inside of a modern Scandinavian hotel – with minimalist tones, and splashes of color. Twin lower beds convert to queen-size beds, and there is a reasonable amount of closet and drawer space, but there is little room to maneuver between the bed and the desk/television unit.

The bathrooms are small but functional. The shower units are small, there is no cabinet for toiletries, and the towels are thin. In the passageways, upbeat artwork depicts musical themes.

Suite-grade accommodation gives you more space and larger bathrooms (some with bathtubs). For the best accommodation, choose the Royal Suite, which comes with a white baby grand piano.

DINING. The two-level Edelweiss Dining Room is attractive and works well as a large restaurant, although the noise level can be high. When you book, choose one of two seatings (fixed for dinner) for dinner or My Time Dining (eat when you want, during dining room hours).

The cuisine is typical of mass banquet catering that offers standard fare comparable to that found in American family-style restaurants ashore. Overall, meals are rather hit and miss – in fact non-memorable. If you want lobster or a decent filet mignon (steak), it's at extra cost. However, a decent selection of light meals is provided; vegetarian and children's menus are also available.

Most meat dishes are disguised with gravies or sauce reductions. Most fish and seafood items tend to be overcooked and lack taste. Green vegetables are rather scarce – they're basically for decoration – but salad items are plentiful, and desserts are good. Rice is often used as a source of carbohydrates.

Breads and pastry items are reasonably decent (these are thawed and then baked from frozen 'starter' dough), although items such as croissants lack any hint of butter.

Other dining venues and eateries are as follows. Some cost extra, but food is mostly cooked to order. Reservations (make them through the digital system) are required; note that menus do not change.

Chops Grille Steakhouse is for premium veal chops and steaks and seafood items. Giovanni's Table is for Italian trattoria-style cuisine. Izumi Asian Cuisine includes a sushi bar and features hot-rock cooking; it is open for lunch and dinner. A la carte menu pricing applies to all three venues.

Chef's Table is a private experience co-hosted by the executive chef and sommelier for a multi-course wine-pairing dinner. Park Café is a casual no-charge market-style eatery for salads, sandwiches, soups, and pastries.

For casual eats, the Windjammer Café – located at the front of the ship with some commanding ocean views – is a large self-serve buffet venue (like a food court).

A drinks package is available at all bars, so you can pre-pay for a selection of standard soft drinks and alcoholic drinks; the packages are, however, confusing.

ENTERTAINMENT. The Broadway Melodies Theater is the principal showlounge. It is a large, but well-designed room with main and balcony levels, and good sight lines from most of the banquette seats.

Other cabaret (and late-night comedy) acts are presented in the Shall We Dance Lounge, located aft.

The entertainment, for which RCI gets abundant praise, is upbeat and colorful. However, it's difficult to escape from the background music provided everywhere else – even in the passenger hallways and elevators, and outdoors on the pool deck.

SPA/FITNESS. The Vitality at Sea Spa and Fitness Center is on one of the aft uppermost decks. The decor has Egypt as its theme, with pharaohs lining an indoor/outdoor solarium pool. It is operated by Steiner, a specialist concession with staff providing a wide range of body treatments and hair care.

Other facilities include a rock-climbing wall aft of the funnel, with several climbing tracks.

RIVIERA
★★★★+

A HOMEY, VERY COMFORTABLE, MID-SIZE SHIP WITH A COUNTRY-CLUB FEEL

Size:	Mid-size Ship	Passenger/Crew Ratio (lower beds):	1.5
Tonnage:	66,084	Cabins (total):	629
Cruise Line:	Oceania Cruises	Size Range (sq ft/m):	172.2–2,000/16.0–185.0
Former Names:	none	Cabins (for one person):	0
Builder:	Fincantieri (Italy)	Cabins with balcony:	593
Entered Service:	Jul 2012	Cabins (wheelchair accessible):	6
Length (ft/m):	776.5/236.7	Wheelchair accessibility:	Good
Beam (ft/m):	105.3/32.1	Elevators:	6
Propulsion/Propellers:	diesel-electric/2	Casino (gaming tables):	Yes
Passenger Decks:	11	Swimming Pools:	1
Total Crew:	800	Self-Service Launderette:	Yes
Passengers (lower beds):	1,258	Library:	Yes
Passenger Space Ratio (lower beds):	52.5	Onboard currency:	US$

THE SHIP. *Riviera* is the second newbuild (close sister to *Marina*) for this small premium-ship cruise line. Its profile is quite handsome, with a nicely rounded front, and is topped by a swept-back funnel.

The ship suits mature-age adults who appreciate quality and style, plenty of space and comfort (no lines), and high-level cuisine and service, in a semi-casual country house setting with realistic pricing.

The interior layout is uncomplicated, and the focal point is a stunning wrought-iron and Lalique glass horseshoe-shaped staircase in the main lobby. Differences from *Marina* – there are reportedly 727 of them – include better steps on the lobby staircase, a higher ceiling on one public deck, changes to drawer depth in cabins, a hand-held shower in suites with bathtub, and faster Internet speed.

Public rooms include nine bars and lounges. There is a 2,000-book library, set on the port side of the funnel housing, which also contains the staffed Oceania@Sea computer center, and Barista's coffee bar/lounge (serving illy coffee). The ship also showcases a collection of fine Latin artwork by some of the most renowned artists from Cuba's Vanguard Movement in the second quarter of the 20th century

A Monte Carlo Casino is located between two bars – the Grand Bar and Martinis, with its own soft lavender-colored Casino Bar. Martinis houses a beautiful special-edition Steinway baby grand piano. There are also three boutiques, and several dining venues.

BERLITZ'S RATINGS		
	Possible	Achieved
Ship	500	425
Accommodation	200	170
Food	400	309
Service	400	307
Entertainment	100	77
Cruise Experience	400	313

OVERALL SCORE 1601 points out of 2000

There aren't that many different lounges as such, because most are drinking venues.

A Culinary Center includes a cooking-demonstration kitchen and 24 workstations, with various classes run in conjunction with the US-based *Bon Appétit* magazine – there's a charge for these, but you get to eat your creations.

You can bring your paintbrushes to an Artist's Loft that has constantly changing artists. Other classes may include photography, needlepoint, scrap-booking, drawing, and quilting.

The dress code is 'elegant country club attire' – no pajamas or track suits, but no ties either. A gratuity of 18 percent is added to all bar and spa accounts.

ACCOMMODATION. There are four suite grades and four cabin grades. Price depends on size and location, but all have one thing in common – a good-sized bathroom with tub and separate shower enclosure, plus his 'n' hers toiletry cabinets. All suites/cabins have dark wood cabinetry with rounded edges. The decor includes chocolate brown, cream, and white – earthy colors that don't jar the senses. Around 96 percent of all accommodation has teak-decked balconies.

Standard veranda cabins. These measure 282 sq ft (26 sq m).

Penthouse Suites. These measure 420 sq ft (39 sq m).

Oceania Suites. These measure about 1,030 sq ft (96 sq m).

Vista Suites. These range from 1,200 to 1,500 sq ft (111–139 sq m).

Owner's Suite. At more than 2,000 sq ft (186 sq m), this spans the entire beam of the ship (about 105ft/32m). It is decked out in furniture, fabrics, lighting, and bedding from the Ralph Lauren Home collection with interior design by New York-based Tocar Inc. It is outfitted with a Yamaha baby grand piano, private fitness room, laptop computers, Bose audio system, and a teak-decked balcony with Jacuzzi tub.

Suite-category occupants get niceties including Champagne on arrival, 1,000-thread-count bed linen, 42ins (107cm) plasma TVs, Hermès and Clarins bath amenities, butler service, and en suite delivery from any of the ship's restaurants. Amenities include Tranquillity beds, Wi-Fi laptop computer, refrigerated mini-bar with unlimited free soft drinks and bottled water replenished daily, personal safe, writing desk, cotton bathrobes, slippers, and marble and granite bathroom. Priority check-in and early embarkation and priority luggage delivery are extra perks.

Some grades get access to an Executive or Concierge Lounge, with sofas, Internet-connect computers, Continental breakfast items, soft drinks, magazines, and more. Self-service launderettes are on each accommodation deck – useful for long voyages.

DINING. This ship uses good-quality ingredients and has a number of dining venues, providing plenty of choice, even for long cruises. Particularly good are the breads, rolls, croissants, and brioches – all made on board from French flour and Isigny butter.

The Grand Dining Room is elegant. It has 566 seats, and a domed central ceiling. Versace bone china, Christofle silver, and fine linens are used. Canyon Ranch Spa dishes are available for all meals.

However, banquette seating in some venues does not evoke the image of premium dining as much as individual seating does.

Other dining/eatery options include: Jacques, with 124 seats – the second seagoing restaurant for French celebrity chef Jacques Pépin, Oceania's executive culinary director. With antique oak flooring, antique flatware, and Lalique glassware, it provides fine dining in an elegant but informal setting, with

roast free-range meats, nine classic French dessert items, and a choice of 12 AOC cheeses.

Polo Grill, with about 130 seats, serves steaks and seafood, including Oceania's signature 32oz (907g) bone-in King's Cut prime rib. The setting is traditional steakhouse, with dark wood paneling and classic white tablecloths, although the tables are close together.

Toscana is a 124-seat venue for Italian-style cuisine (including some tasty desserts), and Versace china.

Privée, with seating for up to 10 in a private setting, invites exclusivity for its seven-course dégustation menu.

La Réserve is an intimate, 24-seat venue for wine and food with small-portion, wine-paired dégustation menus.

The Terrace Café is the casual self-serve buffet-style venue. Outdoors, as an extension of the café, is Tapas on the Terrace, good for light bites – although the ceiling is low and tables are close together, so it can be noisy.

Red Ginger offers 'classic and contemporary' Asian cuisine. The setting is visually refined, with ebony and dark wood finishes, but the banquette-style seating lets the venue down. You'll be asked by the waiter to choose your chopsticks from a lacquered presentation box.

Waves Grill, located poolside and shaded from the sun, is for burgers (including fishburgers and veggie burgers), seafood, and other fast food, cooked to order. Baristas coffee bar overlooks the pool deck and has excellent, free *illy* Italian coffee – though, sadly, it's served in paper cups.

ENTERTAINMENT. The 600-seat Marina Lounge spans two decks, with tiered amphitheater-style seating. It's more cabaret-style entertainment than big production shows. Overall, the entertainment is poor.

SPA/FITNESS. The Canyon Ranch SpaClub provides wellness and personal spa treatments (at high prices). The facility includes a fitness center, beauty salon, several treatment rooms (including a couples room), sauna and steam rooms, and a large thalassotherapy pool. Treatments incur an automatic 18 percent gratuity – almost one-fifth of the treatment price. A jogging track is located aft of the funnel.

ROALD AMUNDSEN
NYR

THIS SHIP IS FOR HARDY OUTDOOR TYPES WHO DON'T MIND FAIRLY BASIC FACILITIES

Size:	Small Ship
Tonnage:	20,000
Cruise Line:	Hurtigruten
Former Names:	*none*
Builder:	Kleven Verft (Norway)
Entered Service:	Jul 2018
Length (ft/m):	459.3/140.0
Beam (ft/m):	77.4/23.6
Propulsion/Propellers:	diesel-electric/ 2 azimuthing pods
Passenger Decks:	9
Total Crew:	120
Passengers (lower beds):	530
Passenger Space Ratio (lower beds):	37.7
Passenger/Crew Ratio (lower beds):	4.4
Cabins (total):	265
Size Range (sq ft/m):	161.4–398.2/15.0–37.0
Cabins (for one person):	0
Cabins with balcony:	139
Cabins (wheelchair accessible):	0
Wheelchair accessibility:	Poor
Elevators:	2
Casino (gaming tables):	No
Swimming Pools:	1
Self-Service Launderette:	No
Library:	Yes
Onboard currency:	Norwegian Krona

THE SHIP. Based somewhat on the company's *Fram*, this new expedition-style ship is larger, more up to date, with almost upright bows and a tender-loading platform. Outdoors, a small infinity pool is located aft, and a half-ship walking deck encircles the front of the ship. Public areas include an observation lounge and outdoor viewing area, a lecture hall, shop, Internet corner, lobby with reception and shore-excursion counters, and a video games room. The interior design is Scandinavian, and minimalist, but includes artwork depicting the polar Arctic and Antarctic regions.

Note that when on expedition voyages, many things cost extra (such as kayaking in Antarctica).

ACCOMMODATION. There are numerous accommodation price grades (15, actually). The price you pay depends on the size, location, and grade you

BERLITZ'S RATINGS		
	Possible	Achieved
Ship	500	NYR
Accommodation	200	NYR
Food	400	NYR
Service	400	NYR
Entertainment	100	NYR
Cruise Experience	400	NYR

OVERALL SCORE NYR points out of 2000

choose. From the smallest cabin to the largest suite (sleeping up to four), they are fairly utilitarian and rather sparing in their appointments.

DINING. The T. Aune Restaurant is the main dining room, with open seating. It has seats by the windows, while a self-serve buffet section resides in the center. Most meals are buffet-style, while with some dinners will be served by waiters.

The Fredheim Restaurant is an extra-cost venue, with better, cooked-to-order food. There's also the Lindstrøm Restaurant.

ENTERTAINMENT. Lectures are held on board for all voyages.

SPA/FITNESS. Facilities include a fitness room, two saunas (on an outdoor pool deck), and hot tubs.

ROTTERDAM
★★★+

DUTCH HERITAGE AND DECOR ABOUND FOR CRUISERS OF AN UPPER-AGE

Size:	Mid-size Ship	Passenger/Crew Ratio (lower beds):	2.3
Tonnage:	59,855	Cabins (total):	702
Cruise Line:	Holland America Line	Size Range (sq ft/m):	184.0–1,124.8/17.1–104.5
Former Names:	none	Cabins (for one person):	0
Builder:	Fincantieri (Italy)	Cabins with balcony:	192
Entered Service:	Dec 1997	Cabins (wheelchair accessible):	25
Length (ft/m):	777.5/237.0	Wheelchair accessibility:	Best
Beam (ft/m):	105.8/32.2	Elevators:	12
Propulsion/Propellers:	diesel-electric (37,500kW)/2	Casino (gaming tables):	Yes
Passenger Decks:	12	Swimming Pools:	2 (1 w/sliding glass door)
Total Crew:	600	Self-Service Launderette:	Yes
Passengers (lower beds):	1,404	Library:	Yes
Passenger Space Ratio (lower beds):	42.6	Onboard currency:	US$

THE SHIP. Now 20 years old, *Rotterdam* is the sixth HAL ship to bear the same name. It has a nicely raked bow and a more rounded exterior. Also retained are the familiar interior flow and design style, and twin-funnel.

Two decks – Promenade Deck and Upper Promenade Deck – house most of the public rooms, and are sandwiched between several accommodation decks. The layout is quite easy to learn, and the signage is good.

The interior decor is restrained, with much wood accenting, and lots of the traditional ocean liner detailing so loved by HAL's frequent passengers. A three-deck-high atrium has an oval shape. Its focal point is a huge 'one-of-a-kind' custom-made clock, based on an antique Flemish original that includes an astrolabe, an astrological clock, and 14 other clocks.

One room has a glass ceiling similar to that aboard a former *Statendam*, while the Ambassador's Lounge has an interesting brass dance floor, similar to the dance floor that adorned the Ritz-Carlton room aboard the previous *Rotterdam*.

Rotterdam has three main stairways – good from the viewpoint of safety, passenger accessibility, and evacuation. A pool, on the Lido Deck (between the mast and the ship's twin funnels), is covered by a glass dome.

Popcorn is available at the Wajang Theatre for moviegoers, while adjacent is the popular Java Café. The casino, located in the middle of a major passen-

BERLITZ'S RATINGS		
	Possible	Achieved
Ship	500	376
Accommodation	200	142
Food	400	250
Service	400	268
Entertainment	100	73
Cruise Experience	400	276
OVERALL SCORE 1385 points out of 2000		

ger flow, has blackjack, roulette, poker, and dice tables alongside the requisite rows of slot machines.

HAL has a long legacy in Dutch maritime history. The $2 million worth of artwork here consists of a collection of 17th-century Dutch and Japanese artifacts, together with contemporary works specially created for the ship, although there seems little linkage between some of the items.

HAL's Signature of Excellence program has created 'Mix,' a new open area with comfortable sofa and armchair seating in small alcove-like setting adjacent to a shopping area. The trendy, upbeat space combines three specialty theme bars: Champagne (serving Champagne and sparkling wines), Martinis, and Spirits & Ales (a sports bar). Microsoft Surface touch-screen technology enhances checkers and chess, air hockey, and other sports games.

With one whole deck of suites – and a dedicated, private Concierge Lounge – the company has a two-class environment. Passenger niggles include poor room service and staff communication, and the charge to use the washing machines and dryers in the self-service launderette – petty and irritating.

In a 2009 refit, 23 Veranda Deck cabins were converted into 'Spa Cabins,' while new lanai-style cabins were created on Lower Promenade Deck.

Overall, this fairly contemporary ship has light, bright decor and is extremely comfortable, with elegant decorative features. But these plus points are marred by the poor quality of the dining room food and service, and a lack of understanding of what it takes to make the 'luxury' cruise experience touted in the company's brochures.

ACCOMMODATION. There are several categories, priced by grade, size and location. Accommodation is spread over five decks, and some cabins have full or partially obstructed views. No cabin is more than 144ft (44m) from a stairway, which makes it easier to get from cabins to public rooms. All cabin doors have a bird's-eye maple look, and hallways have framed fabric panels to make them less clinical.

All standard inside and outside cabins are tastefully furnished, with twin beds that convert to a queen-size one, though space is tight for walking between beds and vanity unit. There is a decent amount of closet and drawer space, but this will prove tight for longer voyages.

The fully tiled bathrooms are disappointingly small, particularly for long cruises, and have small shower tubs, utilitarian toiletries cupboards, and exposed under-sink plumbing. There is no detailing to distinguish them significantly from bathrooms aboard the S-class ships.

There are 36 full Veranda Suites on Navigation Deck, including four Penthouse Suites, which share a private Concierge Lounge and concierge to handle such things as special dining arrangements, shore excursions, and other requests – although strangely there are no butlers for these suites, as aboard many ships with similar facilities. Each suite has a separate steward's entrance and separate bedroom, dressing, and living areas. Suite passengers get personal stationery, complimentary laundry and ironing, cocktail-hour hors d'oeuvres, and other goodies, as well as priority embarkation and disembarkation. The Concierge Lounge, with its latticework teak detailing and private library is accessible only by private key-card.

Disabled passengers have a choice of 20 cabins, including two of the Penthouse Suites that include concierge services. However, there are different cabin configurations, and it is wise to check with your booking agent.

DINING. The ship's La Fontaine Dining Room seats 747, spans two decks, and has are tables for four, six, or eight, but only nine tables for two. Both open seating and assigned seating are available, while breakfast and lunch are open seating, where you'll be taken to your table by restaurant staff when you enter. Fine Rosenthal china and good cutlery are provided.

With a few exceptions, the cuisine is rather unmemorable, and is missing passion and taste, because it's all about mass catering in large batches. There's a distinct lack of variety of green vegetables, and too much use of rice, canned fruit, and already sliced and diced cheese. Still, you get friendly service from Indonesian and Filipino stewards, and the plates are nice.

Pinnacle Grill is an extra-cost (reservations-required) 88-seat restaurant that is more upscale and more intimate than the main dining room. It also features higher-quality ingredients and better presentation than the main dining room. It is on Promenade Deck and fronts onto the second level of the atrium lobby. Pacific Northwest cuisine is featured, plus an array of premium-quality steaks. There are good table settings, china, and silverware, and leather-bound menus. The wine list consists mostly of American wines. For casual meals, the Lido Restaurant is a self-serve buffet venue. A section of this restaurant turns into the Canaletto Restaurant by night, when Italian dishes are featured (reservations are required and a cover charge applies).

Also, a Lido Deck poolside 'Dive-In at the Terrace Grill' features signature burgers, hot dogs, and fries; on certain days, barbeques and other culinary treats may be featured.

ENTERTAINMENT. The 577-seat Showroom at Sea is the venue for all production shows, the strongest of which is cabaret, and other entertainment. It is two decks high, with seating on both main and balcony levels. The decor includes umbrella-shaped gold ceiling lamps made from Murano glass (from Venice), and the stage has hydraulic lifts and three video screens, as well as a closed-loop system for the hearing-impaired.

SPA/FITNESS. The Ocean Spa is one deck above the navigation bridge at the very forward part of the ship. It includes a gymnasium with all the latest muscle-pumping exercise machines, including an abundance of treadmills, with forward views over the ship's bows. There's an aerobics exercise area, beauty salon with ocean-view windows to the port side, several treatment rooms, and men's and women's sauna, steam room, and changing areas.

ROYAL CLIPPER
★★★★

THIS FINE SAIL-CRUISE SHIP EXUDES ABUNDANT CHARACTER AND CHARM

Size:	Boutique Ship	Passenger/Crew Ratio (lower beds):	2.1
Tonnage:	5,061	Cabins (total):	114
Cruise Line:	Star Clippers	Size Range (sq ft/m):	100.0–320.0/9.3–29.7
Former Names:	*none*	Cabins (for one person):	0
Builder:	De Merwede (Holland)	Cabins with balcony:	14
Entered Service:	Oct 2000	Cabins (wheelchair accessible):	0
Length (ft/m):	439.6/134.0	Wheelchair accessibility:	None
Beam (ft/m):	54.1/16.5	Elevators:	0
Propulsion/Propellers:	diesel (3,700kW)/1	Casino (gaming tables):	No
Passenger Decks:	5	Swimming Pools:	3
Total Crew:	106	Self-Service Launderette:	No
Passengers (lower beds):	228	Library:	Yes
Passenger Space Ratio (lower beds):	22.1	Onboard currency:	Euros

THE SHIP. The culmination of an owner's childhood dream, *Royal Clipper* is a stunning sight under sail. It's the world's largest true fully rigged sailing ship and has five masts, whereas the company's two other, smaller ships (*Star Clipper* and *Star Flyer*) have just four. The vessel best suits couples and solo travelers who would probably never consider a 'normal' cruise ship, but who enjoy sailing and the thrill of ocean and wind and want a package that includes accommodation, food, like-minded companions, and interesting destinations, without the bother of owning or chartering their own yacht. This is the bee's knees.

Royal Clipper's design is based on the only other five-masted sailing ship ever to be built, the 1902-built German tall ship *Preussen*. It has approximately the same dimensions, albeit 46ft (14m) shorter.

The construction time for this ship was remarkably short, because its hull had almost been completed (at Gdansk shipyard, Poland) for another owner, before becoming available to Star Clippers. It is instantly recognizable due to its geometric blue-and-white hull markings. Power winches, as well as hand winches, are employed in deck fittings, as well as a mix of horizontal furling for the square sails and hydraulic power assist to roll the square sails along the yardarm. The sail-handling system, designed by the owner Mikael Krafft, is such that the vessel can quickly be converted from a full rigger to a schooner.

BERLITZ'S RATINGS		
	Possible	Achieved
Ship	500	401
Accommodation	200	154
Food	400	288
Service	400	296
Entertainment	100	80
Cruise Experience	400	312
OVERALL SCORE 1531 points out of 2000		

The masts reach 197ft (60m) above the waterline, and the top 19ft (5.8m) can be hinged over 90 degrees to clear bridges, cable lines, and other port-based obstacles. Watching the sailors manipulate ropes, rigging, and sails is like watching a ballet – the precision and cohesion of a group of men, who make it all look so simple.

Passengers may be allowed to climb to special lookout points aloft, and on the bridge at any time – but they cannot go in the galley or engine room.

The ship has a large amount of open deck space and sunning space – something most tall ships lack – although, naturally, this is laid with rigging ropes. An aft marina platform can be lowered, so that passengers can use surfboards, sailing dinghies, take a ride on the banana boat, or go waterskiing or swimming. Snorkeling gear is available free, but there is a charge for scuba gear. You will be asked to sign a waiver if you use the water-sports equipment.

Inside, a small midships atrium three decks high sits under one of the ship's three swimming pools, and sunlight streams down through a piano lounge on the uppermost level inside the ship and into the lower level dining room. A forward observation lounge is a real plus – it's connected to the piano lounge via a central corridor. An Edwardian library/card room includes a Belle Epoque fireplace. The Captain Nemo Club lets you observe fish and marine life when the ship is at anchor, through thick glass portholes; it's floodlit from underneath at night to attract the fish.

The ship operates cruises in the Grenadines and Lower Windward Islands of the Caribbean in winter and Mediterranean cruises in summer. Officers navigate using both traditional (sextant) and contemporary methods (advanced electronic positioning system).

This being a tall ship with true sailing traditions, there is, naturally, a parrot (it is sometimes kept in a gilded cage, but it may be seen around the ship on someone's shoulder); it's considered to be part of the crew. The ambience is extremely relaxed, friendly, and unpretentious. The dress code is always casual (shorts and casual tops are the order of the day – yachting wear), with no ties needed ever.

The suites and cabins are, in general, smaller than aboard *Sea Cloud* and *Sea Cloud II*. I do not include the Windstar Cruises ships (*Wind Spirit*, *Wind Star*, *Wind Surf*), because they are not tall ships. *Royal Clipper*, however, is exactly that – a real, working, wind-and-sails-in-your-face tall ship.

This vessel is not for the physically impaired, or for children. The steps of the internal stairs are steep, as in most sailing vessels. Any gratuities you give are pooled and divided among all crew members. What gives the ship a little extra in the scoring department is the fact that many water sports are included in the price.

ACCOMMODATION. There are several accommodation grades, priced according to size, type and location: Owner's Suites (2), Deluxe Suites (14), and categories 1–6. All have polished wood-trimmed cabinetry and wall-to-wall carpeting, personal safe, full-length mirror, small TV set with audio channels and 24-hour text-based news, and private bathroom. All have twin beds (86 of which convert into a queen-size bed, while 28 are fixed queen-size beds), hairdryer, and satellite-linked telephone. The six interior cabins and a handful of other cabins have a permanently fixed double bed.

Most cabins have a privacy curtain, so that you can't be seen from the hallway when the cabin attendant opens the door – useful if you're undressed. Additionally, 27 cabins can sleep three.

Two Owner's Suites, located aft, provide the most lavish accommodation, and have one queen-size bed and one double bed, a living area with semicircular sofa, vanity desk, mini-bar/refrigerator, marble-clad bathroom with whirlpool bathtub, plus one guest bathroom, and butler service. They have an interconnecting door, so a combined super-suite can sleep eight.

The 'Deck Suites' have interesting names, including Ariel, Cutty Sark, Doriana, Eagle Wing, Flying Cloud, France, Gloria, Golden Gate, Great Republic, Passat, Pommern, Preussen, and Thermopylae. However, they are not actually suites, as the sleeping area can't be separated from the lounge – they are simply larger cabins with a nicer interior, more storage space, and a larger bathroom. Each has two lower beds convertible to a queen-size one, small lounge area, mini-bar/refrigerator, writing desk, small private balcony, and marble-clad bathroom with combination whirlpool tub/shower, washbasin, and toilet. The door to the balcony can be opened, so that fresh air floods the room; note that there is a 12ins (30cm) threshold to step over. There are no curtains, only roll-down shades for the windows and balcony door. The balcony itself typically has two white chairs and drinks table. The balconies are not particularly private, and most have ship's tenders or Zodiacs overhanging them, or some rigging obscuring the views.

Two other named cabins (Lord Nelson and Marco Polo) are located aft. Their facilities are similar to those of the Deck Suites, but they lack private balconies.

The interior cabins and the lowest grades of outside-view cabins are extremely small and tight, with little room to move around the beds. So take only the minimum amount of clothing and luggage. When in cabins where beds are linked together to form a double bed, you need to clamber up over the front of the bed, as both sides have built-in storm barriers (this applies in inclement weather conditions only).

There is a small room service menu (all items cost extra).

DINING. The Dining Room is on several connecting levels (getting used to the steps is not easy), and seats all passengers at one seating under a three-deck-high atrium dome. You can sit with whom you wish at tables for four to 10. However, it is noisy, due to the numerous waiter stations. Some tables are badly positioned, so that correct waiter service is impossible; much reaching over has to be done in order to serve everyone.

One corner can be closed off for private parties. Breakfasts and lunches are self-serve buffets, while dinner is a sit-down affair with table service; the ambience is always friendly and lighthearted. The wine list consists of young wines, and prices are high. The cuisine, although perfectly acceptable, is nothing to write home about.

ENTERTAINMENT. There are no shows, nor are any expected by passengers aboard a tall ship such as this, where sailing is the main purpose. There is, however, live music, provided by a single lounge pianist/singer.

SPA/FITNESS. The Royal Spa is located on the lowest passenger deck and, although not large, incorporates a beauty salon, an extra-charge Moroccan steam room, and a small gymnasium.

ROYAL PRINCESS
★★★★

THIS IS A LARGE, FAMILY-FRIENDLY, MULTI-CHOICE CONTEMPORARY RESORT-STYLE SHIP

Size:	Large Resort Ship	Passenger/Crew Ratio (lower beds):	2.6
Tonnage:	142,229	Cabins (total):	1,780
Cruise Line:	Princess Cruises	Size Range (sq ft/m):	161.4–554.3/15–51.5
Former Names:	none	Cabins (for one person):	0
Builder:	Fincantieri (Italy)	Cabins with balcony:	1,438
Entered Service:	Jun 2013	Cabins (wheelchair accessible):	36
Length (ft/m):	1,082.6/330.0	Wheelchair accessibility:	Best
Beam (ft/m):	126.3/38.6	Elevators:	14
Propulsion/Propellers:	diesel-electric (52,000kW)/2	Casino (gaming tables):	Yes
Passenger Decks:	17	Swimming Pools:	2
Total Crew:	1,346	Self-Service Launderette:	Yes
Passengers (lower beds):	3,560	Library:	Yes
Passenger Space Ratio (lower beds):	39.9	Onboard currency:	US$

THE SHIP. *Royal Princess* has an almost streamlined look. Sadly, there is no complete walk-around promenade deck. An aft-deck swimming pool was added in a retro-fit. Although this reduced some open deck space, it is a much-appreciated facility. Lifeboats are located outside the main public room areas, so that they don't impair the view from balcony cabins.

One notable innovation are two 'over-the-water' SeaWalks, top-deck glass-floor enclosed walkways on both sides; these extend almost 30ft (9.1m) beyond the vessel's edge. Go there for dramatic views of the sea – some 128ft (39m) below.

For real escapees, an extra-cost adults-only retreat called The Sanctuary is larger than aboard the Grand-class ships and has more amenities. It includes four rentable cabanas and two extra-cost Lotus Spa-operated 'couples' cabanas, and has its own retreat pool and relaxation areas (in both sunny and shaded positions). The adjacent Retreat area has grown in size, and so other passengers have less open deck space.

The Piazza Atrium is the ship's multi-faceted social hub. It combines specialty eateries, for light meals, snacks, pastries, beverages, entertainment, shopping, and passenger services all in one area, with multi-level horseshoe-shaped 'flowing' stairways, mood lighting effects, and a small dance floor. The atrium's base level includes a large International Café, for coffees, teas, panini, and pastries;

BERLITZ'S RATINGS

	Possible	Achieved
Ship	500	401
Accommodation	200	139
Food	400	268
Service	400	293
Entertainment	100	82
Cruise Experience	400	296

OVERALL SCORE 1479 points out of 2000

Sabatini's (adjacent to the atrium), a Tuscan specialty extra-cost restaurant, has both regular and à la carte menus; and a gift shop. Upstairs, level two includes a 121-seat Alfredo's Pizzeria (pizzas are free), Bellini's (featuring Bellini drinks), a photo gallery, and the reception and shore-excursion counters. On the third level is Crooners Bar, with solo pianist entertainers, and a small Seafood Bar.

One serious design fault is the complete lack of a central stairway above the two main restaurants (between decks 7 and 16 – a design fault because stairs are only at the forward and aft elevator banks); this leads to severe crowding of the forward and aft elevators, and the Berlitz Rating score reflects this omission.

Passenger niggles include the user-unfriendly automated telephone system, the small cabin towels, the extra cost for items such as ice cream, and the (coins-needed) charge for the washers and dryers in self-service launderettes.

Overall, however, Princess Cruises delivers a consistently fine, comfortable, well-packaged product, always with a good degree of style, at a competitive price, so passengers keep returning.

ACCOMMODATION. There are five main types of accommodation and a bewildering number of different price grades: (a) Grand Suite; (b) 40 suites with balcony; (c) 306 mini-suites with balcony; (d) 360 deluxe outside-view balcony cabins; (e) 732 outside-view cabins with balcony; and (f) 342 interior cabins. Pricing depends on two things: size and location. Outside-view cabins account for about 81 percent of all accommodation, and have a balcony; those located at the stern are the quietest. Some 68 cabins have lifeboat-obstructed views, and 52 cabins on Deck 8 above the showlounge are subject to noise pollution from the shows until late in the evening.

All grades have energy-efficient lighting and key card readers that automatically turn off lights when occupants leave. All cabins have beds, upholstered headboards, wall-mounted TV sets, 220v electrical sockets, turndown service and heart-shaped chocolates on pillows nightly, bathrobes (on request unless you are in suite-grade accommodation), and toiletries. A hairdryer is sensibly located at the vanity desk unit in the living area. Bathrooms generally have a good amount of open shelf storage space for toiletries.

Suite- and mini-suite-grade occupants have access to their own Concierge Lounge, more amenities, larger TV sets, larger towels, and two washbasins.

Some of the most sought-after suites are located aft, occupying the corner (port and starboard) positions. Be aware that the balconies of cabins on Marina Deck 15 can be seen by anyone on the overhanging Skywalk on the deck above (so pick your cabin wisely).

DINING. There are three 'formal' main dining rooms: Allegro, Concerto, and Symphony. Choose either traditional two-seating dining (typically 6pm and 8.15pm for dinner), or 'anytime dining' – where you choose when and with whom you want to eat. However, if you want to see a show in the evening, your dining time will be dictated by the time of the show, which limits your choice.

A 12-seat circular table is located within the Wine Cellar of the Allegro and Symphony dining rooms. This extra-cost, reservations-required venue is for private functions and celebrations. Also available is a private Chef's Table Lumière; it's within the Concerto dining room. It has a custom-made glass dining table and fine-dining utensils.

Although portions are generous, the food and its presentation are disappointing, and quite standardized. Fish is often disguised by a crumb or batter coating, the choice of fresh green vegetables is limited, few garnishes are used, and cheese is already sliced and diced. But, this is big-ship banquet catering, with all its attendant standardization and 'batch' cooking. Pasta dishes are acceptable (though voluminous), typically served by section headwaiters, who may also make 'something special for you' – in search of favorable comments and gratuities. If you like desserts, order a sundae at dinner (most other items are just so-so).

Extra-cost, reservations-required Sabatini's (adjacent to Vines Bar off the lower atrium level, is an Italian restaurant with Tuscan decor. Named after Trattoria Sabatini, the historic institution in Florence, it serves Italian-style pasta dishes with a choice of sauces, all provided with flair and entertainment by energetic waiters. This venue also hosts Italian wine tasting.

Alfredo's is a sit-down pizzeria named after Alfredo Marzi, corporate chef for Princess Cruises; the venue specializes in 'authentic,' family-friendly-size pizzas.

Ocean Terrace, located on the upper level of the three-deck-high atrium lobby, is a seafood bar. International Café, on the lowest level of the Piazza Atrium, is the place for extra-cost coffees, pastries, paninis, and more.

Vines Wine Bar is close to Sabatini's and provides an escape from all the noise and hubbub elsewhere – for a glass of extra-cost wine and tapas. It's a pleasant area in which to while away a late afternoon, trying out new wines.

Crown Grill is an extra-cost, reservations-required venue, serving premium-quality steaks and grilled seafood. It is close to the aft stairway, and adjacent to the Wheelhouse Bar, which can be noisy at times.

For casual meals, the self-serve buffet Horizon Court (it seats 900 indoors and 350 outdoors) has multiple 'active' cooking stations, but few beverage stations. Sections highlight specific themes, such as Mediterranean, Asian, and Italian cuisine; there's also a deli section. At night, the aft section becomes the Horizon Bistro, for casual dinners. Some evenings feature themes, such as British pub food or as a Brazilian churrascaria (for carved meat dishes). A hibachi grill and other active cooking stations (for regional specialties) are part of the scenario. It's a flexible large-scale eatery – but useful as a change to the main dining rooms. Additionally, Horizon Court has its own bakery.

Outside, the poolside Trident Grill (for burgers, hot dogs, and other fast-food grilled items during the day) becomes a smokehouse barbeque in the evenings. Meanwhile, Mexican-style eats can be obtained from the Outrigger Bar.

ENTERTAINMENT. The 1,000 seat Princess Theater is the showlounge. Two decks high, it is designed for the large-scale production shows for which Princess Cruises is renowned, and has good views from all seats – there are no pillars to spoil the view, which is an outstanding achievement in such a large room.

SPA/FITNESS. The large Lotus Spa is forward of the atrium's lower level, so it doesn't take away premium outdoor-view real estate space. Separate facilities for men and women include a sauna, steam room, and changing rooms; common facilities include a relaxation/waiting zone and body-pampering treatment rooms. A gymnasium packed with high-tech equipment is located aft on a higher deck.

RUBY PRINCESS
★★★★

THIS FAMILY-FRIENDLY RESORT SHIP HAS PLEASANT DECOR AND DINING OPTIONS

Size:	Large Resort Ship	Passenger/Crew Ratio (lower beds):	2.5
Tonnage:	113,561	Cabins (total):	1,557
Cruise Line:	Princess Cruises	Size Range (sq ft/m):	163–1,279/15.1–118.8
Former Names:	none	Cabins (for one person):	0
Builder:	Fincantieri (Italy)	Cabins with balcony:	881
Entered Service:	Sep 2008	Cabins (wheelchair accessible):	25
Length (ft/m):	951.4/290.0	Wheelchair accessibility:	Good
Beam (ft/m):	118.1/36.0	Elevators:	14
Propulsion/Propellers:	diesel-electric (42,000kW)/2	Casino (gaming tables):	Yes
Passenger Decks:	15	Swimming Pools:	3
Total Crew:	1,200	Self-Service Launderette:	Yes
Passengers (lower beds):	3,114	Library:	Yes
Passenger Space Ratio (lower beds):	36.4	Onboard currency:	US$

THE SHIP. *Ruby Princess* has the same profile, interior layout, and public rooms as sister ships *Crown Princess* (2006) and *Emerald Princess* (2007). The ship accommodates over 500 more passengers than earlier half-sisters (such as *Diamond Princess*), but the outdoor deck space remains the same, as do the number of elevators.

The Sanctuary, an extra-cost adults-only retreat, is worth paying extra for in warm-weather areas. Forward on the uppermost deck, it is a 'private' place to relax and unwind. Attendants provide chilled face towels and light bites; there are also two cabanas.

There's a good sheltered faux wood promenade strolling deck – it's actually painted steel – which almost wraps around the front and aft areas of the ship; three times round is equal to 1 mile (1.6km). Movies Under the Skies and major sporting events are shown on a 300-sq-ft (28-sq-m) screen located at the pool forward of the large funnel structure.

The main public bars and lounges are located off a double-width promenade deck. The main lobby is the focal meeting point. Called The Plaza, it's like a town square, and includes a 44-seat International Café (patisserie/deli) and lots of nice cakes and pastries, and Vines, a combination wine/cheese and sushi/tapas counter.

The library is in a little corner adjacent to the wood-paneled Wheelhouse Bar. There are many other pleasant bars and lounges to enjoy, including

BERLITZ'S RATINGS		
	Possible	Achieved
Ship	500	373
Accommodation	200	135
Food	400	247
Service	400	285
Entertainment	100	81
Cruise Experience	400	284
OVERALL SCORE 1405 points out of 2000		

Crooners, an intimate New York-style piano bar, with around 70 seats on the upper level of the lobby, but perhaps the nicest of all is Adagio's.

The casino, Gatsby's, has over 260 slot machines (linked slot machines provide a combined payout), and blackjack, craps, and roulette tables for serious gamers.

Passenger niggles include the user-unfriendly automated telephone system, the small cabin towels, the extra cost for items such as ice cream, and the (coins-needed) charge for the washers and dryers in self-service launderettes.

Overall, however, Princess Cruises delivers a consistently fine, comfortable, well-packaged product, always with a good degree of style, at a competitive price.

ACCOMMODATION. There are six main types of cabins and configurations: (a) Grand Suite, (b) suite, (c) mini-suite, (d) outside-view double cabins with balcony, (e) outside-view double cabins, and (f) interior (no-view) double cabins. These come in a multitude of different brochure price categories. Pricing depends on size and location. Two family suites have an interconnecting door, plus a large balcony. These can sleep up to 10, if at least four are children, or up to eight adults.

By comparison, the largest suite is slightly smaller, and the smallest interior cabin is slightly larger than the equivalent suites/cabins aboard *Golden*, *Grand*, and *Star Princess*. Almost all balcony suites and cabins can be overlooked both from the navigation bridge wing, as well as from the port and starboard sections of Skywalkers, high above the ship at the stern. Suites C401, 402, 404, 406, 408, 410, 412, 401, 405, 411, 415, and 417 on Riviera Deck 14, and D105 and D106 (Dolphin Deck 9) have only semi-private balconies that can be seen from above, so there is little privacy. Also, most outside-view cabins on Emerald Deck have views obstructed by lifeboats.

Some cabins can accommodate a third and fourth person in upper berths, but, in these, the lower beds can't be pushed together to make a queen-size bed.

Cabin bath towels are small, and drawer space is tight. There are no butlers – even for the top-grade suites, which are not large in comparison to similar suites aboard some other similarly sized ships. Suite-grade occupants get better service, personal amenities, and other perks.

The largest accommodation is a Grand Suite (A750); it is located at the stern. It has a large bedroom with queen-size bed, huge walk-in closets, two bathrooms, a lounge with fireplace, sofa bed, wet bar, refrigerator, and a large private balcony on the port side, with a hot tub accessible from both balcony and bedroom.

Wheelchair-accessible cabins measure 250–385 sq ft (23–35.8 sq m), but there's no mirror for dressing, and no full-length hanging space.

DINING. There are several dining options, including three main dining rooms, plus a Crown Grill, and Sabatini's Trattoria.

The three main dining rooms are Botticelli, Da Vinci, and Michelangelo. The Botticelli Dining Room has traditional two seating dining (typically 6pm and 8.15pm for dinner), while 'Anytime Dining' – where you choose when and with whom you want to eat – is offered in Da Vinci and Michelangelo. They are split into various sections in a non-symmetrical design that presents smaller sections for better ambience; each has its own galley.

Although portions are generous, the food and its presentation are disappointing, and quite standardized. Fish is often disguised by a crumb or batter coating, the choice of fresh green vegetables is limited, few garnishes are used, and cheese is already sliced and diced. But, this is big-ship banquet catering, with all its attendant standardization and reliance on batch cooking. Pasta dishes are acceptable (though voluminous), served by section headwaiters, who may also make 'something special just for you' – in search of favorable comments and gratuities. If you like desserts, order a sundae at dinner (most other items are just so-so).

The extra-cost SHARE by Curtis Stone and Crown Grill, both require reservations. The former is located on a high deck aft of the funnel, and features a degustation menu. The latter is a 138-seat restaurant serving premium steaks, chops, and grilled seafood items (everything is cooked to order); it is located off the main indoor Deck 7 promenade. Seating is mainly in semi-private alcoves, and there's a show kitchen, so you can watch the action.

The 312-seat Horizon Court, with its indoor-outdoor seating, is open almost 24 hours a day for casual meals (on plastic plates), and has large ocean-view windows on both sides. The central display sections are often crowded.

Other casual eateries include a poolside burger grill and pizza bar. Note that extra charges apply if you order items to eat at the coffee bar/patisserie, or the caviar/Champagne bar.

There's also the International Café, on Deck 5 in The Plaza – the place for coffees and specialty coffees, pastries, light lunches, and delightful afternoon cakes, most at no extra cost.

ENTERTAINMENT. The Princess Theater spans two decks and has comfortable seating on both levels. It has a live orchestra for backing colorful production shows and major cabaret acts. The ship has a resident troupe of singers and dancers, plus an army of audio-visual support staff.

SPA/FITNESS. The Lotus Spa is located forward on Sun Deck. Separate facilities for men and women include a sauna, steam room, and changing rooms; common facilities include a relaxation/waiting zone, body-pampering treatment rooms, and a gymnasium with high-tech muscle-pumping equipment, and great ocean views. Some fitness classes are free, while others cost extra.

SAGA PEARL II
★★★+

THIS COMFORTABLE SMALL SHIP IS GOOD FOR DISCOVERY-STYLE CRUISING

Size:	Small Ship
Tonnage:	18,591
Cruise Line:	Saga Cruises
Former Names:	Quest for Adventure, Saga Pearl II, Astoria, Arkona, Astor
Builder:	Howaldtswerke Deutsche Werft (Germany)
Entered Service:	Dec 1981/May 2013
Length (ft/m):	539.2/164.3
Beam (ft/m):	74.1/22.6
Propulsion/Propellers:	diesel (13,200kW)/2
Passenger Decks:	8
Total Crew:	252
Passengers (lower beds):	456
Passenger Space Ratio (lower beds):	40.7
Passenger/Crew Ratio (lower beds):	1.8
Cabins (total):	258
Size Range (sq ft/m):	150.0–725.0/13.4–65.3
Cabins (for one person):	60
Cabins with balcony:	40
Cabins (wheelchair accessible):	0
Wheelchair accessibility:	Fair
Elevators:	3
Casino (gaming tables):	No
Swimming Pools:	2
Self-Service Launderette:	Yes
Library:	Yes
Onboard currency:	UK£

THE SHIP. *Saga Pearl II* is best suited to English-speaking couples, and solo travelers of mature years. Saga Cruises staff go out of their way to ensure you have an excellent time. The vessel itself is a traditional-looking cruise ship. A multi-million pound 2009 refit added a superb 3,000-book library, an array of balcony cabins, and new galleys. There is a good amount of open deck and sunbathing space, with some teakwood decks, polished wood railings, and cushioned pads for sunloungers. There is no walk-around promenade deck outdoors, but a small walking area under the lifeboats exists on both sides.

ACCOMMODATION. The accommodation consists of many different price categories, including several for solo travelers in single-occupancy cabins, and it is spread over four decks.

Grand Suites. Two Boat Deck suites (725 sq ft/67 sq m) provide really large spaces, and have just about everything needed for refined, private shipboard living. There's a separate bedroom with double bed, and a living room with sofa, dining table, and chairs. The tiled bathroom has a large tub, separate shower, and plenty of storage space for toiletries.

Suites. Some 34 suites (269 sq ft/25 sq m) have separate bedrooms with twin beds, and living rooms with sofa, dining table, and chairs. The tiled bathrooms have large tubs, separate shower enclosures, and plenty of space for toiletries.

BERLITZ'S RATINGS

	Possible	Achieved
Ship	500	320
Accommodation	200	128
Food	400	255
Service	400	277
Entertainment	100	72
Cruise Experience	400	265

OVERALL SCORE 1317 points out of 2000

Outside-view cabins/interior cabins. The standard cabins (140 sq ft/13 sq m) are quite well appointed and decorated, and all are in crisp, clean colors. The bathrooms are quite compact units, although there is a decent-size shower.

DINING. The Dining Room has ocean-view picture windows. It has dark wood paneling and restful decor. There's a single, open seating, at tables for four, six, or eight. Two small wings, each with one 12-seat table, can be used for small groups. The wine list has a decent selection of wines from many regions. Self-serve buffets, for breakfast and lunch, and as a casual alternative to dinner in the Dining Room, can be taken in the Verandah Restaurant, which overlooks the aft pool and open deck area.

ENTERTAINMENT. The Discovery Lounge is the main entertainment space. It is a single-level room, although 14 pillars obstruct the sight lines from many seats. The stage also acts as the dance floor and cannot be raised for shows. The entertainment consists of cabaret-style performances. It can also be used as a lecture room.

SPA/FITNESS. The spa is located on the lowest passenger deck, and contains a sauna (but no steam room), solarium, indoor swimming pool, treatment rooms, and changing areas.

SAGA SAPPHIRE
★★★★

A SMALL, ELEGANT SHIP FOR BRITISH CRUISERS OF A CERTAIN AGE

Size:	Small Ship	Passenger/Crew Ratio (lower beds):	1.7
Tonnage:	37,301	Cabins (total):	374
Cruise Line:	Saga Cruises	Size Range (sq ft/m):	161.4–678.1/15.0–63.0
Former Names:	Bleu de France, Holiday Dream,	Cabins (for one person):	56
	SuperStar Aries, SuperStar Europe, Europa	Cabins with balcony:	19
Builder:	Bremer Vulkan (Germany)	Cabins (wheelchair accessible):	2
Entered Service:	Jan 1982/Mar 2012	Wheelchair accessibility:	Good
Length (ft/m):	654.9/199.6	Elevators:	4
Beam (ft/m):	93.8/28.6	Casino (gaming tables):	No
Propulsion/Propellers:	diesel (21,270kW)/2	Swimming Pools:	2
Passenger Decks:	10	Self-Service Launderette:	Yes
Total Crew:	415	Library:	Yes
Passengers (lower beds):	706	Onboard currency:	UK£
Passenger Space Ratio (lower beds):	49.6		

THE SHIP. *Saga Sapphire* was originally built as the fifth incarnation of *Europa* for Hapag-Lloyd Cruises, and was for many years the pride of the German cruise industry. It was originally to have twin side-by-side funnels, but the idea was dropped in favor of a single funnel. The ship is in remarkably fine shape, despite the fact that it is now over 30 years old. Saga Cruises tailored the ship to British tastes when it took delivery in April 2012.

It has a deep blue hull and white upper structure, and a sponson stern – a kind of 'skirt' added in order to comply with the latest stability regulations. But it still maintains its moderately handsome, balanced profile. There is a really decent amount of open outdoor deck space. The ship has both outdoor and outdoor/indoor pools. While there is no walk-around outdoors promenade deck, there are half-length teak port and starboard promenades.

The interior focal point is a three-deck high lobby, which has a 'floating' fish sculpture. (I counted over 1,000 fish, including one red herring!) There is a good range of good-size public rooms, most of which have high ceilings, and wide interior stairways that create a feeling of spaciousness on a grand – but human – scale. Contemporary yet restful colors have been applied to many public rooms and cabins, and subtle, hidden lighting is used throughout, particularly on the stairways. The public rooms are positioned aft in a 'cake-layer' stacking, with all the accommodation

BERLITZ'S RATINGS		
	Possible	Achieved
Ship	500	385
Accommodation	200	143
Food	400	274
Service	400	289
Entertainment	100	71
Cruise Experience	400	281

OVERALL SCORE 1443 points out of 2000

located forward, thus separating potentially noisy areas from quieter ones.

Facilities include a delightful observation lounge (The Drawing Room), and an integral, extensive library plus several Internet-connected computer stations (iPads can also be provided), and chess and draughts tables; light entertainment is presented here in the evenings, and excellent Lavazza coffees are available here at almost any time, with delightful cakes in mid-morning (free). Quirky table lamps are made from old clarinets and fishing rods.

For a delightful, neat hideaway, head to Cooper's, named after the British comedian and magician Tommy Cooper. There are numerous black-and-white photos on the wall of some of the UK's best-known comedians of yesteryear and today, including Spike 'Milligna' – the well-known typing error. The table lamps are topped by Tommy Cooper's trademark – a fez. Then there's Aviators – a cute little pre-dining room bar with models of splendid Spitfire aircraft (from World War II), with, of course, Spitfire draft beer as the featured bar beverage.

The ship, which has some rather amusing and quirky artwork, provides an informal, relaxed, yet elegant setting, with many public rooms that have a high ceiling. Saga Cruises includes many things other UK-based operators charge extra for – that's why its cruises may appear to cost more – such as private car transfers to the ship (check brochure for details), all gratuities, shuttle buses in ports of call where possible, and newspapers in the library in each port of call, when available. Saga also provides excellent user-friendly port and shore-excursion information booklets.

Saga Sapphire is best suited to couples and solo travelers, almost all of whom tend to be British, seeking a holiday afloat in spacious, classy surroundings. It provides decent accommodation, good food, and friendly service, plus interesting itineraries and destinations. Passengers must be over 50, but spouses and partners can be as young as 45.

ACCOMMODATION. There is a wide range of suites and cabins (including many for solo travelers), in a multitude of price grades. All of the original cabins are quite spacious, and have illuminated closets, dark wood cabinetry with rounded edges, full-length mirrors, color TV/DVD player, mini-bar/refrigerator, personal safe, hairdryer, and good cabin insulation. They are also laid out in a very practical design. Some suites/cabins have table lamps made from old cameras such as the Kodak Brownie and similar 'box' cameras – delightfully quirky!

Most of the bathrooms (163 to be precise) have deep tubs (cabins without a bathtub have large shower enclosures), a three-head shower unit, two deep washbasins (not all cabins), useful toiletries cabinet, and handsome toiletries – Citrus, created exclusively for Saga Cruises by Clarity, an organization that provides employment for blind persons.

The largest living spaces are the suites. However, because of their location – they were created from former bridge officers' cabins in a 1999 refit – they have lifeboat-obstructed views. Six other suites had private balconies added, and all provide generous living spaces. There is a separate bedroom with either a queen-size or twin beds, illuminated closets, and a vanity/writing desk. The lounge includes a wet bar with refrigerator and glass cabinets and large audio-visual center complete with large-screen infotainment screen. The marble-clad bathroom has a large shower enclosure, with retractable clothesline.

Even the standard, lower-priced cabins are very comfortable, the ship having been designed for long voyages.

DINING. Pole to Pole, the main restaurant, seats 620 diners and has ocean-view windows on two sides, yet still manages to have an intimate, clubby feel thanks to different areas styled to the theme of four continents: Africa, the Americas, Asia, and Europe. Both self-serve buffet and full-service meals are provided. There is open seating, so you can dine wherever you choose. For dinner, a number of tables can be reserved for fixed dining times when you book.

The Grill and Verandah, an indoor/outdoor venue, provides lighter, healthier grilled meals, with food cooked to order in a show kitchen. It's open for breakfast, lunch, and relaxed dinner. The 'spider's web' alcove seating partitions are novel – I haven't found any big spiders yet! One neat feature is a slicing machine to produce cold cuts of meat, so you know it's fresh.

Asian-fusion cuisine (Indian, Sri Lankan, and Thai) is served in the intimate 64-seat East to West restaurant, where the decor includes traditional wood carvings, reflecting the mood of the East. Adjacent is The Grill, specializing in steaks and seafood, in a room with an open kitchen.

The Beach, adjacent to the indoor/outdoor pool, provides fish and chips and other light British fare, traditional desserts, and ice cream (the machine is inside a blue-and-white-striped beach hut, and there are jars and jars of boiled sweets in a second beach hut – all very British and a pleasant throwback to yesteryear).

ENTERTAINMENT. The Britannia Lounge is the venue for major social events and shows. The sight lines are mostly good, although some thin pillars present problems from some seats – the room was originally built more for use as a single-level concert salon than a room for shows – but the setting is elegant. The productions are performed by a small troupe of female dancers, plus a number of cabaret acts. There is live music for listening or dancing to in various bars and lounges. Male dance hosts are aboard each cruise for the many solo women passengers.

SPA/FITNESS. An area of about 8,611 sq ft (800 sq m) is host to a rather nice, homey retreat – an indoor wellness center. It includes an indoor swimming pool (few ships have them today). Adjacent facilities include a sauna and steam room, a fitness/exercise area, several treatment rooms, and a beauty salon. Sporting facilities include St. Andrews, a crazy-golf course located outdoors.

SAPPHIRE PRINCESS
★★★+

THIS IS A MULTI-CHOICE LARGE SHIP FOR INFORMAL FAMILY-FRIENDLY CRUISING

Size:	Large Resort Ship	Passenger/Crew Ratio (lower beds):	2.1
Tonnage:	115,875	Cabins (total):	1,337
Cruise Line:	Princess Cruises	Size Range (sq ft/m): 168–1,329.3/15.6–123.5	
Former Names:	none	Cabins (for one person):	0
Builder:	Mitsubishi Heavy Industries (Japan)	Cabins with balcony:	750
Entered Service:	May 2004/May 2004	Cabins (wheelchair accessible):	28
Length (ft/m):	951.4/290.0	Wheelchair accessibility:	Good
Beam (ft/m):	123.0/37.5	Elevators:	14
Propulsion/Propellers: diesel-electric (42,000kW)/2		Casino (gaming tables):	Yes
Passenger Decks:	13	Swimming Pools:	3
Total Crew:	1,238	Self-Service Launderette:	Yes
Passengers (lower beds):	2,674	Library:	Yes
Passenger Space Ratio (lower beds):	43.3	Onboard currency:	US$

THE SHIP. *Sapphire Princess* is quite a grand playground in which to roam and play when you're not ashore. Princess Cruises delivers a fine, well-packaged holiday product, with some sense of style, at an attractive, highly competitive price, and this ship will appeal to those who really enjoy big-city life with all the trimmings.

The vessel has an instantly recognizable funnel due to two jet engine-like pods that sit high up on its structure, but really they are mainly for decoration. The ship is similar in size and internal layout to *Golden Princess*, *Grand Princess*, and *Star Princess*, although of a greater beam. Unlike its half-sister ships, all of which had a 'spoiler' containing a disco located aft of the funnel, this has been removed from both *Diamond Princess* and *Sapphire Princess*, being replaced by a more sensible aft-facing nightclub/disco, Skywalkers Nightclub.

Several areas focus on swimming pools. One has a giant poolside movie screen, one is two decks high and is covered by a retractable glass dome, itself an extension of the funnel housing, and one pool lies within The Sanctuary – an adults-only, extra-cost relaxation area.

The interiors were overseen and outfitted by the Okura Group, whose Okura Hotel is one of Tokyo's finest. Fit and finish quality is superior to that of the Italian-built *Golden Princess*, *Grand Princess*, and *Star Princess*. Unlike the outside decks, there is plenty of space inside the ship – but there are also plenty of passengers – and a wide array of public rooms, with

BERLITZ'S RATINGS

	Possible	Achieved
Ship	500	350
Accommodation	200	139
Food	400	247
Service	400	289
Entertainment	100	76
Cruise Experience	400	286

OVERALL SCORE 1387 points out of 2000

many 'intimate' (this being a relative term) spaces and places to enjoy. The passenger flow has been well thought out, and there's little congestion.

The interior focal point is a piazza-style atrium lobby, with Vines (wine bar), an International Café (for coffee, pastries, panini, etc.), library/Internet-connect center, and Alfredo's sit-down pizzeria.

A Wedding Chapel has a live web-cam to relay ceremonies via the Internet. The ship's captain can legally marry American couples, due to the ship's Bermuda registry and a dispensation that should be verified in advance according to where you reside. Princess Cruises offers three wedding packages – Pearl, Emerald, and Diamond.

The Grand Casino has gaming tables and over 260 slot machines (some of which are linked and may provide a combined payout). Other facilities include a library/computer room, and a card room. The wood-paneled Wheelhouse Bar is finely decorated with memorabilia and ship models tracing part of the history of sister company P&O. The Wake View Bar has a spiral stairway leading down to a great viewing spot for those who want to watch the ship's wake.

A high-tech hospital has live SeaMed telemedicine linkups to the Cedars-Sinai Medical Center in Los Angeles, with specialists available for emergency help.

The ship is full of revenue centers. Expect to be subjected to flyers advertising daily art auctions, designer watches, and the like.

The dress code is formal or smart casual – interpreted by many as jeans and trainers. Gratuities to staff are added to your account, with gratuities for children charged at the same rate. If you want to pay less, you can have these charges adjusted at the reception desk.

Lines form for many things aboard large ships, but particularly so for the information office, and for open-seating breakfast and lunch in the four main dining rooms. Long lines for shore excursions and shore tenders are also a fact of life, as is waiting for elevators at peak times, and embarkation and disembarkation – though an 'express check-in' option is available for embarkation if you fill in some forms 40 days before your cruise.

The many extra-charge items include ice cream and freshly squeezed orange juice. Yoga, group exercise cycling, and kick-boxing classes cost extra. There's an hourly rate for group babysitting services, and a charge for using washers and dryers in the self-service launderettes.

ACCOMMODATION. Everyone receives turndown service and nightly chocolates on pillows, bathrobes on request, and toiletries. A hairdryer is provided in all cabins. All bathrooms are tiled and have a decent amount of open shelf storage space for toiletries.

Most outside cabins on Emerald Deck have views obstructed by the lifeboats. Sadly, there are no cabins for solo travelers. Your name is typically placed outside your suite or cabin – handy for delivery service personnel but eroding your privacy. Most balcony suites and cabins can be overlooked from the navigation bridge wing. There is 24-hour room service, though some menu items aren't available during early morning hours.

Note that cabins with balconies on Baja, Caribe, and Dolphin decks are overlooked by passengers on balconies on the deck above. Cabin bath towels are small, and drawer space is limited. There are no butlers, even for the top-grade suites – which aren't really large in comparison to similar suites aboard some other ships.

DINING. All dining rooms are located on one of two decks in the ship's center. There are five principal dining rooms with themed decor and cuisine: Sterling Steakhouse for steak and grilled meats; Vivaldi for Italian fare; Santa Fe for cuisine from the US Southwest; Pacific Moon for Asian cuisine; and International, the largest, located aft, with two seatings and 'traditional' cuisine. These offer a mix of two seatings and 'Anytime Dining,' where you choose when and with whom you want to eat. All dining rooms are split into sections in a non-symmetrical design that breaks what are quite large spaces into many smaller sections, for better ambience and less noise pollution.

Specially designed dinnerware and good-quality linens and silverware are used. Note that 15 percent is added to all beverage bills, including wines.

Although portions are generous, the food and its presentation are quite standardized. Fish is often disguised by coatings, the choice of fresh green vegetables is limited, few garnishes are used, and cheese is already sliced and diced. But, this is big-ship banquet catering, with all its attendant standardization and batch cooking. Pasta dishes are very decent (though voluminous), typically served by section headwaiters, who may also make 'something special just for you' – in search of favorable comments and gratuities. If you like desserts, order a sundae at dinner (most other items are just so-so).

Sabatini's is an informal eatery (reservations required; cover charge). It features an eight-course meal, including Italian-style pizzas and pastas, with a variety of sauces, as well as Italian-style entrées (mains) including tiger prawns and lobster tail. Its cuisine is prepared with better-quality ingredients and more attention to presentation and taste than the food in the other dining rooms.

A poolside hamburger grill and a pizza bar (no additional charge) are additional dining spots for casual bites. You have to pay extra if you order items to eat at either the coffee bar/patisserie, or the caviar/Champagne bar.

Other casual meals can be taken in the Horizon Court, open 24 hours a day, with large ocean view on the port and starboard sides and direct access to the two principal swimming pools and Lido Deck.

ENTERTAINMENT. The Princess Theater, spanning two decks, has comfortable seating on both main and balcony levels. It has $3 million in sound and light equipment, plus a nine-piece orchestra.

Princess Cruises has glamorous all-American production shows, and the two or three shows on a typical seven-day cruise should not disappoint.

A second large entertainment lounge, Club Fusion, presents cabaret acts at night, and lectures, bingo, and horse racing during the day. A third entertainment lounge also hosts cabaret acts and dance bands. Most lounges and bars have live music, and a number of male dance hosts act as partners for women traveling alone.

SPA/FITNESS. The Lotus Spa is forward on Sun Deck – one of the uppermost decks. Separate facilities for men and women include a sauna, steam room, and changing rooms; common facilities include a relaxation/waiting zone, body-pampering treatment rooms, and a gymnasium packed with high-tech muscle-pumping equipment, and great views. Some fitness classes are free, while others cost extra.

The Lotus Spa is operated by Steiner Leisure (online reservations can be made for any spa treatments).

SCENIC ECLIPSE
NYR

THIS SHIP IS DESIGNED SPECIFICALLY FOR IN-DEPTH 'SOFT' EXPEDITION ADVENTURES

Size:	Boutique Ship	Passenger/Crew Ratio (lower beds):	1.2/1
Tonnage:	17,085	Cabins (total):	114
Cruise Line:	Scenic	Size Range (sq ft/m):	344.4-2,099.0/32.0-195.0
Former Names:	none	Cabins (for one person):	0
Builder:	Uljanik Group (Croatia)	Cabins with balcony:	114
Entered Service:	Aug 2018	Cabins (wheelchair accessible):	0
Length (ft/m):	551.1/168.0	Wheelchair accessibility:	Poor
Beam (ft/m):	70.5/21.5	Elevators:	1
Propulsion/Propellers:	diesel-electric/2 azimuthing pods	Casino (gaming tables):	No
		Swimming Pools:	1 (plunge pool)
Passenger Decks:	8	Self-Service Launderette:	No
Total Crew:	178	Library:	Yes
Passengers (lower beds):	228	Onboard currency:	Euros
Passenger Space Ratio (lower beds):	72.3		

THE SHIP. This smart-looking specialist expedition ship – designed from the ground up to operate in Arctic and Antarctic regions – and described by Scenic as 'the world's first discovery yacht' – is powered by Azipods, marine propulsion units that provide ample operational flexibility.

The ship carries a ROV (submersible, remotely operated vehicle – for extra-cost use), has underwater cameras, and a helicopter. A fleet of Zodiacs and kayaks are also on board, plus scuba-diving and snorkeling equipment.

Public rooms include an observation lounge, library, and lecture theater. At the time this book was completed, few details of the expedition leaders had been announced, but these will be vitally important to the success of the ship, which is launching in 2018.

ACCOMMODATION. There are numerous accommodation price grades, but all are designated

BERLITZ'S RATINGS		
	Possible	Achieved
Ship	500	NYR
Accommodation	200	NYR
Food	400	NYR
Service	400	NYR
Entertainment	100	NYR
Cruise Experience	400	NYR

OVERALL SCORE NYR points out of 2000

as suites (all with butler service). The price you pay depends on the size, location, and grade you choose. From the largest owner's suites to the smallest, they all feature contemporary design and fittings. However, for expedition-style cruises, you won't be in your cabin much, because of the destination-immersive nature of the voyages.

DINING. There are several dining options (all at no extra cost), which include a French fine-dining venue, an Italian/Steak restaurant, and a pan-Asian eatery.

ENTERTAINMENT. The Theatre is the venue for expedition lectures, and small revue shows.

SPA/FITNESS. The ship has the Spa Sanctuary with wellness facilities, gym, exercise studio for yoga and Pilates, and indoor and outdoor pools.

SEA ADVENTURER
★★

A HARDY BUT DATED EXPEDITION SHIP SUITED TO CRUISING IN POLAR REGIONS

Size:	Boutique ship	Passenger/Crew Ratio (lower beds):	1.4
Tonnage:	5,750	Cabins (total):	61
Cruise Line:	Quark Expeditions	Size Range (sq ft/m):	119.0–211.0/11.0-19.6
Former Names:	*Clipper Adventurer, Alla Tarasova*	Cabins (for one person):	0
Builder:	Brodgradiliste Uljanik, (Yugoslavia)	Cabins with balcony:	0
Entered Service:	1976/2011	Cabins (wheelchair accessible):	0
Length (ft/m):	328.0/100.0	Wheelchair accessibility:	None
Beam (ft/m):	53.2/16.2	Elevators:	0
Propulsion/Propellers:	diesel (3,884kW)/2	Casino (gaming tables):	No
Passenger Decks:	5	Swimming Pools:	0
Total Crew:	72	Self-Service Launderette:	No
Passengers (lower beds):	122	Library:	Yes
Passenger Space Ratio (lower beds):	47.1	Onboard currency:	US$

THE SHIP. *Sea Adventurer* is a solidly built small ship that rides well. It has an ice-strengthened (A1 ice classification), royal blue hull, and white funnel, bow-thruster, and stabilizers. It is best suited to couples and solo travelers who enjoy nature and wildlife up close. However, even with an ice classification, the ship got stuck in an ice field in the Antarctic's Bellingshausen Sea in 2000. It also ran aground in 2010 in the Canadian Arctic. But all is now back to normal, helped by the ship's very tough, deep-draft hull.

There are 10 Zodiac rigid inflatable craft for landings and in-depth excursions, and a covered promenade deck. This cozy ship caters to travelers rather than mere passengers. The dress code is casual during the day, although at night many passengers wear jackets and ties. The public spaces are a little limited, with just one main lounge and bar. There is a small library, with high wingback chairs.

There is no observation lounge with forward-facing views, although there is an outdoor observation area directly below the bridge. The ship is operated under charter by Quark Expeditions, who provide the food, expedition staff and experienced geologists. Naturalist lecturers accompany all cruise expeditions. Smoking is permitted only on the outside decks.

The passageways are narrow, and outer deck stairways are rather steep.

BERLITZ'S RATINGS	Possible	Achieved
Ship	500	219
Accommodation	200	99
Food	400	190
Service	400	211
Entertainment	100	40
Cruise Experience	400	186

OVERALL SCORE 945 points out of 2000

ACCOMMODATION. There are seven grades of cabin, including a dedicated price for single occupancy. All cabins have outside views and twin lower beds, with private bathroom with shower, and toilet. The bathrooms are really tiny, although they have all the basics. Several double-occupancy cabins can be booked by single travelers, but special rates apply.

All cabins have a lockable drawer for valuables, telephone, and individual temperature control. Some have picture windows, while others have portholes. Two larger cabins (called suites in the brochure, which they really are not) are quite well equipped for the size of the vessel.

DINING. The dining room, with deep ocean-view windows, accommodates all passengers at a single seating. The food, a combination of American and Continental European cuisine, is prepared freshly by chefs trained at some of America's best culinary institutions. Unfortunately, though, the food is quite disappointing. There are limited menu choices and too much use of canned fruits and juices, particularly for breakfasts, which are repetitive. Casual, self-service breakfast and luncheon buffets are taken in the main lounge.

ENTERTAINMENT. After-dinner conversation in the lounge/bar is the main evening event.

SPA/FITNESS. There is a small sauna.

SEA CLOUD
★★★★★

THIS IS QUITE SIMPLY THE MOST BEAUTIFUL SAIL-CRUISE SHIP IN THE WORLD

Size:	Boutique Ship	Passenger Space Ratio (lower beds):	39.5
Tonnage:	2,532	Passenger/Crew Ratio (lower beds):	1.1
Cruise Line:	Sea Cloud Cruises	Cabins (total):	32
Former Names:	Sea Cloud of Grand Cayman, IX-99,	Size Range (sq ft/m):	102.2–409.0/9.5–38.0
	Antama, Patria, Angelita, Sea Cloud, Hussar	Cabins (for one person):	0
Builder:	Krupp Werft (Germany)	Cabins with balcony:	0
Entered Service:	1931/1979	Cabins (wheelchair accessible):	0
Length (ft/m):	359.2/109.5	Wheelchair accessibility:	None
Beam (ft/m):	48.2/14.9	Elevators:	0
Propulsion/Propellers:	sail power + diesel	Casino (gaming tables):	No
	(4,476kW)/2	Swimming Pools:	0
Passenger Decks:	3	Self-Service Launderette:	No
Total Crew:	60	Library:	Yes
Passengers (lower beds):	64	Onboard currency:	Euros

THE SHIP. *Sea Cloud* is a completely authentic 1930s barque whose 85th birthday was in 2016. It is the largest private yacht ever built – three times the size of Captain Cook's *Endeavour* – and a stunningly beautiful ship when under sail in both the Caribbean and European/Mediterranean waters. Its four masts are almost as high as a 20-story building, the main one being 178ft (54m) above the

BERLITZ'S RATINGS		
	Possible	Achieved
Ship	500	432
Accommodation	200	174
Food	400	336
Service	400	336
Entertainment	100	91
Cruise Experience	400	333

OVERALL SCORE 1702 points out of 2000

Main Deck, and, with its full complement of 30 sails (measuring some 32,292 sq ft (3,000 sq m) billowing in the wind, it really is a sight to behold.

This was the largest private yacht ever built when completed in 1931 by Edward F. Hutton for his wife, Marjorie Merriweather Post, the American cereal heiress. Originally constructed for $1 million as *Hussar* in the Germany's Krupp shipyard in Kiel, the steel-hulled vessel saw action during World War II as a weather-observation ship, under the code name IX-99.

There is plenty of deck space (but lots of ropes on deck, and other nautical equipment), even under the vast expanse of white sail, and the Promenade Deck outdoors still has wonderful varnished sea chests. The decks themselves are made of mahogany and teak, and wooden steamer-style sunloungers are provided.

One of the most delightful aspects of sailing aboard this ship is its 'Blue Lagoon,' located at the stern. Weather permitting, you can lie down on the thick blue padding and gaze up at the stars and

night sky – it's glorious, particularly when the ship is under sail, with engines turned off.

The original engine room, with diesel engines, is still in operation for the rare occasions when sail power can't be used. An open-bridge policy is the norm, except during poor weather or navigational maneuvers. Passengers are not, however, allowed to climb the rigging. This is because the mast rigging on this vintage sailing ship is of a very different type to more modern sailing vessels such as *Royal Clipper, Star Clipper, Star Flyer,* and *Sea Cloud II.*

In addition to the retained and refurbished original suites and cabins, some newer, smaller cabins were added in 1979 when a consortium of German yachtsmen and businessmen bought the ship and spent $7.5 million refurbishing it. The interiors exude warmth and are finely hand-crafted. There is much antique mahogany furniture, fine original oil paintings, gorgeous carved oak paneling, parquet flooring, and burnished brass everywhere, as well as some finely detailed ceilings. Marjorie Merriweather Post had been accustomed to the very finest things in life.

A cruise aboard the intimate *Sea Cloud* is really exhilarating. A kind of stately home afloat, it remains one of the world's best travel experiences. The activities are few, and so relaxation is the key, in a setting that provides fine service and style, but in an unpretentious way. The only dress-up nights are the Welcome Aboard, and Farewell dinners, but otherwise, smart casual clothing is all that is needed.

Bear in mind that a big sailing vessel such as this can heel to one side occasionally, so flat shoes are preferable to high heels. Note that shorter skirts are not the most practical garments for climbing some of the ship's steep staircases.

White and red wines and beer are included for lunch and dinner, and soft drinks, espresso and cappuccino coffees are included at any time. Shore excursions are an optional extra, as are gratuities, which can be charged to your onboard account.

Although now aged 85 years – I doubt if any modern cruise ship will last this long – Sea Cloud is so lovingly maintained and operated that anyone who sails aboard it cannot fail to be impressed. The food and service are good, as is the interaction between passengers and mixed-nationality crew, many of whom have worked aboard the ship for many, many years. Once a cruise, a sailors' choir (made up of officers and crew members) sings seafaring songs. One bonus is the fact that the doctor on board is available at no charge for medical emergencies or seasickness medication.

Sea Cloud is the most romantic sailing ship afloat. It is best suited to couples and solo travelers (not children) who would probably never consider a 'normal' cruise ship, but who would enjoy sailing aboard a real tall ship that is packaged to include accommodation, good food, like-minded companions, and interesting destinations. It operates under charter to various travel companies for much of the year, as well for individual bookings.

Hamburg-based Sea Cloud Cruises also operates companion sailing ship, Sea Cloud II, with 23 sails.

ACCOMMODATION. Because Sea Cloud was built as a private yacht, there is a wide variation in cabin sizes and configurations. Some cabins have double beds, while some have twins (side by side or in an L-shaped configuration) that are fixed and cannot be placed together. Many of the original cabins have a fireplace, now with an electric fire.

All the cabins are very comfortable, but those on Main Deck (cabins 1–8) were part of the original accommodation. Of these, the two Owner's Suites (cabins 1 and 2) are really opulent, and have original Chippendale furniture, fine gilt detailing, a real fireplace, French canopy bed, and large Italian Carrara marble bathrooms with gold fittings.

Owner's Cabin Number 1 is decorated in white throughout, and has a French double bed, a marble fireplace, and Louis Philippe chairs; the bathroom is appointed in Carrara marble, with cut-glass mirrors,

and faucets (taps) in the shape of swans. Owner's Cabin Number 2, completely paneled in rich woods, retains the mahogany secretary used 60 years ago by Edward F. Hutton, with its dark wood decor reminiscent of the 1930s.

Other cabins – both the original ones, and some newer additions – are beautifully furnished. All were refurbished in 1993 and are surprisingly large for the size of the ship. There is a good amount of closet and drawer space, and all cabins have a personal safe and telephone. The cabin bathrooms, too, are quite luxurious, and equipped with everything you might need, including bathrobes and hairdryer, and an assortment of toiletries. There is a 110-volt AC shaver socket in each bathroom, and toilets are of the 'quiet flush' type. The 'new' cabins are rather small for two persons, so it's best to take minimal luggage.

There is no cabin food or beverage service. Also, if you occupy one of the original cabins on Main Deck, you may be subjected to some noise when the motorized capstans are used to raise and lower or trim the sails. On one day each cruise, an 'open-house' cocktail party is held on the Main Deck, with cabins available for passengers to see.

DINING. The exquisitely elegant dining room, created from the original owner's living room/saloon, is in the center of the vessel, and also houses the ship's library. It has beautiful wood-paneled walls and a wood beam ceiling.

There is ample space at each table for open-seating meals. German chefs are in charge, and the high-quality cuisine is very international, with a good balance of nouvelle cuisine and regional dishes, although there is little choice, due to the size of the galley. There is always excellent seafood and fish, which are purchased locally, when available, as are most other ingredients.

For breakfast and lunch, there are self-serve buffets. Wines accompany lunch and dinner. Soft drinks and bottled water are included in the fare, while alcoholic drinks cost extra.

ENTERTAINMENT. A keyboard player/singer is available for the occasional soirée, but after-dinner conversation constitutes the main entertainment each evening.

SPA/FITNESS. There are no spa or fitness facilities. However, for recreation (particularly at night), there is the Blue Lagoon, an area of seating with blue cushioned pads at the very aft of the ship, where you can lie down and watch the heavens.

SEA CLOUD II
★★★★★

THIS FINE SHIP PROVIDES EXCLUSIVE, RELAXING SAIL-CRUISES FOR COUPLES

Size:	Boutique Ship
Tonnage:	3,849
Cruise Line:	Sea Cloud Cruises
Former Names:	none
Builder:	Astilleros Gondan, Figueras (Spain)
Entered Service:	Feb 2001
Length (ft/m):	383.8/117.0
Beam (ft/m):	52.9/16.1
Propulsion/Propellers:	sail power + diesel (2,500kW)/2
Passenger Decks:	4
Total Crew:	60
Passengers (lower beds):	94
Passenger Space Ratio (lower beds):	40.9
Passenger/Crew Ratio (lower beds):	1.6
Cabins (total):	47
Size Range (sq ft/m):	215.2–322.9/20.0–30.0
Cabins (for one person):	0
Cabins with balcony:	0
Cabins (wheelchair accessible):	0
Wheelchair accessibility:	None
Elevators:	0
Casino (gaming tables):	No
Swimming Pools:	0
Self-Service Launderette:	No
Library:	Yes
Onboard currency:	Euros

THE SHIP. This three-mast tall ship (called a barque) is slightly longer and beamier than the original *Sea Cloud*, and has the look, ambience, and feel of a 1930s sailing vessel (think polished woods, brass elements, gold fittings, and marble fireplaces), while benefiting from the latest high-tech navigational aids. It complements the company's original, 1931-built *Sea Cloud* in almost every way, including its external appearance – except for a very rounded stern in place of the counter stern of the original ship.

The interior designers have managed to replicate the same beautiful traditional look and special decorative touches, so anyone who has sailed aboard *Sea Cloud* will feel instantly at home. Whether the modern materials used in this ship (which entered service in 2001) will stand up to 85 years of use like those of the original remains to be seen, but it's certainly quality. The main lounge is truly elegant, with sofa and large individual tub chair seating around oval drinks tables. The ceiling is ornate, with an abundance of wood detailing, and an oval centerpiece is set around skylights to the open deck above. A bar is set into the aft port side of the room, which has audio-visual aids built in for lectures and presentations.

A treasured aspect of sailing aboard this ship is its 'Blue Lagoon', at the very stern – part of the Lido outdoor bar and casual dining area. Weather permitting, you can lie on thick blue padding and gaze up at the stars and warm night sky – it's a huge pleasure,

BERLITZ'S RATINGS		
	Possible	Achieved
Ship	500	432
Accommodation	200	173
Food	400	339
Service	400	335
Entertainment	100	90
Cruise Experience	400	332

OVERALL SCORE 1701 points out of 2000

particularly when the ship is under sail, with engines off.

In terms of interior design, degree of luxury in appointments, the passenger flow, fabrics, food, service, the ceiling height of public rooms, larger cabins, great open deck space, and excellent passenger/space ratio and crew per passenger ratio, there is none better than *Sea Cloud II*. I have sailed aboard both this and its sister vessel, and I can promise you a memorable sail-cruise experience.

A small water-sports platform is built into the aft quarter of the starboard side (with adjacent shower), and the ship carries four inflatable craft for close-in shore landings, as well as snorkeling equipment.

There are three masts and 30 sails, measuring a billowing 32,292 sq ft (3,000 sq m). There are: Bowsprit, flying jib, fore topgallant staysail, outer jib, inner jib; fore topmast staysail, fore mast, fore royal, fore topgallant, fore upper topsail, fore lower topsail, fore course; main royal staysail, main topgallant staysail, main mast, sky sail, main royal, main topgallant, main upper topsail, main lower topsail, main course, mizzen topgallant staysail, mizzen topmast staysail; mizzen mast, upper spanker, lower spanker, mizzen spanker boom, middle gaff, and upper gaff.

This is just about as exclusive as it gets – sailing in the lap of luxury aboard one of the world's finest true sailing ships – although your experience will depend on which company is operating the ship (it may be under charter) when you sail, and what is included in the package.

ACCOMMODATION. The decor in the cabins is very tasteful 1920s retro, with lots of bird's-eye maple wood paneling, brass accenting, and beautiful molded white ceilings. All cabins have a vanity desk, hairdryer, refrigerator (typically stocked with soft drinks and bottled water), and a combination TV/DVD unit. Comparisons are bound to be made between this and its sister ship, and if you have sailed aboard the original *Sea Cloud*, you may be disappointed with the smaller space and decoration of the equivalent cabins aboard this ship.

All cabins have a private bathroom with shower enclosure (or tub/shower combination), and plenty of storage space for products. Toilets are of the quiet, gentle flush type. The cabin current is 220 volts, although bathrooms also include a 110-volt socket for shavers.

There are two suites. Naturally, these have more space – but not as much space as the two Owner's Suites aboard *Sea Cloud*. They comprise a completely separate bedroom, with four-poster bed, and living room, while the marble-clad bathroom has a full-size tub.

There are 16 Junior Suites. These provide a living area and sleeping area with twin beds that convert to a queen-size bed. The marble-clad bathroom is quite opulent, and has a small tub/shower combination, with lots of cubbyholes to store toiletries.

DINING. The one-sitting dining room is open-seating, so you can dine with whom you wish. It is decorated in a light, modern maritime style, with wood and carpeted flooring, comfortable chairs with armrests, and circular light fixtures. The gold-rimmed plates used for the captain's dinner – typically a candlelit affair – have the ship's crest embedded in the white porcelain; they are extremely elegant and highly collectible (purchase on-board is available). The place settings for dinner, also often by candlelight, are green and white.

There is always excellent seafood and fish, purchased fresh, locally, when available, as are many other ingredients. For breakfast and lunch, there are self-serve buffets. These are really good, and beautifully presented – usually indoors for breakfast, and outdoors on the Promenade Deck for lunch. Meal times are announced by the ringing of a bell.

European wines typically accompany lunch and dinner – mostly young vintages. Soft drinks and bottled water are included in the fare, while alcoholic drinks cost extra.

ENTERTAINMENT. There is a keyboard player/singer for the occasional soirée, but nothing else – nothing else is needed since the thrill of sailing is the entertainment. Dinner and after-dinner conversation with fellow passengers really becomes the main evening activity. So, if you are feeling anti-social and don't want to talk to your fellow passengers, take a good book or two.

SPA/FITNESS. There is a health/fitness area, with a small gymnasium, and sauna. Massage and facials are available.

SEA EXPLORER
★★★+

A FAIRLY STYLISH , VERY COMFORTABLE POCKET-SIZED SHIP FOR DISCOVERY CRUISES

Size:	Boutique Ship	Passenger/Crew Ratio (lower beds):	1.5
Tonnage:	4,200	Cabins (total):	53
Cruise Line:	Oceanwide Expeditions	Size Range (sq ft/m):	234.6–353.0/21.8–32.8
Former Names:	Renai I, Regina Renaissance	Cabins (for one person):	0
Builder:	Cantieri Navali Baglietto (Italy)	Cabins with balcony:	0
Entered Service:	2014	Cabins (wheelchair accessible):	0
Length (ft/m):	297.2/90.6	Wheelchair accessibility:	None
Beam (ft/m):	50.1/15.3	Elevators:	1
Propulsion/Propellers:	diesel/2	Casino (gaming tables):	No
Passenger Decks:	5	Swimming Pools:	0
Total Crew:	70	Self-Service Launderette:	No
Passengers (lower beds):	106	Library:	Yes
Passenger Space Ratio (lower beds):	39.6	Onboard currency:	US$

THE SHIP. *Sea Explorer* is for going to out-of-the-way ports and destinations with a focus on destination discovery. Originally built for the long-defunct Renaissance Cruises as *Renaissance VII* (*Caledonian Sky* – originally *Renaissance VI* – is a sister ship). It is a classy little vessel with interior decor that is reminiscent of a small, traditional country club (with lots of faux wood and brass accenting). The ship is now owned by the UK's Noble Caledonia and Australia's APT Touring.

The public rooms are cozy, with (faux) wood paneling and brass in evidence throughout.

Inspector Hercule Poirot would be very much at home here. However, several pillars – needed for structural support – create obstructions in some public rooms and hallways.

ACCOMMODATION. There are several accommodation price grades, with the price dependent on the size and location. From the smallest to the largest (with balcony), they all have ample closet space,

BERLITZ'S RATINGS		
	Possible	Achieved
Ship	500	351
Accommodation	200	158
Food	400	225
Service	400	252
Entertainment	100	60
Cruise Experience	400	266

OVERALL SCORE 1312 points out of 2000

although drawer and other storage space is limited. Bathrooms (there is a step between bedroom and bathroom) are of a decent size, and marble-clad; towels and plush bathrobes are cotton, as is the bed linen. Note that announcements cannot be turned off in your cabin.

DINING. The Restaurant has ocean-view portholes, and operates a single seating with table assignments for dinner, and in an open-seating arrangement for breakfast and lunch. It is an elegant, pleasant room, with wood paneling, fine furnishings, subtle lighting, and plenty of space around each table. A mix of chairs with and without armrests is provided. There are tables for two to eight.

ENTERTAINMENT. This consists of recaps and after-dinner conversation with fellow adventurous participants.

SPA/FITNESS. There is a small beauty salon, and one hot tub on the uppermost open deck.

SEA PRINCESS
★★★+

THIS FAMILY-FRIENDLY MID-SIZE SHIP IS VERY COMFORTABLE FOR GENERAL CRUISING

Size:	Mid-size Ship	Passenger/Crew Ratio (lower beds):	2.2
Tonnage:	77,690	Cabins (total):	1,008
Cruise Line:	Princess Cruises	Size Range (sq ft/m):	158.2–610.3/14.7–56.7
Former Names:	Adonia, Sea Princess	Cabins (for one person):	0
Builder:	Fincantieri (Italy)	Cabins with balcony:	411
Entered Service:	Dec 1998/Apr 2005	Cabins (wheelchair accessible):	19
Length (ft/m):	857.2/261.3	Wheelchair accessibility:	Good
Beam (ft/m):	105.6/32.2	Elevators:	11
Propulsion/Propellers:	diesel-electric (46,080kW)/2	Casino (gaming tables):	Yes
Passenger Decks:	10	Swimming Pools:	3
Total Crew:	850	Self-Service Launderette:	Yes
Passengers (lower beds):	2,016	Library:	Yes
Passenger Space Ratio (lower beds):	39.3	Onboard currency:	US$

THE SHIP. *Sea Princess, like its sister, Sun Princess,* cruises in Australasian and South Pacific waters.

The all-white ship has a profile balanced by a large, swept-back funnel, with a deck-tennis/basketball/volleyball court in its sheltered base. There is a wide, teak walk-around promenade deck outdoors, some real teak steamer-style deck chairs with cushioned pads, and lots of outdoor space. An extra cost adults-only sunbathing and pool retreat, The Sanctuary, provides 'me' space away from kids.

Sea Princess absorbs passengers well and has a decent passenger/space ratio. Some areas have an intimate feel. The interiors are attractive and welcoming with pastel colors and decor that includes countless wall murals and other artwork. There is a wide range of public rooms, bars, and lounges. The interior focal and social meeting point is a four-deck-high atrium lobby, with winding double stairways and two panoramic glass-walled elevators.

The Grand Casino is slightly out of the main passenger flow and so doesn't generate the 'walk-through' factor found aboard so many ships.

Perhaps the most popular drinking venue is the Wheelhouse Bar, with decor that is a pleasing mix of traditional and modern, a bandstand and dance floor; it's like a gentleman's club, with its wood paneling and comfortable seating. For families with children, plenty of space is provided in The Fun Zone

BERLITZ'S RATINGS		
	Possible	Achieved
Ship	500	359
Accommodation	200	148
Food	400	249
Service	400	278
Entertainment	100	77
Cruise Experience	400	281

OVERALL SCORE 1392 points out of 2000

children's center, on the starboard side of Riviera Deck.

A captain's cocktail party is normally held in the four-deck-high open-flow main atrium.

Niggles include the disjointed layout and number of dead ends. Also, the cabin-numbering system is illogical, the accommodation hallways are plain, the automated telephone system is user-unfriendly, the cabin towels are small, as are the swimming pools, and the pool deck is cluttered with white plastic sunloungers (no cushioned pads). Extra cost include ice creams, except in the restaurant, and bottled water; these can add up to a considerable amount on a long cruise. Overall, however, Princess Cruises delivers a consistently decent, comfortable, well-packaged product, always with a decent degree of style, at a competitive price.

ACCOMMODATION. There are numerous accommodation price grades, designated as suites with private balcony, mini-suites with private balcony, outside-view twin-bedded cabins with balcony, and interior twin-bedded cabins. Standard outside-view and interior cabins are a little small, but they are functional. Proportionately, there are quite a lot of interior (no-view) cabins. The cabin-numbering system is illogical, and the room service menu is poor.

Many outside-view cabins have narrow private balconies, and there is no outside light. Some cabins have third- and fourth-person upper bunk beds, which is good for families.

The storage space is adequate for a seven-night cruise, but challenging for longer cruises. Also provided is a refrigerator, and each night a chocolate will appear on your pillow. Bathrooms are practical units, with all the facilities one needs – although, again, they really are tight spaces. Fortunately, they have a decent shower enclosure, real glasses, a hairdryer, and a small shelf for toiletries.

DINING. Rigoletto and Traviata are the two main, asymmetrically designed, dining rooms; each seats about 500. They are located on the two lower levels of the atrium lobby (your cabin location determines which you are assigned to). Each has its own galley and is split into multi-tier sections that help create a feeling of intimacy. Breakfast and lunch are open seating, and dinner is in two seatings.

Although portions are generous, the food and its presentation are disappointing, and quite standardized. Fish is often disguised by a crumb or batter coating, the choice of fresh green vegetables is limited, few garnishes are used, and cheese is already sliced and diced. But, this is big-ship banquet catering, with all its attendant standardization. Pasta dishes are acceptable (though voluminous), typically served by section headwaiters, who may also make 'something special just for you' – in search of favorable comments and gratuities. If you like desserts, order a sundae at dinner; most other items are just so-so.

Horizon Court is an almost 24-hour casual, self-serve buffet. At night, one section becomes the Steakhouse, with cooked-to-order premium steaks.

Outdoors, with a sheltered view over the Riviera Pool, the Terrace Grill has fast-food items for sunbathers. In the evening, the grill offers steaks, seafood, and a 'white sisters' mixed grill (a cover charge applies for dining under the stars).

Café Corniche, on the upper atrium level, is good for extra-cost premium coffees, teas, and pastries.

ENTERTAINMENT. The Princess Theater, located forward, is a 550-seat, theater-style show-lounge, where the main production shows are staged and movies can be shown. The second theater, Vista Lounge, located aft, is a 480-seat lounge and bar for cabaret and lectures.

The ship also has an array of cabaret acts, and although many are not what you would call headliners, they regularly travel the cruise ship circuit.

SPA/FITNESS. The Lotus Spa has facilities contained in a glass-walled complex located on Lido Deck aft. It includes an ocean-view fitness room with muscle-pumping equipment, an exercise room, sauna and steam room, and several body-treatment rooms.

Forming part of the outside area of the spa complex, one swimming pool is 'suspended' aft between two decks. Two other pools are located in another area in the center of the ship, although they are small.

Joggers can exercise on the wraparound open Promenade Deck.

SEA SPIRIT
★★★+

THIS CHARTERED SHIP OPERATES ON 'SOFT' BUT COMFORTABLE EXPEDITION VOYAGES

Size:	Boutique Ship	Passenger Space Ratio (lower beds):	35
Tonnage:	4,200	Passenger/Crew Ratio (lower beds):	1.0
Cruise Line:	Poseidon Expeditions	Cabins (total):	60
Former Names:	Spirit of	Size Range (sq ft/m):	215.2–430.5/20.0–40.0
Oceanus, Megastar Sagittarius, Sun Viva, Renaissance		Cabins (for one person):	0
5, Hanseatic Renaissance		Cabins with balcony:	6
Builder:	Nuovi Cantieri Appaunia (Italy)	Cabins (wheelchair accessible):	0
Entered Service:	1991/2015	Wheelchair accessibility:	None
Length (ft/m):	296.2/90.3	Elevators:	1
Beam (ft/m):	49.8/15.2	Casino (gaming tables):	No
Propulsion/Propellers:	diesel/2	Swimming Pools:	0
Passenger Decks:	5	Self-Service Launderette:	No
Total Crew:	120	Library:	Yes
Passengers (lower beds):	120	Onboard currency:	US$

THE SHIP. This ship is good for couples and solo travelers looking for nature and wildlife up close and personal but in surroundings that are quite comfortable. It's for anyone who wouldn't dream of cruising aboard anything larger. The ageing ship has quite a smart, chic, mega-yacht-like profile. It was originally built as one of a series of eight similar ships for the long-defunct Renaissance Cruises. There is a narrow teak walk-around promenade deck outdoors, and a good amount of open deck and observation space. The ship has a fleet of Zodiac inflatables for shore landings, and an open bridge policy (so you can visit whenever you want, although note that some navigation officers smoke inside the bridge).

Inside, nothing jars the senses, and the decor is quite elegant, with polished (faux) wood-finish paneling throughout. The ambience is warm and intimate. There are, however, several pillars throughout the public areas, which spoil the decor and sight lines.

ACCOMMODATION. The cabins (all were refurbished in 2017) are quite spacious and combine highly polished imitation rosewood paneling with lots of mirrors, hand-crafted furniture, illuminated walk-in

BERLITZ'S RATINGS		
	Possible	Achieved
Ship	500	331
Accommodation	200	138
Food	400	221
Service	400	252
Entertainment	100	50
Cruise Experience	400	264

OVERALL SCORE 1256 points out of 2000

closets, three-sided vanity mirrors – there are a lot of mirrored surfaces in the decor – and just about everything you need, including a refrigerator, a TV, and (extra-cost) Wi-Fi access. The bathrooms are extremely compact; they have real teakwood floors and marble vanities, and shower enclosures, but none has tubs.

DINING. The dining room operates with open seating for all meals. Small, but comfortable and quite attractive, it has tables for two to eight. You sit where you like, and with whom you like. The meals are self-service, buffet-style affairs for breakfast and lunch, with hot foods chosen from a table menu and served properly for dinner. The food quality and choice are all adequate for hearty expeditioners.

ENTERTAINMENT. There is no entertainment other than evening recaps, dinner, and after-dinner conversation with fellow passengers in the ship's lounge/bar. Six pillars obstruct sight lines to the small stage area.

SPA/FITNESS. Facilities include an aft platform, and Zodiac inflatable craft. There are no spa facilities.

SEABOURN ENCORE
★★★★+

THIS IS A SMALL, ELEGANT SHIP FOR WELL-TRAVELLED, HIGH-COMFORT SEEKERS

Size:	Small Ship	Passenger/Crew Ratio (lower beds):	1.3
Tonnage:	40,350	Cabins (total):	302
Cruise Line:	Seabourn	Size Range (sq ft/m):	295.0–438.1/27.5–133.6
Former Names:	none	Cabins (for one person):	0
Builder:	Mariotti (Italy)	Cabins with balcony:	199
Entered Service:	Dec 2016	Cabins (wheelchair accessible):	7
Length (ft/m):	650.0/198.1	Wheelchair accessibility:	Good
Beam (ft/m):	83.9/25.6	Elevators:	3
Propulsion/Propellers:	diesel-electric/2	Casino (gaming tables):	Yes
Passenger Decks:	10	Swimming Pools:	2
Total Crew:	450	Self-Service Launderette:	Yes
Passengers (lower beds):	604	Library:	Yes
Passenger Space Ratio (lower beds):	67.2	Onboard currency:	US$

THE SHIP. *Seabourn Encore* has two outdoor pools, midships and aft; the aft ('dip' only) pool is in a delightful area, although there's little open sunbathing space. For stargazing, the hot tub located by the ship's bows is a delight; it's dimly lit and peaceful. By day it's a great place to sit and chill out when the ship is underway, just in front of the navigation bridge. The top deck Retreat has 15 extra-cost cabanas for rent in the most peaceful part of the ship, shielded from the sun.

The front of the ship houses the accommodation section, with public rooms located aft, in a vertical stacking that is not so user-friendly.

Seabourn Square is the focal social gathering point, and has a relaxed, club-like ambience. It includes a library, shops, eight computers (Internet use is chargeable – at high cost – a major source of passenger complaints), an outdoor terrace, and a coffee bar. Its 'concierges' can provide in-port shopping tips, set up shore excursions, and make dinner reservations in ports of call, etc. There's a private diamond showroom, called The Collection. Drinks, wines with meals, and all gratuities are included, though premium brands and high-quality wines cost extra.

While real teak is used in most outdoor areas, faux teak (called Flexteak) is used in some others. Cabin doors are narrow, and other doors inside the cabins are of varying heights and sizes, and feel utilitarian. Most public rooms are of a single deck height, so

BERLITZ'S RATINGS		
	Possible	Achieved
Ship	500	428
Accommodation	200	178
Food	400	315
Service	400	328
Entertainment	100	76
Cruise Experience	400	308

OVERALL SCORE 1633 points out of 2000

there's not such a good feeling of spaciousness, and support pillars are everywhere.

ACCOMMODATION. Seabourn markets all accommodation as suites, but the smaller ones are really large cabins, not suites. However, there are six grades spread over seven decks, and all have a 'private' balcony. The price you pay depends on the size, location, and grade you choose. From the smallest (Verandah suite) to the largest (Wintergarden suite), all are comfortable. Note that the Wintergarden suite's balcony is tiny. For a larger balcony, try a Signature suite.

The suites are contemporary, homey living spaces, although the walls are plain and the decor is unimaginative. The beds are high enough off the floor to enable even the largest suitcases to be stowed underneath, and all drawers are fitted with soft gel for quiet closing.

DINING. The Restaurant has open-seating dining at tables for two to eight. It has white-on-white decor (think weddings) and a double-height ceiling in its central section; the port and starboard sides sections have windows, but the ceiling height is low, making it feel cramped.

The Grill by Thomas Keller (reservations required) is a classic American steak and seafood house, with under 100 (indoor and outdoor) seats on Deck 8. The decor is designed as a tribute to the Big Band era.

There's also a venue for sushi on the same deck, with sushi counter and table seating (and bento boxes at lunchtime).

The casual self-serve Colonnade eatery, located aft, has indoor/outdoor seating, although its free-flow design is quite poor, because there's too little outdoor seating for the demand in warm-weather cruise areas.

Patio Grill is in a casual poolside setting outdoors – it's enjoyable on a balmy evening, as a change to the air-conditioned interior venues.

Also, a 24-hour, in-suite menu offers the à la carte items served in the main dining room during dinner hours. Extra-cost Silver or Gold 'connoisseur' wine packages provide a choice of red and white vintage wines for a set amount – perhaps a good idea for longer cruises.

ENTERTAINMENT. The Grand Salon is the venue for shows, cabaret performances, social dancing, and for use as a cinema. It has a gently sloping main and tiered balcony banquette seating.

Small production shows (remember this is a small ship) and a live six-piece band complete the picture.

Another venue, The Club, is a large, cool, trendy, but high-volume nightclub/disco with a wooden dance floor, large bar, and minimalist design. Located beneath the Grand salon, it incorporates a small casino, plus 15 slot machines.

SPA/FITNESS. The Spa at Seabourn, operated by Elemis (Steiner Leisure), occupies the aft section of two decks, and is quite large, at 11,500 sq ft (1,068 sq m). It offers full services in a pleasant setting that includes a two-deck-high waterfall at the entrance and seven indoor/outdoor treatment rooms, a Kneipp 'walk-in-the-water' experience, an extra-cost thermal suite, and salon facilities, with a hot tub and relaxation area on the deck above accessible by a spiral staircase. Separate saunas and steam rooms for men and women are provided, but they are really small. In the gymnasium, personal-training sessions, yoga classes, mat Pilates, and body-composition analysis are available at extra cost, but some basic exercise programs are free.

SEABOURN ODYSSEY
★★★★+

THIS SMALL SHIP HAS COMFORTABLE DECOR FOR THE STYLISH AND WELL-TRAVELED

Size:	Small Ship	Passenger/Crew Ratio (lower beds):	1.3
Tonnage:	32,000	Cabins (total):	225
Cruise Line:	Seabourn	Size Range (sq ft/m):	295.0–438.1/27.5–133.6
Former Names:	none	Cabins (for one person):	0
Builder:	Mariotti (Italy)	Cabins with balcony:	199
Entered Service:	Jun 2009	Cabins (wheelchair accessible):	7
Length (ft/m):	650.0/198.1	Wheelchair accessibility:	Good
Beam (ft/m):	83.9/25.6	Elevators:	3
Propulsion/Propellers:	diesel-electric (23,040kwW)/2	Casino (gaming tables):	Yes
Passenger Decks:	10	Swimming Pools:	2
Total Crew:	330	Self-Service Launderette:	Yes
Passengers (lower beds):	450	Library:	Yes
Passenger Space Ratio (lower beds):	71.1	Onboard currency:	US$

THE SHIP. *Seabourn Odyssey*, the first of a new series of ships for Seabourn, looks like an up-sized version of its three former (smaller) vessels. However, this and sister ships *Seabourn Ovation*, *Seabourn Quest*, and *Seabourn Sojourn* have passenger/space ratios that are among the highest in the cruise industry – so there's no crowded feeling anywhere.

There are two outdoor pools, midships and aft; the aft pool is in a more secluded area, although there's not a lot of sunbathing space, and the steel-mesh sunloungers are not comfortable. One of the most pleasing outdoor areas is the Sky Bar. For stargazing, a hot tub located by the ship's bow is a delight. While real teak decking is used in most outdoor areas, faux teak is used in some locations.

Accommodation areas are in the forward section, with most public rooms aft, so the accommodation is quiet, but you'll need to pass through several decks to get to some public rooms. An Observation Lounge, which has great views, is a well-laid-out, very comfortable room. A Marina, at the stern, has a staging area from which water sports are organized. The interior decor uses light woods, tame colors, and rich soft furnishings to create a contemporary, restrained, relaxing environment, which is good considering the low ceiling height in most public rooms.

Seabourn Square is a relaxed, club-like area designed to encourage sociability; it includes a library,

BERLITZ'S RATINGS		
	Possible	Achieved
Ship	500	426
Accommodation	200	178
Food	400	315
Service	400	328
Entertainment	100	76
Cruise Experience	400	307

OVERALL SCORE 1630 points out of 2000

computer terminals, an outdoor terrace, and a coffee bar that's good for late-riser coffees and pastries. Wi-Fi is available throughout.

Drinks, wines with meals, and all gratuities are included, though premium brands and high-quality wines do cost extra.

This is a ship with a yacht-like ambience. Strong points include the staff, decent service levels, some attention to detail, and the wellness facilities. Passenger niggles include the high charge for Internet-connectivity. The ship's 'vertical stacking' layout is not particularly user-friendly. The cabin doors are rather narrow; doors within cabins are of varying heights and sizes, and feel utilitarian. Most public rooms are of a single deck height, making them feel somewhat cramped. There are support pillars everywhere, and many fire doors protrude outside bulkheads instead of being integral to them.

ACCOMMODATION. There are several different grades of suites in many price categories, although the smaller 'suites' are really large cabins. However, the ship has a lot of balcony cabins (about 90 percent, in fact), giving you plenty of personal privacy. Even the smallest cabin measures a comfortable 269 sq ft (25 sq m). All cabins have a separate tub and shower enclosure in a granite bathroom setting, twin beds convertible to a queen-size bed, flat-screen infotainment system, mini-bar, vanity desk with hairdryer, world atlas, personalized stationery, and large walk-in closet with personal safe.

The interior designers have crafted homey, contemporary living spaces in the suites and cabins, although walls and celings are bland. The beds are high enough off the floor to enable even the largest suitcases to be stowed underneath. All drawers are fitted with soft gel, which means they are quiet – no more slamming contests with your next-door neighbor.

The cabinetry has many seams and strips covering joints, which suggest that the ship's outfitters would benefit from a joinery course. One neat, very creative feature is a leather-clad vanity stool/table that converts into a backgammon table.

Seabourn Suites and Veranda Suites are quite narrow, and feel cramped, with little space between the bed and the opposite wall. However, the bathrooms are generously proportioned, and have gray/chocolate-brown decor, two washbasins, a bathtub, and a separate shower enclosure.

Some size examples (excluding balcony): Grand Suites 1,135 sq ft (105 sq m), including two-bedrooms; Signature Suites 819 sq ft (76 sq m); Wintergarden Suites 914 sq ft (85 sq m) – rather neat suites within a glass-enclosed solarium, set in front of the funnel, with a side balcony; Owner's Suites 611–675 sq ft (57–63 sq m); Penthouse Suites 436–611 sq ft (41–57 sq m); Veranda Suites 269–298 sq ft (25–28 sq m); and Seabourn Suites, measuring 295 sq ft (27 sq m).

Four Penthouse Spa Suites were added in a 2013 refit. These are located directly above the spa (and connect to it via a spiral stairway), and measure between 688 sq ft (64 sq m) and 710 sq ft (66 sq m), including a balcony. Plus, there's free access to the spa's Serene Area.

DINING. There are three dining venues plus a poolside grill: The Restaurant has open-seating dining at tables for two to eight. It is a large venue that feels more clinical than classical, with white-on-white decor and double-height ceiling in its central section. The most-sought-after seats are located in the center, rather than along the port and starboard sides, which have a window but low ceilings. Extra-cost Silver or Gold 'connoisseur' wine packages provide a choice of red and white vintage wines for a set amount – perhaps a good idea for longer cruises.

As an alternative, The Grill by Thomas Keller has 44 seats; it is a classic American steak and seafood house, located adjacent to The Colonnade. The food is cooked to order, and the extra cost is probably worth it, because of higher-quality ingredients. However, the ceiling height is rather low, which makes it feel rather cramped. Reservations are required.

The casual self-serve Colonnade eatery, located aft, has indoor/outdoor seating and is nicely decorated, although its free-flow design could be better; there's too little outdoor seating for the demand in warm-weather areas, when many passengers like to eat outdoors. During dinner on designated formal nights, passengers who are dressed accordingly have to share the space with those who are casually dressed.

The Patio Grill is located in a casual poolside setting outdoors – and is most enjoyable on balmy evenings, as a change to the air-conditioned interior dining venues.

In addition, a 24-hour, in-suite menu offers the à la carte items served in the main dining room during dinner hours.

ENTERTAINMENT. The Grand Salon is for shows, cabaret, social dancing, and for use as a cinema. However, the stage is small – large enough for a live band, but the performers must use the dance floor area. Nine thick pillars that make it awkward to see anything at all, although the room's floor is gently sloped. In the central section hangs an unattractive black, 'decorative,' steel ceiling grating. There's banquette seating in the front and mid-section, and, strangely, sofa-style leather seating along the side walls to the rear, which means you actually sit with your back to the stage – a stupid arrangement!

Another venue, The Club, is a large, cool, trendy but high-volume nightclub/disco with a wooden dance floor, large bar, and minimalist design. Located beneath the Grand Salon, it incorporates a comfortable casino.

SPA/FITNESS. The Spa at Seabourn, operated by Elemis, occupies the aft section of two decks. At 11,500 sq ft (1,068 sq m), it is quite large, and offers full services in a very pleasant setting that includes a two-deck-high waterfall at the entrance. Facilities include seven indoor/outdoor treatment rooms, a Kneipp 'walk-in-the-water' experience, a thermal suite (for which a pass costs extra), salon facilities, and gymnasium, while a hot tub and relaxation area on the deck above are accessed by a spiral staircase. Small, separate saunas and steam rooms for men and women are also provided. Personal training sessions, yoga classes, mat Pilates, and body-composition analysis are available at extra cost, but some basic exercise programs are free.

SEABOURN OVATION
NYR

A HIGHLY COMFORTABLE SMALL SHIP WITH PREMIUM STYLE FOR MATURE TRAVELERS

Size:	Small Ship	Passenger/Crew Ratio (lower beds):	1.3
Tonnage:	40,350	Cabins (total):	225
Cruise Line:	Seabourn	Size Range (sq ft/m):	295.0–438.1/27.5–133.6
Former Names:	none	Cabins (for one person):	0
Builder:	Mariotti (Italy)	Cabins with balcony:	199
Entered Service:	May 2018	Cabins (wheelchair accessible):	7
Length (ft/m):	688.9/210.00	Wheelchair accessibility:	Good
Beam (ft/m):	91.8/28.00	Elevators:	3
Propulsion/Propellers:	diesel-electric/2	Casino (gaming tables):	Yes
Passenger Decks:	10	Swimming Pools:	2
Total Crew:	330	Self-Service Launderette:	Yes
Passengers (lower beds):	604	Library:	Yes
Passenger Space Ratio (lower beds):	67.2	Onboard currency:	US$

THE SHIP. *Seabourn Ovation* is the fifth ship of the similar size and layout for Seabourn (a division of Holland America Line). The outside decks house two small outdoor pools, midships, and aft; the aft ('dip' only) pool is in a pleasant area, but there's little space for sunbathing. For stargazing, a hot tub located near the ship's bows is really pleasant, being peaceful and dimly lit. By day it's good for sitting and chilling out when the ship is underway, located as it is just in front of the navigation bridge. On the top deck, The Retreat has 15 cabanas for rent in the most peaceful part of the ship, shielded from the sun and elements; they are rather expensive, however.

The front section houses the accommodation section, with public rooms located aft, in a vertical stacking that is not so much user-friendly as elevator-friendly.

Inside, the social gathering point – with its relaxed, club-like ambience – is called Seabourn Square. It includes a library, several shops (including a private diamond showroom called The Collection – do people really go to ships to buy diamonds?), computer terminals (Internet use is chargeable), an outdoor terrace, and a coffee bar. 'Concierges' can provide in-port shopping tips, set up shore excursions, and make dinner reservations in ports of call, etc. Alcoholic drinks, wines with meals, and all gratuities are included, though premium brands and high-quality wines cost extra.

BERLITZ'S RATINGS

	Possible	Achieved
Ship	500	NYR
Accommodation	200	NYR
Food	400	NYR
Service	400	NYR
Entertainment	100	NYR
Cruise Experience	400	NYR

OVERALL SCORE NYR points out of 2000

Overall impressions? Although some outdoor deck areas have teak wood, faux teak is used for most. Narrow doors and other doors inside the cabins are of different heights and sizes, and feel utilitarian. Most public rooms are of a single deck height, so there's no feeling of spaciousness, and there are many support pillars, and the showlounge is poorly designed.

ACCOMMODATION. Although the company markets all accommodation as suites, the smaller ones are simply large cabins, although all of them do have a 'private' balcony. Six category grades are spread over seven decks. The price depends on the size, location, and grade you choose. From the smallest to the largest grade, all are very comfortable.

The larger suites are contemporary, homey living spaces, but with walls that are quite plain. The beds are high off the floor, so even the largest suitcases can be stowed underneath. All drawers are fitted with soft gel for quiet closing.

DINING. There is one main dining room, plus a few alternatives. The Restaurant (main dining room) has open-seating dining at tables for two to eight. It feels clinical with its white-on-white decor and double-height ceiling in its central section; the port and starboard sides sections have windows, but the ceiling height of those areas is low, so it feels rather cramped.

The Grill by Thomas Keller (reservations needed) is a classic American steak and seafood venue, with comfortable, contemporary decor, and fewer than 100 seats – including several in an alfresco area. However, it has a low ceiling height, and feels cramped – although some might view this as 'intimate.'

Other dining options include a sushi venue on the same deck, with sushi counter, table seating, and bento boxes at lunchtime, while the casual, self-serve Colonnade eatery, located aft (adjacent to The Grill), has indoor/outdoor seating. Its free-flow design could be better, and there is too little outdoor seating for the demand in warm-weather cruising areas.

Patio Grill, in a casual poolside setting, is enjoyable on a balmy evening, as a change to the air-conditioned interior venues.

A 24-hour, in-suite menu offers the à la carte items served in the main dining room during dinner hours. Extra-cost Silver or Gold 'connoisseur' wine packages provide a choice of red and white vintage wines for a set amount – perhaps a good idea for longer cruises.

ENTERTAINMENT. The Grand Salon (it's not grand at all) is for shows, cabaret performances, social dancing, and movies. The stage is small – enough for a live band – but performers must use the dance floor.

Sadly, nine thick pillars make it awkward to see anything at all, although the floor is gently sloped. There's banquette seating at the front and in the mid-section, and, strangely, sofa-style leather seating along the side walls to the rear, which means you actually sit with your back to the stage – a poor arrangement.

Small production shows (remember this is a small ship) are performed to pre-recorded background, and the audio equipment and sound dispersion are good.

Another venue, The Club, is a large, high-volume nightclub/disco with a wooden dance floor, large bar, and minimalist design. Located beneath the Grand Salon, it incorporates a small casino with gaming tables and slot machines.

SPA/FITNESS. The Spa at Seabourn, operated by Elemis, is aft on two decks, and occupies 11,500 sq ft (1,068 sq m) of space. The entrance has a delightful two-deck-high waterfall. Facilities include seven indoor/outdoor treatment rooms, a Kneipp 'walk-in-the-water' foot bath, an extra-cost thermal suite, and salon facilities, and a hot tub and relaxation area one deck above, with a spiral staircase access. Small, separate saunas and steam rooms for men and women are provided. In the gymnasium, most classes and personal-training sessions cost extra, although some basic exercise programs are free.

SEABOURN QUEST
★★★★+

AN ELEGANT, INCLUSIVE SMALL SHIP FOR DISCOVERY-STYLE CRUISES

Size:	Small Ship	Passenger/Crew Ratio (lower beds):	1.3
Tonnage:	32,346	Cabins (total):	225
Cruise Line:	Seabourn	Size Range (sq ft/m):	295.0–438.1/27.5–133.6
Former Names:	none	Cabins (for one person):	0
Builder:	Mariotti (Italy)	Cabins with balcony:	199
Entered Service:	Jun 2011	Cabins (wheelchair accessible):	7
Length (ft/m):	650.0/198.1	Wheelchair accessibility:	Good
Beam (ft/m):	83.9/25.6	Elevators:	3
Propulsion/Propellers:	diesel-electric (23,040kW)/2	Casino (gaming tables):	Yes
Passenger Decks:	10	Swimming Pools:	2
Total Crew:	330	Self-Service Launderette:	Yes
Passengers (lower beds):	450	Library:	Yes
Passenger Space Ratio (lower beds):	71.1	Onboard currency:	US$

THE SHIP. *Seabourn Quest's* attractions are its staff, service levels, and wellness facilities. Like its sister ships, *Seabourn Odyssey* and *Seabourn Sojourn*, it has one of the highest passenger space ratios in the cruise industry, so there's no sense of being crowded anywhere.

It has two small outdoor pools, midships and aft; the aft pool is in a pleasant area, although there's little sunbathing space, and the pool is just a 'dip' pool. One popular outdoor area is the Sky Bar, good for balmy evenings. For stargazing, the hot tub located by the ship's bow is a delight; it's a dimly lit area and peaceful. By day it's a space for sitting and chilling out when the ship is underway, and for watching the rest of the ship's rounded front section below the navigation bridge. The Marina, aft, has a staging area for expedition equipment, Zodiac shore-landing craft, a boot-washing station, and storage area.

All the accommodation areas are in the forward section, with most public rooms located aft, so the accommodation areas are quiet; however, you'll need to traverse through several decks to get to some of the public rooms.

Seabourn Square, the focal social gathering point of the ship and 'concierge lounge,' has a relaxed, club-like ambience. The area includes a library, shops, eight computers (Internet use is chargeable – at high cost – a major source of passenger complaints), an outdoor terrace, and a coffee bar. Its

BERLITZ'S RATINGS		
	Possible	Achieved
Ship	500	427
Accommodation	200	178
Food	400	315
Service	400	329
Entertainment	100	76
Cruise Experience	400	308

OVERALL SCORE 1633 points out of 2000

'concierges' can provide in-port shopping tips, set up shore excursions, and make dinner reservations in ports of call, etc. There's a private diamond showroom, called The Collection. Drinks, wines with meals, and all gratuities are included, though premium brands and high-quality wines cost extra. Wi-Fi is available throughout the ship.

The 'vertical stacking' layout is not user-friendly. While real teak is used in most outdoor areas, faux teak is used in other areas. The cabin doors are narrow, and doors within the cabins are of varying heights and sizes, and feel utilitarian. Most public rooms are of a single deck height, so there's not such a good feeling of spaciousness, and support pillars are everywhere.

ACCOMMODATION. There are 13 grades of suites in many price categories, although note that the smaller 'suites' are really large cabins, not suites. However, there are many balcony cabins, which are good for personal privacy.

All cabins have a separate tub and shower enclosure in a granite bathroom setting, twin beds convertible to a queen-size bed, flat-screen TV plus CD and DVD player, mini-bar, vanity desk with hairdryer, world atlas, personalized stationery, and large walk-in closet with personal safe.

The interior designers have created homey, contemporary living spaces, although the walls are rather plain and unimaginative. It's good to see that the beds are high enough off the floor to enable even the largest suitcases to be stowed underneath. All drawers are fitted with soft gel, which means they are quiet.

The cabinetry has many seams and strips covering joints, which suggest that the ship's outfitters would benefit from joinery lessons. One neat, creative feature is a leather-clad vanity stool/table that converts into a backgammon table. The design of a 'cube table' that can be inserted under a glass-topped table when not being used as a footrest is a smart idea for making more space.

The Seabourn Suites and Veranda Suites are quite narrow, and feel cramped, with little space between the bed and the opposite wall. However, the bathrooms are generously proportioned, with gray and chocolate-brown decor, two washbasins, a bathtub, and a separate shower enclosure.

Some size examples (excluding balcony): Grand Suites 1,135 sq ft (105 sq m), including two-bedrooms; Signature Suites 819 sq ft (76 sq m); Wintergarden Suites 914 sq ft (85 sq m) – rather neat suites within a glass-enclosed solarium, set in front of the funnel, with a side balcony; Owner's Suites 611–675 sq ft (57–63 sq m); Penthouse Suites 436–611 sq ft (41–57 sq m); Veranda Suites 269–298 sq ft (25–28 sq m); and Seabourn Suites, measuring 295 sq ft (27 sq m).

Four Penthouse Spa Suites were added in a 2013 refit; they are located directly above the spa (and connect to it via a spiral stairway), and measure between 688 sq ft (64 sq m) and 710 sq ft (66 sq m), including balcony. They have a living and dining area seating four, a separate bedroom, walk-in closet, a bathroom with tub and shower, and balcony. Plus, there's free access to the spa's Serene Area.

DINING. There are three venues, plus a Poolside Grill. The Restaurant has open-seating dining at tables for two, four, six, or eight. It is a large venue that actually feels more clinical than classical with its white-on-white decor and double-height ceiling in its central section. The most-sought-after seats are in the center rather than along the port and starboard sides, which have windows, but the ceiling height is low.

The Grill (with 94 seats) by Thomas Keller is a classic American steak and seafood house, located aft on Deck 8. The food is cooked to order, so the extra cost may be worth it, because of higher-quality ingredients. The wine list consists of around 90 selections. However, the venue's ceiling height is rather low, which makes it feel cramped.

The casual Colonnade self-serve eatery, located aft, has indoor/outdoor seating and is nicely decorated, although its free-flow design could be better;

there's too little outdoor seating for the demand in warm-weather cruising areas, when many passengers like to eat outdoors. During dinner, passengers who are dressed formally on designated formal nights have to share the space with those who are more casually dressed.

The Patio Grill is in a casual poolside setting outdoors – and most enjoyable on a balmy evening, as a change to the air-conditioned interior dining venues.

In addition, a 24-hour, in-suite menu offers the à la carte items served in the main dining room during dinner hours.

Extra-cost Silver or Gold 'connoisseur' wine packages provide a choice of red and white vintage wines for a set amount – perhaps a good idea for a longer cruise.

ENTERTAINMENT. The Grand Salon is the main entertainment venue for shows, cabaret performances, social dancing, and for use as a cinema. However, the stage is small – large enough for a live band, but performers need to use the dance floor area – and the room has nine thick pillars that make it awkward to see anything at all, although the room has a gentle slope. On the ceiling of the central section there is a decorative steel grating, which is black, cold-looking, and unappealing. The room has banquette seating in the front and mid-section, and, strangely, sofa-style leather seating along the side walls to the rear, which means you actually sit with your back to the stage – a rather unhelpful arrangement. Small-scale shows (remember this is a small ship) are performed well to pre-recorded tracks, and the audio equipment and sound dispersion are extremely good.

Another venue, The Club, is a large, cool, trendy, but high-volume nightclub/disco with a wooden dance floor, large bar and minimalist design. Located beneath the Grand salon, it incorporates a comfortable casino.

SPA/FITNESS. The Spa at Seabourn, operated by Elemis, occupies the aft section of two decks, and is quite large, at 11,500 sq ft (1,068 sq m). It offers full services in a very pleasant setting that includes a two-deck-high waterfall at the entrance and seven indoor/outdoor treatment rooms, as well a Kneipp 'walk-in-the-water' experience, a thermal suite (for which a pass costs extra), and complete salon facilities, while a hot tub and relaxation area on the deck above are accessed by a spiral staircase. Separate saunas and steam rooms for men and women are provided, but they are very small. In the gymnasium, personal-training sessions, yoga classes, mat Pilates, and body-composition analysis are available at extra cost, but some basic exercise programs are free.

SEABOURN SOJOURN
★★★★+

THIS IS AN UPSCALE, ELEGANT SMALL SHIP FOR THE WELL-TRAVELED

Size:	Small Ship	Passenger/Crew Ratio (lower beds):	1.3
Tonnage:	32,346	Cabins (total):	225
Cruise Line:	Seabourn	Size Range (sq ft/m):	295.0–438.1/27.5–133.6
Former Names:	none	Cabins (for one person):	0
Builder:	Mariotti (Italy)	Cabins with balcony:	199
Entered Service:	Jun 2010	Cabins (wheelchair accessible):	7
Length (ft/m):	650.0/198.1	Wheelchair accessibility:	Good
Beam (ft/m):	83.9/25.6	Elevators:	3
Propulsion/Propellers:	diesel-electric (23,040kW)/2	Casino (gaming tables):	Yes
Passenger Decks:	10	Swimming Pools:	2
Total Crew:	330	Self-Service Launderette:	Yes
Passengers (lower beds):	450	Library:	Yes
Passenger Space Ratio (lower beds):	71.8	Onboard currency:	US$

THE SHIP. *Seabourn Sojourn*, the second of Seabourn's three larger ships (the three former boutique-sized ships – *Seabourn Legend*, *Seabourn Pride*, and *Seabourn Spirit* – were sold to Windstar Crusies in 2014), has two small outdoor swimming pools, midships and aft; the aft pool is in a delightful area, although there's not a lot of sunbathing space. One of the most pleasing outdoor areas is the Sky Bar, and, for stargazing, the hot tub located on the ship's foredeck is a peaceful delight.

All the accommodation areas are in the forward section, with most public rooms located aft, but you'll need to traverse through several decks to get to some of the public rooms. The Marina, at the stern, has a staging area from which water sports are organized.

Seabourn Square, the focal social gathering point of the ship, is a 'concierge lounge,' with a relaxed, club-like ambience. The area includes a library, shops, eight computers (Internet connection is chargeable), an outdoor terrace, and a coffee bar. Its 'concierges' can provide in-port shopping tips, set up shore excursions, and make dinner reservations in ports of call, etc. There's a private diamond showroom, called The Collection. Drinks, wines with meals, and all gratuities are included, though premium brands and high-quality wines cost extra. Wi-Fi is available throughout the ship.

There's plenty of space per passenger, so there is no hint of it being crowded. Minus points? The

BERLITZ'S RATINGS		
	Possible	Achieved
Ship	500	424
Accommodation	200	178
Food	400	315
Service	400	328
Entertainment	100	78
Cruise Experience	400	307

OVERALL SCORE 1628 points out of 2000

'vertical stacking' layout is not really user-friendly. While real teak is used in most outdoor areas, faux teak is used in other areas. The cabin doors are rather narrow, and doors within the cabins vary in height and size, and feel utilitarian. The canapés provided each evening need to be improved.

Most public rooms are of a single deck height, so there's not such a good feeling of spaciousness, and support pillars are everywhere – Mariotti, the shipbuilder, should look at *Europa* to see that it's not necessary to have so many pillars.

ACCOMMODATION. There are several grades of suites in multiple price categories. The smaller 'suites' are really large cabins, and not true suites. However, there are many balcony cabins, for personal privacy (about 90 percent of all suites/cabins have them).

All cabins have a separate tub and shower enclosure in a granite bathroom setting, twin beds convertible to a queen-size bed, flat-screen TV plus CD and DVD player, mini-bar, vanity desk with hairdryer, world atlas, personalized stationery, and large walk-in closet with personal safe.

The interior designers have created very cozy, contemporary living spaces in the suites and cabins, although the walls are rather plain and unimaginative. It's good to see that the beds are high enough off the floor to enable even the largest suitcases to be stowed underneath. All drawers are fitted with soft gel, which means they are quiet – no more slamming contests with your next-door neighbor.

The cabins are bathed in soft earthy tones, although a splash of color wouldn't go amiss. The cabinetry has many seams and strips covering joints, which suggest that the ship's outfitters would benefit from a joinery course. It's also strange that several internal doors are of different sizes, widths, and heights. One neat, very creative feature is a leather-clad vanity stool/table that converts into a backgammon table. The design of a 'cube table' that can be inserted under a glass-topped table when not being used as a footrest is a smart idea for making more space.

Seabourn Suites and Veranda Suites are quite narrow, and feel cramped, with little space between the bed and the opposite wall. However, the bathrooms are generously proportioned, with gray and chocolate-brown decor; there are two washbasins, a bathtub, and a separate shower enclosure.

Some size examples (excluding balcony): Grand Suites 1,135 sq ft (105 sq m), including two-bedrooms; Signature Suites 819 sq ft (76 sq m); Wintergarden Suites 914 sq ft (85 sq m) – rather neat suites within a glass-enclosed solarium, set in front of the funnel, with a side balcony; Owner's Suites 611–675 sq ft (57–63 sq m); Penthouse Suites 436–611 sq ft (41–57 sq m); Veranda Suites 269–298 sq ft (25–28 sq m); and Seabourn Suites, measuring 295 sq ft (27 sq m).

Four Spa Suites were added in a 2013 refit. These are located directly above the spa itself (connected to it via a spiral stairway), and measure between 688 sq ft (64 sq m) and 710 sq ft (66 sq m), including a balcony. The suites have a living and dining area with seating for four, a separate bedroom, walk-in closet, a bathroom with tub and shower, and balcony. Occupants get free use of the 'Serene' relaxation area of the spa.

DINING. There are three venues, plus a poolside grill. The Restaurant has open-seating dining at tables for two, four, six, or eight, with menus designed by American celebrity chef Charlie Palmer. It is a large venue that actually feels more clinical than classical with its white-on-white decor and double-height ceiling in its central section. The most-sought-after seats are in the center rather than along the port and starboard sides, which have a window, but low ceiling height.

The Grill by Thomas Keller has 44 seats and is a ship's classic American steak and seafood house, located adjacent to The Colonnade. The food is cooked to order, and the extra cost is probably worth it, because of the higher-quality ingredients. However, the ceiling height is rather low, which makes the feeling cramped.

The self-serve Colonnade eatery, located aft, has indoor/outdoor seating and is nicely decorated, although its free-flow design could be better; there's too little outdoor seating for the demand in warm-weather areas, when many passengers like to eat outdoors. During dinner on designated formal nights passengers who are dressed accordingly have to share the space with those who are more casually dressed. The venue is also adjacent to one of the fine dining restaurants.

The Patio Grill is located in a casual poolside setting outdoors; it is at its most enjoyable on balmy evenings, as a change to the air-conditioned interior dining venues.

In addition, a 24-hour, in-suite menu offers the à la carte items served in the main dining room during dinner hours.

Extra-cost Silver or Gold 'connoisseur' wine packages provide a choice of red and white vintage wines for a set amount – perhaps a good idea for a longer cruise.

ENTERTAINMENT. The Grand Salon is the main entertainment venue for shows, cabaret performances, and social dancing, and is used as a cinema. However, the stage is small – large enough for a live band, but performers need to use the dance floor area – and the room has nine thick pillars that make it awkward to see anything at all, although the room has a gentle slope. On the ceiling of the central section there is a decorative steel grating, which is black, cold-looking, and unappealing. The room has banquette seating in the front and mid-section, and, strangely, sofa-style leather seating along the side walls to the rear, which means you actually sit with your back to the stage – a rather unhelpful arrangement!

Small production shows (remember this is a small ship) are performed well to pre-recorded tracks, and the audio equipment and sound dispersion are extremely good. Just don't expect big ship entertainment, though.

Another venue, The Club, is a large, cool, trendy, but high-volume nightclub/disco with a wooden dance floor, large bar, and minimalist design. Located beneath the Grand salon, it incorporates a comfortable casino.

SPA/FITNESS. The Spa at Seabourn, operated by Elemis, occupies the aft section of two decks, and is quite large, at 11,500 sq ft (1,068 sq m). It offers full services in a very relaxing setting that includes a two-deck-high waterfall at the entrance and seven indoor/outdoor treatment rooms, as well as a thalassotherapy wave pool; there's also a thermal suite (a pass for this costs extra), and complete salon facilities, while a hot tub and relaxation area on the deck above are accessed by a spiral staircase. Separate saunas and steam rooms for men and women are provided, but they are extremely small. In the gymnasium, personal-training sessions, yoga classes, mat Pilates, and body-composition analysis are available at extra cost, but some of the basic exercise programs are free.

SEADREAM I
★★★★★

THIS IS ABOUT ULTRA-STYLISH CRUISING ON AN INFORMAL, POCKET-SIZED SHIP

Size:	Boutique Ship	Passenger/Crew Ratio (lower beds):	1.1
Tonnage:	4,253	Cabins (total):	56
Cruise Line:	SeaDream Yacht Club	Size Range (sq ft/m):	195.0–446.7/18.1–41.4
Former Names:	Seabourn Goddess I, Sea Goddess I	Cabins (for one person):	0
Builder:	Wartsila (Finland)	Cabins with balcony:	0
Entered Service:	Apr 1984/May 2002	Cabins (wheelchair accessible):	0
Length (ft/m):	343.8/104.8	Wheelchair accessibility:	None
Beam (ft/m):	47.9/14.6	Elevators:	1
Propulsion/Propellers:	diesel (3,540kW)/2	Casino (gaming tables):	Yes
Passenger Decks:	5	Swimming Pools:	1
Total Crew:	95	Self-Service Launderette:	No
Passengers (lower beds):	112	Library:	Yes
Passenger Space Ratio (lower beds):	37.9	Onboard currency:	US$

THE SHIP. *SeaDream I* is for sophisticated, well-traveled couples. Rejecting today's huge standard resort cruise ships, its clientele is looking for a small ship with excellent food approaching gourmet standards, and fine European-style service in surroundings that border on the elegant and refined, while remaining informal.

SeaDream I (and sister ship *SeaDream II*) were originally funded by about 800 investors, and operated under the Norske Cruise banner, and named *Sea Goddess I* and *Sea Goddess II*. They have an ultra-sleek profile, with deep blue hull and white superstructure, and the ambience of a private club. Purchased by SeaDream Yacht Club in 2001, they were completely refurbished, with many changes to public rooms and outdoor areas. Some new features were added to create contemporary, chic, and desirable, if aging, vessels.

A 'Top of the Yacht' bar, crafted in warm wood, was added to both ships. So were eight special alcoves set to the port and starboard sides of the funnel, equipped with two-person sunloungers with thick pads (and two equipped for one person); however, there is quite a bit of noise from the adjacent funnel. You are encouraged to sleep under the stars, if you wish, and cotton sleep suits are provided.

At the front part of the deck there are more sunloungers and a couple of large hammocks, as well as a golf simulator with a choice of 30 courses.

BERLITZ'S RATINGS		
	Possible	Achieved
Ship	500	419
Accommodation	200	173
Food	400	344
Service	400	360
Entertainment	100	81
Cruise Experience	400	338
OVERALL SCORE 1706 points out of 2000		

Inside, there is a feeling of unabashed but discreet sophistication. Elegant public rooms have flowers and potpourri everywhere. The main social gathering places are the lounge, a delightful library/living room with a selection of about 1,000 books, a piano bar – which can be more like a karaoke bar at times – and a small casino with two blackjack tables and five slot machines.

All drinks (including good-quality Champagne, but not premium drink brands and connoisseur wines), farmed caviar, and gratuities are included, but port charges and insurance are not.

ACCOMMODATION. There are four types – in six price categories (depending on location, size, and grade). From the smallest to the largest these are : Yacht Club (standard) Cabin; Commodore Club Suite; Admiral Suite; and Owner's Suite.

Incorrectly called 'suites' in the brochure, Yacht Club Cabins are, more correctly, fully equipped mini-suites with an outside view through windows or portholes, depending on deck and price category. Each measures 195 sq ft (18 sq m), which is not large by today's cruise ship standards; however, it is large compared to cabins aboard many private motor yachts, and extremely large when compared to oceangoing racing yachts. The sleeping area has twin beds that can be put together to form a queen-size bed, positioned next to the window or porthole, so you can entertain in the living area without going past the sleeping area, as you must aboard the slightly larger Seabourn or Silversea ships. A curtain separates the sleeping and lounge areas. All cabinetry and furniture is of thick blond wood, with nicely rounded edges.

In the lounge area, a long desk has six drawers, plus a vertical cupboard unit that houses a sensible safe, refrigerator, and drinks cabinet stocked with your choice of drinks. There is also a 20-ins (51-cm) flat-screen television, CD and DVD player, and an MP3 audio player with more than 100 selections. The beds have the finest linens, including thick cotton duvets, and hypoallergenic pillows are also available. There's little room under the beds for luggage, although this can be taken away and stored.

One drawback is the fact that the insulation between cabins is not particularly good, although rarely does this present a problem, as most passengers are generally quiet, considerate types, who are allergic to noise. Incidentally, a sleep suit is supplied in case you want to sleep out on deck under the stars in one of the on-deck two-person beds.

For larger accommodation, choose one of 16 Commodore Club Suites. These consist of two standard cabins with an interconnecting door, thus providing you with a healthy 380 sq ft (35 sq m) of living space. One cabin is made into a lounge and dining room, with table and up to four chairs, while the other becomes your sleeping area. The advantage is that you get two bathrooms. One disadvantage is that the soundproofing between cabins could be better.

For the largest living space, go for the Owner's Suite. This measures a grand 490 sq ft (46 sq m). It's the only accommodation with a bathroom that has a full-size tub; there's also a separate shower enclosure and lots of space for toiletries.

Added in 2008–9, the Admiral Suite occupies space previously devoted to the ship's boutique, adjacent to the piano bar/library. It's a little smaller than the Owner's Suite, but is well laid out and extremely comfortable.

When the ships became SeaDream I and II, all the bathrooms were totally refurbished. The cheerful decor is chic, with soft colors and large (beige) marble tiles. The former tiny sit-in bathtubs were taken out – these are missed by some passengers – and replaced by a multi-jet power glassed-in shower enclosure. A washbasin set in a marble-look surround and two glass shelves make up the facilities, and an under-sink cupboard provides further space for larger toiletries.

However, the bathrooms really are small, particularly for anyone of larger-than-average build. Also, the bathroom door opens inwards, so space inside is at a premium. The toilet is located in an awkward position, and, unless you close the door, you can see yourself in the mirror of the closets opposite the bathroom door.

DINING. The Restaurant is elegant and inviting, and has bird's-eye maple wood-paneled walls and alcoves showcasing beautiful handmade glass creations. It is cozy, yet with plenty of space around each table for fine service, and the ship provides a culinary celebration in an open-seating arrangement, so you can dine whenever, and with whomever, you want. Course-by-course meals can also be served on the open deck.

Tables can be configured for two, four, six, or eight. They are laid with a classic setting of a real glass base (show) plate, Porsgrund china, pristine white monogrammed table linen, and fresh flowers.

Candlelit dinners and leather-bound menus are part of the inviting setting. There's even a box of spare spectacles for reading the menu, should you forget your own.

The SeaDream Yacht Club experience really is all about good food. Only the freshest and finest-quality ingredients are used. Fine, unhurried European service is provided. Additionally, good-quality Champagne is available whenever you want it, and so is caviar – American farmed Hackleback sturgeon malossol caviar, sadly, and not Russian caviar, whose purchase and supply today is limited. The ice cream, which is made on board, however, is excellent.

Everything is prepared individually to order for dinner, and the cuisine is extremely creative, and special orders are possible. You can also dine course by course in your suite for any meal, at any time during meal hours. The dining room isn't open for lunch, which disappoints those who don't want to eat outside, particularly in hot climates.

Good-quality table wines are included in the cruise fare for lunch and dinner. Wine connoisseurs, however, will appreciate the availability of an extra wine list, full of special vintages and premier crus at extra cost. If you want to do something different with a loved one, you can also arrange to dine one evening on the open (but covered) deck, overlooking the swimming pool and stern – it is a rather romantic setting.

The Topside Restaurant is an informal open-air eatery with roll-down sides (in case of inclement weather), and is open for breakfast, lunch, or the occasional dinner. Teak tables and chairs add a touch of class.

ENTERTAINMENT. There is no evening entertainment as such (it's not needed), other than a duo or solo musician to provide music for listening and dancing to in the lounge. Dinner is the main event; DVDs are available to take to your cabin.

SPA/FITNESS. The holistic approach to wellbeing plays a big part in relaxation and body pampering aboard SeaDream I. The Asian Spa/Wellness Centre has three massage rooms, a small sauna, and steam shower enclosure.

SEADREAM II
★★★★★

IT'S LIKE HAVING YOUR OWN MEGA-YACHT FOR STYLISH, RELAXING CRUISES

Size:	Boutique Ship	Passenger/Crew Ratio (lower beds):	1.1
Tonnage:	4,333	Cabins (total):	56
Cruise Line:	SeaDream Yacht Club	Size Range (sq ft/m):	195.0–446.7/18.1–41.5
Former Names:	Seabourn Goddess II, Sea Goddess II	Cabins (for one person):	0
Builder:	Wartsila (Finland)	Cabins with balcony:	0
Entered Service:	May 1985/Jan 2002	Cabins (wheelchair accessible):	0
Length (ft/m):	343.8/104.8	Wheelchair accessibility:	None
Beam (ft/m):	47.9/14.6	Elevators:	1
Propulsion/Propellers:	diesel (3,540kW)/2	Casino (gaming tables):	Yes
Passenger Decks:	5	Swimming Pools:	1
Total Crew:	95	Self-Service Launderette:	No
Passengers (lower beds):	112	Library:	Yes
Passenger Space Ratio (lower beds):	37.9	Onboard currency:	US$

THE SHIP. *SeaDream II* is best suited to sophisticated and well-traveled couples who are typically over 40 – in fact anyone looking for a small ship with excellent food approaching gourmet standards, and fine European-style service in surroundings that border on the elegant and refined while remaining trendy.

SeaDream II (and sister ship *SeaDream I*) were originally funded by about 800 investors, and operated under the Norske Cruise banner as *Sea Goddess I* and *Sea Goddess II*. They have a sleek profile, with deep blue hull and white superstructure, and the ambience of a private club. After they were bought by SeaDream Yacht Club in 2001, they were completely refurbished, with many changes to public rooms and outdoor areas, and several new features added to create what are contemporary, chic, and desirable, if aging, vessels.

These ships are popular for small company charters, so you may find that the date and itinerary you want will not be available (you may be asked to change to the sister ship and a different itinerary).

A 'Top of the Yacht' bar, crafted in warm wood, was added to both ships. So were eight special alcoves set to the port and starboard sides of the funnel, equipped with two-person sunloungers with thick pads (and two equipped for one person); however, there is quite a bit of noise from the adjacent funnel. You can sleep under the stars if you wish (cotton sleep suits are provided).

BERLITZ'S RATINGS

	Possible	Achieved
Ship	500	418
Accommodation	200	164
Food	400	344
Service	400	358
Entertainment	100	81
Cruise Experience	400	336

OVERALL SCORE 1701 points out of 2000

Inside, there is unabashed but discreet sophistication, and the public rooms have flowers everywhere. The main social gathering places are the lounge, a delightful library/living room with a selection of about 1,000 books, a piano bar (more like a karaoke bar at times), and a small casino with blackjack tables and slot machines.

SeaDream II really is like having your own private yacht, in which hospitality, anticipation, and personal recognition are art forms practiced to a high level. The staff is delightful and accommodating, and the dress code is resort (no tie) casual. Fine-quality furnishings and fabrics are used throughout, with marble and blond wood accents that make it warm.

SeaDream II is a good choice for you if you don't like the idea of regular cruise ships, with glitzy lounges and a platoon of people running around, or dressing up – no tuxedos or gowns are allowed, and ties aren't needed. It's all about personal indulgence and refined, unstructured living at sea, in a casual setting akin to that on a private mega-yacht. One delightful feature of each cruise in warm-weather areas is a 'caviar in the surf' beach barbecue.

SeaDream I and *II* were the first of the mega-yacht-style ships when built, and none of the cabins has a private balcony – but anyway, yachts don't have balconies. Embarkation never starts before 3pm, in case you are eager to get aboard.

ACCOMMODATION. There are four types – in six price categories (depending on location, size, and grade) – which, from the largest to the smallest, are: Owner's Suite; Admiral Suite; Commodore Club Suite; and Yacht Club (standard) Cabin.

For the largest living space, go for the Owner's Suite. This measures a grand 490 sq ft (46 sq m). It's the only accommodation with a bathroom that incorporates a real full-size tub; there's also a separate shower enclosure and lots of space for toiletries.

Added in 2008–9, the Admiral Suite is adjacent to the piano bar/library. It's a little smaller than the Owner's Suite, but is well laid out and extremely comfortable.

For accommodation larger than standard, choose one of the 16 Commodore Club Suites. These consist of two standard cabins with an interconnecting door, thus providing you with a healthy 380 sq ft (35 sq m) of living space. One cabin is made into a lounge and dining room, with table and up to four chairs, while the other becomes your sleeping area. The advantage is that you get two bathrooms. One disadvantage is that the soundproofing between cabins could be better.

Incorrectly called 'suites' in the brochure, Yacht Club Cabins are, more correctly, fully equipped mini-suites with an outside view through windows or portholes, depending on deck and price category. Each measures 195 sq ft (18 sq m) . The sleeping area has twin beds that can be put together to form a queen-size configuration; a curtain separates the sleeping and lounge areas.

In the lounge area, a vertical cupboard unit houses a safe, refrigerator, and drinks cabinet stocked with your choice of drinks. There is also a 20-ins (51-cm) flat-screen television, CD and DVD player, and an MP3 audio player with more than 100 selections. The beds have the finest linens, including thick cotton duvets; hypoallergenic pillows are also available. There's little room under the beds for luggage, although this can be taken away and stored. Note that the insulation between cabins is not particularly good, although this rarely presents a problem.

When the ships became *SeaDream I* and *II*, all bathrooms were totally refurbished. The cheerful decor is nicer than before, with soft colors and large marble tiles. The former tiny sit-in bathtubs were taken out and replaced by multi-jet power glassed-in shower enclosures. Bulgari toiletries are provided, as are gorgeously plush cotton SeaDream-logo bathrobes and towels. However, despite their having been completely rebuilt, the bathrooms are small, particularly for those of larger-than-average build. Also, the bathroom door opens inward, so space inside is at a premium.

DINING. The dining salon, called The Restaurant, is elegant and inviting. It is cozy, yet with plenty of space around each table for fine service, and the open-seating arrangement means you can dine whenever, and with whomever, you want. Course-by-course meals can also be served out on deck. Tables can be configured for two to eight.

There's even a box of spare spectacles for reading the menu, in case you forget your own. You get leather-bound menus, and close-to-impeccable personalized European service.

The SeaDream Yacht Club experience really is all about dining, and culinary excellence prevails, using the freshest and finest-quality ingredients possible. Fine, unhurried European service is provided. Additionally, good-quality Champagne is available whenever you want it, and so is caviar. The ice cream, which is made on board, is excellent. In addition to the regular menus, some beautifully prepared and presented 'raw food' menu items have been introduced.

SeaDream II provides extremely creative cuisine. Everything is prepared individually to order, and special orders are possible. You can also dine course by course in your suite for any meal, at any time during meal hours. The dining room isn't open for lunch, which disappoints those who don't want to eat outside, particularly in hot climates.

Good-quality table wines are included in the cruise fare for lunch and dinner. Wine connoisseurs, however, will appreciate the availability of an extra wine list, full of special vintages and premier crus at extra cost. If you want to do something different with a loved one, you can also arrange to dine one evening on the open (but covered) deck.

The Topside Restaurant is an informal open-air eatery and has roll-down sides (in case of inclement weather), and is open for breakfast, lunch, or the occasional dinner.

ENTERTAINMENT. There is no evening entertainment as such (it's not needed), other than a duo or solo musician to provide music for listening and dancing to in the lounge. Dinner is the main event, and DVDs are available to take to your cabin.

SPA/FITNESS. The holistic approach to wellbeing plays a big part in relaxation and body pampering aboard *SeaDream II*. There are three massage rooms, a small sauna, and steam shower enclosure. The Spa, located in a private area, is operated as a concession by Universal Maritime Services. Massage on the beach is available when the ship stages its famous beach party.

For golfers, there's an electronic golf simulator, and choice of several golf courses to play. There is a small, retractable water sports platform at the stern. Equipment carried includes a water-ski boat, sailboat, wave runners (jet skis), kayaks, wake boards, snorkeling equipment, and two Zodiacs – all included in the price of a cruise. Ten mountain bikes are also carried; these can be used on shore visits.

SERENADE OF THE SEAS
★★★+

THIS MID-SIZE SHIP IS GOOD FOR CASUAL, FAMILY-FRIENDLY CRUISING

Size:	Mid-size Ship	Passenger/Crew Ratio (lower beds):	2.4
Tonnage:	90,090	Cabins (total):	1,050
Cruise Line:	Royal Caribbean International	Size Range (sq ft/m):	165.8–1,216.3/15.4–113.0
Former Names:	none	Cabins (for one person):	0
Builder:	Meyer Werft (Germany)	Cabins with balcony:	577
Entered Service:	Aug 2003	Cabins (wheelchair accessible):	14
Length (ft/m):	961.9/293.2	Wheelchair accessibility:	Best
Beam (ft/m):	105.6/32.2	Elevators:	9
Propulsion/Propellers:	gas turbine (40,000kW)/ 2 azimuthing pods	Casino (gaming tables):	Yes
		Swimming Pools:	2
Passenger Decks:	12	Self-Service Launderette:	No
Total Crew:	858	Library:	Yes
Passengers (lower beds):	2,100	Onboard currency:	US$
Passenger Space Ratio (lower beds):	42.9		

THE SHIP. *Serenade of the Seas* uses gas and steam turbine power, as do sister ships *Brilliance of the Seas, Jewel of the Seas,* and *Radiance of the Seas*, instead of the conventional diesel or diesel-electric combination.

As aboard all Royal Caribbean International (RCI) vessels, the navigation bridge is fully enclosed. In the very front of the ship is a helipad, which also acts as a viewing platform for passengers (it makes for a good photo opportunity). One of two swimming pools can be covered by a glass dome, and there's a large poolside screen for screening movies in the open air.

A contemporary ship, it has a two-deck-high walk-around structure in the forward section of the funnel. Along the starboard side, is a protruding central glass wall, which affords great views; cabins with balconies occupy the space directly opposite on the port side. The gently rounded stern has nicely tiered decks, which gives the ship a well-balanced look.

The interior focal point is the Centrum (city center), a nine-deck-high atrium lobby with glass-walled elevators (on the port side of the ship only) that travel through 12 decks, face the sea, and provide a link with nature and the ocean. Centrum is the focal point, and *the* social meeting place. It houses an R Bar (for some creative cocktails), several passenger service counters, art gallery, and Café Latte-tudes (for coffees and specialty coffees). Close by is Casino Royale (for gamers and slot-machine lovers), and

BERLITZ'S RATINGS

	Possible	Achieved
Ship	500	363
Accommodation	200	132
Food	400	242
Service	400	258
Entertainment	100	73
Cruise Experience	400	258

OVERALL SCORE 1326 points out of 2000

the Schooner Bar, with its nautical-themed decor and maritime art. Aerial entertainment takes place in the Centrum, too.

Other facilities include a delightful, but small, library. There's also a little screening room for movies, as well as a 194-seat conference center and a business center.

A Viking Crown Lounge, an RCI trademark, is set around the base of the funnel. It is an observation lounge by day, with views forward over the pool deck. In the evening, it morphs into a dance club, as well as a more intimate and relaxed entertainment venue for softer mood music.

Serenade of the Seas is a ship that all the family can enjoy. Many 'private' balcony cabins aren't private, however, as they can be overlooked by anyone standing in the port and starboard wings of the Solarium, and from other locations. There are no cushioned pads for sunloungers, and the deck towels provided are small and thin. It is virtually impossible to escape background music.

ACCOMMODATION. There is a wide range of suites and standard outside-view and interior cabins, in many different categories.

Apart from the largest suites (six Owner's Suites), which have king-size beds, almost all other cabins have twin beds that convert to a queen. All cabins have rich (but faux) wood cabinetry, including a vanity desk with hairdryer, drawers that close silently (hooray), a television, personal safe, and three-sided mirrors. Some cabins have ceiling-recessed, pull-down berths for third and fourth persons, although closet and drawer space is extremely tight for four people, even if two of them are children.

Most cabin bathrooms have tiled accenting and a terrazzo-style tiled floor, a rather small shower enclosure in a half-moon shape, 100 percent Egyptian cotton towels, a small cabinet for toiletries, and a small shelf. In reality, there is little space to stow toiletries for two or more people.

The largest accommodation consists of a family suite with two bedrooms. One bedroom has twin beds that convert to a queen, while a second has two lower beds and two upper Pullman berths, a combination that can sleep up to eight people – this would suit large families.

Occupants of accommodation designated as suites also get the use of a private Concierge Lounge, where priority dining reservations, shore-excursion bookings, and beauty salon/spa appointments can be made.

DINING. Reflections, the main dining room, seats 1,096 at tables for two to 10 persons. With a water-themed decor, it spans two decks; the upper deck level has floor-to-ceiling windows, while the lower level has picture windows. It is a pleasant but inevitably noisy dining hall, reminiscent of those aboard the ocean liners of yesteryear, although eight thick pillars obstruct sight lines. Two small private dining rooms – Illusions with 94 seats and Mirage with 30 seats – are adjacent. You can choose one of two seatings, or My Time Dining (to eat when you want during dining room hours).

Main dining room cuisine is all about standardized banquet catering and batch cooking. The menu descriptions sound tempting, but the food, although prepared well, is just so-so. Vegetarian and children's menus are also available. Note that there are no wine waiters.

Most meat dishes are disguised with gravies or heavy sauce reductions; rice is often used as a source of carbohydrates. Green vegetables are scarce, but basic salad items are plentiful, and the desserts are very decent. Breads and pastry items are also plentiful (though these are thawed and then baked from frozen 'starter' dough), but the croissants lack any hint of butter.

Other dining venues and eateries (some of which cost extra, but the food is mostly cooked to order) include favorites such as Chops Grille Steakhouse (for premium veal chops, steaks, and seafood items),

Portofino (for Italian-American cuisine), and Giovanni's Table (for Italian trattoria-style dishes). Reservations (make them through the digital system) are required; note that menus do not change.

Windjammer Marketplace is a cavernous, casual self-serve buffet eatery, but note that plastic plates for hot items are mildly warm, at best. Breakfast buffet items and lunchtime salad items are pretty repetitive. Beverage stations have just the basics. Burgers and hot dogs in self-serve buffet locations are displayed in steam dishes. If you are disabled or have mobility difficulties, do ask for help.

Izumi: an extra-cost Asian-style eatery with a sushi bar and hot-rocks cooking (open for lunch and dinner, with a small cover charge plus à la carte menu pricing).

Extra-cost Chef's Table: for a private experience, typically co-hosted by the executive chef and sommelier for a multi-course wine-pairing dinner.

Park Café is a casual, no-charge market-style eatery for salads, sandwiches, soups, and pastries.

ENTERTAINMENT. Facilities include the three-level, 874-seat Tropical Theater, which also has 24 stations for wheelchairs, and good sight lines from most seats. Strong cabaret acts are also presented in this main showlounge.

A second entertainment venue is Safari Club, for more casual cabaret shows, including late-night adult comedy. Entertainment is always upbeat – in fact, it is almost impossible to get away from music and noise. There is even background music in all corridors and elevators, and constant music on the pool deck. If you want a quiet vacation, choose another cruise line.

SPA/FITNESS. The Vitality Spa and Fitness center has themed decor. It includes a 10,176-sq-ft (945-sq-m) solarium, a gym with 44 cardiovascular machines, a 50-person aerobics room, sauna and steam rooms, and therapy treatment rooms. The climate-controlled, Balinese-themed indoor/outdoor solarium has a sliding glass dome roof that can be closed in cool or inclement weather conditions, and includes a whirlpool and counter-current swimming.

For sporty types, there is activity galore – including a 30ft (9m) rock-climbing wall with five separate climbing tracks. It is located outdoors at the aft end of the funnel. Other sports facilities include a nine-hole miniature golf course, and an indoor/outdoor country club with golf simulator, a jogging track, and basketball court.

SERENISSIMA
★★+

DATED BUT TOUGH, THIS CASUAL LITTLE SHIP IS GOOD FOR COASTAL CRUISING

Size:	Boutique Ship	
Tonnage:	2,632	
Cruise Line:	Premier Cruises	
Former Names:	Andrea, Harald Jarl	
Builder:	Trondheims Mek (Norway)	
Entered Service:	Jun 1960/Dec 2012	
Length (ft/m):	286.7/87.4	
Beam (ft/m):	43.6/13.2	
Propulsion/Propellers:	diesel/2	
Passenger Decks:	5	
Total Crew:	55	
Passengers (lower beds):	107	
Passenger Space Ratio (lower beds):	24.5	
Passenger/Crew Ratio (lower beds):	2.1	
Cabins (total):	59	
Size Range (sq ft/m):	66.0-236.8/6.1-22.0	
Cabins (for one person):	0	
Cabins with balcony:	4	
Cabins (wheelchair accessible):	0	
Wheelchair accessibility:	None	
Elevators:	1	
Casino (gaming tables):	No	
Swimming Pools:	0	
Self-Service Launderette:	No	
Library:	Yes	
Onboard currency:	Euros	

THE SHIP. This intimate ship is best for cruising in coastal regions. It is suited to couples and solo travelers of mature years who enjoy nature and wildlife at close range, and who would not dream of cruising in the mainstream sense aboard ships with large numbers of people. This is for the hardy, adventurous types who don't need constant entertainment or parlor games.

The 107-passenger *Serenissima* began her career as *Harald Jarl*, cruising the Norwegian coastline and fjords. Extensively renovated in 2003, she began her career as a classic cruise ship. In spring 2012 the ship was purchased by the owner of the Russian rivership *Volga Dream*, and renamed *Serenissima*. After a thorough renovation, this charming ship commenced cruise operations in April 2013. With her small size she is able to dock close to the heart of Europe's historic centers and is able to navigate into smaller, remote ports inaccessible to large resort ships.

Serenissima has a good amount of outdoors space (including a forward-viewing and observation platform), and the rather nice semi-covered aft area of the Boat Deck. The ship also now has stabilizers to counteract her well-known rolling motion.

ACCOMMODATION. Several different grades of cabins are arranged over five decks, and, with the exception of the five interior cabins, all have either windows or portholes. Because of the nature of this

BERLITZ'S RATINGS		
	Possible	Achieved
Ship	500	253
Accommodation	200	109
Food	400	231
Service	400	241
Entertainment	100	54
Cruise Experience	400	211

OVERALL SCORE 1099 points out of 2000

eclectic ship, the cabins do vary in shape and size, giving the ship more character: from dimensionally challenged interior cabins of approximately 108 sq ft (10 sq m), to 'executive suites' of 273 sq ft (25.4 sq m) with small balconies, minibar, and other amenities. Two Owner's Suites are located at the front, directly under the navigation bridge, with forward-facing views; they measure 244 sq ft (22.7 sq m). Dedicated standard single-occupancy cabins range in size from 107 to 137 sq ft (9.9 to 12.7 sq m). The cabins are very nicely furnished.

Cabin 407 is designated for mobility-limited passengers (an adjacent elevator serves decks 3 to 6).

DINING. There is a cozy, one-seating Venice Restaurant, but the chairs do not have armrests, so lingering over a meal is not as comfortable as it could be. The food is tasty and well presented, and there is a good variety. Casual eats can be taken in the aft-facing open-deck Café.

ENTERTAINMENT. With this kind of ship, it's the after-dinner conversation that creates most of the evening's entertainment, although there is usually a solo pianist or other musical unit.

SPA/FITNESS. A small fitness center has only a limited amount of equipment (treadmills, bicycles, and free weights), plus an adjacent massage room.

SEVEN SEAS EXPLORER
★★★★+

AN ELEGANT AND EXTREMELY SPACIOUS CONTEMPORARY SHIP WITH STYLE

Size:	Small Ship	Passenger/Crew Ratio (lower beds):	1.3
Tonnage:	56,000	Cabins (total):	375
Cruise Line:	Regent Seven Seas Cruises	Size Range (sq ft/m):	301.3–3,875.1/3,875.1–360.0
Former Names:	none	Cabins (for one person):	0
Builder:	Fincantieri (Italy)	Cabins with balcony:	375
Entered Service:	Jul 2016	Cabins (wheelchair accessible):	3
Length (ft/m):	731.6/223.0	Wheelchair accessibility:	Best
Beam (ft/m):	102.0/31.0	Elevators:	6
Propulsion/Propellers:	diesel-electric/2	Casino (gaming tables):	Yes
Passenger Decks:	10	Swimming Pools:	1
Total Crew:	542	Self-Service Launderette:	Yes
Passengers (lower beds):	750	Library:	Yes
Passenger Space Ratio (lower beds):	74.6	Onboard currency:	US$

THE SHIP. This all-suite, all-balcony ship is the flagship of Regent Seven Seas Cruises, although its exterior design is not particularly handsome. It is most suited to couples and solo travelers who appreciate space, creature comforts, and stylish surroundings.

Incorporating many of the design features for which the company is known, *Seven Seas Explorer* is another example of the evolution of spacious, small-capacity ships. Sadly, there's no wrap-around outdoor promenade deck (although there is a jogging track atop ship).

Inside, the main focus point is a two-deck high atrium lobby, with a sweeping grand stairway. Facilities include an Observation Lounge (with retro decor reminiscent of a 1920s speakeasy), Connoisseur Club (for cigar enthusiasts – cigars cost extra), library, card room, business center, and coffee bar (with illy Italian coffees).

So, is it the 'most luxurious ship ever built,' as claimed by this cruise line? No, although some aspects are certainly in keeping with the word luxury; it is, however, an extremely comfortable ship. It's not just the hardware, but the software (crew, hospitality, training, service finesse, and communication skills) that are important in the overall picture of perceived luxury.

ACCOMMODATION. With 16 accommodation categories, the price you pay depends on the size,

BERLITZ'S RATINGS		
	Possible	Achieved
Ship	500	426
Accommodation	200	171
Food	400	299
Service	400	323
Entertainment	100	78
Cruise Experience	400	320

OVERALL SCORE 1617 points out of 2000

location, and features you want. Some suites have interconnecting doors – good for an extended family cruising together. All suites have a mini-bar replenished daily, walk-in closet, personal safe, hairdryer, marble-clad bathroom with bathtub or shower enclosure (or both), L'Occitane products, bathrobe and slippers, 24-hour room service, and balconies with teak decking.

The smallest accommodation units are Verandah Suites (approximately 215.2 sq ft/20 sq m without balcony, and 307 sq ft/29 sq m including balcony).

The most expansive of all is the opulent 3,875 sq ft (360 sq m) – or 4,443 sq ft (412.7 sq m), if you add a second adjoining bedroom – Regent Suite, which spans the whole beam of the front of the ship on the uppermost deck. It has an in-built Spa Retreat (including sauna, steam shower, two heated relaxation loungers – unlimited private spa treatments included), as well as an Arabesque baby grand Steinway piano (not to mention a Savoir No. 1 bed). However, unless you are considering a longer cruise and don't plan to go ashore much (if you do, note that a private car and driver will be available in every port), it may not be worth it.

DINING. With a choice of one main dining room, three other specialty dining venues, and casual eateries, it's tempting to try them all. Compass Rose Restaurant is the ship's main dining room; its focal point is a cascading aqua-blue chandelier. It has over 30 tables for two; the others seat either four or eight.

Restaurant Chartreuse is a romantically stylish venue for experiencing some classic French cuisine, cooked to order and presented on fine Bernardaud china. Seating is in small, intimate moon-shaped alcoves and at tables for two or four. There is some banquette seating.

Richly decorated Prime 7 is a premium-quality steakhouse, with banquette and individual seating, plus intimate alcoves. It is open for dinner only, and reservations are required.

Pacific Rim features pan-Asian cuisine (outside is a Tibetan-style prayer wheel). The decor of La Verandah relives the 1960s glamour of the Italian Riviera, with mahogany detailing, terrazzo flooring, and brushed-brass marine accents. It's open for self-serve breakfast and lunch, and transforms into a modestly elegant restaurant, Sette Mari La Veranda, each evening for dinner.

The casual Pool Grill, for burgers, fresh grilled seafood, sandwiches, and fresh salads, has open-air and glass-enclosed seating, with fine views. Milk shakes, malts, and ice-cream desserts are also available.

You can also order meals in your suite 24 hours a day.

ENTERTAINMENT. The 694-seat Constellation Theater (showlounge) spans two decks, with seating on both levels. It is an amphitheatre-style showlounge with a thrust stage, and is the venue for production shows and cabaret acts, with music provided by a 9-piece showband. During the day, it also acts as a cooking school (extra cost), with 18 preparation stations.

Live music is provided by a number of artists in various lounges such as the Horizon Lounge and Observation Lounge.

SPA/FITNESS. The Canyon Ranch Spa Club occupies space partly along the starboard side and at the aft of the ship – an open-air relaxation zone with its own dip pool. Facilities include seven body-treatment rooms plus one for couples. A circular stairway leads to the fitness studio on the deck above. A personal trainer is also available. Sports facilities include a bocce court, shuffleboard, paddle tennis, a putting green, and a jogging track.

SEVEN SEAS MARINER
★★★★

THIS ALL-INCLUSIVE, VERY SPACIOUS PREMIUM SHIP IS FOR SENIOR-AGE TRAVELERS

Size:	Small Ship	Passenger/Crew Ratio (lower beds):	1.6
Tonnage:	48,075	Cabins (total):	354
Cruise Line:	Regent Seven Seas Cruises	Size Range (sq ft/m):	301.3–2,002.0/28.0–186.0
Former Names:	none	Cabins (for one person):	0
Builder:	Chantiers de l'Atlantique (France)	Cabins with balcony:	354
Entered Service:	Mar 2001	Cabins (wheelchair accessible):	6
Length (ft/m):	713.0/217.3	Wheelchair accessibility:	Best
Beam (ft/m):	95.1/29.0	Elevators:	6
Propulsion/Propellers:	diesel-electric (16,000kW)/ 2 azimuthing pods	Casino (gaming tables):	Yes
Passenger Decks:	9	Swimming Pools:	1
Total Crew:	445	Self-Service Launderette:	Yes
Passengers (lower beds):	708	Library:	Yes
Passenger Space Ratio (lower beds):	67.9	Onboard currency:	US$

THE SHIP. *Seven Seas Mariner* is best suited to well-traveled couples and solo travelers, typically over 50, who seek excellent itineraries, fine food, and good service, with some entertainment, wrapped up in a contemporary, elegant ship. Its passenger/space ratio is among the highest in the cruise industry.

This was the first ship in the fleet to have a pod propulsion system, replacing the traditional shaft and rudder. The ship was extensively refurbished in 2014.

There is a wide range of public rooms, almost all located under the accommodation decks. With three sets of stairways (forward, center, and aft) it is easy to find your way around. An atrium lobby spans nine decks, with the lowest level opening directly onto the tender landing stage.

Facilities include a comfortable observation lounge, a small casino (with gaming tables and slot machines), a shopping concourse with 'open market' area, a garden lounge/promenade arcade, a large library (incorporating several computer workstations) and adjacent room with 14 Internet-connect computers, coffee lounge, card player's room, conference room, cigar-smoking lounge (Connoisseur Club), and a Park West art gallery.

Seven Seas Mariner loses a few points because the dining service ranges from excellent to patchy and inconsistent.

Basic gratuities are included, as are all alcoholic and non-alcoholic beverages and table wines for lunch and dinner. Premium and connoisseur selections are available at extra cost, and Internet-connection charges are high. Shore excursions and pre- or post-cruise hotel stays are also included, depending on the itinerary.

BERLITZ'S RATINGS

	Possible	Achieved
Ship	500	400
Accommodation	200	164
Food	400	296
Service	400	308
Entertainment	100	77
Cruise Experience	400	303

OVERALL SCORE 1548 points out of 2000

ACCOMMODATION. There are several accommodation categories. *Seven Seas Mariner* was the cruise industry's first all-suite, all-balconies ship – though that's not technically correct, as not all accommodation has sleeping areas completely separated from living areas.

Most grades have private, marble-clad bathrooms with tub or half-tub, and suite entrances are neatly recessed away from the passenger hallways to provide quiet (refreshingly there's no music in the hallways, although there is some in the elevators).

In terms of sizing, accommodation is as follows:

Concierge Suites and Deluxe Suites: 301 sq ft (28 sq m).

Penthouse Suites: 449 sq ft (41.7 sq m).

Horizon Suites: 627 sq ft (58 sq m). There are 12 of these; they overlook the stern and have very large balconies.

Seven Seas Suites: 600–697 sq ft (56–65 sq m). They also overlook the ship's stern.

Grand Suites: 707 sq ft (66 sq m).

Mariner Suites: 739 sq ft (69 sq m).

Master Suites: 1,580 sq ft (147 sq m).

Six wheelchair-accessible suites are located as close to an elevator as one could possibly get, and provide ample living space, together with a large roll-in shower and all bathroom fittings located at the correct height.

DINING. Four dining venues all operate on an open-seating basis, so you can dine when and with whomever you choose. Reservations are required in two of the four venues. In general, the cuisine is good to very good, with creative presentation and a wide variety of food choices (Kosher meals can be provided).

The main dining room, the 570-seat Compass Rose Restaurant, has a light, fresh decor, and seating at tables for two, four, six, or eight – although tables for six or eight predominate. With a one-and-a-half deck height, the restaurant has a nice open feeling, and there's plenty of space around most tables for decent service to be provided.

The 80-seat Prime 7 Steakhouse is the smallest of the specialty dining venues. It features a range of superb USDA prime, dry-aged steaks as well as chops, oven-roasted half chicken, Alaskan king crab legs, and Maine lobster. It's the most intimate dining spot – though, again, the single-deck ceiling height makes it feel busy – and it can get noisy (call it lively ambience). There is seating for two, four, or six, and reservations are required.

Signatures is a 120-seat 'supper club' with ocean views along the room's port side. It is directed and staffed by chefs wearing the white toque and blue riband of Le Cordon Bleu, the prestigious culinary society for classic French cuisine. Doors open onto a covered area outdoors, with small stage and dance floor. Seating is at tables of two, four, or six, and reservations are required. However, the single-deck ceiling height robs the room of the grandeur that suits fine classic French cuisine best.

For more casual meals, La Veranda is a large self-serve indoor/outdoor café with seats for 450 and fresh, light decor. This eatery has several food islands and substantial counter display space. At night, it is transformed into Sette Mari – an Italian eatery with some excellent pasta-based dishes.

The outdoor Pool Grill and ice cream bar, adjacent to the swimming pool, is a popular eatery. It features a creative list of burgers (a choice of 11, to be exact), including Black Angus beefburger, Philly beefburger, southwestern beefburger, pesto beefburger, Portobello and feta cheese burger, Asian salmon burger, tofu veggie burger, roasted garlic teriyaki mushroom turkey burger – and others – as well as various sandwiches.

ENTERTAINMENT. The Constellation Theater spans two decks and is delightful, with good sight lines from almost all seats. The proscenium arch stage also has a front thrust stage – useful for presenting more intimate cabaret acts – and an LED backdrop for dramatic show scenery images.

The Horizon Lounge, located aft, is a combination day lounge with bar, and the venue for afternoon tea and daily quizzes. A number of bands, small musical units, and solo pianists provide live music in lounges and bars.

There is also Stars nightclub, with an oval-shaped dance floor, and a stairway connecting it to the casino on the deck above.

SPA/FITNESS. Canyon Ranch Spa facilities include an extensive health spa with gymnasium and aerobics room, beauty parlor, and separate changing, sauna, and steam rooms for men and women.

Sports devotees can play on the paddle-tennis court and in the golf driving and practice cages.

SEVEN SEAS NAVIGATOR
★★★+

A MOSTLY PREMIUM, ALL-INCLUSIVE SHIP FOR MATURE-AGE CRUISERS

Size:	Small Ship	Passenger/Crew Ratio (lower beds):	1.5
Tonnage:	28,550	Cabins (total):	245
Cruise Line:	Regent Seven Seas Cruises	Size Range (sq ft/m):	301.3–1,173.3/28.0–109.0
Former Names:	*none*	Cabins (for one person):	0
Builder:	T. Mariotti (Italy)	Cabins with balcony:	196
Entered Service:	Aug 1999	Cabins (wheelchair accessible):	4
Length (ft/m):	559.7/170.6	Wheelchair accessibility:	Good
Beam (ft/m):	71.5/21.8	Elevators:	5
Propulsion/Propellers:	diesel (13,000kW)/2	Casino (gaming tables):	Yes
Passenger Decks:	8	Swimming Pools:	1
Total Crew:	325	Self-Service Launderette:	Yes
Passengers (lower beds):	490	Library:	Yes
Passenger Space Ratio (lower beds):	58.2	Onboard currency:	US$

THE SHIP. *Seven Seas Navigator* was built using a hull already constructed in St. Petersburg, Russia, as the research vessel *Akademik Nikolay Pilyugin*. The superstructure was incorporated into the hull in an Italian shipyard – the result being that, in effect, a new ship was delivered in record time. The result is less than handsome – particularly at the stern – but it's large enough to be stable over long stretches of water, and there is an excellent amount of space per passenger. In 2009, a 'ducktail' stern was added to aid stability and buoyancy.

The interiors (refreshed in a 2016 makeover) have a mix of classical and modern Italian styling and decor, with warm, soft colors and fine-quality soft furnishings and fabrics. The Galileo Lounge features a Steinway piano, and has good views over the stern. A Navigator's Lounge has warm mahogany and cherry wood paneling and large, comfortable, mid-back tub chairs. Next door, cigars and cognac can be taken in the Connoisseur's Club. An extensive library, with a faux fireplace, also has several computers with Internet access.

There is no walk-around promenade deck outdoors, although there's a jogging track high atop the aft section around the funnel housing. Two of the upper, outer decks are laid with green Astroturf, which cheapens the look of the ship – they would be better in teak. The ceilings in several public rooms, including the main restaurant, are quite low, which makes

BERLITZ'S RATINGS		
	Possible	Achieved
Ship	500	325
Accommodation	200	155
Food	400	277
Service	400	287
Entertainment	100	68
Cruise Experience	400	282

OVERALL SCORE 1394 points out of 2000

the ship feel smaller and more closed-in than it is. It still suffers from a considerable amount of vibration, which detracts from the comfort level when compared with other vessels of the same size.

The ship is best suited to well-traveled couples and solo travelers, typically over 50, who seek excellent itineraries, fine food, and good service, with some entertainment, all wrapped up in a contemporary ship that's elegant and comfortable. Designed for worldwide cruise itineraries, this is one of the upscale ships in the diverse Regent Seven Seas Cruises fleet.

Basic gratuities are included in the fare, as are alcoholic and non-alcoholic beverages, plus table wines for lunch and dinner (premium wines are available at extra cost). Shore excursions and any pre- or post-cruise hotel stays are also included.

ACCOMMODATION. There are several different price grades, and the company markets this as an 'all-suites' ship. Even the smallest suite is quite large, and all have outside views (all were refreshed in the 2016 revamp). Almost 90 percent of all suites have a private balcony, with floor-to-ceiling sliding glass doors, while 10 suites are interconnecting, and 38 have an extra bed for a third occupant. By comparison, even the smallest suite is more than twice the size of the smallest cabin aboard the world's largest cruise ships, Royal Caribbean International's *Oasis*-class ships.

All accommodation grades have a walk-in closet, European king-size bed or twin beds, wooden cabinetry with nicely rounded edges, plenty of drawer space, mini-bar/refrigerator stocked with complimentary soft drinks and bar set-up on embarkation, infotainment system, and personal safe. The marble-appointed bathroom has a full-size tub, as well as a separate shower enclosure, cotton bathrobe and towels, and hairdryer. Balconies benefit from real teak decking.

The largest living spaces are in four Grand and Master Suites. Then there's Navigator Suites, which are located in the ship's center, directly underneath the pool deck, although this means that they are subject to early morning noise attacks – when deck cleaning is carried out, and chairs are dragged across the deck. Despite this, they are delightful living spaces.

Four suites aimed at passengers with physical disabilities have private balconies, and are ideally located adjacent to the elevators. However, while they are generally very practical, it is almost impossible to access the balcony because of the high threshold at the bottom of the sliding glass door.

DINING. The 384-seat Compass Rose Dining Room has large ocean-view picture windows and open-seating dining, which means that you can choose your companions. There are a few tables for two, but most are for four, six, or eight persons. With a low ceiling height and noisy waiter stations, the overall feeling is cramped and unbecoming in terms of the lack of space and grace. Complimentary wines are served during dinner, and a connoisseur wine list is available at extra cost. The company also promotes 'heart healthy' cuisine.

La Veranda is the casual self-serve eatery for breakfast and lunch. Each evening, it is transformed into Sette Mari, for informal dining, and serves dinners with an emphasis on Italian cuisine (reservations required for dinner). Alfresco dining is also available.

The 70-seat Prime 7 is the place for steaks and seafood, is in an elegant setting for dinner only (reservations required). For fast food, there is a small outdoor Grill one deck above.

You can also dine in your cabin. There is a 24-hour room service menu and, during regular dinner hours, you can choose from the full dining room menu. For coffee lovers, there's Coffee Connection (for illy coffees), close to the Navigator Lounge.

ENTERTAINMENT. The Seven Seas Lounge, a two-deck-high showlounge, has reasonable sight lines from most seats on both main and balcony levels, although pillars obstruct views from some side balcony seats. *Seven Seas Navigator* puts on both production shows and cabaret acts. Bands, small musical units, and solo pianist entertainers provide live music in the lounges and bars.

SPA/FITNESS. The spa, fitness center, and beauty salon are in the most forward part of the top deck. Canyon Ranch SpaClub operates the spa and beauty services as a concession, provides the staff, and sells its own beauty products. An 18 percent gratuity is included in treatment and beauty salon services prices.

SEVEN SEAS VOYAGER
★★★★+

A PREMIUM ALL-INCLUSIVE CRUISE SHIP WITH OODLES OF SPACE AND STYLE

Size:	Small Ship
Tonnage:	42,363
Cruise Line:	Regent Seven Seas Cruises
Former Names:	none
Builder:	T. Mariotti (Italy)
Entered Service:	Mar 2003
Length (ft/m):	669.2/204.0
Beam (ft/m):	94.5/28.8
Propulsion/Propellers:	diesel-electric (16,000kW)/ 2 azimuthing pods
Passenger Decks:	9
Total Crew:	445
Passengers (lower beds):	708
Passenger Space Ratio (lower beds):	59.8
Passenger/Crew Ratio (lower beds):	1.6
Cabins (total):	354
Size Range (sq ft/m):	356.0–1,399.3/33.0–130.0
Cabins (for one person):	0
Cabins with balcony:	354
Cabins (wheelchair accessible):	4
Wheelchair accessibility:	Best
Elevators:	6
Casino (gaming tables):	Yes
Swimming Pools:	1
Self-Service Launderette:	Yes
Library:	Yes
Onboard currency:	US$

THE SHIP. *Seven Seas Voyager* was built in 32 blocks, with the same basic hull design as *Seven Seas Mariner*, with a few modifications. Following a 2016 multi-million dollar makeover, the ship has been refreshed and has a more elegant feel. There is a complete outdoor teak walk-around deck, and a keyhole-shaped pool with two adjacent hot tubs.

Inside, there is a good array of public rooms, almost all located below the accommodation decks. Three sets of stairways mean it is easy to find your way around. An atrium lobby spans eight decks, with the lowest level opening directly onto the tender landing stage.

Facilities include five bars, a showlounge that spans two decks, an observation lounge (with heavy, but very comfortable white chairs), a Horizon Lounge (strangely, at the back of the ship), a small casino (with gaming tables and slot machines), a shopping concourse, a large library, Internet-connect center (Club.com), business center (Coffee.com), card room, and small conference room. There is also a nightclub, Voyager, with an oval-shaped dance floor, a cigar-smoking lounge (Connoisseur Club), for cigars and cognacs, and an 'art' gallery.

Seven Seas Voyager is ideally suited to well-traveled couples and solo travelers, typically over 50, seeking excellent itineraries, good food and service, with some entertainment, in a contemporary ship that's elegant and very comfortable. (Only several pillars and low ceilings in public rooms mar

BERLITZ'S RATINGS

	Possible	Achieved
Ship	500	409
Accommodation	200	168
Food	400	298
Service	400	312
Entertainment	100	77
Cruise Experience	400	309

OVERALL SCORE 1574 points out of 2000

the feeling of spaciousness.) It's an 'all-inclusive' ship, although the company chooses the drink brands, not you.

ACCOMMODATION. There are about a dozen different accommodation price grades. As the ship was built with a central hallway design, it allowed for larger suites and bathrooms than sibling *Seven Seas Mariner*. Regent Seven Seas Cruises says it's an 'all-suites, all-balconies' ship – although that's incorrect, as not all sleeping areas are completely separated from living areas. Electrical outlets are both US and European-style.

All accommodation grades have private, marble-clad bathrooms with tub, walk-in closet with personal safe, and most suite entrances are recessed away from passenger hallways to provide extra quiet. All have a small private balcony, although all except those in the Master Suites and Grand Suites measure only 50 sq ft (4.6 sq m); all have teak decking. Partitions are of the partial type, except for the Master Suites and Grand Suites, which have full floor-to-ceiling partitions, and are completely private. From the smallest to the largest:

Deluxe Suites measure 356 sq ft (33 sq m) and have twin beds that convert to a queen-size bed, but the sleeping area is separated from the living area only by partial room dividers, and therefore they are cabins – albeit good-size ones – not suites.

654 SEVEN SEAS VOYAGER

Horizon Suites measure 522 sq ft (48.4 sq m) and overlook the stern.

Category 'A' and Category 'B' Penthouse Suites measure 370 sq ft (34.3 sq m).

Seven Seas Suites measure 657 sq ft (61 sq m). Located aft, they have a generous wraparound balcony, although these can be partly overlooked.

Voyager Suites measure 603 sq ft (56 sq m), and are located on the port and starboard sides of the atrium on three decks.

Grand Suites (1104, 1005) are one deck above the navigation bridge; each measures 876 sq ft (81 sq m).

Two Master Suites measure 1,162 sq ft (108 sq m). These suites, 1100 and 1001, each expand to 1,403 sq ft (130 sq m) when paired with one Grand Suite via an interconnecting door, while 700 and 701 measure 1,335 sq ft (124 sq m).

Four wheelchair-accessible suites (761, 762, 859, and 860) are all close to an elevator, and provide ample living space, together with a large roll-in shower and all bathroom fittings at the correct height.

DINING. The 570-seat Compass Rose Restaurant is the main dining room. It has tables for two to 10, and dining is on an open seating basis, so you can dine with whomever you like, when you choose. In general, the cuisine is very good, and there's plenty of choice, although it lacks the wow factor you might expect. It is a shame, too, to find packets of sugar and jams on an elegant ship.

Chartreuse is an intimate, stylish venue for experiencing some classic French cuisine, cooked to order and presented on fine Bernardaud china.

Prime 7 Steakhouse is the smallest of the specialty dining venues, with 80 seats. It features a range of USDA prime, dry-aged steaks as well as chops,

oven-roasted half chicken, Alaskan king crab legs, and Maine lobster. It's the most intimate dining spot – although the single-deck ceiling height makes it feel busy – and it can get noisy. There is seating for two, four, or six, and reservations are required.

Signatures 'supper club' seats 120, and has ocean views along the room's port side. It is directed and staffed by chefs wearing the white toque and blue riband of Le Cordon Bleu, the prestigious culinary society for classic French cuisine. Seating is at tables of two, four, or six, and reservations are required.

For more casual meals, La Veranda is a large self-serve indoor/outdoor café with seats for 450, and fresh, light decor. This eatery has several food islands and substantial counter display space. At night, it morphs into Sette Mari – an Italian-style eatery featuring pasta-based dishes.

The outdoor Pool Grill and ice cream bar, adjacent to the swimming pool, is a popular eatery. It features a creative list of burgers and various sandwiches.

ENTERTAINMENT. The Constellation Showlounge spans two decks, and sight lines are very good from almost all of the (mostly banquette) seats. A troupe of singers/dancers provides colorful (mini) Vegas-style revues and production shows. Cabaret acts provide stand-alone evening shows. The ship carries a main showband, several small musical groups, and soloists.

SPA/FITNESS. Canyon Ranch SpaClub facilities include an extensive health spa with gymnasium and aerobics room, beauty parlor, and separate changing, sauna, and steam rooms for men and women.

An 18 percent gratuity is included in the price of treatments and beauty salon services.

SILVER CLOUD
★★★★

AN INCLUSIVE, UPMARKET BUT DATED SMALL SHIP FOR DISCOVERY CRUISING

Size: .... Small Ship	Passenger/Crew Ratio (lower beds): 1.2
Tonnage: 16,927	Cabins (total): 148
Cruise Line: ....Silversea Cruises	Size Range (sq ft/m): 240.0–1,314.0/22.2–122.0
Former Names: .... *none*	Cabins (for one person): 0
Builder: .... Visentini/Mariotti (Italy)	Cabins with balcony: 110
Entered Service: ....Apr 1994	Cabins (wheelchair accessible): 2
Length (ft/m): 514.4/155.8	Wheelchair accessibility: .... Fair
Beam (ft/m): 70.62/21.4	Elevators: 4
Propulsion/Propellers: .... diesel (11,700kW)/2	Casino (gaming tables): .... Yes
Passenger Decks: 6	Swimming Pools: 1
Total Crew: 204	Self-Service Launderette: .... Yes
Passengers (lower beds): 260	Library: .... Yes
Passenger Space Ratio (lower beds): 62.6	Onboard currency: .... US$

THE SHIP. *Silver Cloud*, now well over 20 years old, has fairly handsome profile, with a sloping stern reminiscent of an Airstream trailer. Following a 2017 conversion to make it more like an expedition-style ship, *Silver Cloud* carries 18 Zodiac landing craft, and now has a deep blue hull. The ship has an ice-class hull modification for sailing in more remote areas (including Antarctica), and now carries a maximum of 260 passengers (200 on Antarctic voyages). But it's not a real expedition ship (it lacks properly designed 'mud' rooms, boot-washing areas, and storage rooms).

The vertical cake-layer stacking of public rooms aft and the location of accommodation forward ensures quiet cabins. There is a synthetic turf-covered (this doesn't equate with luxury) walk-around promenade deck outdoors, and a pool deck with teak/aluminum deck furniture.

The spacious interior has bland decor, but fine-quality soft furnishings accented by the gentle use of brass fittings, fine woods, and creative ceilings.

An excellent amount of space per passenger means there is no hint of a line anywhere in this unhurried environment.

All drinks, gratuities, and port taxes are included, and no further tipping is necessary – though it is not prohibited.

Niggles? Some vibration is evident when bow thrusters or the anchors are used, particularly in the forward-most cabins. The self-service launderette is

BERLITZ'S RATINGS		
	Possible	Achieved
Ship	500	340
Accommodation	200	157
Food	400	294
Service	400	309
Entertainment	100	66
Cruise Experience	400	286

OVERALL SCORE 1452 points out of 2000

not large enough for longer cruises. Crew facilities are minimal, leading to a high crew turnover, which undermines service.

ACCOMMODATION. There are several price grades in this 'all-suites' ship. The all-outside-view suites, three-quarters of which have fine private teakwood balconies, have convertible queen-to-twin beds, and are beautifully fitted out. They have large floor-to-ceiling windows, large walk-in closets, dressing table, writing desk, stocked mini-bar/refrigerator (no charge), and fresh flowers.

Marble-floored bathrooms have a tub, fixed showerhead, single washbasin, and plenty of high-quality towels.

The walk-in closets don't provide much hanging space, particularly for such items as full-length dresses, and it would be better for the door to open outward instead of inward. The drawers themselves are poorly positioned, but several other drawers and storage areas are provided in the living area.

Although the cabin insulation above and below is good, the insulation between cabins is not – a privacy curtain installed between entry door and sleeping area would be most useful. Light from the passageway leaks into the cabin, so it's hard to achieve a dark room.

Top-grade suites have teak balcony furniture, while other suites do not, but all balconies have teak floors. Suites with balconies on the lowest deck can suffer from sticky salt spray when the ship is moving, so the balconies need lots of cleaning. Each evening, the stewardesses bring plates of canapés to your suite – just right for a light bite with cocktails. In the Grand, Royal, Rossellini, or Owner's suites, you get unobtrusive butler service from butlers certified by London's Guild of Professional Butlers.

DINING. The Restaurant provides open-seating dining in somewhat elegant surroundings. It has an attractive arched gazebo center and a wavy ceiling design as its focal point, and is set with fine Eschenbach china and well-balanced Christofle silverware. Meals are served in an open seating, which means you can eat when the dining room is open, and with whom you like.

Standard table wines are included for lunch and dinner, and there is a 'connoisseur list' of premium wines at extra charge. All meals are prepared à la minute, with little of the pre-preparation that used to exist.

La Saletta, adjacent to the main dining room, is an intimate 24-seat specialty dining salon. Dégustation menus include dishes designed for Silversea Cruises by chefs from Relais & Châteaux and paired with selected wines. Reservations are required, and there's a cover charge.

La Terrazza provides self-serve breakfast and lunch buffets and informal evening dining with different regional Italian dishes nightly. Both indoor and outdoor seating is at teakwood tables and chairs.

There is a 24-hour in-cabin dining service. Full course-by-course dinners are available, although the balcony tables in the standard suites are rather low for dining outdoors.

ENTERTAINMENT. The Showlounge hosts entertainment events and some social functions. The room spans two decks and has a sloping floor; banquette and individual seating are provided, with good sight lines.

Although Silversea Cruises places more emphasis on food than entertainment, what is provided is quite tasteful and not overbearing, as aboard some larger ships. A decent array of cabaret acts does the Silversea circuit, and small colorful production shows have been re-introduced.

Most of the cabaret acts provide intelligent entertainment that is generally appreciated by the well-traveled international clientele, and there's more emphasis now on classical music ensembles. A band provides live music in the evenings in The Bar, and Panorama Lounge.

SPA/FITNESS. The Spa at Silversea is quite small compared to those on other so-called luxury ships.

Facilities include a separate sauna for men and women, several treatment rooms, and a beauty salon. Massage and other body-pampering treatments, facials, pedicures, and beauty salon treatments cost extra.

A separate gymnasium (formerly an observation lounge), located atop the ship, provides sea views.

SILVER DISCOVERER
★★★★

A SMALL EXPEDITION-STYLE SHIP THAT IS BUILT FOR DISCOVERY CRUISES

Size:	Boutique Ship	Passenger/Crew Ratio (lower beds):	1.7
Tonnage:	5,218	Cabins (total):	62
Cruise Line:	Silversea Cruises	Size Range (sq ft/m):	182.9–258.3/17–24
Former Names:	Clipper Odyssey, Oceanic Odyssey,	Cabins (for one person):	0
	Oceanic Grace	Cabins with balcony:	8
Builder:	NKK Tsu Shipyard (Japan)	Cabins (wheelchair accessible):	1
Entered Service:	Apr 1989/May 2014	Wheelchair accessibility:	Fair
Length (ft/m):	337.9/103.0	Elevators:	1
Beam (ft/m):	50.5/15.4	Casino (gaming tables):	No
Propulsion/Propellers:	diesel (5,192kW)/2	Swimming Pools:	1
Passenger Decks:	5	Self-Service Launderette:	No
Total Crew:	70	Library:	Yes
Passengers (lower beds):	120	Onboard currency:	US$
Passenger Space Ratio (lower beds):	43.4		

THE SHIP. *Silver Discoverer* is liked by couples and solo travellers who seek nature and wildlife up close and personal, but in highly comfortable surroundings, and who wouldn't dream of cruising aboard anything larger.

The ship has quite a smart, chic, mega-yacht-like profile, with a flared bow, square stern, and twin funnels that sweep up from each of the ship's sides. Designed in Holland and built in Japan, it tried to copy the *SeaDream* small ship/ultra-yacht concept, originally for the Japanese market. Operated by Japan's Showa Line, it wasn't suited to Japan's often choppy seas, so, after 10 years, it was sold to Clipper Cruise Line and managed by International Shipping Partners. In 2013 it was purchased by Silversea Cruises and renamed following a substantial refit and refurbishment program.

There are expansive areas outdoors for its size, and these are excellent for viewing nature and wildlife. A small swimming pool is just a 'dip' pool, but there is a wide teakwood outdoor jogging track. Snorkeling equipment is available, as is a fleet of 12 Zodiacs for shore landings, and a glass-bottom boat for marine-life exploration.

Inside, nothing jars the senses, as the interior design concept is balanced. The ambience is warm and intimate. There are, however, several pillars throughout the public areas, which spoil the decor and sight lines. The ship concentrates on exploring

BERLITZ'S RATINGS		
	Possible	Achieved
Ship	500	324
Accommodation	200	135
Food	400	305
Service	400	313
Entertainment	100	59
Cruise Experience	400	295
OVERALL SCORE 1431 points out of 2000		

regions such as Australia's Kimberley, the Russian Far East, and the Bering Sea area.

ACCOMMODATION. There are several cabin categories, and the all-outside cabins are tastefully furnished with blond wood cabinetry, twin- or queen-size beds, living area with sofa, personal safe, minibar/refrigerator, TV and three-sided mirror. Some cabins have private balconies; but these are very small, with awkward door handles. All bathrooms have shower enclosures; note that the toilet seats are extremely high.

There is one suite, which is the size of two cabins. It provides more room, of course, than a standard cabin, with a lounge area, and more storage space.

DINING. The dining room has large ocean-view picture windows. It is quite warm and inviting, and all passengers eat in a single seating. The cuisine includes fresh foods from local ports where possible.

ENTERTAINMENT. There is no entertainment as such, although evening recaps, dinner and after-dinner conversation with fellow passengers in the ship's lounge/bar really is the entertainment.

SPA/FITNESS. There is a tiny beauty salon, and an adjacent massage/body-treatment room. A small fitness room is located on a different deck.

SILVER EXPLORER
★★★★

THIS SMALL 'SOFT' EXPEDITION SHIP HAS SOME PREMIUM CHARACTERISTICS

Size:	Boutique Ship	Passenger Space Ratio (lower beds):	60.7
Tonnage:	6,072	Passenger/Crew Ratio (lower beds):	0.8
Cruise Line:	Silversea Cruises	Cabins (total):	66
Former Names:	*Prince Albert II, World Discoverer,*	Size Range (sq ft/m):	172.2–785.7/16.0–73.0
	Dream 21, Baltic Clipper, Sally Clipper, Delfin Star,	Cabins (for one person):	0
	Delfin Clipper, World Adventurer, Delfin Clipper	Cabins with balcony:	6 + 14 French balconies
Builder:	Rauma-Repola (Finland)	Cabins (wheelchair accessible):	0
Entered Service:	Jul 1989/Jun 2008	Wheelchair accessibility:	None
Length (ft/m):	354.3/108.0	Elevators:	2
Beam (ft/m):	51.1/15.6	Casino (gaming tables):	No
Propulsion/Propellers:	diesel (4,500kW)/2	Swimming Pools:	0
Passenger Decks:	5	Self-Service Launderette:	No
Total Crew:	117	Library:	No
Passengers (lower beds):	100	Onboard currency:	US$

THE SHIP. Twin swept-back outboard funnels highlight the semi-smart exterior design of this small specialist expedition cruise ship. It has a dark ice-hardened hull, carries a fleet of eight Zodiac inflatable landing craft for shore landings and exploration, and has one boot-washing station, the Mud Room, with six bays. There is no walk-around promenade deck outdoors.

The accommodation is located forward, with all public rooms aft except for an observation lounge, an arrangement that helps keep noise to a minimum in the accommodation areas. The interior has many European design elements, including warm color combinations. Public rooms include an observation lounge, which, following a 2017 refurbishment, now incorporates reference books that were in the former library, plus a panorama lounge (a strange name for a room at the back of the ship), large lecture room/cinema with bar, and boutique.

Silver Explorer has many of the creature comforts of much larger vessels and will provide a very comfortable expedition-style cruise experience in tasteful and elegant surroundings. All passengers receive a pre-cruise amenities package that typically includes a field guide, backpack, carry-on travel bag, and luggage tags.

The ship is best suited to adventurous couples and solo travelers of mature years who enjoy seeing

BERLITZ'S RATINGS		
	Possible	Achieved
Ship	500	354
Accommodation	200	144
Food	400	295
Service	400	322
Entertainment	100	58
Cruise Experience	400	289

OVERALL SCORE 1462 points out of 2000

nature at close range, but want an extremely comfortable setting, plus good food and service.

ACCOMMODATION. There is a range of accommodation and price grades. The cabins, which are quite large for such a small ship, are outfitted to a good standard, with ample closet and drawer space. All have outside views and twin beds that convert to a queen-size bed, flat-screen TV, telephone, hairdryer, refrigerator, and lockable drawer. The bathrooms have rainshowers.

Although only six suites have a large private balcony (they're really not needed in cold-weather regions), several 'suites' have glass doors that open onto a few inches of space outdoors. The Owner's Suites have two rooms, linked by an interconnecting door, to provide a separate lounge, bedroom, and two bathrooms.

DINING. The spacious dining room, with pastel-colored decor, accommodates all passengers in one seating. Casual alfresco bites can be had at the outdoor grill.

ENTERTAINMENT. Daily recaps and after-dinner conversation make up the onboard entertainment.

SPA/FITNESS. Facilities include a small gymnasium, sauna, and treatment room for massage.

SILVER GALAPAGOS
★★★+

A FINE SHIP TO USE AS A FLOATING BASE IN THE GALÁPAGOS

Size:	Boutique Ship	Passenger/Crew Ratio (lower beds):	1.3
Tonnage:	4,077	Cabins (total):	50
Cruise Line:	Silversea Cruises	Size Range (sq ft/m):	231.4–282.0/21.5–26.2
Former Names:	Renaissance Three,	Cabins (for one person):	0
	Galapagos Explorer II	Cabins with balcony:	24
Builder:	Cantieri Navale Ferrari (Italy)	Cabins (wheelchair accessible):	0
Entered Service:	Aug 1990/Sep 2013	Wheelchair accessibility:	None
Length (ft/m):	293.1/89.3	Elevators:	1
Beam (ft/m):	50.1/15.3	Casino (gaming tables):	No
Propulsion/Propellers:	diesel (3,514kW)/2	Swimming Pools:	0
Passenger Decks:	5	Self-Service Launderette:	No
Total Crew:	75	Library:	Yes
Passengers (lower beds):	100	Onboard currency:	US$
Passenger Space Ratio (lower beds):	40.7		

THE SHIP. *Silver Galápagos* operates two specific Galápagos cruise itineraries year-round from Baltra, Ecuador. It suits couples and solo travelers who want to cruise around the islands in comfortable, stylish surroundings.

It is an inviting ship, built as one of a series of eight similar small ships for the defunct Renaissance Cruises. While the vessel is in good condition, maintenance could be better. Its looks are quite contemporary in the style of a mega-yacht, and there is a wooden promenade deck outdoors. The limited number of public rooms have smart and restful, non-glitzy decor. The main lounge doubles as a lecture room, but perhaps it is the piano bar that provides the best place to relax after dinner in the evening. A doctor is carried at all times.

This ship (first operated by Silversea Cruises in 2013) provides a destination-intensive, refined, quiet, and relaxed cruise for those who don't like crowds or dressing up. Trained naturalist guides lead the shore excursions (included in the fare); the ship carries two glass-bottom boats, plus wetsuits and snorkeling equipment.

All drinks, bottled water, and soft drinks are included in the fare. Also included are guided visits to the islands. The brochure rates may or may not include the Galápagos Islands visitor tax, which must be paid in cash.

Sunbathing space is cramped. Plastic wood is everywhere (although it looks good). The service lacks finesse, but the crew is willing. The small library is attractive, but the book selection is poor.

ACCOMMODATION. This is located forward, with public rooms aft. Pleasant, all-outside suites have a large picture window, hand-crafted Italian furniture, and wet bar. All cabins have a queen-size bed, a sitting area, a minibar/refrigerator, TV, DVD player, and hairdryer. The small bathrooms have showers with a fold-down seat, real teakwood floors, and marble vanities.

DINING. The small, elegant, intimate dining room has open seating and tables for two, four, six, and eight. The meals are dinner is à la carte, while lunch is buffet-style (sometimes on the open deck), with local Ecuadorian delicacies and meat.

ENTERTAINMENT. After-dinner conversation with fellow passengers forms the entertainment each evening.

SPA/FITNESS. There is a small sauna. Snorkel gear is also available.

BERLITZ'S RATINGS		
	Possible	Achieved
Ship	500	338
Accommodation	200	150
Food	400	259
Service	400	292
Entertainment	100	50
Cruise Experience	400	267
OVERALL SCORE 1356 points out of 2000		

SILVER MUSE
★★★★+

THIS SHIP WOULD BE A GOOD CHOICE FOR SOPHISTICATED INTERNATIONAL TRAVELERS

Size:	Small Ship	Passenger/Crew Ratio (lower beds):	1.4/1
Tonnage:	40,700	Cabins (total):	298
Cruise Line:	Silversea Cruises	Size Range (sq ft/m):	387.5–1,969.8/36.0–183.0
Former Names:	none	Cabins (for one person):	0
Builder:	Fincantieri (Italy)	Cabins with balcony:	298
Entered Service:	Apr 2017	Cabins (wheelchair accessible):	4
Length (ft/m):	698.8/213.0	Wheelchair accessibility:	Best
Beam (ft/m):	88.5/27.0	Elevators:	6
Propulsion/Propellers:	diesel/2	Casino (gaming tables):	Yes
Passenger Decks:	8	Swimming Pools:	1
Total Crew:	411	Self-Service Launderette:	Yes
Passengers (lower beds):	596	Library:	Yes
Passenger Space Ratio (lower beds):	78.8	Onboard currency:	US$

THE SHIP. An evolution of *Silver Spirit*, *Silver Muse* has more space, more dining options, larger public rooms, and more passengers. It has nicely tiered aft decks, and there is a good amount of open deck space. Public rooms include an observation lounge, panorama lounge, Connoisseur's Corner (for cigar-smokers), Dolce Vita (a main lounge and social gathering place), an Arts Café, library, and children's center.

BERLITZ'S RATINGS		
	Possible	Achieved
Ship	500	429
Accommodation	200	181
Food	400	326
Service	400	338
Entertainment	100	85
Cruise Experience	400	325

OVERALL SCORE 1684 points out of 2000

A high degree of comfort and style, together with 'Italian flair' go hand in hand with good culinary offerings for a cosmopolitan clientele. Silversea Cruises has 'all-inclusive' pricing (although it doesn't include things such as shore excursions or spa treatments), except for premium drink brands and really good vintage wines.

Overall, it's the largest ship in the fleet, but the interior design, colors, and furnishings are far superior to those on all the other Silversea ships. There are more dining and food choices, and the suites (particularly the smallest ones) are better designed.

ACCOMMODATION. There are numerous accommodation price grades, with the price dependent on the size, location, and grade you choose. From the smallest to the largest (Owner's Suites – four of them), this all-suite ship has some delightfully spacious accommodation. Note that balconies have faux teak decking.

DINING. There is no single main restaurant. Instead, Atlantide (for seafood and grills) and Indochine (for Indian, Thai, Vietnamese, etc.) are the two largest dining venues. This is all about open-seating dining, in attractive surroundings, with unhurried, unobtrusive service, and seating with whomever you wish. The restaurants are open for all meals; tables are set with fine china, silverware, and Riedel wine glasses.

Other restaurants and eateries include: La Dame by Relais & Châteaux, an extra-cost, reservations-required finer-dining venue; Silver Note, a dinner/dancing venue, for tapas-style bites in an elegant, jazz-themed setting; Kaiseki, an extra-cost, reservations-required Japanese-style venue; and a Teppanyaki grill in the evening. La Terrazza is an indoor/outdoor self-serve casual eatery for breakfast and lunch. The casual Spaccanapoli is the venue for pizzas, while Hot Rocks is an outdoor venue for steaks and grilled seafood items.

In case you want to be private, you can eat, course-by-course, in the privacy of your suite.

ENTERTAINMENT. The showlounge has a classic thrust stage. It spans two decks and has a sloping floor and tiered seating levels. Colorful small-cast song-and-dance shows and cabaret acts are featured.

SPA/FITNESS. Zagara Spa, operated by Steiner Leisure, has saunas and steam rooms for men and women, a thermal suite (day passes are at extra cost), an outdoor relaxation area (with hot tub and loungers), and a fitness center with cardiovascular equipment.

SILVER SHADOW
★★★★+

THIS ALL-INCLUSIVE PREMIUM SHIP IS A GOOD CHOICE FOR MATURE-AGE CRUISERS

Size:	Small Ship	Passenger/Crew Ratio (lower beds):	1.3
Tonnage:	28,258	Cabins (total):	194
Cruise Line:	Silversea Cruises	Size Range (sq ft/m):	287.0–1,435.0/26.6–133.3
Former Names:	none	Cabins (for one person):	0
Builder:	Visentini/Mariotti (Italy)	Cabins with balcony:	166
Entered Service:	Sep 2000	Cabins (wheelchair accessible):	2
Length (ft/m):	610.2/186.0	Wheelchair accessibility:	Good
Beam (ft/m):	81.8/24.8	Elevators:	5
Propulsion/Propellers:	diesel/2	Casino (gaming tables):	Yes
Passenger Decks:	7	Swimming Pools:	1
Total Crew:	295	Self-Service Launderette:	Yes
Passengers (lower beds):	388	Library:	Yes
Passenger Space Ratio (lower beds):	72.8	Onboard currency:	US$

THE SHIP. This ship is best suited to discerning, well-traveled couples, typically over 50, who seek a small ship with excellent food that approaches gourmet standards, and fine service in surroundings bordering on the elegant and luxurious.

Silver Shadow is one of the second generation of ships in the Silversea Cruises fleet, and slightly larger than *Silver Cloud* and *Silver Wind*, with a more streamlined forward profile and large, sleek single funnel. However, the ship's stern is not particularly handsome. There is a generous amount of open deck and sunbathing space, and aluminum/teak deck furniture is provided.

The company's many international passengers react well to the ambience, food, service, and the helpful staff. The cruise line has 'all-inclusive' fares, including gratuities and many things that cost extra aboard many rivals' ships, but the fares don't include vintage wines, massage, or other personal services.

Although the ship shows signs of wear, the onboard product is very good, particularly the cuisine and its presentation. Shuttle buses are provided in most ports of call, and all the little extras that passengers receive make this an extremely pleasant experience, in surroundings that are comfortable and contemporary without being extravagant, with open-seating dining and drinks included, cold canapés and hot hors d'oeuvres served in the bars in the pre-dinner cocktail hour, a captain's welcome aboard, and farewell cocktail party.

BERLITZ'S RATINGS		
	Possible	Achieved
Ship	500	405
Accommodation	200	178
Food	400	314
Service	400	318
Entertainment	100	78
Cruise Experience	400	313

OVERALL SCORE 1606 points out of 2000

The swimming pool is surprisingly small, as is the fitness room, although it was expanded in 2007. The Humidor by Davidoff (a cigar lounge) has 25 seats and is in the style of an English smoking club. There is a Champagne bar and a four-terminal computer center (Wi-Fi costs extra).

ACCOMMODATION. There are eight price grades in this all-suites ship. Each suite has a double vanity, tub, and separate shower enclosure in its marble-floored bathroom. All grades receive Silversea-monogrammed Frette bed linen, an eight-pillow menu (from soft down to memory foam), 100 percent cotton bathrobes, a range of Acqua di Parma bathroom products, and personalized stationery. Stay in the Grand, Royal, Rossellini, or Owner's suites and you also receive unobtrusive service from butlers certified by London's Guild of Professional Butlers.

The Vista Suites measure 287 sq ft (27 sq m); they don't have a private balcony.

Verandah Suites (really Vista Suites plus a veranda) measure 345 sq ft (32 sq m).

Silver Suites are 701 sq ft (65 sq m).

Owner's Suites measure 1,208 sq ft (112 sq m).

Royal Suites are either 1,312 sq ft (122 sq m) or 1,352 sq ft (126 sq m).

There are two Grand Suites, one measuring 1,286 sq ft (119 sq m), and the other (including an adjoining suite with interconnecting door) 1,435 sq ft (133 sq m).

There are also two Disabled Suites (535 and 537), both adjacent to an elevator and next to each other; these measure a generous 398 sq ft (37 sq m). They are well equipped with an accessible hanging rail, and roll-in bathroom with roll-in shower unit.

DINING. The main dining room, The Restaurant, has open seating in elegant surroundings. Three grand chandeliers provide an upward focal point. Meals can also be served, course-by-course, in your suite, although the balcony tables are rather low for dining outdoors. The cuisine is very good, with a choice of formal and informal areas. Standard table wines are included for lunch and dinner, with an extra-cost 'connoisseur list' of premium wines. Once each cruise, there's a Galley Brunch when the galley is transformed into a large 'chef's kitchen.'

For something special, Le Champagne is a more intimate extra-cost venue that allows diners to sample highly specialized dégustation menus marrying international cuisine with vintage wines selection by Relais & Châteaux sommeliers. Reservations are needed, and the wines also cost extra.

For more informal meals, La Terrazza provides self-serve breakfast and lunch buffets; outdoor seating is at teakwood tables and chairs. The buffet design and set-up presents flow problems during breakfast, and 'active' stations for cooking eggs or pasta to order would help.

Adjacent to La Terazza is a wine bar and a cigar-smoking room. A poolside grill provides a casual alternative daytime bistro-style eatery, for grilled and fast-food items, and becomes The Grill for evening dining, with food cooked on hot stones.

ENTERTAINMENT. The Showlounge, the venue for entertainment and some social functions, spans two decks and has a sloping floor; both banquette and individual seating are provided, with good sight lines from almost all seats.

Although Silversea Cruises places more emphasis on food than entertainment, what is provided is quite tasteful. A decent array of cabaret acts does the Silversea circuit, and small, colorful production shows have been reintroduced. More emphasis is placed on classical music ensembles. There is a band and several small musical units for live music in the evenings in The Bar and the Panorama Lounge.

SPA/FITNESS. The Spa at Silversea health/fitness facility, just behind the Observation Lounge, high atop the ship, had a complete makeover in 2007. It includes a gymnasium, beauty salon, and separate saunas and steam rooms for men and women, plus several treatment rooms.

SILVER SPIRIT
★★★★+

A STYLISH UPPER-CLASS SHIP FOR SOPHISTICATED CRUISING AND GOOD FOOD

Size:	Small Ship	Passenger/Crew Ratio (lower beds):	1.4
Tonnage:	36,009	Cabins (total):	270
Cruise Line:	Silversea Cruises	Size Range (sq ft/m):	312.1–1,614.6/29–150
Former Names:	none	Cabins (for one person):	0
Builder:	Fincantieri (Italy)	Cabins with balcony:	258
Entered Service:	Dec 2009	Cabins (wheelchair accessible):	4
Length (ft/m):	642.3/195.8	Wheelchair accessibility:	Best
Beam (ft/m):	86.9/26.5	Elevators:	6
Propulsion/Propellers:	diesel-electric (26,100kW)/2	Casino (gaming tables):	Yes
Passenger Decks:	8	Swimming Pools:	1
Total Crew:	370	Self-Service Launderette:	Yes
Passengers (lower beds):	540	Library:	Yes
Passenger Space Ratio (lower beds):	66.6	Onboard currency:	US$

THE SHIP. *Silver Spirit*, larger than *Silver Shadow* and *Silver Whisper*, is the newest 'all-inclusive' addition to the Silversea Cruises fleet – although 'all-inclusive' doesn't include the two specialty dining venues. It represents a substantial investment in new tonnage. Sharing its name with a famous Rolls-Royce car, *Silver Spirit* has a similar profile to the smaller *Silver Shadow* and *Silver Whisper*, with a nicely shaped stern with tiered aft decks, but exudes more style and provides more choice than the line's other ships.

Although there's a main pool and hot tub deck, there's little shade, and no hot tubs on any other deck. Also, because there are so many balcony suites/cabins, there's no walk-around outdoor promenade deck.

The interior layout has a cake-layer stacking of almost all the public rooms in the aft section, and the accommodation located forward, so there is minimal noise in passenger accommodation, although it means there are more stairs and no flow-through horizontal deck where passengers can parade. But regular Silversea Cruises passengers are used to this arrangement, and it's good exercise. The decor is elegant and understated, with muted colors; style-wise, it's a mix of Art Deco and modern, but not contemporary.

The Observation Lounge, at the front of the ship with access from a central passageway, has fine ocean views, and is a very comfortable place in which to relax and read. A Panorama Lounge, at the stern, is a comfortable multi-function room. Non-

BERLITZ'S RATINGS		
	Possible	Achieved
Ship	500	417
Accommodation	200	178
Food	400	316
Service	400	328
Entertainment	100	83
Cruise Experience	400	317
OVERALL SCORE 1639 points out of 2000		

smokers should note that smoking is allowed on the port side. A cigar lounge, with doors that open in to the casino, has a pleasing list of cigars. The casino has five blackjack tables, an American Roulette table, and 52 slot machines.

The company's 'all-inclusive' fares include gratuities, drinks with meals, and many things that cost extra on competitor ships. Vintage wines, massage, and other personal services do cost extra, though. Passengers appreciate open-seating dining, cold canapés and hot hors d'oeuvres served in the bars in the pre-dinner cocktail hour, a captain's welcome aboard, and a farewell cocktail party. Shuttle buses are provided in most ports of call.

The passenger mix includes many nationalities, which makes for a more interesting experience, although most passengers are North American. Children are sometimes seen aboard, but they are not really welcomed by most people.

The ship suits discerning, well-traveled couples and solo travelers, typically over 50, who are looking for a smaller ship with fine food and European-style service in surroundings bordering on the elegant and luxurious without being extravagant. All the little extras passengers receive make a cruise an extremely pleasant experience.

Passenger niggles include the lack of electrical sockets in the cabins; there are almost no shaded outdoor areas; and the butler service is sometimes poor, not least because each butler has about 15 cabins to look after.

ACCOMMODATION. *Silver Spirit*, like other Silversea Cruises ships, has 'all-suites' accommodation. Some suites can accommodate a third person. Eight suites have interconnecting doors, so families and friends can be adjacent.

Accommodation (from largest to smallest) consists of: two Owner's Suites, approx. 1,292 sq ft (120 sq m) for one bedroom and 1,614 sq ft (150 sq m) for two bedrooms; Grand Suites in the front of the ship (990 sq ft/92 sq m for one bedroom and 1,302 sq ft/121 sq m for two bedrooms); Royal Suites in the front of the ship, and Silver Suites (742 sq ft/69 sq m); Midship Veranda Suites (376 sq ft/35 sq m); Veranda Suites (376 sq ft/35 sq m); and Vista Suites (312 sq ft/29 sq m). The Owner's, Grand, and Royal suites all have interconnecting doors for an available second bedroom.

All accommodation comes with personalized stationery, a menu with a choice of eight pillows from soft down to memory foam, bathrobes, and an array of Bulgari bathroom amenities. All have walk-in closets with personal safe, TV set, DVD unit, and vanity desk with hairdryer. Suite bathrooms are marble-clad, with marble and wood floors, and contain a toilet, one or two washbasins, a full-size tub, and a shower enclosure with both a fixed 'rain shower' and a separate hand-held shower. Occupants of the Owner's Suites or Grand Suites receive unobtrusive service from 21 butlers certified by London's Guild of Professional Butlers.

The suites have recessed lighting in the ceiling – a nice touch that allows a little diffused mood lighting when needed. Balconies have sliding doors that can move if not securely locked when not in use. Non-smokers should be aware that Silversea Cruises allows smoking in cabins.

DINING. There are several dining choices, but some venues cost extra. While Silversea's cuisine has, in the past been very good, many passengers have noticed a decrease in the quality and in the variety of the dishes provided lately, and service has become more hurried.

The Restaurant is the name of the ship's main dining room – it's a light, airy venue, although the low height of the ceiling is disappointing. It seats up to 456, and has an integral dance floor. This is open-seating dining in quite elegant surroundings, with unhurried, unobtrusive service. It is open for breakfast, lunch, and dinner; tables are set with fine china, silverware, and Riedel wine glasses. For complete privacy, meals can also be served, course-by-course, in your suite.

Le Champagne, adjacent to The Restaurant, is an intimate, extra-cost, reservations-required, dinner-only venue offering a six-course mini-dégustation menu based on Relais & Châteaux menus. Sadly, the banquette seating along the outer walls detracts from the otherwise very comfortable, uncluttered, intimate dining spot, which has a small walk-in wine room as its central, focal point.

Seishin Restaurant, also adjacent to The Restaurant, is an extra-cost reservations-required venue, with just 24 seats. It serves Kobe beef, sushi, and Asian seafood, and an octagonal display counter is the focal point to the venue. It is open for dinner only, and there's a cover charge.

La Terrazza is the venue for self-serve buffet-style items for breakfast and lunch. Each evening, it turns into an Italian-themed dining spot, with waiter service and regional Italian cuisine cooked to order. Reservations are required for dinner (not open for lunch).

Stars Supper Club, with 58 seats and a dance floor, is designed in the manner of an English supper club of the 1920s to provide an intimate, club-like ambience and all-night (volume-intrusive) entertainment. Reservations are required for dinner (not open for lunch).

The Pool Grill is a casual outside eatery serving steaks, seafood, and pizza. Meals are served on hot stones that act as plates, so you can't touch them. Additionally, a lobby bar serves Lavazza Italian coffees, wines, spirits, and pastries.

ENTERTAINMENT. The Showlounge, in the aft section, has a main stage and two side stages. It seats about 320 passengers, and there are good sight lines from all seats but no beverage service. It's a lovely room, and seating consists of two-person love seats, and each has a small table for personal items. Production shows have been re-introduced, and these, together with cabaret acts, provide a balanced entertainment program.

SPA/FITNESS. The Spa at Silversea, with 8,300 sq ft (770 sq m) of space, is quite large for this size of ship, and includes a sanctuary for total relaxation and detox. Located at the stern of the ship, one deck below La Terrazza, it is a haven for me-time and personal treatments.

SILVER WHISPER
★★★★+

'INCLUSIVE' CRUISING WITH SPACE, STYLE, SOME GOOD FOOD, AND COMFORT

Size:	Small Ship	Passenger/Crew Ratio (lower beds):	1.4/1
Tonnage:	28,258	Cabins (total):	194
Cruise Line:	Silversea Cruises	Size Range (sq ft/m):	287.0–1,435.0/26.6–133.3
Former Names:	none	Cabins (for one person):	0
Builder:	Visentini/Mariotti (Italy)	Cabins with balcony:	166
Entered Service:	Jul 2001	Cabins (wheelchair accessible):	2
Length (ft/m):	610.2/186.0	Wheelchair accessibility:	Good
Beam (ft/m):	81.8/24.8	Elevators:	5
Propulsion/Propellers:	diesel/2	Casino (gaming tables):	Yes
Passenger Decks:	7	Swimming Pools:	1
Total Crew:	302	Self-Service Launderette:	Yes
Passengers (lower beds):	388	Library:	Yes
Passenger Space Ratio (lower beds):	72.8	Onboard currency:	US$

THE SHIP. *Silver Whisper*, which Russia's Vladimir Putin chartered in 2003 to host guests for the three-day celebrations of St. Petersburg's 300th anniversary, is the second generation of vessels in the Silversea Cruises fleet. It is sister to *Silver Shadow*, and is slightly larger than the line's first two ships, *Silver Cloud* and *Silver Wind*, but with a more streamlined profile and a large, sleek single funnel.

BERLITZ'S RATINGS		
	Possible	Achieved
Ship	500	403
Accommodation	200	178
Food	400	314
Service	400	318
Entertainment	100	78
Cruise Experience	400	313
OVERALL SCORE 1604 points out of 2000		

The ship has 'all-inclusive' fares, including gratuities (although additional tips are not expected, they are not prohibited). The fares do not include vintage wines, or massage, or other personal services, but they do include many things that are extra-cost items compared with ships of some other cruise lines. Shuttle buses are provided in most ports of call.

The passenger mix includes many nationalities, although the majority of passengers are North American. Children are sometimes seen aboard, but not really welcomed by most passengers.

Silversea Cruises' emphasis on quality has earned it a good reputation, particularly for cuisine, and all the little extras that passengers receive make sailing on this ship an extremely pleasant experience. The surroundings are very comfortable and contemporary without being extravagant, there is open-seating dining with drinks included, cold canapés and hot hors d'oeuvres are served in the bars in the pre-dinner cocktail hour, and there are captain's welcome aboard and farewell cocktail parties.

Aluminum/teak deck furniture is placed by the swimming pool, but the pool itself is quite small. The Humidor, by Davidoff, a 25-seat cigar-smoking lounge, has been styled like an English smoking club. There's a wine bar and computer-learning center.

This ship suits discerning, well-traveled couples who like a small ship, good food, and European-style service in elegant, highly comfortable surroundings. Silversea Cruises promotes its Italian Heritage theme, and its many international passengers respond well to the ambience, food, and the staff, most of whom go out of their way to please.

ACCOMMODATION. This 'all-suites' ship has several price categories. All grades have double vanities in the marble-floored bathrooms, plus tub and separate shower enclosure. Premium Italian bed linen is provided in all grades, as is an eight-pillow menu from soft down to memory foam, 100 percent cotton bathrobes, a fine array of Acqua di Parma bathroom amenities, and personalized stationery. In the Grand, Royal, Rossellini (named after the Italian actress), or Owner's suites, you get unobtrusive service from butlers certified by London's Guild of Professional Butlers.

Vista Suites measure 287 sq ft (27 sq m) and don't have a private balcony. Veranda Suites (really Vista Suites plus a veranda) measure 345 sq ft (32 sq m).

Silver Suites measure 701 sq ft (65 sq m). Owner's Suites each measure 1,208 sq ft (112 sq m). Royal

Suites measure 1,312 sq ft (122 sq m) or 1,352 sq ft (126 sq m). Grand Suites: one measures 1,286 sq ft (119 sq m); the other, including an adjoining suite with interconnecting door, 1,435 sq ft (133 sq m).

There are two adjacent suites for passengers with disabilities (535 and 537), both beside an elevator. They measure a generous 398 sq ft (37 sq m) and are well equipped with an accessible hanging rail, and roll-in bathroom with roll-in shower unit.

DINING. The Restaurant (the main dining room) has open-seating dining in elegant surroundings. Three grand chandeliers provide an upward focal point. Meals can also be served, course-by-course, in your suite, although the balcony tables are rather low for dining outdoors. The cuisine is good throughout the ship, with a choice of formal and informal areas, and Cristofle silverware is provided. 'Standard' table wines are included for lunch and dinner, and there is an extra-cost 'connoisseur list' of premium wines.

As an alternative, the extra-cost Le Champagne offers a more intimate, reservation-only dining spot. Here, passengers can enjoy highly specialized dégustation menus marrying international cuisine with vintage wines selected by Relais & Châteaux sommeliers.

La Terrazza is for self-serve breakfast and lunch buffets. The buffet design and set-up presents flow problems during breakfast, however, and 'active' stations for cooking eggs or pasta to order would help. In the evening, this room serves regional Italian cuisine, and has softer lighting to create a more intimate atmosphere.

Adjacent to the café is a wine bar and a cigar-smoking room. A poolside grill provides a casual alternative daytime dining spot; in the evening it turns into The Grill, with food cooked using the Black Rock (hot stone) method.

ENTERTAINMENT. The Showlounge spans two decks and has a sloping floor; both banquette and individual seating are provided, with good sight lines from almost all seats.

A decent array of cabaret acts does the Silversea circuit, most providing intelligent entertainment; colourful productions are also featured. Musically, more emphasis is placed on classical music ensembles. A band and small groups/ensembles perform in the evenings in The Bar and the Panorama Lounge.

SPA/FITNESS. The Spa at Silversea health/fitness facility, just behind the Observation Lounge, includes a gymnasium, beauty salon, separate saunas and steam rooms for men and women, plus several treatment rooms. A range of body-pampering services is offered to men and women. Massage and other treatments, facials, pedicures, and beauty treatments cost extra.

SILVER WIND
★★★★

AN INCLUSIVE, BUT DATED SMALL SHIP FOR THE SOPHISTICATED AND WELL-TRAVELED

Size:	Small Ship	Passenger/Crew Ratio (lower beds):	1.3
Tonnage:	17,400	Cabins (total):	151
Cruise Line:	Silversea Cruises	Size Range (sq ft/m):	240.0–1,314.0/22.2–122.0
Former Names:	none	Cabins (for one person):	0
Builder:	Visentini/Mariotti (Italy)	Cabins with balcony:	123
Entered Service:	Jan 1995	Cabins (wheelchair accessible):	2
Length (ft/m):	514.4/155.8	Wheelchair accessibility:	Fair
Beam (ft/m):	70.62/21.4	Elevators:	4
Propulsion/Propellers:	diesel (11,700kW)/2	Casino (gaming tables):	Yes
Passenger Decks:	6	Swimming Pools:	1
Total Crew:	222	Self-Service Launderette:	Yes
Passengers (lower beds):	302	Library:	Yes
Passenger Space Ratio (lower beds):	57.6	Onboard currency:	US$

THE SHIP. This ship is best suited to discerning couples, typically over 50, who seek a small ship with fine cuisine, European-style service, and surroundings that border on the elegant. An announcement-free ambience prevails, and there is no pressure or hype, and an enthusiastic staff knows how to pamper you.

Silver Wind has a quite handsome profile, with a sloping stern reminiscent of an Airstream trailer. The size is just about ideal for personalized cruising in an elegant environment. The vertical cake-layer stacking of public rooms aft and the location of accommodation units forward ensures quiet cabins. There is a synthetic turf-covered (not quite equating with luxury) walk-around promenade deck outdoors – which should be upgraded to teak or Bolidt – and a fairly spacious swimming pool and sunbathing deck with teak/aluminum deck furniture. Little touches such as cold towels, water sprays, and fresh fruit provide poolside pampering on hot days.

The ship has had several makeovers (in 2003, 2009, and 2014), which have made it more user-friendly by adding a proper, if small, observation lounge with bookcases and a covered walkway to access it, as well as a relocated and enlarged health spa. The spacious interior is well planned, with elegant decor and fine-quality soft furnishings throughout, accented by brass fittings, fine woods, and creative ceilings. There is an excellent amount of space per passenger, and no hint of a line anywhere. There is a useful

BERLITZ'S RATINGS		
	Possible	Achieved
Ship	500	344
Accommodation	200	158
Food	400	294
Service	400	301
Entertainment	100	67
Cruise Experience	400	307

OVERALL SCORE 1471 points out of 2000

Internet center, a 24-hour library, and a cigar lounge.

Before your cruise, good documentation is provided in a high-quality document wallet and presentation box. Insurance, once included in the fare, now costs extra. All drinks, gratuities, and port taxes are included, and no further tipping is necessary (although not prohibited). Not included, however, are vintage wines, spa treatments, or other personal services. It would be hard not to have a good cruise aboard this ship, albeit at a fairly high price. The company's many international passengers like the ambience, food, service, and the staff, who generally go out of their way to please.

Shuttle buses are provided in most ports of call, and all the little extras that passengers receive aboard this ship makes it an extremely pleasant experience, in surroundings that are comfortable and contemporary without being extravagant, with open seating dining, cold canapés and hot hors d'oeuvres served in the bars in the pre-dinner cocktail hour, a captain's welcome aboard, and a farewell cocktail party.

Silversea Cruises has a defined product based on an Italian Heritage theme. While the past few years sometimes saw the delivery of a tarnished service, this has been recognized, and Silversea Cruises is now polishing the silver again.

The passenger mix includes many nationalities, although most passengers are North American. Children are sometimes seen aboard.

Passenger niggles include the fact that some vibration is evident when bow thrusters or the anchors are used, particularly in the forward-most suites. The self-service launderette is poor and not large enough for longer cruises, when passengers like to wash their own small items. Crew facilities are minimal, so crew turnover is quite high, making it difficult to maintain consistency.

ACCOMMODATION. There are seven price grades. The all-outside suites, 75 percent with fine private teakwood-floor balconies, have convertible queen-to-twin beds, and are nicely fitted out. They include large floor-to-ceiling windows, large walk-in closets, dressing table, writing desk, stocked minibar/refrigerator (no charge), and fresh flowers. The marble floor bathrooms have a tub, fixed shower head, single washbasin, and plenty of high-quality towels. Personalized stationery, an eight-pillow menu from soft down to memory foam, bathrobes, and an array of Acqua di Parma bathroom amenities are provided.

In the Grand, Royal, Rossellini or Owner's suites, you get unobtrusive service from butlers certified by London's Guild of Professional Butlers.

All suites have infotainment systems. However, walk-in closets don't provide much hanging space, particularly for such items as full-length dresses; it would be better for the door to open outward instead of inward. Drawers are poorly positioned, although several other drawers and storage areas are provided in the living area. Although the cabin insulation above and below each suite is good, insulation between them is not – a privacy curtain installed between entry door and sleeping area would be useful – and light from the passageway leaks into the suite, making it hard to achieve a dark room.

The top suite grades have teak balcony furniture, while others don't – but all balconies have teak floors. Suites with balconies on the lowest deck can suffer from sticky salt spray when the ship is moving, so the balconies need lots of cleaning. Each evening, the stewardesses bring canapés to your suite – just right for a light bite with cocktails.

DINING. The main dining room, The Restaurant, provides open-seating dining in elegant surroundings. It has a wood floor, an attractive arched gazebo center, and a wavy ceiling design as its focal point, and is set with fine Limoges china and well-balanced Christofle silverware. Meals are served in an open seating, which means you can eat when you like within the given dining room opening times, and with whom you like.

The cuisine/dining experience is good, with a choice of three dining salons. Standard table wines are included for lunch and dinner, but there is also a 'connoisseur list' of premium wines at extra charge. All meals are prepared as à la carte items, with almost none of the pre-preparation that used to exist. Special orders are also possible.

A specialty dining salon, the intimate 24-seat La Saletta, adjacent to the main dining room, has dégustation menus that include dishes designed for Silversea Cruises by chefs from Relais & Châteaux Gourmands (the cuisine-oriented division of Relais & Châteaux); these are paired with selected wines. Reservations are required, and there's a cover charge.

For more casual dining, La Terrazza offers self-serve breakfast and lunch buffets. In the evening it serves Italian regional dishes and has softer lighting, with both indoors and outdoors seating at teakwood tables and chairs.

There is a 24-hour in-cabin dining service; full course-by-course dinners are available, although the balcony tables in the standard suites are rather low for dining outdoors.

ENTERTAINMENT. The Showlounge is the venue for all entertainment events and some social functions. The room spans two decks and has a sloping floor; both banquette and individual seating are provided, with good sight lines from almost all seats.

Although Silversea Cruises places more emphasis on food than entertainment, what is provided is quite tasteful and not overbearing, as aboard some larger ships. A decent array of cabaret acts does the Silversea circuit. Most of the cabaret acts provide intelligent entertainment.

Also, more emphasis is now placed on classical music ensembles. There is also a band, as well as several small musical units for live music in the evenings in The Bar and the Panorama Lounge.

SPA/FITNESS. Although The Spa at Silversea facility isn't large, it underwent a sea change in 2007 with redesigned, more welcoming, decor, and an updated range of treatments and spa packages for both men and women. Massage and other body-pampering treatments, facials, pedicures, and beauty treatments cost extra.

Facilities include a mixed sauna for men and women, several treatment rooms, and a beauty salon. A separate gymnasium, formerly an observation lounge, located atop the ship, provides sea views.

SIRENA
★★★★

THIS INFORMAL SMALLER SHIP IS GOOD FOR THOSE OF A MATURE-AGE

Size:	Small Ship	Passenger/Crew Ratio (lower beds):	1.8
Tonnage:	30,277	Cabins (total):	344
Cruise Line:	Oceania Cruises	Size Range (sq ft/m):	145.3–968.7/13.5–90.0
Former Names:	*Tahitian Princess, R Four*	Cabins (for one person):	0
Builder:	Chantiers de l'Atlantique (France)	Cabins with balcony:	232
Entered Service:	Nov 1999/Dec 2002	Cabins (wheelchair accessible):	3
Length (ft/m):	593.7/181.0	Wheelchair accessibility:	Good
Beam (ft/m):	83.5/25.5	Elevators:	4
Propulsion/Propellers:	diesel-electric (18,600kW)/2	Casino (gaming tables):	Yes
Passenger Decks:	9	Swimming Pools:	1
Total Crew:	373	Self-Service Launderette:	Yes
Passengers (lower beds):	688	Library:	Yes
Passenger Space Ratio (lower beds):	44.1	Onboard currency:	US$

THE SHIP. This ship is perhaps best suited to mature-age couples, and older solo travelers who like to mingle in a small ship setting with pleasing, sophisticated surroundings, and lifestyle, and are happy with reasonably good entertainment, and fairly decent food and service, all at an affordable price.

Formerly *Ocean Princess* (known as *Tahitian Princess* until 2009), *Sirena* is an ideal size for smaller ports. The value for money is good, and gives you a chance to cruise in comfort aboard a small ship with some attractive dining choices.

The interior decor is easy on the eye, with the traditional touches of a grand hotel, and a throwback to ship decor of the ocean liners of the 1920s and '30s. This includes detailed ceiling cornices, both real and faux wrought-iron staircase railings, leather- and cherry wood-paneled walls, trompe l'oeil ceilings, rich carpeting in hallways with an Oriental rug-look center section, and many other interesting and expensive-looking decorative touches. The staircase in the main, two-deck-high foyer may remind you of the one in the movie *Titanic*.

The public rooms are spread over three decks. The reception hall has a staircase with intricate wrought-iron railings. The Nightclub, with forward-facing views, sits high in the ship and has Polynesian-inspired decor and furniture.

There are plenty of bars – including one in the entrance to each restaurant. Perhaps the nicest can be found in the casino bar/lounge, a beautiful room reminiscent of London's grand hotels and understated gaming clubs. It has an inviting marble fireplace, comfortable sofas, and individual chairs. There is also a large card room, which incorporates an Internet center, with eight stations.

The Library, a grand room designed in the Regency style by the Scottish interior designer John McNeece, has a fireplace, a high, indented trompe l'oeil ceiling, and an excellent selection of books, plus some comfortable wingback chairs with footstools, and sofas you can easily fall asleep on – it's the most relaxing room aboard.

There is no walk-around promenade deck outdoors, though there's a small jogging track around the perimeter of the swimming pool, and port and starboard side decks. There are no wooden decks outdoors; instead, they are covered by a sand-colored rubberized material. There is no sauna. Stairways, although carpeted, are tinny. To keep prices low, the air routing to get to and from your ship is often not the most direct. There is a charge for using machines in the self-service launderette, and you have to obtain tokens from the reception desk – a change machine in the launderette itself would be better. Drinks prices are extremely high.

ACCOMMODATION. There are several different cabin types. The standard interior and outside-view

BERLITZ'S RATINGS

	Possible	Achieved
Ship	500	378
Accommodation	200	145
Food	400	252
Service	400	286
Entertainment	100	71
Cruise Experience	400	287

OVERALL SCORE 1419 points out of 2000

cabins are extremely tight for two persons, particularly for cruises longer than seven days. Cabins have twin beds (convertible to a queen-size one), with good under-bed storage areas, personal safe, vanity desk with large mirror, good closet and drawer space in rich, dark woods, and a bathrobe. The infotainment television system carries a variety of programming, including round-the-clock movies. The bathrooms, which have tiled floors and plain walls, are compact, standard units, and include a shower enclosure with a removable, strong hand-held shower unit, hairdryer, cotton towels, storage shelves for toiletries, and a retractable clothesline.

The suites/cabins with private balconies (66 percent of all accommodation) have partial, and not full, balcony partitions, and sliding glass doors. Due to good design and layout, only 14 cabins on Deck 6 have lifeboat-obstructed views. The balcony floor is covered in thick plastic matting – teak would be nicer.

Mini-Suites are simply larger cabins than the standard cabins, because the sleeping and lounge areas aren't divided. While not overly large, the bathrooms have a good-size tub and ample space for storing toiletries. The living area has a mini-fridge/mini-bar, lounge area with breakfast table, and a balcony with two plastic chairs and a table.

There are 10 Owner's Suites, the most spacious accommodation. These fine, large living spaces are located in the forward-most and aft-most sections; particularly nice are those that overlook the stern, on decks 6, 7, and 8. They have more extensive balconies that can't be overlooked by anyone from the decks above. There is an entrance foyer, living room, bedroom, bathroom with Jacuzzi tub, as well as a small guest bathroom. The bed faces the sea, which can be seen through the floor-to-ceiling windows and sliding glass door.

The accommodation at the stern may suffer from vibration and noise, particularly when the ship is close to full speed, or maneuvering in port.

DINING. Flexibility and choice are what this mid-size ship's dining facilities are all about. There is a choice of four different dining spots, including a self-serve buffet:

The Grand Dining Room has 338 seats (all with armrests), and a large raised central section. There are large windows on three sides, and several prime tables overlooking the stern. The noise level can be high, due to its single deck height ceiling. It is operated in two seatings, with dinner typically at 6pm and 8.15pm, while the other venues have open dining hours.

Red Ginger is a Pan-asian restaurant, with windows along two sides.

The Tuscan Steakhouse is an extra-charge, reservations-required venue featuring a mix of an American-style steak house and a rustic Tuscan eatery, complete with hardwood floor (but contemporary platinum/silver decor). The 98 seats all have armrests, and there are windows along two sides, but few tables for two.

The Lido Café has indoor and outdoor seating (white plastic patio furniture outdoor). It is open for breakfast, lunch, and casual dinners. As the ship's self-serve buffet restaurant, it incorporates a small pizzeria and grill. Salads, a meat-carving station, and a selection of cheeses are provided daily. There is also a Poolside Grill and Bar for fast-food items.

ENTERTAINMENT. The 345-seat Cabaret Lounge has a stage, and circular hardwood dance floor with banquette and individual tub chair seating, and raised sections on port and starboard sides. It is not large, and not really designed for production shows, so cabaret acts form the main focus, with mini-revue style shows presented by a troupe of resident singer/dancers.

A band, small musical units, and solo entertaining pianists provide live music for shows and dancing in the various lounges and bars before and after dinner.

SPA/FITNESS. A gymnasium has ocean-view windows, high-tech muscle-toning equipment and treadmills, steam rooms (no sauna), changing areas for men and women, and a beauty salon with ocean views. The spa is operated by a specialist concession. A lido deck has a swimming pool, and good sunbathing space, while an aft deck has a thalassotherapy pool. A jogging track circles the pool deck, but one deck above. The uppermost outdoors deck includes a golf driving net and shuffleboard court.

SKYSEA GOLDEN ERA
★★★

A FAIRLY MODERN MID-SIZE SHIP WITH COLORFUL DECOR FOR CHINESE FAMILIES

Size:	Mid-size Ship	Passenger/Crew Ratio (lower beds):	2.0
Tonnage:	71,545	Cabins (total):	907
Cruise Line:	SkySea Cruises	Size Range (sq ft/m):	168.9–1,514.5/15.7–140.7
Former Names:	Celebrity Century, Century	Cabins (for one person):	0
Builder:	Meyer Werft (Germany)	Cabins with balcony:	386
Entered Service:	Dec 1995/May 2015	Cabins (wheelchair accessible):	8
Length (ft/m):	807.1/246.0	Wheelchair accessibility:	Good
Beam (ft/m):	105.6/32.2	Elevators:	9
Propulsion/Propellers:	diesel (29,250kW)/2	Casino (gaming tables):	Yes
Passenger Decks:	10	Swimming Pools:	2
Total Crew:	858	Self-Service Launderette:	No
Passengers (lower beds):	1,814	Library:	Yes
Passenger Space Ratio (lower beds):	39.4	Onboard currency:	Renminbi

THE SHIP. *SkySea Golden Era* is aimed at Chinese-speaking families and operates short cruises from Shanghai, China. A niggle is the overload of annoying announcements.

The exterior profile is well balanced, despite a squared-off stern. With a decent passenger/space ratio, there is no sense of crowding. There is a good amount of open deck space, a three-quarter, two-level teakwood promenade deck, and a jogging track atop the ship. The atrium lobby is calm and refreshing and not at all glitzy. Many of the public rooms have high ceilings, providing a sense of space. Anyone who likes gambling will find a large casino tightly packed with slot machines and gaming tables.

In 2015, the ship underwent an extensive makeover that also saw several public rooms renamed. During the refit, a trampoline at sea and mini-golf were added, together with a trendy ice bar, and many other items designed for active Asian cruisers. Children and teens have several playrooms and areas of their own.

ACCOMMODATION. There are numerous different grades of cabins, including family cabins, and ones for couples, with many different configurations for extended groups. All cabins have wood cabinetry, a safe, minibar/refrigerator, and interactive

BERLITZ'S RATINGS		
	Possible	Achieved
Ship	500	311
Accommodation	200	130
Food	400	234
Service	400	234
Entertainment	100	57
Cruise Experience	400	221

OVERALL SCORE 1166 points out of 2000

flat-screen TVs and entertainment systems; beds have duvets. Suites with private balconies have floor-to-ceiling windows.

DINING. A grand staircase connects the upper and lower levels of the two-level Grand Restaurant. Huge windows overlook the stern. The cuisine is almost totally geared to Chinese tastes. Tables are for two to 10.

Other dining options include Murano, a reservations-only specialty restaurant for fine-dining; Silk Harvest (Asian cuisine); Tuscan Grille (Italian cuisine); The Porch (for casual, self-serve eats); and Happy Sea Sushi Bar.

ENTERTAINMENT. The Celebrity Theater is the ship's two-level, 1,000-seat showlounge, with balcony alcoves on two sides. It has a large stage and a split orchestra pit (hydraulic).

SPA/FITNESS. The fitness facility has 9,040 sq ft (840 sq m) of space dedicated to wellbeing and body treatments, all set in a calming environment. It includes a large fitness/exercise area, thalassotherapy pool, and 10 treatment rooms. The spa includes an acupuncture clinic, and a Rasul chamber.

SOVEREIGN
★★+

THIS DATED MID-SIZE SHIP IS GOOD FOR SPANISH-SPEAKING FAMILY CRUISING

Size:	Mid-size Ship	Passenger/Crew Ratio (lower beds):	2.8
Tonnage:	73,192	Cabins (total):	1,153
Cruise Line:	Pullmantur Cruises	Size Range (sq ft/m):	118.4–670.0/11.0–62.2
Former Names:	*Sovereign of the Seas*	Cabins (for one person):	0
Builder:	Chantiers de l'Atlantique (France)	Cabins with balcony:	62
Entered Service:	Jan 1988/Mar 2009	Cabins (wheelchair accessible):	6
Length (ft/m):	879.9/268.2	Wheelchair accessibility:	Fair
Beam (ft/m):	105.9/32.3	Elevators:	13
Propulsion/Propellers:	diesel (21,844kW)/2	Casino (gaming tables):	Yes
Passenger Decks:	11	Swimming Pools:	2
Total Crew:	820	Self-Service Launderette:	No
Passengers (lower beds):	2,306	Library:	Yes
Passenger Space Ratio (lower beds):	31.7	Onboard currency:	Euros

THE SHIP. This ship is best suited to Spanish-speaking families, young couples, and solo travelers seeking a first cruise at an all-inclusive price that even covers drinks. The high-density ship is well run and highly programmed, and is geared to families with children.

Sovereign has a smart profile and nicely rounded lines. The ship has a lounge and bar that is wrapped around the blue funnel and provides a stunning view. Open deck space isn't generous, but there's a wide walk-around polished wood promenade deck. The interior layout is unusual in that most of the public rooms are located aft in a stack, like layers on a cake, with the accommodation situated forward.

There's an array of spacious public rooms, including a library, and card players' room, plus a Monte Carlo Casino. Children and teens are well catered for, and there's a whole team of youth-activity staff, together with a range of rooms for children and teens. The dress code is very casual. All gratuities and port taxes are included in the cruise fare.

ACCOMMODATION. There are several cabin price grades. The price depends on size, grade and location. Some cabins have interconnecting doors, which is useful for families. Thirteen suites on Bridge Deck, the largest of which is the Royal Suite, are reasonably large and nicely furnished, with separate living and sleeping spaces.

BERLITZ'S RATINGS		
	Possible	Achieved
Ship	500	273
Accommodation	200	104
Food	400	232
Service	400	232
Entertainment	100	56
Cruise Experience	400	221
OVERALL SCORE 1088 points out of 2000		

The standard outside-view and interior cabins are very small, although arched windows and colorful soft furnishings give the illusion of more space. Almost all cabins have twin beds that convert to a queen-size or double-bed configuration. There is little closet and drawer space. All cabins have a private bathroom, with shower, toilet, and washbasin.

DINING. El Guardiana and El Duero, two dining rooms off the Centrum (lobby), have tables for four, six, or eight persons but none for two. Both have two seatings, with table wines included in the fare. An additional restaurant offers better menus (à la carte) at an extra cost. For casual meals and snacks, the two-level Buffet Panorama is open almost 24 hours a day, although it is usually congested at peak times.

ENTERTAINMENT. The Broadway Showlounge has both main and balcony levels, with banquette seating. A smaller venue for late-night dancing or chilling out is the Disco Zoom.

SPA/FITNESS. In the Spa del Mar, you'll find a gym with fine ocean views, full of cardiovascular equipment. There's also an aerobics studio, a salon, and sauna, as well as 11 treatment rooms, including one for couples' massages. An outdoor rock-climbing wall, located on the aft of the ship's blue funnel, has several climbing tracks.

STAR BREEZE
★★★★

THIS IS A CONTEMPORARY, HANDY-SIZED SHIP FOR MATURE-AGE CRUISERS

Size:	Boutique Ship	Passenger/Crew Ratio (lower beds):	1.3/1
Tonnage:	9,975	Cabins (total):	106
Cruise Line:	Windstar Cruises	Size Range (sq ft/m):	277.0–575.0/25.7–53.4
Former Names:	*Seabourn Spirit*	Cabins (for one person):	0
Builder:	Seebeckwerft (Germany)	Cabins with balcony:	6
Entered Service:	Nov 1989/Apr 2015	Cabins (wheelchair accessible):	4
Length (ft/m):	439.9/134.1	Wheelchair accessibility:	None
Beam (ft/m):	62.9/19.2	Elevators:	3
Propulsion/Propellers:	diesel (5,355kW)/2	Casino (gaming tables):	Yes
Passenger Decks:	6	Swimming Pools:	1
Total Crew:	160	Self-Service Launderette:	Yes
Passengers (lower beds):	212	Library:	Yes
Passenger Space Ratio (lower beds):	47.0	Onboard currency:	US$

THE SHIP. The intimate *Star Breeze* is best suited to sophisticated and well-traveled couples. The ship's big advantage is being able to cruise where large cruise ships can't, thanks to its ocean-yacht size, creating a sense of intimate camaraderie.

The ship (nicely refurbished after being acquired by Wind Star cruises) has sleek yacht-like exterior styling, and a handsome profile with rounded lines. It is an identical twin to *Star Pride.* An aft water-sports platform and marina can be used in suitably calm warm-water areas (typically only once per cruise). Water-sports facilities include a small, enclosed 'dip' pool, sea kayaks, snorkel equipment, windsurfers, and water-ski boat (their use is complimentary).

Inside, a wide central passageway divides port and starboard accommodation. The inviting public rooms have quiet, non-jarring colors and fine fixtures. They include a main lounge (The Lounge), a nightclub (Compass Rose), a Yacht Club (observation lounge) with bar, a library, card room, shop, computer room, and a mini-casino with gaming tables and a few slot machines.

Star Breeze provides friendly personal service and a relaxing cruise experience. Open-seating dining and use of equipment for water sports are included, as are soft drinks and bottled water (alcoholic drinks cost extra). Gratuities, port charges, and insurance are not included, and internet use also costs extra.

Passenger niggles: there is no walk-around promenade deck outdoors; there is only one dryer in the self-service launderette; and the beverage service staff in the dining room are lacking in training. Overall, this is a premium (not luxury) ship that provides a pleasant, relaxing experience, but the food is decidedly underwhelming, and there are fewer crew members than when the ship was operated by previous owner Seabourn.

BERLITZ'S RATINGS		
	Possible	Achieved
Ship	500	378
Accommodation	200	169
Food	400	287
Service	400	304
Entertainment	100	71
Cruise Experience	400	295
OVERALL SCORE 1504 points out of 2000		

ACCOMMODATION. This is spread over three decks, with nine price categories. The all-outside cabins (called suites in brochure-speak) are comfortably large and nicely equipped with everything one could reasonably need. Electric blackout blinds are provided for the large windows, in addition to curtains. Cabinetry is made of blond woods, with softly rounded edges, and cabin doors are neatly angled away from the passageway.

All suites have a sleeping area, with duvets and fine linens. A separate lounge area has a Bose Wave audio unit, DVD player and flat-screen TV, vanity desk with hairdryer, world atlas, minibar/refrigerator, and 110/220-volt power outlets. A large walk-in closet illuminates automatically when you open the door. Other items include wooden hangers, personal safe, umbrella, and wall-mounted clock and barometer.

Marble-clad bathrooms have one or two washbasins, depending on the accommodation grade, a decent but small bathtub (four suites have a shower enclosure only – no tub), plenty of storage areas, thick cotton towels, terrycloth bathrobe, designer soaps, and L'Occitane personal amenities.

Suites on two out of three accommodation decks have French balconies. These are not balconies in the true sense of the word, but have two doors that open onto a tiny teakwood balcony that is just 10.6ins (27cm) wide. The balconies allow you to have fresh sea air (and salt spray).

Course-by-course in-cabin dining is available during dinner hours, and the cocktail table can be raised to form a dining table. There is 24-hour room service. Four Owner's Suites (King Haakon/King Magnus, each measuring 530 sq ft (49 sq m), and Amundsen/Nansen, each 575 sq ft (53 sq m), and two Classic Suites (King Harald/King Olav), each 400 sq ft (37 sq m), offer fine living spaces.

DINING. The 'AmphorA' Restaurant is a part-marble, part-carpeted dining room with portholes and restful decor. Open-seating dining means that you can dine when you want, with whom you wish. The lighting, however, is far too bright, and the chairs are not very comfortable.

The menus are decent enough, and feature some regional specialties. Overall, the meals are nothing special, and could really do with some improvement. Kosher meals can be provided, if ordered in advance. There is now only a limited selection of fruits and cheeses. The wine list is sound, with prices ranging from moderate to high.

Breakfasts and lunch buffets (plus some à la carte items) are provided at Candles (offering indoor seating at just eight tables) or the adjacent outdoor Veranda Café. At night the indoor/outdoor venue becomes Candles Grill, a reservations-required steakhouse.

The Star Bar provides an above-poolside setting for candlelit dining. It specializes in sizzling steaks and seafood.

ENTERTAINMENT. The Lounge has a sloping floor that provides good sight lines from almost all seats. The shows are of limited scope, as dinner is usually the main event. You can, however, expect to see the occasional cabaret act. Singers also tend to do mini-cabaret performances in The Club, one deck above the showlounge, the gathering place for the late-night set. Non-American passengers should note that almost all entertainment and activities are geared towards North American tastes, despite the increasingly international passenger mix.

SPA/FITNESS. The Spa is a small but well-equipped health center. It has sauna and steam rooms (separate facilities for men and women), an equipment-packed gymnasium – but the ceiling height is low – and a beauty salon.

The spa is staffed and operated by concession Elemis by Steiner. Treatment prices equal those in an expensive land-based spa. The beauty salon has hair-beautifying treatments and conditioning.

STAR CLIPPER
★★★+

THIS SHIP OFFERS A REAL TALL-SHIP EXPERIENCE THAT PUTS WIND IN YOUR SAILS

Size:	Boutique Ship	Passenger/Crew Ratio (lower beds):	2.3/1
Tonnage:	2,298	Cabins (total):	85
Cruise Line:	Star Clippers	Size Range (sq ft/m):	95.0–225.0/8.8–21.0
Former Names:	none	Cabins (for one person):	0
Builder: Scheepswerven van Langerbrugge (Belgium)		Cabins with balcony:	0
Entered Service:	May 1992	Cabins (wheelchair accessible):	0
Length (ft/m):	378.9/115.5	Wheelchair accessibility:	None
Beam (ft/m):	49.2/15.0	Elevators:	0
Propulsion/Propellers:	sail power + diesel (1,030kW)/1	Casino (gaming tables):	No
		Swimming Pools:	2
Passenger Decks:	4	Self-Service Launderette:	No
Total Crew:	72	Library:	Yes
Passengers (lower beds):	170	Onboard currency:	Euros
Passenger Space Ratio (lower beds):	13.5		

THE SHIP. This tall sail-cruise ship suits couples and solo travelers who would probably never even consider a 'normal' cruise ship, but who enjoy sailing and the thrill of ocean and wind, with everything packaged to include accommodation, decent food, like-minded companions, interesting destinations, and an almost unstructured lifestyle.

Star Clipper is one of a pair of almost identical sailing ships (sister ship to *Star Flyer*, the first clipper sailing ship to be built for 140 years and the first commercial sailing vessel to cross the North Atlantic in 90 years). It is, first and foremost, a sailing vessel with cruise accommodation that evokes memories of the 19th-century clipper sailing ships. This is an accurate four-mast, barquentine-rigged schooner with graceful lines, a finely shaped hull and masts that are 206ft (63m) tall. Some amenities found aboard large cruise vessels are provided, such as air conditioning, cashless cruising, occasional live music, a small shop, and two pools to 'dip' in.

Breathtaking when under full sail, the ship displays excellent sea manners – heeling is kept to a very comfortable 6 degrees. This working sailing ship relies on the wind about 80 percent of the time. During a typical cruise, you may be able to climb the main mast to a platform 75ft (23m) above the sea and help with the ropes and sails at appropriate times – this could be an unnerving experience, if you're not used to heights, but it is exhilarating when the ship is moving under sail. One really neat chill-out pleasure is to

BERLITZ'S RATINGS		
	Possible	Achieved
Ship	500	363
Accommodation	200	134
Food	400	245
Service	400	271
Entertainment	100	78
Cruise Experience	400	281
OVERALL SCORE 1372 points out of 2000		

lie in the netting at the front of the ship's bows, watching the bow wake as it streams along the ship's sides.

A diesel engine provides the propulsion when the ship is not under sail (in poor wind conditions), and two generators supply electrical power and help desalinate 40 or so tons of seawater each day for shipboard needs. The crew performs almost every task, including hoisting, trimming, winching, and repairing the sails, helped by electric winches. Water-sports facilities include a water-ski boat, sunfish, scuba and snorkel equipment, and eight Zodiac inflatables. Sports directors provide basic dive instruction for a fee.

Inside the vessel, classic Edwardian nautical decor throughout is clean, warm, intimate, and inviting. The paneled library has a fireplace and comfortable chairs. There are no lines and no hassle. Sailing a Square Rigger and other nautical classes are a part of every cruise, as is stargazing at night.

Depending on the itinerary and region, passengers may gather for 'captain's storytime,' normally held on an open deck area adjacent to the bridge, or in the bar – which, incidentally, has a collection of single malt whiskies. The captain may explain sailing maneuvers when changing the rigging or directing the ship as it sails into port, and note the important events of the day.

The sail-ship promotes total informality and provides a carefree sailing experience in an unstructured and relaxed setting at a fair price. Take minimal clothing: short-sleeved shirts and shorts for men, shorts and tops for women are the order of the day (smart casual at night). No jackets, ties, high-heeled shoes, cocktail dresses, or formal wear are needed. Take flat shoes because there are lots of ropes and sailing rig to negotiate on deck, not to mention the high thresholds to climb over and steps to negotiate – this is, after all a tall ship, not a cruise ship. The deck crew consists of real sailors, brought up with yachts and tall ships – most wouldn't set foot aboard a 'normal' cruise ship.

The steps of the internal stairways are short and steep, as in all sailing vessels, and so this ship cannot be recommended for anyone with walking disabilities. Also, there is no doctor on board, although there is a nurse.

For yachting enthusiasts, sailing aboard *Star Clipper* is like finding themselves in heaven, as there is plenty of sailing during a typical one-week cruise. The whole experience evokes the feeling of sailing aboard some famous private yacht, and even the most jaded traveler should enjoy the feel of the wind and sea close at hand. Just don't expect fine food to go with what is decidedly a fine sailing experience – which is what *Star Clipper* is all about. Note that a 12.5 percent gratuity is added to all beverage purchases.

For the nautically minded, the sailing rig consists of 16 manually furled sails, measuring a billowing 36,221 sq ft (3,365 sq m). These include: fore staysail, inner jib, outer jib, flying jib, fore course, lower topsail, upper topsail, lower topgallant, upper topgallant, main staysail, upper main staysail, mizzen staysail, main fisherman, jigger staysail, mizzen fisherman, and spanker. The square sails are furled electronically by custom-made winches.

ACCOMMODATION. There are six cabin price grades plus one Owner's Suite. Generally, the higher the deck, the more expensive a cabin. The cabins are quite well equipped and comfortable, with rosewood-trimmed cabinetry and wall-to-wall carpeting, two-channel audio, color TV and DVD player, personal safe, and full-length mirrors. The bathrooms are very compact but practical units, and have gray marble tiling, glazed rosewood toiletries cabinet and paneling, some under-shelf storage space, washbasin, shower stall, and toilet. There is no 'lip' to prevent water from the shower from moving over the bathroom floor.

The cabins in the lowest price grade are interior cabins with upper and lower berths, and not two lower beds – so someone will need to be agile to climb a ladder to the upper berth. A handful of cabins have a third, upper Pullman-style berth – good for families with children, but closet and drawer space will be at a premium with three persons in a cabin. Larger luggage can be stored under the bed.

There is no cabin food or beverage service.

The deluxe cabins (called 'deck cabins') are larger, with additional features including a full-size Jacuzzi tub or corner tub, flat-screen television and DVD player, and minibar/refrigerator. However, these cabins are subject to noise pollution from the same-deck Tropical Bar's music at night (typically until midnight), from the electric winches during sail maneuvers, and from noisy walkabout exercisers in the early morning.

DINING. The dining room is cozy and quite attractive. There are self-serve buffet breakfasts and lunches, together with a mix of buffet and à la carte dinners, generally with a choice of three entrées (mains), in an open-seating environment.

The seating, mostly at tables of six, adjacent to a porthole or inboard, makes it difficult for waiters to serve properly – food is passed along the tables that occupy a porthole position. However, you can dine with whomever you wish, and this is supposed to be a casual experience, after all.

While cuisine aboard the ship is perhaps less than the advertised 'gourmet' excellence as far as presentation and choice are concerned, it is fairly creative – and there's plenty of it. Also, one has to take into account the small galley. Passenger niggles include repetitious breakfasts and lunchtime salad items, because lack of space prevents more choices. But most passengers are happy with the dinners, which tend to be good, although there is a lack of green vegetables. There's a good choice of bread rolls, pastry items, and fruit.

Tea and coffee is available 24 hours a day in the lounge – mugs, tea cups, and saucers are provided. There is no cabin food service.

ENTERTAINMENT. There are no shows as such, except for an occasional local folklore show from ashore, nor are any expected by passengers aboard a tall ship such as this. Live music is typically provided by a solo lounge pianist/singer. Otherwise, dinner is the main evening event, as well as 'captain's storytime,' recapping the day's events, and conversation with fellow passengers.

During the day, when the ship is sailing, passengers can learn about the sails and their repair, and the captain or chief officer will give briefings as the sails are being furled and unfurled. The closest this tall ship comes to any kind of 'show' is perhaps one provided by members of the crew, plus a few traditional sea shanties.

SPA/FITNESS. There are no fitness facilities, or beauty salon, although a masseuse provides Oriental massage. For recreation, the ship does have a program for water sports. Facilities include kayaks, a water-ski boat, sunfish, scuba and snorkel equipment, and eight Zodiac inflatable craft. The use of scuba facilities costs extra.

STAR FLYER
★★★+

THIS PROPER SAILING SHIP PROVIDES AN ANTIDOTE TO 'NORMAL' CRUISE SHIPS

Size:	Boutique Ship	Passenger/Crew Ratio (lower beds):	2.3/1
Tonnage:	2,298	Cabins (total):	85
Cruise Line:	Star Clippers	Size Range (sq ft/m):	95.0–225.9/8.8–21.0
Former Names:	none	Cabins (for one person):	0
Builder: Sheepswerven van Langerbrugge (Belgium)		Cabins with balcony:	0
Entered Service:	Jul 1991	Cabins (wheelchair accessible):	0
Length (ft/m):	378.9/115.5	Wheelchair accessibility:	None
Beam (ft/m):	49.2/15.0	Elevators:	0
Propulsion/Propellers:	sail power + diesel	Casino (gaming tables):	No
	(1,030kW)/1	Swimming Pools:	2
Passenger Decks:	4	Self-Service Launderette:	No
Total Crew:	72	Library:	Yes
Passengers (lower beds):	170	Onboard currency:	Euros
Passenger Space Ratio (lower beds):	13.5		

THE SHIP. The first clipper sailing ship to be built for 140 years, *Star Flyer* became the first commercial sailing vessel in more than 90 years to cross the North Atlantic. It suits those who would never consider a 'normal' cruise ship.

Star Flyer is one of a pair of almost identical tall ships – its sister ship is *Star Clipper*. It is, first and foremost, a sailing vessel with cruise accommodation that evokes memories of the 19th-century clipper sailing ships. This is an accurate four-mast, barquentine-rigged schooner with graceful lines, a finely shaped hull, masts that are 206ft (63m) tall, and 16 manually furled sails totaling 36,221 sq ft (3,364 sq m). Some amenities found aboard large cruise vessels are provided, such as air conditioning, cashless cruising, live music, a small shop, and two pools to 'dip' in.

Breathtaking when under full sail, the ship displays excellent sea manners and relies on the wind about 80 percent of the time, and heeling is kept to a very comfortable 6 degrees.

During the cruise, you'll be able to climb the main mast to a platform 75ft (23m) above the sea and help with the ropes and sails at appropriate times. One really neat chill-out pleasure is to lie in the netting at the front of the ship's bows.

A diesel engine provides propulsion when the ship is not under sail (in poor wind conditions), and two generators supply electrical power and help desalinate 40 or so tons of seawater each day for shipboard

BERLITZ'S RATINGS		
	Possible	Achieved
Ship	500	363
Accommodation	200	134
Food	400	249
Service	400	271
Entertainment	100	78
Cruise Experience	400	287
OVERALL SCORE 1382 points out of 2000		

needs. Engine-room visits may be offered for anyone interested. Water-sports facilities include a water-ski boat, sunfish, scuba and snorkel equipment, and eight Zodiac inflatables. Sports directors provide basic dive instruction for a fee.

Inside, classic Edwardian nautical decor throughout is clean, warm, intimate, and inviting. The paneled library has a fireplace and comfortable chairs. There are no lines and no hassle. Sailing a Square Rigger and other nautical classes are a part of every cruise, as is stargazing at night.

Depending on the itinerary and region, passengers may gather for 'captain's storytime,' normally held on an open deck area adjacent to the bridge, or in the bar – which, incidentally, has a collection of single malt whiskies. The captain may explain sailing maneuvers when changing the rigging or directing the ship as it sails into port, and notes the important events of the day.

The sail-ship promotes total informality and provides a carefree sailing experience in a totally unstructured and relaxed setting at a reasonable price. Take minimal clothing: short-sleeved shirts and shorts for men, shorts and tops for women are the order of the day (smart casual at night). No jackets, ties, high-heeled shoes, cocktail dresses, or formal wear are needed. Take flat shoes because there are lots of ropes and sailing rig to negotiate on deck, not to mention the high thresholds to climb over and steps to negotiate – this is, after all a tall ship, not a cruise ship.

The steps of the internal stairways are short and steep, as in all sailing vessels, and so this ship cannot be recommended for anyone with walking disabilities. Also, there is no doctor on board, although there is a nurse.

For yachting enthusiasts, sailing aboard *Star Flyer* is like finding themselves in heaven, as there is plenty of sailing during a typical one-week cruise. The whole experience evokes the feeling of sailing aboard some famous private yacht, and even the most jaded passenger should enjoy the feel of the wind and sea close at hand. Just don't expect fine food to go with what is decidedly a fine sailing experience – which is what *Star Flyer* is all about. Note that a 12.5 percent gratuity is added to all beverage purchases.

For the nautically minded, the sailing rig consists of 16 manually furled sails: fore staysail, inner jib, outer jib, flying jib, fore course, lower topsail, upper topsail, lower topgallant, upper topgallant, main staysail, upper main staysail, mizzen staysail, main fisherman, jigger staysail, mizzen fisherman, and spanker. The square sails are furled electronically by custom-made winches.

ACCOMMODATION. There are six cabin price grades plus one Owner's Suite. Generally, the higher the deck, the more expensive a cabin. The cabins are quite well equipped and comfortable; they have rosewood-trimmed cabinetry and wall-to-wall carpeting, two-channel audio, color TV and DVD player, personal safe, and full-length mirrors. The bathrooms are very compact but practical units, and have gray marble tiling, glazed rosewood toiletries cabinet and paneling, some under-shelf storage space, washbasin, shower stall, and toilet. There is no 'lip' to prevent water from the shower from moving over the bathroom floor.

Individual European 100 percent individual cotton duvets are provided. There is no cabin food or beverage service.

The deluxe cabins (called 'deck cabins') are larger, and additional features include a full-size Jacuzzi tub or corner tub, flat-screen television and DVD player, and minibar/refrigerator. However, these cabins are subject to noise pollution from the same-deck Tropical Bar's music at night (typically until midnight), from the electric winches during sail maneuvers, and from noisy walkabout exercisers in the early morning.

The cabins in the lowest price grade are interior cabins with upper and lower berths, and not two lower beds – so someone will need to be agile to climb a ladder to the upper berth. A handful of cabins have a third,

upper Pullman-style berth, which is good for families with children, although closet and drawer space will be at a premium with three people in a cabin.

DINING. The dining room is quite attractive, and has lots of wood and brass accenting and nautical decor. There are self-serve buffet breakfasts and lunches, together with a mix of buffet meals and dining à la carte, generally with a choice of three entrées (mains), in an open-seating environment.

The seating is mostly at tables of six, and either adjacent to a porthole or inboard; it makes it difficult for waiters to serve properly – so the food is passed along the tables that occupy a porthole position. However, you can dine with whomever you wish, and this is supposed to be a casual experience, after all.

While cuisine aboard the ship is perhaps less than the advertised 'gourmet' excellence as far as presentation and choice are concerned, it is fairly creative – and there's plenty of it. Also, one has to take into account the small galley. Passenger niggles include repetitious breakfasts and lunchtime salad items, because lack of space prevents more choices. But most passengers are happy with the dinners, which tend to be good, although there is a lack of green vegetables. There's a good choice of bread rolls, pastry items, and fruit.

Tea and coffee is available 24 hours a day in the lounge – mugs, tea cups, and saucers are provided. There is no cabin food service.

ENTERTAINMENT. There are no shows as such, except for an occasional local folklore show from ashore, nor are any expected by passengers aboard a tall ship such as this. Live music is typically provided by a solo lounge pianist/singer. Otherwise, dinner is the main evening event, as well as 'captain's storytime,' recapping the day's events, and conversation with fellow passengers.

During the day, when the ship is sailing, passengers can learn about the sails and their repair, and the captain or chief officer will give briefings, as the sails are being furled and unfurled. The closest this tall ship comes to any kind of 'show' is perhaps one provided by members of the crew, plus a few traditional sea shanties.

SPA/FITNESS. There are no fitness facilities, or beauty salon, although a masseuse provides Oriental massage. For recreation, the ship has a water-sports program. Facilities include kayaks, a water-ski boat, scuba and snorkel equipment, and eight Zodiac inflatable craft. The use of scuba facilities costs extra.

STAR LEGEND
★★★★

A POCKET-SIZED, COZY, AND ELEGANT SHIP FOR MATURE-AGE CRUISERS

Size:	Boutique Ship
Tonnage:	9,961
Cruise Line:	Windstar Cruises
Former Names:	Seabourn Legend, Queen Odyssey, Royal Viking Queen
Builder:	Schichau Seebeckwerft (Germany)
Entered Service:	Mar 1992/May 2015
Length (ft/m):	442.9/135.0
Beam (ft/m):	62.9/19.2
Propulsion/Propellers:	diesel (7,280kW)/2
Passenger Decks:	6
Total Crew:	160
Passengers (lower beds):	212
Passenger Space Ratio (lower beds):	46.9

Passenger/Crew Ratio (lower beds):	1.3/1
Cabins (total):	106
Size Range (sq ft/m):	277.0–575.8/25.7–53.5
Cabins (for one person):	0
Cabins with balcony:	6
Cabins (wheelchair accessible):	4
Wheelchair accessibility:	None
Elevators:	3
Casino (gaming tables):	Yes
Swimming Pools:	1
Self-Service Launderette:	Yes
Library:	Yes
Onboard currency:	US$

THE SHIP. *Star Legend* can cruise to places where large cruise ships can't, thanks to its ocean-yacht size. For a grand, boutique-size ship vacation in premium surroundings, with just over 100 other couples as neighbors. it's hard to beat. It is best suited to sophisticated, well-traveled couples who want to relax.

Star Legend is a contemporary gem of a ship with a handsome profile, almost identical in looks and size to sisters *Star Breeze* and *Star Pride*, but younger and built to a higher standard, with streamline 'decorator' bars made by Mercedes-Benz located along the side of the upper superstructure and a slightly different swept-over funnel design.

An aft water-sports platform and marina can be used in suitably calm warm-water areas. Watersports facilities include a small, enclosed 'dip' pool, sea kayaks, snorkel equipment, windsurfers, and water-ski boat (use of water-sports equipment is complimentary).

Inside, a wide central passageway divides port and starboard side accommodation. High-quality interior fixtures, fittings, and fabrics are combined in its sumptuous public areas, including a main lounge, observation lounge, nightclub, screening room, library, reception desk, shop and mini-casino (with tables and a few slot machines). There is no glitz anywhere, and the dress code is always relaxed.

Passenger gripes: There is no walk-around promenade deck. Gratuities are not included, and Internet

BERLITZ'S RATINGS

	Possible	Achieved
Ship	500	386
Accommodation	200	171
Food	400	287
Service	400	305
Entertainment	100	71
Cruise Experience	400	297

OVERALL SCORE 1517 points out of 2000

use costs extra. Almost all entertainment and activities are geared towards American tastes. Overall, this is a premium ship that provides a relaxing experience, but don't expect any 'wow' factor from the food – it's disappointing and lacks flair. Also, there are fewer crew members than when operated by the previous owner.

ACCOMMODATION. This is spread over three decks, and there are several price categories. All suites are comfortably sized and comprehensively equipped. They are, for example, larger than those aboard the smaller *SeaDream I* and *SeaDream II*, but then the ship is also larger, with almost twice as many passengers. All suites have a sleeping area with premium bedding, duvets and high-quality linens, a large walk-in closet that illuminates automatically when you open the door, digital safe, umbrella, wall-mounted clock and barometer, and 110/220-volt power outlets.

Marble-clad bathrooms have one or two washbasins, depending on accommodation grade, a decent but not full-size tub (four suites have a shower enclosure only – no bathtub), plenty of storage areas, thick cotton towels, plush terrycloth bathrobe, and designer soaps.

In 2001, 36 French balconies were added to suites on two out of three accommodation decks. These are not balconies, but have two doors that open wide onto a tiny teakwood 'balcony' that is just 10.6ins (27cm) deep – just enough for your toes. The balconies do allow you to have fresh sea air, however, together with some salt spray.

The largest accommodation are four Owner's Suites (Ibsen/Grieg, each 530 sq ft/49 sq m, and Eriksson/Heyerdahl, each 575 sq ft/53 sq m), and two Classic Suites (Queen Maud/Queen Sonja, each 400 sq ft/37 sq m) – these are superb, private living spaces. There is a fully secluded, forward- or side-facing balcony, with sun lounge chairs and wooden drinks table (Ibsen and Grieg don't have balconies).

DINING. 'AmphorA' Restaurant is a part-marble, part-carpeted dining room that has portholes and elegant decor. Open-seating dining means that you can dine when you want, with whom you wish.

The menus are creative and quite well balanced, with a decent selection of dishes, including some regional specialties. The food is nicely presented, with some items cooked to order, but it's not life-changing. The selection of fruit and cheese is small. The wine list is quite sound, with prices ranging from moderate to high. Overall, while the accommodation is good, the meals are disappointing, and experienced staff members are lacking.

Breakfasts and lunch buffets (plus some à la carte items) are provided in Candles (which has indoor seating at just eight tables) or the adjacent outdoor Veranda Café. At night the indoor/outdoor venue becomes Candles Grill, a reservations-required steakhouse.

Additionally, the Star Bar provides an above-poolside setting for candlelit dining (steaks and seafood).

ENTERTAINMENT. The Lounge is the venue for shows, cabaret acts, lectures, and most social functions. It has a sloping floor that provides good sight lines. This is a small, premium ship, so shows are small scale.

SPA/FITNESS. The Spa is a small but well-equipped health spa/fitness center, located just aft of the navigation bridge. It provides sauna and steam rooms with separate facilities for men and women, an integral changing room, and a beauty salon.

STAR PRIDE
★★★★

AN INTIMATE, INCLUSIVE SHIP FOR STYLISH, INFORMAL CRUISING

Size:	Boutique Ship	Passenger/Crew Ratio (lower beds):	1.3
Tonnage:	9,975	Cabins (total):	106
Cruise Line:	Windstar Cruises	Size Range (sq ft/m):	277.0–575.0/25.7–53.4
Former Names:	*Seabourn Pride*	Cabins (for one person):	0
Builder:	Seebeckwerft (Germany)	Cabins with balcony:	6
Entered Service:	Dec 1988/May 2014	Cabins (wheelchair accessible):	4
Length (ft/m):	439.9/134.1	Wheelchair accessibility:	None
Beam (ft/m):	62.9/19.2	Elevators:	3
Propulsion/Propellers:	diesel (5,355kW)/2	Casino (gaming tables):	Yes
Passenger Decks:	6	Swimming Pools:	1
Total Crew:	160	Self-Service Launderette:	Yes
Passengers (lower beds):	212	Library:	Yes
Passenger Space Ratio (lower beds):	47.09	Onboard currency:	US$

THE SHIP. *Star Pride* is best for sophisticated, well-traveled couples seeking an informal small ship experience. The ship's big advantage is being able to cruise where larger ships can't, thanks to its handy ocean-yacht size. You sail with only 210 others, creating a sense of intimate camaraderie.

Pleasantly appointed, the ship has sleek exterior styling, a handsome profile with swept-back, rounded lines, and is an identical twin to *Star Breeze*. It has two fine mahogany water taxis for use as shore tenders. An aft water sports platform and marina can be used in suitably calm warm-water areas. Water sports facilities include a small, enclosed 'dip' pool, sea kayaks, snorkel equipment, windsurfers, water-ski boat, and Zodiac inflatable boats.

A wide central passageway divides the port and starboard accommodation. Inviting, warm public areas have high-quality interior fixtures and fittings. For a small ship, there's a wide range of public rooms, all updated by Windstar Cruises. These include a main lounge (for shows), a nightclub, and The Yacht Club (observation lounge-cum-lifestyle lounge and coffee bar). There is a library, shop, small screening room, and a mini-casino with roulette and blackjack tables and a few slot machines.

The ship was acquired by Xanterra Parks & Resorts, parent company of Windstar Cruises, in May 2014. Two sister ships *Star Breeze and Star Legend* joined the fleet in 2015.

BERLITZ'S RATINGS

	Possible	Achieved
Ship	500	378
Accommodation	200	169
Food	400	287
Service	400	303
Entertainment	100	71
Cruise Experience	400	295

OVERALL SCORE 1503 points out of 2000

Passenger niggles? There is no outdoor walk-around deck. Gratuities are not included, and internet use costs extra. Overall, this is a premium (not luxury) ship that provides a relaxing environment – just don't expect great food. There are also far fewer crew members than when operated by the previous owner.

ACCOMMODATION. This is spread over three decks, with several different price categories. The all-outside cabins (called suites in brochure-speak) are comfortably large and beautifully equipped with everything one could reasonably need. Electric blackout blinds are provided for the large windows in addition to curtains, and beds have premium bedding, duvets, and fine drapes. The cabinetry is made of blond woods and has softly rounded edges, and cabin doors are neatly angled away from the passageway.

A large walk-in closet is illuminated automatically when you open the door; wooden hangers, personal safe, umbrella, wall-mounted clock and barometer, and 110/220-volt power outlets are also provided. The decor is contemporary, but warm, in blues and beiges.

Marble-clad bathrooms have one or two washbasins, depending on the accommodation grade, a decent, but not full-size, bathtub (four suites have a shower enclosure only – no tub), plenty of storage areas, cotton towels, bathrobe, and personal amenities.

On two out of three accommodation decks, some 36 suites have French balconies. These are not balconies in the true sense of the word, but they do have two doors that open wide onto a tiny teakwood balcony that is 10.6ins (27cm) wide (just enough for your feet). The balconies allow you to have fresh sea air, and salt spray.

Four Owner's Suites, each measuring between 530 sq ft (49 sq m) and 575 sq ft (53 sq m), and two Classic Suites, each 400 sq ft (37 sq m), offer superb, private living spaces. Each is named after a Windstar destination (Bora-Bora Suite, for example). Each has a walk-in closet, second closet, full bathroom plus a guest toilet with washbasin. There is a fully secluded forward- or side-facing balcony, with sunloungers and drinks table.

DINING. 'AmphorA' Restaurant, the main dining room, has portholes and restful decor. Open-seating dining means that you can dine when you want, with whom you wish.

The menus sound appealing, with a selection of contemporary cuisine and regional foods, but there's little taste and a lack of green vegetables – overall, it's underwhelming. Fruit and cheese selections are poor, as are salads. The wine list is fairly decent, with prices ranging from moderate to high.

Alternative dining can be found at Candles (indoor seating at just eight tables) or the adjacent outdoor Veranda Café. At night the indoor/outdoor venue becomes Candles Grill, a reservations-required steakhouse.

The Star Bar provides an above-poolside setting for candlelit dining. It specializes in sizzling steaks and seafood.

ENTERTAINMENT. The Lounge has a sloping floor that provides good sight lines from almost all seats. Small-scale shows, and the occasional cabaret act, are presented here. Non-American passengers should note that almost all entertainment and activities are geared towards North American tastes.

SPA/FITNESS. The Spa is a small but well-equipped health spa, with a small fitness room. It has sauna and steam rooms (separate facilities for men and women), an equipment-packed gymnasium (with a low ceiling) and a beauty salon.

The spa is staffed and operated by concession Elemis by Steiner. Treatment prices equal those in an expensive land-based spa. The beauty salon has hair-beautifying treatments and conditioning. In the gymnasium, personal training sessions and some classes may be at extra cost.

STAR PRINCESS
★★★+

THIS LARGE, MULTIPLE-CHOICE, RESORT SHIP IS GOOD FOR THE WHOLE FAMILY

Size:	Large Resort Ship	Passenger/Crew Ratio (lower beds):	2.3/1
Tonnage:	108,977	Cabins (total):	1,301
Cruise Line:	Princess Cruises	Size Range (sq ft/m):	161.4–1,314.0/15.0–122.0
Former Names:	none	Cabins (for one person):	0
Builder:	Fincantieri (Italy)	Cabins with balcony:	711
Entered Service:	Feb 2002	Cabins (wheelchair accessible):	28
Length (ft/m):	951.4/290.0	Wheelchair accessibility:	Best
Beam (ft/m):	118.1/36.0	Elevators:	14
Propulsion/Propellers:	diesel-electric (42,000kW)/2	Casino (gaming tables):	Yes
Passenger Decks:	13	Swimming Pools:	3
Total Crew:	1,200	Self-Service Launderette:	Yes
Passengers (lower beds):	2,602	Library:	Yes
Passenger Space Ratio (lower beds):	41.8	Onboard currency:	US$

THE SHIP. *Star Princess* is a grand resort playground, with many choices and 'small' rooms to enjoy. It is extremely well designed and competitively priced. The odds are that you'll have a fine time, in a controlled, well-packaged way.

The design for this large cruise ship, whose close sister ships are *Golden Princess* and *Grand Princess* (and slightly larger half-sister *Caribbean Princess*), presents a bold, forthright profile, with a racy 'spoiler' effect at its galleon-like transom stern (the 'spoiler' acts as a stern observation lounge by day, and a stunning disco by night).

There is a good sheltered faux teak promenade deck – it's actually painted steel – which almost wraps around (three times round is equal to 1 mile/2km) and a walkway, which goes right to the ship's enclosed bow. The outdoor pools have beach-like surroundings. One lap pool has a pumped 'current' to swim against.

Unlike on the outside decks, there is plenty of space inside the ship – but there are also plenty of passengers – and a wide array of public rooms, with many 'intimate' (this being a relative word) spaces and places to play. The passenger flow has been well thought-out, and works well. The decor is attractive, with lots of muted earth tones.

Four areas center on swimming pools, one of which is two decks high and is covered by a glass dome, itself an extension of the funnel housing.

The Grand Casino has more than 260 slot machines; there are blackjack, craps, and roulette ta-

BERLITZ'S RATINGS		
	Possible	Achieved
Ship	500	350
Accommodation	200	139
Food	400	247
Service	400	284
Entertainment	100	75
Cruise Experience	400	284

OVERALL SCORE 1379 points out of 2000

bles, plus other games. But the highlight could well be the specially linked slot machines that provide a combined payout.

Other facilities include a decent library/computer room, and a separate card room. Ship lovers should enjoy the wood-paneled Wheelhouse Bar, finely decorated with memorabilia and ship models tracing part of the history of sister company P&O; this ship highlights the 1950-built cargo ship *Ganges*. A sports bar, Shooters, has two billiard tables, as well as eight television screens.

The dress code is formal or 'smart casual,' the latter interpreted by many as jeans and trainers. Daily per-person gratuities are automatically added to your account, for both adults and children. To have these charges adjusted, you'll need to go to the reception desk.

Passenger niggles include the user-unfriendly automated telephone system, the small cabin towels, and having to pay extra for items such as ice cream; also, the charge (coins needed) for the washers and dryers in self-service launderettes.

Overall, however, Princess Cruises delivers a consistently fine, comfortable, well-packaged product, always with a good degree of style, at a competitive price.

ACCOMMODATION. There are six principal types of cabins and configurations: (a) grand suite, (b) suite, (c) mini-suite, (d) outside-view double cabin with balcony, (e) outside-view double cabin, and (f) interior double cabin. These come in many different price categories, and the choice is bewildering. Note that the interior (no-view) cabins and standard ocean-view cabins are extremely small. Some cabins can accommodate a third and fourth person in upper berths, although the lower beds cannot then be pushed together to make a queen-size bed.

All accommodation comes with morning and evening turndown service (with chocolates on pillows each night), bathrobes on request, and toiletry kits (larger for suite/mini-suite occupants). A hairdryer is provided in all cabins, sensibly located at the vanity desk unit in the living area. All bathrooms have tiled floors, and there is a decent amount of open shelf storage space for toiletries, although the plain beige decor is very basic and unappealing. Princess Cruises typically carries CNN, CNBC, ESPN, and TNT, when available, on the in-cabin television system.

Lifeboats obstruct most outside-view cabins on Emerald Deck. Your name is placed outside your suite or cabin in a documents holder – making it simple for delivery service personnel but privacy-insensitive. There is 24-hour room service, though some items on the menu are not available during early morning hours.

Almost all balcony suites and cabins can be overlooked both from the navigation bridge wing, as well as from the port and starboard sections of the ship's disco – located high above the ship at the stern. Cabins with balconies on Dolphin, Caribe, and Baja decks are also overlooked by passengers on balconies on the deck above, and are hence not at all private. However, perhaps the least-desirable balcony cabins are eight ones located forward on Emerald Deck – the balconies don't extend to the side of the ship and can be passed by walkers and gawkers on the adjacent Upper Promenade walkway, so occupants need to keep their curtains closed most of the time. Also, passengers in some the most expensive suites with balconies at the stern may experience vibration during certain ship maneuvers.

DINING. For formal meals there are three principal dining rooms: Amalfi, with 504 seats; Capri, with 486 seats; and Portofino, with 486 seats. Seating is assigned according to your cabin location. There are two seatings in Amalfi, while Capri and Portofino offer 'Anytime Dining' – so you choose when and with whom you want to eat. All three are split into multi-tier sections in a non-symmetrical design that breaks them into small sections. Each dining room has its own galley.

While four elevators go to Fiesta Deck, where the Amalfi and Portofino restaurants are located, only two elevators go to Plaza Deck 5, where the Capri Restaurant is located; this can cause long wait problems at peak times, particularly for anyone in a wheelchair.

Specially designed dinnerware (by Dudson of England), high-quality Frette Egyptian cotton table linens, and silverware by Hepp of Germany are used in the main dining rooms. Note that 15 percent is automatically added to all beverage bills, including wines.

Although portions are generous, the food and its presentation are disappointing, and quite standardized. Fish is often disguised by a crumb or batter coating, the choice of fresh green vegetables is limited, few garnishes are used, and cheese is already sliced and diced. But, this is big-ship mass catering, with all its attendant standardization. Pasta dishes are acceptable (though voluminous), typically served by section headwaiters, who may also make 'something special just for you' – in search of favorable comments and gratuities. If you like desserts, order a sundae at dinner (most other items are just so-so).

There are two extra-charge restaurants: Sabatini's and Tequila's, both open for lunch and dinner on days at sea. Sabatini's, with colorful tiled Mediterranean-style decor, serves Italian-style pizzas and pastas, with a variety of sauces, plus Italian-style entrées (mains) including tiger prawns and lobster tail. All are provided with flair and entertainment by the waiters. Reservations are required.

Tequila's features food from the American Southwest (a cover charge applies for lunch or dinner) on sea days only. The restaurant is spread over the ship's entire width, and two walkways intersect it, which means that it's a very open area, with people walking through it as you eat – not a comfortable arrangement. Reservations are needed.

A poolside hamburger grill and a pizza bar (no additional charge) are dining spots for casual bites. Note that it costs extra to eat at the coffee bar/patisserie, or the caviar/Champagne bar.

Other casual meals can be taken in the Horizon Court, open 24 hours a day. It has large ocean-view windows on port and starboard sides and direct access to the two main swimming pools and Lido Deck. There is no real finesse in presentation, however, as plastic plates (no trays) are provided.

ENTERTAINMENT. The Princess Theater is the showlounge; it spans two decks and has comfortable seating on both levels. It has $3 million worth of sound and light equipment, and a live showband to accompany the colorful production shows for which Princess Cruises is well known.

The Vista Lounge, a second entertainment lounge, has cabaret acts such as magicians, comedy jugglers, and ventriloquists at night, and lectures, bingo, and horse racing during the day. Explorers, a third lounge, can also host cabaret acts and dance bands. Various other lounges and bars have live music, and Princess Cruises has a number of male dance hosts as partners for women traveling alone.

SPA/FITNESS. The Lotus Spa has Japanese-style decor, and surrounds one of the swimming pools. You can have a massage or other spa treatment in an ocean-view treatment room. Some of the massage-treatment rooms are located directly underneath the jogging track.

SUN PRINCESS
★★★+

THIS LARGE, FAMILY-FRIENDLY RESORT SHIP HAS FAIRLY MODERN DECOR

Size:	Mid-size Ship	Passenger/Crew Ratio (lower beds):	2.0
Tonnage:	77,499	Cabins (total):	975
Cruise Line:	Princess Cruises	Size Range (sq ft/m):	134.5–753.4/12.5–70.0
Former Names:	none	Cabins (for one person):	0
Builder:	Fincantieri (Italy)	Cabins with balcony:	410
Entered Service:	Dec 1995	Cabins (wheelchair accessible):	19
Length (ft/m):	857.2/261.3	Wheelchair accessibility:	Good
Beam (ft/m):	105.6/32.2	Elevators:	11
Propulsion/Propellers:	diesel-electric (28,000kW)/2	Casino (gaming tables):	Yes
Passenger Decks:	10	Swimming Pools:	3
Total Crew:	900	Self-Service Launderette:	Yes
Passengers (lower beds):	1,950	Library:	Yes
Passenger Space Ratio (lower beds):	39.7	Onboard currency:	Australian $

THE SHIP. This all-white ship, which is now over 20 years old (it's the oldest in the fleet), has a fairly decent profile that is well balanced by its large funnel (this contains a deck tennis/basketball/volleyball court in its sheltered aft base). There is a wide, teakwood walk-around promenade deck outdoors, some real teak steamer-style deck chairs with royal blue cushioned pads, and 93,000 sq ft (8,640 sq m) of space outdoors. An extensive glass area on the upper decks provides plenty of light and connection with the outside world.

Sun Princess absorbs passengers well, and has a quasi-intimate feel, with warm, welcoming decor. A wide array of public rooms includes several intimate rooms and spaces, so that you don't feel overwhelmed by large spaces. The interior focal point (and always a good place to arrange to meet others) is a pleasant four-deck-high atrium lobby with winding, double staircases, and two panoramic glass-walled elevators.

The main entertainment rooms are located underneath three decks of cabins. There is plenty of space, the flow is good, and the ship absorbs people well. There are two showlounges, one at each end of the ship; one is a pleasant theater-style space, where movies are also shown, and the other is a cabaret-style lounge, complete with bar.

The library is a warm, welcoming room with ocean-view windows, and it has six large buttery

BERLITZ'S RATINGS	Possible	Achieved
Ship	500	350
Accommodation	200	128
Food	400	249
Service	400	276
Entertainment	100	68
Cruise Experience	400	276

OVERALL SCORE 1347 points out of 2000

leather chairs for listening to CDs. There is a conference center for up to 300, as well as a business center. The collection of artwork is good, particularly on the stairways, and it helps to make the ship feel smaller than it is, although in places it doesn't always seem coordinated.

The most traditional room aboard (a standard on all Princess ships) is the Wheelhouse Lounge/Bar, decorated in the style of a late 19th-century gentleman's club, complete with wood paneling and comfortable seating. Its focal point is a large ship model from the P&O archives.

One nice feature is the captain's cocktail party; it is held in the four-deck-high main atrium, so you can come and go as you please. There's no standing in line to have your photograph taken with the captain, if you don't want to.

Niggles include the layout: there are a number of dead ends in the interior, so it's not as user-friendly as a ship this size should be. The cabin-numbering system is extremely illogical, with numbers going through several hundred series on the same deck. The walls of the passenger accommodation decks are very plain. The swimming pools are small for the number of passengers carried, and the pool deck is cluttered with white plastic sunloungers that lack cushioned pads.

ACCOMMODATION. There are many different cabin grades. Although the standard outside-view and interior cabins are small, they are well designed, with a functional layout, and are in earth tones accentuated by splashes of color from the bedspreads. Many of the outside-view cabins have private balconies, and all are quite well soundproofed, although the balcony partition is not floor-to-ceiling type, so you can hear your neighbors clearly. The balconies are very narrow, just large enough for two small chairs.

A reasonable amount of closet and abundant drawer and other storage space is provided in all cabins – just about adequate for a seven-night cruise – as are a TV set and refrigerator. However, for longer voyages, the cabin closet space could prove to be much too small. Each night a chocolate will appear on your pillow.

The cabin bathrooms are practical, and come complete with all the details one needs, although they really are tight spaces, one-person-at-a-time units. They have a decent shower enclosure, real glasses, a hairdryer and bathrobe, and a small amount of shelving for toiletries.

The largest accommodation is in six suites, two on each of three decks at the stern, with large private balcony (536–754 sq ft/50–70 sq m, including balcony). Mini-suites (374–536 sq ft/35–50 sq m) typically have two lower beds that convert to a queen-size bed. Some are 19 wheelchair-accessible cabins, which measure 213–305 sq ft (20–28 sq m), in a mix of seven outside-view and 12 interior cabins.

DINING. There are two main dining rooms of asymmetrical design – Marquis and Regency – located adjacent to the two lower levels of the four-deck-high atrium lobby. Each seats around 500, has its own galley, and is split into multi-tier sections that help create a feeling of intimacy, although there is a lot of noise from the waiter stations adjacent to many tables. Breakfast and lunch are provided in an open-seating arrangement, while dinner is in two seatings.

The wine list is reasonable, but there are no wine waiters. A 15 percent is automatically added to all beverage bills, including for wines.

Although portions are generous, the food and its presentation are disappointing, and quite standardized. Fish is often disguised by a crumb or batter coating, the choice of fresh green vegetables is limited, few garnishes are used, and cheese is already sliced and diced. But, this is big-ship banquet catering, which means cooking in large batches. Pasta dishes are acceptable (though voluminous), typically served by sec-

tion headwaiters, who may also make 'something special just for you' – in search of favorable comments and gratuities. If you like desserts, order a sundae at dinner (most other items are just so-so).

'SHARE' by Curtis Stone, located on the upper level of the atrium lobby, features a multi-course degustation menu.

For some really good meat, consider the extra-cost Sterling Steakhouse; there are four different cuts of Angus beef – Filet Mignon, New York Strip, Porterhouse, and Rib-Eye, first presented on a silver tray. This is available as an alternative to the dining rooms between 6.30pm and 9.30pm, but, instead of being a separate, intimate room, it is located in a section of the Horizon Buffet, with its own portable bar and some decorative touches to set it apart from the regular buffet area.

The Horizon Buffet itself is open almost around the clock, and, at night, has an informal dinner setting with sit-down waiter service. The buffet displays are, for the most part, fairly repetitious. There is no real finesse in presentation, however (plastic plates are provided, instead of trays).

There is also a patisserie (for extra-cost cappuccino/espresso coffees and pastries), a wine/caviar bar, and a pizzeria (complete with cobblestone floors and wrought-iron decorative features), and a choice of pizzas.

ENTERTAINMENT. There are two showlounges, both theater- and cabaret-style. The main one, the Princess Theater, has a sloping floor, with aisle-style seating that is well tiered, and with good sight lines to the raised stage from most of the 500 seats.

The 480-seat Vista Lounge, at the aft end, has cabaret entertainment, and also acts as a lecture and presentation room. Princess Cruises has a good stable of regular cabaret acts to draw from, so there should be something for most tastes.

SPA/FITNESS. A glass-walled Lotus Spa is located in an aft area of Riviera deck, and includes a gymnasium with high-tech machines, several massage/body-treatment rooms, and a beauty salon. The facility is staffed and operated by a specialist spa concession.

Sports facilities are located in an open-air sports deck inside the funnel and adaptable for basketball, volleyball, badminton, or paddle tennis. Joggers can exercise on the walk-around open Promenade Deck.

SUPERSTAR AQUARIUS
★★★

THIS FAMILY-FRIENDLY, CASUAL CRUISE SHIP IS GOOD FOR CASINO GAMERS

Size:	Mid-size Ship	Passenger/Crew Ratio (lower beds):	1.7/1
Tonnage:	50,764	Cabins (total):	765
Cruise Line:	Star Cruises	Size Range (sq ft/m):	139.9–349.8/13.0–32.5
Former Names:	Norwegian Wind, Windward	Cabins (for one person):	0
Builder:	Chantiers de l'Atlantique (France)	Cabins with balcony:	74
Entered Service:	Jun 1993/May 2007	Cabins (wheelchair accessible):	11
Length (ft/m):	754.0/229.8	Wheelchair accessibility:	Fair
Beam (ft/m):	93.5/28.5	Elevators:	10
Propulsion/Propellers:	diesel (18,480kW)/2	Casino (gaming tables):	Yes
Passenger Decks:	10	Swimming Pools:	1
Total Crew:	889	Self-Service Launderette:	No
Passengers (lower beds):	1,529	Library:	Yes
Passenger Space Ratio (lower beds):	33.1	Onboard currency:	Hong Kong $

THE SHIP. *SuperStar Aquarius* was transferred from Norwegian Cruise Line to the Star Cruises fleet in 2007 to operate overnight and short cruises from Hong Kong. The dress code is strictly casual. Several cabins are specially equipped for the hearing-impaired. All gratuities for staff are included.

The exterior design emphasizes a clever use of large windows that helps to create a sense of open spaces, but there are many smaller public rooms. There is no big atrium lobby, and the ceiling height is low.

Public rooms include bars and lounges, including Skyline Karaoke, which has five private karaoke rooms. There's a Mahjong/card room, childcare center, video arcade, Genting Club for invited gaming guests, business meeting rooms, an Internet-connect center/library, cigar lounge, and a small boutique. There is a blue rubber-covered walk-around promenade deck outdoors. Outdoor stairways are numerous and confusing, while the carpeted steel interior stairwell steps are tinny.

ACCOMMODATION. There are several different cabin price grades. No cabin includes the number '4,' as this signifies 'death' in China. Most cabins have outside views and wood-trimmed cabinetry and warm decor, but there's almost no drawer space (although the closets have open shelves), so be minimalist when packing. All cabins have a sitting area. The bathrooms are small but practical.

BERLITZ'S RATINGS		
	Possible	Achieved
Ship	500	284
Accommodation	200	119
Food	400	237
Service	400	247
Entertainment	100	60
Cruise Experience	400	232

OVERALL SCORE 1179 points out of 2000

There are 18 suites (12 with a private entrance and a small, private balcony), each with separate living room and bedroom, and plenty of closet and drawer space. Occupants of suites receive 'concierge' service. In addition, 16 suites and 70 cabins have interconnecting doors.

DINING. Freestyle Dining venues include the 280-seat Dynasty Restaurant, for Chinese family-style food. It has some prime tables at ocean-view window seats in a section that extends from the ship's port and starboard sides in half-moon shapes. There's also Spices Restaurant, an Asian specialty buffet venue with 180 seats; Oceana Barbeque, an outdoor buffet venue; Blue Lagoon, a 24-hour bistro, with 80 seats; and Mariner's Buffet, an international self-service buffet.

ENTERTAINMENT. The 700-seat Stardust Lounge is two decks high, but the banquette and individual tub chair seating is only on the main level. There is no live showband, only recorded music. High-volume razzle-dazzle shows are presented to a pre-recorded track, as well as special individual cabaret acts.

SPA/FITNESS. A gymnasium has high-tech muscle-toning equipment, reflexology lounge, and Oscar Hair and Beauty Salon. There's a ping-pong table, basketball/volleyball court, golf driving range, and a jogging track.

SUPERSTAR GEMINI
★★★

THIS CASUAL, FAMILY-FRIENDLY SHIP IS POPULAR WITH ASIAN CRUISERS

Size:	Mid-size Ship	Passenger/Crew Ratio (lower beds):	1.7/1
Tonnage:	50,764	Cabins (total):	765
Cruise Line:	Star Cruises	Size Range (sq ft/m):	139.9–349.8/13.0–32.5
Former Names:	Norwegian Dream, Dreamward	Cabins (for one person):	0
Builder:	Chantiers de l'Atlantique (France)	Cabins with balcony:	74
Entered Service:	Dec 1992/Jan 2013	Cabins (wheelchair accessible):	11
Length (ft/m):	754.0/229.8	Wheelchair accessibility:	Fair
Beam (ft/m):	93.5/28.5	Elevators:	10
Propulsion/Propellers:	diesel (18,480kW)/2	Casino (gaming tables):	Yes
Passenger Decks:	10	Swimming Pools:	1
Total Crew:	889	Self-Service Launderette:	No
Passengers (lower beds):	1,529	Library:	Yes
Passenger Space Ratio (lower beds):	33.1	Onboard currency:	Hong Kong $

THE SHIP. *SuperStar Gemini* is a mid-sized ship that is popular with Asian families and couples looking for a general cruise experience in fairly contemporary surroundings.

Although its funnel is large and looks square, the ship has a profile that is balanced; this is because it underwent a 'chop-and-stretch' operation, in which a new 131ft (40m) mid-section was added in 1998. This gave the ship not only more cabins, but also a larger number of public rooms and places in which to play.

The tiered pool deck aft is neat, as are the multi-deck aft sun terraces and all the fore and aft connecting exterior stairways. The overall exterior design emphasizes a clever and extensive use of large windows that create a sense of open spaces. However, there is no big atrium lobby, as one might expect.

Public rooms include a Mahjong room, an activity center, several shops (including a duty-free store, a tea corner for premium teas, and a jewelry store), an Observatory Lounge (Karaoke Lounge), Genting Club, and Star Club (casino with gaming tables and slot machines).

ACCOMMODATION. There are several grades of cabins (the price you pay will depend on the grade, size, and location you choose). Most cabins have outside views, wood-trimmed cabinetry, and warm

BERLITZ'S RATINGS		
	Possible	Achieved
Ship	500	295
Accommodation	200	119
Food	400	237
Service	400	247
Entertainment	100	60
Cruise Experience	400	234

OVERALL SCORE 1192 points out of 2000

decor, with multi-colored soft furnishings. But there is almost no drawer space (the closets have open shelves). All cabins benefit from a sitting area, but this takes away any free space, making movement pretty tight. The bathrooms are small but practical.

DINING. There are plenty of choices when it comes to dining. The main full-service dining room is Bella Vista (the nicest, with prime tables and ocean-view window seats); Dynasty (a self-serve Chinese buffet); Mariners Restaurant (a self-serve buffet); Oceana Barbecue (outdoors, for grilled specialties and buffet-style eats); and Blue Lagoon (à la carte and open 24-hours). The cuisine is Asian, and quite decent.

ENTERTAINMENT. The Stardust Lounge is the ship's main showlounge. Two decks high, it is located in the ship's center, with cabins in front of it, and other public rooms and dining spots behind it.

SPA/FITNESS. Spa/fitness facilities are located in the forward section of Sports Deck 12 (just aft of the observation lounge), and include a gymnasium with high-tech muscle-toning equipment, a beauty salon, several massage and associated treatment rooms, and men's and women's saunas and changing rooms.

SUPERSTAR LIBRA
★★★

THIS CASUAL, FAMILY-FRIENDLY ASIAN SHIP IS GOOD FOR CASINO GAMERS

Size:	Mid-size Ship	Passenger/Crew Ratio (lower beds):	2.1/1
Tonnage:	42,276	Cabins (total):	732
Cruise Line:	Star Cruises	Size Range (sq ft/m):	109.7–269.1/10.2–25.0
Former Names:	Norwegian Sea, Seaward	Cabins (for one person):	0
Builder:	Wartsila (Finland)	Cabins with balcony:	0
Entered Service:	Jun 1988/Oct 2005	Cabins (wheelchair accessible):	4
Length (ft/m):	708.6/216.0	Wheelchair accessibility:	Fair
Beam (ft/m):	95.1/29.0	Elevators:	6
Propulsion/Propellers:	diesel (21,120kW)/2	Casino (gaming tables):	Yes
Passenger Decks:	9	Swimming Pools:	2
Total Crew:	700	Self-Service Launderette:	No
Passengers (lower beds):	1,472	Library:	No
Passenger Space Ratio (lower beds):	28.0	Onboard currency:	Hong Kong $

THE SHIP. Based at Penang in Malaysia, this ship is suited to couples and solo travelers seeking a short cruise in surroundings tailored specifically for them. It was built before balcony cabins came into vogue, so there aren't any.

SuperStar Libra is an angular yet reasonably attractive ship that has a contemporary European cruise-ferry profile with a sharply raked bow and sleek mast and funnel added. It is quite well designed, with generally sound passenger flow. The interior decor, stressing corals, blues, and mauves, reminds you of sea and sky.

The two-deck-high lobby is pleasing without being overwhelming. There is a decent selection of public rooms, bars, and lounges, including an inviting wood-paneled Admiral's Lounge, a Star Club casino, a disco (Boomer's), and The Bollywood karaoke lounge. Gratuities are included.

The open decks are cluttered and badly dented, and scuffed panels in the accommodation hallways are unattractive. The steps on the stairways are quite tinny. The constant background music in the hallways is irritating. There is too much use of synthetic turf on the upper outdoors decks – this gets soggy when wet.

ACCOMMODATION. There are numerous suite/cabin price categories. No cabin includes the number '4,' which signifies 'death' in China. Although the cabins are of average size, they are tastefully appointed and comfortable. Audio channels are avail-

BERLITZ'S RATINGS		
	Possible	Achieved
Ship	500	276
Accommodation	200	119
Food	400	227
Service	400	246
Entertainment	100	61
Cruise Experience	400	228
OVERALL SCORE 1157 points out of 2000		

able via the TV set, although the picture can't be turned off with the audio function on. The bathrooms are well designed, but the hairdryers are weak.

A suite or one of two upper-grade cabins offers a little more space, a lounge area with table and sofa that converts into another bed, European duvets, and a refrigerator (top categories only). The bathrooms also have a tub, shower, and retractable clothesline.

DINING. There are no assigned dining rooms, tables, or seats. Some eateries cost extra, including: the Four Seasons Restaurant, the principal dining room, serving Continental Cuisine; The Saffron; Two Trees Restaurant (exclusive lounge/restaurant); Taj by the Bay; Blue Lagoon for 24-hour casual refreshments; and Coconut Willy's, a poolside refreshment center.

ENTERTAINMENT. The 770-seat Stardust Lounge is the venue for shows and major cabaret acts, but 12 thick pillars obstruct many sight lines. The Galaxy of the Stars Lounge is for cabaret acts. A number of bands and solo entertaining musicians provide live music for listening and dancing in several lounges and bars.

SPA/FITNESS. There's a decent fitness center, located around the mast. It is accessible from the outside deck only, which is inconvenient when it rains.

SUPERSTAR VIRGO
★★★+

THIS FAMILY-FRIENDLY SHIP IS FOR ULTRA-CASUAL CRUISING AND ENERGETIC ENTERTAINMENT

Size:	Mid-size Ship	Passenger/Crew Ratio (lower beds):	1.4/1
Tonnage:	75,338	Cabins (total):	935
Cruise Line:	Star Cruises	Size Range (sq ft/m):	150.6–638.3/14.0–59.3
Former Names:	none	Cabins (for one person):	0
Builder:	Meyer Werft (Germany)	Cabins with balcony:	390
Entered Service:	Aug 1999	Cabins (wheelchair accessible):	4
Length (ft/m):	879.2/268.0	Wheelchair accessibility:	Good
Beam (ft/m):	105.6/32.2	Elevators:	9
Propulsion/Propellers:	diesel (50,400kW)/2	Casino (gaming tables):	Yes
Passenger Decks:	10	Swimming Pools:	2
Total Crew:	1,225	Self-Service Launderette:	No
Passengers (lower beds):	1,870	Library:	Yes
Passenger Space Ratio (lower beds):	41.7	Onboard currency:	Hong Kong $

THE SHIP. This ship, now almost 20 years old, is for couples, solo travelers, and families with children who want to cruise aboard a contemporary floating resort with decent facilities and Asian cuisine.

SuperStar Virgo was the second new Star Cruises ship for the Asian market. The all-white ship has a distinctive red-and-blue funnel with gold star logo, and decorative hull art. There are three classes. As you check in, you get a colored boarding card to denote Admiral Class passengers (yellow), Balcony Class (red), or World Cruisers (blue).

There is a walk-around promenade deck outdoors, which is good for strolling. Inside are two boulevards, and a stunning, large, two-deck-high central atrium lobby with three glass-walled elevators and space to peruse the shops and cafés.

The casino complex is at the forward end of the atrium boulevard on Deck 7. This includes a large, brightly lit casino, called Oasis, with abundant gaming tables and slot machines. There's a smaller members-only gaming club, plus VIP gaming rooms, one of which has private access to the showlounge's upper level. The 450-seat Galaxy of the Stars Lounge is an observation lounge by day and a nightclub at night, with live music.

Three stairways are each carpeted in a different color, which helps new cruise passengers find their way around easily.

Other facilities include a business center with six

BERLITZ'S RATINGS

	Possible	Achieved
Ship	500	355
Accommodation	200	137
Food	400	238
Service	400	244
Entertainment	100	64
Cruise Experience	400	263

OVERALL SCORE 1301 points out of 2000

meeting rooms, a large library and writing room, plus private Mahjong and karaoke rooms, and a smoking room. A shopping concourse includes a wine shop.

Star Cruises has established a Southeast Asian regional cruise audience for its diverse fleet. *SuperStar Virgo* is good for the active local market, and is the most comprehensive ship sailing year-round in this popular region.

Lots of choices, more dining options, and Asian hospitality all add up to an attractive package suitable for families with children, in a floating resort. The dress code is ultra-casual (no jacket and tie needed), and a no-tipping policy applies. While the initial cruise fare seems very reasonable, extra costs and charges soon mount up when you indulge in more than the basics. Although service levels and finesse are inconsistent, the smile-rich hospitality is good.

There are many extra-cost items in addition to the à la carte dining spots, such as for morning and afternoon tea, most cabaret shows (except a crew show), and childcare. Finding your way around many areas blocked by portable 'crowd containment' ribbon barriers is frustrating.

ACCOMMODATION. There are seven types of accommodation, in a number of different price categories. Three entire decks of cabins have private balconies, while two-thirds of all cabins have outside views. Both the standard outside-view and interior cabins really are very small, particularly since all cabins have extra berths for a third/fourth person. So pack minimally, as there's almost no storage space for luggage.

All cabins have a personal safe, cotton towels, and duvets or sheets. Bathrooms have a good-size shower enclosure, and include toiletries such as Burberry soap, conditioning shampoo, and body lotion.

For more space, choose one of 13 suites. Each has a separate lounge/dining room, bedroom, and bathroom, and an interconnecting door to an ocean-view cabin with private balcony. The bedroom is still small, completely filled by its queen-size bed; there is a reasonable amount of drawer space, but the drawers are very small. The closet space is rather tight – it contains two personal safes. A large en-suite bathroom is part of the bedroom, and has a gorgeous mosaic tiled floor, tub, two basins, separate shower enclosure with floor-to-ceiling ocean-view window, and separate toilet with glass door. There are TV sets in the lounge, bedroom, and bathroom.

For even more space, choose one of the six largest suites (Boracay, Nicobar, Langkawi, Majorca, Phuket, and Sentosa) and you'll have a generous amount of private living space, with a separate lounge, dining area, bedroom, large bathroom, and private lit balcony. The facilities are similar to those in the suites already described. There are TV sets in the lounge, bedroom, and bathroom.

Room service offers a small menu, to which you need to add a 15 percent service charge plus a gratuity.

DINING. There's certainly no lack of choice, with eight venues, plus a café:

Bella Vista (perhaps the equivalent of a main dining room) seats over 600 in an open-seating arrangement, but in effect it operates two seatings. The aft section is two decks high, and huge cathedral-style windows set in three sections looking aft.

Mediterranean Buffet is a large self-serve buffet restaurant with indoor/outdoor seating for 400.

The Pavilion Room has traditional Cantonese Chinese cuisine, including dim sum at lunchtime.

The following are (extra-cost) à la carte dining spots:

Noble House: a Chinese Restaurant, with traditional Hong Kong-themed decor and items such as dim sum. There are also two small private dining rooms.

Palazzo: a beautiful, if slightly ostentatious, Italian restaurant. It has fine food, and a genuine Renoir painting well protected by cameras and alarms.

Samurai: a Japanese restaurant and sushi bar (for sashimi and sushi). There are two Teppanyaki grills, each with 10 seats, where the chef cooks in front of you.

The Taj: an Indian/vegetarian dining spot that offers a range of food in a self-serve buffet set-up.

Blue Lagoon: a casual 24-hour street café with noodle dishes, fried rice, and other Southeast Asian dishes.

Out of Africa: a casual karaoke café and bar, where coffees, teas, and pastries are available.

ENTERTAINMENT. The Lido showlounge, with 934 seats, spans two decks. It has main and balcony levels, with the balcony level reserved for VIP 'gaming club' members. The room has almost no support columns to obstruct the sight lines, and a revolving stage for revues and other production shows, with recorded music – there is no live showband. It can also be used as a large-screen cinema, with superb surround sound.

In addition, local specialty cabaret acts are brought on board, as are revue-style shows complete with topless dancers. Bands and small musical units provide plenty of live music for dancing and listening in the various lounges.

SPA/FITNESS. The Roman Spa and Fitness Center is on one of the uppermost decks, just forward of the Tivoli Pool. It has a gymnasium full of high-tech muscle-toning equipment, plus an aerobics exercise room, hair and beauty salon, and saunas, steam rooms, changing rooms for men and women, several treatment rooms, and aqua-swim pools that provide counter-flow jets. There is an extra charge for use of the sauna and steam rooms.

Thai massage is the specialty – you can have it in the spa, outdoors on deck, in your cabin, or on your private balcony, space permitting. Sports facilities include a jogging track, golf driving range, basketball and tennis courts, and there are four levels of sunbathing decks.

THOMSON CELEBRATION
★★★

A DATED, 'INCLUSIVE' FAMILY-FRIENDLY SHIP FOR A LOW-BUDGET FIRST CRUISE

Size:	Mid-size Ship	Passenger/Crew Ratio (lower beds):	2.4/1
Tonnage:	33,930	Cabins (total):	627
Cruise Line:	Thomson Cruises	Size Range (sq ft/m):	140.0–430.0/13.0–40.0
Former Names:	*Noordam*	Cabins (for one person):	0
Builder:	Chantiers de l'Atlantique (France)	Cabins with balcony:	26
Entered Service:	Apr 1984/May 2005	Cabins (wheelchair accessible):	4
Length (ft/m):	704.2/214.6	Wheelchair accessibility:	Fair
Beam (ft/m):	89.4/27.2	Elevators:	7
Propulsion/Propellers:	diesel (21,600kW)/2	Casino (gaming tables):	Yes
Passenger Decks:	10	Swimming Pools:	2
Total Crew:	520	Self-Service Launderette:	Yes
Passengers (lower beds):	1,254	Library:	Yes
Passenger Space Ratio (lower beds):	27.0	Onboard currency:	UK£

THE SHIP. This ship suits couples and solo travelers taking their first or second cruise, seeking a fairly modern but not glitzy ship. It is exclusively chartered by Thomson Cruises, so most passengers will be British, typically over 55. *Thomson Celebration* has a good amount of open deck space, and traditional teakwood decks outdoors, including a walk-around promenade deck. The ship, however, is dated and can suffer from vibration. It has a spacious interior layout. Public lounges include an Explorers' Lounge, Library, and Horizon's observation lounge. There are many interior cabins, and standing in line is inevitable. Gratuities are included, linen changes are minimal, and the dress code is not enforced, leading to many complaints.

ACCOMMODATION. There are four accommodation grades: suite-grade, deluxe, outside, and interior (no view). Four cabins with great forward-facing views are designated for the passengers with disabilities. You can pre-book your preferred cabin for an extra fee. Cabins are adequately appointed and practically laid out. There is good counter but limited storage space, a large mirror, and a small bathroom. Some cabins have bathtubs; others have shower enclosures only. Some cabins have additional upper berths for a third/fourth person (useful for families with small children). Room service is provided 24/7, at extra cost. Note that cabin insulation is poor. Some cabins on Mariner and Bridge decks have lifeboat-obstructed views.

BERLITZ'S RATINGS

	Possible	Achieved
Ship	500	290
Accommodation	200	126
Food	400	223
Service	400	241
Entertainment	100	60
Cruise Experience	400	235

OVERALL SCORE 1175 points out of 2000

DINING. The 600-seat Meridian Restaurant has warm decor, and operates in an open-seating arrangement. Although there are a few tables for two, most are for four to eight. Dinners typically include a choice of four mains. Children have their own menu. Dessert and pastry items will usually be of good quality, made for British tastes.

A small à la carte restaurant, Mistral's, is an intimate dining spot; reservations are required, and there's a per-person cover charge. It has superior food and service plus a more refined atmosphere. The Kora La restaurant features Asian cuisine.

The casual self-serve Lido Restaurant is active 24 hours a day. Each week a themed buffet may be offered. However, self-serve buffets are quite repetitive. On Lido Deck, the outdoor Terrace Grill provides fast-food grilled items, pasta at lunchtime, and pizza.

ENTERTAINMENT. The Broadway Show Lounge, located mid-ship, is a 600-seat venue for production shows. It is two decks high, and several pillars obstruct sight lines. Liberties is a multi-functional room for quizzes, dancing, karaoke, and a late-night disco. Bands and musical units provide live music in several lounges and bars.

SPA/FITNESS. Oceans Health Club has good ocean views. Facilities include an exercise room, a gym, men's and women's saunas, and body-treatment rooms.

THOMSON DREAM
★★★

THIS NOW QUITE DATED MID-SIZE SHIP IS FOR FRUGAL, FAMILY-FRIENDLY CRUISES

Size:	Mid-size Ship	Passenger/Crew Ratio (lower beds):	2.5/1
Tonnage:	54,763	Cabins (total):	753
Cruise Line:	Thomson Cruises	Size Range (sq ft/m):	129.1–425.1/12.0–39.5
Former Names:	... Costa Europa, Westerdam, Homeric	Cabins (for one person):	18
Builder:	Meyer Werft (Germany)	Cabins with balcony:	0
Entered Service:	May 1986/Dec 2010	Cabins (wheelchair accessible):	4
Length (ft/m):	797.9/243.2	Wheelchair accessibility:	Fair
Beam (ft/m):	95.1/29.0	Elevators:	7
Propulsion/Propellers:	diesel (23,830kW)/2	Casino (gaming tables):	Yes
Passenger Decks:	9	Swimming Pools:	2
Total Crew:	600	Self-Service Launderette:	Yes
Passengers (lower beds):	1,506	Library:	Yes
Passenger Space Ratio (lower beds):	36.3	Onboard currency:	UK£

THE SHIP. *Thomson Dream* suits couples and solo travelers taking their first or second cruise, and families with children of all ages. The ship was acquired by Thomson Cruises in 2009, when it was extensively refurbished to cater to Thomson's mainly British clientele.

There is good teak decking on the exterior decks, and a walk-around promenade deck, plus a decent amount of space for sunbathing. There is also a swimming pool deck, although the pool itself is small. There are several bars and lounges, and shops, plus lots of nooks and crannies to relax in, including a library/Internet lounge, and card room.

Thomson Dream allots a decent amount of space to children's facilities, which suits the increasing number of families who choose this ship. Some larger cabins have a sofa that turns into a bed.

Passenger niggles include poor maintenance of exterior areas, too few elevators for the number of passengers, irritating announcements, expensive shore excursions, and the lack of an observation lounge.

ACCOMMODATION. There are several grades, including suites, mini-suites, outside-view cabins, and interior (no-view) cabins, priced according to grade, size, and location. You can pre-book your preference for a per cabin fee of £42 (around $60). Except for suite-category cabins, almost all other cabins are of a similar size. In general, they are fairly well equipped. Soundproofing is poor, however. Most cabins have twin beds, but some

BERLITZ'S RATINGS		
	Possible	Achieved
Ship	500	300
Accommodation	200	122
Food	400	226
Service	400	248
Entertainment	100	61
Cruise Experience	400	238
OVERALL SCORE 1195 points out of 2000		

have berths (useful for families). There are four cabins for passengers with disabilities located on higher decks, close to elevators.

DINING. The Orion Restaurant is a traditional dining room with port and starboard side portholes. Open seating is the norm, but be aware that tables are close together and it cna be noisy. The cuisine is British-Continental, and there's plenty of it, but the quality and presentation are poor. However, it's all provided at a low price point: you get what you pay for.

The Grill is an extra-cost, reservations-required, à la carte steak and seafood restaurant, with white tablecloths and candlelight dining. Andromeda Restaurant and Sirens Restaurant provide meals in a self-serve buffet setting, while the poolside Terrace Grill is for fast food such as barbeque items, pizzas, pasta, and salads.

ENTERTAINMENT. Facilities include the Atlante Theatre, a two-deck-high showlounge. Pillars obstruct sight lines from some seats. A resident troupe present colorful, high-energy production shows. For nights when there's no show, the showlounge presents cabaret acts. A number of bands and small musical units provide live music in many lounges and bars.

SPA/FITNESS. Oceans Spa includes a gymnasium, saunas, and massage rooms. The facility is really small, given the number of passengers carried. It is operated by Flair, a specialist concession with clinical therapists.

TUI DISCOVERY
★★★+

TRY THIS LIVELY MID-SIZED SHIP FOR BRITISH FAMILY-FRIENDLY CRUISING

Size:	Mid-size Ship	Passenger/Crew Ratio (lower beds):	2.5
Tonnage:	69,130	Cabins (total):	902
Cruise Line:	Thomson Cruises	Size Range (sq ft/m):	137.7–1,147.4/12.8–106.6
Former Names:	none	Cabins (for one person):	0
Builder:	Chantiers de l'Atlantique (France)	Cabins with balcony:	355
Entered Service:	Mar 1996/Jun 2016	Cabins (wheelchair accessible):	17
Length (ft/m):	867.0/264.2	Wheelchair accessibility:	Good
Beam (ft/m):	105.0/32.0	Elevators:	11
Propulsion/Propellers:	diesel (40,200kW)/2	Casino (gaming tables):	Yes
Passenger Decks:	11	Swimming Pools:	2 (1 w/sliding glass dome)
Total Crew:	720	Self-Service Launderette:	No
Passengers (lower beds):	1,804	Library:	Yes
Passenger Space Ratio (lower beds):	38.3	Onboard currency:	UK£

THE SHIP. *TUI Discovery*, now over 20 years old, has a fairly contemporary profile with a wavy blue-and-white paint job on the hull, and a nicely shaped stern. The pool deck amidships overhangs the hull to provide an extremely wide deck, originally designed so that the ship could transit the Panama Canal. With engines placed amidships, there's little noise and little vibration.

The ship was transferred to Thomson Cruises (a division of TUI Cruises) from Royal Caribbean International in spring 2016 and modified to suit British family cruising tastes, and British-Continental cuisine.

Inside, finger-touch digital screens to help you navigate your way around the ship. Natural light is brought inside in many places, with lots of of glass for a feeling of connection with the sea. A single-level sliding glass roof over one of two pools provides a multi-activity all-weather indoor/outdoor area (the Glass House). It provides shelter for the Roman-style pool, spa, and fitness facilities, and slides aft to cover a miniature golf course when required – though both can't be covered simultaneously.

Two full entertainment decks are sandwiched between five decks of cabins, so there are plenty of public rooms to lounge and drink in (and separate children's facilities). A seven-deck-high atrium lobby is the focal point – and *the* social meeting place. On its various levels it houses reception and destination-services counters, the Atrium Bar, and the Photo

BERLITZ'S RATINGS		
	Possible	Achieved
Ship	500	342
Accommodation	200	127
Food	400	235
Service	400	254
Entertainment	100	68
Cruise Experience	400	257

OVERALL SCORE 1283 points out of 2000

Gallery, while adjacent is the Live Casino (for table gaming and slot machines), and Coffee Port.

Niggles include the fact that Thomson charges for shuttle buses in some ports of call, and the cost of bottled water is high. Overall, however, it's a very pleasant ship for families who don't need all the bells and whistles of the latest ships, but want several dining choices.

ACCOMMODATION. There are 15 different cabin price grades, depending on size and location. All cabins have a flat-screen TV, a sitting area, beds that convert to double configuration, and ample closet and drawer space, although there's little room around the bed. Also, the showers could have been better designed.

The largest accommodation, Cabin 8500, is a fine living space. It is beautifully designed and decorated, and has a baby grand piano and whirlpool bathtub. Quiet sitting areas are located adjacent to the best cabins amidships.

Some cabins on Deck 8 have a larger door for wheelchair access in addition to the cabins for passengers with disabilities, and the ship is very accessible, with ample ramped areas and sloping decks.

DINING. The unimaginatively named Main Restaurant has two-deck-high glass side walls so that many passengers can see both the ocean and each other in reflection. The food is similar to what you'd get in a decent family restaurant, but with better presentation, table settings, and service.

Gallery 47o is located upstairs in the main dining room and features carbohydrate-rich 'contemporary' Italian cuisine.

A La Carte is an extra-cost restaurant; part of the Sky Lounge, it features so-called 'International' cuisine.

For casual eats, Islands is a large self-serve buffet venue with indoor-outdoor seating. It has good forward views (it's located at the front of the ship), but it can be cramped when busy. Outside on deck is a snack bar, creatively called Snack Shack.

ENTERTAINMENT. The 802-seat Broadway Show Lounge is a single-level height room, with tiered seating levels and decent sight lines from almost all seats. A neat feature is that the orchestra pit can be raised or lowered as required. Some cabaret acts are featured in the 338-seat Lounge. A number of other bars and lounges have live music of differing types.

SPA/FITNESS. Oceans Spa is located on Deck 9, aft of the funnel. It includes a fitness center with a small selection of muscle-pumping equipment, an aerobics area, a beauty salon, a sauna, and several rooms for body treatments. The facilities are small, but they are adequate. There is also an outdoor rock-climbing wall (on the aft wall of the funnel), with several separate climbing tracks. For golfers, there's a 6,000-sq-ft (557-sq-m) 18-hole mini-golf course, with lighting for night play; the holes are 155 to 230 sq ft (14 to 21 sq m).

TUI DISCOVERY 2
★★★+

A FAMILY-FRIENDLY SHIP WITH EUROPEAN DECOR FOR BRITISH CRUISERS

Size:	Mid-size Ship	Passenger/Crew Ratio (lower beds):	2.4/1
Tonnage:	69,472	Cabins (total):	902
Cruise Line:	Thomson Cruises	Size Range (sq ft/m):	137.7–1,147.4/12.8–106.6
Former Names:	Legend of the Seas	Cabins (for one person):	0
Builder:	105.0/32.0	Cabins with balcony:	231
Entered Service:	Apr-17	Cabins (wheelchair accessible):	17
Length (ft/m):	867.0/264.2	Wheelchair accessibility:	Good
Beam (ft/m):	105.0/32.0	Elevators:	11
Propulsion/Propellers:	diesel/2	Casino (gaming tables):	Yes
Passenger Decks:	11	Swimming Pools:	2
Total Crew:	726	Self-Service Launderette:	No
Passengers (lower beds):	1,804	Library:	Yes
Passenger Space Ratio (lower beds):	38.4	Onboard currency:	UK£

THE SHIP. *TUI Discovery 2* has a fairly modern profile and a nicely tiered stern, although its 'duck-tail' stern, fitted to aid stability, is not particularly handsome. The pool deck amidships overhangs the hull to provide an extremely wide deck, while still allowing the ship to navigate the Panama Canal. With engines placed midships, there is little noise and no noticeable vibration, and the ship has an operating speed of up to 24 knots.

BERLITZ'S RATINGS		
	Possible	Achieved
Ship	500	1286
Accommodation	200	127
Food	400	235
Service	400	255
Entertainment	100	68
Cruise Experience	400	344

OVERALL SCORE 1286 points out of 2000

The outside light is brought inside in many places. There's a single-level sliding glass roof over the more formal setting of one of two swimming pools, providing an all-weather indoor-outdoor area called the Solarium. Inside, two full entertainment decks are sandwiched between five decks full of cabins, so there are plenty of public rooms to lounge and drink in. A seven-deck-high Atrium (lobby) is the main focal point, and *the* social meeting place. On its various levels it houses an Atrium Bar, Cocktail and Piano Bar, several passenger-service counters, and a casino (for table gaming and slot machines). Set around the base of the funnel is a Sky Lounge, bar,and an extra-cost à la carte restaurant..

Overall, *TUI Discovery 2* should provide you with a very pleasant cruise experience if you don't need all the bells and whistles of the latest ships, but like to have the choice of several dining options and various contemporary bars and lounge. However, the ship is showing its age in some areas.

ACCOMMODATION. There are many different cabin price grades. Some cabins on Deck 8 have a larger door for wheelchair access, and there are other cabins that are suitable for less-mobile passengers; the ship's open layout makes it easy to get around.

All cabins have a sitting area and a queen-sized bed, and there is ample closet and drawer space. Generally, there is very little space around the bed, though, and the showers could have been better designed (bathrooms are mostly really small, too).

The largest accommodation is the Royal Suite, which is beautifully designed and nicely decorated, and even has a baby grand piano.

DINING. The 1,050-seat Main Restaurant has dramatic two-deck-high glass side walls. Part of the upper level is an Italian restaurant, Gallery 47o, for carbohydrate-rich cuisine.

Other eateries include an extra–cost, reservations–required, à la carte restaurant (part of the Sky Lounge – with great views high atop the ship).

A large Islands self-serve eatery – like a food court – has good ocean views on three sides. However, there are mainly large tables, so table sharing is part of the experience, and the food selection is adequate, nothing more.

ENTERTAINMENT. The Broadway Show Lounge seats 802 and is a single-level showlounge with tiered seating levels and good sight lines from al-most all seats. Strong cabaret acts are also pre-sented here. A second entertainment lounge, the Lounge, is where cabaret acts, including late-night adult comedy are presented.

Entertainment throughout the ship is upbeat – in fact, it is difficult to get away from music and noise. There is even background music in all corridors and elevators, and constant music outdoors on the pool deck. If you want a quiet relaxing holiday, choose an-other ship.

SPA/FITNESS. Oceans Spa and Fitness Center has a small workout room, aft of the funnel, with a small selection of muscle-pumping equipment. There is also an aerobics studio, a beauty salon, and saunas for men and women, plus rooms for body-pampering treatments. While the facili-ties are quite small compared with those aboard the company's newer ships, they are adequate for short cruises.

An outdoor rock-climbing wall, with several sepa-rate climbing tracks, is located aft of the funnel.

VEENDAM
★★★

A MID-SIZE SHIP WITH DUTCH HERITAGE AND DECOR FOR MATURE-AGE TRAVELERS

Size:	Mid-size Ship	Passenger/Crew Ratio (lower beds):	2.2
Tonnage:	57,092	Cabins (total):	674
Cruise Line:	Holland America Line	Size Range (sq ft/m):	186.2–1,124.8/17.3–104.5
Former Names:	none	Cabins (for one person):	0
Builder:	Fincantieri (Italy)	Cabins with balcony:	182
Entered Service:	May 1996	Cabins (wheelchair accessible):	8
Length (ft/m):	719.3/219.3	Wheelchair accessibility:	Fair
Beam (ft/m):	101.0/30.8	Elevators:	8
Propulsion/Propellers:	diesel-electric (34,560kW)/2	Casino (gaming tables):	Yes
Passenger Decks:	10	Swimming Pools:	2 (1 w/ sliding glass dome)
Total Crew:	561	Self-Service Launderette:	Yes
Passengers (lower beds):	1,348	Library:	Yes
Passenger Space Ratio (lower beds):	42.4	Onboard currency:	US$

THE SHIP. *Veendam* is one of four almost identical ships, the others being *Maasdam*, *Pacific Aria* (formerly *Ryndam*), and *Pacific Eden* (formerly *Statendam*). Although the exterior styling is rather angular (some would say boxy – the funnel certainly is), it is balanced somewhat by the black hull. A ducktail sponson stern was added in 2009 for better stability and ride. There is a full walk-around teakwood promenade deck outdoors, which is good for strolling.

The Retreat includes a hot tub, pizzeria (Slices), a bar, sunloungers within a wading pool, and a large movie screen.

Most public rooms are concentrated on two decks, Promenade Deck, and Upper Promenade Deck, which creates a decent, spacious feel. In general, the approach to interior styling is restrained, using a mix of contemporary materials combined with traditional woods and ceramics. There's little glitz anywhere.

The artwork showcases HAL's Dutch heritage. Also noticeable are live flower arrangements, used to good effect to brighten up the otherwise dull decor.

Atop the ship is the Crow's Nest Lounge, an observation lounge with ocean-view windows by day; in the evening it's a nightclub with variable lighting.

A three-deck-high atrium foyer is quite appealing (and a good meeting place), although its sculpted centerpiece makes it feels crowded, leaving little room in front of reception. A hydraulic glass dome covers the swimming pool/whirlpools and central Lido area,

BERLITZ'S RATINGS		
	Possible	Achieved
Ship	500	297
Accommodation	200	125
Food	400	228
Service	400	264
Entertainment	100	60
Cruise Experience	400	245

OVERALL SCORE 1219 points out of 2000

for all-weather use. The pool's focal point is a large dolphin sculpture.

There is a relaxing reference library within the 'Mix' lifestyle area; the space combines three theme bars in one central area: Champagne, Martinis, and Spirits & Ales. Touch-screen technology is available for playing checkers and chess, air hockey, and other games.

A casino features gaming tables and slot machines.

Regular HAL passengers, almost all North American, find its ships comfortable. The company continues its maritime traditions, although maintenance and the food and service components still let down the rest of the cruise experience. The service staff is Indonesian; although they are mostly quite charming, communication can occasionally prove frustrating, and service is inconsistent.

An escalator travels between two of the lower decks (one was originally planned to be the embarkation point). The charge to use the washing machines and dryers in the self-service launderette is petty. The men's public restroom urinals are unusually high.

ACCOMMODATION. The accommodation ranges from small interior cabins to a large Penthouse Suite, in many different price categories.

The interior and outside-view standard cabins have twin beds that convert to a queen-size bed, and there is a separate living space with sofa and coffee table. Although the drawer space is generally good, closet space is tight, particularly for long cruises, but adequate for seven nights. The tiled bathrooms are compact but practical. Bathrobes, hairdryers, and a small number of toiletries are provided for all suites/cabins. The bathrooms are quite well laid out, but the bathtubs are very small units (better described as shower tubs). Some cabins have interconnecting doors.

On Navigation Deck, the suites can accommodate four persons and offer in-suite dining as an alternative to dining in public. They are spacious, tastefully decorated, and well laid-out, with a separate living room, bedroom with two lower beds that convert to a king-size bed, a good-size living area, dressing room, plenty of closet and drawer space, and marble bathroom with Jacuzzi tub.

The largest accommodation is the Penthouse Suite, on the starboard side of Navigation Deck at the forward staircase.

DINING. The Rotterdam Dining Room spans two decks aft, and has two grand staircases to connect each level, and panoramic views on three sides. Both open seating and assigned-table seating are available, although breakfast and lunch are just open seating (you'll be taken to a free table by restaurant staff when you enter). There are tables for two to eight, and Rosenthal china and good-quality cutlery are provided. The waiter stations are noisy for anyone seated near them.

With just a few exceptions, the cuisine is rather unmemorable, and is missing passion and taste, because it's all about production (batch) cooking. There's a distinct lack of variety of green vegetables, and too heavy a use of rice, canned fruit, and already sliced and diced cheese. Still, you get friendly service from Indonesian and Filipino stewards, and the plates are nice.

A more intimate, extra-cost, reservations-required Pinnacle Grill is located just forward of the balcony level of the main dining room on the starboard side. The 66-seat venue features premium steaks and seafood. A Bulgari show plate, Rosenthal china, Riedel wine glasses, and Frette table linen are used.

For more casual evening eating, the self-serve Lido Buffet is open for dinners on all except the last night of each cruise, in an open-seating arrangement. Tables are set with crisp linens, flatware, and stemware. A set menu is featured, with a choice of four entreés (mains). This is also the place for casual breakfasts and lunches. Each evening, a section transforms into Canaletto (reservations required) for casual Italian meals.

You may need to eat in the Lido Buffet on days when the dining room is closed for lunch – typically once or twice per cruise, depending on the itinerary.

Also, a Lido Deck poolside 'Dive-In at the Terrace Grill' features burgers, hot dogs, and fries, and, occasionally, barbeques and other culinary treats.

ENTERTAINMENT. The Showroom at Sea, forward, spans two decks, with banquette seating on both the main and upper levels. The ceiling is low, and sight lines from the balcony level are quite poor.

SPA/FITNESS. The Ocean Spa is one deck below the navigation bridge. It includes a gymnasium with all the latest muscle-pumping exercise machines, including an abundance of treadmills. It has ocean views, a large beauty salon with ocean-view windows to the port side, several treatment rooms, a sauna, steam room, and changing areas.

VENTURA
★★★+

THIS LARGE, FAMILY-FRIENDLY SHIP IS AIMED AT THOSE WITH BRITISH TASTES

Size:	Large Resort Ship	Passenger/Crew Ratio (lower beds):	2.4/1
Tonnage:	116,017	Cabins (total):	1,546
Cruise Line:	P&O Cruises	Size Range (sq ft/m):	134.5–534.0/12.5–49.6
Former Names:	none	Cabins (for one person):	18
Builder:	Fincantieri (Italy)	Cabins with balcony:	880
Entered Service:	Apr 2008	Cabins (wheelchair accessible):	25
Length (ft/m):	951.4/290.0	Wheelchair accessibility:	Good
Beam (ft/m):	118.1/36.0	Elevators:	12
Propulsion/Propellers:	diesel-electric (42,000kW)/2	Casino (gaming tables):	Yes
Passenger Decks:	15	Swimming Pools:	3
Total Crew:	1,239	Self-Service Launderette:	Yes
Passengers (lower beds):	3,074	Library:	Yes
Passenger Space Ratio (lower beds):	37.7	Onboard currency:	UK£

THE SHIP. *Ventura* (now almost 10 years old) is suited best to British families with children and adult couples looking for a big-ship environment with comfortable but unstuffy surroundings and lots of options. This is the P&O version of Princess Cruises' *Grand*-class ships, along with sister ship *Azura*.

There are promenade walking decks to the port and starboard sides, underneath the lifeboats. You can't walk completely around, however, unless you use the steps at the front (which is often closed); it's narrow in some places, and you have to weave past a number of deck lounge chairs. There are three pools: two on the pool deck, one of which can be covered by a glass-roof, and one aft. There's not a lot of outdoor deck space – unless you pay extra to go into a covered, adults-only, quiet zone called The Retreat (located above the spa), with private cabanas and waiter service.

Inside, a three-deck atrium is the focal social meeting point. Designed on a gateway theme, central to which are four towering black granite archways sourced from India, it's the place to see and be seen, and a good location to arrange to meet friends. The upper-deck public room layout is challenging, because you can't go from one end of the ship to the other without first going down, along, and up – poor for anyone with mobility problems.

Public rooms include a perfume shop, a small library, a Cruise Sales Centre, the (small) Fortunes Casino, and several bars, including The Exchange (an

BERLITZ'S RATINGS

	Possible	Achieved
Ship	500	370
Accommodation	200	142
Food	400	246
Service	400	283
Entertainment	100	68
Cruise Experience	400	263

OVERALL SCORE 1372 points out of 2000

'urban warehouse' bar), and The Beach House (outside with great aft views and views along the ship's sides – over everyone's balcony), and Red bar.

Passenger niggles include the push for on-board revenue, low passenger/space ratio, lack of a dedicated card room, mediocre self-service buffet food, and charge for shuttle buses in some ports.

Smoking is permitted only in designated spots on the open decks. Gratuities are automatically charged to your onboard account.

It's possible to get married on board, with the captain officiating.

ACCOMMODATION. There are many different accommodation price grades, according to location chosen, from suites with balcony to outside-view twin/queen (no balcony) and interior no-view cabins.

Over one-third of the accommodation is comprised of interior (no-view) cabins Some cabins have extra berths that fold down from the ceiling. While suites are quite spacious, they are small when compared to those aboard many other cruise lines, such as Celebrity Cruises or Holland America Line. There are 18 solo-occupancy cabins (12 outside and six interior), as aboard *Azura*.

Standard in all cabins: bed runners, Slumberland sprung mattresses, and Egyptian cotton towels. Basic tea/coffee-making facilities and packets of UHT milk, not fresh milk, are provided. Bathrobes are available only for passengers occupying grades A, B, and D accommodation. Three-pin UK and US-style 110-volt sockets are provided for electrical devices.

Cabins have open closets (no doors = no money wasted), providing easy access. Some balcony cabins have teak patio furniture, and an outside light.

Wheelchair-accessible cabins have a shower enclosure, except R415, which has a bathtub with integral shower. To take breakfast in the self-serve Waterside casual eatery, wheelchair users (mostly accommodated in the ship's forward section) must go across the decks containing the Beachcomber and Laguna pools and past many deck chairs – not easy. Alternatively, room service breakfast – typically cold items only – can be ordered. (Note that there is no room service breakfast on disembarkation day.)

DINING. P&O's marketing blurb claims there are 10 restaurants. There really aren't. There are five genuine restaurants (Bay Tree, Cinnamon, Saffron, The Epicurian, and Sindhu); the rest are more casual eateries.

The three main dining rooms, Bay Tree, Cinnamon, and Saffron, have standard à la carte menus. Bay Tree offers fixed seating dining, with assigned tables and seating times (typically 6.30pm or 8.30pm). In the other two, you can dine when you want, with whom you want, between 6pm and 10pm (Freedom Dining), but there can be long wait times for a table.

Special themed dinners are provided in the main dining rooms (one is a 'Chaîne des Rôtisseurs' event). The wine list is ho-hum average.

Specialty dining venues include the Epicurian, located high above the children's play area, with a quarter of the tables on an adjacent open deck. It features modern European dishes in an environment that is intimate and attentive but unstuffy – good for families. Reservations are needed, and there's a cover charge. The food is cooked to order, unlike in the main dining rooms. For complete privacy, private balcony dining, with selections from the Epicurean menu, is available as a pricey (but worthwhile, if the budget allows) extra-cost option.

The cuisine is straightforward, no-nonsense British food, reasonably well presented on nice Wedg-wood china. But it tends to be rather bland and uninspiring. It is typical of mass-banquet catering with standard fare comparable to that found in a family hotel in a classic English seaside town.

The Waterside is a large, self-serve, 'seaside chic' buffet with indoor-outdoor seating. Unfortunately, the cramped seating is poorly designed, and the food selection is poor (better for lunch than for breakfast or dinner).

On the same deck, adjacent to the forward pool, are Frankie's Grill and Frankie's Pizzeria.

Tazzine, a coffee lounge by day, turns into a cocktail bar in the evening.

The Beach House is a casual dining spot for families, open 24 hours. Marco's roof-side café serves gourmet pizzas, grills, and interesting ice cream flavors such as chocolate truffle and prune and Armagnac. Children's cutlery, bibs, and beakers are available.

East is an Asian fusion eatery on the main indoor promenade. In addition, 24-hour room service is available in cabins.

ENTERTAINMENT. The 785-seat Arena Theatre, at the front, spans two decks. Havana, the main nightclub and entertainment venue, where movies are sometimes shown, is an activities room by day and a sultry Cuba-inspired club by night, but the sight lines are extremely poor from many seats.

A cool wall in the Metropolitan Club lounge screens real-time footage of seven of the world's most famous city skylines – Hong Kong, Las Vegas, London, New York, Paris, Rio de Janeiro, and Sydney.

SPA/FITNESS. The Oasis Spa is located forward, almost atop the ship. It includes a gymnasium, aerobics room, beauty salon, men's and women's saunas and steam rooms, and 11 rooms for body treatments. An internal stairway connects to the deck below, which contains an extra-charge Thermal Suite. The spa staff and services are provided by Harding Brothers. Treatments include special packages for couples, and the SilverSpa Generation, and a whole range of individual treatments.

VIKING SEA
★★★★+

A SMART-LOOKING PREMIUM SHIP FOR THE EXPERIENCED TRAVELER

Size:	Mid-size Ship	Passenger/Crew Ratio (lower beds):	1.7/1
Tonnage:	47,800	Cabins (total):	465
Cruise Line:	Viking Cruises	Size Range (sq ft/m):	312.1-1,668.4/29.0-155.0
Former Names:	none	Cabins (for one person):	0
Builder:	Fincantieri (Italy)	Cabins with balcony:	465
Entered Service:	May 2016	Cabins (wheelchair accessible):	2
Length (ft/m):	745.4/227.2	Wheelchair accessibility:	Good
Beam (ft/m):	94.5/28.8	Elevators:	6
Propulsion/Propellers:	diesel-electric / 2	Casino (gaming tables):	No
Passenger Decks:	9	Swimming Pools:	1
Total Crew:	545	Self-Service Launderette:	Yes
Passengers (lower beds):	930	Library:	Yes
Passenger Space Ratio (lower beds):	51.5	Onboard currency:	US$

THE SHIP. *Viking Sea* is a handsome contemporary ship with Scandinavian attitude. It is excellent for grown-ups who want to experience destinations in comfort. There are numerous public areas and dining options for its size, plus an abundance of glass walls that help connect you with the sea on every level.

The ship is powered by hybrid energy-efficient engines, solar panels, and equipment for minimizing air pollution. Viking Ocean Cruises focuses on enhancing the destination experience (rather than the ship being your only destination), so throughout the ship you'll find interactive stations that provide a wealth of destination information. The interior design leaves an uncluttered impression, so you won't find overly opulent surroundings – it's more Hyatt (premium) than Four Seasons (luxe).

A walk-around promenade deck is on a lower deck (Deck 2), so it's fairly well sheltered from any wind, and is good for a stroll. Meanwhile, on the largest upper open deck, a sliding glass dome covers the main pool deck on the deck below, just forward of the main pool; aft of the pool is a spacious Wintergarden, with wood cladding around its support pillars. There's also a large screen for poolside movies. A second pool (and adjacent hot tub) on the same deck, but at the aft of the ship, is an infinity pool that forms part of an alfresco casual eatery with fine ocean views – the Aquavit Terrace.

BERLITZ'S RATINGS		
	Possible	Achieved
Ship	500	460
Accommodation	200	171
Food	400	338
Service	400	325
Entertainment	100	76
Cruise Experience	400	322
OVERALL SCORE 1692 points out of 2000		

One neat feature of all the sun-loungers is that they have retractable footrests, while the square drinks tables have a thick wood top – very smart and practical. Inside, the main focal point is a delightful, elegant, rectangular atrium lobby that is three decks high and features light woods and clean Scandinavian design that lets in plenty of natural light. There is an abundance of inviting seating on all levels.

An Explorer's Lounge spans two decks. It is a fine, comfortable observation lounge with great views, and incorporates a library, practical seating, and a deli counter called Viking Café – so it's rather like an all-in-one living space, or lifestyle lounge. The upper level is certainly reminiscent of the popular Polaris (observation) Lounge aboard the ships of the former Royal Viking Line, and includes glass cabinets displaying items connected with exploration and discovery, as well as models of historic ships.

Viking Ocean Cruises is the sister company of the well-established and highly experienced Viking River Cruises. It has certainly concentrated on devising itineraries that are very destination-rich and immersive, so the shore-excursion program is focused much more on the cultural experience.

Overall, the company is positioned against Azamara Club Cruises and Oceania Cruises – with much larger shower enclosures, lower pricing, and with more included. *Viking Sea* is an almost all-inclusive ship, with the fare covering Wi-Fi, a shore excursion in each port of call, overnight stays in embarkation or disembarkation ports, and complimentary beer and wine with lunch and dinner.

ACCOMMODATION. There are just five accommodation categories, but with many different price grades, according to deck and location.

The company keeps things such as interior decor simple, which is typical of the efficient Scandinavian design approach and a philosophy that has worked very well for its river cruise division. It is comfortable and practical, but perhaps a little minimalist for some. All cabins feature a private balcony (Viking calls them 'verandas') and a *king*-size bed, and even the smallest cabin has a shower enclosure spacious enough to bathe in (only suites have bathtubs). If you like more space, the Explorer Suites, located at the very front or back of the ship, are the ones to go for; most of these have a wrap-around balcony.

The largest accommodation is a superb Owner's Suite, which is conveniently positioned adjacent to the Explorer's Lounge. It includes a master bedroom, lounge, dining area, walk-in closet, wet room, and private sauna.

DINING. There are several restaurants and eateries to choose from, all of which operate on an open-seating basis, so you can dine with whom you like, when you like, and all of which are included in the cruise price. Most venues also have an alfresco option (there is a great emphasis on dining in the fresh air).

The main dining room is called, quite simply, The Dining Room. It has a sliding glass wall that can open onto the wrap-around promenade deck aft, with a few tables for alfresco dining, weather permitting.

The cuisine is decidedly international, but with some 'always available' comfort classics. The focus is on regional and sustainably sourced ingredients.

There are other dining options, the first three of which are located on the deck below the Dining Room. Manfredi's Italian Restaurant features Italian food with a focus on Tuscany; its decoration includes real accordions (the national instrument of Italy).

The Chef's Table is for a food-and-wine-paired specialty dining experience. The Kitchen Table is an intimate venue for chef's selections at night, while during the daytime the venue can be used for cooking classes.

Viking Café is part of the Explorer's Lounge, on its lower level. World Café (Lido Café) also has an outdoor area known as the Aquavit Terrace (a term borrowed from the sister company's riverships). Adjacent is an infinity pool and hot tub.

Additionally, complimentary specialty coffees and teas are available around-the-clock, as is 24-hour room service, while an afternoon 'High Tea' can be experienced in the Wintergarden.

ENTERTAINMENT. The 250-seat Star Theater is a single-deck-height showlounge, designed more for cabaret acts, recitals, and lectures than for large production shows. This is because most of the experience aboard this ship involves the destinations (including overnight visits in some), so there's little need for entertainment on a grand scale.

SPA/FITNESS. The Spa is expansive and beautifully designed. Located indoors, on the lowest passenger deck, it includes a beauty salon, workout center, 'snow' room, and a salt-water thermal pool (with swim-against-the-flow feature), in a delightfully relaxing backdrop that includes glass-fronted fireplaces. Separate men's and women's areas include a sauna, plunge bath, changing rooms, cupboards for clothes, and a relaxation space. Operated by LivNordic, the whole spa is precisely that – Nordic – and elegant, with well-trained staff, who refreshingly don't push for sales of expensive bodycare items.

VIKING SKY
★★★★+

A WELL-PROPORTIONED SHIP WITH PREMIUM STYLE FOR EXPERIENCED TRAVELERS

Size:	Mid-size Ship	Passenger/Crew Ratio (lower beds):	1.7/1
Tonnage:	47,800	Cabins (total):	465
Cruise Line:	Viking Ocean Cruises	Size Range (sq ft/m):	270.0–1,163.0/25.0–108.0
Former Names:	none	Cabins (for one person):	0
Builder:	Fincantieri (Italy)	Cabins with balcony:	464
Entered Service:	Feb 2017	Cabins (wheelchair accessible):	7
Length (ft/m):	754.5/230.0	Wheelchair accessibility:	Good
Beam (ft/m):	94.5/28.8	Elevators:	8
Propulsion/Propellers:	diesel-electric/2	Casino (gaming tables):	No
Passenger Decks:	9	Swimming Pools:	2
Total Crew:	545	Self-Service Launderette:	Yes
Passengers (lower beds):	928	Library:	Yes
Passenger Space Ratio (lower beds):	51.5	Onboard currency:	US$

THE SHIP. *Viking Sky* is a very smart-looking contemporary ship (delightfully reminiscent of the former Royal Viking Line's *Royal Viking Sky*). It exudes style, and is aimed squarely at adults who want comfort and some elements of luxe without glitz. It has a lot of public areas and dining options for its size, plus an abundant glass walls that connect you with the sea on every level, providing the feeling that you are cruising in a floating residence.

The sleek, uncluttered design of this ship – powered by hybrid energy-efficient engines, solar panels, and equipment for minimizing air pollution – is focused on destination experiences (rather than the ship being the destination), so you'll find interactive stations that provide a wealth of destination information. What you won't find is overly opulent surroundings – the result of design elements that are more Hyatt (premium) than Four Seasons (luxe), and approaching *Europa 2*'s beautiful interior design.

On a lower deck (Deck 2), there's a walk-around promenade deck that is fairly well sheltered from any wind, which is good for a stroll. On the largest upper open deck, a sliding glass dome covers the main pool deck (and adjacent rectangular hot tub with its fine geometric-design tile surround) on the deck below, just forward of the main pool; aft of the pool is a large screen for poolside movies. Another pool on the same deck, but at the aft of the ship, is an infinity pool (with adjacent tiled hot tub), which is cantile-

BERLITZ'S RATINGS

	Possible	Achieved
Ship	500	460
Accommodation	200	170
Food	400	325
Service	400	325
Entertainment	100	76
Cruise Experience	400	323

OVERALL SCORE 1692 points out of 2000

vered off the ship's stern; it is part of the Aquavit Terrace, an alfresco casual eatery with fine ocean views. Sunloungers include retractable footrests, while square drinks tables have thick wooden tops, which is both smart and practical.

Viking uses the interior space well, which provides a restrained wow factor. The main focal point is an elegant rectangular atrium lobby, called The Living Room. Three decks high, its clean Scandinavian design, with light woods, lets in plenty of natural light. There is excellent, inviting seating on all levels, while a coffee bar, large lounge chairs, sofas, and low tables add to the comfortable and spacious living room ambience. A grand stairway, located forward, is wide, with a large LED backdrop screen projecting constantly changing images of Norway; underneath it is a lichen garden.

The two-deck, split-level Explorer's Lounge is an extremely comfortable observation lounge with fine views; the soft furnishings include an abundance of cushions. The room incorporates library books, and Mamsen's deli counter for Nordic treats including Norwegian waffles and fresh berries for a breakfast snack –the teacups and coffee mugs here are the same as the ones used in the the family home of Torstein Hagen, Viking's CEO. The Explorer Lounge's upper level is reminiscent of the Polaris Lounge (the observation lounge) aboard the ships of the former Royal Viking Line; it has glass cabinets displaying items connected with exploration and discovery by

Norwegians Roald Amundsen, Leif Erikson, and Thor Heyerdahl, and models of historic ships, and is a delightful spot to chill-out and relax.

Viking Ocean Cruises is the first new start-up cruise line to build new ships since 1998, when Disney Cruise Line built two. It's the sister company of the well-established and highly experienced Viking River Cruises. The company has concentrated on devising itineraries that really are destination-rich and immersive, so the program of shore excursions is focused much more on the cultural experience than most, and on really learning about the destinations.

Despite an initial impression of Scandinavian minimalism, the interior designers have created a beautiful, cozy and warm, homey environment. There are lots of delightful, quirky details – in fact, to find them all, you'll need to take another cruise. You may not find flowers, but you will see bonsai, arrangements of moss, bark, lichen, and other tactile items, including some beautiful fabrics and touchy-feely surfaces.

Viking Ocean Cruises has positioned itself fairly and squarely against Azamara Club Cruises and Oceania Cruises, but with newer ships (with much larger bathrooms and shower enclosures, for example), lower pricing, and with more things included. *Viking Sky* is almost an all-inclusive ship. What's included? Ship-wide Wi-Fi; a shore excursion in each port; overnight stays in embarkation or disembarkation ports; complimentary self-service laundry; specialty coffees and teas (served or self-serve 24/7); no extra charges for any restaurant or eatery; 24-hour room service; stocked mini-bar (in most accommodation grades); and beer and wine with lunch and dinner. Viking Ocean Cruises really straddles the line between premium and luxury and is perhaps the best value in cruising today!

ACCOMMODATION. There are just five accommodation categories, but with many different price grades, according to deck and location.

The decor is simple – a philosophy that has worked well for its river cruise division. It is comfortable and practical (perhaps a little minimalist for some), but typical of the Scandinavian design efficiency approach. All cabins and suites have a private balcony (Viking calls them verandas) and a *king*-size bed, and even the smallest cabin has a spacious shower enclosure (only suites have bathtubs). If you like more space, the Explorer Suites, located at the very front or back of the ship, are the ones to go for; most of these have a wrap-around balcony.

The largest accommodation is a superb Owner's Suite, which is conveniently positioned adjacent to the Explorer's Lounge, and includes a master bedroom, lounge, dining area, walk-in closet, wet room, and private sauna.

DINING. There are several restaurants and eateries from which to choose. All operate on an open-seating basis, so you can dine with whom you like,

when you like. All are included in the cruise price, and most also have an alfresco option (in fact, there is a great emphasis on dining in fresh air).

The principal dining venue is called, quite simply, The Dining Room (with tablecloths for all meals, fine plates, and cutlery that is of an ideal weight). It has a sliding glass wall that can open onto the wrap-around promenade deck aft, with some tables for alfresco dining.

The cuisine is decidedly international, but with some 'always available' comfort classics. The focus is on regional and sustainably sourced ingredients, with everything cooked from scratch (no pre-mixed sauces, soups, or bread purchased from outside sources).

Other restaurants are located on the deck below the main dining room (The Dining Room). Manfredi's Italian Restaurant features Italian food with a focus on Tuscany; its decoration includes real accordions (the national instrument of Italy), and photographs of Italian film stars.

Chef's Table is the venue for a specialty dining experience, where the food and wine are paired. The Kitchen Table is an intimate venue for chef's selections at night, while during the daytime the venue can be used for cooking classes.

Mamsen's (a sort of Norwegian deli) is part of the lower level of the Explorer's Lounge.

World Café is a casual self-serve Lido Café – with open kitchen, and moveable glass doors that open onto an outdoor area called the Aquavit Terrace (a term borrowed from the sister company's river-ships), adjacent to the infinity pool and hot tub.

Additionally, complimentary specialty coffees and loose-leaf teas are available around-the-clock, as is 24-hour room service, while an afternoon High Tea can be taken in the Wintergarden. Do try one of the superb armagnacs, with vintages starting in 1935 – you'll find them in a hide-away bar called Torshavn.

ENTERTAINMENT. The 250-seat Star Theater is the ship's single-deck-height showlounge, designed more for cabaret acts, recitals, and lectures than for large production shows. This is because most of the experience aboard this ship involves the destinations (including overnight visits in some), so there's little need for entertainment on a grand scale.

SPA/FITNESS. The Spa is expansive and beautifully designed. Located indoors on the lowest passenger deck, it includes a beauty salon, workout center, 'snow' room, and a salt-water thermal pool (with swim-against-the-flow feature), in a delightfully relaxing backdrop that includes glass-fronted fireplaces. Separate men's and women's areas include a sauna, plunge bath, changing area, cupboards for clothes, and a relaxation area. Operated by LivNordic, the whole spa area is precisely that – Nordic and elegant, with well-trained staff, who refreshingly don't push for sales of expensive bodycare products.

VIKING STAR
★★★★+

THIS HANDSOME-LOOKING PREMIUM SHIP IS FOR THE WELL-TRAVELED

Size:	Mid-size Ship	Passenger/Crew Ratio (lower beds):	1.7/1
Tonnage:	47,800	Cabins (total):	465
Cruise Line:	Viking Cruises	Size Range (sq ft/m):	312.1-1,668.4/29.0-155.0
Former Names:	none	Cabins (for one person):	0
Builder:	Fincantieri (Italy)	Cabins with balcony:	465
Entered Service:	Apr 2015	Cabins (wheelchair accessible):	2
Length (ft/m):	745.4/227.2	Wheelchair accessibility:	Good
Beam (ft/m):	94.5/28.8	Elevators:	6
Propulsion/Propellers:	diesel-electric / 2	Casino (gaming tables):	No
Passenger Decks:	9	Swimming Pools:	1
Total Crew:	545	Self-Service Launderette:	Yes
Passengers (lower beds):	930	Library:	Yes
Passenger Space Ratio (lower beds):	51.5	Onboard currency:	US$

THE SHIP. *Viking Star* is a very smart-looking contemporary ship (delightfully reminiscent of the former Royal Viking Line's *Royal Viking Star*), exuding style. It is aimed squarely at adults who want comfort and some elements of luxe, but no glitz. It has a lot of public areas and dining options for its size, plus an abundance of glass walls that help connect you with the sea on every level, creating the feeling that you are cruising in a floating residence.

The sleek, uncluttered design of this ship – powered by hybrid energy-efficient engines, solar panels, and equipment for minimizing air pollution – is focused on enhancing the destination experience (rather than the ship being your only destination), so throughout the ship you'll find interactive stations that provide a wealth of destination information. It is uncluttered and extremely comfortable.

A walk-around promenade deck is on a lower deck (Deck 2) and is fairly well sheltered from any wind, which is good for a stroll (and very popular). On the largest upper open deck, a sliding glass dome covers the main pool deck (and adjacent rectangular hot tub with its fine geometric-design tile surround) on the deck below, just forward of the main pool; aft of the pool is a large screen for poolside movies. Another pool on the same deck, but at the aft of the ship, is an infinity pool (and adjacent tiled hot tub) that is cantilevered off the ship's stern; it is part of the Aquavit Terrace, an alfresco casual eatery with fine ocean

BERLITZ'S RATINGS

	Possible	Achieved
Ship	500	460
Accommodation	200	171
Food	400	338
Service	400	325
Entertainment	100	76
Cruise Experience	400	322

OVERALL SCORE 1692 points out of 2000

views. The sunloungers include a retractable footrest, while square drinks tables have a thick wood top – smart – and practical.

Inside, it is clear that Viking uses space efficiently, and provides a restrained 'wow' factor. The main focal point is a stunning, elegant, rectangular atrium lobby called The Living Room. It is three decks high and features clean Scandinavian design, with light woods, that lets in plenty of natural light. There is an abundance of inviting seating on all levels, while a coffee bar, large lounge chairs, sofas, and low tables really do provide a spacious living room ambiance.

At two decks high, the split-level Explorer's Lounge is a supremely comfortable observation lounge with fine views (and tactile seat decoration including furry animal pelts thrown over chairs and sofas, and an abundance of cushions). It incorporates a library, and Mamsen's – a deli counter featuring Nordic treats – including Norwegian waffles and fresh berries for a breakfast snack (the teacups and coffee mugs are the same as used in the family home of the Viking chairman, Torstein Hagen). The upper level is reminiscent of the Polaris Lounge (the observation lounge) aboard the ships of the former Royal Viking Line; it includes glass cabinets displaying items connected with exploration and discovery by Norwegians Roald Amundsen, Leif Erikson, and Thor Heyerdahl, and models of historic ships, and is a delightful spot to relax in.

Viking Ocean Cruises is the first new start-up cruise line to build new ships since 1998, when Disney Cruise Line built two. It's the sister company of the well-established and highly experienced Viking River Cruises. Viking has concentrated on devising itineraries that really are destination-rich and immersive, so the shore-excursion program is focused much more on the cultural experience than most, and really learning about the destinations.

Despite an initial impression of Scandinavian minimalism, the interior designers have created a beautiful, cozy and warm home-like environment. There are lots of delightful, quirky details, including bonsai, some beautiful fabrics and touchy-feely surfaces.

Viking Ocean Cruises appears to have positioned itself squarely against Azamara Club Cruises and Oceania Cruises, but with newer ships (and with much larger bathrooms and shower enclosures, for example), lower pricing, and more things included. *Viking Star* is almost an all-inclusive ship. Together with extremely good value lead-in prices, these are all included: ship-wide Wi-Fi; a shore excursion in each port; overnight stays in embarkation or disembarkation ports; complimentary self-service laundry; specialty coffees and teas (served or self-serve 24/7); no extra charges for any restaurant or eatery; 24-hour room service; stocked mini-bar (in most accommodation grades); and beer and wine with lunch and dinner. Viking Ocean Cruises straddles the line between premium-plus and luxury and is perhaps the best value in cruising today!

ACCOMMODATION. There are just five accommodation categories, plus a superb Owner's Suite that is conveniently positioned adjacent to the Explorer's Lounge - it includes a master bedroom, lounge, dining area, walk-in closet, wet room, and private sauna. There are many different prices, according to deck and location. All accommodation has a private balcony ('veranda').

Viking likes to keep things like interior decor simple - a philosophy that has worked very well for its river cruise division. It is comfortable and practical, but perhaps a little minimalist for some, which is typical of the Scandinavian design approach.

All accommodation grades feature a *king*-size bed, and even the smallest cabin has a shower enclosure spacious enough to bathe in (only suites have bathtubs). If you like more space, the Explorer Suites, located at the very front or back of the ship, are the ones to go for; most of these have a wrap-around balcony.

DINING. There are several restaurants and eateries to choose from, all of which operate on an open-seating basis, so you can dine with whom you like, when you like, and all of which are included in the cruise price. Most also have an alfresco op-

tion (in fact, there is a great emphasis on dining in fresh air).

The principal dining venue is called, quite simply, The Dining Room (with tablecloths for all meals, and fine plates and cutlery that is of an ideal weight). It has a sliding glass wall that can open onto the wraparound promenade deck aft, with some tables for alfresco dining, weather permitting.

The cuisine is decidedly international, but with some 'always available' comfort classics. The focus is on regional and sustainably sourced ingredients, with everything cooked from scratch (no pre-mixed sauces, soups, or bread purchased from outside sources).

In terms of other dining venues, the first three of these are located on the deck below the main dining room. Manfredi's Italian Restaurant features Italian food with a focus on Tuscany; its decoration includes real accordions (the national instrument of Italy), and photographs of Italian film stars.

The Chef's Table is for a specialty dining experience, where the food and wine are paired. The Kitchen Table is an intimate venue for chef's selections at night, while during the daytime the venue can be used for cooking classes. Mamsen's (a sort of Norwegian deli) is part of the lower level of the Explorer's Lounge. World Café is the ship's casual self-serve Lido Café - with open kitchen, and moveable glass doors that can open onto an outdoor area called the Aquavit Terrace that is adjacent to the infinity pool and hot tub.

Additionally, complimentary specialty coffees and loose-leaf teas are available around-the-clock, as is 24-hour room service, while an afternoon High Tea can be taken in The Wintergarden. Do try one of the superb Armagnacs, with vintages starting in 1935 - you'll find them in a hide-away bar called Torshavn.

ENTERTAINMENT. The 250-seat Star Theater is the ship's single-deck-height showlounge, designed more for cabaret acts, recitals, and lectures rather than large production shows. This is because most of the experience aboard this ship involves the destinations (including overnight visits in some), so there's little need for entertainment on a grand scale.

SPA/FITNESS. The Spa is expansive and beautifully designed. It includes a beauty salon, fitness center, 'snow' room, and a salt-water thermal pool (with swim-against-the-flow feature), in a delightfully relaxing backdrop that includes glass-fronted fireplaces. Separate men's and women's areas include a sauna, plunge bath, changing rooms, cupboards for clothes, and a relaxation space. Operated by LivNordic, the whole spa is precisely that - Nordic - and elegant, with well-trained staff, who refreshingly don't push for sales of expensive bodycare items. However, body-pampering treatments are on the pricey side.

VIKING SUN
★★★★+

A WELL-DESIGNED PREMIUM SHIP THAT IS IDEAL FOR STYLISH TRAVELERS

Size:	Mid-size Ship	Passenger/Crew Ratio (lower beds):	1.7/1
Tonnage:	47,800	Cabins (total):	465
Cruise Line:	Viking Ocean Cruises	Size Range (sq ft/m):	270.0–1,163.0/25.0–108.0
Former Names:	none	Cabins (for one person):	0
Builder:	Fincantieri (Italy)	Cabins with balcony:	464
Entered Service:	Nov 2017	Cabins (wheelchair accessible):	7
Length (ft/m):	754.5/230.0	Wheelchair accessibility:	Good
Beam (ft/m):	94.5/28.8	Elevators:	8
Propulsion/Propellers:	diesel-electric/2	Casino (gaming tables):	No
Passenger Decks:	9	Swimming Pools:	2
Total Crew:	545	Self-Service Launderette:	Yes
Passengers (lower beds):	928	Library:	Yes
Passenger Space Ratio (lower beds):	51.5	Onboard currency:	US$

THE SHIP. *Viking Sun* is a very well-proportioned contemporary ship with a host of clean Scandinavian design elements. Step aboard, and it immediately feels homey – like a highly comfortable moving hotel. There are plenty of public areas and dining options, plus an abundance of glass walls that help connect you with the sea on every level.

The ship is powered by energy-efficient hybrid engines, solar panels, and equipment for minimizing air pollution. Viking Ocean Cruises focuses on enhancing the destination experience (rather than the ship being your only destination), and provides interactive touch-screen stations that provide a wealth of destination information. This ship provides an excellent base for the various destinations covered on Viking's itineraries. The interior design is tasteful, and leaves an uncluttered impression, so you won't find overly opulent surroundings – it's more Hyatt (premium) than Four Seasons (luxe).

A walk-around promenade deck is on a lower deck (Deck 2), so it's fairly well sheltered from any wind, and good for a stroll. Meanwhile, on the largest upper open deck, a sliding glass dome covers the main pool deck on the deck below, just forward of the main pool; aft of the pool is a spacious Wintergarden, with wood cladding around its support pillars. There's also a large screen for poolside movies. A second pool (and adjacent hot tub) on the same deck, but at the aft of the ship, is an infinity pool that forms part of the Aquavit Terrace, an alfresco casual eatery with fine ocean

BERLITZ'S RATINGS		
	Possible	Achieved
Ship	500	461
Accommodation	200	171
Food	400	338
Service	400	325
Entertainment	100	76
Cruise Experience	400	322
OVERALL SCORE 1693 points out of 2000		

views. Sunloungers have a retractable footrest, while the drinks tables are square with a thick wood top – both smart and practical.

Inside, the main focal point is a delightful, elegant, rectangular atrium lobby that is three decks high and features light woods and abundant glass that lets in plenty of natural light. There is an abundance of seating on all levels.

An Explorer's Lounge spans two decks. It is a very comfortable observation lounge with great views, and incorporates a library, practical seating, and a deli counter called Viking Café. The upper level is reminiscent of the popular Polaris (observation) Lounge aboard the former Royal Viking Line ships; it features glass cabinets displaying items connected with exploration and discovery, and historic ship models.

Viking Ocean Cruises is expert at concentrating on destination-rich and immersive itineraries, and a program of shore excursions focused on cultural experiences.

Viking Sun is an almost all-inclusive ship; the fare includes ship-wide Wi-Fi, a shore excursion in each port of call, overnight stays in embarkation or disembarkation ports, and complimentary beer and wine with lunch and dinner.

ACCOMMODATION. There are five accommodation categories, but many different price grades, according to deck and location. It is comfortable and practical – perhaps a little too minimalist and not sumptuous enough for some – and typical of the efficient Scandinavian approach to design. All cabins/suites have a private balcony (Viking calls them 'verandas'), a *king*-size bed, and a spacious shower enclosure (the suites have bathtubs), and all bathrooms have heated floors, which is a nice touch. If you like more space, it's worth considering one of the Explorer Suites located at the very front or back of the ship – most have a wrap-around balcony.

The largest accommodation is a superb Owner's Suite, which is conveniently positioned adjacent to the Explorer's Lounge. It includes a master bedroom, lounge, dining area, walk-in closet, wet room, and private sauna.

DINING. There are several restaurants and eateries, all of which operate on an open-seating basis, so you can dine with whom you like, when you like, and all of which are included in the cruise price. Most venues also have an alfresco option (there is a great emphasis on dining in the fresh air).

The Dining Room (an easy name to remember) has a sliding glass wall that can open onto the wraparound promenade deck aft, with a few tables for alfresco dining, weather permitting.

The cuisine is decidedly international and unfussy, and it includes 'always available' comfort classics. The focus is on regional and sustainably sourced ingredients.

Three alternative restaurants are located on the deck below the Dining Room. Manfredi's Italian Restaurant features Italian cuisine with a focus on Tuscany; its decoration includes real accordions (the national instrument of Italy).

The Chef's Table is for a really good food-and-wine-paired dining experience, while the Kitchen Table is an intimate venue for the chef's selections at night; during the daytime the venue is used for cooking classes.

Viking Café is part of the Explorer's Lounge, on its lower level. World Café (Lido Café) also has an outdoor area known as the Aquavit Terrace (a term borrowed from the sister company's riverships).

Additionally, complimentary specialty coffees and teas are available around-the-clock, as is 24-hour room service, while an afternoon High Tea can be taken in The Wintergarden.

ENTERTAINMENT. The 250-seat Sun Theater is a single-deck-height showlounge, designed more for cabaret acts, recitals, and lectures than production shows. This is because most of the experience aboard this ship involves the destinations (including overnight visits in some), so there's little need for entertainment on a grand scale.

SPA/FITNESS. The Spa is expansive and beautifully designed. Located on the lowest passenger deck, it includes a beauty salon, workout center, 'snow' room, and a salt-water thermal pool (with swim-against-the-flow feature), in a delightfully relaxing backdrop that includes glass-fronted fireplaces. Separate areas for men and women include a sauna, plunge bath, changing area, cupboards for clothes, and relaxation space. Operated by LivNordic, the whole spa area is precisely that – Nordic – and elegant, with well-trained staff, who refreshingly don't push for sales of expensive bodycare products.

VISION OF THE SEAS
★★★+

THIS GOOD-LOOKING SHIP HAS SLEEK LINES AND IS VERY COMFORTABLE

Size:	Mid-size Ship	Passenger/Crew Ratio (lower beds):	2.7
Tonnage:	78,491	Cabins (total):	1,000
Cruise Line:	Royal Caribbean International	Size Range (sq ft/m):	135.0–1,270.1/12.5–118.0
Former Names:	none	Cabins (for one person):	0
Builder:	Chantiers de l'Atlantique (France)	Cabins with balcony:	229
Entered Service:	May 1998	Cabins (wheelchair accessible):	14
Length (ft/m):	915.3/279.0	Wheelchair accessibility:	Good
Beam (ft/m):	105.6/32.2	Elevators:	9
Propulsion/Propellers:	diesel-electric (50,400kW)/2	Casino (gaming tables):	Yes
Passenger Decks:	11	Swimming Pools:	2
Total Crew:	735	Self-Service Launderette:	No
Passengers (lower beds):	2,000	Library:	Yes
Passenger Space Ratio (lower beds):	39.2	Onboard currency:	US$

THE SHIP. *Vision of the Seas* (a *Radiance*-class ship), with its slim funnel placed at the very aft, is for the whole family to enjoy, and offers a good choice of restaurants and eateries. The ship shares the design features that make all Royal Caribbean International (RCI) ships identifiable. The ship's stern is beautifully rounded.

There are two swimming pools; the main pool, which also has a large movie screen, and an aft pool, which is within a Solarium indoor/outdoor area (with a retractable dome). There's a decent amount of open-air walking space, although this is cluttered with sunloungers that lack cushioned pads. While not as large as the newer ships in the fleet, the ship is perhaps more suited to couples and families with children that don't need all those bells and whistles, but want to cruise with up-to-date facilities and have multiple dining choices for more convenience. The finger-touch digital 'wayfinder' direction screens are useful.

A multi-level atrium lobby called the Centrum is the focal interior point and *the* social meeting place. In a 2013 makeover, the whole area was revamped, and new features were added. On its various levels, it houses an R Bar (for some creative cocktails), several passenger service counters, an art gallery, and Café Latte-tudes (for coffee). Close by are the flashy Casino Royale (for table gaming and slot machines), the popular Schooner Bar, with its nautical-theme decor and maritime art, and the Centrum shops.

BERLITZ'S RATINGS		
	Possible	Achieved
Ship	500	361
Accommodation	200	137
Food	400	240
Service	400	258
Entertainment	100	73
Cruise Experience	400	257

OVERALL SCORE 1326 points out of 2000

Aerial entertainment happens in the Centrum, too.

Other public rooms include the Library – with its decent array of books, and a neat wooden sculpture of something that looks like the Tin Man from *The Wizard of Oz*.

Take time to look at some of the $6 million worth of artwork throughout the ship's interior – it's both colorful and creative.

ACCOMMODATION. There's a range of suites and cabin types to choose from, and the price you pay depends on the size, grade and location. All cabins/suites have a flat-screen television/infotainment system.

The many standard cabins are of an adequate size, and have just enough functional facilities to make them comfortable. Twin lower beds convert to a queen-size one, and there is a reasonable amount of closet and drawer space, but little room between the bed and desk. The bathrooms are small but functional, the shower units are very small, and there is no cabinet for personal toiletries.

Choose suite-grade accommodation for more space, including a curtained-off sleeping area, a good-size outside balcony with part-partition, lounge with sofa, two chairs and drinks table, three closets, plenty of drawer and storage space, and TV/infotainment system. The bathroom is large and has a full-size tub, integral shower, and dual washbasins/toiletries cabinets.

For the ultimate accommodation, choose the Royal Suite (think Palm Beach apartment), which has a white baby grand piano. It has a separate bedroom with king-size bed, living room with queen-size sofa bed, refrigerator/mini-bar, dining table, infotainment center, and vanity dressing area. Located just under the starboard-side navigation bridge wing is a private balcony.

DINING. The expansive Aquarius Dining Room spans two levels, with large ocean-view windows on two sides and a connecting stairway. Choose either one of two seatings (with fixed times for dinner), or My Time Dining, where you can eat when you want, during dining room hours.

So, what's the food like? It's like you'd get in a smart American family restaurant, although the menu descriptions make the food sound better than it is, and the selection of breads, rolls, fruit, and cheese is poor. Overall, meals are rather hit and miss. Also, if you want lobster or a decent filet mignon (steak), you will be asked to pay extra.

Other eateries include:

The extra-cost Chops Grille (opposite the Schooner Bar): large-size premium-quality steaks and seafood items (reservations are required).

The extra-cost Giovanni's Table (adjacent to Chops Grille): Italian cuisine in a rustic setting (reservations are required).

Izumi: an extra-cost Asian-style eatery with a sushi bar and hot-rocks cooking (it's open for lunch and dinner; reservations required).

The extra-cost, reservations-required Chef's Table (located in one corner of the lower level of the Aquarius main dining room): this is a private experience, typically co-hosted by the executive chef and sommelier for a multi-course wine-pairing dinner. It's expensive, but worth it for a special occasion.

Park Café is a casual no-charge market-style eatery for salads, sandwiches, soups, pastries, and wraps.

A drinks package is also available at all bars, in the form of cards or stickers. This enables you to pre-pay for a selection of standard soft and alcoholic drinks, but the packages are not exactly easy to understand.

The Windjammer Café is the casual dining spot for self-serve buffets (open for all meals and late-night snacks). It is quite large, and, because it's positioned at the front of the ship, has fine ocean views.

ENTERTAINMENT. The Masquerade Theater, the ship's showlounge, is located forward and presents production shows and major cabaret performances. It is a large, but well-designed, room with main and balcony levels, and good sight lines from most of the banquette seating.

Other cabaret acts perform in the Some Enchanted Evening Lounge, located aft. This venue is for cabaret, (smutty) late-night comedy, and live music for dancing.

The entertainment throughout is upbeat, and it's difficult to get away from it. There's even background music in all corridors and elevators, and constant music outdoors on the pool deck.

SPA/FITNESS. The Vitality at Sea Spa and Fitness Center has a solarium, an indoor/outdoor dome-covered pool, Inca- and Mayan-theme decor, sauna/steam rooms, and a gymnasium. Other facilities include a rock-climbing wall with several separate climbing tracks, located outdoors aft of the funnel.

VOLENDAM
★★★

DATED SHIP WITH DUTCH DECOR AND ABUNDANT HERITAGE FOR MATURE-AGE CRUISERS

Size:	Mid-size Ship	Passenger/Crew Ratio (lower beds):	2.5
Tonnage:	61,214	Cabins (total):	720
Cruise Line:	Holland America Line	Size Range (sq ft/m):	113.0–1,126.0/10.5–104.6
Former Names:	none	Cabins (for one person):	0
Builder:	Fincantieri (Italy)	Cabins with balcony:	197
Entered Service:	Nov 1999	Cabins (wheelchair accessible):	23
Length (ft/m):	781.0/238.00	Wheelchair accessibility:	Good
Beam (ft/m):	105.8/32.2	Elevators:	12
Propulsion/Propellers:	diesel-electric (37,500kW)/2	Casino (gaming tables):	Yes
Passenger Decks:	10	Swimming Pools:	2 (1 w/ sliding glass dome)
Total Crew:	561	Self-Service Launderette:	Yes
Passengers (lower beds):	1,440	Library:	Yes
Passenger Space Ratio (lower beds):	42.5	Onboard currency:	US$

THE SHIP. *Volendam* has the flow, artwork and comfortable feeling that repeat passengers will recognize from other Holland America Line ships. The name is taken from a fishing village north of Amsterdam. The hull is dark blue, in keeping with all HAL ships. A glass dome-covered pool on the Lido Deck between the mast and the funnel is located one deck higher than on earlier *Statendam*-class ships, with the positive result that there is direct access between the aft and midships pools.

The interior design theme is flowers, and the interior focal point is a huge crystal sculpture, *Caleido*, in the three-deck-high atrium, by one of Italy's leading contemporary glass artists, Luciano Vistosi.

In the casino bar, which is also known as the sports bar, a cinematic theme gives visions of Hollywood, and includes a collection of costumes, props, photos, and posters of movies and the actors who starred in them. The ship looks somewhat tired.

ACCOMMODATION. This ranges from interior cabins (no view) to a Penthouse Suite. The interior and outside cabins are tastefully furnished, and have twin beds that convert to a queen-size bed, but space is tight. The fully tiled bathrooms are small, and have small shower tubs, utilitarian toiletries cupboards, and exposed under-sink plumbing.

Suite occupants share a private Concierge Lounge. Strangely, there are no butlers. Suite passengers re-

BERLITZ'S RATINGS		
	Possible	Achieved
Ship	500	306
Accommodation	200	125
Food	400	228
Service	400	267
Entertainment	100	60
Cruise Experience	400	241

OVERALL SCORE 1227 points out of 2000

ceive complimentary laundry and ironing services, cocktail-hour hors d'oeuvres and other goodies, as well as priority embarkation and disembarkation, but the bathrooms (except for the Penthouse Suite) are really small . For the ultimate in accommodation choose the Penthouse Suite. It has a bedroom, separate living room with baby grand piano, and a dining room, dressing room, walk-in closet, butler's pantry, and private balcony – though the balcony is still small. Other facilities include an audio-visual center, wet bar, large bathroom with Jacuzzi, and guest bathroom.

All outside-view suites and cabin bathrooms have a tub/shower, while interior cabins have a shower only. The 23 cabins for passengers with limited mobility have a roll-in shower enclosure for wheelchairs – none has bathtubs, no matter the category.

There is a charge to use the washing machines and dryers in the self-service launderette, although it really should be included for the occupants of high-priced suites. Although room service is adequate, it remains a weak point.

DINING. The Rotterdam Dining Room (with 747 seats) is a traditional, grand room spread over two decks. Both open seating and fixed seating with assigned tables and times are available, while breakfast and lunch are open seating. Rosenthal porcelain and good-quality cutlery are provided. Tables are for two, four, six, or eight.

With a few exceptions, the cuisine is rather unmemorable, and is missing passion and taste, because it's all about batch cooking. There's a distinct lack of variety of green vegetables, and too much rice, canned fruit, and already sliced and diced cheese. Still, you get friendly service from Indonesian and Filipino stewards, and the plates are decent ones.

Pinnacle Grill is an extra-cost (reservations required) venue featuring Pacific Northwest cuisine, including premium steaks and seafood (suite occupants get priority reservations).

Lido Buffet is a self-serve café for casual breakfasts and luncheons; it is also open for dinner in an open-seating arrangement. Canaletto (a section of the Lido Buffet) is set aside and features Italian-style cuisine. Reservations are required. The Lido Deck poolside Dive-In at the Terrace Grill does burgers, hot dogs, and fries, and on some days, barbeques.

ENTERTAINMENT. The Frans Hals Showlounge spans two decks and is a fairly well-designed room, but sight lines from the balcony level are poor.

SPA/FITNESS. The Ocean Spa facilities are decent, and include a gym, separate saunas and steam rooms, and several treatment rooms. There are practice tennis courts outdoors, as well as shuffleboard courts, a jogging track, and a full walk-around teakwood promenade deck.

VOYAGER OF THE SEAS
★★★+

THIS LARGE, FAMILY-FRIENDLY SHIP HAS MANY EATING VENUE CHOICES

Size:	Large Resort Ship	Passenger/Crew Ratio (lower beds):	2.6
Tonnage:	137,280	Cabins (total):	1,557
Cruise Line:	Royal Caribbean International	Size Range (sq ft/m):	151.0–1,358.0/14.0–126.1
Former Names:	none	Cabins (for one person):	0
Builder:	Kvaerner Masa-Yards (Finland)	Cabins with balcony:	757
Entered Service:	Nov 1999	Cabins (wheelchair accessible):	26
Length (ft/m):	1,020.6/311.1	Wheelchair accessibility:	Best
Beam (ft/m):	155.5/47.4	Elevators:	14
Propulsion/Propellers:	diesel-electric (28,000kW)/ 2 azimuthing pods	Casino (gaming tables):	Yes
Passenger Decks:	14	Swimming Pools:	3
Total Crew:	1,176	Self-Service Launderette:	No
Passengers (lower beds):	3,114	Library:	Yes
Passenger Space Ratio (lower beds):	44.0	Onboard currency:	US$

THE SHIP. The exterior design is like an enlarged version of the company's *Vision*-class ships. With its larger proportions, it provides more facilities and options, yet manages to maintain a healthy passenger/space ratio.

Embarkation and disembarkation take place through two access points, designed to minimize the inevitable lines at the start and end of the cruise. A four-deck-high Royal Promenade, the interior focal point (in the style of London's chic Burlington Arcade), is a good meeting place. It is 394ft (120m) long – the length of two American football fields – with two internal lobbies that rise through 11 decks, one at each end.

The entrance to one of three levels of the main restaurant, together with shops and entertainment locations spin off from this 'boulevard,' while 'interior promenade-view' cabins, with bay windows, look into it from above. It houses a traditional English pub (the Pig 'n' Whistle, with draft beer and street-front seating), Promenade Café (for Continental breakfast, all-day pizzas, sandwiches, and coffees), Ben & Jerry's Ice Cream (extra cost), Sprinkles (for round-the-clock ice-cream and yoghurt), and Scoreboard (a sports bar). Several themed shops are located here, and a bright red telephone kiosk houses an ATM cash machine. It's a cross between a shopping arcade and an amusement park and a nice place to see and be seen. The RCI company chairman even donated his own treasured Morgan sports car to grace it. The best view of the whole

BERLITZ'S RATINGS

	Possible	Achieved
Ship	500	367
Accommodation	200	132
Food	400	258
Service	400	258
Entertainment	100	73
Cruise Experience	400	257

OVERALL SCORE 1309 points out of 2000

promenade is from one of the cabins that look into it, or from a 'captain's bridge' that crosses above it.

At the forward end is the showlounge. In the center, a stairway connects you to the deck below, for the Schooner Bar (a piano lounge that's a feature on all RCI ships), while gaming tables and slot machines can be found in the Casino Royale. A second showlounge – Studio B – houses a regulation-size ice-skating rink that has real ice – plus arena seating for up to 900 – and broadcast facilities. A number of slim pillars obstruct sight lines, however. If ice-skating doesn't appeal, try the two-deck library; it was the first aboard any modern cruise ship, and is open 24 hours a day.

Drinking places include a gastro pub called The Tavern; the intimate 'R' Bar; and the Golden Room (casino lounge). Jazz fans might like High Notes, an intimate room for cool music atop the ship within the Viking Crown Lounge, or the Schooner Bar piano lounge. For golfers, there's the 19th Hole, a golf bar.

Studio B houses a 400-seat conference center and a 60-seat multimedia screening room. Many decks above, couples can tie the knot in a 'wedding chapel in the sky,' the Skylight Chapel.

Although the ship is large, cabin hallways have a warm and attractive feel, with artwork cabinets and wavy lines that lead you along and break up the monotony. The theme-park, banquet-style regimentation is well organized. You will, however, need to plan, otherwise you'll miss out on some of the things that you might like to include in your vacation.

Because cruise fares are so reasonable, there's always a push for extra-revenue items, drinks packages, and extra-cost dining options, etc. In the end, however, you should have a decent cruise. Facilities for children and teenagers (in four age groupings) are extensive, and include Adventure Beach, an area for all the family, with swimming pools, a water slide, and game areas.

Overall, this is a good all-round ship for everyone.

ACCOMMODATION. The cabin price grades are in four major groupings: premium ocean-view suites and cabins; interior (atrium-view) cabins; ocean-view cabins; and interior cabins. Many cabins are of a similar size – good for incentives and large groups – and 300 have interconnecting doors (good for families).

Standard outside-view and interior (no-view) cabins are of a reasonably adequate size, with just enough facilities to make them comfortable and functional. Twin lower beds convert to queen-size beds, and there is a reasonable amount of closet and drawer space, but the bed(s) take up most of the space. Bathrooms are small but functional, with dimensionally challenged shower enclosures, and no cabinet for personal toiletries. Overall, they're cramped.

Some 138 'interior' cabins have bay windows that look into an interior horizontal atrium – a cruise industry first, when the ship debuted. (You'll need to keep the curtains closed in the bay windows if you are changing, because you can be seen.) Regardless of which cabin grade you choose, all except for the Royal Suite and Owner's Suite have twin beds that convert to a queen-size unit, TV, radio and telephone, personal safe, vanity unit, hairdryer, and private bathroom.

Some accommodation grades have a refrigerator/mini-bar. If you take anything from it on the day of embarkation in Miami, sales tax is added to your bill.

Note that cabins with 'private' balconies aren't so private. The balcony decking is made of Bolidt – a sort of rubberized sand – though the balcony rail is wood. If you have a cabin with a connecting door to another cabin, be aware that you'll probably be able to hear everything your next-door neighbors say and do. The bathroom vacuum toilets are explosively noisy. Cabin bath towels are small and skimpy. The menus from room service are basic.

DINING. Sapphire, the main dining room, is very large and set on three levels, each with an operatic name and theme: Carmen, La Bohème, and Magic Flute. A stunning staircase connects the three levels, but fat support pillars obstruct sight lines from many seats. All three have the same menus and food. Choose one of two seatings, or My Time Dining, which allows you to eat when you want during dining room hours. The tables are for four to 12, and the place settings, china, and cutlery are of good quality.

The food in the main dining room is all about standardized catering and batch cooking. The menu descriptions sound tempting, but the food, although prepared well, is just so-so. Vegetarian and children's menus are also available. Note that there are no wine waiters.

Most meat dishes are disguised with gravies or heavy sauce reductions; rice is often used as a source of carbohydrates. Green vegetables are scarce, but basic salad items are plentiful, and the desserts are very decent. Breads and pastry items are plentiful too (though these are thawed and then baked from frozen 'starter' dough), but the croissants lack any hint of butter.

Other dining venues and eateries (some cost extra, but the food is mostly cooked to order) include favorites such as Chops Grille Steakhouse (for premium veal chops, steaks, and seafood dishes), Portofino (for Italian-American cuisine), and Giovanni's Table (for Italian trattoria-style dishes). Reservations (make them through the digital system) are required; note that menus do not change.

Windjammer Marketplace is a cavernous, casual self-serve buffet eatery, but note that the plastic plates for hot items are mildly warm, at best. Breakfast buffet items and lunchtime salad items are pretty repetitive. Beverage stations have just the basics. Burgers and hot dogs in self-serve buffet locations are displayed in steam dishes. If you are disabled, do ask for help.

Johnny Rockets is a retro 1950s all-day, all-night diner-style eatery that has burgers and malt shakes. All indoor tables have a mini-jukebox with dimes provided to make your selection of vintage records. There's a cover charge, whether you eat in or take out.

Promenade Café is for Continental breakfast, all-day pizzas, sandwiches, and coffees in paper cups, while Sprinkles has round-the-clock ice cream and free yoghurt, pastries, and coffee.

ENTERTAINMENT. The 1,347-seat La Scala Theater, a fine showlounge, is located at the front and spans five decks, with a few slim pillars and almost no disruption of sight lines. The room has a hydraulic orchestra pit and huge stage areas, together with rather loud sound, and superb lighting equipment.

In addition, the ship has an array of cabaret acts. There is also late-night adults-only comedy. Arguably, however, the best shows are the Ice Spectaculars.

SPA/FITNESS. The Voyager Day Spa and Fitness Center is reasonably large, and measures 15,000 sq ft (1,400 sq m). It has a main and an upper level, and includes an aerobics room, fitness center, several treatment rooms, and men's and women's sauna/steam rooms. Another 10,000 sq ft (930 sq m) of space is provided for a Solarium (with sliding glass-dome roof) to relax in after you've exercised.

Aft is a 32.8ft (10m) rock-climbing wall, with five climbing tracks. Other sports facilities include a roller-blading track, a dive-and-snorkel shop, a basketball court, and a nine-hole, par 26 golf 'course.'

WESTERDAM
★★★+

THIS MID-SIZED SHIP FEATURES LOTS OF TRADITIONAL DUTCH DECOR AND ARTIFACTS

Size:	Mid-size Ship	Passenger/Crew Ratio (lower beds):	2.3
Tonnage:	82,348	Cabins (total):	958
Cruise Line:	Holland America Line	Size Range (sq ft/m):	170.0–1,318.6/15.7–122.5
Former Names:	none	Cabins (for one person):	0
Builder:	Fincantieri (Italy)	Cabins with balcony:	641
Entered Service:	Apr 2004	Cabins (wheelchair accessible):	28
Length (ft/m):	935.0/285.0	Wheelchair accessibility:	Good
Beam (ft/m):	105.6/32.2	Elevators:	14
Propulsion/Propellers:	diesel-electric (35,240kW)/2 azimuthing pods	Casino (gaming tables):	Yes
		Swimming Pools:	2 (1 w/ sliding glass dome)
Passenger Decks:	11	Self-Service Launderette:	No
Total Crew:	817	Library:	Yes
Passengers (lower beds):	1,916	Onboard currency:	US$
Passenger Space Ratio (lower beds):	41.9		

THE SHIP. *Westerdam* is one of what is known as a series of *Vista*-class vessels, designed to appeal to younger, active vacationers. It has two funnels, placed close together, one in front of the other, the result of the configuration of the machinery. The ship has, in effect, two engine rooms – one with three diesels, and one with two diesels and a gas turbine. Pod propulsion is provided, powered by a diesel-electric system (there's almost no vibration), and a small gas turbine in the funnel helps reduce emissions.

There's a complete walk-around exterior teak promenade deck, with teak steamer-style sunloungers. A jogging track is located around the mast and the forward third of the ship. Exterior glass elevators, mounted midships on both sides, provide ocean views. There are two centrally located swimming pools outdoors, one of which can be used in poor weather thanks to its retractable sliding glass roof. Two adjacent whirlpool tubs are abridged by a bar. Another smaller pool is for children.

A 'Retreat' is available at extra cost; it has 14 cabanas (at even more cost per day).

An entrance lobby spans three decks, and is topped by a beautiful, rotating Waterford crystal globe of the world. The interior decor is interesting; the ceilings are particularly noticeable in the public decor, the colors are muted and warm. The information desk is small and removed from the main passenger flow.

BERLITZ'S RATINGS		
	Possible	Achieved
Ship	500	361
Accommodation	200	144
Food	400	233
Service	400	254
Entertainment	100	67
Cruise Experience	400	266

OVERALL SCORE 1325 points out of 2000

There are two whole entertainment/public room decks. The most dramatic room is the showlounge, which spans three decks in the forward part of the ship. Other facilities include a winding shopping street with boutique stores and logo shops, an Internet center, a decent library, card room, an art gallery, photo gallery, and several small meeting rooms. The casino is large – one has to walk through it to get from the restaurant to the showlounge on one of the entertainments decks.

In a 2007 refit, an Explorations Café was added to the Crow's Nest (a HAL trademark observation lounge atop the ship). This encompasses the ship's library, and a lounge area with fine ocean views, and is nice when it's not too busy.

On lower decks is a Queen's Lounge, which acts as a lecture room and a Culinary Arts Center. There are also a number of other bars and lounges, including an Explorer's Lounge. The ship also has a small 40-seat movie-screening room. Niggles include several pillars that obstruct the flow and lines of sight throughout the ship; there are no self-service launderettes, although special laundry packages are available; and the air conditioning cannot be turned off in cabins or bathrooms.

ACCOMMODATION. There are many price categories. From largest to smallest: Penthouse Verandah Suites measure 1,318 sq ft (122 sq m), including balcony; Deluxe Verandah Suites measure 563 sq ft (52 sq m); Verandah Suites measure 284 sq ft (26 sq m); outside-view cabins are 197 sq ft (18 sq m); interior (no-view) cabins are slightly smaller, at 183 sq ft (17 sq m).

Lifeboats obstruct the view from some cabins on the lowest accommodation deck. Some cabins that can accommodate a third and fourth person have little closet space and only one personal safe. Some cabins have interconnecting doors. Occupants of suites have exclusive use of a concierge lounge and service, priority embarkation and disembarkation, and other benefits. In many suites and cabins with private balconies the balconies aren't really private (many can be overlooked from above).

DINING. Options range from full-service meals in the main dining room and à la carte restaurant to casual, self-serve buffet-style meals and fast-food outlets. The 1,045-seat Vista Dining Room, located aft, is two decks high, with seating provided on the main and balcony levels. Both open seating and assigned seating are available, while breakfast and lunch are open seating, where you'll be taken to a table by restaurant staff when you enter.

There are tables for two to eight. The waiter stations can be noisy for anyone seated adjacent to them. Rosenthal porcelain and decent cutlery are used, but there are no fish knives. Lighter-option meals are available for the nutrition-conscious. HAL can provide Kosher meals, although these are prepared ashore, frozen, and brought to the table sealed in their original containers.

With a few exceptions, the cuisine is unmemorable, and is missing passion and taste, because it's all about catering for the masses. There's a distinct lack of variety of green vegetables, heavy use of rice, canned fruit, and already sliced and diced cheese. Still, you get friendly service from Indonesian and Filipino stewards, and the plates are nice.

Pinnacle Grill (including Pinnacle Bar) is an intimate 130-seat venue with higher-quality ingredients and smarter presentation than in the main dining room. It is on Lower Promenade Deck, and fronts onto the second level of the atrium lobby. Pacific Northwest cuisine and premium-quality steaks, shown to you at your table, are featured. Reservations are required, and there's a cover charge (the steaks are worth it).

An extensive self-serve Lido Café (buffet) wraps around the funnel housing and extends aft. It includes a pizzeria counter, a salad bar, Asian stir-fry counter, deli sandwiches, and a dessert section. Movement around it can be slow, particularly at peak times. In the evenings, one side of this venue is turned into an extra-cost, 72-seat Canaletto Restaurant – a quasi-Italian informal eatery with waiter service.

Also, the poolside Dive-In at the Terrace Grill does several signature burgers (with special Dive-In sauce), hot dogs, and fries, and, on certain days, barbeques.

Meanwhile, the Windsurf Café in the atrium lobby is open most of the day for extra-cost coffees, pastries, snack foods, deli sandwiches, and, in the evening, liqueur coffees.

ENTERTAINMENT. The 846-seat Vista Lounge is for revue shows and major cabaret presentations. It spans three decks in the forward section. The main floor level has a bar in its starboard aft section. Spiral stairways at the back of the lounge connect all levels. The upper levels have better sight lines.

SPA/FITNESS. The large, two-deck-high Greenhouse Spa is located directly above the navigation bridge. Facilities include a solarium, hydrotherapy pool, and a unisex thermal suite – an area incorporating saunas and steam rooms. There's also a beauty salon, several massage/therapy rooms (including one for couples), and a gym with ocean views and high-tech equipment.

Sports facilities include a basketball court, volleyball court, and golf simulator.

WIND SPIRIT
★★★+

THIS MODERN SAIL-CRUISE SHIP HAS CHIC, CONTEMPORARY STYLE

Size:	Boutique Ship	Passenger/Crew Ratio (lower beds):	1.6
Tonnage:	5,350	Cabins (total):	74
Cruise Line:	Windstar Cruises	Size Range (sq ft/m):	185.0–220.0/17.0–22.5
Former Names:	none	Cabins (for one person):	0
Builder:	Ateliers et Chantiers du Havre	Cabins with balcony:	0
Entered Service:	Apr 1988	Cabins (wheelchair accessible):	0
Length (ft/m):	439.6/134.0	Wheelchair accessibility:	None
Beam (ft/m):	51.8/15.8	Elevators:	0
Propulsion/Propellers:(a) diesel-electric (1,400kW)/1;		Casino (gaming tables):	Yes
	(b) sails	Swimming Pools:	1
Passenger Decks:	5	Self-Service Launderette:	No
Total Crew:	88	Library:	Yes
Passengers (lower beds):	148	Onboard currency:	US$
Passenger Space Ratio (lower beds):	36.1		

THE SHIP. *Wind Spirit*, an identical twin to *Wind Star*, is a sleek-looking craft that is part-yacht, part-cruise ship, with four masts that tower 170ft (52m) above the deck, and with computer-controlled sails. The masts, sails, and rigging cost $5 million, when the ship was built. A computer keeps the ship on an even keel via the movement of a water hydraulic ballast system of 142,653 US gallons (540,000 liters), so there is no rolling over 6 degrees. You may be under sail for less than 40 percent of the time, depending on the conditions and cruise area winds prevailing.

Because of the amount of complex sail machinery, there is little open deck space. At the stern is a small water-sports platform for use when at anchor, but only in really calm sea conditions. Water-sports toys include a banana boat, kayaks, sunfish sailboats, windsurf boards, water-ski boat, scuba and snorkel equipment, and four Zodiacs. You will need to sign a waiver if you wish to use the water-sports equipment.

The ship has a finely crafted interior with pleasing, blond woods, and soft, complementary colors and decor that is chic, even elegant, but a little cold. Note that the main lounge aboard this ship is of a slightly different design from that aboard *Wind Star*.

No scheduled activities help to make this a really relaxing, unregimented 'get away from it all' vacation. It's about an unstructured environment.

Niggles? The swimming pool is just a tiny 'dip' pool. Be prepared for the whine of the generators, which

BERLITZ'S RATINGS		
	Possible	Achieved
Ship	500	355
Accommodation	200	160
Food	400	267
Service	400	271
Entertainment	100	73
Cruise Experience	400	257

OVERALL SCORE 1383 points out of 2000

are needed to run the air-conditioning and lighting systems 24 hours a day. Beverage prices are a little high. The library is small and needs more hardback fiction. Members of staff, though friendly, are generally casual and a little sloppy at times in the finer points of service.

This sail-cruise ship is ideally suited to youthful couples and solo travelers seeking contemporary facilities and some water sports in a relaxed but chic setting that's different from 'normal' cruise ships.

The dress code is casual, with no jackets and ties, even for dinner. Gratuities are added to your account daily, and 15 percent is added to bar and wine accounts.

ACCOMMODATION. All cabins are nicely equipped, have a mini-bar/refrigerator (stocked when you embark, but all drinks cost extra), 24-hour room service, personal safe, and plenty of storage space. The TV rotates so that it is viewable from both bed and bathroom. All cabins have two outside-view portholes, and deadlights (steel covers that can be closed in poor weather conditions). The decor is a pleasant mix of rich woods, natural fabrics and colorful soft furnishings, and hi-tech yacht-style amenities. A basket of fruit is replenished daily.

The bathrooms are compact units, designed in a figure of eight, with a teakwood floor in the central section. There is decent storage space for toiletries in two cabinets, as well as under-sink cupboard space. A wall-mounted hairdryer is also provided. The shower enclosure (no cabins have bathtubs) is circular and has both a hand-held as well as a fixed shower. L'Occitane bathroom products are provided, as are a vanity kit and shower cap.

The lighting is not strong enough for make-up application – for this it's better to use the vanity desk in the cabin, which has more powerful overhead (halogen) lighting. Bathrobes and towels are 100 percent cotton.

DINING. The elegant 'AmphorA' Restaurant has ocean views from large, picture windows, a lovely wood ceiling and wood-paneled walls. California-style nouvelle cuisine is served, with attractively presented dishes. Also, signature dishes created by master chefs Joachim Splichal and Jeanne Jones are featured. It's open seating, so you can dine when you want and with whomever you wish.

The service staff are mostly Indonesians and Filipinos, who struggle sometimes at communicating, although their service is friendly. The selection of breads, cheeses, and fruits could be better. There is a big push to sell wines, but prices are high, as they are for most alcoholic drinks – and even for bottled water.

There is often casual dinner on the open deck under the stars, with grilled seafood and steaks. At the bars, hot and cold hors d'oeuvres appear at cocktail times.

Fancy something quiet and romantic? At no extra charge, a 'Cuisine de l'Amour' romantic dinner for two can be served to you in your cabin, complete with candle.

ENTERTAINMENT. There is no showlounge, shows, or cabaret. However, these are not needed, because a cruise aboard this high-tech sailing ship provides an opportunity to get away from all that noise and 'entertainment.' The main lounge, a corner of which houses a small casino, has a small dance floor, and, typically, a trio plays there.

The main lounge is also used for social functions. Otherwise, it's down to more personal entertainment, such as a DVD in your cabin late at night – or, much more romantic, after-dinner hours spent outside strolling or simply lounging on deck.

SPA/FITNESS. A gymnasium (with a modicum of muscle-toning equipment, treadmills, and exercycles) and sauna are located aft, adjacent to the water-sports platform. Extra-cost spa packages can be pre-booked before you arrive at the ship.

WIND STAR
★★★+

A CONTEMPORARY SAIL-CRUISE SHIP FOR SMART-CASUAL CRUISING

Size:	Boutique Ship	
Tonnage:	5,350	
Cruise Line:	Windstar Cruises	
Former Names:	none	
Builder:	Ateliers et Chantiers du Havre	
Entered Service:	Dec 1986	
Length (ft/m):	439.6/134.0	
Beam (ft/m):	51.8/15.8	
Propulsion/Propellers:	(a) diesel-electric (1,400kW)/1; (b) sails	
Passenger Decks:	5	
Total Crew:	88	
Passengers (lower beds):	148	
Passenger Space Ratio (lower beds):	36.1	

Passenger/Crew Ratio (lower beds):	1.6
Cabins (total):	74
Size Range (sq ft/m):	185.0–220.0/17.0–22.5
Cabins (for one person):	0
Cabins with balcony:	0
Cabins (wheelchair accessible):	0
Wheelchair accessibility:	None
Elevators:	0
Casino (gaming tables):	Yes
Swimming Pools:	1
Self-Service Launderette:	No
Library:	Yes
Onboard currency:	US$

THE SHIP. *Wind Star* is a long, sleek-looking craft that is part-yacht, part-cruise ship, with four masts towering 170ft (52m) above the deck, and with computer-controlled sails. The computer keeps the ship on an even keel via the movement of a water hydraulic ballast system of 142,653 US gallons (540,000 liters), so there is no rolling over 6 degrees. You may be under sail for less than 40 percent of the time, depending on the conditions and cruise area winds. Because of the amount of sail machinery, there is little open deck space when the ship is full. A small, aft water-sports platform can be used when at anchor. Water-sports facilities include a banana boat, kayaks, sunfish sailboats, windsurf boards, water-ski boat, scuba and snorkel equipment, and four Zodiacs.

The ship has a nicely crafted interior with blond woods, together with soft, complementary colors and decor that is chic, but a little cold. This ship had a complete makeover in 2012.

No scheduled activities help to make this a relaxing, unregimented 'get away from it all' vacation. Windstar ships offer cruising in very comfortable surroundings bordering on the luxurious, in an unstructured environment.

The dress code is casual, with no jackets and ties. Gratuities are charged to your onboard account, and 15 percent is added to bar, wine and spa accounts.

BERLITZ'S RATINGS		
	Possible	Achieved
Ship	500	355
Accommodation	200	160
Food	400	267
Service	400	271
Entertainment	100	73
Cruise Experience	400	257
OVERALL SCORE 1383 points out of 2000		

Niggles? The swimming pool is really only a tiny 'dip' pool. Be prepared for the whine of the vessel's generators. You'll hear it at night in your cabin; it takes some passengers a day or two to get used to. Beverage prices are a little high. The library is small. The staff, though friendly, is a little sloppy at times in the finer points of service.

Overall, *Wind Star* is suited to youthful couples and solo travelers who want contemporary facilities and some water sports in a relaxed but chic setting.

ACCOMMODATION. The cabins are nicely equipped, have crisp, inviting decor and a mini-bar/refrigerator (stocked when you embark, but all drinks cost extra), 24-hour room service, personal safe, and plenty of storage space. The TV rotates so that it is viewable from the bed and the bathroom. All cabins all have two portholes. The bathrooms are compact with a teakwood floor. There is a good amount of storage space for toiletries in two cabinets, as well as under-sink cupboard space. A wall-mounted hairdryer is also provided. The shower enclosure (no cabins have bathtubs) is circular and has both a hand-held as well as a fixed shower unit. L'Occitane toiletries are provided.

DINING. The main dining room, the 'AmphorA' Restaurant is chic, and has ocean views. California-style cuisine is served, with attractively presented dishes. Additionally, signature dishes created by master chefs Joachim Splichal and Jeanne Jones are offered. Open seating means you dine when and with whom you want to.

The service staff members are mostly Indonesians and Filipinos, who struggle sometimes at communicating, although their service is pleasant. The selection of breads, cheeses, and fruits could be better. There is a big push to sell wines, although the prices are extremely high, as they are for most drinks – even bottled water is the highest in the industry, at $7 per liter bottle.

There is often casual dinner on the open deck under the stars, with grilled seafood and steaks. At the bars, hot and cold hors d'oeuvres appear at cocktail times. For something quiet and romantic, a 'Cuisine de l'Amour' romantic dinner for two can be served to you in your cabin. The menu offers a choice of appetizer, a set soup, choice of salad, and two entrée (main) options, and a set dessert to finish.

ENTERTAINMENT. There is no showlounge, so no shows, or cabaret. The main lounge, a corner of which houses a small casino, has a small dance floor, and, typically, a trio plays there. Otherwise, it's down to more personal entertainment, such as a movie in your cabin late at night – or, much more romantic, after-dinner hours spent outside strolling or simply lounging on deck.

SPA/FITNESS. A fitness room and sauna are located aft. The spa is operated by a specialist concession. Special spa packages can be pre-booked.

WIND SURF
★★★★

ELEGANT DECOR FOR SMART-CASUAL SAIL-CRUISING IN RELAXED COMFORT

Size:	Small Ship	Passenger/Crew Ratio (lower beds):	1.9
Tonnage:	14,745	Cabins (total):	156
Cruise Line:	Windstar Cruises	Size Range (sq ft/m):	188.0–500.5/17.5–46.5
Former Names:	*Club Med I*	Cabins (for one person):	0
Builder:	Ateliers et Chantiers du Havre	Cabins with balcony:	0
Entered Service:	Feb 1990/May 1998	Cabins (wheelchair accessible):	0
Length (ft/m):	613.5/187.0	Wheelchair accessibility:	None
Beam (ft/m):	65.6/20.0	Elevators:	2
Propulsion/Propellers:(a) diesel-electric (1,400kW)/1;		Casino (gaming tables):	Yes
	(b) sails	Swimming Pools:	2
Passenger Decks:	8	Self-Service Launderette:	No
Total Crew:	163	Library:	Yes
Passengers (lower beds):	312	Onboard currency:	US$
Passenger Space Ratio (lower beds):	47.2		

THE SHIP. This sail-cruise ship is a good choice for couples seeking informality (no jackets or ties), but who don't want the inconvenience of the workings of a real tall ship. It cruises in the Caribbean (Nov–Mar) and in the Mediterranean (May–Oct).

Wind Surf, one of a pair of the world's largest sail-cruisers, is part-cruise ship, part-yacht – its sister ship operates as *Club Med II*. This is a larger, grander sister to the original three Windstar Cruises vessels. Five huge masts of 164ft (50m), rising 221ft (67m) above sea level, carry seven triangular, self-furling Dacron sails, with a total surface area of 26,881 sq ft (2,497 sq m).

No human hands touch the sails – instead, everything is handled electronically by computer control from the bridge, which some might think is a little boring. Also, because European sailings take place at night, with days spent in port, there seems little point to having the sails, as you won't get to experience them.

A computer keeps the ship on an even keel via the movement of a water hydraulic ballast system of 266,800 US gallons (1 million liters), so there is no heeling over 6 degrees. When the ship isn't using the sails, four diesel-electric motors propel it at up to approximately 12 knots. The ship is very quiet when moving.

Swimming from the aft water-sports platform isn't allowed. But extensive water sports facilities include

BERLITZ'S RATINGS		
	Possible	Achieved
Ship	500	369
Accommodation	200	160
Food	400	280
Service	400	282
Entertainment	100	73
Cruise Experience	400	285

OVERALL SCORE 1449 points out of 2000

windsurfers, sailboats, water-ski boats, scuba tanks, snorkels, fins, masks, and inflatable Zodiac motorized boats for water-skiing – all at no extra charge, except for the scuba tanks.

There are two salt-water swimming pools – little more than 'dip' pools. One is amidships on the uppermost deck; the other is aft, together with two hot tubs, and an adjacent bar. There are no showers at either of the pools, so passengers get into the pools or hot tubs while covered in oil or lotion, an unhygienic arrangement.

A meeting room can accommodate 30–60 people. The casino/main lounge has four blackjack tables, one roulette table, and 21 slot machines. It has an unusually high ceiling for the size of the ship.

A Yacht Club includes books and DVDs for in-cabin use and provides comfortable seating for relaxation or listening to music loaded for you on iPods available from reception. An espresso bar offers extra-cost Lavazza coffee, plus other drinks and deli sandwiches. Eight computers have Internet access, and there's Wi-Fi access.

Hotel service is provided mostly by Filipino and Indonesian staff. Gratuities are charged to your onboard account, and 15 percent is added to bar and wine accounts, and to all spa treatments and services. The quality of food and its presentation is a definite plus, as is the policy of no music in passenger hallways or elevators.

ACCOMMODATION. There are just three price categories. Unusually, the cabin numbers (port side: even numbers; starboard side: odd numbers) are sequenced with lower numbers aft, while higher numbers are forward. All cabins are very nicely equipped, with crisp, inviting decor. They have a mini-bar/refrigerator (stocked when you embark, but all drinks are at extra cost), 24-hour room service, personal safe, a flat-screen TV set viewable from the bed or sofa, depending on cabin configuration, plenty of storage space, and two portholes. There are six four-person cabins; 35 doubles are fitted with an extra Pullman berth, and several cabins have an interconnecting door – good for families. Spa Suite packages are available at extra cost. All cabins have Wi-Fi access, at extra cost.

The bathrooms are compact, designed in a figure of eight, with a teakwood floor in the central section. There is a good amount of storage space for toiletries in two cabinets, as well as under-basin storage space, and a wall-mounted hairdryer. The circular shower enclosure has both a hand-held and a fixed shower. The lighting is not strong enough for applying make-up – this is better applied at the cabin's vanity desk.

Almost all suites have two bathrooms, a separate living/dining area, a sleeping area that can be curtained off, two vanity/writing desks, and four portholes instead of two. There are two TV sets (one in the lounge, one in the sleeping area), video player and CD player, and Bose SoundDock for iPods. Popcorn for movie viewing is available from room service. Bathrooms have granite countertops, open shelving, toiletries cabinets, and magnifying mirror.

A further two Bridge Deck suites (around 495 sq ft/46 sq m) would be delightful for a honeymoon; each has a bedroom, separate living/dining room, and marble bathroom with Jacuzzi tub, two washbasins, separate toilet, and a walk-in closet.

Spa Suite packages, introduced in 2010, also include a queen-size bed with microfiber bed linen, bathrobes, an orchid flower arrangement, two bathrooms, a flat-screen TV with DVD player, and Bose SoundDock speakers for iPods. A pillow menu provides several choices, including a 'snore-no-more' hypoallergenic pillow.

Tea collections include wellbeing, herbal, or exotic teas. Brewing service includes contemporary porcelain tea-ware and is available from room service 24 hours a day. Berlitz tip: ask for it to be made with mineral water, not the standard chlorinated ship's water.

DINING. The 'AmphorA' Restaurant seats 272 and has tables for two, four, or six. It has open seating with no pre-assigned tables, and is open only for dinner, typically 7.30–9.30pm. California-style nouvelle cuisine is served, with dishes attractively presented.

The 124-seat Degrees Bistro, a specialty dining venue, features Mediterranean cuisine. Located atop the ship, on Star Deck, it has picture windows on port and starboard sides, an open kitchen, and tables for two to six. Reservations are required for dinner, although there's no extra charge.

The Veranda, amidships on Star Deck, has an open terrace for informal, self-serve breakfast and lunch buffets. It is pleasant to be outside, eating an informal breakfast or lunch. Do try the bread pudding, available daily at lunch – the ship is famous for it, and each day has a variation on the theme.

The Compass Rose, an indoor/outdoor casual eatery, provides deli-style snack items plus some pastries and coffee for breakfast, lunch, and afternoon tea. At night, it turns into Candles for alfresco dining around the aft pool. A permanent outdoor barbeque offers fresh grilled items.

Windstar Cruises food is generally good, and geared toward American tastes. Europeans and other nationals should note that items such as bacon may be overcooked, and the choice of cheeses and teas is limited. Service in the dining room is also quite fast – geared towards those who haven't yet learned to unwind.

A nice feature is a 'Cuisine de l'Amour' romantic candlelight dinner for two, served in your cabin at no extra charge. The menu, with seductive-sounding selections, offers a choice of appetizer, a set soup, choice of salad, two entrée (main) options, and a set dessert to finish.

Finally, there's quite an extensive room service menu.

ENTERTAINMENT. There is no showlounge as such (this is a yachting-style experience, after all), although the main lounge (with a wooden dance floor), which incorporates a small casino, serves as an occasional cabaret room, and is also used for cocktail parties and other social functions.

SPA/FITNESS. The Health Spa has a unisex sauna (bathing suits required), beauty salon, and several treatment rooms for massage, facials, and body wraps. There is a decent gymnasium – on a separate deck, with ocean views – and an aerobics workout room. Unfortunately, the spa facilities are split over three separate decks, making them rather disjointed. Special spa packages can be pre-booked through your travel agent. The spa is operated by the UK's Onboard Spa Company.

WORLD DREAM
NYR

THIS FAMILY-FRIENDLY SHIP IS FOR PREMIUM ASIA CRUISING IN HIGH-TECH SURROUNDINGS

Size:	Large Resort Ship	Passenger/Crew Ratio (lower beds):	1.6/1
Tonnage:	151,300	Cabins (total):	1,680
Cruise Line:	Dream Cruises	Size Range (sq ft/m):	150.6-1,969.8/14.0-183.0
Former Names:	none	Cabins (for one person):	0
Builder:	Meyer Werft (Germany)	Cabins with balcony:	1,188
Entered Service:	Nov-17	Cabins (wheelchair accessible):	32
Length (ft/m):	1,100.0/335.3	Wheelchair accessibility:	Good
Beam (ft/m):	130.2/39.7	Elevators:	16
Propulsion/Propellers:	diesel-electric/	Casino (gaming tables):	Yes
	2 azimuthing pods	Swimming Pools:	2
Passenger Decks:	18	Self-Service Launderette:	No
Total Crew:	2,030	Library:	Yes
Passengers (lower beds):	3,360	Onboard currency:	RMB
Passenger Space Ratio (lower beds):	45		

THE SHIP. *World Dream* is the second of two stunning large resort ships for Dream Cruises – the 'premium' brand created in 2015, owned by Genting Hong Kong, operator of Star Cruises. The attention-grabbing hull is painted in flamboyant red and gold (it was conceived by Chinese Pop artist Jacky Tsai, and features a story involving a mermaid and an astronaut); the ship's exterior comes to life with LED lighting at night.

This large, family-friendly resort ship has upper exterior decks filled with sports and active waterpark attractions that are good for all ages. There is a complete, 2,000-ft- (610-m-) long walk-around outside promenade deck (with indoor-outdoor seaside eateries), multiple pools (including a private extra-cost adults-only pool and relaxation area), and the Wet 'n' Wild Water Park, in the ship's center (adjacent to the main pool), with six water slides for children and teens. Zouk Beach and bar, music lounge, and a sports bar are located aft of the funnel.

Inside, the decor is decidedly upbeat, with an abundance of colors. There are numerous bars, lounges, karaoke and mahjong rooms, large duty-free shopping street, entertainment facilities including large showlounges (for lavish shows), as well as a large Genting Casino filled with gaming tables and slot machines (plus private gaming rooms), Resorts World Casino, Resorts World Premium Club, and Maxim's – for card games. Other facilities include

BERLITZ'S RATINGS		
	Possible	Achieved
Ship	500	NYR
Accommodation	200	NYR
Food	400	NYR
Service	400	NYR
Entertainment	100	NYR
Cruise Experience	400	NYR
OVERALL SCORE NYR points out of 2000		

a business center, meeting rooms. Also, there's a special night street 'market' with hawker stalls featuring Asian delicacies.

While the facilities are really extensive, it may take time to make reservations for the various restaurants because there are many choices – particularly for cruise under seven days long.

ACCOMMODATION. There are numerous accommodation grades, from the smallest interior (no-view) cabin (measuring 150 sq ft/14 sq m) to the largest Dream Suite, measuring 1,970 sq ft/183 sq m and spread over two decks. The price you pay depends on the size, location, and grade you choose.

Occupants of Dream Palace get a private-access VIP area located in a touch-card accessible section at the front above the navigation bridge (similar to, but more expansive than, MSC Cruises' Yacht Club and Norwegian Cruise Line's The Haven), with access to a private outdoor pool, hot tubs, relaxation area, and cabanas, Horizons Lounge (observation lounge), and a private club for gaming (so there's no need to go downstairs to the busier and noisier Resorts World and other casino areas).

Over 100 family-friendly cabins have interconnecting doors, so parents can take their young ones and feel comfortable that they'll be well looked after (actually, they won't want to leave the ship after the cruise).

DINING. With an abundance of dining, eatery and drinking options, the ship is able to cater to almost any dietary and ethnic persuasion and taste. The largest dining venues include Windows, a bi-level dining hall, located aft, with ocean views from huge windows (a window table is definitely one to have). Another large restaurant is Genting Palace. The culinary emphasis throughout the ship is, naturally, on the Asia-Pacific region; this includes the Chinese lunchtime favorite – dim-sum (whose meaning, literally, is: to touch the heart).

Noted Australian chef Mark Best has a 'Bistro' venue (his second at sea) with a menu that focuses on small producer Australian beef, lamb, river fish and the freshest seafood.

Some other indoor and outdoor venues (some are at extra cost) include:

Silk Road: for à la carte Chinese regional and provincial cuisine (with tablecloths).

Blue Lagoon: for tuck-in Chinese street (finger) food and clay pot cuisine.

Umi-Uma: this Japanese cuisine venue has Teppanyaki grills, and a sushi bar.

Positano: this Italian eatery, with lots of pasta dishes, may remind you of the Amalfi coast.

Genting Palace: this restaurant features traditional Cantonese-style Chinese dishes.

Makan Makan: for south-east Asian cuisine, including Chinese and Malaysian specialties.

World Buffet: this is an ultra-casual international food court-style area with serve-yourself food from various display counters and active cooking stations, while adjacent and outside on deck is a pool bar and grill.

Bread Box and Tiffin Café: this 'see and be seen' venue is for coffees/teas and light bites.

Drinking places include a Red Lion Pub, Johnny Walker bar (with a wall full of decorative bottles of JW and a special-edition Dream Cruises JW whisky), a Martini bar, Bar City, Boba Cha, and Bar 360, among others. The ship also features a Penfolds (the celebrated Australian winery) Wine Vault.

ENTERTAINMENT. The multi-deck 1,000-seat Zodiac Theater is the principal showlounge. It features glamorous production shows including aerial acrobatics, and major cabaret acts.

Silk Road: this extra-cost supper club/nightclub features a colorful Burlesque (topless) show; adjacent are several bookable karaoke rooms.

SPA/FITNESS. Crystal Life Spa has two sections - one for Asians (for whom the 'flow-through' is much more important than the range of treatments offered), and one is for Westerners. The spa (the largest at sea) has its own spa café for 'healthy' food and drinks (some at extra cost). World Dream is only the second cruise ship with an MRI scanner (the first being sister ship Genting Dream). Sports facilities in various locations include a bowling alley, basketball court, a climbing wall, and an extensive Dreamcatcher rope-climbing course – great for kids and adults alike.

ZAANDAM
★★★

THIS SHIP FEATURES DUTCH-STYLE DECOR FOR CRUISERS OF A CERTAIN AGE

Size:	Mid-size Ship	Passenger/Crew Ratio (lower beds):	2.5
Tonnage:	61,396	Cabins (total):	720
Cruise Line:	Holland America Line	Size Range (sq ft/m):	113.0–1,126.3/10.5–104.6
Former Names:	none	Cabins (for one person):	0
Builder:	Fincantieri (Italy)	Cabins with balcony:	197
Entered Service:	May 2000	Cabins (wheelchair accessible):	23
Length (ft/m):	777.5/237.0	Wheelchair accessibility:	Good
Beam (ft/m):	105.8/32.2	Elevators:	12
Propulsion/Propellers:	diesel-electric (37,500kW)/2	Casino (gaming tables):	Yes
Passenger Decks:	10	Swimming Pools:	2 (1 w/sliding glass dome)
Total Crew:	561	Self-Service Launderette:	Yes
Passengers (lower beds):	1,440	Library:	Yes
Passenger Space Ratio (lower beds):	42.6	Onboard currency:	US$

THE SHIP. *Zaandam*'s hull is dark blue, in keeping with all HAL ships, with a single funnel.

It has three principal passenger stairways, which is better than two stairways from the viewpoints of safety, accessibility, and passenger flow. A glass-covered pool is located on the Lido Deck between the mast and the funnel.

The interior decor is restrained, with traditional ocean liner detailing and wood accenting. The design theme is music. Most of the memorabilia on show was acquired from the 'Pop and Guitars' auction at Christie's in London in 1997. It includes a Fender Squier Telecaster guitar signed by Mick Jagger, Keith Richards, Charlie Watts, Ronnie Wood, and Bill Wyman of The Rolling Stones; a Conn saxophone signed on the mouthpiece by former US president Bill Clinton; an Ariana acoustic guitar signed by David Bowie and Iggy Pop; a Fender Stratocaster guitar signed in silver ink by the members of the rock band Queen; a Bently Les Paul-style guitar signed by artists including Carlos Santana, Eric Clapton, B.B. King, Robert Cray, Keith Richards, and Les Paul. Perhaps the ship should be named *Rockerdam*.

The Oasis outdoor relaxation areas aft of the funnel include a waterfall and family-gathering areas. Explorations is an excellent combination of café, Internet connection center, and library. There are children's and teens' play areas. Popcorn is provided at the Wajang Theater for moviegoers, and this location

BERLITZ'S RATINGS

	Possible	Achieved
Ship	500	310
Accommodation	200	127
Food	400	228
Service	400	267
Entertainment	100	63
Cruise Experience	400	246

OVERALL SCORE 1241 points out of 2000

incorporates a kitchen for HAL's Culinary Arts program, for interactive cooking and tasting demonstrations. The casino has gaming tables and slot machines. Adjacent is a sports bar.

The ship's focal point is a three-deck-high atrium, with the reception desk, shore-excursions desk, photo shop, and photo gallery grouped around it. It also houses a real showpiece – a fancy 22-ft- (6.7-m-) high pipe organ with puppets that move with the music. One of the largest such Dutch band organs ever built, it was custom-made for the ship in Hilversum in the Netherlands.

As on *Volendam*, the Lido Deck swimming pool is located one deck higher than on the *Statendam*-class ships, so that you can have direct access between the aft and midships pools (not so aboard the S-class ships). This has created more space for extra cabins on the Navigation Deck below.

With one whole deck of suites and a private concierge lounge for them, the company has in effect created a two-class ship.

Niggles include that the charge to use the washing machines and dryers in the self-service launderette is petty and irritating, particularly for the occupants of suites, who pay high prices for their cruises. Communication in English with many of the staff, particularly in the dining room and buffet areas, can be frustrating. Room service is poor. Standing in line for embarkation, disembarkation, shore tenders, and for self-serve buffet meals is inevitable aboard large ships.

ACCOMMODATION. The range is comparable to that found aboard the similarly sized *Rotterdam*, and there are many different price categories. There is one Penthouse Suite, 28 suites, and 168 mini-suites, with the rest of the accommodation a mixture of outside-view and interior cabins. All passenger hallways now include pleasing artwork.

All standard interior and outside cabins are tastefully furnished, with twin beds that convert to a queen-size bed, though space is tight for walking between beds and vanity unit. There is a decent amount of closet and drawer space, but this will be tight for longer voyages. The tiled bathrooms are disappointingly small, particularly for long cruises, and have small shower tubs, utilitarian toiletries cupboards, and exposed under-sink plumbing. Occupants of the Verandah Suites and the Penthouse Suite – with a separate steward's entrance – share a private concierge lounge (Neptune Lounge, accessible by private key card). Each suite has a separate bedroom, dressing, and living area. Strangely, there are no butlers.

Other facilities include an audio-visual center, wet bar with refrigerator, large bathroom with Jacuzzi tub, separate toilet with bidet, and a guest bathroom with toilet and washbasin.

Except in the Penthouse Suite (forward on the starboard side), the bathrooms in the other suites and mini-suites are disappointingly small and not as opulent as one might expect. All outside-view suites and cabin bathrooms have a tub/shower, while interior cabins have only a shower. Some 23 cabins for the mobility-limited are, however, very spacious and have a large roll-in shower enclosure for wheelchair users (some also have a bathtub), and ramped access to the balcony.

DINING. The Rotterdam Dining Room, a grand, traditional room, spans two aft decks, with ocean views on three sides and an imposing staircase connecting the upper and lower levels. Both open seating and assigned seating are available, while breakfast and lunch are open seating. You'll be taken to a table by restaurant staff when you enter. Tables are for two to eight.

With a few exceptions, the cuisine is unmemorable, missing passion and taste, because it's mass catering. There's a distinct lack of variety of green vegetables, too heavy a use of rice, canned fruit, and already sliced and diced cheese. Still, you get friendly service from the Indonesian and Filipino stewards, and the Rosenthal plates are nice. Lighter-option meals are available for the nutrition- and weight-conscious, as are Kosher (pre-prepared) meals.

Pinnacle Grill features Pacific Northwest cuisine and seats 88. There's a cover charge, and reservations are required (suite-grade occupants qualify for priority reservations).

The Lido Buffet is a casual, self-serve café for casual breakfasts and luncheons. A poolside grill, Terrace Café, has hamburgers, hot dogs, and other fast-food items. Canaletto is open in the evening in a section of the Lido Buffet and features popular Italian dishes. Waiter service is provided, and reservations are required.

Also, a Lido Deck poolside 'Dive-In at the Terrace Grill' features signature burgers, hot dogs, and fries, and, on certain days, barbecues and other culinary treats may be featured.

ENTERTAINMENT. The Mondriaan Show Lounge, located forward, spans two decks and has banquette seating on both the main and upper levels. It is basically a well-designed room, but the ceiling is low, and the sight lines from the balcony level are quite poor.

SPA/FITNESS. The Greenhouse Spa facilities are quite extensive and include a gymnasium with good muscle-toning equipment, separate saunas and steam rooms for men and women, and several treatment rooms, each with a shower and toilet. Outdoor facilities include basketball and shuffleboard courts, a jogging track, and a full walk-around teakwood promenade deck for strolling.

ZENITH
★★★+

THIS FAMILY-FRIENDLY, CASUAL SHIP IS FOR SPANISH SPEAKING CRUISERS

Size:	Mid-size Ship	Passenger/Crew Ratio (lower beds):	2.0
Tonnage:	52,090	Cabins (total):	670
Cruise Line:	CDF Croisieres de France	Size Range (sq ft/m):	172.2–500.5/16–46.5
Former Names:	none	Cabins (for one person):	0
Builder:	Meyer Werft (Germany)	Cabins with balcony:	110
Entered Service:	Apr 1992/Jun 2007	Cabins (wheelchair accessible):	4
Length (ft/m):	682.4/208.0	Wheelchair accessibility:	Good
Beam (ft/m):	95.1/29.0	Elevators:	7
Propulsion/Propellers:	diesel (19,960kW)/2	Casino (gaming tables):	Yes
Passenger Decks:	10	Swimming Pools:	2
Total Crew:	670	Self-Service Launderette:	No
Passengers (lower beds):	1,340	Library:	Yes
Passenger Space Ratio (lower beds):	37.3	Onboard currency:	Euros

THE SHIP. *Zenith* was originally operated by Celebrity Cruises. Although now 20-plus years old, it has a contemporary, angular profile that gives the impression of power and speed. Inside there is elegant and restrained decor. The Art Deco-style hotel-like lobby, reminiscent of hotels in Miami Beach, has a spacious feel.

The main deck containing many of the public entertainment rooms has a double-width indoor promenade. There is a good-size library. Other facilities include a cigar-smoking lounge; an Internet-connect center; and the Plaza Café for coffee. A large, elegantly appointed casino has its own bar. The hospitality and the range of food have been tailored to its French-speaking family clientele. You will usually find a lot of smokers aboard.

Passenger niggles? Standing in line is inevitable. Public restroom doors are rather heavy. There are no cushioned pads for poolside sunloungers.

ACCOMMODATION. There are several different price grades, including outside-view suites and cabins, and interior cabins. Many outside-view cabins on one deck have lifeboat-obstructed views.

All cabins have good-quality fittings with lots of wood accenting, are tastefully decorated, and are of an above-average size, with an excellent closet and drawer space. All have twin beds that convert to a queen-size one. Soundproofing is quite good, but depends on location – some cabins are located opposite crew-access doors, which can be noisy. Bathrooms have a generous shower

BERLITZ'S RATINGS		
	Possible	Achieved
Ship	500	337
Accommodation	200	131
Food	400	222
Service	400	261
Entertainment	100	61
Cruise Experience	400	251

OVERALL SCORE 1263 points out of 2000

area, although towels are small. The lowest-grade outside-view cabins have a porthole, but all others have picture windows, while suites are larger, but suffer from noise on the swimming pool deck directly above.

DINING. The Caravelle Dining Room has several tables for two, as well as for four, six, or eight (in banquettes). There are two seatings for dinner, and open seating for breakfast and lunch. The cuisine, its presentation, and service are more notable for quantity than quality, and green vegetables are hard to come by.

For informal meals, the Windsurf Buffet has a traditional single-line self-service buffet for breakfast and lunch. At peak times, the buffet is simply too small, too crowded, and very noisy. The Grill, located outdoors, serves fast food such as pizzas.

ENTERTAINMENT. The two-level Showlounge, with main and balcony levels, has good sight lines from most seats, although a railing at the front of the balcony level impedes the view. Shows consist of a troupe of showgirl dancers, whose routines are amateurish. Cabaret acts are the main feature and are geared to a family audience. There is also plenty of live music for dancing in bars and lounges, plus the inevitable discotheque.

SPA/FITNESS. The Spa is high in the ship, aft of the funnel. It has a gym with ocean-view windows and therapy treatment rooms including a Rasul chamber.

ZUIDERDAM
★★★+

THERE IS DUTCH HERITAGE AND DECOR ABOARD THIS FAMILY-FRIENDLY CRUISE SHIP

Size:	Mid-size Ship	Passenger/Crew Ratio (lower beds):	2.3
Tonnage:	82,305	Cabins (total):	924
Cruise Line:	Holland America Line	Size Range (sq ft/m):	185.0–1,318.6/17.1–122.5
Former Names:	none	Cabins (for one person):	0
Builder:	Fincantieri (Italy)	Cabins with balcony:	623
Entered Service:	Dec 2002	Cabins (wheelchair accessible):	28
Length (ft/m):	935.0/285.0	Wheelchair accessibility:	Good
Beam (ft/m):	105.6/32.2	Elevators:	14
Propulsion/Propellers:	diesel-electric (35,240kW)/ 2 azimuthing pods	Casino (gaming tables):	Yes
		Swimming Pools:	2 (1 w/ sliding glass dome)
Passenger Decks:	11	Self-Service Launderette:	No
Total Crew:	800	Library:	Yes
Passengers (lower beds):	1,848	Onboard currency:	US$
Passenger Space Ratio (lower beds):	44.5		

THE SHIP. *Zuiderdam* has two funnels, placed close together, one in front of the other, and not side by side, as aboard the smaller *Amsterdam* and *Rotterdam*. This placement is because the ship has two engine rooms – one with three diesels, and one with two diesels and a gas turbine. Pod propulsion is provided, powered by a diesel-electric system, so there's almost no discernible vibration.

Several glass elevators provide ocean views. There are two centrally located swimming pools outdoors, and one of the pools can be used in inclement weather conditions due to its retractable glass-domed cover. Two whirlpool tubs, adjacent to the swimming pools, are abridged by a bar, while another (smaller) pool is provided for children.

The lobby space is small, and spans just three decks. It has a stairway, and the lobby's focal point is a 10-ft- (3-m-) high transparent Waterford crystal 'seahorse.' The decor is extremely bright for a Holland America Line ship, with an eclectic color and pattern mix that assails you from all directions.

There are two entertainment/public room decks, the upper of which has an exterior promenade deck – something new for this traditional cruise line. Although it doesn't go around the whole ship, it's long enough for walking. There is also a jogging track outdoors.

The most dramatic public room is the Vista Lounge, which spans three decks in the forward section of the ship. The casino is equipped with all the gaming para-

BERLITZ'S RATINGS

	Possible	Achieved
Ship	500	362
Accommodation	200	144
Food	400	233
Service	400	255
Entertainment	100	67
Cruise Experience	400	266

OVERALL SCORE 1327 points out of 2000

phernalia and slot machines you can think of, and it is so large that you have to walk through it to get from the restaurant to the showlounge.

The Crow's Nest is a multi-function 'lifestyle' area, encompassing the ship's library, a lounge area with fine ocean views, and an Explorations Café.

The ship is designed to appeal to young, vibrant, family-oriented passengers, with a good array of public rooms, bars, and lounges.

Niggles include the fact that many of the 'private' balconies aren't so private, and can be overlooked from various public locations. Also, some pillars obstruct the passenger flow and lines of sight on the main public decks. It can sometimes be difficult to escape from smokers, and from those walking around in unsuitable clothing.

ACCOMMODATION. There are numerous accommodation price grades. The price you pay depends on the size, location, and grade you choose. From largest to smallest: Penthouse Verandah Suites (1,318 sq ft/122 sq m, including balcony); Deluxe Verandah Suites (563 sq ft/52 sq m); Verandah Suites (284 sq ft/26 sq m); outside-view cabins (197 sq ft/18 sq m); and interior (no-view) cabins, which are slightly smaller, at 183 sq ft (17 sq m).

A number of cabins on Main Deck have views obstructed by lifeboats. Some cabins that can accommodate a third and fourth person have very little closet space, and only one personal safe. Audio channels are provided on the in-cabin TV system.

Each morning, an eight-page edition of *The New York Times* (Times Fax) is provided for each cabin. Fresh fruit is available on request. Shoe-shine service and evening turndown service are also provided, as is a small range of toiletries.

DINING. The 1,045-seat Vista Dining Room is aft. Spanning two decks, it is a pleasant room, with seating on the main and balcony levels. Both open seating (you may have to wait a considerable time for a table), and fixed seating (assigned tables and times) are available; you'll be taken to a table by restaurant staff when you enter. With a few exceptions, the cuisine is best described as uneventful and unmemorable, and is missing passion and taste, because it's all about cooking in quantity. There's a distinct lack of variety of green vegetables, and an overuse of rice, canned fruit and already sliced and diced cheese. Still, you get friendly service from smiling Indonesian and Filipino stewards, and the plates are nice.

Breakfast and lunch are open-seating, so you'll be seated by restaurant staff. Tables are for two to eight. The waiter stations can be noisy if you are seated adjacent to them. Live music is provided for dinner. Lighter-option meals are always available for the nutrition- and weight-conscious, as are Kosher meals, although these are prepared ashore, frozen, and brought to your table sealed in their original containers.

A 130-seat Pinnacle Grill is an upscale dining spot with higher-quality ingredients cooked to order. Located on Lower Promenade Deck, it fronts onto the second level of the atrium lobby. The cuisine is Pacific Northwest, plus premium-quality steaks from hand-selected cuts of beef. Reservations are needed, and there's a cover charge, but the steaks are worth it.

For casual eating, there's an extensive Lido Café, which includes a pizzeria/Italian specialties counter, salad bar, Asian stir-fry counter, deli sandwiches, and a separate dessert buffet. Movement through the buffet area can be very slow, particularly at peak times. In the evenings, one side of this venue is turned into an extra-cost, 72-seat Canaletto Restaurant – a quasi-Italian informal eatery with waiter service.

Also, a poolside 'Dive-In at the Terrace Grill' features multi-choice signature burgers (with special Dive-In sauce), hot dogs, fries, and, on certain days, barbecues and other culinary treats.

The Windsurf Café in the atrium lobby (open 20 hours a day) serves extra-cost coffees, pastries, snack foods, deli sandwiches, and, in the evenings, liqueur coffees.

ENTERTAINMENT. The 867-seat Vista Lounge is the venue for Las Vegas-style revue shows and major cabaret presentations. It spans three decks in the forward section, and the main floor level has a bar in its starboard aft section. Spiral stairways at the back of the lounge connect all levels. Stage shows are best seen from the upper levels, from where the sight lines are quite good.

SPA/FITNESS. The Greenhouse Spa is a large, two-decks-high health spa area, set above the navigation bridge. Facilities include a solarium, and an extra-cost thermal suite – a unisex area incorporating a Laconium, Hammam, and Chamomile Grotto, plus a swim-against-the-current Hydropool. There's also a beauty salon and several private treatment rooms, including one for couples. A large gymnasium with floor-to-ceiling windows has the latest equipment.

SHIPS RATED BY SCORE

Ship	Score	Rating	Ship	Score	Rating
Europa 2	★★★★★+	1863	Le Soleal	★★★★	1522
Europa	★★★★★+	1852	Artania	★★★★	1521
Hanseatic	★★★★★	1716	Deutschland	★★★★	1521
SeaDream I	★★★★★	1706	L'Austral	★★★★	1517
Sea Cloud	★★★★★	1702	Le Boreal	★★★★	1517
Sea Cloud II	★★★★★	1701	Star Legend	★★★★	1517
SeaDream II	★★★★★	1701	Star Breeze	★★★★	1504
Viking Sun	★★★★+	1693	Anthem of the Seas	★★★★	1503
Viking Sea	★★★★+	1692	Star Pride	★★★★	1503
Viking Sky	★★★★+	1692	National Geographic Orion	★★★★	1498
Viking Star	★★★★+	1692	Bremen	★★★★	1495
Crystal Serenity	★★★★+	1686	Celebrity Reflection	★★★★	1493
Silver Muse	★★★★+	1684	Nippon Maru	★★★★	1488
Queen Mary 2	★★★★+	1683	Mein Schiff 2	★★★★	1487
Crystal Symphony	★★★★+	1677	Quantum of the Seas	★★★★	1486
Hebridean Princess	★★★★+	1669	Celebrity Solstice	★★★★	1485
Asuka II	★★★★+	1662	Celebrity Equinox	★★★★	1484
Mein Schiff 6	★★★★+	1661	Paul Gauguin	★★★★	1484
Mein Schiff 5	★★★★+	1659	Celebrity Eclipse	★★★★	1483
Mein Schiff 4	★★★★+	1649	Celebrity Silhouette	★★★★	1483
Mein Schiff 3	★★★★+	1647	Majestic Princess	★★★★	1482
Silver Spirit	★★★★+	1639	Nautica	★★★★	1482
Seabourn Encore	★★★★+	1633	Regal Princess	★★★★	1480
Seabourn Quest	★★★★+	1633	Royal Princess	★★★★	1479
Seabourn Odyssey	★★★★+	1630	Ovation of the Seas	★★★★	1477
Seabourn Sojourn	★★★★+	1628	Regatta	★★★★	1477
Seven Seas Explorer	★★★★+	1617	Insignia	★★★★	1476
Silver Shadow	★★★★+	1606	Koningsdam	★★★★	1473
Silver Whisper	★★★★+	1604	Norwegian Escape	★★★★	1473
Riviera	★★★★+	1601	Norwegian Joy	★★★★	1472
Caledonian Sky	★★★★+	1587	Silver Wind	★★★★	1471
Marina	★★★★+	1587	Britannia	★★★★	1462
Genting Dream	★★★★+	1585	Silver Explorer	★★★★	1462
MSC Meraviglia	★★★★+	1585	AIDAperla	★★★★	1458
Seven Seas Voyager	★★★★+	1574	Mein Schiff 1	★★★★	1457
Queen Elizabeth	★★★★+	1572	AIDAPrima	★★★★	1452
Queen Victoria	★★★★+	1566	Silver Cloud	★★★★	1452
Island Sky	★★★★+	1561	MSC Magnifica	★★★★	1451
Azamara Journey	★★★★+	1551	Wind Surf	★★★★	1449
Azamara Quest	★★★★+	1551	MSC Poesia	★★★★	1446
Amadea	★★★★	1547	MSC Orchestra	★★★★	1445
MSC Preziosa	★★★★	1548	Disney Fantasy	★★★★	1443
Seven Seas Mariner	★★★★	1548	Saga Sapphire	★★★★	1443
MSC Divina	★★★★	1544	Disney Dream	★★★★	1442
MSC Fantasia	★★★★	1536	MSC Musica	★★★★	1441
Le Lyrial	★★★★	1534	Norwegian Getaway	★★★★	1441
MSC Splendida	★★★★	1532	Oasis of the Seas	★★★★	1440
Royal Clipper	★★★★	1531	Norwegian Breakaway	★★★★	1438

Ship	Score	Rating	Ship	Score	Rating
Harmony of the Seas	★★★★	1436	Pacific Explorer	★★★+	1356
Allure of the Seas	★★★★	1435	Silver Galapagos	★★★+	1356
Silver Discoverer	★★★★	1431	Brilliance of the Seas	★★★+	1352
Hebridean Sky	★★★★	1429	AIDAdiva	★★★+	1350
Fifty Years of Victory	★★★★	1424	AIDAluna	★★★+	1350
Sirena	★★★★	1419	Norwegian Sun	★★★+	1347
Celebrity Constellation	★★★★	1418	Sun Princess	★★★+	1347
Celebrity Infinity	★★★★	1416	Enchantment of the Seas	★★★+	1346
Diamond Princess	★★★★	1416	Norwegian Star	★★★+	1346
Celebrity Millennium	★★★★	1415	Freedom of the Seas	★★★+	1344
Celebrity Summit	★★★★	1412	Norwegian Gem	★★★+	1344
Crystal Esprit	★★★★	1406	Norwegian Dawn	★★★+	1343
Norwegian Epic	★★★★	1406	Oriana	★★★+	1343
Ruby Princess	★★★★	1405	Norwegian Sky	★★★+	1342
Emerald Princess	★★★★	1404	Norwegian Jade	★★★+	1341
Crown Princess	★★★★	1402	Norwegian Pearl	★★★+	1339
Caribbean Princess	★★★+	1399	Norwegian Spirit	★★★+	1338
MSC Opera	★★★+	1399	Adventure of the Seas	★★★+	1337
Seven Seas Navigator	★★★+	1394	Norwegian Jewel	★★★+	1337
MSC Lirica	★★★+	1392	Arcadia	★★★+	1336
Sea Princess	★★★+	1392	Explorer of the Seas	★★★+	1334
Azura	★★★+	1391	Le Ponant	★★★+	1332
Pearl Mist	★★★+	1391	Eurodam	★★★+	1328
Amsterdam	★★★+	1387	Zuiderdam	★★★+	1327
Sapphire Princess	★★★+	1387	Serenade of the Seas	★★★+	1326
Disney Wonder	★★★+	1386	Vision of the Seas	★★★+	1326
Rotterdam	★★★+	1385	Oosterdam	★★★+	1325
Wind Spirit	★★★+	1383	Westerdam	★★★+	1325
Wind Star	★★★+	1383	AIDAvita	★★★+	1324
Star Flyer	★★★+	1382	Radiance of the Seas	★★★+	1323
Disney Magic	★★★+	1381	Pacific Venus	★★★+	1322
Nieuw Amsterdam	★★★+	1381	AIDAaura	★★★+	1321
Coral Princess	★★★+	1380	Mariner of the Seas	★★★+	1321
Star Princess	★★★+	1379	Golden Princess	★★★+	1320
Noordam	★★★+	1377	Prinsendam	★★★+	1317
Island Princess	★★★+	1376	Saga Pearl II	★★★+	1317
MSC Armonia	★★★+	1373	Grand Princess	★★★+	1315
Star Clipper	★★★+	1372	Navigator of the Seas	★★★+	1315
Ventura	★★★+	1372	Costa Diadema	★★★+	1312
MSC Sinfonia	★★★+	1371	Sea Explorer	★★★+	1312
AIDAblu	★★★+	1365	Costa Deliziosa	★★★+	1311
AIDAbella	★★★+	1363	Voyager of the Seas	★★★+	1309
Aurora	★★★+	1363	Oceana	★★★+	1307
Balmoral	★★★+	1363	Rhapsody of the Seas	★★★+	1307
Jewel of the Seas	★★★+	1361	SuperStar Virgo	★★★+	1301
Independence of the Seas	★★★+	1360	Costa Fascinosa	★★★+	1299
Pacific Princess	★★★+	1359	Costa Luminosa	★★★+	1299
Liberty of the Seas	★★★+	1358	Grandeur of the Seas	★★★+	1299
AIDAmar	★★★+	1357	Costa Favolosa	★★★+	1297
AIDAstella	★★★+	1357	Costa Fortuna	★★★+	1295
AIDAsol	★★★+	1356	Costa Pacifica	★★★+	1293

Ship	Score	Rating	Ship	Score	Rating
Costa Serena	★★★+	1293	Thomson Dream	★★★	1195
Pacific Jewel	★★★+	1293	SuperStar Gemini	★★★	1192
Pacific Dawn	★★★+	1288	Costa Victoria	★★★	1189
AIDAcara	★★★+	1286	Carnival Victory	★★★	1187
TUI Discovery 2	★★★+	1286	Astor	★★★	1183
Aegean Odyssey	★★★+	1284	SuperStar Aquarius	★★★	1179
Costa Magica	★★★+	1284	Columbus	★★★	1175
TUI Discovery	★★★+	1283	Thomson Celebration	★★★	1175
Black Watch	★★★+	1277	SkySea Golden Era	★★★	1166
Boudicca	★★★+	1277	Carnival Elation	★★★	1165
Carnival Vista	★★★+	1275	Carnival Inspiration	★★★	1165
Club Med 2	★★★+	1273	Carnival Fascination	★★★	1164
Braemar	★★★+	1269	Carnival Paradise	★★★	1164
Costa Mediterranea	★★★+	1268	Carnival Ecstasy	★★★	1161
Adonia	★★★+	1265	Carnival Imagination	★★★	1161
Celebrity Xpedition	★★★+	1263	Carnival Magic	★★★	1161
Zenith	★★★+	1263	Carnival Fantasy	★★★	1158
Horizon	★★★+	1261	Carnival Sensation	★★★	1157
Pacific Eden	★★★+	1260	SuperStar Libra	★★★	1157
Pacific Aria	★★★+	1258	Kapitan Khlebnikov	★★★	1153
Sea Spirit	★★★+	1256	Magellan	★★★	1148
Costa Atlantica	★★★+	1253	Ocean Endeavour	★★★	1120
Fram	★★★	1245	Ocean Diamond	★★+	1099
Carnival Breeze	★★★	1241	Majesty of the Seas	★★+	1089
Zaandam	★★★	1241	Monarch	★★+	1089
Maasdam	★★★	1240	Serenissima	★★+	1099
Celestyal Cristal	★★★	1236	Sovereign	★★+	1088
Hamburg	★★★	1236	Astoria	★★+	1080
Carnival Dream	★★★	1235	National Geographic Explorer	★★+	1077
Celestyal Olympia	★★★	1234	Marco Polo	★★+	1067
Costa neoRiviera	★★★	1234	Expedition	★★+	1059
Costa neoRomantica	★★★	1230	Empress of the Seas	★★+	1028
Volendam	★★★	1227	Grand Celebration	★★+	1012
Carnival Freedom	★★★	1223	American Star	★★+	1000
Carnival Conquest	★★★	1220	National Geographic Endeavour	★★+	972
Costa neoClassica	★★★	1220	Ortelius	★★+	966
Veendam	★★★	1219	Independence	★★+	952
Celestyal Nefeli	★★★	1216	Sea Adventurer	★★	945
Pride of America	★★★	1215	Grande Mariner	★★	840
Berlin	★★★	1212	American Constellation	NYR	NYR
Carnival Glory	★★★	1211	Carnival Horizon	NYR	NYR
Carnival Spirit	★★★	1210	Flying Clipper	NYR	NYR
Carnival Splendor	★★★	1209	Le Champlain	NYR	NYR
Carnival Sunshine	★★★	1208	Le Lapérouse	NYR	NYR
Carnival Legend	★★★	1207	MSC Seaside	NYR	NYR
Carnival Miracle	★★★	1207	National Geographic Quest	NYR	NYR
Carnival Pride	★★★	1205	Norwegian Bliss	NYR	NYR
Carnival Liberty	★★★	1203	Roald Amundsen	NYR	NYR
Albatros	★★★	1200	Scenic Eclipse	NYR	NYR
Carnival Valor	★★★	1197	Seabourn Ovation	NYR	NYR
Carnival Triumph	★★★	1195	World Dream	NYR	NYR

Credits

Photo Credits

AIDA Cruises 126/127, 193, 195, 197, 199, 201, 203
Alamy 178
All Leisure Holidays 69, 82, 146
American Cruise Lines 215, 216, 426
Aurora Expeditions 83
Ayako Ward 11, 70, 76, 77, 158
Azamara Club Cruises 141
Bahnfrend 571
Bo Randstedt 467
Carnival Cruises 23, 24, 60, 129, 178/179, 256, 258, 260, 262, 264, 266, 268, 270, 272, 274, 276, 278, 280, 282, 284, 286, 288, 290, 292, 294, 296, 298, 300, 302, 304, 306
Carnival/Andy Newman 29, 130
Celebrity Cruises 49, 160
Celebrity/Michel Verdure 100, 131
Celebrity/Quentin Bacon 120
Celebrity/Steve Beaudet 132
Celestyal Cruises 95, 328, 329, 330
Christopher Michel 401
Costa Cruises 133, 337, 339, 341, 343, 345, 347, 349, 351, 353, 355, 359, 361, 363, 365, 371
Cruise & Maritime Voyages 226, 333
Crystal Cruises 103, 142
Crystal Yacht Cruises 368
Cunard 22, 64, 143, 175, 589, 591, 594
Cunard/Indusfoto 166
Dennis Jarvis 582
Didier Descouens 239
Disney Cruise Line 20, 37, 57, 107, 108, 121, 144, 377, 379, 381, 383
Douglas Ward 9, 12, 19, 27, 33, 43, 45, 55, 71, 72, 75, 84, 86, 89, 90/91, 97, 99, 101, 106, 113, 123, 138, 148, 151, 153, 162, 163, 164, 167, 171, 173, 185, 187, 189, 191, 204/205, 207, 221, 224, 227, 229, 231, 244, 246, 369, 392, 413, 416, 421, 424, 441, 454, 469, 479, 491, 516, 518, 519, 600, 613, 638, 640, 644, 661, 667, 692, 714
Dream Cruises 406, 724
Eirik Berger 398
Ester Kokmeijer 403
Fred Olsen Cruise Lines 237, 240, 242
Getty Images 31, 66, 81, 104, 118
Hapag-Lloyd Cruises 4/5, 10, 13, 21, 30, 32, 35, 53, 58, 78, 94, 122, 145, 168, 174, 177, 395, 417
Hebridean Island Cruises 102
Holland America Line 134, 217, 390, 437, 452, 562, 585, 607, 698, 712, 716, 726, 729
Hurtigruten 606
iStock 96
Jesse Chandler 578
Linbald Expeditions 507, 508, 509, 511
Lindblad/Sisse Brimberg & Cotton Coulson 46
Louis Cruises 147
Mark Jones/Roving Tortoise Photography/Aurora Expeditions 140
Ming Tang-Evans/Apa Publications 92
MSC Cruises 54, 65, 67, 135, 159, 481, 483, 484/485, 487, 489, 493, 495, 497, 499, 501, 503, 505
NCL 16, 26, 40, 63, 73, 110, 112, 115, 119, 136, 521, 523, 526, 528, 531, 534, 536, 539, 541, 543, 545, 547, 549, 551, 553, 583
NCL/Susan Seubert 114
Noble Caledonia 252, 423, 433
Norbert Nagel 410
Oceania Cruises 429, 461, 512, 604, 668/669
Oceanwide Expeditions 566, 626
P&O Cruises Australia 569, 570, 572, 574
P&O Cruises 88, 235, 250, 560, 564, 700
Paul Gauguin Cruises 8, 150, 580
Phoenix Reisen 209, 213, 223, 373
Piergiuliano Chesi 357
Pjotr Mahhonin 332, 459, 646
Ponant 439, 443, 444, 445, 447, 448
Poseidon Expeditions 629
Princess Cruises 1, 38, 61, 137, 254, 335, 366, 375, 385, 408, 411, 430/431, 455, 576, 598, 611, 618, 627, 681, 683, 685
Public domain 387, 671
Pullmantur Cruises 477, 672, 728
Quark Expeditions 436, 558, 559, 621
Regent Seven Seas Cruises 36, 50, 125, 152, 647, 649, 651, 653
Regent Seven Seas Cruises/Michel Verdure 25
Royal Caribbean 3MR, 6/7, 17, 44, 48, 62, 68, 98, 109, 139, 172, 181, 210, 219, 233, 248, 308, 310, 312, 314, 316, 318, 321, 323, 325, 327, 388, 398/399, 404, 414, 419, 427, 434, 450, 457, 463, 514, 555, 567, 587, 596, 602, 710
Saga Group Limited 615, 616
Scenic 620
Sea Cloud Cruises 85, 622, 624
Seabourn 154, 630, 632, 634, 636
SeaDream Yacht Club 116, 642
Shutterstock 34, 165, 702, 704
Silversea Cruises 156, 655, 657, 658, 659, 660, 663, 665
Star Clippers 402, 609, 675
Star Cruises 687, 688, 689, 690
Steve Dunlop Photographer/P&O Cruises 149
Thomson Cruises 693
TUI Cruises 465, 471, 473, 475, 694, 696
Viking Cruises 39, 157, 176, 706, 708
Voyages to Antiquity 183
Windstar Cruises 673, 677, 679, 718, 720, 722

Cover Credits

Front cover: Ships in Nice, iStock
Back cover: The EUROPA 2 off the San Blas islands, Hapag-Lloyd Cruises; Splashaway Bay on the Liberty of the Seas, Royal Caribbean; *Grease* on Harmony of the Seas, Royal Caribbean

Berlitz/Insight Guide Credits

Distribution

UK, Ireland and Europe
Apa Publications (UK) Ltd
sales@insightguides.com

United States and Canada
Ingram Publisher Services
ips@ingramcontent.com

Australia and New Zealand
Woodslane
info@woodslane.com.au

Southeast Asia
Apa Publications (SN) Pte
singaporeoffice@insightguides.com

Hong Kong, Taiwan and China
Apa Publications (HK) Ltd
hongkongoffice@insightguides.com

Worldwide
Apa Publications (UK) Ltd
sales@insightguides.com

Special Sales, Content Licensing and CoPublishing
Insight Guides can be purchased in bulk quantities at discounted prices. We can create special editions, personalised jackets and corporate imprints tailored to your needs.
sales@insightguides.com;
www.insightguides.biz

www.berlitzpublishing.com

Author
Douglas Ward

Managing Editor
Sarah Clark

Copyeditor
Clare Peel

Picture Editor
Tom Smyth

Head of Production
Rebeka Davies

TELL US YOUR THOUGHTS

Dear Cruiser,

I hope you have found this edition of Berlitz Cruising and Cruise Ships both enjoyable and useful. If you have any comments or queries, or experiences of cruising that you would like to pass on, or perhaps some ideas for subjects that could be included in the future, I would be delighted to read them. With your help, I can improve and expand the guide in future editions.

The world of cruising is evolving fast and certain facts and figures may have changed since this guide went to print, so if you have found any outdated information in these pages, please do let me know and I will make sure it is corrected as soon as possible.

You can write to me by email at:
shipratings@hotmail.com

Or by post to:
APA Publications
PO Box 7910
London SE1 1WE
United Kingdom

Thank you,
Douglas Ward

Index